exciting new resources for instructors.

Do you assign cases in your marketing courses?

Bookmark: www.prenhall.com/custombusiness

It's where you'll find over 1,000 marketing-specific cases from today's leading case institutions. Search by key word, company, length, author, and even year.

Harvard Business School has suggested 100 cases for use with Kotler's *Marketing Management.*
View the list at
www.prenhall.com/kotler

It's as easy as 1-2-3. You select the cases. We publish your custom casebooks

Questions Call: 1.800.877.6872

Do you use videos in your classroom?

Make your classroom "newsworthy". PH and BusinessNow have partnered together to create a completely new Marketing Management video library for the Eleventh Edition.

Using today's popular news magazine format, students are taken on location and behind closed doors. Each news story profiles well-known companies or rising companies that are leaders in their industries. Issue-focused footage includes interviews with top executives, objective reporting by real news anchors and industry research analysts, marketing and advertising campaign excerpts, and more.

This exciting new library is available to adopters of the Eleventh Edition.

ELEVENTH EDITION

MARKETING MANAGEMENT

Prentice Hall Marketing

What's on Your Shelf?   www.prenhall.com/marketing

Albaum/Strandskov	International Marketing and Export Management 4/e
Active Learning Technology	Mastering Marketing CD-ROM 1.0
Anderson/Narus	Business Market Management: Understanding, Creating and Delivering Value 2/e
Armstrong/Kotler	Marketing: An Introduction 6/e
Ballou	Business Logistics Management 4/e
Batra/Myers/Aaker	Advertising Management 6/e
Berman/Evans	Retail Management: A Strategic Approach 8/e
Best	Market Based Management: Strategies for Growing Customer Value and Profitability 3/e
Bloomberg/LeMay/Hanna	Logistics
Brierty/Eckles/Reeder	Business Marketing
Burns/Bush	Marketing Research with SPSS 4/e
Center/Jackson	Public Relations Practices 6/e
Chopra/Meindl	Supply Chain Management: Strategy, Planning and Operation
Clow/Baack	Integrated Advertising, Promotion and Marketing Communications
Coughlan/Anderson/Stern/El-Ansary	Marketing Channels 6/e
Coupey	Marketing and the Internet
Cutlip/Center/Broom	Effective Public Relations 8/e
D'Andrea/Quelch	Cases in Strategic Marketing Management: Business Strategies in Latin America
Hair/Anderson/Tatham/Black	Multivariate Data Analysis 5/e
Harrell	Marketing: Connecting with Customers 2/e
Keegan	Global Marketing Management 7/e
Keegan/Green	Global Marketing 3/e
Keller	Strategic Brand Management: Building, Measuring and Managing Brand Equity 2/e
Kerin/Peterson	Strategic Marketing Problems: Cases and Comments 9/e
Kotler	Marketing Management 11/e
Kotler	Framework for Marketing Management 2/e
Kotler/Andreasen	Strategic Marketing for NonProfit Organizations 5/e
Kotler/Armstrong	Principles of Marketing 9/e
Kotler/Armstrong	ActiveBook: Principles of Marketing
Kotler/Chin-Tiong/Swee-Hoon/Siew-Meng	Marketing Management: An Asian Perspective 2/e
Kumar	International Marketing Research
Frost/Strauss	Building Effective Websites
Hanna/Wozniak	Consumer Behavior: An Applied Approach
Johnson/Wood/Wardlow/Murphy	Contemporary Logistics 7/e
Kardes	Consumer Behavior and Managerial Decision Making 2/e
Lilien/Rangaswamy	Marketing Engineering: Computer-Assisted Marketing Analysis and Planning 2/e
Lovelock	Services Marketing: People, Technology, Strategy 4/e
Lovelock/Wright	Principles of Services Marketing 2/e
Malhotra	Marketing Research 3/e
Malhotra	Basic Marketing Research: Application to Contemporary Issues with SPSS
Manning/Reece	Selling Today 8/e
McEnally	Cases in Consumer Behavior, Volumes I & II
Mohr	Marketing of High Technology Products and Innovation
Mowen/Minor	Consumer Behavior 5/e
Mowen/Minor	Consumer Behavior: A Framework
Nagle/Holden	The Strategy and Tactics of Pricing: A Guide to Profitable Decision Making 3/e
Palo Alto Software	Advertising PlanPro
Palo Alto Software	Marketing Plan Pro 4.0
Quelch	Cases in Strategic Marketing Management: Business Strategies in Muslim Countries
Quelch	Global Marketing Management
Roberts/Berger	Direct Marketing
Rosenthal/Brown	Cases in Strategic Marketing
Russell/Lane	Kleppner's Advertising Procedure 15/e
Schiffman/Kanuk	Consumer Behavior 7/e
Seitel	Practice of Public Relations 8/e
Shank	Sports Marketing 2/e
Solomon	Consumer Behavior 5/e
Solomon/Stuart	Marketing: Real People, Real Choices 3/e
Strauss/Frost	E-Marketing 2/e
Wells/Burnett/Moriarty	Advertising: Principles and Practices 6/e
Winer	Marketing Management
Wood	The Marketing Plan: A Handbook

Need Cases, Articles, Resources? Visit www.prenhall.com/custombusiness

ELEVENTH EDITION

MARKETING MANAGEMENT

Philip Kotler
Northwestern University

*"The marketer's watchwords
are quality, service, and value."*
— **Philip Kotler**

Prentice
Hall
Upper Saddle River, New Jersey 07458

Library of Congress Cataloging-in-Publication Data
Kotler, Philip.
    Marketing management / Philip Kotler.–11th ed.
    Various multi-media instructional aids, including a web site, are available to
    supplement the text.
     Includes bibliographical references and indexes.
     ISBN 0-13-033629-7 (alk. paper)
      1. Marketing—Management. I. Title.
HF5415.13.K64   2003
658.8—dc21

Senior Editor: Wendy Craven
Editor-in-Chief: Jeff Shelstad
Assistant Editor: Melissa Pellerano
Editorial Assistant: Danielle Serra
Senior Developmental Editor: Jeannine Ciliotta
Media Project Manager: Anthony Palmiotto
Senior Marketing Manager: Michelle O'Brien
Marketing Assistant: Christine Genneken
Managing Editor (Production): Judy Leale
Production Editor: Cindy Spreder
Production Assistant: Dianne Falcone
Permissions Supervisor: Suzanne Grappi
Associate Director, Manufacturing: Vinnie Scelta
Production Manager: Arnold Vila
Manufacturing Buyer: Diane Peirano
Design Manager: Patricia Smythe
Art Directror: Kevin Kall
Interior Design: Amanda Kavanagh
Cover Design: Fong Yoo
Illustrator (Interior): Accurate Art
Manager, Print Production: Christy Mahon
Page Formatter: Ashley Scattergood
Composition: Carlisle Communications
Full-Service Project Management: Lynn Steines, Carlisle Communications
Printer/Binder: Courier

Credits and acknowledgments borrowed from other sources and reproduced, with
permission, in this textbook appear on appropriate page within text and on page C1.

Pearson Education LTD.
Pearson Education Australia PTY, Limited
Pearson Education Singapore, Pte. Ltd
Pearson Education North Asia Ltd
Pearson Education, Canada, Ltd
Pearson Educacion de Mexico, S.A. de C.V.
Pearson Education–Japan
Pearson Education Malaysia, Pte. Ltd

10 9 8 7 6 5 4 3 2 1
ISBN 0-13-0336297

Dedication

This book is dedicated to my wife and best friend, Nancy, with love.

about the **author**

Philip Kotler is one of the world's leading authorities on marketing. He is the S. C. Johnson & Son Distinguished Professor of International Marketing at the Kellogg School of Management, Northwestern University. He received his master's degree at the University of Chicago and his Ph.D. at MIT, both in economics. He did postdoctoral work in mathematics at Harvard University and in behavioral science at the University of Chicago.

Dr. Kotler is the co-author of *Principles of Marketing* and *Marketing: An Introduction*. His *Strategic Marketing for Nonprofit Organizations*, now in its fifth edition, is the best seller in that specialized area. Dr. Kotler's other books include *Marketing Models; The New Competition; Marketing Professional Services; Strategic Marketing for Educational Institutions; Marketing for Health Care Organizations; Marketing Congregations; High Visibility; Social Marketing; Marketing Places; The Marketing of Nations; Marketing for Hospitality and Tourism; Standing Room Only—Strategies for Marketing the Performing Arts; Museum Strategy and Marketing; Marketing Moves;* and *Kotler on Marketing.*

In addition, he has published more than one hundred articles in leading journals, including the *Harvard Business Review, Sloan Management Review, Business Horizons, California Management Review,* the *Journal of Marketing,* the *Journal of Marketing Research, Management Science,* the *Journal of Business Strategy,* and *Futurist.* He is the only three-time winner of the coveted Alpha Kappa Psi award for the best annual article published in the *Journal of Marketing.*

Professor Kotler was the first recipient of the American Marketing Association's (AMA) Distinguished Marketing Educator Award (1985). The European Association of Marketing Consultants and Sales Trainers awarded him their Prize for Marketing Excellence. He was chosen as the Leader in Marketing Thought by the Academic Members of the AMA in a 1975 survey. He also received the 1978 Paul Converse Award of the AMA, honoring his original contribution to marketing. In 1995, the Sales and Marketing Executives International (SMEI) named him Marketer of the Year. In 2002, Professor Kotler received the Distinguished Educator Award from The Academy of Marketing Science. He has received honorary doctoral degrees from Stockholm University, the University of Zurich, Athens University of Economics and Business, DePaul University, the Cracow School of Business and Economics, Groupe H.E.C. in Paris, the Budapest School of Economic Science and Public Administration, and the University of Economics and Business Administration in Vienna.

Professor Kotler has been a consultant to many major U.S. and foreign companies, including IBM, General Electric, AT&T, Honeywell, Bank of America, Merck, SAS Airlines, Michelin, and others in the areas of marketing strategy and planning, marketing organization, and international marketing.

He has been Chairman of the College of Marketing of the Institute of Management Sciences, a Director of the American Marketing Association, a Trustee of the Marketing Science Institute, a Director of the MAC Group, a member of the Yankelovich Advisory Board, and a member of the Copernicus Advisory Board. He is a member of the Board of Governors of the School of the Art Institute of Chicago and a member of the Advisory Board of the Drucker Foundation. He has traveled extensively throughout Europe, Asia, and South America, advising and lecturing to many companies about global marketing opportunities.

brief **contents**

contents

Recently the CEO of a major corporation told me he still likes to refer to the first edition of *Marketing Management*, published in 1967, a book he used in graduate school. When he asked me to sign his copy, I obliged but told him I would be signing an antique. So much has changed since I first wrote it. Granted it introduced the concept that companies must be customer-and-market driven, but it left out today's marketplace dynamics. There was no mention of segmentation, targeting, and positioning. The Internet did not exist, nor did, for example, debit cards, smart cards, cellular phones, personal digital assistants, hypercompetition, cyberconsumers, customer equity, customer value analysis, customer relationship management, price transparency, value networks, hybrid channels, supply chain management, viral marketing, integrated marketing communication, and mobile marketing.

Even if some people question the existence of a new economy, they need to acknowledge the new elements in today's marketplace. The Internet has multiplied the number of ways consumers buy and companies sell and how companies carry on their businesses. The Internet has increased customer price sensitivity. Cellular phones have enabled people to exchange messages and buy and sell on the go. Companies face competitors from a growing number of countries, who offer lower prices and equal quality for their products and services. We are witnessing a precipitous decline in the effectiveness of mass advertising as a result of the explosion of communication channels. Companies are trying to reduce their sales forces (the most expensive way to sell) by encouraging customers to use lower-cost channels (telephone and online ordering). Store-based retailers, such as small bookstores, music stores, and travel agents, are in a daily struggle against online competitors. All industries are experiencing hypercompetition, dog-eat-dog pricing. Company margins have thinned considerably, and power is clearly shifting to customers, who are increasingly telling companies what product features they want, what communications they will tolerate, what incentives they expect, and what prices they will pay.

In response, companies are shifting gears from managing product portfolios to managing customer portfolios. The focus today is on Customer Relationship Management (CRM). Companies emphasize keeping and growing customers instead of finding new ones. They are compiling databases on individual customers so they can understand them better and construct individualized offerings and messages. They are doing less product and service standardization and more niching and customization. They are replacing monologues with customer dialogues. They are improving their methods of measuring customer profitability and customer lifetime value. They are intent on measuring the return on their marketing investment and its impact on shareholder value.

Companies have stopped thinking of the Internet as an information channel or a sales channel. The Internet requires a complete rethinking of a company's marketing strategy and the models on which it builds its business. Every company occupies a position in a long value chain connecting customers, employees, suppliers, distributors, and dealers. Today Intranets improve internal communication and Extranets facilitate communicating with partners.

As markets change, so does marketing. Marketing is no longer a company department charged with a limited number of tasks: managing advertising, sending out direct mail, finding sales leads, providing customer service. Marketing must be a company-wide undertaking. It must drive the company's vision, mission, and strategic planning. Marketing is about deciding who the company wants as its customers; which needs to satisfy; what products and services to offer; what prices to set; what communications to send and receive; what channels of distribution to use; and what partnerships to develop.

Marketing deals with the whole process of entering markets, establishing profitable positions, and building loyal customer relationships. This can happen only if all departments work together: engineering designs the right products, finance furnishes the required funds, purchasing buys quality materials, production makes quality products on time, and accounting measures the profitability of different customers, products, and areas.

this edition

Marketing is of interest to everyone, whether they are marketing goods, services, properties, persons, places, events, information, ideas, or organizations. So the eleventh edition is dedicated to helping companies, groups, and individuals adapt their marketing strategies and management to the new technological and global realities.

This edition emphasizes:

- The Internet and its uses and effects
- Demand chain and supply chain management
- Customer relationship management and partner relationship management
- Alternative go-to-market channels
- Brand building and brand asset management

At the same time, it builds on the fundamental strengths of past editions:

- **Managerial Orientation.** This book focuses on the major decisions marketing managers and top management face in their efforts to harmonize the organization's objectives, capabilities, and resources with marketplace needs and opportunities.
- **Analytical Approach.** This book presents a framework for analyzing recurrent problems in marketing management. Cases and examples illustrate effective marketing principles, strategies, and practices.
- **Multidisciplinary Perspective.** This book draws on the rich findings of various scientific disciplines—economics, behavioral science, management theory, and mathematics—for fundamental concepts and tools.
- **Universal Applications.** This book applies marketing thinking to the complete spectrum of marketing: products and services, consumer and business markets, profit and nonprofit organizations, domestic and foreign companies, small and large firms, manufacturing and intermediary businesses, and low- and high-tech industries.
- **Comprehensive and Balanced Coverage.** This book covers all the topics an informed marketing manager needs to understand to carry out strategic, tactical, and administrative marketing.

features of the eleventh edition

This edition has been both streamlined and expanded to bring essentials and classic examples into sharper focus while covering new concepts and ideas in depth.

new topics, new organization

Chapter 2, "Adapting Marketing to the New Economy," is an entirely new chapter dealing with the impact of the Internet on marketing and consumers. What are the major forces driving the new economy? How is business theory and practice changing as a result? How are marketers using the Internet, customer databases, and customer relationship management? This new chapter focuses on these questions, and examples of online companies and marketing have been added throughout the book. Chapter 19, "Managing Advertising, Sales Promotion, and Public Relations," and Chapter 21, "Managing Direct and On-line Marketing" have been combined because both deal with marketing's communication function.

new concepts and ideas

A large number of concepts have been added or explored in greater detail: the new economy, Internet marketing, reverse marketing, experiential marketing, buzz marketing, viral marketing, guerrilla marketing, high-tech product marketing, industry convergence, cyberconsumers, customer relationship management, customization and customerization, customer equity, customer lifetime value, customer share, customer activity cycles, customer value analysis, database marketing and datamining, telemarketing, shareholder value, value chains, brand building, brand asset management, self-service technologies, mobile marketing, gain-and-risk sharing pricing, dynamic pricing, tiered loyalty programs, hybrid channels, demand chains. New published research findings have been added to every topic.

boxed features

This edition also has three box series. Marketing Memos, which appear in the margins, present tips and suggestions for managers at all stages of the marketing management process. Marketing Insights highlight current research findings in marketing management. **New!** Marketing for the New Economy boxes focus on the effects of market and technological changes on marketing and marketing management.

New and updated **Marketing Memo** boxes focus on such topics as "Succeeding with Electronic Commerce," "A Guide to Generation Y," "Why Developing Hi-Tech Products Is Especially Difficult," "Ten Rules of Radical Marketing," "Questionnaire Do's and Don'ts," "Biotech: Unleashing Unlimited Market Opportunities," "Internet Ethics for Targeting Kids," "Going After Poor Markets around the Globe," "The Ten Commandments of Global Branding," "Buzz Marketing," and "Designing a Customer-Driven Distribution System."

New and updated **Marketing Insight** boxes include such topics as "Ride the Cluetrain Manifesto," "Using Observational Research," "Tracking Consumer Trends," "Cause Marketing," "Can You Build a Cult Brand," and "Drug Salespeople Rely on New Technology to Reach Doctors."

Marketing for the New Economy boxes include such topics as "M-Commerce," "Snapshots of a Country on the Move," " Customer Service Live and On-Line," "The Network Economy," "Smart Cards," "The Elusive Goal of Branding on the World Wide Web," "Technologies of Customer Empowerment," "Extreme Retailing."

text examples and minicases

In-text examples and minicase and have been replaced, updated, and added to focus on e-commerce companies, uses of the Internet, and service businesses, as well as classic cases. Over 100 new examples of good and bad company marketing practices have been added to supplement or replace older examples. New minicases include PlasticsNet.com, Earthlink.com, GAP, Palm Computing, GM, DaimlerChrysler, Compaq, CEOExpress.com, Abercrombie & Fitch, Selfridges, Heublein, Verizon, IKEA, Cemex, boo.com, and Blue Man Group. Updated minicases include Dell, Saturn, Nike, Wal-Mart, Caterpillar, McDonald's, Kinko's, A&E Network, Snapple, Club Med. Classic minicases such as Swatch, UPS, Absolut vodka, and Kodak have been retained.

end-of-chapter exercises

The Applications section includes several new types of extremely practical exercises to challenge students:

- *New!* **Marketing Debate** in each chapter now features a question asking students to take sides on a marketing issue covered in that chapter.

- **Marketing and Advertising** exercises focus on real companies and include the ads being discussed. They give the student practice in analyzing the marketing objectives advertising is trying to realize.

- *New!* **Online Marketing Today** exercises focus on e-business and e-commerce, and send students to the company Web site to complete the assignment.

- **You're the Marketer** asks students to make a formal marketing plan using the Sonic PDA hypothetical example from Chapter 4. It is linked to the *Marketing Plan Pro* software and *The Marketing Plan: A Handbook,* offered as supplements in a value-priced package.

coursecomplete – www.prenhall.com/custombusiness

Prentice Hall Custom Business Resources can provide you and your students with all of the texts, cases and articles needed to enhance and maximize the learning in your unique marketing course. Create your own Custom CoursePacks or Custom CaseBooks or use our QuickPacks, which include pre-selected resources that correlate with chapters in the text. Our resources include top tier cases from Darden, Harvard, Ivey, Nacra and Thunderbird, plus full access to the wealth of articles in the ProQuest and XanEdu databases. Students have access to both the print and online resources. For details on how to order these value-priced packages, contact your local rep or visit the **The Prentice Hall Custom Business Resources** Web site at *www.prenhall.com/custombusiness.*

the teaching and learning package

This edition of *Marketing Management* includes a number of professor and student ancillaries designed to make the marketing management course an exciting, dynamic, interactive experience.

- **Instructor Course Organizer CD-ROM.** One source for all of your supplement needs. This Instructor CD contains all the print and technology supplements on a single CD-ROM. Enjoy the freedom to transport the entire supplements package from office, to home, to classroom. The Instructor CD-ROM enables you to customize any of the ancillaries, print only the chapters or materials you wish to use, or access any item from the package within the classroom.

- A comprehensive, extensively revised *Instructor's Resource Manual,* prepared by Dale Shook and Marian Burk Wood, includes chapter/summary overviews, key teaching objectives, answers to all end-of-chapter Applications exercises, supplementary resource suggestions, exercises, and detailed lecture outlines. Portions of the manual may be downloaded as an electronic file from the Prentice Hall Web site at *www.prenhall.com/kotler.*

- **The Test Item File,** prepared by Betty Pritchett, contains more than 2,000 multiple-choice, true-false, and essay questions. Each question includes a text page reference. Prentice Hall Electronic Test Manager, available in both Mac and Windows format, creates exams and evaluates and tracks student results. Instructors without access to computers can use Prentice Hall's complimentary test preparation service by dialing 1-800-550-1701.

- **PowerPoint Files.** With up to 40 slides per chapter, this set of lecture aids follows the chapter outline, highlights key concepts, and includes key figures from the text. These files may be downloaded from the Prentice Hall Web site at *www.prenhall.com/kotler* and are also available on the Instructor Course Organizer CD-ROM. A select number of slides are also available as transparency acetates.

- **Custom Case Videos.** *Prentice Hall Video Gallery: Marketing Management 03.* Make your classroom "newsworthy." PH and BusinessNow have partnered to create a completely new Marketing Management video library for the Eleventh Edition. Using today's popular newsmagazine format, students are taken on location and behind closed doors. Each news story profiles a well-known or up-and-coming company leading the way in its industry. Highlighting over 20 companies, including Starbucks, Intel, Accenture, DoubleClick, P&O NEDLLOYD and more, the issue-focused footage includes interviews with top executives, objective reporting by real news anchors, industry research analysts and marketing and advertising campaign excerpts. Extensive teaching materials are available to accompany the video library.

- **Companion Web Site** at *www.prenhall.com/kotler.* Our acclaimed Web resource provides professors and students with a customized course Web site that features a complete array of teaching and learning material. For instructors: downloadable versions of the Instructor's Resource Manual and PowerPoint slides, plus additional resources such as current events and Internet exercises. Or, try the syllabus builder to plan your own course! For students: an interactive student Study Guide with quizzes plus in-depth information about many of the major companies mentioned in each chapter. Also includes a brand new interactive case tool, which teaches the fundamentals of case study analysis.

- **Marketing PlanPro and *NEW Marketing Plan: A Handbook*.** Marketing PlanPro is a highly rated commercial software program that guides students through the entire marketing plan process. The software is totally interactive and features ten sample marketing plans, step-by-step guides, and customizable charts. Customize your marketing plan to fit your marketing needs by following easy-to-use plan wizards. Follow the clearly outlined steps from strategy to implementation. Click to print, and your text, spreadsheet, and charts come together to create a powerful marketing plan. The new *Marketing Plan: A Handbook,* by Marian Burk Wood, supplements the in-text marketing plan material with an in-depth guide to what student marketers really need to know. A structured learning process leads to a complete and actionable marketing plan. Also included are timely, real-world examples that illustrate key points, sample marketing plans, and Internet resources. The Handbook and Marketing PlanPro software are available as value-pack items at a discounted price. Contact your local Prentice Hall representative for more information.

- **Innovative Online Courses.** Standard Online Courses in WebCT, CourseCompass, and BlackBoard. No technical expertise needed! Teach a complete online course or a web enhanced course. Add your own course materials, take advantage of online testing and Gradebook opportunities, and utilize the bulletin board and discussion board functions. Free to your students with purchase of the text.

- **CourseCompass with EBook.** Students receive the benefits of both an online course *and* 24/7 online access to their textbook from any computer. Available at a nominal charge.

acknowledgments

The eleventh edition bears the imprint of many people. My colleagues and associates at the Kellogg Graduate School of Management at Northwestern University continue to have an important impact on my thinking: James C. Anderson, Robert C. Blattberg, Bobby J. Calder, Gregory S. Carpenter, Alex Chernev, Anne T. Coughlan, Dawn Iacobucci, Dipak C. Jain, Robert Kozinets, Lakshman Krishnamurti, Angela Lee, Ann L. McGill, Vincent Nijs, Christie Nordhielm, Mohanbir S. Sawhney, John F. Sherry Jr., Louis W. Stern, Brian Sternthal, Alice M. Tybout, and Andris A. Zoltners. I also want to thank the S. C. Johnson Family for the generous support of my chair at the Kellogg School. Completing the Northwestern team is my former dean, Donald P. Jacobs, and my current dean, Dipak Jain, both of whom have provided generous support for my research and writing.

Several former faculty members of the marketing department had a great influence on my thinking when I first joined the Kellogg marketing faculty, specifically Richard M. Clewett, Ralph Westfall, Harper W. Boyd, and Sidney J. Levy. I also want to acknowledge Gary Armstrong for our work on *Principles of Marketing*.

In preparing this edition, I want to give special acknowledgment to Professor Kevin Lane Keller of Dartmouth. Kevin, one of the major thought leaders in brand management, not only gave the manuscript a scrupulous critical reading, but added many examples and ideas to improve this edition.

I am indebted to the following coauthors of international editions of *Marketing Management* and *Principles of Marketing* who have taught me a great deal as we worked together to adapt marketing management thinking to the problems of different nations:

- Swee-Hoon Ang and Siew-Meng Leong: National University of Singapore
- Chin-Tiong Tan: Singapore Management University
- Friedhelm W. Bliemel: Universitat Kaiserslautern (Germany)
- Peter Chandler, Linden Brown, and Stewart Adam: Monash and RMIT University (Australia)
- Bernard Dubois: Groupe HEC School of Management (France)
- John Saunders (Loughborough University) and Veronica Wong (Warwick University, United Kingdom)
- Jacob Hornick: Tel Aviv Univesity (Israel)
- Walter Giorgio Scott: Universita Cattolica del Sacro Cuore (Italy)
- Ronald E. Turner and Peggy Cunningham: Queen's University (Canada)

I also want to acknowledge how much I have learned from working with coauthors on more specialized marketing subjects: Alan Andreasen, Christer Asplund, Paul N. Bloom, John Bowen, Roberta C. Clarke, Karen Fox, Michael Hamlin, Thomas Hayes, Dipak Jain, Somkid Jatusripitak, Hermawan Kartajaya, Neil Kotler, Nancy Lee, Suvit Maesincee, James Maken, Gustave Rath, Irving Rein, Eduardo Roberto, Joanne Scheff, Norman Shawchuck, Martin Stoller, and Bruce Wrenn.

I am indebted to the following colleagues at other universities who reviewed this new edition:

- Brent Cunningham, Ph.D.: Jacksonville State University
- Ralph Gaedeke: California State University, Sacramento

- Bill Gray: Keller Graduate School of Management
- Ron Lennon: Barry University
- Kenneth P. Mead: Central Connecticut State University
- Hank Pruden: Golden Gate University
- Scott D. Roberts: Northern Arizona University
- Alex Sharland: Hofstra University
- Michael Swenson: Brigham Young University, Marriott School
- Dr. R. Venkatesh: University of Pittsburgh—Katz Graduate School of Business

I would also like to thank colleagues who have reviewed previous editions of *Marketing Management*:

Hiram Barksdale, University of Georgia
Boris Becker, Oregon State University
Sunil Bhatla, Case Western Reserve University
John Burnett, University of Denver
Surjit Chhabra, DePaul University
Dennis Clayson, University of Northern Iowa
John Deighton, University of Chicago
Ralph Gaedeke, California State University, Sacramento
Dennis Gensch, University of Wisconsin, Milwaukee
David Georgoff, Florida Atlantic University
Bill Gray, Keller Graduate School of Management
Arun Jain, State University of New York, Buffalo
Ron Lennon, Barry University
H. Lee Matthews, Ohio State University
Paul McDevitt, University of Illinois, Springfield
Mary Ann McGrath, Loyola University, Chicago
Henry Metzner, University of Missouri, Rolla
Pat Murphy, University of Notre Dame
Jim Murrow, Drury College
Nicholas Nugent, Boston College
Donald Outland, University of Texas, Austin
Albert Page, University of Illinois, Chicago
Christopher Puto, Arizona State University
Robert Roe, University of Wyoming
Dean Siewers, Rochester Institute of Technology
Greg Wood, Canisius College

The talented staff at Prentice Hall deserves praise for their roles in shaping the eleventh edition. My editor of many years, Whitney Blake, offered excellent advice and direction for this eleventh edition, as she has done for past editions. Bruce Kaplan and Wendy Craven, my new editors, have done the same. I benefited greatly from the superb editorial help of Jeannine Ciliotta, who lent her considerable talents as a development editor to improve this edition. I also want to acknowledge the fine production work of Cindy Spreder, the creative design work of Kevin Kall, and the editorial assistance of Danielle Serra. I thank Anthony Palmiotto and Melissa Pellerano for their work on the supplements and media packages. I'd also like to thank my marketing manager, Michelle O'Brien. And finally, thanks to Marian Burk Wood for providing the new end-of-chapter application exercises.

My overriding debt continues to be to my lovely wife, Nancy, who provided me with the time, support, and inspiration needed to prepare this edition. It is truly our book.

Philip Kotler
S. C. Johnson Distinguished Professor of International Marketing
Kellogg School of Management
Northwestern University
Evanston, Illinois

C H A P T E R

1

defining marketing for the twenty-first century

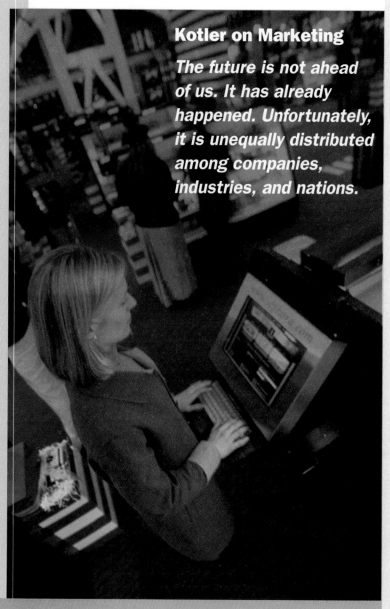

Kotler on Marketing

The future is not ahead of us. It has already happened. Unfortunately, it is unequally distributed among companies, industries, and nations.

In this chapter we will address the following questions:

- What is the new economy like?
- What are the tasks of marketing?
- What are the major concepts and tools of marketing?
- What orientations do companies exhibit in the marketplace?
- How are companies and marketers responding to the new challenges?

Today it is fashionable to talk about the new economy. We hear that businesses are operating in a globalized economy; that things are moving at a nanosecond pace; that our markets are characterized by hyper-competition; that disruptive technologies are challenging every business; and that business must adapt to the empowered consumer.

The old economy seemed simpler. It was based on the Industrial Revolution and on managing manufacturing industries. Manufacturers applied certain principles and practices for the successful operation of their factories. They standardized products in order to bring down costs. They aimed to continually expand their market size to achieve economies of scale. They tended to replicate their procedures and policies in every

1

geographic market. The goal was efficiency; and to accomplish this the firm was managed hierar-chically, with a boss on top issuing orders to middle managers, who in turn guided the workers.

The new economy, in contrast, is based on the Digital Revolution and the management of information. Information has a number of attributes. It can be infinitely differentiated, cus-tomized, and personalized. It can be dispatched to a great number of people who are on a net-work and it can reach them with great speed. To the extent that the information is public and accessible, people will be better informed and able to make better choices.

the new economy

The digital revolution has placed a whole new set of capabilities in the hands of con-sumers and businesses. Consider what consumers have today that they didn't have yesterday:

- *A substantial increase in buying power.* Buyers today are only a click away from comparing competitor prices and product attributes. They can get answers on the Internet in a mat-ter of seconds. They don't need to drive to stores, park, wait on line, and hold discussions with salespeople. On Priceline.com, consumers can even name the price they want to pay for a hotel room, airline ticket, or mortgage, and see if there are any willing suppliers. Business buyers can run a reverse auction where sellers compete during a given time period to capture the buyer's business. Buyers can join with others to aggregate their purchases to achieve deeper volume discounts.
- *A greater variety of available goods and services.* Today a person can order almost anything over the Internet: furniture (Ethan Allen), washing machines (Sears), management con-sulting ("Ernie"), medical advice (cyberdocs). Amazon.com advertises itself as the world's largest bookstore, with over 3 million books; no physical bookstore can match this. Furthermore, buyers can order these goods from anywhere in the world, which helps people living in countries with very limited local offerings to achieve great savings. It also means that buyers in countries with high prices can reduce their costs by ordering in countries with lower prices.
- *A great amount of information about practically anything.* People can read almost any news-paper in any language from anywhere in the world. They can access on-line encyclope-dias, dictionaries, medical information, movie ratings, consumer reports, and countless other information sources.
- *A greater ease in interacting and placing and receiving orders.* Today's buyers can place orders from home, office, or mobile phone 24 hours a day, 7 days a week, and the orders will be delivered to their home or office quickly.
- *An ability to compare notes on products and services.* Today's customers can enter a chat room centered on some area of common interest and exchange information and opinions. Women can visit iVillage to discuss common family problems; movie lovers can visit any number of movie chat rooms to share ideas.

Today's companies also have a new set of capabilities:

- Companies can operate a powerful new information and sales channel with augmented geographical reach to inform and promote their businesses and products. By establishing one or more Web sites, a company can list its products and services, its history, its busi-ness philosophy, its job opportunities, and other information of interest to visitors. Unlike the ads and brochures of the past, the Internet permits them to transmit an almost unlimited amount of information. Companies such as Grainger are putting huge catalogs on their Web sites, making it easy for customers to search for and order products. Each company has the option of turning its Web site into a sales channel as well as an infor-mation channel. Furthermore, since the Internet is worldwide, people from anywhere in the world can learn about the company and place orders.

- Companies can collect fuller and richer information about markets, customers, prospects, and competitors. Not only can companies find abundant information, but they can also conduct fresh marketing research using the Internet. They can arrange for focus groups, send out questionnaires, and gather primary data in several other ways.
- Companies can facilitate and speed up internal communication among their employees. By using the Internet as a private intranet, employees can query one another, seek advice, and download or upload needed information from and to the company's main computer.
- Companies can have two-way communications with customers and prospects, and more efficient transactions. The Internet makes it easy for individuals to send e-mail messages to companies and receive replies, and more companies today are developing extranets with suppliers and distributors for sending and receiving information, placing orders, and making payments more efficiently.
- Companies are now able to send ads, coupons, samples, and information to customers who have requested these items or have given the company permission to send them.
- Companies can customize offerings and services to individual customers. Companies can know the number of visitors to their Web sites and visit frequency. By putting this information into a database and enhancing it with other information, they are in a better position to customize messages, offerings, and services.
- Companies can improve purchasing, recruiting, training, and internal and external communications. All companies are buyers as well as sellers; they can achieve substantial savings in using the Internet to compare sellers' prices, and to purchase materials at auction or by posting their own terms. Companies can recruit new employees through the Internet. Many are also preparing Internet training products that can be downloaded to employees, dealers, and agents so that they can easily be kept up to date.
- Companies can substantially improve logistics and operations for substantial cost savings while improving accuracy and service quality. The Internet provides a more accurate and faster way to send and receive information, orders, transactions, and payments between companies, their business partners, and their customers.

The new capabilities unleashed by the Information Age will lead to substantially new forms of marketing and business. The Industrial Age was characterized by mass-production and mass-consumption, stores overstuffed with inventory, ads everywhere, and rampant discounting. The Information Age promises to lead to more accurate levels of production, more targeted communications, and more relevant pricing.

Here are the views of three leading CEOs on the Internet's impact:

> Every now and then, a technology comes along that is so profound, so universal, that its impact will change everything. It will transform every institution in the world. It will create winners and losers, it will change the way we do business, the way we teach our children, communicate and interact as individuals. —Lou Gerstner, Chairman of IBM.

> The Internet ranks as priority No. 1, 2, 3, and 4! . . . Embrace the Internet. Bring me a plan for how you are going to transform your business beyond adding an Internet site. —Jack Welch, former CEO of GE.

> Will e-commerce change everything—or just add another small sales channel? The Internet is not just another sales channel. It will transform your business. The future company will operate with a digital nervous system. —Bill Gates, Chairman of Microsoft.

In this book, we want to consider how marketing will change under the impact of these new forces.

Marketing deals with identifying and meeting human and social needs. One of the shortest definitions of marketing is "meeting needs profitably." Whether the marketer is Procter & Gamble, who noticed that people feel overweight and want tasty but less fatty foods, and invented Olestra; or CarMax, who noted that people want more certainty when they buy a used automobile and invented a new system for selling used cars; or IKEA, who noticed that people want good furniture at a substantially lower price and created knock-down furniture—all are motivated to turn a private or social need into a profitable business opportunity. However, marketing is tricky and it has been the Achilles' heel of many formerly prosperous companies. Seemingly invincible businesses such as Sears, Levi's, General Motors, Kodak, and Xerox have confronted newly empowered customers and new competitors, and have had to rethink their business models. Even information-savvy companies such as Cisco Systems, Wal-Mart, Intel, and AOL cannot afford to relax. Jack Welch, GE's brilliant former CEO, repeatedly warned his company: "Change or die."

The companies at greatest risk are those that fail to monitor their customers and competitors and to continuously improve their value offerings. Too many companies have not carefully defined their target market or their value proposition and they compensate by spending an inordinate amount on acquiring new customers, only to lose them. They take a short-term, sales-driven view of their business and ultimately, they fail to satisfy their stockholders, their employees, their suppliers, and their channel partners.

marketing tasks

A recent book entitled *Radical Marketing* praises companies such as Harley-Davidson, Virgin Atlantic Airways, and Boston Beer for succeeding by breaking all the rules of marketing.[1] Instead of commissioning expensive marketing research, spending huge sums on mass advertising, and operating large marketing departments, these companies stretched their limited resources, stayed in close contact with their customers, and created more satisfying solutions to customer needs. They formed buyers' clubs, used creative public relations, and focused on delivering high product quality and winning long-term customer loyalty. (See "Marketing Insight: The Ten Rules of Radical Marketing.")

We can distinguish three stages through which marketing practice might pass:

1. *Entrepreneurial marketing*: Most companies are started by individuals who live by their wits. They visualize an opportunity and knock on every door to gain attention. Jim Koch, founder

marketing **insight**

The Ten Rules of Radical Marketing

In their book *Radical Marketing*, Sam Hill and Glenn Rifkin lay out a set of prescriptive guidelines that can help other companies emulate the radical marketers.

1. *The CEO must own the marketing function.* CEOs of radical marketers never delegate marketing responsibility; they typically act like de facto chief marketing officers.

2. *Make sure the marketing department starts small and flat and stays small and flat.* In order to stay involved with marketing, CEOs must not allow layers of management to grow so numerous that they distance them from the market.

3. *Get face-to-face with the people who matter most—the customers.* For radical marketers, " 'face-to-face' is a mantra." They know the advantages of direct interaction with customers.

4. *Use market research cautiously.* Market research typically tells a marketer what the average customer wants. Radical marketers prefer grassroots techniques.

5. *Hire only passionate missionaries.* Radical marketers "don't have marketers, they have missionaries."

6. *Love and respect your customers.* Radical marketers respect customers as individuals, not as numbers on a spreadsheet.

They recognize that the core customers are responsible for the bulk of their companies' successes.

7. *Create a community of consumers.* Radical marketers "encourage their customers to think of themselves as a community, and of the brand as a unifier of that community."

8. *Rethink the marketing mix.* Radical marketers' marketing techniques often differ dramatically from those used by traditional marketers. For example, traditional marketers seek to reach broad audiences via large-scale advertising, while radical marketers use "surgical strike advertising" characterized by short, targeted ad campaigns.

9. *Celebrate common sense.* Smaller companies with limited resources cannot hope to compete with larger competitors without fresh and different marketing ideas. So radical marketers, for example, limit distribution in order to create loyalty and commitment among their distributors and among their customers.

10. *Be true to the brand.* Radical marketers "are obsessive about brand integrity, and they are fixated on quality."

Source: Sam Hill and Glenn Rifkin, *Radical Marketing* (New York: HarperCollins, 1999), pp. 19–31.

of Boston Beer Company, whose Samuel Adams beer has become a top-selling "craft" beer, started out in 1984 carrying bottles of Samuel Adams from bar to bar to persuade bartenders to carry it. For 10 years he couldn't afford an advertising budget; he sold his beer through direct sales and grassroots public relations. Today his business pulls in $210 million, making it the leader in the craft beer market.

2. *Formulated marketing*: As small companies achieve success, they inevitably move toward more formulated marketing. Boston Beer now spends considerable sums on TV advertising, employs dozens of salespeople, and carries on sophisticated marketing research. It has discovered that continued success requires setting up and managing a capable marketing department.

3. *Intrepreneurial marketing*: Many large companies get stuck in formulated marketing, poring over the latest Nielsen numbers, scanning market research reports, trying to fine-tune dealer relations and advertising messages. These companies lack the creativity and passion of the guerrilla marketers in the entrepreneurial stage.[2] Their brand and product managers need to get out of the office, start living with their customers, and visualize new ways to add value to their customers' lives.

The bottom line is that effective marketing can take many forms. There will be a constant tension between the formulated side of marketing and the creative side. It is easier to learn the formulated side, which will occupy most of our attention in this book; but we will also describe how real creativity and passion operate in many companies.

the scope of marketing

Marketing is typically seen as the task of creating, promoting, and delivering goods and services to consumers and businesses. Marketers are skilled in stimulating demand for a company's products, but this is too limited a view of the tasks marketers perform. Just as production and logistics professionals are responsible for supply management, marketers are responsible for demand management. Marketing managers seek to influence the level, timing, and composition of demand to meet the organization's objectives. Table 1.1 distinguishes eight different states of demand and the corresponding tasks facing marketing managers.

Marketing people are involved in marketing 10 types of entities: goods, services, experiences, events, persons, places, properties, organizations, information, and ideas.

GOODS   Physical goods constitute the bulk of most countries' production and marketing effort. Each year U.S. companies alone market billions of canned and frozen food products, millions of tons of steel, millions of hair dryers, cars, television sets, machines, and various other mainstays of a modern economy. Not only do companies market their goods, but thanks to the Internet, even individuals can market goods.

eBay   Today eBay is the world's largest person-to-person online trading community. It offers efficient one-to-one trading in an auction format on the Web. Individuals can use eBay to sell or buy items in thousands of categories: paintings, stamps, coins, sports memorabilia, toys, dolls. Each day over 400,000 new items are offered, and more than 3.5 million auctions are in progress.

SERVICES   As economies advance, a growing proportion of their activities is focused on the production of services. The U.S. economy today consists of a 70–30 services-to-goods mix. Services include the work of airlines, hotels, car rental firms, barbers and beauticians, maintenance and repair people, dog kennels and dog therapists, as well as professionals working within or for companies, such as accountants, lawyers, engineers, doctors, software programmers, and management consultants. Many market offerings consist of a variable mix of goods and services. At the pure services end would be a psychiatrist listening to a patient or a quartet performing Mozart; at another level would be the telephone call that is supported by a huge investment in plant and equipment; and at a more tangible level would be a fast-food establishment where the customer consumes both a product and a service.

table **1.1**		
Demand States and Marketing Tasks	1. *Negative demand.*	A major part of the market dislikes the product and may even pay a price to avoid it—vaccinations, dental work, vasectomies, and gallbladder operations, for instance. Employers have a negative demand for ex-convicts and alcoholics as employees. The marketing task is to analyze why the market dislikes the product and whether a marketing program consisting of product redesign, lower prices, and more positive promotion can change beliefs and attitudes.
	2. *No demand.*	Target consumers may be unaware of or uninterested in the product. Farmers may not be interested in a new farming method, and college students may not be interested in foreign-language courses. The marketing task is to find ways to connect the benefits of the product with people's natural needs and interests.
	3. *Latent demand.*	Consumers may share a strong need that cannot be satisfied by any existing product. There is a strong latent demand for harmless cigarettes, safer neighborhoods, and more fuel-efficient cars. The marketing task is to measure the size of the potential market and develop goods and services to satisfy the demand.
	4. *Declining demand.*	Every organization, sooner or later, faces declining demand for one or more of its products. Churches have seen membership decline; private colleges have seen applications fall. The marketer must analyze the causes of the decline and determine whether demand can be restimulated by new target markets, by changing product features, or by more effective communication. The marketing task is to reverse declining demand through creative remarketing.
	5. *Irregular demand.*	Many organizations face demand that varies on a seasonal, daily, or even hourly basis. Much mass-transit equipment is idle during off-peak hours and insufficient during peak travel hours. Museums are undervisited on weekdays and overcrowded on weekends. The marketing task, called **synchromarketing**, is to find ways to alter the pattern of demand through flexible pricing, promotion, and other incentives.
	6. *Full demand.*	Organizations face full demand when they are pleased with their volume of business. The marketing task is to maintain the current level of demand in the face of changing consumer preferences and increasing competition. The organization must maintain or improve its quality and continually measure consumer satisfaction.
	7. *Overfull demand.*	Some organizations face a demand level that is higher than they can or want to handle. Yosemite National Park is terribly overcrowded in the summer. The marketing task, called **demarketing**, requires finding ways to reduce demand temporarily or permanently. General demarketing seeks to discourage overall demand and includes such steps as raising prices and reducing promotion and service. Selective demarketing consists of trying to reduce demand from those parts of the market that are less profitable.
	8. *Unwholesome demand.*	Unwholesome products will attract organized efforts to discourage their consumption. Unselling campaigns have been conducted against cigarettes, alcohol, hard drugs, handguns, X-rated movies, and large families. The marketing task is to get people who like something to give it up, using such tools as fear messages, price hikes, and reduced availability.

Sources: See Philip Kotler, "The Major Tasks of Marketing Management," *Journal of Marketing* (October 1973): 42–49; and Philip Kotler and Sidney J. Levy, "Demarketing, Yes, Demarketing," *Harvard Business Review* (November–December 1971): 74–80.

EXPERIENCES   By orchestrating several services and goods, a firm can create, stage, and market experiences. Walt Disney World's Magic Kingdom represents experiential marketing: customers visit a fairy kingdom, a pirate ship, or a haunted house. So does the Hard Rock Café. There is also a market for customized experiences, such as spending a week at a baseball camp playing with some retired baseball greats, paying to conduct the Chicago Symphony Orchestra for five minutes, or climbing Mount Everest.[3]

EVENTS   Marketers promote time-based events, such as the Olympics, company anniversaries, major trade shows, sports events, and artistic performances. There is a whole profession of meeting planners who work out the details of an event and make sure it comes off perfectly.

PERSONS   Celebrity marketing is a major business. Years ago, someone seeking fame would hire a press agent to plant stories in newspapers and magazines. Today every major film star has an agent, a personal manager, and ties to a public relations agency. Artists, musicians, CEOs, physicians, high-profile lawyers and financiers, and other professionals are also getting help from celebrity marketers.[4] People like Madonna and the late Andy Warhol have done a masterful job of marketing themselves. Management consultant Tom Peters, himself a master at self-branding, has advised each person to become a "brand."

PLACES   Places—cities, states, regions, and whole nations—compete actively to attract tourists, factories, company headquarters, and new residents.[5] Stratford, Ontario, in Canada was a fairly run-down city with one asset: its name and a river called Avon. This became the basis for an annual Shakespeare festival that put Stratford on the tourist map. Ireland has been an outstanding place marketer, having attracted more than 500 companies to locate their plants there. It operates the Irish Development Board, the Irish Tourist Board, and the Irish Export Board, responsible for inward investment, tourists, and exports, respectively. Place marketers include economic development specialists, real estate agents, commercial banks, local business associations, and advertising and public relations agencies.

PROPERTIES   Properties are intangible rights of ownership of either real property (real estate) or financial property (stocks and bonds). Properties are bought and sold, and this requires marketing. Real estate agents work for property owners or sellers or buy residential or commercial real estate. Investment companies and banks are involved in marketing securities to both institutional and individual investors.

ORGANIZATIONS   Organizations actively work to build a strong, favorable image in the minds of their target publics. Companies spend money on corporate identity ads. Philips, the Dutch electronics company, puts out ads with the tag line "Let's Make Things Better." The Body Shop and Ben & Jerry's gained attention by promoting social causes. Other companies owe their visibility to a dramatic leader, such as Virgin's Richard Branson or Nike's Phil Knight. Universities, museums, and performing arts organizations all use marketing to boost their public images and to compete for audiences and funds.

INFORMATION   Information can be produced and marketed as a product. This is essentially what schools and universities produce and distribute at a price to parents, students, and communities. Encyclopedias and most nonfiction books market information. Magazines such as *Road and Track* and *Byte* supply information about the car and computer worlds, respectively. We buy software and CDs and we visit the Internet for information. The production, packaging, and distribution of information is one of our society's major industries.[6]

IDEAS   Every market offering includes a basic idea. Charles Revson of Revlon observed: "In the factory, we make cosmetics; in the store we sell hope." Products and services are

Marketing
MEMO

Marketers' Frequently Asked Questions

1. How can we spot and choose the right market segment(s) to serve?
2. How can we differentiate our offering from competitive offerings?
3. How should we respond to customers who press us for a lower price?
4. How can we compete against lower-cost, lower-price competitors from here and abroad?
5. How far can we go in customizing our offering for each customer?
6. What are the major ways in which we can grow our business?
7. How can we build stronger brands?
8. How can we reduce the cost of customer acquisition?
9. How can we keep our customers loyal for a longer period?
10. How can we tell which customers are more important?
11. How can we measure the payback from advertising, sales promotion, and public relations?
12. How can we improve sales force productivity?
13. How can we establish multiple channels and yet manage channel conflict?
14. How can we get the other company departments to be more customer-oriented?

platforms for delivering some idea or benefit. Social marketers are busy promoting such ideas as "Say no to drugs," "Save the rainforest," "Exercise daily," or "Avoid fatty foods."

the decisions marketers make

Marketing managers face a host of decisions, from major ones such as what product features to design into a new product, how many salespeople to hire, or how much to spend on advertising, to minor decisions such as the exact wording or color for new packaging. The "Marketing Memo: Marketers' Frequently Asked Questions" lists many of the questions marketing managers ask, which will be examined in this book.

These questions vary in importance in different marketplaces. Consider the following four markets: consumer, business, global, and nonprofit.

CONSUMER MARKETS   Companies selling mass consumer goods and services such as soft drinks, toothpaste, television sets, and air travel spend a great deal of time trying to establish a superior brand image. This requires getting a clear sense of their target customers and what need(s) their product will meet, and communicating brand positioning forcefully and creatively. Much of a brand's strength depends on developing a superior product and packaging and backing it with promotion and reliable service. Consumer marketers decide on the features, quality level, distribution coverage, and promotion expenditures that will help their brand achieve a number-one or -two position in their target market.

BUSINESS MARKETS   Companies selling business goods and services face well-trained and well-informed professional buyers who are skilled in evaluating competitive offerings. Business buyers buy goods for their utility in enabling them to make or resell a product to others, and they purchase products to make profits. Business marketers must demonstrate how their products will help customers achieve higher revenue or lower costs. Advertising plays a role, but a stronger role is played by sales force, price, and the company's reputation for reliability and quality.

GLOBAL MARKETS   Companies selling goods and services in the global marketplace face additional decisions and challenges. They must decide which countries to enter; how to enter each country (as an exporter, licenser, joint venture partner, contract manufacturer, or solo manufacturer); how to adapt their product and service features to each country; how to price their products in different countries in a narrow enough band to avoid creating a gray market for their goods; and how to adapt their communications to fit the cultural practices of each country. These decisions must be made in the face of a different legal system; different styles of negotiation; different requirements for buying, owning, and disposing of property; a currency that might fluctuate in value; a different language; and conditions of corruption or political favoritism.

NONPROFIT AND GOVERNMENTAL MARKETS   Companies selling their goods to nonprofit organizations such as churches, universities, charitable organizations, or government agencies need to price carefully because these organizations have limited purchasing power. Lower prices affect the features and quality that the seller can build into the offering. Much government purchasing calls for bids, with the lowest bid being favored, in the absence of extenuating factors.

marketing concepts and tools

Marketing boasts a rich array of concepts and tools. We will first define marketing, then describe its major concepts and tools.

defining marketing

We can distinguish between a social and a managerial definition of marketing. A social definition shows the role marketing plays in society. One marketer said that marketing's role is to "deliver a higher standard of living." Here is a social definition that serves our purpose: **Marketing** is a societal process by which individuals and groups obtain what they need and want through creating, offering, and freely exchanging products and services of value with others. For a managerial definition, marketing has often been described as "the art of selling products," but people are surprised when they hear that the most important part of marketing is not selling! Selling is only the tip of the marketing iceberg.

Peter Drucker, a leading management theorist, puts it this way:

> There will always, one can assume, be need for some selling. But the aim of marketing is to make selling superfluous. The aim of marketing is to know and understand the customer so well that the product or service fits him and sells itself. Ideally, marketing should result in a customer who is ready to buy. All that should be needed then is to make the product or service available.[7]

When Sony designed its Walkman, when Nintendo designed a superior video game, and when Toyota introduced its Lexus automobile, these manufacturers were swamped with orders because they had designed the "right" product based on careful marketing homework.

The American Marketing Association offers the following definition: Marketing is the process of planning and executing the conception, pricing, promotion, and distribution of ideas, goods, and services to create exchanges that satisfy individual and organizational goals.[8] Coping with exchange processes calls for a considerable amount of work and skill. Marketing management takes place when at least one party to a potential exchange thinks about the means of achieving desired responses from other parties. We see **marketing management** as the art and science of choosing target markets and getting, keeping, and growing customers through creating, delivering, and communicating superior customer value.

core marketing concepts

Marketing can be further understood by defining several of its core concepts.

TARGET MARKETS AND SEGMENTATION   A marketer can rarely satisfy everyone in a market. Not everyone likes the same soft drink, hotel room, restaurant, automobile, college, and movie. Therefore, marketers start by dividing up the market. They identify and profile distinct groups of buyers who might prefer or require varying product and services mixes. *Market segments* can be identified by examining demographic, psychographic, and behavioral differences among buyers. The marketer then decides which segments present the greatest opportunity—which are its **target markets**. For each chosen target market, the firm develops a *market offering*. The offering is positioned in the minds of the target buyers as delivering some central benefit(s). For example, Volvo develops its cars for buyers to whom automobile safety is a major concern. Volvo, therefore, positions its car as the safest a customer can buy.

Traditionally, a "market" was a physical place where buyers and sellers gathered to buy and sell goods. Economists now describe a market as a collection of buyers and sellers who transact over a particular product or product class (the housing market or grain market); but marketers view the sellers as constituting the industry and the buyers as constituting the market. Figure 1.1 shows the relationship between the industry and the market. Sellers and buyers are connected by four flows. The sellers send goods and services and communications (ads, direct mail) to the market; in return they receive money and information (attitudes, sales data). The inner loop shows an exchange of money for goods and services; the outer loop shows an exchange of information.

MARKETPLACE, MARKETSPACE, AND METAMARKET   Businesspeople often use the term *market* to cover various groupings of customers. They talk about need markets (the diet-seeking market), product markets (the shoe market), demographic markets (the youth market), and geographic markets (the French market); or they extend the concept to cover other markets, such as voter markets, labor markets, and donor markets.

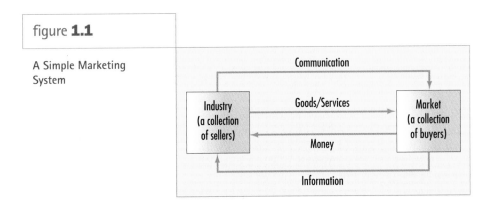

figure **1.1**

A Simple Marketing System

Modern economies abound in markets. Five basic markets and their connecting flows are shown in Figure 1.2. Manufacturers go to resource markets (raw-material markets, labor markets, money markets), buy resources and turn them into goods and services, and then sell finished products to intermediaries, who sell them to consumers. Consumers sell their labor and receive money with which they pay for goods and services. The government collects tax revenues to buy goods from resource, manufacturer, and intermediary markets and uses these goods and services to provide public services. Each nation's economy and the global economy consist of complex interacting sets of markets linked through exchange processes.

Today we can distinguish between a *marketplace* and *marketspace*. The **marketplace** is physical, as when one goes shopping in a store; **marketspace** is digital, as when one goes shopping on the Internet. Many observers believe that an increased amount of purchasing will shift into marketspace.[9]

Mohan Sawhney has proposed the concept of a **metamarket** to describe a cluster of complementary products and services that are closely related in the minds of consumers but are spread across a diverse set of industries. The automobile metamarket consists of automobile manufacturers, new car and used car dealers, financing companies, insurance companies, mechanics, spare parts dealers, service shops, auto magazines, classified auto ads in newspapers, and auto sites on the Internet. In purchasing a car, a buyer

figure **1.2**

Structure of Flows in a Modern Exchange Economy

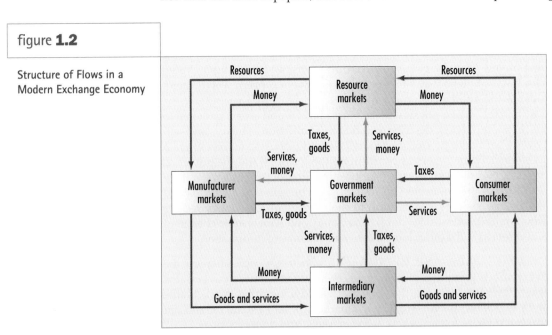

will get involved in many parts of this metamarket, and this has created an opportunity for metamediaries to assist buyers to move seamlessly through these groups, although they are disconnected in physical space. One example is Edmund's (*www.edmunds.com*), a Web site where a car buyer can find the stated features and prices of different automobiles and easily click to other sites to search for the lowest-price dealer, for financing, for car accessories, and for used cars at bargain prices. Metamediaries can also serve other metamarkets such as the home ownership market, the parenting and baby care market, and the wedding market.[10]

MARKETERS AND PROSPECTS   A **marketer** is someone seeking a response (attention, a purchase, a vote, a donation) from another party, called the **prospect**. If two parties are seeking to sell something to each other, we call them both marketers.

NEEDS, WANTS, AND DEMANDS   The marketer must try to understand the target market's needs, wants, and demands. **Needs** are the basic human requirements. People need food, air, water, clothing, and shelter to survive. People also have strong needs for recreation, education, and entertainment. These needs become **wants** when they are directed to specific objects that might satisfy the need. An American needs food but wants a hamburger, French fries, and a soft drink. A person in Mauritius needs food but wants a mango, rice, lentils, and beans. Wants are shaped by one's society. **Demands** are wants for specific products backed by an ability to pay. Many people want a Mercedes; only a few are able and willing to buy one. Companies must measure not only how many people want their product but also how many would actually be willing and able to buy it.

These distinctions shed light on the frequent criticism that "marketers create needs" or "marketers get people to buy things they don't want." Marketers do not create needs: Needs preexist marketers. Marketers, along with other societal factors, influence wants. Marketers might promote the idea that a Mercedes would satisfy a person's need for social status. They do not, however, create the need for social status.

PRODUCT, OFFERING, AND BRAND   Companies address needs by putting forth a **value proposition**, a set of benefits they offer to customers to satisfy their needs. The intangible value proposition is made physical by an **offering**, which can be a combination of products, services, information, and experiences.

A **brand** is an offering from a known source. A brand name such as McDonald's carries many associations in the minds of people: hamburgers, fun, children, fast food, Golden Arches. These associations make up the **brand image**. All companies strive to build brand strength—that is, a strong, favorable brand image.

VALUE AND SATISFACTION   The offering will be successful if it delivers value and satisfaction to the target buyer. The buyer chooses between different offerings on the basis of which is perceived to deliver the most value. Value can be seen as primarily a combination of quality, service, and price (QSP), called the **customer value triad**. Value increases with quality and service and decreases with price.

More specifically, we can define **value** as a ratio between what the customer gets and what he gives. The customer gets benefits and assumes costs. The benefits include functional benefits and emotional benefits. The costs include monetary costs, time costs, energy costs, and psychic costs. Thus value is given by:

$$\text{Value} = \frac{\text{Benefits}}{\text{Costs}} = \frac{\text{Functional benefits} + \text{Emotional benefits}}{\text{Monetary costs} + \text{Time costs} + \text{Energy costs} + \text{Psychic costs}}$$

The marketer can increase the value of the customer offering in several ways:

- Raise benefits
- Reduce costs
- Raise benefits and reduce costs
- Raise benefits by more than the raise in costs
- Lower benefits by less than the reduction in costs

The customer who is choosing between two value offerings, V1 and V2, will examine the ratio V1:V2. She will favor V1 if the ratio is larger than one; she will favor V2 if the ratio is smaller than one; and she will be indifferent if the ratio equals one.

EXCHANGE AND TRANSACTIONS   Exchange is only one of four ways in which a person can obtain a product. One can self-produce the product or service, as when one hunts, fishes, or gathers fruit. One can use force to get a product, as in a holdup or burglary. One can beg, as happens when a homeless person asks for food. Or one can offer a product, a service, or money in exchange for something he or she desires.

Exchange, which is the core concept of marketing, is the process of obtaining a desired product from someone by offering something in return. For exchange potential to exist, five conditions must be satisfied:

1. There are at least two parties.
2. Each party has something that might be of value to the other party.
3. Each party is capable of communication and delivery.
4. Each party is free to accept or reject the exchange offer.
5. Each party believes it is appropriate or desirable to deal with the other party.

Whether exchange actually takes place depends on whether the two parties can agree on terms that will leave them both better off (or at least not worse off) than before. Exchange is a value-creating process because it normally leaves both parties better off.

Two parties are engaged in exchange if they are negotiating—trying to arrive at mutually agreeable terms. When an agreement is reached, we say that a transaction takes place. A **transaction** is a trade of values between two or more parties: A gives X to B and receives Y in return. Smith sells Jones a television set and Jones pays $400 to Smith. This is a classic monetary transaction; but transactions do not require money as one of the traded values. A **barter** transaction involves trading goods or services for other goods or services, as when lawyer Jones writes a will for physician Smith in return for a medical examination.

A transaction involves several dimensions: at least two things of value, agreed-upon conditions, a time of agreement, and a place of agreement. A legal system supports and enforces compliance on the part of the transactors. Without a law of contracts, people would approach transactions with some distrust, and everyone would lose.

A transaction differs from a transfer. In a **transfer**, A gives X to B but does not receive anything tangible in return. Gifts, subsidies, and charitable contributions are all transfers. Transfer behavior can also be understood through the concept of exchange. Typically, the transferer expects to receive something in exchange for his or her gift—for example, gratitude or seeing changed behavior in the recipient. Professional fundraisers provide benefits to donors, such as thank-you notes, donor magazines, and invitations to events. Marketers have broadened the concept of marketing to include the study of transfer behavior as well as transaction behavior.

In the most generic sense, marketers seek to elicit a **behavioral response** from another party. A business firm wants a purchase, a political candidate wants a vote, a church wants an active member, and a social-action group wants the passionate adoption of some cause. Marketing consists of actions undertaken to elicit desired responses from a target audience.

To make successful exchanges, marketers analyze what each party expects from the transaction. Simple exchange situations can be mapped by showing the two actors and the wants and offerings flowing between them. Suppose Caterpillar, the world's largest manufacturer of earth-moving equipment, researches the benefits that a typical construction company wants when it buys earth-moving equipment. These benefits, listed at the top of the exchange map in Figure 1.3, include high-quality equipment, a fair price, on-time delivery, good financing terms, and good parts and service. The items on this want list are not equally important and may vary from buyer to buyer. One of Caterpillar's tasks is to discover the relative importance of these different wants to the buyer.

Caterpillar also has a want list. It wants a good price for the equipment, on-time payment, and good word of mouth. If there is a sufficient match or overlap in the want

figure **1.3**

Two–Party Exchange Map Showing Want Lists of Both Parties

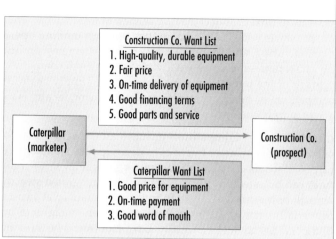

Construction Co. Want List
1. High-quality, durable equipment
2. Fair price
3. On-time delivery of equipment
4. Good financing terms
5. Good parts and service

Caterpillar (marketer)

Construction Co. (prospect)

Caterpillar Want List
1. Good price for equipment
2. On-time payment
3. Good word of mouth

lists, a basis for a transaction exists. Caterpillar's task is to formulate an offer that motivates the construction company to buy Caterpillar equipment. The construction company might in turn make a counteroffer. This process of negotiation leads to mutually acceptable terms or a decision not to transact.

RELATIONSHIPS AND NETWORKS   Transaction marketing is part of a larger idea called relationship marketing. **Relationship marketing** has the aim of building mutually satisfying long-term relations with key parties—customers, suppliers, distributors—in order to earn and retain their business.[11] Marketers accomplish this by promising and delivering high-quality products and services at fair prices to the other parties over time. Relationship marketing builds strong economic, technical, and social ties among the parties. It cuts down on transaction costs and time. In the most successful cases, transactions move from being negotiated each time to being a matter of routine.

The ultimate outcome of relationship marketing is the building of a unique company asset called a marketing network. A **marketing network** consists of the company and its supporting stakeholders (customers, employees, suppliers, distributors, retailers, ad agencies, university scientists, and others) with whom it has built mutually profitable business relationships. Increasingly, competition is not between companies but between marketing networks, with the prize going to the company that has built the better network. The operating principle is simple: Build an effective network of relationships with key stakeholders, and profits will follow.[12]

MARKETING CHANNELS   To reach a target market, the marketer uses three kinds of marketing channels. *Communication channels* deliver and receive messages from target buyers, and include newspapers, magazines, radio, television, mail, telephone, billboards, posters, fliers, CDs, audiotapes, and the Internet. Beyond these, communications are conveyed by facial expressions and clothing, the look of retail stores, and many other media. Marketers are increasingly adding dialogue channels (e-mail and toll-free numbers) to counterbalance the more normal monologue channels (such as ads).

The marketer uses *distribution channels* to display, sell, or deliver the physical product or service(s) to the buyer or user. They include distributors, wholesalers, retailers, and agents.

The marketer also uses *service channels* to carry out transactions with potential buyers. Service channels include warehouses, transportation companies, banks, and insurance companies that facilitate transactions. Marketers clearly face a design problem in choosing the best mix of communication, distribution, and service channels for their offerings.

SUPPLY CHAIN Whereas marketing channels connect the marketer to the target buyers, the **supply chain** describes a longer channel stretching from raw materials to components to final products that are carried to final buyers. The supply chain for women's purses starts with hides, and moves through tanning operations, cutting operations, manufacturing, and the marketing channels bringing products to customers. The supply chain represents a value delivery system. Each company captures only a certain percentage of the total value generated by the supply chain. When a company acquires competitors or moves upstream or downstream, its aim is to capture a higher percentage of supply chain value.

COMPETITION **Competition** includes all the actual and potential rival offerings and substitutes that a buyer might consider. Suppose an automobile company is planning to buy steel for its cars. Figure 1.4 shows several levels of competitors. The car manufacturer can buy steel from U.S. Steel or other integrated steel mills in the United States or abroad; or buy steel from a minimill such as Nucor at a cost savings; or buy aluminum for certain parts of the car to lighten the cars' weight; or buy engineered plastics for bumpers instead of steel. Clearly, U.S. Steel would be thinking too narrowly of competition if it thought only of other integrated steel companies. In fact, U.S. Steel is more likely to be hurt in the long run by substitute products than by its immediate steel company rivals. It must also consider whether to make substitute materials or stick only to those applications where steel offers superior performance.

We can broaden the picture further by distinguishing four levels of competition, based on the degree of product substitutability:

1. *Brand competition.* A company sees its competitors as other companies offering similar products and services to the same customers at similar prices. Volkswagen might see its major com-

figure **1.4**

U.S. Steel Radar Screen

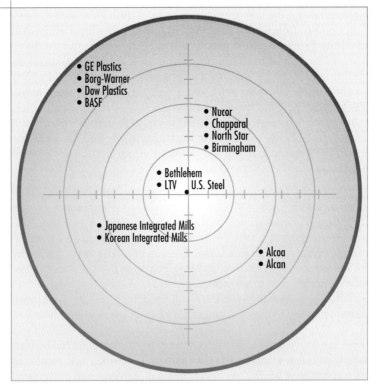

Source: Adrian V. Slywotzky, *Value Migration* (Boston: Harvard Business School Press, 1996), p. 99

petitors as Toyota, Honda, Renault, and other manufacturers of medium-priced automobiles. It would not see itself as competing with Mercedes or with Hyundai.

2. *Industry competition.* A company sees its competitors as all companies making the same product or class of products. Volkswagen would see itself as competing against all other automobile manufacturers.

3. *Form competition.* A company sees its competitors as all companies manufacturing products that supply the same service. Volkswagen would see itself competing against not only other automobile manufacturers, but also against manufacturers of motorcycles, bicycles, and trucks.

4. *Generic competition.* A company sees its competitors as all companies that compete for the same consumer dollars. Volkswagen would see itself competing with companies that sell major consumer durables, foreign vacations, and new homes.

MARKETING ENVIRONMENT   Competition represents only one force in the environment in which the marketer operates. The marketing environment consists of the task environment and the broad environment.

The **task environment** includes the immediate actors involved in producing, distributing, and promoting the offering. The main actors are the company, suppliers, distributors, dealers, and the target customers. Included in the supplier group are material suppliers and service suppliers such as marketing research agencies, advertising agencies, banking and insurance companies, transportation, and telecommunications companies. Included with distributors and dealers are agents, brokers, manufacturer representatives, and others who facilitate finding and selling to customers.

The **broad environment** consists of six components: demographic environment, economic environment, natural environment, technological environment, political-legal environment, and social-cultural environment. These environments contain forces that can have a major impact on the actors in the task environment. Market actors must pay close attention to the trends and developments in these environments and make timely adjustments to their marketing strategies. (See "Marketing for the New Economy: A Snapshot of a Country on the Move.")

MARKETING PROGRAM   The marketer's task is to build a marketing program or plan to achieve the company's desired objectives. The **marketing program** consists of numerous decisions on the mix of marketing tools to use. The **marketing mix** is the set of marketing tools the firm uses to pursue its marketing objectives in the target market.[13]

marketing for the **new economy**

A Snapshot of a Country on the Move

The 2000 U.S. census provides an in-depth look at the population swings, demographic groups, regional migrations, and changing family structure of 281,421,906 people. In addition to its great social and political significance, the census is also an invaluable marketing planning tool. Census marketer Claritas cross-references census figures with consumer surveys and its own grassroots research for clients such as Procter & Gamble Co., Dow Jones & Co., and Ford Motor Co. Partnering with "list houses" that provide customer phone and address information, Claritas can help firms select and purchase mailing lists with specific clusters.

Hyundai relies heavily on census data to develop targeted marketing that maximizes its advertising budget. Working with Claritas software, Hyundai is able to target areas of the country with the most promising customer makeup. For instance, the software enabled Hyundai to determine which zip codes across the country were likely to be interested in a test-drive offer mailing. Within weeks of the mailing, the number of test drives increased, as did sales. More important, the targeted marketing reduced Hyundai's cost per sale by half.

More companies than ever before are turning to the census for clues about consumers. Starbucks uses census data as part of the calculations for site selection for new stores. Blockbuster decides what types of movies and video games to stock in a particular store based on the results of the census. As statistical models and computer algorithms become more sophisticated, the U.S. census is likely to become an indispensable marketing tool.

Source: Amy Merrick, "Counting on the Census," *Wall Street Journal*, February 14, 2001, B1.

figure **1.5**

The Four P Components
of the Marketing Mix

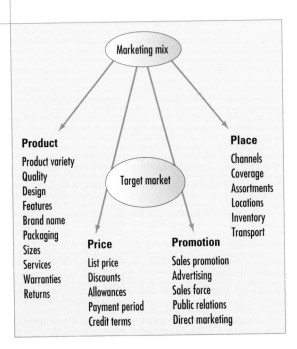

McCarthy classified these tools into four broad groups that he called the four Ps of marketing: product, price, place, and promotion.[14]

The particular marketing variables under each P are shown in Figure 1.5. Marketing-mix decisions must be made for influencing the trade channels as well as the final consumers. Figure 1.6 shows the company preparing an offering mix of products, services, and prices, and utilizing a promotion mix of sales promotion, advertising, sales force, public relations, direct mail, telemarketing, and Internet to reach the trade channels and the target customers.

The firm can change its price, sales force size, and advertising expenditures in the short run. It can develop new products and modify its distribution channels only in the

figure **1.6**

Marketing–Mix Strategy

Promotion mix

Offering mix		Sales promotion
Company	Products Services Prices	Advertising
		Sales force
		Public relations
		Direct mail, telemarketing, and Internet

Distribution channels → Target customers

long run. Thus the firm typically makes fewer period-to-period marketing-mix changes in the short run than the number of marketing-mix decision variables might suggest.

Note that the four Ps represent the sellers' view of the marketing tools available for influencing buyers. From a buyer's point of view, each marketing tool is designed to deliver a customer benefit. Robert Lauterborn suggested that the sellers' four Ps correspond to the customers' four Cs.[15]

Four Ps	**Four Cs**
Product	Customer solution
Price	Customer cost
Place	Convenience
Promotion	Communication

Winning companies will be those that can meet customer needs economically and conveniently and with effective communication.

company orientations toward the marketplace

We have defined *marketing management* as the conscious effort to achieve desired exchange outcomes with target markets, but what philosophy should guide a company's marketing efforts? What relative weights should be given to the interests of the organization, the customers, and society? Very often these interests conflict.

Dexter   One of Dexter Corporation's most popular products was a profitable grade of paper that prevented tea bags from disintegrating in hot water. Unfortunately, the materials used to produce the paper accounted for 98 percent of Dexter's annual hazardous wastes. Dexter assigned an employee task force representing the company's environmental, legal, R&D, and marketing departments to solve the problem. The task force succeeded, and the company increased its market share and virtually eliminated hazardous waste in the process.[16]

Clearly, marketing activities should be carried out under a well-thought-out philosophy of efficiency, effectiveness, and social responsibility. However, there are six competing concepts under which organizations conduct marketing activities: the production concept, product concept, selling concept, marketing concept, customer concept, and societal marketing concept.

the production concept

The production concept is one of the oldest concepts in business. The **production concept** holds that consumers will prefer products that are widely available and inexpensive. Managers of production-oriented businesses concentrate on achieving high production efficiency, low costs, and mass-distribution. They assume that consumers are primarily interested in product availability and low prices. This orientation makes sense in developing countries, where consumers are more interested in obtaining the product than in its features. It is also used when a company wants to expand the market.

Intel   In a 1965 edition of the journal *Electronics*, Intel cofounder Gordon Moore identified Moore's Law, which states that the density of transistors per square inch of a computer microprocessor doubles every 18 months. The more transistors contained by a chip, the more powerful the chip is. For Intel to stay on schedule with the Moore's Law cycle required investment in research and technology, as well as construction of new factories for each successive generation of microprocessor. Over the next 35 years, the company's computer chip production cycles obeyed Moore's Law. Production increased tremendously, prices came down, and Intel generated enormous profits as a result. By the mid-1990s, its processors could be found in more than 80 percent of the world's PCs.[17]

Some service organizations also operate on the production concept. Many medical and dental practices are organized on assembly-line principles, as are some government agencies (such as unemployment offices and license bureaus). Although this management orientation can handle many cases per hour, it is open to charges of impersonal and poor-quality service.

the product concept

Other businesses are guided by the **product concept**, which holds that consumers will favor those products that offer the most quality, performance, or innovative features. Managers in these organizations focus on making superior products and improving them over time. They assume that buyers admire well-made products and can evaluate quality and performance. However, these managers are sometimes caught up in a love affair with their products. Management might commit the "better-mousetrap" fallacy, believing that a better mousetrap will lead people to beat a path to its door. Such was the case when WebTV was launched during Christmas 1996 to disappointing results.

WebTV   It seemed like a couch potato's dream: A TV with a set-top box that allows you to surf the Web and watch TV. Yet, despite a $50-million promotional blitz by WebTV and partners Sony and Philips Electronics, only 50,000 subscribers signed up. Nothing was wrong with the product; the problem was the wrong marketing message. Couch potatoes want to be entertained, whereas computer users want to surf the Web and make use of multimedia, which the underpowered processor in the WebTV box had difficulty handling. A revamped campaign emphasized entertainment over education, and attracted over one million total subscribers by 2000. After the successful debut of digital video recorders that same year, Microsoft, now owner of WebTV, switched to a more interactive strategy. The company offered a new service, called UltimateTV, which combined satellite TV technology and a video recorder unit to provide interactive features for game shows, sports broadcasts, and advertising, as well as e-mail and Internet access.[18]

Product-oriented companies often trust that their engineers can design exceptional products. They get little or no customer input, and very often they will not even examine competitors' products. A General Motors executive said years ago: "How can the public know what kind of car they want until they see what is available?" GM's designers and engineers would design the new car. Then manufacturing would make it. The finance department would price it. Finally, marketing and sales would try to sell it. No wonder the car required such a hard sell! Today GM asks customers what they value in a car and includes marketing people in the very beginning stages of design.

The product concept can lead to what Theodore Levitt called "marketing myopia."[19] He pointed out that customers do not buy drill bits—they buy ways to make holes. Railroad management thought that travelers wanted trains and overlooked the growing competition for transportation from airlines, buses, trucks, and automobiles. Coca-Cola, focused on its soft-drink business, missed seeing the market for coffee bars and fresh-fruit juice bars that eventually impinged on its soft-drink business. McDonald's is in danger of overfocusing on its hamburger business while many diners are turning to sandwiches, pizza, tacos, and other fast foods. These organizations are looking into a mirror when they should be looking out of the window.

the selling concept

The selling concept is another common business orientation. The **selling concept** holds that consumers and businesses, if left alone, will ordinarily not buy enough of the organization's products. The organization must, therefore, undertake an aggressive selling and promotion effort. This concept assumes that consumers typically show buying inertia or resistance and must be coaxed into buying. It also assumes that the company has a whole battery of effective selling and promotion tools to stimulate more buying. The selling concept is epitomized by the thinking of Sergio Zyman, Coca-Cola's former vice president of marketing: The purpose of marketing is to sell more stuff to more people more often for more money in order to make more profit.[21]

The selling concept is practiced most aggressively with unsought goods, goods that buyers normally do not think of buying, such as insurance, encyclopedias, and funeral plots. These industries have perfected various sales techniques to locate prospects and hard sell them on their products' benefits. The selling concept is also practiced in the nonprofit area by fund-raisers, college admissions offices, and political parties.

A political party "sells" its candidate to voters. The candidate moves through voting precincts from early morning to late evening, shaking hands, kissing babies, meeting donors, and making speeches. Countless dollars are spent on radio and television advertising, posters, and mailings. The candidate's flaws are concealed from the public because the aim is to make the sale, not worry about postpurchase satisfaction. After the election, the new official continues to take a sales-oriented view. There is little research into what the public wants and a lot of selling to get the public to accept policies the politician and the party want.[21]

Most firms practice the selling concept when they have overcapacity. Their aim is to sell what they make rather than make what the market wants. In modern industrial economies, productive capacity has been built up to a point where most markets are buyer markets (the buyers are dominant) and sellers have to scramble for customers. Prospects are bombarded with TV commercials, newspaper ads, direct mail, and sales calls. At every turn, someone is trying to sell something. As a result, the public often identifies marketing with hard selling and advertising.

However, marketing based on hard selling carries high risks. It assumes that customers who are coaxed into buying a product will like it; and that if they do not, they will not bad-mouth it or complain to consumer organizations and will forget their disappointment and buy it again. These are indefensible assumptions. One study showed that dissatisfied customers may bad-mouth the product to 10 or more acquaintances; today bad news travels even faster and further with the Internet.[22]

the marketing concept

The marketing concept emerged in the mid-1950s and challenged the preceding concepts.[23] Instead of a product-centered, "make-and-sell" philosophy, we shift to a customer-centered, "sense-and-respond " philosophy. Instead of "hunting," marketing is "gardening." The job is not to find the right customers for your product, but the right products for your customers. As stated by the famed direct marketer Lester Wunderman, "The chant of the Industrial Revolution was that of the manufacturer who said, 'This is what I make, won't you please buy it.' The call of the Information Age is the consumer asking, 'This is what I want, won't you please make it.' "

The **marketing concept** holds that the key to achieving its organizational goals consists of the company being more effective than competitors in creating, delivering, and communicating superior customer value to its chosen target markets. It crystallized in the mid-1950s and has been expressed in many colorful ways:

- "Meeting needs profitably."
- "Find wants and fill them."
- "Love the customer, not the product."
- "Have it your way." (Burger King)
- "You're the boss." (United Airlines)
- "Putting people first." (British Airways)
- "Partners for profit." (Milliken & Company)

figure 1.7

Contrast Between the Sales
Concept and the
Marketing Concept

Theodore Levitt of Harvard drew a perceptive contrast between the selling and marketing concepts:

> Selling focuses on the needs of the seller; marketing on the needs of the buyer.
> Selling is preoccupied with the seller's need to convert his product into cash;
> marketing with the idea of satisfying the needs of the customer by means of the
> product and the whole cluster of things associated with creating, delivering
> and finally consuming it.[24]

The marketing concept rests on four pillars: target market, customer needs, integrated marketing, and profitability. They are illustrated in Figure 1.7, where they are contrasted with a selling orientation. The selling concept takes an inside-out perspective. It
starts with the factory, focuses on existing products, and calls for heavy selling and promoting to produce profitable sales. The marketing concept takes an outside-in perspective. It starts with a well-defined market, focuses on customer needs, coordinates all the
activities that will affect customers, and produces profits by satisfying customers.

TARGET MARKET   Companies do best when they choose their target market(s) carefully and prepare tailored marketing programs. Terra Lycos is an example.

> **Terra Lycos**   Madrid-based Terra Lycos became a top Internet service provider by
> aiming at the neglected Hispanic market segment. The company developed tailored
> marketing programs for the most prosperous one-fifth of Hispanics across eight dif-
> ferent markets. As one company executive said: "Our Brazilian product doesn't
> have anything to do with our Mexican product other than it's under the same
> brand. Our U.S. product is not targeted to Latin America—it's targeted to the U.S."
> After a $5-billion merger with Lycos in October 2000, Terra Lycos's stated mission
> was "to hold the number one or two position in each of the markets in which it
> operates by delivering services in a highly targeted, localized manner."[25]

CUSTOMER NEEDS   A company can define its target market but fail to correctly
understand the customers' needs. Consider the following example:

> A major chemical company invented a new substance that hardened into a
> marble-like material. Looking for an application, the marketing department
> decided to target the bathtub market. The company created a few model bath-

tubs and exhibited them at a trade show. It hoped to convince manufacturers to produce bathtubs with the new material. Although bathtub manufacturers thought the tubs were attractive, none signed up. The reason soon became obvious. The bathtub would have to be priced at $2,000, whereas most bathtubs sold in the $500 range. For the higher price, consumers could buy tubs made out of real marble or onyx. In addition, the bathtubs were so heavy that home-owners would have to reinforce their floors.

Understanding customer needs and wants is not always simple. Some customers have needs of which they are not fully conscious, or they cannot articulate these needs, or they use words that require some interpretation. What does it mean when the customer asks for an "inexpensive" car, a "powerful" lawnmower, a "fast" lathe, an "attractive" bathing suit, or a "restful" hotel?

Consider the customer who says he wants an inexpensive car. The marketer must probe further. We can distinguish among five types of needs:

1. Stated needs (the customer wants an inexpensive car)
2. Real needs (the customer wants a car whose operating cost, not its initial price, is low)
3. Unstated needs (the customer expects good service from the dealer)
4. Delight needs (the customer would like the dealer to include an onboard navigation system)
5. Secret needs (the customer wants to be seen by friends as a savvy consumer)

Even the idea of meeting or responding to people's needs is too limited a view of a company's role in the marketplace. Many consumers do not know what they want in a product. Consumers did not know much about cellular phones when they were first introduced. Nokia and Ericsson fought to shape consumer perceptions of cellular phones. Consumers were in a learning mode and companies forged strategies to shape their wants. As stated by Carpenter, "Simply giving customers what they want isn't enough any more—to gain an edge companies must help customers learn what they want."[26]

Responding only to the stated need may shortchange the customer. Consider a woman who enters a hardware store and asks for a sealant to seal glass window panes. This customer is stating a solution, not a need. The salesperson might suggest that tape would provide a better solution. The customer may appreciate that the salesperson met her need, not her stated solution.

A distinction needs to be drawn between responsive marketing, anticipative marketing, and creative marketing. A *responsive* marketer finds a stated need and fills it. An *anticipative* marketer looks ahead into what needs customers may have in the near future. A *creative* marketer discovers and produces solutions customers did not ask for but to which they enthusiastically respond. Hamel and Prahalad believe that companies must go beyond just asking consumers what they want:

> Customers are notoriously lacking in foresight. Ten or 15 years ago, how many of us were asking for cellular telephones, fax machines, and copiers at home, 24-hour discount brokerage accounts, multivalve automobile engines, compact disc players, cars with on-board navigation systems, hand-held global satellite positioning receivers, automated teller machines, MTB, or the Home Shopping Network?[27]

Sony exemplifies creative marketing in its introduction of many successful new products that customers never asked for or even thought were possible: Walkmans, VCRs, videocameras, CDs. Sony is a *market-driving firm*, not just a *market-driven firm*. Akio Morita, its founder, once proclaimed that Sony doesn't serve markets; Sony creates markets.[28] The Walkman is a classic example: In the late 1970s Akio Morita was working on a pet project that would revolutionize the way people listened to music: a portable cassette player he called the Walkman. Engineers at the company insisted there was little demand for such a product, but Morita refused to part with his vision. By the twentieth anniversary of the Walkman, Sony had sold over 250 million in nearly 100 different models.[29]

In the past, "responding to customer needs" meant studying customer needs and making a product that fit these needs on the average, but some of today's companies instead respond to each customer's *individual* need. Dell Computer does not prepare a perfect computer for its target market. Rather, it provides product platforms on which each customer customizes the features he or she desires in the computer. This is a change from a "make-and-sell" philosophy to a philosophy of "sense and respond." Ford too has recently changed its priorities.

Ford   The cover of Ford's 1999 annual report is titled "Connecting with Customers" to reflect the heightened priority that Ford was placing on becoming a customer-driven company. The report noted: "A customer-driven company must be relentless in its focus. It must listen to customers, find ways to fill their needs, and continually seek feedback on how well it is satisfying those needs." Ford expresses its intent as to have customers who "trust our company, love our brands, and delight in our services." To achieve this goal, Ford employs management techniques such as Consumer-Driven Six Sigma. Sigma is the Greek symbol used to represent one standard deviation. The goal of Consumer-Driven Six Sigma is to achieve a value of six sigma, which corresponds to only 3.4 defects per million. Although Ford experienced several setbacks with product recalls and a highly publicized split with long-time tire supplier Firestone in 2001, company management vowed that a strong customer focus would still be the key to turning the company's fortunes around.[30]

Why is it supremely important to satisfy target customers? Because a company's sales each period come from two groups: new customers and repeat customers. One estimate is that attracting a new customer can cost five times as much as pleasing an existing one.[31] Also, it might cost 16 times as much to bring the new customer to the same level of profitability as the lost customer. Customer retention is thus more important than customer attraction.

Although the company must focus on its present customers, it can learn a great deal from its noncustomers in its target market. Why are they buying competitors' products? What is their image of this company? Many new ideas can be garnered in this way.

INTEGRATED MARKETING   When all the company's departments work together to serve the customer's interests, the result is **integrated marketing**. Unfortunately, not all employees are trained and motivated to work for the customer. An engineer once complained that the salespeople are "always protecting the customer and not thinking of the company's interest"! He went on to blast customers for "asking for too much." The following example highlights the coordination problem:

> The marketing vice president of a major European airline wants to increase the airline's traffic share. His strategy is to build up customer satisfaction through providing better food, cleaner cabins, better-trained cabin crews, and lower fares; yet he has no authority in these matters. The catering department chooses food that keeps down food costs; the maintenance department uses cleaning services that keep down cleaning costs; the human resources department hires people without regard to whether they are naturally friendly; the finance department sets the fares. Because these departments generally take a cost or production point of view, the vice president of marketing is stymied in creating an integrated marketing mix.

Integrated marketing takes place on two levels. First, the various marketing functions—sales force, advertising, customer service, product management, marketing research—must work together. Too often the sales force thinks product managers set prices or sale quotas "too high"; or the advertising director and a brand manager cannot agree on an advertising campaign. All these marketing functions must be coordinated from the customer's point of view.

figure **1.8**   Traditional Organization Chart Versus Modern Customer–Oriented Company Organization Chart

Second, marketing must be embraced by the other departments; they must also "think customer." According to David Packard of Hewlett-Packard: "Marketing is far too important to be left only to the marketing department!" Marketing is not a department so much as a company orientation. Xerox goes so far as to include in every job description an explanation of how that job affects the customer. Xerox factory managers know that visits to the factory can help sell a potential customer if the factory is clean and efficient. Xerox accountants know that customer attitudes are affected by Xerox's billing accuracy and promptness in returning calls.

To foster teamwork among all departments, the company carries out internal marketing as well as external marketing. **External marketing** is marketing directed at people outside the company. **Internal marketing** is the task of hiring, training, and motivating able employees who want to serve customers well. In fact, internal marketing must precede external marketing. It makes no sense to promise excellent service before the company's staff is ready to provide it.

Managers who believe the customer is the company's only true "profit center" consider the traditional organization chart in Figure 1.8(a)—a pyramid with the president at the top, management in the middle, and front-line people and customers at the bottom—obsolete. Master marketing companies invert the chart, as shown in Figure 1.8(b). At the top are the customers; next in importance are the front-line people who meet, serve, and satisfy the customers; under them are the middle managers, whose job is to support the front-line people so they can serve the customers well; and at the base is top management, whose job is to hire and support good middle managers. We have added customers along the sides of Figure 1.8(b) to indicate that all the company's managers must be personally involved in knowing, meeting, and serving customers.

PROFITABILITY   The ultimate purpose of the marketing concept is to help organizations achieve their objectives. In the case of private firms, the major objective is long-run profitability; in the case of nonprofit and public organizations, it is surviving and attracting enough funds to perform useful work. Private firms should not aim for profits as such, but rather to achieve profits as a consequence of creating superior customer value. A company makes money by satisfying customer needs better than its competitors. Consider Frank Perdue's philosophy.

Perdue Chicken Farms   Perdue Farms is America's third largest chicken producer, with margins substantially above the industry average. Market shares in its major markets reach 50 percent, and the product is chicken—a commodity if there ever was one! Yet its colorful founder, Frank Perdue, does not believe that "a chicken is a chicken is a chicken," nor do his customers. The company has always aimed to produce chickens for which discriminating customers will pay a premium price. Perdue raises its chickens on a chemical-free diet to produce quality birds with distinct characteristics. Ads featuring Frank Perdue and the tag line "It takes a tough man to make a tender chicken" were the company's signature line from 1971 until 1995. When Frank Perdue stepped down, a new advertising campaign introduced his son Jim to the country. "After three generations, the Perdues know more about breeding chickens than chickens do," says one of the ads. Under new leadership, the privately held company has continued to prosper. Perdue currently ships 50 million pounds of chicken every week to more than 50 countries across the globe.[32]

Only a handful of companies stand out as master marketers: Procter & Gamble, Kraft, Southwest Airlines, Home Depot, Disney, Nordstrom, Wal-Mart, Milliken & Company, McDonald's, Marriott Hotels, American Airlines, and several Japanese (Sony, Toyota, Canon) and European companies (IKEA, Club Med, Bang & Olufsen, Electrolux, Nokia, ABB, Lego, Tesco). These companies focus on the customer and are organized to respond effectively to changing customer needs. They all have well-staffed marketing departments, and all their other departments—manufacturing, finance, research and development, personnel, purchasing—also accept the concept that the customer is king.

Several scholars have found that companies who embrace the marketing concept achieve superior performance.[33] This was first demonstrated for companies practicing a *reactive market orientation*—understanding and meeting customers' expressed needs; but some critics say this means that companies develop only low-level innovations. Narver and his colleagues argue that high-level innovation is possible if the focus is on customers' latent needs. He calls this a *proactive marketing orientation*.[34] Companies such as 3M, HP, and Motorola have made a practice of researching or imagining latent needs through a "probe-and-learn" process. Companies that practice both a reactive and proactive marketing orientation are implementing a *total market orientation* and are likely to be the most successful.

However, most companies do not embrace the marketing concept until driven to it by circumstances. Various developments prod them to take the marketing concept to heart:

- *Sales decline:* When sales fall, companies panic and look for answers. Today, newspapers are experiencing declining circulation as more people rely on radio, TV, and the Internet for their news. Some publishers now realize that they know little about why people read newspapers. These publishers are commissioning consumer research and attempting to redesign newspapers to be contemporary, relevant, and interesting to readers. They have also set up Web pages.
- *Slow growth:* Slow sales growth leads some companies to search for new markets. They realize they need marketing skills to identify and select new opportunities. Wanting new sources of revenue, Dow Chemical entered consumer markets and invested heavily to acquire consumer marketing expertise to perform well in these markets.
- *Changing buying patterns:* Many companies operate in markets characterized by rapidly changing customer wants. These companies need more marketing know-how if they are to track buyers' changing values.

- *Increasing competition:* Complacent companies may suddenly be attacked by powerful competitors. AT&T was a regulated, marketing-naive telephone company until the 1970s, when the government began allowing other companies to sell telecommunications equipment. AT&T hired the best marketers it could find to help it compete. Companies in deregulated industries all find it necessary to build up marketing expertise.[35]
- *Increasing marketing expenditures:* Companies may find that their expenditures for advertising, sales promotion, marketing research, and customer service are yielding poor results. Management then decides it is time to undertake a serious marketing audit to improve its marketing.[36]

In the course of converting to a marketing orientation, a company faces three hurdles: organized resistance, slow learning, and fast forgetting. Some company departments (often manufacturing, finance, and R&D) believe a stronger marketing function threatens their power in the organization. The nature of the threat is illustrated in Figure 1.9(a) through (e). Initially, the marketing function is seen as one of several equally important functions in a check-and-balance relationship. Lack of demand leads marketers to argue that their function is more important. A few enthusiasts go further and say marketing is the major function of the enterprise, for without customers there would be no company. Enlightened marketers clarify the issue by putting the customer rather than marketing at the center of the company. They argue for a customer orientation in which all functions work together to respond to, serve, and satisfy the customer. Some marketers say that marketing still needs to command a central position if customers' needs are to be correctly interpreted and efficiently satisfied.[37] (See "Marketing Memo: Reasons to Embrace the Marketing Concept.")

Resistance is especially strong in industries where marketing is being introduced for the first time—for instance, in law offices, colleges, deregulated industries, and government agencies; but in spite of resistance, many companies manage to introduce some marketing thinking into their organization. The company president establishes a marketing department; marketing talent is hired; key managers attend marketing seminars; the marketing budget is substantially increased; marketing planning and control systems are introduced. Even with these steps, however, learning comes slowly.

Once marketing has been installed, management must fight a tendency to forget basic principles, especially in the wake of success. For example, look at what happened to Intel.

Intel   In June 1994, technicians at Intel discovered a flaw in the newest line of Pentium chips. The problems surfaced only rarely, and Intel management chose to keep knowledge of the flaw from the public. Eventually, the story broke in the national press, and Pentium owners expressed concern. Intel proposed selective replacement to those who had experienced the problem, and the result was a PR nightmare. By December, Intel was offering replacements to all customers who asked for them. Andy Grove referred to the company's handling of the problem as his "biggest mistake"; by not immediately offering replacements, Intel "basically defied [its] consumer population." But despite the negative media attention and the dissatisfied customer responses, Intel managed to avert a major crisis in terms of lost customers and damaged brand image by spending $475 million on replacement chips, issuing a reassuring document to the press explaining the problem, and hiring hundreds of customer service people to handle questions and complaints.

Companies face a particularly difficult task in adapting ad slogans to international markets. Perdue's slogan—"It takes a tough man to make a tender chicken"—was rendered into Spanish as "It takes a sexually excited man to make a chick affectionate." Even when the language is the same, words carry different meanings: Electrolux's British ad line for its vacuum cleaners—"Nothing sucks like an Electrolux"—would certainly not lure customers in the United States![38]

figure **1.9**

Evolving Views of Marketing's Role in the Company

(a) Marketing as an equal function

(b) Marketing as a more important function

(c) Marketing as the major function

(d) The customer as the controlling function

(e) The customer as the controlling function and marketing as the integrative function

the customer concept

Today many companies are moving beyond the marketing concept to the customer concept. The **customer concept** is illustrated in Figure 1.10.

Whereas companies practicing the marketing concept work at the level of customer segments, a growing number of today's companies are now shaping separate offers, services, and messages to individual customers. These companies collect information on each customer's past transactions, demographics, psychographics, and media and distribution preferences. They hope to achieve profitable growth through capturing a larger share of each customer's expenditures by building high customer loyalty and focusing on customer lifetime value.

The ability of a company to deal with customers one at a time has become practical as a result of advances in factory customization, computers, the Internet, and database marketing software. Yet the practicing of a one-to-one marketing is not for every company: The required investment in information collection, hardware, and software may exceed the payout. It works best for companies that normally collect a great deal of individual customer information, carry a lot of products that can be cross-sold, carry products that need periodic replacement or upgrading, and sell products of high value.

the societal marketing concept

Some have questioned whether the marketing concept is an appropriate philosophy in an age of environmental deterioration, resource shortages, explosive population growth, world hunger and poverty, and neglected social services. Are companies that do an excellent job of satisfying consumer wants necessarily acting in the best long-run interests of consumers and society? The marketing concept sidesteps the potential conflicts among consumer wants, consumer interests, and long-run societal welfare.

Consider the following criticism:

> The fast-food hamburger industry offers tasty but unhealthy food. The hamburgers have a high fat content, and the restaurants promote fries and pies, two products high in starch and fat. The products are wrapped in convenient packaging, which leads to much waste. In satisfying consumer wants, these restaurants may be hurting consumer health and causing environmental problems.

Situations like this one call for a new term that enlarges the marketing concept. Among those suggested are "humanistic marketing" and "ecological marketing." We propose calling it the societal marketing concept. The **societal marketing concept** holds that the organization's task is to determine the needs, wants, and interests of target mar-

---

figure **1.10**

The Customer Concept

Starting point	Focus	Means	Ends
Individual customer	Customer needs and values	One-to-one marketing integration and value chain	Profitable growth through capturing customer share, loyalty, and lifetime value

kets and to deliver the desired satisfactions more effectively and efficiently than competitors in a way that preserves or enhances the consumer's and the society's well-being.

The societal marketing concept calls upon marketers to build social and ethical considerations into their marketing practices. They must balance and juggle the often conflicting criteria of company profits, consumer want satisfaction, and public interest. Yet a number of companies—including the Body Shop, Ben & Jerry's, and Patagonia—have achieved notable sales and profit gains by adopting and practicing the societal marketing concept. Consider Patagonia.[39]

Patagonia   Patagonia world-class climber Yvon Chouinard founded Patagonia in 1966 by selling rock climbing hardware from the trunk of his car. By the time the company changed its focus to selling soft goods and apparel in the mid-1970s, Patagonia was committed to two main goals: provid[ing] the highest quality gear for outdoor enthusiasts, and "implement[ing] solutions to the environmental crisis." The company gave an "earth tax" of one percent of sales or ten percent of pre-tax profits (whichever is greater) to "activists who take radical and strategic steps to protect habitat, wilderness, and biodiversity." However, as Patagonia expanded, many aspects of its operations contributed to the environmental pollution the company worked so hard to counter. After an internal study in the early 1990s, the company sought to use materials and fabrics that would minimize its impact on the environment, such as Synchilla fleece made from recycled plastic bottles and the 100 percent organic cotton used in every cotton product. The corporate culture avidly supports activism, as evidenced by a company program through which employees receive pay to work up to two months in an environmental organization. Patagonia sent 70 of its 900 employees abroad on such trips in 1999.[40]

Patagonia is practicing a form of the societal marketing concept called **cause-related marketing**. Pringle and Thompson define this as activity by which a company with an image, product, or service to market builds a relationship or partnership with a "cause," or a number of "causes," for mutual benefit."[41]

Companies see cause-related marketing as an opportunity to enhance their corporate reputation, raise brand awareness, increase customer loyalty, build sales, and increase press coverage. They believe that customers will increasingly look for signs of good corporate citizenship that go beyond supplying rational and emotional benefits.

how business and marketing are changing

We can say with some confidence that "the marketplace isn't what it used to be." It is changing radically as a result of major societal forces such as technological advances, globalization, and deregulation. These major forces have created new behaviors and challenges:

- *Customers* increasingly expect higher quality and service and some customization. They perceive fewer real product differences and show less brand loyalty. They can obtain extensive product information from the Internet and other sources, which permits them to shop more intelligently. They are showing greater price sensitivity in their search for value.
- *Brand manufacturers* are facing intense competition from domestic and foreign brands, which is resulting in rising promotion costs and shrinking profit margins. They are being further buffeted by powerful retailers who command limited shelf space and are putting out their own store brands in competition with national brands.
- *Store-based retailers* are suffering. Small retailers are succumbing to the growing power of giant retailers and "category killers." Store-based retailers are facing growing competition from catalog houses; direct-mail firms; newspaper, magazine, and TV direct-to-customer ads; home shopping TV; and e-commerce on the Internet. As a result, they are experiencing shrinking margins. In response, entrepreneurial retailers are building entertainment into stores with coffee bars, lectures, demonstrations, and performances. They are marketing an "experience" rather than a product assortment.

company responses and adjustments

Companies are doing a lot of soul-searching, and many highly respected companies are changing in a number of ways. Here are some current trends:

- *Reengineering:* From focusing on functional departments to reorganizing by key processes, each managed by a multidiscipline team.
- *Outsourcing:* From making everything inside the company to buying more goods and services from outside if they are cheaper and better. More companies are preferring to own brands rather than physical assets; they are decapitalizing. A few companies are moving toward outsourcing everything, making them virtual companies owning very few assets and, therefore, earning extraordinary rates of return.
- *E-commerce:* From attracting customers to stores and having salespeople call on offices to making virtually all products available on the Internet. Consumers can access pictures of products, read the specs, shop among on-line vendors for the best prices and terms, and click to order and pay. Business-to-business purchasing is growing fast on the Internet. Personal selling can increasingly be conducted electronically, with buyer and seller seeing each other on their computer screens in real time.
- *Benchmarking:* From relying on self-improvement to studying "world-class performers" and adopting "best practices."
- *Alliances:* From trying to win alone to forming networks of partner firms.
- *Partner-suppliers:* From using many suppliers to using fewer but more reliable suppliers who work closely in a "partnership" relationship with the company.
- *Market-centered:* From organizing by products to organizing by market segment.
- *Global and local:* From being local to being both global and local, called "glocal."
- *Decentralized:* From being managed from the top to encouraging more initiative and "intrepreneurship" at the local level.

marketer responses and adjustments

Marketers also are rethinking their philosophies, concepts, and tools. Here are the major marketing themes in the new economy:

- *Customer relationship marketing:* From focusing on transactions to building long-term, profitable customer relationships. Companies focus on their most profitable customers, products, and channels.
- *Customer lifetime value:* From making a profit on each sale to making profits by managing lifetime sales. Some companies offer to deliver a constantly needed product on a regular basis at a lower price per unit because they will capture the customer's business for a longer period.
- *Customer share:* From a focus on gaining market share to a focus on building customer share. A bank aims to increase its share of the customer's wallet; the supermarket aims to capture a larger share of the customer's "stomach." Companies build customer share by offering a larger variety of goods to existing customers. They train their employees in cross-selling and up-selling.
- *Target marketing:* From selling to everyone to trying to be the best firm serving well-defined target markets. Target marketing is being facilitated by the proliferation of special-interest magazines, TV channels, and Internet newsgroups.
- *Customization:* From selling the same offer in the same way to everyone in the target market to individualizing and customizing messages and offerings.
- *Customer database:* From collecting sales data to building a rich data warehouse of information about individual customers' purchases, preferences, and demographics, and profitability. Companies can then apply datamining techniques to discover new segments and trends hidden in the data.
- *Integrated marketing communications:* From heavy reliance on one communication tool such as advertising or sales force to blending several tools to deliver a consistent brand image to customers at every brand contact.
- *Channels as partners:* From thinking of intermediaries as customers to treating them as partners in delivering value to final customers.

- *Every employee a marketer:* From thinking that marketing is done only by marketing, sales, and customer support personnel to recognizing that every employee must be customer-focused.
- *Model-based decision making:* From basing decisions on intuition or slim data to basing decisions on models and facts on how the marketplace works.

These major themes will be examined throughout this book to help marketers and companies sail safely through the rough but promising waters ahead. Successful companies will be those who can keep their marketing changing with the changes in their marketplace—and marketspace.

summary

1. Businesses today face three major challenges and opportunities: globalization, the effects of advances in technology, and deregulation.

2. Marketing is typically seen as the task of creating, promoting, and delivering goods and services to consumers and businesses. Effective marketing can take many forms: It can be entrepreneurial, formulated, or intrepreneurial; and marketers are involved in marketing many types of entities: goods, services, experiences, events, persons, places, properties, organizations, information, and ideas.

3. Marketers are skilled at managing demand: They seek to influence the level, timing, and composition of demand. To do this, they face a host of decisions, from major ones such as what features a new product should have to minor ones such as the color of packaging. They also operate in four different marketplaces: consumer, business, global, and nonprofit.

4. For each chosen target market, a firm develops a market offering that is positioned in the minds of buyers as delivering some central benefits. Marketers must try to understand the target market's needs, wants, and demands: A product or offering will be successful if it delivers value and satisfaction to the target buyer. The term *markets* covers various groupings of customers. Today there are both physical marketplaces and digital marketspaces, as well as megamarkets.

5. Exchange involves obtaining a desired product from someone by offering something in return. A transaction is a trade of values between two or more parties: It involves at least two things of value, agreed-upon conditions, a time of agreement, and a place of agreement. In the most generic sense, marketers seek to elicit a behavioral response from another party: a purchase, a vote, active membership, adoption of a cause.

6. Relationship marketing has the aim of building long-term, mutually satisfying relations with key parties—customers, suppliers, and distributors—in order to earn and retain their long-term preference and business. The ultimate outcome of relationship marketing is the building of a unique company asset called a marketing network.

7. Marketers reach their markets through various channels—communication, distribution, and selling. Marketers operate in a task environment and a broad environment. They face competition from actual and potential rival offerings and substitutes. The set of tools marketers use to elicit the desired responses from their target markets is called the marketing mix.

8. There are six competing concepts under which organizations can choose to conduct their business: the production concept, product concept, selling concept, marketing concept, customer concept, and societal marketing concept. The first three are of limited use today. The marketing concept holds that the key to achieving organizational goals consists of determining the needs and wants of target markets and delivering the desired satisfactions more effectively and efficiently than competitors. It starts with a well-defined market, focuses on customer needs, coordinates all the activities that will affect customers, and produces profits by satisfying customers. The customer concept addresses the individual needs of specific customers and aims to build customer loyalty and lifetime value.

9. The societal marketing concept holds that the organization's task is to determine the needs, wants, and interests of target markets and to deliver the desired satisfactions more effectively and efficiently than competitors, in a way that preserves or enhances the consumer's and the society's well-being. The concept calls upon marketers to balance three considerations: company profits, consumer want satisfaction, and the public interest.

applications

marketing debate – does marketing create or satisfy needs?

Marketing has often been defined in terms of satisfying customers' needs and wants. Critics, however, maintain that marketing does much more than that and creates needs and wants that did not exist before. According to these critics, marketers encourage consumers to spend more money than they should on goods and services they really do not need.

Take a position: Marketing shapes consumer needs and wants versus Marketing merely reflects the needs and wants of consumers.

marketing and advertising

1. The T. K. Maxx ad shown in Figure 1 stresses the money-saving aspect of shopping for brand-name merchandise at the chain's stores in the United Kingdom. T. K. Maxx in the United States, operated by the same corporate parent, also attracts shoppers by promoting low prices on well-known brands.

    a. How is the combination of brand-name products at low prices likely to affect the customers' perceptions of value at T. K. Maxx?

    b. What else is T. K. Maxx stressing in its advertising to affect customers' perceptions of value?

    c. How might T. K. Maxx use the other aspects of its four Ps (product, place, price, promotion) to enhance customers' perceptions of the value of its total offer?

2. Canada-based Nexen focuses on exploration and production of natural gas and crude oil in locations around the world. Its success depends on a complex network of customers, employees, suppliers, distributors, investors, and other stakeholders. Yet the ad shown in Figure 2 focuses on Nexen's commitment to social responsibility.

    a. Why would Nexen advertise its socially responsible activities in a business magazine?

    b. What effect does the company expect this ad to have on its relationships with various stakeholders?

    c. How can Nexen build on strong stakeholder relationships to compete more effectively in the energy industry?

Figure 1

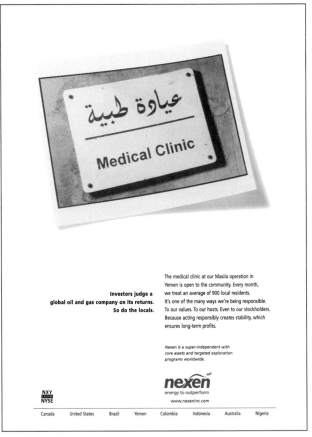

Figure 2

online marketing today

Tesco, the largest supermarket chain in Great Britain, is also the world's most successful online grocery retailer. Tesco rings up $32 billion in annual sales through 900 stores in the United Kingdom, Eastern Europe, and Southeast Asia, and through its profitable Tesco.com Web site *www.tesco.com*, which processes 70,000 orders every week. From appliances to apples, garbage bags to gifts, Tesco.com will deliver whatever its one million customers order, adding a per-order fee of $7. Tesco is now bringing its proven online system to the United States through a partnership with the Safeway chain and Dallas-based GroceryWorks.com.[a] Visit both sites to see what they offer. What benefits might customers perceive in ordering groceries from Texco.com or GroceryWorks.com? What costs might customers perceive? How might the value equation differ for a customer shopping in a local Safeway store?

Source: ᵃGregory Katz, "British Grocer Tesco Tries to Succeed Where Others Have Failed," *Dallas Morning News,* August 2, 2001, *www.dallasnews.com.*

notes

1. Sam Hill and Glenn Rifkin, *Radical Marketing* (New York: HarperBusiness, 1999).

2. Jay Conrad Levinson and Seth Godin, *The Guerrilla Marketing Handbook* (Boston: Houghton Mifflin, 1994).

3. Philip Kotler, "Dream Vacations: The Booming Market for Designed Experiences," *The Futurist* (October 1984): 7–13; B. Joseph Pine II and James Gilmore, *The Experience Economy* (Boston: Harvard Business School Press, 1999); and Bernd Schmitt, *Experience Marketing* (New York: Free Press, 1999).

4. Irving J. Rein, Philip Kotler, and Martin Stoller, *High Visibility* (Chicago: NTC Publishers, 1998).

5. Philip Kotler, Irving J. Rein, and Donald Haider, *Marketing Places: Attracting Investment, Industry, and Tourism to Cities, States, and Nations* (New York: Free Press, 1993); and *Marketing Places Europe* (London: Financial Times Prentice-Hall, 1999).

6. Carl Shapiro and Hal R. Varian, "Versioning: The Smart Way to Sell Information," *Harvard Business Review* (November–December 1998): 106–14.

7. Peter Drucker, *Management: Tasks, Responsibilities, Practices* (New York: Harper and Row, 1973), pp. 64–65.

8. *Dictionary of Marketing Terms*, 2nd ed., ed. Peter D. Bennett (Chicago: American Marketing Association, 1995).

9. Jeffrey Rayport and John Sviokla, "Managing in the Marketspace," *Harvard Business Review* (November–December 1994): 141–50. Also see their "Exploring the Virtual Value Chain," *Harvard Business Review* (November–December 1995): pp. 75–85.

10. Mohan Sawhney, *Seven Steps to Nirvana* (New York: McGraw-Hill, 2001).

11. Evert Gummesson, *Total Relationship Marketing* (Boston: Butterworth-Heinemann, 1999); Regis McKenna, *Relationship Marketing* (Reading, MA: Addison-Wesley, 1991); Martin Christopher, Adrian Payne, and David Ballantyne, *Relationship Marketing: Bringing Quality, Customer Service, and Marketing Together* (Oxford, U.K: Butterworth-Heinemann, 1991).

12. James C. Anderson, Hakan Hakansson, and Jan Johanson, "Dyadic Business Relationships within a Business Network Context," *Journal of Marketing* (October 15, 1994): 1–15.

13. Neil H. Borden, "The Concept of the Marketing Mix," *Journal of Advertising Research* 4 (June): 2–7. For another framework, see George S. Day, "The Capabilities of Market-Driven Organizations," *Journal of Marketing* 58, no. 4 (October 1994): 37–52.

14. E. Jerome McCarthy, *Basic Marketing: A Managerial Approach,* 12th ed. (Homewood, IL: Irwin, 1996). Two alternative classifications are worth noting. Frey proposed that all marketing decision variables could be categorized into two factors: the offering (product, packaging, brand, price, and service) and methods and tools (distribution channels, personal selling, advertising, sales promotion, and publicity). See Albert W. Frey, *Advertising,* 3rd ed. (New York: Ronald Press, 1961), p. 30. Lazer and Kelly proposed a three-factor classification: goods and services mix, distribution mix, and communications mix. See William Lazer and Eugene J. Kelly, *Managerial Marketing: Perspectives and Viewpoints,* rev. ed. (Homewood, IL: Irwin, 1962), p. 413.

15. Robert Lauterborn, "New Marketing Litany: 4P's Passe; C-Words Take Over," *Advertising Age,* October 1, 1990, p. 26.

16. Kathleen Dechant and Barbara Altman, "Environmental Leadership: From Compliance to Competitive Advantage," *Academy of Management Executive* 8, no. 3 (1994): 7–19. Also see Gregory R. Elliott, "The Marketing Concept—Necessary, but Sufficient?: An Environmental View," *European Journal of Marketing* 24, no. 8 (1990): 20–30 see also Ajay Menon and Anil Menon, "Enviropreneurial Marketing Strategy: The Emergence of Corporate Environmentalism as Marketing Strategy," *Journal of Marketing* 61, no. 1 (January 1997): 51–67.

17. David Kirkpatrick, "Intel's Amazing Profit Machine," *Fortune,* February 17, 1997, pp. 60–63.

18. Paul C. Judge, "Are Tech Buyers Different?" *BusinessWeek,* January 26, 1998, pp. 64–65, 68; B. G. Yovovich, "Webbed Feat," *Marketing News,* January 19, 1998, pp. 1, 18.

19. Theodore Levitt's classic article, "Marketing Myopia," *Harvard Business Review* (July–August 1960): 45–56.

20. Sergio Zyman, *The End of Marketing as We Know It* (New York: Harper Business, 1999).

21. Bruce I. Newman, ed., *Handbook of Political Marketing* (Thousand Oaks, CA: Sage Publications, 1999); and Bruce I. Newman, *The Mass Marketing of Politics* (Thousand Oaks, CA: Sage Publications, 1999).

22. Karl Albrecht and Ron Zemke, *Service America!* (Homewood, IL: Dow Jones-Irwin, 1985), pp. 6–7.

23. John B. McKitterick, "What Is the Marketing Management Concept?" In *The Frontiers of Marketing Thought and Action* (Chicago: American Marketing Association, 1957), pp. 71–82; Fred J. Borch, "The Marketing Philosophy as a Way of Business Life," *The Marketing Concept: Its Meaning to Management* (Marketing series, no. 99) (New York: American Management Association, 1957), pp. 3–5; Robert J. Keith, "The Marketing Revolution," *Journal of Marketing* (January 1960): 35–38.

24. Levitt, "Marketing Myopia," p. 50.

25. David J. Lynch, "Net Company Terra Aims for Hispanic Connection," *USA Today,* January 20, 2000, p. B1–2.

26. Private conversation with Carpenter.

27. Gary Hamel and C. K. Prahalad, *Competing for the Future* (Boston: Harvard Business School Press, 1994).

28. Akio Morita, *Made in Japan* (New York: Dutton, 1986), ch. 1.

29. Jonathan Glancey, "The Private World of the Walkman," *The Guardian*, October 11, 1999.

30. Joann Muller, "Ford: Why It's Worse Than You Think," *Business Week*, June 25, 2001; Ford *1999 Annual Report*; Greg Keenan, "Six Degrees of Perfection." *The Globe and Mail*, December 20, 2000.

31. Patricia Sellers, "Getting Customers to Love You," *Fortune*, March 13, 1989, pp. 38–49.

32. Christopher Thorne, "Q&A: Jim Perdue Faces Challenges to Chicken Empire," *AP Newswire*, March 11, 2001.

33. Ajay K. Kohli and Bernard J. Jaworski, "Market Orientation: The Construct, Research Propositions, and Managerial Implications," *Journal of Marketing (*April 1990): pp. 1–18; John C. Narver and Stanley F. Slater, "The Effect of a Market Orientation on Business Profitability," *Journal of Marketing* (October 1990): pp. 20–35; Stanley F. Slater and John C. Narver, "Market Orientation, Customer Value, and Superior Performance," *Business Horizons,* March–April 1994, 22–28; A. Pelham and D. Wilson, "A Longitudinal Study of the Impact of Market Structure, Firm Structure, Strategy and Market Orientation Culture on Dimensions of Business Performance," *Journal of the Academy of Marketing Science* 24, no. 1, (1996): pp. 27–43; Rohit Deshpande and John U. Farley, "Measuring Market Orientation: Generalization and Synthesis," *Journal of Market-Focused Management* 2 (1998): 213–32.

34. John C. Narver, Stanley F. Slater, and Douglas L. MacLachlan, "Total Market Orientation, Business Performance, and Innovation," Working Paper Series, Marketing Science Institute, Report No. 00-116, 2000, pp. 1–34. See also Ken Matsuno and John T. Mentzer. "The Effects of Strategy Type on the Market Orentation—Performance Relationship," *Journal or Marketing* (October 2000): pp. 1–16.

35. Bro Uttal, "Selling Is No Longer Mickey Mouse at AT&T," *Fortune*, July 17, 1978, pp. 98–104.

36. Thomas V. Bonoma and Bruce H. Clark, *Marketing Performance Assessment* (Boston: Harvard Business School Press, 1988); Robert Shaw, *Measuring and Valuing Customer Relationships* (London; Business Intelligence, 1999).

37. Christian Honburg, John P. Workman Jr., and Harley Krohmen, "Marketings Influence Within the Firm," *Journal of Marketing* (January 1999): pp. 1–15.

38. Richard Barnet, *Global Dreams: Imperial Corporations and the New World Order* (New York: Simon & Schuster, 1994), pp. 170-71; Michael R. Czinkota, Ilka A. Ronkainen, and John J. Tarrant, *The Global Marketing Imperative* (Chicago: NTC Business Books, 1995), p. 249.

39. Constance L. Hays, "Getting Serious at Ben & Jerry's," *New York Times*, May 22, pp. D1–2; Anita Roddick, *Business as Unusual* (London: Thomsons, 2001).

40. Roger Rosenblatt, "Heroes for the Planet," *Time*, October 18, 1999; Peter Carlin, "Pure Profit for Small Companies that Stress Social Values as Much as the Bottom Line," *Los Angeles Times Magazine*, February 5, 1995; Natalie Southworth, "Patagonia's Perks Have Workers Turning Green," *The Globe and Mail*, August 23, 2000.

41. Hanish Pringle and Marjorie Thompson, *Brand Soul: How Cause-Related Marketing Builds Brands* (New York: John Wiley & Sons, 1999); Richard Earle, *The Art of Cause Marketing* (Lincolnwood, IL: NTC, 2000).

2

adapting marketing to the new economy

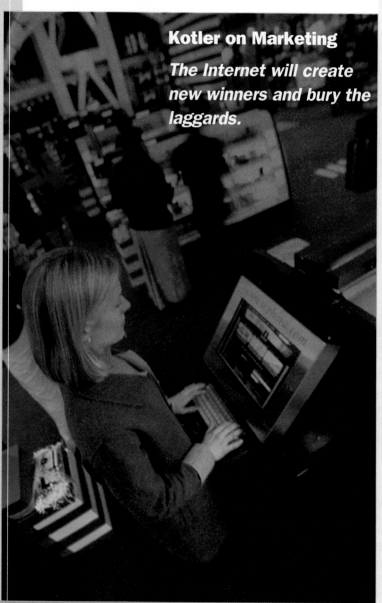

Kotler on Marketing

The Internet will create new winners and bury the laggards.

In this chapter, we will address the following questions:

- What are the major forces driving the new economy?
- How are business and marketing practices changing as a result of the new economy?
- How are marketers using the Internet, customer databases, and customer relationship management in the new economy?

Today's companies need fresh thinking about how to operate and compete in the new economy. In this book, we are using the term new economy to describe a whole set of forces that have appeared in the last decade and that call for new marketing and business practices. Today's economy is made up of old and new elements and is essentially a hybrid. In this chapter, we want to emphasize new elements such as the following:

- Companies are increasingly subcontracting activities to outsourcing firms. Their maxim: Outsource those activities that others can do cheaper and better, retain core activities.

- Companies are increasingly benchmarking their performance against best-of-class companies anywhere in the world.

- *Companies are deepening their partnering arrangements with key suppliers and distributors.*
- *Companies are emphasizing interdepartmental teamwork to manage key processes rather than relying on traditional departmental systems.*
- *Companies are inventing new advantages rather than relying on their existing advantages.*
- *Companies are recognizing that much of their market value comes from intangible assets, particularly their brands, customer base, employees, distributor and supplier relations, and intellectual capital.*
- *Companies are making substantial investments in information systems as the key to lowering their costs and gaining a competitive edge.*
- *Companies are increasingly organizing their activities around customer groups, not just around products.*

Many standard marketing practices—mass media advertising, sales promotion, sales force calls—were part of the old economy. They will continue to be important, but today's businesses will have to answer such questions as: "Is too much money being spent on mass advertising and not enough on one-to-one customer relationship management?" "Will companies need as many salespeople as before in an information-rich economy?" "Should companies reduce their huge sales promotion expenditures and move to everyday low prices?"

In this chapter, we will first describe the key drivers of the new economy. Then we will examine how business and marketing practices are changing.[1] Following this, we will look at how today's companies are using the Internet, customer databases and datamining, and customer relationship management (CRM) to improve their marketing performance.

the major drivers of the new economy

Many forces play a major role in reshaping the world economy, among them technology, globalization, and market deregulation. Here we will describe four specific drivers that underpin the new economy:

- Digitalization and connectivity
- Disintermediation and reintermediation
- Customization and customerization
- Industry convergence

digitalization and connectivity

In the past, most appliances and systems—such as the telephone, the wrist watch, recorded music, and panel gauges—operated with analog information. Analog information is continuously variable in response to physical stimuli: thus a phonograph plays music by responding to the physical grooves in the record. Today most appliances and systems operate with digital information, which converts text, data, sound, and images into a stream of zeros and ones that can be combined into bits and transmitted from appliance to appliance. Software is essentially digital instructions for operating systems, games, storage, and other applications.

But bits will not reside in separate appliances unless connectivity is established. For bits to flow from one appliance and location to another, a wired or wireless communications network is necessary. The Internet, the "information highway," can dispatch bits at incredible speeds from one location to another. Much of today's business is carried over networks connecting people and companies. These networks are called Intranets when they connect people within a company to one another and to the company mainframe; Extranets when they connect a company with its suppliers and distributors; and the

marketing for the **new economy**

M-Commerce Opens Up New Opportunities for Marketers

Consumers and businesspeople no longer need to be near a computer to send and receive information. All they need is a cellular phone or personal digital assistant (PDA, such as a Palm). While they are on the move, they can connect with the Internet to check stock prices, the weather, sports scores, or send and receive email messages. They can place online orders by simply using a phone or a PDA. A whole field called *telematics* involves placing wireless Internet-connected computers in the dashboards of cars and trucks, and making more home appliances (such as computers) wireless so that they can be used anywhere in or near the home. Many see a big future in what is now called *m-commerce* (*m* for mobile). Consider the fast growth of Internet-connected phones.

NTT DoCoMo   In Japan, two million teenagers carry DoCoMo phones available from NTT (Nippon Telephone and Telegraph). They view manga cartoons, haiku poetry, and pictures of snow falling on the Hokkaido mountains. They spend a lot of time sending and receiving instant messages from friends. They can also use the phone to order goods. They scan a list of some thousand companies that sell things. A person wanting a new pair of running shoes can look up shoes, then Nike, then the style and size, and order a pair of shoes. The person's address is in the system and the shoes will be sent to the 7-11 store nearest their home or office. The person can pick up the shoes at that store or pay the store to deliver the shoes. Each month, the subscriber will receive a bill from NTT listing the monthly subscriber

fee, the usage fee, and the cost of all the transactions. The person can then pay the bill at the nearest 7-11 store.

According to IDC, a technology research company, the market for location-based services is forecasted to approach $5 billion by 2004. Here are some possibilities:

- Getting a Coke by pointing and clicking the phone at a vending machine. The bottle drops down and an appropriate amount is deducted from the owner's bank account.
- Using the phone to search for a nearby restaurant that meets the customer's entered criteria.
- Watching stock prices while sitting in the restaurant and deciding to place a purchase order.
- Clicking the phone to pay the bill for the meal; the cellular phone replaces the credit card.
- Coming home and clicking a combination of keys on the phone to open the door.

Some see positive benefits, such as locating people making emergency 911 calls or checking on the whereabouts of one's children late at night. Others worry about privacy issues. What if an employer learns that an employee is being treated for AIDS at a local clinic, or a wife finds out her husband is out clubbing? Like so many new technologies, location-based services have potential for good or harm, and ultimately they will warrant public scrutiny and regulation.

Source: Douglas Lamont, *Conquering the Wireless World: The Age of M-Commerce* (New York: Wiley, 2001).

Internet when they connect users to a large worldwide "information repository." Connectivity is further enhanced by wireless communication. (See "Marketing for the New Economy: M-Commerce Opens Up New Opportunities for Marketers.")

A survey by Jupiter Communications found that most Americans wouldn't use or pay for m-commerce because they didn't see a "killer application," because the mobile Internet is slow, and because the appliance screens are too small. In contrast, Europe and Japan have and are using better wireless service. M-commerce entrepreneurs need to focus on converting specific groups to m-commerce; they will make faster inroads by promoting separate service packages for, teenagers, mothers, investors, and executives than by trying to attract the mass market.

disintermediation and reintermediation

The new technological capabilities have led thousands of entrepreneurs to launch a dot-com in the hope of striking gold. The amazing success of early online dot-coms such as AOL, Amazon, Yahoo, eBay, Etrade, and dozens of others struck terror in the hearts of many established manufacturers and retailers. For example, Compaq had its hands tied because it sold its computers through retailers, whereas Dell Computer grew faster by choosing to sell online. Established store-based retailers—notably bookstores, music stores, travel agents, stockbrokers, and car dealers—began to doubt their future as more businesses went into direct online marketing. They feared, and rightly so, being *disintermediated* by the new e-tailers.

But disintermediation was only half the story. Although some established middlemen lost their businesses, new middlemen sprang up to supply Internet services to both businesses and consumers. *Reintermediation* took place on a grand scale. New online middlemen appeared such as mySimon.com, Evenbetter.com, Buy.com, ShopBest.com, Bestbook.com, Smartshop.com, and StreetPrices.com.

mySimon.com   This Web site acts as an *intelligent shopping agent* (sometimes called a "bot," short for "robot") for consumers looking for the best buys in several categories including books, toys, computers, and electronics. A person who wants a digital camera can go to mySimon, click on cameras, then digital cameras, then (say) Fuji MX700, and find which of several merchants offers the camera at the lowest price. Competing bots include buy.com and compare.com.

Priceline.com   This Web site allows people to state a price they would pay for an airplane trip, hotel, mortgage, car purchase, etc. In the case of a car purchase, Priceline faxes a potential purchase order to dealers and reports back the best deal for the buyer, who then can confirm the purchase. Buyers pay $25; dealers pay $75 for this service.

Lifeshopper.com   This Web site allows consumers to specify the type and amount of life insurance they are interested in. Lifeshopper sends back the prices offered by different insurance companies.

As for the traditional "brick-only" firms— such as Compaq, Barnes & Noble, and Merrill Lynch—they dragged their feet, hoping that the assault of "pure click" (online only) firms would falter or disappear. Then they started their own online sales channels, becoming "brick-and-click" competitors. They had to do this carefully in order to retain the loyalty of retailers, brokers, and agents. The irony is twofold. First, many brick-and-click competitors became stronger contenders than the pure-click firms, since they had a larger pool of resources to work with and well-established brand names. And second, many formidable pure-click dot-coms started to falter as investors sensed a bubble, and began to disinvest, dropping the value of dot-com stocks, causing mass staff layoffs, and sending many—such as Pets.com, Mothernature.com, Boo.com, Garden.com, Eve.com— into bankruptcy. At the same time, many other pure-click dot-coms are surviving and even prospering in today's marketplace.

customization and customerization

The old economy revolved around manufacturing companies whose main drive was to standardize production, products, and business processes. They invested large sums in brand building to tout the advantages of their standard market offerings. Through standardization and branding, manufacturers hoped to grow and take advantage of economies of scale. And the key to managing their assets was to establish a command-and-control system that would run the business like a machine.

In contrast, the new economy is supported by information businesses. Information has the advantages of being easy to differentiate, customize, personalize, and dispatch over networks at incredible speed. As companies grew proficient at gathering information about individual customers and business partners (suppliers, distributors, retailers), and as their factories were designed more flexibly, they increased their ability to individualize their market offerings, messages, and media. For example, Dell Computer invites customers to specify exactly what they want in a computer and delivers a custom-built one in a few days. P&G, on its Reflect.com site, allows a person to specify needs for a shampoo by answering a set of questions, and then P&G formulates a unique shampoo for the person. Levi's is now able to produce customized jeans based on a person's measurements.

Procter & Gamble's Reflect.com site allows customers to design their own beauty products.

In this process, we can distinguish between customization and customerization. *Customization* means that the company is able to produce individually differentiated goods whether ordered in person, on the phone, or online. By going online, companies essentially enable consumers to design their own goods; in effect, it enables them to be *prosumers*, namely self-producing consumers. The company is essentially providing a workshop where each individual can design what he or she wants.

The company also acquired the capacity to interact with each customer personally, namely to *personalize* messages, services, and the relationship. The customer can request customization of products, services, prices, and delivery channels. The combination of operational customization and marketing customization has been called **customerization**. A company is customerized when it is able to dialogue with individual customers and respond by customizing its products, services, and messages on a one-to-one basis.[2]

Customization is not for every company: There are several downsides. Customization may be very difficult to implement for complex products such as automobiles. Customization can raise the cost of goods by more than the customer is willing to pay. Some customers do not know what they want until they see actual products. Customers cannot cancel the order after the company has started to work on the product. The product may be hard to repair and have little sales value. In spite of this, customization has worked well for some products—laptop computers, apparel, skincare products, and vitamins—and is an opportunity worth investigating.

industry convergence

Industry boundaries are blurring at an incredible rate. Pharmaceutical companies, at one time essentially chemical companies, are now adding biogenetic research capacities in order to formulate new drugs, new cosmetics (cosmoneuticals) and new foods (nutriceuticals). Film companies such as Kodak are also chemical companies, but they are moving into electronics to digitize their image-making capabilities. Shiseido, the Japanese cosmetics firm, now markets a portfolio of dermatology drugs. Disney is not only into cartoons and theme parks, but it makes major films, licenses characters, and manages retail stores, hotels, cruise ships, and educational facilities. The merger of AOL and Time-Warner has created an online and traditional media hybrid that opens up a host of new marketing communication options. In all these cases, companies are recognizing that new opportunities lie at the intersection of two or more industries. Capitalizing on these opportunities can be challenging, however, as firms are having to learn about new markets and competitors as well as how to achieve maximum synergy across the different parts of their business.

how business practices are changing

The changes in technology and economy are eliciting a new set of beliefs and practices on the part of business firms. Let's look at the major business beliefs in the old economy and how these beliefs are shifting (see Table 2.1).

FROM ORGANIZING BY PRODUCT UNITS TO ORGANIZING BY CUSTOMER SEGMENTS   A company making two or more products normally assigns product managers or product divisions to manage them. GE's Appliance Division would assign different people or business units to manage their washing machines, dryers, refrigerators, and stoves. This makes sense, but it also makes sense to add marketing groups that address the needs of different customer groups, such as households and building contractors, who buy differently. This would mean a switch from being product-centered to being customer-segment centered.

FROM FOCUSING ON PROFITABLE TRANSACTIONS TO FOCUSING ON CUSTOMER LIFETIME VALUE   Companies normally focus on individual transactions with the aim of making a profit on each transaction. New economy companies add a focus on estimating individual customer lifetime value and designing their market offerings and prices to make a profit over the customer's lifetime. The company will sometimes underprice to gain new customers and will be generous in its pricing and services to existing customers with an eye toward retaining them for the long run.

FROM FOCUSING ON JUST THE FINANCIAL SCORECARD TO FOCUSING ALSO ON THE MARKETING SCORECARD   Most senior managers will judge the company's performance by financial results as reflected on the profit and loss statement and the balance sheet. Top management in new economy companies will also examine the marketing scorecard to interpret what is happening to market share (not just sales revenue), customer loss rate, customer satisfaction, product quality relative to competitors, and other measures. They recognize that changes in marketing indicators predict changes in financial results.

FROM FOCUSING ON SHAREHOLDERS TO FOCUSING ON STAKEHOLDERS   Top management sees its primary mission as making profits for shareholders. The costs of working with other stakeholders, such as employees, suppliers, and distributors, are kept under tight rein. They treat business as a zero-sum game, where by paying the least

table **2.1** Old Economy Versus New Economy	Old Economy	New Economy
	Organize by product units	Organize by customer segments
	Focus on profitable transactions	Focus on customer lifetime value
	Look primarily at financial scorecard	Look also at marketing scorecard
	Focus on shareholders	Focus on stakeholders
	Marketing does the marketing	Everyone does the marketing
	Build brands through advertising	Build brands through performance
	Focus on customer acquisition	Focus on customer retention
	No customer satisfaction measurement	Measure customer satisfaction and retention rate
	Overpromise, underdeliver	Underpromise, overdeliver

to employees, suppliers, and distributors, the company will be left with the most profit. Top management in new economy companies respects the importance of creating co-prosperity among all the business partners and customers. These managers carefully define their stakeholders and develop policies and strategies to balance the returns to all the key stakeholders. They believe business success depends on high-level performance by employees and business partners.

FROM MARKETING DOES THE MARKETING TO EVERYONE DOES THE MARKETING Companies generally establish a marketing department to be responsible for creating and delivering customer value. Unfortunately, this leads other departments in the company to feel less responsible for company performance vis-á-vis customers. But as the late David Packard of Hewlett-Packard observed, "Marketing is far too important to leave to the marketing department." Every employee has an impact on the customer and must see the customer as the source of the company's prosperity.

FROM BUILDING BRANDS THROUGH ADVERTISING TO BUILDING BRANDS THROUGH PERFORMANCE Relying on heavy advertising to build brand knowledge and preference in the target public's mind certainly worked well in the old economy. But brands, ultimately, are built by the customer's experience with the brand and by word-of-mouth. Companies are recognizing that a whole set of tools can help build brands, including sponsorships, event management, public relations, and charitable gifts.

FROM FOCUSING ON CUSTOMER ACQUISITION TO FOCUSING ON CUSTOMER RETENTION Most companies seek growth and reward salespeople handsomely for finding new customers. As a consequence, salespeople spend less time ensuring the satisfaction of existing customers, with the result that some current customers defect. New economy companies place much more emphasis on customer retention. Attracting a new customer may cost five times as much as doing a good job to retain existing customers.

FROM NO CUSTOMER SATISFACTION MEASUREMENT TO IN-DEPTH CUSTOMER SATISFACTION MEASUREMENT Many companies fail to systematically measure and track customer satisfaction and the factors shaping it. Instead they rely on anecdotal information that is not reliable. An increasing number of companies are making customer satisfaction a major priority. For example, IBM systematically measures how satisfied customers are with each IBM salesperson they encounter, and makes this a factor in each salesperson's compensation.

FROM OVER-PROMISE, UNDER-DELIVER TO UNDER-PROMISE, OVER-DELIVER To get the order, salespeople frequently over-promise on quality or delivery, and worry later about the repercussions. This is true of ads that exaggerate the performance of company products. New economy companies recognize that customer satisfaction is a function of the match between customer expectations and company performance. These companies want their messages and promises to be accurate. Some would even prefer that their salespeople under-promise and over-deliver, as a way to create customer delight.

THE NEW HYBRID The fact is that today's economy and most companies are a hybrid of the old economy and the new economy. Companies need to retain skills and competencies that have worked in the past, but they will also need to add new understandings and competencies if they hope to grow and prosper. Today's marketplace is made up of traditional consumers (who do not buy online), cyberconsumers (who mostly buy online), and hybrid consumers (who do both).[3]

Most consumers are hybrid: They shop in grocery stores but occasionally order from Peapod; they buy books in Barnes & Noble bookstores and sometimes order books from bn.com. People still like to squeeze the tomatoes, touch the fabric, smell the perfume, and interact with salespeople. Consumers are motivated by other needs than only shopping efficiency. Most companies will need a presence both offline and online to cater to these hybrid consumers. The task today is for companies to rethink and revise their overall company strategy and within that, their marketing strategy. We will even argue that marketing should play the lead role in shaping company strategy.

Companies are adjusting their marketing practices to meet new conditions. We will examine two newer practices that companies and their marketers are getting involved in: E-business and customer relationship management.

how marketing practices are changing: e–business

E-business describes the use of electronic means and platforms to conduct a company's business. The advent of the Internet has greatly increased the ability of companies to conduct their business faster, more accurately, over a wider range of time and space, at reduced cost, and with the ability to customize and personalize customer offerings. Countless companies have set up Web sites to inform and promote their products and services. They have created Intranets to facilitate employees communicating with one another and to facilitate downloading and uploading information to and from the company's computers. Companies have also set up Extranets with major suppliers and distributors to facilitate information exchange, orders, transactions, and payments. Bill Gates of Microsoft claims that Microsoft is almost entirely run electronically; there is hardly any paper flowing through the company because everything is on the computer screen.[4]

E-commerce is more specific than e-business; it means that in addition to providing information to visitors about the company, its history, policies, products, and job opportunities, the company or site offers to transact or facilitate the selling of products and services online. Most company sites are still just providing information, not doing e-commerce. Amazon.com, CDNow, eToys, e-Steel, and e-Plasticsnet are examples of e-commerce sites.

E-commerce has given rise in turn to e-purchasing and e-marketing. **E-purchasing** means companies decide to purchase goods, services, and information from various online suppliers. Smart e-purchasing has already saved companies millions of dollars. **E-marketing** describes company efforts to inform, communicate, promote, and sell its products and services over the Internet. The *e* term is also used in terms such as e-finance, e-learning, and e-service. But as someone observed, the *e* will eventually be dropped when most business practice is online.

E-business and e-commerce take place over four major Internet domains: B2C (business to consumer), B2B (business to business), C2C (consumers to consumers), and C2B (consumers to businesses). (We will omit government relations like G2C, G2B, B2G, and C2G.)

internet domains: B2C (business to consumer)

The popular press has paid the most attention to consumer Web sites. In 2000, more than 106 million Americans went online, with 80 percent looking for information, 73 percent researching a product or service before buying it, 68 percent looking for travel information, and 65 percent looking for information on movies, books, and leisure activities.[5]

The most frequent online consumer purchases (in terms of the percentage of online buyers saying they have purchased in the category) have been books (58%), music (50%), software (44%), air tickets (29%), PC peripherals (28%), clothing (26%), videos (24%), hotel reservations (20%), toys (20%), flowers (17%), and consumer electronics (12%). The Internet is most useful for products and services when the shopper seeks greater ordering convenience (e.g., books and music) or lower cost (e.g., stock trading or news reading). It is also useful when buyers need information about product features and prices (e.g., automobiles or computers). Individuals are also using the Internet to search for others to meet or date on such sites as Match.com, Americansingles.com, or Virtuallydating.com. Companies must set up and operate their e-commerce Web sites carefully, as the "Marketing Memo: Succeeding with Electronic Commerce" shows.

The Internet is less useful for products that must be touched or examined in advance. But even this has exceptions. People can order furniture from EthanAllen.com, major

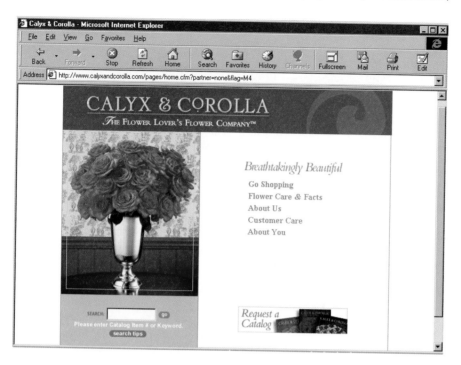

Customers can shop online at Calyx & Corolla or ask for a catalog and shop by phone.

appliances from Sears.com, and expensive computers from Dell or Gateway without trying them in advance. People order flowers, wine, and even home mortgages online.

Calyx & Corolla (C&C) C&C is a direct floral retailer started by a visionary entrepreneur, Ruth M. Owades. Customers can order fresh flowers and bouquets from a four-color catalog by phoning 1-800-877-0998 or by placing an order on the Web site at www.calyxandcorolla.com, which also shows floral bouquets, plants, preserved designs, and corporate gifts. The fresh flower order goes immediately to one of 25 growers in the C&C network, who picks and packages the flowers and ships them via FedEx. The flowers arrive fresher and last about 10 days longer than flowers ordered from store-based retailers. Owades credits her success to a sophisticated information system and her strong alliances with FedEx and the growers.

Wine.com Wine.com is the brainchild of master sommelier Peter Granoff and Silicon Valley engineer Robert Olson. The idea behind the site is to make it easy to locate and purchase hard-to-find wine, food, and gifts from artisan producers. Wine.com features wines from California and European wineries, and food and gift items. It makes the often intimidating topic of wine congenial for those who might be afraid to ask what "carbonic maceration" means. Wine.com hosts five monthly wine clubs. It features Q&A sections on the characteristics of wine, serving and storing wine, and wine and food pairing suggestions. There is also a "Wine Basics" page with sections on wine types, wineries, appellations, etc.

Homeowners.com Prospective home buyers can research home mortgage rates and interest rate trends, use financial tools to analyze loans, and sign up for RateWatch, an e-mail service that keeps them informed of trends in loan rates. They can apply online for a home mortgage from a variety of home mortgage providers and obtain responses within one business day. In addition, they can connect with realtors in specific locations and neighborhoods.

marketing **insight**

Ride the Cluetrain Manifesto

In 1999, four academics—Christopher Locke, Rick Levine, Doc Searls, and David Weinberger—published *The Cluetrain Manifesto*, a short book with a huge message aiming to change the way companies think about consumers and about marketing to them. The authors see the Internet as producing a profound humanistic change in the relation between businesses and consumers. The book presents 95 theses, starting with "Markets are conversations" (thesis 1) and "Markets consist of human beings, not demographic sectors (thesis 2). "The Internet is enabling conversations among human beings that were simply not possible in the era of mass media" (thesis 5). "As a result, markets are getting smarter, more informed, more organized" (thesis 10). "People in networked markets have figured out that they get far better information and support from each other than from vendors" (thesis 11). "And whether the news is good or bad, they tell everyone" (thesis 12). "Companies that speak in the lan-

guage of the pitch, the dog-and-pony show, are no longer speaking to anyone" (thesis 16). "People will not settle for the 4-color brochure, for web sites...with eye candy but lacking any substance" (thesis 65). "If you (the company) want us to talk to you, tell us something. Make it something interesting for a change" (thesis 75). "We want you (the company) to drop your trip, come out of your neurotic self-involvement, join the party" (thesis 79).

The Cluetrain Manifesto charges that companies are too bureaucratic, too artificial, too manipulative, too given to one-way rhetoric. Companies which do not recognize that today's markets are conversations are destined to flounder.

Source: Christopher Locke, Rick Levine, Doc Searls, and David Weinberger, *The Cluetrain Manifesto: The End of Business as Usual.* (Cambridge, MA: Perseus Books, 2000); also www.cluetrain.com

Online consumers tend to be younger, more affluent, and better educated than the general population. But as more people find their way onto the Internet, the cyberspace population is becoming more mainstream and diverse. Younger users are more likely to use the Internet for entertainment and socializing. Yet 45 percent of users are 40 years of age or older, and use the Internet for investments and more serious matters.

The exchange process in the age of information has become customer-initiated and customer-controlled. Marketers and their representatives must wait until customers invite them to participate in the exchange. Even after marketers enter the exchange process, customers define the rules of engagement, and insulate themselves with the help of agents and intermediaries. Customers define what information they need, what offerings they are interested in, and what prices they are willing to pay. (To better understand the new power of consumers opened up by the Internet, see the "Marketing Insight: Ride the Cluetrain Manifesto.")

internet domains: B2B (business to business)

Although the popular press has given the most attention to business-to-consumer (B2C) Web sites, even more activity is being conducted on business-to-business (B2B) sites. The B2B sites are changing the supplier-customer relationship in profound ways (see Figure 2.1). Forrester and Gartner, major research firms on online commerce, estimate that B2B commerce is 10 to 15 times greater than B2C commerce. Gartner estimates that by 2005, more than 500,000 enterprises will participate in e-markets as buyers, sellers, or both. These firms are using B2B auction sites, spot exchanges, online product catalogues, barter sites, and other online resources to obtain better prices. Many major enterprises, including Chevron, Ford Motor Company, GE, and Merck, have invested millions in Web procurement systems. The result: Invoices that used to cost $100 to process now cost as little as $20.

GE is now requiring all its partners to join its Web procurement network—the Trading Process Network (TPN)—in an initiative that could save GE as much as $200 million per year by 2003. Here are three examples of B2B sites:

figure **2.1**

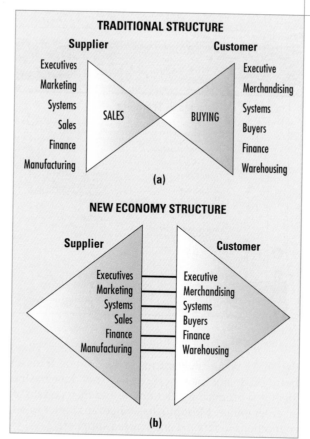

The Supplier–Customer
Relationship:
The Traditional Structure
and the New Economy
Structure

PlasticsNet.com   This is a vertical hub for the plastic products industry bringing together more than 90,000 monthly visitors with over 200 suppliers. In addition to facilitating online transactions, the site provides a supplier directory, material data sheets, an industry publication, and a list of educational programs, books, and seminars of relevance to the plastics industry.

SoluMed.com   One feature of this Web site is Medical EquipNet™, which serves as a clearinghouse for companies, doctors offices, and hospitals in the market to buy and sell used or refurbished medical equipment. Because this secondary market is transaction-oriented and geographically scattered, the site opens up a cost-effective sales channel for the purchase of second-hand medical equipment.

FreeMarkets   FreeMarkets is an online trading network connecting over 150,000 industrial suppliers with over 100 corporate buyers all over the world in more than 165 goods and services categories. Since its founding in 1995, this Pittsburgh-based firm has conducted nearly 10,000 auctions and currently operates offices in 13 countries.

Company purchasing agents initially favored shifting their commodity purchases to digital marketplaces that bring together many buyers and sellers in one place. However, www.transora.com: global online marketplace for the consumer packaged goods industry.

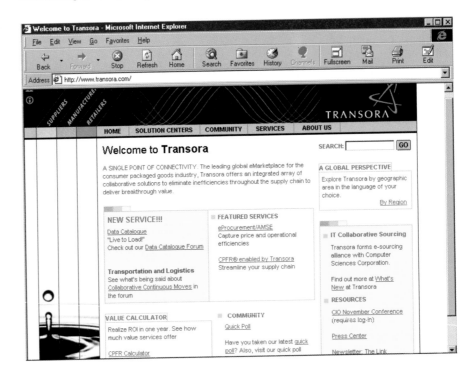

they have been reluctant to finalize online transactions with companies they never heard of, do not know well, or have not done business with in the past. They prefer to identify a promising seller online and then go into offline negotiation rather than place an order online. Most purchasing groups prefer to set up their own portal with Extranet connections to favored and trusted suppliers.

In several industries, companies have formed *buying alliances* to secure even deeper volume discounts from suppliers. GM, Ford, and DaimlerChrysler formed Covisint, and they believe they can save as much as $1,200 a car by combining their purchases. Coca-Cola, Sara Lee, Kraft, and several other consumer packaged goods companies formed Transora to effect cost savings in raw material and logistical procurement. Much work has to be done before these buying alliances begin to work, but when they do, sellers will be under even more price pressure.

The impact of B2B sites is to make markets more efficient. In the past, buyers had to exert a lot of effort to gather information on worldwide suppliers. With the Internet, buyers have access to much greater information. They can get information from: (1) supplier Web sites, (2) *infomediaries*, third parties that add value by aggregating information about alternatives; (3) *market makers*, third parties who create markets linking buyers and sellers, and (4) *customer communities*, that swap stories about suppliers' products and services.[6]

The net impact of these mechanisms is to make prices more transparent. In the case of undifferentiated products, price pressure will increase. In the case of highly differentiated products, buyers will gain a better picture of their true value. Suppliers of superior products will be able to offset price transparency with value transparency; suppliers of undifferentiated products will have to drive down their costs in order to compete.

internet domains: C2C (consumer to consumer)

There is considerable consumer-to-consumer communication on the Web on a whole range of subjects. AOL boasts some 14,000 chat rooms covering such topics as healthy eating, caring for your Bonsai tree, and exchanging views about the latest soap opera happenings. AOL recently introduced "buddy lists," which alert members when friends are online, allowing them to exchange instant messages. ParentSoup.com is an online community of more than 200,000 parents who spend time online gathering information, chatting with other parents, and linking to related sites. On Agriculture.com, farmers can find commodity prices, recent farm news, and chat rooms of all types. The site is attracting as many as five million hits per month. The Web hosts many bulletin boards where people can post messages. The most prominent C2C channel is e-mail, which functions as a digital post office.

C2C means that online visitors increasingly create product information, not just consume it. They join Internet interest groups to share information, so that "word of web" is joining "word of mouth" as an important buying influence. Words about good companies travel fast; and words about bad companies travel even faster.

---

eBay   eBay is a person-to-person online trading community with more than 23 million registered users. The company's Web site hosts more than two million auctions each month for items in more than 1,000 categories, from jewelry to stamps, and from antiques to electronics. eBay also maintains auction sites in several foreign countries, including Japan, the United Kingdom, and Germany.

WebMD   This online health network provides a wealth of B2B and B2C services linking patients, doctors, and healthcare industry companies. Aside from these services, an important aspect of its consumer-health homepage is a network connecting consumers who have interests in similar health issues. WebMD hosts a variety of daily chats on topics such as prostate cancer and nutrition, offers health journal forums, and finds "diet buddies" for weight-conscious consumers.

internet domains C2B (consumer to business)

Consumers are also finding it easier to communicate with companies. Companies often encourage communication by inviting prospects and customers to send in questions, suggestions, and even complaints via e-mail. Some sites even include a call-me button—the customer clicks on it and his or her phone rings with a customer representative ready to answer a question. Customer service representatives can in principle respond quickly to these messages. Yet many online merchants are guilty of considerably slow responses to consumer mail. Smart online marketers will answer quickly, by sending out newsletters, special product or promotion offers based on purchase histories, reminders of service requirements or warranty renewals, or announcements of special events.

pure-click versus brick-and-click companies

We can distinguish between **pure-click** companies, those that launched a Web site without any previous existence as a firm, and **brick-and-click** companies, existing companies that added an online site for information and/or e-commerce.

PURE-CLICK COMPANIES   There are several kinds of pure-click companies: Search engines, Internet Service Providers (ISPs), commerce sites, transaction sites, content sites, and enabler sites.

Search engines and portals such as Yahoo! and Alta Vista started as search engines and later added services such as news, weather, stock reports, entertainment, and storefronts hoping to become the user's point of entry on the Internet. ISPs such as AOL and Compuserv provide Internet and e-mail connections for a fee. Commerce sites sell books, music, toys, insurance, stocks, clothes, financial services, and so on. Among the most prominent ones are Amazon, CDNow, and Buy.com. Transaction sites such as auctions and brokerages like eBay and ETrade take a commission for transactions conducted on their sites. Content sites such as The Street, New York Times, and Encyclopaedia

CarPoint, leading metamediary for car buying, is a pure click company: It exists only on the Web.

Britannica provide financial, research, and other information. Enabler sites provide the hardware and software that enable Internet communication and commerce.

These sites compete using various strategies: CarPoint, a leading metamediary of car buying and related services; Travelocity, the information leader in air travel; Buy.com, the low price leader; Mercata, the demand aggregator leader; Winespectator, the single category specialist; and Reflect.com, the most personalized site for skin and hair care.

Pure-click Web businesses reached astronomical capitalization levels in the late 1990s, in some cases far exceeding the capitalization of major companies such as United Airlines or Pepsi-Cola. They were considered a major threat to traditional businesses until the investing frenzy collapsed in 2000.

Dot-coms failed for a variety of reasons: Many rushed into the market without proper research or planning. They had poorly designed Web sites with problems of complexity, poor navigation, and downtime. They lacked adequate infrastructures for shipping on time and for answering customer inquiries. They believed that the first company entering a category would win category leadership. These companies wanted to exploit network economies, namely the fact that the value of a network to each of its members is proportional to the number of other users (Metcalfe's Law). Some just rushed into the market in the hope of launching an initial public offering (IPO) while the market was hot.

To acquire customers, dot-coms spent large amounts on mass marketing and offline advertising. They relied on spin and buzz instead of using target marketing and word-of-mouth marketing, and they devoted too much effort to acquiring customers instead of building loyal and more frequent users among their current customers. They did not understand customer behavior when it came to online surfing and purchasing.

Many dot-coms did not build a sound business model that would deliver eventual profits. The ease of entry of competitors and the ease of customers switching Web sites in search of better prices forced dot-coms to accept margin-killing low prices. Webvan, the online grocer, illustrates how dot-coms failed to understand their marketplace.

Webvan   Webvan began operations in 1999, and its stock zoomed to $34 from an offering price of $15. Although Webvan raised $1.2 billion in start-up capital, by February 2001 its stock had fallen to $.31 a share. Some households liked the convenience of ordering groceries online and receiving the goods at home, but the average Webvan customer used the service less than twice every three months, and many dropped out. Webvan found that its trucks did 2.3 deliveries per hour, with an average order size around $70. Instead of carefully working out the economics of this business in its initial San Francisco location, Webvan expanded aggressively into many cities and built automated warehouses that operated far below their breakeven point. Webvan also botched a $1.2 billion merger with its rival, Home-Grocer. On July 9, 2001, Webvan ceased operations and filed for bankruptcy.

At the same time, many pure-click dot-coms are surviving and even prospering. Others are showing losses today, but their business plans are fundamentally good. Consider Earthlink.com:

Earthlink.com   Earthlink is an ISP that sells Internet and e-mail connection time for a $20 monthly fee. Its customer maintenance expenses amount to $9 a month, leaving an $11 contribution margin. It costs Earthlink an average of $100 to acquire a new customer, and it takes 11 months before it breaks even with a new customer (= $100/9). Earthlink keeps its customers for an average of 31 months, which leaves it with 20 months of net income. At a $9 contribution margin a month, Earthlink makes $180 (= 20 months × $9…undiscounted) on that customer. When Sky Dayton, Earthlink's founder, was asked why Earthlink is still losing money, he answered that Earthlink is acquiring so many new customers it will take awhile for the $100 acquisition cost to be covered by the subsequent inflow of contribution margin.

BRICK–AND–CLICK COMPANIES   Many incumbent companies moved quickly to open Web sites describing their business but resisted adding e-commerce to their sites. They felt that selling their products or services online would produce channel conflict—they would be competing with their offline retailers and agents. For example, Compaq feared that its retailers would drop its line of computers if Compaq offered to sell the same computers directly online. Merrill Lynch hesitated to introduce online stock trading to compete with ETrade, Schwab, and other online brokerages fearing that its own brokers would rebel. Even the store-based bookseller Barnes & Noble delayed opening an online site to challenge Amazon.

These companies struggled with the question of how to conduct online sales without cannibalizing their own stores, resellers, or agents. Here are examples of how some companies resolved this conflict.[7]

Gibson Guitars   Gibson Guitars found that although its dealers were outraged when it tried to sell guitars directly to consumers, the dealers did not object to direct sales of accessories such as guitar strings and parts.

Liberty Mutual   Liberty Mutual asks its online customers whether they prefer to buy directly or through a financial advisor. In the case of through an advisor, customers are told that information about their needs will be relayed to an advisor.

Avon   Avon did not want to cannibalize Avon ladies who had close relations with customers. Fortunately, Avon's research showed little overlap between existing customers and potential Web customers, so Avon went ahead. Meanwhile, Avon also offered to help its reps set up their own Web sites.

J. C. Penney   J. C. Penney uses its Web site to offer online coupons that can be printed and redeemed at its stores. It even sells some offerings online that would not be profitable to sell through its stores.

Although brick-and-click firms face channel conflict issues, they probably will have more online success than their pure-click competitors. First, companies such as Compaq, Merrill Lynch, and Barnes & Noble have better known brand names; their cost of acquiring a new customer is $12 compared to the $82 that pure click e-tailers spend to acquire a new customer.[8] Second, they have greater financial resources and access to funds. Third, they have deeper industrial knowledge and experience, good relationships with key suppliers, and a large customer base. Fourth, they can now be reached 24 hours a day, 7 days a week and merchandise can be returned to their 9 to 5 stores. And fifth, the Internet allows them to reach and serve additional customers who may be far away from their store locations. Gap illustrates the advantages of a brick-and-click operation over a pure-click operation.

Gap.com   Gap.com draws more than one million visitors per month. The site mirrors the clean, functional image of Gap stores, and works seamlessly with the stores. Online purchases can be returned to any store, and Gap stores mention Gap.com on signage, receipts, and even shopping bags. Gap.com offers some sizes and colors not available in stores and also provides e-mail gift reminders and wish-list registries.

how marketing practices are changing: setting up web sites

Clearly all companies need to move into e-marketing and e-purchasing. In deciding to set up and operate their own Web sites, they face many questions, such as those listed in Table 2.2.

Many of these questions will be answered throughout the book. Here we address only three: Designing an attractive Web site; placing ads and promotion online; and building a revenue and profit model.

designing an attractive web site

A key challenge is designing a site that is attractive on first viewing and interesting enough to encourage repeat visits. Early text-based Web sites have increasingly been replaced by sophisticated sites that provide text, sound, and animation (see www.gap.com or www.1800flowers.com).

Rayport and Jaworski have proposed that effective Web sites feature seven design elements that they call the 7Cs:[9]

- *Context:* Layout and design.
- *Content:* Text, pictures, sound, and video the site contains.
- *Community:* How the site enables user-to-user communication.
- *Customization:* Site's ability to tailor itself to different users or to allow users to personalize the site.
- *Communication:* How the site enables site-to-user, user-to-site, or two-way communication.
- *Connection:* Degree that the site is linked to other sites.
- *Commerce:* Site's capabilities to enable commercial transactions.

To encourage repeat visits, companies need to pay attention to context and content factors.

CONTEXT FACTORS   Visitors will judge a site's performance on its ease-of-use and its physical attractiveness. Ease-of-use breaks down into three attributes: (1) the Web site downloads quickly, (2) the first page is easy to understand, and (3) the visitor finds it easy to navigate to other pages that open quickly. The site's physical attractiveness is determined by the following factors: (1) the individual pages are clean looking and not

table **2.2**

Setting Up a Dot–com
Presence

Attracting and Keeping Visitors

How can we get more prospects to know and visit our site?

How can we use marketing to spread word-of-mouth?

How can we convert visitors into repeaters?

How do we make our site more experiential and real?

How can we build a strong relationship with our customers?

How can we build a customer community?

How can we capture and exploit customer data for up-selling and cross-selling?

How much should we spend on building and marketing our site?

Advertising on the Internet

What are the various ways that we can advertise on the Internet?

How do we choose the right sites for placing our ads or sponsorship?

Dealing with Retailers

How can we sell direct and yet keep our retailers happy?

How can we coordinate our online commerce and own-store sales and service?

How much will our retail operations be hurt by our online sales and by other e-tailers?

Putting the Site Together and Making It Profitable

How do we pick and manage suppliers and partners?

Should the site be set up inside or outside of the company?

How do we get management buy-in and funding?

How can we fight price pressure and price transparency on the Internet?

Which revenue and profit model makes the most sense?

Source: www.Customers.com

overly crammed with content, (2) the type faces and font sizes are very readable, and (3) the site makes good use of color (and sound).

CONTENT FACTORS   Context factors facilitate repeat visits, but they do not ensure that this happens. Returning to a site depends on content. The content must be interesting, useful, and continuously changing. Certain types of content function well to attract first-time visitors and to bring them back again: (1) deep information with links to related sites, (2) changing news of interest, (3) changing free offers to visitors, (4) contests and sweepstakes, (5) humor and jokes, and (6) games.

GETTING FEEDBACK   From time to time, a company needs to reassess its site's attractiveness and usefulness. One way to do this is to ask site design experts. But the most important source of feedback is users who can be asked what they like and dislike about the site and for suggestions for improvement.

Here are examples of well-designed company Web sites:

Clinique.com   This Web site provides excellent information about cosmetics, beauty tips, new-products, and pricing. It offers a tool to evaluate skin type, a bulletin board, a bridal guide, and visiting experts. It also offers online purchasing.

Lands' End   Lands' End engaged IBM to use datamining techniques to cluster its customers. IBM identified 5,200 different market cells. One market cell consisted of 850 customers who had purchased a blue shirt and red tie. This alerted Lands' End to the possible interest of these customers in buying a dark blue jacket, at which point it sent them a special offer.

placing ads and promotion online

The Internet will not become a major advertising medium like television, radio, and print media. Internet users generally do not welcome advertising. Yet advertising does appear on the Internet. A company has to decide which forms will be most cost-effective in achieving their advertising objectives.

Banner ads, small boxes containing text and perhaps a picture, are the most extensively used Internet advertising tool. Companies pay to place their banner ads on relevant Web sites. The larger the audience reached, the more the placement will cost. Popular portals such as Yahoo! and AOL are able to charge large fees because they have huge audiences. But the fees may be coming down. Some banners on Web sites are not paid for, but instead are accepted on a barter basis.

In the early days of the Internet, viewers probably clicked on 2 to 3 percent of the banner ads they saw. More recently they are clicking on less than ½ of 1 percent of banner ads. Companies placing banner ads would be wise to pay not simply for banner placements, nor even only for click-throughs, but instead only for sales resulting from the click-throughs. Yet those offering sites for banner ads are not likely to accept this riskier type of pricing. In the meantime, advertisers are pressing online sites to accept larger ads than banners if they want more payment, but the sites are uncertain as to how their viewers will react.

Many companies get their name on the Internet by sponsoring special content on Web sites that carry news, financial information, and so on. **Sponsorships** are best placed in well-targeted sites where they can offer relevant information or service. The sponsor pays for showing the content and in turn receives acknowledgment as the sponsor of that particular service on the Web site.

A **microsite** is a limited area on the web managed and paid for by an external advertiser/company. Microsites are particularly relevant for companies selling low-interest products such as insurance. People rarely visit an insurance company's Web site. However, the insurance company can create a microsite on used-car sites, offering advice for buyers of used cars and at the same time offering a good insurance deal.

Interstitials are advertisements that pop-up between changes on a Web site. At the website www.msnbc.com, advertising can be seen if viewers go to the sports page. At www.blender.com, users can download a special Blenderbrowser to view full-screen advertisements in the form of 10-second interstitials with sound. Ads for Johnson & Johnson's Tylenol headache reliever pop up on brokers' Web sites whenever the stock market falls by 100 points or more. **Browser ads** pay a viewer to watch them. For example, Alladvantage.com downloads a view bar which displays ads targeted to the users. Viewers earn $20 to $1 per hour in return.

Companies can set up **alliances** and **affiliate programs**. When one Internet company works with another one, they end up advertising each other. AOL has created many successful alliances with other companies. Amazon has more than 350,000 affiliates that post Amazon banners on their Web sites. Companies can also undertake guerrilla marketing actions to publicize the site and generate word-of-mouth. When Yahoo! started its Denmark site, it distributed apples in the busiest train station in Denmark with the message that in the next hours a trip to New York could be won on the Yahoo! site; it also managed to get this mentioned in Danish newspapers. Companies can offer to **push** content and ads to targeted audiences who agree to receive them. Infogate (www.infogate.com) and Ifusion (www.ifusion.com) automatically download customized information and ads to recipients' PCs. The advantage is

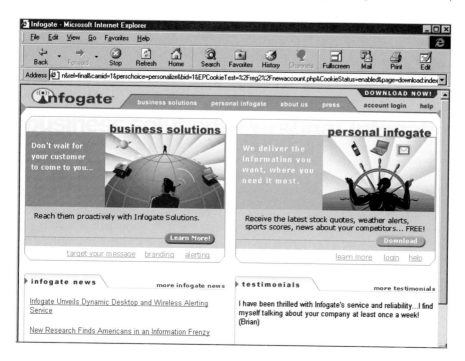

Infogate.com "pushes" targeted content and ads to those who are interested in a product or product category.

that the targeted content and ads reach users who are interested in the product or product category.

Web advertising is showing double-digit growth. Costs are reasonable compared with those of other advertising media. For example, Web advertising on ESPN.com (www.espn.com), which attracts more than 500,000 Web surfers and 20 million hits per week, costs about $300,000 per year. Yahoo! employs 100 salespeople who demonstrate how online ads can reach people with certain interests or who live in specific zip codes.

building a revenue and profit model

Dot-com companies need to tell their investors how they will eventually make profits. They need to have a **revenue and profit model**, a business model that specifies the main revenue sources, and the projected revenue, costs, and income the dot-com expects to achieve.

The company's revenue stream may come from several sources:

- *Advertising income:* Sales of banner ads could provide a major source of revenue. Buy.com gets so much revenue from carrying banner ads that it is able to sell many products at cost.
- *Sponsorship income:* A dot-com can solicit sponsors for some of its content and collect sponsor fees to help cover costs.
- *Alliance income:* A company can invite business partners to share costs in setting up the Web site and offer them free advertising.
- *Membership and subscription income:* Web sites can charge a subscription fee to receive a password to use the site. Many online newspapers (e.g., the *Wall Street Journal* and the *Financial Times*) require a subscription for their online services. Auto-By-Tel gets its income from selling subscriptions to auto dealers who want to receive hot buyer leads from Auto-By-Tel's Web site.
- *Profile income:* Web sites that have accumulated the profiles of a particular target group can sell these profiles if they get permission. At the same time, there is a code of ethics that warns against the wrongful sale or misuse of customer information.
- *Product and service sales income:* E-commerce Web sites draw a good portion of their revenue from marking up the prices of their goods and services.

- *Transaction commissions and fees:* Dot-coms charge commission fees on transactions between other parties. For example, eBay puts buyers in touch with sellers and takes from a 1.25 to 5 percent commission on each transaction.
- *Market research/information:* Companies can charge for special market information or intelligence. NewsLibrary charges a dollar or two to download copies of archived news stories. LifeQuote provides price comparisons from approximately 50 different life insurance companies and gets a commission of 50 percent of the first year's premium from the company chosen by the consumer.
- *Referral income:* Companies can collect revenue by referring customers to others. Edmund's receives a finder's fee every time a customer fills out an Auto-By-Tel form at Edmund's Web site, regardless of whether a deal is consummated. Marketplace.com charges a fee for the names of corporate customers who want to sell or buy a business.

Many dot-coms failed because they overestimated the revenue and underestimated the costs of starting up and maintaining momentum. And venture capital funders were also at fault for committing funds without requiring better business models from dot-com entrepreneurs.

How many dot-coms are profitable today? McKinsey & Company studied more than 200 B2C e-businesses and found that 20 percent are making an operating profit. The best performers were transaction sites, with media and content sites lagging behind.[10]

how marketing practices are changing: customer relationship marketing

In addition to e-marketing, companies are becoming more skillful in customer relationship marketing and database marketing. **Customer relationship marketing (CRM)** enables companies to provide excellent real-time customer service by developing a relationship with each valued customer through the effective use of individual account information. Based on what they know about each customer, companies can customize market offerings, services, programs, messages, and media.

Customer relationship marketing holds that a major driver of company profitability is the aggregate value of the company's customer base.[11]

Winning companies are more productive in acquiring, keeping, and growing customers. These companies improve the value of their customer base by excelling at the following customer strategies:

- Reducing the rate of customer defection.
- Increasing the longevity of the customer relationship.
- Enhancing the growth potential of each customer through "share-of-wallet, " cross-selling, and upselling.
- Making low-profit customers more profitable or terminating them.
- Focusing disproportionate effort on high value customers.

Table 2.3 lists the main differences between mass marketing and one-to-one marketing. Some of the groundwork for customer relationship marketing was laid by Don Peppers and Martha Rogers in their book, *The One-to-One Future.*[12] Peppers and Rogers use a four-step framework for one-to-one marketing:

- Identify your prospects and customers. Do not go after everyone.
- Differentiate customers in terms of (1) their needs and (2) their value to your company. As for customer value, companies should spend proportionately more effort on their most valuable customers (MVCs). Customer value is estimated as the net present value of all future profits coming from purchases, margin levels, and referrals, less customer-specific servicing costs.
- Interact with individual customers to improve your learning about their individual needs and to build stronger relationships.
- Customize products, services, and messages to each customer.

Mass Marketing	One-to-One Marketing
Average customer	Individual customer
Customer anonymity	Customer profile
Standard product	Customized market offering
Mass production	Customized production
Mass distribution	Individualized distribution
Mass advertising	Individualized message
Mass promotion	Individualized incentives
One-way message	Two-way messages
Economies of scale	Economies of scope
Share of market	Share of customer
All customers	Profitable customers
Customer attraction	Customer retention

table 2.3

Mass Marketing Versus One-to-One Marketing

Source: Adapted from Don Peppers and Martha Rogers, *The One-to-One Future* (New York: Doubleday/Currency, 1993). See their Web site *www.1to1.com.*

customer databases and database marketing

The important point is to know the customer. And in order to know the customer, the company must collect information and store it in a customer database and do database marketing: A **customer database** is an organized collection of comprehensive information about individual customers or prospects that is current, accessible, and actionable for such marketing purposes as lead generation, lead qualification, sale of a product or service, or maintenance of customer relationships. **Database marketing** is the process of building, maintaining, and using customer databases and other databases (products, suppliers, resellers) for the purpose of contacting, transacting, and building relationships.

Many companies confuse a customer mailing list with a customer database. A **customer mailing list** is simply a set of names, addresses, and telephone numbers. A customer database contains much more information. Companies accumulate this information through customer transactions, registration information, telephone queries, cookie information, and information from every contact with a customer (a touchpoint).

A customer database ideally would contain the consumer's past purchases, demographics (age, income, family members, birthdays), psychographics (activities, interests, and opinions), mediagraphics (preferred media), and other useful information. For example, the catalog company Fingerhut possesses some 1,400 pieces of information about each of the 30 million households in its massive customer database. And the Royal Bank of Canada has individual data on its 9 million customers and is able to model the lifetime value of individual customers, their potential interest in different offerings, and their vulnerability to attrition.

A **business database** ideally would contain past purchases of business customers; past volumes, prices, and profits; buyer team member names (and their ages, birthdays, hobbies, and favorite foods); status of current contracts; an estimate of the supplier's share of the customer's business; competitive suppliers; assessment of competitive strengths and weaknesses in selling and servicing the account; and relevant buying practices, patterns, and policies. For example, a Latin American unit of the Swiss pharmaceutical firm

Novartis keeps data on 100,000 of Argentina's farmers, knows their crop protection chemical purchases, groups them by value, and treats each group differently.

data warehouses and datamining

Savvy companies are capturing information every time a customer comes into contact with any of its departments. The touch points include a customer purchase, a customer-requested service call, an online query, or a mail-in rebate card. These data are collected by the company's contact center and organized into a **data warehouse**. Company personnel can capture, query, and analyze the data. Inferences can be drawn about an individual customer's needs and responses. Telemarketers can respond to customer inquiries based on a total picture of the customer relationship.

Through **datamining**, marketing statisticians can extract useful information about individuals, trends, and segments from the mass of data. Datamining involves the use of sophisticated statistical and mathematical techniques such as cluster analysis, automatic interaction detection, predictive modeling, and neural networking. A company that wants to learn the most from its database needs to engage the services of a person or company skilled in datamining.

USING THE DATABASE   In general, companies can use their databases in five ways:

1. *To identify prospects.* Many companies generate sales leads by advertising their product or service. The ads generally contain a response feature, such as a business reply card or toll-free phone number. The database is built from these responses. The company sorts through the database to identify the best prospects, then contacts them by mail, phone, or personal call in an attempt to convert them into customers.

2. *To decide which customers should receive a particular offer.* Companies are interested in selling, up-selling, and cross-selling their products and services. Companies set up criteria describing the ideal target customer for a particular offer. Then they search their customer databases for those who most closely resemble the ideal type.

US West   Twice a year US West sifts through its customer list looking for customers that have the potential to be more profitable. The company's database contains as many as 200 observations about each customer's calling patterns. By looking at demographic profiles, plus the mix of local versus long-distance calls or whether a consumer has voice mail, US West can estimate potential spending. Next, the company determines how much of the customer's likely telecom budget is already coming its way. Armed with that knowledge, US West sets a cutoff point for how much to spend marketing to this customer.

Royal Caribbean   Royal Caribbean uses its database to offer spur-of-the-moment cruise packages to fill all the berths on its ships. It focuses on retired people and single people because they are more able to make quick commitments. Fewer empty berths mean maximized profits for the cruise line.

By noting response rates, a company can improve its targeting precision over time. Following a sale, it can set up an automatic sequence of activities: One week later, send a thank-you note; five weeks later, send a new offer; ten weeks later (if customer has not responded), phone the customer and offer a special discount.

3. *To deepen customer loyalty.* Companies can build interest and enthusiasm by remembering customer preferences; by sending appropriate gifts, discount coupons, and interesting reading material. Here are some examples:

Fingerhut   The skillful use of database marketing and relationship building has made catalog house Fingerhut one of the nation's largest direct-mail marketers. Not only is its database full of demographic details such as age, marital status, and number of children, but it also tracks customers' hobbies, interests, birthdays. Fingerhut tailors mail offers based on what each customer is likely to buy. Fingerhut stays in continuous touch with customers through regular and special promotions, such as annual sweepstakes, free gifts, and deferred billing. Now the company has applied its database marketing to its Web sites.

Mars   Mars is a market leader not only in candy, but also in pet food. In Germany, Mars has compiled the names of virtually every cat-owning German family by contacting veterinarians and also advertising a free booklet titled "How to Take Care of Your Cat." Those who request the booklet fill out a questionnaire, so Mars knows the cat's name, age, and birthday. Mars now sends a birthday card to each cat each year, along with a new-cat-food sample or money-saving coupons for Mars brands. Do the cat owners appreciate this? You bet!

4. *To reactivate customer purchases.* Companies can install automatic mailing programs (automatic marketing) that send out birthday or anniversary cards, Christmas shopping reminders, or off-season promotions. The database can help the company make attractive or timely offers.

5. *To avoid serious customer mistakes.* A major bank confessed to a number of mistakes that it had made by not using its customer database well. In one case, the bank charged a customer a penalty for late payment on his mortgage, failing to note that he headed a company that was a major depositor in this bank. He quit the bank. In a second case, two different staff members of the bank phoned the same mortgage customer offering a home equity loan at different prices. Neither knew that the other had made the call. In a third case, a bank gave a premium customer only standard service in another country.

THE DOWNSIDE OF DATABASE MARKETING   Having described the good news about database marketing, we also have to describe the bad news. Three problems can deter a firm from effectively using CRM. The first is that building and maintaining a customer database requires a large investment in computer hardware, database software, analytical programs, communication links, and skilled personnel. It is difficult to collect the right data, especially to capture all the occasions of company interaction with individual customers. Building a customer database would not be worthwhile in the following cases: (1) where the product is a once in a-lifetime purchase (e.g., a grand piano), (2) where customers show little loyalty to a brand (i.e., there is lots of customer churn), (3) where the unit sale is very small (e.g., a candy bar), and (4) where the cost of gathering information is too high.

The second problem is the difficulty of getting everyone in the company to be customer-oriented and to use the available information. Employees find it far easier to carry on traditional transaction marketing than to practice customer relationship marketing.

The third problem is that not all customers want a relationship with the company, and they may resent knowing that the company has collected that much personal information about them. Marketers must be concerned about customer attitudes toward privacy and security. American Express, long regarded as a leader on privacy issues, does not sell information on specific customer transactions. However, American Express found itself the target of consumer outrage when it announced a partnership with KnowledgeBase Marketing, Inc. that would have made data on 175 million Americans available to any merchant who accepts American Express cards. American Express killed the partnership. AOL, also targeted by privacy advocates, junked a plan to sell subscribers' telephone numbers. Online companies would be smart to explain their privacy policies, and give consumers the right not to have their information stored in a database.

European countries do not look favorably upon database marketing. The European Union just passed a law handicapping the growth of database marketing in its 15 member countries. Europeans are more protective of their private information than are U.S. citizens.

It turns out that database marketing is not for everyone. Database marketing is most frequently used by business marketers and service providers (hotels, banks, and airlines) that normally and easily collect a lot of customer data. It is used less often by packaged-goods retailers and consumer packaged-goods companies, though some companies (Kraft, Quaker Oats, Ralston Purina, and Nabisco) have built databases for certain brands.

At CNA Insurance, five programmers worked for nine months loading five years of claims data into a computer, only to discover that the data had been miscoded. Even if coded correctly, the data must be updated continuously because people move, drop out, or change their interests. Deloitte Consulting reported in 1999 that 70 percent of firms found little or no improvement through CRM implementation. The reasons are many: The system was poorly designed, it became too expensive, users didn't make much use of it or report much benefit, and collaborators ignored the system. All this points to the need for each company to determine how much to invest in building and using database marketing to conduct its customer relationships.

summary

1. New technological advances and new market forces are creating a new economy. Companies and marketers need to add new tools and practices if they hope to be successful.

2. Four specific drivers of the new economy are digitalization and connectivity, disintermediation and reintermediation, customization and customerization, and industry convergence. Digitalization in particular has introduced exciting new capabilities for consumers and for businesses.

3. The new economy is shifting several old economy business practices toward organizing by customer segments (instead of only by products), focusing on customer lifetime value (instead of only transactions), focusing on stakeholders (and not only shareholders), getting everyone to do the

marketing, building brands through behavior (not just advertising), focusing on customer retention (as much as customer acquisition), measuring customer satisfaction, and underpromising and overdelivering.

4. Companies face many questions in adopting e-marketing. Three of them are knowing how to design an attractive Web site, knowing how to advertise on the Web, and knowing how to build a sound revenue and profit model for their dot-com business.

5. Companies are also becoming skilled in Customer Relationship Management (CRM), which focuses on meeting the individual needs of valued customers. The skill requires building a customer database and doing datamining to detect trends, segments, and individual needs.

applications

marketing debate – napster

A major benefit of the Internet is its ability to link computer users together so they may share information rapidly and easily. Because it requires shared resources, peer-to-peer technology enables groups of computer users to assemble networks and share information without using servers and expensive infrastructure. The music file sharing program Napster is a famous example of this type of exchange. Napster connects millions of music lovers together and allows them to share music in the form of digitized sound files called mp3s. Napster sparked a veritable revolution in the way people listen to music. Millions of music fans around the world used the software to search for and download digitized music from a virtual library supported and stocked by other users, all

without paying a cent. Some recording artists and record industry representatives have argued that Napster facilitates the pirating of copyrighted material, while other artists applaud the program for building new audiences and hail the file-sharing concept as the next wave of music distribution. A recent court decision sided with those seeking to limit Napster, and the company was ordered to prohibit the exchange of copyrighted material.

Take a position: File-sharing services such as Napster need to be closely regulated to satisfy all laws versus File sharing services such as Napster satisfy unfulfilled consumer needs and should be given more freedom.

marketing and advertising

1. The ePad ad in Figure 1, targeted to consumers, highlights one aspect of the boom in electronic payment: The legality of electronic signatures for completing a variety of sales transactions. Interlink Electronics is positioning the ePad as a simple yet technologically advanced method of securely and permanently documenting a consumer's signature on a paperless real estate contract or any other electronic transaction.

   a. How does Interlink Electronics build on the major drivers of the new economy in marketing the ePad?

   b. If Interlink wanted to expand from this B2C ad to a B2B ad, who might the company target and with what benefits?

   c. How might Interlink Electronics enhance its revenue stream by targeting business buyers for ePad purchases?

2. The ad for Garmin StreetPilot in-vehicle satellite navigation system in Figure 2 focuses on New Economy connectivity. At the same time, it suggests access to the burgeoning world of m-commerce, in which customers will be able to locate and buy goods and services in the vast virtual marketspace, not just the marketplace.

   a. Which core marketing concepts are reflected in the text of this ad?

   b. If Garmin collected data about customer use of the StreetPilot, how might it use this information for relationship marketing?

   c. What concerns might customers have if Garmin decided to track their use of the StreetPilot? How could Garmin respond to such concerns?

Figure 1

Figure 2

online marketing today

While some resellers fear that pure click e-tailers will steal their customers, they also worry about losing business to big suppliers who can afford to establish flashy e-commerce sites. For their part, suppliers want to ensure proper attention and emphasis from resellers who handle a variety of brands and products. With these issues in mind, Hewlett-Packard set up the AisleOnline e-commerce framework—complete with ordering, inventory, and fulfillment functions—as a free service for resellers of its DesignJet printers. Smaller HP resellers simply post a link to the main AisleOnline e-commerce site; larger resellers get their own customized versions, complete with logos and pricing. Visit the site of Laser-Life Technologies *www.laser-life.com* and follow the HP DesignJet link to see a customized AisleOnline site. How does AisleOnline help HP build supply-chain relationships and deliver value to final buyers? Which of the new economy practices is HP applying with the AisleOnline program?

Source: Jim Sterne, "United We Stand," *Inc. Tech 2001,* June 15, 2001, pp. 87–88.

notes

1. George S. Day and David B. Montgomery, "Charting New Directions for Marketing." *Journal of Marketing* (Special Issue 1999) pp. 3–13, and Donna L. Hoffman "The Revolution Will Not Be Televised: Introduction to the Special Issue on Marketing Science and the Internet," *Marketing Science* (Winter 2000): pp. 1–3.

2. Yoram J. Wind and Vijay Mahajan with Robert E. Gunther, *Convergence Marketing: Strategies for Reaching the New Hybrid Consumer* (Upper Saddle River, NJ: Prentice Hall PTR, 2002).

3. Wind, op. cit.

4. Bill Gates with Collins Hemingway, *Business at the Speed of Thought: Using a Digital Nervous System* (New York: Warner Books, 1999).

5. *Pew Internet and American Life Project Survey,* November–December 2000.

6. Ralph A. Oliva, "Nowhere to Hide," *Marketing Management,* July/August 2001, pp. 44–46.

7. Chuck Martin, *Net Future* (New York: McGraw-Hill, 1999).

8. J. Timothy Hunt, "Beyond Point and Click," *Financial Post—Canada,* May 1, 2001.

9. Jeffrey F. Rayport and Bernard J. Jaworski, *e-commerce* (New York: McGraw-Hill, 2001), p. 116.

10. Tilman Kemmler, Monika Kubicová, Robert Musslewhite, and Rodney Prezeau, "E-Performance II—The Good, the Bad, and the Merely Average," an exclusive to *mckinseyquarterly.com,* 2001.

11. George S. Day, "Capabilities for Forging Customer Relationships," *Working Paper Series, Marketing Science Institute,* Report No. 00-118, 2000.

12. Don Peppers and Martha Rogers, *The One-to-One Future* (New York: Doubleday/Currency, 1993).

building customer satisfaction, value, and retention

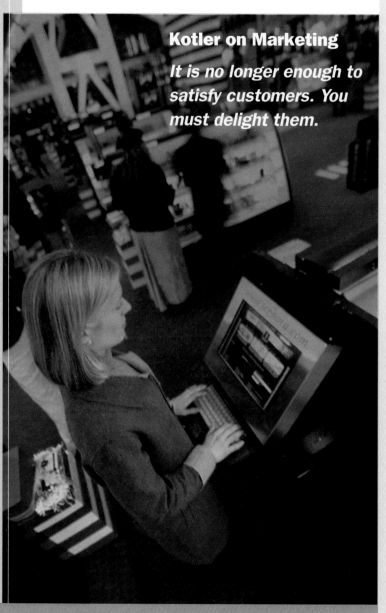

Kotler on Marketing

It is no longer enough to satisfy customers. You must delight them.

In this chapter, we will address the following questions:

- What are customer value and satisfaction, and how can companies deliver them?
- What makes a high-performance business?
- How can companies both attract and retain customers?
- How can companies improve both customer and company profitability?
- How can companies deliver total quality?

Today's companies are facing their toughest competition ever. We argued in Chapter 1 that companies can outperform the competition if they can move from a product and sales philosophy to a marketing philosophy. John Chambers, CEO of Cisco Systems, put it well: "Make your customer the center of your culture." In Chapter 2, we showed that companies need to move rapidly into the new economy and employ Internet, wireless, and other technologies to achieve a competitive advantage.

In this chapter, we spell out in detail how companies can go about winning customers and outperforming competitors. The answer lies in doing a better job of meeting or exceeding customer expectations. Customer-centered

*companies are adept at building customers, not just products; they are skilled in market engi-
neering, not just product engineering.*

*Too many companies think that it is the marketing or sales department's job to acquire and
manage customers, but, in fact, marketing is only one factor in attracting and keeping customers. The best marketing department in the world cannot sell products that are poorly made
or fail to meet a need. The marketing department can be effective only in companies whose
employees have implemented a competitively superior customer value-delivery system.*

*For example, take McDonald's. Every day an average of 45 million people visit its 29,000
restaurants in 121 countries. People do not swarm to McDonald's outlets solely because they
love the hamburgers; other restaurants make better-tasting hamburgers. People are flocking to
a system, not a hamburger. Throughout the world, this fine-tuned system of suppliers, franchise
owners, and employees delivers a high standard of what McDonald's calls QSCV—quality, service, cleanliness, and value.[1] This chapter describes and illustrates the philosophy of the
customer-focused firm and value marketing.[2]*

defining customer value and satisfaction

Over 38 years ago, Peter Drucker observed that a company's first task is "to create customers." However, customers face a vast array of product and brand choices, prices,
and suppliers. How do they make their choices?

We believe that customers estimate which offer will deliver the most value. Customers
are value-maximizers, within the bounds of search costs and limited knowledge, mobility,
and income. They form an expectation of value and act on it. Whether or not the offer lives
up to the value expectation affects both satisfaction and repurchase probability.

customer perceived value

Our premise is that customers will buy from the firm that they see as offering the highest
perceived value (Figure 3.1): **Customer perceived value (CPV)** is the difference between
the prospective customer's evaluation of all the benefits and all the costs of an offering
and the perceived alternatives. **Total customer value** is the perceived monetary value of
the bundle of economic, functional, and psychological benefits customers expect from a
given market offering. **Total customer cost** is the bundle of costs customers expect to
incur in evaluating, obtaining, using, and disposing of the given market offering.

An example will help here. Suppose the buyer for a large construction company
wants to buy a tractor from Caterpillar or Komatsu. The competing salespeople carefully
describe their respective offers. The buyer wants to use the tractor in residential construction work. He would like the tractor to deliver certain levels of reliability, durability,
performance, and resale value. He evaluates the tractors and decides that Caterpillar has
a higher product value based on perceived reliability, durability, performance, and resale
value. He also perceives differences in the accompanying services—delivery, training,
and maintenance—and decides that Caterpillar provides better service and more knowledgeable and responsive personnel. Finally, he places higher value on Caterpillar's corporate image. He adds up all the values from these four sources—product, services, personnel, and image—and perceives Caterpillar as delivering greater customer value.

Does he buy the Caterpillar tractor? Not necessarily. He also examines his total cost
of transacting with Caterpillar versus Komatsu, which consists of more than the money.
As Adam Smith observed over two centuries ago, "The real price of anything is the toil
and trouble of acquiring it." Total customer cost includes the buyer's time, energy, and
psychic costs. The buyer evaluates these elements together with the monetary cost to
form a total customer cost. Then the buyer considers whether Caterpillar's total cus-

---

figure **3.1**

Determinants of Customer-
Delivered Value

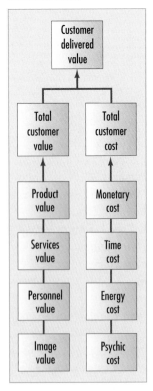

tomer cost is too high in relation to the total customer value Caterpillar delivers. If it is, the buyer might choose the Komatsu tractor. The buyer will buy from whichever source he thinks delivers the highest perceived customer value.

Now let us use this decision-making theory to help Caterpillar succeed in selling to this buyer. Caterpillar can improve its offer in three ways. First, it can increase total customer value by improving product, services, personnel, and/or image benefits. Second, it can reduce the buyer's nonmonetary costs by reducing the time, energy, and psychic costs. Third, it can reduce its product's monetary cost to the buyer.

Suppose Caterpillar concludes that the buyer sees its offer as worth $20,000. Further, suppose Caterpillar's cost of producing the tractor is $14,000. This means that Caterpillar's offer potentially generates $6,000 over the company's cost so Caterpillar needs to charge a price between $14,000 and $20,000. If it charges less than $14,000, it won't cover its costs; if it charges more than $20,000, it will price itself out of the market.

The price Caterpillar charges will determine how much value will be delivered to the buyer and how much will flow to Caterpillar. For example, if Caterpillar charges $19,000, it is creating $1,000 of customer perceived value and keeping $5,000 for itself. The lower Caterpillar sets its price, the higher the customer perceived value and, therefore, the higher the customer's incentive to purchase. To win the sale, Caterpillar must offer more customer perceived value than Komatsu does.[3]

Some marketers might argue that the process we have described is too rational. Suppose the customer chose the Komatsu tractor. How can we explain this choice? Here are three possibilities:

1. The buyer might be under orders to buy at the lowest price. The Caterpillar salesperson's task is to convince the buyer's manager that buying on price alone will result in lower long-term profits.
2. The buyer will retire before the company realizes that the Komatsu tractor is more expensive to operate. The buyer will look good in the short run; he is maximizing personal benefit. The Caterpillar salesperson's task is to convince other people in the customer company that Caterpillar delivers greater customer value.
3. The buyer enjoys a long-term friendship with the Komatsu salesperson. In this case, Caterpillar's salesperson needs to show the buyer that the Komatsu tractor will draw complaints from the tractor operators when they discover its high fuel cost and need for frequent repairs.

The point of these examples is clear: Buyers operate under various constraints and occasionally make choices that give more weight to their personal benefit than to the company's benefit. However, customer perceived value is a useful framework that applies to many situations and yields rich insights. Here are its implications: First, the seller must assess the total customer value and total customer cost associated with each competitor's offer in order to know how his or her offer rates in the buyer's mind. Second, the seller who is at a customer perceived value disadvantage has two alternatives: to increase total customer value or to decrease total customer cost. The former calls for strengthening or augmenting the offer's product, services, personnel, and image benefits. The latter calls for reducing the buyer's costs by reducing the price, simplifying the ordering and delivery process, or absorbing some buyer risk by offering a warranty.[4]

total customer satisfaction

Whether the buyer is satisfied after purchase depends on the offer's performance in relation to the buyer's expectations. In general, **satisfaction** is a person's feelings of pleasure or disappointment resulting from comparing a product's perceived performance (or outcome) in relation to his or her expectations. If the performance falls short of expectations, the customer is dissatisfied. If the performance matches the expectations, the customer is satisfied. If the performance exceeds expectations, the customer is highly satisfied or delighted.[5]

The link between customer satisfaction and customer loyalty is not proportional. Suppose customer satisfaction is rated on a scale from one to five. At a very low level of customer satisfaction (level one), customers are likely to abandon the company and even bad-mouth it. At levels two to four, customers are fairly satisfied but still find it easy to switch when a better offer comes along. At level five, the customer is very likely to repurchase and even spread good word of mouth about the company. High satisfaction or delight creates an emotional bond with the brand or company, not just a rational preference. Xerox's senior management found out that its "completely satisfied" customers are six times more likely to repurchase Xerox products over the following 18 months than its "very satisfied" customers.[6]

CUSTOMER EXPECTATIONS   How do buyers form their expectations? From past buying experience, friends' and associates' advice, and marketers' and competitors' information and promises. If marketers raise expectations too high, the buyer is likely to be disappointed. However, if the company sets expectations too low, it won't attract enough buyers (although it will satisfy those who do buy).[7]

Some of today's most successful companies are raising expectations and delivering performances to match. These companies are aiming for TCS—total customer satisfaction. Xerox, for example, guarantees "total satisfaction" and will replace at its expense any dissatisfied customer's equipment within a period of three years after purchase. Cigna advertises, "We'll never be 100% satisfied until you are, too," and one of Honda's ads says, "One reason our customers are so satisfied is that we aren't." Nissan invites potential Infiniti buyers to drop in for a "guest drive" (not a "test drive"), because the Japanese word for customer is "honored guest." Look at what high satisfaction can do.

Saturn   About a decade ago, Saturn (General Motors' newest car division) changed the whole buyer–seller relationship with a New Deal for car buyers: There would be a fixed price (none of the traditional haggling); a 30-day guarantee or money back; and salespeople on salary, not on commission (none of the traditional hard sell). Once a sale is made, the sales staff surrounds the new owner for a commemorative photo. "The company celebrated its tenth anniversary in 2000 when more than 40,000 Saturn owners visited company headquarters in Spring Hill, Tennessee, to attend the annual Homecoming."[8] Saturn enjoys customer loyalty rates in the 60 percent range, compared with overall industry rates below 40 percent.

A customer's decision to be loyal or to defect is the sum of many small encounters with the company. Consulting firm Forum Corporation says that in order for all these small encounters to add up to customer loyalty, companies need to create a "branded customer experience." Here is how San Francisco's Joie de Vivre chain does this.

Joie de Vivre   Joie de Vivre Hospitality Inc., operates a chain of boutique hotels, restaurants, and resorts in the San Francisco area. Each property's unique décor, quirky amenities, and thematic style are often loosely based on popular magazines. For example, the Hotel del Sol—a converted motel bearing a yellow exterior and surrounded by palm trees wrapped with festive lights—is described as "kind of *Martha Stewart Living* meets *Islands* magazine."[9] Two Silicon Valley hotels offer guests high-speed Internet connections in their rooms and by the pool.[10] The boutique concept enables the hotels to offer personal touches such as vitamins in place of chocolates on pillows. Joie de Vivre now owns the largest number of independent hotel properties in the Bay Area.

DELIVERING HIGH CUSTOMER VALUE   The key to generating high customer loyalty is to deliver high customer value. According to Michael Lanning, in his *Delivering Profitable Value*, a company must design a competitively superior value proposition aimed at a specific market segment, backed by a superior value-delivery system.[11]

The **value proposition** consists of the whole cluster of benefits the company promises to deliver; it is more than the core positioning of the offering. For example, Volvo's core positioning is "safety," but the buyer is promised more than just a safe car; other benefits include a long-lasting car, good service, and a long warranty period. Basically, the value proposition is a statement about the resulting experience customers will gain from the company's market offering and from their relationship with the supplier. The brand must represent a promise about the total experience customers can expect. Whether the promise is kept depends on the company's ability to manage its value-delivery system. The **value-delivery system** includes all the experiences the customer will have on the way to obtaining and using the offering.

A similar theme is emphasized by Simon Knox and Stan Maklan in their *Competing on Value*.[12] Too many companies create a value gap by failing to align brand value with customer value. Brand marketers try to distinguish their brand from others by a slogan ("washes whiter") or a unique selling proposition ("A Mars a day helps you work, rest, and play"), or by augmenting the basic offering with added services ("Our hotel will provide a computer upon request"). Yet, they are less successful in delivering distinctive customer value, primarily because their marketing people focus on brand development. Whether customers will actually receive the promised value proposition will depend on the marketer's ability to influence various core business processes. Knox and Maklan want company marketers to spend as much time influencing the company's core processes as they do designing the brand profile. Here is a company that is a master at delivering customer value.

Superquinn   Superquinn is Ireland's largest supermarket chain and its founder, Feargal Quinn, is Ireland's master marketer. A greeter is posted at the store entrance to welcome and help customers and even offer coffee, to provide umbrellas in case of rain and carryout service to customers' cars. Department managers post themselves in the aisles to interact with customers and answer questions. There is a high-quality salad bar, fresh bread baked every four hours, and indications of when produce arrived, including the farmers' pictures. Superquinn operates a child-care center. It offers a loyalty program that gives points for the amount purchased and also for discovering anything wrong with the store, such as dented cans or bad tomatoes. The loyalty card is recognized by a dozen other firms (a bank, gas station, etc.) who give points for purchasing at their establishments. Because everything is done to exceed normal customer expectations, Superquinn stores enjoy an almost cult following.[13]

In addition to tracking customer value expectations and satisfaction, companies need to monitor their competitors' performance in these areas. One company was pleased to find that 80 percent of its customers said they were satisfied. Then the CEO found out that its leading competitor attained a 90 percent customer satisfaction score. He was further dismayed when he learned that this competitor was aiming for a 95 percent satisfaction score.

Table 3.1 describes four methods companies use to track customer satisfaction.

For customer-centered companies, customer satisfaction is both a goal and a marketing tool. Companies that achieve high customer satisfaction ratings make sure that their target market knows it. The Honda Accord received the number-one rating in customer satisfaction from J. D. Powers for several years, and Honda's advertising of this fact helped it sell more Accords. Dell Computer's meteoric growth in the computer systems industry can be partly attributed to achieving and advertising its number-one rank in customer satisfaction. For more information on how Dell Computer Corporation gets closer to customers, see "Marketing Insight: Customer Configured: How Dell Computer Corporation Clicks with Customers."

MEASURING SATISFACTION   Although the customer-centered firm seeks to create high customer satisfaction, that is not its main goal. If the company increases customer satisfaction by lowering its price or increasing its services, the result may be lower profits.

table **3.1**		
Tools for Tracking and Measuring Customer Satisfaction	*Complaint and suggestion systems:*	A customer-centered organization makes it easy for customers to register suggestions and complaints. Some customer-centered companies—P&G, General Electric, Whirlpool—establish hot lines with toll-free numbers. Companies are also using Web sites and e-mail for quick, two-way communication.
	Customer satisfaction surveys:	Studies show that although customers are dissatisfied with one out of every four purchases, less than 5 percent will complain. Most customers will buy less or switch suppliers. Responsive companies measure customer satisfaction directly by conducting periodic surveys. While collecting customer satisfaction data, it is also useful to ask additional questions to measure repurchase intention and to measure the likelihood or willingness to recommend the company and brand to others.
	Ghost shopping:	Companies can hire people to pose as potential buyers to report on strong and weak points experienced in buying the company's and competitors' products. These mystery shoppers can even test how the company's sales personnel handle various situations. Managers themselves should leave their offices from time to time, enter company and competitor sales situations where they are unknown, and experience firsthand the treatment they receive. A variant of this is for managers to phone their own company with questions and complaints to see how the calls are handled.
	Lost customer analysis:	Companies should contact customers who have stopped buying or who have switched to another supplier to learn why this happened. Not only is it important to conduct exit interviews when customers first stop buying; it is also necessary to monitor the customer loss rate.

The company might be able to increase its profitability by means other than increased satisfaction (for example, by improving manufacturing processes or investing more in R&D). Also, the company has many stakeholders, including employees, dealers, suppliers, and stockholders. Spending more to increase customer satisfaction might divert funds from increasing the satisfaction of other "partners." Ultimately, the company must operate on the philosophy that it is trying to deliver a high level of customer satisfaction subject to delivering acceptable levels of satisfaction to the other stakeholders, given its total resources.

When customers rate their satisfaction with an element of the company's performance—say, delivery—the company needs to recognize that customers vary in how they define good delivery. It could mean early delivery, on-time delivery, order completeness, and so on. Yet if the company had to spell out every element in detail, customers would face a huge survey questionnaire. The company must also realize that two customers can report being "highly satisfied" for different reasons. One may be easily satisfied most of the time and the other might be hard to please but was pleased on this occasion.[14]

Claes Fornell has developed the American Customer Satisfaction Index (ACSI) to measure the perceived satisfaction consumers feel with different firms, industries, economic sectors, and national economies. Some companies and brands with high ACSI scores in 2001 include H. J. Heinz Company (89), Colgate-Palmolive (85), Cadillac (88), and Dell (78).[15]

Companies need to be especially concerned today with their customer satisfaction level because the Internet provides a tool for consumers to spread bad word of mouth—as well as good word of mouth—to the rest of the world.

marketing **insight**

Customer Configured: How Dell Computer Corporation Clicks with Customers

"We have a tremendously clear business model," says Michael Dell, "There's no confusion about what the value proposition is, what the company offers, and why it's great for customers." Dell is now the number one computer systems company.

Dell is extremely responsive. Buyers go on Dell's Web site and design their own computer. They give their payment authorization, which means that Dell receives the money in advance and can use the funds to pay for the supplies needed to build the computer. Because its computers are built-to-order, Dell carries an industry-leading four days of inventory. It takes delivery of components just minutes before they are needed. At its Austin, Texas, factories, a Dell System can in some cases be built, have the software installed, be tested, and be packed in eight hours. Dell's costs are lower, allowing it to price its computers lower than competitors' prices if it wishes.

Yet speed is only one part of the Dell equation. Service is the other. In fact, it was through veering away from its successful business model that Dell discovered the importance of customer service. In 1993, the company began trying to sell to retailers, mainly because everyone else was. Customers were disgruntled because of poor retail service. Dell ultimately abandoned the retail channel.

Most important, Michael Dell decided that "there would be more things we'd have to do besides build a PC." He knew his company had two kinds of customers, corporate and consumer. Whereas the consumer would buy mainly because of price, the corporate buyer needed a carefully developed relationship. Like most successful companies, Dell put the most resources into building relationships with its most profitable customers.

Corporate customers make up about 80 percent of Dell's business, and the company manages its corporate accounts with a top-notch sales team. Dell also installs custom software and keeps track of business customers' inventory for them. Through the use of Premier Dell.com, cus-

tomized customer Web pages at the Dell site, the company has created a 24-hour order-entry system. Big customers can click on the site to see all kinds of information about their preferences and needs. The site can be accessed worldwide by any company subsidiary; and employees, not just purchasing agents, can use the Premier Dell.com to purchase computers according to an automated policy. "It's the ultimate network," Michael Dell says, "and a fabulous way for us to interact with our customers."

The normal practice of companies is to "build to stock." This is a guessing game that companies often lose by building too much or too little. In the auto industry, cars will sit unsold in dealers' lots for 60 days, tying up working capital. Why have auto and other companies not moved from the inefficient "build to stock" model of production to Dell's "build to order" model? Auto manufacturers have invited Michael Dell to speak to them on several occasions. The consensus seems to be that Dell works with 50 main suppliers to put together a $1,000 PC, but a car manufacturer may have to work with 900 suppliers to put together a $20,000 car. In addition to the technical challenge, the auto industry faces dealer and legislative hurdles.

Premier Dell.com is a special business-oriented part of the Dell Web site that allows customers to interact with Dell and customize all phases of doing business with Dell.

Sources: Michele Marchetti, "Dell Computer," *Sales & Marketing Management* (October 1997) 50–53; Evan Ramstad, "Dell Fights PC Wars by Emphasizing Customer Service—Focus Wins Big Clients and Gives IBM and Compaq a Run for Their Money," *Wall Street Journal*, August 15, 1997, p. B4; Saroja Girishankar, "Dell's Site Has Business in Crosshairs," *Internetweek*, April 13, 1998, p. 1; "The *Internetweek* Interview—Michael Dell, Chairman and CEO, Dell Computer," *Internetweek*, April 13, 1998, p. 8; Dale Buss, "Custom Cars Stuck in Gridlock," *The Industry Standard*, October 23, 2000, pp. 90–97; and "A Revolution of One," *The Economist*, April 14, 2001; Betsy Morris, "Can Michael Dell Escape the Box?" *Fortune*, October 16, 2000; Gary McWilliams, "Dell Computer Has a Midlife Crisis," *Wall Street Journal*, August 31, 2000; "Dell Increases Its Market Share as PC Sales Slow," *New York Times*, January 22, 2001; Leah Beth Ward, "Dell Sales Overtake Compaq," *Dallas Morning News*, January 24, 2000.

the nature of high-performance businesses

Some companies navigate all these pitfalls to reach their customer value and satisfaction goals. We call these companies **high-performance businesses**. The consulting firm of Arthur D. Little proposed a model of the characteristics of a high-performance business. It pointed to the four factors shown in Figure 3.2 as keys to success: stakeholders, processes, resources, and organization.[16]

stakeholders

As its first stop on the road to high performance, the business must define its stakeholders and their needs. Traditionally, most businesses focused on their stockholders. Today's businesses are increasingly recognizing that unless they nurture other stakeholders—customers, employees, suppliers, distributors—the business may never earn sufficient profits for the stockholders.

A company can aim to deliver satisfaction levels above the minimum for different stakeholders. For example, it might aim to delight its customers, perform well for its employees, and deliver a threshold level of satisfaction to its suppliers. In setting these levels, a company must be careful not to violate the various stakeholder groups' sense of fairness about the relative treatment they are getting.[17]

There is a dynamic relationship connecting the stakeholder groups. A smart company creates a high level of employee satisfaction, which leads to higher effort, which leads to higher-quality products and services, which creates higher customer satisfaction, which leads to more repeat business, which leads to higher growth and profits, which leads to high stockholder satisfaction, which leads to more investment, and so on. This is the virtuous circle that spells profits and growth.

processes

A company can accomplish its stakeholder goals only by managing and linking work processes. High-performance companies are increasingly focusing on the need to manage core business processes such as new-product development, customer attraction and retention, and order fulfillment. They are reengineering the work flows and building cross-functional teams responsible for each process.[18]

figure **3.2**

The High Performance Business

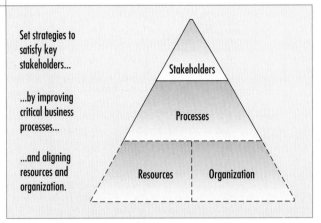

Source: P. Ranganath Nayak, Erica Drazen, and George Kastner, "The High-Performance Business: Accelerating Performance Improvement," *Prism* (First Quarter 1992), p. 6. Reprinted by permission of Arthur D. Little, Inc.

For example, at Xerox a Customer Operations Group links sales, shipping, installation, service, and billing so that these activities flow smoothly into one another. Winning companies will be those that achieve excellent capabilities in managing core business processes through cross-functional teams. A McKinsey & Company study reported:

> High-performing companies emphasize a set of skills notably different from their less successful counterparts. They value cross-functional skills, while other companies pride themselves on their functional strengths. High performers boast, "We've got the best project managers in the world." Low performers say, "We've got the best circuit designers."[19]

AT&T, Polaroid, and Motorola are companies that have reorganized their employees into cross-functional teams; but cross-functional teams are also found in nonprofits and government organizations as well.

San Diego Zoo   As the San Diego Zoo's mission changed from simple exhibition to conservation to education, it changed its organization. The revamped zoo consists of bioclimatic zones, exhibits that immerse zoogoers in an environment of predator and prey and flora and fauna from different parts of the world. Because the zones themselves are more interdependent, the employees who manage them must work together. Gardeners, groundskeepers, and animal care experts are no longer separated by traditional boundaries.[20]

resources

To carry out its business processes, a company needs resources—labor power, materials, machines, information, and energy. Traditionally, companies owned and controlled most of the resources that entered their businesses, but this situation is changing. Some resources under their control are not performing as well as those that they could obtain from outside. Many companies today outsource less critical resources if they can be obtained at better quality or lower cost. Frequently, outsourced resources include cleaning services, landscaping, and auto fleet management. Kodak even turned over the management of its data processing department to IBM. Here are two examples of successful outsourcing.

Palm Computing   According to Donna Dubinsky, president of Palm Computing, her company outsources services whenever they can be done better and more cheaply. This includes outsourcing manufacturing, logistics, services, and customer support systems. Her staff is a group of talented product designers, inventors, and engineers, along with a senior group who manage the outsourced infrastructure organizations.

Topsy-Tail   Tomima Edmark, inventor of the plastic hairstyling piece called Topsy-Tail, grew her company's sales to $80 million in 1993 with only two employees. Instead of hiring 50 or more employees, Edmark and her two employees set up a network of 20 vendors who handled everything from product manufacturing to servicing the retail accounts. Yet Edmark has been careful to follow the first rule of effective outsourcing: She keeps control of new-product development and marketing strategy, the core competencies that make up the heart of her company.[21]

The key, then, is to own and nurture the core resources and competencies that make up the essence of the business. Nike, for example, does not manufacture its own shoes, because certain Asian manufacturers are more competent in this task; but Nike nurtures its superiority in shoe design and shoe merchandising, its two core competencies. We can say that a **core competency** has three characteristics: (1) It is a source of competitive advantage in that it makes a significant contribution to perceived customer benefits, (2) it has a breadth of applications to a wide variety of markets, and (3) it is difficult for competitors to imitate.[22]

Competitive advantage also accrues to companies that possess distinctive capabilities. Whereas core competencies tend to refer to areas of special technical and production expertise, **distinctive capabilities** tend to describe excellence in broader business processes. For example, Wal-Mart has a distinctive capability in product replenishment, based on several core competencies including information system design and logistics. George Day sees market-driven organizations as excelling in three distinctive capabilities: market sensing, customer linking, and channel bonding.[23]

Competitive advantage ultimately derives from how well the company has "fitted" its core competencies and distinctive capabilities into tightly interlocking "activity systems." Competitors find it hard to imitate companies such as Southwest Airlines, Dell, or IKEA because they are unable to copy their activity systems.

organization and organizational culture

A company's **organization** consists of its structures, policies, and corporate culture, all of which can become dysfunctional in a rapidly changing business environment. Whereas structures and policies can be changed (with difficulty), the company's culture is very hard to change. Yet changing a corporate culture is often the key to successfully implementing a new strategy.

What exactly is a **corporate culture**? Most businesspeople would be hard-pressed to find words to describe this elusive concept, which some define as "the shared experiences, stories, beliefs, and norms that characterize an organization." Yet, walk into any company and the first thing that strikes you is the corporate culture—the way people are dressed, how they talk to one another, the way they greet customers.

Sometimes corporate culture develops organically and is transmitted directly from the CEO's personality and habits to the company employees. Such is the case with computer giant Microsoft, which began as an entrepreneurial upstart. Even as it has grown to a $23-billion company, Microsoft has not lost the hard-driving culture perpetuated by founder Bill Gates. In fact, most feel that Microsoft's ultracompetitive culture is the biggest key to its success and to its much-criticized dominance in the computing industry.[24]

Microsoft   Do not let the relaxed, low-rise campus buildings, plush lawns, shaded copses, and strictly casual dress code fool you. Microsofties, as Microsoft employees refer to themselves, are fueled with a take-no-prisoners competitive drive that mirrors Gates's own persona. Rivals from Silicon Valley refer to them as "microserfs." Like Gates, who founded the company as a teenager, Microsofties are young; nearly one-third are age 29 or younger, with an average age of 34. Their casual dress code also stems from Gates, who used to fall asleep on the floor of his garage after an all-night code-writing session and go to work in his rumpled clothing the next morning. Although you would not know it to look at the T-shirt-clad employees, many of them are rolling in money from Microsoft stock options. Part of the competitive zeal is due to the drive to sustain a lofty share price, which traded in multiples at or near twice the S&P's 500 until the recent technology stock slide. Insiders own over one-third of the company, and there are more millionaires on staff than in any other firm on earth.

What happens when entrepreneurial companies grow and need to create a tighter structure? What happens when companies with clashing cultures enter a joint venture or merger? In a study by Coopers & Lybrand of 100 companies with failed or troubled mergers, 855 of executives polled said that differences in management style and practices were the major problem.[25] This was the case when Germany's Daimler merged with Chrysler in 1998.

DaimlerChrysler   Daimler-Benz AG and Chrysler Corp. merged in 1998 to form DaimlerChrysler. Executives from both companies thought a host of synergies would enable DaimlerChrysler to swiftly build a global automotive empire. Fundamental differences in the way the two corporations did business, however, contributed to early departures by executives, a stock price slide, management restructuring, and even considerable losses by the American manufacturer. The two companies had contrasting management styles, Daimler preferring to operate a classic bureaucracy and Chrysler traditionally giving decision-making ability to managers lower in the ranks. After restructuring the company in 1999 to give more autonomy to the American division, DaimlerChrysler CEO Jürgen Schrempp angered Chrysler employees anew when he announced that he always intended to make Chrysler a division of Daimler. What began as a highly-touted global "merger of equals" turned into a disaster as the losses piled up at Chrysler and DaimlerChrysler stock languished at more than half off its peak. The company announced 26,000 layoffs in February 2001.[26]

The question of what accounts for the success of long-lasting, high-performance companies was addressed in a six-year study by Collins and Porras called *Built to Last*.[27] The Stanford researchers identified two companies in each of 18 industries, one that they called a "visionary company" and one that they called a "comparison company." The visionary companies were acknowledged as the industry leaders and widely admired; they set ambitious goals, communicated them to their employees, and embraced a high purpose beyond making money. They also outperformed the comparison companies by a wide margin. The visionary companies included General Electric, Hewlett-Packard, and Boeing; the corresponding comparison companies were Westinghouse, Texas Instruments, and McDonnell Douglas.

The authors found three commonalities among the 18 market leaders. First, the visionary companies each held a distinctive set of values from which they did not deviate. Thus, IBM has held to the principles of respect for the individual, customer satisfaction, and continuous quality improvement throughout its history;[28] and Johnson & Johnson holds to the principle that its first responsibility is to its customers, its second to its employees, its third to its community, and its fourth to its stockholders. The second commonality is that visionary companies express their purpose in enlightened terms. Xerox wants to improve "office productivity" and Monsanto wants to "help end hunger in the world." According to Collins and Porras, a company's core purpose should not be confused with specific business goals or strategies and should not be simply a description of a company's product line. (See "Marketing Memo: Why Do You Exist and What Do You Stand For?") The third commonality is that visionary companies have developed a vision of their future and act to implement it. IBM is now working to establish leadership as a "network-centric" company and not simply as the leading computer manufacturer.

Successful companies may need to adopt a new view of how to craft their strategy. The traditional view is that senior management hammers out the strategy and hands it down. Gary Hamel offers the contrasting view that imaginative ideas on strategy exist in many places within a company.[29] Senior management should identify and encourage fresh ideas from three groups who tend to be underrepresented in strategy making: employees with youthful perspectives; employees who are far removed from company headquarters; and employees who are new to the industry. Each group is capable of challenging company orthodoxy and stimulating new ideas.

Strategy must be developed by identifying and selecting among different views of the future. The Royal Dutch/Shell Group has pioneered scenario analysis. A **scenario analysis** consists of developing plausible representations of a firm's possible future that make different assumptions about forces driving the market and include different uncertainties. Managers need to think through each scenario with the question: "What

---

will we do if it happens?" They need to adopt one scenario as the most probable and watch for signposts as time passes that might confirm or disconfirm that scenario.[30]

High-performance companies are set up to create and deliver superior customer value and satisfaction. Let us see how this is done.

delivering customer value and satisfaction

In a hypercompetitive economy with increasingly rational buyers, a company can only win by creating and delivering superior value. This involves the following five capabilities: understanding customer value; creating customer value; delivering customer value; capturing customer value; and sustaining customer value. To succeed, a company needs to use the concepts of a value chain and a value-delivery network.

value chain

Michael Porter of Harvard proposed the **value chain** as a tool for identifying ways to create more customer value (see Figure 3.3).[31] Every firm is a synthesis of activities that are performed to design, produce, market, deliver, and support its product. The value chain identifies nine strategically relevant activities that create value and cost in a specific business. These nine value-creating activities consist of five primary activities and four support activities.

The primary activities represent the sequence of bringing materials into the business (inbound logistics), converting them into final products (operations), shipping out final products (outbound logistics), marketing them (marketing and sales), and servicing them (service). The support activities—procurement, technology development, human resource management, and firm infrastructure—are handled in certain specialized departments, but not only there. For example, several departments may do some procurement and hiring of people. The firm's infrastructure covers the costs of general management, planning, finance, accounting, legal, and government affairs that are borne by all the primary and support activities.

The firm's task is to examine its costs and performance in each value-creating activity and to look for ways to improve it. The firm should estimate its competitors' costs

---

figure **3.3**

The Generic Value Chain

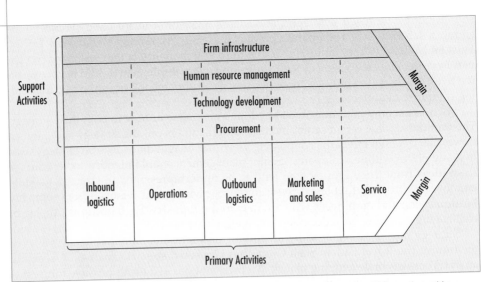

Source: Reprinted with the permission of The Free Press, an imprint of Simon & Schuster, from Michael E. Porter, *Competitive Advantage. Creating and Sustaining Superior Performance.* Copyright 1985 by Michael E. Porter.

and performances as **benchmarks** against which to compare its own costs and performances. It should go further and study the "best of class" practices of the world's best companies.[32]

The firm's success depends not only on how well each department performs its work, but also on how well the various departmental activities are coordinated. Too often, company departments act to maximize their interests. A credit department may take a long time to check a prospective customer's credit so as not to incur bad debts. Meanwhile, the customer waits and the salesperson is frustrated. A traffic department chooses to ship the goods by rail to save money and again the customer waits. Each department has erected walls that slow down the delivery of quality customer service. The solution to this problem is to place more emphasis on the smooth management of core business processes.[33]

These core business processes include:

- *The market sensing process:* All the activities involved in gathering market intelligence, disseminating it within the organization, and acting on the information.
- *The new offering realization process:* All the activities involved in researching, developing, and launching new high-quality offerings quickly and within budget.
- *The customer acquisition process:* All the activities involved in defining target markets and prospecting for new customers.
- *The customer relationship management process:* All the activities involved in building deeper understanding, relationships, and offerings to individual customers.
- *The fulfillment management process:* All the activities involved in receiving and approving orders, shipping the goods on time, and collecting payment.

Strong companies develop superior capabilities in managing their core processes. For example, Wal-Mart has superior strength in its stock replenishment process. As Wal-Mart stores sell their goods, sales information flows via computer not only to Wal-Mart's headquarters, but also to Wal-Mart's suppliers, who ship replacement merchandise to the stores almost at the rate it moves off the shelf.[34] The idea is not to manage stocks of goods, but flows of goods, and Wal-Mart has turned over this responsibility to its leading vendors in a system known as **vendor-managed inventories (VMI)**.

the value-delivery network

To be successful a firm also needs to look for competitive advantages beyond its own operations, into the value chains of its suppliers, distributors, and customers. Many companies today have partnered with specific suppliers and distributors to create a superior **value-delivery network** (also called a **supply chain**).[35]

Bailey Controls   An Ohio-headquartered, $300-million-a-year manufacturer of control systems for big factories, Bailey Controls treats some of its suppliers as if they were departments within Bailey. The company recently plugged two of its suppliers directly into its inventory-management system. Every week Bailey electronically sends Montreal-based Future Electronics its latest forecasts of the materials it will need for the next six months. Whenever a bin of parts falls below a designated level, a Bailey employee passes a laser scanner over the bin's bar code, alerting Future to send the parts at once. Although arrangements like this shift inventory costs to the suppliers, the suppliers expect those costs to be more than offset by the gain in volume. It is a win–win partnership.

Betz Laboratories   Betz Laboratories, a Pennsylvania-based maker of industrial water-treatment chemicals, sells chemicals to keep the water in its customers' plants from gunking up pipes or corroding machinery. Today Betz provides its large customers with

figure **3.4**

Levi Strauss's Value–Delivery
Network

Competition is between
networks, not companies.
The winner is the company
with the better network.

both goods and expertise. High-level teams composed of Betz's and its customers' engineers and managers examine all the water in the customers' plants. They ask and answer such questions as: Is the water safe for the equipment? Does it meet environmental standards? Is it being used in the most cost-effective way? In less than one year the Betz team in one AlliedSignal plant pinpointed $2.5 million in potential cost savings.

Another excellent example of a value-delivery network is the one that connects Levi Strauss & Company, the famous maker of blue jeans, with its suppliers and distributors (see Figure 3.4). One of Levi's major retailers is Sears. Every night Levi's learns the sizes and styles of its blue jeans sold through Sears and other major outlets. Levi's then electronically orders more fabric for next-day delivery from Milliken & Company, its fabric supplier. Milliken, in turn, relays an order for more fiber to DuPont, its fiber supplier. In this way, the partners in the supply chain use the most current sales information to manufacture what is selling, rather than for a forecast that may not match current demand. In this system, the goods are pulled by demand rather than pushed by supply.

attracting and retaining customers

In addition to working with partners—called **partner relationship management (PRM)**—many companies are intent on developing stronger bonds with their customers—called **customer relationship management (CRM)**. This is the process of managing detailed information about individual customers and carefully managing all the customer "touchpoints" with the aim of maximizing customer loyalty.

attracting customers

Today's customers are becoming harder to please. They are smarter, more price conscious, more demanding, less forgiving, and they are approached by many more competitors with equal or better offers. The challenge, according to Jeffrey Gitomer, is not to produce satisfied customers; several competitors can do this. The challenge is to produce delighted and loyal customers.[36]

Companies seeking to expand their profits and sales have to spend considerable time and resources searching for new customers. To generate leads, the company develops ads and places them in media that will reach new prospects; it sends direct mail and makes phone calls to possible new prospects; its salespeople participate in trade shows where they might find new leads; and so on. All this activity produces a list of suspects. The next task is to identify which suspects are really good prospects, by interviewing them, checking on their financial standing, and so on. Then it is time to send out the salespeople.

computing the cost of lost customers

It is not enough to be skillful in attracting new customers; the company must keep them and increase their business. Too many companies suffer from high **customer churn**—namely, high customer defection. It is like adding water to a leaking bucket. Cellular carriers, for example, are plagued with "spinners," customers who switch carriers at least three times a year looking for the best deal. Many lose 25 percent of their subscribers each year at an estimated cost of $2 billion to $4 billion.

There are steps a company can take to reduce the defection rate. First, the company must define and measure its retention rate. For a magazine, the renewal rate is a good measure of retention. For a college, it could be the first- to second-year retention rate, or the class graduation rate. Second, the company must distinguish the causes of customer attrition and identify those that can be managed better. (See "Marketing Memo: Asking Questions When Customers Leave.") The Forum Corporation analyzed the customers lost by 14 major companies for reasons other than leaving the region or going out of business: 15 percent switched because they found a better product; another 15 percent found a cheaper product; and 70 percent left because of poor or little attention from the supplier. Not much can be done about customers who leave the region or go out of business, but much can be done about those who leave because of poor service, shoddy products, or high prices.[37]

Third, the company needs to estimate how much profit it loses when it loses customers. In the case of an individual customer, the lost profit is equal to the customer's **lifetime value**—that is, the present value of the profit stream that the company would have realized if the customer had not defected prematurely (see the discussion of lifetime value, under "Measuring Customer Lifetime Value"). For a group of lost customers, one major transportation carrier estimated its lost profit as follows:

1. The company had 64,000 accounts.
2. The company lost 5 percent of its accounts this year due to poor service: This was a loss of 3,200 accounts (.05 × 64,000).
3. The average lost account represented a $40,000 loss in revenue. Therefore, the company lost $128,000,000 in revenue (3,200 × $40,000).
4. The company's profit margin is 10 percent. Therefore, the company lost $12,800,000 (.10 × $128,000,000) this year. Because the customers left prematurely, the actual loss over time is much greater.

Fourth, the company needs to figure out how much it would cost to reduce the defection rate. As long as the cost is less than the lost profit, the company should spend the money.

Finally, nothing beats listening to customers. Some companies have created an ongoing mechanism that keeps senior managers permanently plugged in to front-line customer feedback. MBNA, the credit-card giant, asks every executive to listen in on telephone conversations in the customer service area or customer recovery units. Deere & Company, which makes John Deere tractors and has a superb record of customer loyalty—nearly 98 percent annual retention in some product areas—uses retired employees to interview defectors and customers.[38] (See "Marketing for the New Economy: Customer Service Live and Online," for another example.)

the need for customer retention

Unfortunately, most marketing theory and practice centers on the art of attracting new customers rather than on retaining and cultivating existing ones. The emphasis traditionally has been on making sales rather than building relationships; on preselling and selling rather than caring for the customer afterward. A company would be wise to measure customer satisfaction regularly, because the key to customer retention is customer satisfaction.

A highly satisfied customer stays loyal longer, buys more as the company introduces new products and upgrades existing products, talks favorably about the company and its products, pays less attention to competing brands and is less sensitive to price, offers product or service ideas to the company, and costs less to serve than new customers because transactions are routine.

Some companies think they are getting a sense of customer satisfaction by tallying customer complaints, but 96 percent of dissatisfied customers don't complain; many just stop buying.[39] The best thing a company can do is to make it easy for the customer to complain. Suggestion forms and toll-free numbers and e-mail addresses serve this purpose. The 3M Company claims that over two-thirds of its product-improvement ideas come from listening to customer complaints.

Listening is not enough, however. The company must respond quickly and constructively to the complaints:

Of the customers who register a complaint, between 54 and 70% will do business again with the organization if their complaint is resolved. The figure goes up to a staggering 95% if the customer feels that the complaint was resolved quickly. Customers who have complained to an organization and had their complaints satisfactorily resolved tell an average of five people about the good treatment they received.[40]

Marketing
MEMO

Asking Questions When Customers Leave

To create effective retention programs, marketing managers need to identify patterns among customer defections. This analysis should start with internal records, such as sales logs, pricing records, and customer survey results. The next step is extending defection research to outside sources, such as benchmarking studies and statistics from trade associations. Some key questions to ask:

1. Do customers defect at different rates during the year?
2. Does retention vary by office, region, sales representative, or distributor?
3. What is the relationship between retention rates and changes in prices?
4. What happens to lost customers, and where do they usually go?
5. What are the retention norms for your industry?
6. Which company in your industry retains customers the longest?

Source: Reprinted from William A. Sherden, "When Customers Leave," *Small Business Reports* (November 1994): 45.

marketing for the **new economy**

Customer Service Live and Online

E-commerce companies looking to attract and retain customers are discovering that personalization goes beyond creating customized information. For example, the Lands' End Live Web site offers visitors the opportunity to talk with a customer service representative. Nordstrom takes a similar approach with its Web site to ensure that online buyers are as satisfied with the company's customer service as the in-store visitors; and, with the click of a button, Eddie Bauer's e-commerce site connects shoppers to customer service representatives (CSRs) with a text-based chat feature.

Research from a 1999 survey by Boston Consulting group and Shop.org revealed that 65 percent of online shoppers abandon their purchase before finishing checkout. Worse, only 1.8 percent of visits to online retailers lead to sales, compared with 5 percent of visits to department stores. Analysts attribute this behavior partly to a general absence of interactive customer service in e-commerce. Customers looking for help are often sent to a text help file rather than a live sales representative. This can be frustrating and may prompt a customer to exit the site without buying. Another benefit of providing live sales assistance is the ability to sell additional items. When a representative is involved in the sale, the average amount per order is typically higher.

Not all customer service features involve live personnel. Both Macys.com and gap.com offer prerecorded customer service information. Gap's Web site includes a "zoom" feature, which shoppers can use to get a close look at every detail of a garment, from elastic waistbands to fabric prints. Lands' End Live allows customers to "try on" clothes online using virtual models based on measurements supplied by customers.

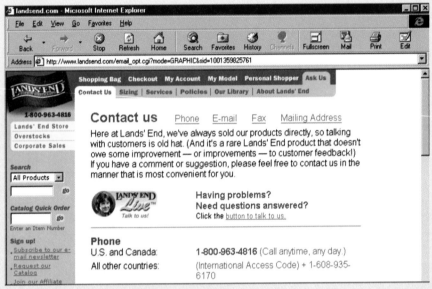

On the Lands' End Web site, customers can click a button to talk with a customer service representative.

Sources: Susan Stellin, "For Many Online Companies, Customer Service Is Hardly a Priority," *New York Times*, February 19, 2001; Michelle Johnson, "Getting Ready for the Onslaught," *Boston Globe*, November 4, 1999.

One company long recognized for its emphasis on customer satisfaction is Maine's L.L. Bean, Inc., which runs a mail-order catalog business in clothing and equipment for rugged living. Bean once refunded the money on a pair of two-year-old shoes because the customer said the pair did not wear as well as expected. L.L. Bean has carefully blended its external and internal marketing programs. To its customers, it offers the following:[41]

100% Guarantee

All of our products are guaranteed to give 100% satisfaction in every way. Return anything purchased from us at any time if it proves otherwise. We will replace it, refund your purchase price or credit your credit card, as you wish. We do not want you to have anything from L.L. Bean that is not completely satisfactory.

To motivate its employees to serve the customers well, it displays the following poster prominently around its offices:[42]

What Is a Customer?

A Customer is the most important person ever in this office . . . in person or by mail.

A Customer is not dependent on us . . . we are dependent on him.

A Customer is not an interruption of our work . . . he is the purpose of it. We are not doing a favor by serving him . . . he is doing us a favor by giving us the opportunity to do so.

A Customer is not someone to argue or match wits with. Nobody ever won an argument with a Customer.

A Customer is a person who brings us his wants. It is our job to handle them profitably to him and to ourselves.

Today, more companies are recognizing the importance of satisfying and retaining customers. Satisfied customers constitute the company's relationship capital. If the company were to be sold, the acquiring company would have to pay not only for the plant and equipment and the brand name, but also for the delivered customer base, namely, the number and value of the customers who would do business with the new firm. Here are some interesting facts bearing on customer retention:[43]

1. Acquiring new customers can cost five times more than the costs involved in satisfying and retaining current customers. It requires a great deal of effort to induce satisfied customers to switch away from their current suppliers.

2. The average company loses 10 percent of its customers each year.

3. A 5 percent reduction in the customer defection rate can increase profits by 25 percent to 85 percent, depending on the industry.

4. The customer profit rate tends to increase over the life of the retained customer.

measuring customer lifetime value

The case for increasing the customer retention rate is captured in the concept of customer lifetime value (CLV). **Customer lifetime value (CLV)** describes the present value of the stream of future profits expected over the customer's lifetime purchases. The company must subtract from the expected revenues the expected costs of attracting, selling, and servicing that customer. Various estimates have been made for different products and services.

- Carl Sewell, in *Customers for Life* (with Paul Brown), estimated that a customer entering his dealership for the first time represents a potential lifetime value of over $300,000.[44] If the customer is satisfied and buys several automobiles from the dealership over his or her buying lifetime, and subtracting the cost of selling and serving the customer, this may be the figure. If the satisfied customer brings in other customers, the figure would be higher.

- Mark Grainer, former chairman of the Technical Assistance Research Programs Institute (TARP), estimated that a loyal supermarket customer is worth $3,800 annually.[45]

Of course, a company needs, in addition to an average customer estimate, a way of estimating CLV for each individual customer. This is because the company must decide on how much to invest in each customer.

We can work out an example of estimating CLV. Suppose a company analyzes its new-customer acquisition cost:

Cost of an average sales call (including salary, commission, benefits, and expenses)	$300
Average number of sales calls to convert an average prospect into a customer	×4
Cost of attracting a new customer	$1,200

This is an underestimate because we are omitting the cost of advertising and promotion, plus the fact that only a fraction of all pursued prospects end up being converted into customers.

Now suppose the company estimates average customer lifetime value as follows:

Annual customer revenue	$5,000
Average number of loyal years	×2
Company profit margin	.10
Customer lifetime value	$1,000

This company is spending more to attract new customers than they are worth. Unless the company can sign up customers with fewer sales calls, spend less per sales call, stimulate higher new-customer annual spending, retain customers longer, or sell them higher-profit products, it is headed for bankruptcy.

There are two ways to strengthen customer retention. One is to erect high switching barriers. Customers are less inclined to switch to another supplier when this would involve high capital costs, high search costs, or the loss of loyal-customer discounts. The better approach is to deliver high customer satisfaction. This makes it harder for competitors to offer just lower prices or switching inducements. The task of creating strong customer loyalty is called customer relationship management.

customer relationship management (crm): the key

The aim of **customer relationship management (CRM)** is to produce high customer equity. **Customer equity** is the total of the discounted lifetime values of all of the firm's customers. Clearly, the more loyal the customers, the higher the customer equity. Rust, Zeithaml, and Lemon distinguish three drivers of customer equity: value equity, brand equity, and relationship equity.[46]

- *Value equity* is the customer's objective assessment of the utility of an offering based on perceptions of its benefits relative to its costs. The subdrivers of value equity are quality, price, and convenience. Each industry has to define the specific factors underlying each subdriver in order to find programs to improve value equity. An airline passenger might define quality as seat width; a hotel guest might define quality as room size. Value equity makes the biggest contribution to customer equity when products are differentiated and when they are more complex and need to be evaluated. Value equity especially drives customer equity in business markets.
- *Brand equity* is the customer's subjective and intangible assessment of the brand, above and beyond its objectively perceived value. The subdrivers of brand equity are customer brand awareness, customer attitude toward the brand, and customer perception of brand ethics. Companies use advertising, public relations, and other communication tools to affect these subdrivers. Brand equity is more important than the other drivers of customer equity where products are less differentiated and have more emotional impact.
- *Relationship equity* is the customer's tendency to stick with the brand, above and beyond objective and subjective assessments of its worth. Subdrivers of relationship equity include loyalty programs, special recognition and treatment programs, community building programs, and knowledge-building programs. Relationship equity is especially important where personal relationships count for a lot and where customers tend to continue with suppliers out of habit or inertia.

This formulation integrates *value management*, *brand management*, and *relationship management* within a customer-centered focus. Companies can decide which driver(s) to strengthen for the best payoff. The researchers believe they can measure and compare the financial return of alternative investments. Companies now have a better framework for choosing strategies and actions based on which would provide the best return on marketing investments.

Figure 3.5 shows the main steps in the process of attracting and keeping customers. The starting point is everyone who might conceivably buy the product or service (suspects). From these the company determines the most likely prospects, which it hopes to convert into first-time customers, and then into repeat customers, and then into clients—people whom the company treats very specially and knowledgeably. The next

figure **3.5**

The Customer–Development Process

Source: See Jill Griffin, *Customer Loyalty: How to Earn It, How to Keep It* (New York: Lexington Books, 1995), p. 36. Also see Murray Raphel and Neil Raphel, *Up the Loyalty Ladder: Turning Sometime Customers into Full-Time Advocates of Your Business* (New York: HarperBusiness, 1995).

challenge is to turn clients into members by starting a membership program that offers benefits to customers who join, and then into advocates, customers who enthusiastically recommend the company and its products and services to others. The ultimate challenge is to turn advocates into partners.

Some customers inevitably become inactive or drop out. The challenge is to reactivate dissatisfied customers through win-back strategies. It is often easier to reattract ex-customers (because the company knows their names and histories) than to find new ones. The key is to analyze the causes of customer defection through exit interviews and lost customer surveys. The aim is to win back only those customers who have strong profit potential.

How much should a company invest in building loyalty so that the costs do not exceed the gains? We need to distinguish five different levels of investment in customer-relationship building:

1. *Basic marketing:* The salesperson simply sells the product.
2. *Reactive marketing:* The salesperson sells the product and encourages the customer to call if he or she has questions, comments, or complaints.
3. *Accountable marketing:* The salesperson phones the customer to check whether the product is meeting expectations. The salesperson also asks the customer for any product- or service-improvement suggestions and any specific disappointments.
4. *Proactive marketing:* The salesperson contacts the customer from time to time with suggestions about improved product uses or new products.
5. *Partnership marketing:* The company works continuously with its large customers to help improve their performance. (General Electric, for example, has stationed engineers at large utilities to help them produce more power.)

Most companies practice only basic marketing when their markets contain many customers and their unit profit margins are small. Whirlpool is not going to phone each washing machine buyer to express appreciation. At best, it may set up a customer hot line. At the other extreme, in markets with few customers and high profit margins, most sellers will move toward partnership marketing. Boeing, for example, works closely with American Airlines in designing airplanes that fully satisfy American's requirements. As Figure 3.6 shows, the likely level of relationship marketing depends on the number of customers and the profit margin level.

The best relationship marketing going on today is driven by technology. GE Plastics could not target its e-mail effectively to different customers if it were not for advances in database software. Dell Computer could not customize computer ordering for its global corporate customers without advances in Web technology. Companies are using e-mail, Web sites, call centers, databases, and database software to foster continuous contact

figure **3.6**

	High Margin	Medium Margin	Low Margin
Many customers/ distributors	Accountable	Reactive	Basic or reactive
Medium number of customers/ distributors	Proactive	Accountable	Reactive
Few customers/ distributors	Partnership	Proactive	Accountable

Levels of Relationship Marketing

between company and customer. Here is how one company used technology to build customer value:

> **Ameritrade**   The discount brokerage service Ameritrade provides detailed information to its customers, which helps to create strong bonds. It provides customized alerts to the device of the customer's choice, detailing stock movements and analysts' recommendations. The company's Web site permits online trading and provides access to a variety of research tools. Ameritrade developed an investing tutorial called Darwin that it offered free on CD-ROM to its customers. Customers responded to this new focus on their needs: Ameritrade grew from fewer than 100,000 accounts in 1997 to 1.3 million in 2000.[47]

forming strong customer bonds: the basics

Companies that want to form strong customer bonds need to attend to the following basics:

- Get cross-departmental participation in planning and managing the customer satisfaction and retention process.
- Integrate the Voice of the Customer in all business decisions.
- Create superior products, services, and experiences for the target market.
- Organize and make accessible a database of information on individual customer needs, preferences, contacts, purchase frequency, and satisfaction.
- Make it easy for customers to reach appropriate company personnel and express their needs, perceptions, and complaints.
- Run award programs recognizing outstanding employees.

Berry and Parasuraman have gone beyond these basics and identified three retention-building approaches:[48] adding financial benefits, adding social benefits, and adding structural ties.

ADDING FINANCIAL BENEFITS   Two financial benefits that companies can offer are frequency programs and club marketing programs. **Frequency programs (FPs)** are designed to provide rewards to customers who buy frequently and in substantial amounts. Frequency marketing is an acknowledgment of the fact that 20 percent of a company's customers might account for 80 percent of its business.

American Airlines was one of the first companies to pioneer a frequency program in the early 1980s, when it decided to offer free mileage credit to its customers. Hotels next adopted FPs, with Marriott taking the lead with its Honored Guest Program. Shortly thereafter, car rental firms sponsored FPs. Then credit-card companies began to offer points based on card usage level. Sears offers rebates to its Discover cardholders. Today most supermarket chains offer price club cards, which provide member customers with discounts on particular items.

Typically, the first company to introduce an FP gains the most benefit, especially if competitors are slow to respond. After competitors respond, FPs can become a financial burden to all the offering companies, but some companies are more efficient and creative in managing an FP. For example, airlines are running tiered loyalty programs in which they offer different levels of rewards to different travelers. They may offer one frequent-flier mile for every mile flown to occasional travelers and two frequent-flier miles for every mile flown to top customers.

Many companies have created club membership programs to bond customers closer to the company. Club membership can be open to everyone who purchases a product or service, or it can be limited to an affinity group or to those willing to pay a small fee. Although open clubs are good for building a database or snagging customers from competitors, limited membership clubs are more powerful long-term loyalty builders. Fees and membership conditions prevent those with only a fleeting interest in a company's products from joining. These clubs attract and keep those customers who are responsible for the largest portion of business. Some highly successful clubs include the following:

Apple   Apple encourages owners of its computers to form local Apple-user groups. By 2001, there were over 600 groups ranging in size from fewer than 25 members to over 1,000 members. The user groups provide Apple owners with opportunities to learn more about their computers, share ideas, get product discounts, and they sponsor special activities and events and perform community service. A visit to Apple's Web site will help a customer find a nearby user group.[49]

Harley–Davidson   The world-famous motorcycle company sponsors the Harley Owners Group (H.O.G.), which now numbers 600,000 members in over 1,200 chapters. The first-time buyer of a Harley-Davidson motorcycle gets a free one-year membership. H.O.G. benefits include a magazine called *Hog Tales*, a touring handbook, emergency road service, a specially designed insurance program, theft reward service, discount hotel rates, and a Fly & Ride program enabling members to rent Harleys while on vacation. The company also maintains an extensive Web site devoted to H.O.G., which includes information on club chapters, events, and a special members-only section.[50]

ADDING SOCIAL BENEFITS   Company personnel work on increasing social bonds with customers by individualizing and personalizing customer relationships. Table 3.2 contrasts a socially sensitive approach with a socially insensitive approach to customers. In essence, thoughtful companies turn their customers into clients. Donnelly, Berry, and Thompson draw this distinction:

Customers may be nameless to the institution; clients cannot be nameless. Customers are served as part of the mass or as part of larger segments; clients are served on an individual basis. Customers are served by anyone who happens to be available; clients are served by the professional assigned to them.[51]

The H.O.G. Web site presents the benefits of joining.

table **3.2**	Good Things	Bad Things
Social Actions Affecting Buyer–Seller Relationships	Initiate positive phone calls	Make only callbacks
	Make recommendations	Make justifications
	Candor in language	Accommodative language
	Use phone	Use correspondence
	Show appreciation	Wait for misunderstandings
	Make service suggestions	Wait for service requests
	Use "we" problem-solving language	Use "owe-us" legal language
	Get to problems	Only respond to problems
	Use jargon or shorthand	Use long-winded communications
	Personality problems aired	Personality problems hidden
	Talk of "our future together"	Talk about making good on the past
	Routinize responses	Fire drill and emergency responsiveness
	Accept responsibility	Shift blame
	Plan the future	Rehash the past

Source: Theodore Levitt, *The Marketing Imagination* (New York: Free Press, 1983), p. 119. Reprinted by permission of the *Harvard Business Review.* An exhibit from Theodore Levitt, "After the Sale Is Over," *Harvard Business Review* (September–October 1983): p. 119. Copyright 1983 by the President and Fellows of Harvard College, all rights reserved.

ADDING STRUCTURAL TIES   The company may supply customers with special equipment or computer linkages that help customers manage orders, payroll, and inventory. A good example is McKesson Corporation, a leading pharmaceutical wholesaler, which invested millions of dollars in EDI capabilities to help independent pharmacies manage inventory, order-entry processes, and shelf space. Another example is Milliken & Company, which provides proprietary software programs, marketing research, sales training, and sales leads to loyal customers.

Lester Wunderman, one of the most astute observers of contemporary marketing, thinks talk about "loyalizing" customers misses the point.[52] People can be loyal to their country, family, and beliefs, but less so to their toothpaste, soap, or even beer. The marketer's aim should be to increase the consumer's *proclivity to repurchase* the company's brand.

Here are his suggestions for creating structural ties with the customer:

1. *Create long-term contracts.* A newspaper subscription replaces the need to buy a newspaper each day. A 20-year mortgage replaces the need to re-borrow the money each year. A home heating oil agreement assures continual delivery without renewing the order.

2. *Charge a lower price to consumers who buy larger supplies.* Offer lower prices to people who agree to be supplied regularly with a certain brand of toothpaste, detergent, or beer.

3. *Turn the product into a long-term service.* Daimler-Chrysler is considering selling miles of reliable transportation instead of cars, with the consumer able to order different cars at different times, such as a station wagon for shopping and a convertible for the weekend. Gaines, the dog food company, could offer a Pet Care service that includes kennels, insurance, and veterinary care along with food.

customer profitability, company profitability, and total quality management
measuring profitability

Ultimately, marketing is the art of attracting and keeping profitable customers. According to James V. Putten of American Express, the best customers outspend others by ratios of 16 to 1 in retailing, 13 to 1 in the restaurant business, 12 to 1 in the airline business, and 5 to 1 in the hotel and motel industry.[53] Yet every company loses money on some of its customers. The well-known 20–80 rule says that the top 20 percent of the customers may generate as much as 80 percent of the company's profits. Sherden suggested amending the rule to read 20–80–30, to reflect the idea that the top 20 percent of customers generate 80 percent of the company's profits, half of which are lost serving the bottom 30 percent of unprofitable customers.[54] The implication is that a company could improve its profits by "firing" its worst customers.

Furthermore, it is not necessarily the company's largest customers who yield the most profit. The largest customers demand considerable service and receive the deepest discounts. The smallest customers pay full price and receive minimal service, but the costs of transacting with small customers reduce their profitability. The midsize customers receive good service and pay nearly full price and are often the most profitable. This fact helps explain why many large firms are now invading the middle market. Major air express carriers, for instance, are finding that it does not pay to ignore small and midsize international shippers. Programs geared toward smaller customers provide a network of drop boxes, which allow for substantial discounts over letters and packages picked up at the shipper's place of business. In addition, United Parcel Service (UPS) conducts seminars to instruct exporters in the finer points of shipping overseas.[55]

What makes a customer profitable? A **profitable customer** is a person, household, or company that over time yields a revenue stream that exceeds by an acceptable amount the company's cost stream of attracting, selling, and servicing that customer. Note that the emphasis is on the lifetime stream of revenue and cost, not on the profit from a particular transaction. Here are two illustrations of customer lifetime value.

GM   When car buyers look at cars on the lot, they often experience sticker shock. $15,000 may seem like a lot of money to pay for a Cavalier, but that sum is nothing compared to the $276,000 that General Motors estimates its lifetime customers to be worth on average. The six-figure value is a graphic illustration of the importance of keeping the customer satisfied for the life of the automobile to better the chances of a repeat purchase.[56]

Taco Bell   When tacos cost less than a dollar each, you would not think Taco Bell would fret over lost customers. However, executives at Taco Bell have determined that a repeat customer is worth as much as $11,000. By sharing such estimates of customer lifetime value with its employees, Taco Bell's managers help employees understand the value of keeping customers satisfied.[57]

Although many companies measure customer satisfaction, most companies fail to measure individual customer profitability. Banks claim that this is a difficult task because a customer uses different banking services and the transactions are logged in different departments. However, banks that have succeeded in linking customer transactions have been appalled by the number of unprofitable customers in their customer base. Some banks report losing money on over 45 percent of their retail customers. There are only two solutions to handling unprofitable customers: raise fees or reduce service support.[58]

figure **3.7**

Customer–Product
Profitability Analysis

A useful type of profitability analysis is shown in Figure 3.7.[59] Customers are arrayed along the columns and products along the rows. Each cell contains a symbol for the profitability of selling that product to that customer. Customer 1 is very profitable; he buys three profit-making products (P1, P2, and P4). Customer 2 yields a picture of mixed profitability; he buys one profitable product and one unprofitable product. Customer 3 is a losing customer because he buys one profitable product and two unprofitable products.

What can the company do about customers 2 and 3? (1) It can raise the price of its less profitable products or eliminate them, or (2) it can try to sell them its profit-making products. Unprofitable customers who defect should not concern the company. In fact, the company should encourage these customers to switch to competitors.

Customer profitability analysis (CPA) is best conducted with the tools of an accounting technique called Activity-Based Costing (ABC). The company estimates all revenue coming from the customer, less all costs. The costs should include not only the cost of making and distributing the products and services, but also such costs as taking phone calls from the customer, traveling to visit the customer, entertainment and gifts— all the company's resources that went into serving that customer. When this is done for each customer, it is possible to classify customers into different profit tiers: platinum customers (most profitable), gold customers (profitable), iron customers (low profitability but desirable), and lead customers (unprofitable and undesirable).

The company's job is to move iron customers into the gold tier and gold customers into the platinum tier, while dropping the lead customers or making them profitable by raising their prices or lowering the cost of serving them. The company's marketing investment ought to be higher in the higher profit tiers (see Figure 3.8).

increasing company profitability

Companies must not only be able to create high absolute value, but also high value relative to competitors at a sufficiently low cost. **Competitive advantage** is a company's ability to perform in one or more ways that competitors cannot or will not match. Michael Porter urged companies to build a sustainable competitive advantage.[60] But few competitive advantages are sustainable. At best, they may be leverageable. A *leverageable advantage* is one that a company can use as a springboard to new advan-

figure 3.8

Allocating marketing investment according to customer value

tages, much as Microsoft has leveraged its operating system to Microsoft Office and then to networking applications. In general, a company that hopes to endure must be in the business of continuously inventing new advantages.

Any competitive advantage must be seen by customers as a *customer advantage*. For example, if a company delivers faster than its competitors, this will not be a customer advantage if customers do not value speed. Companies must focus on building customer advantages. Then they will deliver high customer value and satisfaction, which leads to high repeat purchases and ultimately to high company profitability. (For a cogent view of how to measure profitability, see "Marketing Insight: Marketing's Goal: To Increase Shareholder Value.")

marketing **insight**

Marketing's Goal: To Increase Shareholder Value

Companies normally focus on profit maximization rather than on shareholder value maximization. Doyle, in his *Value-Based Marketing*, charges that profit maximization leads to short-term planning and underinvestment in marketing. It leads to a focus on building sales, market share, and current profits. It leads to cost cutting and shedding assets to produce quick improvements in earnings, and erodes a company's long-term competitiveness by neglecting to invest in new market opportunities.

Companies normally measure their profit performance using ROI (return on investment, calculated by dividing profits by investment). This has two problems:

1. Profits are arbitrarily measured and subject to manipulation. Cash flow is more important. As someone observed: "Profits are a matter of opinion; cash is a fact."

2. Investment ignores the real value of the firm. More of a company's value resides in its marketing assets—brands, market knowledge, customer relationships, and partner relationships—than in its balance sheet. These are the drivers of long-term profits.

Doyle argues that marketing will not mature as a profession until it can demonstrate the impact of marketing on **shareholder value,** the market value of a company minus its debt. The market value is the share price times the number of shares outstanding. The share price reflects what investors estimate is the present value of the future lifetime earnings of a company. When management is choosing a marketing strategy, Doyle wants it to apply shareholder value analysis (SVA) to see which alternative course of action will maximize shareholder value.

If Doyle's arguments are accepted, marketing will finally get the attention it deserves in the boardroom. Instead of seeing marketing as a specific function concerned only with increasing sales or market share, senior management will see it as an integral part of the whole management process. It will judge marketing by how much it contributes to shareholder value.

Source: Peter Doyle, *Value-Based Marketing: Marketing Strategies for Corporate Growth and Shareholder Value* (Chichester, England: John Wiley & Sons, 2000).

implementing total quality management

One of the major values customers expect from vendors is high product and service quality. Most will no longer accept or tolerate average quality. If companies want to stay in the race, let alone be profitable, they have no choice but to adopt total quality management (TQM). **Total quality management (TQM)** is an organizationwide approach to continuously improving the quality of all the organization's processes, products, and services.

According to GE's former chairman, John F. Welch Jr., "Quality is our best assurance of customer allegiance, our strongest defense against foreign competition, and the only path to sustained growth and earnings."[61] The drive to produce goods that are superior in world markets has led some countries—and groups of countries—to recognize or award prizes to companies that exemplify the best quality practices.

Japan: In 1951, Japan became the first country to award a national quality prize, the Deming prize (named after W. Edwards Deming, the American statistician who taught the importance and methodology of quality improvement to postwar Japan). Deming's work forms the basis of many TQM practices.

United States: In the mid-1980s, the United States established the Malcolm Baldrige National Quality Award in honor of the late secretary of commerce. The Baldrige award criteria consist of seven measures: customer focus and satisfaction, quality and operational results, management of process quality, human resource development and management, strategic quality planning, information and analysis, and senior executive leadership. Past winners include Xerox, Motorola, Federal Express, IBM, Texas Instruments, and Ritz-Carlton hotels. One of the latest quality awards went to Custom Research, a highly regarded marketing research firm in Minneapolis.

Europe: The European Quality Award was established in 1993. It is awarded to companies that have achieved high grades on certain criteria: leadership, people management, policy and strategy, resources, processes, people satisfaction, customer satisfaction, impact on society, and business results. It established the ISO 9000, which has become a set of generally accepted principles for documenting quality. Earning the ISO 9000 certification involves a quality audit every six months from a registered ISO (International Standards Organization) assessor.[62]

Product and service quality, customer satisfaction, and company profitability are intimately connected. Higher levels of quality result in higher levels of customer satisfaction, which support higher prices and (often) lower costs. The well-known PIMS studies show a high correlation between relative product quality and company profitability.[63]

What exactly is quality? Various experts have defined it as "fitness for use," "conformance to requirements," "freedom from variation," and so on.[64] We will use the American Society for Quality Control's definition: **Quality** is the totality of features and characteristics of a product or service that bear on its ability to satisfy stated or implied needs.[65] This is clearly a customer-centered definition. We can say that the seller has delivered quality whenever the seller's product or service meets or exceeds the customers' expectations. A company that satisfies most of its customers' needs most of the time is called a quality company, but it is important to distinguish between *conformance* quality and *performance* quality (or grade). A Mercedes provides higher performance quality than a Hyundai: The Mercedes rides smoother, goes faster, and lasts longer. Yet both a Mercedes and a Hyundai can be said to deliver the same conformance quality if all the units deliver their respective promised quality.

Total quality is the key to value creation and customer satisfaction. Total quality is everyone's job, just as marketing is everyone's job. This idea was expressed well by Daniel Beckham:

> Marketers who don't learn the language of quality improvement, manufacturing, and operations will become as obsolete as buggy whips. The days of functional marketing are gone. We can no longer afford to think of ourselves as market researchers, advertising people, direct marketers, strategists—we have

to think of ourselves as customer satisfiers—customer advocates focused on whole processes.[66]

Marketing managers have two responsibilities in a quality-centered company. First, they must participate in formulating strategies and policies to help the company win through total quality excellence. Second, they must deliver marketing quality alongside production quality. Each marketing activity—marketing research, sales training, advertising, customer service, and so on—must be performed to high standards.

Marketers play several roles in helping their companies define and deliver high-quality goods and services to target customers. First, they bear the major responsibility for correctly identifying the customers' needs and requirements. Second, they must communicate customer expectations properly to product designers. Third, they must make sure that customers' orders are filled correctly and on time. Fourth, they must check that customers have received proper instructions, training, and technical assistance in the use of the product. Fifth, they must stay in touch with customers after the sale to ensure that they are satisfied and remain satisfied. Sixth, they must gather customer ideas for product and service improvements and convey them to the appropriate departments. When marketers do all this, they are making substantial contributions to total quality management and customer satisfaction, as well as to customer and company profitability.

summary

1. Customers are value-maximizers. They form an expectation of value and act on it. Buyers will buy from the firm that they perceive to offer the highest customer-delivered value, defined as the difference between total customer value and total customer cost.

2. A buyer's satisfaction is a function of the product's perceived performance and the buyer's expectations. Recognizing that high satisfaction leads to high customer loyalty, many companies today are aiming for TCS—total customer satisfaction. For such companies, customer satisfaction is both a goal and a marketing tool.

3. Strong companies develop superior capabilities in managing core business processes such as new-product realization, inventory management, and customer acquisition and retention. Managing these core processes effectively means creating a marketing network in which the company works closely with all parties in the production and distribution chain, from suppliers of raw materials to retail distributors. Companies no longer compete—marketing networks do.

4. Losing profitable customers can dramatically affect a firm's profits. The cost of attracting a new customer is estimated to be five times the cost of keeping a current customer happy. The key to retaining customers is relationship marketing. To keep customers happy, marketers can add financial or social benefits to products, or create structural ties between the company and its customers.

5. Quality is the totality of features and characteristics of a product or service that bear on its ability to satisfy stated or implied needs. Today's companies have no choice but to implement total quality management programs if they are to remain solvent and profitable. Total quality is the key to value creation and customer satisfaction.

6. Marketing managers have two responsibilities in a quality-centered company. First, they must participate in formulating strategies and policies designed to help the company win through total quality excellence. Second, they must deliver marketing quality alongside production quality. Each marketing activity—marketing research, sales training, advertising, customer service, and so on—must be performed to high standards.

applications

marketing debate – online versus off-line privacy?

As more and more firms practice relationship marketing and develop databases of customer information, privacy issues are emerging as an important topic. Consumers and public interest groups are scrutinizing—and sometimes criticizing—the privacy policies of firms. Concerns are also being raised about potential theft of online credit-card information or other potentially sensitive or confidential financial information. Others maintain that the online privacy fears are unfounded and that security issues are every bit as much a concern in the off-line world. They argue that the opportunity to steal information exists virtually everywhere and that it is up to the consumer to protect his or her interests.

Take a position: (1) Privacy is a bigger issue in the online world than the off-line world versus Privacy is no different online than off-line. (2) Consumers on the whole receive more benefit than risk from marketers knowing their personal information.

marketing and advertising

1. Doubletree targets both vacationers and business travelers for its hotels and resort accommodations. The ad in Figure 1 shows how this hotel chain seeks to build relationships with business travelers by adding value in a variety of ways.

   a. What types of benefits are being emphasized in Doubletree's relationship-building efforts with business travelers? Why are these appropriate for the target market?

   b. Which of the customer value and customer cost factors are being addressed in this ad? How do they affect the customer's determination of delivered value?

   c. How else does Doubletree use this ad to stress benefits that appeal to customers as value-maximizers?

2. Blue Martini in Figure 2 makes software that enables people in different locations to move through a Web site at the same time, shopping or chatting as they progress through the pages. By facilitating collaboration between individuals or groups, Blue Martini enhances users' online experience, according to this ad. How does this help customer satisfaction?

   a. If a company using Blue Martini software allowed two sisters to simultaneously browse the same retailing Web site, how would this be likely to affect the sisters' perception of value?

   b. Would Blue Martini be part of the primary or support activities of a business customer's value chain?

   c. What else might Blue Martini do in its advertising to stress the value of its software to its customers' customers?

Figure 1

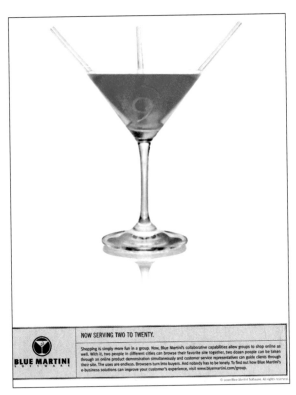

Figure 2

online marketing today

Any time a company registers a Web site ending in .com or .net, Verisign makes money as the administrator of these U.S. Internet domain names. Verisign also manages electronic payments for Bank of America as well as signature security—allowing legal documents to be signed and exchanged over the Internet—for Ford, Microsoft, and 3,000 other corporations. Quality is therefore very important to the satisfaction of Verisign's business customers, who value both security and accuracy.[a] Visit Verisign's Web site *<www.verisign.com>*, follow the link to its products page, and read about SSL Certificates or Web Site Trust Services. What are the benefits of this bundle of services? Would customers who buy this service be seeking conformance or performance quality? How does this set of services contribute to Verisign's competitive advantage?

---

[a]Fred Vogelstein, "The Man Who Bought the Internet," *Fortune*, June 25, 2001, pp. 126–127.

notes

1. "Mac Attacks," *USA Today*, March 23, 1998, p. B1.
2. See, for example, "Value Marketing: Quality, Service, and Fair Pricing Are the Keys to Selling in the '90s," *BusinessWeek*, November 11, 1991, pp. 132–40.
3. Irwin P. Levin and Richard D. Johnson, "Estimating Price-Quality Tradeoffs Using Comparative Judgments," *Journal of Consumer Research* (June 11, 1984): 593–600. Customer perceived value can be measured as a difference or as a ratio. If total customer value is $20,000 and total customer cost is $16,000, then the customer perceived value is $4,000 (measured as a difference) or 1.25 (measured as a ratio). Ratios that are used to compare offers are often called *value-price ratios*.
4. For more on customer perceived value, see David C. Swaddling and Charles Miller, *Customer Power* (Dublin, OH: The Wellington Press, 2001).
5. For some provocative analysis, see Susan Fournier and David Glenmick, "Rediscovering Satisfaction," *Journal of Marketing*, (October 1999): pp. 5–23.
6. Thomas O. Jones and W. Earl Sasser, Jr., "Why Satisfied Customers Defect," *Harvard Business Review* (November–December 1995): 88–99.
7. For an interesting analysis of the effects of different types of expectations, see William Boulding, Ajay Kalra, and Richard Staelin, "The Quality Double Whammy," *Marketing Service*, 18(4), 1999, pp. 463–484.
8. <www.saturn.com>; "Saturn Illustrates Value of Customer Loyalty," *Louisville Courier-Journal*, September 5, 1999.
9. As quoted in Templin, Neal. "Boutique-Hotel Group Thrives on Quirks," *Wall Street Journal*, March 18, 1999.
10. As quoted in Carlsen, Clifford. "Joie de Vivre Resorts to New Hospitality Strategy," *San Francisco Business Times*, June 18, 1999.
11. Michael J. Lanning, *Delivering Profitable Value* (Oxford, UK: Capstone, 1998).
12. Simon Knox and Stan Maklan, *Competing on Value: Bridging the Gap Between Brand and Customer Value* (London, UK: Financial Times, 1998). See also Richard A. Spreng, Scott B. MacKenzie, and Richard W. Olshawskiy, "A Reexamination of the Determinants of Consumer Satisfaction," *Journal of Marketing*, no. 3 (July 1996): 15–32.
13. Fred Crawford and Ryan Mathews, *The Myth of Excellence: Why Great Companies Never Try to Be the Best of Everything* (New York: Crown Business), pp. 85–100.
14. Companies should also note that managers and salespeople can manipulate customer satisfaction ratings. They can be especially nice to customers just before the survey. They can also try to exclude unhappy customers. Another danger is that if customers know the company will go out of its way to please customers, some may express high dissatisfaction in order to receive more concessions.
15. Claes Fornell, Michael D. Johnson, Eugene W. Anderson, Jaaesung Cha, and Barbara Everitt Bryant, "The American Customer Satisfaction Index: Nature, Purpose, and Findings," *Journal of Marketing*, October 1996, pp. 7–18; and Eugene W. Anderson and Claes Fornell, "Foundations of the American Customer Satisfaction Index," *Total Quality Management*, 11, no. 7, 2000, pp. S869–S882.
16. Tamara J. Erickson and C. Everett Shorey, "Business Strategy: New Thinking for the '90s," *Prism* (Fourth Quarter 1992): 19–35.
17. Robert S. Kaplan and David P. Norton, *The Balanced Scorecard: Translating Strategy into Action* (Boston: Harvard Business School Press, 1996), as a tool for monitoring stakeholder satisfaction.
18. Jon R. Katzenbach and Douglas K. Smith, *The Wisdom of Teams: Creating the High-Performance Organization* (Boston: Harvard Business School Press, 1993); Michael Hammer and James Champy, *Reengineering the Corporation* (New York: HarperBusiness, 1993).
19. T. Michael Nevens, Gregory L. Summe, and Bro Uttal, "Commercializing Technology: What the Best Companies Do," *Harvard Business Review*, (May–June 1990): 162.
20. David Glines, "Do You Work in a Zoo?" *Executive Excellence* 11, no. 10 (October 1994): 12–13.
21. Echo Montgomery Garrett, "Outsourcing to the Max," *Small Business Reports* (August 1994): 9–14. The case for more outsourcing is ably spelled out in James Brian Quinn, *Intelligent Enterprise* (New York: The Free Press, 1992).
22. C. K. Prahalad and Gary Hamel, "The Core Competence of the Corporation," *Harvard Business Review*, (May–June 1990): 79–91.
23. George S. Day, "The Capabilities of Market-Driven Organizations," *Journal of Marketing* (October 1994): 38.
24. "Business: Microsoft's Contradiction," *The Economist* (January 31, 1998): 65–67; Andrew J. Glass, "Microsoft Pushes Forward, Playing to Win the Market," *Atlanta Constitution*, June 24, 1998, p. D12.
25. Daniel Howe, "Note to DaimlerChrysler: It's Not a Small World after All," *Detroit News*, May 19, 1998, p. B4; Bill Vlasic, "The First Global Car Colossus," *BusinessWeek*, May 18, 1998, pp. 40–43; Pamela Harper, "Business 'Cultures' at War," *Electronic News*, August 3, 1998, pp. 50, 53.
26. Bill Vlasic, and Bradley Stertz. "Taken for a Ride," *Business Week*, June 5, 2000; Jeffrey Ball, and Scott Miller,. "DaimlerChrysler Isn't Living up to Its Promise," *Wall Street Journal*, July 26, 2000; Eric Reguly, "Daimler, Chrysler Still a Cutture Clash," *The Globe and Mail*, January 30, 2001.
27. James C. Collins and Jerry I. Porras, *Built to Last: Successful Habits of Visionary Companies* (New York: HarperBusiness, 1994).
28. F. G. Rodgers and Robert L. Shook, *The IBM Way: Insights into the World's Most Successful Marketing Organization* (New York: Harper and Row, 1986).
29. Gary Hamel, "Strategy as Revolution," *Harvard Business Review*, (July–August 1996): 69–82.
30. Paul J. H. Shoemaker, "Scenario Plannning: A Tool for Strategic Thinking," *Sloan Management Review*, (Winter 1995): 25–40.
31. Michael E. Porter, *Competitive Advantage: Creating and Sustaining Superior Performance* (New York: The Free Press, 1985).
32. Robert Hiebeler, Thomas B. Kelly, and Charles Ketteman, *Best Practices: Building Your Business with Customer-Focused Solutions* (New York: Simon and Schuster, 1998).
33. Hammer and Champy, *Reengineering the Corporation*.
34. George Stalk, "Competing on Capability: The New Rules of Corporate Strategy," *Harvard Business Review* (March–April 1992): 57–69; Benson P. Shapiro, V. Kasturi Rangan, and John J. Sviokla, "Staple Yourself to an Order," *Harvard Business Review* (July–August 1992): 113–22.
35. Myron Magnet, "The New Golden Rule of Business," *Fortune*, November 28, 1994, pp. 60–64.

36. Jeffrey Gitomer, *Customer Satisfaction Is Worthless: Customer Loyalty Is Priceless: How to Make Customers Love You, Keep Them Coming Back and Tell Everyone They Know* (Austin, TX: Bard Press, l998).

37. Frederick F. Reichheld, "Learning from Customer Defections," *Harvard Business Review* (March–April 1996): 56–69.

38. Ibid.

39. Technical Assistance Research Programs (Tarp), *U.S Office of Consumer Affairs Study on Complaint Handling in America*, 1986.

40. Karl Albrecht and Ron Zemke, *Service America!* (Homewood Il: Dow Jones-Irwin, 1985), pp. 6–7.

41. Courtesy L.L. Bean, Freeport, Maine.

42. Ibid.

43. Frederick F. Reichheld, *The Loyalty Effect* (Boston: Harvard Business School Press, 1996).

44. Carl Sewell and Paul Brown, *Customers for Life* (New York: Pocket Books, 1990), p. 162.

45. Cited in Don Peppers and Martha Rogers, *The One to One Future* (New York: Currency, 1993), pp. 37–38.

46. Roland T. Rust, Valerie A. Zeithaml, and Katherine A. Lemon, *Driving Customer Equity* (New York Free Press 2000).

47. www.ameritrade.com; Rebecca Buckman, "Ameritrade Unveils Index That Tracks Customer Trends," *Wall Street Journal*, December 2, 1999. For a contrast, see Susan Stellin, "For Many Online Companies, Customer Service Is Hardly a Priority," *New York Times*, February 19, 2001.

48. Leonard L. Berry and A. Parasuraman, *Marketing Services: Computing through Quality* (New York: The Free Press, 1991), pp. 136–42. See also Richard Cross and Janet Smith, *Customer Bonding: Pathways to Lasting Customer Loyalty* (Lincolnwood, IL: NTC Business Books, 1995).

49. www.apple.com

50. www.hog.com

51. James H. Donnelly Jr., Leonard L. Berry, and Thomas W. Thompson, *Marketing Financial Services—A Strategic Vision* (Homewood, IL: Dow Jones–Irwin, 1985), p. 113.

52. From a privately circulated paper, Lester Wunderman, "The Most Elusive Word in Marketing," June 2000. Also see Lester Wunderman, *Being Direct* (NewYork: Random House 1996).

53. Quoted in Don Peppers and Martha Rogers, *The One-to-One Future: Building Relationships One Customer at a Time* (New York: Currency Doubleday, 1993), p. 108.

54. William A. Sherden, *Market Ownership: The Art and Science of Becoming #1* (New York: Amacom, 1994), p. 77.

55. Robert J. Bowman, "Good Things, Smaller Packages," *World Trade* 6, no. 9 (October 1993): 106–10.

56. Greg Farrel, "Marketers Put a Price on Your Life." *USA Today*, July 7, 1999.

57. Stephan A. Butscher, "Welcome to the Club: Building Customer Loyalty," *Marketing News*, September 9, 1996, p. 9.

58. Rakesh Niraj, Mahendra Gupta, and Chakravarthi Narasimhan, "Customer Profitability in a Supply Chain," *Journal of Marketing*, July 2001, pp. 1–16.

59. Thomas M. Petro, "Profitability: The Fifth 'P' of Marketing," *Bank Marketing* (September 1990): 48–52; and "Who Are Your Best Customers?" *Bank Marketing* (October 1990): 48–52.

60. Michael E. Porter, *Competitive Strategy: Techniques for Analyzing Industries and Competitors* (New York: Free Press, 1980).

61. "Quality: The U.S. Drives to Catch Up," *Business Week*, November 1982, pp. 66–80. For a more recent assessment of progress, see "Quality Programs Show Shoddy Results," *Wall Street Journal*, May 14, 1992, p. B1. See also Roland R. Rust, Anthony J. Zahorik, and Timothy L. Keiningham, "Return on Quality (ROQ): Making Service Quality Financially Accountable," *Journal of Marketing* 59, no. 2 (April 1995): 58–70.

62. "Quality in Europe," *Work Study* (January–February 1993): 30; Ronald Henkoff, "The Hot New Seal of Quality," *Fortune*, June 28, 1993, pp. 116–20; Amy Zukerman, "One Size Doesn't Fit All," *Industry Week*, January 9, 1995, pp. 37–40; and "The Sleeper Issue of the '90s," *Industry Week*, August 15, 1994, pp. 99–100, 108.

63. Robert D. Buzzell and Bradley T. Gale, *The PIMS Principles: Linking Strategy to Performance* (New York: The Free Press, 1987), ch. 6. (PIMS stands for Profit Impact of Market Strategy.)

64. "The Gurus of Quality: American Companies Are Heading the Quality Gospel Preached by Deming, Juran, Crosby, and Taguchi," *Traffic Management* (July 1990): 35–39.

65. Cyndee Miller, "U.S. Firms Lag in Meeting Global Quality Standards," *Marketing News*, February 15, 1993.

66. J. Daniel Beckham, "Expect the Unexpected in Health Care Marketing Future," *The Academy Bulletin* (July 1992): 3.

C H A P T E R

4

winning markets through market-oriented strategic planning

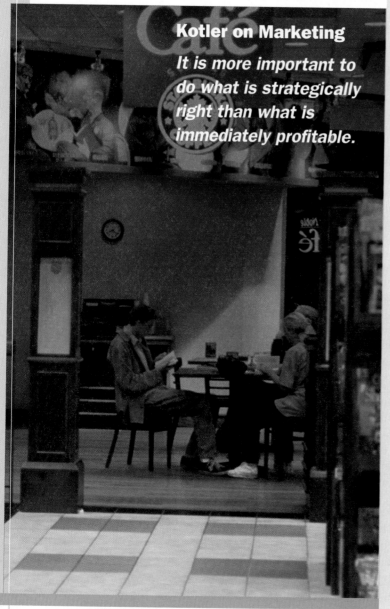

Kotler on Marketing

It is more important to do what is strategically right than what is immediately profitable.

In this chapter, we will address the following questions:

- How is strategic planning carried out at the corporate and division levels?
- How is planning carried out at the business unit level?
- What are the major steps in the marketing process?
- How is planning carried out at the product level?
- What does a marketing plan include?

In Chapters 1, 2, and 3 we asked the question: How do companies compete successfully in today's marketplace? One part of the answer is a commitment to creating and delivering superior value to target customers. We can now add a second part: Successful companies know how to adapt to a continuously changing marketplace. They practice the art of market-oriented strategic planning, *the managerial process of developing and maintaining a viable fit between the organization's objectives, skills, and resources and its changing market opportunities. The aim of strategic planning is to shape the company's businesses, products, services, and messages so that they achieve targeted profits and growth.*

strategic planning: three key areas and four organizational levels

Strategic planning calls for action in three key areas: The first is managing a company's businesses as an investment portfolio. The second involves assessing each business's strength by considering the market's growth rate and the company's position and fit in that market. The third is establishing a strategy. For each business, the company must develop a game plan for achieving its long-run objectives.

Marketing plays a critical role in the strategic-planning process. According to General Electric:

> The marketing manager is the most significant functional contributor to the strategic-planning process, with leadership roles in defining the business mission; analysis of the environmental, competitive, and business situations; developing objectives, goals, and strategies; and defining product, market, distribution, and quality plans to implement the business's strategies. This involvement extends to the development of programs and operating plans that are fully linked with the strategic plan.[1]

To understand marketing management, we must understand strategic planning. Most large companies consist of four organizational levels: the corporate level, the division level, the business unit level, and the product level. Corporate headquarters is responsible for designing a corporate strategic plan to guide the whole enterprise; it makes decisions on the amount of resources to allocate to each division, as well as on which businesses to start or eliminate. Each division establishes a division plan covering the allocation of funds to each business unit within the division. Each business unit develops a strategic plan to carry that business unit into a profitable future. Finally, each product level (product line, brand) within a business unit develops a marketing plan for achieving its objectives in its product market.

The marketing plan operates at two levels: strategic and tactical. The **strategic marketing plan** lays out the target markets and the value proposition that will be offered, based on an analysis of the best market opportunities. The **tactical marketing plan** specifies the marketing tactics, including product features, promotion, merchandising, pricing, sales channels, and service.

The **marketing plan** is the central instrument for directing and coordinating the marketing effort. Today, the marketing department does not set the marketing plan by itself. Plans are developed by teams, with inputs and sign-offs from every important function. These plans are then implemented at the appropriate levels of the organization. Results are monitored, and corrective action is taken when necessary. The complete planning, implementation, and control cycle is shown in Figure 4.1.

corporate and division strategic planning

By preparing statements of mission, policy, strategy, and goals, headquarters establishes the framework within which the divisions and business units prepare their plans. Some corporations give a lot of freedom to their business units to set their own sales and profit goals and strategies. Others set goals for their business units but let them develop their own strategies. Still others set the goals and participate in developing individual business unit strategies.[2]

All corporate headquarters undertake four planning activities:

1. Defining the corporate mission
2. Establishing strategic business units (SBUs)
3. Assigning resources to each SBU
4. Planning new businesses, downsizing, or terminating older businesses

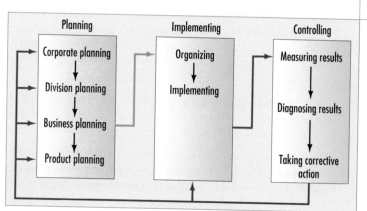

figure **4.1**

The Strategic–Planning, Implementation, and Control Processes

defining the corporate mission

An organization exists to accomplish something: to make cars, lend money, provide a night's lodging, and so on. Its specific mission or purpose is usually clear when the business starts. Over time the mission may change, to take advantage of new opportunities or respond to new market conditions. Amazon.com changed its mission from being the world's largest online bookstore to aspiring to become the world's largest online store. eBay changed its mission from running online auctions for collectors to running online auctions covering all kinds of goods.

To define its mission, the company should address Peter Drucker's classic questions:[3] What is our business? Who is the customer? What is of value to the customer? What will our business be? What should our business be? These simple-sounding questions are among the most difficult the company will ever have to answer. Successful companies continuously raise these questions and answer them thoughtfully and thoroughly.

Organizations develop **mission statements** to share with managers, employees, and (in many cases) customers. A clear, thoughtful mission statement provides employees with a shared sense of purpose, direction, and opportunity. The statement guides geographically dispersed employees to work independently and yet collectively toward realizing the organization's goals.

Mission statements are at their best when they are guided by a vision, an almost "impossible dream" that provides a direction for the company for the next 10 to 20 years. Sony's former president, Akio Morita, wanted everyone to have access to "personal portable sound," so his company created the Walkman and portable CD player. Fred Smith wanted to deliver mail anywhere in the United States before 10:30 A.M. the next day, so he created FedEx.

Here are examples of mission statements:

Rubbermaid Commercial Products, Inc. "Our Vision is to be the Global Market Share Leader in each of the markets we serve. We will earn this leadership position by providing to our distributor and end-user customers innovative, high-quality, cost-effective and environmentally responsible products. We will add value to these products by providing legendary customer service through our Uncompromising Commitment to Customer Satisfaction."[4]

Motorola   "The purpose of Motorola is to honorably serve the needs of the community by providing products and services of superior quality at a fair price to our customers; to do this so as to earn an adequate profit which is required for the total enterprise to grow; and by so doing provide the opportunity for our employees and shareholders to achieve their reasonable personal objectives."

eBay   "We help people trade practically anything on earth. We will continue to enhance the online trading experiences of all—collectors, dealers, small businesses, unique item seekers, bargain hunters, opportunity sellers, and browsers."

Good mission statements have three major characteristics. First, they focus on a limited number of goals. The statement, "We want to produce the highest-quality products, offer the most service, achieve the widest distribution, and sell at the lowest prices" claims too much. Second, mission statements stress the major policies and values the company wants to honor. Policies define how the company will deal with its various stakeholders and narrow the range of individual discretion so that employees act consistently on important issues. Third, they define the major competitive scopes within which the company will operate:

■ *Industry scope:* The range of industries in which a company will operate. Some companies will operate in only one industry; some only in a set of related industries; some only in industrial goods, consumer goods, or services; and some in any industry. For example, DuPont prefers to operate in the industrial market, whereas Dow is willing to operate in the industrial and consumer markets. 3M will get into almost any industry where it can make money.

■ *Products and applications scope:* The range of products and applications that a company will supply. St. Jude Medical aims to "serve physicians worldwide with high-quality products for cardiovascular care."

■ *Competence scope:* The range of technological and other core competencies that a company will master and leverage. Japan's NEC has built its core competencies in computing, communications, and components. These competencies support its production of laptop computers, television receivers, and handheld telephones.

■ *Market-segment scope:* The type of market or customers a company will serve. Some companies will serve only the upscale market. For example, Porsche makes only expensive cars. Gerber serves primarily the baby market.

■ *Vertical scope:* The number of channel levels from raw material to final product and distribution in which a company will participate. At one extreme are companies with a large vertical scope; at one time Ford owned its own rubber plantations, sheep farms, glass manufacturing plants, and steel foundries. At the other extreme are "hollow corporations" or "pure marketing companies" consisting of a person with a phone, fax, computer, and desk who contracts out for every service, including design, manufacture, marketing, and physical distribution.[5]

■ *Geographical scope:* The range of regions, countries, or country groups in which a company will operate. At one extreme are companies that operate in a specific city or state. At the other extreme are multinationals such as Unilever and Caterpillar, which operate in almost every country in the world.

Mission statements should not be revised every few years in response to every new turn in the economy. However, a company must redefine its mission if that mission has lost credibility or no longer defines an optimal course for the company.[6]

establishing strategic business units

Most companies operate several businesses. They often define their businesses in terms of products: They are in the "auto business" or the "clothing business"; but Levitt argued that market definitions of a business are superior to product definitions.[7]

Company	Product Definition	Market Definition
Missouri-Pacific Railroad	We run a railroad.	We are a people-and-goods mover.
Xerox	We make copying equipment.	We help improve office productivity.
Standard Oil	We sell gasoline.	We supply energy.
Columbia Pictures	We make movies.	We market entertainment.
Encyclopaedia Britannica	We sell encyclopedias.	We distribute information.
Carrier	We make air conditioners and furnaces.	We provide climate control in the home.

A business must be viewed as a customer-satisfying process, not a goods-producing process. Products are transient, but basic needs and customer groups endure forever. Transportation is a need; the horse and carriage, the automobile, the railroad, the airline, and the truck are products that meet that need. Levitt encouraged companies to redefine their businesses in terms of needs, not products. Kodak, for example, redefined itself from a film company to an image company so it could add digital imaging. IBM redefined itself from a hardware and software manufacturer to a "builder of networks." On September 29, 1997, Sara Lee announced an abrupt shift in strategy and focus: It would outsource its manufacturing operations and become a marketer of brands. [8]

Table 4.1 gives several examples of companies that have moved from a product to a market definition of their business. It highlights the difference between a target market definition and a strategic market definition of a business. A *target market definition* tends to focus on selling a product or service. Thus, Pepsi will define its target market as everyone it hopes it can get to drink a cola beverage; but this limits Pepsi to seeing competitors as other cola companies. A *strategic market definition* would be everyone who might drink something to quench thirst. Suddenly, Pepsi will see its competition as including noncola soft drinks, bottled water, fruit juices, tea, and coffee. This will help broaden Pepsi's view of its competition. In fact, Pepsi might decide to sell additional beverages whose growth rate appears to be promising.

A business can be defined in terms of three dimensions: customer groups, customer needs, and technology. [9] Consider, for example, a small company that defines its business as designing incandescent lighting systems for television studios. Its customer group is television studios; the customer need is lighting; and the technology is incandescent lighting. The company might want to expand into additional businesses. For example, it could make lighting for other customer groups, such as homes, factories, and offices; or it could supply other services needed by television studios, such as heating, ventilation, or air conditioning. It could design other lighting technologies for television studios, such as infrared or ultraviolet lighting.

Large companies normally manage quite different businesses, each requiring its own strategy. General Electric classified its businesses into 49 **strategic business units (SBUs)**. An SBU has three characteristics:

1. It is a single business or collection of related businesses that can be planned separately from the rest of the company.
2. It has its own set of competitors.
3. It has a manager who is responsible for strategic planning and profit performance and who controls most of the factors affecting profit.

The purpose of identifying the company's strategic business units is to develop separate strategies and assign appropriate funding. Senior management knows that its portfolio of businesses usually includes a number of "yesterday's has-beens" as well as "tomorrow's breadwinners." Yet it cannot rely on impressions; it needs analytical tools to classify its businesses by profit potential. Two of the best-known business portfolio evaluation models are the Boston Consulting Group model and the General Electric model.[10]

the boston consulting group approach

The Boston Consulting Group (BCG), a leading management consulting firm, developed and popularized the growth-share matrix shown in Figure 4.2. The eight circles represent the current sizes and positions of eight business units in a hypothetical company. The size of the circle depends on the dollar volume of each business. Thus, the two largest businesses are 5 and 6. The location of each business unit indicates its market growth rate and relative market share.

THE GROWTH–SHARE MATRIX   The market growth rate on the vertical axis indicates the annual growth rate of the market in which the business operates. In Figure 4.2, it ranges from 0 percent to 20 percent. A market growth rate above 10 percent is considered high. **Relative market share**, which is measured on the horizontal axis, refers to the SBU's market share relative to that of its largest competitor in the segment. It serves as a measure of the company's strength in that market segment. A relative market share of 0.1 means that the company's sales volume is only 10 percent of the leader's; a relative share of 10 means that the company's SBU is the leader and has 10 times the sales of the next-strongest competitor in that market. Relative market share is divided into high and low share, using 1.0 as the dividing line. Relative market share is drawn in log scale, so that equal distances represent the same percentage increase.

figure **4.2**

The Boston Consulting Group's Growth–Share Matrix

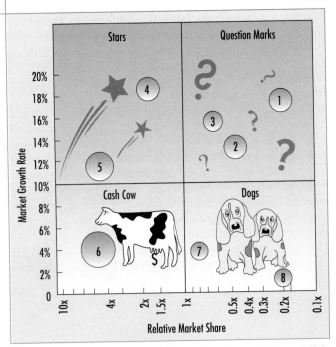

Source: Reprinted from *Long Range Planning* (February 1977): 12. Copyright 1977 with kind permission from Elsevier Science Ltd.

The growth-share matrix is divided into four cells, each indicating a different type of business:

1. *Question marks:* Businesses that operate in high-growth markets but have low relative market shares. A question mark requires a lot of cash because the company has to spend money on plant, equipment, and personnel to keep up with the fast-growing market, and because it wants to overtake the market leader. The company has to think hard about whether to keep pouring money into this business. The company in Figure 4.2 operates three question-mark businesses, and this may be too many.
2. *Stars:* The market leaders in a high-growth market. A star does not necessarily produce a positive cash flow for the company. The company must spend substantial funds to keep up with the high market growth, and to fight off competitors' attacks. In Figure 4.2, the company has two stars.
3. *Cash cows:* Stars with a falling growth rate that still have the largest relative market share and produce a lot of cash for the company. The company does not have to finance expansion because the market's growth rate has slowed. Because the business is the market leader, it enjoys economies of scale and higher profit margins. The company uses its cash cows to pay bills and support other businesses. The company in Figure 4.2 has only one cash cow and is therefore highly vulnerable. If this cash cow starts losing relative market share, the company will have to pump money back into it to maintain market leadership.
4. *Dogs:* Businesses that have weak market shares in low-growth markets. The company in Figure 4.2 holds two dogs, and this may be two too many. The company should consider whether it is holding on to these businesses for good reasons (such as an expected turnaround in the market growth rate or a new chance at market leadership).

After plotting its various businesses in the growth-share matrix, a company must determine whether its portfolio is healthy. An unbalanced portfolio would have too many dogs or question marks and too few stars and cash cows.

SBU STRATEGIES The company's next task is to determine what objective, strategy, and budget to assign to each SBU. Four strategies can be pursued: build, hold, harvest, or divest. Building is appropriate for question marks whose market shares must grow if they are to become stars. The hold strategy is appropriate for strong cash cows if they are to continue yielding large positive cash flows.

The objective of the harvest strategy is to increase short-term cash flow regardless of long-term effect. Harvesting involves a decision to cash in on its "crop," to "milk its business." Harvesting generally involves eliminating R&D expenditures, not replacing the physical plant, not replacing salespeople, reducing advertising expenditures, and so on. This strategy is appropriate for weak cash cows whose future is dim and from which more cash flow is needed. Harvesting can also be used with question marks and dogs. The objective of the divest strategy is to sell or liquidate the business because resources can be better used elsewhere. This strategy is appropriate for dogs and question marks that are acting as a drag on the company's profits.

Companies must decide whether harvesting or divesting is a better strategy for a weak business. Harvesting reduces the business's future value and therefore the price at which it could be sold later. An early decision to divest, in contrast, is likely to produce fairly good bids if the business is in relatively good shape and of more value to another firm.

THE SBU LIFE CYCLE As time passes, SBUs change their position in the growth-share matrix. Successful SBUs have a life cycle. They start as question marks, become stars, then cash cows, and finally dogs. For this reason, companies should examine not only their businesses' current positions in the growth-share matrix (as in a snapshot) but also their moving positions (as in a motion picture). If a given SBU's expected trajectory is not satisfactory, the corporation should ask its manager to propose a new strategy and the likely resulting trajectory.

The worst mistake a company could make would be to require all its SBUs to aim for the same growth rate or return level. The very point of SBU analysis is that each business has a different potential and requires its own objective. Other mistakes include: leaving cash cows with too little in retained funds (in which case they grow weak) or leaving them with too much in retained funds (in which case the company fails to invest enough in new businesses with growth potential); making major investments in dogs in hopes of turning them around, but failing each time; and maintaining too many question marks and underinvesting in each. Question marks should either receive enough support to achieve segment dominance or be dropped.

the general electric model

An SBU's appropriate objective cannot be determined solely by its position in the growth-share matrix. If additional factors are considered, the growth-share matrix can be seen as a special case of a multifactor portfolio matrix such as that pioneered by General Electric (GE). This model is shown in Figure 4.3(a), where one company's seven businesses are plotted. This time the size of each circle represents the size of the relevant market rather than the size of the company's business. The dark brown shaded part of the circle represents that business's market share. Thus, the company's clutch business operates in a moderate-sized market and enjoys approximately a 30 percent market share.

| figure **4.3** | Market Attractiveness-Competitive-Position Portfolio Classification and Strategies |

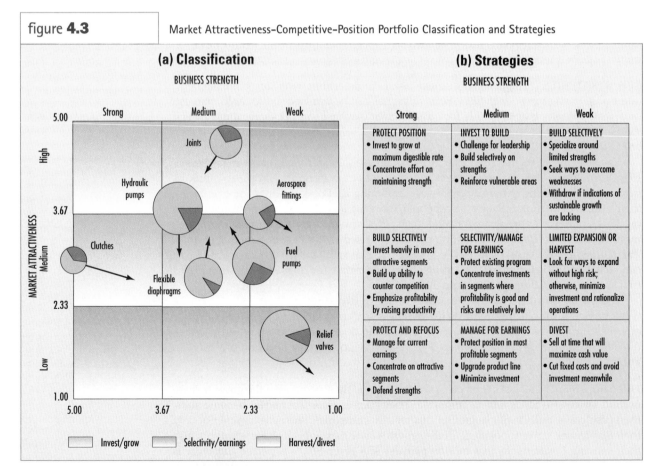

Each business is rated in terms of two major dimensions, market attractiveness and business strength (Figure 4.3[b]). These two factors make excellent marketing sense for rating a business. Companies are successful to the extent that they enter attractive markets and possess the required business strengths to succeed in those markets. If one of these factors is missing, the business will not produce outstanding results. Neither a strong company operating in an unattractive market nor a weak company operating in an attractive market will do very well.

To measure these two dimensions, strategic planners must identify the factors underlying each dimension and find a way to measure them and combine them into an index. Table 4.2 lists two possible sets of factors making up the two dimensions for the hydraulic-pumps business in Figure 4.3. (Each company has to decide on its own list of factors.) For the hydraulic-pumps business, market attractiveness varies with the market's size, annual market growth rate, historical profit margins, and so on. Business strength varies with the company's market share, share growth, product quality, and so on. Note that the

table **4.2**

Factors Underlying Market Attractiveness and Competitive Position in GE Multifactor Portfolio Model: Hydraulic–Pumps Market

		Weight	Rating = (1–5)	Value
	Overall market size	0.20	4	0.80
	Annual market growth rate	0.20	5	1.00
	Historical profit margin	0.15	4	0.60
Market	Competitive intensity	0.15	2	0.30
Attractiveness	Technological requirements	0.15	4	0.60
	Inflationary vulnerability	0.05	3	0.15
	Energy requirements	0.05	2	0.10
	Environmental impact	0.05	3	0.15
	Social-political-legal	Must be acceptable		
		1.00		3.70

		Weight	Rating = (1–5)	Value
	Market share	0.10	4	0.40
	Share growth	0.15	2	0.30
	Product quality	0.10	4	0.40
	Brand reputation	0.10	5	0.50
	Distribution network	0.05	4	0.20
Business	Promotional effectiveness	0.05	3	0.15
Strength	Productive capacity	0.05	3	0.15
	Productive efficiency	0.05	2	0.10
	Unit costs	0.15	3	0.45
	Material supplies	0.05	5	0.25
	R&D performance	0.10	3	0.30
	Managerial personnel	0.05	4	0.20
		1.00		3.40

Source: Adapted from La Rue T. Hosmer, *Strategic Management* (Upper Saddle River, NJ: Prentice Hall, 1982), p. 310.

two BCG factors—market growth rate and market share—are subsumed under the two major variables of the GE model. The GE model leads strategic planners to look at more factors in evaluating an actual or potential business than the BCG model does.

How does the company arrive at the data in Table 4.2 and the circles in Figure 4.3(a)? Management rates each factor from 1 (very unattractive) to 5 (very attractive). The hydraulic-pumps business is rated 4 on overall market size, indicating that the market size is pretty large (a 5 would be very large). The ratings are then multiplied by weights reflecting the factors' relative importance, to arrive at the values, which are summed for each dimension. The hydraulic-pumps business scored a 3.70 on market attractiveness and a 3.40 on business strength, out of a maximum possible score of 5.00 for each. The analyst places a point representing this business in the multifactor matrix in Figure 4.3(a) and draws a circle around it whose size is proportional to the size of the relevant market. The company's market share of approximately 14 percent is shaded in. Clearly, the hydraulic-pumps business is in a fairly attractive part of the matrix.

In fact, the GE matrix is divided into nine cells, which in turn fall into three zones (Figure 4.3[a]). The three cells in the upper-left corner indicate strong SBUs in which the company should invest or grow. The diagonal cells stretching from the lower left to the upper right indicate SBUs that are medium in overall attractiveness. The company should pursue selectivity and manage for earnings in these SBUs. The three cells in the lower-right corner indicate SBUs that are low in overall attractiveness: The company should give serious thought to harvesting or divesting these companies. For example, the relief-valves business represents an SBU with a small market share in a fair-sized market that is not very attractive and in which the company has a weak competitive position: It is a fit candidate for harvest or divest.[11]

Management should also forecast each SBU's expected position in the next three to five years given current strategy. Making this determination involves analyzing where each product is in its product life cycle as well as expected competitor strategies, new technologies, economic events, and so on. The results are indicated by the length and direction of the arrows in Figure 4.3(a). For example, the hydraulic-pumps business is expected to decline slightly in market attractiveness, and the clutches business is expected to decline strongly.

The company's objective is not always to build sales in each SBU. Rather, the objective might be to maintain the existing demand with fewer marketing dollars or to take cash out of the business and allow demand to fall. Thus, the task of marketing management is to manage demand or revenue to the target level negotiated with corporate management. Marketing contributes to assessing each SBU's sales and profit potential, but once the SBU's objectives and budget are set, marketing's job is to carry out the plan efficiently and profitably.

critique of portfolio models

In addition to the BCG and GE models, other portfolio models have been developed, particularly the Arthur D. Little model and the Shell directional-policy model.[12] Portfolio models have helped managers to think more strategically, understand the economics of their businesses better, improve the quality of their plans, improve communication between business and corporate management, pinpoint information gaps and important issues, eliminate weaker businesses, and strengthen their investment in more promising businesses.

However, portfolio models must be used cautiously. They may lead the company to place too much emphasis on market-share growth and entry into high-growth businesses or to neglect its current businesses. The results are sensitive to the ratings and weights and can be manipulated to produce a desired location in the matrix.

Furthermore, because these models use an averaging process, two or more businesses may end up in the same cell position but differ greatly in underlying ratings and weights. Many businesses will end up in the middle of the matrix as a result of averaging the ratings, and this makes it hard to know what the appropriate strategy should be. Finally, the models fail to show the synergies between two or more businesses. Companies need to focus on customer segments that buy from several of the company's business units, rather than those that sell one product at a time. There is a danger of terminating a losing business unit that actually provides an essential core competence or market offering needed by several other business units.[13]

planning new businesses, downsizing older businesses

The company's plans for its existing businesses allow it to project total sales and profits. Often, these are less than what corporate management wants them to be. If there is a gap between future desired sales and projected sales, corporate management will have to develop or acquire new businesses to fill it.

Figure 4.4 illustrates this strategic-planning gap for a major manufacturer of audio-cassette tapes called Musicale (name disguised). The lowest curve projects the expected sales over the next five years from the current business portfolio. The highest curve describes desired sales over the next five years. Evidently, the company wants to grow much faster than its current businesses will permit. How can it fill the strategic-planning gap?

Three options are available. The first is to identify opportunities to achieve further growth within current businesses (intensive growth opportunities). The second is to identify opportunities to build or acquire businesses that are related to current businesses (integrative growth opportunities). The third is to identify opportunities to add attractive businesses that are unrelated to current businesses (diversification growth opportunities).

INTENSIVE GROWTH   Corporate management's first course of action should be a review of whether any opportunities exist for improving its existing businesses' performance. Ansoff has proposed a useful framework for detecting new intensive growth opportunities called a "product–market expansion grid" (Figure 4.5).[14]

The company first considers whether it could gain more market share with its current products in their current markets (market-penetration strategy). Next it considers whether it can find or develop new markets for its current products (market-development strategy). Then it considers whether it can develop new products of potential interest to

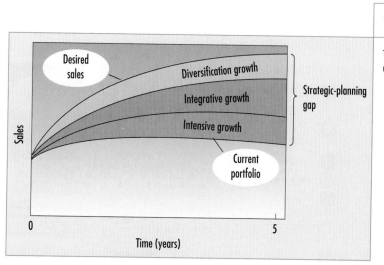

figure **4.4**

The Strategic–Planning Gap

figure **4.5**

Three Intensive Growth
Strategies: Ansoff's
Product–Market
Expansion Grid

	Current Products	New Products
Current Markets	1. Market-penetration strategy	3. Product-development strategy
New Markets	2. Market-development strategy	(Diversification strategy)

its current markets (product-development strategy). Later it will also review opportunities to develop new products for new markets (diversification strategy). Starbucks is a good example.

Starbucks   Starbucks got its start in Seattle in the 1970s as a gourmet coffee retailer, selling fresh ground coffee beans to local coffee lovers. When Howard Schultz, Starbucks' CEO until 2000, came to the company in 1982, he recognized an unfilled niche for cafés serving gourmet coffee directly to customers. This became Starbucks' market-penetration strategy, and helped the company attain a loyal customer base in Seattle. The market-development strategy marked the next phase in Starbucks' growth: It applied the same successful formula that had worked wonders in Seattle first to other cities in the Pacific Northwest, then throughout North America, and finally, across the globe. Once the company established itself as a presence in thousands of cities internationally, Starbucks sought to increase the number of purchases

Starbucks' home page: Customers can request a catalog of Starbucks products, subscribe to a newsletter, and shop online.

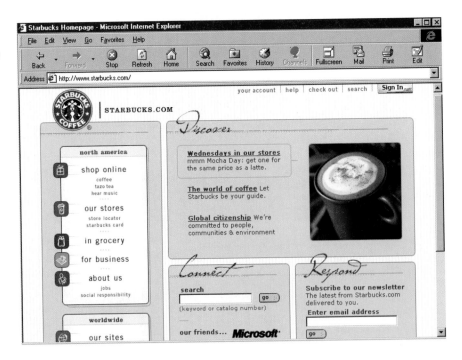

by existing customers with a product-development strategy that led to new in-store merchandise, including compilation CDs and *Joe* lifestyle magazine. Finally, Starbucks pursued diversification into grocery store aisles with Frappuccino® bottled drinks, Starbucks brand ice cream, and the purchase of tea retailer Tazo® Tea.[15]

How might Musicale use these three major intensive growth strategies to increase its sales? There are three major approaches to a market-penetration strategy. Musicale could try to encourage its current customers to buy more. This could work if its customers could be shown the benefits of using more cassettes for music recording or dictation. Musicale could try to attract competitors' customers. This could work if Musicale noticed major weaknesses in competitors' product or marketing programs. Finally, Musicale could try to convince nonusers of cassettes to start using them. This could work if there are still many people who do not own tape recorders.

How can Musicale use a product-development strategy? First, it might try to identify potential user groups in the current sales areas. If Musicale has been selling cassette tapes only to consumer markets, it might go after office and factory markets. Second, Musicale might seek additional distribution channels in its present locations. If it has been selling its tapes only through stereo-equipment dealers, it might add mass-merchandising channels. Third, the company might consider selling in new locations in its home country or abroad. Thus, if Musicale sold only in the United States, it could consider entering the European market.

Management should also consider new-product possibilities. Musicale could develop new features, such as a longer-playing tape and a tape that buzzes at the end of its play. It could offer the tape at two or more quality levels, or it could research an alternative technology such as compact disks (CDs) and digital audiotape.

By examining these three intensive growth strategies, management may discover several ways to grow. Still, that growth may not be enough. In that case, management must also examine integrative growth opportunities.

INTEGRATIVE GROWTH   Often a business's sales and profits can be increased through backward, forward, or horizontal integration within its industry. Musicale might acquire one or more of its suppliers (such as plastic-material producers) to gain more control or generate more profit (backward integration). It might acquire some wholesalers or retailers, especially if they are highly profitable (forward integration). Finally, Musicale might acquire one or more competitors, provided that the government does not bar this move (horizontal integration). However, these new sources may still not deliver the desired sales volume. In that case, the company must consider diversification.

DIVERSIFICATION GROWTH   Diversification growth makes sense when good opportunities can be found outside the present businesses. A good opportunity is one in which the industry is highly attractive and the company has the mix of business strengths to be successful. Three types of diversification are possible. The company could seek new products that have technological or marketing synergies with existing product lines, even though the new products themselves may appeal to a different group of customers (concentric diversification strategy). It might start a computer-tape manufacturing operation because it knows how to manufacture audiocassette tape.

Second, the company might search for new products that could appeal to current customers even though the new products are technologically unrelated to its current product line (horizontal diversification strategy). Musicale might produce cassette-holding trays, even though producing them requires a different manufacturing process. Finally, the company might seek new businesses that have no relationship to its current technology, products, or markets (conglomerate diversification strategy). Musicale might want to consider such new businesses as making application software or personal organizers.

DOWNSIZING OLDER BUSINESSES   Companies must not only develop new businesses, but must also carefully prune, harvest, or divest tired old businesses in order to release needed resources and reduce costs. Weak businesses require a disproportionate amount of managerial attention. Managers should focus on growth opportunities, not fritter away energy and resources trying to salvage hemorrhaging businesses.

business unit strategic planning

The business unit strategic-planning process consists of the eight steps shown in Figure 4.6. We examine each step in the sections that follow.

business mission

Each business unit needs to define its specific mission within the broader company mission. Thus, a television studio-lighting-equipment company might define its mission as, "The company aims to target major television studios and become their vendor of choice for lighting technologies that represent the most advanced and reliable studio lighting arrangements." Notice that this mission does not attempt to win business from smaller television studios, win business by being lowest in price, or venture into non-lighting products.

swot analysis

The overall evaluation of a company's strengths, weaknesses, opportunities, and threats is called SWOT analysis.

EXTERNAL ENVIRONMENT ANALYSIS (OPPORTUNITY AND THREAT ANALYSIS) In general, a business unit has to monitor key *macroenvironment forces* (demographic-economic, technological, political-legal, and social-cultural) and significant *microenvironment actors* (customers, competitors, distributors, suppliers) that affect its ability to earn profits. The business unit should set up a marketing intelligence system to track trends and important developments. For each trend or development, management needs to identify the associated opportunities and threats.

A major purpose of environmental scanning is to discern new marketing opportunities. A **marketing opportunity** is an area of buyer need or potential interest in which a company can perform profitably. Opportunities can take many forms and marketers have to be good at spotting them:

- A company may make a buying process more convenient or efficient. Example: Consumers can now use the Internet to find more books than ever and search for the lowest price with a few clicks.
- A company can meet the need for more information and advice. Example: Guru.com facilitates finding professional experts in a wide range of fields.

figure 4.6   The Business Strategic-Planning Process

- A company can customize a product or service that was formerly offered only in a standard form. Example: P&G's Reflect.com Web site is capable of producing a customized skin care or hair care product to meet a customer's need.
- A company can introduce a new capability. Example: Consumers can now create and edit digital "iMovies" with the new iMac and upload them to an Apple Web server to share with friends around the world.
- A company may be able to deliver a product or a service faster. Example: FedEx discovered a way to deliver mail and packages much more quickly than the U.S. Post Office.
- A company may be able to offer a product at a much lower price. Example: Pharmaceutical firms have created generic versions of brand-name drugs.

The company now applies **Market Opportunity Analysis (MOA)** to determine the attractiveness and success probability of any opportunity. Five questions are asked:

1. Can the benefits involved in the opportunity be articulated convincingly to a defined target market(s)?
2. Can the target market(s) be located and reached with cost-effective media and trade channels?
3. Does the company possess or have access to the critical capabilities and resources needed to deliver the customer benefits?
4. Can the company deliver the benefits better than any actual or potential competitors?
5. Will the financial rate of return meet or exceed the company's required threshold for investment?

In the opportunity matrix in Figure 4.7(a), the best marketing opportunities facing the TV-lighting-equipment company are listed in the upper-left cell (#1); management should pursue these opportunities. The opportunities in the lower-right cell (#4) are too minor to consider. The opportunities in the upper-right cell (#2) and lower-left cell (#3) should be monitored in the event that any improve in attractiveness and success probability.

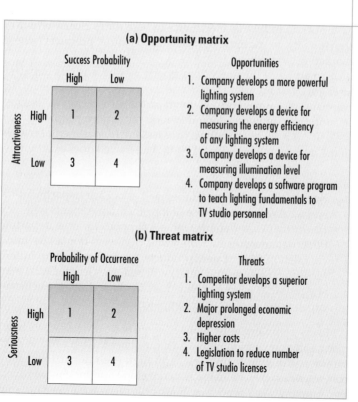

figure **4.7**

Opportunity and Threat Matrices

Some developments in the external environment represent threats. An **environmental threat** is a challenge posed by an unfavorable trend or development that would lead, in the absence of defensive marketing action, to deterioration in sales or profit. Threats should be classified according to seriousness and probability of occurrence. Figure 4.7(b) illustrates the threat matrix facing the TV-lighting-equipment company. The threats in the upper-left cell are major threats, because they can seriously hurt the company and they have a high probability of occurrence. To deal with these threats, the company needs to prepare contingency plans that spell out changes it can make before or during the threat. The threats in the lower-right cell are very minor and can be ignored. The threats in the upper-right and lower-left cells do not require contingency planning but need to be monitored carefully in the event that they grow more serious.

Once management has identified the major threats and opportunities facing a specific business unit; it can characterize that business's overall attractiveness. Four outcomes are possible:

- An ideal business is high in major opportunities and low in major threats.
- A speculative business is high in both major opportunities and threats.
- A mature business is low in major opportunities and low in threats.
- A troubled business is low in opportunities and high in threats.

INTERNAL ENVIRONMENT ANALYSIS (STRENGTHS/WEAKNESSES ANALYSIS) It is one thing to discern attractive opportunities and another to be able to take advantage of these opportunities. Each business needs to evaluate its internal strengths and weaknesses. It can do so by using a form like the one shown in the "Marketing Memo: Checklist for Performing Strengths/Weaknesses Analysis."

Clearly, the business does not have to correct all its weaknesses, nor should it gloat about all its strengths. The big question is whether the business should limit itself to those opportunities where it possesses the required strengths or whether it should consider better opportunities where it might have to acquire or develop certain strengths. For example, managers at Texas Instruments (TI) were split between those who wanted TI to stick to industrial electronics (where it has clear strength) and those who wanted the company to continue introducing consumer products (where it lacks some required marketing strengths).

Sometimes a business does poorly not because its departments lack the required strengths, but because they do not work together as a team. In one major electronics company, the engineers look down on the salespeople as "engineers who couldn't make it," and the salespeople look down on the service people as "salespeople who couldn't make it." It is therefore critical to assess interdepartmental working relationships as part of the internal environmental audit. Honeywell does exactly this.

Honeywell Each year, Honeywell asks each department to rate its own strengths and weaknesses and those of the other departments with which it interacts. The notion is that each department is a supplier to some departments and a customer of other departments. If Honeywell engineers frequently underestimate the cost and completion time of new products, for example, their "internal customers" (manufacturing, finance, and sales) will be hurt. George Stalk, a leading BCG consultant, suggests that winning companies are those that have achieved superior in-company capabilities, not just core competencies.[16]

Every company must manage some basic processes, such as new-product development, sales generation, and order fulfillment. Each process creates value and requires interdepartmental teamwork. Although each department may possess specific core competencies, the challenge is to develop superior competitive capability in managing the company's key processes. Stalk calls this *capabilities-based competition.*

Marketing
MEMO

Checklist for Performing Strengths/Weaknesses Analysis

	PERFORMANCE					IMPORTANCE		
	MAJOR STRENGTH	MINOR STRENGTH	NEUTRAL	MINOR WEAKNESS	MAJOR WEAKNESS	HI	MED	LOW
MARKETING								
1. Company reputation	____	____	____	____	____	____	____	____
2. Market share	____	____	____	____	____	____	____	____
3. Customer satisfaction	____	____	____	____	____	____	____	____
4. Customer retention	____	____	____	____	____	____	____	____
5. Product quality	____	____	____	____	____	____	____	____
6. Service quality	____	____	____	____	____	____	____	____
7. Pricing effectiveness	____	____	____	____	____	____	____	____
8. Distribution effectiveness	____	____	____	____	____	____	____	____
9. Promotion effectiveness	____	____	____	____	____	____	____	____
10. Sales force effectiveness	____	____	____	____	____	____	____	____
11. Innovation effectiveness	____	____	____	____	____	____	____	____
12. Geographical coverage	____	____	____	____	____	____	____	____
FINANCE								
13. Cost or availability of capital	____	____	____	____	____	____	____	____
14. Cash flow	____	____	____	____	____	____	____	____
15. Financial stability	____	____	____	____	____	____	____	____
MANUFACTURING								
16. Facilities	____	____	____	____	____	____	____	____
17. Economies of scale	____	____	____	____	____	____	____	____
18. Capacity	____	____	____	____	____	____	____	____
19. Able, dedicated workforce	____	____	____	____	____	____	____	____
20. Ability to produce on time	____	____	____	____	____	____	____	____
21. Technical manufacturing skill	____	____	____	____	____	____	____	____
ORGANIZATION								
22. Visionary, capable leadership	____	____	____	____	____	____	____	____
23. Dedicated employees	____	____	____	____	____	____	____	____
24. Entrepreneurial orientation	____	____	____	____	____	____	____	____
25. Flexible or responsive	____	____	____	____	____	____	____	____

goal formulation

Once the company has performed a SWOT analysis, it can proceed to develop specific goals for the planning period. This stage of the process is called *goal formulation*. Managers use the term *goals* to describe objectives that are specific with respect to magnitude and time.

Most business units pursue a mix of objectives including profitability, sales growth, market-share improvement, risk containment, innovation, and reputation. The business unit sets these objectives and then manages by objectives (MBO). For an MBO system to work, the unit's various objectives must meet four criteria:

1. They must be arranged hierarchically, from the most to the least important. For example, the business unit's key objective for the period may be to increase the rate of return on investment. This can be accomplished by increasing the profit level and reducing the amount of invested capital. Profit itself can be increased by increasing revenue and reducing expenses. Revenue can be increased by increasing market share and prices. By proceeding this way, the business can move from broad to specific objectives for specific departments and individuals.

2. Objectives should be stated quantitatively whenever possible. The objective "increase the return on investment (ROI)" is better stated as the goal "increase ROI to 15 percent within two years."

3. Goals should be realistic. They should arise from an analysis of the business unit's opportunities and strengths, not from wishful thinking.

4. Objectives must be consistent. It is not possible to maximize both sales and profits simultaneously.

Other important trade-offs include short-term profit versus long-term growth, deep penetration of existing markets versus developing new markets, profit goals versus nonprofit goals, and high growth versus low risk. Each choice in this set of trade-offs calls for a different marketing strategy.

Many believe that adopting the goal of strong market share growth may mean having to forego strong short-term profits. For years, Compaq priced aggressively in order to build its market share in the computer market. More recently, Compaq decided to pursue profitability at the expense of growth.

Yet Charan and Tichy believe that most businesses can be a growth business and can grow profitably.[17] They cite success stories such as GE Medical, Allied Signal, Citibank, and GE Capital, all enjoying profitable growth. Some so-called trade-offs may not be trade-offs at all.

strategic formulation

Goals indicate what a business unit wants to achieve; **strategy** is a game plan for getting there. Every business must design a strategy for achieving its goals, consisting of a *marketing strategy,* and a compatible *technology strategy* and *sourcing strategy.*

PORTER'S GENERIC STRATEGIES   Michael Porter has proposed three generic strategies that provide a good starting point for strategic thinking: overall cost leadership, differentiation, and focus.[18]

- *Overall cost leadership:* The business works hard to achieve the lowest production and distribution costs so that it can price lower than its competitors and win a large market share. Firms pursuing this strategy must be good at engineering, purchasing, manufacturing, and physical distribution. They need less skill in marketing. Texas Instruments is a leading practitioner of this strategy. The problem with this strategy is that other firms will usually compete with still lower costs and hurt the firm that rested its whole future on cost.

- *Differentiation:* The business concentrates on achieving superior performance in an important customer benefit area valued by a large part of the market. The firm cultivates those strengths that will contribute to the intended differentiation. Thus the firm seeking quality leadership, for example, must make products with the best components, put them together expertly, inspect them carefully, and effectively communicate their quality. Intel has established itself as a technology leader by introducing new microprocessors at breakneck speed.

- *Focus:* The business focuses on one or more narrow market segments. The firm gets to know these segments intimately and pursues either cost leadership or differentiation within the target segment. Airwalk shoes came to fame by focusing on the very narrow extreme-sports segment.

The online air travel industry provides a good example of these three strategies.

Travelocity's Web site helps the consumer plan the whole vacation—flights, lodging, and car rental.

Travelocity.com, Lowestfare.com, and Lastminute.com   Travelocity is pursuing a differentiation strategy by offering the most comprehensive range of services to the traveler. Lowestfare is pursuing a lowest-cost strategy; and Lastminute is pursuing a niche strategy in focusing on travelers who have the flexibility to travel on very short notice.

OPERATIONAL EFFECTIVENESS AND STRATEGY   According to Porter, firms pursuing the same strategy directed to the same target market constitute a **strategic group**. The firm that carries out that strategy best will make the most profits. Firms that do not pursue a clear strategy and try to be good on all strategic dimensions do the worst. International Harvester went out of the farm equipment business because it did not stand out in its industry as lowest in cost, highest in perceived value, or best in serving some market segment. Porter drew a distinction between operational effectiveness and strategy.[19]

Many companies believe they can win by performing the same activities more effectively than their competitors; but competitors can quickly copy the operationally effective company using benchmarking and other tools, thus diminishing the advantage of operational effectiveness. Porter defines strategy as "the creation of a unique and valuable position involving a different set of activities." A company can claim that it has a strategy when it "performs different activities from rivals or performs similar activities in different ways." Companies such as IKEA, Southwest Airlines, Dell Computer, Saturn, and Home Depot run their businesses much differently from their competitors; and these competitors would find it hard to copy and synchronize all the different activities that a strategically differentiated company carries out.

STRATEGIC ALLIANCES   Companies are also discovering that they need strategic partners if they hope to be effective. Even giant companies—AT&T, IBM, Philips, Siemens—often cannot achieve leadership, either nationally or globally, without forming alliances

marketing for the **new economy**

The Network Economy

In the new global environment, with greater competition from more and more products and choices, alliances are not just a planning option but a strategic necessity. As Jim Kelly, CEO of UPS, which has a number of global alliances, puts it, "The old adage 'If you can't beat 'em, join 'em' is being replaced by 'Join 'em and you can't be beat.'" In fact, new technology companies in software, biotechnology, or telecommunications are now usually "born global." HDM, a computer-mapping company, had a joint venture in Japan and development groups in Canada and Russia within two years of its formation. "Virtually everything we do is partnerships," says Tom Parmeter, president of Protein Polymer Technologies, Inc., a biomaterials manufacturer in San Diego. Alliances are crucial because Protein Polymer cannot build markets on its own.

Strategic alliances are booming across the entire spectrum of industries and services and for a wide variety of purposes. According to Booz, Allen, and Hamilton, the number of U.S. firms with partners in Europe, Asia, and Latin America is growing at a rate of 25 percent annually. Why the boom? Here are several strategic reasons companies enter into alliances:

- Fill gaps in current market and technology
- Turn excess manufacturing capacity into profits
- Reduce risk and entry costs into new markets
- Accelerate product introductions
- Achieve economies of scale
- Overcome legal and trade barriers
- Extend the scope of existing operations
- Cut exit costs when divesting operations

Even multinational giants are forging alliances. Recently, Coca-Cola partnered with several other global companies. In May 2000, Coke formed a marketing alliance with AOL TimeWarner designed to both bolster Coke's online marketing presence and promote AOL's image off-line. Coke partnered with Interpublic ad agency in December 2000 to coordinate its $1 billion annual global marketing effort. With these deals, Coke sought to capitalize on many of the strategic reasons for alliances listed above.

Sources: Julie Cohen Mason, "Strategic Alliances: Partnering for Success," *Management Review*, (May 1993): 10–15; John Naisbitt, *The Global Paradox* (New York: William Morrow, 1994), pp. 18–21; Rosabeth Moss Kantner, "The Power of Partnering," *Sales & Marketing Management* (June 1997): 26–28; Roberta Maynard, "Striking the Right Match," *Nation's Business* (May 1996): 18.

with domestic or multinational companies that complement or leverage their capabilities and resources. The Star Alliance, for example, brings together 15 airlines—Lufthansa, United Airlines, Mexicana, Air Canada, ANA, Austrian Airlines, British Midland, Singapore Airlines, Tyrolean, Lauda, SAS, Thai Airways, Varig, Air New Zealand, and Ansett Australia—into a huge global partnership that allows travelers to make nearly seamless connections to about 700 destinations.

Just doing business in another country may require the firm to license its product, form a joint venture with a local firm, or buy from local suppliers to meet "domestic content" requirements. As a result, many firms are rapidly developing global strategic networks, and victory is going to those who build the better global network. For more details, see "Marketing for the New Economy: The Network Economy."

MARKETING ALLIANCES Many strategic alliances take the form of marketing alliances. These fall into four major categories.

1. *Product or service alliances:* One company licenses another to produce its product, or two companies jointly market their complementary products or a new product. For instance, H&R Block and Hyatt Legal Services—two service businesses—have also joined together in a marketing alliance.
2. *Promotional alliances:* One company agrees to carry a promotion for another company's product or service. McDonald's, for example, has often teamed up with Disney to offer products related to current Disney films to people buying its food.
3. *Logistics alliances:* One company offers logistical services for another company's product. For example, Abbott Laboratories warehouses and delivers all of 3M's medical and surgical products to hospitals across the United States.
4. *Pricing collaborations:* One or more companies join in a special pricing collaboration. It is common for hotel and rental car companies to offer mutual price discounts.

Marketing
MEMO

Strategic Alliances

Despite the many good reasons for pursuing alliances, a high percentage end in failure. A study by McKinsey & Company revealed that roughly one-third of 49 alliances failed to live up to the partners' expectations. Yet such painful lessons are teaching companies how to craft a winning alliance. Three keys seem to be:

1. *Strategic fit:* Before even considering an alliance, companies need to assess their own core competencies. Then they need to find a partner that will complement them in business lines, geographic positions, or competencies. A good example of strategic fit is AT&T and Sovintel, a Russian telephone company. The two joined forces to offer high-speed ISDN services for digitized voice, data, and video communications between the two countries. By joining together, the two telecommunications companies can offer new services for more business customers than either could do alone.

2. *A focus on the long term:* Rather than joining forces to save a few dollars, strategic partners should focus more on gains that can be harvested for years to come. Corning, the $5-billion-a-year glass and ceramics maker, is renowned for making partnerships. It has derived half of its products from joint ventures and even defines itself as a "network of organizations." That network includes German and Korean electronics giants Siemens and Samsung, and Mexico's biggest glassmaker, Vitro.

3. *Flexibility:* Alliances can last only if they are flexible. One example of a flexible partnership is Merck's alliance with AB Astra of Sweden. Merck started out simply with U.S. rights to its partner's new drugs. For the next phase, Merck set up a new corporation to handle the partnership's $500-million-a-year business and sold half the equity to Astra.

Sources: Stratford Sherman, "Are Strategic Alliances Working?" *Fortune*, September 21, 1992, pp. 77–78; Stephen D. Moore, "Astra and Merck Agree to Revamp U. S. Affiliate," *Wall Street Journal*, June 22, 1998.

Companies need to give creative thought to finding partners that might complement their strengths and offset their weaknesses. Well-managed alliances allow companies to obtain a greater sales impact at less cost. To keep their strategic alliances thriving, corporations have begun to develop organizational structures to support them and have come to view the ability to form and manage partnerships as core skills in and of themselves (called **Partner Relationship Management, PRM**). Companies can designate a core group in charge of partnerships, even if it is not formal, to manage and monitor alliances.[20]

program formulation and implementation

Once the business unit has developed its principal strategies, it must work out detailed supporting programs. If the unit has decided to attain technological leadership, it must plan programs to strengthen its R&D department, gather technological intelligence, develop leading-edge products, train the technical sales force, and develop ads to communicate its technological leadership.

Once the marketing programs are formulated, the marketing people must estimate their costs. Questions arise: Is participating in a particular trade show worth it? Will a specific sales contest pay for itself? Will hiring another salesperson contribute to the bottom line? Activity-based cost (ABC) accounting should be applied to each marketing program to determine whether it is likely to produce sufficient results to justify the cost.[21]

A great marketing strategy can be sabotaged by poor implementation. Copernicus, a leading marketing research and consulting firm, studied 82 different marketing programs and found many cases of poor implementation.[22]

According to McKinsey & Company, strategy is only one of seven elements in successful business practice.[23] McKinsey's 7-S framework for business success is shown in Figure 4.8. The first three elements—strategy, structure, and systems—are considered the "hardware" of success. The next four—style, skills, staff, and shared values—are the "software."

The first "soft" element, *style,* means that company employees share a common way of thinking and behaving. McDonald's employees smile at the customer, and IBM employees are very professional in their customer dealings. The second, *skills,* means that the employees have the skills needed to carry out the company's strategy. The third,

figure **4.8**

McKinsey 7–S Framework

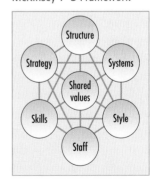

Source: McKinsey 7-S Framework from Thomas J. Peters and Robert H. Waterman Jr., *In Search of Excellence: Lessons from America's Best Run Companies.* Copyright © 1982 by Thomas J. Peters and Robert H. Waterman Jr. Reprinted by permission of HarperCollins Publishers, Inc.

staffing, means that the company has hired able people, trained them well, and assigned them to the right jobs. The fourth, *shared values,* means that the employees share the same guiding values. When these elements are present, companies are usually more successful at strategy implementation.[24]

feedback and control

As it implements its strategy, the firm needs to track the results and monitor new developments. Some environments are fairly stable from year to year. Other environments evolve slowly in a fairly predictable way. Still other environments change rapidly in major and unpredictable ways. Nonetheless, the company can count on one thing: The marketplace will change; and when it does, the company will need to review and revise its implementation, programs, strategies, or even objectives. Compaq is a good example.

Compaq   Compaq was the world's number-one computer seller in 1997. That position was under heavy assault from Dell, which had achieved remarkable success by employing a direct-sales strategy. Fearful that Dell would leave it in the dust, Compaq decided to adopt a direct-sales strategy of its own. By February 1999, Compaq's new line of direct-sales computers was selling $1 million worth per day. Although Dell overtook Compaq as the top seller in the United States for 1999, Compaq defended its global lead and regained the top spot domestically the next year.[25]

A company's strategic fit with the environment will inevitably erode because the market environment changes faster than the company's 7-Ss. Thus, a company might remain efficient while it loses effectiveness. Peter Drucker pointed out that it is more important to "do the right thing" (effectiveness) than "to do things right" (efficiency). The most successful companies excel at both.

Once an organization fails to respond to a changed environment, it becomes increasingly hard to recapture its lost position. This happened to the once-unassailable Motorola when it responded too slowly to the new digital technology and kept rolling out analog phones. Also consider what happened to Lotus Development Corporation. Its Lotus 1-2-3 software was once the world's leading software program, and now its market share in desktop software has slipped so low that analysts do not even bother to track it.

Lotus   Sales of the original IBM-PC were driven by Lotus 1-2-3, which combined an accounting spreadsheet with a program that could turn rows of numbers into charts and graphs. Yet Lotus ultimately did not keep pace as the PC evolved. It was late to market with a version of 1-2-3 for the Apple Macintosh. It was late again when Microsoft Windows took off, and it was late once more when the market turned to bundles of applications called suites.

Following IBM's acquisition of the company in 1995, Lotus capitalized on the growing popularity of corporate e-mail systems with its Notes software, but Microsoft's ability to tie applications to operating systems gave it an unbeatable advantage. The company now works in concert with Microsoft to make sure its latest Smart Suite software takes full advantage of the Windows 98, Windows NT, and domestically, the next year.[26]

Organizations, especially large ones, are subject to inertia. They are set up as efficient machines, and it is difficult to change one part without adjusting everything else. Yet organizations can be changed through strong leadership, preferably in advance of a crisis. The key to organizational health is willingness to examine the changing environment and to adopt new goals and behaviors. High-performance organizations continuously monitor the environment and use flexible strategic planning to maintain a fit with that environment as it evolves.

the marketing process

Planning at the corporate, division, and business unit levels is an integral part of the marketing process; but to fully understand that process, we must first look at how a company defines its business.

The task of any business is to deliver customer value at a profit. There are at least two views of the *value-delivery process*.[27] The traditional view is that the firm makes something and then sells it (Figure 4.9[a]). For example, Thomas Edison invents the phonograph and then hires people to make and sell it. In this view, marketing takes place in the second half of the process. The traditional view assumes that the company knows what to make and that the market will buy enough units to produce profits for the company.

the value-delivery sequence

Companies that subscribe to this traditional view have the best chance of succeeding in economies marked by goods shortages where consumers are not fussy about quality, features, or style. However, the traditional view of the business process will not work in more competitive economies where people face abundant choices. The "mass-market" is actually splintering into numerous micromarkets, each with its own wants, perceptions, preferences, and buying criteria. Therefore, the smart competitor must design and deliver offerings for well-defined target markets. This belief is at the core of the new view of business processes, which places marketing at the beginning of the planning process. Instead of emphasizing making and selling, companies see themselves as part of a value creation and delivery sequence (Figure 4.9[b]). This sequence consists of three parts.

The first phase, choosing the value, represents the "homework" that marketing must do before any product exists. The marketing staff must segment the market, select the appropriate market target, and develop the offering's value positioning. The formula "segmentation, targeting, positioning (STP)" is the essence of strategic marketing. Once the business unit has chosen the value, the second phase is providing the value. Marketing must determine specific product features, prices, and distribution as part of tactical marketing. The task in the third phase is communicating the value. Here further tactical marketing occurs in utilizing the sales force, sales promotion, advertising, and other promotional tools to inform and promote the product.

figure **4.9**	Two Views of the Value–Delivery Process

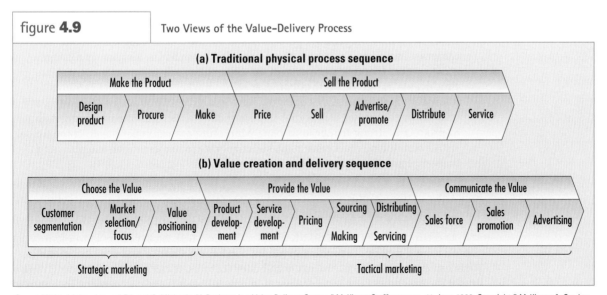

(a) Traditional physical process sequence

Make the Product / Sell the Product

Design product › Procure › Make › Price › Sell › Advertise/promote › Distribute › Service

(b) Value creation and delivery sequence

Choose the Value / Provide the Value / Communicate the Value

Customer segmentation › Market selection/focus › Value positioning › Product development › Service development › Pricing › Sourcing › Distributing › Making › Servicing › Sales force › Sales promotion › Advertising

Strategic marketing / Tactical marketing

Source: Michael J. Lanning and Edward G. Michaels, "A Business Is a Value Delivery System," McKinsey Staff paper no. 41, June 1988. Copyright © McKinsey & Co., Inc.

Nike   Critics of Nike often complain that its shoes cost almost nothing to make yet cost the consumer so much. True, the raw materials and manufacturing costs involved in the making of a sneaker are relatively cheap, but the process of selling the product to the consumer is expensive. Materials, labor, shipping, equipment, import duties, and suppliers' costs generally total fewer than $25 for a pair of shoes. Nike must compensate its sales team, its distributors, its administration, and its endorsers, as well as pay for advertising and R&D. This adds an additional $15 or so to the total. Finally, Nike sells its product to retailers to make a profit of $7. The retailer therefore pays roughly $47 in order to put a pair of Nikes on the shelf. When the retailer's overhead (typically $30 covering personnel, lease, and equipment) is factored in along with a $10 profit, the shoe costs the consumer over $80.[28]

As Figure 4.9(b) shows, the marketing process begins before there is a product and continues while it is being developed and after it becomes available. The Japanese have further developed this view by promulgating the following concepts:

- *Zero customer feedback time:* Customer feedback should be collected continuously after purchase to learn how to improve the product and its marketing.
- *Zero product-improvement time:* The company should evaluate all improvement ideas and introduce the most valued and feasible improvements as soon as possible.
- *Zero purchasing time:* The company should receive the required parts and supplies continuously through just-in-time arrangements with suppliers. By lowering its inventories, the company can reduce its costs.
- *Zero setup time:* The company should be able to manufacture any of its products as soon as they are ordered, without facing high setup time or costs.
- *Zero defects:* The products should be of high quality and free of flaws.

steps in the planning process

To carry out their responsibilities, marketing managers—whether at the corporate, division, business, or product level—follow a marketing process. Working within the plans set by the levels above them, product managers come up with a marketing plan for individual products, lines, brands, channels, or customer groups.

The **marketing process** consists of analyzing marketing opportunities; researching and selecting target markets; designing marketing strategies; planning marketing programs; and organizing, implementing, and controlling the marketing effort.

We will illustrate each step here in connection with the following situation:

Zeus, Inc. (name disguised) operates in several industries, including chemicals, cameras, and film. The company is organized into SBUs. Corporate management is considering what to do with its Atlas camera division. At present, Atlas produces a range of 35 mm cameras. The market for standard cameras is intensely competitive. On a growth-share matrix, this business is becoming a weak cash cow. Zeus's corporate management wants Atlas's marketing group to produce a strong turnaround plan. Marketing management has to come up with a convincing marketing plan, sell corporate management on the plan, and then implement and control it.

The sections that follow apply to marketing planning at all levels of the organization. Later in this chapter, we will examine the components of a specific marketing plan developed to support a product line.

ANALYZING MARKET OPPORTUNITIES   The first task facing Atlas is to identify its potential long-run opportunities given its market experience and core competencies. Atlas can develop its film cameras with better features. It can also consider designing a line of digital cameras or video cameras, or it can use its core competency in optics to design a line of binoculars and telescopes.

To evaluate its opportunities, Atlas needs a reliable marketing research and information system (see Chapter 5). Marketing research is an indispensable marketing tool for assessing buyer wants and behavior and market size. The marketing people can research secondary sources, run focus groups, and conduct telephone, mail, and personal surveys. By analyzing the collected data, Atlas will gain a better picture of the size of each market opportunity.

Marketing research gathers significant information about the marketing environment (see Chapter 6). Atlas's microenvironment consists of all the players who affect the company's ability to produce and sell cameras—suppliers, marketing intermediaries, customers, and competitors. Its macroenvironment consists of demographic, economic, physical, technological, political-legal, and social-cultural forces that affect its sales and profits. An important part of gathering environmental information includes measuring market potential and forecasting future demand.

Atlas needs to understand consumer markets (see Chapter 7). How many households plan to buy cameras? Who buys and why do they buy? What are they looking for in the way of features and prices? Where do they shop? What are their images of different brands? Atlas also sells cameras to business markets, including large corporations, professional firms, retailers, and government agencies (see Chapter 8). Purchasing agents or buying committees make the decisions. Atlas needs to gain a full understanding of how organizational buyers buy. It needs a sales force that is well trained in presenting product benefits.

Atlas must also pay close attention to competitors (see Chapter 9), anticipating its competitors' moves and knowing how to react quickly and decisively. It may want to initiate some surprise moves, in which case it needs to anticipate how its competitors will respond.

Once Atlas has analyzed its market opportunities, it is ready to select target markets. Modern marketing practice calls for dividing the market into major market segments, evaluating each segment, and targeting those market segments that the company can best serve (see Chapter 10).

DEVELOPING MARKETING STRATEGIES   Suppose Atlas decides to focus on the consumer market and develop a positioning strategy (see Chapter 11). Should Atlas position its cameras as the "Cadillac" brand, offering a superior camera at a premium price with excellent service and strong advertising? Should it build a simple, low-price camera aimed at more price-conscious consumers? Should it develop a medium-quality, medium-price camera? Once Atlas decides on its product positioning, it must initiate new-product development, testing, and launching (see Chapter 12).

After launch the product's strategy will need modification at the different stages in the product life cycle: introduction, growth, maturity, and decline (see Chapter 11). Furthermore, strategy choice will depend on whether the firm is a market leader, challenger, follower, or nicher (see Chapter 9). Finally, strategy will have to take into account changing global opportunities and challenges (see Chapter 13).

PLANNING MARKETING PROGRAMS   To transform marketing strategy into marketing programs, marketing managers must make basic decisions on marketing expenditures, marketing mix, and marketing allocation. First, Atlas must decide what level of marketing expenditures will achieve its objectives. Companies typically establish their marketing budgets as a percentage of the sales goal. A particular company may spend more than normal in the hope of achieving a higher market share. Second, the company has to decide how to divide the total marketing budget among the various tools in the marketing mix: product, price, place, and promotion.[29]

Finally, marketers must decide on the allocation of the marketing budget to the various products, channels, promotion media, and sales areas. How many dollars should support Atlas's two or three camera lines? Direct versus distributor sales? Direct-mail advertising versus trade-magazine advertising? East Coast markets versus West Coast markets? To make these allocations, marketing managers use sales-response functions that show how sales and profits would be affected by the amount of money spent in each application.

The basic marketing-mix tool is product—the firm's tangible offering to the market, which includes the product quality, design, features, branding, and packaging (see Chapter 14). As part of its product offering, Atlas may provide various services, such as leasing, delivery, repair, and training (see Chapter 15). Such support services can provide a competitive advantage in the global marketplace.

A critical marketing-mix tool is price (see Chapter 16). Atlas has to decide on wholesale and retail prices, discounts, allowances, and credit terms. Its price should be commensurate with the offer's perceived value; otherwise, buyers will turn to competitors' products.

Place includes the various activities the company undertakes to make the product accessible and available to target customers (see Chapters 17 and 18). Atlas must identify, recruit, and link various marketing facilitators to supply its products and services efficiently to the target market. It must understand the various types of retailers, wholesalers, and physical-distribution firms and how they make their decisions.

Promotion includes all the activities the company undertakes to communicate and promote its products to the target market (see Chapters 19 to 21). Atlas has to hire, train, and motivate salespeople. It has to set up communication and promotion programs consisting of advertising, sales promotion, public relations, and direct and online marketing.

MANAGING THE MARKETING EFFORT   The final step in the marketing process is organizing the marketing resources and then implementing and controlling the marketing plan. The company must build a marketing organization that is capable of implementing the marketing plan (see Chapter 22). In a small company, one person might carry out all the marketing tasks. Divisions of large companies such as Atlas will have several marketing specialists: salespeople, sales managers, marketing researchers, advertising personnel, product and brand managers, market-segment managers, and customer service personnel.

Marketing departments are typically headed by a marketing vice president who performs three tasks. The first is to coordinate the work of all the marketing personnel. The second task is to work closely with the other functional vice presidents. The third is selecting, training, directing, motivating, and evaluating marketing personnel. Because of surprises and disappointments that can occur as marketing plans are implemented, the company needs feedback and control.[30] There are three types of marketing control:

1. *Annual-plan* control is the task of ensuring that the company is achieving its current sales, profits, and other goals. First, management must state well-defined goals for each month or quarter. Second, management must measure its performance in the marketplace. Third, management must determine the underlying causes of any serious performance gaps. Fourth, management must choose corrective actions to close gaps between goals and performance.

2. *Profitability control* is the task of measuring the actual profitability of products, customer groups, trade channels, and order sizes. This is not a simple task. A company's accounting system is seldom designed to report the real profitability of different marketing entities and activities. Marketing profitability analysis measures the profitability of different marketing activities. Marketing efficiency studies try to determine how various marketing activities could be carried out more efficiently.

3. *Strategic control* is the task of evaluating whether the company's marketing strategy is appropriate to market conditions. Because of rapid changes in the marketing environment, each company needs to reassess its marketing effectiveness periodically, through a control instrument known as the marketing audit.

Figure 4.10 presents a grand summary of the marketing process and the forces shaping the company's marketing strategy.

figure **4.10**

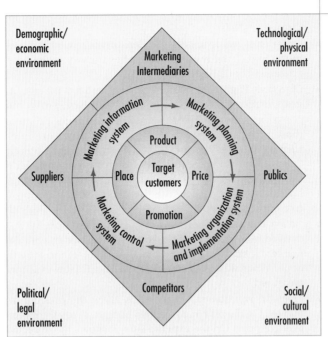

Factors Influencing
Company Marketing
Strategy

product planning: the nature and contents of a marketing plan

Each product level (product line, brand) must develop a **marketing plan** for achieving its goals. The marketing plan is one of the most important outputs of the marketing process.

Marketing plans are becoming more customer- and competitor-oriented and better reasoned and more realistic than in the past. The plans draw more inputs from all the functions and are team-developed. Marketing executives increasingly see themselves as professional managers first, and specialists second. Planning is becoming a continuous process to respond to rapidly changing market conditions. The trends we have discussed so far are in full force in the world of marketing!

At the same time, marketing planning procedures and content vary considerably among companies. The plan is variously called a "business plan," a "marketing plan," and sometimes a "battle plan." Most marketing plans cover one year. The plans vary in length from under 5 to over 50 pages. Some companies take their plans very seriously, whereas others see them only as a rough guide to action. Eisenhower once observed: "In preparing for battle I have always found that plans are useless but planning is indispensable." The most frequently cited shortcomings of current marketing plans, according to marketing executives, are lack of realism, insufficient competitive analysis, and a short-run focus.

What, then, does a marketing plan look like? What does it contain?

contents of the marketing plan

■ *Executive summary and table of contents:* The marketing plan should open with a brief summary of the main goals and recommendations. The executive summary permits senior management to grasp the plan's major thrust. A table of contents should follow the executive summary.

- *Current marketing situation:* This section presents relevant background data on sales, costs, profits, the market, competitors, channels, and the forces in the macroenvironment. This information is used to carry out on a SWOT (strengths, weaknesses, opportunities, threats) analysis.

- *Opportunity and issue analysis:* Here, management reviews the main opportunities found in the SWOT analysis and identifies the key issues likely to affect the organization's attainment of its objectives.

- *Objectives:* Here, the product manager outlines the plan's major financial and marketing goals, expressed in sales volume, market share, profit, and other relevant terms.

- *Marketing strategy:* Here the product manager defines the target segments, namely, those groups and needs the market offerings are intended to satisfy. The manager then establishes the product line's competitive positioning, which will inform the "game plan" to accomplish the plan's objectives. All this is done with inputs from other organizational areas, such as purchasing, manufacturing, sales, finance, and human resources, to ensure that the company can provide proper support for effective implementation.

- *Action programs:* The marketing plan must specify the actual marketing programs, derived from the marketing strategy, to be used in achieving the business objectives. Each marketing strategy element must be elaborated to answer these questions: What will be done? When will it be done? Who will do it? How much will it cost? How will progress be measured?

- *Financial projections:* Action plans allow the product manager to build a supporting budget. On the revenue side, this budget shows the forecasted sales volume in units and average price. On the expense side, it shows the expected costs of production, distribution, and marketing, broken down into finer categories. The difference between revenues and sales is projected profit. Once approved, the budget is the basis for developing plans and schedules for material procurement, production scheduling, employee recruitment, and marketing operations.

- *Implementation controls:* The last section of the marketing plan outlines the controls for monitoring and adjusting implementation of the plan. Typically, the goals and budget are spelled out for each month or quarter so management can review each period's results and take corrective action as needed. Some organizations include contingency plans outlining the steps management would take in response to specific environmental developments, such as price wars or strikes.

sample marketing plan: sonic personal digital assistant

Sonic, a hypothetical start-up company, is getting ready to introduce a new multifunction personal digital assistant (PDA), also known as a handheld computer. Sonic's new product is entering a marketplace crowded with offerings from Palm, Handspring, and other PDA makers. The following is excerpted from the marketing plan that Jane Melody, Sonic's chief marketing officer, has prepared for the coming year.

CURRENT MARKETING SITUATION   The $3.7 billion PDA market is dominated by Palm, which sold 13 million units in its first five years. Industrywide sales are expected to accelerate for at least the next five years, with multifunction devices attracting an ever-increasing market share. Analysts predict 4 million units in total PDA sales for this year and 5 million for the next year.

Market leader Palm offers a range of PDAs for consumer and business use, from a low-end, non-Web-enabled, monochrome model to a slimmer, lighter, high-end model equipped for Web access and e-mail notification. Handspring, an aggressive number two in the market, attracted a 21 percent share in its first year and drove Palm's share to below 70 percent. It licenses the Palm operating system for its Visor PDAs, which are lower-priced and generally more versatile than Palm's PDAs. PDAs made by Compaq, Hewlett-Packard, and Casio—all of which are based on the Windows CE operating system—currently account for less than 10 percent of the market.

Despite intense competition, Sonic can rely on numerous strengths. First, its PDA has a superior handwriting recognition system, which simplifies use. Second, it bundles valuable features found only on higher-priced rival products. Third, Sonic's PDA can accept any Palm-compatible peripheral; and fourth, it is priced lower than competing models. However, its weaknesses include: lack of brand awareness and image; lack of color display screen; and slightly heavier weight than most competing models.

In addition, there are broad macroenvironmental factors that affect Sonic's product.

OPPORTUNITY AND ISSUE ANALYSIS   Sonic licenses Palm's operating system rather than using Microsoft's Windows CE operating system. This allows its PDA to work with thousands of Palm-compatible applications and peripherals such as cameras, phones, and global positioning systems—greatly expanding the appeal of its PDA for both consumers and business buyers. Yet increased competition from hybrids such as the cell phone–PDA combinations offered by Mitsubishi, Kyocera, and Samsung could slow acceptance of Sonic's model, which can use the optional Palm-compatible cell-phone attachment. Increased competition will complicate Sonic's ability to differentiate the Sonic PDA from competing models. Another threat is the ongoing downward pressure on pricing caused by the proliferation of PDA and hybrid products.

Among the issues Sonic must address are: (1) Should it develop a proprietary operating system, switch to the Windows CE system, or continue to pay licensing fees for the Palm system? (2) Should Sonic offer customized applications for business users? (3) Should it create a game-playing peripheral to make the Sonic PDA compatible with Sony's PlayStation 2?

OBJECTIVES   Sonic's financial objectives are to:

- Earn an annual rate of return on investment of 15 percent after taxes over the next five years.
- Produce net profits of $6 million next year with a target profit margin of 10 percent on total sales.
- Achieve first-year total sales revenue of $60 million, based on an average price of $250 per unit.

Sonic's marketing objectives are to:

- Achieve a first-year unit sales volume of 240,000, which represents a projected market share of 6 percent with one model in product line.
- Increase second-year share to 10 percent, based on sales of two models in product line.
- Generate 40 percent brand awareness within the consumer target market and 50 percent brand awareness within the business target market by the end of next year.
- Arrange for distribution through Amazon.com and through the leading computer retailers in the top 50 U.S. markets within three months, followed by distribution coverage in the remaining major metropolitan areas within six months.

MARKETING STRATEGY   On the consumer side, the target market is middle- to upper-income professionals who need one portable device to coordinate their busy schedules and communicate with family and colleagues. These consumers prefer lower-priced PDAs with expandable memory and functionality. On the business side, the target market is mid- to large-sized corporations that want to help their workforce stay in touch and input or access critical data on the go. These buyers want durable, powerful, easy-to-use PDAs that can operate customized business applications.

Highlights of Sonic's marketing strategy:

- *Positioning:* Sonic's is the most versatile PDA for personal and professional use.
- *Product management:* Basic model, to be introduced next year, incorporates wireless Web access and MP3 downloading capabilities, with slots for expanded memory and functionality. Focus research and development on a more compact, higher-power, top-end model for introduction the following year.

- *Pricing:* First-year average product price of $350 is in the mid-range of the market, offering unusually high value for advanced features. Expect to lower price of first model when higher-end model is introduced in second year.
- *Distribution:* Should be through the best-known Internet and computer retailers, starting with the top 50 U.S. markets.
- *Marketing communications:* Create an advertising campaign to build brand awareness and differentiate the product from competitors; emphasize trade sales promotion to support distribution strategy; and develop a high-profile product-launch strategy to generate publicity and media coverage.
- *Marketing research:* Measure brand awareness before, during, and after marketing campaigns; study customer satisfaction and identify opportunities for future product development efforts.

ACTION PROGRAMS   Sonic will carry out its marketing strategy and achieve its objectives through a variety of scheduled programs. In January, it plans to initiate a $500,000 trade sales promotion to educate dealers and generate excitement for the product launch in February. As part of this trade push, Sonic will exhibit at the major consumer electronics trade show. In February, it will kick off its consumer advertising with an integrated print/radio/Internet campaign supported by point-of-sale signage. In March. . . .

FINANCIAL PROJECTIONS   Total first-year sales revenue is projected at $60 million, with an average wholesale price of $250 per unit, variable cost per unit of $150 on unit sales volume of 240,000, and target profit margin of 10 percent. On a quarterly basis, Sonic projects sales of $8 million, $12 million, $11 million, and $29 million, based on cumulatively higher business sales and a spike in year-end consumer sales. Each action program carries its own financial assumptions, as well as managerial assignments and scheduling details. In turn, these financial projections lay the foundation for planning in the manufacturing, human resources, research and development, and finance and accounting departments.

IMPLEMENTATION CONTROLS   This marketing plan includes a detailed budget, schedule, and managerial assignment for every action program. For control purposes, the plan also allows for month-by-month comparison of actual versus projected sales and expenses. A contingency plan, attached, has been developed for implementation in the case of severe downward pricing pressure.[31]

summary

1. Market-oriented strategic planning is the managerial process of developing and maintaining a viable fit between the organization's objectives, skills, and resources and its changing market opportunities. The aim of strategic planning is to shape the company's businesses and products so that they yield target profits and growth. Strategic planning takes place at four levels: corporate, division, business unit, and product.

2. Corporate headquarters is responsible for setting the strategic-planning process in motion. The corporate strategy establishes the framework within which the divisions and business units prepare their strategic plans. Setting a corporate strategy entails four activities: defining the corporate mission, establishing strategic business units (SBUs), assigning resources to each SBU based on its market attractiveness and business strength, and planning new businesses and downsizing older businesses.

3. Strategic planning for individual businesses entails the following activities: defining the business mission, analyzing external opportunities and threats, analyzing internal strengths and weaknesses, formulating goals, formulating strategy, formulating supporting programs, implementing the programs, and gathering feedback and exercising control.

4. The marketing process consists of four steps: analyzing market opportunities; developing marketing strategies; planning marketing programs; and organizing, implementing, and controlling the marketing effort.

5. Each product level within a business unit must develop a marketing plan for achieving its goals. The marketing plan is one of the most important outputs of the marketing process, and it should contain the following elements: an executive summary and table of contents; an overview of the current marketing situation; an analysis of the opportunities and issues facing the product; a summary of the plan's financial and marketing objectives; an overview of the marketing strategy to be used to achieve the plan's objectives; a description of the action programs to be implemented to achieve the plan's objectives; a projected profit-and-loss statement; and a summary of the controls to be used in monitoring the plan's progress.

applications

marketing debate – what good is a mission statement?

Virtually all firms have mission statements to help guide and inspire employees as well as signal what is important to the firm to those outside the firm. Mission statements are often the product of much deliberation and discussion. At the same time, critics claim that mission statements sometimes lack "teeth" and lack specificity. Moreover, critics also maintain that in many cases, mission statements do not vary much from firm to firm and make the same empty promises.

Take a position: Mission statements are critical to a successful marketing organization, *or* Mission statements rarely provide useful marketing value.

marketing and advertising

1. Strategic alliances are extremely common in the airline industry. The ad in Figure 1, which appeared in a business magazine, promotes the North American alliance between AeroMexico and Delta Airlines. This alliance allows business travelers and vacationers to conveniently fly between many destinations in Mexico and the United States.

   a. In which of the four major categories does this strategic alliance fit?

   b. What benefits does this alliance offer the two partners? What benefits does it offer the partners' customers?

   c. What threats and opportunities might confront the partners in this alliance?

2. Ernst & Young's specialists are equipped to "more than just advise on the tax implications of doing international business," as the ad in Figure 2 explains. In today's global economy, more and more companies need professional help to be sure their accounting and financial activities comply with the regulations of every country where they do business.

   a. Is the strategy being used by Ernst & Young one of cost leadership, differentiation, or focus? How does this ad support the company's strategy?

   b. What feedback mechanisms might Ernst & Young use to learn about the effect of the campaign that includes this ad?

   c. Which factors in the macroenvironment might exert the most influence on Ernst & Young's plans to market its foreign tax services?

Figure 1

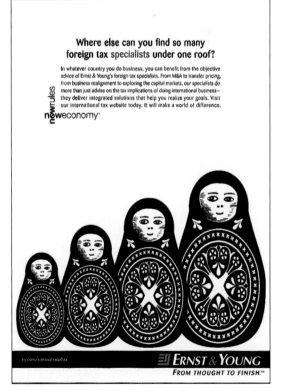

Figure 2

online marketing today

Reflect.com, set up by Procter & Gamble, is applying customization to take advantage of a new economy opportunity in beauty products. Instead of selling standard, branded products, Reflect.com invites customers to log on, get beauty advice, and then click to customize cosmetics and fragrances for their individual needs and tastes. The company even allows customers to personalize the packaging and choose from different logos. A P&G manufacturing plant in New York formulates products according to customer specifications, and a service center in Ohio handles customer inquiries. Visit Reflect.com <www.reflect.com> and follow the "About us"[a] link to read about the company's background and offerings. Also browse the other sections of the site. What environmental threats might influence Reflect.com's ability to fully exploit its market opportunity? What strengths can Reflect.com build on to overcome these threats? What weaknesses should Reflect.com bear in mind as it formulates its marketing strategy?

[a]Based on Fara Warner, "Don't Shout, Listen," *Fast Company*, August 2001, pp. 130–39.

you're the marketer: sonic pda marketing plan

Marketing Plan Pro

Every marketing plan must include the company's mission and financial and marketing objectives to guide the implementation of specific strategies and programs during the period covered by the plan. The marketing plan should also indicate the major competitive scopes within which the business will operate.

As shown in the sample marketing plan on pages 116–118, Sonic is a start-up company that will soon introduce a new multi-function personal digital assistant (PDA) to compete with established products made by Palm, Handspring, and others. As an assistant to Jane Melody, Sonic's chief marketing officer, you have been assigned to draft a mission statement for top management's review. You are also expected to suggest how Sonic should define its competitive scopes and recommend an appropriate generic competitive strategy for the business. Using your knowledge of marketing, the information you have about Sonic, and library or Internet resources, answer the following questions:

- What should Sonic's mission be?

- In what competitive scopes (industry, products and applications, competence, market-segment, vertical, and geographic) should Sonic operate?
- Which of Porter's generic competitive strategies would you recommend that Sonic follow in formulating overall strategy? How would this strategy help the firm compete within a crowded marketplace?
- How do the firm's marketing and financial objectives fit with your recommended mission and strategy?

As your instructor directs, enter Sonic's mission statement, overall strategy, and objectives in a written marketing plan or type them into the Your Company and Mission sections of the *Marketing Plan Pro* software. Also enter information on the competitive scope and generic strategy in the Executive Summary and Current Situation sections of the marketing plan.

notes

1. Steve Harrell, in a speech at the plenary session of the American Marketing Association's Educators' Meeting, Chicago, August 5, 1980.
2. "The New Breed of Strategic Planning," *BusinessWeek*, September 7, 1984, pp. 62–68.
3. Peter Drucker, *Management: Tasks, Responsibilities and Practices* (New York: Harper and Row, 1973), ch. 7.
4. Rubbermaid, *Annual Report*, 1997.
5. See "The Hollow Corporation," *BusinessWeek*, March 3, 1986, pp. 57–59. Also see William H. Davidow and Michael S. Malone, *The Virtual Corporation* (New York: HarperBusiness, 1992).
6. For more discussion, see Laura Nash, "Mission Statements—Mirrors and Windows," *Harvard Business Review* (March–April 1988): 155–56.
7. Theodore Levitt, "Marketing Myopia," *Harvard Business Review* (July–August 1960): 45–56.
8. "Sara Lee to Build Brand through Outsourcing, Marketing," *Discount Store News*, October 20, 1997, p. A4.

9. Derek Abell, *Defining the Business: The Starting Point of Strategic Planning* (Upper Saddle River, NJ: Prentice Hall, 1980), ch. 3.
10. See Roger A. Kerin, Vijay Mahajan, and P. Rajan Varadarajan, *Contemporary Perspectives on Strategic Planning* (Boston: Allyn & Bacon, 1990).
11. A hard decision must be made between harvesting and divesting a business. Harvesting a business will strip it of its long-run value, in which case it will be difficult to find a buyer. Divesting, on the other hand, is facilitated by maintaining a business in a fit condition in order to attract a buyer.
12. Peter Patel and Michael Younger, "A Frame of Reference for Strategy Development," *Long Range Planning* (April 1978): 6–12; S. J. Q. Robinson et al., "The Directional Policy Matrix—Tool for Strategic Planning," *Long Range Planning* (June 1978): 8–15.
13. For a contrary view, however, see J. Scott Armstrong and Roderick J. Brodie, "Effects of Portfolio Planning Methods on Decision Making: Experimental Results," *International Journal of Research in Marketing* (1994): 73–84.

14. The same matrix can be expanded into nine cells by adding modified products and modified markets. See S. J. Johnson and Conrad Jones, "How to Organize for New Products," *Harvard Business Review* (May–June 1957): 49–62.

15. <www.starbucks.com>; Howard Schultz, *Pour Your Heart into It* (New York: Hyperion, 1997).

16. George Stalk, Philip Evans, and Lawrence E. Shulman, "Competing Capabilities: The New Rules of Corporate Strategy," *Harvard Business Review* (March–April 1992): 57–69.

17. Ram Charan and Noel M. Tichy, *Every Business Is a Growth Business: How Your Company Can Prosper Year after Year* (New York: Times Business, Random House, 1998).

18. Michael E. Porter, *Competitive Strategy: Techniques for Analyzing Industries and Competitors* (New York: The Free Press, 1980), ch.2.

19. Michael E. Porter, "What Is Strategy?" *Harvard Business Review* (November–December 1996): 61–78.

20. For readings on strategic alliances, see Peter Lorange and Johan Roos, *Strategic Alliances: Formation, Implementation and Evolution* (Cambridge, MA: Blackwell, 1992); Jordan D. Lewis, *Partnerships for Profit: Structuring and Managing Strategic Alliances* (New York: The Free Press, 1990).

21. Robin Cooper and Robert S. Kalpan, "Profit Priorities from Activity-Based Costing," *Harvard Business Review* (May–June 1991): 130–35.

22. Conversation with Kevin Clancy, CEO of Copernicus, March 2001.

23. Thomas J. Peters and Robert H. Waterman Jr., *In Search of Excellence: Lessons from America's Best-Run Companies* (New York: Harper and Row, 1982), pp. 9–12.

24. Terrence E. Deal and Allan A. Kennedy, *Corporate Cultures: The Rites and Rituals of Corporate Life* (Reading, MA: Addison-Wesley, 1982); "Corporate Culture," *BusinessWeek*, October 27, 1980, pp. 148–60; Stanley M. Davis, *Managing Corporate Culture* (Cambridge, MA: Ballinger, 1984); John P. Kotter and James L. Heskett, *Corporate Culture and Performance* (New York: The Free Press, 1992).

25. Gary McWilliams, "Compaq Says Sales of New PC Top $1 Million a Day," *Wall Street Journal*, February 1, 1999; Peter Burrows, "Can Compaq Catch Up?" *BusinessWeek*, May 3, 1999.

26. Lawrence M. Fisher, "With a New Smart Suite, Lotus Catches Its Rivals' Success," *New York Times*, June 15, 1998, p. 6.

27. Michael J. Lanning and Edward G. Michaels, "A Business Is a Value Delivery System," McKinsey Staff Paper, no. 41, June 1988 (McKinsey & Co., Inc.)

28. Ed. Blitz, "How Can a $9 Sneaker Cost $70?" *San Diego Union-Tribune*, April 25, 1998.

29. E. Jerome McCarthy, *Basic Marketing: A Managerial Approach*, 12th ed. (Homewood, IL: Irwin, 1996).

30. Matrik G. Dekimpe and Dominique M. Hanssens, "Sustained Spending and Persistent Response: A New Look at Long-Term Profitability," *Journal of Marketing Research* (November 1999): pp. 397–412.

31. Based on Marian Burk Wood, *The Marketing Plan: A Handbook* (Upper Saddle River, NJ: Prentice Hall, 2003), Appendix 2.

5

gathering information and measuring market demand

In this chapter, we will address the following questions:

- What are the components of a modern marketing information system?
- What constitutes good marketing research?
- How can marketing decision support systems help marketing managers make better decisions?
- How can demand be more accurately measured and forecasted?

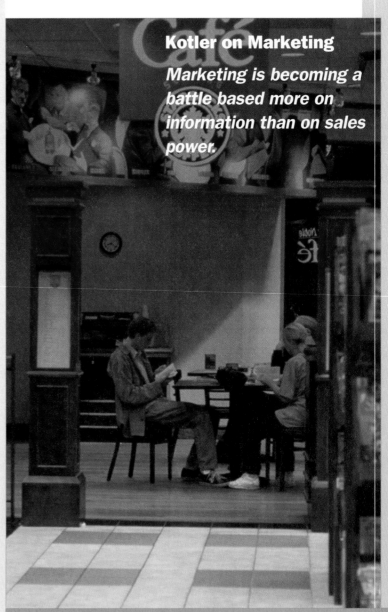

Kotler on Marketing

Marketing is becoming a battle based more on information than on sales power.

The marketing environment is changing at an accelerating rate, so the need for real-time market information is greater than at any time in the past. The shifts are dramatic: from local to national to global marketing, from buyer needs to buyer wants, from price to non-price competition. As companies expand their geographical market coverage, their managers need more information more quickly. As incomes improve, buyers become more selective in their choices of goods. To predict buyers' responses to different features, styles, and other attributes, sellers must turn to marketing research. As sellers increase their use of branding, product differentiation, advertising, and sales promotion, they require information on the effectiveness of these marketing tools.

Fortunately, the exploding information requirements have given rise to impressive new information technologies: computers, cable television, copy machines, fax machines, scanners, audio and video recorders, videodisc players, CD-ROMs, camcorders, cellular phones, and most impressive of all, the Internet.[1]

the components of a modern marketing information system

Some firms have developed marketing information systems that provide management with rapid and incredible detail about buyer wants, preferences, and behavior. For example, the Coca-Cola Company knows that we put 3.2 ice cubes in a glass, see 69 of its commercials every year, and prefer cans to pop out of vending machines at a temperature of 35 degrees. Kimberly-Clark, which makes Kleenex, has calculated that the average person blows his or her nose 256 times a year. Hoover learned that we spend about 35 minutes each week vacuuming, sucking up about 8 pounds of dust each year and using 6 bags to do so.[2]

Marketers also have extensive information about consumption patterns in other countries. On a per capita basis within Western Europe, for example, the Swiss consume the most chocolate, the Greeks eat the most cheese, the Irish drink the most tea, and the Austrians smoke the most cigarettes.[3]

Nevertheless, many business firms lack information sophistication. Many lack a marketing research department. Others have departments that limit work to routine forecasting, sales analysis, and occasional surveys. In addition, many managers complain about not knowing where critical information is located in the company; getting too much information that they cannot use and too little that they really need; getting important information too late; and doubting the information's accuracy. In today's information-based society, companies with superior information enjoy a competitive advantage. The company can choose its markets better, develop better offerings, and execute better marketing planning.

Every firm must organize and distribute a continuous flow of information to its marketing managers. Companies study their managers' information needs and design marketing information systems (MIS) to meet these needs. A **marketing information system (MIS)** consists of people, equipment, and procedures to gather, sort, analyze, evaluate, and distribute needed, timely, and accurate information to marketing decision makers.

The company's marketing information system should represent a cross between what managers think they need, what managers really need, and what is economically feasible. An internal MIS committee can interview a cross-section of marketing managers to discover their information needs. Some useful questions are:

1. What decisions do you regularly make?
2. What information do you need to make these decisions?
3. What information do you regularly get?
4. What special studies do you periodically request?
5. What information would you want that you are not getting now?
6. What information would you want daily? Weekly? Monthly? Yearly?
7. What magazines and trade reports would you like to see on a regular basis?
8. What topics would you like to be kept informed of?
9. What data analysis programs would you want?
10. What are the four most helpful improvements that could be made in the present marketing information system?

A marketing information system is developed from internal company records, marketing intelligence activities, marketing research, and marketing decision support analysis.

internal records system

Marketing managers rely on internal reports on orders, sales, prices, costs, inventory levels, receivables, payables, and so on. By analyzing this information, they can spot important opportunities and problems.

the order-to-payment cycle

The heart of the internal records system is the order-to-payment cycle. Sales representatives, dealers, and customers dispatch orders to the firm. The sales department prepares invoices and transmits copies to various departments. Out-of-stock items are back ordered. Shipped items are accompanied by shipping and billing documents that are sent to various departments.

Today's companies need to perform these steps quickly and accurately. Customers favor firms that can promise timely delivery. Customers and sales representatives fax or e-mail their orders. Computerized warehouses fill these orders quickly. The billing department sends out invoices as quickly as possible. An increasing number of companies are using the Internet and extranets to improve the speed, accuracy, and efficiency of the order-to-payment cycle. Retail giant Wal-Mart tracks the stock levels of its products daily and its computers send automatic replenishment orders to its vendors.[4]

sales information systems

Marketing managers need timely and accurate reports on current sales. Wal-Mart, for example, knows the sales of each product by store and total each evening. This enables it to transmit nightly orders to suppliers for new shipments of replacement stock. Wal-Mart shares its sales data with its larger suppliers such as P&G and expects P&G to re-supply Wal-Mart stores in a timely manner. Wal-Mart has entrusted P&G with the management of its inventory.

Companies must carefully interpret the sales data so as not to get the wrong signals. Michael Dell gave this illustration: "If you have three yellow Mustangs sitting on a dealer's lot and a customer wants a red one, the salesman is really good at figuring out how to sell the yellow Mustang. So the yellow Mustang gets sold, and a signal gets sent back to the factory that, hey, people want yellow Mustangs."

Here are two companies that are using computer technology to design fast and comprehensive sales reporting systems.

Ascom Timeplex, Inc.   Before heading out on a call, sales reps at this telecommunications equipment company use their laptop computers to dial into the company's worldwide data network. They can retrieve the latest price lists, engineering and configuration notes, status reports on previous orders, and e-mail from anywhere in the company; and when deals are struck, the laptop computers record each order, double-check the order for errors, and send it electronically to Timeplex headquarters in Woodcliff Lake, New Jersey.[5]

Montgomery Security   In 1996, San Francisco–based Montgomery Security was in a bind. To remain competitive in the financial sector, this NationsBank subsidiary had to find a way for more than 400 finance, research, and sales or trading employees to share information about companies whose stock they were considering taking public. The company solved the problem with Sales Enterprise Software from Siebel Systems. With a common database format, everyone could share information and keep confidential information secure.[6]

databases, data warehouses, and data-mining

Today companies organize their information in databases—customer databases, product databases, salesperson databases, and so forth—and then combine data from the different databases. For example, the customer database will contain every customer's name, address, past transactions, and even demographics and psychographics (activities, interests, and opinions) in some instances. Instead of a company sending a mass "carpet bombing" mailing of a new offer to every customer in its database, it will score the different customers according to their purchase recency, frequency, and monetary value. It will send the offer only to the highest scoring customers. Besides saving on mailing expenses, this will often achieve a double-digit response rate.

Companies warehouse these data and make them easily accessible to decision makers. Furthermore, by hiring analysts skilled in sophisticated statistical methods, they can "mine" the data and garner fresh insights into neglected customer segments, recent customer trends, and other useful information. The customer information can be cross-tabbed with product and salesperson information to yield still deeper insights. (See "Marketing for the New Economy: Companies Turn to Data Warehousing and Data Mining: Exercise Care.")

the marketing intelligence system

Whereas the internal records system supplies results data, the marketing intelligence system supplies happenings data. A **marketing intelligence system** is a set of procedures and sources used by managers to obtain everyday information about developments in the marketing environment. Marketing managers collect marketing intelligence by reading books, newspapers, and trade publications; talking to customers, suppliers, and distributors; and meeting with other company managers. A company can take several steps to improve the quality of its marketing intelligence.

First, it can train and motivate the sales force to spot and report new developments. Sales representatives are positioned to pick up information missed by other means. Yet they are very busy and often fail to pass on that information. The company must "sell" its sales force on their importance as intelligence gatherers. Sales reps should know which types of information to send to which managers. For instance, the Prentice Hall sales reps who sell this textbook let their editors know what is going on in each discipline, who is doing exciting research, and who plans to write cutting-edge textbooks.

Second, the company can motivate distributors, retailers, and other intermediaries to pass along important intelligence. Consider the following example.

Parker Hannifin Corporation   A major fluid-power-products manufacturer, Parker Hannifin requires each of its distributors to forward to Parker's marketing research division a copy of all invoices containing sales of its products. Parker analyzes these invoices to learn about end users, and shares its findings with the distributors.[7]

Many companies hire specialists to gather marketing intelligence. Retailers often send mystery shoppers to their stores to assess how employees treat customers. The city of Dallas hired Feedback Plus, a professional shopper agency, to see how carpound employees treat citizens picking up their cars. Neiman Marcus employs the same agency to shop at its 26 stores nationwide. "Those stores that consistently score high on the shopping service," says a Neiman Marcus senior VP, "not so coincidentally have the best sales." The stores will tell salespeople that they've "been shopped" and give them copies of the mystery shopper's report. Typical questions on the report are: How long before a sales associate greeted you? Did the sales associate act as if he or she wanted your business? Was the sales associate knowledgeable about products in stock?[8]

marketing for the **new economy**

Companies Turn to Data Warehousing and Data Mining: Exercise Care

Companies are using data mining to extract patterns from large masses of data organized in what is called a data warehouse. Banks and credit-card companies, telephone companies, catalog marketers, and many other companies have a great deal of information about their customers, including not only addresses and phone numbers, but also their transactions and enhanced data on age, family size, income, and other demographic information.

Some observers believe that a proprietary database can provide a company with a significant competitive advantage. It is no wonder that, at its secret location in Phoenix, security guards watch over American Express's 500 billion bytes of data on how its customers have used the company's 35 million green, gold, and platinum charge cards. Amex uses the database to include precisely targeted offers in its monthly mailing of millions of customer bills. MCI Communications Corporation, the long-distance carrier, sifts through 1 trillion bytes of customer phoning data to craft new discount calling plans for different types of customers.

Marriott's Vacation Club International has managed to reduce its volume of mail and yet increase its response rate by developing a model showing which customers in its database are most likely to respond to specific vacation offerings.

Tesco, the British supermarket chain, notifies different groups when there will be a special sale on items they buy. Lands' End can tell which of its 2 million customers should receive special mailings of specific clothing items that would fit their wardrobe needs.

These benefits do not come without heavy cost, not only in collecting the original customer data but also in maintaining them and mining them. Yet when it works, a data warehouse yields more than it costs. A 1996 study by DWI estimated that the average return on investment for a data warehouse over the course of three years is more than 400 percent, but the data have to be in good condition, and the discovered relationships must be valid. British Columbia Telecom wanted to invite 100 of its best customers to a Vancouver Grizzlies basketball game and selected customers who were heavy 900-number users. The invitations were already at the printer when the marketing staff discovered that heavy 900-number users included sex-line enthusiasts. They quickly added other criteria to search for a revised list of guests.

The Marriott Vacation Club International Web site gives interested consumers the opportunity to sell themselves on the Marriott offerings.

Sources: Peter R. Peacock, "Data Mining in Marketing: Part 1," *Marketing Management* (Winter 1998): 9–18, and "Data Mining in Marketing: Part 2," *Marketing Management* (Spring 1998): 15–25; Ginger Conlon, "What the !@#!*?!! Is a Data Warehouse?" *Sales & Marketing Management* (April 1997): 41–48; Skip Press, "Fool's Gold? As Companies Rush to Mine Data, They May Dig Up Real Gems—Or False Trends," *Sales & Marketing Management* (April 1997): 58, 60, 62; John Verity, "A Trillion-Byte Weapon," *BusinessWeek*, July 31, 1995, pp. 80–81.

CEOExpress.com is a portal to information: a user clicks on a listing and is then connected to that site.

Third, companies can collect competitive intelligence by purchasing competitors' products; attending open houses and trade shows; reading competitors' published reports; attending stockholders' meetings; talking to employees, dealers, distributors, suppliers, and freight agents; collecting competitors' ads; and looking up news stories about competitors on the Internet.

Ceoexpress.com   This site serves as a portal offering the researcher a comprehensive listing of the sites of newspapers, magazines, television stations, government agencies, financial sites, statistical sites, legal sites, and so on. The user simply clicks on any listing and is immediately connected to that site.

Fourth, a company can set up a customer advisory panel made up of representative customers or the company's largest customers or its most outspoken or sophisticated customers. For example, Hitachi Data Systems holds a three-day meeting with its customer panel of 20 members every 9 months. They discuss service issues, new technologies, and customers' strategic requirements. The discussion is free-flowing, and both parties gain: The company gains valuable information about customer needs, and the customers feel more bonded to a company that listens closely to their comments.[9]

Fifth, a company can purchase information from outside suppliers such as the A. C. Nielsen Company and Information Resources, Inc. (see Table 5.1, part D; and "Marketing Memo: Secondary Sources of Data Online" on pages 130–131). These research firms gather consumer-panel data at a much lower cost than the company could manage on its own.

Sixth, some companies circulate marketing intelligence. The staff scans the Internet and major publications, abstracts relevant news, and disseminates a news bulletin to marketing managers. It collects and files relevant information and assists managers in evaluating new information.

table **5.1**

Secondary-Data
Sources

A. Internal Sources

Company profit-loss statements, balance sheets, sales figures, sales-call reports, invoices, inventory records, and prior research reports.

B. Government Publications

- *Statistical Abstract of the United States*
- *County and City Data Book*
- *Industrial Outlook*
- *Marketing Information Guide*
- Other government publications include the *Annual Survey of Manufacturers; Business Statistics;* Census of Manufacturers; Census of Population; Census of Retail Trade, Wholesale Trade, and Selected Service Industries; Census of Transportation; *Federal Reserve Bulletin*; *Monthly Labor Review*; *Survey of Current Business*; and *Vital Statistics Report.*

C. Periodicals and Books

- *Business Periodicals Index*
- *Standard and Poor's Industry*
- *Moody's Manuals*
- *Encyclopedia of Associations*
- Marketing journals include the *Journal of Marketing, Journal of Marketing Research,* and *Journal of Consumer Research.*
- Useful trade magazines include *Advertising Age, Chain Store Age, Progressive Grocer, Sales & Marketing Management,* and *Stores.*
- Useful general business magazines include *BusinessWeek, Fortune, Forbes, The Economist,* and *Harvard Business Review.*

D. Commercial Data

- Nielsen Company: Data on products and brands sold through retail outlets (Retail Index Services), supermarket scanner data (Scantrack), data on television audiences (Media Research Services), magazine circulation data (Neodata Services, Inc.), and others.
- MRCA Information Services: Data on weekly family purchases of consumer products (National Consumer Panel) and data on home food consumption (National Menu Census).
- Information Resources, Inc.: Supermarket scanner data (InfoScan) and data on the impact of supermarket promotions (PromotioScan).
- SAMI/Burke: Reports on warehouse withdrawals to food stores in selected market areas (SAMI reports) and supermarket scanner data (Samscam).
- Simmons Market Research Bureau (MRB Group): Annual reports covering television markets, sporting goods, and proprietary drugs, with demographic data by sex, income, age, and brand preferences (selective markets and media reaching them).
- Other commercial research houses selling data to subscribers include the Audit Bureau of Circulation; Arbitron, Audits and Surveys; Dun & Bradstreet's; National Family Opinion; Standard Rate & Data Service; and Starch.

marketing research system

Marketing managers often commission formal marketing studies of specific problems and opportunities. They may request a market survey, a product-preference test, a sales forecast by region, or an advertising evaluation. It is the job of the marketing researcher to produce customer insight into the problem. We define **marketing research** as the systematic design, collection, analysis, and reporting of data and findings relevant to a specific marketing situation facing the company.

suppliers of marketing research

A company can obtain marketing research in a number of ways. Most large companies have their own marketing research departments.[10]

Procter & Gamble   P&G assigns marketing researchers to each product operating division to conduct research for existing brands. There are two separate in-house research groups, one in charge of overall company advertising research and the other in charge of market testing. Each group's staff consists of marketing research managers, supporting specialists (survey designers, statisticians, behavioral scientists), and in-house field representatives to conduct and supervise interviewing. Brand managers commission annual brand awareness and tracking studies, consumer-use tests, continuous retail audits, and laboratory research studies. Each year, P&G calls or visits over one million people in connection with about 1,000 research projects.

Small companies can hire the services of a marketing research firm or conduct research in creative and affordable ways, such as:

1. Engaging students or professors to design and carry out projects: One Boston University MBA project helped American Express develop a successful advertising campaign geared toward young professionals. The cost: $15,000.
2. Using the Internet: A company can collect considerable information at very little cost by examining competitors' Web sites, monitoring chat rooms, and accessing published data.
3. Checking out rivals: Many small companies routinely visit their competitors. Tom Coohill, a chef who owns two Atlanta restaurants, gives managers a food allowance to dine out and bring back ideas. Atlanta jeweler Frank Maier Jr., who often visits out-of-town rivals, spotted and copied a dramatic way of lighting displays.[11]

Companies normally budget marketing research at one to two percent of company sales. A large percentage is spent on the services of outside firms. Marketing research firms fall into three categories:

1. *Syndicated-service research firms:* These firms gather consumer and trade information, which they sell for a fee. Examples: Nielsen Media Research, SAMI/Burke.
2. *Custom marketing research firms:* These firms are hired to carry out specific projects. They design the study and report the findings.
3. *Specialty-line marketing research firms:* These firms provide specialized research services. The best example is the field-service firm, which sells field interviewing services to other firms.

the marketing research process

Effective marketing research involves the six steps shown in Figure 5.1. We will illustrate these steps with the following situation:

American Airlines (AA) is constantly looking for new ways to serve its passengers; it was one of the first companies to install phone handsets. Now it is reviewing many new ideas, especially to cater to its first-class passengers on

figure **5.1**

The Marketing Research Process

Marketing
MEMO

Secondary Sources of Data Online

The number of online government and business information sources is truly overwhelming. Here is a sample of several that should prove useful when conducting online market research, and many offer information free or for a reasonable fee. Note that because the Web is changing at such a rapid rate, the addresses may change.

Associations:

- American Marketing Association (*www.ama.org*).
- The American Society of Association Executives (*www.asaenet.org*).
- CommerceNet—industry association for Internet commerce (*www.commerce.net*).
- Gale's Encyclopedia of Associations (*www.gale.com*).

Business Information:

- A Business Researcher's Interests—provides links to business directories, media sites, marketing-related resources, and much more (*www.brint.com*).
- Bloomberg Personal—timely news and financial services (*www.bloomberg.com*).
- C/Net—journalistic coverage of high technology, computers, and the Internet (*www.cnet.com*).
- Company Link—free basic directory data, press releases, stock prices, and SEC data on 45,000 U.S. firms and more information available to subscribers (*www.companylink.com*).
- EDGAR—public company financial filings (*www.sec.gov/edgarhp.htm*).
- Hoover's—directory of company information (*www.hoovers.com*).
- National Trade Data Bank—free access to over 18,000 market research reports analyzing trends and competition in scores of industries and for hundreds of products (*www.stat-usa.gov*).

continued...

very long flights, many of whom are business people whose high-priced tickets pay most of the freight. Among these ideas are: (1) to supply a power plug in first class so that the business person could work on the computer longer than the two hours normally provided by a battery; (2) to supply an Internet connection with limited access to Web pages and e-mail messaging; (3) to offer 24 channels of satellite cable TV; and (4) to offer a 50-CD audio system that lets each passenger create a customized play list of music and movies to enjoy during the flight. The marketing research manager was assigned to investigate how first-class passengers would rate these services and how much extra they would be willing to pay if a charge was made. He was asked to focus specifically on the Internet connection. One estimate says that airlines might realize revenues of $70 billion over the next decade from in-flight Internet access, if enough first-class passengers would be willing to pay $25 for it. AA could thus recover its costs in a reasonable time. Making the connection available would cost the airline $90,000 per plane.[12]

STEP 1: DEFINE THE PROBLEM, THE DECISION ALTERNATIVES, AND THE RESEARCH OBJECTIVES   Marketing management must be careful not to define the problem too broadly or too narrowly for the marketing researcher. A marketing manager who instructs the marketing researcher to "Find out everything you can about first class air travelers' needs," will collect a lot of unnecessary information. Similarly, a marketing manager who says, "Find out if enough passengers aboard a B747 flying direct between Chicago and Tokyo would be willing to pay $25 for an Internet connection so that American Airlines would break even in one year on the cost of offering this service," is taking too narrow a view of the problem. The marketing researcher might even raise this question: "Why does the Internet connection have to be priced at $25 as opposed to $10, $50, or some other price? Why does American have to break even on the cost of the service, especially if it attracts new users to AA?"

In discussing the problem, American's managers discovered another issue. If the new service were successful, how fast could other airlines copy it? Airline marketing research is replete with examples of new services that have been so quickly copied by competitors that no airline has gained a sustainable competitive advantage. How important is it to be first and how long could the lead be sustained?

The marketing manager and marketing researcher agreed to define the problem as follows: "Will offering an in-flight Internet service create enough incremental preference and profit for American Airlines to justify its cost against other possible investments American might make?" To help think about designing the research, management should first spell out the decisions it might face and then work backward. Suppose management spells out the following decisions: (1) Should American offer an Internet connection? (2) If so, should the service be offered to first-class only, or include business class, and possibly economy class? (3) What price(s) should be charged? (4) On what types of planes and lengths of trips should it be offered?

Now management and marketing researchers are ready to set specific research objectives: (1) What types of first-class passengers would respond most to using an in-flight Internet service? (2) How many first-class passengers are likely to use the Internet service at different price levels? (3) How many extra first-class passengers might choose American because of this new service? (4) How much long-term goodwill will this service add to American Airlines' image? (5) How important is Internet service to first-class passengers relative to providing other services such as a power plug, or enhanced entertainment?

Not all research projects can be this specific. Some research is exploratory—its goal is to shed light on the real nature of the problem and to suggest possible solutions or new ideas. Some research is descriptive—it seeks to ascertain certain magnitudes, such as how many first-class passengers would purchase in-flight Internet service at $25. Some research is causal—its purpose is to test a cause-and-effect relationship.

STEP 2: DEVELOP THE RESEARCH PLAN   The second stage of marketing research calls for developing the most efficient plan for gathering the needed information. The marketing manager needs to know the cost of the research plan before approving it. Suppose the company made a prior estimate that launching the in-flight Internet service would yield a long-term profit of $50,000. The manager believes that doing the research would lead to an improved pricing and promotional plan and a long-term profit of $90,000. In this case, the manager should be willing to spend up to $40,000 on this research. If the research would cost more than $40,000, it is not worth doing.[13] Designing a research plan calls for decisions on the data sources, research approaches, research instruments, sampling plan, and contact methods.

Data Sources   The researcher can gather secondary data, primary data, or both. Secondary data are data that were collected for another purpose and already exist somewhere. Primary data are data freshly gathered for a specific purpose or for a specific research project.

Researchers usually start their investigation by examining secondary data to see whether the problem can be partly or wholly solved without collecting costly primary data. (Table 5.1 on page 128 shows the rich variety of secondary-data sources available in the United States.)[14] Secondary data provide a starting point for research and offer the advantages of low cost and ready availability. See "Marketing Memo: Secondary Sources of Data Online" for a mini-directory of sites where you can conduct free or at least inexpensive market research.

When the needed data do not exist or are dated, inaccurate, incomplete, or unreliable, the researcher will have to collect primary data. Most marketing research projects involve some primary-data collection. The normal procedure is to interview some people individually or in groups, to get a sense of how people feel about the topic in question, and then develop a formal research instrument, debug it, and carry it into the field.

Research Approaches   Primary data can be collected in five ways: through observation, focus groups, surveys, behavioral data, and experiments.

- *Observational research:* Fresh data can be gathered by observing the relevant actors and settings. The American Airlines researchers might meander around first-class lounges to hear how travelers talk about the different carriers and their features. The researchers can fly on competitors' planes to observe their in-flight service. This exploratory research might yield some useful hypotheses about how travelers feel about different air carriers and their services. (For another application of observational research, see "Marketing Insight: Using Observational Research to Study Shopping Behavior.")

- *Focus-group research:* A **focus group** is a gathering of six to ten people who are invited to spend a few hours with a skilled moderator to discuss a product, service, organization, or other marketing entity (see Figure 5.2). The moderator needs to be objective, knowledgeable on the issue, and skilled in group dynamics. Participants are normally paid a small sum for attending. The meeting is typically held in pleasant surroundings and refreshments are served.

  In the American Airlines research, the moderator might start with a broad question, such as "How do you feel about first-class air travel?" Questions then move to how people regard the different airlines, different existing services, different proposed services, and specifically, Internet service. The moderator encourages free and easy discussion, hoping that the group dynamics will reveal deep feelings and thoughts. At the same time, the moderator "focuses" the discussion. The discussion, recorded through note taking or on audiotape or videotape or behind a one-way mirror, is subsequently studied to understand consumer beliefs, attitudes, and behavior.

- Public Register's Annual Report Service—allows searches of 3,200 public companies by company name or industry and offers annual reports via e-mail (*www.prars.com/index.html*).
- Quote.Com—access to a wide range of business wires, companies' directories, and stock quotes (*www.quote.com*).

Government Information:
- Census Bureau (*www.census.gov*).
- FedWorld—a clearinghouse for over 100 federal government agencies (*www.fedworld.gov*).
- Thomas—indexes federal government sites (*thomas.loc.gov*).
- Trade/Exporting/business: Stat-USA (*www.stat-usa.gov*).
- US Business Advisor (*www.business.gov*).

International Information:
- CIA World Factbook—a comprehensive statistical and demographic directory covering 264 countries around the world (*www. odic.gov/cia/publications*).
- The Electronic Embassy (*www.embassy.org*).
- I-Trade—free and fee-based information services for firms wishing to do business internationally (*www.i-trade.com*).
- The United Nations (*www.un.org*).

Sources: Based on information from Robert I. Berkman, *Find It Fast: How to Uncover Expert Information on Any Subject in Print or Online* (New York: HarperCollins, 1997); Christine Galea, "Surf City: The Best Places for Business on the Web," *Sales & Marketing Management*, January 1997, pp. 69–73; David Curle, "Out-of-the-Way Sources of Market Research on the Web," *Online* (January–February 1998): 63–68. See also Jan Davis Tudor, "Brewing Up: A Web Approach to Industry Research," *Online* (July–August 1996): 12.

marketing **insight**

Using Observational Research to Study Shopping Behavior

Paco Underhill runs a firm called Environsell that has been snooping on shoppers for over 20 years. His clients include McDonald's, Starbucks, Estee Lauder, and Blockbuster. His researchers enter different retail settings and use unobtrusive methods to record the movements of shoppers. They use clipboards, track sheets, video equipment, and keen eyes to describe every nuance of shopping behavior, including how people circulate through the store and interact with store personnel. These "retail anthropologists" observe over 70,000 shoppers a year in their "natural habitat"; and they carry out post-shopping exit interviews to confirm their observations. Here are some findings in Underhill's book *Why We Buy: The Science of Shopping*:

- The faster people walk, the narrower their field of vision becomes.
- Shoppers slow down when they see reflective surfaces and speed up when they see blanks.

- Shoppers invariably walk to the right.
- Experiential in-store information has more weight than company advertising.
- Men who take jeans into fitting rooms are more likely to buy than females.
- Women are more likely to avoid narrow aisles than men.
- A Harley-Davidson showroom is filled with three types of shoppers: "well-off male menopause victims looking to recover their virility by buying bikes; blue-collar gear heads who are there for spare parts; and teenage dreamers interested in Harley-logo fashions."

Source: Paco Underhill, *Why We Buy: The Science of Shopping* (New York: Simon & Schuster, 1999).

Focus-group research is a useful exploratory step. Consumer-goods companies have been using focus groups for many years, and an increasing number of newspapers, law firms, hospitals, and public-service organizations are discovering their value. However, researchers must avoid generalizing the reported feelings of the focus-group participants to the whole market, because the sample size is too small and the sample is not drawn randomly.[15]

With the development of the Web, many companies are now conducting online focus groups.[16]

figure **5.2**

Focus–group Research

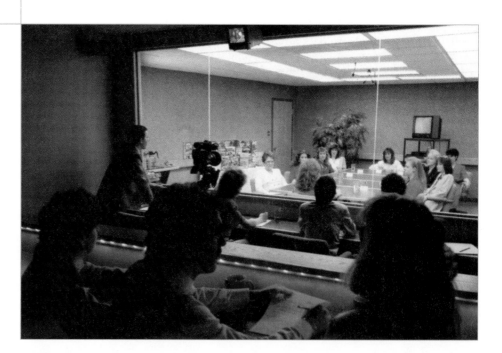

Cyber dialogue   Janice Gjersten of WPStudio, an online entertainment company, found that online focus-group respondents could be much more honest than those in her traditional, in-person focus groups. Gjersten contacted Cyber Dialogue, which provided focus-group respondents drawn from its 10,000-person database. The focus group was held in a chat room that Gjersten "looked in on" from her office computer. Gjersten could interrupt the moderator at any time with flash e-mails unseen by the respondents. Although the online focus group lacked voice and body cues, the cost was one-third that of a traditional focus group, and a full report came to her in one day, compared to four weeks.

- *Survey research:* Surveys are best suited for descriptive research. Companies undertake surveys to learn about people's knowledge, beliefs, preferences, and satisfaction, and to measure these magnitudes in the general population. A company such as American Airlines might prepare its own survey instrument to gather the information it needs, or it might add questions to an omnibus survey that carries the questions of several companies at a much lower cost. It can also put the questions to an ongoing consumer panel run by itself or another company or it may do a mall intercept study by approaching people in a shopping mall who might volunteer to answer questions.

- *Behavioral data:* Customers leave traces of their purchasing behavior in store scanning data, catalog purchases, and customer databases. Much can be learned by analyzing these data. Customers' actual purchases reflect preferences and often are more reliable than statements they offer to market researchers. People may report preferences for popular brands, and yet the data show them actually buying other brands. For example, grocery shopping data show that high-income people do not necessarily buy the more expensive brands, contrary to what they might state in interviews; and many low-income people buy some expensive brands. Clearly, American Airlines can learn many useful things about its passengers by analyzing ticket purchase records.

- *Experimental research:* The most scientifically valid research is experimental research. The purpose of experimental research is to capture cause-and-effect relationships by eliminating competing explanations of the observed findings. To the extent that the design and execution of the experiment eliminate alternative hypotheses that might explain the results, research and marketing managers can have confidence in the conclusions. It calls for selecting matched groups of subjects, subjecting them to different treatments, controlling extraneous variables, and checking whether observed response differences are statistically significant. To the extent that extraneous factors are eliminated or controlled, the observed effects can be related to the variations in the treatments.

American Airlines might introduce in-flight Internet service on one of its regular flights from Chicago to Tokyo. It might charge $25 one week and charge only $15 the next week. If the plane carried approximately the same number of first-class passengers each week and the particular weeks made no difference, any significant difference in the number of calls made could be related to the different prices charged. The experimental design could be elaborated by trying other prices and including other air routes.

Research Instruments   Marketing researchers have a choice of three main research instruments in collecting primary data: questionnaires, psychological tools, and mechanical devices.

1. *Questionnaires.* A questionnaire consists of a set of questions presented to respondents. Because of its flexibility, the questionnaire is by far the most common instrument used to collect primary data. Questionnaires need to be carefully developed, tested, and debugged before they are administered on a large scale.

   In preparing a questionnaire, the researcher carefully chooses the questions and their form, wording, and sequence. The form of the question asked can influence the response. Marketing researchers distinguish between closed-end and open-end questions. Closed-end questions specify all the possible answers and provide answers that are easier to interpret and tabulate.

Open-end questions allow respondents to answer in their own words and often reveal more about how people think. They are especially useful in exploratory research, where the researcher is looking for insight into how people think rather than measuring how many people think a certain way. Table 5.2 provides examples of both types of questions; and see "Marketing Memo: Questionnaire Dos and Don'ts."

2. *Psychological tools*. Marketing researchers can probe a buyer's deeper beliefs and feelings using psychological tools such as laddering techniques, depth interviews, and Rorshach tests. Laddering involves asking a male consumer, for example, "Why do you want to buy an SUV vehicle?" He may answer, "It is a good-looking car." He is asked a follow-up question: "Why do you want a good-looking car?" Upon receiving his answer, another question is put: "Why is this important to you?" This continues until the researcher arrives at a deeper reason, such as "People will be more impressed with me."

Depth interviewing involves going deeply into the thoughts that an individual may have about a product or service. The late Ernest Dichter was a master of depth interviewing and came out with many surprising findings: People do not like prunes because their wrinkled appearance makes them think of old age; and women do not respond to cake mixes that do not include adding an egg because they see baking as an act of giving birth. Whatever the validity, his findings gave his corporate clients many ideas. Dichter held that qualitative research ("head shrinking") gave far more insight than questionnaire-based, quantitative research ("nose counting").

Zaltman recently introduced a psychological instrument called the Zaltman Metaphoric Elicitation Technique (ZMET), which uses metaphors to access nonverbal images.[17] One study probed what women thought of panty hose. Twenty hose-wearing women were asked to collect pictures that captured their feelings about wearing panty hose. Some of the pictures showed fence posts encased in plastic wrap or steel bands strangling trees, suggesting that panty hose are tight and inconvenient. On the other hand, another picture showed tall flowers in a vase, suggesting that the product made a woman feel thin, tall, and sexy. This technique gets at associations that are less likely to emerge during normal interviewing.

3. *Mechanical devices*. Mechanical devices are occasionally used in marketing research. Galvanometers measure the interest or emotions aroused by exposure to a specific ad or picture. The tachistoscope flashes an ad to a subject with an exposure interval that may range from less than one hundredth of a second to several seconds. After each exposure, the respondent describes everything he or she recalls. Eye cameras study respondents' eye movements to see where their eyes land first, how long they linger on a given item, and so on. An audiometer is attached to television sets in participating homes to record when the set is on and to which channel it is tuned.[18]

4. *Qualitative measures*. Some marketers prefer more qualitative methods for gauging consumer opinion because consumer actions do not always match their answers to survey questions. New tools such as videos, pagers, and informal interviewing will help marketers overcome the limitations of traditional research methods. In 1999, the ad agency Ogilvy & Mather created the Discovery Group, a research unit that creates documentary-style videos by sending researchers with handheld videocameras into consumers' homes. Hours of footage are edited to a 30-minute "highlight reel" which the company uses to analyze consumer behavior for its clients. Other researchers equip consumers with pagers and instruct them to write down what they are doing whenever prompted, or hold more informal interview sessions at a café or bar.

In addition to new qualitative research tools, marketers have developed new methodologies to help them understand target consumers. Two of these are prototyping and articulative interviewing. Customer prototyping attempts to paint a realistic portrait of an individual by describing a specific customer type (e.g., "ideal customer" or "nonuser") in qualitative terms. To arrive at a prototype, marketers strive to answer questions such as "What is important to this person?" and "How does this person want others to view him or her?" The process is repeated until the prototypes begin to overlap. The areas of overlap describe the marketer's target customers. Articulative interviewing is designed to determine what social values interviewees hold dear by having them talk about broad topics such as their various roles in life and their daily activities. The broad format enables the marketer to draw out relevant information; the interviewee is also table **5.2**   Types of Questions

A. Closed-end Questions

Name	Description	Example
Dichotomous	A question with two possible answers.	In arranging this trip, did you personally phone American? Yes No
Multiple choice	A question with three or more answers.	With whom are you traveling on this flight? ☐ No one ☐ Children only ☐ Spouse ☐ Business associates/friends/relatives ☐ Spouse and children ☐ An organized tour group
Likert scale	A statement with which the respondent shows the amount of agreement/disagreement.	Small airlines generally give better service than large ones. Strongly disagree Disagree Neither agree nor disagree Agree Strongly agree 1___ 2___ 3___ 4___ 5___
Semantic differential	A scale connecting two bipolar words. The respondent selects the point that represents his or her opinion.	American Airlines Large - - - - - - - - - - - - - - - - - - - Small Experienced - - - - - - - - - - - - - - - - - Inexperienced Modern - - - - - - - - - - - - - - - - - - Old-fashioned
Importance scale	A scale that rates the importance of some attribute.	Airline food service to me is Extremely important Very important Somewhat important Not very important Not at all important 1___ 2___ 3___ 4___ 5___
Rating scale	A scale that rates some attribute from "poor" to "excellent."	American food service is Excellent Very Good Good Fair Poor 1___ 2___ 3___ 4___ 5___
Intention-to-buy scale	A scale that describes the respondent's intention to buy.	If an in-flight telephone were available on a long flight, I would Definitely buy Probably buy Not sure Probably not buy Definitely not buy 1___ 2___ 3___ 4___ 5___

B. Open-end Questions

Name	Description	Example
Completely unstructured	A question that respondents can answer in an almost unlimited number of ways.	What is your opinion of American Airlines?
Word association	Words are presented, one at a time, and respondents mention the first word that comes to mind.	What is the first word that comes to your mind when you hear the following? Airline _____ American _____ Travel _____
Sentence completion	An incomplete sentence is presented and respondents complete the sentence.	When I choose an airline, the most important consideration in my decision is _____.
Story completion	An incomplete story is presented, and respondents are asked to complete it.	"I flew American a few days ago. I noticed that the exterior and interior of the plane had very bright colors. This aroused in me the following thoughts and feelings. . . . " Now complete the story.
Picture	A picture of two characters is presented, with one making a statement. Respondents are asked to identify with the other and fill in the empty balloon.	
Thematic Apperception Test (TAT)	A picture is presented and respondents are asked to make up a story about what they think is happening or may happen in the picture.	

Marketing
MEMO

Questionnaire Dos and Don'ts

1. *Ensure that questions are without bias.* Do not lead the respondent into an answer.
2. *Make the questions as simple as possible.* Questions that include multiple ideas or two questions in one will confuse respondents.
3. *Make the questions specific.* Sometimes it is advisable to add memory cues. For example, it is good practice to be specific with time periods.
4. *Avoid jargon or shorthand.* Trade jargon, acronyms, and initials not in everyday use should be avoided.
5. *Steer clear of sophisticated or uncommon words.* Only use words in common speech.
6. *Avoid ambiguous words.* Words such as "usually" or "frequently" have no specific meaning.
7. *Avoid questions with a negative in them.* It is better to say "Do you ever . . . ?" than "Do you never . . . ?"
8. *Avoid hypothetical questions.* It is difficult to answer questions about imaginary situations. Answers cannot necessarily be trusted.
9. *Do not use words that could be misheard.* This is especially important when the interview is administered over the telephone. "What is your opinion of sects?" could yield interesting but not necessarily relevant answers.
10. *Desensitize questions by using response bands.* For questions that ask people their age or companies their turnover, it is best to offer a range of response bands.
11. *Ensure that fixed responses do not overlap.* Categories used in fixed response questions should be sequential and not overlap.
12. *Allow for "others" in fixed response questions.* Pre-coded answers should always allow for a response other than those listed.

Source: Adapted from Paul Hague and Peter Jackson, *Market Research: A Guide to Planning, Methodology, and Evaluation* (London: Kogan Page, 1999). See also Hans Baumgartner and Jan Benedict E. M. Steen Kamp, "Response Styles in Marketing Research: A Cross-National Investigation," May 2001, pp. 143–156.

likely to reveal valuable information regarding core beliefs and other social factors that may influence product decisions.[19]

Sampling Plan   After deciding on the research approach and instruments, the marketing researcher must design a sampling plan. This calls for three decisions:

1. *Sampling unit: Who is to be surveyed?* The marketing researcher must define the target population that will be sampled. In the American Airlines survey, should the sampling unit be only first-class business travelers, first-class vacation travelers, or both? Should travelers under age 18 be interviewed? Should both husbands and wives be interviewed? Once the sampling unit is determined, a sampling frame must be developed so that everyone in the target population has an equal or known chance of being sampled.

The Food & Brand Lab page of Brian Wansink's consumer psychology Web site.

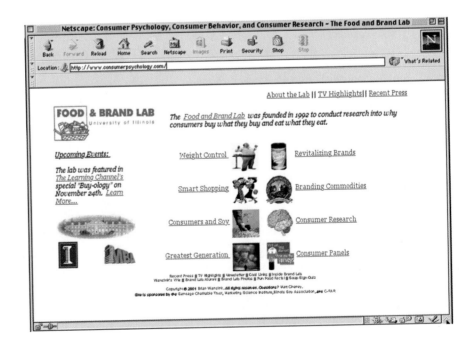

table **5.3**

Probability and
Nonprobability
Samples

A. Probability Sample

Simple random sample	Every member of the population has an equal chance of selection
Stratified random sample	The population is divided into mutually exclusive groups (such as age groups), and random samples are drawn from each group
Cluster (area) sample	The population is divided into mutually exclusive groups (such as city blocks), and the researcher draws a sample of the groups to interview

B. Nonprobability Sample

Convenience sample	The researcher selects the most accessible population members
Judgment sample	The researcher selects population members who are good prospects for accurate information
Quota sample	The researcher finds and interviews a prescribed number of people in each of several categories

2. *Sample size: How many people should be surveyed?* Large samples give more reliable results than small samples. However, it is not necessary to sample the entire target population or even a substantial portion to achieve reliable results. Samples of less than 1 percent of a population can often provide good reliability, with a credible sampling procedure.

3. *Sampling procedure: How should the respondents be chosen?* To obtain a representative sample, a probability sample of the population should be drawn. Probability sampling allows the calculation of confidence limits for sampling error. Thus, one could conclude after the sample is taken that "the interval 5 to 7 trips per year has 95 chances in 100 of containing the true number of trips taken annually by first-class passengers flying between Chicago and Tokyo." Three types of probability sampling are described in Table 5.3 part A. When the cost or time involved in probability sampling is too high, marketing researchers will take nonprobability samples. Table 5.3, part B describes three types. Some marketing researchers feel that nonprobability samples are very useful in many circumstances, even though they do not allow sampling error to be measured.

Contact Methods   Once the sampling plan has been determined, the marketing researcher must decide how the subject should be contacted: mail, telephone, personal, or online interview.

The *mail questionnaire* is the best way to reach people who would not give personal interviews or whose responses might be biased or distorted by the interviewers. Mail questionnaires require simple and clearly worded questions. Unfortunately, the response rate is usually low or slow. Telephone interviewing is the best method for gathering information quickly; the interviewer is also able to clarify questions if respondents do not understand them. The response rate is typically higher than in the case of mailed questionnaires. The main drawback is that the interviews have to be short and not too personal. Telephone interviewing is getting more difficult because of answering machines and people becoming suspicious of telemarketing.

Personal interviewing is the most versatile method. The interviewer can ask more questions and record additional observations about the respondent, such as dress and body language. Brian Wansink has developed a customer profiling technique based on personal interviews that generates interesting hypotheses which can be further tested or used in communication strategy.[20] At the same time, personal interviewing is the most expensive method and requires more administrative planning and supervision than the other three. It is also subject to interviewer bias or distortion. Personal interviewing takes two forms. In *arranged interviews,* respondents are contacted for an appointment, and often a small payment or incentive is offered. *Intercept interviews* involve stopping people at a shopping mall or busy street corner and requesting an interview. Intercept interviews have the drawback of being nonprobability samples, and the interviews must not require too much time.

There is increased use of *online methods.* Online product testing is expected to grow and provide information faster than traditional marketing research techniques. A company can include a questionnaire on its Web site and offer an incentive to answer the questionnaire; or it can place a banner on some frequently visited site such as Yahoo!, inviting people to answer some questions and possibly win a prize. The company can enter a target chat room and seek volunteers for a survey, or sponsor a chat room and introduce questions from time to time. A company can learn about individuals who visit its site by following how they *clickstream* through the Web site and move to other sites. Computers contain *cookies* that capture this data. By analyzing the clickstreams of different visitors, the company can make inferences about consumer behavior. A company can post different prices, use different headlines, offer different product features on different Web sites or at different times to learn the relative effectiveness of its offerings.

Not everyone is on the Web, however, and online market researchers must find creative ways to reach certain population segments, such as older Americans, the disabled, and Hispanics. One option is to combine off-line sources with the online findings. Providing temporary Internet access at locations such as malls and recreation centers is another strategy. Some research firms use statistical models to fill in the gaps in market research left by off-line consumer segments. Knowledge Networks is an example.

Knowledge Networks   Menlo Park–based Knowledge Networks was founded by two Stanford University professors in 1998. To ensure consistent results, the company distributes WebTV interactive television boxes complete with Internet connections to all respondents. The interactive televisions operate with remote controls in exactly the same fashion as normal TVs, so Internet literacy is not required for participation. It has a network of more than 100,000 Web-ready panelists. Knowledge Networks seeks to become a one-stop marketing research company, performing television- and Internet-usage tracking studies, brand management diagnostics and tracking, product and advertising evaluations, and traditional survey applications. Knowledge Networks calls this a "360-degree view of the consumer."[21]

Many companies are now using *automated telephone surveys* to solicit market research information. One popular approach is to distribute prepaid phone cards as an incentive. A survey is programmed into an interactive call system that not only administers the survey, but also sorts the results virtually any way the client wants them. When the call users place their free calls, a voice prompt asks them if they would like to gain additional minutes by taking a short survey. NBC, Coca-Cola, and Amoco are some of the companies that have used prepaid phone cards to survey their customers.[22]

STEP 3: COLLECT THE INFORMATION   The data collection phase of marketing research is generally the most expensive and the most prone to error. In the case of surveys, four major problems arise. Some respondents will not be at home and must be recontacted or replaced. Other respondents will refuse to cooperate. Still others will give biased or dishonest answers. Finally, some interviewers will be biased or dishonest.

Yet data collection methods are rapidly improving, thanks to computers and telecommunications. Some research firms interview from a centralized location.

Professional interviewers sit in booths and draw telephone numbers at random. When the phone is answered, the interviewer reads a set of questions from a monitor and types the respondents' answers into a computer. This procedure eliminates editing and coding, reduces errors, saves time, and produces all the required statistics. Other research firms have set up interactive terminals in shopping centers. Persons willing to be interviewed sit at a terminal, read the questions from the monitor, and type in their answers. Most respondents enjoy this form of "robot" interviewing.

Several recent technical advances have permitted marketers to research the sales impact of ads and sales promotion. Information Resources, Inc., recruits a panel of supermarkets equipped with scanners and electronic cash registers. Scanners read the universal product code on each product purchased, recording the brand, size, and price for inventory and ordering purposes. Meanwhile, the firm has recruited a panel of store customers who have agreed to charge their purchases with a special Shopper's Hotline ID card, which holds information about household characteristics, lifestyle, and income. These same customers have also agreed to let their television-viewing habits be monitored by a black box. All consumer panelists receive their programs through cable television, and Information Resources controls the advertising messages being sent to their homes. The firm can then capture through store purchases which ads led to more purchasing and by which customers.[23]

STEP 4: ANALYZE THE INFORMATION The next-to-last step in the marketing research process is to extract findings from the collected data. The researcher tabulates the data and develops frequency distributions. Averages and measures of dispersion are computed for the major variables. The researcher will also apply some advanced statistical techniques and decision models in the hope of discovering additional findings. (Techniques and models are described later in this chapter.)

STEP 5: PRESENT THE FINDINGS As the last step, the researcher presents the findings. The researcher should present findings that are relevant to the major marketing decisions facing management. The main survey findings for the American Airlines case show that:

1. The chief reasons for using in-flight Internet service are to pass the time surfing, and to send and receive messages from colleagues and family. The charge would be put on passengers' charge accounts and paid by their company.
2. About 5 first-class passengers out of every 10 during a flight would use the Internet service at $25; about 6 would use it at $15. Thus, a charge of $15 would produce less revenue ($90 = 6 × $15) than $25 ($125 = 5 × $25). By charging $25, AA would collect $125 per flight. Assuming that the same flight takes place 365 days a year, AA would annually collect $45,625 (= $125 × 365). Since the investment is $90,000, it will take approximately two years before American Airlines breaks even.
3. Offering in-flight service would strengthen the public's image of American Airlines as an innovative and progressive airline. American would gain some new passengers and customer goodwill.

STEP 6: MAKE THE DECISION The managers who commissioned the research need to weigh the evidence. They know that the findings could suffer from a variety of errors. If their confidence in the findings is low, they may decide against introducing the in-flight Internet service. If they are predisposed to launching the service, the findings support their inclination. They may even decide to study the issues further and do more research. The decision is theirs, but hopefully the research provided them with insight into the problem. (See Table 5.4)[24]

overcoming barriers to the use of marketing research

In spite of the rapid growth of marketing research, many companies still fail to use it sufficiently or correctly, for several reasons:

table **5.4**		
The Seven Characteristics of Good Marketing Research	1. Scientific method.	Effective marketing research uses the principles of the scientific method: careful observation, formulation of hypotheses, prediction, and testing.
	2. Research creativity.	At its best, marketing research develops innovative ways to solve a problem: a clothing company catering to teenagers gave several young men video cameras, then used the videos for focus groups held in restaurants and other places teens frequent.
	3. Multiple methods.	Marketing researchers shy away from overreliance on any one method. They also recognize the value of using two or three methods to increase confidence in the results.
	4. Interdependence of models and data.	Marketing researchers recognize that data are interpreted from underlying models that guide the type of information sought.
	5. Value and cost of information.	Marketing researchers show concern for estimating the value of information against its cost. Costs are typically easy to determine, but the value of research is harder to quantify. It depends on the reliability and validity of the findings and management's willingness to accept and act on those findings.
	6. Healthy skepticism.	Marketing researchers show a healthy skepticism toward glib assumptions made by managers about how a market works. They are alert to the problems caused by "marketing myths."
	7. Ethical marketing.	Marketing research benefits both the sponsoring company and its customers. The misuse of marketing research can harm or annoy consumers, increasing resentment at what consumers regard as an invasion of their privacy or a disguised sales pitch.

- *A narrow conception of the research:* Many managers see marketing research as a fact-finding operation. They expect the researcher to design a questionnaire, choose a sample, conduct interviews, and report results, often without a careful definition of the problem or of the decisions facing management. When fact-finding fails to be useful, management's idea of the limited usefulness of marketing research is reinforced.

- *Uneven caliber of researchers:* Some managers view marketing research as little more than a clerical activity and treat it as such. Less competent marketing researchers are hired, and their weak training and deficient creativity lead to unimpressive results. The disappointing results reinforce management's prejudice against marketing research. Management continues to pay low salaries to its market researchers, thus perpetuating the basic problem.

- *Poor framing of the problem:* In the famous case where Coca-Cola introduced the New Coke after much research, the failure of the New Coke was largely due to not setting up the research problem correctly from a marketing perspective. The issue is how consumers felt about Coca-Cola as a brand and not necessarily the taste in isolation.

- *Late and occasionally erroneous findings:* Managers want results that are accurate and conclusive. They may want the results tomorrow. Yet good marketing research takes time and money. Managers are disappointed when marketing research costs too much or takes too much time.

■ *Personality and presentational differences:* Differences between the styles of line managers and marketing researchers often get in the way of productive relationships. To a manager who wants concreteness, simplicity, and certainty, a marketing researcher's report may seem abstract, complicated, and tentative. Yet in the more progressive companies, marketing researchers are more often being included as members of the product management team, and their influence on marketing strategy is growing.

marketing decision support system

A growing number of organizations are using a marketing decision support system to help their marketing managers make better decisions. John Little defines a **marketing decision support system (MDSS)** as a coordinated collection of data, systems, tools, and techniques with supporting software and hardware by which an organization gathers and interprets relevant information from business and environment and turns it into a basis for marketing action.[25] Table 5.5 describes the major statistical tools, models, and optimization routines that comprise a modern MDSS. Lilien and Rangaswamy recently published *Marketing Engineering: Computer-Assisted Marketing Analysis and Planning*, which includes a disk with widely used modeling software tools.[26]

Once a year, *Marketing News* lists hundreds of current marketing and sales software programs that assist in designing marketing research studies, segmenting markets, setting prices and advertising budgets, analyzing media, and planning sales force activity. Here are examples of decision models that have been used by marketing managers:

BRANDAID: A flexible marketing-mix model focused on consumer packaged goods whose elements are a manufacturer, competitors, retailers, consumers, and the general environment. The model contains submodels for advertising, pricing, and competition. The model is calibrated with a creative blending of judgment, historical analysis, tracking, field experimentation, and adaptive control.[27]

CALLPLAN: A model to help salespeople determine the number of calls to make per period to each prospect and current client. The model takes into account travel time as well as selling time. The model was tested at United Airlines with an experimental group that managed to increase its sales over a matched control group by 8 percentage points.[28]

DETAILER: A model to help salespeople determine which customers to call on and which products to represent on each call. This model was largely developed for pharmaceutical detail people calling on physicians, where they could represent no more than three products on a call. In two applications, the model yielded strong profit improvements.[29]

GEOLINE: A model for designing sales and service territories that satisfies three principles: The territories equalize sales workloads; each territory consists of adjacent areas; and the territories are compact. Several successful applications were reported.[30]

MEDIAC: A model to help an advertiser buy media for a year. The media planning model includes market-segment delineation, sales potential estimation, diminishing marginal returns, forgetting, timing issues, and competitor media schedules.[31]

Some models now claim to duplicate the way expert marketers normally make their decisions. Some recent expert system models include:

PROMOTER evaluates sales promotions by determining baseline sales (what sales would have been without promotion) and measuring the increase over baseline associated with the promotion.[32]

ADCAD recommends the type of ad (humorous, slice of life, and so on) to use given the marketing goals, product characteristics, target market, and competitive situation.[33]

COVERSTORY examines a mass of syndicated sales data and writes an English-language memo reporting the highlights.[34]

table **5.5**		
Quantitative Tools Used in Marketing Decision Support Systems	**Statistical Tools**	
	1. Multiple regression:	A statistical technique for estimating a "best fitting" equation showing how the value of a dependent variable varies with changing values in a number of independent variables. *Example:* A company can estimate how unit sales are influenced by changes in the level of company advertising expenditures, sales force size, and price.
	2. Discriminant analysis:	A statistical technique for classifying an object or persons into two or more categories. *Example:* A large retail chain store can determine the variables that discriminate between successful and unsuccessful store locations.[a]
	3. Factor analysis:	A statistical technique used to determine the few underlying dimensions of a larger set of intercorrelated variables. *Example:* A broadcast network can reduce a large set of TV programs down to a small set of basic program types.[b]
	4. Cluster analysis:	A statistical technique for separating objects into a specified number of mutually exclusive groups such that the groups are relatively homogeneous. *Example:* A marketing researcher might want to classify a set of cities into four distinct groups.
	5. Conjoint analysis:	A statistical technique whereby respondents' ranked preferences for different offers are decomposed to determine the person's inferred utility function for each attribute and the relative importance of each attribute. *Example:* An airline can determine the total utility delivered by different combinations of passenger services.
	6. Multidimensional scaling:	A variety of techniques for producing perceptual maps of competitive products or brands. Objects are represented as points in a multidimensional space of attributes where their distance from one another is a measure of dissimilarity. *Example:* A computer manufacturer wants to see where his brand is positioned in relation to competitive brands.
	Models	
	1. Markov-process model:	This model shows the probability of moving from a current state to any future state. *Example:* A branded packaged-goods manufacturer can determine the period-to-period switching and staying rates for her brand and, if the probabilities are stable, the brand's ultimate brand share.
	2. Queuing model:	This model shows the waiting times and queue lengths that can be expected in any system, given the arrival and service times and the number of service channels. *Example:* A supermarket can use the model to predict queue lengths at different times of the day given the number of service channels and service speed.
	3. New-product pretest models:	This model involves estimating functional relations between buyer states of awareness, trial, and repurchase based on consumer preferences and actions in a pretest situation of the marketing offer and campaign. Among the well-known models are ASSESSOR, COMP, DEMON, NEWS, and SPRINTER.[c]

4. Sales-response models:	This is a set of models that estimate functional relations between one or more marketing variables—such as sales force size, advertising expenditure, sales-promotion expenditure, and so forth—and the resulting demand level.

Optimization Routines

1. Differential calculus:	This technique allows finding the maximum or minimum value along a well-behaved function.
2. Mathematical programming:	This technique allows finding the values that would optimize some objective function that is subject to a set of constraints.
3. Statistical decision theory:	This technique allows determining the course of action that produces the maximum expected value.
4. Game theory:	This technique allows determining the course of action that will minimize the decision maker's maximum loss in the face of the uncertain behavior of one or more competitors.
5. Heuristics:	This involves using a set of rules of thumb that shorten the time or work required to find a reasonably good solution in a complex system.

[a] S. Sands, "Store Site Selection by Discriminant Analysis," *Journal of the Market Research Society* (1981): 40–51.
[b] V. R. Rao, "Taxonomy of Television Programs Based on Viewing Behavior," *Journal of Marketing Research* (August 1975): 355–58.
[c] See Kevin J. Clancy, Robert Shulman, and Marianne Wolf, *Simulated Test Marketing* (New York: Lexington Books, 1994).

forecasting and demand measurement

One major reason for undertaking marketing research is to identify market opportunities. Once the research is complete, the company must measure and forecast the size, growth, and profit potential of each market opportunity. Sales forecasts are used by finance to raise the needed cash for investment and operations; by the manufacturing department to establish capacity and output levels; by purchasing to acquire the right amount of supplies; and by human resources to hire the needed number of workers. Marketing is responsible for preparing the sales forecasts. If its forecast is far off the mark, the company will be saddled with excess inventory or have inadequate inventory. Sales forecasts are based on estimates of demand. Managers need to define what they mean by market demand. Here is a good example of the importance of defining the market correctly:

Coca-Cola   When Roberto Goizueta became CEO of Coca-Cola, many people thought that Coke's sales were maxed out. Goizueta, however, reframed the view of Coke's market share. He said Coca-Cola accounted for less than 2 ounces of the 64 ounces of fluid that each of the world's 4.4 billion people drank on average every day. "The enemy is coffee, milk, tea, water," he told his people at Coke, and he ushered in a huge period of growth.

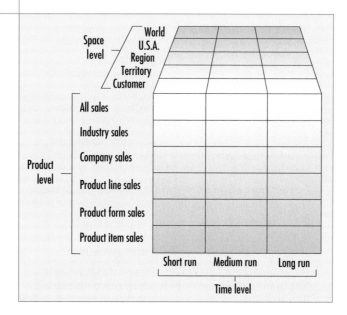

the measures of market demand

Companies can prepare as many as 90 different types of demand estimates (see Figure 5.3). Demand can be measured for six different product levels, five different space levels, and three different time levels.

Each demand measure serves a specific purpose. A company might forecast short-run demand for a particular product for the purpose of ordering raw materials, planning production, and borrowing cash. It might forecast regional demand for its major product line to decide whether to set up regional distribution.

which market to measure?

Marketers talk about potential markets, available markets, served markets, and penetrated markets. Let us start with the definition of market: A **market** is the set of all actual and potential buyers of a market offer. The size of a market hinges on the number of buyers who might exist for a particular market offer. The **potential market** is the set of consumers who profess a sufficient level of interest in a market offer.

However, consumer interest is not enough to define a market. Potential consumers must have enough income and must have access to the product offer. The **available market** is the set of consumers who have interest, income, and access to a particular offer. For some market offers, the company or government may restrict sales to certain groups. For example, a particular state might ban motorcycle sales to anyone under 21 years of age. The eligible adults constitute the *qualified available market*—the set of consumers who have interest, income, access, and qualifications for the particular market offer.

A company can go after the whole available market or concentrate on certain segments. The **target market** (also called the **served market**) is the part of the qualified available market the company decides to pursue. The company, for example, might decide to concentrate its marketing and distribution effort on the East Coast. The company will end up selling to a certain number of buyers in its target market. The **penetrated market** is the set of consumers who are buying the company's product.

These market definitions are a useful tool for market planning. If the company is not satisfied with its current sales, it can take a number of actions. It can try to attract a larger percentage of buyers from its target market. It can lower the qualifications of potential buyers. It can expand its available market by opening distribution elsewhere or lowering its price; or it can reposition itself in the minds of its customers. Consider the case of Target Stores.

Target Facing stiff competition from top retailers Wal-Mart and Kmart, Target Stores decided to reach more affluent shoppers and woo them away from department stores. The Midwestern discount retailer ran an unusual advertising campaign in some unusual spots: the Sunday magazines of the *New York Times*, the *Los Angeles Times*, and the *San Francisco Examiner*. One ad showed a woman riding a vacuum cleaner through the night sky. The ad simply said "Fashion and Housewares," with the Target logo in the lower right-hand corner. These hip spots gained Target Stores a reputation as the "upstairs" mass retailer, or "Kmart for Yuppies," as one shopper put it. In 2001, Target brought "fashion to food" by adding grocery sections to its retail concept and creating 175,000-square-foot SuperTargets.[35] The company added 14 SuperTarget supercenters in 2000, while revenues for that year rose 12.3 percent to $29.3 billion. Target's success prompted parent company Dayton-Hudson Corporation to change its name to Target Corporation in 2000.

a vocabulary for demand measurement

The major concepts in demand measurement are market demand and company demand. Within each, we distinguish among a demand function, a sales forecast, and a potential.

MARKET DEMAND As we have seen, the marketer's first step in evaluating marketing opportunities is to estimate total market demand. **Market demand** for a product is the total volume that would be bought by a defined customer group in a defined geographical area in a defined time period in a defined marketing environment under a defined marketing program.

Market demand is not a fixed number, but rather a function of the stated conditions. For this reason, it can be called the *market demand function*. The dependence of total market demand on underlying conditions is illustrated in Figure 5.4(a). The horizontal axis shows different possible levels of industry marketing expenditure in a given time period. The vertical axis shows the resulting demand level. The curve represents the estimated market demand associated with varying levels of industry marketing expenditure.

Some base sales (called the *market minimum*, labeled $Q1$ in the figure) would take place without any demand-stimulating expenditures. Higher levels of industry marketing expenditures would yield higher levels of demand, first at an increasing rate, then at a decreasing rate. Marketing expenditures beyond a certain level would not stimulate much further demand, thus suggesting an upper limit to market demand called the *market potential* (labeled $Q2$ in the figure).

The distance between the market minimum and the market potential shows the overall *marketing sensitivity of demand*. We can think of two extreme types of markets, the expansible and the nonexpansible. An *expansible market*, such as the market for racquetball playing, is very much affected in its total size by the level of industry marketing expenditures. In terms of Figure 5.4(a), the distance between $Q1$ and $Q2$ is relatively large. A *nonexpansible market*—for example, the market for opera—is not much affected by the level of marketing expenditures; the distance between $Q1$ and $Q2$ is relatively small. Organizations selling in a nonexpansible market must accept the market's size (the level of *primary demand* for the product class) and direct their efforts to winning a larger **market share** for their product (the level of selective demand for the company's product).

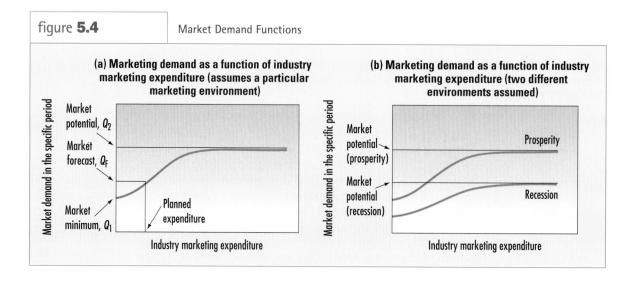

figure **5.4**   Market Demand Functions

(a) Marketing demand as a function of industry marketing expenditure (assumes a particular marketing environment)

Market demand in the specific period

Market potential, Q_2
Market forecast, Q_F
Market minimum, Q_1
Planned expenditure

Industry marketing expenditure

(b) Marketing demand as a function of industry marketing expenditure (two different environments assumed)

Market demand in the specific period

Market potential (prosperity)
Market potential (recession)
Prosperity
Recession

Industry marketing expenditure

It pays to compare the current level of market demand to the potential demand level. The result is called the **market penetration index**. A low market penetration index indicates substantial growth potential for all the firms. A high market penetration index suggests that there will be increased costs in attracting the few remaining prospects. Generally, price competition increases and margins fall when the market penetration index is already high.

A company should also compare its current market share to its potential market share. The result is called the company's **share penetration index**. A low share penetration index indicates that the company can greatly expand its share. The underlying factors holding it back could be many: low brand awareness, low brand availability, benefit deficiencies, too high a price. A firm should calculate the share penetration increases that would occur with investments to remove each deficiency, to see which investments would produce the greatest improvement in share penetration.[36]

It is important to remember that the market demand function is not a picture of market demand over time. Rather, the curve shows alternative current forecasts of market demand associated with alternative possible levels of industry marketing effort in the current period.

MARKET FORECAST   Only one level of industry marketing expenditure will actually occur. The market demand corresponding to this level is called the **market forecast**.

MARKET POTENTIAL   The market forecast shows expected market demand, not maximum market demand. For the latter, we have to visualize the level of market demand resulting from a "very high" level of industry marketing expenditure, where further increases in marketing effort would have little effect in stimulating further demand. **Market potential** is the limit approached by market demand as industry marketing expenditures approach infinity for a given marketing environment.

The phrase "for a given market environment" is crucial. Consider the market potential for automobiles in a period of recession versus a period of prosperity. The market potential is higher during prosperity. The dependence of market potential on the environment is illustrated in Figure 5.4(b). Market analysts distinguish between the position of the market demand function and movement along it. Companies cannot do anything about the position of the market demand function, which is determined by the marketing environment. However, companies influence their particular location on the function when they decide how much to spend on marketing.

Companies interested in market potential have a special interest in the **product penetration percentage**, which is the percentage of ownership or use of a product or service in a population. Here are some U.S. percentages: television (98%), health insurance (84%), car (81%), home ownership (67%), PC (54%), stock ownership (48%), gun ownership (41%), and fax (12%).[37] Companies assume that the lower the product penetration percentage, the higher the market potential, although this assumes that everyone will eventually be in the market for every product.

COMPANY DEMAND   We are now ready to define company demand: **Company demand** is the company's estimated share of market demand at alternative levels of company marketing effort in a given time period. The company's share of market demand depends on how its products, services, prices, communications, and so on are perceived relative to the competitors'. If other things are equal, the company's market share would depend on the size and effectiveness of its market expenditures relative to competitors. Marketing model builders have developed sales-response functions to measure how a company's sales are affected by its marketing expenditure level, marketing mix, and marketing effectiveness.[38]

COMPANY SALES FORECAST   Once marketers have estimated company demand, their next task is to choose a level of marketing effort. The chosen level will produce an expected level of sales. The **company sales forecast** is the expected level of company sales based on a chosen marketing plan and an assumed marketing environment.

The company sales forecast is represented graphically with company sales on the vertical axis and company marketing effort on the horizontal axis, as in Figure 5.4. Too often the sequential relationship between the company forecast and the company marketing plan is confused. One frequently hears that the company should develop its marketing plan on the basis of its sales forecast. This forecast-to-plan sequence is valid if "forecast" means an estimate of national economic activity or if company demand is nonexpansible. The sequence is not valid, however, where market demand is expansible or where "forecast" means an estimate of company sales. The company sales forecast does not establish a basis for deciding what to spend on marketing. On the contrary, the sales forecast is the result of an assumed marketing expenditure plan.

Two other concepts are worth mentioning in relation to the company sales forecast. A **sales quota** is the sales goal set for a product line, company division, or sales representative. It is primarily a managerial device for defining and stimulating sales effort. Management sets sales quotas on the basis of the company sales forecast and the psychology of stimulating its achievement. Generally, sales quotas are set slightly higher than estimated sales to stretch the sales force's effort.

A **sales budget** is a conservative estimate of the expected volume of sales and is used primarily for making current purchasing, production, and cashflow decisions. The sales budget is based on the sales forecast and the need to avoid excessive risk. Sales budgets are generally set slightly lower than the sales forecast.

COMPANY SALES POTENTIAL   **Company sales potential** is the sales limit approached by company demand as company marketing effort increases relative to that of competitors. The absolute limit of company demand is, of course, the market potential. The two would be equal if the company got 100 percent of the market. In most cases, company sales potential is less than the market potential, even when company marketing expenditures increase considerably, relative to competitors'. The reason is that each competitor has a hard core of loyal buyers who are not very responsive to other companies' efforts to woo them.

estimating current demand

We are now ready to examine practical methods for estimating current market demand. Marketing executives want to estimate total market potential, area market potential, and total industry sales and market shares.

TOTAL MARKET POTENTIAL   **Total market potential** is the maximum amount of sales that might be available to all the firms in an industry during a given period, under a given level of industry marketing effort and environmental conditions. A common way to estimate total market potential is as follows: Estimate the potential number of buyers times the average quantity purchased by a buyer times the price.

If 100 million people buy books each year, and the average book buyer buys three books a year, and the average price of a book is $20, then the total market potential for books is $6 billion (100 million $\times 6 \times$ $10). The most difficult component to estimate is the number of buyers for the specific product or market. One can always start with the total population in the nation, say 261 million people. The next step is to eliminate groups that obviously would not buy the product. Let us assume that illiterate people and children under 12 do not buy books, and they constitute 20 percent of the population.

This means that only 80 percent of the population, or approximately 209 million people, would be in the suspect pool. We might do further research and find that people of low income and low education do not read books, and they constitute over 30 percent of the suspect pool. Eliminating them, we arrive at a prospect pool of approximately 146.3 million book buyers. We would use this number of potential buyers to calculate total market potential.

A variation on this method is the *chain-ratio method*. It involves multiplying a base number by several adjusting percentages. Suppose a brewery is interested in estimating the market potential for a new light beer. An estimate can be made by the following calculation:

Demand for the new light beer = Population X personal discretionary income per capita X average percentage of discretionary income spent on food X average percentage of amount spent on food that is spent on beverages X average percentage of amount spent on beverages that is spent on alcoholic beverages X average percentage of amount spent on alcoholic beverages that is spent on beer X expected percentage of amount spent on beer that will be spent on light beer.

AREA MARKET POTENTIAL   Companies face the problem of selecting the best territories and allocating their marketing budget optimally among these territories. Therefore, they need to estimate the market potential of different cities, states, and nations. Two major methods of assessing area market potential are available: the market-buildup method, which is used primarily by business marketers, and the multiple-factor index method, which is used primarily by consumer marketers.

Market-Buildup Method   The **market-buildup method** calls for identifying all the potential buyers in each market and estimating their potential purchases. This method produces accurate results if we have a list of all potential buyers and a good estimate of what each will buy. Unfortunately, this information is not always easy to gather.

Consider a machine-tool company that wants to estimate the area market potential for its wood lathe in the Boston area. Its first step is to identify all potential buyers of wood lathes in the area. The buyers consist primarily of manufacturing establishments that have to shape or ream wood as part of their operation, so the company could compile a list from a directory of all manufacturing establishments in the Boston area. Then it could estimate the number of lathes each industry might purchase based on the number of lathes per thousand employees or per $1 million of sales in that industry.

An efficient method of estimating area market potentials makes use of the *Standard Industrial Classification (SIC) System* developed by the U.S. Bureau of the Census. The SIC classifies all manufacturing into 20 major industry groups, each with a two-digit code. Thus number 25 is furniture and fixtures. Each major industry group is further subdivided into about 150 groups designated by a three-digit code (number 251 is household furniture, and number 252 is office furniture). Each industry is further subdivided into approximately 450 product categories designated by a four-digit code (number 2521 is wood office furniture, and number 2522 is metal office furniture). For each four-digit SIC number, the Census of Manufacturers provides the number of establishments, subclassified by location, number of employees, annual sales, and net worth.

The SIC System is being changed to the new North American Industry Classification System (NAICS), which was developed by the United States, Canada, and Mexico to provide statistics that are comparable across the three countries. It includes 350 new industries, such as casino hotels, diet and weight reducing centers, HMO medical centers, and software publishers. It uses 20 instead of the SIC's 10 broad sectors of the economy, changes reflecting how the economy has changed. Industries are identified by a six-digit rather than a four-digit code, with the last digit changing depending on the country.

To use the SIC, the lathe manufacturer must first determine the four-digit SIC codes that represent products whose manufacturers are likely to require lathe machines. To get a full picture of all four-digit SIC industries that might use lathes, the company can (1) determine past customers' SIC codes; (2) go through the SIC manual and check off all the four-digit industries that might have an interest in lathes; (3) mail questionnaires to a wide range of companies inquiring about their interest in wood lathes.

The company's next task is to determine an appropriate base for estimating the number of lathes that will be used in each industry. Suppose customer industry sales are the most appropriate base. For example, in SIC number 2511, 10 lathes may be used for every $1 million worth of sales. Once the company estimates the rate of lathe ownership relative to the customer industry's sales, it can compute the market potential.

Table 5.6 shows a hypothetical computation for the Boston area involving two SIC codes. In number 2511 (wood household furniture), there are six establishments with annual sales of $1 million and two establishments with annual sales of $5 million. It is estimated that 10 lathes can be sold in this SIC code for every $1 million in customer sales. The six establishments with annual sales of $1 million account for $6 million in sales, which is a potential of 60 lathes (6310). Altogether, it appears that the Boston area has a market potential for 200 lathes.

The company can use the same method to estimate the market potential for other areas in the country. Suppose the market potentials for all the markets add up to 2,000 lathes. This means that the Boston market contains 10 percent of the total market potential, which might warrant the company's allocating 10 percent of its marketing expenditures to the Boston market. In practice, SIC information is not enough. The lathe manufacturer also needs additional information about each market, such as the extent of market saturation, the number of competitors, the market growth rate, and the average age of existing equipment.

table **5.6**

Market–Buildup Method Using SIC Codes

SIC	(a) Annual Sales in Millions of $	(b) Number of Establishments	(c) Potential Number of Lathe Sales per $1 Million Customer Sales	Market Potential (a × b × c)
2511	1	6	10	60
	5	2	10	100
2521	1	3	5	15
	5	1	5	25
			30	200

If the company decides to sell lathes in Boston, it must know how to identify the best-prospect companies. In the old days, sales reps called on companies door to door; this was called *bird-dogging* or *smokestacking*. Cold calls are far too costly today. The company should get a list of Boston companies and qualify them by direct mail or telemarketing to identify the best prospects. The lathe manufacturer can access Dun's Market Identifiers, which lists 27 key facts for over 9.3 million business locations in the United States and Canada.

Multiple-Factor Index Method   Like business marketers, consumer companies also have to estimate area market potentials, but the customers of consumer companies are too numerous to be listed. Thus the method most commonly used in consumer markets is a straightforward index method. A drug manufacturer, for example, might assume that the market potential for drugs is directly related to population size. If the state of Virginia has 2.28 percent of the U.S. population, the company might assume that Virginia will be a market for 2.28 percent of total drugs sold. A single factor, however, is rarely a complete indicator of sales opportunity. Regional drug sales are also influenced by per capita income and the number of physicians per 10,000 people. Thus it makes sense to develop a multiple-factor index with each factor assigned a specific weight.

The numbers are the weights attached to each variable. For example, suppose Virginia has 2.00 percent of the U.S. disposable personal income, 1.96 percent of U.S. retail sales, and 2.28 percent of U.S. population, and the respective weights are 0.5, 0.3, and 0.2. The buying-power index for Virginia would be

$$0.5(2.00) + 0.3(1.96) + 0.2(2.28) = 2.04$$

Thus 2.04 percent of the nation's drug sales might be expected to take place in Virginia.

The weights used in the buying-power index are somewhat arbitrary. Other weights can be assigned if appropriate. Furthermore, a manufacturer would want to adjust the market potential for additional factors, such as competitors' presence in that market, local promotional costs, seasonal factors, and local market idiosyncrasies.

Many companies compute other area indexes as a guide to allocating marketing resources. Suppose the drug company is reviewing the six cities listed in Table 5.7. The first two columns show its percentage of U.S. brand and category sales in these six cities. Column 3 shows the **brand development index (BDI)**, which is the index of brand sales to category sales. Seattle, for example, has a BDI of 114 because the brand is relatively more developed than the category in Seattle. Portland has a BDI of 65, which means that the brand in Portland is relatively underdeveloped. Normally, the lower the BDI, the higher the market opportunity, in that there is room to grow the brand. However, other marketers would argue the opposite, that marketing funds should go into the brand's strongest markets—where it might be easy to capture more brand share.[39]

table **5.7**			
Calculating the Brand Development Index (BDI)			
Territory	(a) Percent of U.S. Brand Sales	(b) Percent of U.S. Category Sales	BDI (a ÷ b) × 100
Seattle	3.09	2.71	114
Portland	6.74	10.41	65
Boston	3.49	3.85	91
Toledo	.97	.81	120
Chicago	1.13	.81	140
Baltimore	3.12	3.00	104

After the company decides on the city-by-city allocation of its budget, it can refine each city allocation down to census tracts or zip+4 code centers. Census tracts are small, locally defined statistical areas in metropolitan areas and some other counties. They generally have stable boundaries and a population of about 4,000. Zip+4 code centers (which were designed by the U.S. Post Office) are a little larger than neighborhoods. Data on population size, median family income, and other characteristics are available for these geographical units. Marketers have found these data extremely useful for identifying high-potential retail areas within large cities or for buying mailing lists to use in direct-mail campaigns.

INDUSTRY SALES AND MARKET SHARES   Besides estimating total potential and area potential, a company needs to know the actual industry sales taking place in its market. This means identifying its competitors and estimating their sales.

The industry's trade association will often collect and publish total industry sales, although it usually does not list individual company sales separately. Using this information, each company can evaluate its performance against the whole industry. Suppose a company's sales are increasing by 5 percent a year, and industry sales are increasing by 10 percent. This company is actually losing its relative standing in the industry.

Another way to estimate sales is to buy reports from a marketing research firm that audits total sales and brand sales. For example, Nielsen Media Research audits retail sales in various product categories in supermarkets and drugstores and sells this information to interested companies. These audits can give a company valuable information about its total product-category sales as well as brand sales. It can compare its performance to the total industry or any particular competitor to see whether it is gaining or losing share.

Business-goods marketers typically have a harder time estimating industry sales and market shares. Business marketers have no Nielsens to rely on. Distributors typically will not supply information about how much of competitors' products they are selling. Business-goods marketers therefore operate with less knowledge of their market-share results.

estimating future demand

We are now ready to examine methods of estimating future demand. Very few products or services lend themselves to easy forecasting; those that do generally involve a product whose absolute level or trend is fairly constant and where competition is nonexistent (public utilities) or stable (pure oligopolies). In most markets, total demand and company demand are not stable. Good forecasting becomes a key factor in company success. The more unstable the demand, the more critical is forecast accuracy, and the more elaborate is forecasting procedure.

Companies commonly use a three-stage procedure to prepare a sales forecast. They prepare a macroeconomic forecast first, followed by an industry forecast, followed by a company sales forecast. The macroeconomic forecast calls for projecting inflation, unemployment, interest rates, consumer spending, business investment, government expenditures, net exports, and other variables. The end result is a forecast of gross national product, which is then used, along with other environmental indicators, to forecast industry sales. The company derives its sales forecast by assuming that it will win a certain market share.

How do firms develop their forecasts? Firms may do it internally or buy forecasts from outside sources such as marketing research firms, which develop a forecast by interviewing customers, distributors, and other knowledgeable parties; and specialized forecasting firms, which produce long-range forecasts of particular macroenvironmental components, such as population, natural resources, and technology. Some examples are Data Resources, Wharton Econometric Forecasting Associates, Forrester Research, and the Gartner Group. Futurist research firms produce speculative scenarios; two examples are the Hudson Institute and the Futures Group.

All forecasts are built on one of three information bases: what people say, what people do, or what people have done. The first basis—what people say—involves surveying the opinions of buyers or those close to them, such as salespeople or outside experts. It encompasses three methods: surveys of buyer's intentions, composites of sales force opinions, and expert opinion. Building a forecast on what people do involves another method—putting the product into a test market to measure buyer response. The final basis—what people have done—involves analyzing records of past buying behavior or using time-series analysis or statistical demand analysis.

survey of buyers' intentions

Forecasting is the art of anticipating what buyers are likely to do under a given set of conditions. Because buyer behavior is so important, buyers should be surveyed. For major consumer durables (for example, major appliances), several research organizations conduct periodic surveys of consumer buying intentions. These organizations ask questions like the following:

Do you intend to buy an automobile within the next six months?

0.00	0.20	0.40	0.60	0.80	1.00
No chance	Slight possibility	Fair possibility	Good possibility	High possibility	Certain

This is called a **purchase probability scale**. The various surveys also inquire into consumers' present and future personal finances and their expectations about the economy. The various bits of information are then combined into a consumer sentiment measure (Survey Research Center of the University of Michigan) or a consumer confidence measure (Sindlinger and Company). Consumer durable-goods producers subscribe to these indexes in the hope of anticipating major shifts in consumer buying intentions so that they can adjust their production and marketing plans accordingly.

Some surveys measuring purchase probability are geared toward getting feedback on specific new products before they are released in the marketplace.

AcuPOLL's home page shows the range of services it offers.

Acupoll   Cincinnati-based AcuPOLL® is one of the nation's largest screeners of new products. In 2000 the company sifted through more than 25,000 new products, picking 400 of the most innovative to test on 100 nationally represented primary grocery store shoppers. The consumers see a photo and brief description and are asked (1) whether they would buy the product and (2) whether they think it is new and different. Products deemed both unique and "buys" are dubbed "pure gold." Products that are unique but not desired by customers are dubbed "fool's gold." AcuPOLL's pure gold list for 2000 included StarKist Tuna in a Pouch, Band-Aid Advanced Healing Bandages, and Downy Wrinkle Release wrinkle-removing spray. Fool's gold products included Bisurkey, a meat patty made from bison and turkey meat; IncrEdibles, portable processed foods in a "push-up" style packaging; and Oishii Kaori, a Japanese air freshener offered in coffee or tea scents.[40]

For business buying, various agencies carry out buyer-intention surveys regarding plant, equipment, and materials. The better-known agencies are McGraw-Hill Research and Opinion Research Corporation. Their estimates tend to fall within a 10 percent error band of the actual outcomes. Buyer-intention surveys are particularly useful in estimating demand for industrial products, consumer durables, product purchases where advanced planning is required, and new products. The value of a buyer-intention survey increases to the extent that the cost of reaching buyers is small, the buyers are few, they have clear intentions, they implement their intentions, and they willingly disclose their intentions.

COMPOSITE OF SALES FORCE OPINIONS   Where buyer interviewing is impractical, the company may ask its sales representatives to estimate their future sales. Each sales representative estimates how much each current and prospective customer will buy of each of the company's products.

Few companies use their sales force's estimates without making some adjustments. Sales representatives might be pessimistic or optimistic, or they might go from one extreme to another because of a recent setback or success. Furthermore, they are often unaware of larger economic developments and do not know how their company's marketing plans will influence future sales in their territory. They might deliberately underestimate demand so that the company will set a low sales quota, or they might lack the time to prepare careful estimates or might not consider the effort worthwhile.

To encourage better estimating, the company could supply certain aids or incentives. For example, sales reps might receive a record of their past forecasts compared with their actual sales and also a description of company assumptions on the business outlook, competitor behavior, and marketing plans.

Involving the sales force in forecasting brings a number of benefits. Sales reps might have better insight into developing trends than any other single group. After participating in the forecasting process, sales reps might have greater confidence in their sales quotas and more incentive to achieve them.[41] Also, a "grassroots" forecasting procedure provides very detailed estimates broken down by product, territory, customer, and sales rep.

EXPERT OPINION   Companies can also obtain forecasts from experts, including dealers, distributors, suppliers, marketing consultants, and trade associations. Large appliance companies periodically survey dealers for their forecasts of short-term demand, as do car companies. Dealer estimates are subject to the same strengths and weaknesses as sales force estimates. Many companies buy economic and industry forecasts from well-known economic-forecasting firms. These specialists are able to prepare better economic forecasts than the company because they have more data available and more forecasting expertise.

Occasionally, companies will invite a group of experts to prepare a forecast. The experts exchange views and produce a group estimate (*group-discussion method*); or the experts supply their estimates individually, and an analyst combines them into a single estimate (*pooling of individual estimates*). Alternatively, the experts supply individual estimates and assumptions that are reviewed by the company, then revised. Further rounds of estimating and refining follow (Delphi method).[42]

PAST-SALES ANALYSIS   Sales forecasts can be developed on the basis of past sales. *Time-series analysis* consists of breaking down past time series into four components (trend, cycle, seasonal, and erratic) and projecting these components into the future. *Exponential smoothing* consists of projecting the next period's sales by combining an average of past sales and the most recent sales, giving more weight to the latter. *Statistical demand analysis* consists of measuring the impact level of each of a set of causal factors (e.g., income, marketing expenditures, price) on the sales level. Finally, *econometric analysis* consists of building sets of equations that describe a system, and proceeding to fit the parameters statistically.

MARKET-TEST METHOD   When buyers do not plan their purchases carefully or experts are not available or reliable, a direct-market test is desirable. A direct-market test is especially desirable in forecasting new-product sales or established product sales in a new distribution channel or territory. (We discuss market testing in detail in Chapter 12.)

summary

1. Three developments make the need for marketing information greater now than at any time in the past: the rise of global marketing, the new emphasis on buyers' wants, and the trend toward nonprice competition.

2. To carry out their analysis, planning, implementation, and control responsibilities, marketing managers need a marketing information system (MIS). The role of the MIS is to assess the managers' information needs, develop the needed information, and distribute that information in a timely manner.

3. An MIS has four components: (a) an internal records system, which includes information on the order-to-payment cycle and sales reporting systems; (b) a marketing intelligence system, a set of procedures and sources used by managers to obtain everyday information about pertinent developments in the marketing environment; (c) a marketing research system that allows for the systematic design, collection, analysis, and reporting of data and findings relevant to a specific marketing situation; and (d) a computerized marketing decision support system that helps managers interpret relevant information and turn it into a basis for marketing action.

4. Companies can conduct their own marketing research or hire other companies to do it for them. Good marketing research is characterized by the scientific method, creativity, multiple research methods, accurate model building, cost-benefit analysis, healthy skepticism, and an ethical focus.

5. The process consists of defining the problem and research objective, developing the research plan, collecting the information, analyzing the information, and presenting the findings to management. In conducting research, firms must decide whether to collect their own data or use data that already exist. They must also decide which research approach (observational, focus-group, survey, behavioral data, or experimental) and which research instrument (questionnaire or mechanical instruments) to use. In addition, they must decide on a sampling plan and contact methods.

6. One major reason for undertaking marketing research is to discover market opportunities. Once the research is complete, the company must carefully evaluate its opportunities and decide which markets to enter. Once in the market, it must prepare sales forecasts based on estimates of demand.

7. There are two types of demand: market demand and company demand. To estimate current demand, companies attempt to determine total market potential, area market potential, industry sales, and market share. To estimate future demand, companies survey buyers' intentions, solicit their sales force's input, gather expert opinions, or engage in market testing. Mathematical models, advanced statistical techniques, and computerized data collection procedures are essential to all types of demand and sales forecasting.

applications

marketing debate – what is the best type of marketing research?

Many market researchers have their favorite research approaches or techniques, although different researchers often have different preferences. For example, some researchers maintain that the only way to really learn about consumers or brands is through in-depth, qualitative research. Others contend that the only legitimate and defensible form of marketing research involves quantitative measures.

Take a position: Marketing research shapes consumer needs and wants versus Marketing research merely reflects the needs and wants of consumers.

marketing and advertising

1. American Beef Producers sponsored the print ad in Figure 1 promoting the nutritional benefits of beef. The ad addresses misconceptions that U.S. consumers have about beef's nutritional value, as revealed in survey research conducted for the National Cattleman's Beef Promotion and Research Board.

   a. When measuring market demand for beef, what space and product levels would the National Cattleman's Beef Promotion and Research Board be most interested in?

   b. Is this ad seeking to increase primary or selective demand for beef? Why?

   c. If the beef producers group needed a relatively accurate measure of market response to this ad, would you recommend that it use a probability or a nonprobability sample?

2. As advertised in Figure 2, Mutual of America wants to help companies of all sizes and types handle their retirement and insurance needs. According to the copy, all business customers "receive the same quality service and care" and "the same freedom of choice" regardless of size.

   a. Which research approaches would be most helpful in identifying any problems that customers might have experienced in working with Mutual of America consultants?

   b. If company marketers decide to collect primary data, would you recommend they use closed-end or open-end questions? Why?

   c. Draft a brief questionnaire that Mutual of America could use to identify additional needs that the company might try to satisfy with new financial services products or services.

Source: Kristin Harmel, "Who Eats Beef? Consumption Depends on Age, Education, UF Study Shows," *ScienceDaily,* September 28, 2000, *www.sciencedaily.com/releases/2000/000914104820.htm*

Figure 1

Figure 2

online marketing today

Research conducted by Purdue University shows that up to 75 percent of consumers fail to complete their online purchases, primarily because of sluggish Web sites, poor site design, and related factors. Seeking to learn what online visitors do and do not do at its Web site, Northwest Airlines has added a new software tool to its online operations. "The success of our online business comes down to our customers and how satisfied they are with our products and services," says Northwest's manager of e-commerce. This new tool, he says, "makes it very easy to determine where we should focus our efforts," by analyzing the online behavior of visitors, finding out which affiliates send the most visitors to the site, and tracking response to online promotions. With this information, the airline will be able to make the site function more efficiently and more effectively to increase sales and customer satisfaction.[43]

Browse Northwest's home page *www.nwa.com* and then follow the link to the "Talk to us" page. Sample several of the links on this page to see how customers can submit questions and feedback. Would such data be included as part of Northwest's marketing information system, marketing intelligence system, or marketing research system? Where would the airline store the primary data about online visitor behavior that its new software tool is collecting? What kind of research approach does this primary data represent? How else might Northwest use its Web site to gather primary data?

you're the marketer: sonic pda marketing plan

Marketing Plan Pro

Marketing information systems, marketing intelligence systems, and marketing research systems are used to gather and analyze data for various parts of the marketing plan. These systems can help marketers examine changes and trends in markets, competition, consumer needs, product usage, and distribution channels, among other areas. They can also turn up evidence of important opportunities and threats that must be addressed.

You are continuing as Jane Melody's assistant at Sonic. She has collected a considerable amount of marketing intelligence about the market and the competitive situation, but you believe Sonic needs more data in preparation for launching the first product. Based on the marketing plan contents discussed in Chapter 4, answer the following questions about how you can use MIS and marketing research to support the development and implementation of Sonic's marketing plan for its new PDA:

■ For which sections will you need secondary data? Primary data? Both? Why do you need the information for each section?

■ Where can you find suitable secondary data? Identify two non-Internet sources and two Internet sources; describe what you plan to draw from each source, and indicate how you will use the data in your marketing planning.

■ What surveys, focus groups, observation, behavioral data, or experiments will Sonic need to support its marketing strategy, including product management, pricing, distribution, and marketing communication? Be specific about the questions or issues that Sonic should seek to resolve using market research data.

Enter your answers about Sonic's use of marketing data and research in the appropriate sections of a written marketing plan or in the Marketing Research, Market Analysis, and Market Trends sections of the *Marketing Plan Pro* software.

notes

1. James C. Anderson and James A. Narus, *Business Market Management: Understanding, Creating and Delivering Value* (Upper Saddle River, NJ: Prentice Hall, 1998), ch. 2.

2. John Koten, "You Aren't Paranoid if You Feel Someone Eyes You Constantly," *Wall Street Journal*, March 29, 1985, pp. 1, 22; "Offbeat Marketing," *Sales & Marketing Management* (January 1990): 35; and Erik Larson, "Attention Shoppers: Don' Look Now but You Are Being Tailed," *Smithsonian Magazine*, January 1993, pp. 70–79.

3. From Consumer Europe 1993, a publication of Euromonitor, pnc. London: Tel 14471 251 8021; U.S. offices: (312) 541-8024.

4. "The dot.com within Ford," *U.S. News & World Report*, February 7, 2000, p. 34.

5. John W. Verity, "Taking a Laptop on a Call," *BusinessWeek*, October 25, 1993, pp. 124–25.

6. Stannie Holt, "Sales-Force Automation Ramps Up," *InfoWorld*, March 23, 1998, pp. 29, 38.

7. James A. Narus and James C. Anderson, "Turn Your Industrial Distributors into Partners," *Harvard Business Review* (March–April 1986): 66–71.

8. Kevin Helliker, "Smile: That Cranky Shopper May Be a Store Spy," *Wall Street Journal*, November 30, 1994, pp. B1, B6. Edward F. McQuarrie, *Customer Visits: Building a Better Market Focus*, 2nd ed. (Newbury Park, CA: Sage Press, 1998).

9. Don Peppers, "How You Can Help Them," *Fast Company* (October–November 1997): 128–36.

10. *1994 Survey of Market Research*, eds. Thomas Kinnear and Ann Root (Chicago: American Marketing Association, 1994).

11. Kevin J. Clancy and Robert S. Shulman, *Marketing Myths That Are Killing Business*, (New York: McGraw-Hill, 1994), p. 58; Phaedra Hise, "Comprehensive CompuServe," *Inc.* (June 1994): 109; "Business Bulletin: Studying the Competition," *Wall Street Journal*, p. A1-5.

12. For some background information on in-flight Internet service, see "In-Flight Dogfight," *Business2.Com*, January 9, 2001, pp. 84–91.

13. For a discussion of the decision-theory approach to the value of research, see Donald R. Lehmann, Sunil Gupta, and Joel Steckel, *Market Research* (Reading, MA: Addison-Wesley, 1997).

14. For an excellent annotated reference to major secondary sources of business and marketing data, see Gilbert A. Churchill Jr., *Marketing Research: Methodological Foundations*, 7th ed. (Fort Worth, TX: Dryden, 1998).

15. Thomas L. Greenbaum, *The Handbook for Focus Group Research* (New York: Lexington Books, 1993).

16. Sarah Schafer, "Communications: Getting a Line on Customers," *Inc. Tech* (1996), p. 102; see also Alexia Parks, "On-Line Focus Groups Reshape Market Research Industry," *Marketing News*, May 12, 1997, p. 28.

17. Kevin Lane Keller, *Strategic Brand Management* (Upper Saddle River, NJ: Prentice Hall, 1998), pp. 317–18; Daniel H. Pink, "Metaphor Marketing," *Fast Company* (April 1998): 214.

18. Roger D. Blackwell, James S. Hensel, Michael B. Phillips, and Brian Sternthal, *Laboratory Equipment for Marketing Research* (Dubuque, IA: Kendall/Hunt, 1970); Wally Wood, "The Race to Replace Memory," *Marketing and Media Decisions* (July

1986): 166–67. See also Gerald Zaltman, "Rethinking Market Research: Putting People Back In," *Journal of Marketing Research* 34, no. 4 (November 1997): 424–37.

19. David Goetzl, "O&M Turns Reality TV into Research Tool," *Advertising Age*, July 10, 2000; Brian Wansink, "New Techniques to Generate Key Marketing Insights," *American Marketing Association: Marketing Research* (Summer 2000).

20. Brian Wansink, "Developing Useful and Accurate Customer Profiles," in *Values, Lifestyles, and Psychographics*, edited by Lynn R. Kahle and Larry Chiagouris (Mahwah, NJ: Lawrence Erlbaum Associates, 1997).

21. <*www.knowledgenetworks.com*>; Peter Sinton, "Polling Using the Internet Seeks to Improve Accuracy," *San Francisco Chronicle*, October 28, 2000.

22. G. K. Sharman, "Sessions Challenge Status Quo," *Marketing News*, November 10, 1997, p. 18; "Prepaid Phone Cards Are Revolutionizing Market Research Techniques," *Direct Marketing* (March l998): 12.

23. For further reading, see Joanne Lipman, "Single-Source Ad Research Heralds Detailed Look at Household Habits," *Wall Street Journal*, February 16, 1988, p. 39; Joe Schwartz, "Back to the Source," *American Demographics* (January 1989): 22–26; Magid H. Abraham and Leonard M. Lodish, "Getting the Most Out of Advertising and Promotions," *Harvard Business Review*, (May–June 1990): 50–60.

24. Kevin J. Clancy and Peter C. Krieg, *Counterintuitive Marketing: How Great Results Come from Uncommon Sense* (New York: The Free Press, 2000).

25. John D. C. Little, "Decision Support Systems for Marketing Managers," *Journal of Marketing* (Summer 1979): 11. See "Special Issue on Managerial Decision Making," *Marketing Science*, 18(3), 1999 for some contemporary perspectives.

26. Gary L. Lilien and Arvind Rangaswamy, *Marketing Engineering: Computer-Assisted Marketing Analysis and Planning* (Reading, MA: Addison-Wesley, 1998). Also see their *Marketing Management and Strategy: Marketing Engineering Applications* (Reading, MA: Addison-Wesley, 1999).

27. John D. C. Little, "BRANDAID: A Marketing Mix Model, Part I: Structure; Part II: Implementation," *Operations Research* 23 (1975): 628–73.

28. Leonard M. Lodish, "CALLPLAN: An Interactive Salesman's Call Planning System," *Management Science* (December 1971): 25–40.

29. David B. Montgomery, Alvin J. Silk, and C. E. Zaragoza, "A Multiple-Product Sales-Force Allocation Model," *Management Science* (December 1971): 3–24.

30. S. W. Hess and S. A. Samuels, "Experiences with a Sales Districting Model: Criteria and Implementation," *Management Science* (December 1971): 41–54.

31. John D. C. Little and Leonard M. Lodish, "A Media Planning Calculus," *Operations Research* (January–February 1969): 1–35.

32. Magid M. Abraham and Leonard M. Lodish, "PROMOTER: An Automated Promotion Evaluation System," *Marketing Science* (Spring 1987): 101–23.

33. Raymond R. Burke, Arvind Rangaswamy, Jerry Wind, and Jehoshua Eliashberg, "A Knowledge-Based System for Advertising Design," *Marketing Science* 9, no. 3 (1990): 212–29.

34. John D. C. Little, "Cover Story: An Expert System to Find the News in Scanner Data," Sloan School, MIT Working Paper, 1988.

35. *Sources*: "Hitting the Bulls-Eye: Target Sets Its Sights on East Coast Expansion," *Newsweek*, October 11, 1999; Janet Moore and Ann Merrill, "Target Market," *Minneapolis-St. Paul Star Tribune*, July 27, 2001; Clarke Canfield, "Anticipation Builds as Fast-Growing Target Enters Another State," AP Newswire, August 6, 2001.

36. For a good discussion and illustration, see Roger J. Best, *Market-Based Management*, 2nd ed. (Upper Saddle River, NJ: Prentice Hall, 2000), pp. 71–75.

37. "Will the Have-Nots Always Be With Us?" *Fortune*, December 20, 1999, pp. 288–89.

38. For further discussion, see Gary L. Lilien, Philip Kotler, and K. Sridhar Moorthy, *Marketing Models* (Upper Saddle River, NJ: Prentice Hall, 1992).

39. For suggested strategies related to the market area's BDI standing, see Don E. Schultz, Dennis Martin, and William P. Brown, *Strategic Advertising Campaigns* (Chicago: Crain Books, 1984), p. 338.

40. <*www.acupoll.com*>

41. Jacob Gonik, "Tie Salesmen's Bonuses to Their Forecasts," *Harvard Business Review* (May–June 1978): 116–23.

42. Norman Dalkey and Olaf Helmer, "An Experimental Application of the Delphi Method to the Use of Experts," *Management Science* (April 1963): 458–67. Also see Roger J. Best, "An Experiment in Delphi Estimation in Marketing Decision Making," *Journal of Marketing Research* (November 1974): 447–52. For an excellent overview of market forecasting, see Scott Armstrong, ed., *Principles of Forecasting: A Handbook for Researchers and Practitioners* (Norwell, MA: Kluwer Academic Publishers, 2001).

43. Erika Morphy, "Airlines Adopt Intelligence Tool For Online Customer Service," *CRM Daily.com*, August 24, 2001; <*http://www.crmdaily.com/perl/story/13070.html*>; "What Do E-Consumers Want?" *USA Today Magazine*, May 2001, p. 8.

6

scanning the marketing environment

In this chapter, we will address the following questions:

- What are the key methods for tracking and identifying opportunities in the macroenvironment?
- What are the key demographic, economic, natural, technological, political, and cultural developments?

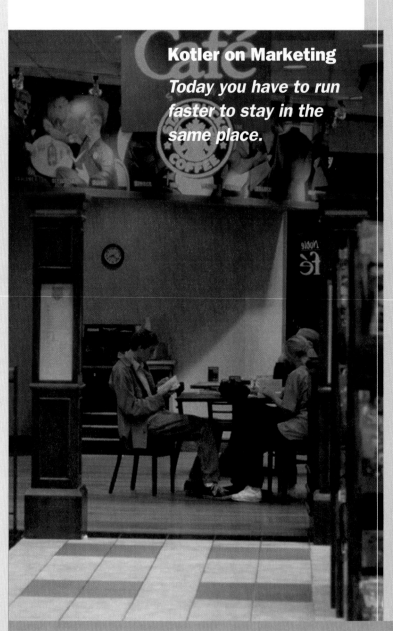

Kotler on Marketing

Today you have to run faster to stay in the same place.

Successful companies take an outside-inside view of their business. They recognize that the marketing environment is constantly presenting new opportunities and threats, and they understand the importance of continuously monitoring and adapting to that environment. One company that has continually reinvented one of its brands to keep up with the changing marketing environment is Mattel with its Barbie doll.[1]

Many companies fail to see change as opportunity. They ignore or resist changes until it is too late. Their strategies, structures, systems, and organizational culture grow increasingly obsolete and dysfunctional. Corporations as mighty as General Motors, IBM, and Sears have passed *through difficult times because they ignored macroenvironmental changes. One critic of Sears recently said, "Sears is slowly sinking into irrelevance. . . Older corporations need to find a way to die gracefully."[2]*

The major responsibility for identifying significant marketplace changes falls to the company's marketers. More than any other group in the company, they must be the trend trackers and opportunity seekers. Although every manager in an organization needs to observe the outside environment, marketers have two advantages: They have disciplined methods—marketing intelligence and marketing research—for collecting information about the marketing environment. They also spend more time with customers and more time watching competitors.

In this and the next four chapters, we examine the firm's external environment—the macroenvironment forces that affect it, its consumer markets, its business markets, and its competitors.

analyzing needs and trends in the macroenvironment

Successful companies recognize and respond profitably to unmet needs and trends. Companies could make a fortune if they could solve any of these problems: a cure for cancer, chemical cures for mental diseases, desalinization of seawater, nonfattening, tasty nutritious food, practical electric cars, and affordable housing.

Enterprising individuals and companies manage to create new solutions to unmet needs. Club Med emerged to meet the needs of single people for exotic vacations; the Walkman and CD Man were created for active people who wanted to listen to music; Nautilus was created for men and women who wanted to tone their bodies; FedEx was created to meet the need for next-day mail delivery.

Many opportunities are found by identifying trends. A **trend** is a direction or sequence of events that has some momentum and durability.

Blockbuster and Satellite TV   The cocooning trend led to a boom in home-video rentals in the 1980s. Blockbuster Video rode this trend to become the world's leading renter of videos, DVDs, and video games. Today, Blockbuster conducts business with approximately 7,700 stores on five continents.[3] While renting videos required consumers to leave their homes, Satellite TV offers the option to view hundreds of television channels without having to leave the house. Companies such as DirecTV capitalized on this consumer need by developing satellite television service that offered a wealth of programming options from around the world. By the end of 2000, DirecTV boasted 9.5 million U.S. subscribers.[4]

We can draw distinctions among fads, trends, and megatrends. A **fad** is "unpredictable, short-lived, and without social, economic, and political significance."[5] A company can cash in on a fad such as Pet Rocks, Beanie Babies, or Pokemon, but this is more a matter of luck and good timing than anything else. Trends are more predictable and durable. A trend reveals the shape of the future. Futurist Faith Popcorn runs BrainReserve, a marketing consulting firm that monitors cultural trends and advises companies such as AT&T, Black & Decker, Hoffman-LaRoche, Nissan, and Rubbermaid. According to Popcorn, a trend has longevity, is observable across several market areas and consumer activities, and is consistent with other significant indicators occurring or emerging at the same time.[6] Popcorn and her associates have identified major cultural trends affecting the U.S. economy. How many of these trends have you noticed in your own life? (See "Marketing Memo: Faith Popcorn: Trends in the Economy.")

Marketing
MEMO

Faith Popcorn: Trends in the Economy

1. *Anchoring.* The tendency to use ancient practices as anchors or support for modern lifestyles: aromatherapy, meditation, yoga, and Eastern religions.
2. *Being alive.* The desire to lead longer and more enjoyable lives: vegetarianism, low-tech medicine, meditation.
3. *Cashing out.* The desire for a simpler, less hectic lifestyle: a nostalgic return to small-town values.
4. *Clanning.* The need to join groups in order to confront a more chaotic world: Harley-Davidson's Harley Owners Group (HOG).
5. *Cocooning.* The impulse to stay inside when outside gets too tough and scary: redecorating, watching TV and rental movies, ordering from catalogs.
6. *Down-aging.* The tendency for older people to act and feel younger than their ages: youthful clothes and hair coloring, adult toys, adventure vacations.
7. *Egonomics.* The wish to individualize oneself through possessions and experience: customized goods, services, experiences.
8. *Fantasy adventure.* The need to find emotional escapes: safari vacations, exotic foods.
9. *99 lives.* Doing many things at once; "multitasking": cluster marketing enterprises—all-in-one service stops.
10. *S.O.S. (save our society).* The desire to make society more socially responsible: education, ethics, the environment.
11. *Female think.* The recognition that men and women act and think differently.
12. *Mancipation.* The emancipation of men from stereotypical male roles of being macho and strong, and instead showing them as nurturing dads and concerned husbands.
13. *Small indulgences.* The desire to indulge in small-scale splurges to obtain an occasional emotional lift.
14. *Pleasure revenge.* The proud and public pursuit of pleasure as a rebellion against self-control and self-deprivation.
15. *Icon toppling.* The return to interest in smaller and more local organizations and products.
16. *The vigilant consumer.* Intolerance for shoddy products and poor service.

Source: This summary is drawn from various pages of Faith Popcorn's *The Popcorn Report* (New York: HarperBusiness, 1992), and Faith Popcorn and Lys Marigold, *Clicking* (New York: HarperCollins, 1996).

John Naisbitt, another futurist, prefers to talk about **megatrends**, which are "large social, economic, political and technological changes [that] are slow to form, and once in place, they influence us for some time–between seven and ten years, or longer."[7] Naisbitt and his staff spot megatrends by counting the number of times hard-news items on different topics appear in major newspapers. Naisbitt has identified such trends as the Rise of the Pacific Rim, the Age of Biology, and Global Lifestyles and Cultural Nationalism.

Some futurists are now giving predictions for the year 2025 that are worth noting, even if their feasibility remains uncertain: Ryan Mathews, a futurist at First Matter LLC in Detroit, predicts that consumers will enjoy *continuous household replenishment* of common household products (paper towels, soft drinks) because their computers will sense when they are running low and automatically reorder them or even find a cheaper substitute; and Procter & Gamble's Gary Wright predicts that retailers will be delivering lowest-cost bundles of our desired products to our doors via powerful alliances between giant supermarkets and logistics firms.[8]

Trends and megatrends merit close attention. A new product or marketing program is likely to be more successful if it is in line with strong trends rather than opposed to them, but detecting a new market opportunity does not guarantee success, even if it is technically feasible. For example, today some companies sell portable "electronic books"; but there may not be a sufficient number of people interested in reading a book on a computer screen or willing to pay the required price. This is why market research is necessary to determine an opportunity's profit potential.

To help marketers spot cultural shifts that might bring new opportunities or threats, several firms offer social-cultural forecasts. The Yankelovich Monitor interviews 2,500 people each year and tracks 35 social trends, such as "antibigness," "mysticism," "living for today," "away from possessions," and "sensuousness." It describes the percentage of the population who share the attitude as well as the percentage who do not. For exam-

marketing **insight**

Tracking Consumer Trends

At the dawn of the twenty-first century, Yankelovich looked back to capture some of the lessons from the 1990s, as well as to offer some insight into the "2000s." Its researchers documented the following eight major consumer themes and developments from the 1990s.

1. "Paradox" (e.g., 82 percent of public agrees that "Life is getting better and worse at the same time").
2. "Trust not" (e.g., great confidence in doctors, public schools, TV news, newspapers, federal government, and corporations drops sharply).
3. "Go it alone" (e.g., more people agree with "I rely more on my own instincts than experts").
4. "Smarts really count" (e.g., fewer people agree with "It's risky to buy a brand you are not familiar with").
5. "No sacrifices" (e.g., many people claim that looks are important, but not at any price; keeping house for show instead of comfort is over; and giving up taste for nutrition is no longer acceptable).
6. "Stress hard to beat" (e.g., more people claim that they are "concerned about getting enough rest").

7. "Reciprocity is the way to go" (e.g., more people agree that "Everybody should feel free to do their own thing").
8. "Me.2" (e.g., people express need to live in a world that is built by "me," not by you).

Yankelovich maintains that the decade drivers for the 2000's will primarily come from baby boomers and Generation X'ers. Baby boomers (born between 1946 and 1964) will be driven by four factors: "adventure" (fueled by a sense of youthfulness), "smarts" (fueled by a sense of empowerment and willingness to accept change), "intergenerational support" (caring for younger and older, often in nontraditional arrangements), and "retreading" (embracing early retirement with a second career or phase of their work life). Generation X'ers (born between 1965 and 1976) will be driven by three factors: "redefining the good life" (highly motivated to improve their economic well-being and remain in control), "new rituals" (returning to traditional values but with a tolerant mind-set and active lifestyle), and "cutting and pasting" (balancing work, play, sleep, family, etc.).

Source: Yankelovich conference presentation.

ple, the percentage of people who value physical fitness and well-being has risen steadily over the years, especially in the under-30 group, the young women and upscale group, and people living in the West. Marketers of health foods and exercise equipment cater to this trend with appropriate products and communications. (See "Marketing Insight: Tracking Consumer Trends.")

identifying and responding to the major macroenvironment forces

Companies and their suppliers, marketing intermediaries, customers, competitors, and publics all operate in a macroenvironment of forces and trends that shape opportunities and pose threats. These forces represent "noncontrollables," to which the company must monitor and respond. In the economic arena, companies and consumers are increasingly affected by global forces. These include:

1. The substantial speedup of international transportation, communication, and financial transactions, leading to the rapid growth of world trade and investment, especially tripolar trade (North America, Western Europe, Far East).
2. The movement of manufacturing capacity and skills to lower-cost countries.
3. The rising economic power of several Asian countries in world markets.
4. The rise of trade blocs such as the European Union and the NAFTA signatories.
5. The severe debt problems of a number of countries, along with the increasing fragility of the international financial system.
6. The increasing use of barter and countertrade to support international transactions.

7. The move toward market economies in formerly socialist countries along with rapid privatization of publicly owned companies.

8. The rapid dissemination of global lifestyles.

9. The gradual opening of major new markets, namely, China, India, Eastern Europe, the Arab countries, and Latin America.

10. The increasing tendency of multinationals to transcend their locational and national characteristics and become transnational firms.

11. The increasing number of cross-border corporate strategic alliances—for example, MCI and British Telecom, and Texas Instruments and Hitachi.

12. The increasing ethnic and religious conflicts in certain countries and regions.

13. The growth of global brands in autos, food, clothing, and electronics.

Colgate-Palmolive   Colgate-Palmolive test-marketed Total, its antibacterial plaque-fighting toothpaste, in six countries: the Philippines, Australia, Colombia, Greece, Portugal, and the United Kingdom. The team in charge of the global launch was a veritable corporate United Nations of operations, logistics, and marketing strategists. Their efforts paid off handsomely: Total was soon a $150-million brand worldwide, selling in 75 countries, with virtually identical packaging, positioning, and advertising (See Figure 6.1).[9]

Within the rapidly changing global picture, the firm must monitor six major forces: demographic, economic, natural, technological, political-legal, and social-cultural. Although these forces will be described separately, marketers must pay attention to their interactions, because these will lead to new opportunities and threats. For example, explosive population growth (demographic) leads to more resource depletion and pollution (natural), which leads consumers to call for more laws (political-legal), which stimulate new technological solutions and products (technological), which, if they are affordable (economic), may actually change attitudes and behavior (social-cultural).

figure **6.1**

Colgate–Palmolive's Total Global Branding Strategy

Colgate-Palmolive has had global success with its Colgate line of tooth-care products. The products and their packaging design do not vary from country to country; the only thing that changes is the language on the packages.

demographic environment

The first macroenvironmental force that marketers monitor is population, because people make up markets. Marketers are keenly interested in the size and growth rate of population in cities, regions, and nations; age distribution and ethnic mix; educational levels; household patterns; and regional characteristics and movements.

WORLDWIDE POPULATION GROWTH   The world population is showing "explosive" growth: it totaled 6.1 billion in 2000 and will exceed 7.9 billion by the year 2025.[10] Here is an interesting picture:

> If the world were a village of 1,000 people, it would consist of 520 women and 480 men, 330 children and 60 people over age 65, 10 college graduates and 335 illiterate adults. The village would contain 52 North Americans, 55 Russians, 84 Latin Americans, 95 Europeans, 134 Africans, and 584 Asians. Communication would be difficult because 165 people would speak Mandarin, 86 English, 83 Hindi, 64 Spanish, 58 Russian, and 37 Arabic, and the rest would speak one of over 200 other languages. There would be 329 Christians, 178 Moslems, 132 Hindus, 62 Buddhists, 3 Jews, 167 nonreligious, 45 atheists, and 84 others.[11]

The world population explosion has been a source of major concern, for two reasons. The first is the fact that certain resources needed to support this much human life (fuel, foods, and minerals) are limited and may run out at some point. First published in 1972, *The Limits to Growth* presented an impressive array of evidence that unchecked population growth and consumption would eventually result in insufficient food supply, depletion of key minerals, overcrowding, pollution, and an overall deterioration in the quality of life.[12] One of the study's strong recommendations is the worldwide social marketing of family planning.[13]

The second cause for concern is that population growth is highest in countries and communities that can least afford it. The less developed regions of the world currently account for 76 percent of the world population and are growing at 2 percent per year, whereas the population in the more developed countries is growing at only 0.6 percent per year. In the developing countries, the death rate has been falling as a result of modern medicine, but the birthrate has remained fairly stable. Feeding, clothing, and educating children while also providing a rising standard of living is nearly impossible in these countries.

Explosive population growth has major implications for business. A growing population does not mean growing markets unless these markets have sufficient purchasing power. Nonetheless, companies that carefully analyze their markets can find major opportunities. For example, to curb its skyrocketing population, the Chinese government has passed regulations limiting families to one child. One consequence of these regulations: These children are spoiled and fussed over as never before. Known in China as "little emperors," Chinese children are being showered with everything from candy to computers as a result of the "six pocket syndrome." As many as six adults—parents, grandparents, great-grandparents, and aunts and uncles—may be indulging the whims of each child. This trend has encouraged toy companies such as Japan's Bandai Company (famous for its Mighty Morphin' Power Rangers), Denmark's Lego Group, and Mattel to enter the Chinese market.[14]

POPULATION AGE MIX   National populations vary in their age mix. At one extreme is Mexico, a country with a very young population and rapid population growth. At the other extreme is Japan, a country with one of the world's oldest populations. Milk, diapers, school supplies, and toys would be important products in Mexico. Japan's population would consume many more adult products.

A population can be subdivided into six age groups: preschool, school-age children, teens, young adults age 25 to 40, middle-aged adults age 40 to 65, and older adults age 65 and up. For marketers, the most populous age groups shape the marketing environment.

In the United States, the "baby boomers," the 78 million people born between 1946 and 1964, are one of the most powerful forces shaping the marketplace. Baby boomers are fixated on their youth, not their age, and ads geared to them tend to capitalize on nostalgia from their past, such as those for the newly redesigned Volkswagen Beetle. Boomers grew up with TV advertising, so they are an easier market to reach than the 45 million born between 1965 and 1976, dubbed Generation X (and also the shadow generation, twenty-somethings, and baby busters). Generation-Xers are typically cynical about hard-sell marketing pitches that promise more than they can deliver. Ads created to woo this market often puzzle older people, because they often do not seem to "sell" at all.[15]

VW Volkswagen sales have risen over 600 percent since 1994, partly a result of the company's new "Drivers Wanted" campaign targeting fun-loving or youth drivers. Recent ads for Volkswagen include a television spot in which two young men are seen trying to retrieve an object stuck in a tree by throwing shoes and other objects into the branches. When they finally succeed, a Volkswagen Golf GTI tumbles out of the tree and the words "The GTI. Use Your Power Wisely" appear on the screen.[16]

Mountain Dew Pepsi initially marketed Mountain Dew with the countrified tagline "Yahoo Mountain Dew! It'll tickle your innards." After an unsuccessful attempt in the early 1980s to bring urban teenage drinkers to the brand by advertising on MTV, the company switched its focus to using outdoor action scenes. Mountain Dew updated this outdoors image in the 1990s by using extreme sports such as skydiving, skateboarding, and snowboarding. The brand's aggressive pursuit of young soda drinkers helped Mountain Dew's market share rise from 2.7 percent in 1980 to 7.2 percent in 2000, good enough for fourth place in the soft drink category.[17]

Both baby boomers and Generation-Xers will be passing the torch to the latest demographic group, the echo boomers (or baby boomlet), born between 1977 and 1994. Now numbering 72 million, this group is almost equal in size to baby boomers. One distinguishing characteristic of this age group is their utter fluency and comfort with computer and Internet technology. Don Tapscott has christened them "Net-Gens" for this reason. He says: "To them, digital technology is no more intimidating than a VCR or a toaster."[18] (See "Marketing Memo: Tapping into the Internet Generation.")

Do marketers have to create separate ads for each generation? J. Walker Smith, co-author of *Rocking the Ages: The Yankelovich Report on Generational Marketing*, says that marketers do have to be careful about turning off one generation each time they craft a message that appeals effectively to another. "I think the idea is to try to be broadly inclusive and at the same time offer each generation something specifically designed for it. Tommy Hilfiger has big brand logos on his clothes for teenagers and little pocket polo logos on his shirts for baby boomers. It's a brand that has a more inclusive than exclusive strategy."[19]

ETHNIC AND OTHER MARKETS Countries also vary in ethnic and racial makeup. At one extreme is Japan, where almost everyone is Japanese; at the other is the United States, where people from come virtually all nations. The United States was originally called a "melting pot," but there are increasing signs that the melting didn't occur. Now people call the United States a "salad bowl" society with ethnic groups maintaining their ethnic differences, neighborhoods, and cultures. The U.S. population (276.2 million in 2000) is 72 percent white. African Americans constitute another 13 percent, and Latinos another 11 percent. The Latino population has been growing fast, with the largest subgroups of Mexican (5.4 percent), Puerto Rican (1.1 percent), and Cuban (0.4 percent) descent. Asian Americans constitute 3.8 percent of the U.S. population, with the Chinese

Marketing
MEMO

Tapping into the Internet Generation

Net-Gens already influence adult purchases more than any preceding generation. The Alliance for Converging Technologies estimates that American preteens and teens spend $130 billion of their own dollars annually and influence upward of $500 billion of their parents' spending. How do you market to this group? Don Tapscott, author of *Growing Up Digital: The Rise of the Net Generation* (www.growingupdigital.com), advises marketers to keep five things in mind:

1. Options are a must—choice is one of their most deeply held values.
2. Customize. These are the kids who build their own levels in video games and write their own Web pages, and they want things their way.
3. Let them have the option of changing their minds. They're growing up in a world where fixing mistakes takes a stroke of the mouse, and they believe that changing their minds should be equally painless.
4. Let them try before they buy. They're users and doers. They reject expert opinions in favor of forming their own.
5. Never forget that they will choose function over form. "Unlike baby boomers, who witnessed the technological revolution," Tapscott says, "N-Geners have no awe of new technology. They have grown up with computers and treat them like any other household appliance. This is an audience that cares about what the technology will do, not the technology itself."

Source: Excerpted from Lisa Krakowka, "In the Net," *American Demographics* (August 1998): p. 56; Don Tapscott, *Growing Up Digital: The Rise of the Net Generation* (New York: McGraw Hill, 1997).

constituting the largest group, followed by the Filipinos, Japanese, Asian Indians, and Koreans, in that order. Latino and Asian American consumers are concentrated in the far western and southern parts of the country, although some dispersal is taking place. Moreover, there are nearly 25 million people living in the United States—more than 9 percent of the population—who were born in another country.

Each group has certain specific wants and buying habits. Several food, clothing, and furniture companies have directed their products and promotions to one or more of these groups.[20] For instance, Sears is taking note of the preferences of different ethnic groups.

Sears If a Sears, Roebuck and Company store has a shopping base that is at least 20 percent Latino, it is designated as a Hispanic store for the purpose of Sears's Hispanic marketing program. More than 130 stores in southern California, Texas, Florida, and New York have earned this label. "We make a special effort to staff those stores with bilingual sales personnel, to use bilingual signage, and to support community programs," says a Sears spokesperson. Choosing merchandise for the Latino marketplace is primarily a color and size issue. "What we find in Hispanic communities is that people tend to be smaller than the general market, and that there is a greater demand for special-occasion clothing and a preference for bright colors. In hardlines, there isn't much difference from the mainstream market."

Yet marketers must be careful not to overgeneralize about ethnic groups. Within each ethnic group are consumers who are quite different from each other. "There is really no such thing as an Asian market," says Greg Macabenta, whose ethnic advertising agency specializes in the Filipino market. Macabenta emphasizes that the five major Asian American groups have their own very specific market characteristics, speak different languages, consume different cuisines, practice different religions, and represent very distinct national cultures.[21]

Diversity goes beyond ethnic and racial markets. More than 52 million Americans have disabilities, and they constitute a market for home delivery companies such as Peapod, and for various medical services.

EDUCATIONAL GROUPS   The population in any society falls into five educational groups: illiterates, high school dropouts, high school degrees, college degrees, and professional degrees. In Japan, 99 percent of the population is literate, whereas in the United States 10 percent to 15 percent of the population may be functionally illiterate. However, the United States has one of the world's highest percentages of college-educated citizens, around 36 percent. The high number of educated people in the United States spells a high demand for quality books, magazines, and travel, and a high supply of skills.

HOUSEHOLD PATTERNS   The "traditional household" consists of a husband, wife, and children (and sometimes grandparents). Yet, in the United States today, one out of eight households is "diverse" or "nontraditional," and includes single live-alones, adult live-togethers of one or both sexes, single-parent families, childless married couples, and empty-nesters. More people are divorcing or separating, choosing not to marry, marrying later, or marrying without the intention to have children. Each group has a distinctive set of needs and buying habits. For example, people in the SSWD group (single, separated, widowed, divorced) need smaller apartments; inexpensive and smaller appliances, furniture, and furnishings; and smaller-size food packages. Marketers must increasingly consider the special needs of nontraditional households, because they are now growing more rapidly than traditional households.

The gay market, in particular, is a lucrative one. Compared to the average American, respondents are 11.7 times more likely to be in professional jobs, almost twice as likely to own a vacation home, eight times more likely to own a computer notebook, and twice as likely to own individual stocks.[22] Insurance, financial, and other companies are waking up to the needs and potential of this market and the nontraditional household market as a whole.

Absolut   Since 1981, Absolut Vodka has targeted members of the gay and lesbian market segment with a variety of marketing efforts. The spirits company, considered a pioneer in marketing to the gay and lesbian community, has advertised in magazines that cover gay and lesbian culture, sponsored gay and lesbian film festivals, among other marketing activities. Absolut became a founding sponsor in 1989 of the annual Gay and Lesbian Alliance Against Defamation (GLAAD) Media Awards. In February 2001, the company ran an ad honoring GLAAD in *The Advocate* and *New York* magazines.[23]

GEOGRAPHICAL SHIFTS IN POPULATION   This is a period of great migratory movements between and within countries. Since the collapse of Soviet Eastern Europe, nationalities are reasserting themselves and forming independent countries. The new countries are making certain ethnic groups unwelcome (such as Russians in Latvia or Muslims in Serbia), and many of these groups are migrating to safer areas. As foreign groups enter other countries for political sanctuary, some local groups start protesting. In the United States, there has been opposition to the influx of immigrants from Mexico, the Caribbean, and certain Asian nations. Yet many immigrants have done very well. Forward-looking companies and entrepreneurs are taking advantage of the growth in immigrant populations and marketing their wares specifically to these new members of the population.

Boreal Ski Area   Boreal Ski Area near Lake Tahoe, California, increased its customer base by marketing to San Francisco's sizable Chinese population. Market research had shown that family activities were popular among Chinese and that Chinese immigrant parents regarded skiing as an activity to help children assimilate. Boreal ran ads in local Chinese-language newspapers, advertised on Chinese TV, and began a PR campaign targeting the Chinese press. By 1999, the number of Asian visitors to Boreal had risen 10 percent.[24]

Population movement also occurs as people migrate from rural to urban areas, and then to suburban areas. The U.S. population has now undergone another shift, which demographers call "the rural rebound." Nonmetropolitan counties that lost population to cities for most of this century are now attracting large numbers of urban refugees. Between 1990 and 1998, rural areas gained 2 million people due to migration from the city.[25]

Cashing Out   Wanda Urbanska and her husband Frank Levering moved from the media grind of Los Angeles to a simpler life in Mount Airy, North Carolina (population 7,200). Urbanska's former job as a reporter for the *Los Angeles Herald Examiner* and Levering's former job as a screenwriter for B movies had taken up so much of their time and energy that they could not really enjoy the money they were making. When Levering's father had a heart attack, the couple packed up and moved to Mount Airy to help him with his fruit orchard. They still help him run the orchard while doing freelance writing on the side, such as two books about seeking a better life: *Simple Living* and *Moving to a Small Town*.[26]

Businesses with potential to cash in on the rural rebound might be those that cater to the growing SOHO (small office—home office) segment. For instance, makers of RTA (ready to assemble) furniture might find a strong consumer base among all the cashed-out former city residents setting up offices in small towns or telecommuting from there to larger companies.

Location makes a difference in goods and service preferences. Over 12 million U.S. households (more than one out of every 10) move each year, and the shift has been toward the Sunbelt states, away from the Midwest and Northeast.[27] The movement to the Sunbelt states has lessened the demand for warm clothing and home heating equipment and increased the demand for air conditioning. Those who live in large cities such as New York, Chicago, and San Francisco account for most of the sales of expensive furs, perfumes, luggage, and works of art. These cities also support the opera, ballet, and other forms of culture. Americans living in the suburbs lead more casual lives, do more outdoor living, and have greater neighbor interaction, higher incomes, and younger families. Suburbanites buy vans, home workshop equipment, outdoor furniture, lawn and gardening tools, and outdoor cooking equipment. There are also regional differences: People in Seattle buy more toothbrushes per capita than people in any other U.S. city; people in Salt Lake City eat more candy bars; people from New Orleans use more ketchup; and people in Miami drink more prune juice.

FROM A MASS MARKET TO MICROMARKETS   The effect of all these changes is fragmentation of the mass market into numerous *micromarkets* differentiated by age, sex, ethnic background, education, geography, lifestyle, and other characteristics. Each group has strong preferences and is reached through increasingly targeted communication media and distribution channels. Companies are abandoning the "shotgun approach" that aimed at a mythical "average" consumer and are increasingly designing their products and marketing programs for specific micromarkets, many of which can be reached through specialized magazines, direct mail, or Web sites.

Demographic trends are highly reliable for the short and intermediate run. There is little excuse for a company's being suddenly surprised by demographic developments. The Singer Company should have known for years that its sewing machine business would be hurt by smaller families and more working wives, yet it was slow in responding. In contrast, think of the rewards marketers reap when they focus on a demographic development. Some marketers are actively courting the lucrative SOHO market. Nearly 40 million Americans are working out of their homes with the help of electronic conveniences like computers, cell phones, fax machines, and personal organizers. One company that is shifting gears to appeal to this micromarket is Kinko's Copy Centers.

Kinko's Copy Centers   Founded in the 1970s as a campus photocopying business, Kinko's is now reinventing itself as the well-appointed office outside the home. Where once there were copy machines, the 902 Kinko's stores in this country and abroad now feature a mix of fax machines, ultra-fast color printers, and networks of computers equipped with popular software programs and high-speed Internet connections. Kinko's is now a $2-billion company that offers an unprecedented array of office services. People can come to a Kinko's store to do all their office jobs: copy, send, and receive faxes, use various programs on the computer, go on the Internet, order stationery and other printed supplies, and even teleconference; and as more people work at home, Kinko's offers an escape from the isolation of the home office. At the same time, Kinko's seeks to make it easier for consumers to access its services from home. In March 2000, Kinko's teamed with Alexandria, Virginia–based LivePrint.com to develop Kinkos.com, a site that allows customers to print, bind, and ship documents.[28]

economic environment

Markets require purchasing power as well as people. The available purchasing power in an economy depends on current income, prices, savings, debt, and credit availability. Marketers must pay close attention to major trends in income and consumer-spending patterns.

INCOME DISTRIBUTION   Nations vary greatly in level and distribution of income and industrial structure. There are four types of industrial structures: subsistence economies (few opportunities for marketers); raw-material-exporting economies like Zaire (copper) and Saudi Arabia (oil), with good markets for equipment, tools, supplies, and luxury goods for the rich; industrializing economies, like India, Egypt, and the Philippines, where a new rich class and a growing middle class demand new types of goods; and industrial economies, which are rich markets for all sorts of goods.

Marketers often distinguish countries with five different income-distribution patterns: (1) very low incomes; (2) mostly low incomes; (3) very low, very high incomes; (4) low, medium, high incomes; and (5) mostly medium incomes. Consider the market for Lamborghinis, an automobile costing more than $150,000. The market would be very small in countries with type (1) or (2) income patterns. One of the largest single markets for Lamborghinis turns out to be Portugal [income pattern (3)]—one of the poorer countries in Western Europe, but one with enough wealthy families to afford expensive cars.

Over the past three decades, the rich have grown richer, the middle class has shrunk, and the poor have remained poor. From 1973 to 1999, earnings for U.S. households in the top 5 percent of the income distribution grew 65 percent, compared with income growth of 11 percent for the middle fifth households during the same period. This is leading to a two-tier U.S. market, with affluent people buying expensive goods and working-class people spending more carefully, shopping at discount stores and factory outlet malls, and selecting less expensive store brands. Conventional retailers who offer medium-priced goods are the most vulnerable to these changes. Companies that respond to the trend by tailoring their products and pitches to these two very different Americas stand to gain.[29]

GAP   The GAP pursues a segmented market strategy with three tiers of retail clothing stores: the upscale Banana Republic, the mid-market GAP, and the budget-priced Old Navy. Jeans sell for $70 at Banana Republic stores and for as much as $50 at GAP stores, and Old Navy jeans sell for under $25. Each store has its own look, its own clothing lines, and its own in-house advertising. This segmented strategy helped The GAP grow from a $7 billion to a $14 billion business between 1996 and 2001.[30]

The Walt Disney Company   The Walt Disney Company, which owns the rights to A. A. Milne's Winnie-the-Pooh and his make-believe friends, is marketing two distinct Poohs. The original line-drawn figures appear on fine china, pewter spoons, and expensive kids' stationery found in upscale specialty and department stores like Nordstrom and Bloomingdale's. A plump, cartoonlike Pooh, clad in a red T-shirt and a goofy smile, adorns plastic key chains, polyester bedsheets, and animated videos. This downscaled Pooh sells at Wal-Mart and other discount stores.

SAVINGS, DEBT, AND CREDIT AVAILABILITY   Consumer expenditures are affected by savings, debt, and credit availability. The Japanese, for example, save about 13.1 percent of their income, whereas U.S. consumers save about 4.7 percent. The result has been that Japanese banks were able to loan money to Japanese companies at a much lower interest rate than U.S. banks could offer to U.S. companies. Access to lower interest rates helped Japanese companies expand faster. U.S. consumers also have a high debt-to-income ratio, which slows down further expenditures on housing and large-ticket items. Credit is very available in the United States but at fairly high interest rates, especially to lower-income borrowers. Here the Internet can offer a helping hand: Consumers seeking a mortgage can go to lendingtree.com, fill out a single loan application, and receive several loan package proposals from competing banks within 48 hours.

The bottom line is that marketers must pay careful attention to major changes in incomes, cost of living, interest rates, savings, and borrowing patterns because they can have a strong impact on business, especially for companies whose products are geared to high-income and price-sensitive consumers.

natural environment

The deterioration of the natural environment is a major global concern. In many world cities, air and water pollution have reached dangerous levels. There is great concern about "greenhouse gases" in the atmosphere due to the burning of fossil fuels, about the depletion of the ozone layer due to certain chemicals, and about growing shortages of water. In Western Europe, "green" parties have vigorously pressed for public action to reduce industrial pollution. In the United States, experts have documented ecological deterioration, and watchdog groups such as the Sierra Club and Friends of the Earth carry these concerns into political and social action.

New regulations hit certain industries very hard. Steel companies and public utilities have had to invest billions of dollars in pollution-control equipment and more environmentally friendly fuels. The auto industry has had to introduce expensive emission controls in cars. The soap industry has had to increase its products' biodegradability.

Marketers need to be aware of the threats and opportunities associated with four trends in the natural environment: the shortage of raw materials, especially water; the increased cost of energy; increased pollution levels; and the changing role of governments.

SHORTAGE OF RAW MATERIALS   The earth's raw materials consist of the infinite, the finite renewable, and the finite nonrenewable. Infinite resources, such as air and water, are becoming a problem. Water shortages are already a political issue, and the danger is no longer long term. Environmental groups have lobbied for a ban on certain propellants used in aerosol cans because of the potential damage they can cause to the ozone layer.

Finite *renewable* resources, such as forests and food, must be used wisely. Forestry companies are required to reforest timberlands in order to protect the soil and to ensure sufficient wood to meet future demand. Because the amount of arable land is fixed and urban areas are constantly encroaching on farmland, food supply can also be a major problem. Finite *nonrenewable* resources—oil, coal, platinum, zinc, silver—will pose a serious problem as the point of depletion approaches. Firms making products that require these increasingly scarce minerals face substantial cost increases. They may not find it easy to pass these cost increases on to customers. Firms engaged in research and development have an excellent opportunity to develop substitute materials.

INCREASED ENERGY COSTS   One finite nonrenewable resource, oil, has created serious problems for the world economy. In October 2000, oil prices shot up again to $34 a barrel, creating a renewed search for alternative energy forms. Companies are searching for practical means to harness solar, nuclear, wind, and other forms of energy. In the solar energy field alone, hundreds of firms introduced first-generation products to harness solar energy for heating homes and other uses. Other firms are engaged in building practical electric automobiles, with a potential prize of billions for the winner. Practical combination vehicles, like the Toyota Prius, are already available.

ANTI-POLLUTION PRESSURES   Some industrial activity will inevitably damage the natural environment. Consider the dangerous mercury levels in the ocean, the quantity of DDT and other chemical pollutants in the soil and food supply, and the littering of the environment with bottles, plastics, and other packaging materials.

About 42 percent of U.S. consumers are willing to pay higher prices for "green" products. This willingness creates a large market for pollution-control solutions, such as scrubbers, recycling centers, and landfill systems. It leads to a search for alternative ways to produce and package goods. 3M runs a Pollution Prevention Pays program that has led to a substantial reduction in pollution and costs. Dow Chemical built a new ethylene plant in Alberta that uses 40 percent less energy and releases 97 percent less wastewater. AT&T uses a special software package to choose the least harmful materials, cut hazardous waste, reduce energy use, and improve product recycling in its operations. McDonald's and Burger King eliminated polystyrene cartons and now use recyclable paper wrappings and paper napkins.[31]

CHANGING ROLE OF GOVERNMENTS   Governments vary in their concern and efforts to promote a clean environment. For example, the German government is vigorous in its pursuit of environmental quality, partly because of the strong green movement in Germany and partly because of the ecological devastation in the former East Germany. Many poor nations are doing little about pollution, largely because they lack the funds or the political will. It is in the richer nations' interest to help the poorer nations control their pollution, but even the richer nations today lack the necessary funds.

The major hope is that companies will increasingly adopt practices that will protect the natural environment. In their book *Natural Capitalism*, Paul Hawken and Amory and Hunter Lovins call upon companies to practice "a new type of industrialism" that will create profits and jobs while saving the environment.[32] They envision hybrid cars that will get 80 miles per gallon, manufacturers relentlessly recyling their products, super-efficient buildings, alternative energy sources, and other developments that will reduce energy and materials consumption by 90 percent. Great opportunities await companies and marketers who can create new solutions that promise to reconcile prosperity with environmental protection.

technological environment

One of the most dramatic forces shaping people's lives is technology. Technology has released such wonders as penicillin, open-heart surgery, and the birth control pill. It has released such horrors as the hydrogen bomb, nerve gas, and the submachine gun. It has also released such mixed blessings as the automobile and video games.

Every new technology is a force for "creative destruction." Transistors hurt the vacuum-tube industry, xerography hurt the carbon paper business, autos hurt the railroads, and television hurt the newspapers. Instead of moving into the new technologies, many old industries fought or ignored them, and their businesses declined. Yet it is the essence of market capitalism to be dynamic and tolerate the creative destructiveness of technology as the price of progress.

Encyclopaedia Britannica (EB). The two-hundred-year-old Encyclopaedia Britannica company is struggling to adapt to the digital age. It still publishes its 32-volume set costing over a thousand dollars. In 1993, Microsoft took the initiative and introduced its Encarta Encyclopedia CD-ROM, which was bundled with more than 50 million computers sold around the world. Reluctantly, and a little later, EB offered a CD-ROM version of its encyclopedia. EB finally went on the Web in 1994 with Britannica Online as a subscription service for colleges and universities. The next year it extended the service to consumers at a $150 a year. It subsequently lowered the price to $50 a year and then in 1999 offered it free, relying on advertising revenues. In 2000, Britannica.com turned itself into a portal to include weather and stock information. In 2001, it attempted to return to a subscription model. The print edition has never recovered from the digital assault, and EB is still trying to figure out what it wants to be on the Web.[33]

The economy's growth rate is affected by how many major new technologies are discovered. Unfortunately, technological discoveries do not arise evenly through time—the railroad industry created a lot of investment, and then investment petered out until the auto industry emerged. Later, radio created a lot of investment, which then petered out until television appeared. In the time between major innovations, an economy can stagnate. In the meantime, minor innovations fill the gap: freeze-dried coffee, combination shampoo and conditioner, antiperspirants and deodorants, and the like. They involve less risk, but they also divert research effort away from major breakthroughs.

New technology also creates major long-run consequences that are not always foreseeable. The contraceptive pill, for example, led to smaller families, more working wives, and larger discretionary incomes—resulting in higher expenditures on vacation travel, durable goods, and luxury items.

The marketer should monitor the following trends in technology: the pace of change, the opportunities for innovation, varying R&D budgets, and increased regulation.

ACCELERATING PACE OF CHANGE   Many of today's common products were not available 40 years ago. John F. Kennedy did not know personal computers, digital wristwatches, video recorders, fax machines, personal digital assistants, or the Internet; nor has the pace of technological change slowed down. The Human Genome project promises to usher in the Biological Century as biotech workers create new medical cures, new foods, and new materials (see "Marketing Memo: Biotech is Unleashing Unlimited Opportunities"). Electronic researchers are building smarter chips to make our cars, homes, and offices more responsive to changing conditions. The blending of personal computers, scanners, fax and copy machines, wireless phones, the Internet, and e-mail has made it possible for people to *telecommute*—that is, work at home or on the road instead of traveling to an office. This trend may reduce auto pollution, bring the family closer together, and create more home-centered shopping and entertainment.

An increasing number of ideas are being worked on, and the time between the appearance of new ideas and their successful implementation is all but disappearing. So is the time between introduction and peak production. Ninety percent of all the scientists who ever lived are alive today, and technology feeds upon itself.

However, bio-research companies will face challenging decisions. The investment cost and risks are extremely high, and the gain is extremely uncertain. Investors face *market uncertainties:* Witness the strong negative response to genetically modified food (GMF). They face *technological uncertainties:* Will the bio-product perform as promised and be ready on time? Investors face *regulatory uncertainty:* Governments might withhold approval of certain bio-products. This makes it imperative for companies to carry

Marketing
MEMO

Biotech is Unleashing Unlimited Opportunities

Many futurists are calling the new century the Biotech Century. Consider the following:

- *Faster computers:* Bio-researchers hope to build faster computers that replace solid-state transistors with molecules that alternate between binary states.
- *Customized medicine:* DNA chips will facilitate *personalized medicine.* Viviometrics' Life Shirt has enough electrodes and sensors to track over 40 of the wearer's vital signs.
- *Security techniques:* Biometric methods will identify people via fingerprint, iris, or facial scans.
- *New skin care products:* New skin care products reduce acne and wrinkles.
- *New enriched food products:* Genetically altered common foods will deliver nutritional or medical benefits. Altered bananas can deliver a hepatitis vaccine.
- *New materials:* There will be new materials for body-parts replacement, such as vascular grafts, intraocular lenses, hip implants, heart valves. Corrosion-resistant paints and resilient automotive panels retain their shape after dents.
- *Improved environmental cleanup:* Microorganisms will remove or render harmless pollutants and hazardous waste.
- *Improved seeds:* Genetically engineered seeds will create food that offers more nutrition or health solutions.

out marketing research to reduce the amount of uncertainty and to prepare marketing strategies aimed at gaining public and government support.

UNLIMITED OPPORTUNITIES FOR INNOVATION Scientists today are working on a startling range of new technologies that will revolutionize products and production processes. Some of the most exciting work is being done in biotechnology, computers, microelectronics, telecommunications, robotics, and designer materials. Researchers are working on AIDS cures, happiness pills, painkillers, totally safe contraceptives, and nonfattening foods. They are designing robots for firefighting, underwater exploration, and home nursing. In addition, scientists also work on fantasy products, such as small flying cars, three-dimensional television, and space colonies. The challenge in each case is to develop affordable versions of these products.

Companies are already harnessing the power of *virtual reality (VR)*, the combination of technologies that allows users to experience three-dimensional, computer-generated environments through sound, sight, and touch (see Figure 6.2). Virtual reality

figure **6.2**

Virtual Reality
Applications in Marketing

Virtual reality technology lets users interact with computer-generated worlds through sight, sound, and touch. A handset and some sort of handheld input device are necessary for many current VR applications. (left) CyberSim's VR program allows prospective home buyers to simulate their future homes and move around inside as if they were actually living in the as-yet-unbuilt house. (right) Another VR program allows prospective car buyers to simulate driving around town in the car of their choice.

marketing for the new economy

Smart Cards and Electronic Devices Will Revolutionize Payment

Today many people make their payments with credit or debit cards from Visa, Mastercharge, American Express, and other card issuers. In the United States alone, consumers have over 1 billion credit cards. Each card has a magnetic strip containing a limited amount of information.

Some years ago, telephone companies started to issue prepaid phone cards which stored a specified amount of value and could be inserted into slots in public phones to make phone calls. Consumers benefited by not needing coins when making a phone call. The issuers benefited by investing the prepaid money into earning assets.

Smart cards have moved beyond such single-use prepaid cards. Smart cards carry a computer chip that can store up to 32 kilobytes of data. They have the advantage of housing data on the card's chip with no need to access the store's computer in a time-consuming, dial-up connection. Many applications can be loyalty-based:

- A cardholder pays for his coffee by putting his smart card in his favorite coffee shop's smart card reader and a slip comes out saying that this coffee is his twentieth cup and therefore free.
- A cardholder uses his smart card to pay for his dress shirt purchase at a favorite department store and a slip comes out offering a 20 percent discount on any ties that he buys.

Smart cards mean that consumers no longer need to carry multiple cards and can use them for both online and off-line shopping. Consumers can install a smart card "reader" that enables them to make secure online purchases from home. They insert the smart card into the reader, type in their password, and complete the transaction. Smart cards can even be used for low-cost purchases, such as fast-food, vending machine, and public transportation purchases.

The use of smart cards is growing fast, particularly in Asia and Europe. In Germany, over 70 million smart cards serve as identification and payment methods for health insurance holders. Consumers in England and France use smart cards to decipher scrambled television signals from subscription services. In America, American Express had issued 6 million of its smart-equipped Blue cards by 2001, and Visa had issued 1.5 million smart cards.

An alternative to the smart card is the use of cellular phones or Palm-like appliances to send an infrared signal to complete a transaction. The consumer pays a restaurant bill by clicking the appliance in the direction of the restaurant's terminal, thus transferring funds from his or her bank account to the restaurant's bank account; or the consumer approaches a Coke vending machine, clicks a Palm, and a Coke drops out.

Sources: Patricia Sabatini, "Getting Smarter for Years, All-In-One Smart Cards Have Been on the Horizon," *Pittsburgh Post-Gazette*, July 1, 2001; "Europeans Prove Themselves Adept with Smart Cards," *Associated Press*, February 2, 2001; "Visa Issued 42m Smart Cards Worldwide," *New Straits Times*, April 13, 2001.

---

has already been applied to gathering consumer reactions to new automobile designs, kitchen layouts, exterior home designs, and other potential offerings. (For another innovation, see "Marketing for the New Economy: Smart Cards and Electronic Devices Will Revolutionize Payment.")

VARYING R&D BUDGETS   The United States leads the world in annual R&D expenditures, $264 billion in 2000, but nearly 60 percent of these funds are still earmarked for defense. There is a need to transfer more of this money into research on material science, biotechnology, and micromechanics. Japan has increased its R&D expenditures much faster than has the United States and is spending it mostly on nondefense-related research in physics, biophysics, and computer science.[34]

A growing portion of U.S. R&D expenditures is going into the development side of R&D, raising concerns about whether the United States can maintain its lead in basic science. Many companies are content to put their money into copying competitors' products and making minor feature and style improvements. Even basic-research companies such as DuPont, Bell Laboratories, and Pfizer are proceeding cautiously, and more research directed toward major breakthroughs is being conducted by consortiums of companies rather than by single companies.

INCREASED REGULATION OF TECHNOLOGICAL CHANGE   As products become more complex, the public needs to be assured of their safety. Consequently, government agencies' powers to investigate and ban potentially unsafe products have been expanded. In the United States, the Federal Food and Drug Administration must approve all drugs before they can be sold. Safety and health regulations have also increased in the areas of food, automobiles, clothing, electrical appliances, and construction. Marketers must be aware of these regulations when proposing, developing, and launching new products.

political-legal environment

Marketing decisions are strongly affected by developments in the political and legal environment. This environment is composed of laws, government agencies, and pressure groups that influence and limit various organizations and individuals. Sometimes these laws also create new opportunities for business. For example, mandatory recycling laws have given the recycling industry a major boost and spurred the creation of dozens of new companies making new products from recycled materials.

Wellman In 1993, Wellman introduced EcoSpun post consumer recycled (PCR) fiber, made from recycled soda bottles, and sold 800,000 pounds in that first year alone. At the Outdoor Retailer Winter Market in 1998, Wellman introduced its EcoSpun®, 100 percent certified recycled polyester fiber, which has moisture-management properties and was designed specifically for a performance-apparel market anxious to jump aboard the recycling bandwagon. Today, Wellman is an international corporation and one of the world's largest recyclers of plastics, with capacity to reclaim almost 3 billion bottles and containers annually.

LEGISLATION REGULATING BUSINESS Business legislation has three main purposes: to protect companies from unfair competition, to protect consumers from unfair business practices, and to protect the interests of society from unbridled business behavior. A major purpose of business legislation and enforcement is to charge businesses with the social costs created by their products or production processes. A central concern about business legislation is: At what point do the costs of regulation exceed the benefits? The laws are not always administered fairly; regulators and enforcers may be lax or overzealous. Although each new law may have a legitimate rationale, it may have the unintended effect of sapping initiative and retarding economic growth.

Legislation affecting business has steadily increased over the years. The European Commission has been active in establishing a new framework of laws covering competitive behavior, product standards, product liability, and commercial transactions for the 15 member nations of the European Union. Ex-Soviet nations are rapidly passing laws to promote and regulate an open-market economy. The United States has many laws on its books covering such issues as competition, product safety and liability, fair trade and credit practices, and packaging and labeling.[35] Several countries have gone farther than the United States in passing strong consumer-protection legislation. Norway bans several forms of sales promotion—trading stamps, contests, premiums—as inappropriate or "unfair" instruments for promoting products. Thailand requires food processors selling national brands to market low-price brands also, so that low-income consumers can find economy brands. In India, food companies need special approval to launch brands that duplicate what already exists on the market, such as another cola drink or brand of rice.

Marketers must have a good working knowledge of the major laws protecting competition, consumers, and society. Companies generally establish legal review procedures and promulgate ethical standards to guide their marketing managers, and as more business takes place in cyberspace, marketers must establish new parameters for doing electronic business ethically.

Publishers Clearing House Beginning in 1999, attorneys general in 24 states and the District of Columbia filed class action lawsuits alleging that Publishers Clearing House engaged in deceptive marketing practices. The suits claimed that the company used deceptive sweepstakes promotions to entice customers to buy magazine subscriptions. Fine print in promotional mailings informs customers of their limited chances of winning and the fact that they are under no obligation to buy. The print, lawyers claimed, was too fine, especially for elderly customers. One Illinois man spent $19,000 over five years on subscriptions in order to "stay in the sweepstakes." In August 2000 the company agreed to reform its business practices and refund $16 million to its customers.[36]

GROWTH OF SPECIAL-INTEREST GROUPS   The number and power of special-interest groups have increased over the past three decades. Political action committees (PACs) lobby government officials and pressure business executives to pay more attention to consumers' rights, women's rights, senior citizens' rights, minority rights, and gay rights. Many companies have established public affairs departments to deal with these groups and issues. An important force affecting business is the **consumerist movement**—an organized movement of citizens and government to strengthen the rights and powers of buyers in relation to sellers. Consumerists have advocated and won the right to know the true interest cost of a loan, the true cost per standard unit of competing brands (unit pricing), the basic ingredients in a product, the nutritional quality of food, the freshness of products, and the true benefits of a product.

In response, several companies have established consumer affairs departments to help formulate policies and respond to consumer complaints. Companies are careful to answer their e-mail and to resolve and learn from any customer complaints. If they fail to do so, angry customers can spread bad word of mouth through chat rooms and other means.

Clearly, new laws and growing numbers of pressure groups have put more restraints on marketers. Marketers have to clear their plans with the company's legal, public-relations, public-affairs, and consumer-affairs departments. Insurance companies directly or indirectly affect the design of smoke detectors; scientific groups affect the design of spray products by condemning aerosols. In essence, many private marketing transactions have moved into the public domain.

social-cultural environment

Society shapes our beliefs, values, and norms. People absorb, almost unconsciously, a worldview that defines their relationships to themselves, to others, to organizations, to society, to nature, and to the universe.

- *Views of themselves:* People vary in the relative emphasis they place on self-gratification. In the United States during the 1960s and 1970s, "pleasure seekers" sought fun, change, and escape. Others sought "self-realization." People bought dream cars and dream vacations and spent more time in health activities (jogging, tennis), in introspection, and in arts and crafts. Today, some people are adopting more conservative behaviors and ambitions. Marketers must recognize that there are many different groups with different views of themselves.

- *Views of others:* People are concerned about the homeless, crime and victims, and other social problems. They would like to live in a more humane society. At the same time, people are seeking out their "own kind" and avoiding strangers. They hunger for serious and long-lasting relationships with a few others. These trends portend a growing market for social-support products and services that promote direct relations between human beings, such as health clubs, cruises, and religious activity. They also suggest a growing market for "social surrogates," things that allow people who are alone to feel that they are not, such as television, home video games, and chat rooms on the Internet.

- *Views of organizations:* People vary in their attitudes toward corporations, government agencies, trade unions, and other organizations. Most people are willing to work for these organizations, but there has been an overall decline in organizational loyalty. The massive wave of company downsizings has bred cynicism and distrust. Many people today see work not as a source of satisfaction, but as a required chore to earn money to enjoy their nonwork hours.

marketing **insight**

Cause-Related Marketing

The 1980s saw the advent of "cause-related marketing." Varadarajan and Menon define **cause–related marketing** as "the process of formulating and implementing marketing activities that are characterized by an offer from the firm to contribute a specified amount to a designated cause when customers engage in revenue-providing exchanges that satisfy organizational and individual objectives." The distinctive feature of cause-related marketing is the firm's contribution to a designated cause being linked to customers' engaging in revenue-producing transactions with the firm.

Many observers credit American Express with raising awareness of the mutual benefits of cause-related marketing through its 1983 campaign to help restore the Statue of Liberty. Donating a penny for every credit-card transaction and a dollar for each new card issued, American Express gave $1.7 million to the Statue of Liberty—Ellis Island Foundation. In the process, transactions for American Express rose 30 percent, and new cards issued increased by 15 per cent during this period. Later, American Express initiated the "Charge Against Hunger" campaign in 1993. The campaign, which raised $5 million in its first year, contributed three cents to feed the hungry every time members used their American Express cards during the months of November and December.

Cause-related marketing comes in many forms. Consider some of the range of programs evident in the United Kingdom. Tesco, a leading retailer, has created a "Computer for Schools" program whereby customers receive vouchers for every 10 pounds spent, which can be donated to the school of their choice; the school can then exchange them for new computer equip-

ment. Andrex, a leading brand of toilet paper, leverages its advertising symbol of a global Labrador puppy to develop on-pack promotions and other marketing inducements to benefit Guide Dogs for the Blind. Austin Reed menswear introduced a "Suit Exchange" program whereby customers received a discount on a new suit for donating an old suit to benefit the homeless. Birds Eye frozen foods has provided financial support via consumer promotions for years to support the life-saving efforts of the Royal National Lifeboat Institution. Flora, a leading brand of margarine with a long-term positioning as a healthier alternative to butter, has been a long-term sponsor of the London Marathon.

The danger is that the promotional efforts behind a cause-related marketing program could backfire if cynical consumers question the link between the product and the cause and see the firm as being self-serving and exploitative as a result. Perhaps the most important benefit of cause-related marketing is that it humanizes the firm, and consumers may develop a strong, unique bond with the firm that transcends normal marketplace transactions.

Sources: P. Rajan Varadarajan and Anil Menon, "Cause-Related Marketing: A Coalignment of Marketing Strategy and Corporate Philanthropy," *Journal of Marketing* 52 (July 1988): 58–74; Richard Earle, *The Art of Cause Marketing: How to Use Advertising to Change Personal Behavior and Public Policy* (Lincolnwood, Il.: NTC Business Books, 2000); Hamish Pringle and Marjorie Thompson, *How Cause Related Marketing Builds Brands* (New York: John Wiley & Sons, 1999); Greg Goldin, "Cause-Related Marketing Grows Up," *ADWEEK*, November 17, 1987, pp. 20–22; Ronald Alsop, "More Firms Push Promotion Aimed at Consumers' Hearts," *Wall Street Journal*, August 29, 1985, p. 23; Yumiko Ono, "Do-Good Ads Aim for Sales That Do Better," *Wall Street Journal*, September 2, 1994, p. B-8.

This outlook has several marketing implications. Companies need to find new ways to win back consumer and employee confidence. They need to make sure that they are good corporate citizens and that their consumer messages are honest.

- *Views of society:* People vary in their attitudes toward their society. Some defend it (preservers), some run it (makers), some take what they can from it (takers), some want to change it (changers), some are looking for something deeper (seekers), and some want to leave it (escapers).[37] Consumption patterns often reflect social attitude. Makers tend to be high achievers who eat, dress, and live well. Changers usually live more frugally, driving smaller cars and wearing simpler clothes. Escapers and seekers are a major market for movies, music, surfing, and camping.
- *Views of nature:* People vary in their attitudes toward nature. Some feel subjugated by it, others feel in harmony with it, and still others seek mastery over it. A long-term trend has been humankind's growing mastery of nature through technology. More recently, however, people have awakened to nature's fragility and finite resources. They recognize that nature can be destroyed by human activities.

Business has responded to increased interest in camping, hiking, boating, and fishing with hiking boots, tenting equipment, and other gear. Tour operators are packaging tours to wilderness areas. Food producers have found growing markets for "natural" products: Two natural-food grocery stores, Whole Foods Markets and Fresh Fields, merged in 1997 with sales of $1.1 billion.

■ *Views of the universe:* People vary in their beliefs about the origin of the universe and their place in it. Most Americans are monotheistic, although religious conviction and practice have been waning through the years. Certain evangelical movements are reaching out to bring people back into organized religion. Some of the religious impulse has been redirected into an interest in Eastern religions, mysticism, the occult, and the human potential movement.

As people lose their religious orientation, they seek self-fulfillment and immediate gratification. At the same time, every trend seems to breed a countertrend, as indicated by a worldwide rise in religious fundamentalism. Here are some other cultural characteristics of interest to marketers: the persistence of core cultural values, the existence of subcultures, and shifts of values through time.

HIGH PERSISTENCE OF CORE CULTURAL VALUES   The people living in a particular society hold many *core beliefs* and values that tend to persist. Most Americans still believe in work, in getting married, in giving to charity, and in being honest. Core beliefs and values are passed on from parents to children and are reinforced by major social institutions—schools, churches, businesses, and governments. *Secondary beliefs* and values are more open to change. Believing in the institution of marriage is a core belief; believing that people ought to get married early is a secondary belief. Thus family-planning marketers could make some headway arguing that people should get married later, rather than that they should not get married at all.

Marketers have some chance of changing secondary values but little chance of changing core values. For instance, the nonprofit organization Mothers Against Drunk Drivers (MADD) does not try to stop the sale of alcohol, but it does promote the idea of appointing a designated driver who will not drink that evening. The group also lobbies to raise the legal drinking age.

EXISTENCE OF SUBCULTURES   Each society contains **subcultures**, groups with shared values emerging from their special life experiences or circumstances. *Star Trek* fans, Black Muslims, and Hell's Angels all represent subcultures whose members share common beliefs, preferences, and behaviors. To the extent that subcultural groups exhibit different wants and consumption behavior, marketers can choose particular subcultures as target markets.

Marketers sometimes reap unexpected rewards in targeting subcultures. For instance, marketers have always loved teenagers because they are society's trendsetters in fashion, music, entertainment, ideas, and attitudes. Marketers also know that if they attract someone as a teen, there is a good chance they will keep the person as a customer in the years ahead. Frito-Lay, which draws 15 percent of its sales from teens, said it saw a rise in chip-snacking by grown-ups. "We think it's because we brought them in as teenagers," said Frito-Lay marketing director.[38]

SHIFTS OF SECONDARY CULTURAL VALUES THROUGH TIME   Although core values are fairly persistent, cultural swings do take place. In the 1960s, hippies, the Beatles, Elvis Presley, and other cultural phenomena had a major impact on young people's hairstyles, clothing, sexual norms, and life goals. Today's young people are influenced by new heroes and new activities: U2's Bono, Tiger Woods, and extreme sports.

summary

1. Successful companies realize that the marketing environment presents a never-ending series of opportunities and threats. The major responsibility for identifying significant changes in the macroenvironment falls to a company's marketers. More than any other group in the company, marketing managers must be the trend trackers and opportunity seekers.

2. Many opportunities are found by identifying trends (directions or sequences of events that have some momentum and durability) and megatrends (major social, economic, political, and technological changes that have long-lasting influence).

3. Within the rapidly changing global picture, marketers must monitor six major environmental forces: demographic, economic, natural, technological, political-legal, and social-cultural.

4. In the demographic environment, marketers must be aware of worldwide population growth; changing mixes of age, ethnic composition, and educational levels; the rise of nontraditional families; large geographic shifts in population; and the move to micromarketing and away from mass marketing.

5. In the economic arena, marketers need to focus on income distribution and levels of savings, debt, and credit availability.

6. In the natural environment, marketers need to be aware of raw materials shortages, increased energy costs and pollution levels, and the changing role of governments in environmental protection.

7. In the technological arena, marketers should take account of the accelerating pace of technological change, opportunities for innovation, varying R&D budgets, and the increased governmental regulation brought about by technological change.

8. In the political-legal environment, marketers must work within the many laws regulating business practices and with various special-interest groups.

9. In the social-cultural arena, marketers must understand people's views of themselves, others, organizations, society, nature, and the universe. They must market products that correspond to society's core and secondary values, and address the needs of different subcultures within a society.

applications

marketing debate

Is consumer behavior more a function of a person's age or generation?

One of the widely debated issues in developing marketing programs that target certain age groups is how much consumers change over time. Some marketers maintain that age differences are critical and that the needs and wants of a 25-year-old in 2002 is not that different from those of a 25-year-old

in 1972. Others dispute that contention and argue that cohort and generation effects are critical and that marketing programs must therefore suit the times.

Take a position: Age differences are fundamentally more important than cohort effects versus cohort effects can dominate age differences.

marketing and advertising

1. Coppertone in Figure 1 is always alert to demographic changes that can affect the marketing of its sunscreen products. As this Italian ad demonstrates, the company offers products for both adults and children. In planning the marketing approach for these products, Coppertone managers had to examine Italy's population growth, age mix, and household patterns.

   a. What sources of information can you identify for data about the demographic environment in Italy?

   b. Assume that the birth rate has been dropping, reducing the average household size in Italy. What are the implications for Coppertone's marketing efforts?

   c. What other environmental factors should Coppertone pay particular attention to when planning its advertising for sunscreen products in Italy?

2. Nearly every state in the United States conducts ongoing marketing campaigns to bring businesses to the area. This ad in Figure 2 which appeared in *Inc.* magazine, seeks to attract businesses to Colorado. Most of the copy focuses on the state's natural environment, although it also mentions the labor force and an existing cluster of high-tech companies.

   a. Why would a business consider the natural environment of a state when making a decision about relocation or expansion? How does Colorado's ad address these considerations?

   b. What view of nature does this ad imply through its use of graphics and copy? Relate this view to the company's relocation/expansion decision discussed in (a).

   c. What other environmental elements are mentioned in the ad that would be meaningful to a business making a relocation decision? Can you suggest additional environmental elements that Colorado marketers should incorporate into this type of campaign?

Figure 1

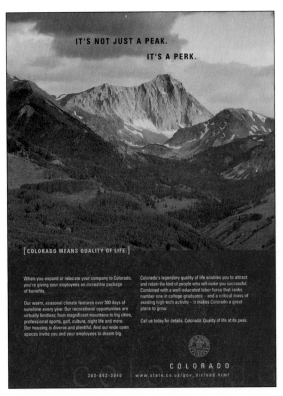

Figure 2

online marketing today

Peapod, one of the pioneers of online grocery retailing, has learned to use changes in the marketing environment to its advantage. Increased diversity is opening new opportunities to offer online shopping and home delivery of groceries to Americans with disabilities. In addition, the company closely follows the economic environment, which influences its customers as well as its competitors. Peapod entered the metropolitan Washington, DC, market by buying the distribution center of failed competitor Streamline.com, which ran out of money during the start of an economic downturn. When venture capital funding ran out for Homeruns.com, a second competitor, Peapod quickly expanded to cover customers in areas that Homeruns.com had once served. Peapod is itself influenced by the economic environment, as well: In search of higher profits, the company has stopped offering free delivery in most markets.[39]

Visit Peapod's home page www.peapod.com, examine the listing of markets served, and read about the benefits for customers. Then follow the "About Peapod" link to learn more about the company's history, goals, and links with employees and affiliates. How has the demographic environment influenced Peapod's choice of markets? How has the economic environment influenced its choice? How do the benefits cited on the home page relate to current trends in the marketing environment?

you're the marketer: sonic pda marketing plan

Every company has to examine its macroenvironment to understand the key developments that shape market opportunities and pose threats to marketing effectiveness. This environmental scanning uncovers emerging trends and changes that can potentially affect the needs and responses of customers, the competition, and the firm's markets.

Jane Melody asks you to scan Sonic's external environment for signs of change that indicate opportunities and threats for the company's PDA product. Review Sonic's current situation and then, using library or Internet resources (or both), locate information to answer the following questions about Sonic's macroenvironment:

■ What demographic changes are likely to affect Sonic's two target markets, middle- to upper-income professionals and mid- to large-sized corporations? One source for this kind of data is the government's annual *Statistical Abstract of the United States* publication <*www.census.gov/prod/www/ statistical-abstract-us.html*>.

- What economic trends might influence the future of the PDA market? Check the Commerce Department's Stat-USA site *<www.stat-usa.gov>*, especially key topics within the General Economic Indicators section under the "State of the Nation" heading, looking for statistics about changes and trends in consumer buying power and related economic topics.
- What technological changes can potentially affect PDA development, buyer acceptance of PDAs, and the development of substitute products? One online source to search is TechNews World *<www.technewsworld.com>*, which reviews national and international technology developments.
- What current or emerging political-legal issues are likely to affect PDAs? Growing concerns over exposure to cell-phone radiation may lead to new legislation for Web-enabled cell phones that compete with Sonic's PDA. CNET's wireless information site *<www.wireless.cnet.com>* is only one of many sites to check for updates on this situation.

Once you have completed your environmental scan, analyze the results and their implications for Sonic's marketing efforts. Summarize your findings and conclusions in a written marketing plan or enter them into the Macroenvironment, Market Analysis, and SWOT Analysis sections of a plan prepared with *Marketing Plan Pro* software.

notes

1. Gene Del Vecchio, "Keeping It Timeless, Trendy," *Advertising Age*, March 23, l998, p. 24.
2. Said by Flip Filipowski, who is described in Howard Wolinsky, "The Prophet of the Silicon Prairie," *The Industry Standard*, December 13-20, 1999, p. 90.
3. Jeff Manning, "Hollywood Forecasts Bright Video Future," *The Oregonian*, January 16, 2000.
4. "Hughes Electronics Earnings—3: DirecTV Subscribers at 9.5 Million," Dow Jones News Service, January 16, 2001.
5. Gerald Celente, *Trend Tracking* (New York: Warner Books, 1991).
6. Faith Popcorn, *The Popcorn Report* (New York: HarperBusiness, 1992).
7. John Naisbitt and Patricia Aburdene, *Megatrends 2000* (New York: Avon Books, 1990).
8. Jennifer Lach, "Dateline America: May 1, 2025," *American Demographics* (May 1999): 19–20.
9. Pam Weisz, "Border Crossings: Brands Unify Image to Counter Cult of Culture," *Brandweek*, October 31, 1994, pp. 24–28.
10. World POPClock, U.S. Census Bureau, *<www.census.gov>*, September 1999.
11. Taken from The World Village Project Web site, *<www.WorldVillage.org>*, March 2000.
12. Donella H. Meadows, Dennis L. Meadows, Jorgen Randers, and William W. Behrens III, *The Limits to Growth* (New York: New American Library, 1972), p. 41.
13. Philip Kotler and Eduardo Roberto, *Social Marketing: Strategies for Changing Public Attitudes* (New York: The Free Press, 1989) and Philip Kotler, Ned Roberts, and Nancy Lee, *Social Marketing: Improving the Quality of Life* (Thousand Oaks, CA: Sage, 2002).
14. Sally D. Goll, "Marketing: China (Only) Children Get the Royal Treatment," *Wall Street Journal*, February 8, 1995, p. B1.
15. Bill Stoneman, "Beyond Rocking the Ages: An Interview with J. Walker Smith," *American Demographics* (May 1998): 45–49; Margot Hornblower, "Great X," *Time*, June 9, l997, pp. 58–59; Bruce Horowitz, "Gen X in a Class by Itself," *USA Today*, September 23, 1996, p. B1.
16. "Striking a Chord," *Brandweek*, April 17, 2000.
17. Michael J. McCarthy, "Mountain Dew Goes Urban to Revamp Country Image," *Wall Street Journal*, April 19, 1989; "Top-10 U.S. Soft Drink Companies and Brands for 2000," *Beverage Digest*, February 15, 2001.
18. David Leonhardt, "Hey Kids, Buy This," *BusinessWeek*, June 30, 1997, pp. 62–67; Don Tapscott, *"Growing up Digital; The Rise of the Net Generation* (New York: McGraw Hill 1997).
19. J. Walker Smith and Ann Clurman, *Rocking the Ages: The Yankelovich Report on Generational Marketing* (New York: HarperBusiness, 1998).
20. For descriptions on the buying habits and marketing approaches to African Americans and Latinos, see Chester A. Swenson, *Selling to a Segmented Market: The Lifestyle Approach* (Lincolnwood, IL: NTC Business Books, 1992).
21. Jacquelyn Lynn, "Tapping the Riches of Bilingual Markets," *Management Review* (March 1995): 56–61; Mark R. Forehand and Rohit Deshpandé "What We See Makes Us Who We Are: Priming Ethnic Self-Awareness and Advertising Response," *Journal of Marketing Research*, August 2001, pp. 336–48.
22. Laura Koss-Feder, "Out and About," *Marketing News*, May 25, 1998, pp. 1, 20.
23. Susan Kastner, "A Tiny Agency's Ingenious Campaign Has Turned the Vodka into a Cult for both Drinkers and Advertisers," *Toronto Star*, January 26, 1997; Stuart Elliot, "Absolut Customizes a Campaign to Salute GLAAD," *New York Times*, February 22, 2001.
24. Barbara Hetzer, "Find a Niche and Start Scratching," *BusinessWeek*, September 14, 1998. "Population Reference Bureau Issues Report on 'The Rural Rebound,' " *US Newswire*, September 29, 1999.
25. Kenneth M. Johnson and Calvin L. Beale, "The Rural Rebound," *The Wilson Quarterly* (Spring 1998): 16–27.
26. Robert Kelly, "It Felt Like Home—More Are Making Move to Small Towns," *St. Louis Post-Dispatch*, April 27, 1997, p. D6.
27. Dan Fost, "Americans on the Move," *American Demographics* (Tools Supplement, January–February 1997): 10–13.
28. Lauri J. Flynn, "Not Just a Copy Shop Any Longer, Kinko's Pushes Its Computer Services," *New York Times*, July 6, 1998, p. D1; *<www.kinkos.com>*.

29. David Leonhardt, "Two-Tier Marketing," *BusinessWeek*, March 17, 1997, pp. 82–90; and Robert H. Franc, "Yes the Rich Get Richer, But There's More to the Story," *Columbia Journalism Review*, November 1, 2000.

30. Barbara Lippert, "Tailor-Made," *Adweek*, May 10, 1999; *<www.gap.com>*; *<www.oldnavy.com>*.

31. Francoise L. Simon, "Marketing Green Products in the Triad," *The Columbia Journal of World Business* (Fall and Winter 1992): 268–85; and Jacquelyn A. Ottman, *Green Marketing: Responding to Environmental Consumer Demands* (Lincolnwood, IL: NTC Business Books, 1993); Ajay Menon and Anil Menon, "Enviropreneurial Marketing Strategy: The Emergence of Corporate Environmentalism as Market Strategy, *Journal of Marketing* (January 1997): 51–67; Michael Rothschild (1999), "Carrots, Sticks, and Promises: A Conceptual Framework for the Management of Public Health and Social Issue Behaviors," *Journal of Marketing*, (October 1999): 29–37.

32. Paul Hawken, Amory B. Lovins, and L. Hunter Lovins, *Natural Capitalism: Creating the Next Industrial Revolution* (Boston: Little, Brown, 1999).

33. Ronna Abramson, "Look Under 'M' for Mess," *The Industry Standard*, April 9, 2001, pp. 56–57.

34. "U.S. R&D Expenditures Have Increased," *Advanced Materials and Processes*, Feb. 1, 2001.

35. See Dorothy Cohen, *Legal Issues on Marketing Decision Making* (Cincinnati: South-Western, 1995).

36. Paul Wenske, "You Too Could Lose $19,000!" *Kansas City Star*, October 31, 1999; "Clearing House Suit Chronology," Associated Press, January 26, 2001.

37. Arnold Mitchell of the Stanford Research Institute, private publication.

38. Laura Zinn, "Teens: Here Comes the Biggest Wave Yet," *BusinessWeek*, April 11, 1994, pp. 76–86.

39. "Peapod Halts Free Delivery," *Supermarket News*, August 27, 2001, p. 6; "Peapod Expands Service," *CNNfn*, August 7, 2001, *<www.cnnfn.com>*.

7

analyzing consumer markets and buyer behavior

In this chapter, we will address the following questions:

- How do the buyer's characteristics—cultural, social, personal, and psychological—influence buying behavior?
- How does the buyer make purchasing decisions?

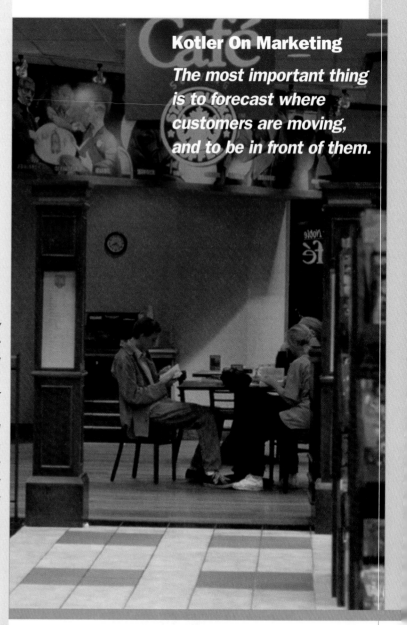

Kotler On Marketing

The most important thing is to forecast where customers are moving, and to be in front of them.

The aim of marketing is to meet and satisfy target customers' needs and wants. The field of consumer behavior studies how individuals, groups, and organizations select, buy, use, and dispose of goods, services, ideas, or experiences to satisfy their needs and desires.

Understanding consumer behavior and "knowing customers" is never simple. Customers may say one thing but do another. They may not be in touch with their deeper motivations. They may respond to influences that change their minds at the last minute. Small companies, such as a corner grocery store, and huge corporations, such as Whirlpool, stand to profit from understanding how and why their customers buy:

Whirlpool Corporation   In the appliance industry, consumer brand loyalties are built up over decades and passed from generation to generation. To shake up entrenched market shares and tap into consumers' often unexpressed needs, appliance giant Whirlpool Corporation hired an anthropologist. The anthropologist went to people's homes, observed how they used their appliances, and talked with all the household members. Whirlpool found that in busy families, women are not the only ones doing the laundry. Armed with this knowledge, company engineers came up with color-coded washer and dryer controls to make it easier for kids and men to pitch in.[1]

Net-Temps   Net-Temps, an online recruiting service for the staffing industry headquartered in Chelmsford, Massachusetts, installed monitoring and tracking tools on its Website to better understand the behavior of its customers. The tools measure the frequency of visits to the Net-Temps site, determine repeat visits, and track advertising. Monitoring software helps the company figure out which temp jobs are in the greatest demand. Net-Temps was recently named the number-one job board for contract professionals in the 2000 Electronic Recruiting Index.[2]

Not understanding your customers' motivations, needs, and preferences can hurt. Consider what happened when Wal-Mart opened its stores in Latin America. Sales have been disappointing, and the question has been raised as to whether Wal-Mart's magic can work in Latin America.

Wal-Mart designed its Latin American stores like those in the United States: narrow aisles crowded with merchandise, huge parking lots, many products with red, white, and blue banners, and so on. However, Latin American shoppers expect wider aisles since they come with larger families; many do not have a car and need door-to-door bus transportation, and the red/white/blue banners seem like Yankee imperialism. Even the Sam's Clubs flopped because the company's huge multipack items were too large for shoppers with small apartments and small disposable incomes. Wal-Mart forgot to study the customer.[3]

Studying customers provides clues for developing new products, product features, prices, channels, messages, and other marketing-mix elements. This chapter explores individual consumers' buying dynamics; the next chapter explores the buying dynamics of business buyers.

influencing buyer behavior

The starting point for understanding buyer behavior is the stimulus-response model shown in Figure 7.1. Marketing and environmental stimuli enter the buyer's consciousness. The buyer's characteristics and decision processes lead to certain purchase decisions. The marketer's task is to understand what happens in the buyer's consciousness between the arrival of outside stimuli and the purchase decisions.

A consumer's buying behavior is influenced by cultural, social, personal, and psychological factors. Cultural factors exert the broadest and deepest influence.

cultural factors

Culture, subculture, and social class are particularly important in buying behavior. **Culture** is the fundamental determinant of a person's wants and behavior. The growing child acquires a set of values, perceptions, preferences, and behaviors through his or her family and other key institutions. A child growing up in the United States is exposed to the following values: achievement and success, activity, efficiency and practicality, progress, material comfort, individualism, freedom, external comfort, humanitarianism, and youthfulness.[4]

Each culture consists of smaller **subcultures** that provide more specific identification and socialization for their members. Subcultures include nationalities, religions, racial groups, and geographic regions. When subcultures grow large and affluent

Model of Buyer Behavior

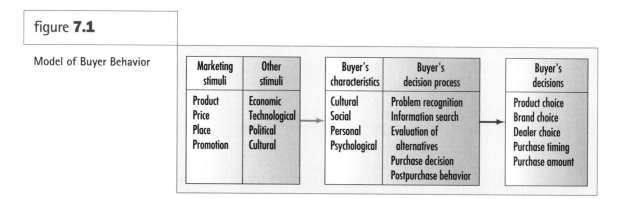

Marketing stimuli	Other stimuli		Buyer's characteristics	Buyer's decision process		Buyer's decisions
Product	Economic		Cultural	Problem recognition		Product choice
Price	Technological		Social	Information search		Brand choice
Place	Political		Personal	Evaluation of		Dealer choice
Promotion	Cultural		Psychological	alternatives		Purchase timing
				Purchase decision		Purchase amount
				Postpurchase behavior		

enough, companies often design specialized marketing programs to serve them. Such programs are known as **diversity marketing**, a practice which was pioneered during the 1980s by large companies like AT&T, Sears Roebuck, and Coca-Cola. Diversity marketing grew out of careful marketing research, which revealed that different ethnic and demographic niches did not always respond favorably to mass-market advertising. (See "Marketing Insight: Marketing to Latinos, African Americans, and Seniors.")

Virtually all human societies exhibit social stratification. Stratification sometimes takes the form of a caste system where the members of different castes are reared for certain roles and cannot change their caste membership. More frequently, it takes the form of **social classes**, relatively homogeneous and enduring divisions in a society, which are hierarchically ordered and whose members share similar values, interests, and behavior.

Social classes reflect not only income, but other indicators such as occupation, education, and area of residence. Social classes differ in dress, speech patterns, recreational preferences, and many other characteristics. Table 7.1 describes the seven U.S. social classes identified by social scientists.

Social classes have several characteristics. First, those within each class tend to behave more alike than persons from two different social classes. Second, persons are perceived as occupying inferior or superior positions according to social class. Third, social class is indicated by a cluster of variables—for example, occupation, income, wealth, education, and value orientation—rather than by any single variable. Fourth, individuals can move up or down the social-class ladder during their lifetimes. The extent of this mobility varies according to how rigid the social stratification is in a given society.

Social classes show distinct product and brand preferences in many areas, including clothing, home furnishings, leisure activities, and automobiles. Social classes differ in media preferences, with upper-class consumers preferring magazines and books and lower-class consumers preferring television. Even within a media category such as TV, upper-class consumers prefer news and drama, and lower-class consumers prefer soap operas and sports programs. There are also language differences among the social classes. Advertising copy and dialogue must ring true to the targeted social class.

social factors

In addition to cultural factors, a consumer's behavior is influenced by such social factors as reference groups, family, and social roles and statuses.

REFERENCE GROUPS A person's **reference groups** consist of all the groups that have a direct (face-to-face) or indirect influence on the person's attitudes or behavior. Groups having a direct influence on a person are called **membership groups**. Some membership groups are **primary groups**, such as family, friends, neighbors, and co-workers, with whom the person interacts fairly continuously and informally. People also belong

marketing **insight**

Marketing to Latinos, African Americans, and Seniors

Latinos

Expected to account for a quarter of the U.S. population by 2050, Latinos (also called Hispanic Americans) are the fastest growing minority, and soon will be the largest minority in the country. Annual Latino purchasing power is $630 billion on everything from cars to computers. The top five markets for Latinos in the United States are located in Los Angeles, New York City, Miami, Chicago, and San Francisco.

The Latino segment is difficult for marketers. Roughly two dozen nationalities can be classified as "Latino," including Cuban, Mexican, Puerto Rican, Dominican, and other Central and South American groups. The Latino group contains a mix of cultures, physical types, racial backgrounds, and aspirations. Yet despite their differences, Latinos often share strong family values, a need for respect, product loyalty, and a strong interest in product quality. Of course, the main common denominator is language: Marketers that reach out to Latinos with targeted Spanish-language promotions or ads stand to reap big benefits. The best medium for reaching Latinos is Spanish-language TV. Hispanics tend to watch more TV than the average American, and they prefer viewing in their native language.

African Americans

The purchasing power of the country's 34 million African Americans exploded during the prosperous 1990s. African American purchasing power was over $500 billion in 2000. What did African Americans spend their money on? Boys' clothing, athletic footwear, personal care services, and auto rentals. They tend to be strongly motivated by quality and selection, and shop more at neighborhood stores.

Many companies have been successful at tailoring products to meet the needs of African Americans. In 1987, Hallmark Cards, Inc. launched its Afrocentric brand, Mahogany, with only 16 cards; it offers 800 cards today. Other companies offer more inclusive product lines within the same brand. Sara Lee Corporation's L'eggs discontinued its separate line of pantyhose for black women and now offers shades and styles popular among black women as half of the company's general-focus sub-brands. Unfortunately, many marketers think that targeting African Americans simply means serving up images of black superstars and idols such as Michael Jordan, Shacquille O'Neal, and actress Halle Berry. African American media and marketing specialists advise marketers to partner with black-owned media and the black community, and to hire more African Americans.

The 50-Plus Market

The magnitude—and wealth—of the mature market should be important to marketers if they want to profit in the new century. The population of mature consumers, those 50 and older, will swell to 115 million in the next 25 years. With a baby boomer turning 50 every 7 seconds, the size of this group will be even bigger by the time you finish reading this paragraph. The 50-plus market represents a whopping $2 trillion in buying power, and this figure is expected to increase by 29 percent in the next few years.

Not only have youth-obsessed marketers traditionally neglected this huge market, but they have also turned them off with stereotypes of grandmas and grandpas living on fixed incomes. Seniors, particularly boomers-turned-seniors, make buying decisions based on lifestyle, not age, and it is an active lifestyle at that. Pfizer ads feature seniors who now live their lives to the fullest, thanks to Pfizer medications. In one ad, a woman is shown traveling the world; in another, a senior former swimming champion tells how he was able to compete again. A Nike commercial features a senior weight lifter who proudly proclaims, "I'm not strong for my age. I'm strong!"

Yet despite their claims to youth, seniors do have less visual acuity and manual dexterity, and marketers must take this into account when packaging products. Pet packaging peeves for seniors include tiny, condensed type on pharmaceutical labels, heat-sealed inner cereal bags or snack food bags that are difficult to pry open, and shrink wrap that is impossible to remove.

Sources: (Latinos) Leon E. Wynter, "Business & Race: Hispanic Buying Habits Become More Diverse," *Wall Street Journal*, January 8, 1997, p. B1; Lisa A. Yorgey, "Hispanic Americans," *Target Marketing* (February 1998): 67; Carole Radice, "Hispanic Consumers: Understanding a Changing Market," *Progressive Grocer* (February 1997): 109–14. See also Brad Edmondson, "Hispanic Americans in 2001," *American Demographics* (January 1997): 16–17, and "Targeting the Hispanic Market," *Advertising Age*, special section, March 31, 1997, pp. A1–A12. (African-Americans) Valerie Lynn Gray, "Going After Our Dollars," *Black Enterprise* (July 1997): 68–78; David Kiley, "Black Surfing," *Brandweek*, November 17, 1997, p. 36; "L'eggs Joins New Approach in Marketing to African-American Women," *Supermarket Business* (June 1998): 81; Beth Belton, "Black Buying Power Soaring," *USA Today*, July 30, 1998, p. 1B; Dana Canedy, "The Courtship of Black Consumers," *New York Times*, August 11, 1998, p. D1. (50-Plus) Rick Adler, "Stereotypes Won't Work with Seniors Anymore," *Advertising Age*, November 11, 1996, p. 32; Richard Lee, "The Youth Bias in Advertising," *American Demographics* (January 1997): 47–50; Cheryl Russell, "The Ungraying of America," *American Demographics* (July 1997): 12–15; Sharon Fairley, George P. Moschis, Herbert M. Myers, and Arnold Thiesfeldt, "Senior Smarts: The Experts Sound Off," *Brandweek*, August 4, 1997, pp. 24–25; Candace Corlett, "Senior Theses," *Brandweek*, August 4, 1997, pp. 22–23.

table **7.1**		
Characteristics of Major U.S. Social Classes	1. *Upper Uppers* (less than 1%)	The social elite who live on inherited wealth. They give large sums to charity, run the debutante balls, maintain more than one home, and send their children to the finest schools. They are a market for jewelry, antiques, homes, and vacations. They often buy and dress conservatively. Although small as a group, they serve as a reference group to the extent that their consumption decisions are imitated by the other social classes.
	2. *Lower Uppers* (about 2%)	Persons, usually from the middle class, who have earned high income or wealth through exceptional ability in their professions or business. They tend to be active in social and civic affairs and to buy the symbols of status for themselves and their children. They include the nouveau riche, whose pattern of conspicuous consumption is designed to impress those below them.
	3. *Upper Middles* (12%)	These persons possess neither family status nor unusual wealth and are primarily concerned with "career." They are professionals, independent businesspersons, and corporate managers who believe in education and want their children to develop professional or administrative skills. Members of this class are civic-minded and home-oriented. They are the quality market for good homes, clothes, furniture, and appliances.
	4. *Middle Class* (32%)	Average-pay white- and blue-collar workers who live on "the right side of town." Often, they buy popular products to keep up with trends. Twenty-five percent own imported cars, and most are concerned with fashion. The middle class believes in spending more money on "worthwhile experiences" for their children and steering them toward a college education.
	5. *Working Class* (38%)	Average-pay blue-collar workers and those who lead a working-class lifestyle, whatever their income, school background, or job. The working class depends heavily on relatives for economic and emotional support, for tips on job opportunities, for advice, and for assistance. A working-class vacation means staying in town, and "going away" means to a lake or resort no more than two hours away. The working class tends to maintain sharp sex-role divisions and stereotyping.
	6. *Upper Lowers* (9%)	Upper lowers are working, although their living standard is just above poverty. They perform unskilled work and are very poorly paid. Often, upper lowers are educationally deficient.
	7. *Lower Lowers* (7%)	Lower lowers are on welfare, visibly poverty stricken, and usually out of work. Some are not interested in finding a permanent job, and most are dependent on public aid or charity for income.

Sources: Richard P. Coleman, "The Continuing Significance of Social Class to Marketing," *Journal of Consumer Research* (December 1983): 265–80; Richard P. Coleman and Lee P. Rainwater, *Social Standing in America: New Dimension of Class* (New York: Basic Books, 1978).

to **secondary groups**, such as religious, professional, and trade-union groups, which tend to be more formal and require less continuous interaction.

People are significantly influenced by their reference groups in at least three ways. Reference groups expose an individual to new behaviors and lifestyles, and influence attitudes and self-concept; they create pressures for conformity that may affect actual product and brand choices. People are also influenced by groups to which they do not belong. **Aspirational groups** are those a person hopes to join; **dissociative groups** are those whose values or behavior an individual rejects.

Marketers try to identify target customers' reference groups. However, level of reference-group influence varies among products and brands. Reference groups appear to strongly influence both product and brand choice only in the case of automobiles and color televisions; brand choice mainly in such items as furniture and clothing; and product choice mainly in such items as beer and cigarettes.

Manufacturers of products and brands where group influence is strong must determine how to reach and influence opinion leaders in these reference groups. An **opinion leader** is the person in informal, product-related communications who offers advice or information about a specific product or product category, such as which of several brands is best or how a particular product may be used.[5] Marketers try to reach opinion leaders by identifying demographic and psychographic characteristics associated with opinion leadership, identifying the media read by opinion leaders, and directing messages at opinion leaders. The hottest trends in teenage music, language, and fashion start in America's inner cities. Clothing companies like Levi Strauss, that hope to appeal to the fickle and fashion-conscious youth market, have made a concerted effort to monitor urban opinion leaders' style and behavior:

Levi Strauss & Company   Levi Strauss & Co. invented blue jeans 150 years ago. Today, it faces a growing field of competitors. Levi's® SILVERTAB® brand is designed and marketed to reach the 15- to 24-year-old male consumer who is influenced by urban styles. The SILVERTAB® marketing team and creative agency developed integrated marketing programs and brand imagery to appeal this consumer. In 2001 and 2002, this program included the use of hip hop and R & B celebrities Fredro Starr, the Black Eyed Peas, City

Levi-Strauss's Web site also targets the youth market.

High and Product G & B as models and performers. Additionally, SILVERTAB® used on-line movies, games, sweepstakes and other forms of outreach to drive awareness of the brand, and sales at key retailers. As a reality check, the SILVERTAB® marketing teams literally "check in" with their consumers in focus groups and closet studies. These initiatives have made SILVERTAB® the 5th largest jeanswear brand.[6]

Other clothing companies like Abercrombie and Fitch appeal to a different youth market.

Abercrombie and Fitch   To ensure that its stores reflect the lifestyle of the core customer base, Abercrombie fills its sales staff with college students who look the part. The company recruits 75 percent of its salespeople, or "brand representatives," from college campuses near each store location. The visual appeal of the sales staff is vital to creating the right in-store environment. "We're not interested in salespeople or clerks," said one Abercrombie & Fitch representative. "We're interested in finding people who represent the brand's lifestyle, which is the college lifestyle—leaders who have charisma, who portray the image of the brand."[7]

FAMILY   The family is the most important consumer-buying organization in society, and family members constitute the most influential primary reference group. The family has been researched extensively.[8] We can distinguish between two families in the buyer's life. The **family of orientation** consists of parents and siblings. From parents a person acquires an orientation toward religion, politics, and economics and a sense of personal ambition, self-worth, and love.[9] Even if the buyer no longer interacts very much with his or her parents, their influence on the buyer's behavior can be significant. In countries where parents live with grown children, their influence can be substantial. A more direct influence on everyday buying behavior is the **family of procreation**—namely, one's spouse and children.

Marketers are interested in the roles and relative influence of the husband, wife, and children in the purchase of a large variety of products and services. These roles vary widely in different countries and social classes. Vietnamese Americans, for example, are more likely to adhere to the traditional model in which the man makes the decisions for any large purchase. Similarly, successful ads for Korean Americans usually feature a man in his thirties or forties unless the ad is for a specifically female product, such as jewelry.[10]

In the United States, husband–wife involvement has traditionally varied widely by product category. The wife has traditionally acted as the family's main purchasing agent, especially for food, sundries, and staple-clothing items. In the case of expensive products and services like vacations or housing, husbands and wives have engaged in more joint decision making. Women are rapidly gaining purchasing power in the household. Business guru Tom Peters cites women as the number-one business marketing opportunity, and says:

> The market research is clear: Women make or greatly influence most purchasing decisions. Homes. . . . Medical care. Cars. Vacations. And hammers and nails in the huge DIY (do-it-yourself) industry: One (rare) female DIY-chain exec remarked to me about her male colleagues' amazement that 60% of their customers were women. . . . Women are where the real bucks are. Now close to 8 million women own enterprises in America, up from about 400,000 in 1970. They employ about 18.5 million of us . . . 40% more than old Forbes 500 industrials. About 22% of working wives outearn their hubbies, and women constitute about half the population of those with $500,000 or more in net worth.[11]

Given women's great strides in the workplace, especially in nontraditional jobs, traditional household purchasing patterns are gradually changing. Shifts in social values regarding the division of domestic labor have also weakened such standard conceptions as "women buy all the household goods." Recent research has shown that although traditional buying patterns still hold, baby boomer husbands and wives are more willing to shop jointly for products traditionally thought to be under the separate control of one spouse or the other.[12] Convenience-goods marketers are making a mistake if they think of women as the main or only purchasers of their products. Similarly, marketers of products traditionally purchased by men may need to start thinking of women as possible purchasers.

This is already happening in the car business.

Cadillac   Women now account for 50 percent of the luxury car market, and automakers are paying attention. Male car designers at Cadillac are going about their work with paper clips on their fingers to simulate what it feels like to operate buttons, knobs, and other interior features with longer fingernails. The Cadillac Catera features an air-conditioned glove box to preserve such items as lipstick and film. This greater attention to detail has led to a rise in the number of female Cadillac owners to 28 percent in 2000. For Cadillac's luxury SUV, the Escalade, the percentage of women buyers was 36 percent in 2000.[13]

Another shift in buying patterns is an increase in the amount of dollars spent and the influence wielded by children and teens.[14] The indirect influence on parental spending of kids age 2 to 14 accounted for $300 billion of household purchases in 1997. Indirect influence means that parents know the brands, product choices, and preferences of their children without hints or outright requests. Direct influence describes children's hints, requests, and demands—"I want to go to McDonald's." Direct influence peaked around $290 billion in 2000. Nontraditional marketers are now figuring out that the fastest route to Mom's and Dad's wallets may be through Junior.

Mattel   In 2000, Mattel targeted mothers, instead of young girls, with a print advertising campaign that emphasized Barbie merchandise in new-product categories. The ads were intended to raise awareness among mothers for such Barbie products as apparel and nail polish. "In the case of apparel in particular, mothers are the ones buying the clothes," says Mattel girl's division president Adrienne Fontanella. "When a mother is alone and has to decide between the GAP and Barbie, she's more familiar with the GAP."[15]

General Motors   In the May 1997 issue of *Sports Illustrated for Kids*, a magazine targeted to 8- to 14-year-old boys, the inside cover featured a brightly colored, two-page spread advertising the Chevy Venture minivan. This was GM's first attempt to woo what it calls "backseat consumers." The Venture's brand manager sent the minivan into malls and showed previews of Disney's *Hercules* on a VCR inside it. These days, kids often play a tie-breaking role in deciding what car to buy.[16]

Today companies are more likely to use the Internet to show off their products to children and solicit marketing information from them. Millions of kids under the age of 17 are online. Marketers have jumped online with them, offering freebies in exchange for personal information. Many have come under fire for this practice and for not clearly differentiating ads from games or entertainment. The Direct Marketing Association has taken a strong stand on marketing to children on the Internet. For its guidelines, see "Marketing Memo: What Every Marketer Needs to Know: Internet Ethics for Targeting Kids."

ROLES AND STATUSES   A person participates in many groups—family, clubs, organizations. The person's position in each group can be defined in terms of role and status. A **role** consists of the activities a person is expected to perform. Each role carries a **status**. A Supreme Court justice has more status than a sales manager, and a sales manager has

Marketing
MEMO

What Every Marketer Needs to Know: Internet Ethics for Targeting Kids

The Children's Online Privacy Protection Act, which took effect in April 2000, requires certain Web sites to obtain parental consent before collecting, using, or disclosing personal information from children under 13. In addition to adhering to this act, online marketers should follow the guidelines for ethical marketing to children suggested by the Direct Marketing Association:

1. Promote an online privacy statement.
2. Offer opt-out/opt-in options in which users have a choice of whether to stop or accept unwanted e-mail solicitation.
3. Utilize technology options such as Web site filtering programs like SurfWatch.
4. Take into account the target market's age, knowledge, sophistication, and maturity when making decisions whether to collect data from or communicate with children online.
5. Be sensitive to parents' concerns about the collection of children's data, and support the ability of parents to limit the collection of this data.
6. Limit the use of data collected from children in the course of their online activities to the promotion, sale, or delivery of goods or services; the performance of market research; and other appropriate marketing activities.
7. Explain that the information is being requested for marketing purposes. Implement strict security measures to ensure against unauthorized access, alteration, or dissemination of the data collected from children online.

Source: Adapted from Rob Yoegel, "Reaching Youth on the Web," *Target Marketing* (November 1997): 38–41; "New Rule Will Protect Privacy of Children Online," Press release, www.ftc.gov, October 20, 1999.

more status than an office clerk. People choose products that communicate their role and status in society. Company presidents often drive Mercedes, wear expensive suits, and drink Chivas Regal scotch. Marketers must be aware of the status-symbol potential of products and brands.

personal factors

A buyer's decisions are also influenced by personal characteristics. These include the buyer's age and stage in the life cycle, occupation, economic circumstances, lifestyle, and personality and self-concept.

AGE AND STAGE IN THE LIFE CYCLE   People buy different goods and services over a lifetime. They eat baby food in the early years, most foods in the growing and mature years, and special diets in the later years. Taste in clothes, furniture, and recreation is also age related.

Consumption is shaped by the **family life cycle**. Nine stages of the family life cycle are listed in Table 7.2, along with the financial situation and typical product interests of each group. Marketers often choose life-cycle groups as their target markets. Yet target households are not always family based: There are also single households, gay households, and cohabitor households. In addition, some recent research has identified *psychological* life-cycle stages. Adults experience certain "passages" or "transformations" as they go through life.[17] Marketers pay close attention to changing life circumstances—divorce, widowhood, remarriage—and their effect on consumption.

OCCUPATION AND ECONOMIC CIRCUMSTANCES   Occupation also influences consumption patterns. A blue-collar worker will buy work clothes, work shoes, and lunchboxes. A company president will buy expensive suits, air travel, and country club membership. Marketers try to identify the occupational groups that have above-average interest in their products and services. A company can even tailor its products for certain occupational groups: Computer software companies, for example, design different products for brand managers, engineers, lawyers, and physicians.

Product choice is greatly affected by economic circumstances: spendable income (level, stability, and time pattern), savings and assets (including the percentage that is

table **7.2**

Stages in Family Life Cycle

1. *Bachelor stage*:	Young, single, not living at home. Few financial burdens. Fashion opinion leaders. Recreation oriented. Buy: basic home equipment, furniture, cars, equipment for the mating game, vacations.
2. *Newly married couples*:	Young, no children. Highest purchase rate and highest average purchase of durables: cars, appliances, furniture, vacations.
3. *Full nest I*:	Youngest child under six. Home purchasing at peak. Liquid assets low. Interested in new products, advertised products. Buy: washers, dryers, TV, baby food, chest rubs and cough medicines, vitamins, dolls, wagons, sleds, skates.
4. *Full nest II*:	Youngest child six or over. Financial position better. Less influenced by advertising. Buy larger-size packages, multiple-unit deals. Buy: many foods, cleaning materials, bicycles, music lessons, pianos.
5. *Full nest III*:	Older married couples with dependent children. Financial position still better. Some children get jobs. Hard to influence with advertising. High average purchase of durables: new, more tasteful furniture, auto travel, unnecessary appliances, boats, dental services, magazines.
6. *Empty nest I*:	Older married couples, no children living with them, head of household in labor force. Home ownership at peak. Most satisfied with financial position and money saved. Interested in travel, recreation, self-education. Make gifts and contributions. Not interested in new products. Buy: vacations, luxuries, home improvements.
7. *Empty nest II*:	Older married. No children living at home, head of household retired. Drastic cut in income. Keep home. Buy: medical appliances, medical-care products.
8. *Solitary survivor*:	In labor force. Income still good but likely to sell home.
9. *Solitary survivor*:	Retired. Same medical and product needs as other retired group; drastic cut in income. Special need for attention, affection, and security.

Sources: William D. Wells and George Gubar, "Life-Cycle Concepts in Marketing Research," *Journal of Marketing Research* (November 1966): 362. Also see Patrick E. Murphy and William A. Staples, "A Modernized Family Life Cycle," *Journal of Consumer Research* (June 1979): 12–22; Frederick W. Derrick and Alane E. Linfield, "The Family Life Cycle: An Alternative Approach," *Journal of Consumer Research* (September 1980): 214–17.

liquid), debts, borrowing power, and attitudes toward spending and saving. Marketers of income-sensitive goods continuously monitor trends in personal income, savings, and interest rates. If economic indicators point to a recession, marketers can take steps to redesign, reposition, and reprice their products so they continue to offer value to target customers.

LIFESTYLE   People from the same subculture, social class, and occupation may lead quite different lifestyles. A **lifestyle** is a person's pattern of living in the world as expressed in activities, interests, and opinions. Lifestyle portrays the "whole person" interacting with his or her environment. Marketers search for relationships between their products and lifestyle groups. For example, a computer manufacturer might find that most computer buyers are achievement-oriented. The marketer may then aim the brand more clearly at the achiever lifestyle.

Psychographics is the science of using psychology and demographics to better understand consumers. One of the most popular commercially available classification systems based on psychographic measurements is SRI Consulting Business Intelligence's (SRIC-BI) VALS™ framework. VALS classifies all U.S. adults into eight primary groups based on psychological attributes and key demographics. The segmentation system is based on responses to a questionnaire featuring 4 demographic and 35 attitudinal questions. The VALS system is continually updated with new data from more then 80,000 surveys per year.[18] (see Figure 7.2).

The major tendencies of the four groups with high resources are:

1. *Actualizers:* Successful, sophisticated, active, "take-charge" people. Purchases often reflect cultivated tastes for relatively upscale, niche-oriented products.
2. *Fulfilleds:* Mature, satisfied, comfortable, reflective. Favor durability, functionality, and value in products.
3. *Achievers:* Successful, career- and work-oriented. Favor established, prestige products that demonstrate success to their peers.
4. *Experiencers:* Young, vital, enthusiastic, impulsive, and rebellious. Spend a comparatively high proportion of income on clothing, fast food, music, movies, and video.

figure **7.2**

The VALS Segmentation System: An 8-Part Typology

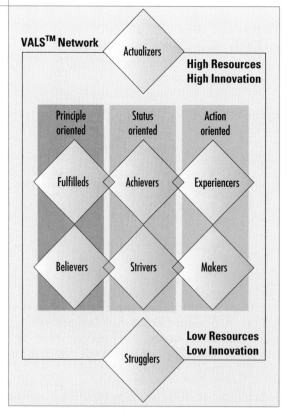

Source: ©2001 by SRI Consulting Business Intelligence. All rights reserved. Printed by permission.

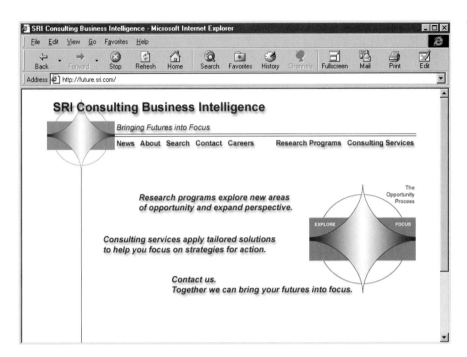

SRI Consulting Business Intelligence's Web site.

The major tendencies of the four groups with lower resources are:

1. *Believers:* Conservative, conventional, and traditional. Favor familiar products and established brands.
2. *Strivers:* Uncertain, insecure, approval-seeking, resource constrained. Favor stylish products that emulate the purchases of those with greater material wealth.
3. *Makers:* Practical, self-sufficient, traditional, family-oriented. Favor only products with a practical or functional purpose such as tools, utility vehicles, fishing equipment.
4. *Strugglers:* Elderly, resigned, passive, concerned, resource constrained. Cautious consumers who are loyal to favorite brands.

You can find out which VALS type you are by going to SRIC-BI's Web site (www. future.sri.com).

Lifestyle segmentation schemes are by no means universal. McCann-Erickson London, for example, identified the following British lifestyles: Avant-Gardians (interested in change); Pontificators (traditionalists, very British); Chameleons (follow the crowd); and Sleepwalkers (contented underachievers). The advertising agency D'Arcy, Masius, Benton & Bowles published *The Russian Consumer: A New Perspective and a Marketing Approach*, which revealed five categories of Russian consumers: Merchants, Cossacks, Students, Business Executives, and Russian Souls.[19] There are even lifestyle segmentation frameworks for classifying people according to their technology orientation. (See "Marketing for the New Economy: Are You a Mouse Potato or a Techno-Striver?")

PERSONALITY AND SELF-CONCEPT   Each person has personality characteristics that influence his or her buying behavior. By **personality**, we mean a set of distinguishing human psychological traits that lead to relatively consistent and enduring responses to environmental stimuli. Personality is often described in terms of such traits as self-confidence, dominance, autonomy, deference, sociability, defensiveness, and adaptability.[20] Personality can be a useful variable in analyzing consumer brand choices. The idea is that brands also have personalities, and that consumers are likely to choose brands whose personalities match their own. We define **brand personality** as the specific mix of human traits that may be attributed to a particular brand.

marketing for the new economy

Traditional market research may tell you who is buying a computer for the household. It may even tell you the kind of lifestyle she or he has. However, it will not tell you who in the household is using the computer and why. It will not tell you that the wife is using the PC to take a distance-learning course, that the son is using it to download computer games from various Web sites, that the daughter is using it to log on to about a dozen chat groups, or that the husband, a confirmed technophobe, logs on to get stock quotes.

Marketers of technology products can segment consumers based on technology types. Forrester Research, Inc.'s "Technographics" segments consumers into nine categories according to motivation, desire, and ability to invest in technology (see table below).

Both Technographics and the SRI-BI VALS™ systems reinforce the idea of a Consumer resource dimension based on knowledge as well as income. Some people who are computer-savvy are good prospects for home banking to pay bills, switch money between accounts, and check their balances. VALS points out that not all computer-savvy people are good home-banking prospects—the key is knowing which ones. Non-computer-literate people will still write checks by hand, send payments through "snail mail," and stand in line for a bank teller. The new market research tools also reveal many shades in the spectrum between "the knows" and "the know nots."

Sources: Based on Andy Hines, "Do You Know Your Technology Type?" *The Futurist* (September–October 1997): 10–11; Rebecca Piirto Heath, "The Frontiers of Psychographics," *American Demographics* (July 1996): 38–43; Paul C. Judge, "Are Tech Buyers Different?" *Business Week*, January 26, 1998, pp. 64–65, 68.

	MORE AFFLUENT — LESS AFFLUENT		
	CAREER	**FAMILY**	**ENTERTAINMENT**
OPTIMISTS	**Fast Forwards** These consumers are the biggest spenders, and they are early adopters of new technology for home, office, and personal use.	**New Age Nurturers** Also big spenders, but focused on technology for home uses, such as a family PC.	**Mouse Potatoes** They like the online world for entertainment and are willing to spend for the latest in "technotainment."
OPTIMISTS	**Techno-Strivers** Use technology from cell phones and pagers to online services primarily to gain a career edge.	**Digital Hopefuls** Families with a limited budget but still interested in new technology. Good candidates for under-$1,000 PC.	**Gadget-Grabbers** They also favor online entertainment but have less cash to spend on it.
PESSIMISTS	**Hand-Shakers** Older consumers—typically managers—who do not touch their computers at work. They leave that to younger assistants.	**Traditionalists** Willing to use technology but slow to upgrade. Not convinced upgrades and other add-ons are worth paying for.	**Media Junkies** Seek entertainment and cannot find much of it online. Prefer TV and other older media.
	SIDELINED CITIZENS (not interested in technology)		

Source: Paul C. Judge, "Are Tech Buyers Different," *Business Week*, January 26, 1998, p. 65; Data Forrester Research, Inc.

Jennifer Aaker conducted research into brand personalities and identified the following five traits:[21]

1. Sincerity (down-to-earth, honest, wholesome, and cheerful)
2. Excitement (daring, spirited, imaginative, and up-to-date)
3. Competence (reliable, intelligent, and successful)
4. Sophistication (upper-class and charming)
5. Ruggedness (outdoorsy and tough)

She proceeded to analyze some well-known brands and found that a number of them tended to be strong on one particular trait: Levi's with "ruggedness"; MTV with "excitement"; CNN with "competence"; and Campbell's with "sincerity." The implication is that these brands will attract persons who are high on the same personality traits.

Marketers attempt to develop brand personalities that will attract consumers with the same **self-concept**, but self-concept is somewhat slippery. A *person's actual self-concept* (how she views herself) may differ from her *ideal self-concept* (how she would like to view herself) and from her *others-self-concept* (how she thinks others see her). Which self will she try to satisfy in choosing a brand? Self-concept theory has had a mixed record of success in predicting consumer responses to brand images.[22]

psychological factors

A person's buying choices are influenced by four major psychological factors—motivation, perception, learning, and beliefs and attitudes.

MOTIVATION   A person has many needs at any given time. Some needs are *biogenic*; they arise from physiological states of tension such as hunger, thirst, or discomfort. Other needs are *psychogenic*; they arise from psychological states of tension such as the need for recognition, esteem, or belonging. A need becomes a motive when it is aroused to a sufficient level of intensity. A **motive** is a need that is sufficiently pressing to drive the person to act.

Psychologists have developed theories of human motivation, and three of the best known—those of Sigmund Freud, Abraham Maslow, and Frederick Herzberg—carry quite different implications for consumer analysis and marketing strategy.

Freud's Theory   Sigmund Freud assumed that the psychological forces shaping people's behavior are largely unconscious, and that a person cannot fully understand his or her own motivations. A technique called *laddering* can be used to trace a person's motivations from the stated instrumental ones to the more terminal ones. Then the marketer can decide at what level to develop the message and appeal.[23]

When a person examines specific brands, he or she will react not only to their stated capabilities, but also to other, less conscious cues. Shape, size, weight, material, color, and brand name can all trigger certain associations and emotions.

Motivation researchers often collect "in-depth interviews" with a few dozen consumers to uncover deeper motives triggered by a product. They use various *projective techniques* such as word association, sentence completion, picture interpretation, and role playing. Many of these techniques were pioneered by Ernest Dichter, a Viennese psychologist who settled in America. His research produced interesting and occasionally bizarre hypotheses:

- Consumers resist prunes because prunes are wrinkled looking and remind people of old age.
- Men smoke cigars as an adult version of thumb sucking.
- Women prefer vegetable shortening to animal fats because the latter arouse a sense of guilt over killing animals.
- Women don't trust cake mixes unless they require adding an egg, because this helps them feel they are giving "birth."

Today motivational researchers continue the tradition of Freudian interpretation. Jan Callebaut identifies different motives that a product can satisfy. For example, whisky can meet the need for social relaxation, status, or fun. Different whisky brands need to be motivationally positioned in one of these three appeals.[24] Another motivation researcher, Clotaire Rapaille, works on breaking the code behind a lot of product behavior. He claims that the code for coffee in the United States is "home" and therefore coffee advertising must use the home theme. The code for cheese in France is "alive," but when you go to America, cheese is "dead." He advises cheese producers to make cheese "alive."[25]

figure **7.3**

Maslow's Hierarchy of
Needs

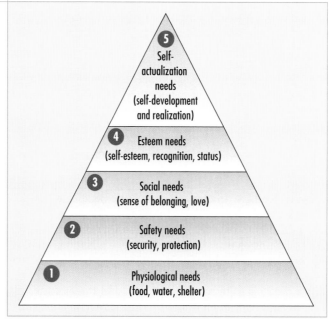

Source: *Motivation and Personality,* 2nd ed., by A. H. Maslow, 1970. Reprinted by
permission of Prentice Hall, Inc., Upper Saddle River, New Jersey.

Maslow's Theory   Abraham Maslow sought to explain why people are driven by particular needs at particular times.[26] Why does one person spend considerable time and energy on personal safety and another on pursuing the high opinion of others? Maslow's answer is that human needs are arranged in a hierarchy, from the most pressing to the least pressing. In order of importance, they are physiological needs, safety needs, social needs, esteem needs, and self-actualization needs (see Figure 7.3). People will try to satisfy their most important needs first. When a person succeeds in satisfying an important need, he or she will then try to satisfy the next-most-important need. For example, a starving man (need 1) will not take an interest in the latest happenings in the art world (need 5), nor in how he is viewed by others (need 3 or 4), nor even in whether he is breathing clean air (need 2); but when he has enough food and water, the next-most-important need will become salient.

Maslow's theory helps marketers understand how various products fit into the plans, goals, and lives of consumers.

Herzberg's Theory   Frederick Herzberg developed a two-factor theory that distinguishes *dissatisfiers* (factors that cause dissatisfaction) and *satisfiers* (factors that cause satisfaction).[27] The absence of dissatisfiers is not enough; satisfiers must be actively present to motivate a purchase. For example, a computer that does not come with a warranty would be a dissatisfier. Yet the presence of a product warranty would not act as a satisfier or motivator of a purchase, because it is not a source of intrinsic satisfaction with the computer. Ease of use would be a satisfier.

Herzberg's theory has two implications. First, sellers should do their best to avoid dissatisfiers (for example, a poor training manual or a poor service policy). Although these things will not sell a product, they might easily unsell it. Second, the manufacturer should identify the major satisfiers or motivators of purchase in the market and then supply them. These satisfiers will make the major difference as to which brand the customer buys.

PERCEPTION   A motivated person is ready to act. How the motivated person actually acts is influenced by his or her perception of the situation. **Perception** is the process by which an individual selects, organizes, and interprets information inputs to create a meaningful picture of the world.[28] Perception depends not only on the physical stimuli, but also on the stimuli's relation to the surrounding field and on conditions within the individual. The key point is that perceptions can vary widely among individuals exposed to the same reality. One person might perceive a fast-talking salesperson as aggressive and insincere; another, as intelligent and helpful. Each will respond differently to the salesperson. In marketing, people's perceptions are more important than the reality.

People can emerge with different perceptions of the same object because of three perceptual processes: selective attention, selective distortion, and selective retention.

Selective Attention   People are exposed to a tremendous amount of daily stimuli: The average person may be exposed to over 1,500 ads a day. Because a person cannot possibly attend to all of these, most stimuli will be screened out—a process called **selective attention**. Selective attention means that marketers have to work hard to attract consumers' notice. The real challenge is to explain which stimuli people will notice. Here are some findings:

1. *People are more likely to notice stimuli that relate to a current need.* A person who is motivated to buy a computer will notice computer ads; he or she will probably not notice DVD ads.
2. *People are more likely to notice stimuli that they anticipate.* You are more likely to notice computers than radios in a computer store because you do not expect the store to carry radios.
3. *People are more likely to notice stimuli whose deviations are large in relation to the normal size of the stimuli.* You are more likely to notice an ad offering $100 off the list price of a computer than one offering $5 off.

Although people screen out much of the surrounding stimuli, they are influenced by unexpected stimuli, such as sudden offers in the mail, over the phone, or from a salesperson. Marketers may attempt to promote their offers intrusively to bypass selective attention filters.

Selective Distortion   Even noticed stimuli do not always come across in the way the senders intended. **Selective distortion** is the tendency to twist information into personal meanings and interpret information in a way that will fit our preconceptions. Unfortunately, there is not much marketers can do about selective distortion.

Selective Retention   People will forget much that they learn but will tend to retain information that supports their attitudes and beliefs. Because of **selective retention**, we are likely to remember good points mentioned about a product we like and forget good points mentioned about competing products. Selective retention explains why marketers use drama and repetition in sending messages to their target market.

LEARNING   When people act, they learn. **Learning** involves changes in an individual's behavior arising from experience. Most human behavior is learned. Learning theorists believe that learning is produced through the interplay of drives, stimuli, cues, responses, and reinforcement.

A **drive** is a strong internal stimulus impelling action. **Cues** are minor stimuli that determine when, where, and how a person responds. Suppose you buy an IBM computer. If your experience is rewarding, your response to computers and IBM will be positively reinforced. Later on, when you want to buy a printer, you may assume that because IBM makes good computers, IBM also makes good printers. In other words, you *generalize* your response to similar stimuli. A countertendency to generalization is discrimination. **Discrimination** means that the person has learned to recognize differences in sets of similar stimuli and can adjust responses accordingly.

Learning theory teaches marketers that they can build up demand for a product by associating it with strong drives, using motivating cues, and providing positive reinforcement. A new company can enter the market by appealing to the same drives that competitors use and by providing similar cue configurations, because buyers are more likely to transfer loyalty to similar brands (generalization); or the company might design its brand to appeal to a different set of drives and offer strong cue inducements to switch (discrimination).

BELIEFS AND ATTITUDES   Through doing and learning, people acquire beliefs and attitudes. These in turn influence buying behavior. A **belief** is a descriptive thought that a person holds about something. People's beliefs about a product or brand influence their buying decisions. A study of the influence of brand beliefs found that consumers were equally split in their preference for Diet Coke versus Diet Pepsi when tasting both on a blind basis.[29] When tasting the branded versions, consumers preferred Diet Coke by 65 percent and Diet Pepsi by only 23 percent (with the remainder seeing no difference). This example highlights the role brand beliefs play in product choice.

Marketers are interested in the beliefs people carry in their heads about their products and brands. Brand beliefs exist in consumers' memory. The associative network memory model posits that memory is a network of nodes and connecting links. The nodes represent stored information (verbal, visual, abstract, or contextual) and the links represent the associations between nodes. Retrieval occurs through a process of *spreading activation*. When a particular node is activated, the information is recalled and further associative information is recalled through the links. Thus a particular brand that is triggered in a node, say, Apple Computer, will activate other nodes carrying such information as "innovative," "user-friendly," "Apple-logo," and "MacIntosh."

Marketers can study the memory networks of different consumers concerning a particular brand and map the main associations that are triggered and their relative strength and frequency. One of these associations can be with a product's country of origin. (See "Marketing Memo: How a Product's Country of Origin Shapes Consumer Brand Beliefs.")

A company has several options when its products are competitively priced but their place of origin turns consumers off. The company can consider co-production with a foreign company that has a better name: South Korea could make a fine leather jacket that it sends to Italy for finishing; or the company can adopt a strategy to achieve world-class quality in the local industry, as is the case with Belgian chocolates, Polish ham, and Colombian coffee. This is what South African wineries are attempting to do.

Marketing
MEMO

How a Product's Country of Origin Shapes Consumer Brand Beliefs

Global marketers know that buyers hold distinct beliefs about brands or products from different countries. Several studies have found the following:

- The impact of country of origin varies with the type of product. Consumers want to know where a car was made but not the lubricating oil.
- Certain countries enjoy a reputation for certain goods: Japan for automobiles and consumer electronics; the United States for high-tech innovations, soft drinks, toys, cigarettes, and jeans; France for wine, perfume, and luxury goods.
- Sometimes country-of-origin perception can encompass an entire country's products. In one study, Chinese consumers in Hong Kong perceived American products as prestigious, Japanese products as innovative, and Chinese products as cheap.
- The more favorable a country's image, the more prominently the "Made in . . ." label should be displayed.
- Attitudes toward country of origin can change over time. Before World War II, Japan had a poor quality image.

Sources: Johnny K. Johansson, "Determinants and Effects of the Use of 'Made In' Labels," *International Marketing Review* (UK) 6, iss. 1 (1989): 47–58; Warren J. Bilkey and Erik Nes, "Country-of-Origin Effects on Product Evaluations," *Journal of International Business Studies* (Spring–Summer 1982): 89–99; P. J. Cattin et al., "A Cross-Cultural Study of 'Made-In' Concepts," *Journal of International Business Studies* (Winter 1982): 131–41; Wai-Sum Siu and Carmen Hau-Ming Chan, "Country-of-Origin Effects on Product Evaluation: The Case of Chinese Consumers in Hong Kong," *Journal of International Marketing and Marketing Research* (October 1997): 115–22; "Old Wine in New Bottles," *The Economist*, February 21, 1998, p. 45; Zeynep Gigrhan-Canli and Durairaj "Cultural Variations in Country of Origin Effects," *Journal of Marketing Research* (August 2000): 309–17.

South African Wineries   South African wines compete for shelf space in European supermarkets, but they are handicapped by the perception that South African vineyards are primitive in comparison to those in Australia and Chile. They are also dogged by South African wine farmers' ugly record of crude labor practices and shady deals. Wine farmers at Nelson's Creek and Fairview have now improved the lives of their workers and given them a stake in the industry. "Wine is such a product of origin that we cannot succeed if South Africa doesn't look good," says Willem Barnard, chief executive of the Ko-operatieve Wijnbouwers Vereniging (KWV), the 80-year-old farmers' co-op that dominates the industry.

Just as important as beliefs are attitudes. An **attitude** is a person's enduring favorable or unfavorable evaluations, emotional feelings, and action tendencies toward some object or idea.[30] People have attitudes toward almost everything: religion, politics, clothes, music, food. Attitudes put them into a frame of mind of liking or disliking an object, moving toward or away from it. Attitudes lead people to behave in a fairly consistent way toward similar objects. People do not have to interpret and react to every object in a fresh way. Because attitudes economize on energy and thought, they are very difficult to change. A person's attitudes settle into a consistent pattern: To change a single attitude may require major adjustments in other attitudes.

Thus a company would be well-advised to fit its product into existing attitudes rather than to try to change people's attitudes. Of course, there are exceptions, where the cost of trying to change attitudes might pay off. Here are two examples of organizations that used ad campaigns to change consumer attitudes, with handsome results:

California Milk Processor Board   After a 20-year decline in milk consumption among Californians, milk processors from across the state formed the California Milk Processor Board (CMPB) in 1993 with one goal in mind: to get people to drink more milk. The ad agency commissioned by the CMPB developed a novel approach to pitching milk's benefits. Research had shown that the majority of consumers already believed milk was good for them. So the campaign would remind consumers of the inconvenience and annoyance of running out of milk, which became known as "milk deprivation." The "Got Milk?" tagline served to remind consumers to make sure they had milk in their refrigerators. Within the first year of the campaign, the number of consumers who reported consuming milk at least "several times a week" jumped from 72 to 78 percent. In 1995, the "Got Milk?" campaign was licensed to the National Dairy Board. In 1998, the National Fluid Milk Processor Education Program, which had been using the "milk mustache" campaign since 1994 to boost sales, bought the rights to the "Got Milk?" tagline. By 1998, "Got Milk?" was being advertised across the country with a combined annual budget of $180 million.[31]

Wood Promotion Network   With a campaign similar in purpose to "Got Milk?", more than 80 wood-products companies joined forces to promote the benefits of wood with a campaign urging consumers to "Be Constructive: Use Wood." Although wood is used by 90 percent of the residential construction market, recent promotional campaigns by steel and concrete manufacturers threatened to erode some of wood's market share. The wood campaign seeks to encourage consumers to choose wood by emphasizing its durability, affordability, and ease of use.[32]

A "Got Milk?" ad from the
National Fluid Milk Processor
Promotion Board's campaign
using mustachioed
celebrities—here the cast of the
TV sitcom Frasier.

the buying decision process

Marketers have to go beyond the various influences on buyers and develop an understanding of how consumers actually make their buying decisions. Specifically, marketers must identify who makes the buying decision, the types of buying decisions, and the steps in the buying process.

buying roles

It is easy to identify the buyer for many products. In the United States, men normally choose their shaving equipment, and women choose their pantyhose; but even here marketers must be careful in making their targeting decisions, because buying roles change. When ICI, the giant British chemical company, discovered that women made 60 percent of the decisions on the brand of household paint, it decided to advertise its DuLux brand to women.

We can distinguish five roles people play in a buying decision:

- *Initiator:* The person who first suggests the idea of buying the product or service.
- *Influencer:* The person whose view or advice influences the decision.
- *Decider:* The person who decides on any component of a buying decision: whether to buy, what to buy, how to buy, or where to buy.
- *Buyer:* The person who makes the actual purchase.
- *User:* The person who consumes or uses the product or service.

buying behavior

Consumer decision making varies with the type of buying decision. The decisions to buy toothpaste, a tennis racket, a personal computer, and a new car are all very different. Complex and expensive purchases are likely to involve more buyer deliberation

table **7.3**

	High Involvement	Low Involvement
Significant Differences between Brands	Complex buying behavior	Variety-seeking buying behavior
Few Differences between Brands	Dissonance-reducing buying behavior	Habitual buying behavior

Four Types of Buying Behavior

Source: Modified from Henry Assael, *Consumer Behavior and Marketing Action* (Boston: Kent Publishing Co., 1987), p. 87. Copyright 1987 by Wadsworth, Inc. Printed by permission of Kent Publishing Co., a division of Wadsworth, Inc.

and more participants. Henry Assael distinguished four types of consumer buying behavior, based on the degree of buyer involvement and the degree of differences among brands[33] (see Table 7.3).

COMPLEX BUYING BEHAVIOR   Complex buying behavior involves a three-step process. First, the buyer develops beliefs about the product. Second, he or she develops attitudes about the product. Third, he or she makes a thoughtful choice. Consumers engage in complex buying behavior when they are highly involved in a purchase and aware of significant differences among brands. This is usually the case when the product is expensive, bought infrequently, risky, and highly self-expressive, like an automobile.

The marketer of a high-involvement product must understand consumers' information-gathering and evaluation behavior. The marketer needs to develop strategies that assist the buyer in learning about the product's attributes and their relative importance, and which call attention to the high standing of the company's brand on the more important attributes. The marketer needs to differentiate the brand's features, use print media to describe the brand's benefits, and motivate sales personnel and the buyer's acquaintances to influence the final brand choice.

DISSONANCE-REDUCING BUYER BEHAVIOR   Sometimes the consumer is highly involved in a purchase but sees little difference in brands. The high involvement is based on the fact that the purchase is expensive, infrequent, and risky. In this case, the buyer will shop around to learn what is available. If the consumer finds quality differences in the brands, he or she might go for the higher price. If the consumer finds little difference, he or she might simply buy on price or convenience.

After the purchase, the consumer might experience dissonance that stems from noticing certain disquieting features or hearing favorable things about other brands, and will be alert to information that supports his or her decision. In this example, the consumer first acted, then acquired new beliefs, then ended up with a set of attitudes. Marketing communications should supply beliefs and evaluations that help the consumer feel good about his or her brand choice.

HABITUAL BUYING BEHAVIOR   Many products are bought under conditions of low involvement and the absence of significant brand differences. Consider salt. Consumers have little involvement in this product category. They go to the store and reach for the brand. If they keep reaching for the same brand, it is out of habit, not strong brand loyalty. There is good evidence that consumers have low involvement with most low-cost, frequently purchased products.

With these products, consumer behavior does not pass through the normal sequence of belief, attitude, and behavior. Consumers do not search extensively for information, evaluate characteristics, and make a decision. Instead, they are passive recipients of information in television or print ads. Ad repetition creates *brand familiarity* rather than *brand conviction*. After purchase, they may not even evaluate the choice. For low-involvement products, the buying process begins with brand beliefs formed by passive learning and is followed by purchase behavior, which may be followed by evaluation.

Marketers of such products find it effective to use price and sales promotions to stimulate product trial. Television advertising is more effective than print because it is a low-involvement medium that is suitable for passive learning.[34]

Marketers use four techniques to try to convert a low-involvement product into one of higher involvement. First, they can link the product to some involving issue, as when Crest toothpaste is linked to avoiding cavities. Second, they can link the product to some involving personal situation—for instance, by advertising a coffee brand early in the morning when the consumer wants to shake off sleepiness. Third, they might design advertising to trigger strong emotions related to personal values or ego defense. Fourth, they might add an important feature (for example, fortifying a plain drink with vitamins). These strategies at best raise consumer involvement from a low to a moderate level; they do not propel the consumer into highly involved buying behavior. (See "Marketing Memo: How to Derive Fresh Consumer Insights to Differentiate Products and Services.")

VARIETY-SEEKING BUYING BEHAVIOR Some buying situations are characterized by low involvement but significant brand differences. Here consumers often do a lot of brand switching. Think about cookies. The consumer has some beliefs about cookies, chooses a brand of cookies without much evaluation, and evaluates the product during consumption. Next time, the consumer may reach for another brand out of a wish for a different taste. Brand switching occurs for the sake of variety rather than dissatisfaction.

The market leader and the minor brands in this product category have different marketing strategies. The market leader will try to encourage habitual buying behavior by dominating the shelf space, avoiding out-of-stock conditions, and sponsoring frequent reminder advertising. Challenger firms will encourage variety seeking by offering lower prices, deals, coupons, free samples, and advertising that presents reasons for trying something new.

stages of the buying decision process

Smart companies will immerse themselves in trying to understand the customer's overall experience in learning about a product, making a brand choice, using the product, and even disposing of it. Honda engineers took videos of shoppers loading groceries into car trunks to observe their frustrations and generate possible design solutions. Intuit, the maker of Quicken financial software, watched first-time buyers try to learn Quicken to sense their problems in learning how to use the software. Benson Shapiro and his co-authors urged companies to "staple yourself to an order" to appreciate everything that occurs or might go wrong in the ordering process.[35]

How can marketers learn about the stages in the buying process for their product? They can think about how they themselves would act (*introspective method*). They can interview a small number of recent purchasers, asking them to recall the events leading to their purchase (*retrospective method*). They can locate consumers who plan to buy the product and ask them to think out loud about going through the buying process (*prospective method*); or they can ask consumers to describe the ideal way to buy the product (*prescriptive method*). Each method yields a picture of the steps in the process.

The Edmunds.com home page shows the variety of services this Web company offers those shopping for a car.

Trying to understand the customer's behavior in connection with a product has been called mapping the customer's *consumption system*,[36] *customer activity cycle*,[37] or *customer scenario*.[38] This can be done for such activity clusters as doing laundry, preparing for a wedding, or buying a car. Buying a car, for example, involves a whole cluster of activities, including choosing the car, financing the purchase, buying insurance, buying accessories, and so on. Professor Sawhney views these activities as constituting a **metamarket,** and calls firms that help customers navigate through these activities **metamediaries.**[39] As an example of an online metamediary, consider Edmunds.com:

Edmunds.com   This site provides unbiased, third-party information and advice on buying autos and related services. Here is how it works:

- Auto buyers can read about features, quality, and dealer costs for any automobile on Edmunds' site. They can narrow their search to a few makes and models, and conduct side-by-side comparisons. They can request Edmunds, in collaboration with the manufacturers, to mail them customized brochures with information on selected makes and models.
- They can seek advice by entering the Edmunds Town Hall discussion area to interact with consumers who have bought or owned these autos. They may visit Web sites that present complaints from those who have had negative experiences with a particular seller (see fordsucks.com or bmwlemon.com for examples).
- Soon, buyers will be able to sign up for appointments to test-drive multiple brands and models at a predefined place and time, sponsored by Edmunds and partners like CarMax or AutoNation. They will be able to "kick the tires" for their favorite brands side-by-side, with no sales pressure from dealers and without ever visiting a brand-specific dealer. The appointments will be prearranged, so that buyers will have exactly the models they want to test-drive.
- When buyers decide on a brand and make, they can define the features and options they want, and click on Edmunds' partner Autobytel.com to act as their buying

figure **7.4**

Five-Stage Model of the Consumer Buying Process

agent. Autobytel informs several local car dealers that there is a "hot" prospect for the particular auto and invites those who have it in stock to bid for the business.

■ Buyers can round out the transaction by clicking on other Edmunds business partners. They can prequalify for financing from NationsBank; get extended warranties from Warranty Gold; buy auto insurance from GEICO; and accessorize their auto with items from J. C. Whitney.

Marketing scholars have developed a "stages model" of the buying decision process (see Figure 7.4). The consumer passes through five stages: problem recognition, information search, evaluation of alternatives, purchase decision, and postpurchase behavior. Clearly, the buying process starts long before the actual purchase and has consequences long afterward.[40]

The model in Figure 7.4 implies that consumers pass through all five stages in buying a product, but this is not the case: Consumers may skip or reverse some stages. A woman buying her regular brand of toothpaste goes directly from the need for toothpaste to the purchase decision, skipping information search and evaluation. However, we will use the model in Figure 7.4 because it captures the full range of considerations that arise when a consumer faces a highly involving new purchase.[41]

problem recognition

The buying process starts when the buyer recognizes a problem or need. The need can be triggered by internal or external stimuli. With an internal stimulus, one of the person's normal needs—hunger, thirst, sex—rises to a threshold level and becomes a drive; or a need can be aroused by an external stimulus. A person passes a bakery and sees freshly baked bread that stimulates her hunger; she admires a neighbor's new car; or she sees a television ad for a Hawaiian vacation.

Marketers need to identify the circumstances that trigger a particular need. By gathering information from a number of consumers, marketers can identify the most frequent stimuli that spark an interest in a product category. They can then develop marketing strategies that trigger consumer interest.

information search

An aroused consumer will be inclined to search for more information. We can distinguish between two levels of arousal. The milder search state is called *heightened attention*. At this level a person simply becomes more receptive to information about a product.

At the next level, the person may enter an *active information search*: looking for reading material, phoning friends, and visiting stores to learn about the product. Of key interest to the marketer are the major information sources to which the consumer will turn and the relative influence each will have on the subsequent purchase decision. Consumer information sources fall into four groups:

■ *Personal sources:* Family, friends, neighbors, acquaintances
■ *Commercial sources:* Advertising, salespersons, dealers, packaging, displays
■ *Public sources:* Mass media, consumer-rating organizations
■ *Experiential sources:* Handling, examining, using the product

The relative amount and influence of these information sources vary with the product category and the buyer's characteristics. Generally speaking, the consumer receives the most information about a product from commercial sources—that is, marketer-dominated sources. However, the most effective information comes from personal sources. Each information source performs a different function in influencing the buying decision. Commercial information normally performs an informing function, and personal sources perform a legitimizing or evaluation function. For example, physicians often learn of new drugs from commercial sources but turn to other doctors for evaluative information.

figure **7.5**

Successive Sets Involved in Consumer Decision Making

Through gathering information, the consumer learns about competing brands and their features. The first box in Figure 7.5 shows the *total set* of brands available to the consumer. The individual consumer will come to know only a subset of these brands (*awareness set*). Some brands will meet initial buying criteria (*consideration set*). As the person gathers more information, only a few will remain as strong contenders (*choice set*). The brands in the choice set might all be acceptable. The person makes a final choice from this set.[42]

Figure 7.5 makes it clear that a company must strategize to get its brand into the prospect's awareness set, consideration set, and choice set. The company must also identify the other brands in the consumer's choice set so that it can plan competitive appeals. In addition, the company should identify the consumer's information sources and evaluate their relative importance. Consumers should be asked how they first heard about the brand, what information came in later, and the relative importance of the different information sources. The answers will help the company prepare effective communications for the target market.

evaluation of alternatives

How does the consumer process competitive brand information and make a final value judgment? There is no single process used by all consumers or by one consumer in all buying situations. There are several decision evaluation processes, the most current models of which see the process as cognitively oriented. That is, they see the consumer as forming judgments largely on a conscious and rational basis.

Some basic concepts will help us understand consumer evaluation processes: First, the consumer is trying to satisfy a need. Second, the consumer is looking for certain benefits from the product solution. Third, the consumer sees each product as a bundle of attributes with varying abilities for delivering the benefits sought to satisfy this need. The attributes of interest to buyers vary by product:

1. *Cameras:* Picture sharpness, camera speeds, camera size, price
2. *Hotels:* Location, cleanliness, atmosphere, price
3. *Mouthwash:* Color, effectiveness, germ-killing capacity, price, taste/flavor
4. *Tires:* Safety, tread life, ride quality, price

Consumers vary as to which product attributes they see as most relevant and the importance they attach to each attribute. They will pay the most attention to attributes

Computer	Attribute			
	Memory Capacity	Graphics Capability	Size and Weight	Price
A	10	8	6	4
B	8	9	8	3
C	6	8	10	5
D	4	3	7	8

Note: Each attribute is rated from 0 to 10, where 10 represents the highest level on that attribute. Price, however, is indexed in a reverse manner, with a 10 representing the lowest price, because a consumer prefers a low price to a high price.

that deliver the sought benefits. The market for a product can often be segmented according to attributes that are salient to different consumer groups.

The consumer develops a set of *brand beliefs* about where each brand stands on each attribute. The set of beliefs about a brand make up the **brand image**. The consumer's brand image will vary with his or her experiences as filtered by the effects of selective perception, selective distortion, and selective retention.

The consumer arrives at attitudes (judgments, preferences) toward the various brands through an attribute evaluation procedure.[43] Suppose that Linda Brown has narrowed her choice set to four computers (A, B, C, D). Assume that she is interested in four attributes: memory capacity, graphics capability, size and weight, and price. Table 7.4 shows her beliefs about how each brand rates on the four attributes. If one computer dominated the others on all the criteria, we could predict that Linda would choose it, but her choice set consists of brands that vary in their appeal. If Linda wants the best memory capacity, she should buy A; if she wants the best graphics capability, she should buy B; and so on.

Most buyers consider several attributes in their purchase decision. If we knew the weights that Linda Brown attaches to the four attributes, we could more reliably predict her computer choice. Suppose Linda assigned 40 percent of the importance to the computer's memory capacity, 30 percent to its graphics capability, 20 percent to its size and weight, and 10 percent to its price. To find Linda's perceived value for each computer, we multiply her weights by her beliefs about each computer's attributes. This computation leads to the following perceived values:

$$\text{Computer A} = 0.4(10) + 0.3(8) + 0.2(6) + 0.1(4) = 8.0$$
$$\text{Computer B} = 0.4(8) + 0.3(9) + 0.2(8) + 0.1(3) = 7.8$$
$$\text{Computer C} = 0.4(6) + 0.3(8) + 0.2(10) + 0.1(5) = 7.3$$
$$\text{Computer D} = 0.4(4) + 0.3(3) + 0.2(7) + 0.1(8) = 4.7$$

We would predict that Linda will favor computer A, which (at 8.0) has the highest perceived value.[44]

Suppose most computer buyers form their preferences the same way. Knowing this, a computer manufacturer can do a number of things to influence buyer decisions. The marketer of computer C, for example, could apply the following strategies to stimulate greater interest in brand C:

■ *Redesign the computer:* This technique is called real repositioning.
■ *Alter beliefs about the brand:* Attempting to alter beliefs about the brand is called psychological repositioning.
■ *Alter beliefs about competitors' brands:* This strategy, called competitive depositioning, makes sense when buyers mistakenly believe a competitor's brand has more quality than it actually has.

- *Alter the importance weights:* The marketer could try to persuade buyers to attach more importance to the attributes in which the brand excels.
- *Call attention to neglected attributes:* The marketer could draw buyers' attention to neglected attributes, such as styling or processing speed.
- *Shift the buyer's ideals:* The marketer could try to persuade buyers to change their ideal levels for one or more attributes.[45]

purchase decision

In the evaluation stage, the consumer forms preferences among the brands in the choice set. The consumer may also form an intention to buy the most preferred brand. However, two factors can intervene between the purchase intention and the purchase decision (Figure 7.6).[46]

The first factor is the *attitudes of others.* The extent to which another person's attitude reduces one's preferred alternative depends on two things: (1) the intensity of the other person's negative attitude toward the consumer's preferred alternative and (2) the consumer's motivation to comply with the other person's wishes.[47] The more intense the other person's negativism and the closer the other person is to the consumer, the more the consumer will adjust his or her purchase intention. The converse is also true: A buyer's preference for a brand will increase if someone he or she respects favors the same brand strongly. The influence of others becomes complex when several people close to the buyer hold contradictory opinions and the buyer would like to please them all.

Related to the attitudes of others is the role played by **infomediaries** who publish their evaluations. Examples include *Consumer Reports*; *Zagats* (which publishes customer reviews of restaurants); professional movie, book, and music reviewers; customer reviews of books and music in Amazon.com; and the increasing number of chat rooms where people discuss products, services, and companies. Consumers are undoubtedly influenced by these evaluations.

The second factor is *unanticipated situational factors* that may erupt to change the purchase intention. Jack Hamilton might lose his job, some other purchase might become more urgent, or a store salesperson may turn him off. Preferences and even purchase intentions are not completely reliable predictors of purchase behavior.

A consumer's decision to modify, postpone, or avoid a purchase decision is heavily influenced by *perceived risk.*[48] The amount of perceived risk varies with the amount of money at stake, the amount of attribute uncertainty, and the amount of consumer self-confidence. Consumers develop routines for reducing risk, such as decision avoidance, information gathering from friends, and preference for national brand names and warranties. Marketers must understand the factors that provoke a feeling of risk in consumers and provide information and support to reduce the perceived risk.

In executing a purchase intention, the consumer may make up to five purchase subdecisions: a *brand decision* (brand A), *vendor decision* (dealer 2), *quantity decision* (one computer), *timing decision* (weekend), and *payment-method decision* (credit card). Purchases of everyday products involve fewer decisions and less deliberation. For example, in buying sugar, a consumer gives little thought to the vendor or payment method.

figure **7.6**

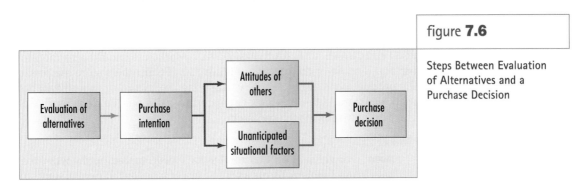

Steps Between Evaluation of Alternatives and a Purchase Decision

postpurchase behavior

After purchasing the product, the consumer will experience some level of satisfaction or dissatisfaction. The marketer's job does not end when the product is bought. Marketers must monitor postpurchase satisfaction, postpurchase actions, and postpurchase product uses.

POSTPURCHASE SATISFACTION   What determines whether the buyer will be highly satisfied, somewhat satisfied, or dissatisfied with a purchase? The buyer's satisfaction is a function of the closeness between the buyer's expectations and the product's perceived performance.[49] If performance falls short of expectations, the customer is *disappointed*; if it meets expectations, the customer is *satisfied*; if it exceeds expectations, the customer is *delighted*. These feelings make a difference in whether the customer buys the product again and talks favorably or unfavorably about it to others.

Consumers form their expectations on the basis of messages received from sellers, friends, and other information sources. The larger the gap between expectations and performance, the greater the consumer's dissatisfaction. Here the consumer's coping style comes into play. Some consumers magnify the gap when the product is not perfect, and they are highly dissatisfied; others minimize the gap and are less dissatisfied.[50]

The importance of postpurchase satisfaction suggests that product claims must truthfully represent the product's likely performance. Some sellers might even understate performance levels so that consumers experience higher-than-expected satisfaction with the product.

POSTPURCHASE ACTIONS   Satisfaction or dissatisfaction with the product will influence a consumer's subsequent behavior. If the consumer is satisfied, he or she will exhibit a higher probability of purchasing the product again. For example, data on automobile brand choice show a high correlation between being highly satisfied with the last brand bought and intention to buy the brand again. One survey showed that 75 percent of Toyota buyers were highly satisfied and about 75 percent intended to buy a Toyota again; 35 percent of Chevrolet buyers were highly satisfied and about 35 percent intended to buy a Chevrolet again. The satisfied customer will also tend to say good things about the brand to others. Marketers say: "Our best advertisement is a satisfied customer."[51]

Dissatisfied consumers may abandon or return the product. They may seek information that confirms its high value. They may take public action by complaining to the company, going to a lawyer, or complaining to other groups (such as business, private, or government agencies). Private actions include making a decision to stop buying the product (*exit option*) or warning friends (*voice option*).[52] In all these cases, the seller has done a poor job of satisfying the customer.[53]

Postpurchase communications to buyers have been shown to result in fewer product returns and order cancellations.[54] Computer companies, for example, can send a letter to new owners congratulating them on having selected a fine computer. They can place ads showing satisfied brand owners. They can solicit customer suggestions for improvements and list the location of available services. They can write intelligible instruction booklets. They can send owners a magazine containing articles describing new computer applications. In addition, they can provide good channels for speedy redress of customer grievances.

POSTPURCHASE USE AND DISPOSAL   Marketers should also monitor how buyers use and dispose of the product (Figure 7.7). If consumers store the product in a closet, the product is probably not very satisfying, and word of mouth will not be strong. If they sell or trade the product, new-product sales will be depressed. Consumers may also find new uses for the product:

Avon   For years Avon's customers have been spreading the word that Skin-So-Soft bath oil and moisturizer is a terrific insect repellent. Whereas some consumers sim-

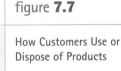

figure **7.7**

How Customers Use or Dispose of Products

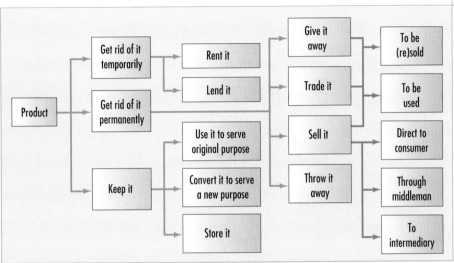

Source: From Jacob Jacoby, Carol K. Berning, and Thomas F. Dietvorst, "What about Disposition?" *Journal of Marketing* (July 1977): 23. Reprinted with permission of the American Marketing Association.

ply bathed in water scented with the fragrant oil, others carried it in their backpacks to mosquito-infested campsites or kept a bottle on the deck of the beach house. After receiving approval by the Environmental Protection Agency, Avon began touting its Skin-So-Soft Moisturizing Suncare Plus as a triple-action product that provided insect repellent and waterproof SPF 15 sun protection, as well as moisturizers. Joey Green, an author of five books on unusual household uses for everyday products, found another use for Skin-So-Soft: removing lime deposits from shower doors.[55]

If consumers throw the product away, the marketer needs to know how they dispose of it, especially if it can hurt the environment (as in the case with beverage containers and disposable diapers). Increased public awareness of recycling and ecological concerns as well as consumer complaints about having to throw away beautiful bottles led French perfume maker Rochas to think about introducing a new refillable fragrance line.

other models of the buying decision process

The five-stage model of the buying decision process shown in Figure 7.4 is one of several models for understanding the buyer's decision process. Here are two other models that marketers have found useful.

HEALTH MODEL   Social marketers in the health field are interested in how patients adopt healthful behaviors, such as stopping smoking or starting a new diet or exercise program. A useful model called Stages of Change distinguishes five stages:[56]

- *Precontemplation:* Not recognizing the problem or the need to change.
- *Contemplation:* Seriously thinking about the problem and the possibility of change.
- *Preparation:* Making a commitment to change and taking steps to prepare for that change.
- *Action:* Successful modification of behavior for a period from 1 day to 6 months.
- *Maintenance:* Continuation of change from 6 months to an indefinite period.

Persons contemplating a change, such as stopping smoking or losing weight, need to pass through these stages. The social marketer's task is to find appeals and tools to help people move from one stage to the next.

figure **7.8**

Activity cycle for IBM customers in the global electronic networking capability market space.

Source: Sandra Vandermerwe, *Customer Capitalism: Increasing Returns in New Market Spaces* (London: Nicholas Brealey, 1999), p. 92, figure 5. Reprinted by permission.

CUSTOMER ACTIVITY CYCLE MODEL   Professor Sandra Vandermerwe focuses on mapping the *pre, during,* and *post* phases of a consumer's behavior toward a particular task.[57]

The *pre* phase is deciding what to do, the *during* phase is doing it, and the *post* phase is keeping it going. Figure 7.8 shows a *customer activity cycle* for a bank customer contemplating whether to purchase a new software system from IBM or another vendor. IBM's task is to add value at each stage to facilitate the buyer's favoring IBM as the vendor. Figure 7.9

figure **7.9**

Value adds for IBM customers in the global electronic networking capability market space.

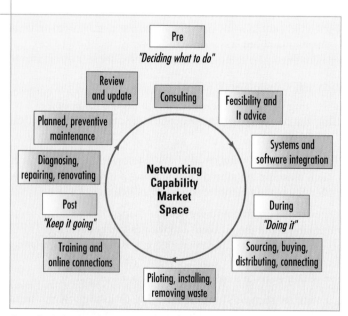

Source: Sandra Vandermerwe, *Customer Capitalism: Increasing Returns in New Market Spaces* (London: Nicholas Brealey, 1999), p. 94, figure 7. Reprinted by permission.

shows the value add-ons that IBM can assemble in order to win the bank's business. Essentially, IBM is putting together a turnkey system to make it easy for the bank to get maximum value. In this way, IBM has created *customer lock-in*. If IBM focused on *product lock-in*, such as only selling the software, customers could have gone elsewhere for the missing services; but with customer lock-in, the bank has little choice but to buy from IBM.

summary

1. Consumer behavior is influenced by four factors: cultural (culture, subculture, and social class); social (reference groups, family, and social roles and statuses); personal (age, stage in the life cycle, occupation, economic circumstances, lifestyle, personality, and self-concept); and psychological (motivation, perception, learning, beliefs, and attitudes). Research into all these factors can provide clues to reach and serve consumers more effectively.

2. To understand how consumers actually make buying decisions, marketers must identify who makes and has input into the buying decision; people can be initiators, influencers, deciders, buyers, or users, and different marketing campaigns might be targeted to each type of person. Marketers must also examine buyers' levels of involvement

and the number of brands available to determine whether consumers are engaging in complex buying behavior, dissonance-reducing buying behavior, habitual buying behavior, or variety-seeking buying behavior.

3. The typical buying process consists of the following sequence of events: problem recognition, information search, evaluation of alternatives, purchase decision, and postpurchase behavior. The marketers' job is to understand the buyer's behavior at each stage. The attitudes of others, unanticipated situational factors, and perceived risk may all affect the decision to buy, as will consumers' levels of postpurchase satisfaction and postpurchase actions on the part of the company.

4. Other models of the buying decision process include the health model and the customer activity cycle model.

applications

marketing debate – is target marketing ever bad?

As marketers increasingly develop marketing programs tailored to certain target market segments, some critics have denounced these efforts as exploitative. For example, the preponderance of billboards advertising cigarettes, alcohol, and other vices in low-income urban areas is seen as taking advantage of a vulnerable market segment. Critics can be especially harsh in evaluating marketing programs that target African Americans and other minority groups, claiming

that they often employ clichéd stereotypes and inappropriate depictions. Others counter with the point of view that targeting and positioning is critical to marketing and that these marketing programs are an attempt to be relevant to a certain consumer group.

> **Take a position:** Targeting minorities is exploitative versus Targeting minorities is a sound business practice.

marketing and advertising

1. This ad in Figure 1 for Quaker Toasted Oatmeal Squares appeals to personal factors that influence consumer buying behavior, including lifestyle and self-concept. It also provides information so that the targeted segment will recognize and understand the bundle of attributes that this cereal product offers to solve the problem of how to eat a "nice, healthy breakfast."

    a. Who is the target audience for this ad, and how does Quaker use the concept of consumer lifestyle to effectively communicate with the target?

    b. Does this ad appeal to the consumer's actual self-concept, ideal self-concept, or others-self-concept? Which is the most appropriate for this product? Explain.

    c. What bundle of attributes does this ad present for the consumer's consideration? What are the benefits associated with each attribute?

2. Businesspeople also have specific needs and buying behavior when they act as consumers. The BlackBerry ad in Figure 2 targets businesspeople who want to avoid losing touch—even momentarily—with colleagues, clients, and other important contacts. Understanding the nuances of this consumer market's buying behavior, BlackBerry presents its wireless device as a convenient solution to the problem of staying connected at all times.

    a. What personal and psychological factors in the buying process have been incorporated into this ad?

    b. What role or roles are being addressed by this ad?

    c. Toward which stage of the consumer buying decision process is this ad most likely geared? Why?

Figure 1

Figure 2

online marketing today

Who would buy pet health insurance—let alone buy it online? Tom Kurtz founded Premier Pet Insurance a few years ago, after his cat needed $2,000 worth of veterinary treatment. Although pet health insurance has long been accepted in Europe, the U.S. market for it remains largely untapped. Fewer than 2 percent of all American cat and dog pets have health insurance, compared with up to 50 percent in Great Britain and Sweden. Now rising costs for sophisticated life-saving procedures such as chemotherapy and kidney transplants are causing more U.S. consumers to consider this type of insurance for their pets. As with other insurance products, many consumers like to shop around and compare policies and rates before making a purchase. That is why Premier maintains an informative, easy-to-navigate Web site.[58]

Visit the Premier Pet Insurance site <*www.ppins.com*>, review the home page, then follow the links to find out more about the various insurance plans, how much buyers can save, FAQs (frequently asked questions), and online quotes and ordering. How does the company address the social and personal factors most likely to affect the purchase of this product? What attitudes and beliefs about this purchase does Premier directly address on its Web site? What type of buying behavior would you expect consumers to follow when buying pet health insurance, and how does the company's online marketing reflect a good understanding of this buying behavior?

you're the marketer: sonic pda marketing plan

Marketing Plan Pro

Every company has to study consumer markets and behavior prior to developing a marketing plan for its products. This enables marketers to understand who constitutes the market, what and why the market buys, who participates in and influences the buying process, and how, when, and where consumers buy.

You are responsible for researching and analyzing the consumer market for Sonic's forthcoming PDA. Look again at the data you have already entered about the company's current situation and macroenvironment, especially the market being targeted. Now answer these questions about the market and buyer behavior:

- What cultural, social, personal, and psychological factors have the most influence on consumers buying PDAs? What research tools would help you better understand the effect on buyer attitudes and behavior?
- Which specific factors should Sonic's marketing plan emphasize and why?

- What consumer buying roles and buying behaviors are particularly relevant for PDA products?
- What kind of marketing activities should Sonic plan to coincide with each stage of the consumer buying process?

After you have analyzed your markets and consumer behavior, consider the implications for Sonic's marketing efforts supporting the launch of its PDA. Finally, document your findings and conclusions in a written marketing plan or type them into the Market Analysis, Situation Analysis, Target Markets, and Market Summary sections of the *Marketing Plan Pro* software.

notes

1. Tobi Elkin, "Product Pampering," *Brandweek*, June 16, 1997, pp. 38–40.
2. <*www.net-temps.com*>; Judith N. Mottl, "Customer Tracking; It's Not Just Website Hits," *InformationWeek*, February 7, 2000.
3. Adrienne Sanders, "Yankee Imperialism, " *Forbes*, December 13, 1999, p.56.
4. Leon G. Schiffman and Leslie Lazar Kanuk, *Consumer Behavior*, 6th ed. (Upper Saddle River, NJ: Prentice Hall, 1997).
5. Ibid.
6. Courteny Kane, "Advertising: TBWA/Chiat Day Brings Street Culture to a Campaign for Levi Strauss Silver Tab Clothing," *New York Times*, August 14, 1998, p. D8.
7. Abigail Goodman, "Store Most Likely to Succeed," *Los Angeles Times*, April 3, 1999.
8. Rosann L. Spiro, "Persuasion in Family Decision Making," *Journal of Consumer Research* (March 1983): 393–402; Lawrence H. Wortzel, "Marital Roles and Typologies as Predictors of Purchase Decision Making for Everyday Household Products: Suggestions for Research," in Jerry C. Olsen, (ed.), *Advances in Consumer Research*, Vol. 7 (Chicago: American Marketing Association, 1989), pp. 212–15; David J. Burns, "Husband-Wife Innovative Consumer Decision Making: Exploring the Effect of Family Power," *Psychology & Marketing* (May–June 1992): 175–89; Robert Boutilier, "Pulling the Family's Strings," *American Demographics* (August 1993): 44–48. For cross-cultural comparisons of husband-wife buying roles, see John B. Ford, Michael S. LaTour, and Tony L. Henthorne, "Perception of Marital Roles in Purchase-Decision Processes: A Cross-Cultural Study,"*Journal of the Academy of Marketing Science* (Spring 1995): 120–31.
9. George Moschis, "The Role of Family Communication in Consumer Socialization of Children and Adolescents," *Journal of Consumer Research* (March 1985): 898–913.
10. John Steere, "How Asian-Americans Make Purchase Decisions," *Marketing News*, March 13, 1995, p. 9.
11. Tom Peters, "Opportunity Knocks," *Forbes*, June 2, 1997, p. 132.
12. Marilyn Lavin, "Husband-Dominant, Wife-Dominant, Joint: A Shopping Typology for Baby Boom Couples?" *Journal of Consumer Marketing* 10, no. 3 (1993): 33–42.
13. Alan Alder, "Purchasing Power: Women's Buying Muscle Shops Up in Car Design, Marketing," *Chicago Tribune*, September 29, 1996, p. 21A; Matt Nauman, "Cadillac Attracts New Buyer Groups with Escalade Sport-Utility," *San Jose Mercury News*, January 19, 2001.
14. James U. McNeal, "Tapping the Three Kids' Markets," *American Demographics* (April 1998): 37–41.
15. Lisa Bannon, "Mattel's Print Ads Will Play Up to Moms to Boost Barbie Brand," *Wall Street Journal*, September 19, 2000.
16. David Leonhardt, "Hey Kid, Buy This," *BusinessWeek*, June 30, 1997, pp. 62–67.
17. Lawrence Lepisto, "A Life Span Perspective of Consumer Behavior," in Elizabeth Hirshman and Morris Holbrook (eds.), *Advances in Consumer Research*, Vol. 12 (Provo, UT: Association for Consumer Research, 1985), p. 47. Also see Gail Sheehy, *New Passages: Mapping Your Life Across Time* (New York: Random House, 1995).
18. Arnold Mitchell, *The Nine American Lifestyles* (New York: Warner Books), pp. viii–x, 25–31; Personal communication from the VALS Program, Business Intelligence Center, SRI Consulting, Menlo Park, CA, February 1, 1996. See also Wagner A. Kamakura and Michel Wedel, "Lifestyle Segmentation with Tailored Interviewing," *Journal of Marketing Research* 32, no. 3 (August 1995): 308–17.
19. Stuart Elliott, "Sampling Tastes of a Changing Russia," *New York Times*, April 1, 1992, pp. D1, D19.
20. Harold H. Kassarjian and Mary Jane Sheffet, "Personality and Consumer Behavior: An Update," in Harold H. Kassarjian and Thomas S. Robertson (eds.), *Perspectives in Consumer Behavior* (Glenview, IL: Scott, Foresman, 1981), pp. 160–80.
21. Jennifer Aaker, "Dimensions of Measuring Brand Personality," *Journal of Marketing Research* 34 (August 1997): 347–56.
22. M. Joseph Sirgy, "Self-Concept in Consumer Behavior: A Critical Review," *Journal of Consumer Research* (December 1982): 287–300. Jennifer L. Aaker, "The Malleable Self: The Role of Self-expression in Persuasion," *Journal of Marketing Research* (May 1999): pp. 45–57.
23. Thomas J. Reynolds and Jonathan Gutman, "Laddering Theory, Method, Analysis, and Interpretation," *Journal of Advertising Research* (February–March 1988): 11–34.
24. Jan Callebaut et al., *The Naked Consumer: The Secret of Motivational Research in Global Marketing* (Antwerp, Belgium: Censydiam Institute, 1994).
25. Jack Hitt, "Does the Smell of Coffee Brewing Remind You of Your Mother?" *New York Times Magazine*, May 7, 2000, pp. 71–74.
26. Abraham Maslow, *Motivation and Personality* (New York: Harper and Row, 1954), pp. 80–106.
27. See Frederick Herzberg, *Work and the Nature of Man* (Cleveland: William Collins, 1966); Henk Thierry and Agnes M. Koopman-Iwerna, "Motivation and Satisfaction," in P. J. Drenth (ed.), *Handbook of Work and Organizational Psychology* (New York: John Wiley, 1984), pp. 141–42.
28. Bernard Berelson and Gary A. Steiner, *Human Behavior: An Inventory of Scientific Findings* (New York: Harcourt, Brace Jovanovich, 1964), p. 88.
29. Leslie de Chernatony and Simon Knox, "How an Appreciation of Consumer Behavior Can Help in Product Testing," *Journal of Market Research Society*, (July 1990): 333. See also Chris Janiszewski and Stiju M. J. Osselar, "A Connectionist Model Of Brand-Quality Association," *Journal of Marketing Research*, August 2000, pp. 331–51.

30. David Krech, Richard S. Crutchfield, and Egerton L. Ballachey, *Individual in Society* (New York: McGraw-Hill, 1962), ch. 2.

31. Jill Venter, "Milk Mustache Campaign Is a Hit with Teens," *St. Louis Post-Dispatch*, April 1, 1998, p. E1; Dave Fusaro, "The Milk Mustache," *Dairy Foods* (April 1997): 75; Judann Pollack, "Milk: Kurt Graetzer," *Advertising Age*, June 30, 1997, p. S1; Kevin Lane Keller, "Milk: Branding a Commodity," *Strategic Brand Management* (Upper Saddle River, NJ: Prentice Hall, 1998).

32. Chad Terhune, "Wood Folks Hope for 'Got Milk?' Success," *Wall Street Journal*, February 9, 2001.

33. See Henry Assael, *Consumer Behavior and Marketing Action* (Boston: Kent, 1987), ch. 4.

34. Herbert E. Krugman, "The Impact of Television Advertising: Learning without Involvement," *Public Opinion Quarterly* (Fall 1965): 349–56.

35. Benson Shapiro, V. Kasturi Rangan, and John Sviokla, "Staple Yourself to an Order," *Harvard Business Review* (July–August 1992): 113–22. See also Carrie M. Heilman, Douglas Bowman, and Gordon P. Wright, "The Evolution of Brand Preferences and Choice Behaviors of Consumers New to a Market," *Journal of Marketing Research* (May 2000), pp.139–55.

36. Harper W. Boyd Jr. and Sidney Levy, "New Dimensions in Consumer Analysis," *Harvard Business Review* 163 (November–December): 129–40.

37. Sandra Vandermerwe, *Customer Capitalism: Increasing Returns in New Market Spaces* (London: Nicholas Brealey Publishing), ch. 11.

38. Patricia B. Seybold, "Get Inside the Lives of Your Customers," *Harvard Business Review* (May 2001): 81–89.

39. Mohanbir Sawhney, "Making New Markets," *Business 2.0* (May 1999): 116–21.

40. Marketing scholars have developed several models of the consumer buying process. See John A. Howard and Jagdish N. Sheth, *The Theory of Buyer Behavior* (New York: Wiley, 1969); James F. Engel, Roger D. Blackwell, and Paul W. Miniard, *Consumer Behavior*, 8th ed. (Fort Worth, TX: Dryden, 1994); Mary Frances Luce, James R. Bettman, and John W. Payne, *Emotional Decisions: Tradeoff Difficulty and Coping in Consumer Choice*, (Chicago, IL: University of Chicago Press, 2001).

41. William P. Putsis Jr. and Narasimhan Srinivasan, "Buying or Just Browsing? The Duration of Purchase Deliberation," *Journal of Marketing Research* (August 1994): 393–402.

42. Chem L. Narayana and Rom J. Markin, "Consumer Behavior and Product Performance: An Alternative Conceptualization," *Journal of Marketing* (October 1975): 1–6. See also Wayne S. DeSarbo and Kamel Jedidi, "The Spatial Representation of Heterogeneous Consideration Sets," *Marketing Science* 14, no.3, pt. 2 (1995): 326–42; Lee G. Cooper and Akihiro Inoue, "Building Market Structures from Consumer Preferences," *Journal of Marketing Research* 33, no. 3 (August 1996): 293–306.

43. See Paul E. Green and Yoram Wind, *Multiattribute Decisions in Marketing: A Measurement Approach* (Hinsdale, IL: Dryden, 1973), ch. 2; Leigh McAlister, "Choosing Multiple Items from a Product Class," *Journal of Consumer Research* (December 1979): 213–24.

44. This expectancy-value model was developed by Martin Fishbein, "Attitudes and Prediction of Behavior," in Martin Fishbein (ed.), *Readings in Attitude Theory and Measurement* (New York: John Wiley, 1967), pp. 477–92. For a critical review, see Paul W. Miniard and Joel B. Cohen, "An Examination of the Fishbein-Ajzen Behavioral-Intentions Model's Concepts and Measures," *Journal of Experimental Social Psychology* (May 1981): 309-39. Other models of consumer evaluation include the ideal-brand model, which assumes that a consumer compares actual brands to her ideal brand and chooses the brand that comes closest to her ideal brand; the conjunctive model, which assumes that a consumer sets minimum acceptable levels on all the attributes and considers only the brands that meet all the minimum requirements; and the disjunctive model, which assumes that a consumer sets minimum acceptable levels on only a few attributes and eliminates those brands falling short. For a discussion of these and other models, see Green and Wind, *Multiattribute Decisions in Marketing A Measurement Approach.*

45. Harper W. Boyd Jr., Michael L. Ray, and Edward C. Strong, "An Attitudinal Framework for Advertising Strategy," *Journal of Marketing* (April 1972): 27–33.

46. Jagdish N. Sheth, "An Investigation of Relationships among Evaluative Beliefs, Affect, Behavioral Intention, and Behavior," in John U. Farley, John A. Howard, and L. Winston Ring (eds.), *Consumer Behavior: Theory and Application* (Boston: Allyn & Bacon, 1974), pp. 89–114.

47. Fishbein, "Attitudes and Prediction of Behavior."

48. Raymond A. Bauer, "Consumer Behavior as Risk Taking," in Donald F. Cox (ed.), *Risk Taking and Information Handling in Consumer Behavior* (Boston: Division of Research, Harvard Business School, 1967); James W. Taylor, "The Role of Risk in Consumer Behavior," *Journal of Marketing* (April 1974): 54–60.

49. Priscilla A. La Barbera and David Mazursky, "A Longitudinal Assessment of Consumer Satisfaction/Dissatisfaction: The Dynamic Aspect of the Cognitive Process," *Journal of Marketing Research* (November 1983): 393–404.

50. Ralph L. Day, "Modeling Choices among Alternative Responses to Dissatisfaction," *Advances in Consumer Research*, Vol. 11 (1984): 496–99. Also see Philip Kotler and Murali K. Mantrala, "Flawed Products: Consumer Responses and Marketer Strategies," *Journal of Consumer Marketing* (Summer 1985): 27–36.

51. Barry L. Bayus, "Word of Mouth: The Indirect Effects of Marketing Efforts," *Journal of Advertising Research* (June-July 1985): 31–39.

52. Albert O. Hirschman, *Exit, Voice, and Loyalty* (Cambridge, MA: Harvard University Press, 1970).

53. Mary C. Gilly and Richard W. Hansen, "Consumer Complaint Handling as a Strategic Marketing Tool," *Journal of Consumer Marketing* (Fall 1985): 5–16.

54. James H. Donnelly Jr. and John M. Ivancevich, "Post-Purchase Reinforcement and Back-Out Behavior," *Journal of Marketing Research* (August 1970): 399–400.

55. Pam Weisz, "Avon's Skin-So-Soft Bugs Out," *Brandweek*, June 6, 1994, p. 4; Beverly Beyette,"Strange but True: Cheez Whiz Works in Laundry," *Los Angles Times*, October 22, 2000.

56. C.C DiClemente and J. O.Prochaska, "Processes and Stages of Self-Change: Coping and Competence in Smoking Behavior Change," in S.Shiffman and T. A. Willis (eds.), *Coping and Substance Abuse I* (San Diego, CA: Academic Press, 1985), pp. 319–43.

57. Sandra Vandermerwe, *Customer Capitalism: Increasing Returns in New Market Spaces* (London: Nicholas Brealey, 1999), pp. 91–95.

58. Michelle Leder, "How Much Is That $100 Deductible in the Window?" *New York Times*, July 22, 2001, sec.3, p.10; Monica Khemsurov, "Smart City Navigator," *New York*, September 11, 2000, <*www.newyorkmag.com/page.cfm?page_id=3752*>.

analyzing business markets and business buying behavior

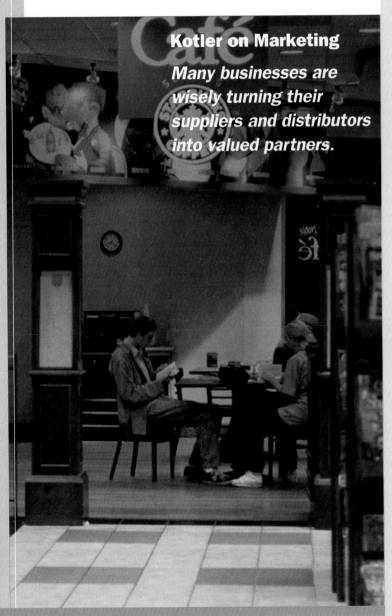

Kotler on Marketing

Many businesses are wisely turning their suppliers and distributors into valued partners.

In this chapter, we will address the following questions:

- What is the business market, and how does it differ from the consumer market?
- What buying situations do organizational buyers face?
- Who participates in the business-to-business buying process?
- What are the major influences on organizational buyers?
- How do business buyers make their decisions?
- How do institutional buyers and government agencies do their buying?

Business organizations do not only sell. They also buy vast quantities of raw materials, manufactured components, plant and equipment, supplies, and business services. There are over 13 million buying organizations in the United States alone. Sellers need to understand these organizations' needs, resources, policies, and buying procedures.

what is organizational buying?

Webster and Wind define **organizational buying** as the decision-making process by which formal organizations establish the need for purchased products and services and identify, evaluate, and choose among alternative brands and suppliers.[1]

the business market versus the consumer market

The **business market** consists of all the organizations that acquire goods and services used in the production of other products or services that are sold, rented, or supplied to others. The major industries making up the business market are agriculture, forestry, and fisheries; mining; manufacturing; construction; transportation; communication; public utilities; banking, finance, and insurance; distribution; and services.

More dollars and items are involved in sales to business buyers than to consumers. Consider the process of producing and selling a simple pair of shoes. Hide dealers must sell hides to tanners, who sell leather to shoe manufacturers, who sell shoes to wholesalers, who sell shoes to retailers, who finally sell them to consumers. Each party in the supply chain also has to buy many other goods and services.

Business markets have several characteristics that contrast sharply with those of consumer markets.

- *Fewer buyers:* The business marketer normally deals with far fewer buyers than the consumer marketer does. Goodyear Tire Company's fate depends on getting contracts from a few major automakers.
- *Larger buyers:* A few large buyers do most of the purchasing in such industries as aircraft engines and defense weapons.
- *Close supplier–customer relationship:* Because of the smaller customer base and the importance and power of the larger customers, suppliers are frequently expected to customize their offerings to individual business customer needs. Sometimes buyers require sellers to change their practices and performance. In recent years, relationships between customers and suppliers have been changing from downright adversarial to close and integrated.

Motoman Inc., and Stillwater Technologies   Motoman Inc., a leading supplier of industry robotic systems, and Stillwater Technologies, a contract tooling and machinery company and a key supplier to Motoman, are tightly integrated. Not only do they occupy office and manufacturing space in the same facility, but their telephone and computer systems are linked, and they share a common lobby, conference room, and employee cafeteria. Philip V. Morrison, chairman and CEO of Motoman, says it is like "a joint venture without the paperwork." Short delivery distances are just one benefit of the unusual partnership. Also key is the fact that employees of both companies have ready access to one another and can share ideas on improving quality and reducing costs. This close relationship has opened the door to new opportunities. Both companies had been doing work for Honda Motor Company, and Honda suggested that the two work together on systems projects. The symbiotic relationship makes the two bigger than they are individually.[2]

- *Geographically concentrated buyers:* More than half of U.S. business buyers are concentrated in seven states: New York, California, Pennsylvania, Illinois, Ohio, New Jersey, and Michigan. The geographical concentration of producers helps to reduce selling costs. At the same time, business marketers need to monitor regional shifts of certain industries.
- *Derived demand:* The demand for business goods is ultimately derived from the demand for consumer goods. For this reason, the business marketer must closely

monitor the buying patterns of ultimate consumers. For instance, a report in *Purchasing* magazine indicated that the Big Three automakers in Detroit are driving the boom in demand for steel-bar products. Much of that demand is derived from consumers' continued love affair with minivans and other light trucks, which consume far more steel than cars.

■ *Inelastic demand:* The total demand for many business goods and services is inelastic— that is, not much affected by price changes. Shoe manufacturers are not going to buy much more leather if the price of leather falls, nor will they buy much less leather if the price rises, unless they can find satisfactory substitutes. Demand is especially inelastic in the short run because producers cannot make quick changes in production methods. Demand is also inelastic for business goods that represent a small percentage of the item's total cost, such as shoelaces.

■ *Fluctuating demand:* The demand for business goods and services tends to be more volatile than the demand for consumer goods and services. A given percentage increase in consumer demand can lead to a much larger percentage increase in the demand for plant and equipment necessary to produce the additional output. Economists refer to this as the *acceleration effect*. Sometimes a rise of only 10 percent in consumer demand can cause as much as a 200 percent rise in business demand for products in the next period; a 10 percent fall in consumer demand may cause a complete collapse in business demand.

■ *Professional purchasing:* Business goods are purchased by trained purchasing agents, who must follow their organization's purchasing policies, constraints, and requirements. Many of the buying instruments—for example, requests for quotations, proposals, and purchase contracts—are not typically found in consumer buying.

Professional buyers spend their careers learning how to buy better. Many belong to the National Association of Purchasing Managers (NAPM), which seeks to improve professional buyers' effectiveness and status. This means that business marketers have to provide greater technical data about their product and its advantages over competitors' products. Business marketers now put their products, prices, and other information on the Internet. Purchasing agents and brokers are able to access more information, more easily, than ever before. Here is how some sellers are making the Internet friendly to buyers:

Cisco Systems, Inc.   When Cisco first offered routers and switches over its Web site, Cisco Connection Online, customers quickly recognized the advantage of seeing prices and configuring products electronically. They simply click onto a program called Configuration Agent, which walks them through the dozen major components that go into a router. If they choose the wrong combination of circuit boards, the program posts an error message and guides them to an acceptable choice. Once the right item is selected, its current price pops up automatically. At Sprint, a major customer of Cisco, it used to take 60 days from the signing of a contract to complete a networking project. Now, thanks partly to the efficiency of ordering Cisco equipment online, it takes 35 to 45 days.[3]

Blue Shield of California   Blue Shield of California created a buzz in the health care industry with its Individual and Family Plans Online Sales system for selling health insurance over the Internet. The system lets brokers run rate quotes, choose a plan, and submit customers' applications in Web form. Blue Shield hopes to build loyalty among its brokers by being the first insurer to offer such a system.[4] In addition, its mylifepath Web site provides a decision support tool that allows individuals looking for an individual and family or medicare plan to answer a few simple questions about their health preferences and to receive recommendations for a plan that meets their needs. Individuals seeking short-term health plan coverage can apply online, receive immediate approval, and obtain coverage effective within 24 hours.

Blue Shield of California's
mylifepath™.

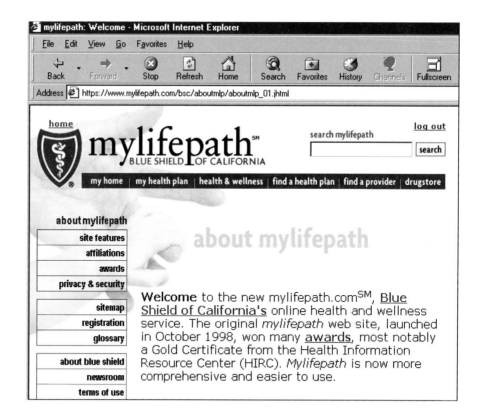

■ *Several buying influences:* More people typically influence business buying decisions. Buying committees consisting of technical experts and even senior management are common in the purchase of major goods. Business marketers have to send well-trained sales representatives and sales teams to deal with the well-trained buyers. Cutler-Hammer uses sales teams.

Cutler–Hammer Pittsburgh-based Cutler-Hammer supplies circuit breakers, motor starters, and other electrical equipment to heavy industrial manufacturers such as Ford Motor Company. In response to the growing complexity and proliferation of its products, C-H developed "pods" of salespeople focused on a particular geographical region, industry, or market concentration. Each person brings a degree of expertise about a product or service that the other members of the team could take to the customer. Now the salespeople could leverage the knowledge of co-workers to sell to increasingly sophisticated buying teams instead of working in isolation.[5]

■ *Multiple sales calls:* Because more people are involved in the selling process, it takes multiple sales calls to win most business orders, and some sales cycles can take years. A study by McGraw-Hill found that it takes four to four and a half calls to close an average industrial sale. In the case of capital equipment sales for large projects, it may take multiple attempts to fund a project, and the sales cycle—between quoting a job and delivering the product—is often measured in years.[6]

■ *Direct purchasing:* Business buyers often buy directly from manufacturers rather than through intermediaries, especially items that are technically complex or expensive (such as mainframes or aircraft).

- *Reciprocity:* Business buyers often select suppliers who also buy from them. An example would be a paper manufacturer that buys chemicals from a chemical company that buys a considerable amount of its paper.
- *Leasing:* Many industrial buyers lease instead of buy heavy equipment like machinery and trucks. The lessee gains a number of advantages: conserving capital, getting the latest products, receiving better service, and gaining some tax advantages. The lessor often ends up with a larger net income and the chance to sell to customers who could not afford outright purchase.

buying situations

The business buyer faces many decisions in making a purchase. The number of decisions depends on the buying situation. Patrick Robinson and others distinguish three types of buying situations: the straight rebuy, modified rebuy, and new task.[7]

- *Straight rebuy:* The straight rebuy is a buying situation in which the purchasing department reorders on a routine basis (e.g., office supplies, bulk chemicals). The buyer chooses from suppliers on an "approved list." These suppliers make an effort to maintain product and service quality. They often propose automatic reordering systems so that the purchasing agent will save reordering time. The "out-suppliers" attempt to offer something new or to exploit dissatisfaction with a current supplier. Out-suppliers try to get a small order and then enlarge their purchase share over time.
- *Modified rebuy:* The modified rebuy is a situation in which the buyer wants to modify product specifications, prices, delivery requirements, or other terms. The modified rebuy usually involves additional decision participants on both sides. The in-suppliers become nervous and have to protect the account. The out-suppliers see an opportunity to propose a better offer to gain some business.
- *New task:* The new task is a buying situation in which a purchaser buys a product or service for the first time (e.g., office building, new security system). The greater the cost or risk, the larger the number of decision participants and the greater their information gathering—and therefore the longer the time to decision completion.[8]

New-task buying passes through several stages: awareness, interest, evaluation, trial, and adoption.[9] The effectiveness of communication tools varies at each stage. Mass media are most important during the initial awareness stage; salespeople have their greatest impact at the interest stage; and technical sources are the most important during the evaluation stage.

The business buyer makes the fewest decisions in the straight-rebuy situation and the most in the new-task situation. In the new-task situation, the buyer has to determine product specifications, price limits, delivery terms and times, service terms, payment terms, order quantities, acceptable suppliers, and the selected supplier. Different decision participants influence each decision, and the order in which these decisions are made varies. The new-task situation is the marketer's greatest opportunity and challenge. The marketer tries to reach as many key buying influencers as possible and provide helpful information and assistance. Because of the complicated selling involved, many companies use a *missionary sales force* consisting of their most effective salespeople.

systems buying and selling

Many business buyers prefer to buy a total solution to their problem from one seller. Called **systems buying**, this practice originated with government purchases of major weapons and communications systems. The government would solicit bids from *prime contractors*, who would assemble the package or system. The contractor who was awarded the contract would be responsible for bidding out and assembling the system's subcomponents from *second-tier contractors*. The prime contractor would thus provide a **turnkey solution**, so-called because the buyer simply had to turn one key to get the job done.

Ford   Ford has transformed itself from being mainly a car manufacturer to being mainly a car assembler. Ford has substantially reduced the number of its suppliers and relies primarily on a few major systems suppliers to provide seating systems, braking systems, door systems, and other major assemblies. In designing a new automobile, Ford works closely with (say) its seat manufacturer and creates a *black box specification* of the basic seat dimensions and performance that it needs, and then waits for the seat supplier to propose the most cost-effective design. When they agree, the seat supplier subcontracts with many parts suppliers to produce and deliver the needed components.

Sellers have increasingly recognized that buyers like to purchase in this way, and many have adopted **systems selling** as a marketing tool. One variant of systems selling is *systems contracting*, where a single supplier provides the buyer with his or her entire requirement of MRO (maintenance, repair, operating) supplies. The supplier takes full responsibility during the contract period to manage the customer's inventory. For example, Shell Oil manages the oil inventory of many of its business customers and knows when it requires replenishment. The customer benefits from reduced procurement and management costs and from price protection over the term of the contract. The seller benefits from lower operating costs because of a steady demand and reduced paperwork.

Systems selling is a key industrial marketing strategy in bidding to build large-scale industrial projects, such as dams, steel factories, irrigation systems, sanitation systems, pipelines, utilities, and even new towns. Project engineering firms must compete on price, quality, reliability, and other attributes to win contracts. Consider the following example.

Japan and Indonesia   The Indonesian government requested bids to build a cement factory near Jakarta. A U.S. firm made a proposal that included choosing the site, designing the cement factory, hiring the construction crews, assembling the materials and equipment, and turning over the finished factory to the Indonesian government. A Japanese firm, in outlining its proposal, included all of these services, plus hiring and training the workers to run the factory, exporting the cement through its trading companies, and using the cement to build roads and new office buildings in Jakarta. Although the Japanese proposal involved more money, it won the contract. Clearly, the Japanese viewed the problem not just as one of building a cement factory (the narrow view of systems selling) but as one of contributing to Indonesia's economic development. They took the broadest view of the customer's needs. This is true systems selling.

---

participants in the business buying process

Who does the buying of the trillions of dollars' worth of goods and services needed by business organizations? Purchasing agents are influential in straight-rebuy and modified-rebuy situations, whereas other department personnel are more influential in new-buy situations. Engineering personnel usually have a major influence in selecting product components, and purchasing agents dominate in selecting suppliers.[10]

Webster and Wind call the decision-making unit of a buying organization the **buying center**. The buying center is composed of "all those individuals and groups who participate in the purchasing decision-making process, who share some common goals and the risks arising from the decisions."[11] The buying center includes all members of the organization who play any of seven roles in the purchase decision process.[12]

1. *Initiators:* Those who request that something be purchased. They may be users or others in the organization.
2. *Users:* Those who will use the product or service. In many cases, the users initiate the buying proposal and help define the product requirements.
3. *Influencers:* People who influence the buying decision. They often help define specifications and also provide information for evaluating alternatives. Technical personnel are particularly important influencers.
4. *Deciders:* People who decide on product requirements or on suppliers.
5. *Approvers:* People who authorize the proposed actions of deciders or buyers.
6. *Buyers:* People who have formal authority to select the supplier and arrange the purchase terms. Buyers may help shape product specifications, but they play their major role in selecting vendors and negotiating. In more complex purchases, the buyers might include high-level managers.
7. *Gatekeepers:* People who have the power to prevent sellers or information from reaching members of the buying center. For example, purchasing agents, receptionists, and telephone operators may prevent salespersons from contacting users or deciders.

The average number of people involved in a buying decision ranges from about three (for services and items used in day-to-day operations) to almost five (for such high-ticket purchases as construction work and machinery). To target their efforts properly, business marketers have to figure out: Who are the major decision participants? What decisions do they influence? What is their level of influence? What evaluation criteria do they use? Consider the following example:

> A company sells nonwoven disposable surgical gowns to hospitals. The hospital personnel who participate in this buying decision include the vice president of purchasing, the operating-room administrator, and the surgeons. The vice president of purchasing analyzes whether the hospital should buy disposable gowns or reusable gowns. If the findings favor disposable gowns, then the operating-room administrator compares various competitors' products and prices and makes a choice. This administrator considers absorbency, antiseptic quality, design, and cost, and normally buys the brand that meets the functional requirements at the lowest cost. Surgeons influence the decision retroactively by reporting their satisfaction with the particular brand.

When a buying center includes many participants, the business marketer will not have the time or resources to reach all of them. Small sellers concentrate on reaching the *key buying influencers.* Larger sellers go for *multilevel in-depth selling* to reach as many participants as possible. Their salespeople virtually "live" with their high-volume customers. Companies will have to rely more heavily on their communications program to reach hidden buying influences and keep their current customers informed.[13]

Business marketers must periodically review their assumptions about buying center participants. For years, Kodak sold X-ray film to hospital lab technicians. Kodak did not notice that the decision was increasingly being made by professional administrators. As sales declined, Kodak hurriedly revised its market target strategy.

major influences on buying decisions

Business buyers respond to many influences when they make their decisions. When supplier offerings are similar, business buyers can satisfy the purchasing requirements with any supplier, and they place more weight on the personal treatment they receive. Where supplier offerings differ substantially, business buyers are more accountable for their choices and pay more attention to economic factors.

Business buyers respond to four main influences: environmental, organizational, interpersonal, and individual (See Figure 8.1).[14]

figure **8.1**

Major Influences on
Industrial Buying Behavior

figure **8.1**

Major Influences on Industrial Buying Behavior

environmental factors

Business buyers pay close attention to current and expected economic factors, such as the level of production, investment, consumer spending, and the interest rate. In a recession, business buyers reduce their investment in plant, equipment, and inventories. Business marketers can do little to stimulate total demand in this environment. They can only fight harder to increase or maintain their share of demand.

Companies that fear a shortage of key materials are willing to buy and hold large inventories. They will sign long-term contracts with suppliers to ensure a steady flow of materials. DuPont, Ford, and several other major companies regard long-term *supply planning* as a major responsibility of their purchasing managers.

Business buyers actively monitor technological, political-regulatory, and competitive developments. For example, environmental concerns cause changes in business buyer behavior. A printing firm might favor paper suppliers that carry a wide selection of recycled papers or ink vendors who use environmentally safe ink. One buyer claimed, "We push suppliers with technical expertise to be more socially conscious."

organizational factors

Every organization has specific purchasing objectives, policies, procedures, organizational structures, and systems. Business marketers need to be aware of the following organizational trends in the purchasing area.

PURCHASING–DEPARTMENT UPGRADING   In the past, purchasing departments occupied a low position in the management hierarchy, in spite of often managing more than half the company's costs. The typical firm spends about 60 percent of its net sales on purchased goods and services. Recent competitive pressures have led many companies to upgrade their purchasing departments and elevate administrators to vice presidential rank. Today's purchasing departments are staffed with MBAs who aspire to be CEOs—like Thomas Stallkamp, Chrysler's former executive vice president of procurement and supply, who cut costs and streamlined the automaker's manufacturing processes.[15]

These new, more strategically oriented purchasing departments have been changed, from old-fashioned "purchasing departments" with an emphasis on buying at the lowest cost, to "procurement departments" with a mission to seek the best value from fewer and better suppliers. Some multinationals have even elevated them to "strategic supply departments" with responsibility for global sourcing and partnering. At Caterpillar, for example, purchasing, inventory control, production scheduling, and traffic have been combined into one department.

The upgrading of purchasing means that business marketers must correspondingly upgrade their sales personnel to match the higher caliber of the business buyers.

CROSS-FUNCTIONAL ROLES   Most purchasing professionals describe their job as less clerical, more strategic, technical, team-oriented, and involving more responsibility than ever before. "Purchasing is doing more cross-functional work than it did in the past," says David Duprey, a buyer for Anaren Microwave Inc. Sixty-one percent of buyers surveyed said the buying group was more involved in new-product design and development than it was five years ago; and more than half of the buyers participate in cross-functional teams, with suppliers well represented.[16]

CENTRALIZED PURCHASING   In multidivisional companies, most purchasing is carried out by separate divisions because of their differing needs. Some companies, however, have started to centralize their purchasing. Headquarters identifies materials purchased by several divisions and buys them centrally, thereby gaining more purchasing clout. The individual divisions can buy from another source if they can get a better deal, but in general, centralized purchasing produces substantial savings. For the business marketer, this development means dealing with fewer and higher-level buyers and using a national account sales group to deal with large corporate buyers.

DECENTRALIZED PURCHASING OF SMALL-TICKET ITEMS   At the same time, companies are decentralizing some purchasing operations by empowering employees to purchase small-ticket items such as special binders, coffeemakers, or Christmas trees. This has come about through the availability of corporate purchasing cards issued by credit-card organizations. Companies distribute the cards to foremen, clerks, and secretaries; the cards incorporate codes that set credit limits and restrict where they can be used. National Semiconductor's purchasing chief has noted that the cards have cut processing costs from $30 an order to a few cents. The additional benefit is that buyers and suppliers now spend less time on paperwork, so purchasing departments have more time for building partnerships.[17]

INTERNET PURCHASING   Forrester Research estimates that B2B transactions over the net will reach $2.7 trillion in 2004. The move to Internet purchasing has far-reaching implications for suppliers and will change the shape of purchasing for years to come. (See "Marketing for the New Economy: The Business-to-Business Cyberbuying Bazaar.")

Although the dot-com crash took its toll on the e-commerce industry, many brick-and-mortar companies wanted ways to expand their online presence: Often they looked to build their business-to-business operations by targeting small businesses, which account for 98 percent of all U.S. employers. Office supply megastores, which had traditionally courted small businesses at their retail locations, aggressively developed online e-commerce ventures in search of profits.

Office Max, Office Depot, Staples   With the launch of OfficeMax.com in 1995, this office supply retailer became the first business in its segment to offer e-commerce solutions for small businesses. In addition to an online catalog of over 30,000 items, the site offers @MaxSolutions, a small business resource center. In 1998, OfficeMax.com ranked as the top office supply superstore e-commerce venture in terms of traffic; in 2000, *BtoB* magazine rated the site number one among B2B Web sites. In 1998, Office Depot opened officedepot.com, and Staples developed a B2B Web site called Staples.com, specifically tailored for small businesses. Both sites have a complete searchable product catalog, online order tracking, and free next-day delivery for orders exceeding $50. In 2000, Staples reported that average yearly spending of small business customers increased 367 percent if the customers shopped online instead of in store locations."[18]

marketing for the **new economy**

The Business-to-Business (B2B) Cyberbuying Bazaar

With all the buzz about consumer online shopping, it is easy to lose sight of one of the most significant trends in e-commerce: the tremendous growth of business-to-business e-*procurement*. Experts estimate the B2B e-procurement will be 10 to 15 times larger in dollar volume than B2C buying. In addition to companies posting their own Web pages on the Internet, they have established intranets for company members to communicate with one another, and extranets to link a company's communications and data with its regular suppliers and distributors.

So far, most of the products businesses are buying electronically are *MRO materials* (maintenance, repair, and operations) and travel and entertainment services. MRO materials make up 30 percent of business purchases, and the transaction costs for order processing are high, which means there is a huge incentive to streamline the process. Here are some examples: Los Angeles County purchases everything from chickens to condoms over the Internet. National Semiconductor has automated almost all of the company's 3,500 monthly requisitions to buy materials ranging from the sterile booties worn in its fabrication plants to state-of-the-art software. GE buys not only general operating supplies, but also industrial supplies online. Now that GE Information Services (GEIS) has opened its buying site to other companies, the company is well on its way to creating a vast electronic clearinghouse. Hundreds of thousands of firms will exchange trillions of dollars of industrial inputs—with GEIS running the show. The state of Pennsylvania wanted to buy rock salt and went on FreeMarkets.com; 615 bids came in from 9 bidders during the day, reducing the cost of rock salt by 7 percent and saving $2.5 million for the taxpayers of Pennsylvania.

Over 54 percent of companies now purchase over the Internet. They are utilizing electronic marketplaces that are popping up in several forms:

- *Catalog sites.* Companies can order thousands of items through electronic catalogs, such as Grainger's.
- *Vertical markets.* Companies buying industrial products such as plastics, steel, or chemicals, or buying services such as logistics or media can go to specialized Web sites (called *e-hubs*). For example, Plastics.com allows thousands of plastics buyers to search for the best prices from the thousands of plastics sellers.

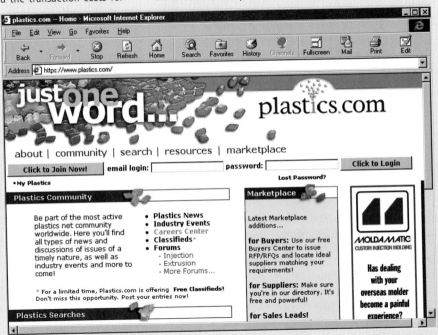

The e-hub Plastics.com home page offers buyers and sellers of plastics a marketplace plus news and information.

OTHER ORGANIZATIONAL FACTORS **Long-Term Contracts** Business buyers are increasingly initiating or accepting long-term contracts with reliable suppliers. For example, General Motors wants to buy from fewer suppliers who are willing to locate close to its plants and produce high-quality components. In addition, business marketers are using the Internet to set up extranets with important customers to facilitate and lower the cost of transactions. Their customers enter orders directly on the computer, and these orders are automatically transmitted to the supplier. Some companies go further and shift the ordering responsibility to their suppliers in systems called *vendor-managed inventory*. These suppliers are privy to the customer's inventory levels and take responsibility to replenish it automatically through *continuous replenishment programs*.

- *Auction sites.* Many auction sites exist for industrial goods, especially those that are surplus.
- *Spot (or exchange) markets.* Many commodities are sold on spot electronic markets where prices change by the minute. CheMatch.com is an *exchange* for buyers and sellers of bulk chemicals such as benzine.
- *Barter markets.* In these markets, participants offer to trade goods or services.
- *Buying alliances.* Several companies buying the same goods join together to gain deeper discounts on volume purchases. Several consumer companies (including Coca-Cola, Sara Lee, Kraft, PepsiCo, Gillette, and P&G) formed a buying alliance called Transora that will use its leverage to obtain lower prices for raw materials and shipping costs. Several major car manufacturers (GM, Ford, and DaimlerChrysler) formed Covisint to obtain lower prices for auto parts. They believe they may save as much as $1,200 per car.

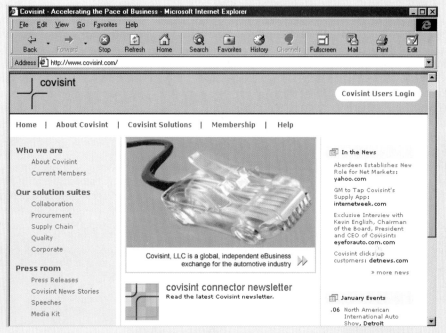

Covisint's Web site offers both services and information.

The online business buying juggernaut promises mostly good and some bad effects:

- Shave transaction costs for both buyers and suppliers
- Reduce time between order and delivery
- Consolidate purchasing systems
- Reduce drudgery and paperwork
- Forge more intimate relationships between partners and buyers
- Erode supplier–buyer loyalty
- Create potential security disasters

Sources: Robert Yoegel, "The Evolution of B-to-B Selling on the 'Net,'" *Target Marketing* (August 1998): 34; Andy Reinhardt, "Extranets: Log On, Link Up, Save Big," *BusinessWeek,* June 22, 1998, p. 134; "To Byte the Hand that Feeds," *The Economist,* June 17, 1998, pp. 61–62; John Evan Frook, "Buying Behemoth—By Shifting $5B in Spending To Extranets, GE Could Ignite a Development Frenzy," *Internetweek,* August 17, 1998, p. 1; John Jesitus, "Procuring an Edge," *Industry Week,* June 23, 1997, pp. 56–62.

Purchasing-Performance Evaluation and Buyers' Professional Development Many companies have set up incentive systems to reward purchasing managers for good buying performance, in much the same way that sales personnel receive bonuses for good selling performance. These systems are leading purchasing managers to increase pressure on sellers for the best terms.

Improved Supply Chain Management Purchasing executives are increasingly involved in working with marketing and other company executives in building a seamless supply chain management system from the purchase of raw materials to the on-time arrival of finished goods to the end users.

marketing **insight**

Just-in-Time II (JIT II): The Next Level of Customer–Supplier Partnerships

The Bose Corporation, in Framingham, Massachusetts, has won numerous awards for the streamlined design of its minuscule, but powerful, stereo systems. The company is equally revered for having streamlined the world of purchasing and materials planning with a home-grown process called Just-in-Time II.

In 1987, Lance Dixon, the company's director of purchasing and logistics, came up with a startling idea. Why not remove the salesperson, buyer, and planner from the typical relationship Bose had with suppliers? In striving to answer this question, Dixon created JIT II, a refinement of the JIT inventory system. Rather than concentrating on reducing inventory, as JIT does, JIT II's focus is on reducing the costs and time involved in day-to-day transactions with suppliers.

The central concept of JIT II is that the supplier, at his or her own expense, places one or more full-time employees at its customer's site. These "inplants" work full-time at the customer's location and take the place of the customer's buyer and materials planner and of the supplier's sales representative. Three relationships have been streamlined into one. According to Dixon, "You no longer have information being handed off from a material planner to a buyer, who then hands it off to a salesman, who eventually hands it off back to his plant. Three or four of those transactions are now occurring within the mind of one individual with the authority to act. It's seamless."

The key ingredient that greases the wheels of JIT II is "trust." Says Christ Labonte, materials manager for G&F Industries, Bose's first inplant supplier, "It's a fresh, nontraditional agreement based on trust. After people get comfortable in their partnering, they start turning up rocks they wouldn't have turned up and revealing causes that were sacred cows."

In addition to saving time, the use of inplants also adds value. Bose found that its inplanted suppliers provided welcome expertise in the creation of audio equipment. At the same time, Bose employees profit from the stimulus of imaginative suggestions for improved product design and engineering. Intrigued by the obvious benefits of JIT II, many other companies have since implemented it. Among them are IBM, JLG Industries, Intel's New Mexico plant, S. C. Johnson Wax, and Motorola Automotive Electronics.

Sources: Robert Hiebeler, Thomas B. Kelly, and Charles Ketteman, *Best Practices: Building Your Business with Customer-Focused Solutions* (New York: Arthur Andersen/Simon & Schuster, 1998), pp. 94–96; "Professional Profile: Intel," *Purchasing,* February 13, 1997, p. 33; Lance Dixon, "JLG Industries Offers JIT II advice," *Purchasing,* January 15, 1998, p. 39.

Lean Production Many manufacturers have moved toward a new way of manufacturing called lean production, which enables them to produce a greater variety of high-quality products at lower cost, in less time, using less labor. Among the elements of this new system are just-in-time (JIT) production, stricter quality control, frequent and reliable delivery from suppliers, suppliers locating closer to major customers, computerized purchasing systems, stable production schedules made available to suppliers, and single sourcing with early supplier involvement.

The linchpin of lean production, just-in-time (JIT) inventory has dramatically changed the way companies purchase products. **Just-in-time** is a method pioneered by Japanese companies in which the goal is zero inventory with 100 percent quality. JIT brings together all materials and parts needed at each stage of production at the precise time they are required. JIT has now given way to JIT II and a further streamlining of the purchasing process. (See "Marketing Insight: Just-in-Time II (JIT II): The Next Level of Customer–Supplier Partnerships.")

interpersonal and individual factors

Buying centers usually include several participants with differing interests, authority, status, empathy, and persuasiveness. The business marketer is not likely to know what kind of group dynamics take place during the buying decision process, although whatever information he or she can discover about personalities and interpersonal factors would be useful.

Each buyer carries personal motivations, perceptions, and preferences, which are influenced by the buyer's age, income, education, job position, personality, attitudes toward risk, and culture. Buyers definitely exhibit different buying styles. There are "keep-it-simple" buyers, "own-expert" buyers, "want-the-best" buyers, and "want-everything-done" buyers. Some younger, highly educated buyers are computer experts who conduct rigorous analyses of competitive proposals before choosing a supplier. Other buyers are "toughies" from the old school and pit the competing sellers against one another.

cultural factors

Buying factors vary from one country to another. Here are some rules of social and business etiquette that marketers should understand when doing business in other countries:[19]

- *France:* If you do not speak French, apologize for your lack of knowledge. The French are quite proud of their language and believe that everyone should feel privileged to speak it.
- *Germany:* Germans are sticklers for titles. Try to introduce people using their full, correct title, no matter how long it is. Also, Germans shake hands at both the beginning and the end of business meetings.
- *Japan:* Most Japanese businesspeople know what will be discussed at a meeting, how everyone feels about it, and how it will affect their business before they even get there. The purpose of a meeting is to reach consensus. A flexible agenda is necessary so that discussions flow more freely. Foreigners should not try to adhere religiously to a set agenda.
- *Korea:* While doing business with Koreans, Americans need to be sensitive to Korea's historical relationship with Japan, which made a virtual colony of the Korean peninsula. Koreans do not like foreigners to assume that their culture is the same as Japan's. However, Koreans do have great respect for Japanese business acumen, and like the Japanese, they still observe Confucian ethics based on respect for authority and the primacy of the group over the individual.
- *Latin America:* In Latin America, it is common to make initial face-to-face contact through an outside liaison who knows the customer's company well. The liaison, or *enchufe*, introduces the salespeople or business representatives to key players. Some time is spent in getting to know each other before talking business.

the purchasing/procurement process

Business buyers buy goods and services to make money or to reduce operating costs or to satisfy a social or legal obligation. A steel company will add another furnace if it sees a chance to make more money. It will computerize its accounting system to reduce the costs of doing business. It will add pollution-control equipment to meet legal requirements.

In principle, business buyers seek to obtain the highest benefit package (economic, technical, service, and social) in relation to a market offering's costs. A business buyer's *incentive to purchase* will be greater in proportion to the ratio of perceived benefits to costs—that is, the greater the perceived value. The marketer's task is to construct a profitable offering that delivers superior customer value to the target buyers.

We can distinguish three company purchasing orientations:[20]

- *Buying Orientation:* The purchaser's focus is short-term and tactical. Buyers are rewarded on their ability to obtain the lowest price from suppliers for the given level of quality and availability. Buyers use two tactics: *commoditization*, where they imply that the product is a commodity and care only about price; and *multisourcing*, where they use several sources and make them compete for shares of the company's purchases.
- *Procurement Orientation:* Here buyers simultaneously seek quality improvements and cost reductions. Buyers develop collaborative relationships with major suppliers and seek savings through better management of acquisition, conversion, and disposal costs. They encourage early supplier involvement in materials handling, inventory levels, just-in-time management, and even product co-design. They negotiate long-term contracts with major suppliers to ensure the timely flow of materials. They work closely with their manufacturing group on *materials requirement planning (MRP)* to make sure that supplies arrive on time.

- *Supply Chain Management Orientation:* Here purchasing's role is further broadened to become a more strategic, value-adding operation. The firm focuses on how to improve the whole value chain from raw materials to end users. Here is how one company is trying to optimize every link on the value chain.

Pioneer Hi-Bred   Des Moines, Iowa–based Pioneer Hi-Bred is a major supplier of corn seed and other agricultural commodities. Its patented hybrid seeds yield 10 percent more corn than its major competitors' seeds and earn a price premium. Still, Pioneer recognizes that seeds account for only 21 cents of the farm operator's value chain. In order to gain a larger share of that value chain, Pioneer can explore three alternatives: (1) It can produce a more disease-resistant seed and charge more because this reduces farmers' need for chemicals. (2) It can bundle fertilizers and chemicals in addition to seeds, but this might require certain competencies and scale it does not presently have. (3) It can provide value-added services. Pioneer decided on the third choice and equipped representatives with notebook computers to provide farmers with customized reports and recommendations. As a result of an investment Pioneer made in this two-way information flow, Pioneer Hi-Bred's share of the North American retail corn seed market has grown from 35 percent during the mid 1980's to 42 percent in 2000.[21]

types of purchasing processes

Marketers need to understand how business purchasing departments work. These departments purchase many types of products, using different purchasing processes. Peter Kraljic distinguished four product-related purchasing processes:[22]

1. *Routine products:* These products have low value and cost to the customer and involve little risk (e.g., office supplies). Customers will seek the lowest price and emphasize routine ordering. Suppliers will offer to standardize and consolidate orders through blanket contracts and facilities management.

2. *Leverage products:* These products have high value and cost to the customer but involve little risk of supply (e.g., engine pistons) because many companies make them. The supplier knows that the customer will compare market offerings and costs, and it needs to show that its offering minimizes the customer's total cost.

3. *Strategic products:* These products have high value and cost to the customer and also involve high risk (e.g., mainframe computers). The customer will want a well-known and trusted supplier and be willing to pay more than the average price. The supplier should seek strategic alliances taking the form of early supplier involvement, co-development programs, and co-investment.

4. *Bottleneck products:* These products have low value and cost to the customer but they involve some risk (e.g., spare parts). The customer will want a supplier who can guarantee a steady supply. The supplier should propose standard parts and offer a tracking system, delivery on demand, and a help desk.

Clearly, the purchasing process will vary with different types of products. Business marketers need to adapt to the buyers' normal steps in a specific buying decision in order to win and maintain the account.

stages in the buying process

At this point we are ready to describe the general stages in the business buying decision process. Robinson and Associates have identified eight stages and called them *buyphases.*[23] The stages are shown in Table 8.1. This model is called the *buygrid* framework.

PROBLEM RECOGNITION   The buying process begins when someone in the company recognizes a problem or need that can be met by acquiring a good or service. The recognition can be triggered by internal or external stimuli. Internally, some common

table **8.1**

		Buyclasses		
		New Task	Modified Rebuy	Straight Rebuy
Buyphases	1. Problem recognition	Yes	Maybe	No
	2. General need description	Yes	Maybe	No
	3. Product specification	Yes	Yes	Yes
	4. Supplier search	Yes	Maybe	No
	5. Proposal solicitation	Yes	Maybe	No
	6. Supplier selection	Yes	Maybe	No
	7. Order-routine specification	Yes	Maybe	No
	8. Performance review	Yes	Yes	Yes

Buygrid Framework: Major Stages (Buyphases) of the Industrial Buying Process in Relation to Major Buying Situations (Buyclasses)

events lead to problem recognition. The company decides to develop a new product and needs new equipment and materials. A machine breaks down and requires new parts. Purchased material turns out to be unsatisfactory, and the company searches for another supplier. A purchasing manager senses an opportunity to obtain lower prices or better quality.

Externally, the buyer may get new ideas at a trade show, see an ad, or receive a call from a sales representative who offers a better product or a lower price. Business marketers can stimulate problem recognition by direct mail, telemarketing, and calling on prospects.

GENERAL NEED DESCRIPTION AND PRODUCT SPECIFICATION Next, the buyer determines the needed item's general characteristics and required quantity. For standard items, this is simple. For complex items, the buyer will work with others—engineers, users—to define characteristics like reliability, durability, or price. Business marketers can help by describing how their products meet the buyer's needs.

The buying organization now develops the item's technical specifications. Often, the company will assign a product-value-analysis (PVA) engineering team to the project. **Product value analysis** is an approach to cost reduction in which components are studied to determine if they can be redesigned or standardized or made by cheaper methods of production. The PVA team will examine the high-cost components in a given product—usually 20 percent of the parts account for 80 percent of the costs of manufacturing it. The team will also identify overdesigned components that last longer than the product itself, then decide on the optimal characteristics. Tightly written specifications will allow the buyer to refuse components that are too expensive or that fail to meet specified standards. Suppliers can use product value analysis as a tool for positioning themselves to win an account.

SUPPLIER SEARCH The buyer now tries to identify the most appropriate suppliers. The buyer can examine trade directories, contact other companies for recommendations, watch trade advertisements, and attend trade shows. However, these days the most likely place to look is on the Internet. Web sites are organized around two types of e-hubs: *vertical hubs* centered on industries (plastics, steel, chemicals, paper) and *functional hubs* (logistics, media buying, advertising, energy management). Besides doing e-procurement on these Web sites, companies can do e-procurement in three other ways:

- *Direct extranet links to major suppliers.* A company can set up extranet links to its major suppliers. For example, it can set up a direct e-procurement account at Dell or Office Depot, and its employees can make their purchases this way.
- *Buying alliances.* Coca-Cola, Sara Lee, Kraft, PepsiCo, Gillette, P&G, and several other companies joined forces to form a buying alliance called Transora to use their combined leverage to obtain lower prices for raw materials. Transora members also share data on less expensive ways to ship products and track inventory. Several auto companies (GM, Ford, DaimlerChrysler) formed Covisint to use leverage to obtain lower prices for auto parts.
- *Company buying sites.* General Electric formed the Trading Process Network (TPN) where it posts *requests for proposals (RFPs),* negotiates terms, and places orders.

Normally, major companies do their purchasing locally and by division, but moving into e-procurement involves more than acquiring software; it requires changing purchasing strategy and structure. However, the benefits are many: Aggregating purchasing across multiple departments gains larger, centrally negotiated volume discounts. There is less buying of substandard goods from outside the approved list of suppliers, and a smaller purchasing staff is required for e-procurement.

Many types of purchases can be made directly and safely on the Internet. If the information is rich enough to satisfy the buyer, there is no further stage to purchasing. When this is not the case, the buyer proceeds to request proposals from some of the business buyers he has identified on the Web.

The supplier's task is to get listed in major online catalogs or services, develop a strong advertising and promotion program, and build a good reputation in the marketplace. Suppliers who lack the required production capacity or suffer from a poor reputation will be rejected. Those who qualify may be visited by the buyer's agents, who will examine the suppliers' manufacturing facilities and meet their personnel. After evaluating each company, the buyer will end up with a short list of qualified suppliers.

PROPOSAL SOLICITATION The buyer invites qualified suppliers to submit proposals. If the item is complex or expensive, the buyer will require a detailed written proposal from each qualified supplier. After evaluating the proposals, the buyer will invite a few suppliers to make formal presentations.

Business marketers must be skilled in researching, writing, and presenting proposals. Written proposals should be marketing documents that describe value and benefits in customer terms, not just technical documents. Oral presentations should inspire confidence, and position their company's capabilities and resources so that they stand out from the competition.

Consider the hurdles that Campbell Soup and Xerox have set up in qualifying suppliers.

Campbell Soup Company The Campbell Qualified Supplier Program requires would-be suppliers to pass through three stages: qualified supplier, approved supplier, and select supplier. To become qualified, the supplier has to demonstrate technical capabilities, financial health, cost-effectiveness, high-quality standards, and innovativeness. A supplier that satisfies these criteria then applies for approval, which is granted only after the supplier has attended a Campbell Vendor seminar, accepted an implementation team visit, and agreed to make certain changes and commitments. Once approved, the supplier becomes a select supplier when it demonstrates high product uniformity, continuous quality improvement, and just-in-time delivery capabilities.

Xerox   Xerox qualifies only suppliers who meet the ISO 9000 quality standards (see Chapter 3), but to win the company's top award—certification status—a supplier must first complete the Xerox Multinational Supplier Quality Survey. The survey requires the supplier to issue a quality assurance manual, to adhere to continuous improvement principles, and to demonstrate effective systems implementation. Once qualified, a supplier must participate in Xerox's Continuous Supplier Involvement process: The two companies work together to create specifications for quality, cost, delivery times, and process capability. The final step toward certification requires a supplier to undergo additional, rigorous quality training and an evaluation based on the same criteria as the Malcolm Baldridge National Quality Award. Not surprisingly, only 176 suppliers worldwide have achieved the 95 percent rating required for certification as a Xerox supplier.[24]

SUPPLIER SELECTION   Before selecting a supplier, the buying center will specify desired supplier attributes and indicate their relative importance. It will then rate suppliers on these attributes and identify the most attractive suppliers. Buying centers often use a supplier-evaluation model such as the one shown in Table 8.2.

In practice, business buyers use a variety of methods to assess supplier value. Business marketers need to do a better job of understanding how business buyers arrive at their valuations. Anderson, Jain, and Chintagunta conducted a study of the main methods business marketers use to assess customer value and found eight different *customer value assessment (CVA)* methods. Companies tended to use the simpler methods, although the more sophisticated ones promise to produce a more accurate picture of customer perceived value. (See "Marketing Memo: Methods of Assessing Customer Value.")

The choice and importance of different attributes varies with the type of buying situation.[25] Delivery reliability, price, and supplier reputation are important for *routine-order products*. For *procedural-problem products*, such as a copying machine, the three most important attributes are technical service, supplier flexibility, and product reliability. For *political-problem products* that stir rivalries in the organization (such as the choice of a computer system), the most important attributes are price, supplier reputation, product reliability, service reliability, and supplier flexibility.

The buying center may attempt to negotiate with its preferred suppliers for better prices and terms before making the final selection. Despite moves toward strategic sourcing, partnering, and participation in cross-functional teams, buyers still spend a

table **8.2**

An Example of Vendor Analysis

Attributes		Rating Scale			
	Importance Weights	Poor (1)	Fair (2)	Good (3)	Excellent (4)
Price	.30				x
Supplier reputation	.20			x	
Product reliability	.30				x
Service reliability	.10		x		
Supplier flexibility	.10			x	
Total score: .30(4) + .20(3) + .30(4) + .10(2) + .10(3) = 3.5					

Marketing
MEMO

Methods of Assessing Customer Value

1. *Internal engineering assessment:* Company engineers use laboratory tests to estimate the product's performance characteristics. If the performance is one and a half times better than the closest competitor's performance, the company feels that it can charge up to one and a half times more. Weakness: Ignores the fact that in different applications, the product will have different economic value.
2. *Field value-in-use assessment:* Customers are interviewed about cost elements associated with using the new-product offering compared to an incumbent product and assign money values to these cost elements. An example would be pricing a Caterpillar tractor against a competitor. Caterpillar tractors have less downtime, quicker repair time, and more resale value. The task is to assess how much each element is worth to the buyer.
3. *Focus-group value assessment:* Customers in a focus group are asked what value they would put on potential market offerings.
4. *Direct survey questions:* Customers are asked to place a direct dollar value on one or more changes in the market offering.
5. *Conjoint analysis:* Customers are asked to rank their preference for alternative market offerings or concepts. Statistical analysis is used to estimate the implicit value placed on each attribute of the offering.
6. *Benchmarks:* Customers are shown a "benchmark" offering and then a new market offering. They are asked how much more they would pay for the new offering. They can also be asked how much less they would pay if certain features were removed from the benchmark offering.
7. *Compositional approach:* Customers are asked to attach a monetary value to each of three alternative levels of a given attribute. This is repeated for other attributes. The values are then added together for any offer configuration.
8. *Importance ratings:* Customers are asked to rate the importance of different attributes. They are also asked to rate the supplier firms with respect to their performance on these attributes. The company can then estimate the relative value of each competitor's offer.

Source: James C. Anderson, Dipak C. Jain, and Pradeep K. Chintagunta, "A Customer Value Assessment in Business Markets: A State-of-Practice Study," *Journal of Business-to-Business Marketing* 1, no. 1 (1993): 3–29.

large chunk of their time haggling with suppliers on price. In 1998, 92 percent of buyers responding to a *Purchasing* magazine survey cited negotiating price as one of their top responsibilities. Nearly as many respondents said price remains a key criterion they use to select suppliers.[26] Marketers can counter the request for a lower price in a number of ways. They may be able to show evidence that the "life-cycle cost" of using their product is lower than that of competitors' products. They can also cite the value of the services the buyer now receives, especially where those services are superior to those offered by competitors. Here is an example of how two suppliers are using value-added services to gain a competitive edge.

Hewlett-Packard Hewlett-Packard's marketing division has developed a concept called "trusted advisor." The marketers felt HP needed to move beyond selling systems to selling itself as an advisor and had to offer customers specific solutions to unique problems. What HP discovered is that some companies want a partner and others simply want a product that works. HP assumes an advisory role when it sells complex products like a network computer system. HP estimates that the new way of selling has contributed to a 60 percent growth of the high-end computer business. The company has increased its consulting business and is working on enterprisewide projects through a series of partnerships with systems integrators and software companies.[27]

Even service companies can add value by offering an extra personal touch.

Advanced Travel Management Service with a personal touch has helped a corporate travel agency, Advanced Travel Management (ATM), recruit a roster of high-profile, demanding clients—including NatWest Markets and DDB Needham

Worldwide Inc. ATM encourages its agents to confirm hotel reservations, check weather reports to predict canceled flights, and ask if travelers need driving instructions generated from mapping software or the Internet. ATM also has written city guides with information on local restaurants, sporting events, hospitals, and even dentists. If a hotel that ATM has booked forgets to give a client a wake-up call and the client complains, partners Michael Share or Frank Kogen call both the hotel and the person in charge of travel at the customer's company to see if they can make the client happy; and they send flowers to the client. Without spending money on an organized sales and marketing effort, this small, boutique-style agency has stolen business from the likes of industry leader American Express Travel Related Services Company, Inc.[28]

Other approaches may also be used to counter intense price pressure. Consider the following example.

Lincoln Electric   Lincoln Electric has instituted a Guaranteed Cost Reduction Program for its distributors. When a customer insists that a Lincoln distributor lower prices to match Lincoln's competitors, the company and the particular distributor may guarantee that, during the coming year, they will find cost reductions in the customer's plant that meet or exceed the price difference between Lincoln's products and the competition's. If they fail, they will rebate the difference. Lincoln sends in its expert production team to identify and propose specific customer cost savings. If an independent audit at the end of the year does not reveal the promised cost savings, Lincoln Electric and the distributor compensate the customer for the difference, with Lincoln paying 70 percent and the distributor paying the rest.[29]

As part of the buyer selection process, buying centers must decide how many suppliers to use. In the past, many companies preferred a large supplier base to ensure adequate supplies and to obtain price concessions. These companies would insist on annual negotiations for contract renewal and would often shift the amount of business they gave to each supplier from year to year. The company would normally place most of the year's order with a prime supplier, and the rest with secondary suppliers. The prime supplier would make an effort to protect its position, whereas the secondary suppliers would try to expand their share. Out-suppliers would try to get a foot in the door by offering an especially low price.

However, companies are increasingly reducing the number of suppliers. Companies such as Ford, Motorola, and AlliedSignal have cut the number of suppliers by anywhere from 20 to 80 percent. These companies want their chosen suppliers to be responsible for a larger component system; they want them to achieve continuous quality and performance improvement while at the same time lowering the supply price each year by a given percentage. These companies expect their suppliers to work closely with them during product development, and they value their suggestions. There is even a trend toward single sourcing.

The *Knoxville News-Sentinel;* **the** *New York Daily News*   The *Knoxville News-Sentinel* and the *New York Daily News* rely on a single source for their newsprint. With single sourcing, it is easier to control newsprint inventories, and there is only one supplier to check with. Using one source not only can translate into more consistency of product, but also allows pressrooms to configure themselves for one particular kind of newsprint rather than changing presses for papers with different attributes.[30]

Companies who use multiple sources often cite the threat of a labor strike as the biggest deterrent to single sourcing. Another reason companies may be reluctant to use a single source is the tendency to become complacent. These companies fear they will become too comfortable in the relationship and lose their competitive edge. Some shrewd value-added marketers have come up with ways to counter this fear.

GC Electronics   GC Electronics of Rockford, Illinois, has a "one source lowest price guarantee program," which plays up the reduced transaction and purchasing costs of using it as a single source. However, if, after being with the program for a while, distributors think they could have gotten a better deal elsewhere, GC offers them a 6 percent rebate if they have the quotes to back up their claims.[31]

ORDER-ROUTINE SPECIFICATION   After selecting suppliers, the buyer negotiates the final order, listing the technical specifications, the quantity needed, the expected time of delivery, return policies, warranties, and so on. In the case of maintenance, repair, and operating items, buyers are moving toward blanket contracts rather than periodic purchase orders. A **blanket contract** establishes a long-term relationship in which the supplier promises to resupply the buyer as needed, at agreed-upon prices, over a specified period of time. Because the stock is held by the seller, blanket contracts are sometimes called **stockless purchase plans**. The buyer's computer automatically sends an order to the seller when stock is needed.

Blanket contracting leads to more single-source buying and ordering of more items from that single source. This system locks suppliers in tighter with the buyer and makes it difficult for out-suppliers to break in unless the buyer becomes dissatisfied with the in-supplier's prices, quality, or service.

PERFORMANCE REVIEW   The buyer periodically reviews the performance of the chosen supplier(s). Three methods are commonly used. The buyer may contact the end users and ask for their evaluations; the buyer may rate the supplier on several criteria using a weighted score method; or the buyer might aggregate the cost of poor supplier performance to come up with adjusted costs of purchase, including price. The performance review may lead the buyer to continue, modify, or end the relationship with the supplier. The supplier should monitor the same variables that are monitored by the product's buyers and end users.

We have described the buying stages involved in a new-task buying situation. In modified-rebuy or straight-rebuy situations, some stages would be compressed or bypassed. For example, in a straight-rebuy situation, the buyer normally has a favorite supplier or a ranked list of suppliers. Thus the supplier search and proposal solicitation stages would be skipped.

The eight-stage buyphase model describes the major steps in the business buying process. Tracing out a **buyflow map** can provide many clues to the business marketer. A buyflow map for the purchase of a packaging machine in Japan is shown in Figure 8.2. The numbers within the icons are defined at the right. The italicized numbers between icons show the flow of events. Over 20 people in the purchasing company were involved, including the production manager and staff, new-product committee, company laboratory, marketing department, and the department for market development. The entire decision-making process took 121 days.

institutional and government markets

Our discussion has concentrated largely on the buying behavior of profit-seeking companies. Much of what we have said also applies to the buying practices of institutional and government organizations. However, we want to highlight certain special features found in these markets.

| figure **8.2** | Organizational Buying Behavior in Japan: Packaging-Machine Purchase Process |

1 President
2 Financial department
3 Sales headquarters
4 Production chief
5 Decision
6 Discussion of production and sales plans
7 Production department
8 Production of packing process plan
9 New products development committee
10 Request for consultation
11 Production of new product marketing plan
12 Product development department
13 Discussion of design of prototype machines
14 Prototype machine
15 Placement of orders
16 Makers design and technical staff
17 Supplier A
18 Supplier B
19 Supplier C
20 Overseas machine exhibitions
21 Request for testing of prototype machines
22 Research staff
23 Production of basic design
24 Foreman
25 Production of draft plans
26 Marketing department

Source: "Japanese Firms Use Unique Buying Behavior," *The Japan Economic Journal*, December 23, 1980, p. 29. Reprinted by permission.

The **institutional market** consists of schools, hospitals, nursing homes, prisons, and other institutions that must provide goods and services to people in their care. Many of these organizations are characterized by low budgets and captive clienteles. For example, hospitals have to decide what quality of food to buy for patients. The buying objective here is not profit, because the food is provided as part of the total service package; nor is cost minimization the sole objective, because poor food will cause patients to complain and hurt the hospital's reputation. The hospital purchasing agent has to search for institutional-food vendors whose quality meets or exceeds a certain minimum standard and whose prices are low. In fact, many food vendors set up a separate division to sell to institutional buyers because of these buyers' special needs and characteristics. Thus, Heinz will produce, package, and price its ketchup differently to meet the different requirements of hospitals, colleges, and prisons.

Being a supplier of choice for the nation's schools or hospitals means big business.

Allegiance Healthcare A spinoff of Baxter Healthcare Corporation, Allegiance Healthcare has become the largest supplier of medical, surgical, and laboratory products in the United States. The company's stockless inventory program, known as ValueLink, was cited as a "best practice" by Arthur Andersen's business consulting practice. Currently in service at over 150 acute-care hospitals in the United States, this program supplies hospital personnel with the products they need when and where they need them. An integrated system meets the needs of customers who deal with life-and-death situations every minute. In the old system, an 18-wheeler simply dropped off a week's or a month's worth of supplies at the back door of a hospital. It inevitably turned out that the items most in demand were the ones in short supply, whereas the ones the hospital never used were available in great number. Allegiance estimates that its ValueLink system saves customers an average of $500,000 or more each year.[32]

In most countries, government organizations are a major buyer of goods and services. Government organizations typically require suppliers to submit bids, and normally they award the contract to the lowest bidder. In some cases, the government unit will make allowance for the supplier's superior quality or reputation for completing contracts on time. Governments will also buy on a negotiated contract basis, primarily in the case of complex projects involving major R&D costs and risks and in cases where there is little competition. Government organizations tend to favor domestic suppliers over foreign suppliers. A major complaint of multinationals operating in Europe was that each country showed favoritism toward its nationals in spite of superior offers that were available from foreign firms. The European Union is removing this bias.

Because their spending decisions are subject to public review, government organizations require considerable paperwork from suppliers, who often complain about excessive paperwork, bureaucracy, regulations, decision-making delays, and frequent shifts in procurement personnel. Given all the red tape, why would any firm want to do business with the U.S. government? Here is how Paul E. Goulding, a Washington, DC–based consultant who has helped clients obtain more than $30 billion in government contracts, answers that question:[33]

> When I hear that question, I tell the story of the businessman who buys a hardware store after moving to a small town. He asks his new employees who the biggest hardware customer in town is. He is surprised to learn that the customer isn't doing business with his store. When the owner asks why not, his employees say the customer is difficult to do business with and requires that a lot of forms be filled out. I point out that the same customer is probably very wealthy, doesn't bounce his checks, and usually does repeat business when satisfied. That's the type of customer the federal government can be.

The U.S. government buys goods and services valued at $200 billion. That makes Uncle Sam the largest customer in the world. It is not just the dollar figure that is large, but the number of individual acquisitions. According to the General Sources Administration Procurement Data Center, over 20 million individual contract actions are processed every year. Although most items purchased are between $2,500 and $25,000, the government also makes purchases in the billions, often of technology. But government decision makers often think that technology vendors have not done their homework. One common mistake is to talk to government officials about product applications and technical features. In addition, vendors do not pay enough attention to cost justification, which is a major activity for government procurement professionals. Companies hoping to be government contractors need to help government agencies see the bottom-line impact of products. Here is how one company does just that.

Cabletron Systems Inc. This Rochester, New Hampshire–based company distributes a free CD to prospects. The CD uses wizards that ask questions about the agency's network. The tool then automatically recommends specific Cabletron products and produces a return-on-investment summary and cost-justification report for its recommendations.[34]

Just as companies provide government agencies with guidelines on how best to purchase and use their products, governments provide would-be suppliers with detailed guidelines describing how to sell to the government. Yet suppliers still have to master the system and find ways to cut through the red tape. Goulding says that it requires an investment of time, money, and resources not unlike what is required for entering a new market overseas. Perhaps it is even more frustrating.

ADI Technology The federal government has always been ADI Technology Corporation's most important client: Federal contracts account for about 90 percent of its nearly $6 million in annual revenues. Yet managers at this professional services company often shake their heads at all the work that goes into winning the coveted government contracts. A comprehensive bid proposal will run from 500 to 700 pages because of federal paperwork requirements. The company's president estimates that the firm has spent as much as $20,000, mostly in worker hours, to prepare a single bid proposal.

Fortunately for businesses of all sizes, the federal government has been putting reforms in place to simplify the contracting procedure and make bidding more attractive. Some reforms place more emphasis on buying commercial off-the-shelf items instead of items built to the government's specs; online communication with vendors to eliminate the massive paperwork; and a "debriefing" from the appropriate government agency for vendors who lose a bid, enabling them to increase their chances of winning the next time around.[35] The government's goal is to get all purchases online. To do this, the government is likely to bet on Web-based forms, digital signatures, and electronic procurement cards (P-cards).[36] Several federal agencies that act as purchasing agents for the rest of the government have launched Web-based catalogs that allow authorized defense and civilian agencies to buy everything from medical and office supplies to clothing online. The General Services Administration, for example, not only sells stocked merchandise through its Web site, but also creates direct links between buyers and contract suppliers.

In spite of these reforms, many companies that sell to the government have not used a marketing orientation—for a number of reasons. The government's procurement policies have traditionally emphasized price, leading suppliers to invest considerable effort in bringing costs down. Where product characteristics are carefully specified, product differentiation is not a marketing factor; nor are advertising and personal selling of much consequence in winning bids.

Some companies have pursued government business by establishing separate government marketing departments. Gateway 2000 is one example.

Gateway 2000 Inc. Gateway markets particular products specifically to the government. The Destination PC is an example. Aimed at the K–12 education market, the Destination combines a big-screen TV with a PC that includes a wireless keyboard and remote. Salespeople who call on education departments discuss the product in terms of case studies, rather than megahertz rates and technical specifications. At the end of one year, Gateway's government sales were an estimated 41 percent of its $155 million total for that year.[37]

Companies such as Gateway, Rockwell, Kodak, and Goodyear anticipate government needs and projects, participate in the product specification phase, gather competitive intelligence, prepare bids carefully, and produce strong communications to describe and enhance their companies' reputations.

summary

1. Organizational buying is the decision-making process by which formal organizations establish the need for purchased products and services, then identify, evaluate, and choose among alternative brands and suppliers. The business market consists of all the organizations that acquire goods and services used in the production of other products or services that are sold, rented, or supplied to others.

2. Compared to consumer markets, business markets generally have fewer and larger buyers, a closer customer–supplier relationship, and more geographically concentrated buyers. Demand in the business market is derived from demand in the consumer market and fluctuates with the business cycle. Nonetheless, the total demand for many business goods and services is quite price-inelastic. Business marketers need to be aware of the role of professional purchasers and their influencers, the need for multiple sales calls, and the importance of direct purchasing, reciprocity, and leasing.

3. The buying center is the decision-making unit of a buying organization. It consists of initiators, users, influencers, deciders, approvers, buyers, and gatekeepers. To influence these parties, marketers must be aware of environmental, organizational, interpersonal, and individual factors.

4. The buying process consists of eight stages called buyphases: (1) problem recognition, (2) general need description, (3) product specification, (4) supplier search, (5) proposal solicitation, (6) supplier selection, (7) order-routine specification, and (8) performance review.

5. The institutional market consists of schools, hospitals, nursing homes, prisons, and other institutions that must provide goods and services to people in their care. Buyers for government organizations tend to require a great deal of paperwork from their vendors and tend to favor open bidding and domestic companies. Suppliers must be prepared to adapt their offers to the special needs and procedures found in institutional and government markets.

applications

marketing debate – how different is business-to-business marketing?

Many business-to-business marketing executives lament the challenges of business-to-business marketing, maintaining that many traditional marketing concepts and principles do not apply. For a number of reasons, they assert that selling products and services to a company is fundamentally different from selling to individuals. Others disagree, claiming that marketing theory is still valid and only involves some adaptation in the marketing tactics.

Take a position: Business-to-business marketing requires a special, unique set of marketing concepts and principles versus Business-to-business marketing is really not that different and the basic marketing concepts and principles apply.

marketing and advertising

1. As the ad in Figure 1 shows, Ford Credit provides commercial lending services for businesses buying Ford vehicles. The Ford logo is prominently featured in this ad, which invites businesspeople to call toll-free or visit the Web site (*www.commtruck.ford.com*) for more information about financing Ford truck and car purchases.

   a. Would an established business with an existing truck fleet be making a straight-rebuy, a modified-rebuy, or a new-task purchase when it orders a new Ford truck? How might Ford Credit use this information to create a suitable advertising campaign to encourage usage of its commercial lending services?

   b. Which members of a business's buying center are most likely to be involved in decisions about choosing and using a commercial lending service to finance a vehicle purchase? What are the implications for Ford Credit's marketing planning?

   c. People who participate in business buying decisions also make consumer buying decisions in private life. Which stages of the business buying process are likely to be most influenced by a business buyer's personal perceptions of and experience with Ford consumer vehicles and

   financing? What should Ford do to leverage positive impressions (or counter negative impressions) among consumers who participate in business buying decisions?

2. The Cessna ad in Figure 2 combines a dramatic photograph with descriptive copy focusing on attributes and benefits that are important to buyers of corporate aircraft. It also makes a head-to-head comparison with a competitive product to establish its superiority with specific evidence that is meaningful to the target market.

   a. Which environmental and interpersonal factors are likely to have the strongest influence on a company's purchase of a new aircraft? How can Cessna incorporate the influence of these factors in its marketing planning?

   b. Toward which stage of the business buying decision process is this ad most likely geared. Why would Cessna want to emphasize that stage in its advertising efforts? In what other stages might advertising be a particularly important part of Cessna's marketing efforts?

   c. What attributes might be most critical for a company that is assessing aircraft suppliers prior to a purchase? Explain.

Figure 1

Figure 2

online marketing today

Germany-based Bayer, which markets chemicals, polymers, and health care products around the world, has created a series of Web sites to connect with its business customers. The strategy is to combine "our traditional strengths—a comprehensive product portfolio, R&D expertise, and customer contact—with the new opportunities offered by the Internet," says Werner Spinner, a member of Bayer's management board. BayerONE, the company's main portal for chemical and polymer products, is available to business customers in North America and Europe, complete with multilingual options. Customers can place orders, track shipments, and examine as many as 50 account reports generated on the site or delivered by e-mail. The specialized Web sites, such as BayerRubberOne, offer more detailed information about products, applications, and industry news.[38]

Visit BayerOne (*www.bayerone.com*) and review the look and contents of the welcome screen. Then go to the BayerRubberOne site (*www.bayerrubberone.com*). Examine the home page and follow the links to see the product information, applications, news, and services areas. Which members of the buying center would probably be most interested in each site? Would these sites be most useful for straight-rebuy, modified-rebuy, or new-task purchasing situations? How does BayerRubberOne address some of the organizational, interpersonal, and individual factors that influence business buying behavior?

you're the marketer: sonic pda marketing plan

Like their counterparts on the consumer side, business-to-business marketers have to understand their markets and the behavior of members of the buying center in order to develop appropriate marketing plans.

At Sonic, you are learning more about the business market for the company's PDA products. Jane Melody has defined this market as mid- to large-sized corporations that need to help their workforce stay in touch and input or access important data from any location. Given Sonic's current situation and your knowledge of business marketing, answer the following questions about this business market:

- What specific types of businesses appear to fit Melody's market definition? How can you research the number of employees and find other data about these types of businesses? Check the U.S. Census Bureau online listing of NAICS business classifications (*www.census.gov/epcd/www/naics.html*) as part of your research.

- What specific needs could Sonic's PDA product address for these businesses?
- What type of purchase would a Sonic system represent for these businesses? Who would participate in and influence this type of purchase?
- Which environmental, interpersonal, and individual influences are likely to be most important to business buyers of PDA products—and why?

Think about the opportunities, threats, and issues represented by the business markets you have researched. Also consider how this information could affect Sonic's marketing efforts in targeting prospective customers in each stage of the business buying process. Now report your findings and conclusions in a written marketing plan or type them into the Market Analysis, Situation Analysis, Target Markets, and Market Summary sections of the *Marketing Plan Pro* software.

notes

1. Frederick E. Webster Jr. and Yoram Wind, *Organizational Buying Behavior* (Upper Saddle River, NJ: Prentice Hall, 1972), p. 2.
2. John H. Sheridan, "An Alliance Built on Trust," *Industry Week*, March 17, 1997, pp. 66–70.
3. Shawn Tully, "How Cisco Mastered the Net," *Fortune*, August 17, 1998, pp. 107–10.
4. Justin Hibbard, "Online Health Insurance," *Information Week*, August 10, 1998, p. 26.
5. Robert Hiebeler, Thomas B. Kelly, and Charles Ketteman, *Best Practices: Building Your Business with Customer-Focused Solutions* (New York: Arthur Andersen/Simon & Schuster, 1998), pp. 122–24.
6. Michael Collins, "Breaking into the Big Leagues," *American Demographics* (January 1996): 24.
7. Patrick J. Robinson, Charles W. Faris, and Yoram Wind, *Industrial Buying and Creative Marketing* (Boston: Allyn & Bacon, 1967).
8. Daniel H. McQuiston, "Novelty, Complexity, and Importance as Causal Determinants of Industrial Buyer Behavior," *Journal of Marketing* (April 1989): 66–79; Peter Doyle, Arch G. Woodside, and Paul Mitchell, "Organizational Buying in New Task and Rebuy Situations," *Industrial Marketing Management* (February 1979): 7–11.
9. Urban B. Ozanne and Gilbert A. Churchill Jr., "Five Dimensions of the Industrial Adoption Process," *Journal of Marketing Research* (August 1971): 322–28.
10. Donald W. Jackson Jr., Janet E. Keith, and Richard K. Burdick, "Purchasing Agents' Perceptions of Industrial Buying Center Influence: A Situational Approach," *Journal of Marketing* (Fall 1984): 75–83.
11. Webster and Wind, *Organizational Buying Behavior*, p. 6.
12. Ibid., pp. 78–80.
13. Ibid.
14. Webster and Wind, *Organizational Buying Behavior*, pp. 33–37.
15. Sara Lorge, "Purchasing Power," *Sales & Marketing Management* (June 1998): pp. 43–46.
16. Tim Minahan, "OEM Buying Survey-Part 2: Buyers Get New Roles but Keep Old Tasks," *Purchasing*, July 16, 1998, pp. 208–9.
17. Shawn Tully, "Purchasing's New Muscle," *Fortune*, February 20, 1995; Mark Fitzgerald, "Decentralizing Control of Purchasing," *Editor and Publisher*, June 18, 1994, pp. 8, 10.
18. "Office Depot Online Opens for Business," *Business Wire*, January 15, 1998; Chris Reidy, "B2B, That Is Staples' Quest," *Boston Globe*, February 18, 2000.
19. (France, Germany, Japan) Teresa C. Morrison, Wayne A. Conaway, and Joseph J. Douress, *Dun & Bradstreet's Guide to Doing Business Around the World* (New York: Prentice Hall, 1997). (Korean) "Tips, Tricks and Pitfalls to Avoid When Doing Business in the Tough but Lucrative Korean Market,"

Business America (June 1997): 7. (Latin America) Dana May Casperson, "Minding Your Manners in Latin America," *Sales & Marketing Management* (March 1998): 96; Valerie Frazee, "Getting Started in Mexico," *Workforce* (January 1997): 16–17.
20. James C. Anderson and James A. Narus, *Business Market Management: Understanding, Creating and Delivering Value* (Upper Saddle River, NJ: Prentice Hall, 1998).
21. Patricia Van Arnum, "Pioneer Hi-Bred to Appeal Ruling Over Insect-Resistant Corn Seed," *Chemical Market Reporter*, September 4, 2000.
22. Adapted from Peter Kraljic, "Purchasing Must Become Supply Management," *Harvard Business Review* (September–October 1993): 109–17.
23. Robinson, Faris, and Wind.
24. "Xerox Multinational Supplier Quality Survey," *Purchasing*, January 12, 1995, p. 112.
25. Donald R. Lehmann and John O'Shaughnessy, "Differences in Attribute Importance for Different Industrial Products," *Journal of Marketing* (April 1974): 36–42.
26. Minahan, "OEM Buying Survey-Part 2: Buyers Get New Roles but Keep Old Tasks."
27. Rick Mullin, "Taking Customer Relations to the Next Level," *The Journal of Business Strategy* (January–February 1997): 22–26.
28. Chad Kaydo, "Good Service Travels Fast," *Sales & Marketing Management* (May 1998): 22–24.
29. See James A. Narus and James C. Anderson, "Turn Your Industrial Distributors into Partners," *Harvard Business Review* (March–April 1986): 66–71.
30. Donna Del Moro, "Single-Source Newsprint Supply," *Editor and Publisher*, October 25, 1997, pp. 42–45.
31. Kitty Vineyard, "Trends . . . in Single Sourcing," *Electrical Apparatus* (November 1996): 12.
32. Robert Hiebeler, Thomas B. Kelly, and Charles Ketteman, *Best Practices: Building Your Business with Customer-Focused Solutions* (New York: Arthur Andersen/Simon & Schuster, 1998), pp. 124–26.
33. Paul E. Goulding, "Q & A: Making Uncle Sam Your Customer," *Financial Executive* (May–June 1998): 55–57.
34. Julie Bort, "Selling High Technology to Uncle Sam," *Electronic Business* (February 1998): 28.
35. Laura M. Litvan, "Selling to Uncle Sam: New, Easier Rules," *Nation's Business* (March 1995): 46–48.
36. Ellen Messmer, "Feds Do E-commerce the Hard Way," *Network World*, April 13, 1998, pp. 31–32.
37. Bort, "Selling High Technology to Uncle Sam"; Larry Light and Lisa Sanders, "Uncle Sam's PC Shopping Binge," *BusinessWeek*, October 28, 1996, p. 8.
38. Bo Glasgow, "Bayer's Channel Mix Strategy Offers a Bevy of B2B Options," *Chemical Market Reporter*, August 20, 2001.

9

dealing with
the competition

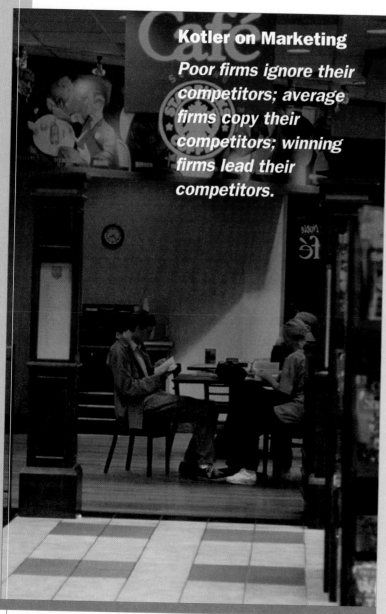

Kotler on Marketing

Poor firms ignore their competitors; average firms copy their competitors; winning firms lead their competitors.

In this chapter, we will address the following questions:

- Who the primary competitors are
- How to ascertain their strategies, objectives, strengths and weaknesses, and reaction patterns
- How to design a competitive intelligence system
- Whether to position as market leader, challenger, follower, or nicher
- How to balance a customer versus competitor orientation

I n the two previous chapters we examined the dynamics of consumer and business markets. This chapter examines the role competition plays and how companies position themselves relative to competitors.

Today, competition is not only rife but growing more intense every year. Many U.S., European, and Japanese companies are setting up production in lower-cost countries and bringing cheaper goods to market. Because markets have become so competitive, understanding customers is no longer enough. Companies must start paying keen attention to their competitors. Successful companies design and operate systems for gathering continuous intelligence about competitors.[1]

competitive forces

Michael Porter has identified five forces that determine the intrinsic long-run profit attractiveness of a market or market segment: industry competitors, potential entrants, substitutes, buyers, and suppliers. His model is shown in Figure 9.1. The threats these forces pose are as follows:

1. *Threat of intense segment rivalry:* A segment is unattractive if it already contains numerous, strong, or aggressive competitors. It is even more unattractive if it is stable or declining, if plant capacity additions are done in large increments, if fixed costs are high, if exit barriers are high, or if competitors have high stakes in staying in the segment. These conditions will lead to frequent price wars, advertising battles, and new-product introductions, and will make it expensive to compete.

2. *Threat of new entrants:* A segment's attractiveness varies with the height of its entry and exit barriers.[2] The most attractive segment is one in which entry barriers are high and exit barriers are low (see Figure 9.2). Few new firms can enter the industry, and poor-performing firms can easily exit. When both entry and exit barriers are high, profit potential is high, but firms face more risk because poorer-performing firms stay in and fight it out. When both entry and exit barriers are low, firms easily enter and leave the industry, and the returns are stable and low. The worst case is when entry barriers are low and exit barriers are high: Here firms enter during good times but find it hard to leave during bad times. The result is chronic overcapacity and depressed earnings for all.

3. *Threat of substitute products:* A segment is unattractive when there are actual or potential substitutes for the product. Substitutes place a limit on prices and on profits. The company has to monitor price trends closely. If technology advances or competition increases in these substitute industries, prices and profits in the segment are likely to fall.

4. *Threat of buyers' growing bargaining power:* A segment is unattractive if the buyers possess strong or growing bargaining power. Buyers' bargaining power grows when they become more concentrated or organized, when the product represents a significant fraction of the buyers' costs, when the product is undifferentiated, when the buyers' switching costs are low, when buyers are price sensitive because of low profits, or when buyers can integrate upstream. To protect

---

figure **9.1**

Five Forces Determining Segment Structural Attractiveness

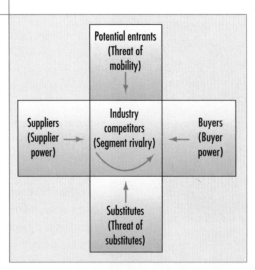

Source: Reprinted with the permission of the Free Press, an imprint of Simon & Schuster, from Michael E. Porter, *Competitive Advantage: Creating and Sustaining Superior Performance.* Copyright 1985 by Michael E. Porter.

figure **9.2**

		Exit Barriers	
		Low	High
Entry Barriers	Low	Low, stable returns	Low, risky returns
	High	High, stable returns	High, risky returns

Barriers and Profitability

themselves, sellers might select buyers who have the least power to negotiate or switch suppliers. A better defense consists of developing superior offers that strong buyers cannot refuse.

5. *Threat of suppliers' growing bargaining power:* A segment is unattractive if the company's suppliers are able to raise prices or reduce quantity supplied. Suppliers tend to be powerful when they are concentrated or organized, when there are few substitutes, when the supplied product is an important input, when the costs of switching suppliers are high, and when the suppliers can integrate downstream. The best defenses are to build win–win relations with suppliers or use multiple supply sources.

identifying competitors

It would seem a simple task for a company to identify its competitors. Coca-Cola knows that PepsiCo is its major competitor; Sony knows that Matsushita is a major competitor;[3] and Petsmart.com knows that Petco.com is a major competitor. However, the range of a company's actual and potential competitors is in reality much broader. A company is more likely to be hurt by emerging competitors or new technologies than by current competitors.

In recent years, many businesses failed to look to the Internet for their most formidable competitors. A few years back, Barnes & Noble and Borders bookstore chains were competing to see who could build the most megastores, where book browsers could sink into comfortable couches and sip cappuccino. While they were deciding which products to stock, Jeffrey Bezos was building an online empire called Amazon.com. Bezos's cyber bookstore had the advantage of offering an almost unlimited selection of books without the expense of stocking inventory. Now both Barnes & Noble and Borders are playing catch-up in building their own online stores. Yet, "competitor myopia"—a focus on current competitors rather than latent ones—has rendered some businesses extinct:[4]

Encyclopaedia Britannica   In 1996, 230-year-old Encyclopaedia Britannica dismissed its entire home sales force after the arrival of its $5-per-month subscription Internet site made the idea of owning a 32-volume set of books for $1,250 less appealing to parents. Britannica decided to create an online site after realizing that computer-savvy kids most often sought information online or on CD-ROMs such as Microsoft's Encarta, which sold for $50. What really smarts is that Britannica had the opportunity to partner with Microsoft in providing content for Encarta but refused. In 1999, Britannica made its entire encyclopedia available online at no cost and began earning revenues via Web advertising sales.[5]

Other publishing businesses feel similarly threatened by the Internet. Web sites that offer jobs, real estate listings, and automobiles online threaten newspapers,

marketing for the **new economy**

Displaced but Not Discouraged: What Happens When E-Commerce Edges Out the Middleman

Belair/Empress Travel in Bowie, Maryland, typifies the kind of business most threatened by the advent of online selling. In addition to having seen airline commissions drop from 62 percent of its revenue to 30 percent, Belair/Empress must now compete against giant online travel sites, such as Expedia or Travelocity, which allow consumers to surf the Web for rock-bottom ticket prices. Airlines joined the online sales fray as well. Every major airline now has a Web site offering online reservations, as well as information on routes and schedules, special deals, and other travel arrangements.

www.owners.com: "The smart way to buy or sell a home."

By facilitating direct contact between buyers and sellers, the Internet is displacing the travel agents, insurance brokers, car dealers, real estate brokers, stockbrokers, and headhunters who have traditionally been the intermediaries. There is even a fancy 17-letter word to describe the demise of the middleman: disintermediation. Here is a short list of some online pioneers that have helped bring it about.

www.expedia.com www.travelocity.com	Not only offer no-hassle ways to purchase airline tickets but also have links to and information about restaurants, hotels, car rentals, and local sights pertinent to a particular destination.
www.carpoint.com www.autobytel.com www.edmunds.com	Provide services ranging from pricing reports and test-drive reviews to leasing options and links to financing sites.
www.owners.com	Real estate sellers enter basic price and property data and even extras like pictures for a small fee, and buyers search over 200,000 listings in all 50 states. If buyer and seller link up, the price for both sides reflects savings on the commission.
www.lifequote.com	Visitors to the site can request life insurance quotes from a number of national insurance companies, compare policies and prices, and choose the best insurance plan.
www.monster.com	This online job market network connects employers with prospective employees. The site lists over 450,000 jobs and attracts more than 4 million unique visitors every quarter.

What can traditional businesses do when facing digital competition? At one end are those who wholeheartedly embrace the Internet. Palo Alto travel agent Bruce Yoxsimer teamed with Internet guru Dan Whaley to set up shop on the Web and launched Internet Travel Network (www.itn.net). In 1995, the first Web site for making travel reservations. Since then, the company (now called GetThere and owned by Sabre Holdings), has helped people book more than 10 million trips over the Internet. Others completely reject the Internet business model. Judy McLoughlin, owner of children's bookstore Reading in the

which derive a huge portion of their revenue from classified employment, real estate, and automobile ads. When you can get free news content online, why should you buy a newspaper? The businesses with the most to fear from Internet technology are the world's middlemen. (See "Marketing for the New Economy: Displaced but Not Discouraged: What Happens When E-Commerce Edges Out the Middleman.")

We can examine competition from both an industry and a marketing point of view.

Park in suburban Detroit says, "I won't want to buy or sell a book I cannot touch." McLoughlin tries to gain an edge through attentiveness to customers. Most businesses fall somewhere in between. Belair/Empress owner Phil Davidoff is now a market nicher specializing in cruises, package tours, and group vacations. The reformulated business is now replete with a Web address (www.belairtrav.com).

Many, such as brokerage firm Charles Schwab, are using the Web. The nation's largest discount stockbroker jumped onto the Internet to face a horde of price-cutting e-commerce competitors who had been there first, including E-Trade and Ameritrade. Not only did Schwab face cheaper competitors, it also had to cannibalize its own accounts. The gamble paid off because the volume of trades grew tremendously. The key to Schwab's success was providing a wealth of financial and company information to help customers research and manage their accounts. The company acquired more than 7 million customer accounts and propelled Schwab to record revenues, which surpassed $6 billion in 2000.

In truth, most consumers appreciate hand-holding from real persons, especially when purchasing such complex or costly products and services as cars, life insurance, or a three-week vacation that includes stops in the Galapagos Islands and Tierra del Fuego. Although the Internet has created a new breed of competitors for traditional middlemen, it has also opened up a great opportunity for a human intermediary to lead consumers through the maze.

GetThere.com launched as the Internet Travel Network in 1995, was the first company to book trips over the Web.

Sources: Marcia Stepanek, "Rebirth of the Salesman," *BusinessWeek*, June 22, 1998, p. 146; Evan J. Schwartz, "How Middlemen Can Come Out on Top," *BusinessWeek*, February 9, 1998, pp. ENT4–ENT7; Bernard Warner, "Prepare for Takeoff," *Brandweek*, January 19, 1998, pp. 38–40; Ira Lewis, Janjaap Semeijn, and Alexander Talalayevsky, "The Impact of Information Technology on Travel Agents," *Transportation Journal* (Summer 1998): 20–25; Mary J. Cronin, "The Travel Agents' Dilemma," *Fortune*, May 11, 1998, pp. 163–64; John Hughes, "Auto Dealers See Future in Internet," *Marketing News*, March 2, 1998, p. 13; Saroja Girishankar, "Virtual Markets Create New Roles for Distributors," *Internetweek*, April 6, 1998, p. S10; Laurie J. Flynn, "Eating Your Young," *Context* (Summer 1998): 45–51; <www.schwab.com>.

industry concept of competition

What exactly is an industry? An **industry** is a group of firms that offer a product or class of products that are close substitutes for one another. Industries are classified according to number of sellers; degree of product differentiation; presence or absence of entry, mobility, and exit barriers; cost structure; degree of vertical integration; and degree of globalization.

NUMBER OF SELLERS AND DEGREE OF DIFFERENTIATION   The starting point for describing an industry is to specify the number of sellers and whether the product is homogeneous or highly differentiated. These characteristics give rise to four industry structure types:

1. *Pure monopoly:* Only one firm provides a certain product or service in a certain country or area (local electricity or gas company). An unregulated monopolist might charge a high price, do little or no advertising, and offer minimal service. If partial substitutes are available and there is some danger of competition, the monopolist might invest in more service and technology. A regulated monopolist is required to charge a lower price and provide more service as a matter of public interest.

2. *Oligopoly:* A small number of (usually) large firms produce products that range from highly differentiated to standardized. *Pure oligopoly* consists of a few companies producing essentially the same commodity (oil, steel). Such companies would find it hard to charge anything more than the going price. If competitors match on price and services, the only way to gain a competitive advantage is through lower costs. *Differentiated oligopoly* consists of a few companies producing products (autos, cameras) partially differentiated along lines of quality, features, styling, or services. Each competitor may seek leadership in one of these major attributes, attract the customers favoring that attribute, and charge a price premium for that attribute.

3. *Monopolistic competition:* Many competitors are able to differentiate their offers in whole or in part (restaurants, beauty shops). Competitors focus on market segments where they can meet customer needs in a superior way and command a price premium.

4. *Pure competition:* Many competitors offer the same product and service (stock market, commodity market). Because there is no basis for differentiation, competitors' prices will be the same. No competitor will advertise unless advertising can create psychological differentiation (cigarettes, beer), in which case it would be more proper to describe the industry as monopolistically competitive.

An industry's competitive structure can change over time.

Palm Pilot   When Palm Computing innovated the Palm Pilot, a Personal Digital Assistant (PDA) with a touch-screen interface, it rolled out over 1 million units in 18 months and found itself an instant monopolist. There was simply no other product like it on the market. Soon, however, a few other companies entered the PDA market, turning it into an oligopoly. The market took on a monopolistically competitive structure by 2000, as PDAs proliferated from a variety of companies such as Sony, Handspring, Hewlett-Packard, and Casio. When demand growth slows, however, we can expect some competitors to exit, returning the market to an oligopoly dominated by a few key competitors.[6]

ENTRY, MOBILITY, AND EXIT BARRIERS   Industries differ greatly in ease of entry. It is easy to open a new restaurant but difficult to enter the aircraft industry. Major *entry barriers* include high capital requirements; economies of scale; patents and licensing requirements; scarce locations, raw materials, or distributors; and reputation requirements. Even after a firm enters an industry, it might face *mobility barriers* when it tries to enter more attractive market segments.

Firms often face *exit barriers*,[7] such as legal or moral obligations to customers, creditors, and employees; government restrictions; low asset salvage value due to overspecialization or obsolescence; lack of alternative opportunities; high vertical integration; and emotional barriers. Many firms stay in an industry as long as they cover their variable costs and some or all of their fixed costs. Their continued presence, however, dampens profits for everyone.

Even if some firms do not want to exit the industry, they might decrease their size. Companies can try to reduce shrinkage barriers to help ailing competitors get smaller gracefully.[8]

COST STRUCTURE   Each industry has a certain cost burden that shapes much of its strategic conduct. For example, steelmaking involves heavy manufacturing and raw-material costs; toy manufacturing involves heavy distribution and marketing costs.

Firms strive to reduce their largest costs. The integrated steel company with the most cost-efficient plant will have a great advantage over other integrated steel companies; but even they have higher costs than the new steel minimills.

DEGREE OF VERTICAL INTEGRATION   Companies find it advantageous to integrate backward or forward (**vertical integration**). Major oil producers carry on oil exploration, oil drilling, oil refining, chemical manufacture, and service-station operation. Vertical integration often lowers costs, and the company gains a larger share of the value-added stream. In addition, vertically integrated firms can manipulate prices and costs in different parts of the value chain to earn profits where taxes are lowest. There can be disadvantages, such as high costs in certain parts of the value chain and a lack of flexibility. Companies are increasingly questioning how vertical they should be. Many are outsourcing more activities, especially those that can be done better and more cheaply by specialist firms.

DEGREE OF GLOBALIZATION   Some industries are highly local (such as lawn care); others are global (such as oil, aircraft engines, cameras). Companies in global industries need to compete on a global basis if they are to achieve economies of scale and keep up with the latest advances in technology.[9]

market concept of competition

In addition to the industry approach, we can identify competitors using the market approach: Competitors are companies that satisfy the same customer need. For example, a customer who buys a word-processing package really wants "writing ability"—a need that can also be satisfied by pencils, pens, or typewriters.

The market concept of competition reveals a broader set of actual and potential competitors. Rayport and Jaworski suggest profiling a company's direct and indirect competitors by mapping the buyer's steps in obtaining and using the product. Figure 9.3 illustrates

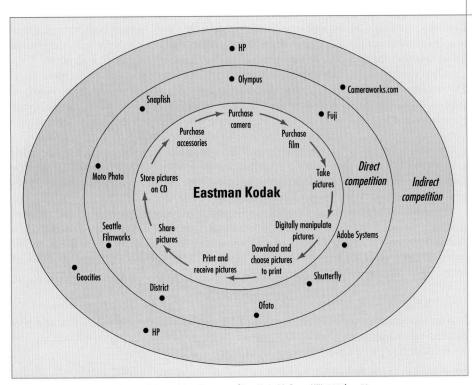

figure **9.3**

Competitor Map –
Eastman Kodak

Source: Jeffrey F. Rayport and Bernard J. Jaworski, *e-Commerce* (New York: McGraw-Hill, 2001), p. 53.

figure **9.4**

Strategic Groups in the Major Appliance Industry

their *competitor map* of Eastman Kodak in the film business. In the center is a listing of consumer activities: buying a camera, buying film, taking pictures, and so on. The first outer ring lists Kodak's main competitors with respect to each consumer activity: Olympus for buying a camera, Fuji for purchasing film, and so on. The second outer ring lists indirect competitors—HP, Intel, cameraworks.com—who may become direct competitors. This type of analysis highlights both the opportunities and the challenges a company faces.[10]

analyzing competitors

Once a company identifies its primary competitors, it must ascertain their characteristics, specifically, their strategies, objectives, strengths and weaknesses, and reaction patterns.

strategies

A group of firms following the same strategy in a given target market is called a **strategic group**.[11] Suppose a company wants to enter the major appliance industry. What is its strategic group? It develops the chart shown in Figure 9.4 and discovers four strategic groups based on product quality and level of vertical integration. Group A has one competitor (Maytag), group B has three (General Electric, Whirlpool, and Sears), group C has four, and group D has two. Important insights emerge from this exercise. First, the height of the entry barriers differs for each group. Second, if the company successfully enters a group, the members of that group become its key competitors.

A company must continuously monitor competitors' strategies. When U.S. automakers just about caught up in mechanical quality, Japanese automakers shifted to sensory qualities. A Ford engineer explained: "It's the turn-signal lever that doesn't wobble . . . the speed of the power window up and down . . . the feel of a climate-control knob . . . this is the next nuance of customer competition."[12]

objectives

Once a company has identified its main competitors and their strategies, it must ask: What is each competitor seeking in the marketplace? What drives each competitor's behavior? Many factors shape a competitor's objectives, including size, history, current management, and financial situation. If the competitor is a division of a larger company, it is important to know whether the parent company is running it for growth, profits, or milking it.[13]

One useful initial assumption is that competitors strive to maximize profits. However, companies differ in the emphasis they put on short-term versus long-term profits. Most U.S. firms operate on a short-run model, largely because current performance is judged by stockholders who might lose confidence, sell their stock, and cause the company's cost of capital to rise. Japanese firms operate largely on a market-share-maximization model. They receive much of their funds from banks at a lower interest rate and in the past have readily accepted lower profits. An alternative assumption is that each competitor pursues some mix of objectives: current profitability, market-share growth, cash flow, technological leadership, service leadership.

Finally, a company must monitor competitors' expansion plans. Figure 9.5 shows a product-market battlefield map for the personal computer industry. Dell, which started out as a strong force in selling personal computers to individual users, is now a major force in the commercial and industrial market. Other incumbents may try to set up mobility barriers to Dell's further expansion.

strengths and weaknesses

A company needs to gather information on each competitor's strengths and weaknesses. According to the Arthur D. Little consulting firm, a company will occupy one of six competitive positions in the target market:[14]

1. *Dominant:* This firm controls the behavior of other competitors and has a wide choice of strategic options.

figure **9.5**

figure **9.5**

A Competitor's Expansion Plans

2. *Strong:* This firm can take independent action without endangering its long-term position and can maintain its long-term position regardless of competitors' actions.
3. *Favorable:* This firm has an exploitable strength and a more-than-average opportunity to improve its position.
4. *Tenable:* This firm is performing at a sufficiently satisfactory level to warrant continuing in business, but it exists at the sufferance of the dominant company and has a less-than-average opportunity to improve its position.
5. *Weak:* This firm has unsatisfactory performance, but an opportunity exists for improvement. The firm must change or else exit.
6. *Nonviable:* This firm has unsatisfactory performance and no opportunity for improvement.

This assessment helped one company decide whom to attack in the programmable-controls market:

> The company faced three entrenched competitors: Allen Bradley, Texas Instruments, and Gould. Its research showed that Allen Bradley had an excellent reputation for technological leadership; Texas Instruments had low costs and engaged in bloody battles for market share; and Gould did a good job but not a distinguished job. The company concluded that its best target was Gould.

Table 9.1 shows the results of a company survey that asked customers to rate its three competitors, A, B, and C, on five attributes. Competitor A turns out to be well-known and respected for producing high-quality products sold by a good sales force. Competitor A is poor at providing product availability and technical assistance. Competitor B is good across the board and excellent in product availability and sales force. Competitor C rates poor to fair on most attributes. This suggests that the company could attack Competitor A

table **9.1**

	Customer Awareness	Product Quality	Product Availability	Technical Assistance	Selling Staff
Competitor A	E	E	P	P	G
Competitor B	G	G	E	G	E
Competitor C	F	P	G	F	F

Note: E = excellent, G = good, F = fair, P = poor.

Customer's Ratings of Competitors on Key Success Factors

table **9.2**

Market Share, Mind
Share, and Heart
Share

	Market Share			Mind Share			Heart Share		
	2000	2001	2002	2000	2001	2002	2000	2001	2002
Competitor A	50%	47%	44%	60%	58%	54%	45%	42%	39%
Competitor B	30	34	37	30	31	35	44	47	53
Competitor C	20	19	19	10	11	11	11	11	8

on product availability and technical assistance and Competitor C on almost anything, but should not attack B, which has no glaring weaknesses.

In general, a company should monitor three variables when analyzing competitors:

1. *Share of market:* The competitor's share of the target market.
2. *Share of mind:* The percentage of customers who named the competitor in responding to the statement "Name the first company that comes to mind in this industry."
3. *Share of heart:* The percentage of customers who named the competitor in responding to the statement "Name the company from which you would prefer to buy the product."

There is an interesting relationship among these three measures. Table 9.2 shows the numbers for these three measures for the three competitors listed in Table 9.1. Competitor A enjoys the highest market share but is slipping. Its mind share and heart share are also slipping, probably because it is not providing good product availability and technical assistance. Competitor B is steadily gaining market share, probably due to strategies that are increasing its mind share and heart share. Competitor C seems to be stuck at a low level of market share, mind share, and heart share, probably because of its poor product and marketing attributes. We could generalize as follows: *Companies that make steady gains in mind share and heart share will inevitably make gains in market share and profitability.*

To improve market share, many companies benchmark their most successful competitors, as well as world-class performers. The technique and its benefits are described in "Marketing Memo: How Benchmarking Helps Improve Competitive Performance."

reaction patterns

Companies react differently to competitive assaults. Some are slow to respond. Others respond only to certain types of attacks, such as price cuts. Still others strike back swiftly and strongly to any assault. Some industries are marked by relative accord among the competitors, and others by constant fighting. Bruce Henderson thinks that much depends on the industry's "competitive equilibrium." Here are his observations:[15]

1. *If competitors are nearly identical and make their living in the same way, then their competitive equilibrium is unstable.* Perpetual conflict characterizes industries such as steel or newsprint, where differentiation is hard to maintain. Equilibrium will be upset if any firm lowers its price to relieve overcapacity. Price wars are frequent.
2. *If a single major factor is the critical factor, then the competitive equilibrium is unstable.* This is the case in industries where cost-differentiation opportunities exist through economies of scale, advanced technology, or experience. Any company that achieves a cost breakthrough can cut its price and win market share at the expense of others, who can defend their market shares only at great cost. Price wars are frequent as a result of cost breakthroughs.
3. *If multiple factors may be critical factors, then it is possible for each competitor to have some advantage and be differentially attractive to some customers. The more factors that may provide an advantage, the more competitors who can coexist. Competitors all have their segment, defined by the preference for the factor trade-offs they offer.* Multiple factors exist in industries that can differentiate quality, service, convenience, and so on.

Marketing
MEMO

How Benchmarking Helps Improve Competitive Performance

Benchmarking is the art of learning from companies that perform certain tasks better than other companies. There can be as much as a tenfold difference in the quality, speed, and cost performance of a world-class company and an average company. The aim of benchmarking is to copy or improve on "best practices," either within an industry or across industries. Benchmarking involves seven steps: (1) Determine which functions to benchmark; (2) identify the key performance variables to measure; (3) identify the best-in-class companies; (4) measure performance of best-in-class companies; (5) measure the company's performance; (6) specify programs and actions to close the gap; and (7) implement and monitor results.

How can companies identify best-practice companies? A good starting point is asking customers, suppliers, and distributors whom they rate as doing the best job. In addition, major consulting firms have built voluminous files of best practices. The accounting and consulting firm Arthur Andersen has invested millions creating a Global Best Practices Knowledge Base to uncover breakthrough thinking at world-class companies. Some of the findings are condensed in the book *Best Practices: Building Your Business with Customer-Focused Solutions*. Data can also be accessed at the Andersen Web site www.globalbestpractices.com

Sources: Robert C. Camp, *Benchmarking: The Search for Industry-Best Practices that Lead to Superior Performance* (White Plains, NY: Quality Resources, 1989); Michael J. Spendolini, *The Benchmarking Book* (New York: Amacom, 1992); Jeremy Main, "How to Steal the Best Ideas Around," *Fortune*, October 19, 1992; A. Steven Walleck et al., "Benchmarking World Class Performance," *McKinsey Quarterly*, no. 1 (1990): 3–24; Otis Port, "Beg, Borrow—and Benchmark," *BusinessWeek*, November 30, 1992, pp. 74–75; Stanley Brown, "Don't Innovate—Imitate!" *Sales & Marketing Management* (January 1995): 24–25; Tom Stemerg, "Spies Like Us," *Inc.* (August 1998): 45–49. See also <www.benchmarking.org>; Michael Hope, "Contrast and Compare," *Marketing*, August 28, 1997, pp. 11–13; Robert Hiebeler, Thomas B. Kelly, and Charles Ketteman, *Best Practices: Building Your Business with Customer-Focused Solutions* (New York: Arthur Andersen/Simon & Schuster, 1998).

4. *The fewer the number of critical competitive variables, the fewer the number of competitors.* If only one factor is critical, then no more than two or three competitors are likely to coexist.

5. *A ratio of 2 to 1 in market share between any two competitors seems to be the equilibrium point at which it is neither practical nor advantageous for either competitor to increase or decrease share.* At this level, the costs of extra promotion or distribution would outweigh the gains in market share.

designing the competitive intelligence system
four main steps

There are four main steps in designing a competitive intelligence system: setting up the system, collecting the data, evaluating and analyzing the data, and disseminating information and responding to queries.

SETTING UP THE SYSTEM   The first step calls for identifying vital types of competitive information, identifying the best sources of this information, and assigning a person who will manage the system and its services. In smaller companies that cannot afford to set up a formal competitive intelligence office, specific executives should be assigned to watch specific competitors. A manager who used to work for a competitor would closely follow that competitor and serve as the in-house expert on that competitor. Any manager who needs to know about a specific competitor would contact the corresponding in-house expert.[16]

COLLECTING THE DATA   The data are collected on a continuous basis from the field (sales force, channels, suppliers, market research firms, trade associations), from people who do business with competitors, from observing competitors, and from published data. In addition, a vast store of data on both domestic and overseas companies is available via CD-ROM and online services.

The Internet is creating a new arsenal for those skilled at gathering intelligence. Now companies place volumes of information on their Web sites to attract customers, partners, suppliers, or franchisees, and that same information is available to competitors at the click of a mouse. Press releases that never made it into the media are published on Web sites, so you can keep abreast of new products and organizational changes. Help wanted ads posted on the Web quickly let you know competitors' expansion priorities.

Marketing
MEMO

Outsmarting the Competition with Guerrilla Marketing Research

Directories, annual reports, brochures, and press releases are good sources of historical information, but they are often not good enough if a company hopes to compete against a recently introduced new product. The following eight techniques could give a company a lead of two or more years on the competition:

1. *Watch the small companies in your industry and related industries.* True innovation often comes from small, inconspicuous companies. Who would have thought, for instance, that Arizona Iced Tea from Ferolito Vultagio & Sons of Brooklyn would make serious inroads in the soft-drink and fruit juice markets?
2. *Follow patent applications.* Not all applications lead to products. Still, patent filings indicate a company's direction. Patent application information can be found in various online and CD-ROM databases.
3. *Track the job changes and other activities of industry experts.* Who have the competitors hired? Have the new hires written papers or made presentations at conferences? What is the value of their expertise to the competitor? If the company gains this expertise, will it affect your firm's position? For instance, when a pulp and paper company hires a marketing director with significant experience in Eastern Europe, the company could be looking toward that market.
4. *Be aware of licensing agreements.* These provide useful information about where, how, and when a company can sell a new product.
5. *Monitor the formation of business contracts and alliances.* These pose new threats to the firm.
6. *Find out about new business practices that are saving your competitors money.* What does it mean if a competing insurance company has bought thousands of laptops and portable printers? Very likely, that its claims adjusters soon will be writing estimates and generating checks on the spot, saving time and overhead.
7. *Follow changes in pricing.* For instance, when luxury items become cheap enough for the mass market, they supplant some of the more expensive equipment, as when camcorders supplanted home movie cameras in the late 1980s.
8. *Be aware of social changes and changes in consumer tastes and preferences that could alter the business environment.* Consumers are fickle. During the past 15 years, jogging has given way to aerobics, and now walking is a preferred leisure activity. By anticipating changing fads, some shoe companies were able to introduce new types of athletic shoes.

Source: Adapted from Ruth Winett, "Guerrilla Marketing Research Outsmarts the Competition," *Marketing News*, January 2, 1995, p. 33.

It is not only company-sponsored Web sites that hold the richest competitor intelligence booty: Trade association sites also hold valuable nuggets of information. When he was controller of Stone Container's specialty-packaging division, Gary Owen visited a trade association Web site and noticed that a rival had won an award for a new process using ultraviolet-resistant lacquers. The site revealed the machines' configuration and run rate, which Stone's engineers used to figure out how to replicate the process.[17]

Although most information-gathering techniques are legal, some involve questionable ethics. Companies have been known to advertise and hold interviews for nonexistent jobs in order to pump competitors' employees for information. Although it is illegal for a company to photograph a competitor's plant from the air, aerial photos are often on file with the U.S. Geological Survey or Environmental Protection Agency. Some companies even buy their competitors' garbage. Once it has left the competitor's premises, refuse is legally considered abandoned property.[18] Companies need to develop ways of acquiring information about competitors without violating legal or ethical standards. (See "Marketing Memo: Outsmarting the Competition with Guerrilla Marketing Research.")

EVALUATING AND ANALYZING THE DATA   The data are checked for validity and reliability, interpreted, and organized.

DISSEMINATING INFORMATION AND RESPONDING   Key information is sent to relevant decision makers, and managers' inquiries are answered. With a well-designed system, company managers receive timely information about competitors via e-mail, phone calls, bulletins, newsletters, and reports. Managers can also contact the market intelligence department or colleagues on the company's intranet when they need help interpreting a competitor's sudden move, when they need to know a competitor's weaknesses and strengths, or when they want to discuss a likely response to a contemplated company move.

selecting competitors

With good competitive intelligence, managers will find it easier to formulate competitive strategies. They can begin with a technique called customer value analysis.

CUSTOMER VALUE ANALYSIS (CVA)   We believe customers choose between competitive brand offerings on the basis of which delivers the most customer value. Customer value is given by:

$$\text{Customer Value} = \text{Customer Benefits} - \text{Customer Costs}$$

Customer benefits include *product benefits, service benefits, personnel benefits,* and *image benefits.* We will assume the customer can judge the relative benefit level or worth of different brands. Suppose the customer is considering three brands, A, B, and C, and judges the customer benefits to be worth $150, $140, and $135, respectively. If the customer costs are the same, the customer would clearly choose brand A.

However, the costs are rarely the same. In addition to *purchase price,* costs include *acquisition costs, usage costs, maintenance costs, ownership costs,* and *disposal costs.* Often a customer will buy a more expensive brand because that particular brand will impose lower costs of the other kinds. Consider Table 9.3. A, the highest-priced brand, also involves a lower total cost than lower-priced brands B and C. Clearly, supplier A has done a good job of reducing customers' other costs.

Now we can compare the customer value of the three brands:

$$\text{Customer value of A} = \$150 - \$130 = \$20$$
$$\text{Customer value of B} = \$140 - \$135 = \$5$$
$$\text{Customer value of C} = \$135 - \$140 = -\$5$$

The customer will prefer brand A both because the benefit level is higher and the customer costs are lower, but this does not have to be the case. Suppose A decided to charge $120 instead of $100 to take advantage of its higher perceived benefit level. Then A's customer cost would have been $150 instead of $130 and just offset its higher perceived benefit. Brand A, because of its greed, would lose the sale to brand B.

Very often, managers conduct a **customer value analysis** to reveal the company's strengths and weaknesses relative to various competitors. The major steps in such an analysis are:

1. *Identify the major attributes customers value.* Customers are asked what attributes and performance levels they look for in choosing a product and vendors.
2. *Assess the quantitative importance of the different attributes.* Customers are asked to rate the importance of the different attributes. If the customers diverge too much in their ratings, they should be clustered into different segments.

table **9.3**

Customer Costs of Three Brands

	A	B	C
Price	$100	$ 90	$ 80
Acquisition costs	15	25	30
Usage costs	4	7	10
Maintenance costs	2	3	7
Ownership costs	3	3	5
Disposal costs	6	5	8
Total Cost	$130	$135	$140

3. *Assess the company's and competitors' performances on the different customer values against their rated importance.* Customers describe where they see the company's and competitors' performances on each attribute.

4. *Examine how customers in a specific segment rate the company's performance against a specific major competitor on an attribute-by-attribute basis.* If the company's offer exceeds the competitor's offer on all important attributes, the company can charge a higher price (thereby earning higher profits), or it can charge the same price and gain more market share.

5. *Monitor customer values over time.* The company must periodically redo its studies of customer values and competitors' standings as the economy, technology, and features change.

CLASSES OF COMPETITORS   After the company has conducted its customer value analysis, it can focus its attack on one of the following classes of competitors: strong versus weak, close versus distant, and "good" versus "bad."

Strong versus Weak   Most companies aim their shots at weak competitors, because this requires fewer resources per share point gained. Yet, in attacking weak competitors, the firm will achieve little in the way of improved capabilities. The firm should also compete with strong competitors to keep up with the best. Even strong competitors have some weaknesses.

Close versus Distant   Most companies compete with competitors who resemble them the most. Chevrolet competes with Ford, not with Jaguar. Yet companies should also recognize distant competitors. Coca-Cola states that its number one competitor is tap water, not Pepsi. U.S. Steel worries more about plastic and aluminum than about Bethlehem Steel; and museums now worry about theme parks and malls.

At the same time, the company should avoid trying to destroy the closest competitor. Porter cites an example of a counterproductive victory:

> Bausch and Lomb in the late 1970s moved aggressively against other soft contact lens manufacturers with great success. However, this led each weak competitor to sell out to larger firms, such as Revlon, Johnson & Johnson, and Schering-Plough, with the result that Bausch and Lomb now faced much larger competitors.

"Good" versus "Bad"   Every industry contains "good" and "bad" competitors.[19] A company should support its good competitors and attack its bad competitors. Good competitors play by the industry's rules; they make realistic assumptions about the industry's growth potential; they set prices in reasonable relation to costs; they favor a healthy industry; they limit themselves to a portion or segment of the industry; they motivate others to lower costs or improve differentiation; and they accept the general level of their share and profits. Bad competitors try to buy share rather than earn it; they take large risks; they invest in overcapacity; and they upset industrial equilibrium.

designing competitive strategies

We can gain further insight by classifying firms by the roles they play in the target market: leader, challenger, follower, or nicher. Suppose a market is occupied by the firms shown in Figure 9.6. Forty percent of the market is in the hands of a *market leader;* another 30 percent is in the hands of a *market challenger;* another 20 percent is in the hands of a *market follower,* a firm that is willing to maintain its market share and not rock the boat. The remaining 10 percent is in the hands of *market nichers,* firms that serve small market segments not being served by larger firms.

market-leader strategies

Many industries contain one firm that is the acknowledged market leader. This firm has the largest market share in the relevant product market, and usually leads the other firms in price changes, new-product introductions, distribution coverage, and promotional intensity. Some of the best-known market leaders are Kodak (photography),

Microsoft (computer software), Intel (microprocessors), Procter & Gamble (consumer packaged goods), Caterpillar (earth-moving equipment), Coca-Cola (soft drinks), McDonald's (fast food), and Gillette (razor blades).

Unless a dominant firm enjoys a legal monopoly, its life is not altogether easy. It must maintain constant vigilance. A product innovation may come along and hurt the leader (Nokia's and Ericsson's digital cell phones taking over from Motorola's analog models). The leader might spend conservatively whereas a challenger spends liberally (Montgomery Ward's loss of its retail dominance to Sears after World War II). The leader might misjudge its competition and find itself left behind (as Sears did when it underestimated Kmart and Wal-Mart). The dominant firm might look old-fashioned against new and peppier rivals (Levi's ceding ground to more stylish megabrands like Tommy Hilfiger, Calvin Klein, and GAP). The dominant firm's costs might rise excessively and hurt its profits.

Remaining number one calls for action on three fronts. First, the firm must find ways to expand total market demand. Second, the firm must protect its current market share through good defensive and offensive actions. Third, the firm can try to increase its market share, even if market size remains constant.

EXPANDING THE TOTAL MARKET The dominant firm normally gains the most when the total market expands. If Americans increase their picture taking, Kodak stands to gain the most because it sells over 80 percent of the country's film. If Kodak can convince more Americans to buy cameras and take pictures, or to take pictures on other occasions besides holidays, or to take more pictures on each occasion, Kodak will benefit considerably. In general, the market leader should look for new users, new uses, and more usage of its products.

New Users Every product class has the potential of attracting buyers who are unaware of the product or who are resisting it because of price or lack of certain features. A company can search for new users among three groups: those who might use it but do not (*market-penetration strategy*), those who have never used it (*new-market segment strategy*), or those who live elsewhere (*geographical-expansion strategy*).

Selfridges London retailer Selfridges, founded in 1909 by an American entrepreneur, undertook a $139 million, seven-year makeover of its Oxford Street flagship store when it became evident that big-spending young fashion enthusiasts had all but abandoned the store. Selfridges restored the interior to reflect the building's classical heritage, eliminated the hardware section, added high-fashion labels like Prada and Valentino, plus displays for wireless devices and other high-tech items. The Oxford Street store reported an 11 percent increase in sales for the first six weeks of 2001, a time during which many competitors suffered.[20]

New Uses Markets can be expanded through discovering and promoting new uses for the product. For example, the average American eats dry breakfast cereal three mornings a week. Cereal manufacturers would gain if they could promote cereal eating on other occasions—perhaps as a snack.

In many cases, customers deserve credit for discovering new uses. Vaseline petroleum jelly started out as a lubricant in machine shops. Over the years, consumers have reported many new uses for the product, including a skin ointment, a healing agent, and a hair dressing. Arm & Hammer, the baking soda brand made by Church and Dwight, had downward-drifting sales for 125 years! Then the company discovered consumers used it as a refrigerator deodorant. It launched a heavy promotion campaign focusing on this single use and succeeded in getting half of the homes in America to place an open box of baking soda in the refrigerator. A few years later, Arm & Hammer discovered consumers who used its product to quell kitchen grease fires, and it promoted this use with great results.

figure **9.6**

Hypothetical Market Structure

More Usage   A third market-expansion strategy is to convince people to use more product per use occasion. Shampoo manufacturers convince consumers to use more shampoo by printing the directions "lather, rinse, and repeat" on every bottle when no one really knows if there is any benefit to washing one's hair twice![21] Consider what Michelin did.

Michelin Tire Company (French)   Michelin wanted to encourage French car owners to drive their cars more miles per year—thus leading to more tire replacement. It conceived the idea of rating French restaurants on a three-star system. Michelin promoted the names of many of the best restaurants in the south of France, leading Parisians to take weekend drives to Provence and the Riviera. Michelin also published guidebooks with maps and lists of sights along the way to encourage additional driving.

Companies have long used a strategy to get people to replace products. Called "planned obsolescence," it is the idea of spurring repeat sales by making goods that break down or wear out. Ever wonder why no one has yet marketed a lightbulb that never burns out or a battery that never wears down? Now manufacturers have taken this concept further by making products that actually "tell" consumers when they are breaking down or wearing out. Gillette's new Mach3 shaving system is a prime example.

Gillette   Each Gillette Mach3 cartridge features a blue stripe that slowly fades with repeated use. After about a dozen shaves, it fades away completely, signaling the user to move on to the next cartridge or in Gillette's more subtle wording, this "alerts men that they're not getting the optimal Mach3 shaving experience," regardless of whether the blade really needs replacing. As Gillette executive Robert King said bluntly, "I wish we could get men to change the cartridge every 4 days. The more they change it, the more we sell."

DEFENDING MARKET SHARE   While trying to expand total market size, the dominant firm must continuously defend its current business. The leader is like a large elephant being attacked by a swarm of bees. Coca-Cola must constantly guard against PepsiCo; Gillette against Bic; Hertz against Avis; McDonald's against Burger King; General Motors against Ford; and Kodak against Fuji.[22] Sometimes the competitor is domestic; sometimes it is foreign.

Kodak and Fuji   For more than 100 years, Eastman Kodak has been known for its easy-to-use cameras, high-quality film, and solid profits. During the past decade, Kodak's sales have flattened and its profits have declined. Kodak has been outpaced by more innovative competitors, many of whom are Japanese, who introduced or improved on 35-mm cameras, videocameras, and digital cameras. Then Fuji Photo Film Company moved in on Kodak's bread-and-butter color film business by offering high-quality color films at prices 10 percent lower than Kodak's. Kodak fought back fiercely, matching Fuji's lower prices, improving its products, and outspending Fuji 20 to 1 on advertising and promotion. Kodak successfully defended its U.S. market position, and by the early 1990s, its share of the domestic film market had stabilized at 80 percent.

But Kodak took the battle a step further by setting up a separate subsidiary—Kodak Japan—to do battle on Fuji's home turf. Kodak bought out a Japanese distributor and set up its own Japanese marketing and sales staff. It invested in a new technology center and research facility. Finally, Kodak greatly increased its Japanese promotion and publicity. Kodak Japan now sponsors everything from Japanese television talk shows to sumo wrestling tournaments.

Kodak sought to take advantage of several benefits of its stepped-up attack on Japan. First, Japan's film and photographic paper market is second only to the

United States in size. Second, much of the new photographic technology originates in Japan. Third, having ownership and joint ventures in Japan helps Kodak to better understand Japanese manufacturing and to better develop new products. As a consequence of Kodak's ramped-up attack, Fuji devoted heavy resources to defending its home turf, and therefore had fewer resources to use against Kodak in the United States. In 1998, Kodak had a 10 percent share of the Japanese color film market, compared with Fuji's two-thirds share.[23]

What can the market leader do to defend its terrain? Twenty centuries ago, in a treatise called *The Art of War*, the famed Chinese military strategist Sun Tsu told his warriors: "One does not rely on the enemy not attacking, but on the fact that he himself is unassailable." The most constructive response is *continuous innovation*. The leader leads the industry in developing new product and customer services, distribution effectiveness, and cost cutting. It keeps increasing its competitive strength and value to customers. *The leader applies the military principle of the offensive: The commander exercises initiative, sets the pace, and exploits enemy weaknesses.* The best defense is a good offense.

IGT   International Game Technology (IGT), a company that manufactures slot machines and video poker machines for casinos around the world, has achieved the feat of maintaining a 64 percent domestic market share. Unlike the people who use its products, the company does not rely on luck. IGT has formed partnerships with casino operators and competitive gaming manufacturers to develop innovative new equipment to replace the old. IGT spends aggressively on R&D, allocating $55 million in 2001 to create new games. Dedication to service is also a company mantra. "We know months, years, in advance what our customers want," says Robert Shay, national product executive for IGT. That is because it involves casino operators throughout the sales process, from initial product development to final placement on the casino floor.[24]

Even when it does not launch offensives, the market leader must not leave any major flanks exposed. It must keep its costs down, and its prices must be consonant

IGT's home page focuses on customer service.

with the value the customers see in the brand. Here is a dramatic example of how a company ignored this vital principle at its peril.

Johnson & Johnson The cardiac stent is a tiny metal scaffold used to prop open obstructed heart vessels. In just 37 months after introducing this breakthrough device, Johnson & Johnson tallied more than $1 billion in sales and garnered more than 90 percent of a remarkably profitable market. In the fall of 1997, Guidant Corporation launched a competing product, and within 45 days it had gained a 70 percent market position. Other competitors moved in, and by the end of that year J&J's share had plummeted to a mere 8 percent. What went wrong? For one thing, J&J was so focused on getting the product to market that it devoted little time or resources to the next generation of the stent. The other stumbling block was its refusal to budge on price or offer discounts. At $1,595, the device was an expensive buy at a time when managed care was putting tremendous pressure on health care providers to keep costs down. With no comparable options on the market, doctors felt gouged.[25]

Clearly, the market leader must consider carefully which terrains are important to defend, even at a loss, and which can be surrendered.[26] The aim of defensive strategy is to reduce the probability of attack, divert attacks to less threatening areas, and lessen their intensity. The defender's speed of response can make an important difference in the profit consequences. Researchers are currently exploring the most appropriate forms of response to price and other attacks. A dominant firm can use the six defense strategies summarized in Figure 9.7 and described in the following paragraphs.[27]

DEFENSE STRATEGIES

Position Defense Position defense involves building superior brand power, making the brand almost impregnable.

Heinz and Hunt's Heinz let Hunt's carry out its massive attack in the ketchup market without striking back. Hunt's attacked Heinz with two new flavors of ketchup; it lowered its price to 70 percent of Heinz's price; it offered heavy trade allowances to retailers; it raised its advertising budget to over twice the level of Heinz's. The strategy failed because Hunt's ketchup did not deliver the same quality and the Heinz brand continued to enjoy consumer preference. Heinz showed great confidence in the superiority of its brand, which as of 2000 has over 50 percent market share in the United States, compared with Hunt's 17 percent.[28]

figure **9.7**

Six Types of Defense Strategies

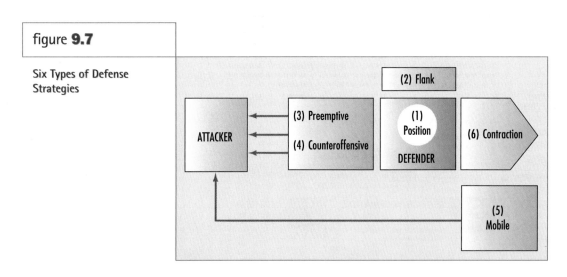

Flank Defense   Although position defense is important, leaders under attack would be foolish to rely on building fortifications around their current product; the market leader should also erect outposts to protect a weak front or possibly serve as an invasion base for counterattack. Here is a good example of a flank defense.

Heublein   Heublein's brand Smirnoff, which had 23 percent of the U.S. vodka market, was attacked by another brand, Wolfschmidt, priced at $1 less per bottle. Instead of lowering the price of Smirnoff by $1, Heublein raised the price by $1 and put the increased revenue into advertising. At the same time, Heublein introduced another brand, Relska, to compete with Wolfschmidt and still another, Popov, to sell for less than Wolfschmidt. This strategy effectively bracketed Wolfschmidt and protected Smirnoff's flanks.

Goodyear   In the 1990s, Goodyear Tire & Rubber Company was faced with fierce competition from the likes of Bridgestone/Firestone and Michelin. To stay ahead of this mounting competition, Goodyear employed a number of flank defenses. The company developed innovative new products, such as the Aquatred, a tire that uses deep grooves to dispel water from the tire's surface, and the Extended Mobility Tire, which, even when completely flat, can be driven 50 miles at 55 miles per hour. Goodyear also acquired other tire companies, such as Debica, the leading tire manufacturer in Poland, and Dunlop, a subsidiary of Sumitomo Rubber Industries, which, in combination with its value-priced Kelly-Springfield brand, provided much competitive breadth and strength. With the Dunlop acquisition, Goodyear once again became the world's largest tire manufacturer.[29]

Preemptive Defense   A more aggressive maneuver is to attack *before* the enemy starts its offense. A company can launch a preemptive defense in several ways. It can wage guerrilla action across the market—hitting one competitor here, another there—and keep everyone off balance; or it can try to achieve a grand market envelopment, as Seiko has done with 2,300 watch models distributed worldwide. It can begin sustained price attacks, as Texas Instruments often did; or it can send out market signals to dissuade competitors from attacking.[30]

Chrysler   In the 1990s, Chrysler had the largest market share of the newly popular minivans. The minivans were priced at $18,000 and highly profitable. Chairman Lee Iacocca knew that competitors would try to enter the market at a lower price, so in an interview with *USA Today*, he indicated that Chrysler was considering introducing a cut-rate minivan. This signal was sent to discourage competitors from thinking they could win by launching a lower-price minivan.

Counteroffensive Defense   When attacked, most market leaders will respond with a counterattack. In a counteroffensive, the leader can meet the attacker frontally or hit its flank or launch a pincer movement. An effective counterattack is to invade the attacker's main territory so that it will have to pull back some troops to defend the territory. One of Northwest Airlines's most profitable routes is Minneapolis to Atlanta. A smaller air carrier launched a deep fare cut and advertised it heavily to expand its share in this market. Northwest retaliated by cutting its fares on the Minneapolis/Chicago route, which the attacking airline depended on for revenue. With its major revenue source hurting, the attacking airline restored its Minneapolis/Atlanta fare to a normal level.

Another common form of counteroffensive is the exercise of economic or political clout. The leader may try to crush a competitor by subsidizing lower prices for the vulnerable product with revenue from its more profitable products; or the leader may prematurely announce that a product upgrade will be available, to prevent customers from buying the competitor's product; or the leader may lobby legislators to take political action that would inhibit or cripple the competition.

Mobile Defense In mobile defense, the leader stretches its domain over new territories that can serve as future centers for defense and offense. It spreads through market broadening and market diversification.

Market broadening involves the company in shifting its focus from the current product to the underlying generic need. The company gets involved in R&D across the whole range of technology associated with that need. Thus "petroleum" companies sought to recast themselves into "energy" companies. Implicitly, this change demanded that they dip their research fingers into the oil, coal, nuclear, hydroelectric, and chemical industries.

Such a strategy should not be carried too far, lest it fault two fundamental military principles—the *principle of the objective* (pursue a clearly defined, decisive, and attainable objective) and the *principle of mass* (concentrate your efforts at a point of enemy weakness). Reasonable broadening, however, makes sense.

Wal-Mart Wal-Mart's supercenters already stock groceries, so the giant chain did not consider it too much of a leap to broaden into the grocery business. In 1998, Wal-Mart Stores Inc., announced plans for three experimental grocery stores in Arkansas. The 40,000-square-foot "Neighborhood Markets" offer traditionally low Wal-Mart prices on a smaller scale with a store modeled after stand-alone grocery chains. The markets use the now-familiar low everyday price concept, while offering more convenience than Wal-Mart supercenters. After initial success in Arkansas, Wal-Mart expanded its Neighborhood Markets into other states. Wal-Mart's move into conventional grocery stores prompted supermarket giants Kroger and Safeway to cut prices and boost service.[31]

Market diversification into unrelated industries is the other alternative. When U.S. tobacco companies like Reynolds and Philip Morris acknowledged the growing curbs on cigarette smoking, they were not content with position defense or even with looking for cigarette substitutes. Instead they moved quickly into new industries, such as beer, liquor, soft drinks, and frozen foods.

Contraction Defense Large companies sometimes recognize that they can no longer defend all of their territory. The best course of action then appears to be *planned contraction* (also called *strategic withdrawal*). Planned contraction means giving up weaker territories and reassigning resources to stronger territories. It is a move to consolidate competitive strength in the market and concentrate mass at pivotal positions. Heinz, General Mills, Del Monte, General Electric, American Can, and Georgia-Pacific are among companies that have significantly pruned their product lines in recent years.

EXPANDING MARKET SHARE   Market leaders can improve their profitability by increasing their market share. In many markets, one share point is worth tens of millions of dollars. A one-share-point gain in coffee is worth $48 million and in soft drinks, $120 million! No wonder normal competition has turned into marketing warfare.

A study by the Strategic Planning Institute (called Profit Impact of Market Strategy, or PIMS) found that a company's profitability, measured by pretax return on investment (ROI), rises with its *relative market share* of its served market,[32] as shown in Figure 9.8(a).[33] The average ROI for businesses with under 10 percent market share was about 11 percent. A difference of 10 percentage points in market share is accompanied by a difference of about 5 points in pretax ROI. The PIMS study shows that businesses with market shares over 40 percent earn an average ROI of 30 percent, or three times that of those with shares under 10 percent.[34] These findings led many companies to pursue market-share expansion and leadership as their objective. General Electric decided it must be number one or two in each market or else get out. GE divested its computer

figure **9.8**	Relationship Between Market Share and Profitability

Source: Figure (a) from Strategic Planning Institute (The PIMS Program) 1030 Massachusetts Avenue, Cambridge, MA 02138.

business and its air-conditioning business because it could not achieve leadership in these industries.

Some critics have attacked the PIMS findings as being either weak or spurious. Hamermesh cited many profitable companies with low market shares.[35] Woo and Cooper identified 40 low-share businesses that enjoyed pretax ROIs of 20 percent or more; these businesses tended to have high relative product quality, medium-to-low prices, narrow product lines, and low total costs.[36] Most of these companies produced industrial components or supplies.

Some industry studies yield a V-shaped relationship between market share and profitability.[37] Figure 9.8(b) shows a V-curve for agricultural-equipment firms. The industry leader, Deere & Company, earns a high return. However, two small specialty firms, Hesston and Steiger, also earn high returns. J. I. Case and Massey-Ferguson are trapped in the valley, and at the time International Harvester commanded substantial market share but earned lower returns. Thus, such industries have one or a few highly profitable large firms, several profitable small and more-focused firms, and several medium-sized firms with poorer profit performance.

How can the two graphs in Figure 9.8 be reconciled? The PIMS findings argue that profitability increases as a business gains share relative to its competitors in its *served (target) market*. The V-shaped curve ignores market segments and looks at profitability relative to size in the *total market*. Mercedes earns high profits because it is a high-share company in its served market of luxury cars, even though it is a low-share company in the total auto market; and it has achieved this high share in its served market because it does many things right, such as producing high relative product quality.

However, gaining increased market share in the served market does not automatically produce higher profits. Much depends on the company's strategy for gaining increased market share.

figure **9.9**

The Concept of Optimal Market Share

McDonald's Since 1987, McDonald's share of fast-food sales in the United States has been slipping. The drop has come even as the company has increased its number of restaurants by 50 percent, far outpacing the industry expansion rate. Ill-fated product innovations took the blame for the market-share drop. Customers were not thrilled about its pizza and veggie burger offerings. When the company tried to expand its way out of the crisis by building thousands of new restaurants, it ended up stealing customers and profits from its own existing franchises. In 2000, the company shifted its focus to providing healthy menu options, improving the ambiance, and changing the food preparation system in its restaurants.

Because the cost of buying higher market share may far exceed its revenue value, a company should consider three factors before pursuing increased market share:

- The first factor is the possibility of provoking antitrust action. Jealous competitors are likely to cry "monopoly" if a dominant firm makes further inroads. This rise in risk would cut down the attractiveness of pushing market-share gains too far. This is what has happened to Verizon.

Verizon Verizon, formed in a merger between Bell Atlantic and GTE, came under fire from consumers and competitors in the state of Pennsylvania for "anti-competitive" practices. Public outcry ensued when Verizon, which controlled 90 percent of local phone lines in the state, announced plans to enter the long-distance market. A 2001 ruling by the state's Public Utilities Commission ordered Verizon to establish "functional structural separation" of its retail and wholesale units, but refrained from breaking the company into two separate parts, as many consumers and competitors had hoped it would do.[39]

- The second factor is economic cost. Figure 9.9 shows that profitability might fall with further market-share gains after some level. In the illustration, the firm's *optimal market share* is 50 percent. The cost of gaining further market share might exceed the value. A company that has, say, 60 percent of the market must recognize that the "holdout" customers may dislike the company, be loyal to competitive suppliers, have unique needs, or prefer dealing with smaller suppliers. The cost of legal work, public relations, and lobbying rises with market share. Pushing for higher market share is less justified when there are few scale or experience economies, unattractive market segments exist, buyers want multiple sources of supply, and exit barriers are high. Some market leaders have even increased profitability by selectively decreasing market share in weaker areas.[40]
- The third factor is that companies might pursue the wrong marketing-mix strategy in their bid for higher market share. Companies that win more market share by cutting price are buying, not earning, a larger share, and their profits may be lower.

Buzzell and Wiersema found that share-gaining companies typically outperform competitors in three areas: new-product activity, relative product quality, and marketing expenditures.[41] Specifically: Share-gaining companies typically develop and add more new products. Companies that increase product quality relative to competitors enjoy greater share gains. Companies that increase marketing expenditures faster than the rate of market growth typically achieve share gains. Increases in sales force expenditures are effective in producing share gains for both industrial and consumer markets. Increased advertising expenditures produce share gains mainly for consumer-goods companies. Increased sales-promotion expenditures are effective in producing share gains for all kinds of companies. Companies that cut prices more deeply than competitors do not achieve significant market-share gains. Presumably, enough rivals meet the price cuts, and others offer other values to buyers, so that buyers do not switch to the price cutter.

two case studies: procter & gamble and caterpillar

Market leaders who stay on top have learned the art of expanding the total market, defending their current territory, and increasing market-share profitably. Here we look at two companies, Procter & Gamble and Caterpillar, which have shown a remarkable ability to protect their market shares against able challengers.

PROCTER & GAMBLE   Procter & Gamble (P&G) is one of the most skilled marketers of consumer packaged goods. It markets the leading brand in 19 of the 39 categories in which it competes. Its average market share is close to 25 percent. Its market leadership rests on several principles:

- *Customer knowledge:* P&G studies its customers—both final consumers and the trade—through continuous marketing research and intelligence gathering. It prints its toll-free 800 number on every product.

- *Long-term outlook:* P&G takes the time to analyze each opportunity carefully and prepare the best product, then commits itself to making this product a success. It struggled with Pringles potato chips for almost a decade before achieving market success.

- *Product innovation:* P&G is an active product innovator, devoting $1.2 billion (3.4 percent of sales) to research and development, an impressively high amount for a packaged-goods company. It holds more than 2,500 active patents protecting 250 proprietary technologies. Part of its innovation process is developing brands that offer new consumer benefits. P&G spent 10 years researching and developing the first effective anticavity toothpaste, Crest.[42]

- *Quality strategy:* P&G designs products of above-average quality and continuously improves them. When P&G announces "new and improved," it means it.

- *Line-extension strategy:* P&G produces its brands in several sizes and forms. This strategy gains more shelf space and prevents competitors from moving in to satisfy unmet market needs.

- *Brand-extension strategy:* P&G often uses its strong brand names to launch new products. The Ivory brand has been extended from a soap to include a liquid soap, a dishwashing detergent, and a shampoo. Launching a new product under a strong existing brand name gives the new brand instant recognition and credibility with much less advertising outlay.

- *Multibrand strategy:* P&G markets several brands in the same product category. It produces eight brands of hand soap and six shampoo brands. Each brand meets a different consumer want and competes against specific competitors' brands. Each brand manager competes for company resources. More recently, P&G has begun to reduce its vast array of products, sizes, flavors, and varieties to bring down costs.[43]

- *Heavy advertising and media pioneer:* P&G is the nation's second largest consumer-packaged-goods advertiser, spending over $3 billion a year on advertising. A pioneer in using the power of television to create strong consumer awareness and preference, P&G is now taking a leading role in building its brand on the Web. In 1998, P&G hosted a high-powered industry "summit" meeting that brought together some 400 top executives from Internet and consumer marketing companies. The goal: figuring out how to best sell products over the Internet.[44]

- *Aggressive sales force:* In 1998, P&G's sales force was named one of the top 25 sales forces by *Sales & Marketing Management* magazine. A key to P&G's success is the close ties its sales force forms with retailers, notably Wal-Mart. The 150-person team that serves the retail giant works closely with Wal-Mart to improve both the products that go to the stores and the process by which they get there.

- *Effective sales promotion:* P&G's sales-promotion department counsels its brand managers on the most effective promotions to achieve particular objectives. The department develops an expert sense of these deals' effectiveness under varying circumstances. At the same time, P&G tries to minimize the use of sales promotion and move toward "everyday low prices."

- *Competitive toughness:* P&G carries a big stick when it comes to aggressors. It is willing to spend large sums of money to outpromote new competitive brands and prevent them from gaining a foothold.

- *Manufacturing efficiency and cost cutting:* P&G's reputation as a great marketing company is matched by its excellence as a manufacturing company. P&G spends large sums developing and improving production operations to keep its costs among the lowest in the industry; and P&G has recently begun slashing its costs even further, allowing it to reduce the premium prices at which some of its goods sell.
- *Brand-management system:* P&G originated the brand-management system, in which one executive is responsible for each brand. The system has been copied by many competitors but frequently without P&G's success. Recently, P&G modified its general management structure so that each brand category is now run by a category manager with volume and profit responsibility. Although this new organization does not replace the brand-management system, it helps to sharpen strategic focus on key consumer needs and competition in the category.

Thus P&G's market leadership is not based on doing one thing well, but on the successful orchestration of myriad factors that contribute to market leadership.

CATERPILLAR   Caterpillar is the dominant leader in the construction-equipment industry. Its tractors, crawlers, and loaders, painted in the familiar yellow, are a common sight at any construction area. Caterpillar has retained leadership in spite of charging a premium price and being challenged by a number of able competitors, including John Deere, J. I. Case, Komatsu, and Hitachi. Several policies combine to explain Caterpillar's success:

- *Premium performance:* Caterpillar produces high-quality equipment known for its reliability and durability. These are key buyer considerations in the choice of heavy industrial equipment.
- *Extensive and efficient dealership system:* Caterpillar maintains the largest number of independent construction-equipment dealers in the industry. Its 220 dealers throughout the world carry a complete line of Caterpillar equipment. Competitors' dealers normally lack a full line and carry complementary, noncompeting lines. Caterpillar can choose the best dealers and spends the most money in training, servicing, and motivating them.
- *Superior service:* Caterpillar has built a worldwide parts and service system second to none in the industry. Caterpillar can ship replacement parts and deliver service anywhere in the world within 24 hours of equipment breakdown. Competitors would have to make a substantial investment to duplicate this service level and would only neutralize Caterpillar's advantage rather than score a new advantage.
- *Full-line strategy:* Caterpillar produces a full line of construction equipment to enable customers to do one-stop buying.
- *Good financing:* Caterpillar provides a wide range of financial terms for customers who buy its equipment.

In the 1980s, Caterpillar experienced difficulties because of the depressed global construction-equipment market and cutthroat competition from Komatsu, Japan's number-one construction firm, which adopted the internal slogan "Encircle Caterpillar." Komatsu attacked market niches, sometimes pricing its equipment as much as 40 percent lower. Caterpillar fought back by cutting costs and meeting Komatsu's prices and sometimes even initiating price cutting. The price wars drove competitors like International Harvester and Clark Equipment to the brink of ruin. The long and damaging price wars appear to be coming to an end, with both sides settling for improved profits.

market-challenger strategies

Firms that occupy second, third, and lower ranks in an industry are often called runner-up, or trailing firms. Some, such as Colgate, Ford, Avis, and PepsiCo, are quite large in their own right. These firms can adopt one of two postures. They can attack the leader and other competitors in an aggressive bid for further market share (market challengers), or they can play ball and not "rock the boat" (market followers).

Many market challengers have gained ground or even overtaken the leader. Toyota today produces more cars than General Motors, and British Airways flies more international passengers than the former leader, Pan Am, did in its heyday. These challengers set high aspirations and leveraged their smaller resources while the market leaders ran their businesses as usual.

Robert Dolan found that competitive rivalry and price cutting are most intense in industries with high fixed costs, high inventory costs, and stagnant primary demand, such as steel, auto, paper, and chemicals.[45] We will now examine the competitive attack strategies available to market challengers.

DEFINING THE STRATEGIC OBJECTIVE AND OPPONENT(S)   A market challenger must first define its strategic objective. Most aim to increase market share. The challenger must decide whom to attack:

- *It can attack the market leader.* This is a high-risk but potentially high-payoff strategy and makes good sense if the leader is not serving the market well. Miller's "lite beer" campaign was successful because it pivoted on discovering consumers who wanted a less caloric, less filling beer. The alternative strategy is to out-innovate the leader across the whole segment. Xerox wrested the copy market from 3M by developing a better copying process. Later, Canon grabbed a large chunk of Xerox's market by introducing desk copiers.
- *It can attack firms of its own size that are not doing the job and are underfinanced.* These firms have aging products, are charging excessive prices, or are not satisfying customers in other ways.
- *It can attack small local and regional firms.* Several major beer companies grew to their present size by gobbling up smaller firms, or "guppies."

If the attacking company goes after the market leader, its objective might be to wrest a certain share. Bic is under no illusion that it can topple Gillette in the razor market—it is simply seeking a larger share. If the attacking company goes after a small local company, its objective might be to drive that company out of existence.

CHOOSING A GENERAL ATTACK STRATEGY   Given clear opponents and objectives, what attack options are available? We can distinguish among five attack strategies shown in Figure 9.10: frontal, flank, encirclement, bypass, and guerilla attacks.

Frontal Attack   In a pure *frontal attack*, the attacker matches its opponent's product, advertising, price, and distribution. The principle of force says that the side with the greater manpower (resources) will win. The military dogma is that for a frontal attack to succeed against a well-entrenched opponent or one controlling the high ground, the attacking forces must have at least a 3-to-1 advantage in combat firepower. The runner-up razor-blade manufacturer in Brazil attacked Gillette, the market leader. The attacker was asked if it offers the consumer a better razor blade. "No" was the reply. "A lower price?" "No." "A better package?" "No." "A clever advertising campaign?" "No." "Better allowances to the trade?" "No." "Then how do you expect to take share away from Gillette?" "Sheer determination" was the reply. Needless to say, the offensive failed.

A modified frontal attack, such as cutting price vis-à-vis the opponent's, can work if the market leader does not retaliate and if the competitor convinces the market that its product is equal to the leader's. Helene Curtis is a master at convincing the market that its brands—such as Suave and Finesse—are equal in quality but a better value than higher-priced brands.

Flank Attack   The major principle of offensive warfare is concentration of strength against weakness. The enemy's weak spots are natural targets. A *flank attack* can be directed along two strategic dimensions—geographical and segmental. In a geographical attack, the challenger spots areas where the opponent is underperforming. For example, some of IBM's former mainframe rivals, such as Honeywell, chose to set up strong sales branches in medium- and smaller-sized cities that were relatively neglected by IBM. The other flanking strategy is to serve uncovered market needs, as Japanese automakers did

figure **9.10**

Attack Strategies

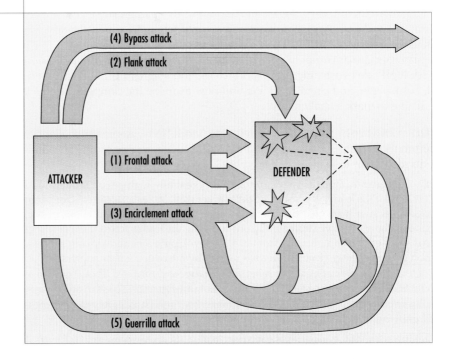

when they developed more fuel-efficient cars, and as Miller Brewing Company did when it introduced light beer.

A flanking strategy is another name for identifying shifts in market segments that are causing gaps to develop, then rushing in to fill the gaps and develop them into strong segments. Flanking is in the best tradition of modern marketing, which holds that the purpose of marketing is to discover needs and satisfy them. Flank attacks are particularly attractive to a challenger with fewer resources than its opponent and are much more likely to be successful than frontal attacks.

Encirclement Attack   The encirclement maneuver is an attempt to capture a wide slice of the enemy's territory through a "blitz." It involves launching a grand offensive on several fronts. Encirclement makes sense when the challenger commands superior resources and believes a swift encirclement will break the opponent's will.

Sun Microsystems Inc.   In making a stand against arch rival Microsoft, Sun Microsystems is licensing its Java software for all sorts of consumer devices. As consumer-electronics products began to go digital, Java started appearing in a wide range of gadgets. Motorola uses Java in everything from pagers and cell phones to fax machines and smartcards. Dallas Semiconductor makes the iButton, a key chain attachment with a Java-encoded chip that provides more secure access to hotel rooms or e-mail stations at public kiosks. As of January 2001, Java was licensed by 200 companies and used by more than 2.5 million software developers.[46]

Bypass Attack   The most indirect assault strategy is the *bypass*. It means bypassing the enemy and attacking easier markets to broaden one's resource base. This strategy offers three lines of approach: diversifying into unrelated products, diversifying into new geographical markets, and leapfrogging into new technologies to supplant existing products. Although PepsiCo and Coca-Cola often go head to head, the bypass attack is also part of their competitive battle plan. Here's how Pepsi used a bypass strategy against Coke:

PepsiCo   In the summer of 1998, many people wondered why PepsiCo paid $3.3 billion for juice giant Tropicana. Unlike soda, juice is a perishable product subject to commodity markets, bad weather, and crop failures. Yet, as the world's largest juice company—with 42 percent of the $3 billion orange juice market—Tropicana armed Pepsi with a powerful new weapon for the war against Coca-Cola, which has only 24 percent of the orange juice market with its own Minute Maid. Pepsi added the dominant player in the sports beverage category to its roster in 2000, when it outbid Coca-Cola and Dannon to buy Quaker Oats, owners of the Gatorade brand, for $14 billion. Gatorade, which boasts over an 80 percent share of the sports drink market, gives Pepsi another non-soft-drink advantage over Coca-Cola, which markets the also-ran sports beverage Powerade.[47]

Technological leapfrogging is a bypass strategy practiced in high-tech industries. The challenger patiently researches and develops the next technology and launches an attack, shifting the battleground to its territory, where it has an advantage. Nintendo's successful attack in the video-game market was precisely about wresting market share by introducing a superior technology and redefining the "competitive space." Then Sega/Genesis did the same with more advanced technology, and now Sony's Playstation is grabbing the technological lead. Here is another example of a technological bypass attack strategy.

SCA   SCA, the Swedish competitor to P&G, has pursued an innovative Internet strategy to outsmart P&G in the baby-diaper market with a much smaller budget. SCA saw an opportunity for real dialogue with expectant and new parents through the Internet, and created the Web site *www.libero.se* as a community for parents. The site contains a large encyclopedia on parenting plus tools like a "baby namefinder." The site also suggests how to choose the right diaper. It hosts debates, encouraging consumers to help each other out. Users can buy and sell child-related equipment free. In its "baby's own Web site," users can upload pictures, write small stories, and make child wish lists, allowing relatives all over the world to follow the child's progress.[48]

Swedish firm SCA's www.libero.se site creates a dialogue with expectant and new parents and even allows users to send pictures, brief stories, and child wish lists to family all over the world.

Guerrilla Warfare   **Guerrilla warfare** consists of waging small, intermittent attacks to harass and demoralize the opponent and eventually secure permanent footholds. The guerrilla challenger uses both conventional and unconventional means of attack. These include selective price cuts, intense promotional blitzes, and occasional legal actions. Here is an example of a very successful guerrilla strategy.

The Princeton Review   In 1938, Stanley H. Kaplan founded Kaplan Educational Centers, which became the largest test-preparation business in the United States. Then a young Princeton graduate named John Katzman created The Princeton Review, and engaged in guerrilla marketing, particularly attacking Kaplan's image. The Princeton Review ads were brash: "Stanley's a wimp," or "Friends don't let friends take Kaplan," while touting the Princeton Review's smaller, livelier classes. Katzman posted horror stories about Kaplan on the Internet, and even picked fights with the Educational Testing Service (ETS), which administers the standardized tests that the test-preparation companies coach students to take. By the 1990s, Princeton Review's guerrilla warfare had paid off. The company is now one of the leading test-preparation companies.

Normally, guerrilla warfare is practiced by a smaller firm against a larger one. The smaller firm launches a barrage of attacks in random corners of the larger opponent's market in a manner calculated to weaken the opponent's market power. Military dogma holds that a continual stream of minor attacks usually creates more cumulative impact, disorganization, and confusion in the enemy than a few major attacks.

A guerrilla campaign can be expensive, although admittedly less expensive than a frontal, encirclement, or flank attack. Guerrilla warfare is more a preparation for war than a war itself. Ultimately, it must be backed by a stronger attack if the challenger hopes to beat the opponent.

CHOOSING A SPECIFIC ATTACK STRATEGY

The challenger must go beyond the five broad strategies and develop more specific strategies:

- *Price discount:* The challenger can offer a comparable product at a lower price. This is the strategy of discount retailers. Three conditions must be fulfilled. First, the challenger must convince buyers that its product and service are comparable to the leader's. Second, buyers must be price sensitive. Third, the market leader must refuse to cut its price in spite of the competitor's attack.
- *Lower price goods:* The challenger can offer an average- or lower-quality product at a much lower price. Little Debbie Snack Cakes is priced lower than Drake's and outsells Drake's by 20 to 1. Firms that establish themselves through a lower-price strategy, however, can be attacked by firms whose prices are even lower.
- *Prestige goods:* A market challenger can launch a higher-quality product and charge a higher price than the leader. Mercedes gained on Cadillac in the U.S. market by offering a car of higher quality at a higher price.
- *Product proliferation:* The challenger can attack the leader by launching a larger product variety, thus giving buyers more choice. Baskin-Robbins achieved its growth in the ice cream business by promoting more flavors—31—than its larger competitors.
- *Product innovation:* The challenger can pursue product innovation. 3M typically enters new markets by introducing a product improvement or breakthrough.
- *Improved services:* The challenger can offer new or better services to customers. Avis's famous attack on Hertz, "We're only second. We try harder," was based on promising and delivering cleaner cars and faster service than Hertz.
- *Distribution innovation:* A challenger might develop a new channel of distribution. Avon became a major cosmetics company by perfecting door-to-door selling instead of battling other cosmetic firms in conventional stores.

- *Manufacturing-cost reduction:* The challenger might achieve lower manufacturing costs than its competitors through more efficient purchasing, lower labor costs, and more modern production equipment.
- *Intensive advertising promotion:* Some challengers attack the leader by increasing expenditures on advertising and promotion. Miller Beer outspent Budweiser in its attempt to increase its share of the U.S. beer market. Substantial promotional spending, however, is usually not a sensible strategy unless the challenger's product or advertising message is superior.

A challenger's success depends on combining several strategies to improve its position over time.

market-follower strategies

Some years ago, Theodore Levitt wrote an article entitled "Innovative Imitation," in which he argued that a strategy of *product imitation* might be as profitable as a strategy of *product innovation.*[49] The innovator bears the expense of developing the new product, getting it into distribution, and informing and educating the market. The reward for all this work and risk is normally market leadership. However, another firm can come along and copy or improve on the new product. Although it probably will not overtake the leader, the follower can achieve high profits because it did not bear any of the innovation expense.

Many companies prefer to follow rather than challenge the market leader. Patterns of "conscious parallelism" are common in capital-intensive, homogeneous-product industries, such as steel, fertilizers, and chemicals. The opportunities for product differentiation and image differentiation are low; service quality is often comparable; and price sensitivity runs high. The mood in these industries is against short-run grabs for market share because that strategy only provokes retaliation. Most firms decide against stealing one another's customers. Instead, they present similar offers to buyers, usually by copying the leader. Market shares show a high stability.

This is not to say that market followers lack strategies. A market follower must know how to hold current customers and win a fair share of new customers. Each follower tries to bring distinctive advantages to its target market—location, services, financing; and because the follower is often a major target of attack by challengers, it must keep its manufacturing costs low and its product quality and services high. It must also enter new markets as they open up. The follower has to define a growth path, but one that does not invite competitive retaliation. Four broad strategies can be distinguished:

1. *Counterfeiter:* The counterfeiter duplicates the leader's product and package and sells it on the black market or through disreputable dealers. Music record firms, Apple Computer, and Rolex have been plagued with the counterfeiter problem, especially in the Far East.
2. *Cloner:* The cloner emulates the leader's products, name, and packaging, with slight variations. For example, Ralcorp Holding Inc. sells imitations of name-brand cereals in lookalike boxes. Its Tasteeos, Fruit Rings, and Corn Flakes sell for nearly a $1 a box less than the leading name brands.[50] In the computer business, clones are a fact of life.
3. *Imitator:* The imitator copies some things from the leader but maintains differentiation in terms of packaging, advertising, pricing, or location. The leader does not mind the imitator as long as the imitator does not attack the leader aggressively.

TelePizza Fernandez Pujals grew up in Fort Lauderdale, Florida, and took Domino's home delivery idea to Spain, where he borrowed $80,000 to open his first store in Madrid. He now operates over 500 stores in Europe, with a business valued at $1.85 billion.

4. *Adapter:* The adapter takes the leader's products and adapts or improves them. The adapter may choose to sell to different markets, but often the adapter grows into the future challenger, as many Japanese firms have done after adapting and improving products developed elsewhere.

S&S Cycle S&S Cycle is the biggest supplier of complete engines and major motor parts to more than 15 companies that build several thousand Harley-like cruiser bikes each year. These cloners charge as much as $30,000 for their customized creations. S&S has built its name by improving on Harley-Davidson's handiwork. Its customers are often would-be Harley buyers frustrated by long waiting lines at the dealers. Other customers simply want the incredibly powerful S&S engines. S&S stays abreast of its evolving market by ordering a new Harley bike every year and taking apart the engine to see what it can improve upon.[51]

What does a follower earn? Normally, less than the leader. For example, a study of food processing companies showed the largest firm averaging a 16 percent return on investment; the number-two firm, 6 percent; the number-three firm, –1 percent, and the number-four firm, –6 percent. In this case, only the top two firms have profits. No wonder Jack Welch, former CEO of GE, told his business units that each must reach the number-one or -two position in its market or else! Followership is often not a rewarding path.

market-nicher strategies

An alternative to being a follower in a large market is to be a leader in a small market, or niche. Smaller firms normally avoid competing with larger firms by targeting small markets of little or no interest to the larger firms. Here is an example.

Logitech International Logitech has become a $750 million global success story by making every variation of computer mouse imaginable. The company turns out mice for left- and right-handed people, cordless mice that use radio waves, mice shaped like real mice for children, and 3-D mice that let the user appear to move behind screen objects. Its global dominance in the mouse category enabled the company to expand into other computer peripherals, such as keyboards, speakers, joysticks, and Internet video cameras.[52]

Even large firms are now setting up business units, or companies, to serve niches. Here are examples of large, profitable companies that have pursued niching strategies.

Beer Industry Microbrewers' specialty beers—such as Pyramid Ale and Pete's Wicked Ale—was the only beer market showing any growth potential in the late 1990s. That fact prompted the Big Four brewers—Anheuser-Busch, Miller, Coors, and Stroh Brewery—to launch their own specialty beers. There is Anheuser's Red Wolf and Killarney's Red, Miller's Red Dog and Icehouse beers, and Coors' George Killian's. However, because some consumers resisted the idea of buying specialty beer from a big player, some companies kept their name off the label. Miller even advertises its Red Dog and Icehouse beers as coming from Plank Road Brewery, with no mention of Miller.[53]

ITW Illinois Tool Works (ITW) manufactures thousands of products, including nails, screws, plastic six-pack holders for soda cans, bicycle helmets, backpacks, plastic buckles for pet collars, resealable food packages, and more. Since the late 1980s, the company has made between 30 and 40 acquisitions each year, which added new products to the product line. ITW has more than 500 highly autonomous and decentralized business units. When one division commercializes a new product, the product and personnel are spun off into a new entity.[54]

Thus, firms with low shares of the total market can be highly profitable through smart niching. Clifford and Cavanagh identified over two dozen highly successful mid-sized companies and studied their success factors.[55] They found that virtually all these companies were nichers. A. T. Cross niched itself in the high-price writing instruments market with its famous gold and silver items. Such companies tend to offer high value, charge a premium price, achieve lower manufacturing costs, and shape a strong corporate culture and vision. Alberto Culver Company is a classic example of a midsized company that has successfully used market-nicher strategies.

Alberto Culver Company　Alberto Culver used market-nicher strategies to grow earnings in 2000 by 13 percent over the previous year to $97.2 million on sales of $2.25 billion. CEO Howard Bernick explains the Alberto Culver philosophy: "We know who we are and, perhaps more importantly, we know who we are not. We know that if we try to out-Procter Procter, we will fall flat on our face." Instead, the company, known mainly for its Alberto VO5 hair products, focused its marketing muscle on acquiring a stable of smaller niche brands, including such nonbeauty items as flavor enhancers Molly McButter and Mrs. Dash, and static-cling fighter Static Guard.[56]

In a study of hundreds of business units, the Strategic Planning Institute found that the return on investment averaged 27 percent in smaller markets, but only 11 percent in larger markets.[57] Why is niching so profitable? The main reason is that the market nicher ends up knowing the target customers so well that it meets their needs better than other firms selling to this niche casually. As a result, the nicher can charge a substantial price over costs. The nicher achieves *high margin*, whereas the mass-marketer achieves *high volume*.

Nichers have three tasks: creating niches, expanding niches, and protecting niches. Niching carries a major risk in that the market niche might dry up or be attacked. The company is then stuck with highly specialized resources that may not have high-value alternative uses. Consider Arm & Hammer.

Arm & Hammer　Church & Dwight Co., makers of Arm & Hammer baking soda, created a new toothpaste category when it unveiled its Arm & Hammer Dental Care toothpaste with baking soda. Arm & Hammer Dental Care was a hit with consumers, and the product quickly became the leading baking soda toothpaste, helping the company capture an 11 percent share of the global toothpaste market in 1993. As major toothpaste brands like Crest, Colgate, and Mentadent all developed baking soda toothpastes, however, Arm & Hammer's market share fell to 7 percent in the global market in 2000, compared with 50 percent for market leader Colgate.[58]

The key idea in nichemanship is specialization. The following specialist roles are open to nichers:

- *End-user specialist:* The firm specializes in serving one type of end-use customer. For example, a *value-added reseller (VAR)* customizes the computer hardware and software for specific customer segments and earns a price premium in the process.[59]
- *Vertical-level specialist:* The firm specializes at some vertical level of the production-distribution value chain. A copper firm may concentrate on producing raw copper, copper components, or finished copper products.
- *Customer-size specialist:* The firm concentrates on selling to either small, medium-sized, or large customers. Many nichers specialize in serving small customers who are neglected by the majors.
- *Specific-customer specialist:* The firm limits its selling to one or a few customers. Many firms sell their entire output to a single company, such as Sears or General Motors.
- *Geographic specialist:* The firm sells only in a certain locality, region, or area of the world.
- *Product or product-line specialist:* The firm carries or produces only one product line or product. A firm may produce only lenses for microscopes. A retailer may carry only ties.
- *Product-feature specialist:* The firm specializes in producing a certain type of product or product feature. Rent-a-Wreck, for example, is a California car-rental agency that rents only "beat-up" cars.

- *Job-shop specialist:* The firm customizes its products for individual customers.
- *Quality-price specialist:* The firm operates at the low- or high-quality ends of the market. Hewlett-Packard specializes in the high-quality, high-price end of the hand-calculator market.
- *Service specialist:* The firm offers one or more services not available from other firms. An example would be a bank that takes loan requests over the phone and hand-delivers the money to the customer.
- *Channel specialist:* The firm specializes in serving only one channel of distribution. For example, a soft-drink company decides to make a very large-sized soft drink available only at gas stations.

Because niches can weaken, the firm must continually create new ones. The firm should "stick to its niching" but not necessarily to its niche. That is why *multiple niching* is preferable to *single niching*. By developing strength in two or more niches, the company increases its chances for survival.

Firms entering a market should aim at a niche initially rather than the whole market. (See "Marketing Insight: Strategies for Entering Markets Held by Incumbent Firms.")

marketing **insight**

Strategies for Entering Markets Held by Incumbent Firms

What marketing strategies can companies use to enter a market held by incumbent firms? Biggadike examined the strategies of 40 invading firms. He found that 10 entered at a lower price, 9 matched incumbents' prices, and 21 entered at a higher price. On quality, 28 claimed superior quality, 5 matched incumbents' quality, and 7 reported inferior product quality. Most entrants offered a specialist product line and served a narrower market segment. Less than 20 percent innovated a new distribution channel. Over half offered a higher level of customer service. Over half spent less than incumbents on sales force, advertising, and promotion. The winning marketing mix was (1) higher prices and higher quality; (2) narrower product line; (3) narrower market segment; (4) similar distribution channels; (5) superior service; and (6) lower expenditure on sales force, advertising, and promotion.

Schnaars examined the strategies of successful invading firms that entered occupied markets and eventually took leadership. He detailed more than 30 cases in which the imitator displaced the innovator, including:

Product	Innovator	Imitator
Word-processing software	Word Star	WordPerfect
Spreadsheet software	Unicalc	Later Word
Credit cards	Diners' Club	Visa and MasterCard
Ball-point pens	Reynolds	Parker
CAT scanners	EMI	General Electric
Hand calculators	Bowmar	Texas Instruments
Food processors	Cuisinart	Black & Decker

The imitators captured the market by offering lower prices, selling an improved product, or using superior market power and resources.

Carpenter and Nakamoto examined strategies for launching a new product into a market dominated by one brand, such as Jell-O or FedEx. (These brands, which include many market pioneers, are particularly difficult to attack because many are the standard against which others are judged.) They identified four strategies that have good profit potential in this situation:

1. *Differentiation:* Positioning away from the dominant brand with a comparable or premium price and heavy advertising spending to establish the new brand as a credible alternative. Example: Honda's motorcycle challenges Harley-Davidson.
2. *Challenger:* Positioning close to the dominant brand with heavy advertising spending and comparable or premium price to challenge the dominant brand as the category standard. Example: Pepsi competing against Coke.
3. *Niche:* Positioning away from the dominant brand with a high price and a low advertising budget to exploit a profitable niche. Example: Tom's of Maine all-natural toothpaste competing against Crest.
4. *Premium:* Positioning near the dominant brand with little advertising spending but a premium price to move "up market" relative to the dominant brand. Examples: Godiva chocolate and Haagen-Dazs ice cream competing against standard brands.

Sources: See Ralph Biggadike, *Entering New Markets: Strategies and Performance* (Cambridge, MA: Marketing Science Institute, 1977), pp. 12–20; Steven P. Schnaars, *Managing Imitation Strategies: How later Entrants Seize Markets from Pioneers* (New York: The Free Press, 1994); Gregory S. Carpenter and Kent Nakamoto, "Competitive Strategies for Late Entry into a Market with a Dominant Brand," *Management Science* (October 1990): 1268–78; Gregory S. Carpenter and Kent Nakamoto, "Competitive Late Mover Strategies," working paper, Northwestern University, 1993.

balancing customer and competitor orientations

We have stressed the importance of a company's positioning itself competitively as a market leader, challenger, follower, or nicher. Yet a company must not spend all its time focusing on competitors. We can distinguish between two types of companies: competitor-centered and customer-centered. A *competitor-centered company* sets its course as follows:

Situation

- Competitor W is going all out to crush us in Miami.
- Competitor X is improving its distribution coverage in Houston and hurting our sales.
- Competitor Y has cut its price in Denver, and we lost three share points.
- Competitor Z has introduced a new service feature in New Orleans, and we are losing sales.

Reactions

- We will withdraw from the Miami market because we cannot afford to fight this battle.
- We will increase our advertising expenditure in Houston.
- We will meet competitor Y's price cut in Denver.
- We will increase our sales-promotion budget in New Orleans.

This kind of planning has some pluses and minuses. On the positive side, the company develops a fighter orientation. It trains its marketers to be on constant alert, to watch for weaknesses in its competitors' and its own position. On the negative side, the company is too reactive. Rather than formulating and executing a consistent, customer-oriented strategy, it determines its moves based on its competitors' moves. It does not move toward its own goals. It does not know where it will end up, because so much depends on what its competitors do.

A *customer-centered company* focuses more on customer developments in formulating its strategies.

Situation

- The total market is growing at 4 percent annually.
- The quality-sensitive segment is growing at 8 percent annually.
- The deal-prone customer segment is also growing fast, but these customers do not stay with any supplier very long.
- A growing number of customers have expressed an interest in a 24-hour hot line, which no one in the industry offers.

Reactions

- We will focus more effort on reaching and satisfying the quality segment of the market. We will buy better components, improve quality control, and shift our advertising theme to quality.
- We will avoid cutting prices and making deals because we do not want the kind of customer that buys this way.
- We will install a 24-hour hot line if it looks promising.

Clearly, the customer-centered company is in a better position to identify new opportunities and set a course that promises to deliver long-run profits. By monitoring customer needs, it can decide which customer groups and emerging needs are the most important to serve, given its resources and objectives. Jeff Bezos, founder of Amazon.com, strongly favors a customer-centered orientation. "Amazon.com's mantra has been that we were going to obsess over our customer and not our competitors. We watch our competitors, learn from them, see the things that they were doing good for customers and copy those things as much as we can. But we were never going to obsess over them."[60]

summary

1. To prepare an effective marketing strategy, a company must study its competitors as well as its actual and potential customers. Companies need to identify competitors' strategies, objectives, strengths, weaknesses, and reaction patterns. They also need to know how to design an effective competitive intelligence system.

2. A company's closest competitors are those seeking to satisfy the same customers and needs and making similar offers. A company should also pay attention to latent competitors, who may offer new or other ways to satisfy the same needs. A company should identify competitors by using both industry and market-based analyses.

3. Competitive intelligence needs to be collected, interpreted, and disseminated continuously. Managers should be able to receive timely information about competitors.

4. Managers need to conduct a customer value analysis to reveal the company's strengths and weaknesses relative to competitors. The aim of this analysis is to determine the benefits customers want and how they perceive the relative value of competitors' offers.

5. A market leader has the largest market share in the relevant product market. To remain dominant, the leader looks for ways to expand total market demand, attempts to protect its current market share, and perhaps tries to increase its market share.

6. A market challenger attacks the market leader and other competitors in an aggressive bid for more market share. Challengers can choose from five types of general attack; challengers must also choose specific strategies: discount prices, produce cheaper goods, produce prestige goods, produce a wide variety of goods, innovate in products or distribution, improve services, reduce manufacturing costs, or engage in intensive advertising.

7. A market follower is a runner-up firm that is willing to maintain its market share and not rock the boat. A follower can play the role of counterfeiter, cloner, imitator, or adapter.

8. A market nicher serves small market segments not being served by larger firms. The key to nichemanship is specialization.

9. As important as a competitive orientation is in today's global markets, companies should not overdo the emphasis on competitors. They should maintain a good balance of consumer and competitor monitoring.

applications

marketing debate – how do you attack a category leader?

Attacking a leader is always difficult. Some strategists recommend attacking a leader "head-on" by targeting its strengths. Other strategists disagree and recommend flanking and attempting to avoid the leader's strengths.

Take a position: The best way to challenge a leader is to attack its strengths versus The best way to attack a leader is to avoid a head-on assault and to adopt a flanking strategy.

marketing and advertising

1. Few product categories have as many competing products and brands as the detergent category. The ad in Figure 1 shows how Surf is responding to competitive pressure from other brands—by suggesting that customers try one of the other Surf products.

   a. What kind of competitive strategy does this ad represent? Explain.

   b. What are the arguments for and against Surf using a price-discount strategy instead of the strategy represented in the ad?

   c. Does Surf appear to have a customer or competitor orientation?

2. This Listerine Essential Care Toothpaste ad (Figure 2) promotes a mouth-care product closely related to Listerine's well-known mouthwash products. The highlighted feature (germ-killing ability) is the same as the main feature of Listerine mouthwash. In this case, however, the highlighted benefit is preventing (or reversing) gingivitis.

   a. Does Listerine appear to be a market leader, challenger, follower, or nicher in the toothpaste category?

   b. How does this ad incorporate competitive strengths and weaknesses?

   c. Colgate is one of the leading toothpaste brands. From its perspective, how can Listerine be classified as a competitor?

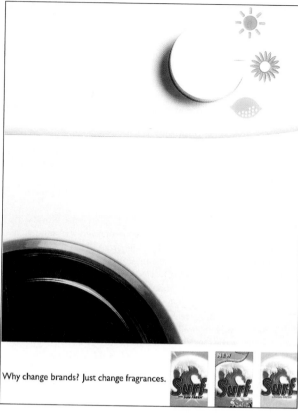

Why change brands? Just change fragrances.

Figure 1

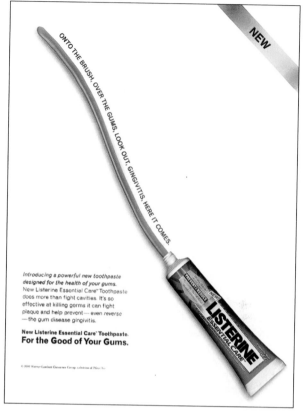

ONTO THE BRUSH, OVER THE GUMS, LOOK OUT, GINGIVITIS, HERE IT COMES

NEW

Introducing a powerful new toothpaste designed for the health of your gums. New Listerine Essential Care™ Toothpaste does more than fight cavities. It's so effective at killing germs it can fight plaque and help prevent — even reverse — the gum disease gingivitis.

New Listerine Essential Care™ Toothpaste. **For the Good of Your Gums.**

Figure 2

online marketing today

NetFlix is a fast-growing DVD rental site that has carved out a popular niche between retail giants like Blockbuster and online retailers like Amazon.com. The company invites movie fans to pay $19.95 per month for all the DVD movies they can see in a month. Although customers can only rent three movies at one time, they can rent up to three more as soon as they return the first three. DVDs arrive in the mail and include a postage-paid envelope for returning rentals. NetFlix does not levy late fees or set deadlines for returns, so customers can watch at their leisure without incurring penalties. This combination of convenience

and value propelled NetFlix into the top five e-commerce sites and helped it attract more than 300,000 regular monthly customers in less than two years of operation.[61]

Go to the NetFlix site (*www.netflix.com*) and read about what the company offers. Next, move to the Customer Service page and browse the top customer questions. As a nicher, which of the specialist roles does NetFlix appear to be adopting? What are the risks of this strategy? What entry, mobility, and exit barriers can you identify for the industry in which NetFlix is currently operating?

you're the marketer: sonic pda marketing plan

Marketing Plan Pro

Competitive strategy comes into play in two areas of the marketing plan. First, in assessing the current marketing situation, businesses must identify their competitors and learn more about each rival's strengths and weaknesses. Second, they have to use competitive intelligence and analysis to shape their overall competitive strategy, which is supported by the marketing mix.

Sonic is a new entrant in an established industry characterized by competitors with relatively high brand identity and strong market positions. In your role of assisting Jane Melody with the development of Sonic's marketing plan, use your

knowledge of competitive strategy to consider the following key issues that will affect the company's ability to successfully introduce a new personal digital assistant product:

- What is the strategic group for Sonic?
- Which firm is the market leader, and what are its objectives, strengths, and weaknesses? What additional competitive intelligence is needed to answer this question more completely?
- How would you classify Sonic's main competitors in terms of strength, closeness, and good versus bad?
- Which competitive strategy would be most effective for Sonic?

Think carefully about how Sonic's competitive strategy will affect its marketing strategy and tactics. Then summarize your ideas in a written marketing plan or enter them into the Competition, SWOT Analysis, Situation Analysis, Market Summary, and Critical Issues sections of the *Marketing Plan Pro* software.

notes

1. Leonard M. Fuld, *The New Competitor Intelligence: The Complete Resource for Finding, Analyzing, and Using Information about Your Competitors* (New York: John Wiley, 1995); John A. Czepiel, *Competitive Marketing Strategy* (Upper Saddle River, NJ: Prentice Hall, 1992).

2. Michael E. Porter, *Competitive Strategy* (New York: The Free Press, 1980), pp. 22–23.

3. Hans Katayama, "Fated to Feud: Sony versus Matsushita," *Business Tokyo* (November 1991): 28–32.

4. Michael Krantz, "Click Till You Drop," *Time*, July 20, 1998, pp. 34–39; Michael Krauss, "The Web Is Taking Your Customers for Itself," *Marketing News*, June 8, 1998, p. 8.

5. Jonathan Gaw, "Britannica Gives in and Gets Online," *Los Angeles Times*, October 19, 2000, p. A-1.

6. Jay Palmer, "Palmed Off: Handy Gadgets Are Hot Today, but the Future Belongs to Wireless Phones," *Barron's*, February 28, 2000.

7. Kathryn Rudie Harrigan, "The Effect of Exit Barriers upon Strategic Flexibility," *Strategic Management Journal* 1 (1980): 165–76.

8. Michael E. Porter, *Competitive Advantage* (New York: The Free Press, 1985), pp. 225, 485.

9. Porter, *Competitive Strategy*, ch. 13.

10. Jeffrey F. Rayport and Bernard J. Jaworski, *e-Commerce* (New York: McGraw-Hill, 2001), p. 53.

11. Porter, *Competitive Strategy*, ch. 7.

12. "The Hardest Sell," *Newsweek*, March 30, 1992, p. 41.

13. William E. Rothschild, *How to Gain (and Maintain) the Competitive Advantage* (New York: McGraw-Hill, 1989), ch. 5.

14. Robert V. L. Wright, *A System for Managing Diversity* (Cambridge, MA: Arthur D. Little, 1974).

15. The following has been drawn from Bruce Henderson's various writings, including "The Unanswered Questions, the Unsolved Problems" (paper delivered in a speech at Northwestern University in 1986); *Henderson on Corporate Strategy* (New York: Mentor, 1982); and "Understanding the Forces of Strategic and Natural Competition," *Journal of Business Strategy* (Winter 1981): 11–15.

16. For more discussion, see Leonard M. Fuld, *Monitoring the Competition* (New York: John Wiley, 1988).

17. "Spy/Counterspy," *Context* (Summer 1998): 20–21.

18. Steven Flax, "How to Snoop on Your Competitors," *Fortune*, May 14, 1984, pp. 29–33.

19. Porter, *Competitive Advantage*, Ch. 6.

20. Ogale Idudu, "London's Once-Stuffy Selfridges Now Woos Hipsters," *Wall Street Journal*, September 19, 2000, p. B1.

21. Paul Lukas, "First: Read Column, Rinse, Repeat," *Fortune*, August 3, 1998, p. 50.

22. Carla Rapoport, "You Can Make Money in Japan," *Fortune*, February 12, 1990, pp. 85–92; Keith H. Hammonds, "A Moment Kodak Wants to Capture," *BusinessWeek*, August 27, 1990, pp. 52–53; Alison Fahey, "Polaroid, Kodak, Fuji Get Clicking," *Advertising Age*, May 20, 1991, p. 18; Peter Nulty, "The New Look of Photography," *Fortune*, July 1, 1991, pp. 36–41.

23. "Kodak Develops Own Strategy," *Nikkei Weekly*, May 15, 2000.

24. Erika Rasmusson, "The Jackpot," *Sales & Marketing Management* (June 1998): 35–41.

25. Ron Winslow, "Missing a Beat: How a Breakthrough Quickly Broke Down for Johnson & Johnson: Its Stent Device Transformed Cardiac Care, Then Left a Big Opening for Rivals: 'Getting Kicked in the Shins,' " *Wall Street Journal*, September 18, 1998, p. A1.

26. The intensified competition that has taken place worldwide in recent years has sparked management interest in models of military warfare; see Sun Tsu, *The Art of War* (London: Oxford University Press, 1963); Miyamoto Mushashi, *A Book of Five Rings* (Woodstock, NY: Overlook Press, 1974); Carl von Clausewitz, *On War* (London: Routledge & Kegan Paul, 1908); B. H. Liddell-Hart, *Strategy* (New York: Praeger, 1967).

27. These six defense strategies, as well as the five attack strategies, are taken from Philip Kotler and Ravi Singh, "Marketing Warfare in the 1980s," *Journal of Business Strategy* (Winter 1981): 30–41. For additional reading, see Gerald A. Michaelson, *Winning the Marketing War: A Field Manual for Business Leaders* (Lanham, MD: Abt Books, 1987); AL Ries and Jack Trout, *Marketing Warfare* (New York: New American Library, 1986); Jay Conrad Levinson, *Guerrilla Marketing* (Boston: Houghton-Mifflin Co., 1984); and Barrie G. James, *Business Wargames* (Harmondsworth, England: Penguin Books, 1984).

28. "Leader of the Pack," *Pittsburgh Post-Gazette*, April 1, 2000.

29. "Goodyear Timeline: 1990s," <www.goodyear.com>.

30. Porter, *Competitive Strategy*, ch. 4.

31. Richard Thomkins, "Wal-Mart Invades Food Chain Turf," *St. Louis Post-Dispatch*, October 7, 1998, p. C1; Maria Halkias, "Wal-Mart to Debut Local Grocery Store," *Dallas Morning News*, August 4, 2000.

32. Relative market share is the business's market share in its served market relative to the combined market share of its three leading competitors, expressed as a percentage. For example, if this business has 30 percent of the market and its three largest competitors have 20 percent, 10 percent, and 10 percent: 30/(20110110)575 percent relative market share.

33. Sidney Schoeffler, Robert D. Buzzell, and Donald F. Heany, "Impact of Strategic Planning on Profit Performance," *Harvard Business Review* (March–April 1974): 137–45; Robert D. Buzzell, Bradley T. Gale, and Ralph G. M. Sultan, "Market Share: A Key to Profitability," *Harvard Business Review* (January–February 1975): 97–106.

34. Buzzell et al., "Market Share," pp. 97, 100. The results held up in more recent PIMS studies, where the database now includes 2,600 business units in a wide range of industries. See Robert D. Buzzell and Bradley T. Gale, *The PIMS Principles: Linking Strategy to Performance* (New York: The Free Press, 1987).

35. Richard G. Hamermesh, M. J. Anderson Jr., and J. E. Harris, "Strategies for Low Market Share Businesses," *Harvard Business Review* (May–June 1978): 95–102.

36. Carolyn Y. Woo and Arnold C. Cooper, "The Surprising Case for Low Market Share," *Harvard Business Review* (November–December 1982): 106–13; also see their "Market-Share Leadership: Not Always So Good," *Harvard Business Review* (January–February 1984): 2–4.

37. This curve assumes that pretax return on sales is highly correlated with profitability and that company revenue is a surrogate for market share. Michael Porter, in his *Competitive Strategy* (p. 43), shows a similar V-shaped curve.

38. Patricia Sellers, "McDonald's Starts Over," *Fortune,* June 22, 1998, pp. 34–35; David Leonhardt, "McDonald's: Can It Regain Its Golden Touch?" *Miami Herald*, August 3, 2000.

39. Yochi J. Dreazen and Shawn Young, "Regulators Stop Short of a Verizon Split," *Wall Street Journal*, March 23, 2001, p. A-3.

40. Philip Kotler and Paul N. Bloom, "Strategies for High Market-Share Companies," *Harvard Business Review* (November–December 1975): 63–72. Also see Porter, *Competitive Advantage*, pp. 221–26.

41. Robert D. Buzzell and Frederick D. Wiersema, "Successful Share-Building Strategies," *Harvard Business Review* (January–February 1981): 135–44.

42. Ronald Henkoff, "P&G: New & Improved," *Fortune*, October 14, 1996, pp. 151–60.

43. Zachary Schiller, "Ed Artzt's Elbow Grease Has P&G Shining," *BusinessWeek*, October 10, 1994, pp. 84–85.

44. Sarah Lorge, "Top of the Charts: Procter & Gamble," *Sales & Marketing Management* (July 1998): 50; Jane Hodges, "P&G Tries to Push Online Advertising," *Fortune*, September 28, 1998, p. 280.

45. Robert J. Dolan, "Models of Competition: A Review of Theory and Empirical Evidence," in Ben M. Enis and Kenneth J. Roering, (eds.), *Review of Marketing* (Chicago: American Marketing Association, 1981), pp. 224–34.

46. Kevin Maney, "Sun Rises on Java's Promise: CEO McNealy Sets Sights on Microsoft," *USA Today*, July 14, 1997, p. B1; Robert D. Hof, "A Java in Every Pot? Sun Aims to Make It the Language of All Smart Appliances," *BusinessWeek*, July 27, 1998, p. 71; Daniel Lyons, "Solar Power," *Forbes*, January 22, 2001, p. 82.

47. Holman W. Jenkins Jr., "Business World: On a Happier Note, Orange Juice," *Wall Street Journal*, September 23, 1998, p. A23; Robert J. O'Harrow Jr., "PepsiCo to Acquire Quaker for $14 Billion," *Washington Post*, December 5, 2000, p. E-01.

48. Martin Linstrom and Tim Frank Andersen, *Brand Building on the Internet* (London: Kogan Page, 2000), p. 44.

49. Theodore Levitt, "Innovative Imitation," *Harvard Business Review* (September–October 1966): 63. Also see Steven P. Schnaars, *Managing Imitation Strategies: How Later Entrants Seize Markets from Pioneers* (New York: The Free Press, 1994).

50. Greg Burns, "A Fruit Look by Any Other Name," *BusinessWeek*, June 26, 1995, pp. 72, 76.

51. Stuart F. Brown, "The Company that Out-Harleys Harley," *Fortune*, September 28, 1998, pp. 56–57.

52. Allen J. McGrath, "Growth Strategies with a '90s Twist," *Across the Board* (March 1995): 43–46; Antonio Ligi, "The Bottom Line: Logitech Plots Its Escape from Mouse Trap," Dow Jones Newswire, February 20, 2001.

53. Richard A. Melcher, "From the Microbrewers Who Brought You Bud, Coors…," *BusinessWeek*, April 24, 1995, pp. 66–70.

54. Melita Marie Garza, "Illinois Tool Works Stock Continues to Suffer Since Acquisition of Firm," *Chicago Tribune*, November 16, 2000.

55. Donald K. Clifford and Richard E. Cavanaugh, *The Winning Performance: How America's High- and Midsize Growth Companies Succeed* (New York: Bantam Books, 1985).

56. Jim Kirk, "Company Finds Itself, Finds Success, Alberto-Culver Adopts Strategy of Knowing Its Strengths and Promoting Small Brands, Rather Than Tackling Giants," *Chicago Tribune*, January 22, 1998, p. 1; Ameet Sachdev, "Melrose Park, Ill.-Based Hair, Skin Firm Sees Shares Surge in 2000," *Chicago Tribune*, January 18, 2001.

57. Reported in E. R. Linneman and L. J. Stanton, *Making Niche Marketing Work* (New York: McGraw-Hill, 1991).

58. Gabriella Stern, "Arm & Hammer Is Losing Lead in Baking-Soda Toothpaste Sales," *Wall Street Journal*, December 28, 1993; p. B-8; Nikhil Deogun,and Emily Nelson, "SmithKline Is a Leading Bidder for Block, *Wall Street Journal*, October 6, 2000, p. B-6.

59. Bro Uttal, "Pitching Computers to Small Businesses," *Fortune*, April 1, 1985, pp. 95–104; also see Stuart Gannes, "The Riches in Market Niches," *Fortune*, April 27, 1987, pp. 227–30.

60. Robert Spector, *Amazon.com: Get Big Fast* (New York: HarperBusiness, 2000), p. 151.

61. "Online Purchases Rebound, Says E-Commerce Index from NextCard," *CnetNews.com*, September 11, 2001, <investor.cnet.com/investor/news/newsitem/)-9900-1028-7128874-0.html>.

10

identifying market segments and selecting target markets

In this chapter, we will address the following questions:

- How can a company identify the segments that make up a market?
- What criteria can a company use to choose the most attractive target markets?

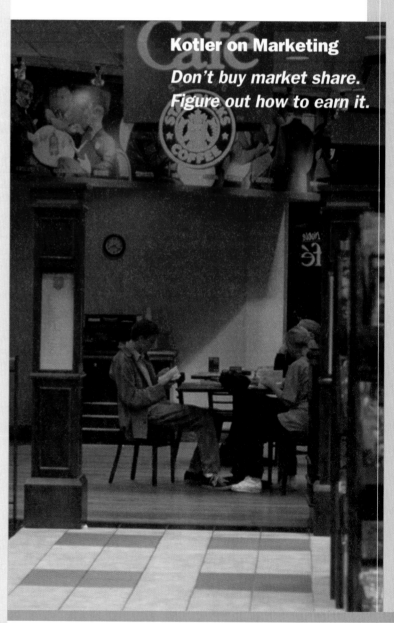

Kotler on Marketing

Don't buy market share. Figure out how to earn it.

A company cannot serve all customers in a broad market such as computers or soft drinks. The customers are too numerous and diverse in their buying requirements. A company needs to identify the market segments it can serve effectively. Here we will examine levels of segmentation, patterns of segmentation, market-segmentation procedures, bases for segmenting consumer and business markets, and requirements for effective segmentation.

Many companies are embracing target marketing. Here sellers distinguish the major market segments, target one or more of these segments, and develop products and marketing programs tailored to each. Instead of scattering *their marketing effort (a "shotgun" approach), they focus on the buyers they have the greatest chance of satisfying (a "rifle" approach).*

Target marketing requires marketers to take three major steps:

1. *Identify and profile distinct groups of buyers who differ in their needs and preferences (market segmentation).*

2. *Select one or more market segments to enter (market targeting).*

3. *For each target segment, establish and communicate the key distinctive benefit(s) of the company's market offering (market positioning).*

This chapter will focus on the first two steps. In the next chapter, we discuss market positioning.

levels and patterns of market segmentation

We begin by examining the various levels and patterns of market segmentation.

levels of market segmentation

The starting point for discussing segmentation is **mass-marketing**. In mass marketing, the seller engages in the mass production, mass distribution, and mass promotion of one product for all buyers. Henry Ford epitomized this marketing strategy when he offered the Model-T Ford "in any color, as long as it is black." Coca-Cola also practiced mass marketing when it sold only one kind of Coke in a 6.5-ounce bottle.

The argument for mass marketing is that it creates the largest potential market, which leads to the lowest costs, which in turn can lead to lower prices or higher margins. However, many critics point to the increasing splintering of the market, which makes mass marketing more difficult. According to Regis McKenna,

> [Consumers] have more ways to shop: at giant malls, specialty shops, and superstores; through mail-order catalogs, home shopping networks, and virtual stores on the Internet. And they are bombarded with messages pitched through a growing number of channels: broadcast and narrow-cast television, radio, on-line computer networks, the Internet, telephone services such as fax and telemarketing, and niche magazines and other print media.[1]

The proliferation of advertising media and distribution channels is making it difficult and increasingly expensive to reach a mass audience. Some claim that mass marketing is dying. Not surprisingly, many companies are turning to **micromarketing** at one of four levels: segments, niches, local areas, and individuals.

SEGMENT MARKETING   A **market segment** consists of a group of customers who share a similar set of wants. Thus we would distinguish between car buyers who are primarily seeking low-cost basic transportation and those seeking a luxurious driving experience. We must be careful not to confuse a *segment* and a *sector*. A car company might say that it will target young, middle-income car buyers. The problem is that young, middle-income car buyers will differ about what they want in a car. Some will want a low-cost car and others will want an expensive car. Young, middle-income car buyers is a **sector**, not a segment.

The marketer does not create the segments; the marketer's task is to identify the segments and decide which one(s) to target. Segment marketing offers several benefits over mass marketing. The company can create a more fine-tuned product or service offering and price it appropriately for the target segment. The company can more easily select the best distribution and communications channels, and it will also have a clearer picture of its competitors, which are the companies going after the same segment.

However, even a segment is partly a fiction, in that not everyone wants exactly the same thing. Anderson and Narus have urged marketers to present flexible market offerings instead of a standard offering to all members of a segment.[2] A **flexible market offering** consists of two parts: a *naked solution* containing the product and service elements that all segment members value, and *discretionary options* that some segment members value. Each option might carry an additional charge. For example, Delta Airlines offers all economy passengers a seat, food, and soft drinks. It charges economy passengers extra for alcoholic beverages and earphones. Seimens sells metal-clad boxes whose price includes free delivery and a warranty, but also offers installation, tests, and communication peripherals as extra-cost options.

NICHE MARKETING   A **niche** is a more narrowly defined group seeking a distinctive mix of benefits. Marketers usually identify niches by dividing a segment into subsegments. For example, the segment of heavy smokers includes two niches: those who are trying to stop smoking and those who do not care.

An attractive niche is characterized as follows: The customers in the niche have a distinct set of needs; they will pay a premium to the firm that best satisfies their needs; the niche is not likely to attract other competitors; the nicher gains certain economies through specialization; and the niche has size, profit, and growth potential.

Whereas segments are fairly large and normally attract several competitors, niches are fairly small and normally attract only one or two. Larger companies, such as IBM, lose pieces of their market to nichers: Dalgic and Leeuw labeled this confrontation "guerrillas against gorillas."[3] Even some large companies have turned to niche marketing. Johnson & Johnson, for example, consists of 170 affiliates (business units), many of which dominate niche markets. Here are some examples of large companies that have moved into niche marketing.

Hallmark   Hallmark rigorously segments its greeting-card business by regularly introducing new card lines. In addition to popular sub-branded card lines like the humorous Shoebox Greetings, Hallmark has introduced lines targeting specific market segments. Fresh Ink targets 18- to 39-year-old women, Hallmark En Espanol targets Hispanic cardgivers, and Mahogany is aimed at African-American consumers. Hallmark also develops cards for new cardgiving occasions, as the company did in 1999 with the debut of Warm Wishes, cards for casual occasions. In 2000, it commanded a 55 percent share of the $7.8 billion global greeting-card market.[4]

Estēe Lauder   The four best-selling prestige perfumes in the United States belong to Estēe Lauder. Seven of the top 10 prestige makeup products are Estēe Lauder's. Of the 10 best-selling prestige skin care products, eight belong to Estēe Lauder, yet few consumers even realize that the product they are buying is Estēe Lauder because the company is expert at marketing brands that appeal to women (and men) of different tastes. The flagship brand, the original Estēe Lauder, appeals to older consumers; Clinique caters to middle-aged women, M.A.C. to youthful hipsters, Aveda to aromatherapy enthusiasts, and Origins to eco-conscious consumers who want cosmetics made from natural ingredients.[5]

Progressive Corporation   Progressive, a Cleveland auto insurer, grew rapidly as a result of filling a niche: The company sells "nonstandard" auto insurance to risky drivers with a record of auto accidents or drunkenness. Progressive charges a high price for coverage, has made a lot of money, and had the field to itself for several years.

The prevalence of niche—and even microniche—marketing can be seen in the magazine world, where new magazines have proliferated. In 1998, for example, there were

1,000 first-edition magazines targeting specific niches, divided and subdivided along lines of ethnicity, gender, or sexual orientation. There are magazines for black gay men, for divers, for Hispanic teenage girls, and almost every other group. Many have short life spans. The same is true of many niche-based Web sites catering to specific groups.

Niche marketers presumably understand their customers' needs so well that the customers willingly pay a premium. Ferrari gets a high price for its cars because loyal buyers feel no other automobile comes close to offering the product-service-membership benefit bundle that Ferrari does. Linneman and Stanton claim that there are "riches in niches" and believe that companies must "niche or be niched."[6] Blattberg and Deighton claim that "niches too small to be served profitably today will become viable as marketing efficiency improves."[7]

The low cost of setting up shop on the Internet has led to many small business start-ups aiming to serve niches. Fifteen percent of the commercial Web sites with fewer than 10 employees take in more than $100,000, and 2 percent even ring up more than $1 million. The recipe for Internet niching success: Choose a hard-to-find product that customers do not need to see and touch. This "Webpreneur" followed the recipe with astonishing results:[8]

Ostrichesonline.com   Whereas Internet giants like Amazon.com have yet to realize a profit, Steve Warrington is earning a six-figure income selling ostriches—and every product derived from them—online (*www.ostrichesonline.com*). Since the site was launched for next to nothing in 1996, Warrington's business has sold to over 10,000 clients in over 100 countries from a catalog of more than 7,000 ostrich-related products. Visitors to the site can buy ostrich meat, feathers, leather jackets, videos, eggshells, and subscribe to a newsletter devoted to ostriches.[9]

In many markets today, niches are the norm. (See "Marketing Insight: Hidden Champions: German Midsized Companies Grow Prosperous Through Niching.")

marketing **insight**

Hidden Champions: German Midsized Companies Grow Prosperous Through Niching

The German economy has more than 300,000 small and mid-sized companies (known as the *Mittelstand*), which collectively account for two-thirds of Germany's gross national product and employ four out of every five workers. Although these companies have fewer than 500 employees, many enjoy over 50 percent market shares in well-defined global niches. Hermann Simon dubbed these global niche leaders *hidden champions* and defines them as businesses that are number one or two in the world market or number one in the European market, earning less than $1 billion in annual sales, and having generally low public visibility. Here are some examples:

- Tetra Food supplies 80 percent of the food for feeding tropical fish.
- Hohner has 85 percent of the world harmonica market.
- Becher has 50 percent of the world's oversized umbrella market.

- Steiner Optical has 80 percent of the world's military field glasses market.

These hidden champions tend to be found in stable markets, are typically family owned or closely held, and are long-lived. They are very dedicated to their customers and offer superior performance, responsive service, and punctual delivery (rather than low price) as well as customer intimacy. Their top management stays in direct and regular contact with top customers, and they emphasize continuous innovation directed at benefiting customers.

Hidden champions are found in many other countries besides Germany. They all share the characteristics of combining high product focus with geographic diversity and establishing the leading reputation in the targeted niche.

Source: Hermann Simon, *Hidden Champions* (Boston: Harvard Business School Press, 1996).

LOCAL MARKETING   Target marketing is leading to marketing programs tailored to the needs and wants of local customer groups (trading areas, neighborhoods, even individual stores). Citibank provides different mixes of banking services in its branches, depending on neighborhood demographics. Kraft helps supermarket chains identify the cheese assortment and shelf positioning that will optimize cheese sales in low-, middle-, and high-income stores, and in different ethnic neighborhoods.

Those favoring localizing a company's marketing see national advertising as wasteful because it fails to address local needs. Those against local marketing argue that it drives up manufacturing and marketing costs by reducing economies of scale. Logistical problems become magnified when companies try to meet local requirements. A brand's overall image might be diluted if the product and message differ in different localities.

INDIVIDUAL CUSTOMER MARKETING   The ultimate level of segmentation leads to "segments of one," "customized marketing," or "one-to-one marketing."[10] Ultimately, every individual has a unique set of wants and preferences. In past centuries, producers customized their offerings to each customer: The tailor fitted a suit and a cobbler made shoes for each individual. The Industrial Revolution ushered in an era of mass-production: Now companies made standard goods in advance of orders and left it to individuals to fit into whatever was available. Producers moved from *built-to-order* marketing to *built-to-stock* marketing. Today the Information Revolution is enabling a growing number of companies to mass-customize their offerings. **Mass-customization** is the ability of a company to prepare on a mass basis individually designed products, services, programs, and communications, to meet each customer's requirements.[11] For examples of mass-customized goods, see "Marketing for the New Economy: Segments of One: Mass-Customization Comes of Age."

Today customers are taking more individual initiative in determining what and how to buy. They log onto the Internet; look up information and evaluations of product or service offers; dialogue with suppliers, users, and product critics; and in many cases, design the product they want. Slywotsky and Morrison noted that more online companies today are offering customers a **Choiceboard**, which is an interactive online system that allows individual customers to design their own products and services by choosing from a menu of attributes, components, prices, and delivery options. The customer's selections send signals to the supplier's manufacturing system that set in motion the wheels of procurement, assembly, and delivery.[12]

Although not every company can use this approach, some companies can achieve an early competitive advantage with it. Here are the advantages:

- The Choiceboard facilitates upselling, cross-selling, and repeat business by opening customers' eyes to further possibilities and by satisfying their preferences.
- The Choiceboard provides real-time market research and insight into customers' current preferences.
- The Choiceboard reduces costs for manufacturers and suppliers by avoiding the production of unwanted goods and discounting to get rid of them.

Wind and Rangaswamy see the Choiceboard as a movement toward "customerizing" the firm.[13] **Customerization** combines operationally driven mass customization with customized marketing in a way that empowers consumers to design the product and service offering of their choice. The firm no longer requires prior information about the customer, nor does the firm need to own manufacturing. The firm provides a platform and tools and "rents" out to customers the means to design their own products. Each business unit will have to decide whether it would gain more by designing its business system to create offerings for *segments* or for *individuals*. Companies that favor segmentation see it as more efficient, requiring less customer information, and permitting more standardization of market offerings. Those who favor individual marketing claim that segments are a fiction, that individuals within so-called segments differ greatly, and that marketers can achieve much more precision and effectiveness by addressing individual needs.

patterns of market segmentation

Here we will consider segment-centered marketing. Market segments can be built up in many ways. One way is to identify *preference segments*. Suppose ice cream buyers are asked how much they value sweetness and creaminess as two product attributes. Three different patterns can emerge.

1. *Homogeneous preferences:* Figure 10.1(a) shows a market where all the consumers have roughly the same preferences. The market shows no natural segments. We would predict that existing brands would be similar and cluster around the middle of the scale in both sweetness and creaminess.

2. *Diffused preferences:* At the other extreme, consumer preferences may be scattered throughout the space (Figure 10.1[b]), indicating that consumers vary greatly in their preferences. The first brand to enter the market is likely to position in the center to appeal to the most people. A second competitor could locate next to the first brand and fight for market share, or it could locate in a corner to attract a customer group that was not satisfied with the center brand. If several brands are in the market, they are likely to position throughout the space and show real differences to match consumer-preference differences.

3. *Clustered preferences:* The market might reveal distinct preference clusters, called *natural market segments* (Figure 10.1[c]). The first firm in this market has three options. It might position in the center, hoping to appeal to all groups. It might position in the largest market segment (*concentrated marketing*). It might develop several brands, each positioned in a different segment. If the first firm developed only one brand, competitors would enter and introduce brands in the other segments.

market-segmentation procedure

How can we identify market segments? One approach would be to classify consumers demographically. A bank, for example, may decide to group its customers by wealth, annual income, and age. Suppose it distinguishes five wealth classes, seven income classes, and six age classes. This alone would create 210 market segments ($5 \times 7 \times 6$). The real question, however, is whether the customers in any one segment really have the same needs, attitudes, and preferences. Probably not!

This has led market researchers to advocate a *needs-based market segmentation approach*. Roger Best proposed the seven-step approach shown in Table 10.1 (on p. 286).

Market segmentation must be done periodically because segments change. At one time the personal computer industry segmented its products purely on speed and power. Later, PC marketers recognized an emerging "Soho" market, named for "small office and home office." Mail-order companies such as Dell and Gateway appealed to this market's requirement for high performance coupled with low price and user-friendliness. Shortly thereafter, PC makers began to see Soho as comprised of smaller segments. "Small-office needs might be very different from home-office needs," says one Dell executive.[14]

One way to discover new segments is to investigate the hierarchy of attributes consumers examine in choosing a brand. This process is called **market partitioning**. Years ago, most car buyers first decided on the manufacturer and then on one of its car divisions (*brand-dominant hierarchy*). A buyer might favor General Motors cars and, within this set, Pontiac. Today, many buyers decide first on the nation from which they want to buy a car (*nation-dominant hierarchy*). Buyers may first decide they want to buy a Japanese car, then Toyota, and then the Corolla model of Toyota. Companies must monitor potential shifts in the consumers' hierarchy of attributes and adjust to changing priorities.

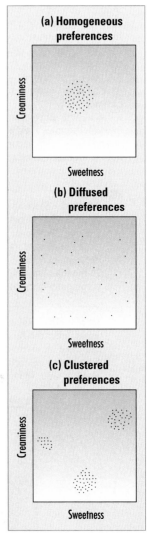

figure **10.1**

Basic Market–Preference Patterns

(a) Homogeneous preferences

Creaminess

Sweetness

(b) Diffused preferences

Creaminess

Sweetness

(c) Clustered preferences

Creaminess

Sweetness

marketing for the **new economy**

Segments of One: Mass-Customization Comes of Age

Imagine walking into a booth that bathes your body in patterns of white light and, in a matter of seconds, determines your exact three-dimensional structure. The digitized measurement data are then collected on a credit card, which you use to order customized clothing. This is the future: A consortium of more than 100 apparel companies, including Levi's, have banded together to develop body scanning technology to make mass-customization commonplace.

A number of companies are already using existing technologies to customize their products to the individual consumer. We all know about Dell and its customer-configured computers, but a host of nontech companies are in the forefront of the mass-customization economy.

Mattel   Starting in 1998, girls were able to log onto Barbie.com and customize "My Design" dolls. They choose the doll's skin tone, eye color, hairdo and hair color, clothes, accessories, and name. They even fill out a questionnaire detailing their doll's likes and dislikes. When the doll arrives in the mail, the doll's name is on the packaging, along with a computer-generated paragraph about her personality.

Levi's   The jeans maker has made measure-to-fit women's jeans under the Personal Pair banner since 1994. It has now launched an in-store customization concept called Original Spin, which will offer even more options and feature men's jeans as well. Today, a fully stocked Levi's store carries 130 ready-to-wear pairs of jeans for a given waist and inseam. With Personal Pair the number jumped to 430, and with Original Spin it will jump to 750.

Acumins   Internet-based vitamin company Acumins blends vitamins, herbs, and minerals according to a customer's instructions, compressing up to 95 ingredients into three to five "personalized pills." The Acumins premise is simple and attractive: Why swallow dozens of pills when you can take three pills with dozens of ingredients of your choosing?

Paris Miki   The Japanese company Paris Miki, one of the largest eyeglass retailers in the world, uses a design tool that takes a digital picture of the customer's face. The customer describes the style he or she wants—sports, elegant, traditional—and the system displays alternatives on the computerized photograph. After selecting the frame, the customer also chooses nosepieces, hinges, and arms. The glasses are ready within an hour.

DeBeers   With DeBeers Design Your Own Engagement Ring program, customers can design their own diamond rings by choosing from any of 189 unique combinations of cut, band, and sidestones and connect with a local jeweler who can help them buy it.

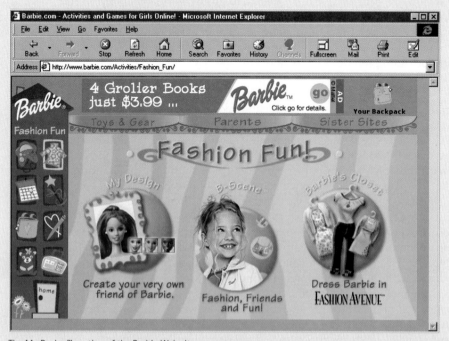

The My Design™ section of the Barbie Web site.

Consumer-goods marketers are not the only ones riding these trends. Business-to-business marketers are also finding that they can provide customers with tailor-made goods and services as cheaply, and in the same amount of time, as it used to take to make standardized products.

Andersen Windows   Andersen Windows of Bayport, Minnesota, the home building industry's leading window and patio door manufacturer, turned to mass-customization after additions to its product line led to fat and unwieldy catalogs and a bewildering array of choices for homeowners and contractors. Andersen developed an interactive computer version of the catalogs for distributors and retailers that is linked directly to the factory. With the system, now in 650 showrooms, salespeople can help customers customize each window, check the design for structural soundness, and generate a price quote. From there Andersen went on to develop a "batch of one" manufacturing process in which every window and door part is made to order, thus reducing its finished parts inventory (a major cost to the company).[a]

ChemStation   Based in Dayton, Ohio, ChemStation offers customized soap formulas to its industrial customers, who range from car washes to the U.S. Air Force. What cleans a car will not clean an airplane or equipment in a mine shaft. Salespeople visit customer sites to gather information. All the data from the company's chemical lab and its field studies are kept in a central database called Tank Management System (TMS). TMS is linked directly to both the lab and the company's 40 plants across the country, where computer-operated machines mix each customer's special formula.

Ross/Flex   Ross Controls, a Troy, Michigan, manufacturer of pneumatic valves, landed a $250 million client, Danly-Komatsu, by offering it a customized valve system under its Ross/Flex program. Using CAD-CAM technology, Ross was able to ship a prototype to Danly-Komatsu's engineers in only two days. Because the system was a custom fit, the engineers were able to install it in their presses in less than half the time it would have taken to assemble and load up standard parts.

Unlike mass production, which eliminates the need for human interaction, mass-customization has made relationships with customers more important than ever. Ross Controls limits the number of clients for which it provides customized valve systems because so much up-front collaboration is necessary. At ChemStation, 95 percent of clients never leave because teaching another company their cleansing needs is not worth the effort. When Levi's sells off-the-shelf jeans, the customer walks out of the store, perhaps never to return. When Levi's sells made-to-order jeans, the company not only captures consumer data in digitized form, but also becomes the customer's "jeans adviser."

Sources: [a]"Creating Greater Customer Value May Require a Lot of Changes," *Organizational Dynamics* (Summer 1998): 26.
Erick Schonfeld, "The Customized, Digitized, Have-It-Your-Way Economy," *Fortune*, September 28, 1998, pp. 115–24; Bruce Fox, "Levi's Personal Pair Prognosis Positive," *Chain Store Age* (March 1996): 35; Jim Barlow, "Individualizing Mass Production," *Houston Chronicle*, April 13, 1997, p. E1; Sarah Schafer, "Have It Your Way," *Inc.*, November 18, 1997, pp. 56–64; <www.levistrauss.com>; Jim Christie, "Mass Customization: The New Assembly Line?" *Investor's Daily*, February 25, 2000.

ChemStation's Web site offers customers solutions to their problems, not just products.

table **10.1**		
Steps in Segmentation Process		**Description**
	1. Needs-Based Segmentation	Group customers into segments based on similar needs and benefits sought by customer in solving a particular consumption problem.
	2. Segment Identification	For each needs-based segment, determine which demographics, lifestyles, and usage behaviors make the segment distinct and identifiable (actionable).
	3. Segment Attractiveness	Using predetermined segment attractiveness criteria (such as market growth, competitive intensity, and market access), determine the overall attractiveness of each segment.
	4. Segment Profitability	Determine segment profitability.
	5. Segment Positioning	For each segment, create a "value proposition" and product-price positioning strategy based on that segment's unique customer needs and characteristics.
	6. Segment "Acid Test"	Create "segment storyboards" to test the attractiveness of each segment's positioning strategy.
	7. Marketing-Mix Strategy	Expand segment positioning strategy to include all aspects of the marketing mix: product, price, promotion, and place.

Source: Adapted from Robert J. Best, *Market-Based Management* (Upper Saddle River, NJ: Prentice Hall, 2000).

The hierarchy of attributes can reveal customer segments. Buyers who first decide on price are price dominant; those who first decide on the type of car (e.g., sports, passenger, station wagon) are type dominant; those who first decide on the car brand are brand dominant. One can identify those who are type/price/brand dominant as making up a segment; those who are quality/service/type dominant as making up another segment. Each segment may have distinct demographics, psychographics, and mediagraphics.[15]

effective segmentation

Not all segmentation is useful. For example, table salt buyers could be divided into blond and brunette customers, but hair color is not relevant to the purchase of salt. Furthermore, if all salt buyers buy the same amount of salt each month, believe all salt is the same, and would pay only one price for salt, this market would be minimally segmentable from a marketing point of view.

To be useful, market segments must be:

- *Measurable:* The size, purchasing power, and characteristics of the segments can be measured.
- *Substantial:* The segments are large and profitable enough to serve. A segment should be the largest possible homogeneous group worth going after with a tailored marketing program. It would not pay, for example, for an automobile manufacturer to develop cars for people who are under four feet tall.
- *Accessible:* The segments can be effectively reached and served.
- *Differentiable:* The segments are conceptually distinguishable and respond differently to different marketing-mix elements and programs. If married and unmarried women respond similarly to a sale on perfume, they do not constitute separate segments.
- *Actionable:* Effective programs can be formulated for attracting and serving the segments.

segmenting consumer and business markets
bases for segmenting consumer markets

Two broad groups of variables are used to segment consumer markets. Some researchers try to form segments by looking at consumer characteristics: geographic, demographic, and psychographic. Then they examine whether these customer segments exhibit different needs or product responses. For example, they might examine the differing attitudes of "professionals," "blue collars," and other groups toward, say, "safety" as a car benefit.

Other researchers try to form segments by looking at consumer responses to benefits, use occasions, or brands. Once the segments are formed, the researcher sees whether different characteristics are associated with each consumer-response segment. For example, the researcher might examine whether people who want "quality" rather than "low price" in buying an automobile differ in their geographic, demographic, and psychographic makeup.

The major segmentation variables—geographic, demographic, psychographic, and behavioral segmentation—are summarized in Table 10.2.

GEOGRAPHIC SEGMENTATION   **Geographic segmentation** calls for dividing the market into different geographical units such as nations, states, regions, counties, cities, or neighborhoods. The company can operate in one or a few geographic areas, or operate in all but pay attention to local variations. For example, Hilton Hotels customizes rooms and lobbies according to the location of its hotels. Northeastern hotels are sleeker and more cosmopolitan. Southwestern hotels are more rustic. Take, for example, Campbell Soup, an experienced regional marketer. Since 1994, the company has marketed its Pace Picante sauce regionally. People in the Southwest do not need to be told that "picante" is a cooking ingredient, whereas northerners confuse it with salsa. The packaging, communication, and marketing effort are more educational in the North. More and more regional marketing means marketing right down to a specific zip code:[16]

> **Pillsbury**   Pillsbury, a $6 billion division of U.K. food giant Diageo, implemented sophisticated statistics software over a network that enables employees all over the world to access and analyze customer data. Using this software, marketers at Pillsbury can instantly sort information like customer preferences, suggestions, and purchase habits by zip code and determine where to target specific marketing campaigns and how grocery stores in a certain area should be stocked.[17]

Many companies use mapping software to show the geographic locations of their customers. Thus a retailer may realize that most of his customers are within only a 10-mile radius of his store, and further concentrated with certain zip+4 areas, enabling him to target his communications more effectively. By mapping the densest areas, he can resort to *customer cloning*, assuming that the best prospects live where most of his customers come from.

DEMOGRAPHIC SEGMENTATION   In **demographic segmentation**, the market is divided into groups on the basis of variables such as age, family size, family life cycle, gender, income, occupation, education, religion, race, generation, nationality, and social class. Demographic variables are the most popular bases for distinguishing customer groups. One reason is that consumer wants, preferences, and usage rates are often associated with demographic variables. Another is that demographic variables are easier to measure. Even when the target market is described in nondemographic terms (say, a personality type), the link back to demographic characteristics is needed in order to estimate the size of the market and the media that should be used to reach it efficiently.

Here is how certain demographic variables have been used to segment markets.

table **10.2**

Major Segmentation
Variables for
Consumer Markets

Geographic	
Region	Pacific, Mountain, West North Central, West South Central, East North Central, East South Central, South Atlantic, Middle Atlantic, New England
City or metro size	Under 5,000; 5,000–20,000; 20,000–50,000; 50,000–100,000; 100,000–250,000; 250,000–500,000; 500,000–1,000,000; 1,000,000–4,000,000; 4,000,000 or over
Density	Urban, suburban, rural
Climate	Northern, southern
Demographic	
Age	Under 6, 6–11, 12–19, 20–34, 35–49, 50–64, 65+
Family size	1-2, 3-4, 5+
Family life cycle	Young, single; young, married, no children; young, married, youngest child under 6; young, married, youngest child 6 or over; older, married, with children; older, married, no children under 18; older, single; other
Gender	Male, female
Income	Under $10,000; $10,000–$15,000; $15,000–$20,000; $20,000–$30,000; $30,000–$50,000; $50,000–$100,000; $100,000 and over
Occupation	Professional and technical; managers, officials, and proprietors; clerical sales; craftspeople; forepersons; operatives; farmers; retired; students; homemakers; unemployed
Education	Grade school or less; some high school; high school graduate; some college; college graduate
Religion	Catholic, Protestant, Jewish, Muslim, Hindu, other
Race	White, Black, Asian, Hispanic
Generation	Baby boomers, Generation Xers
Nationality	North American, South American, British, French, German, Italian, Japanese
Social class	Lower lowers, upper lowers, working class, middle class, upper middles, lower uppers, upper uppers
Psychographic	
Lifestyle	Culture-oriented, sports-oriented, outdoor-oriented
Personality	Compulsive, gregarious, authoritarian, ambitious
Behavioral	
Occasions	Regular occasion, special occasion
Benefits	Quality, service, economy, speed
User status	Nonuser, ex-user, potential user, first-time user, regular user
Usage rate	Light user, medium user, heavy user
Loyalty status	None, medium, strong, absolute
Readiness stage	Unaware, aware, informed, interested, desirous, intending to buy
Attitude toward product	Enthusiastic, positive, indifferent, negative, hostile

Sega's home page: Not just games.

Age and Life-Cycle Stage   Consumer wants and abilities change with age. Gerber realized this and began expanding beyond its traditional baby food line. Its new "Graduates" line is geared for the 1- to 3-year-old. The company is hoping that the parents who buy Gerber's baby food will be receptive to Gerber's Graduates line as their babies grow.[18] Here are some other examples.

Sega   SEGA, the computer games giant, has a similar goal of retaining the loyalty of its main market segment by always delivering the cutting edge of technology. SEGA is expanding its range of products by increasing the emphasis on the Sega Sports brand which appeals to an adult generation of gamers and offering those games across all gaming platforms, online and new wireless devices. SEGA's market lies in the 10-to-18 age range. As the market matures the challenge of advanced gaming devices and content becomes an important factor in retaining customer loyalty.[19]

Eddie Bauer   Clothing retailer Eddie Bauer tested new "electronic poster" window displays for its retail locations in the months leading up to the 2000 holiday season. The posters, which are 50-inch plasma flatscreen televisions, enable Eddie Bauer outlets to customize in-store advertising to target different generational segments, depending on the time of day. For example, a store might post images featuring older models during the morning hours when retirees frequently shop, then change the posters to reflect the younger shopping crowd of the evening. After an initial test of nine weeks, sales at one location rose 56 percent from the previous nine months.[20]

Nevertheless, age and life cycle can be tricky variables. For example, the Ford Motor Company designed its Mustang automobile to appeal to young people who wanted an inexpensive sports car. But Ford found that many Mustangs were purchased by older buyers. It then realized that its target market was not the chronologically young but the psychologically young.

The Neugartens' research indicates that age stereotypes need to be guarded against:

> Age has become a poor predictor of the timing of life events, as well as a poor predictor of a person's health, work status, family status, and therefore, also, of a person's interests, preoccupations, and needs. We have multiple images of persons of the same age: there is the 70-year-old in a wheelchair and the 70-year-old on the tennis court. Likewise, there are 35-year-olds sending children off to college and 35-year-olds furnishing the nursery for newborns, producing in turn, first-time grandparenthood for persons who range in age from 35 to 75.[21]

Life Stage Persons in the same part of the life cycle may differ in their life stage. **Life stage** defines a person's major concern, such as going through a divorce, going into a second marriage, taking care of an older parent, deciding to cohabit with another person, deciding to buy a new home, and so on. These life stages present opportunities for marketers who can help people cope with their major concerns.

Gender Men and women tend to have different attitudinal and behavioral orientations, based partly on genetic makeup and partly on socialization practices. Women tend to be more communal-minded and men tend to be more self-expressive and goal-directed. Women tend to take in more of the data in their immediate environment; men tend to focus on the part of the environment that helps them achieve a goal. Some of these differences have been popularized in books such as John Gray's *Men Are from Mars, Women Are from Venus.* They should be taken into consideration in aiming campaigns at men or women.

Gender differentiation has long been applied in clothing, hairstyling, cosmetics, and magazines. Some products have been positioned as more masculine or feminine. Thus Virginia Slims is addressed to women and accompanied by appropriate flavor, packaging, and advertising cues to reinforce a female image. Burger King is perceived as more masculine than McDonald's and Nike is viewed as more masculine than Reebok.

---

iVillage.com iVillage.com, an online "women's network," reaped the benefits of gender segmentation after initially seeking a broader market. iVillage.com began with a focus on both male and female baby boomers, but offerings geared toward women, such as Parent Soup, where parents (mainly mothers) exchanged advice and parenting tips, attracted the largest audience. Billing itself as a "community of smart, compassionate, real women," iVillage soon evolved into the leading women's online site. Although the company has yet to turn a profit, its popularity helped it float a successful IPO in 1999 and 109 percent revenue growth in 2000.[22]

The automobile industry is beginning to recognize gender segmentation. Since there are now more women car owners, some manufacturers are designing features to appeal to women, although they stop short of advertising the cars as women's cars.

Income Income segmentation is a long-standing practice in such product and service categories as automobiles, boats, clothing, cosmetics, and travel. However, income does not always predict the best customers for a given product. Blue-collar workers were among the first purchasers of color television sets; it was cheaper for them to buy these sets than to go to movies and restaurants. The most economical cars are not bought by the really poor, but rather by those who think of themselves as poor relative to their status aspirations. Medium-priced and expensive cars tend to be purchased by the over-privileged segments of each social class.

Generation Many researchers are now turning to generation segmentation. Each generation is profoundly influenced by the times in which it grows up—the music, movies, politics, and defining events of that period. Demographers call these groups *cohorts*. Members of a cohort share the same major experiences. They have similar outlooks and values. Marketers often advertise to a cohort group by using the icons and images prominent in their experiences.

Meredith Schewe and Karlovich distinguish seven groups:[23]

- *The Depression Cohort*—Shaped by hard times and the Great Depression; aged 79–88 in 2000. This cohort lacked jobs when they were coming of age; financial security is one of their core values.
- *The World War II Cohort*—Shaped by World War II; aged 73–78 in 2000. This cohort focused on defeating a common enemy; they are team-oriented and patriotic.
- *The Postwar Cohort*—Shaped by the optimism and prosperity of the postwar era: aged 55–72 in 2000. This cohort values stability and expects prosperous times to continue.
- *Leading-Edge Baby Boomer Cohort*—Shaped by the assassinations of Kennedy and Martin Luther King and the Vietnam War; aged 46–54 in 2000. This cohort on the one hand champions causes (civil rights, women's rights) and simultaneously is hedonistic and self-indulgent.
- *Trailing-Edge Baby Boomer Cohort*—Shaped by Watergate and the energy crisis; aged 35–45 in 2000. This cohort is less optimistic than the Leading-Edge Boomers.
- *Generation X Cohort*—Shaped by bad economic times, the Challenger explosion, and AIDS awareness; aged 24–34 in 2000. This cohort puts the quality of personal life ahead of work life; they are not team players, and are cynical about advertising.
- *The Generation Y Cohort*—Shaped by economic prosperity and the Internet; aged 23 and under in 2000. This cohort is more idealistic and less cynical than Gen Xers.

The authors have developed a framework called The Lifestage Analytic Matrix that combines information on cohorts, life stages, physiographics, emotional effects, and socioeconomics in analyzing a segment or individual. For example, two individuals from the same cohort may differ in their *life stages* (having a divorce, getting remarried), *physiographics* (coping with hair loss, menopause, arthritis, or osteoporosis), *emotional effects* (nostalgia for the past, wanting experiences instead of things), or *socioeconomics* (losing a job, receiving an inheritance). Schewe and Meredith believe that the use of this analysis will lead to more efficient targeting and messages.

Social Class   Social class has a strong influence on preference in cars, clothing, home furnishings, leisure activities, reading habits, and retailers. Many companies design products and services for specific social classes. The tastes of social classes can change with the years. The 1990s were about greed and ostentation for the upper classes. Affluent tastes now run more toward the utilitarian—a Ford Explorer rather than a Mercedes.[24]

PSYCHOGRAPHIC SEGMENTATION   In *psychographic segmentation*, buyers are divided into different groups on the basis of lifestyle or personality or values. People within the same demographic group can exhibit very different psychographic profiles.

Lifestyle   People exhibit many more lifestyles than are suggested by the seven social classes in Table 10.2. People differ in attitudes, interests, and activities, and these affect the goods and services they consume. Meat, for example, would seem like an unlikely product for lifestyle segmentation, but one forward-looking grocery store found that segmenting its self-service meat products by lifestyle brought a big payoff.

Kroger   Walk by the refrigerated self-service meat cases of most grocery stores and you will usually find the offering grouped by type of meat. Pork is in one case, lamb in another, and chicken in a third. A Nashville, Tennessee–based Kroger supermarket decided to experiment and group meats by lifestyle. For instance, one section was called "Meals in Minutes," one "Cookin' Lite," another, filled with prepared products

---

Marketing
MEMO

A Guide to Generation Y

Generation Y is the term most commonly applied to Americans born between 1977 and 1999, under the broadest definition. Roughly 60 million Americans belong to this group, the largest generational cohort in American history, which is three times the size of Generation X. Generation Y is marked by racial diversity: One out of every three Gen Yers is non-Caucasian. Their technology proficiency will enable them to spend an estimated $1.3 billion online by 2002.

The following are traits often ascribed to Generation Y:

- Optimism and big expectations for the future
- An obsession with achievement
- Technological savvy
- Greater acceptance of racial and ethnic differences
- Media savvy
- Busy schedules
- Higher levels of stress
- A heightened ability to multitask
- A strong sense of community and teamwork
- A wish to make money, but a need to give back
- Emphasis on immediate gratification
- Suspicious of advertising

Sources: J. M. Lawrence, "Trends: X-ed Out: Gen Y Takes Over," *Boston Herald*, February 2, 1999, p. 243. Martha Irvine, "Labels Don't Fit Us, Gen Y Insists," *Denver Post*, April 19, 2001, p. A-9.

like hot dogs and ready-made hamburger patties, "Kids Love This Stuff," and yet another "I Like to Cook." As other Kroger stores adopted a reorganized meat-case policy, the average sales increase was expected to be $10 million over a year.[25]

Lifestyles are shaped partly by whether consumers are *time-constrained* or *money-constrained*. Consumers who experience time famine are prone to **multitasking**, that is, doing two or more things at the same time. They will phone or eat while driving, or bicycle to work to get exercise. They will also pay others to perform tasks because time is more important than money. They prefer cats to dogs because cats are easier to handle. They prefer bagels to breakfast cereals because they are quicker. Companies aiming to serve them will create convenient services for this group. As for the money-constrained individuals, companies aiming to serve them will create lower-cost products and services.

Companies making cosmetics, alcoholic beverages, and furniture are always seeking opportunities in lifestyle segmentation, but lifestyle segmentation does not always work. Nestlé introduced a special brand of decaffeinated coffee for "late nighters," and it failed.

Personality   Marketers have used personality variables to segment markets. They endow their products with a *brand personality* that corresponds to a target consumer personality. A brand may wish to appear *sincere* (Gateway Computer), *exciting* (Nike), *competent* (Hewlett-Parkard), *sophisticated* (Lexus), or *rugged* (Timberland).[26] A brand personality may have several attributes: Levi's suggests a personality that is youthful, rebellious, rugged, authentic, and American. The company utilizes product features, services, and image making to transmit the product's personality.

Values   Some marketers segment by **core values**, the belief systems that underlie consumer attitudes and behaviors. Core values go much deeper than behavior or attitude, and determine, at a basic level, people's choices and desires over the long term. Marketers who segment by values believe that by appealing to people's inner selves, it is possible to influence their outer selves—their purchase behavior. (See "Marketing Memo: Tapping into Core Values Around the Globe.")

BEHAVIORAL SEGMENTATION   In **behavioral segmentation**, buyers are divided into groups on the basis of their knowledge of, attitude toward, use of, or response to a prod-

Marketing
MEMO

Tapping into Core Values Around the Globe

Roper Reports interviewed about 1,000 people in their homes in each of 35 countries. They were asked to rank 56 values by the importance they hold as guiding principles in their lives. Among adults, Roper found six global *values segments* in all 35 countries, but to varying degrees in each.

1. *Strivers:* Strivers (12%) are slightly more likely to be men than women, and they place high emphasis on material and professional goals. One in three people in developing Asia is a Striver.
2. *Devouts:* Devouts (22%) include more women than men, and tradition and duty are very important to them. Devouts are most common in developing Asia and the Middle Eastern and African countries surveyed. They are least common in developed Asia and Western Europe.
3. *Altruists:* Altruists (18%) are interested in social issues and the welfare of society. There are slightly more women than men. With a median age of 44, this group is older. More Altruists live in Latin America and Russia than in other countries.
4. *Intimates:* Intimates (15%) value close personal relationships and family above all else. They are almost as likely to be men as women. One in four Europeans and Americans qualify, compared with just 7 percent of developing Asia.
5. *Fun Seekers:* Fun Seekers (12%) are found in disproportionate numbers in developed Asia. Fun Seekers are the youngest group, with a male–female ratio of 54 to 46.
6. *Creatives:* Creatives (10%) have a strong interest in education, knowledge, and technology. Creatives are more common in Latin America and Western Europe.

Roper's research shows that people in different segments generally pursue different activities, buy different products, and use different media. Knowing which segments dominate in a country helps with marketing efforts and enables advertisers to tailor their message to those parts of the population most likely to buy.

Source: Adapted from Tom Miller, "Global Segments from 'Strivers' to 'Creatives,' " *Marketing News,* July 20, 1998, p. 11.

uct. Many marketers believe that behavioral variables—occasions, benefits, user status, usage rate, loyalty status, buyer-readiness stage, and attitude—are the best starting points for constructing market segments.

Occasions Buyers can be distinguished according to the occasions when they develop a need, purchase a product, or use a product. For example, air travel is triggered by occasions related to business, vacation, or family. An airline can specialize in serving people for whom one of these occasions dominates: Charter airlines serve people who fly to a vacation destination.

Occasion segmentation can help firms expand product usage. For example, orange juice is usually consumed at breakfast. An orange juice company can try to promote drinking orange juice on other occasions—lunch, dinner, midday. Certain holidays—Mother's Day and Father's Day, for example—were established partly to increase the sale of candy and flowers. The Curtis Candy Company promoted the trick-or-treat custom at Halloween.

A company can consider occasions of *critical life events or transitions*—marriage, childbirth, illness, relocation, divorce, career change—as giving rise to new needs. These should alert service providers—banks, lawyers, and marriage, employment, and bereavement counselors—to ways they can help.[27]

Bank of America (BOA) BOA is using "event-based triggers" to help its premier customers. BOA, using NCR's "Relationship Optimizer" solution, monitors large deposits, withdrawals, insufficient funds, and other events that deviate from a customer's normal behavior. Client managers are alerted to these events and phone the client to see if they can be of any assistance. For example, if a client has withdrawn a large sum of money to buy a home, the client manager offers to help the client find the best mortgage. Clients seem to appreciate these offers of assistance.

Benefits Buyers can be classified according to the benefits they seek. People vary considerably in the benefits they seek from the same product. Even car drivers who want to stop for gas may seek different benefits. Through its research, Mobil identified five different benefit segments and their sizes:

1. *Road Warriors:* premium products and quality service. (16%)
2. *Generation F:* fast fuel, fast service, and fast food. (27%)
3. *True Blues:* branded products and reliable service. (16%)
4. *Home Bodies:* convenience. (21%)
5. *Price Shoppers:* low price. (20%)

Surprisingly, although gasoline is largely a commodity, price shoppers constituted only 20 percent of the buyers. Mobil decided to focus on the less price-sensitive segments and rolled out *Friendly Serve*: cleaner property, bathrooms, better lighting, well-stocked stores, and friendlier personnel. Although Mobil charged $.02 per gallon more than its competitors, sales increased by 20 to 25 percent.[28]

User Status Markets can be segmented into nonusers, ex-users, potential users, first-time users, and regular users of a product. Blood banks cannot rely only on regular donors to supply blood; they must also recruit new first-time donors and contact ex-donors, and each will require a different marketing strategy.

Included in the potential user group are consumers who will become users in connection with some life stage or life event. Mothers-to-be are potential users who will turn into heavy users. Producers of infant products and services learn their names and shower them with products and ads to capture a share of their future purchases.

Market-share leaders tend to focus on attracting potential users because they have the most to gain. Smaller firms focus on trying to attract current users away from the market leader.

Usage Rate Markets can be segmented into light, medium, and heavy product users. Heavy users are often a small percentage of the market but account for a high percentage of total consumption. For example, heavy beer drinkers account for 87 percent of the beer consumed—almost seven times as much as the light beer drinkers. Marketers would rather attract one heavy user than several light users. The problem, however, is that heavy users either are extremely loyal to one brand, or never stay loyal to a brand and are always looking for the lowest price.

Loyalty Status Consumers have varying degrees of loyalty to specific brands, stores, and companies. Oliver defines **loyalty** as "A deeply held commitment to re-buy or re-patronize a preferred product or service in the future despite situational influences and marketing efforts having the potential to cause switching behavior."[29]

Buyers can be divided into four groups according to brand loyalty status:

1. *Hard-core loyals:* Consumers who buy one brand all the time.
2. *Split loyals:* Consumers who are loyal to two or three brands.
3. *Shifting loyals:* Consumers who shift from one brand to another.
4. *Switchers:* Consumers who show no loyalty to any brand.[30]

Each market consists of different numbers of the four types of buyers. A *brand-loyal market* is one with a high percentage of hard-core brand-loyal buyers. The toothpaste market and the beer market are fairly high brand-loyal markets. Companies selling in a brand-loyal market have a hard time gaining more market share, and companies that enter such a market have a hard time getting in.

A company can learn a great deal by analyzing the degrees of brand loyalty: (1) By studying its hard-core loyals, the company can identify its products' strengths. (2) By studying its split loyals, the company can pinpoint which brands are most competitive with its own. (3) By looking at customers who are shifting away from its brand, the company can learn about its marketing weaknesses and attempt to correct them.

One caution: What appear to be brand-loyal purchase patterns may reflect habit, indifference, a low price, a high switching cost, or the nonavailability of other brands. Thus a company must carefully interpret what is behind the observed purchase patterns.

Buyer-Readiness Stage A market consists of people in different stages of readiness to buy a product. Some are unaware of the product, some are aware, some are informed, some are interested, some desire the product, and some intend to buy. The relative numbers make a big difference in designing the marketing program.

Suppose a health agency wants to encourage women to have an annual Pap test to detect possible cervical cancer. At the beginning, most women may be unaware of the Pap test. The marketing effort should go into awareness-building advertising using a simple message. Later, the advertising should dramatize the benefits of the Pap test and the risks of not taking it. A special offer of a free health examination might motivate women into actually signing up for the test.

Attitude Five attitude groups can be found in a market: enthusiastic, positive, indifferent, negative, and hostile. Door-to-door workers in a political campaign use the voter's attitude to determine how much time to spend with that voter. They thank enthusiastic voters and remind them to vote; they reinforce those who are positively disposed; they try to win the votes of indifferent voters; they spend no time trying to change the attitudes of negative and hostile voters. To the extent that attitudes are correlated with demographic descriptors, the political party can more efficiently locate the best prospects.

MULTIATTRIBUTE SEGMENTATION (GEOCLUSTERING) Marketers no longer talk about the average consumer or even limit their analysis to only a few market segments. Rather, they are increasingly combining several variables in an effort to identify smaller, better-defined target groups. Thus a bank may not only identify a group of wealthy retired adults, but within that group distinguish several segments depending on current income, assets, savings, and risk preferences.

One of the most promising developments in multiattribute segmentation is called geoclustering. It yields richer descriptions of consumers and neighborhoods than traditional demographics. Claritas, Inc., has developed a geoclustering approach called PRIZM (Potential Rating Index by Zip Markets) that classifies over half a million U.S. residential neighborhoods into 62 distinct lifestyle groupings called PRIZM Clusters.[31] The groupings take into consideration 39 factors in 5 broad categories: (1) education and affluence, (2) family life cycle, (3) urbanization, (4) race and ethnicity, and (5) mobility. The neighborhoods are broken down by zip code, zip+4, or census tract and block group. The clusters have descriptive titles such as *Blue Blood Estates, Winner's Circle, Hometown Retired, Latino America, Shotguns and Pickups,* and *Back Country Folks.* The inhabitants in a cluster tend to lead similar lives, drive similar cars, have similar jobs, and read similar magazines. Here are four PRIZM clusters:

- **American Dreams** This segment represents the emerging, upscale, ethnic, big-city mosaic. People in this segment are likely to buy imported cars, read *Essence* magazine, bank with a home computer, watch pro football, and wear designer jeans. Their annual median household income is $59,000.
- **Rural Industria** This cluster includes young families in heartland offices and factories. Their lifestyle is typified by trucks, *Field and Stream* magazine, fishing trips, and auto racing enthusiasm. Annual median household income is $27,900.
- **Gray Power** These aging baby boomers live the good life in the suburbs. They are likely to belong to a country club, subscribe to *Modern Maturity*, purchase cruise vacations, and watch the Travel Channel. Annual median household income is $41,800.
- **Country Squires** This cluster comprises 1 percent of American households in the primary age group of 35–54 whose lifestyle is characterized by business trips by air, personal computers and personal digital assistants, gourmet coffee, classical radio, Saab 900s, and moderate Republican orientation. Annual median household income is $75,000.

Other PRIZM clusters include *Kids & Cul-de-Sacs*, which covers the baby boomer migration to the suburbs; *Young Literati*, which taps Generation X; and *New Ecotopia*, which focuses on the country's aging hippies.[32]

Marketers can use PRIZM to answer such questions as these: Which geographic areas (neighborhoods or zip codes) contain our most valuable customers? How deeply have we already penetrated these segments? Which distribution channels and promotional media work best in reaching our target clusters in each area? Spiegel, a direct marketer, uses geoclustering information to search for where to mail its catalogs. In marketing its Suave shampoo, Helene Curtis uses PRIZM to identify neighborhoods with high concentrations of young working women. These women responded best to Suave advertising messages.

Geoclustering captures the increasing diversity of the American population. Marketing to microsegments has become accessible even to small organizations as database costs decline, PCs proliferate, software becomes easier to use, data integration increases, and the Internet grows.[33]

TARGETING MULTIPLE SEGMENTS Very often, companies start marketing to one segment, then expand to others. Consider the experiences of one technology company:

Motorola In 1999, Motorola used the results of a 25-nation segmentation research project to create four different sub-brands for its mobile phones: Accompli, Timeport, V., and Talkabout. Accompli is designed for customers seeking leading edge wireless technology; phones come with state-of-the-art features such as office assistant software and a large touchscreen. The Java-based Timeport phone features Internet browsing software as well as a desktop organizer. It is similar to the Accompli, but caters to the business user who views a phone as a tool. V. targets status-seeking phone users with the latest styles as well as high-end technology. Top models come with mini-browsers for Web surfing. Talkabout is made for those who use the phone for everyday calling; these phones offer standard features at good value.[34]

Many consumers are cross-shoppers and cannot be neatly pigeonholed into one segment. Consider the person who buys an expensive Bill Blass suit but shops at Wal-Mart for underwear; or the one who eats a Healthy Choice frozen dinner followed by Ben & Jerry's ice cream for dessert. It is dangerous to interpret segment membership by observing only one purchase. Segmentation ignores the whole customer profile, which becomes clear only with individual profiling.

bases for segmenting business markets

Business markets can be segmented with some of the same variables used in consumer market segmentation, such as geography, benefits sought, and usage rate, but business marketers also use other variables. Bonoma and Shapiro proposed segmenting the business market with the variables shown in Table 10.3. The demographic variables are the

table **10.3**	
Major Segmentation Variables for Business Markets	**Demographic** 1. *Industry:* Which industries should we serve? 2. *Company size:* What size companies should we serve? 3. *Location:* What geographical areas should we serve? **Operating Variables** 4. *Technology:* What customer technologies should we focus on? 5. *User or nonuser status:* Should we serve heavy users, medium users, light users, or nonusers? 6. *Customer capabilities:* Should we serve customers needing many or few services? **Purchasing Approaches** 7. *Purchasing-function organization:* Should we serve companies with highly centralized or decentralized purchasing organizations? 8. *Power structure:* Should we serve companies that are engineering dominated, financially dominated, and so on? 9. *Nature of existing relationships:* Should we serve companies with which we have strong relationships or simply go after the most desirable companies? 10. *General purchase policies:* Should we serve companies that prefer leasing? Service contracts? Systems purchases? Sealed bidding? 11. *Purchasing criteria:* Should we serve companies that are seeking quality? Service? Price? **Situational Factors** 12. *Urgency:* Should we serve companies that need quick and sudden delivery or service? 13. *Specific application:* Should we focus on certain applications of our product rather than all applications? 14. *Size of order:* Should we focus on large or small orders? **Personal Characteristics** 15. *Buyer-seller similarity:* Should we serve companies whose people and values are similar to ours? 16. *Attitudes toward risk:* Should we serve risk-taking or risk-avoiding customers? 17. *Loyalty:* Should we serve companies that show high loyalty to their suppliers?

Source: Adapted from Thomas V. Bonoma and Benson P. Shapiro, *Segmenting the Industrial Market* (Lexington, MA: Lexington Books, 1983).

most important, followed by the operating variables—down to the personal characteristics of the buyer.

The table lists major questions that business marketers should ask in determining which segments and customers to serve. A rubber-tire company should first decide which industries it wants to serve. It can sell tires to manufacturers of automobiles, trucks, farm tractors, forklift trucks, or aircraft. Within a chosen target industry, a company can further segment by company size. The company might set up separate operations for selling to large and small customers. Consider how Dell is organized.

Dell Dell is divided into two direct sales divisions: One sells to consumers and small businesses; another manages the company's corporate accounts. Three key segments are included under the corporate accounts umbrella: the enterprise group (*Fortune* 500 companies), large corporate accounts (multinational companies in what would be the *Fortune* 501 to 2000 range), and preferred accounts (medium businesses with 200 to 2,000 employees). This last segment represents Dell's fastest-growing business, and it serves such customers as Rollerblade and Associated Press.

Small businesses, in particular, have become a Holy Grail for business marketers.[35] In the United States, small businesses are now responsible for 50 percent of the gross national product, according to the U.S. Small Business Administration, and this segment is growing at 11 percent annually, three percentage points higher than the growth of large companies. Here are two examples of how to focus on small businesses.

IBM This $90 billion technology company has already proved that it can market successfully to other corporate giants such as General Motors and Citibank. Now it is trying to prove that it is nimble enough to market to the millions of enterprises with 1,000 or fewer employees. In addition to assigning field salespeople exclusively to small and medium-sized businesses (SMBs), IBM is putting greater emphasis on telesales and service. Within the small business segment, it is targeting minority-owned businesses because small business owners are more likely to be women, black, Asian, Hispanic, gay, or lesbian than white males. IBM executives responsible for targeting each segment have become involved in associations such as the National Black MBA Association or the National Foundation for Women Business Owners.[36]

BB&T BB&T, a Raleigh, North Carolina, bank, is positioning itself as a powerful local bank with a down-home approach. It launched a business-to-business (B2B) advertising campaign depicting various Carolina businesses and their owners. Each entrepreneur is a BB&T small business customer, and the ads reinforce the bank's commitment to small business.[37]

Within a given target industry and customer size, a company can segment by purchase criteria. For example, government laboratories need low prices and service contracts for scientific equipment; university laboratories need equipment that requires little service; and industrial laboratories need equipment that is highly reliable and accurate.

Business marketers generally identify segments through a sequential segmentation process. Consider an aluminum company: The company first undertook macrosegmentation. It looked at which end-use market to serve: automobile, residential, or beverage containers. It chose the residential market, and needed to determine the most attractive product application: semifinished material, building components, or aluminum mobile homes. Deciding to focus on building components, it considered the best customer size and chose large customers. The second stage consisted of microsegmentation. The company distinguished among customers buying on price, service, or quality. Because the aluminum company had a high-service profile, it decided to concentrate on the service-motivated segment of the market.

Business buyers seek different benefit bundles based on their stage in the purchase decision process:[38]

1. *First-time prospects:* Customers who have not yet purchased but want to buy from a vendor who understands their business, who explains things well, and whom they can trust.
2. *Novices:* Customers who are starting their purchasing relationship want easy-to-read manuals, hot lines, a high level of training, and knowledgeable sales reps.
3. *Sophisticates:* Established customers want speed in maintenance and repair, product customization, and high technical support.

These segments may also have different channel preferences. First-time prospects would prefer to deal with a company salesperson instead of a catalog or direct-mail channel, because the latter provides too little information. Sophisticates, on the other hand, may want to conduct more of their buying over electronic channels.

Rangan, Moriarty, and Swartz studied a mature commodity market, steel strapping, and found four business segments:[39]

1. *Programmed buyers:* Buyers who view the product as not very important to their operation. They buy it as a routine purchase item, usually paying full price and receiving below-average service. Clearly, this is a highly profitable segment for the vendor.
2. *Relationship buyers:* Buyers who regard the product as moderately important and are knowledgeable about competitive offerings. They get a small discount and a modest amount of service and prefer the vendor as long as the price is not far out of line. They are the second most profitable group.
3. *Transaction buyers:* Buyers who see the product as very important to their operations. They are price and service sensitive. They receive about a 10 percent discount and above-average service. They are knowledgeable about competitive offerings and are ready to switch for a better price, even at the sacrifice of some service.
4. *Bargain hunters:* Buyers who see the product as very important and demand the deepest discount and the highest service. They know the alternative suppliers, bargain hard, and are ready to switch at the slightest dissatisfaction. The company needs these buyers for volume purposes, but they are not very profitable.

This segmentation scheme can help a company in a mature commodity industry do a better job of figuring out where to apply price and service increases and decreases, because each segment would react differently.[40]

Rackham and Vincentis proposed a segmentation scheme that classifies business buyers into three groups, each warranting a different type of selling:[41]

- *Price-oriented customers (transactional selling).* They want value through lowest price.
- *Solution-oriented customers (consultative selling).* They want value through more benefits and advice.
- *Strategic-value customers (enterprise selling).* They want value through the supplier co-investing and participating in the customer's business.

The authors cite several cases of mismanagement by companies that did not understand the business buyer:

- A packaging manufacturer decided to upgrade and rename sales reps as packaging consultants at a cost of $10 million, but 90 percent of the customers bought transactionally. The company failed and was acquired by a major competitor who reintroduced a transactional selling effort.
- A consulting firm replaced its long-term consultants with salespeople to sell quick consulting projects. They acquired many new clients but lost most of their old clients who wanted consultative selling.
- A container manufacturer selling consultatively to a major food company was asked to join in some risk and gain sharing involving co-development of radically new packaging approaches. It refused and lost the account.

market targeting

Once the firm has identified its market-segment opportunities, it has to decide how many and which ones to target.

evaluating and selecting the market segments

In evaluating different market segments, the firm must look at two factors: the segment's overall attractiveness and the company's objectives and resources. Does a potential segment have characteristics that make it generally attractive, such as size, growth, profitability, scale economies, and low risk? Does investing in the segment make sense given the firm's objectives, competencies, and resources? Some attractive segments may not mesh with the company's long-run objectives, or the company may lack one or more necessary competencies to offer superior value.

Having evaluated different segments, the company can consider five patterns of target market selection, shown in Figure 10.2.

SINGLE-SEGMENT CONCENTRATION　Volkswagen concentrates on the small-car market and Porsche on the sports car market. Through concentrated marketing, the firm gains a strong knowledge of the segment's needs and achieves a strong market presence. Furthermore, the firm enjoys operating economies through specializing its production, distribution, and promotion. If it captures segment leadership, the firm can earn a high return on its investment.

However, concentrated marketing involves risks. A particular market segment can turn sour. When young women suddenly stopped buying sportswear, Bobbie Brooks's earnings fell sharply; or a competitor may invade the segment. For these reasons, many companies prefer to operate in more than one segment.

SELECTIVE SPECIALIZATION　The firm selects a number of segments, each objectively attractive and appropriate. There may be little or no synergy among the segments, but each promises to be a moneymaker. This multisegment strategy has the advantage of diversifying the firm's risk.

Consider a radio broadcaster that wants to appeal to both younger and older listeners. Emmis Broadcasting owns New York's KISS-FM, which describes itself as "smooth R&B [rhythm and blues] and classic soul" and appeals to older listeners, and WQHT-FM ("Hot 97"), which plays hip-hop (urban street music) for listeners in the under-25 crowd.[42]

PRODUCT SPECIALIZATION　The firm makes a certain product that it sells to several segments. An example would be a microscope manufacturer who sells to university, government, and commercial laboratories. The firm makes different microscopes for the different customer groups and builds a strong reputation in the specific product area. The downside risk is that the product may be supplanted by an entirely new technology.

MARKET SPECIALIZATION　The firm concentrates on serving many needs of a particular customer group. An example would be a firm that sells an assortment of products only to university laboratories. The firm gains a strong reputation in serving this customer group and becomes a channel for additional products the customer group can use. The downside risk is that the customer group may suffer budget cuts.

FULL MARKET COVERAGE　The firm attempts to serve all customer groups with all the products they might need. Only very large firms such as IBM (computer market), General Motors (vehicle market), and Coca-Cola (drink market) can undertake a full market coverage strategy. Large firms can cover a whole market in two broad ways: through undifferentiated marketing or differentiated marketing.

In *undifferentiated marketing*, the firm ignores segment differences and goes after the whole market with one offer. It designs a product and a marketing program that will appeal to the broadest number of buyers. It relies on mass-distribution and

figure **10.2**

Five Patterns of Target Market Selection

Single-segment concentration

Selective specialization

Product specialization

Market specialization

Full market coverage

P = Product　M = Market

Source: Adapted from Derek F. Abell, *Defining the Business: The Starting Point of Strategic Planning* (Upper Saddle River, NJ: Prentice Hall, 1980), ch. 8, pp. 192–96.

mass-advertising. It aims to endow the product with a superior image in people's minds. Undifferentiated marketing is "the marketing counterpart to standardization and mass production in manufacturing."[43] The narrow product line keeps down costs of research and development, production, inventory, transportation, marketing research, advertising, and product management. The undifferentiated advertising program keeps down advertising costs. Presumably, the company can turn its lower costs into lower prices to win the price-sensitive segment of the market.

In *differentiated marketing*, the firm operates in several market segments and designs different products for each segment. General Motors does this when it says that it produces a car for every "purse, purpose, and personality." IBM offers many hardware and software packages for different segments in the computer market. Consider the case of American Drug.

American Drug   American Drug, one of the largest U.S. drugstore retailers, had its marketing team assess shopping patterns at hundreds of its Osco and Sav-on Drug Stores on a market-by-market basis. Using scanned data, the company fine-tuned the stores' product mix, revamped store layout, and refocused marketing efforts to be more closely aligned with local consumer demand. Depending on the local demographics, each store unit varies the amount and type of merchandise in such categories as hardware, electrical supplies, automotive supplies, cookware, over-the-counter drugs, and convenience goods.[44]

Differentiated marketing typically creates more total sales than undifferentiated marketing. However, it also increases the costs of doing business. The following costs are likely to be higher:

- *Product modification costs:* Modifying a product to meet different market-segment requirements usually involves R&D, engineering, and special tooling costs.
- *Manufacturing costs:* It is usually more expensive to produce 10 units of 10 different products than 100 units of one product. The longer the production setup time and the smaller the sales volume of each product, the more expensive the product becomes. However, if each model is sold in sufficiently large volume, the higher setup costs may be quite small per unit.
- *Administrative costs:* The company has to develop separate marketing plans for each market segment. This requires extra marketing research, forecasting, sales analysis, promotion, planning, and channel management.
- *Inventory costs:* It is more costly to manage inventories containing many products.
- *Promotion costs:* The company has to reach different market segments with different promotion programs. The result is increased promotion-planning costs and media costs.

Because differentiated marketing leads to both higher sales and higher costs, nothing general can be said regarding this strategy's profitability. Companies should be cautious about oversegmenting their market. If this happens, they may want to turn to *countersegmentation* to broaden the customer base. For example, Johnson & Johnson broadened its target market for its baby shampoo to include adults. Smith Kline Beecham launched its Aquafresh toothpaste to attract three benefit segments simultaneously: those seeking fresh breath, whiter teeth, and cavity protection.

additional considerations

Four other considerations must be taken into account in evaluating and selecting segments: ethical choice of market targets, segment interrelationships and supersegments, segment-by-segment invasion plans, and intersegment cooperation.

ETHICAL CHOICE OF MARKET TARGETS   Market targeting sometimes generates public controversy.[45] The public is concerned when marketers take unfair advantage of vulnerable groups (such as children) or disadvantaged groups (such as inner-city poor people), or promote potentially harmful products. The cereal industry has been heavily criticized for marketing efforts directed toward children. Critics worry that high-powered appeals presented through the mouths of lovable animated characters will overwhelm children's defenses and lead them to eat too much sugared cereal or poorly balanced breakfasts. Toy marketers have been similarly criticized. McDonald's and other chains have drawn criticism for pitching their high-fat, salt-laden fare to low-income, inner-city residents.

Internal documents from R. J. Reynolds and Brown & Williamson Tobacco Corporation (marketer of the Kool brand) have revealed the extent to which these companies target black youths age 16 to 25, particularly with their menthol brands.[46] G. Heileman Brewing drew fire when it extended its Colt 45 malt liquor line with Powermaster, a new high-test malt (5.9 alcohol). Malt liquor is consumed primarily by blacks, and by targeting blacks extensively Heileman was itself targeted by federal officials, industry leaders, black activists, and the media.[47]

Not all attempts to target children, minorities, or other special segments draw criticism. Colgate-Palmolive's Colgate Junior toothpaste has special features designed to get children to brush longer and more often. Golden Ribbon Playthings has developed a highly acclaimed and very successful black character doll named "Huggy Bean" to connect minority consumers with their African heritage. Other companies are responding to the special needs of minority segments. Black-owned ICE theaters noticed that although moviegoing by blacks has surged, there are few inner-city theaters. ICE partners with the black communities in which it operates theaters, using local radio stations to promote films and featuring favorite food items at concession stands.[48] Thus the issue is not who is targeted, but rather, how and for what. Socially responsible marketing calls for targeting that serves not only the company's interests but also the interests of those targeted.

In selecting more than one segment to serve, the company should pay close attention to segment interrelationships on the cost, performance, and technology side. A company carrying a fixed cost (sales force, store outlets) can add products to absorb and share some costs. The sales force will sell additional products, and a fast-food outlet will offer additional menu items. Economies of scope can be just as important as economies of scale.

Companies should try to operate in supersegments rather than in isolated segments. A **supersegment** is a set of segments sharing some exploitable similarity. For example, many symphony orchestras target people who have broad cultural interests, rather than only those who regularly attend concerts.

SEGMENT-BY-SEGMENT INVASION PLANS   A company would be wise to enter one segment at a time without revealing its total expansion plans. Competitors must not know to what segment(s) the firm will move next. Segment-by-segment invasion plans are illustrated in Figure 10.3. Three firms, A, B, and C, have specialized in adapting computer systems to the needs of airlines, railroads, and trucking companies. Company A meets all the computer needs of airlines. Company B sells large computer systems to all three transportation sectors. Company C sells personal computers to trucking companies.

Where should company C move next? Arrows have been added to the chart to show the planned sequence of segment invasions. Company C will next offer midsized computers to trucking companies. Then, to allay company B's concern about losing some large computer business with trucking companies, C's next move will be to sell personal computers to railroads. Later, C will offer midsized computers to railroads. Finally, it may launch a full-scale attack on company B's large computer position in trucking companies. Of course, C's hidden planned moves are provisional in that much depends on competitors' segment moves and responses.

Unfortunately, too many companies fail to develop a long-term invasion plan. PepsiCo is an exception. It first attacked Coca-Cola in the grocery market, then in the vending-machine market, then in the fast-food market, and so on. Japanese firms also plot their invasion sequence. They first gain a foothold in a market, then enter new segments with products. Toyota began by introducing small cars (Tercel, Corolla), then expanded into midsize cars (Camry, Avalon), and finally into luxury cars (Lexus).

figure **10.3**

Segment–by–Segment
Invasion Plan

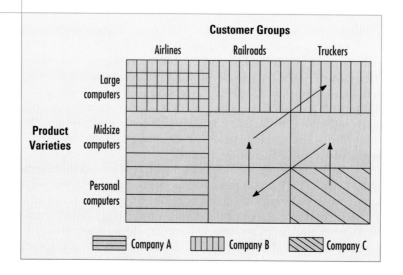

A company's invasion plans can be thwarted when it confronts blocked markets. The invader must then figure out a way to break in. The problem of entering blocked markets calls for a megamarketing approach. **Megamarketing** is the strategic coordination of economic, psychological, political, and public-relations skills, to gain the cooperation of a number of parties in order to enter or operate in a given market.

Pepsi used megamarketing to enter the Indian market.

PepsiCo   After Coca-Cola left India, Pepsi worked with an Indian business group to gain government approval for its entry, over the objections of domestic soft-drink companies and anti-multinational legislators. Pepsi offered to help India export some agricultural products in a volume that would more than cover the cost of importing soft-drink concentrate. Pepsi also promised to help rural areas in their economic development. It further offered to transfer food-processing, packaging, and water-treatment technology to India. Pepsi's bundle of benefits won the support of various Indian interest groups. Instead of relying on the normal four Ps for entering a market, Pepsi added two additional Ps, namely, *politics* and *public opinion*.

Once in, a multinational must be on its best behavior. This calls for well-thought-out *civic positioning*. For example, Olivetti enters new markets by building housing for workers, generously supporting local arts and charities, and hiring and training indigenous managers.[49]

INTERSEGMENT COOPERATION   The best way to manage segments is to appoint segment managers with sufficient authority and responsibility for building their segment's business. At the same time, segment managers should not be so focused as to resist cooperating with other groups in the company. Consider the following situation.

Baxter Baxter operates several divisions selling different products and services to hospitals. Each division sends out its own invoices. Some hospitals complain about receiving as many as seven different Baxter invoices each month. Baxter's marketers finally convinced the separate divisions to send the invoices to headquarters so that Baxter could send one invoice a month to its customers.

summary

1. Target marketing involves three activities: market segmentation, market targeting, and market positioning.

2. Markets can be targeted at four levels: segments, niches, local areas, and individuals. Market segments are large identifiable groups within a market. A niche is a more narrowly defined group. Marketers are localizing their campaigns for trading areas, neighborhoods, and even individual stores. Finally, more companies now practice individual and mass-customization. The future is likely to see more self-marketing, a form of individual marketing in which individual consumers take the initiative in designing products and brands.

3. There are two bases for segmenting consumer markets: consumer characteristics and consumer responses. The major segmentation variables for consumer markets are geographic, demographic, psychographic, and behavioral. These variables can be used singly or in combination. Business marketers use all these variables along with operating variables, purchasing approaches, and situational fac-

tors. To be useful, market segments must be measurable, substantial, accessible, differentiable, and actionable.

4. Once a firm has identified its market-segment opportunities, it has to evaluate the various segments and decide how many and which ones to target. In evaluating segments, it must look at the segment's attractiveness indicators and the company's objectives and resources. In choosing which segments to target, the company can choose to focus on a single segment, several segments, a specific product, a specific market, or the full market. If it decides to serve the full market, it must choose between differentiated and undifferentiated marketing.

5. Marketers must choose target markets in a socially responsible manner. Marketers must also monitor segment interrelationships, and seek economies of scope and the potential for marketing to supersegments. Marketers should develop segment-by-segment invasion plans. Finally, market segment managers should be prepared to cooperate in the interest of overall company performance.

applications

marketing debate – is mass marketing dead?

With marketers increasingly adopting more and more refined market segmentation schemes—fueled by the Internet and other customization efforts—some critics claim that mass-marketing is dead. Others counter that there will always be room for large brands that employ marketing programs targeting the mass-market.

Take a position: Mass-marketing is dead versus Mass-marketing is still a viable way to build a profitable brand.

marketing and advertising

1. With the headline "Adult Entertainment," the ad in Figure 1 beckons to a particular segment of the consumer market. Bahlsen knows that consumers of all ages generally like cookies, yet the company is signaling its segmentation strategy through the headline, body copy, and illustration.

   a. Which variables is Bahlsen using to segment the overall consumer market?

   b. Based on these variables, how would you describe the segment being targeted?

   c. Why would segmentation be effective for identifying market segments in this situation?

2. Hertz is a well-known brand among consumers and business travelers who rent cars. As shown in Figure 2, the company targets specific segments within business markets.

   a. Which of the major segmentation variables does Hertz appear to be using on its business markets?

   b. Which of the three business buyer groups identified by Rackham and Vincentis might Hertz be stressing in this ad?

   c. What personal characteristics might be particularly important in this segment of Hertz's business markets?

Figure 1

We make a big deal out of small business.

Figure 2

online marketing today

For Levi Strauss, the key to successful mass-customization is to make clothing that meets customers' expectations for fit as well as style. Customers can customize an existing Levi's style (such as the 502 button-fly model) or start from scratch to create a one-of-a-kind pair of jeans, khaki pants, and shorts by mixing and matching color, length, and other style choices. Still, the company recognizes that there is no substitute for accurate body measurements. As a result, its Original Spin site allows online visitors to learn about the process, review their options, and even fill out an order form. To complete the transaction and place an order, however, customers must go to a local store to be measured.

Visit the Original Spin site (*www.originalspin.com*) and follow the links to learn how the process works. Also follow the links to find the nearest Original Spin retail site and to examine the order form. Which of the four types of segmentation variables is Levi Strauss applying in its mass-customization strategy? How does the Web site support or reinforce the segmentation strategy? Why would Levi Strauss insist that reorders be funneled through the stores rather than submitted online? What improvements can you suggest to make the Original Spin site more effective in attracting or serving customers?

you're the marketer: sonic pda marketing plan

Marketing Plan Pro

Defining a target marketing strategy through market segmentation is a critical aspect of any marketing plan. The purpose is to identify and describe distinct market segments, target specific segments, and then pinpoint the differentiating benefits to be stressed.

In your role as Jane Melody's assistant, you are responsible for market segmentation and targeting for Sonic's new PDA product. Look back at the SWOT analysis, market needs information, and competitive data you previously documented in the marketing planning process. Then answer the following questions about Sonic's market segments and targeting:

■ Which variables should Sonic use to segment its consumer markets? For example, in addition to income and geography, does Sonic want to focus on consumers who have specific lifestyles, needs, or attitudes?

■ Which variables should Sonic use to segment its business markets?
■ How can Sonic evaluate the attractiveness of each identified segment? Should Sonic market to one consumer segment and one business segment or target more than one in each market? Why?
■ Should Sonic pursue full market coverage, market specialization, product specialization, selective specialization, or single-segment concentration? Why?

Next, consider how your decisions about segmentation and targeting will affect Sonic's marketing efforts. Depending on your instructor's directions, summarize your conclusions in a written marketing plan or enter them in the Market Analysis and Target Markets sections of the *Marketing Plan Pro* software. Also note any additional research you may need in the Marketing Research section of the software.

notes

1. Regis McKenna, "Real-Time Marketing," *Harvard Business Review* (July–August 1995): 87.
2. James C. Anderson and James A. Narus, "Capturing the Value of Supplementary Services," *Harvard Business Review* (January–February 1995): 75–83.
3. Tevfik Dalgic and Maarten Leeuw, "Niche Marketing Revisited: Concept, Applications, and Some European Cases," *European Journal of Marketing* 28, no. 4 (1994): 39–55.
4. Beth Whitehouse, "Season's Greetings," *Newsday,* December 11, 2000, p. B6.
5. <www.esteelauder.com>.
6. Robert E. Linneman and John L. Stanton Jr., *Making Niche Marketing Work: How to Grow Bigger by Acting Smaller* (New York: McGraw-Hill, 1991).
7. Robert Blattberg and John Deighton, "Interactive Marketing: Exploiting the Age of Addressability," *Sloan Management Review* 33, no. 1 (1991): 5–14.
8. Paul Davidson, "Entrepreneurs Reap Riches from Net Niches," *USA Today,* April 20, 1998, p. B3.
9. <www.ostrichesonline.com>.
10. Don Peppers and Martha Rogers, *The One-to-One Future: Building Relationships One Customer at a Time* (New York: Currency/Doubleday, 1993).
11. B. Joseph Pine II, *Mass Customization* (Boston: Harvard Business School Press, 1993); B. Joseph Pine II, Don Peppers, and Martha Rogers, "Do You Want to Keep Your Customers Forever?" *Harvard Business Review* (March–April 1995): 103–14.
12. Adrian J. Slywotzky and David J. Morrison, *How Digital is Your Business?* (New York: Crown Business, 2000), p. 39.
13. Jerry Wind and A. Rangaswamy, "Customerization: The Second Revolution in Mass Customization," Wharton School Working Paper, June 1999.
14. Catherine Arns, "PC Makers Head for 'SoHo,'" *BusinessWeek,* September 28, 1992, pp. 125–26; Gerry Khermouch, "The Marketers Take Over," *Brandweek,* September 27, 1993, pp. 29–35.
15. For a market-structure study of the hierarchy of attributes in the coffee market, see Dipak Jain, Frank M. Bass, and Yu-Min Chen, "Estimation of Latent Class Models with Heterogeneous Choice Probabilities: An Application to Market Structuring," *Journal of Marketing Research* (February 1990): 94–101. For an application of means-end chain analysis to global markets, see Freakel Ter Hofstede, Jan-Benrlict E. M. Steenkamp, and Michel Wedel, "International Market Segmentation Based on Consumer-Product Relations," *Journal of Marketing Research* (February 1999): 1–17.
16. Kate Kane, "It's a Small World," *Working Woman* (October 1997): 22.
17. Roger Crockett, "Pillsbury's New Software Will Let the Food Giant Slice and Dice Reams of Data, Changing Everything about How It Caters to Consumers," *BusinessWeek,* April 3, 2000, p. EB-78.
18. Leah Rickard, "Gerber Trots Out New Ads Backing Toddler Food Line," *Advertising Age,* April 11, 1994, pp. 1, 48.
19. "Sega to Target Adults with Brand Extensions," *Marketing Week,* March 12, 1998, p. 9.
20. Calmetta Y. Coleman "Eddie Bauer's Windows Add Electronics," *Wall Street Journal,* November 28, 2000, p. B10.
21. *America Demographics* (August 1986).
22. Lisa Napoli, "A Focus on Women at iVillage.com," *New York Times,* August 3, 1998, p. D6; Justin Fox, "Net Stock Rules: Masters of a Parallel Universe," *Fortune,* June 7, 1999, p. 66.
23. Geoffrey E. Meredith and Charles D. Schewe with Janice Karlovich, *Defining Markets, Defining Moments* (New York, NY: Hungrey Minds, Inc., 2002).
24. Andrew E. Serwer, "42,496 Secrets Bared," *Fortune,* January 24, 1994, pp. 13–14; Kenneth Labich, "Class in America," *Fortune,* February 7, 1994, pp. 114–26.
25. "Lifestyle Marketing," *Progressive Grocer* (August 1997): 107–10; "Kroger's Tim Brown Predicts $8.5 Billion Dollar Industry Boost from NPPC's Meat Case Initiative," *Business Wire,* April 15, 1996.
26. Jennifer Aaker, "Dimensions of Brand Personality," *Journal of Marketing Research* (August 1997): 347–56.
27. Cathy Goodwin and James W. Gentry, "Life Transition as a Basis for Segmentation," *Journal of Segmentation in Marketing* 4 no. 1 (2000).
28. Allana Sullivan, "Mobil Bets Drivers Pick Cappuccino over Parties," *Wall Street Journal,* January 30, 1995.
29. Richard L. Oliver, *Satisfaction: A Behavioral Perspective on the Consumer* (New York: McGraw-Hill, 1997).
30. This classification was adapted from George H. Brown, "Brand Loyalty: Fact or Fiction?" *Advertising Age,* June 1952–January 1953, a series. See also Peter E. Rossi, R. McCulloch, and G. Allenby, "The Value of Purchase History Data in Target Marketing," *Marketing Science* 15, no. 4 (1996): 321–40.
31. Other leading suppliers of geodemographic data are ClusterPlus (by Donnelly Marketing Information Services) and Acord (C.A.C.I., Inc.).
32. Christina Del Valle, "They Know Where You Live: And How You Buy," *BusinessWeek,* February 7, 1994, p. 89.
33. Michael J. Weiss, *The Clustering of America* (New York: Harper and Row, 1988); *Breaking Up is Hard to Do: The Clustered World* (Boston: Little, Brown & Co., 2000).
34. <www.motorola.com>; Bhanu Pande, "Upwardly Mobiles," *Business Standard,* May 30, 2000, p. 1.
35. Michele Marchetti, "Dell Computer," *Sales & Marketing Management,* (October 1997): 50–53.
36. Geoffrey Brewer, "Lou Gerstner Has His Hands Full," *Sales & Marketing Management* (May 1998): 36–41.
37. Jennifer Porter Gore, "Small Business Is Big at BB&T," *Bank Marketing* (August 1998): 10.
38. Thomas S. Robertson and Howard Barich, "A Successful Approach to Segmenting Industrial Markets," *Planning Forum* (November–December 1992): 5–11.
39. V. Kasturi Rangan, Rowland T. Moriarty, and Gordon S. Swartz, "Segmenting Customers in Mature Industrial Markets," *Journal of Marketing* (October 1992): 72–82.
40. For another interesting approach to segmenting the business market, see John Berrigan and Carl Finkbeiner, *Segmentation Marketing: New Methods for Capturing Business* (New York: HarperBusiness, 1992).
41. Neil Rackham and John DeVincentis, *Rethinking the Sales Force: Redefining Selling to Create and Capture Customer Value* (New York: McGraw-Hill, 1999), ch. 1.

42. Wendy Brandes, "Advertising: Black-Oriented Radio Tunes into Narrower Segments," *Wall Street Journal,* February 13, 1995, p. B5.

43. Wendell R. Smith, "Product Differentiation and Market Segmentation as Alternative Marketing Strategies," *Journal of Marketing* (July 1956): 4.

44. Susan Reda, "American Drug Stores Custom-Fits Each Market," *Stores* (September 1994): 22–24.

45. Bart Macchiette and Roy Abhijit, "Sensitive Groups and Social Issues," *Journal of Consumer Marketing* 11, no. 4 (1994): 55–64.

46. Barry Meier, "Data on Tobacco Show a Strategy Aimed at Blacks," *New York Times*, February 6, 1998, p. A1; Gregory Freeman, "Ads Aimed at Blacks and Children Should Exact a High Price," *St. Louis Post-Dispatch*, p. B1.

47. N. Craig Smith and Elizabeth Cooper-Martin, "Ethics and Target Marketing: The Role of Product Harm and Consumer Vulnerability," *Journal of Marketing* (July 1997): 11–20.

48. Roger O. Crockett, "They're Lining Up for Flicks in the 'Hood," *Business Week,* June 8, 1998, pp. 75–76.

49. Philip Kotler, "Megamarketing," *Harvard Business Review* (March–April 1986): 117–24.

positioning and differentiating the market offering through the product life cycle

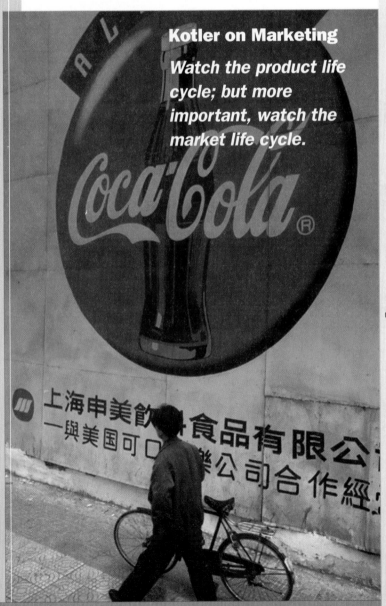

Kotler on Marketing

Watch the product life cycle; but more important, watch the market life cycle.

In this chapter, we will address the following questions:

- How can a firm choose and communicate an effective positioning in the market?
- What are the major differentiating attributes available to firms?
- What marketing strategies are appropriate at each stage of the product life cycle?
- What marketing strategies are appropriate at each stage of the market's evolution?

Today's economies are afflicted with surpluses, not shortages. In a U.S. supermarket, there are not only several brands of toothpaste but one brand, Colgate, offers a dozen varieties—with baking soda or peroxide, or loaded with "sparkling white" or tartar control. Kellogg's Eggo waffles come in 16 flavors, and Kleenex tissue comes in nine varieties. Consider other markets. Investors can choose among 8,000 mutual funds. Students can choose among hundreds of business schools. For the seller, this spells hypercompetition. For the buyer, this spells overchoice.

No company can win if its product and offering resembles every other product and offering. Today, most companies are guilty of strategy convergence—namely, undifferentiated strategies. Companies must pursue meaningful and *relevant positioning and differentiation. Each company and offering must represent a distinctive big idea in the mind of the target market; and each company must dream up new features, services and guarantees, special rewards for loyal users, and new conveniences and enjoyments.*

Yet even when a company succeeds in distinguishing itself, the differences are short-lived. Competitors are quicker than ever in copying good ideas; therefore companies constantly need to think up new value-adding features and benefits to win the attention and interest of choice-rich, price-prone consumers.

Companies normally reformulate their marketing strategies and offerings several times. Economic conditions change, competitors launch new assaults, and the product passes through new stages of buyer interest and requirements. Consequently, strategies appropriate to each stage in the product's life cycle must be developed. The goal is to extend the product's life and profitability, keeping in mind that the product will not last forever. This chapter explores specific ways a company can effectively position and differentiate its offerings to achieve competitive advantage throughout the life cycle of a product or an offering.

developing and communicating a positioning strategy

All marketing strategy is built on STP—Segmentation, Targeting, and Positioning. A company discovers different needs and groups in the marketplace, targets those needs and groups that it can satisfy in a the superior way, and then positions its offering so that the target market recognizes the company's distinctive offering and image. If a company does a poor job of positioning, the market will be confused as to what to expect. If a company does an excellent job of positioning, then it can work out the rest of its marketing planning and differentiation from its positioning strategy.

We define positioning as follows: **Positioning** is the act of designing the company's offering and image to occupy a distinctive place in the mind of the target market. The end result of positioning is the successful creation of a customer-focused **value proposition**, a cogent reason why the target market should buy the product. Table 11.1 shows how three companies—Perdue, Volvo, and Domino's—defined their value proposition given their target customers, benefits, and prices.

table **11.1**	Examples of Value Propositions Demand States and Marketing Tasks			
Company and Product	**Target Customers**	**Benefits**	**Price**	**Value Proposition**
Perdue (chicken)	Quality-conscious consumers of chicken	Tenderness	10% premium	More tender golden chicken at a moderate premium price
Volvo (station wagon)	Safety-conscious "upscale" families	Durability and safety	20% premium	The safest, most durable wagon in which your family can ride
Domino's (pizza)	Convenience-minded pizza lovers	Delivery speed and good quality	15% premium	A good hot pizza, delivered to your door within 30 minutes of ordering, at a moderate price

positioning according to ries and trout

The word *positioning* was popularized by two advertising executives, Al Ries and Jack Trout. They see positioning as a creative exercise done with an existing product:[1]

> Positioning starts with a product. A piece of merchandise, a service, a company, an institution, or even a person. . . . But positioning is not what you do to a product. Positioning is what you do to the mind of the prospect. That is, you position the product in the mind of the prospect.

Ries and Trout argue that well-known products generally hold a distinctive position in consumers' minds. Hertz is thought of as the world's largest auto-rental agency, Coca-Cola as the world's largest soft-drink company, and Porsche as one of the world's best sports cars. These brands own these positions, and it would be hard for a competitor to claim them.

A competitor has three strategic alternatives:

The first is to strengthen its own current position in the consumer's mind. Avis acknowledged its second position in the rental car business and claimed: "We're number two. We try harder." 7-Up capitalized on not being a cola drink by advertising itself as "the Uncola."

The second strategy is to grab an unoccupied position. Three Musketeers chocolate bar advertised itself as having 45 percent less fat than other chocolate bars. United Jersey Bank, noting that giant banks were usually slower in arranging loans, positioned itself as "the fast-moving bank."

The third strategy is to *de-position* or *re-position* the competition in the customer's mind. Most U.S. buyers of dinnerware thought that Lenox and Royal Doulton china both come from England. Royal Doulton de-positioned Lenox china by showing that it is made in New Jersey. BMW attempts to de-position Mercedes Benz with the comparison: "The ultimate sitting machine versus the ultimate driving machine." Popeye cajunstyle fried chicken aims to "save America from bland chicken" (implying an attack on KFC). Wendy's famous commercial, in which a 70-year-old woman named Clara looked at a competitor's hamburger and said "Where's the beef?" showed how an attack could destabilize consumer confidence in the leader.

Ries and Trout argue that, in an overadvertised society, the mind often knows brands in the form of *product ladders*, such as Coke-Pepsi-RC Cola or Hertz-Avis-National. The top firm is remembered best. For example, when asked "Who was the first person to fly alone across the Atlantic Ocean successfully?" we answer "Charles Lindbergh." When asked, "Who was the second person to do it?" we draw a blank. This is why companies fight for the number-one position. The "largest firm" position can be held by only one brand. The second brand should invent and lead in a new category. Thus 7-Up is the number-one Uncola, Porsche is the number-one small sports car, and Dial is the number-one deodorant soap. A fourth strategy is the exclusive-club strategy. For example, a company can promote the idea that it is one of the Big Three. The Big Three idea was invented by the third-largest U.S. auto firm, Chrysler. (The market leader never invents this concept.) The implication is that those in the club are the "best."

Ries and Trout essentially deal with communication strategies for positioning or re-positioning a brand in the consumer's mind. Yet they acknowledge that positioning requires every tangible aspect of product, price, place, and promotion to support the chosen to positioning strategy.

positioning according to treacy and wiersema

Two consultants, Michael Treacy and Fred Wiersema, proposed a positioning framework called *value disciplines*.[2] Within its industry, a firm could aspire to be the *product leader,* the *operationally excellent firm,* or the *customer intimate firm.* This is based on the notion that in every market there is a mix of three types of customers. Some customers favor the firm that is advancing on the technological frontier (product leadership); other customers want highly reliable performance (operational excellence), and still others want high responsiveness in meeting their individual needs (customer intimacy).

Treacy and Wiersema observed that a firm cannot normally be best in all three ways, or even in two ways. It lacks sufficient funds, and each value discipline requires different managerial mind-sets and investments that often conflict. Thus McDonald's excels at operational excellence, but could not afford to slow down its service to prepare hamburgers differently for each customer. Nor could McDonald's lead in new products because each addition would disrupt the smooth functioning of its normal operations. Even within a large company, such as GE, each division might follow a different value discipline: GE's major appliance division pursues operational excellence, its engineered plastics division pursues customer intimacy, and its jet engine division pursues product leadership.

Treacy and Wiersema propose that a business should follow four rules for success:

1. Become best at one of the three value disciplines.
2. Achieve an adequate performance level in the other two disciplines.
3. Keep improving one's superior position in the chosen discipline so as not to lose out to a competitor.
4. Keep becoming more adequate in the other two disciplines, because competitors keep raising customers' expectations.

positioning: how many ideas to promote?

A company must decide how many ideas (e.g., benefits, features) to convey in its positioning to its target customers. Many marketers advocate promoting only one central benefit. Rosser Reeves believes a company should develop a *unique selling proposition* (USP) for each brand and stick to it.[3] Crest toothpaste consistently promotes its anticavity protection, and Mercedes promotes its great engineering. Ries and Trout favor one consistent positioning message.[4] This makes for easier communication to the target market; it results in employees being clearer about what counts; and it makes it easier to align the whole organization with the central positioning.

The brand should tout itself as "number one" on the benefit it selects. Number-one positionings include "best quality," "best performance," "best service," "best styling," "best value," "lowest price," "safest," "fastest," "most customized," "most convenient," "most technological," "most reliable," or "most prestigious." If a company consistently hammers away at one positioning and delivers on it, it will probably be best known and recalled for this benefit. For example, Home Depot has gained a reputation for "best service" among home-improvement product retailers:

Home Depot Since Home Depot opened its first store in 1978 in Atlanta, the company has emphasized exemplary customer service. Its sales staff is trained to offer on-the-spot lessons in tile laying, electrical installations, and other projects; they are experienced tradespersons—plumbers, electricians, and carpenters. In recent years there have been customer complaints about clutter in the aisles and salespeople stocking items instead of providing service, so starting in 2001, Home Depot gave its stores a makeover called Service Performance Improvement (SPI). SPI limits restocking to off-peak hours and prohibits forklifts in store aisles during the day. The program resulted in up to a 70 percent increase in employee interactions with customers. Before SPI was introduced, employees spent as little as 40 percent of their time with customers.[5]

Not everyone agrees that single-benefit positioning is always best. What if the market tires of the benefit or believes that most competitors now deliver it? Today people believe that most cars are safe and that most cars have pretty good quality. Double-benefit positioning may be more distinctive. Steelcase, Inc., a leading office-furniture-systems company, claims two benefits: "best on-time delivery" and "best installation support." Volvo double-positions its automobiles as "safest" and "most durable."

There are even cases of successful triple-benefit positioning. Smith Kline Beecham promotes its Aquafresh toothpaste as offering three benefits: anticavity protection, better breath, and whiter teeth. The challenge is to convince consumers that the brand delivers all three. Smith Kline's solution was to create a toothpaste that squeezes out of the tube in three colors, thus visually confirming the three benefits. In doing this, Smith Kline "countersegmented"; that is, it attracted three segments instead of one.

As companies increase the number of claimed benefits for their brand, they risk disbelief and a loss of clear positioning. In general, a company must avoid four major positioning errors:

1. *Underpositioning:* Some companies discover that buyers have only a vague idea of the brand. The brand is seen as just another entry in a crowded marketplace. When Pepsi introduced its clear Crystal Pepsi in 1993, customers were distinctly unimpressed. They didn't see "clarity" as an important benefit in a soft drink.

2. *Overpositioning:* Buyers may have too narrow an image of the brand. Thus a consumer might think that diamond rings at Tiffany start at $5,000 when in fact Tiffany now offers affordable diamond rings starting at $1,000.

3. *Confused positioning:* Buyers might have a confused image of the brand resulting from the company's making too many claims or changing the brand's positioning too frequently. This was the case with Stephen Jobs's sleek and powerful NeXT desktop computer, which was positioned first for students, then for engineers, and then for businesspeople, all unsuccessfully.

4. *Doubtful positioning:* Buyers may find it hard to believe the brand claims in view of the product's features, price, or manufacturer. When GM's Cadillac division introduced the Cimarron, it positioned the car as a luxury competitor with BMW, Mercedes, and Audi. Although the car featured leather seats, a luggage rack, lots of chrome, and a Cadillac logo stamped on the chassis, customers saw it as a dolled-up version of Chevy's Cavalier and Oldsmobile's Firenza. The car was positioned as "more for more": customers saw it as "less for more."

Solving the positioning problem enables the company to solve the marketing-mix problem. Seizing the "high-quality position" requires the firm to produce high-quality products, charge a high price, distribute through high-class dealers, and advertise in high-quality magazines.

How do companies select their positioning? Consider the following example:

A theme park company wants to build a new park in the Los Angeles area to cater to the large number of tourists. Seven theme parks now operate in this area: Disneyland, Magic Mountain, Knott's Berry Farm, Busch Gardens, Japanese Deer Park, Marineland of the Pacific, and Lion Country Safari.

The company presented tourists with a series of trios (for example, Busch Gardens, Japanese Deer Park, and Disneyland) and asked them to choose the two most similar attractions and the two least similar attractions in each. A statistical analysis led to the *perceptual map* in Figure 11.1 The map contains two features. The seven dots represent the seven tourist attractions. The closer any two attractions are, the more similar they are in tourists' minds. Thus Disneyland and Magic Mountain are perceived as similar, whereas Disneyland and Lion Country Safari are perceived as very different.

The map also shows nine satisfactions that people look for in tourist attractions. These are indicated by arrows. Marineland of the Pacific is perceived as involving the "least waiting time," so it is farthest along the imaginary line of the "little waiting" arrow. Consumers think of Busch Gardens as the most economical choice.[6]

The theme park company can now choose from several different positioning possibilities:[7]

- *Attribute positioning:* A company positions itself on an attribute, such as size or number of years in existence. Disneyland can advertise itself as the largest theme park in the world.

- *Benefit positioning:* The product is positioned as the leader in a certain benefit. Knott's Berry Farm may try to position itself as a theme park that delivers a fantasy experience, such as living in the Old West.

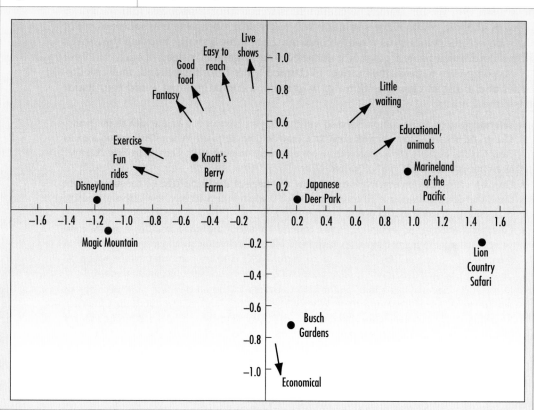

figure **11.1**   Perceptual Map

- *Use or application positioning:* Positioning the product as best for some use or application. Japanese Deer Park can position itself for the tourist who has only an hour to catch some quick entertainment.
- *User positioning:* Positioning the product as best for some user group. Magic Mountain can advertise itself as best for "thrill seekers."
- *Competitor positioning:* The product claims to be better in some way than a named competitor. For example, Lion Country Safari can advertise having a greater variety of animals than Japanese Deer Park.
- *Product category positioning:* The product is positioned as the leader in a certain product category. Marineland of the Pacific can position itself not as a "recreational theme park" but as an "educational institution."
- *Quality or price positioning:* The product is positioned as offering the best value. Busch Gardens can position itself as offering the "best value" for the money.

which positioning to promote?

Suppose a company has identified four alternative positioning platforms: technology, cost, quality, and service (Table 11.2). It has one major competitor. Both companies stand at 8 on technology (1 = low score, 10 = high score), which means they both have good technology. The competitor has a better standing on cost (8 instead of 6). The company offers higher quality than its competitor (8 compared to 6). Finally, both companies provide below-average service.

table **11.2**			Method for Competitive–Advantage Selection			
(1)	**(2)**	**(3)**	**(4)**	**(5)**	**(6)**	**(7)**
			Importance of Improving	Affordability	Competitor's Ability to	
Competitive Advantage	Company Standing	Competitor Standing	Standing (H–M–L)*	and Speed (H–M–L)	Improve Standing (H–M–L)	Recommended Action
Technology	8	8	L	L	M	Hold
Cost	6	8	H	M	M	Monitor
Quality	8	6	L	L	H	Monitor
Service	4	3	H	H	L	Invest

*H=high; M=medium; L=low

It would seem that the company should go after cost or service to improve its market appeal. However, other considerations arise. The first is how target customers feel about improvements in each of these attributes. Column 4 indicates that improvements in cost and service would be of high importance to customers, but can the company afford to make the improvements and how fast can it provide them? Column 5 shows that improving service would have high affordability and speed, but would the competitor be able to match the improved service? Column 6 shows that the competitor's ability to improve service is low. Based on this information, column 7 shows the appropriate actions to take. The one that makes the most sense is for the company to improve its service and promote this improvement. This was the conclusion Monsanto reached in one of its chemical markets. Monsanto hired additional technical service people. When they were trained and ready, Monsanto promoted itself as the "technical service leader."

communicating the company's positioning

To communicate a company or brand positioning, a marketing plan should include a *positioning statement*. The statement should follow the form: To *(target group and need)* our *(Brand)* is *(concept)* that *(point-of-difference)*.[8] For example: "To *busy professionals who need to stay organized, Palm Pilot is an electronic organizer that allows you to back up files on your PC more easily and reliably than competitive products.*" Sometimes the positioning statement is more detailed:

> *Mountain Dew:* To young, active soft-drink consumers who have little time for sleep, Mountain Dew is the soft drink that gives you more energy than any other brand because it has the highest level of caffeine. With Mountain Dew, you can stay alert and keep going even when you haven't been able to get a good night's sleep.[9]

Note that the positioning first states the product's membership in a category (e.g., Mountain Dew is a soft drink) and then shows its point-of-difference from other members of the group (e.g., has more caffeine). The product's membership in the category suggests the points-of-parity that it might have with other products in the category, but the case for the product rests on its points-of-difference. Sometimes the marketer will put the product in a surprisingly different category before indicating the points of difference.

Mountain Dew's Web site supports its positioning.

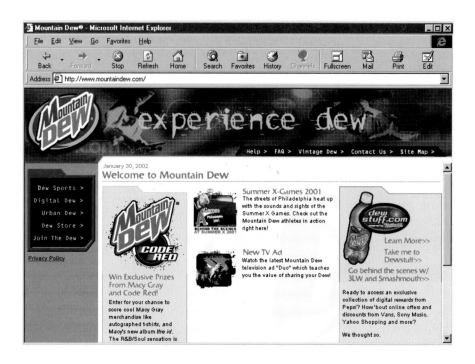

DiGiorno's pizza DiGiorno's is a frozen pizza whose crust rises when the pizza is heated. Instead of putting it in the frozen pizza category, the marketers positioned it in the delivered pizza category. Their ad shows party guests asking which pizza delivery service the host used, but he says: "It's not delivery, its DiGiorno!" This helped highlight DiGiorno's fresh quality and superior taste over the normal frozen pizza.[10]

Once the company has developed a clear positioning statement, it must communicate that positioning effectively through all the elements of the marketing mix. Suppose a company chooses the "best quality" positioning. Quality is communicated by choosing those physical signs and cues that people normally use to judge quality. Here are some examples:

A lawnmower manufacturer claims its lawn mower is "powerful" and has a noisy motor because buyers think noisy lawnmowers are more powerful.

A truck manufacturer undercoats the chassis not because it needs undercoating but because undercoating suggests concern for quality.

A car manufacturer makes cars with good-slamming doors because many buyers slam the doors in the showroom to test how well the car is built.

Ritz Carlton hotels signal high quality by training employees to answer calls within three rings, to answer with a genuine "smile" in their voices, and to be extremely knowledgeable about all hotel services.

Quality is also communicated through other marketing elements. A high price usually signals a premium-quality product. The product's quality image is also affected by packaging, distribution, advertising, and promotion. Here are some cases where a brand's quality image was hurt:

- A well-known frozen-food brand lost its prestige image by being on sale too often.
- A premium beer's image was hurt when it switched from bottles to cans.
- A highly regarded television receiver lost its quality image when mass-merchandise outlets began to carry it.

A manufacturer's reputation also contributes to the perception of quality. Certain companies are sticklers for quality; consumers expect Nestlé and IBM products to be well made. Smart companies communicate their quality to buyers and guarantee "customer satisfaction or your money back."

As important as positioning is to a company's success, most ads fail to communicate the company or the brand's positioning. Kevin Clancy, CEO of Copernicus, a marketing strategy consulting firm, examined 340 commercials and found that only 7 percent communicated any sort of positioning; and only 50 percent mentioned product features. Not only is this a waste of advertising money, but unpositioned brands in overcrowded categories tend to devolve into price-driven brands.[11]

adding further differentiation

The task of positioning is to deliver a central idea about a company or an offering to the target market. Positioning simplifies what we think of the entity. Differentiation goes beyond positioning to spin a complex web of differences characterizing that entity. We define **differentiation** as the process of adding a set of meaningful and valued differences to distinguish the company's offering from competitors' offerings. Consider IKEA.

IKEA   IKEA, the world's largest furniture retailer, is positioned as a company offering "good quality furniture at a low price"; but IKEA has spun further differences to distinguish itself from normal furniture stores. It operates an excellent restaurant in each store (rare among furniture stores); it offers child care services while the parents shop; it offers a membership program entitling members to special discounts on their purchases beyond the normal low price; and it mails out millions of catalogs featuring the latest furniture. All this creates a highly differentiated picture of IKEA in the target market's mind.

All products can be differentiated to some extent,[12] but not all brand differences are meaningful or worthwhile. A difference will be stronger to the extent that it satisfies the following criteria:

- *Important:* The difference delivers a highly valued benefit to a sufficient number of buyers.
- *Distinctive:* The difference is delivered in a distinctive way.
- *Superior:* The difference is superior to other ways of obtaining the benefit.
- *Preemptive:* The difference cannot be easily copied by competitors.
- *Affordable:* The buyer can afford to pay for the difference.
- *Profitable:* The company will find it profitable to introduce the difference.

Many companies have introduced differentiations that failed on one or more of these tests. The Westin Stamford hotel in Singapore advertises that it is the world's tallest hotel, but a hotel's height is not important to many tourists. Polaroid's Polarvision, although distinctive and preemptive, was inferior to another way of capturing motion—namely, video cameras. When the Turner Broadcasting System installed TV monitors to beam Cable News Network (CNN) to bored shoppers in store checkout lines, it did not pass the "superior" test. Customers were not looking for a new source of entertainment in supermarkets, and Turner took a $16 million tax write-down.

Carpenter, Glazer, and Nakamoto posit that brands can sometimes be successfully differentiated on irrelevant attributes.[13] Procter & Gamble differentiates its Folger's instant coffee by its "flaked coffee crystals" created through a "unique patented process." In reality, the coffee particle's shape is irrelevant because the crystal immediately dissolves in the hot water. Saying that a brand of coffee is "mountain grown" is irrelevant because most coffee is mountain grown. Alberto Culver's Alberto Natural Silk shampoo is advertised with the slogan "We put silk in a bottle." However, a company spokesman conceded that silk does not really do anything for hair.

Sony is a good example of a company that constantly comes up with new features and benefits. As soon as Sony develops a new product, it might assemble up to three teams to view the new product as if it were a competitor's. The first team thinks of minor improvements, the second team thinks of major improvements, and the third team thinks of ways to make the product obsolete.

A major chemical company held a brainstorming session and came up with a dozen ways to create extra value for customers, among them were: helping reduce process costs by improving yield and reducing waste; helping reduce inventory by consignments, just-in-time delivery, and reduced cycle time; helping reduce administrative costs by simplified billing and electronic data interchange; improving safety for customer's employees; and reducing price to the customer by substituting components and reducing supplier costs. For more examples of differentiation, see "Marketing for the New Economy: Airlines Show They Aren't Commodities as They Jockey for Position."

Crego and Schiffrin have proposed that customer-centered organizations should study what customers value and then prepare an offering that exceeds their expectations.[14] They see this as a three-step process:

1. *Defining the customer value model:* The company first lists all the product and service factors that might influence the target customers' perception of value.

marketing for the new economy

Airlines Show They Aren't Commodities as They Jockey for Position

It used to be that air travel was regarded as a commodity. In 1978, deregulation kicked off an era of fierce competition. It also opened the way for some upstart "Davids" to differentiate themselves and steal passengers from airline "Goliaths." Two airlines that have been successful at differentiating themselves are Virgin Atlantic and Southwest Airlines.

Virgin Atlantic
Founded in 1983, this classy, iconoclastic airline was widely predicted to follow Laker Airway's Skytrain, a no-frills airline started by British businessman Freddy Laker, as another doomed transatlantic start-up. But in its 18-year history, Virgin has shaken up the airline industry. Richard Branson, the company's founder and current chairman and CEO, is a charismatic and talented entrepreneur. At a press conference where he launched the airline, Branson appeared wearing an old-fashioned leather flying jacket, goggles, and a helmet. When asked why he was going into the airline business, Branson quipped, "If we didn't do it, nobody else would have." Branson's personality has been a point-of-difference for Virgin Airlines. His most daring stunts, including several failed attempts to circumnavigate the globe in a hot air balloon, give the airline a certain cachet.

Southwest Airlines
The Dallas-based airline carved its niche in short-haul flights with low prices and no frills. Two Texans, Rollin King and Herb Kelleher, founded the company, originally called Air Southwest, in 1967. Southwest was a commuter service linking Dallas, Houston, and San Antonio. Eventually, it grew into a national airline operating in 55 cities across 29 states. By flying from smaller airports and avoiding major airport hubs, the airline has avoided direct competition from other airlines. Southwest also offers many short-hop flights connecting nearby cities, and its low prices on those flights lure passengers who would normally drive. The company reduced costs further by offering only basic in-flight service (no meals, no movies), and for many years the transfer of luggage between airlines was the passengers' responsibility.

Southwest knew that it could not differentiate on price alone, because competitors could easily muscle into the market with their own cheaper versions. The airline has distinguished itself as a "fun" airline, noted for humorous in-flight commentary from pilots and cabin crew members. Herb Kelleher has been known to dress up like Elvis Presley to greet passengers on occasion, and even handed out peanuts on a flight one Easter while dressed in a bunny suit. Another popular feature of Southwest flights is the first-come, first-served open seating: Passengers are given numbered cards based on when they arrive at the gate.

Kelleher, who stepped down from his CEO position in 2001, saw the company through unprecedented growth for a start-up airline. Today, Southwest is the nation's seventh-largest airline, and holds the distinction of being the only low-fare airline to achieve long-term success.

Sources: Jane Woolridge, "Baby-boom Airline Is Unknown, Cheap," *San Diego Union-Tribune,* December 30, 1984; Melanie Wells, "Red Baron: The Sun Never Sets on Richard Branson's Empire," *Forbes,* July 3, 2000; Katrina Brooker, "The Chairman of the Board Looks Back," *Fortune,* May 28, 2001.

2. *Building the customer value hierarchy:* The company now assigns each factor to one of four groups: basic, expected, desired, and unanticipated. Consider the set of factors at a fine restaurant:
   - *Basic:* The food is edible and delivered in a timely fashion. (If this is all the restaurant does right, the customer would normally not be satisfied.)
   - *Expected:* There is good china and tableware, a linen tablecloth and napkin, flowers, discreet service, and well-prepared food. (These factors make the offering acceptable, but not exceptional.)
   - *Desired:* The restaurant is pleasant and quiet, and the food is especially good and interesting.
   - *Unanticipated:* The restaurant serves a complimentary sorbet between the courses and places candy on the table after the last course is served.
3. *Deciding on the customer value package:* Now the company chooses that combination of tangible and intangible items, experiences, and outcomes designed to outperform competitors and win the customers' delight and loyalty.

differentiation tools

The number of differentiation opportunities varies with the type of industry. The Boston Consulting Group (BCG) has distinguished four types of industries based on the number of available competitive advantages and their size (see Figure 11.2):

figure **11.2**

The BCG Competitive Advantage Matrix

1. *Volume industry:* One in which companies can gain only a few, but rather large, competitive advantages. In the construction-equipment industry, a company can strive for the low-cost position or the highly differentiated position and win big on either basis. Profitability is correlated with company size and market share.
2. *Stalemated industry:* One in which there are few potential competitive advantages and each is small. In the steel industry, it is hard to differentiate the product or decrease manufacturing costs. Companies can try to hire better salespeople, entertain more lavishly, and the like, but these are small advantages. Profitability is unrelated to company market share.
3. *Fragmented industry:* One in which companies face many opportunities for differentiation, but each opportunity for competitive advantage is small. A restaurant can differentiate in many ways but end up not gaining a large market share. Both small and large restaurants can be profitable or unprofitable.
4. *Specialized industry:* One in which companies face many differentiation opportunities, and each differentiation can have a high payoff. Among companies making specialized machinery for selected market segments, some small companies can be as profitable as some large companies.

Miland Lele observed that companies differ in their potential *maneuverability* along five dimensions: *target market, product, place (channels), promotion,* and *price.*[15] The company's freedom of maneuver is affected by the industry structure and the firm's position in the industry. For each potential maneuver, the company needs to estimate the return. Those maneuvers that promise the highest return define the company's *strategic leverage.* Companies in a stalemated industry have very little maneuverability and strategic leverage, and those in specialized industries enjoy great maneuverability and strategic leverage.

Yet even in stalemated, commodity-type industries, some real or image differentiation is possible. Commodities such as bananas, salt, chicken, and milk can be differentiated. Shoppers look for the Chiquita label on bananas, the Dole label on pineapples, and the Green Giant on frozen vegetables; these brands give them an assurance of quality. Most people buy Morton salt and pay a little more; and they prefer Frank Perdue's chicken because "it takes a tough man to make a tender chicken." There are now several varieties of milk—calcium fortified, lactose free, soymilk, and so on. The marketer must start with the belief that "you can differentiate anything."

Here we will examine how a company can differentiate its market offering along five dimensions: product, services, personnel, channel, and image (see Table 11.3).

table **11.3**

Differentiation
Variables

Product	Services	Personnel	Channel	Image
Form	Ordering ease	Competence	Coverage	Symbols
Features	Delivery	Courtesy	Expertise	Media
Performance	Installation	Credibility	Performance	Atmosphere
Conformance	Customer training	Reliability		Events
Durability	Customer consulting	Responsiveness		
Reliability	Maintenance and repair	Communication		
Repairability	Miscellaneous			
Style				
Design				

product differentiation

Physical products vary in their potential for differentiation. At one extreme we find products that allow little variation: chicken, steel, aspirin. Yet even here, some differentiation is possible. Procter & Gamble makes several brands of laundry detergent, each with a separate brand identity. At the other extreme are products capable of high differentiation, such as automobiles, commercial buildings, and furniture. Here the seller faces an abundance of design parameters, including form, features, performance quality, conformance quality, durability, reliability, repairability, style, and design.[16]

FORM   Many products can be differentiated in *form*—the size, shape, or physical structure of a product. Consider the many possible forms taken by products such as aspirin. Although aspirin is essentially a commodity, it can be differentiated by dosage size, shape, color, coating, or action time.

FEATURES   Most products can be offered with varying features that supplement the product's basic function. Being the first to introduce valued new features is one of the most effective ways to compete. Oral-B managed to differentiate its toothbrush by introducing a blue dye in the center bristles that fades and tells customers when they need a new toothbrush.

General Motors   General Motors offers the OnStar system on selected vehicles. It includes GPS (global positioning system) for locating the car's exact position. The driver can locate the nearest ATM, hospital, convenience store, gas station and hotel, and even book a room. The driver can press a button in case of an emergency to get immediate aid.

McDonald's   McDonald's has added PlayLands at a number of its U.S. and Mexican restaurants to cater to young customers. In Paraguay, McDonald's has installed a number of computer stations to cater to Internet-inclined customers.

How can a company identify and select appropriate new features? It can ask recent buyers: How do you like the product? Are there any features we could add that would improve your satisfaction? How much would you pay for each? How do you feel about the following features that other customers have suggested?

table **11.4**

Feature	Company Cost (a)	Customer Value (b)	Customer Value/ Customer Cost (c=b/a)
Rear-window defrosting	$100	$ 200	2
Cruise control	600	600	1
Automatic transmission	800	2,400	3

Measuring Customer
Effectiveness Value

The next task is to decide which features are worth adding. For each potential feature, the company should calculate *customer value* versus *company cost*. Suppose an auto manufacturer is considering the three possible improvements shown in Table 11.4. Rear-window defrosting would add $100 of cost per car at the factory level. The average customer said this feature was worth $200. The company could therefore generate $2 of incremental customer satisfaction for every $1 increase in company cost. Looking at the other two features, it appears that automatic transmission would create the most customer value per dollar of company cost. The company would also need to consider how many people want each feature, how long it would take to introduce each feature, and whether competitors could easily copy the feature.

Companies must also think in terms of feature bundles or packages. Auto companies often manufacture cars at several "trim levels." This lowers manufacturing and inventory costs. Each company must decide whether to offer feature customization at a higher cost or a few standard packages at a lower cost.

PERFORMANCE QUALITY   Most products are established at one of four performance levels: low, average, high, or superior. **Performance quality** is the level at which the product's primary characteristics operate. The important question here is: Does offering higher product performance produce higher profitability? The Strategic Planning Institute studied the impact of higher relative product quality and found a significantly positive correlation between relative product quality and return on investment (ROI). High-quality business units earned more because premium quality allowed them to charge a premium price; they benefited from more repeat purchasing, consumer loyalty, and positive word of mouth; and their costs of delivering more quality were not much higher than for business units producing low quality.

Quality's link to profitability does not mean that the firm should design the highest performance level possible. The manufacturer must design a performance level appropriate to the target market and competitors' performance levels. A company must also manage performance quality through time. Continuously improving the product often produces the highest return and market share. The second strategy is to maintain product quality at a given level. Many companies leave quality unaltered after its initial formulation unless glaring faults or opportunities occur. The third strategy is to reduce product quality through time. Some companies cut quality to offset rising costs; others reduce quality deliberately in order to increase current profits, although this course of action often hurts long-run profitability. See what happened to Schlitz.

Schlitz   Schlitz, the number-two beer brand in the United States in the 1960s and 1970s, was driven into the dust because management adopted a financially motivated strategy to increase its short-term profits and curry favor with shareholders. When it decided to cut the aging time and use less expensive hops, sales of Schlitz dropped from 17.8 million barrels in 1974 to 7.5 million in 1980. By then, its stock price had plummeted to less than 9 percent of its 1974 value. Heavy marketing expenditures and a product reformulation back to the classic recipe could not revive the brand.[17]

CONFORMANCE QUALITY   Buyers expect products to have a high **conformance quality**, which is the degree to which all the produced units are identical and meet the promised specifications. Suppose a Porsche 944 is designed to accelerate to 60 miles per hour within 10 seconds. If every Porsche 944 coming off the assembly line does this, the model is said to have high conformance quality. The problem with low conformance quality is that the product will disappoint some buyers.

DURABILITY   **Durability**, a measure of the product's expected operating life under natural or stressful conditions, is a valued attribute for certain products. Buyers will generally pay more for vehicles and kitchen appliances that have a reputation for being long lasting. However, this rule is subject to some qualifications. The extra price must not be excessive. Furthermore, the product must not be subject to rapid technological obsolescence, as is the case with personal computers and videocameras.

RELIABILITY   Buyers normally will pay a premium for more reliable products. **Reliability** is a measure of the probability that a product will not malfunction or fail within a specified time period. Maytag, which manufactures major home appliances, has an outstanding reputation for creating reliable appliances.

REPAIRABILITY   Buyers prefer products that are easy to repair. **Repairability** is a measure of the ease of fixing a product when it malfunctions or fails. An automobile made with standard parts that are easily replaced has high repairability. Ideal repairability would exist if users could fix the product themselves with little cost in money or time. Some products include a diagnostic feature that allows service people to correct a problem over the telephone or advise the user how to correct it. Many computer hardware and software companies offer technical support over the phone, or by fax or e-mail. Consider the steps taken by Cisco.

Cisco   Cisco, a major manufacturer of Internet components, now conducts over 85 percent of all sales via the Web. Its customers often need answers to questions about its equipment, and Cisco needs a large staff for its telephone support system. To handle the problem, Cisco put together a Knowledge Base of Frequently Asked Questions (FAQs) on its Web site. Cisco estimates that its Knowledge Base handles about 80 percent of the roughly 4 million monthly requests for information, which saves the company $250 million annually. Each new call and solution goes to a tech writer who adds the solution to the FAQs, thus reducing the number of future phone calls.[18]

STYLE   *Style* describes the product's look and feel to the buyer. Car buyers pay a premium for Jaguars because of their extraordinary look. Aesthetics play a key role in such brands as Absolut vodka, Apple computers, Montblanc pens, Godiva chocolate, and Harley-Davidson motorcycles.[19]

Starbucks   Integrated retail design has played a large role in Starbucks' ability to charge $2 for a cup of coffee. The elements include light wood tones at the counters; polished dark-marble countertops; lamps, walls, and tables imitating coffee tones from green to light and darker browns; comfortable chairs, well-designed cups; and coffee packages smooth and soft to the touch.

Style has the advantage of creating distinctiveness that is difficult to copy. On the negative side, strong style does not always mean high performance. A car may look sensational but spend a lot of time in the repair shop.

We must include packaging as a styling weapon, especially in food products, cosmetics, toiletries, and small consumer appliances. The package is the buyer's first encounter with the product and is capable of turning the buyer on or off. For Arizona Iced Tea, packaging is definitely a turn-on.[20]

Arizona Iced Tea   Arizona Iced Tea marketer Ferolito, Vultaggio & Sons has gained success by taking a rather straightforward drink—tea—and putting it into unusual bottles with elaborate designs. The wide-mouthed, long-necked bottles have been trendsetters in the New Age beverage category, and customers often buy the tea just for the bottle. Because consumers are known to hang on to their empties or convert them into lamps and other household objects, the company uses unique bottle shapes for its line extensions. It uses a ridged grip design on Arizona Rx Elixirs, miniature jugs for Arizona Iced Coffees, and a pint-sized deep-blue urn for Blue Luna Café Latte.[21]

DESIGN: THE INTEGRATING FORCE   As competition intensifies, design offers a potent way to differentiate and position a company's products and services.[22] In increasingly fast-paced markets, price and technology are not enough. Design is the factor that will often give a company its competitive edge. Design is the totality of features that affect how a product looks and functions in terms of customer requirements.

Design is particularly important in making and marketing retail services, apparel, packaged goods, and durable equipment. All the qualities we have discussed are design parameters. The designer has to figure out how much to invest in form, feature development, performance, conformance, durability, reliability, repairability, and style. To the company, a well-designed product is one that is easy to manufacture and distribute. To the customer, a well-designed product is one that is pleasant to look at and easy to open, install, use, repair, and dispose of. The designer has to take all these factors into account.

Here are two companies with products that embody the form-follows-function maxim.

Apple Computers   Who said that computers have to be beige and boxy? Apple's newest computer, the iMac, is anything but. The iMac features a sleek, curvy monitor and hard drive, all in one unit, in a translucent casing. There is no clunky tower or desktop hard drive to clutter up the office area. There is also no floppy drive, simply because Apple feels the floppy is on the verge of extinction. With its one-button Internet access, this machine is designed specifically for cruising the Internet (that is what the "i" in "iMac" stands for). Only one month after the iMac hit the stores in the summer of 1998, it was the number-two best-selling computer. Strong iMac sales contributed to earnings of $309 million in 1998 and $601 million in 1999.[23]

Black & Decker   What could be handier than a flashlight you do not have to hold while probing under the sink for the cause of a leaky faucet? Black & Decker's Snakelight looks just like its name and attaches itself to almost anything, leaving your hands free. It can also stand up like an illuminated cobra to light your workspace. In a market where the average flashlight cost is just $6, consumers are paying $30 for this flashlight, which was a gold medalist in the Industrial Design Excellence Awards (IDEA).[24]

Certain countries are winning on design: Italian design in apparel and furniture; Scandinavian design for functionality, aesthetics, and environmental consciousness. Braun, a German division of Gillette, has elevated design to a high art in its electric shavers, coffeemakers, hair dryers, and food processors. The company's design department enjoys equal status with engineering and manufacturing. The Danish firm Bang & Olufsen has received many kudos for the design of its stereos, TV equipment, and telephones.

services differentiation

When the physical product cannot easily be differentiated, the key to competitive success may lie in adding valued services and improving their quality. The main service differentiators are ordering ease, delivery, installation, customer training, customer consulting, and maintenance and repair.

ORDERING EASE   *Ordering ease* refers to how easy it is for the customer to place an order with the company. Baxter Healthcare has eased the ordering process by supplying hospitals with computer terminals through which they send orders directly to Baxter. Many banks now provide home banking software to help customers get information and do transactions more efficiently. Consumers are now even able to order and receive groceries without going to the supermarket.

Peapod   Peapod (*www.peapod.com*) takes computer orders and delivers groceries to the doors of over 120,000 customers in cities such as Boston, Chicago, and Washington, D.C. As the nation's largest online grocer, Peapod allows consumers to choose from between 8,000 and 10,000 food items online, and then home-delivers customers' orders as soon as the next day after they are placed. While several competitors struggled to avoid the dot-com crash (and most failed), Peapod reported achieving an operating profit in its Chicago market in the first quarter of 2001. It was subsequently purchased by Dutch food retailer Royal Ahold. The service has been integrated with Ahold's brick-and-mortar supermarket companies in the United States.[25]

DELIVERY   *Delivery* refers to how well the product or service is delivered to the customer. It includes speed, accuracy, and care attending the delivery process. Today's customers have grown to expect delivery speed: pizza delivered in one-half hour, film developed in one hour, eyeglasses made in one hour, cars lubricated in 15 minutes. A company such as Deluxe Check Printers, Inc., has built an impressive reputation for shipping out its checks one day after receiving an order—without being late once in 18 years. Levi Strauss, Benetton, and The Limited have adopted computerized *quick*

The home page for Peapod, the nation's largest online grocer.

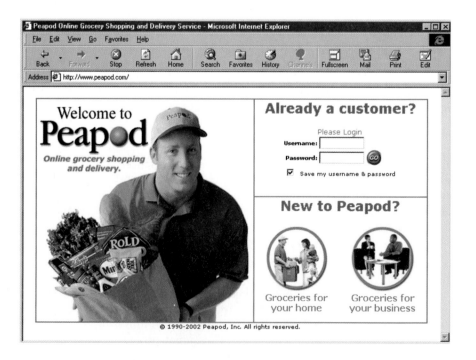

response systems (QRS) that link the information systems of their suppliers, manufacturing plants, distribution centers, and retailing outlets. Buyers will often choose a supplier with a better reputation for speedy or on-time delivery.[26]

Krones   Krones, the world leader in bottle labeling machines, deploys 250 service and installation technicians around the world. The company stores data for each machine, totaling 20,000, in its central computer. These data can be made available at every one of its locations in the world within half a minute. The data are fed directly into numerically controlled machines, and the spare parts are manufactured immediately. Parts ordered before 7:00 A.M. are sent in the afternoon, by truck, to Frankfurt Airport; from there they are air freighted the same evening to their destination. At the same time, the subsidiary receives the flight and freight numbers so that the shipment can be cleared through customs without delay.[27]

Cemex   Cemex, a giant cement company based in Mexico, has transformed the cement business by promising to deliver concrete faster than pizza. Cemex equips every truck with a *global positioning system* (GPS) so that its real-time location is known and full information is available to drivers and dispatchers. Cemex is able to promise that if your load is more than 10 minutes late, you get a 20 percent discount. It has managed to digitalize the cement business; if one can digitalize the cement business, any business can be digitalized![28]

INSTALLATION   *Installation* refers to the work done to make a product operational in its planned location. Buyers of heavy equipment expect good installation service. Differentiating at this point in the consumption chain is particularly important for companies with complex products. Ease of installation becomes a true selling point, especially when the target market is technology novices who are notoriously intolerant of on-screen messages such as "Disk Error 23."

Pacific Bell   Consumers wishing to connect to the Internet using a high-speed digital subscriber line (DSL) often require the help of a trained phone-company technician to help them with the setup. Even with trained assistance, the process can take hours, or in some cases days, to complete. To make installation easier for its new DSL customers, in 2000 Pacific Bell developed installation kits that included an interactive software setup program. The company found that most consumers who used the kits could complete their DSL setup in less than an hour.[29]

CUSTOMER TRAINING   *Customer training* refers to training the customer's employees to use the vendor's equipment properly and efficiently. General Electric not only sells and installs expensive X-ray equipment in hospitals; it also gives extensive training to users of this equipment. McDonald's requires its new franchisees to attend Hamburger University in Oakbrook, Illinois, for two weeks, to learn how to manage their franchise properly.

CUSTOMER CONSULTING   *Customer consulting* refers to data, information systems, and advice services that the seller offers to buyers. One of the best providers of value-adding consulting service is Milliken & Company.

Milliken & Company   Milliken sells shop towels to industrial launderers, who rent them to factories. Although the towels are physically similar to competitors' towels, Milliken charges a higher price and enjoys the leading market share. How can it do this? Milliken adds continuous service enhancements for customers. It trains customers' salespeople, supplies prospect leads and sales-promotional material, supplies online computer-order-entry and route-optimization systems, does marketing research, sponsors quality-improvement workshops, and sends its salespeople to work with customers. Customers are more than willing to pay a price premium because the extra services improve their profitability.[30]

In consumer marketing, Rite Aid drugstores has launched a successful consumer consulting initiative.

Rite Aid   With a mandate to increase sales, Rite Aid lowered prices, and in 1997 the company launched the Vitamin Institute, designed to make consumers more comfortable asking for help at the pharmacy window. Rite Aid pharmacists now provide interested customers with available research to help them make more educated judgments. The Vitamin Institute has been hugely successful, but Rite Aid's approach is actually reminiscent of the "good old days," when people relied on their local druggists, sometimes even more than their doctors. Rite Aid extended its in-store consultation practice to the Internet when it added an "Ask Your Pharmacist" feature to its Web site.[31]

MAINTENANCE AND REPAIR   *Maintenance and repair* describes the service program for helping customers keep purchased products in good working order. Consider Hewlett-Packard's e-support system.

Hewlett-Packard   Hewlett-Packard is one of several PC manufacturers offering online technical support, or "e-support," for their customers. In the event of a service problem, customers can use various online tools to find a solution. Those aware of the specific problem can search an online database for fixes; those unaware can use diagnostic software that finds the problem and searches the online database for an automatic fix. Customers can also seek online help from a technician. "Research suggests PC users want help, but they don't necessarily want problems solved for them," says Bruce Greenwood, a Hewlett-Packard marketing manager. "Many users want to understand the issues and their solutions so they can become more self-sufficient."[32]

Hewlett-Packard's online support page, which allows customers to solve their own problems.

MISCELLANEOUS SERVICES   Companies can find other ways to differentiate customer services. They can offer an improved product warranty or maintenance contract. They can offer rewards.

MacMillan and McGrath say companies have opportunities to differentiate at every stage of the consumption chain. They point out that companies can even differentiate at the point when their product is no longer in use:[33]

Canon   Canon has developed a system that allows customers to return spent printer cartridges at Canon's expense. The cartridges are then rehabilitated and sold as such. Canon makes it easy for customers to return used cartridges: All they need to do is drop the prepaid package off at a United Parcel Service collection station. Canon reported collection of 12,175 tons of toner cartridges worldwide in 1999, which represented a 100 percent recycling ratio. The program has helped build Canon's reputation as an environmentally friendly company.[34]

personnel differentiation

Companies can gain a strong competitive advantage through having better-trained people. Singapore Airlines enjoys an excellent reputation in large part because of its flight attendants. The McDonald's people are courteous, the IBM people are professional, and the Disney people are upbeat. The sales forces of such companies as General Electric, Cisco, Frito-Lay, Northwestern Mutual Life, and Pfizer enjoy an excellent reputation.[35] Better-trained personnel exhibit six characteristics: *Competence*: They possess the required skill and knowledge; *courtesy*: They are friendly, respectful, and considerate; *credibility*: They are trustworthy; *reliability*: They perform the service consistently and accurately; *responsiveness*: They respond quickly to customers' requests and problems; and *communication*: They make an effort to understand the customer and communicate clearly.[36]

In an age when competitors can knock off products or services in an instant, some savvy companies are marketing their employees' unique know-how.

The Orvis Company   The Orvis Company is a mail-order and retail supplier of "country" clothing, gifts, and sporting gear that competes with the likes of L.L. Bean and Eddie Bauer. Orvis, founded in 1856, differentiates itself by selling its long history of fly-fishing expertise. Its fly-fishing schools, all situated in scenic areas from California to Florida, make a tough sport accessible to novices. The schools, not coincidentally, are usually located near Orvis retail outlets. Orvis had sales of less than $1 million in 1968, when it opened its first fly-fishing school. Now company sales are at about $500 million. Although actual fly-fishing products account for only a small portion of this, catalog manager and vice president Tom Rosenbauer says, "Without our fly-fishing heritage, we'd be just another rag vendor."[37]

channel differentiation

Companies can achieve competitive advantage through the way they design their distribution channels' coverage, expertise, and performance. Caterpillar's success in the construction-equipment industry is based partly on superior channel development. Its dealers are found in more locations than competitors' dealers, and they are typically better trained and perform more reliably. Dell in computers and Avon in cosmetics distinguish themselves by developing and managing high-quality direct-marketing channels. Iams pet food provides an instructive case on how developing a different channel can pay off.

Iams Pet Food   Back in 1946, when Paul Iams founded the company in Dayton, Ohio, pet food was cheap, not too nutritious, and sold exclusively in supermarkets and the occasional feed store. Iams went instead to regional veterinarians, breeders, and pet stores. After the company implemented this marketing strategy on a national scale in the early 1970s, annual sales soared from $16 million in 1982 to $800 million in 1999. Procter & Gamble bought Iams for $2.1 billion in 2000 and decided to expand distribution into supermarkets and other major retail outlets, but Iams' premium brand, Eukanuba, would continue to be available only in specialty outlets.[38]

image differentiation

Buyers respond differently to company and brand images. The primary way to account for Marlboro's extraordinary worldwide market share (around 30 percent) is that Marlboro's "macho cowboy" image has struck a responsive chord with much of the cigarette-smoking public. Wine and liquor companies also work hard to develop distinctive images for their brands.

Identity and image need to be distinguished. *Identity* comprises the ways that a company aims to identify or position itself or its product. *Image* is the way the public perceives the company or its products. Image is affected by many factors beyond the company's control, as the case of Vans' counterculture marketing versus Nike, Reebok, and Adidas shows.

Vans   In the 1990s, several shoe companies found success marketing "counterculture" alternatives to established athletic shoe companies like Nike, Reebok, and Adidas. Vans Inc., a Santa Fe Springs, California, shoe and apparel manufacturer, started in 1966 selling handmade shoes from a single retail location. The publicly traded company now does big business in retail centers and company-owned stores throughout the nation; sales topped $274 million in 2000. Its popularity among action sports enthusiasts is bolstered by a marketing program that includes brand name indoor and outdoor skate parks, sponsorship of the Vans Warped Tour summer concert series, signature shoe models associated with famous pro athletes, and offbeat advertising.[39]

An effective identity does three things. First, it establishes the product's character and value proposition. Second, it conveys this character in a distinctive way. Third, it delivers emotional power beyond a mental image. For the identity to work, it must be conveyed through every available communication vehicle and brand contact. It must be worked into ads and media that convey a story, a mood, a claim—something distinctive. It should be diffused in annual reports, brochures, catalogs, packaging, company stationery, and business cards. If "IBM means service," this message must be expressed in symbols, colors and slogans, atmosphere, events, and employee behavior.

SYMBOLS, COLORS, SLOGANS, SPECIAL ATTRIBUTES   Identity can be built by strong symbols. The company can choose a symbol such as the lion (Harris Bank), apple (Apple Computer), or doughboy (Pillsbury). A brand can be built around a famous person, as with Elizabeth Taylor perfumes. Companies may choose a color identifier such as blue (IBM), yellow (Kodak), or red (Campbell Soup), or a specific piece of sound or music.

Every company would benefit by adopting and repeating a short slogan or "tag line" after every mention of its name. AT&T called itself "The Right Choice"; Ford said "Quality is Our Number One Job"; and DuPont described its output as "Better Living Through Chemistry." The slogan must be chosen carefully, however. Holiday Inns once described itself as the "No Surprise" hotel. After several embarrassments, it quickly withdrew this slogan. Philips, the large Dutch electronics firm, used the slogan "From

Sand to Chips" in an effort to convey that it made lightbulbs and silicon chips, all from sand. People not only did not understand this, but the slogan was about the company, not the consumer.

A company can further differentiate its image using its special attributes, such as the company's heritage, its being the first to enter the field, its being the largest or oldest company in its industry, or its being the most preferred according to opinion polls.[40]

PHYSICAL PLANT   The seller's physical space can be another powerful image generator. Hyatt Regency hotels developed a distinctive image through its atrium lobbies. A bank that wants to convey the image of a safe bank must communicate this through the building's architecture, interior design, layout, colors, materials, and furnishings.

Companies can create a strong image by inviting prospects and customers to visit their well-laid-out headquarters and factories. Boeing, Ben & Jerry's, Hershey's, Saturn, and Crayola all sponsor excellent company tours that draw millions of visitors a year.[41] Companies such as Hallmark and Kohler have built corporate museums at their headquarters that display their history and the drama of producing and marketing their products.

EVENTS AND SPONSORSHIPS   A company can build its brand image through creating or sponsoring various events. Event marketers have favored sports events and are now using other venues such as art museums, zoos, or ice shows to entertain clients and employees. AT&T and IBM sponsor symphony performances and art exhibits; Visa is an active sponsor of the Olympics; Harley-Davidson sponsors annual motorcycle rallies; and Perrier sponsors sports events. Companies are searching for better ways to quantify the benefits of sponsorship and they are demanding greater accountability from event owners and organizers.

Companies can also create events designed to surprise the public and create a buzz. Many amount to guerrilla marketing tactics. Here are some examples:

- Driver 2, a new car-chase video game, arranged for a convoy of 20 car wrecks with smoke pouring from their engines to crawl through Manhattan and Los Angeles to attract attention to the new game.
- Ask Jeeves, the Internet search engine, sent 35 actors in British butler's outfits to guide visitors to their seats and answer tennis trivia questions at the U.S. Open tennis tournament.
- Kibu.com pays hundreds of school girls to do "peer marketing" by hanging around with their peers, handing out free lip gloss, and talking up Kibu's cosmetic site.[42]

The increased use of attention-getting events is a response to the fragmentation of media: Consumers can turn to hundreds of cable channels, thousands of magazine titles, and millions of Internet pages. Events can create attention, although whether they have a lasting effect on brand awareness, knowledge, or preference will vary considerably, depending on the quality of the product, the event itself, and its execution.

USING MULTIPLE IMAGE-BUILDING TECHNIQUES   Swatch watch provides an excellent example of how to use multiple image-building techniques to etch a lasting image in the public's mind.

Swatch   Nicholas G. Hayek, Swatch's founder, launched Swatch watches in 1983 by hanging a 500-foot-long sign from the tallest bank in Frankfurt. Within a few weeks, every German knew Swatch. Swatch is a lightweight, water-resistant, shockproof electronic analog watch with a wide variety of colorful faces and bands celebrating famous artists, sports and space events, and anniversaries. Over 200 million Swatches have been sold in over 70 markets worldwide. Here are some examples of Swatch's promotion and advertising:

Swatch issues new watches throughout the year but launches limited editions of "snazzy" watch designs only twice a year. Only Swatch Club members can bid to buy them. Swatch may produce only 40,000 units and yet receive orders from 100,000 or more collectors. The company will sponsor a drawing to choose the lucky collectors who can buy the watch.

Christie's, the auction house, holds periodic auctions of early Swatch watches. One collector paid $60,000 for one of the rarer ones.

Swatch continues to innovate and keep people buzzing about its state-of-the-art products. Alongside the standard plastic watches there are new developments such as the Irony (a metal Swatch), a light-powered Swatch Solar, and a melodious alarm clock called the Swatch Musicall. Swatch has created the world's first pager in a wristwatch, the Swatch the Beep, as well as an "e-watch" equipped with electronic mail and Internet access.

Swatch clearly has written the marketing book on how to build a cult following by applying superior styling, merchandising, and promotion.[43]

product life-cycle marketing strategies

A company's positioning and differentiation strategy must change as the product, market, and competitors change over time. Here we will describe the concept of the product life cycle (PLC) and the normal changes as the product passes through each life-cycle stage.

To say that a product has a life cycle is to assert four things:

1. Products have a limited life.
2. Product sales pass through distinct stages, each posing different challenges, opportunities, and problems to the seller.
3. Profits rise and fall at different stages of the product life cycle.
4. Products require different marketing, financial, manufacturing, purchasing, and human resource strategies in each life-cycle stage.

product life cycles

Most product life-cycle curves are portrayed as bell-shaped (see Figure 11.3). This curve is typically divided into four stages: introduction, growth, maturity, and decline.[44]

1. *Introduction:* A period of slow sales growth as the product is introduced in the market. Profits are nonexistent because of the heavy expenses incurred with product introduction.
2. *Growth:* A period of rapid market acceptance and substantial profit improvement.

figure **11.3**

Sales and Profit Life Cycles

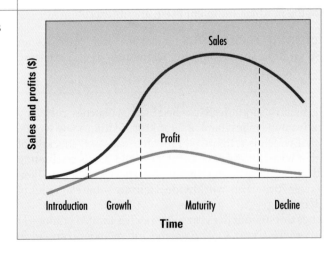

| figure **11.4** | Common Product Life–Cycle Patterns |

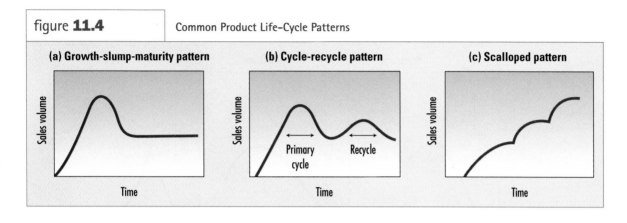

(a) Growth-slump-maturity pattern

Sales volume

Time

(b) Cycle-recycle pattern

Sales volume

Primary cycle

Recycle

Time

(c) Scalloped pattern

Sales volume

Time

3. *Maturity:* A period of a slowdown in sales growth because the product has achieved acceptance by most potential buyers. Profits stabilize or decline because of increased competition.
4. *Decline:* The period when sales show a downward drift and profits erode.

The PLC concept can be used to analyze a product category (liquor), a product form (white liquor), a product (vodka), or a brand (Smirnoff). Not all products exhibit a bell-shaped PLC.[45] Three common alternate patterns are shown in Figure 11.4. Figure 11.4(a) shows a *growth-slump-maturity pattern*, often characteristic of small kitchen appliances. Some years ago, sales of electric knives grew rapidly when the product was first introduced and then fell to a "petrified" level. The petrified level is sustained by late adopters buying the product for the first time and early adopters replacing the product.

The *cycle-recycle pattern* in Figure 11.4(b) often describes the sales of new drugs. The pharmaceutical company aggressively promotes its new drug, and this produces the first cycle. Later, sales start declining and the company gives the drug another promotion push, which produces a second cycle (usually of smaller magnitude and duration).[46]

Another common pattern is the *scalloped PLC* in Figure 11.4(c). Here sales pass through a succession of life cycles based on the discovery of new-product characteristics, uses, or users. Nylon's sales, for example, show a scalloped pattern because of the many new uses—parachutes, hosiery, shirts, carpeting, boat sails, automobile tires—that continue to be discovered over time.[47]

STYLE, FASHION, AND FAD LIFE CYCLES   Three special categories of product life cycles should be distinguished—styles, fashions, and fads (Figure 11.5). A **style** is a basic and distinctive mode of expression appearing in a field of human endeavor. Styles appear in homes (colonial, ranch, Cape Cod); clothing (formal, casual, funky); and art (realistic, surrealistic, abstract). A style can last for generations, and go in and out of vogue. A **fashion** is a currently accepted or popular style in a given field. Fashions pass through four stages:[48] distinctiveness, emulation, mass-fashion, and decline.

The length of a fashion cycle is hard to predict. Chester Wasson believes that fashions end because they represent a purchase compromise, and consumers start looking for missing attributes.[49] For example, as automobiles become smaller, they become less comfortable, and then a growing number of buyers start wanting larger cars. Furthermore, too many consumers adopt the fashion, thus turning others away. William Reynolds suggests that the length of a particular fashion cycle depends on the extent to which the fashion meets a genuine need, is consistent with other trends in the society, satisfies societal norms and values, and does not exceed technological limits as it develops.[50]

Fads are fashions that come quickly into public view, are adopted with great zeal, peak early, and decline very fast. Their acceptance cycle is short, and they tend to attract only a limited following of those who are searching for excitement or want to distinguish

figure **11.5**

Style, Fashion, and Fad
Life Cycles

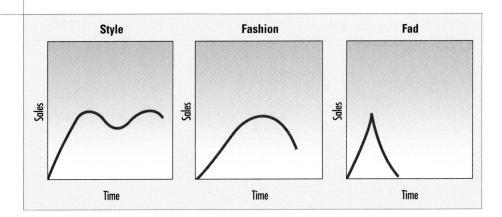

themselves from others. They often have a novel or capricious aspect, such as body piercing and tattooing. Fads do not survive because they do not normally satisfy a strong need. The marketing winners are those who recognize fads early and leverage them into products with staying power. Here is a success story of a company that managed to extend a fad's life span:

Trivial Pursuit   Since its debut at the International Toy Fair in 1982, Trivial Pursuit has sold 65 million copies in 18 languages in 32 countries, and it remains the best-selling adult game. Parker Brothers has kept the product's popularity going by making a new game with updated questions every year. It also keeps creating offshoots—travel packs, a children's version, Trivial Pursuit Genus IV, and an interactive CD-ROM from Virgin Entertainment Interactive. The game has its own Web site (*www.trivialpursuit.com*), which received 100,000 visitors in its initial two-month test period. If you are having trouble making dinner conversation on a date—no problem: NTN Entertainment Network has put Trivial Pursuit in about 3,000 restaurants.[51]

marketing strategies: introduction stage

Because it takes time to roll out a new product and fill dealer pipelines, sales growth tends to be slow at this stage. Robert Buzzell identified several causes for the slow growth: delays in the expansion of production capacity; technical problems ("working out the bugs"); delays in obtaining adequate distribution through retail outlets; and customer reluctance.[52] Sales of expensive new products such as high-definition TV are retarded by additional factors such as product complexity and fewer buyers.

Profits are negative or low in the introduction stage. Promotional expenditures are at their highest ratio to sales because of the need to (1) inform potential consumers, (2) induce product trial, and (3) secure distribution in retail outlets. Firms focus on those buyers who are the readiest to buy, usually higher-income groups. Prices tend to be high because costs are high.

THE PIONEER ADVANTAGE   Companies that plan to introduce a new product must decide when to enter the market. To be first can be highly rewarding, but risky and expensive. To come in later makes sense if the firm can bring superior technology, quality, or brand strength.

Speeding up innovation time is essential in an age of shortening product life cycles. Those companies that first reach practical solutions will enjoy "first-mover" advantages in the market. Being early pays off. One study found that products that came out six months late but on budget earned an average of 33 percent less profit in their first five years; products that came out on time but 50 percent over budget cut their profits by only 4 percent.

Most studies indicate that the market pioneer gains the most advantage. Companies like Amazon.com, Campbell, Coca-Cola, Eastman Kodak, Hallmark, Peapod.com, and Xerox developed sustained market dominance. Robinson and Fornell studied a broad range of mature consumer- and industrial-goods businesses, and found that market pioneers generally enjoy a substantially higher market share than do early followers and late entrants:[53] Glen Urban's study also found a pioneer advantage: It appears that the second entrant obtained only 71 percent of the pioneer's market share, and the third entrant obtained only 58 percent.[54] Carpenter and Nakamoto found that 19 out of 25 companies who were market leaders in 1923 were still the market leaders in 1983, 60 years later.[55]

What are the sources of the pioneer's advantage?[56] Early users will recall the pioneer's brand name if the product satisfies them. The pioneer's brand also establishes the attributes the product class should possess. The pioneer's brand normally aims at the middle of the market and so captures more users. Customer inertia also plays a role; and there are producer advantages: economies of scale, technological leadership, patents, ownership of scarce assets, and other barriers to entry. An alert pioneer, according to Robertson and Gatignon, can maintain its leadership indefinitely by pursuing various strategies.[57]

However, the pioneer advantage is not inevitable. One only has to reflect on the fate of Bowmar (hand calculators), Apple's Newton (personal digital assistant), Netscape (web browser), Reynolds (ballpoint pens), and Osborne (portable computers), market pioneers who were overtaken by later entrants. Steven Schnaars studied 28 industries where the imitators surpassed the innovators.[58] He found several weaknesses among the failing pioneers, including new products that were too crude, were improperly positioned, or appeared before there was strong demand; product-development costs that exhausted the innovator's resources; a lack of resources to compete against entering larger firms; and managerial incompetence or unhealthy complacency. Successful imitators thrived by offering lower prices, improving the product more continuously, or using brute market power to overtake the pioneer.

Golder and Tellis raise further doubts about the pioneer advantage.[59] They distinguish between an *inventor* (first to develop patents in a new-product category), a *product pioneer* (first to develop a working model), and a *market pioneer* (first to sell in the new-product category). They also include nonsurviving pioneers in their sample. They conclude that although pioneers may still have an advantage, a larger number of market pioneers fail than has been reported and a larger number of early market leaders (though not pioneers) succeed. Examples of later entrants overtaking market pioneers are IBM over Sperry in mainframe computers, Matsushita over Sony in VCRs, Texas Instruments over Bowmar in hand calculators, and GE over EMI in CAT scan equipment. Tellis and Golder, in a more recent study, identify the following five factors as underpinning long-term market leadership: vision of a mass market, persistence, relentless innovation, financial commitment, and asset leverage.[60]

The pioneer should visualize the various product markets it could initially enter, knowing that it cannot enter all of them at once. Suppose market-segmentation analysis reveals the product market segments shown in Figure 11.6. The pioneer should analyze the profit potential of each product market singly and in combination and decide on a market expansion path. Thus the pioneer in Figure 11.6 plans first to enter product market P_1M_1, then move the product into a second market (P_1M_2), then surprise the competition by developing a second product for the second market (P_2M_2), then take the second product back into the first market (P_2M_1), and then launch a third product for the first market (P_3M_1). If this game plan works, the pioneer firm will own a good part of the first two segments and serve them with two or three products.

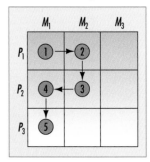

figure **11.6**

Long–Range Product Market Expansion Strategy
(P_i=product i; M_j=Market j)

figure **11.7**

Stages of the Competitive Cycle

Source: John B. Frey, "Pricing Over the Competitive Cycle," speech at the 1982 Marketing Conference. New York: The Conference Board, 1982.

THE COMPETITIVE CYCLE   The pioneer knows that competition will eventually enter and cause prices and its market share to fall. When will this happen? What should the pioneer do at each stage? Frey describes five stages of the *competitive cycle* that the pioneer has to anticipate (Figure 11.7).[61]

1. Initially the pioneer is the *sole supplier*, with 100 percent of production capacity and sales.
2. *Competitive penetration* starts when a new competitor has built production capacity and begins commercial sales. The leader's share of production capacity and share of sales falls. As more competitors enter the market and charge a lower price, the perceived relative value of the leader's offer declines, forcing a reduction in the leader's price premium.
3. Capacity tends to be overbuilt during rapid growth. When a cyclical slowdown occurs, industry overcapacity drives down margins to lower levels. New competitors decide not to enter, and existing competitors try to solidify their positions. This leads to *share stability*.
4. Stability is followed by *commodity competition*. The product is viewed as a commodity, buyers no longer pay a price premium, and the suppliers earn only an average rate of return.
5. At this point, *withdrawal* begins. The pioneer might decide to build share further as other firms withdraw.

marketing strategies: growth stage

The growth stage is marked by a rapid climb in sales. Early adopters like the product, and additional consumers start buying it. New competitors enter, attracted by the opportunities. They introduce new product features and expand distribution.

Prices remain where they are or fall slightly, depending on how fast demand increases. Companies maintain their promotional expenditures at the same or at a slightly increased level to meet competition and to continue to educate the market. Sales rise much faster than promotional expenditures, causing a welcome decline in the promotion–sales ratio. Profits increase during this stage as promotion costs are spread over a larger volume and unit manufacturing costs fall faster than price declines owing to the producer learning effect. Firms have to watch for a change from an accelerating to a decelerating rate of growth in order to prepare new strategies.

During this stage, the firm uses several strategies to sustain rapid market growth:

- It improves product quality and adds new product features and improved styling.
- It adds new models and flanker products (i.e., products of different sizes, flavors, and so forth that protect the main product).
- It enters new market segments.
- It increases its distribution coverage and enters new distribution channels.
- It shifts from product-awareness advertising to product-preference advertising.
- It lowers prices to attract the next layer of price-sensitive buyers.

These market expansion strategies strengthen the firm's competitive position. Consider the following cases.

Starbucks Coffee Company   Starbucks Coffee is one of the best-known brands in the world. Starbucks is able to sell a cup of coffee for $1.40 while the store next door can only get $.50. And if you want the popular café latte, it's $2. Howard Schultz, the genius behind the brand, not only delivers a great-tasting cup of coffee, but serves it in attractive "coffee houses." You can meet friends at Starbucks, or enjoy a moment of solitude. Starbucks consists of more than 3,000 retail outlets in stores, airports, and bookstore chains all over the world. Not surprisingly, competitors have sprung up ranging from Dunkin' Donuts to smaller chains such as Tully's Coffee in Seattle and Coffee Station in New York City. Starbucks is using a number of flank defenses. For one thing, it is trying to push out innovative non-coffee-related products, such as its combo of teas and juice named Tiazzi and its ice cream products. It is also selling its premium beans in supermarkets and is getting into the restaurant business. The first Cafe Starbucks opened to capacity crowds in the fall of 1998, and the company opened another restaurant by the end of the year. Starbucks continues to expand globally, entering China, Kuwait, Korea, and Lebanon in 1999 and opening locations in Hong Kong in 2000.[62]

Yahoo!   Founded in 1994 by Web-surfing grad students, Yahoo! became the number-one place to be on the Web. The company grew into more than just a search engine; it became a portal, offering a full-blown package of information and services. In 1998, Yahoo! stock soared to $200 a share and its market capitalization was $9.1 billion. Yet as the dot-com crash took its toll on Yahoo!'s core stable of advertisers—Internet start-ups—the company began a long earnings and share price slide. It sought to broaden its content and limit its reliance on the previously bulletproof Web advertising model by focusing on e-commerce, licensing, and wireless applications. Still, Yahoo!'s problems worsened. Its stock languished under $25 for much of the first half of 2001 and its CEO (Tim Koogle) resigned in March of that year. The company hired former Warner Bros. Studio chief Terry Semel to replace Koogle, an indication that the company was eager to embrace a future as a media company. As the only portal company not to merge with a giant media company, Yahoo! remained a rugged individualist in spite of its financial difficulties.[63]

A firm in the growth stage faces a trade-off between high market share and high current profit. By spending money on product improvement, promotion, and distribution, it can capture a dominant position. It forgoes maximum current profit in the hope of making even greater profits in the next stage.

marketing strategies: maturity stage

At some point, the rate of sales growth will slow, and the product will enter a stage of relative maturity. This stage normally lasts longer than the previous stages, and poses formidable challenges to marketing management. *Most products are in the maturity stage of the life cycle, and most marketing managers cope with the problem of marketing the mature product.*

The maturity stage divides into three phases: growth, stable, and decaying maturity. In the first phase, the sales growth rate starts to decline. There are no new distribution channels to fill. In the second phase, sales flatten on a per capita basis because of market saturation. Most potential consumers have tried the product, and future sales are governed by population growth and replacement demand. In the third phase, decaying maturity, the absolute level of sales starts to decline, and customers begin switching to other products.

The sales slowdown creates overcapacity in the industry, which leads to intensified competition. Competitors scramble to find niches. They engage in frequent markdowns. They increase advertising and trade and consumer promotion. They increase R&D budgets to develop product improvements and line extensions. They make deals to supply private brands. A shakeout begins, and weaker competitors withdraw. The industry eventually consists of well-entrenched competitors whose basic drive is to gain or maintain market share.

Dominating the industry are a few giant firms—perhaps a quality leader, a service leader, and a cost leader—that serve the whole market and make their profits mainly through high volume and lower costs. Surrounding these dominant firms is a multitude of market nichers, including market specialists, product specialists, and customizing firms. The issue facing a firm in a mature market is whether to struggle to become one of the "big three" and achieve profits through high volume and low cost or to pursue a niching strategy and achieve profits through low volume and a high margin.

Some companies abandon weaker products and concentrate on more profitable products and on new products. Yet they may be ignoring the high potential many mature markets and old products still have. Industries widely thought to be mature— autos, motorcycles, television, watches, cameras—were proved otherwise by the Japanese, who found ways to offer new values to customers. Seemingly moribund brands like Jell-O, Ovaltine, and Arm & Hammer baking soda have achieved major sales revivals several times, through the exercise of marketing imagination.[64] The resurgence in Hush Puppies' popularity in the footwear category is a case study in reviving old, nearly forgotten brands.

Hush Puppies   Once the ruler of the casual footwear industry, the Hush Puppies brand slid into irrelevance in the 1980s when the parent company, Wolverine World, overextended itself by acquiring companies that had nothing to do with footwear. It took a bit of luck, plus some savvy marketing moves, to bring the brand back. In 1994, New York fashion designer John Barrett took some Hush Puppies classic styles and dyed them in colors—purple, green, and orange—to match the clothing in his runway shows. Soon afterword, a menswear trade publication ran a headline saying Hush Puppies were back. Then the company did some smart marketing: It brought out new Hush Puppies in updated colors such as powder blue, lime green, and electric orange and limited distribution to six of the most avant-garde shoe stores in the country. Wolverine also jacked the price up to $70 from $40, and showered free shoes on Hollywood celebrities. Once the shoes had garnered enough buzz, the company made them more widely available by distributing them to better department stores. Hush Puppies sales rose to more than 1.7 million pairs in 1996, from 30,000 pairs in 1994. When fashions shifted a few years later, Hush Puppies expanded into sandals and walking shoes to keep profits going.[65]

MARKET MODIFICATION   The company might try to expand the market for its mature brand by working with the two factors that make up sales volume:

$$\text{Volume} = \text{number of brand users} \times \text{usage rate per user}$$

It can try to expand the number of brand users by (1) *Converting nonusers:* The key to the growth of air freight service is the constant search for new users to whom air carriers can demonstrate the benefits of using air freight rather than ground transportation. (2) *Entering new market segments*: Johnson & Johnson successfully promoted its baby shampoo to adult users. (3) *Winning competitors' customers*: PepsiCo is constantly tempting Coca-Cola users to switch.

Volume can also be increased by convincing current users to increase their brand usage: (1) *Use the product on more occasions.* Serve Campbell's soup for breakfast. Use Heinz vinegar to clean windows. Take Kodak pictures of your pets. (2) *Use more of the product on each occasion.* Drink a larger glass of orange juice. (3) *Use the product in new ways.* Use Arm & Hammer Baking Soda as a refrigerator deodorant or to extinguish grease fires.[66]

PRODUCT MODIFICATION   Managers also try to stimulate sales by modifying the product's characteristics through quality improvement, feature improvement, or style improvement.

Quality improvement aims at increasing the product's functional performance. A manufacturer can often overtake its competition by launching a "new and improved" product. Grocery manufacturers call this a "plus launch" and promote a new additive or advertise something as "stronger," "bigger," or "better." This strategy is effective to the extent that the quality is improved, buyers accept the claim of improved quality, and a sufficient number of buyers will pay for higher quality. However, customers are not always willing to accept an "improved" product, as the classic tale of New Coke illustrates.

Coca-Cola   Battered by competition from the sweeter Pepsi-Cola, Coca-Cola decided in 1985 to replace its old formula with a sweeter variation, dubbed the New Coke. Coca-Cola spent $4 million on market research. Blind taste tests showed that Coke drinkers preferred the new, sweeter formula, but the launch of New Coke provoked a national uproar. Market researchers had measured the taste but had failed to measure the emotional attachment consumers had to Coca-Cola. There were angry letters, formal protests, and even lawsuit threats, to force the retention of "The Real Thing." Ten weeks later, the company withdrew New Coke and reintroduced its century-old formula as "Classic Coke," giving the old formula even stronger status in the marketplace.

Feature improvement aims at adding new features (for example, size, weight, materials, additives, accessories) that expand the product's versatility, safety, or convenience. You would not think one could do much to change a sliced pickle, but Vlasic R&D people worked for years to modify its core product.

Vlasic Foods International   Pickle consumption has been declining about 2 percent a year since the 1980s. Vlasic began its quest for a blockbuster pickle in the mid-1990s, after focus groups revealed that people hate it when pickle slices slither out the sides of hamburgers and sandwiches. At first the company decided to slice its average pickles horizontally into strips and marketed them as "Sandwich Stackers." The only problem was that the strips usually contained the soft seedy part of the cucumber, not the crunchy part. The company then embarked on "Project Frisbee," an effort to create a giant pickle chip. In 1998, after years of research and development, Vlasic created a cucumber 10 times larger than the traditional pickle cucumber. The chips, sold as "Hamburger Stackers," are large enough to cover the entire surface of a hamburger and are stacked a dozen high in jars.[67]

This strategy has several advantages. New features build the company's image as an innovator and win the loyalty of market segments that value these features. They provide an opportunity for free publicity and they generate sales force and distributor enthusiasm. The chief disadvantage is that feature improvements are easily imitated; unless there is a permanent gain from being first, the feature improvement might not pay off in the long run.[68]

A strategy of style improvement aims at increasing the product's aesthetic appeal. The periodic introduction of new car models is largely about style competition, as is the introduction of new packaging for consumer products. A style strategy might give the product a unique market identity. Yet style competition has problems. First, it is difficult to predict whether people—and which people—will like a new style. Second, a style change usually requires discontinuing the old style, and the company risks losing customers. Consumers may become attached to something as seemingly insignificant as a peanut shell. In the United States, eating unshelled peanuts at baseball games is a time-honored tradition. During the 1986 major league baseball season at New York's Shea Stadium, the concessionaire began selling preshelled peanuts in cellophane packages. Sales fell 15 percent and consumers complained strongly.[69]

MARKETING–MIX MODIFICATION Product managers might also try to stimulate sales by modifying other marketing-mix elements. They should ask the following questions:

- *Prices:* Would a price cut attract new buyers? If so, should the list price be lowered, or should prices be lowered through price specials, volume or early-purchase discounts, freight cost absorption, or easier credit terms? Or would it be better to raise the price to signal higher quality?
- *Distribution:* Can the company obtain more product support and display in existing outlets? Can more outlets be penetrated? Can the company introduce the product into new distribution channels? When Goodyear decided to sell its tires via Wal-Mart, Sears, and Discount Tire, it boosted market share from 14 percent to 16 percent in the first year.[70]
- *Advertising:* Should advertising expenditures be increased? Should the message or copy be changed? Should the media mix be changed? Should the timing, frequency, or size of ads be changed?
- *Sales promotion:* Should the company step up sales promotion—trade deals, cents-off coupons, rebates, warranties, gifts, and contests?
- *Personal selling:* Should the number or quality of salespeople be increased? Should the basis for sales force specialization be changed? Should sales territories be revised? Should sales force incentives be revised? Can sales-call planning be improved?
- *Services:* Can the company speed up delivery? Can it extend more technical assistance to customers? Can it extend more credit?

Marketers often debate which tools are most effective in the mature stage. For example, would the company gain more by increasing its advertising or its sales-promotion budget? Sales promotion has more impact at this stage because consumers have reached an equilibrium in their buying habits and preferences, and psychological persuasion (advertising) is not as effective as financial persuasion (sales-promotion deals). Many consumer-packaged-goods companies now spend over 60 percent of their total promotion budget on sales promotion to support mature products. Other marketers argue that brands should be managed as capital assets and supported by advertising. Advertising expenditures should be treated as a capital investment. Brand managers, however, use sales promotion because its effects are quicker and more visible to their superiors; but excessive sales-promotion activity can hurt the brand's image and long-run profit performance.

"Marketing Memo: Breaking Through the Mature-Product Syndrome" shows how *gap analysis* can be used to discover possible growth opportunities in a mature market.

marketing strategies: decline stage

Sales decline for a number of reasons, including technological advances, shifts in consumer tastes, and increased domestic and foreign competition. All lead to overcapacity, increased price cutting, and profit erosion. The decline might be slow, as in the case of oatmeal; or rapid, as in the case of the Edsel automobile. Sales may plunge to zero, or they may petrify at a low level.

Marketing
MEMO

Breaking Through the Mature-Product Syndrome

Managers of mature products need a systematic framework for identifying possible "breakthrough" ideas. Professor John A. Weber of Notre Dame developed the following framework, which he calls gap analysis, to guide the search for growth opportunities. We will apply this to a mature beverage product such as Kool-Aid:

1. *Natural changes in the size of industry market potential*: Will current birth rates and demographics favor more consumption of Kool-Aid? How will the economic outlook affect Kool-Aid consumption?
2. *New uses or new user segments*: Can Kool-Aid be made to appeal to teenagers, young adult singles, young adult parents, and so on?
3. *Innovative product differentiations*: Can Kool-Aid be made in different versions such as low calorie or super-sweet?
4. *Add new product lines*: Can the Kool-Aid name be used to launch a new soft-drink line?
5. *Stimulate nonusers*: Can elderly people be persuaded to try Kool-Aid?
6. *Stimulate light users*: Can children be reminded to drink Kool-Aid daily?
7. *Increase amount used on each use occasion*: Can more Kool-Aid be put in each package at a higher price?
8. *Close existing product and price gaps*: Should new sizes of Kool-Aid be introduced?
9. *Create new product-line elements*: Should Kool-Aid introduce new flavors?
10. *Expand distribution coverage*: Can Kool-Aid distribution coverage be expanded to Europe and the Far East?
11. *Expand distribution intensity*: Can the percentage of convenience stores in the Midwest that carry Kool-Aid be increased from 70 to 90 percent?
12. *Expand distribution exposure*: Can offers to the trade win more shelf space for Kool-Aid?
13. *Penetrate substitutes' positions*: Can consumers be convinced that Kool-Aid is better than other soft drinks?
14. *Penetrate direct competitors' position(s)*: Can consumers of other brands be convinced to switch to Kool-Aid?
15. *Defend firm's present position*: Can Kool-Aid satisfy the current users more so that they remain loyal?

Source: John A. Weber, *Identifying and Solving Marketing Problems with Gap Analysis* (Notre Dame, IN: Strategic Business Systems, 1986).

As sales and profits decline, some firms withdraw from the market. Those remaining may reduce the number of products they offer. They may withdraw from smaller market segments and weaker trade channels, and they may cut their promotion budgets and reduce prices further.

Unfortunately, most companies have not developed a policy for handling aging products. Sentiment often plays a role:

> Putting products to death—or letting them die—is a drab business, and often engenders much of the sadness of a final parting with old and tried friends. The portable, six-sided pretzel was the first product The Company ever made. Our line will no longer be our line without it.[71]

Logic may also play a role. Management believes that product sales will improve when the economy improves, or when the marketing strategy is revised, or when the product is improved; or the weak product may be retained because of its alleged contribution to the sales of the company's other products; or its revenue may cover out-of-pocket costs, even if it is not turning a profit.

Unless strong reasons for retention exist, carrying a weak product is very costly to the firm—and not just by the amount of uncovered overhead and profit: There are many hidden costs. Weak products often consume a disproportionate amount of management's time; require frequent price and inventory adjustments; generally involve short production runs in spite of expensive setup times; require both advertising and sales force attention that might be better used to make the healthy products more profitable; and can cast a shadow on the company's image. The biggest cost might well lie in the future. Failing to eliminate weak products delays the aggressive search for replacement products. The weak products create a lopsided product mix, long on yesterday's bread-winners and short on tomorrow's.

In handling aging products, a company faces a number of tasks and decisions. The first task is to establish a system for identifying weak products. Many companies appoint a product-review committee with representatives from marketing, R&D, manufacturing, and finance. The controller's office supplies data for each product showing trends in market size, market share, prices, costs, and profits. A computer program then analyzes this information. The managers responsible for dubious products fill out rating forms showing where they think sales and profits will go, with and without any changes in marketing strategy. The product-review committee makes a recommendation for each product—leave it alone, modify its marketing strategy, or drop it.[72]

Some firms will abandon declining markets earlier than others. Much depends on the presence and height of exit barriers in the industry.[73] The lower the exit barriers, the easier it is for firms to leave the industry, and the more tempting it is for the remaining firms to stay and attract the withdrawing firms' customers. For example, Procter & Gamble stayed in the declining liquid-soap business and improved its profits as others withdrew.

In a study of company strategies in declining industries, Kathryn Harrigan identified five decline strategies available to the firm:

1. Increasing the firm's investment (to dominate the market or strengthen its competitive position).
2. Maintaining the firm's investment level until the uncertainties about the industry are resolved.
3. Decreasing the firm's investment level selectively, by dropping unprofitable customer groups, while simultaneously strengthening the firm's investment in lucrative niches.
4. Harvesting ("milking") the firm's investment to recover cash quickly.
5. Divesting the business quickly by disposing of its assets as advantageously as possible.[74]

The appropriate strategy depends on the industry's relative attractiveness and the company's competitive strength in that industry. A company that is in an unattractive industry but possesses competitive strength should consider shrinking selectively. A company that is in an attractive industry and has competitive strength should consider strengthening its investment. Boston Market is an example.

Boston Market   Just five years after its 1993 initial public offering, fast-food chain Boston Market declared bankruptcy. McDonald's bought the struggling chain in 2000 for $173 million, planning to convert its locations into new McDonald's franchises. The burger giant soon realized that the Boston Market brand still had value, and decided to try to revitalize the company. Boston Market now grosses more than $700 million a year. Based on successful test-market results, McDonald's plans to give every Boston Market store a makeover that includes warmer décor and more menu options.[75]

If the company were choosing between harvesting and divesting, its strategies would be quite different. *Harvesting* calls for gradually reducing a product or business's costs while trying to maintain its sales. The first step is to cut R&D costs and plant and equipment investment. The company might also reduce product quality, sales force size, marginal services, and advertising expenditures. It would try to cut these costs without letting customers, competitors, and employees know what is happening. Harvesting is an ethically ambivalent strategy, and it is also difficult to execute. Yet many mature products warrant this strategy. Harvesting can substantially increase the company's current cash flow.[76]

Companies that successfully restage or rejuvenate a mature product often do so by adding value to the original product. Consider the experience of Pitney Bowes Inc., the dominant producer of postage meters.

Pitney Bowes   In 1996, critics, and even Pitney Bowes insiders, predicted that faxes would kill regular mail, on which Pitney's business relies. Then they predicted that e-mail would kill faxes and that all these technological advances combined would kill Pitney's profits. As it happens, the surge in direct mail and Internet-related bills has generated more mail, not less, but the Internet also enabled new companies such as e-Stamps and stamps.com to enter Pitney's territory by offering a way to download stamps over the Internet. Pitney recast itself as a messaging company, not merely a mailing company. It developed software products that let customers track incoming materials and outgoing products, convert bills and print files to fax or e-mail, and track when a document has been acted upon. Pitney also provides electronic billing services for e-commerce companies and even added an electronic-stamp business to compete with the stamp start-ups. Pitney's saving view: The Internet is not the enemy; rather, it is a vehicle for becoming a broad-based messaging company.[77]

When a company decides to drop a product, it faces further decisions. If the product has strong distribution and residual goodwill, the company can probably sell it to another firm. If the company can't find any buyers, it must decide whether to liquidate the brand quickly or slowly. It must also decide on how much inventory and service to maintain for past customers.

the product life-cycle concept: critique

The PLC concept helps interpret product and market dynamics. It can be used for planning and control, although as a forecasting tool it is less useful. PLC theory has its share of critics. They claim that life-cycle patterns are too variable in shape and duration. PLCs lack what living organisms have—namely, a fixed sequence of stages and a fixed length of each stage. Critics also charge that marketers can seldom tell what stage the product is in. A product may appear to be mature when actually it has reached a plateau prior to another upsurge. They charge that the PLC pattern is the result of marketing strategies rather than an inevitable course that sales must follow:

> Suppose a brand is acceptable to consumers but has a few bad years because of other factors—for instance, poor advertising, delisting by a major chain, or entry of a "me-too" competitive product backed by massive sampling. Instead of thinking in terms of corrective measures, management begins to feel that its brand has entered a declining stage. It therefore withdraws funds from the promotion budget to finance R&D on new items. The next year the brand does even worse, panic increases. . . . Clearly, the PLC is a dependent variable which is determined by marketing actions; it is not an independent variable to which companies should adapt their marketing programs.[78]

Table 11.5 summarizes the characteristics, marketing objectives, and marketing strategies of the four stages of the PLC.

market evolution

Because the PLC focuses on what is happening to a particular product or brand rather than on what is happening to the overall market, it yields a product-oriented picture rather than a market-oriented picture. Firms need to visualize a market's evolutionary path as it is affected by new needs, competitors, technology, channels, and other developments.

In the course of a product's or brand's existence, its positioning must change to keep pace with market developments. Consider the case of Lego.

LEGO Group LEGO Group, the Danish toy company, enjoyed a 72 percent global market share of the construction toy market; but children were spending more of their spare time with video games, computers, and television and less time with

table **11.5**		Summary of Product Life–Cycle Characteristics, Objectives, and Strategies		
	Introduction	**Growth**	**Maturity**	**Decline**
Characteristics				
Sales	Low sales	Rapidly rising sales	Peak sales	Declining sales
Costs	High cost per customer	Average cost per customer	Low cost per customer	Low cost per customer
Profits	Negative	Rising profits	High profits	Declining profits
Customers	Innovators	Early adopters	Middle majority	Laggards
Competitors	Few	Growing Number	Stable number beginning to decline	Declining number
Marketing Objectives				
	Create product awareness and trial	Maximize market share	Maximize profit while defending market share	Reduce expenditure and milk the brand
Strategies				
Product	Offer a basic product	Offer product extensions, service, warranty	Diversify brands and items models	Phase out weak
Price	Charge cost-plus	Price to penetrate market	Price to match or best competitors'	Cut price
Distribution	Build selective distribution	Build intensive distribution	Build more intensive distribution	Go selective: phase out unprofitable outlets
Advertising	Build product awareness among early adopters and dealers	Build awareness and interest in the mass-market	Stress brand differences and benefits	Reduce to level needed to retain hard-core loyals
Sales Promotion	Use heavy sales promotion to entice trial	Reduce to take advantage of heavy consumer demand	Increase to encourage brand switching	Reduce to minimal level

Sources: Chester R. Wasson, *Dynamic Competitive Strategy and Product Life Cycles* (Austin, TX: Austin Press, 1978); John A. Weber, "Planning Corporate Growth with Inverted Product Life Cycles," *Long Range Planning* (October 1976): 12–29; Peter Doyle, "The Realities of the Product Life Cycle," *Quarterly Review of Marketing* (Summer 1976).

traditional toys. So Lego recognized the need to change or expand its market space. It redefined its market space as "family edutainment," which included toys, education, interactive technology, software, computers, and consumer electronics. All involved exercising the mind and having fun. Part of LEGO Group's plan is to capture an increasing share of customer spending as children become young adults and then parents.

stages in market evolution

Like products, markets evolve through four stages: emergence, growth, maturity, and decline.

EMERGENCE   Before a market materializes, it exists as a latent market. For example, for centuries people have wanted faster means of calculation. This need was successively satisfied through abacuses, slide rules, and large adding machines. Suppose an entrepreneur recognizes this need and imagines a technological solution in the form of a small, handheld electronic calculator. He now has to determine the product attributes,

LEGO GROUP'S "family edutainment" Web site. LEGO is a trademark of the LEGO Group © 2002 The LEGO Group. The LEGO® trademarks and products are used with permission. The LEGO Group does not sponsor or endorse Prentice Hall/Pearson Education.

including physical size and number of mathematical functions. Because he is market-oriented, he interviews potential buyers. He finds that target customers vary greatly in their preferences. Some want a four-function calculator (adding, subtracting, multiplying, and dividing) and others want more functions (calculating percentages, square roots, and logs). Some want a small hand calculator and others want a large one. This type of market, in which buyer preferences scatter evenly, is called a *diffused-preference market*.

The entrepreneur's problem is to design an optimal product for this market. He or she has three options:

1. The new product can be designed to meet the preferences of one of the corners of the market (*a single-niche strategy*).
2. Two or more products can be simultaneously launched to capture two or more parts of the market (*a multiple-niche strategy*).
3. The new product can be designed for the middle of the market (*a mass-market strategy*).

For small firms, a single-niche market strategy makes the most sense. A small firm does not have the resources for capturing and holding the mass-market. A large firm might go after the mass-market by designing a product that is medium in size and number of functions. A product in the center minimizes the sum of the distances of existing preferences from the actual product, thereby minimizing total dissatisfaction. Assume that the pioneer firm is large and designs its product for the mass market. On launching the product, the *emergence* stage begins.

GROWTH   If the new product sells well, new firms will enter the market, ushering in a *market-growth stage*. Where will a second firm enter the market, assuming that the first firm established itself in the center? The second firm has three options:

1. It can position its brand in one of the corners (single-niche strategy).
2. It can position its brand next to the first competitor (mass-market strategy).
3. It can launch two or more products in different, unoccupied corners (multiple-niche strategy).

If the second firm is small, it is likely to avoid head-on competition with the pioneer and to launch its brand in one of the market corners. If the second firm is large, it might

figure **11.8**

Market Fragmentation and
Market Consolidation
Strategies

(a) Market-fragmentation stage

(b) Market-consolidation stage

launch its brand in the center against the pioneer. The two firms can easily end up sharing the mass market; or a large second firm can implement a multiniche strategy and surround and box in the pioneer.

MATURITY Eventually, the competitors cover and serve all the major market segments and the market enters the *maturity stage*. In fact, they go further and invade each other's segments, reducing everyone's profits in the process. As market growth slows down, the market splits into finer segments and high *market fragmentation* occurs. This situation is illustrated in Figure 11.8(a) where the letters represent different companies supplying various segments. Note that two segments are unserved because they are too small to yield a profit.

Market fragmentation is often followed by a *market consolidation* caused by the emergence of a new attribute that has strong appeal. Market consolidation took place in the toothpaste market when P&G introduced Crest, which effectively retarded dental decay. Suddenly, toothpaste brands that claimed whitening power, cleaning power, sex appeal, taste, or mouthwash effectiveness were pushed into the corners because consumers primarily wanted dental protection. Crest won a lion's share of the market, as shown by the X territory in Figure 11.8(b).

However, even a consolidated market condition will not last. Other companies will copy a successful brand, and the market will eventually splinter again. Mature markets swing between fragmentation and consolidation. The fragmentation is brought about by competition, and the consolidation is brought about by innovation.

DECLINE Eventually, demand for the present products will begin to decrease, and the market will enter the *decline stage*. Either society's total need level declines or a new technology replaces the old. Thus an entrepreneur might invent a mouth-rinse liquid that is superior to toothpaste. In this case, the old technology will eventually disappear and a new life cycle will emerge.

AN EXAMPLE: THE PAPER–TOWEL MARKET Consider the evolution of the paper-towel market. Originally, homemakers used cotton and linen dishcloths and towels in their kitchens. A paper company, looking for new markets, developed paper towels. This development crystallized a latent market. Other manufacturers entered the market. The number of brands proliferated and created market fragmentation. Industry overcapacity led manufacturers to search for new features. One manufacturer, hearing consumers complain that paper towels were not absorbent, introduced "absorbent" towels and increased its market share. This market consolidation did not last long because competitors came out with their own versions of absorbent paper towels. The market fragmented again. Then another manufacturer introduced a "superstrength" towel. It was soon copied. Another manufacturer introduced a "lint-free" paper towel, which was subsequently copied. Thus paper towels evolved from a single product to one with various absorbencies, strengths, and applications. Market evolution was driven by the forces of innovation and competition.

dynamics of attribute competition

Competition produces a continuous round of new product attributes. If a new attribute succeeds, several competitors soon offer it. To the extent that many airlines serve in-flight meals, meals are no longer a basis for air-carrier choice. *Customer expectations are progressive.* This fact underlines the strategic importance of a maintaining the lead in introducing new attributes. Each new attribute, if successful, creates a competitive advantage for the firm, leading to temporarily higher-than-average market share and profits. The market leader must learn to routinize the innovation process.

Can a firm look ahead and anticipate the succession of attributes that are likely to win favor and be technologically feasible? How can the firm discover new attributes? There are four approaches.

1. *A customer-survey process:* The company asks consumers what benefits they would like added to the product and their desire level for each. The firm also examines the cost of developing each new attribute and likely competitive responses.

2. *An intuitive process:* Entrepreneurs get hunches and undertake product development without much marketing research. Natural selection determines winners and losers. If a manufacturer has intuited an attribute that the market wants, that manufacturer is considered smart or lucky.

3. *A dialectical process:* Innovators should not march with the crowd. Thus blue jeans, starting out as an inexpensive clothing article, over time became fashionable and more expensive. This unidirectional movement, however, contains the seeds of its own destruction. Eventually, the price falls again or some manufacturer introduces another cheap material for pants.

4. *A needs-hierarchy process:* (See Maslow's theory in Chapter 7.) We would predict that the first automobiles would provide basic transportation and be designed for safety. Later, automobiles would start appealing to social acceptance and status needs. Still later, automobiles would be designed to help people "fulfill" themselves. The innovator's task is to assess when the market is ready to satisfy a higher-order need.

The actual unfolding of new attributes in a market is more complex than simple theories suggest.[79] We should not underestimate the role of technology and societal processes. For example, the strong consumer wish for portable computers remained unmet until miniaturization technology was sufficiently developed. Developments such as inflation, shortages, environmentalism, consumerism, and new lifestyles lead consumers to reevaluate product attributes. Inflation increases the desire for a smaller car, and a desire for car safety increases the desire for a heavier car. The innovator must use marketing research to gauge the demand potency of different attributes in order to determine the company's best move.

summary

1. Many marketers advocate promoting only one product benefit, thus creating a unique selling proposition as they position their product. People tend to remember "number one." Double-benefit position and triple-benefit positioning can also be successful, but must be used carefully.

2. The key to competitive advantage is product differentiation. A market offering can be differentiated along five dimensions: product (form, features, performance quality, conformance quality, durability, reliability, repairability, style, design); services (order ease, delivery, installation, customer training, customer consulting, maintenance and repair, miscellaneous services); personnel, channel, or image (symbols, media, atmosphere, and events). A difference is worth establishing to the extent that it is important, distinctive, superior, preemptive, affordable, and profitable.

3. Because economic conditions change and competitive activity varies, companies normally find it necessary to reformulate their marketing strategy several times during a product's life cycle. Technologies, product forms, and brands also exhibit life cycles with distinct stages. The general sequence of stages in any life cycle is introduction, growth, maturity, and decline. The majority of products today are in the maturity stage.

4. Although many products exhibit a bell-shaped product life cycle (PLC), there are many other patterns, including the growth-slump-maturity pattern, the cycle-recycle pattern, and the scalloped pattern. The PLCs of styles, fashions, and fads can be erratic; the key to success in these areas lies in creating products with staying power.

5. Each stage of the PLC calls for different marketing strategies. The introduction stage is marked by slow growth and minimal profits. If successful, the product enters a growth stage marked by rapid sales growth and increasing profits. There follows a maturity stage in which sales growth slows and profits stabilize. Finally, the product enters a decline stage. The company's task is to identify the truly weak products; develop a strategy for each one; and finally, phase out weak products in a way that minimizes the hardship to company profits, employees, and customers.

6. Like products, markets evolve through four stages: emergence, growth, maturity, and decline.

applications

marketing debate – do brands have finite lives?

Often, after a brand begins to slip in the marketplace or disappears all together, commentators observe, "all brands have their day." Their rationale is that all brands, in some sense, have a finite life and cannot be expected to be leaders forever. Other experts contend, however, that brands can live forever, and their long-term success depends as much on the skill and insight of the marketers involved.

Take a position: Brands cannot be expected to last forever versus There is no reason for a brand to ever become obsolete.

marketing and advertising

1. When T-Fal sells its pans around the world, it takes into account each market's unique characteristics. The headline of the ad in Figure 1 reads, "Pan for the Index Finger," showing how Japanese customers can use one finger to detach the handle so the pan can be used in different ways and stored in tight spaces.

   a. What unique selling proposition is this ad promoting?

   b. Which of the nine product differentiation variables is being communicated in this ad? Why is this variable important to the target market?

   c. State the value proposition suggested by this T-Fal ad.

2. The ad in Figure 2, placed by the U.S. Postal Service for its NetPost Mailing Online service, targets businesses that use direct mail to reach their customers.

   a. Is this ad illustrating attribute, benefit, use, user, competitor, product category, or quality/price positioning?

   b. Which of the main service differentiators is being communicated by this ad? Why would customers value this difference?

   c. The market for postal services is in the maturity stage. Does the U.S. Postal Service appear to be using market modification, product modification, or marketing-mix modification to stimulate sales?

Figure 1

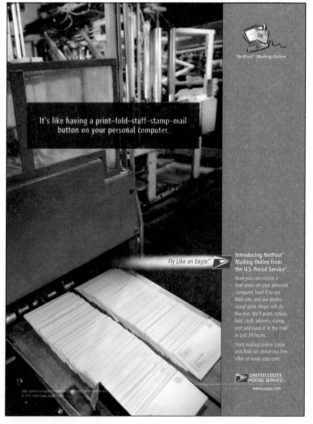

Figure 2

online marketing today

Although pioneering a market can be expensive and difficult, companies that do it effectively will reap first-mover advantages. The online auction site eBay is a good case in point. When the Internet was in its infancy, eBay invented the online auction concept and revolutionized the way consumers buy and sell products among themselves. Now 30 million consumers are registered as eBay buyers or sellers, and 2 million more register every month. In recent years, companies have begun using eBay's auction facilities to sell a range of new products. JCPenney, for example, has auctioned clothing on eBay, while Mitsubishi Electric has auctioned factory automation equipment.[80]

Visit the eBay site (*www.ebay.com*) and see how the company orients new users to its services. Also look at the goods and services featured on the home page; follow the link to eBay Motors or another of the specialty sites; and follow the link to read "About eBay." Based on your observations of eBay's online marketing efforts, does this market appear to be in the emergence, growth, maturity, or decline stage? How are eBay's marketing efforts intended to affect the market? How is eBay using its site to create an effective image?

you're the marketer: sonic pda marketing plan

In the course of developing a marketing strategy, marketers must select and communicate an effective positioning to differentiate their offerings. They also have to plan appropriate marketing strategies for each stage of the product life cycle and the market's evolution.

As before, you are working with Jane Melody on Sonic's marketing plan for launching a new PDA. Review your work on previous sections of the marketing plan. Then answer these questions about positioning and life-cycle strategies for Sonic:

- Which of the differentiation variables related to product, services, personnel, channels, and image are best suited to Sonic's situation, strategy, and goals? Include the rationale for your selection.

- In developing your positioning, identify the benefits most valued by your target customers. Will you stress one or more than one benefit in your positioning? In a sentence, what is the value proposition for Sonic's PDA?

- Knowing the stage of Sonic's PDA in the product life cycle, what are the implications for the marketing mix, product management strategy, service strategy, and R&D strategy?

- In which stage of its evolution does the PDA market appear to be? What does this mean for Sonic's marketing plans?

Once you have answered these questions and considered the effects on Sonic's marketing, either summarize your ideas in a written marketing plan or type them in the Positioning sections of the *Marketing Plan Pro* software. Also note any additional research you may need in the Marketing Research section of the software.

notes

1. Al Ries and Jack Trout, *Positioning: The Battle for Your Mind* (New York: Warner Books, 1982).
2. Michael Treacy and Fred Wiersema, *The Disciplines of Market Leaders* (Reading, MA: Addison-Wesley, 1994).
3. Rosser Reeves, *Reality in Advertising* (New York: Alfred A. Knopf, 1960).
4. Ries and Trout, *Positioning*.
5. Chad Terhune, "Home Depot's Home Improvement," *Wall Street Journal,* March 8, 2001, p. B1.
6. Robert V. Stumpf, "The Market Structure of the Major Tourist Attractions in Southern California," *Proceedings of the 1976 Sperry Business Conference* (Chicago: American Marketing Association, 1976), pp. 101–6.
7. Yoram J. Wind, *Product Policy: Concepts, Methods and Strategy* (Reading, MA: Addison-Wesley, 1982), pp. 79–81; David Aaker and J. Gary Shansby, "Postioning Your Product," *Business Horizons* (May–June 1982): 56–62.
8. Bobby J. Calder and Steven J. Reagan, "Brand Design," in *Kellogg on Marketing,* ed. Dawn Iacobucci (New York: John Wiley & Sons, 2001), p. 61.
9. The Palm Pilot and Mountain Dew examples are taken from Alice M. Tybout and Brian Sternthal, "Brand Positioning," in *Kellogg on Marketing,* ed. Dawn Iacobucci (New York: John Wiley & Sons, 2001), p. 54.
10. Alice M. Tybout and Brian Sternthal, "Brand Positioning," in *Kellogg on Marketing,* ed. Dawn Iacobucci (New York: John Wiley & Sons, 2001), p. 35.
11. Kevin Clancy, Copernicus newsletter, May 2001.
12. Theodore Levitt, "Marketing Success through Differentiation: Of Anything," *Harvard Business Review* (January–February 1980).
13. Gregory S. Carpenter, Rashi Glazer, and Kent Nakamoto, "Meaningful Brands from Meaningless Differentiation: The Dependence on Irrelevant Attributes," *Journal of Marketing Research* (August 1994): 339–50.
14. Edwin T. Crego Jr. and Peter D. Schiffrin, *Customer Centered Reengineering* (Homewood, IL: Irwin, 1995).
15. Miland M. Lele, *Creating Strategic Leverage* (New York: John Wiley, 1992).
16. Some of these bases are discussed in David A. Garvin, "Competing on the Eight Dimensions of Quality," *Harvard Business Review* (November–December 1987): 101–9.
17. David A. Aaker, *Managing Brand Equity* (New York: The Free Press, 1991).
18. Elizabeth Corcoran, "The E Gang," *Forbes,* July 24, 2000, p. 145.
19. Bernd Schmitt and Alex Simonson, *Marketing Aesthetics: The Strategic Management of Brand, Identity, and Image* (New York: The Free Press, 1997).

20. Gerry Khermouch, "Zona Sets Collectible Max-packs," *Brandweek*, April 20, 1998, p. 16.

21. <*www.arizonabev.com*>.

22. Philip Kotler, "Design: A Powerful but Neglected Strategic Tool," *Journal of Business Strategy* (Fall 1984): 16–21. Also see Christopher Lorenz, *The Design Dimension* (New York: Basil Blackwell, 1986).

23. "Hot R.I.P: The Floppy Disk," *Rolling Stone*, August 20, 1998, p. 86; Owen Edwards, "Beauty and the Box," *Forbes*, October 5, 1998, p. 131; Brent Schlender, "Steve Jobs: The Graying Prince of a Shrinking Kingdom," *Fortune*, May 14, 2001, p. 118.

24. Joseph Weber, "A Better Grip on Hawking Tools," *BusinessWeek*, June 5, 1995, p. 99.

25. "Internet Grocer Peapod Achieves Operating Profitability in Chicago," *Business Wire*, April 23, 2001; James Turner, "Online Grocers Try to Extend Their Shelf Life," *Christian Science Monitor*, February 12, 2001, p. 16.

26. For further reading, George Stalk Jr. and Thomas M. Hout, *Competing Against Time* (New York: The Free Press, 1990); Joseph D. Blackburn, *Time-Based Competition* (Homewood, IL: Irwin, 1991); Christopher Meyer, *Fast Cycle Time* (New York: The Free Press, 1993); "The Computer Liked Us," *U.S. News & World Report*, August 14, 1995, pp. 71–72.

27. Hermann Simon, *Hidden Champions* (Boston: Harvard Business School Press, 1996).

28. For a comprehensive discussion of Cemex, see Adrian J. Slywotzky and David J. Morrison, *How Digital Is Your Business* (New York: Crown Business, 2000), ch. 5.

29. "Pac Bell to Offer DSL, You Can Install," *San Francisco Chronicle*, March 20, 2000.

30. Adapted from Tom Peters's description in *Thriving on Chaos* (New York: Alfred A. Knopf, 1987), pp. 56–57.

31. Susan Hirsh, "At Rite Aid, the Medicine 'Is Working'," *Baltimore Sun*, January 10, 2001, p. 1C.

32. Linda Knapp, "A Sick Computer?" *Seattle Times*, January 28, 2001, p. D-8.

33. Ian C. MacMillan and Rita Gunther McGrath, "Discovering New Points of Differentiation," *Harvard Business Review* (July–August 1997): 133–45.

34. *Canon Environmental Report*, 2000.

35. "The 25 Best Sales Forces," *Sales & Marketing Management* (July 1998): 32–50.

36. For a similar list, see Leonard L. Berry and A. Parasuraman, *Marketing Services: Competing Through Quality* (New York: The Free Press, 1991), p. 16.

37. Susan Greco, "Inside-Out Marketing," *Inc.*, January 1998, pp. 51–59; James P. Sterba, "Hunting with the Man Who Made Orvis a Winner," *Wall Street Journal*, November 2, 1999, p. A24.

38. Erin Davies, "Selling Sex and Cat Food," *Fortune*, June 9, 1997, p. 36; Shelly Branch, "P&G Is Out to Fetch Distribution Gains for Iams Pet Food," *Wall Street Journal*, January 6, 2000, p. A6.

39. <*www.vans.com*>.

40. Jack Trout and Steve Rivkin, *Differentiate or Die* (New York: Wiley, 2000).

41. Karen Axelrod and Bruce Brumberg, *Watch It Made in the U.S.A.* (Santa Fe: John Muir Publications, 1997).

42. "Guerrillas in Our Midst," *The Economist*, October 14, 2000, pp. 80–81.

43. "Swatch: Ambitious," *The Economist*, April 18, 1992, pp. 74–75. See also <*www.swatch.com*>.

44. Some authors distinguished additional stages. Wasson suggested a stage of competitive turbulence between growth and maturity. See Chester R. Wasson, *Dynamic Competitive Strategy and Product Life Cycles* (Austin, TX: Austin Press, 1978). Maturity describes a stage of sales growth slowdown and saturation, a stage of flat sales after sales have peaked.

45. John E. Swan and David R. Rink, "Fitting Market Strategy to Varying Product Life Cycles," *Business Horizons* (January–February 1982): 72–76; and Gerald J. Tellis and C. Merle Crawford, "An Evolutionary Approach to Product Growth Theory," *Journal of Marketing* (Fall 1981): 125–34.

46. William E. Cox Jr., "Product Life Cycles as Marketing Models," *Journal of Business* (October 1967): 375–84.

47. Jordan P. Yale, "The Strategy of Nylon's Growth," *Modern Textiles Magazine*, February 1964, p. 32. Also see Theodore Levitt, "Exploit the Product Life Cycle," *Harvard Business Review* (November–December 1965): 81–94.

48. Chester R. Wasson, "How Predictable Are Fashion and Other Product Life Cycles?" *Journal of Marketing* (July 1968): 36–43.

49. Ibid.

50. William H. Reynolds, "Cars and Clothing: Understanding Fashion Trends," *Journal of Marketing* (July 1968): 44–49.

51. Patrick Butters, "What Biggest Selling Adult Game Still Cranks Out Vexing Questions?" *Insight on the News*, January 26, 1998, p. 39.

52. Robert D. Buzzell, "Competitive Behavior and Product Life Cycles," in *New Ideas for Successful Marketing*, ed. John S. Wright and Jack Goldstucker (Chicago: American Marketing Association, 1956), p. 51.

53. William T. Robinson and Claes Fornell, "Sources of Market Pioneer Advantages in Consumer Goods Industries," *Journal of Marketing Research* (August 1985): 305–17.

54. Glen L. Urban et al., "Market Share Rewards to Pioneering Brands: An Empirical Analysis and Strategic Implications," *Management Science* (June 1986): 645–59.

55. Gregory S. Carpenter and Kent Nakamoto, "Consumer Preference Formation and Pioneering Advantage," *Journal of Marketing Research* (August 1989): 285–98.

56. Frank R. Kardes, Gurumurthy Kalyanaram, Murali Chankdrashekaran, and Ronald J. Dornoff, "Brand Retrieval, Consideration Set Composition, Consumer Choice, and the Pioneering Advantage," *Journal of Consumer Research* (June 1993): 62–75. See also Frank H. Alpert and Michael A. Kamins, "Pioneer Brand Advantage and Consumer Behavior: A Conceptual Framework and Propositional Inventory," *Journal of the Academy of Marketing Science* (Summer 1994): 244–53.

57. Thomas S. Robertson and Hubert Gatignon, "How Innovators Thwart New Entrants into Their Market," *Planning Review* (September–October 1991): 4–11, 48.

58. Steven P. Schnaars, *Managing Imitation Strategies* (New York: The Free Press, 1994). See also Jin K. Han, Namwoon Kim, and Hony-Bom Kin, "Entry Barriers: A Oull-, One-, or Two-Edged Sword for Incumbents? Unraveling the Paradox from a Contingency Perspective," *Journal of Marketing* (January 2001): 1–14.

59. Peter N. Golder and Gerald J. Tellis, "Pioneer Advantage: Marketing Logic or Marketing Legend?" *Journal of Marketing*

Research (May 1992): 34–46; Shizhang and Arthur B. Markman "Overcoming the Early Advantge: The Role of Alignable and Nanalignable Differences, *Journal of Marketing Research* (November 1998): 1–15.

60. Gerald Tellis and Peter Golder, *Will & Vision: How Latecomers Can Grow to Dominate Markets* (New York: McGraw-Hill, 2001). Rajesh K. Chanely and Gerald J. Tellis, "The Incumbent's Curse? Incumbency, Size, and Radical Product Innovation," *Journal of Marketing Research* (July 2000): 1–17.

61. John B. Frey, "Pricing Over the Competitive Cycle," speech presented at the 1982 Marketing Conference, Conference Board, New York.

62. Seanna Broder, "Reheating Starbucks," *BusinessWeek*, September 28, 1998, p. A1, <www. Starbucks.com>.

63. Linda Himelstein, "Yahoo! The Company, the Strategy, the Stock," *BusinessWeek*, September 7, 1998, pp. 66–76. Marc Gunther, "The Cheering Fades for Yahoo," *Fortune*, November 12, 2001; Ben Elgin, "Inside Yahoo! The untold story of how arrogance, infighting, and management missteps derailed one of the hottest companies on the Web," *BusinessWeek*, May 21, 2001, p. 114.

64. Joulee Andrews and Daniel C. Smith, "In Search of the Marketing Imagination: Factors Affecting the Creativity of Marketing Programs for Mature Products," *Journal of Marketing Research* (May 1996): 174–87; William Boulding, Eunkyu Lee, and Richard Staelin, "Mastering the Mix: Do Advertising, Promotion, and Sales Force Activities Lead to Differentiation?" *Journal of Marketing Research* (May 1994): 159–72.

65. John Bigness, "New Twists Revive Past Product Hits," *Houston Chronicle*, October 11, 1998, p. 8; Denise Gellene, "An Old Dog's New Tricks: Hush Puppies' Return in the '90s Is No Small Feet," *Los Angeles Times*, August 30, 1997, p. D1; Malcolm Gladwell, "How to Start an Epidemic," *The Guardian*, April 22, 2000.

66. Brian Wansink and Michael L. Ray, "Advertising Strategies to Increase Usage Frequency," *Journal of Marketing* (January 1996): 31–46. Also see Brian Wansink, "Expansion Advertising," in *How Advertising Works*, ed. John Philip Jones (Thousand Oaks, CA: Sage Publications), pp. 95–103.

67. Vanessa O'Connell, "Food: After Years of Trial and Error, a Pickle Slice That Stays Put," *Wall Street Journal*, October 6,

1998, p. B1; "Vlasic's Hamburger-Size Pickles," *Wall Street Journal*, October 5, 1998, p. A26, <www.vlasic.com>.

68. Stephen M. Nowlis and Itamar Simmonson, "The Effect of New Product Features on Brand Choice," *Journal of Marketing Research* (February 1996): 36–46.

69. Donald W. Hendon, *Classic Failures in Product Marketing* (New York: Quorum Books, 1989), p. 29.

70. Allen J. McGrath, "Growth Strategies with a '90s Twist," *Across the Board*, March 1995, pp. 43–46.

71. R. S. Alexander, "The Death and Burial of 'Sick Products,'" *Journal of Marketing* (April 1964): 1.

72. Philip Kotler, "Phasing Out Weak Products," *Harvard Business Review* (March–April 1965): 107–18; Richard T. Hise, A. Parasuraman, and R. Viswanathan, "Product Elimination: The Neglected Management Responsibility," *Journal of Business Strategy* (Spring 1984): 56–63; George J. Avlonitis, "Product Elimination Decision Making: Does Formality Matter," *Journal of Marketing* (Winter 1985): 41–52.

73. Kathryn Rudie Harrigan, "The Effect of Exit Barriers upon Strategic Flexibility," *Strategic Management Journal* 1 (1980): 165–76.

74. Kathryn Rudie Harrigan, "Strategies for Declining Industries," *Journal of Business Strategy*, (Fall 1980): 27.

75. Michael Arndt, "There's Life in the Old Bird Yet," *Business Week*, May 14, 2001, p. 77.

76. Philip Kotler, "Harvesting Strategies for Weak Products," *Business Horizons* (August 1978): 15–22; Laurence P. Feldman and Albert L. Page, "Harvesting: The Misunderstood Market Exit Strategy," *Journal of Business Strategy* (Spring 1985): 79–85.

77. Claudia H. Deutsch, "Pitney Bowes Survives Faxes, E-Mail and the Internet," *New York Times*, August 18, 1998, p. D1; Matthew Lubanko, "Pitney Bowes Faces E-Foes Despite Lion's Share of the Market," *Hartford Courant*, March 18, 2000, p. E1.

78. Nariman K. Dhalla and Sonia Yuspeh, "Forget the Product Life Cycle Concept!" *Harvard Business Review* (January–February 1976): 105.

79. Marnik G. Dekimpe and Dominique M. Hanssens, "Empirical Generalizations about Market Evolution and Stationarity," *Marketing Science* 14, no. 3, pt. 1 (1995): G109–21.

80. Leslie Walker, "Retail's Piece of the Auction: Big-Business Strategy Emerging on eBay," *Washington Post*, July 19, 2001, p. A1.

12

developing new
market offerings

In this chapter, we will address the following questions:

- What challenges does a company face in developing new products?
- What organizational structures are used to manage new-product development?
- What are the main stages in developing new products, and how can they be managed better?
- What factors affect the rate of diffusion and consumer adoption of newly launched products?

Kotler on Marketing

Who should ultimately design the product? The customer, of course.

O nce a company has carefully segmented the market, chosen its target customers, identified their needs, and determined its market positioning, it is better able to develop new products. Marketers play a key role in the new-product process, by identifying and evaluating new-product ideas and working with R&D and others in every stage of development.

Every company must develop new products. New-product development shapes the company's future. Improved or replacement products must be created to maintain or build sales. Customers want new products, and competitors will do their best to supply them. In the year 2000, consumer-product firms churned out 31,000 new products (including line extensions and new brands). Today the typical supermarket stocks 40,000 items.

A company can add new products through acquisition or development. The acquisition route can take three forms. The company can buy other companies, it can acquire patents from other companies, or it can buy a license or franchise from another company. The development route can take two forms. The company can develop new products in its own laboratories, or it can contract with independent researchers or new-product-development firms to develop specific new products.

Booz, Allen, and Hamilton identified six categories of new products:[1]

1. *New-to-the-world products: New products that create an entirely new market.*

2. *New product lines: New products that allow a company to enter an established market for the first time.*

3. *Additions to existing product lines: New products that supplement a company's established product lines (package sizes, flavors, and so on).*

4. *Improvements and revisions of existing products: New products that provide improved performance or greater perceived value and replace existing products.*

5. *Repositionings: Existing products that are targeted to new markets or market segments.*

6. *Cost reductions: New products that provide similar performance at lower cost.*

Less than 10 percent of all new products are truly innovative and new to the world. These products involve the greatest cost and risk because they are new to both the company and the marketplace. Most new-product activity is devoted to improving existing products. At Sony, over 80 percent of new-product activity is undertaken to modify and improve existing Sony products.

Most companies rarely innovate, some innovate occasionally, and a few innovate continuously. In the last category, Sony, 3M, Charles Schwab, Dell Computer, Sun Microsystems, Oracle, Southwest Airlines, Maytag, Costco, and Microsoft are the stock price gain leaders in their respective industries.[2] These companies have decided that they must build innovation into the very fiber of their businesses. They have created a positive attitude toward innovation and risk taking; they have routinized the innovation process; they practice teamwork; and they allow their people to experiment and even fail. They know that in an economy of rapid change, continuous innovation is necessary.

challenges in new-product development

Companies that fail to develop new products are putting themselves at great risk. Their existing products are vulnerable to changing customer needs and tastes, new technologies, shortened product life cycles, and increased domestic and foreign competition. New technologies are especially threatening. Most established companies focus on *incremental innovation*. Newer companies create *disruptive technologies* that are cheaper and more likely to alter the competitive space. Established companies are slow to react or invest in these disruptive technologies because they threaten their investment. Then they suddenly find themselves facing formidable new competitors, and many fail.[3]

At the same time, new-product development is risky. Texas Instruments lost $660 million before withdrawing from the home computer business; RCA lost $500 million on its videodisc players; FedEx lost $340 million on its Zap mail; Ford lost $250 million on its Edsel; DuPont lost an estimated $100 million on a synthetic leather called Corfam; and the British-French Concorde aircraft will never recover its investment.[4] Even these amounts are paltry compared to the $5 billion Iridium fiasco (see "Marketing Insight: Mismarketing: The $5 Billion Iridium Fiasco").

New products continue to fail at a disturbing rate. Recent studies put the failure rate of new consumer products at 95 percent in the United States and 90 percent in Europe.[5]

marketing **insight**

Mismarketing: The $5 Billion Iridium Fiasco

In the late 1990s, Motorola and several partners launched Iridium, a $5 billion global satellite-based wireless telephone system. Motorola's engineers envisioned launching 66 telecommunications satellites to circle the earth that would make it possible for consumers to place and receive calls with one phone anywhere in the world. Motorola's aim was to establish a universal standard for wireless telephony.

Yet in August 1999, Iridium had to file for bankruptcy because it was unable to meet a $90 million bond payment, and in March 2000, a judge ordered that the bankrupt system be shut down. Motorola was forced to pull the plug on the project. It is clear that the project's sponsors did a poor job of thinking through the four Ps and the target market size.

First, the product. The Iridium handset weighed about one pound; most cell phones weigh a couple of ounces. The handset was shaped like a brick and was awkward to carry or pack in a briefcase. The user had to carry a bag of attachments to achieve full functionality. Transmission problems included frequent incomplete calls and lost calls, and the voice quality was poorer than callers were used to on their cellular phones. *Second, the price.* Iridium was originally launched at $3,000 and eventually came down to $1,500. Worse, airtime charges ranged from $4 to $9 a minute, whether the caller was phoning in his own city or calling from a Borneo jungle. No wonder the project never attracted more than 50,000 buyers. *Third, the place.* Although the phone was touted to be workable anywhere, it could not be used inside buildings or in moving cars. Users had to have a clear path between the handset and the orbiting satellites. Furthermore, large areas in Europe, Asia, and Africa lacked service linkages.

Fourth, the promotion. Iridium budgeted $180 million for promotion. Its advertising campaign showed a man in a heavy parka pulling a sled in a desolate snowbound place. His phone suddenly rings: He has contact with the outside world. This ad campaign was supplemented with a direct-mail campaign and a strong public relations program, but all this promotion needed to be followed up by competent personal selling. This was the hardest challenge, because prospects would raise questions about price, service breakdowns, and the bulky handset, and often conclude that the benefits were not worth the price being asked. Furthermore, Motorola chose selling partners in other parts of the world who often lacked marketing skills. Although the promotion campaign generated about 1.5 million inquiries, most were not answered or not answered quickly enough.

Senior management set a drop-dead launch date of September 23, 1998, but had to delay this until November 1. Even then, the company still had problems with the product, service, distribution, support, and finances. The lesson: No amount of promotion can make a success out of a poorly designed product plagued with poor quality and poor service in many areas.

Source: Eric M. Olson, Stanley F. Slater, and Andrew J. Czaplewski, "The Iridium Story: A Marketing Disconnect?" *Marketing Management* (Summer 2000): 54–57.

(See "Marketing Insight: Mr. Failure's Lessons for Sweet Success: Robert McMath's New Product Showcase and Learning Center.")

Why do new products fail?

- A high-level executive pushes a favorite idea through in spite of negative market research findings.
- The idea is good, but the market size is overestimated.
- The product is not well designed.
- The product is incorrectly positioned in the market, not advertised effectively, or overpriced.
- The product fails to gain sufficient distribution coverage or support.
- Development costs are higher than expected.
- Competitors fight back harder than expected.

Here is a product that failed for another reason.

Campbell Soup   Campbell spent $55 million and seven years of research to develop and introduce Intelligent Quisine (IQ), a frozen food line that would help older Americans suffering from high blood pressure or diabetes actually reduce cholesterol and blood pressure. The need was great, the medical community supported it, and many people tried it in test markets. Unfortunately, consumers did not repeat-purchase IQ on a sustainable level. The overwhelming response was that the food did not taste good! They would buy it only for "emergencies." Campbell withdrew it from test markets and is not planning to reintroduce it.

marketing **insight**

Mr. Failure's Lessons for Sweet Success: Robert McMath's New Product Showcase and Learning Center

Strolling the aisles at Robert McMath's New Product Showcase and Learning Center is like being in some nightmare version of a supermarket. There is Gerber food for adults—pureed sweet-and-sour pork and chicken Madeira—microwaveable ice cream sundaes, parsnip chips, aerosol mustard, Ben-Gay aspirin, and Miller Clear Beer. How about Richard Simmons Dijon Viniagrette Salad Spray, garlic cake in a jar, and Farrah shampoo?

McMath's unusual showcase represents $4 billion in product investment. Behind each of the 80,000 products on display are squandered dollars and hopes. From them he has distilled dozens of lessons for an industry that, by its own admission, has a very short memory. McMath, a former marketer for Colgate-Palmolive, has now put his unique insights into a book, *What Were They Thinking?* Here are a few of the marketing lessons McMath espouses:

- The value of a brand is its good name, which it earns over time. People trust it to deliver a consistent set of attributes. Do not squander this trust by attaching your good name to something totally out of character. Louis Sherry No Sugar Added Gorgonzola Cheese dressing was everything that Louis Sherry, known for its rich candies and ice cream, should not be: sugarless, cheese, and salad dressing.

- Me-too marketing is the number-one killer of new products. Pepsi is one of the few survivors among dozens of other brands that have challenged Coke for more than a century. Ever hear of Toca-Cola? Coco-Cola? Yum-Yum Cola? French Wine of Cola? How about King-Cola, "the royal drink"?
- People usually do not buy products that remind them of their shortcomings. Gillette's For Oily Hair Only shampoo flopped because people did not want to confess that they had greasy hair; nor do they wish to advertise their faults and foibles to other people by carrying such products in their grocery carts.
- Some products are too different from the products, services, or experiences consumers normally purchase. You can tell that some innovative products are doomed as soon as you hear their names: Toaster Eggs, Cucumber Antiperspirant spray, Health-Sea Sea Sausage.

Sources: Paul Lukas, "The Ghastliest Product Launches," *Fortune*, March 16, 1996, p. 44; Jan Alexander, "Failure Inc." *Worldbusiness* (May–June 1996): 46; Ted Anthony, "Where's Farrah Shampoo? Next to the Salsa Ketchup," *Marketing News*, May 6, 1996, p. 13; bulleted points are adapted from Robert M. McMath and Thom Forbes, *What Were They Thinking? Marketing Lessons I've Learned from Over 80,000 New-Product Innovations and Idiocies* (New York: Times Business, 1998), pp. 22–24, 28, 30–31, and 129–30.

Several factors tend to hinder new-product development:

- *Shortage of important ideas in certain areas:* There may be few ways left to improve some basic products (such as steel, detergents).
- *Fragmented markets:* Companies have to aim their new products at smaller market segments, and this can mean lower sales and profits for each product.
- *Social and governmental constraints:* New products have to satisfy consumer safety and environmental concerns.
- *Cost of development:* A company typically has to generate many ideas to find just one worthy of development, and often faces high R&D, manufacturing, and marketing costs.
- *Capital shortages:* Some companies with good ideas cannot raise the funds needed to research and launch them.
- *Faster required development time:* Companies must learn how to compress development time by using new techniques, strategic partners, early concept tests, and advanced marketing planning. Alert companies use concurrent new-product development, in which cross-functional teams collaborate to push new products through development to market. Concurrent product development resembles a rugby match rather than a relay race, with team members passing the new product back and forth as they head toward the goal. The Allen-Bradley Corporation (a maker of industrial controls) was able to develop a new electrical control device in just two years, as opposed to six years under its old system.
- *Shorter product life cycles:* When a new product is successful, rivals are quick to copy it. Sony used to enjoy a three-year lead on its new products. Now Matsushita will copy the product within six months, leaving hardly enough time for Sony to recoup its investment.

What can a company do to develop successful new products? Cooper and Kleinschmidt found that the number-one success factor is a unique, superior product.

Such products succeed 98 percent of the time, compared to products with a moderate advantage (58 percent success) or minimal advantage (18 percent success). Another key success factor is a well-defined product concept prior to development. The company carefully defines and assesses the target market, product requirements, and benefits before proceeding. Other success factors are technological and marketing synergy, quality of execution in all stages, and market attractiveness.[6]

Madique and Zirger, in a study of successful product launches in the electronics industry, found eight factors accounting for new-product success. New-product success is greater the deeper the company's understanding of customer needs, the higher the performance-to-cost ratio, the earlier the product is introduced ahead of competition, the greater the expected contribution margin, the more spent on announcing and launching the product, the greater the top management support, and the greater the cross-functional teamwork.[7] (For the special case of high-tech products, see "Marketing Memo: Why Developing Successful High-Tech Products Is Especially Difficult.")

organizational arrangements

New-product development requires senior management to define business domains, product categories, and specific criteria. One company established the following acceptance criteria:

- The product can be introduced within five years.
- The product has a market potential of at least $50 million and a 15 percent growth rate.
- The product would provide at least 30 percent return on sales and 40 percent on investment.
- The product would achieve technical or market leadership.

Marketing
MEMO

Why Developing Successful High-Tech Products Is Especially Difficult

High tech covers a wide range of industries—telecommunications, computers, consumer electronics, biotech, software. Radical innovations carry a high level of risk and typically hurt the company's bottom line at least in the short run. The good news is that success can create a greater sustainable competitive advantage than might come from more ordinary products.

One way to define the scope of high tech is by its common characteristics:

- *High technological uncertainty:* Scientists working on high-tech products are never sure they will function as promised and be delivered on time. Will the new CAD-CAM software be ready when promised?
- *High market uncertainty:* Marketers are not sure what needs the new technology will meet. How will buyers use Interactive TV? Will the WAP standard for wireless phones be adopted in the United States? How quickly will the new microchip be adopted?
- *High competitive volatility:* Will the strongest competition come from within the industry or from outside? Will competitors use common tactics or rewrite the rules? What products will this new technology replace? How large will the market be?
- *High investment cost, low variable cost:* Many high-tech products require a large up-front investment to develop the first unit, but the costs fall rapidly on additional units. The cost of developing a new piece of software is very high, but the cost of distributing it in a CD-ROM is relatively low.
- *Short life:* Most high-tech products must be constantly upgraded. Competitors will come out with better versions, often forcing the innovator to produce a second generation before recouping its investment on the first generation.
- *Finding funding sources* for such risky projects is not easy. Companies must create a strong R&D/marketing partnership to pull it off. For radical innovations, few reliable techniques exist for estimating demand. Focus groups will provide some perspectives on customer interest and need, but high-tech marketers will have to use a *probe and learn* approach based on observing early users and collecting feedback on their experiences.

High-tech marketers also face difficult questions related to the 4 Ps:

- *Product:* What features and functions should they build into the new product? Should manufacturing be done in-house or be outsourced?
- *Price:* Should the price be set high? Would a low price be better in order to sell more quickly and go down the experience curve faster? Should the product be almost given away to accelerate adoption?
- *Place:* Is the product best sold through the company's own sales force or should it be put in the hands of agents, distributors, and dealers? Should the company start with one channel or build multiple sales channels early?
- *Promotion:* What are the best messages to convey the basic benefits and features of the new product? What are the best media for communicating these messages? What sales-promotion incentives would drive early interest and purchase?

Source: For further ideas, see Jakki Mohr, *Marketing of High-Technology Products and Innovations* (Upper Saddle River, NJ: Prentice Hall, 2001).

budgeting for new-product development

Senior management must decide how much to budget for new-product development. R&D outcomes are so uncertain that it is difficult to use normal investment criteria. Some companies solve this problem by financing as many projects as possible, hoping to achieve a few winners. Other companies apply a conventional percentage of sales figures or spend what the competition spends. Still other companies decide how many successful new products they need and work backward to estimate the required investment. The 3M Company, one of the most innovative U.S. companies, has a distinctive approach.

3M   Today 3M makes more than 50,000 products, including sandpaper, adhesives, optical films, fiber optic connectors, and Post-it® notes. Each year 3M launches scores of new products. Its immodest goal is to have each of its divisions generate at least 30 percent of sales from products less than four years on the market.[8] Here is what 3M does:

- 3M's 15 percent rule allows all employees to spend up to 15 percent of their time working on projects of personal interest. Post-it notes, masking tape, and 3M's microreplication technology grew from 15 percent–rule activities.
- 3M expects some failures: "You have to kiss a lot of frogs to find a prince."
- 3M hands out Golden Step awards each year to venture teams whose new product earned more than $2 million in U.S. sales or $4 million in worldwide sales within three years of commercial introduction.

Table 12.1 shows how a company might calculate the cost of new-product development. The new-products manager at a large consumer packaged-goods company reviewed the results of 64 ideas. Only one in four, or 16, passed the screening stage. It cost $1,000 to review each idea at this stage. Half of these ideas, or eight, survived the concept-testing stage, at a cost of $20,000 each. Half of these, or four, survived the product-development stage, at a cost of $200,000 each. Half of these, or two, did well in the test

Innovation is an important part of 3M's Web site.

table **12.1**

Finding One
Successful New
Product (Starting with
64 New Ideas)

Stage	Number of Ideas	Pass Ratio	Cost per Product Idea	Total Cost
1. Idea screening	64	1:4	$ 1,000	$ 64,000
2. Concept testing	16	1:2	20,000	320,000
3. Product development	8	1:2	200,000	1,600,000
4. Test marketing	4	1:2	500,000	2,000,000
5. National launch	2	1:2	5,000,000	10,000,000
			$5,721,000	$13,984,000

market, at a cost of $500,000 each. When these two ideas were launched, at a cost of $5 million each, only one was highly successful. Thus the one successful idea cost the company $5,721,000 to develop.

In the process, 63 other ideas fell by the wayside. The total cost for developing one successful new product was $13,984,000. Unless the company can improve the pass ratios and reduce the costs at each stage, it will have to budget nearly $14 million for each successful new idea it hopes to find. If top management wants four successful new products in the next few years, it will have to budget at least $56 million (4 × $14 million) for new-product development.

organizing new-product development

Companies handle the organizational aspect of new-product development in several ways.[9] Many companies assign responsibility for new-product ideas to *product managers*, but product managers are often so busy managing existing lines that they give little thought to new products other than line extensions. They also lack the specific skills and knowledge needed to develop and critique new products. Kraft and Johnson & Johnson have *new-product managers* who report to category managers. This position professionalizes the new-product function. Some companies have a *high-level management committee* charged with reviewing and approving proposals. Large companies often establish a *new-product department* headed by a manager who has substantial authority and access to top management. The department's major responsibilities include generating and screening new ideas, working with the R&D department, and carrying out field testing and commercialization.

3M, Dow, and General Mills often assign new-product development work to *venture teams*. A **venture team** is a cross-functional group charged with developing a specific product or business. They are "intrapreneurs" relieved of their other duties and given a budget, a time frame, and a "skunkworks" setting. *Skunkworks* are informal workplaces, sometimes garages, where intrapreneurial teams attempt to develop new products. (See "Marketing Memo: The Wisdom of Cross-Functional Teams.")

3M, Hewlett-Packard, Lego and many other companies use the **stage-gate system** to manage the innovation process.[10] The process is divided into several stages. At the end of each stage is a gate or checkpoint. The project leader, working with a cross-functional team, must bring a set of known deliverables to each gate before the project can pass to the next stage. To move from the business plan stage into product development requires a convincing market research study of consumer needs and interest, a competitive analysis, and a technical appraisal. Senior managers review the criteria at each gate to

Marketing
MEMO

The Wisdom of Cross-Functional Teams

Product development teams historically consisted almost exclusively of scientists and engineers. Although this system often reaped brilliant results, it also produced glaring inefficiencies and marketing myopia. Engineers were often driven to create a "better mousetrap" when potential customers did not really need or want one. The venerable tradition of engineers working in isolation finally ended in the late 1980s and early 1990s with the implementation of cross-functional new-product teams.

Don H. Lester, a manager of operations for a Hoechst division with 10 years of experience as a new-product venture team leader, developed the following criteria for staffing cross-functional new-product venture teams:

- *Desired team leadership style and level of expertise:* The more complex the new-product concept, the greater the desired expertise.
- *Team member skills and expertise:* Hoechst new-venture teams contain people with expertise in chemistry, engineering, market research, financial analysis, and manufacturing.
- *Level of interest in the particular new-product concept:* Is there interest or, even better, a high level of ownership and commitment (a "concept champion")?
- *Potential for personal reward:* What motivates individuals to want to participate in this effort?
- *Diversity of team members:* This includes race, gender, nationality, breadth of experience, depth of experience, and personality. The greater the diversity, the greater the range of viewpoints and decision-making potential.

Source: Don H. Lester, "Critical Success Factors for New Product Development," *Research Technology Management* (January–February 1998): 36–43.

judge whether the project deserves to move to the next stage. The gatekeepers make one of four decisions: *go, kill, hold,* or *recycle.* Stage-gate systems put strong discipline into the innovation process, making its steps visible to all involved and clarifying the project leader's and team's responsibilities at each stage.[11]

We will now look at the marketing challenges arising at each of the eight stages of the new-product development process shown in Figure 12.1.

figure **12.1**   The New-Product Development Decision Process

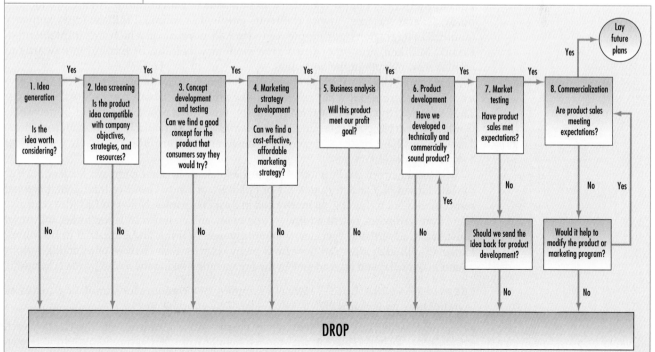

managing the development process: ideas
idea generation

The new-product development process starts with the search for ideas. New-product ideas can come from interacting with various groups and from using creativity generating techniques. (See "Marketing Memo: Ten Ways to Great New-Product Ideas.")

INTERACTING WITH OTHERS   Ideas for new products can come from customers, scientists, competitors, employees, channel members, and top management.

Customer needs and wants are the logical place to start the search for ideas. Here are two examples.

Procter & Gamble   For P&G, consumer understanding is "the heart and start" of everything it does. It has sent camera crews into homes to collect footage on everyday events, such as a mother feeding her baby or a woman washing dishes. It has set up consumer panels on the Web so users can post messages about their experiences with P&G products. P&G also set up a Future Home Lab to study consumer reactions to new household products. In these and other ways, P&G is taking an almost anthropological approach to study consumers.[12]

3M   In an attempt to grab a foothold in steel-wool soap pads, a niche dominated by SOS and Brillo, 3M arranged eight consumer focus groups around the country. The most frequent complaint with traditional soap pads was that the pads scratched expensive cookware. This finding produced the idea for the Scotch-Brite Never Scratch pad, whose sales have exceeded 3M's expectations.[13]

In the case of new industrial products, Eric von Hippel has shown that the highest percentage of ideas originate with customers.[14] Technical companies can learn a great deal by studying those customers who make the most advanced use of the company's products and who recognize the need for improvements before other customers do. Employees throughout the company can be a source of ideas for improving production, products, and services. Toyota claims its employees submit 2 million ideas annually (about 35 suggestions per employee), over 85 percent of which are implemented. Kodak, Milliken, and other firms give monetary, holiday, or recognition awards to employees who submit the best ideas.

Companies can also find good ideas by researching competitors' products and services. They can find out what customers like and dislike about competitors' products. They can buy their competitors' products, take them apart, and build better ones. Company *sales representatives* and *intermediaries* are a particularly good source of ideas. These groups have firsthand exposure to customers and are often the first to learn about competitive developments.

Top management can be another major source of ideas. Some company leaders, such as the late Edwin H. Land, former CEO of Polaroid, or Andy Grove of Intel, took personal responsibility for technological innovation in their companies. New-product ideas can also come from inventors, patent attorneys, university and commercial laboratories, industrial consultants, advertising agencies, marketing research firms, and industrial publications. However, although ideas can flow from many sources, their chances of receiving serious attention often depend on someone in the organization taking the role of *product champion*.

CREATIVITY TECHNIQUES   Here is a sampling of techniques for stimulating creativity in individuals and groups.[15]

- *Attribute listing:* List the attributes of an object, such as a screwdriver. Then modify each attribute, such as replacing the wooden handle with plastic, providing torque power, adding different screw heads, and so on.

Marketing
MEMO

Ten Ways to Great New-Product Ideas

1. Run informal sessions where groups of customers meet with company engineers and designers to discuss problems and needs and brainstorm potential solutions.
2. Allow time off—scouting time—for technical people to putter on their own pet projects. 3M allows 15 percent time off; Rohm & Haas allows 10 percent.
3. Make a customer-brainstorming session a standard feature of plant tours.
4. Survey your customers: Find out what they like and dislike in your and competitors' products.
5. Undertake "fly-on-the-wall" or "camping out" research with customers, as do Fluke and Hewlett-Packard.
6. Use iterative rounds: a group of customers in one room, focusing on identifying problems, and a group of your technical people in the next room, listening and brainstorming solutions. The proposed solutions are then tested immediately on the group of customers.
7. Set up a keyword search that routinely scans trade publications in multiple countries for new-product announcements and so on.
8. Treat trade shows as intelligence missions, where you view all that is new in your industry under one roof.
9. Have your technical and marketing people visit your suppliers' labs and spend time with their technical people—find out what is new.
10. Set up an idea vault, and make it open and easily accessed. Allow employees to review the ideas and add constructively to them.

Source: Adapted from Robert Cooper, *Product Leadership: Creating and Launching Superior New Products* (New York: Perseus Books, 1998).

- *Forced relationships:* List several ideas and consider each one in relation to each other one. In designing new office furniture, for example, consider a desk, bookcase, and filing cabinet as separate ideas. One can then imagine a desk with a built-in bookcase or a desk with built-in files or a bookcase with built-in files.

- *Morphological analysis:* Start with a problem, such as "getting something from one place to another via a powered vehicle." Now think of dimensions, such as the type of platform (cart, chair, sling, bed), the medium (air, water, oil, rails), and the power source (compressed air, electric motor, magnetic fields). By listing every possible combination, one can generate many new solutions.

- *Reverse assumption analysis:* List all the normal assumptions about an entity and then reverse them. Instead of assuming that a restaurant has menus, charges for food, and serves food, reverse each assumption. The new restaurant may decide to serve only what the chef bought that morning and cooked; may provide some food and charge only for how long the person sits at the table; and may design an exotic atmosphere and rent out the space to people who bring their own food and beverages.

- *New contexts:* Take familiar processes, such as human-helping services, and put them into a new context. Imagine helping dogs and cats instead of people with day care service, stress reduction, psychotherapy, animal funerals, and so on. As another example, instead of hotel guests going to the front desk to check in, greet them at curbside and use a wireless device to register them.

- *Mind-mapping:* Start with a thought, such as a car, write it on a piece of paper, then think of the next thought that comes up (say Mercedes), link it to car, then think of the next association (Germany), and do this with all associations that come up with each new word. Perhaps a whole new idea will materialize.

idea screening

A company should motivate its employees through rewards to submit their new ideas to an *idea manager* whose name and phone number are widely circulated. Ideas should be written down and reviewed each week by an *idea committee*. The company then sorts the proposed ideas into three groups: promising ideas, marginal ideas, and rejects. Each promising idea is researched by a committee member, who reports back to the committee. The surviving ideas then move into a full-scale screening process. In screening ideas, the company must avoid two types of errors.

Source: With permisson of Jerold Panas, Young & Partners, Inc.

figure **12.2**

Forces Fighting New Ideas

"I've got a great idea!"

"It won't work here."

"We've tried it before."

"This isn't the right time."

"It can't be done."

"It's not the way we do things."

"We've done all right without it."

"It will cost too much."

"Let's discuss it at our next meeting."

A **DROP-error** occurs when the company dismisses an otherwise good idea. It is extremely easy to find fault with other people's ideas (Figure 12.2). Some companies shudder when they look back at ideas they dismissed: Xerox saw the novel promise of Chester Carlson's copying machine, but IBM and Eastman Kodak did not. IBM thought the market for personal computers was minuscule. RCA saw the opportunity of radio; the Victor Talking Machine Company did not. Marshall Field understood the unique market-development possibilities of installment buying; Endicott Johnson did not. Sears dismissed the importance of discounting; Wal-Mart and Kmart did not.[16]

A **GO-error** occurs when the company permits a poor idea to move into development and commercialization. An *absolute product failure* loses money; its sales do not cover variable costs. A *partial product failure* loses money, but its sales cover all its variable costs and some of its fixed costs. A *relative product failure* yields a profit that is less than the company's target rate of return.

The purpose of screening is to drop poor ideas as early as possible. The rationale is that product-development costs rise substantially with each successive development stage. Most companies require new-product ideas to be described on a standard form that can be reviewed by a new-product committee. The description states the product idea, the target market, and the competition, and roughly estimates market size, product price, development time and costs, manufacturing costs, and rate of return.

The executive committee then reviews each idea against a set of criteria. Does the product meet a need? Would it offer superior value? Can it be distinctively advertised? Does the company have the necessary know-how and capital? Will the new product deliver the expected sales volume, sales growth, and profit? The product criteria are more specific for each company, as in the case of Lego.

LEGO Group   LEGO Group does not accept a new product idea unless it satisfies these questions: "Does the proposed product have the LEGO look? Will children learn while having fun? Will parents approve? Does the product maintain high quality standards? Does it stimulate creativity?"[17]

The surviving ideas can be rated using a weighted-index method like that in Table 12.2. The first column lists factors required for successful product launches, and the second column assigns importance weights. The third column scores the product idea on a scale from 0 to 1.0, with 1.0 the highest score. The final step multiplies each factor's importance by the product score to obtain an overall rating. In this example, the product idea scores .69, which places it in the "good idea" level. The purpose of this basic rating device is to promote systematic evaluation and discussion. It is not supposed to make the decision for management.

As the idea moves through development, the company will constantly need to revise its estimate of the product's overall probability of success, using the following formula:

Overall probability of success	=	Probability of technical completion	×	Probability of commercialization given technical completion	×	Probability of economic success given commercialization

For example, if the three probabilities are estimated as .50, .65, and .74, respectively, the overall probability of success is .24. The company then has to judge whether this probability is high enough to warrant continued development.

table **12.2**

Product-Idea Rating Device

Product Success Requirements	Relative Weight (a)	Product Score (b)	Product Rating (c = a × b)
Unique or superior product	.40	.8	.32
High performance-to-cost ratio	.30	.6	.18
High marketing dollar support	.20	.7	.14
Lack of strong competition	.10	.5	.05
Total	1.00		.69[a]

[a]Rating scale: .00–.30 poor; .31–.60 fair; .61–.80 good. Minimum acceptance rate: .61

managing the development process: concept to strategy
concept development and testing

Attractive ideas must be refined into testable product concepts. A *product idea* is a possible product the company might offer to the market. A *product concept* is an elaborated version of the idea expressed in meaningful consumer terms.

CONCEPT DEVELOPMENT   Let us illustrate concept development with the following situation: A large food processing company gets the idea of producing a powder to add to milk to increase its nutritional value and taste. This is a product idea, but consumers do not buy product ideas; they buy product concepts.

A product idea can be turned into several concepts. The first question is: Who will use this product? The powder can be aimed at infants, children, teenagers, young or middle-aged adults, or older adults. Second, what primary benefit should this product provide? Taste, nutrition, refreshment, energy? Third, when will people consume this drink? Breakfast, midmorning, lunch, midafternoon, dinner, late evening? By answering these questions, a company can form several concepts:

- *Concept 1:* An instant breakfast drink for adults who want a quick nutritious breakfast without preparation.
- *Concept 2:* A tasty snack drink for children to drink as a midday refreshment.
- *Concept 3:* A health supplement for older adults to drink in the late evening before they go to bed.

Each concept represents a *category concept* that defines the product's competition. An instant breakfast drink would compete against bacon and eggs, breakfast cereals, coffee and pastry, and other breakfast alternatives. A tasty snack drink would compete against soft drinks, fruit juices, and other thirst quenchers.

Suppose the instant-breakfast-drink concept looks best. The next task is to show where this powdered product would stand in relation to other breakfast products. Figure 12.3(a) uses the two dimensions of cost and preparation time to create a *product-positioning map* for the breakfast drink. An instant breakfast drink offers low cost and quick preparation. Its nearest competitor is cold cereal; its most distant competitor is bacon and eggs. These contrasts can be utilized in communicating and promoting the concept to the market.

figure **12.3**

Product and Brand Positioning

(a) Product-positioning map (breakfast market)

(b) Brand-positioning map (instant breakfast market)

Next, the product concept has to be turned into a *brand concept*. Figure 12.3(b) is a brand-positioning map showing the current positions of three existing brands of instant breakfast drinks. The company needs to decide how much to charge and how calorific to make its drink. The new brand would be distinctive in the medium-price, medium-calorie market or in the high-price, high-calorie market. The company would not want to position it next to an existing brand, unless that brand is weak or inferior.

CONCEPT TESTING Concept testing involves presenting the product concept to appropriate target consumers and getting their reactions. The concepts can be presented symbolically or physically. The more the tested concepts resemble the final product or experience, the more dependable concept testing is. In the past, creating physical prototypes was costly and time-consuming, but computer-aided design and manufacturing programs have changed that. Today firms can use *rapid prototyping* to design products (for example, small appliances or toys) on a computer, and then produce plastic models of each. Potential consumers can view the plastic models and give their reactions.[18]

Companies are also using *virtual reality* to test product concepts. Virtual reality programs use computers and sensory devices (such as gloves or goggles) to simulate reality.

Gadd International Gadd has developed a research tool called Simul-Shop, a CD-ROM virtual-reality approach that re-creates shopping situations in which researchers can test consumer reactions to factors such as product positioning, store layouts, and package designs. Suppose a cereal marketer wants to test reactions to a new package design and store shelf positioning. Using Simul-Shop on a standard desktop PC, test shoppers begin their shopping spree with a screen showing the outside of a grocery store. They click to enter the virtual store and are guided to the appropriate store section. Once there, they can scan the shelf, pick up various cereal packages, rotate them, study the labels—even look around to see what is on the shelf behind them. A Gadd's research director explains: "Once users move toward the item we want to test, [they] can look at different packaging, shelf layouts, and package colors. Depending on the activity, we can even ask users why they did what they did."[19]

Many companies today use *customer-driven engineering* to design new products. Customer-driven engineering attaches high importance to incorporating customer preferences in the final design. Here is how one company uses the World Wide Web to enhance its customer-driven engineering.

National Semiconductor National Semiconductor has used "applets"—simple multimedia applications written in Java—and parametric search technologies to make its entire product database available on the Web. With the means to track customer searches, National Semiconductor can know when a customer did not find a product. That information helps National Semiconductor shrink the time needed to identify market niches and to develop new products. It is basically high-quality market research—free.[20]

Concept testing entails presenting consumers with an elaborated version of the concept. Here is the elaboration of concept 1 in our milk example:

Our product is a powdered mixture that is added to milk to make an instant breakfast that gives the person all the needed nutrition along with good taste and high convenience. The product would be offered in three flavors (chocolate, vanilla, and strawberry) and would come in individual packets, six to a box, at $2.49 a box.

After receiving this information, researchers measure product dimensions by having consumers respond to the following questions:

figure **12.4**

Samples for Conjoint Analysis

1. *Communicability and believability:* Are the benefits clear to you and believable? If the scores are low, the concept must be refined or revised.
2. *Need level:* Do you see this product solving a problem or filling a need for you? The stronger the need, the higher the expected consumer interest.
3. *Gap level:* Do other products currently meet this need and satisfy you? The greater the gap, the higher the expected consumer interest. The need level can be multiplied by the gap level to produce a *need-gap score*. A high need-gap score means that the consumer sees the product as filling a strong need that is not satisfied by available alternatives.
4. *Perceived value:* Is the price reasonable in relation to the value? The higher the perceived value, the higher the expected consumer interest.
5. *Purchase intention:* Would you (definitely, probably, probably not, definitely not) buy the product? This would be high for consumers who answered the previous three questions positively.
6. *User targets, purchase occasions, purchasing frequency:* Who would use this product, and when and how often will the product be used?

The respondents' answers indicate whether the concept has a broad and strong consumer appeal, what products this new product competes against, and which consumers are the best targets. The need-gap levels and purchase-intention levels can be checked against norms for the product category to see whether the concept appears to be a winner, a long shot, or a loser. One food manufacturer rejects any concept that draws a definitely-would-buy score of less than 40 percent.

CONJOINT ANALYSIS   Consumer preferences for alternative product concepts can be measured through **conjoint analysis**, a method for deriving the utility values that consumers attach to varying levels of a product's attributes. Respondents are shown different hypothetical offers formed by combining varying levels of the attributes, then asked to rank the various offers. Management can identify the most appealing offer and the estimated market share and profit the company might realize.

Green and Wind have illustrated this approach in connection with developing a new spot-removing carpet-cleaning agent for home use.[21] Suppose the new-product marketer is considering five design elements:

- Three package designs (A, B, C—see Figure 12.4)
- Three brand names (K2R, Glory, Bissell)
- Three prices ($1.19, $1.39, $1.59)
- A possible Good Housekeeping seal (yes, no)
- A possible money-back guarantee (yes, no)

Although the researcher can form 108 possible product concepts ($3 \times 3 \times 3 \times 2 \times 2$), it would be too much to ask consumers to rank 108 concepts. A sample of, say, 18 contrasting product concepts can be chosen, and consumers would rank them from the most to the least preferred.

The marketer now uses a statistical program to derive the consumer's utility functions for each of the five attributes (see Figure 12.5). Utility ranges between zero and one; the higher the utility, the stronger the consumer's preference for that level of the attribute. Looking at packaging, we see that package B is the most favored, followed by C and then A (A hardly has any utility). The preferred names are Bissell, K2R, and Glory, in that order. The consumer's utility varies inversely with price. A Good Housekeeping seal is preferred, but it does not add that much utility and may not be worth the effort to obtain it. A money-back guarantee is strongly preferred. Putting these results together, we can see that the consumer's most desired offer would be package design B, with the brand name Bissell, selling at the price of $1.19, with a Good Housekeeping seal and a money-back guarantee.

figure **12.5**

Utility Functions Based
on Conjoint Analysis

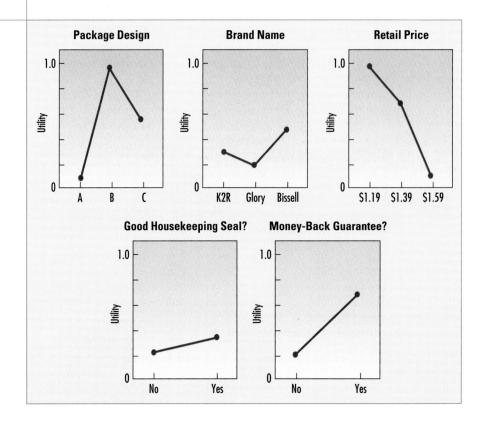

We can also determine the relative importance of each attribute to this consumer—the difference between the highest and lowest utility level for that attribute. The greater the difference, the more important the attribute. Clearly, this consumer sees price and package design as the most important attributes, followed by money-back guarantee, brand name, and last, a Good Housekeeping seal.

When preference data are collected from a sufficient sample of target consumers, the data can be used to estimate the market share any specific offer is likely to achieve, given any assumptions about competitive response. The company, however, may not launch the market offer that promises to gain the greatest market share because of cost considerations. The most customer-appealing offer is not always the most profitable offer to make. Under some conditions, researchers will collect the data not with a full-profile description of each offer, but by presenting two factors at a time. For example, respondents may be shown a table with three price levels and three package types and asked which of the nine combinations they would like most, followed by which one they would prefer next, and so on. They would then be shown a further table consisting of trade-offs between two other variables. The trade-off approach may be easier to use when there are many variables and possible offers. However, it is less realistic in that respondents are focusing on only two variables at a time.

Conjoint analysis has become one of the most popular concept-development and testing tools. Marriott designed its Courtyard hotel concept with the benefit of conjoint analysis. Other applications have included airline travel services, ethical drug design, and credit-card features.

marketing strategy

Following a successful concept test, the new-product manager will develop a preliminary marketing-strategy plan for introducing the new product into the market. The plan consists of three parts. The first part describes the target market's size, structure, and behavior; the planned product positioning; and the sales, market share, and profit goals sought in the first few years:

> The target market for the instant breakfast drink is families with children who are receptive to a new, convenient, nutritious, and inexpensive form of breakfast. The company's brand will be positioned at the higher-price, higher-quality end of the instant-breakfast-drink category. The company will aim initially to sell 500,000 cases or 10 percent of the market, with a loss in the first year not exceeding $1.3 million. The second year will aim for 700,000 cases or 14 percent of the market, with a planned profit of $2.2 million.

The second part outlines the planned price, distribution strategy, and marketing budget for the first year:

> The product will be offered in chocolate, vanilla, and strawberry in individual packets of six to a box at a retail price of $2.49 a box. There will be 48 boxes per case, and the case price to distributors will be $24. For the first two months, dealers will be offered one case free for every four cases bought, plus cooperative-advertising allowances. Free samples will be distributed door to door. Coupons for 20¢ off will appear in newspapers. The total sales-promotional budget will be $2.9 million. An advertising budget of $6 million will be split 50:50 between national and local. Two-thirds will go into television and one-third into newspapers. Advertising copy will emphasize the benefit concepts of nutrition and convenience. The advertising-execution concept will revolve around a small boy who drinks instant breakfast and grows strong. During the first year, $100,000 will be spent on marketing research to buy store audits and consumer-panel information to monitor market reaction and buying rates.

The third part of the marketing-strategy plan describes the long-run sales and profit goals and marketing-mix strategy over time:

> The company intends to win a 25 percent market share and realize an after-tax return on investment of 12 percent. To achieve this return, product quality will start high and be improved over time through technical research. Price will initially be set at a high level and lowered gradually to expand the market and meet competition. The total promotion budget will be boosted each year about 20 percent, with the initial advertising–sales promotion split of 65:35 evolving eventually to 50:50. Marketing research will be reduced to $60,000 per year after the first year.

business analysis

After management develops the product concept and marketing strategy, it can evaluate the proposal's business attractiveness. Management needs to prepare sales, cost, and profit projections to determine whether they satisfy company objectives. If they do, the concept can move to the development stage. As new information comes in, the business analysis will undergo revision and expansion.

ESTIMATING TOTAL SALES Total estimated sales are the sum of estimated first-time sales, replacement sales, and repeat sales. Sales-estimation methods depend on whether the product is a one-time purchase (such as an engagement ring or retirement home), an infrequently purchased product, or a frequently purchased product. For one-time purchased products, sales rise at the beginning, peak, and later approach zero as the number of potential buyers is exhausted (see Figure 12.6[a]). If new buyers keep entering the market, the curve will not go down to zero.

figure **12.6**

Product Life–Cycle Sales for Three Types of Products

Infrequently purchased products—such as automobiles, toasters, and industrial equipment—exhibit replacement cycles dictated by physical wearing out or by obsolescence associated with changing styles, features, and performance. Sales forecasting for this product category calls for estimating first-time sales and replacement sales separately (see Figure 12.6[b]).

Frequently purchased products, such as consumer and industrial nondurables, have product life-cycle sales resembling Figure 12.6(c). The number of first-time buyers initially increases and then decreases as fewer buyers are left (assuming a fixed population). Repeat purchases occur soon, providing that the product satisfies some buyers. The sales curve eventually falls to a plateau representing a level of steady repeat-purchase volume; by this time, the product is no longer a new product.

In estimating sales, the manager's first task is to estimate first-time purchases of the new product in each period. To estimate replacement sales, management has to research the product's *survival-age distribution*—that is, the number of units that fail in year one, two, three, and so on. The low end of the distribution indicates when the first replacement sales will take place. The actual timing will be influenced by a variety of factors. Because replacement sales are difficult to estimate before the product is in use, some manufacturers base the decision to launch a new product solely on the estimate of first-time sales.

For a frequently purchased new product, the seller has to estimate repeat sales as well as first-time sales. A high rate of repeat purchasing means that customers are satisfied; sales are likely to stay high even after all first-time purchases take place. The seller should note the percentage of repeat purchases that take place in each repeat-purchase class: those who rebuy once, twice, three times, and so on. Some products and brands are bought a few times and dropped.[22]

ESTIMATING COSTS AND PROFITS   Costs are estimated by the R&D, manufacturing, marketing, and finance departments. Table 12.3 illustrates a five-year projection of sales, costs, and profits for the instant breakfast drink.

Row 1 shows the projected sales revenue over the five-year period. The company expects to sell $11,889,000 (approximately 500,000 cases at $24 per case) in the first year.

table **12.3**

Projected Five-Year Cash-Flow Statement (in thousands of dollars)

	Year 0	Year 1	Year 2	Year 3	Year 4	Year 5
1. Sales revenue	$ 0	$11,889	$15,381	$19,654	$28,253	$32,491
2. Cost of goods sold	0	3,981	5,150	6,581	9,461	10,880
3. Gross margin	0	7,908	10,231	13,073	18,792	21,611
4. Development costs	−3,500	0	0	0	0	0
5. Marketing costs	0	8,000	6,460	8,255	11,866	13,646
6. Allocated overhead	0	1,189	1,538	1,965	2,825	3,249
7. Gross contribution	−3,500	−1,281	2,233	2,853	4,101	4,716
8. Supplementary contribution	0	0	0	0	0	0
9. Net contribution	−3,500	−1,281	2,233	2,853	4,101	4,716
10. Discounted contribution (15%)	−3,500	−1,113	1,691	1,877	2,343	2,346
11. Cumulative discounted cash flow	−3,500	−4,613	−2,922	−1,045	1,298	3,644

Behind this sales projection is a set of assumptions about the rate of market growth, the company's market share, and the factory-realized price. *Row 2* shows the cost of goods sold, which hovers around 33 percent of sales revenue. This cost is found by estimating the average cost of labor, ingredients, and packaging per case. *Row 3* shows the expected gross margin, which is the difference between sales revenue and cost of goods sold.

Row 4 shows anticipated development costs of $3.5 million, including product-development cost, marketing-research costs, and manufacturing-development costs. *Row 5* shows the estimated marketing costs over the five-year period to cover advertising, sales promotion, and marketing research and an amount allocated for sales force coverage and marketing administration. *Row 6* shows the allocated overhead to this new product to cover its share of the cost of executive salaries, heat, light, and so on.

Row 7, the gross contribution, is found by subtracting the preceding three costs from the gross margin. *Row 8*, supplementary contribution, lists any change in income from other company products caused by the introduction of the new product. It has two components. *Dragalong income* is additional income on other company products resulting from adding this product to the line. *Cannibalized income* is the reduced income on other company products resulting from adding this product to the line.[23] Table 12.3 assumes no supplementary contributions. *Row 9* shows the net contribution, which in this case is the same as the gross contribution. *Row 10* shows the discounted contribution—that is, the present value of each future contribution discounted at 15 percent per annum. For example, the company will not receive $4,716,000 until the fifth year. This amount is worth only $2,346,000 today if the company can earn 15 percent on its money through other investments.[24]

Finally, *row 11* shows the cumulative discounted cash flow, which is the cumulation of the annual contributions in row 10. Two things are of central interest. The first is the maximum investment exposure, which is the highest loss that the project can create. We see that the company will be in a maximum loss position of $4,613,000 in year 1. The second is the payback period, which is the time when the company recovers all of its investment, including the built-in return of 15 percent. The payback period here is approximately three and a half years. Management therefore has to decide whether to risk a maximum investment loss of $4.6 million and a possible payback period of three and a half years.

Companies use other financial measures to evaluate the merit of a new-product proposal. The simplest is **break-even analysis**, in which management estimates how many units of the product the company would have to sell to break even with the given price and cost structure. Or the estimate may be in terms of how many years it will take to break even. If management believes sales could easily reach the break-even number, it is likely to move the project into product development.

The most complex method of estimating profit is **risk analysis**. Here three estimates (optimistic, pessimistic, and most likely) are obtained for each uncertain variable affecting profitability under an assumed marketing environment and marketing strategy for the planning period. The computer simulates possible outcomes and computes a rate-of-return probability distribution showing the range of possible rates of returns and their probabilities.[25]

managing the development process: development to commercialization
product development

Up to now, the product has existed only as a word description, a drawing, or a prototype. This step involves a large jump in investment that dwarfs the costs incurred in the earlier stages. At this stage the company will determine whether the product idea can be translated into a technically and commercially feasible product. If it cannot, the accumulated project cost will be lost except for any useful information gained in the process.

The job of translating target customer requirements into a working prototype is helped by a set of methods known as *quality function deployment* (QFD). The methodology takes the list of desired *customer attributes* (CAs) generated by market research and turns them into a list of *engineering attributes* (EAs) that the engineers can use. For example, customers of a proposed truck may want a certain acceleration rate (CA). Engineers can turn this into the required horsepower and other engineering equivalents (EAs). The methodology permits measuring the trade-offs and costs of providing the customer requirements. A major contribution of QFD is that it improves communication between marketers, engineers, and the manufacturing people.[26]

The R&D department will develop one or more physical versions of the product concept. Its goal is to find a prototype that embodies the key attributes described in the product-concept statement, that performs safely under normal use and conditions, and that can be produced within the budgeted manufacturing costs. Developing and manufacturing a successful prototype can take days, weeks, months, or even years. Sophisticated virtual-reality technology is speeding the process. By designing and testing product designs through simulation, for example, companies achieve the flexibility to respond to new information and to resolve uncertainties by quickly exploring alternatives.

Boeing   Boeing designed its 777 aircraft on a totally digital basis. Engineers, designers, and more than 500 suppliers designed the aircraft on a special computer network without ever making a blueprint on paper. Its partners were connected by an extranet enabling them to communicate, share ideas, and work on the design at a distance. A computer-generated "human" could climb inside the three-dimensional design on-screen to show how difficult maintenance access would be for a live mechanic. Such computer modeling allowed engineers to spot design errors that otherwise would have remained undiscovered until a person began to work on a physical prototype. Avoiding the time and cost associated with building physical prototypes reduced development time and scrappage and rework by 60 to 90 percent.[27]

Maxwell House   Even developing a new taste formula can take time. Maxwell House discovered that consumers wanted coffee that was "bold, vigorous, and deep tasting." Its laboratory technicians spent over four months working with various coffee blends and flavors to formulate a corresponding taste that turned out to be too expensive to produce. The company cost-reduced the blend to meet the target manufacturing cost. The change compromised the taste, and the new brand did not sell well in the market.

With the rise of the World Wide Web, there is a need for more rapid prototyping and more flexible development processes (see "Marketing for the New Economy: Production Cycles in the Internet Age"). Michael Schrage, research associate at MIT's media lab, has correctly predicted: "Effective prototyping may be the most valuable 'core competence' an innovative organization can hope to have."[28] This has certainly been true for software companies such as Microsoft, Netscape, and the hundreds of Silicon Valley start-ups. Although Schrage says that specification-driven companies require that every "i" be dotted and "t" be crossed before anything can be shown to the next level of management, prototype-driven companies—such as Yahoo!, Microsoft, and Netscape—cherish quick-and-dirty tests and experiments.

Lab scientists must not only design the product's functional characteristics, but also communicate its psychological aspects through physical cues. How will consumers react to different colors, sizes, and weights? In the case of a mouthwash, a yellow color supports an "antiseptic" claim (Listerine), a red color supports a "refreshing" claim (Lavoris), and a green or blue color supports a "cool" claim (Scope). Marketers need to supply lab people with information on what attributes consumers seek and how consumers judge whether these attributes are present.

marketing for the **new economy**

Production Cycles in the Internet Age

The PC industry is a good example of a turbulent business environment. The rapid pace of technological innovation during the 1980s and 1990s ushered in an era of unprecedented growth in this industry. Product cycles in the PC industry took about one year to complete during the 1980s; by 1999 they had been reduced to three months. Because of the speed at which technology currently improves, computer components like microprocessors and memory are especially time-sensitive. Today's latest, fastest, and best components will be surpassed by even better components within months. Most computer manufacturers now delay until the end of the production cycle the inclusion of the most time-sensitive components. Dell Computer takes this approach to its logical extreme by building each computer according to the customer's specification and shipping it directly from the factory the moment it is ready. A Dell customer can visit the company's Web site, customize a new PC or laptop, and expect delivery within 10 days.

Lands' End Japan Web site.

With the advent of e-commerce, the expansion of the Internet has even benefited nontechnology companies. Establishing a new e-commerce venture takes considerably less time than building a new brick-and-mortar or, in catalog retailer Lands' End's case, a mail-order business. Using the Internet, Lands' End launched catalog businesses in three different European countries within a year. Before the Internet, it took the company 10 years to launch its first three international catalog businesses.

In light of the troubles recently faced by dot-coms and other tech companies, many of which did business at a breakneck pace, we should remember that speed is just one of many factors that determine a company's ability to compete. These examples demonstrate that companies can achieve marked growth by making speed a priority. If faster production were their only advantage, however, companies like Dell and Lands' End would not likely be as successful.

Source: James Curry and Martin Kenney, "Beating the Clock: Corporate Responses to Rapid Change in the PC Industry," *California Management Review*, October 1, 1999, p. 8.

When the prototypes are ready, they must be put through rigorous functional tests and *customer tests. Alpha testing* is the name given to testing the product within the firm to see how it performs in different applications. After refining the prototype further, the company moves to *beta testing*. It enlists a set of customers to use the prototype and give feedback. Beta testing is most useful when the potential customers are heterogeneous, the potential applications are not fully known, several decision makers are involved in purchasing the product, and opinion leadership from early adopters is sought.[29] Here are some of the functional tests that products go through before they enter the marketplace.

Shaw Industries At Shaw Industries, temps are paid $5 an hour to pace up and down five long rows of sample carpets for up to eight hours a day, logging an average of 14 miles each. One regular reads three mysteries a week while pacing and shed 40 pounds in two years. Shaw Industries counts walkers' steps and figures that 20,000 steps equal several years of average wear.

Apple Computer Apple Computer assumes the worst for its PowerBook customers and submits the computers to a battery of indignities: It drenches the computers in Pepsi and other sodas, smears them with mayonnaise, and bakes them in ovens at temperatures of 140 degrees or more to simulate conditions in a car trunk.

Gillette At Gillette, 200 volunteers from various departments come to work unshaven each day, troop to the second floor of the company's South Boston manufacturing and research plant, and enter small booths with a sink and mirror. There they take instructions from technicians on the other side of a small window as to which razor, shaving cream, or aftershave to use, and then they fill out questionnaires. "We bleed so you'll get a good shave at home," says one Gillette employee.[30]

Consumer testing can take several forms, from bringing consumers into a laboratory to giving them samples to use in their homes. In-home placement tests are common with products ranging from ice cream flavors to new appliances. When DuPont developed its new synthetic carpeting, it installed free carpeting in several homes in exchange for the homeowners' willingness to report their likes and dislikes about the carpeting.

Consumer preferences can be measured in several ways. Suppose a consumer is shown three items—A, B, and C, such as three cameras, three insurance plans, or three advertisements.

- The *rank-order* method asks the consumer to rank the three items in order of preference. The consumer might respond with A>B>C. Although this method has the advantage of simplicity, it does not reveal how intensely the consumer feels about each item nor whether the consumer likes any item very much. It is also difficult to use this method when there are many objects to be ranked.
- The *paired-comparison* method calls for presenting pairs of items and asking the consumer which one is preferred in each pair. Thus the consumer could be presented with the pairs AB, AC, and BC and say that she prefers A to B, A to C, and B to C. Then we could conclude that A>B>C. People find it easy to state their preference between two items, and this method allows the consumer to focus on the two items, noting their differences and similarities.
- The *monadic-rating* method asks the consumer to rate liking of each product on a scale. Suppose a seven-point scale is used, where 1 signifies intense dislike, 4 indifference, and 7 intense like. Suppose the consumer returns the following ratings: A=6, B=5, C=3. We can derive the individual's preference order (i.e., A>B>C), and even know the qualitative levels of the person's preference for each and the rough distance between preferences.

market testing

After management is satisfied with functional and psychological performance, the product is ready to be dressed up with a brand name and packaging, and put into a market test. The new product is introduced into an authentic setting to learn how large the market is and how consumers and dealers react to handling, using, and repurchasing the product.

Not all companies undertake market testing. A company officer at Revlon, Inc., stated: "In our field—primarily higher-priced cosmetics not geared for mass distribution—it would be unnecessary for us to market test. When we develop a new product, say an improved liquid makeup, we know it's going to sell because we're familiar with the field. And we've got 1,500 demonstrators in department stores to promote it." Most companies, however, know that market testing can yield valuable information about buyers, dealers, marketing program effectiveness, and market potential. The main issues are: How much market testing should be done, and what kind(s)?

The amount of market testing is influenced by the investment cost and risk on the one hand, and the time pressure and research cost on the other. High investment–high risk products, where the chance of failure is high, must be market tested; the cost of the market tests will be an insignificant percentage of the total project cost. High-risk products—those that create new-product categories (first instant breakfast drink) or have novel features (first fluoride toothpaste)—warrant more market testing than modified products (another toothpaste brand).

The amount of market testing may be severely reduced if the company is under great time pressure because the season is just starting or because competitors are about to launch their brands. The company may therefore prefer to face the risk of a product failure to the risk of losing distribution or market penetration on a highly successful product.

Here we describe consumer-goods market testing and business-goods market testing.

CONSUMER-GOODS MARKET TESTING   In testing consumer products, the company seeks to estimate four variables: *trial, first repeat, adoption,* and *purchase frequency.* The company hopes to find all these variables at high levels. In some cases, it will find many consumers trying the product but few rebuying it; or it might find high permanent adoption but low purchase frequency (as with gourmet frozen foods).

Here are four major methods of consumer-goods market testing, from the least to the most costly.

Sales-Wave Research   In *sales-wave research,* consumers who initially try the product at no cost are reoffered the product, or a competitor's product, at slightly reduced prices. They might be reoffered the product as many as three to five times (sales waves), with the company noting how many customers selected that product again and their reported level of satisfaction. Sales-wave research can also include exposing consumers to one or more advertising concepts to see the impact of that advertising on repeat purchase.

Sales-wave research can be implemented quickly, conducted with a fair amount of security, and carried out without final packaging and advertising. However, sales-wave research does not indicate the trial rates that would be achieved with different sales-promotion incentives, because the consumers are preselected to try the product; nor does it indicate the brand's power to gain distribution and favorable shelf position.

Simulated Test Marketing   *Simulated test marketing* calls for finding 30 to 40 qualified shoppers and questioning them about brand familiarity and preferences in a specific product category. These people are then invited to a brief screening of both well-known and new commercials or print ads. One ad advertises the new product, but it is not singled out for attention. Consumers receive a small amount of money and are invited into a store where they may buy any items. The company notes how many consumers buy the new brand and competing brands. This provides a measure of the ad's relative effectiveness against competing ads in stimulating trial. Consumers are asked the reasons for their purchases or non-purchases. Those who did not buy the new brand are given a free sample. Some weeks later, they are reinterviewed by phone to determine product attitudes, usage, satisfaction, and re-purchase intention and are offered an opportunity to repurchase any products.

This method gives fairly accurate results on advertising effectiveness and trial rates (and repeat rates if extended) in a much shorter time and at a fraction of the cost of using real test markets. Pretests often take only three months and may cost $250,000.[31] The results are incorporated into new-product forecasting models to project ultimate sales levels. Marketing research firms report surprisingly accurate predictions of sales levels of products that are subsequently launched in the market.[32]

Controlled Test Marketing   In this method, a research firm manages a panel of stores that will carry new products for a fee. The company with the new product specifies the number of stores and geographic locations it wants to test. The research firm delivers the product to the participating stores and controls shelf position; number of facings, displays, and point-of-purchase promotions; and pricing. Sales results can be measured through electronic scanners at the checkout. The company can also evaluate the impact of local advertising and promotions during the test.

Controlled test marketing allows the company to test the impact of in-store factors and limited advertising on buying behavior. A sample of consumers can be interviewed later to give their impressions of the product. The company does not have to use its own sales force, give trade allowances, or "buy" distribution. However, controlled test marketing provides no information on how to sell the trade on carrying the new product. This technique also exposes the product and its features to competitors' scrutiny.

Test Markets   The ultimate way to test a new consumer product is to put it into full-blown test markets. The company chooses a few representative cities, and the sales force tries to sell the trade on carrying the product and giving it good shelf exposure. The company puts on a full advertising and promotion campaign in these markets similar to the one that it would use in national marketing. A full-scale test can cost over $1 million, depending on the number of test cities, the test duration, and the amount of data the company wants to collect.

Management faces several decisions:

1. *How many test cities?* Most tests use between two and six cities. The greater the maximum possible loss, the greater the number of contending marketing strategies, the greater the regional differences, and the greater the chance of test-market interference by competitors, the greater the number of cities that should be used.
2. *Which cities?* Each company must develop selection criteria such as having good media coverage, cooperative chain stores, and average competitive activity.
3. *Length of test?* Market tests last anywhere from a few months to a year. The longer the average repurchase period, the longer the test period necessary.
4. *What information?* Warehouse shipment data will show gross inventory buying but will not indicate weekly sales at the retail level. Store audits will show retail sales and competitors' market shares but will not reveal buyer characteristics. Consumer panels will indicate which people are buying which brands and their loyalty and switching rates. Buyer surveys will yield in-depth information about consumer attitudes, usage, and satisfaction.
5. *What action to take?* If the test markets show high trial and repurchase rates, the product should be launched nationally; if they show a high trial rate and a low repurchase rate, the product should be redesigned or dropped; if they show a low trial rate and a high repurchase rate, the product is satisfying but more people have to try it. This means increasing advertising and sales promotion. If trial and repurchase rates are both low, the product should be abandoned.

Test marketing permits testing the impact of alternative marketing plans:

Colgate   Colgate used a different marketing mix in each of four cities to market a new soap product: (1) an average amount of advertising coupled with free samples distributed door to door, (2) heavy advertising plus samples, (3) an average amount of advertising linked with mailed redeemable coupons, and (4) an average amount of advertising with no special introductory offer. The third alternative generated the best profit level, although not the highest sales level.

In spite of its benefits, many companies today are skipping test marketing and relying on faster and more economical market-testing methods. General Mills now prefers to launch new products in perhaps 25 percent of the country, an area too large for rivals to disrupt. Managers review retail scanner data, which tell them within days how the product is doing and what corrective fine-tuning to do. Colgate-Palmolive often launches a new product in a set of small "lead countries" and keeps rolling it out if it proves successful.

BUSINESS–GOODS MARKET TESTING Business goods can also benefit from market testing. Expensive industrial goods and new technologies will normally undergo alpha testing (within the company) and beta testing (with outside customers). During beta testing, the vendor's technical people observe how test customers use the product, a practice that often exposes unanticipated problems of safety and servicing and alerts the vendor to customer training and servicing requirements. The vendor can also observe how much value the equipment adds to the customer's operation as a clue to subsequent pricing.

The vendor will ask the test customers to express their purchase intention and other reactions after the test. Vendors must carefully interpret the beta test results because only a small number of test customers are used, they are not randomly drawn, and the tests are somewhat customized to each site. Another risk is that test customers who are unimpressed with the product may leak unfavorable reports about it.

A second common test method for business goods is to introduce the new product at trade shows. The vendor can observe how much interest buyers show in the new product, how they react to various features and terms, and how many express purchase intentions or place orders. Book publishers, for instance, regularly launch their fall titles at the American Booksellers Association convention each spring. They display page proofs wrapped in dummy book covers. If a large bookstore chain objects to a cover design or title of a promising new book, the publisher will consider making changes. The disadvantage of trade shows is that they reveal the product to competitors; therefore, the vendor should be ready to launch the product soon after the trade show.

New industrial products can be tested in distributor and dealer display rooms, where they may stand next to the manufacturer's other products and possibly competitors' products. This method yields preference and pricing information in the product's normal selling atmosphere. The disadvantages are that the customers might want to place early orders that cannot be filled, and those customers who come in might not represent the target market.

Industrial manufacturers come close to using full test marketing when they give a limited supply of the product to the sales force to sell in a limited number of areas that receive promotion support and printed catalog sheets.

commercialization

If the company goes ahead with commercialization, it will face its largest costs to date. The company will have to contract for manufacture or build or rent a full-scale manufacturing facility. Plant size will be a critical decision. When Quaker Oats launched its 100 Percent Natural breakfast cereal, it built a smaller plant than called for by the sales forecast. The demand so exceeded the forecast that for about a year it could not supply enough product to stores. Although Quaker Oats was gratified with the response, the low forecast cost it a considerable amount of profit.

Another major cost is marketing. To introduce a major new consumer packaged good into the national market, the company may have to spend between $20 million and $80 million in advertising and promotion in the first year. In the introduction of new food products, marketing expenditures typically represent 57 percent of sales during the first year. Most new-product campaigns rely on a sequenced mix of market communication tools.

In the movie business, companies make and launch "new products" costing $75 to $100 million each without spending much on market research. Hollywood studios believe that films are different from other products and audience size cannot be predicted. Yet Josh Eliashberg and his co-researchers recently created Moviemod, a prerelease market evaluation tool for motion pictures which is designed to generate box office forecasts and to support marketing, advertising, and distribution-related decisions for a new movie after it has been produced but before its public release.[33] This tool is designed to help Hollywood make better use of the $25 million that companies normally spend on marketing. Moviemod incorporates variables for word of mouth, distribution intensity, film advertising, the movie theme, movie quality, and critics' reviews. It draws data by exposing a representative sample of moviegoers to the new film and uses their responses to make a forecast. In two different trials, Moviemod has predicted total sales and revenues to within 5 percent of the actual figures in two different markets. If Moviemod had been applied to *Godzilla,* the story would have been different:

Sony Pictures Entertainment   Sony Pictures spent $125 million to make its blockbuster *Godzilla,* and some $200 million to make sure it was a hit. Actually, 250 marketing partners, such as Taco Bell, put up $150 million of that $200 million for licensing rights to Godzilla backpacks, T-shirts, and other scaly paraphernalia. The huge ad campaign included billboards and buses, buttons and T-shirts, TV and radio. Yet, the only truly big thing about *Godzilla* was that it was a big flop. Critics panned the movie and audiences agreed. When Sony's top brass saw the initial screening and realized *Godzilla* would be a bomb, they went out and spent even more money on marketing to lure as many moviegoers as possible into theaters early. The gamble paid off. Sony would end up grossing more than the $175 million it spent to make and market *Godzilla.*[34]

WHEN (TIMING)   In commercializing a new product, market-entry timing is critical. Suppose a company has almost completed the development work on its new product and learns that a competitor is nearing the end of its development work. The company faces three choices:

1. *First entry:* The first firm entering a market usually enjoys the "first mover advantages" of locking up key distributors and customers and gaining reputational leadership. But, if the product is rushed to market before it is thoroughly debugged, the first entry can backfire.
2. *Parallel entry:* The firm might time its entry to coincide with the competitor's entry. The market may pay more attention when two companies are advertising the new product.
3. *Late entry:* The firm might delay its launch until after the competitor has entered. The competitor will have borne the cost of educating the market. Its product may reveal faults the late entrant can avoid. The late entrant can also learn the size of the market.

The timing decision involves additional considerations. If a new product replaces an older product, the company might delay the introduction until the old product's stock is drawn down. If the product is seasonal, it might be delayed until the right season arrives;[35] and often a product waits for a "killer application" to occur. Microwave ovens began to enjoy explosive growth only after microwave-oven popcorn was developed.

WHERE (GEOGRAPHIC STRATEGY)   The company must decide whether to launch the new product in a single locality, a region, several regions, the national market, or the international market. Most will develop a planned market rollout over time. Coca-Cola launched its new soda, Citra, a caffeine-free, grapefruit-flavored drink, in about half the United States. The multistaged rollout, following test marketing in Phoenix, south Texas, and south Florida, began in January 1998 in Dallas, Denver, and Cincinnati.[36]

Company size is an important factor here. Small companies will select an attractive city and put on a blitz campaign. They will enter other cities one at a time. Large companies will introduce their product into a whole region and then move to the next region. Companies with national distribution networks, such as auto companies, will launch their new models in the national market.

Most companies design new products to sell primarily in the domestic market. If the product does well, the company considers exporting to neighboring countries or the world market, redesigning if necessary. Cooper and Kleinschmidt, in their study of industrial products, found that domestic products designed solely for the domestic market tend to show a high failure rate, low market share, and low growth. In contrast, products designed for the world market—or at least to include neighboring countries—achieve significantly more profits, both at home and abroad. Yet only 17 percent of the products in Cooper and Kleinschmidt's study were designed with an international orientation.[37] The implication is that companies should adopt an international focus in designing and developing new products.

In choosing rollout markets, the major criteria are market potential, company's local reputation, cost of filling the pipeline, cost of communication media, influence of area on other areas, and competitive penetration. The presence of strong competitors will influence rollout strategy. Suppose McDonald's wants to launch a new chain of fast-food pizza parlors. Pizza Hut, a formidable competitor, is strongly entrenched on the East Coast. Another pizza chain is entrenched on the West Coast but is weak. The Midwest is the battleground between two other chains. The South is open, but Shakey's is planning to move in. McDonald's faces a complex decision in choosing a geographic rollout strategy.

With the World Wide Web connecting far-flung parts of the globe, competition is more likely to cross national borders. Companies are increasingly rolling out new products simultaneously across the globe, rather than nationally or even regionally. However, masterminding a global launch provides challenges. Autodesk, the world's leading supplier of PC design software and multimedia tools, has 3 million customers in more than 150 countries. Carol Bartz, chairman and CEO, says that the biggest obstacle to a global launch success is getting all the different marketers to agree with the positioning: "Then the issue is speed—getting the materials out fast enough. We get them to agree on the look (using one image), and then it's a matter of putting a local spin on it. It requires an immense amount of concentration."[38]

Companies will increasingly add the Web as another advertising medium to launch and describe each important new product:

Philips   Philips, the Dutch electronics company, recently launched Pronto, an "Intelligent Remote Control" to replace all other devices that receive infrared signals. Its Web address, *www.pronto.philips.com*, contains several features: About Pronto, A Virtual Tour, Where to Buy, Pronto News, Pronto Communities, and FAQs and Contacts. This is much richer information than any ad could offer.

TO WHOM (TARGET-MARKET PROSPECTS)   Within the rollout markets, the company must target its initial distribution and promotion to the best prospect groups. Presumably, the company has already profiled the prime prospects, who would ideally have the following characteristics: They would be early adopters, heavy users, and

Philips' Pronto Web site.

opinion leaders, and they could be reached at a low cost.[39] Few groups have all these characteristics. The company should rate the various prospect groups on these characteristics and target the best group. The aim is to generate strong sales as soon as possible to attract further prospects. (See "Marketing Insight: Strategies for Launching Technological Innovations.")

marketing **insight**

Strategies for Launching Technological Innovations

Many families still have not purchased a computer, answering machine, cellular phone, palm pilot, or a Web TV set. Even among those who have a home computer, many have resisted using it to order an online education course, or purchase a car online, or apply for a large loan over the Internet. Companies think they can overcome this resistance with conventional marketing approaches, particularly mass-advertising. Parasuraman and Colby believe an entirely different strategy is required. They have been researching "techno-ready consumers" and have identified five segments based on attitudes toward optimism and innovation (which drive adoption) and discomfort and insecurity (which inhibit adoption):

- *Explorers* are extremely high on the drivers of technology readiness and very low on inhibitors such as discomfort and insecurity. They are usually younger, upscale, and male. They comprise the first wave of customer adopters of innovations.
- *Pioneers* desire the benefits of the innovation but are more practical about the difficulties. Pioneers tend to be young, middle class, and success-oriented.
- *Skeptics* are low in optimism and innovation but might buy eventually if they are convinced of the benefits. They are of average age and upper middle class.
- *Paranoids* are optimistic about technology but do not tend to adopt innovations. They exhibit a high degree of discomfort and insecurity. They tend to be middle aged and have lower incomes.
- *Laggards* are pessimistic and have little interest in innovations. They are characterized by discomfort and insecurity. They tend to be older and have lower incomes.

Because consumers vary in their technological readiness, the technology marketer should build a campaign that successively reaches explorers, pioneers, and further groups, with different appeals. Parasuraman and Colby recommend several strategies:

- *Technology evangelism:* Apple Computer users became passionate about the superiority of Apple software and spread the word to others.
- *Future-ready design:* The innovator needs to launch a version that seems to be fairly complete and workable for at least a few years.
- *Proving benefits:* Companies must articulate and demonstrate clear benefits.
- *Market-stage pricing:* Companies must bring down the innovation's price to attract groups with lower techno-readiness.

The authors recommend some additional practices to improve adoption success:

- *Customer-focused design:* The company must design the offering so that it appears easy to use.
- *Responsive customer care:* The company should stand ready to offer help over the phone or by e-mail or in-person.
- *Reassuring communications:* The company should offer demonstrations, reassuring feedback, strong brand names, and guarantees.

Geoffrey Moore, in his *Crossing the Chasm*, focuses on the necessity of changing the marketing messages and tools if the innovation is to move smoothly into new market segments. He sees the potential market as consisting of five adoption groups: innovators, early adopters, early majority, late majority, and laggards, with each group having different motives for adopting or resisting the new product. Unless the company recognizes these differences and adapts its marketing approach, the product is likely to lose momentum and miss the transition to the next segment.

- *Innovators* are *technology enthusiasts* and enjoy tinkering with new products and mastering their intricacies. In return for low prices, they are happy to conduct alpha and beta testing and report on early weaknesses.
- *Early adopters* are *visionaries* who search for new technologies that might give them a dramatic competitive advantage. They are less price-sensitive and willing to adopt the product if given personalized solutions and good service support.
- *Early majority* are *pragmatists* who adopt the new technology when its benefits are proven and a lot of adoption has already taken place. They make up the mainstream market.
- *Late majority* are *conservatives* who are risk averse, technology shy, and price-sensitive.
- *Laggards* are *skeptics* who resist the innovation until they find that the status quo is no longer defensible.

Each of the five groups must be approached with a different type of marketing if the firm wants to move its innovation through the full product life cycle.

Sources: A. Parasuraman and Charles L. Colby, *Techno-Ready Marketing* (New York: The Free Press, 2001); Geoffrey A. Moore, *Crossing the Chasm: Marketing and Selling High-Tech Products to Mainstream Customers* (New York: HarperBusiness, 1999); Jakki Mohr, *Marketing of High-Technology Products and Innovations* (Upper Saddle River, NJ: Prentice Hall, 2001).

HOW (INTRODUCTORY MARKET STRATEGY)   The company must develop an action plan for introducing the new product into the rollout markets. With its debut in 1998, the competitively priced iMac represented Apple Computer's reentry into the computer PC business after a hiatus of 14 years. The company staged a massive marketing blitz to launch the new machine.

Apple Computer   Apple's launch of the iMac, the sleek, egg-shaped computer with one-touch Internet access, was dramatic. For starters, the iMac was a closely guarded secret until May 6, 1998, when Steve Jobs literally unveiled the machine to awestruck reporters. The buzz continued to mount, online and off, until the machine went on sale in August. On the weekend of August 14, computer retailers prepared Midnight Madness sales featuring 20-foot-high inflatable iMacs flying above the stores. Radio stations across the country began an iMac countdown, topped off with iMac giveaways. Jobs personally signed five "golden" tickets and placed them in the boxes of five iMacs, with the winner receiving a free iMac each year for the next five years. Apple augmented these efforts with a $100 million ad campaign, its biggest ever, to promote iMac through TV, print, radio, and billboards. The campaign featured images of the iMac alongside slogans such as "Mental Floss" and "I think, therefore iMac."[40]

To coordinate the many activities involved in launching a new product, management can use network-planning techniques such as critical path scheduling. **Critical path scheduling (CPS)** calls for developing a master chart showing the simultaneous and sequential activities that must take place to launch the product. By estimating how much time each activity takes, the planners estimate completion time for the entire project. Any delay in any activity on the critical path will cause the project to be delayed. If the launch must be completed earlier, the planner searches for ways to reduce time along the critical path.[41]

the consumer–adoption process

How do potential customers learn about new products, try them, and adopt or reject them? (**Adoption** is an individual's decision to become a regular user of a product.) *The consumer-adoption process* is later followed by the *consumer-loyalty process*, which is the concern of the established producer. Years ago, new-product marketers used a *mass-market approach* to launch products. This approach had two main drawbacks: It called for heavy marketing expenditures, and it involved many wasted exposures. These drawbacks led to a second approach, *heavy-user target marketing*. This approach makes sense, provided that heavy users are identifiable and are early adopters. However, even within the heavy-user group, many heavy users are loyal to existing brands. New-product marketers now aim at consumers who are early adopters.

The theory of innovation diffusion and consumer adoption helps marketers identify early adopters.

stages in the adoption process

An **innovation** is any good, service, or idea that is *perceived* by someone as new. The idea may have a long history, but it is an innovation to the person who sees it as new. Innovations take time to spread through the social system. Rogers defines the **innovation diffusion process** as "the spread of a new idea from its source of invention or creation to its ultimate users or adopters."[42] The consumer-adoption process focuses on the mental process through which an individual passes from first hearing about an innovation to final adoption.

Adopters of new products have been observed to move through five stages:

1. *Awareness:* The consumer becomes aware of the innovation but lacks information about it.
2. *Interest:* The consumer is stimulated to seek information about the innovation.
3. *Evaluation:* The consumer considers whether to try the innovation.
4. *Trial:* The consumer tries the innovation to improve his or her estimate of its value.
5. *Adoption:* The consumer decides to make full and regular use of the innovation.

The new-product marketer should facilitate movement through these stages. A portable electric-dishwasher manufacturer might discover that many consumers are stuck in the interest stage; they do not buy because of their uncertainty and the large investment cost, but these same consumers would be willing to use an electric dishwasher on a trial basis for a small monthly fee. The manufacturer should consider offering a trial-use plan with option to buy.

Developers of general-interest interactive CD-ROM titles found that consumers were stuck in the interest or trial stage and moved less rapidly to adoption.

CD-ROMs In the early 1990s, multimedia developers were producing action games and educational software and moving into a hodgepodge of interactive products that ranged from hypertext novels to multimedia music anthologies. Today, few of these products are selling well or even on the market. Most CD-ROMs, particularly reference titles, found a more cost-effective home on the Web, a medium that also enables them to keep up-to-date and link to a community of users. CD-ROMs also faced hundreds of competitors in an extremely fragmented entertainment market. Another problem was the glut of titles with serious quality problems, especially technical glitches. The newer DVD-ROM technology, which has caught on among home movie viewers in particular, is expected to have a greater number of shipments than CD-ROMs in 2002.[43]

factors influencing the adoption process

Marketers recognize the following characteristics of the adoption process: differences in individual readiness to try new products; the effect of personal influence; differing rates of adoption; and differences in organizations' readiness to try new products.

READINESS TO TRY NEW PRODUCTS AND PERSONAL INFLUENCE Everett Rogers defines a person's innovativeness as "the degree to which an individual is relatively earlier in adopting new ideas than the other members of his social system." In each product area, there are pioneers and early adopters. Some people are the first to adopt new clothing fashions or new appliances; some doctors are the first to prescribe new medi-

figure **12.7**

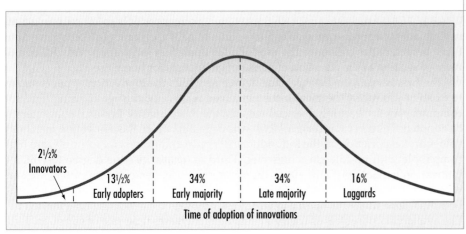

Source: Redrawn from Everett M. Rogers, *Diffusion of Innovations* (New York: The Free Press, 1983).

cines; and some farmers are the first to adopt new farming methods. People can be classified into the adopter categories shown in Figure 12.7. After a slow start, an increasing number of people adopt the innovation, the number reaches a peak, and then it diminishes as fewer nonadopters remain.

Rogers sees the five adopter groups as differing in their value orientations. Innovators are venturesome; they are willing to try new ideas. Early adopters are guided by respect; they are opinion leaders in their communities and adopt new ideas early but carefully. The early majority are deliberate; they adopt new ideas before the average person. The late majority are skeptical; they adopt an innovation only after a majority have tried it. Finally, laggards are tradition-bound; they are suspicious of change, mix with other tradition-bound people, and adopt the innovation only when it takes on a measure of tradition itself.

This classification suggests that an innovating firm should research the demographic, psychographic, and media characteristics of innovators and early adopters and direct communications specifically to them. According to Rogers, earlier adopters tend to be younger in age, have higher social status, and a more favorable financial position. They utilize a greater number of more cosmopolitan information sources than do later adopters.[44]

Personal influence is the effect one person has on another's attitude or purchase probability. Although personal influence is an important factor, its significance is greater in some situations and for some individuals than for others. Personal influence is more important in the evaluation stage of the adoption process than in the other stages. It has more influence on late adopters than early adopters. It also is more important in risky situations.

Companies often target innovators and early adopters with their product rollouts. Here is one example.

Red Bull   When sports/energy drink company Red Bull entered the U. S. market after achieving phenomenal success in Europe, it targeted "small market cells" in California with high percentages of early adopters. Santa Cruz, with a high concentration of young sports enthusiasts and a trend-setting reputation, was the first target market. Next came select areas in San Francisco, followed by test markets in Venice Beach and Santa Monica. In these markets, the company pursues a "seeding program": It uses a small team of marketers to place the product at "in" spots, gradually moving from bars and clubs to convenience stores and restaurants, and finally entering supermarkets.

After seeding programs in smaller test markets produced inspired results, Red Bull moved to larger markets like Miami, Chicago, and Atlanta.[45]

CHARACTERISTICS OF THE INNOVATION Some products catch on immediately (rollerblades), whereas others take a long time to gain acceptance (diesel engine autos). Five characteristics influence the rate of adoption of an innovation. We will consider them in relation to the adoption of personal computers for home use.

The first is *relative advantage*—the degree to which the innovation appears superior to existing products. The greater the perceived relative advantage of using a personal computer, say, for keeping financial records, the more quickly personal computers will be adopted. The second is *compatibility*—the degree to which the innovation matches the values and experiences of the individuals. Personal computers, for example, are highly compatible with middle-class lifestyles. Third is *complexity*—the degree to which the innovation is relatively difficult to understand or use. Personal computers are somewhat complex and will therefore take a slightly longer time to penetrate into home use. Fourth is *divisibility*—the degree to which the innovation can be tried on a limited basis. The availability of rentals or friend's computers increases their rate of adoption. Fifth is *communicability*—the degree to which the beneficial results of use are observable or describable to others. The fact that personal computers lend themselves to easy demonstration and description helps them diffuse faster in the social system.

Other characteristics that influence the rate of adoption are cost, risk and uncertainty, scientific credibility, and social approval. The new-product marketer has to research all these factors and give the key ones maximum attention in designing the new-product and marketing program.[46]

ORGANIZATIONS' READINESS TO ADOPT INNOVATIONS The creator of a new teaching method would want to identify innovative schools. The producer of a new piece of medical equipment would want to identify innovative hospitals. Adoption is associated with variables in the organization's environment (community progressiveness, community income), the organization itself (size, profits, pressure to change), and the administrators (education level, age, sophistication). Other forces come into play in trying to get a product adopted into organizations that receive the bulk of their funding from the government, such as public schools. A controversial or innovative product can be squelched by negative public opinion.

summary

1. Once a company has segmented the market, chosen its target customer groups and identified their needs, and determined its desired market positioning, it is ready to develop and launch appropriate new products. Marketing should participate with other departments in every stage of new-product development.

2. Successful new-product development requires the company to establish an effective organization for managing the development process. Companies can choose to use product managers, new-product managers, new-product committees, new-product departments, or new-product venture teams.

3. Eight stages are involved in the new-product development process: idea generation, screening, concept development and testing, marketing-strategy development, business analysis, product development, market testing, and commercialization. The purpose of each stage is to determine whether the idea should be dropped or moved to the next stage.

4. The consumer-adoption process is the process by which customers learn about new products, try them, and adopt or reject them. Today many marketers are targeting heavy users and early adopters of new products, because both groups can be reached by specific media and tend to be opinion leaders. The consumer-adoption process is influenced by many factors beyond the marketer's control, including consumers' and organizations' willingness to try new products, personal influences, and the characteristics of the new product or innovation.

applications

marketing debate – who should you target with new products?

Many firms target lead users or innovators with their new products, with the assumption that their adoption will trickle down to influence the broader market. Others disagree with this approach and contend that the most efficient and quickest route is to target the broader or even mass-market directly.

Take a position: New products should always target new adopters versus New products should target the broadest market possible.

marketing and advertising

1. The ad in Figure 1 introduces a new blend of seasonings from Mrs. Dash, along with a recipe in which it can be used. The inset showing ripe tomatoes, fresh basil leaves, and garlic cloves highlights the flavors featured in the new product, one in a line of other seasoning blends.

   a. How could this idea have been described as a product concept during the product-development process? Suggest an appropriate concept statement.

   b. What forms of consumer testing would be appropriate for this seasoning product? Why?

   c. Which of the four consumer-goods market testing methods do you think Mrs. Dash should have used to gauge consumer reaction prior to launching this product? Explain your answer.

2. Office furniture manufacturer Steelcase recently introduced the new product shown in Figure 2, an interactive sign system for managing meeting rooms.

   a. Into which of the six categories of new products does this sign system fit? Explain.

   b. In estimating total sales for the RoomWizard sign system, would Steelcase consider this a one-time purchase, an infrequently purchased product, or a frequently purchased product? What are the implications for the product life-cycle sales curve?

   c. Would Steelcase have benefited from alpha testing of this new product? What other market testing methods would you recommend for this product—and why?

Figure 1

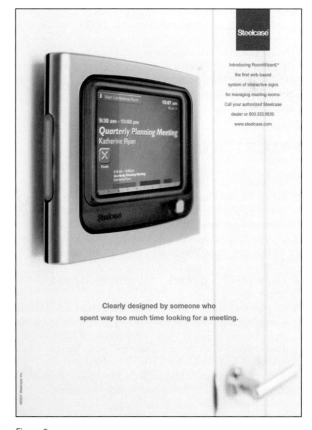

Figure 2

online marketing today

Intuit, which makes Quicken, Quickbooks, and other financial management software packages, is well-known for applying customer-driven engineering in its new-product development process. Many months before a new program is scheduled to be released, the company invites individuals and business users to become beta testers of a "prerelease" version. Then Intuit's marketers and technical specialists ask beta testers to comment on all aspects of the software, including the ease of use and the value of the features.

Visit Intuit's Web site (www.intuit.com) and browse the home page. Follow any visible links to the beta testing page (located at http://beta.intuit.com/public/default.cfm) or use the search function to find the location if this page is not available through a direct link. Why would consumers and business customers want to participate in the beta testing of an Intuit software package? Why does Intuit impose restrictions on prospective beta testers? What does Intuit stand to gain from testers' feedback? How early in the development process do you think Intuit should start beta testing?

you're the marketer: sonic pda marketing plan

Marketing Plan Pro

Product strategy is based on the choices companies make as they segment their markets, research and target customer groups, and create an appropriate market positioning. With this foundation, marketers are ready to plan for new-product development and management.

Now you are considering Sonic's new-product development options for its line of personal digital assistants (PDAs). In light of what you know about the company and the recommendations you have made so far in the marketing-planning process, answer these questions to continue with the Sonic marketing plan:

- What specific needs of the targeted customer segments should Sonic seek to profitably satisfy with a second PDA product?
- Working alone or with other students, generate at least four ideas for new PDA products, and indicate the criteria Sonic should use to screen these ideas.
- Develop the most promising idea into a product concept and explain how Sonic can test this concept. What particular dimensions must be tested?

- Assuming that this idea has tested well, develop a marketing strategy for the introduction of the new product. Include a description of the target market; the product positioning; the estimated sales, profit, and market-share goals for the first year; your channel strategy; and the marketing budget you will recommend for this new-product introduction. If possible, estimate Sonic's costs and conduct a break-even analysis.
- Into which of the six categories of new products identified by Booz, Allen, and Hamilton does Sonic's first PDA product fit? Into which of these categories does your suggested new product fit? What are the implications for Sonic's marketing plan?

As your instructor directs, summarize your ideas in a written marketing plan or enter them in the Marketing Mix, Marketing Research, Break-Even, Sales Forecast, Budgets Analysis, and Milestone sections of the *Marketing Plan Pro* software. Be sure to include your estimates of sales, profits, and budget requirements for the new product, along with a schedule for its introduction.

notes

1. Booz, Allen & Hamilton, *New Products Management for the 1980s* (New York: Booz, Allen & Hamilton, 1982).
2. For details, see Thomas Kuczmarski, Arthur Middlebrooks, and Jeffrey Swaddling, *Innovating the Corporation: Creating Value for Customers and Shareholders* (Lincolnwood, IL: NTC, 2000).
3. Clayton M. Christensen, *The Innovator's Dilemma: When New Technologies Cause Great Firms to Fail* (Boston: Harvard Business School Press, 1997).
4. Christopher Power, "Flops," *BusinessWeek*, August 16, 1993, pp. 76–82.
5. Deloitte and Touche, "Vision in Manufacturing Study," Deloitte Consultng and Kenan-Flagler Business School, March 6, 1998; A. C. Nielsen, "New Product Introduction—Successful Innovation/Failure: Fragile Boundary," A. C. Nielsen BASES and Ernst & Young Global Client Consulting, June 24, 1999.
6. Robert G. Cooper and Elko J. Kleinschmidt, *New Products: The Key Factors in Success* (Chicago: American Marketing Association, 1990).
7. Modesto A. Madique and Billie Jo Zirger, "A Study of Success and Failure in Product Innovation: The Case of the U.S.

Electronics Industry," *IEEE Transactions of Engineering Management* (November 1984): 192–203.
8. Michelle Conlin, "Too Much Doodle?" *Forbes*, October 19, 1998, pp. 54–55; Tim Stevens, "Idea Dollars," *Industry Week*, February 16, 1998, pp. 47–49.
9. David S. Hopkins, *Options in New-Product Organization* (New York: Conference Board, 1974); Doug Ayers, Robert Dahlstrom, and Steven J. Skinner, "An Exploratory Investigation of Organizational Antecedents to New Product Success," *Journal of Marketing Research* (February 1997): 107–16.
10. Robert G. Cooper, "Stage-Gate Systems: A New Tool for Managing New Products," *Business Horizons* (May–June 1990): 44–54. See also "The New Prod System: The Industry Experience," *Journal of Product Innovation Management* 9 (1992): 113–27.
11. Robert Cooper, *Product Leadership: Creating and Launching Superior New Products* (New York: Perseus Books, 1998).
12. "Consumed by the Consumer," *Financial Times*, May 23, 2001, p. 12.

13. Constance Gustke, "Built to Last," *Sales & Marketing Management* (August 1997): 78–83.

14. Eric von Hippel, "Lead Users: A Source of Novel Product Concepts," *Management Science* (July 1986): 791–805. Also see *The Sources of Innovation* (New York: Oxford University Press, 1988); and "Learning from Lead Users," in *Marketing in an Electronic Age*, ed. Robert D. Buzzell (Cambridge, MA: Harvard Business School Press, 1985), pp. 308–17.

15. Michael Michalko, *Cracking Creativity: The Secrets of Creative Genius* (Berkeley, CA: Ten Speed Press, 1998); James M. Higgins, *101 Creative Problem Solving Techniques* (New York: New Management Publishing Company, 1994).

16. Mark Hanan, "Corporate Growth through Venture Management," *Harvard Business Review* (January–February 1969): 44. See also Carol J. Loomis, "Dinosaurs?" *Fortune*, May 3, 1993, pp. 36–42.

17. Kathleen M. Eisenhardt and Donald Sull, "Strategy as Simple Rules," *Harvard Business Review* (January–February 2001): 111.

18. "The Ultimate Widget: 3-D 'Printing' May Revolutionize Product Design and Manufacturing," *U.S. News & World Report*, July 20, 1992, p. 55

19. Tom Dellacave Jr., "Curing Market Research Headaches," *Sales & Marketing Management* (July 1996): 84–85.

20. Dan Deitz, "Customer-Driven Engineering," *Mechanical Engineering* (May 1996): 68; "In Search of e-Success," *Chief Executive*, January, 2000, pp. 54–61.

21. The full-profile example was taken from Paul E. Green and Yoram Wind, "New Ways to Measure Consumers' Judgments," *Harvard Business Review* (July–August 1975): 107–17. © 1975 by the President and Fellows of Harvard College, all rights reserved. Also see Paul E. Green and V. Srinivasan, "Conjoint Analysis in Marketing: New Developments with Implications for Research and Practice," *Journal of Marketing* (October 1990): 3–19; Jonathan Weiner, "Forecasting Demand: Consumer Electronics Marketer Uses a Conjoint Approach to Configure Its New Product and Set the Right Price," *Marketing Research: A Magazine of Management & Applications* (Summer 1994): 6–11; Dick R. Wittnick, Marco Vriens, and Wim Burhenne, "Commercial Uses of Conjoint Analysis in Europe: Results and Critical Reflections," *International Journal of Research in Marketing* (January 1994): 41–52.

22. Robert Blattberg and John Golany, "Tracker: An Early Test Market Forecasting and Diagnostic Model for New Product Planning," *Journal of Marketing Research* (May 1978): 192–202; Glen L. Urban, Bruce D. Weinberg, and John R. Hauser, "Premarket Forecasting of Really New Products," *Journal of Marketing* (January 1996): 47–60; Peter N. Golder and Gerald J. Tellis, "Will It Ever Fly? Modeling the Takeoff of Really New Consumer Durables," *Marketing Science* 16, no. 3 (1997): 256–70.

23. Roger A. Kerin, Michael G. Harvey, and James T. Rothe, "Cannibalism and New Product Development," *Business Horizons* (October 1978): 25–31.

24. The present value (V) of a future sum (I) to be received t years from today and discounted at the interest rate (r) is given by $V5I_t/(11r)^t$. Thus $\$4,761,000/(1.15)^55\$2,346,000$.

25. David B. Hertz, "Risk Analysis in Capital Investment," *Harvard Business Review* (January–February 1964): 96–106.

26. John Hauser, "House of Quality," *Harvard Business Review* (May–June 1988): 63–73. Customer-driven engineering is also called "quality function deployment." See Lawrence R. Guinta and Nancy C. Praizler, *The QFD Book: The Team Approach to Solving Problems and Satisfying Customers through Quality Function Deployment* (New York: AMACOM, 1993); V. Srinivasan, William S. Lovejoy, and David Beach, "Integrated Product Design for Marketability and Manufacturing," *Journal of Marketing Research* (February 1997): 154–63.

27. Marco Iansiti and Alan MacCormack, "Developing Products on Internet Time," *Harvard Business Review* (September–October 1997): 108–17; Srikant Datar, C. Clark Jordan, and Kannan Srinivasan, "Advantages of Time-Based New Product Development in a Fast-Cycle Industry," *Journal of Marketing Research* (February 1997): 36–49; Christopher D. Ittner and David F. Larcker, "Product Development Cycle Time and Organizational Performance," *Journal of Marketing Research* (February 1997): 13–23.

28. Tom Peters, *The Circle of Innovation* (New York: Alfred A. Knopf, 1997), p. 96. For more general discussion, see also Rajesh Sethi, "New Product Quality and Product Development Teams," *Journal of Marketing* (April 2000): 1–14; Christine Moorman and Anne S. Miner, "The Convergence of Planning and Execution Improvisation in New Product Development," *Journal of Marketing* (July 1998): 1–20; and Ravinchoanath MacChavan and Rajiv Graver, "From Embedded Knowledge to Embodied Knowledge: New Product Development as Knowledge Management," *Journal of Marketing* (October 1998): 1–12.

29. Ibid., p. 99.

30. Faye Rice, "Secrets of Product Testing," *Fortune*, November 28, 1994, pp. 172–74; Lawrence Ingrassia, "Taming the Monster: How Big Companies Can Change: Keeping Sharp: Gillette Holds Its Edge by Endlessly Searching for a Better Shave," *Wall Street Journal*, December 10, 1992, p. A1.

31. Christopher Power, "Will It Sell in Podunk? Hard to Say," *Business Week*, August 10, 1992, pp. 46–47.

32. Kevin J. Clancy, Robert S. Shulman, and Marianne Wolf, *Simulated Test Marketing: Technology for Launching Successful New Products* (New York: Lexington Books, 1994); V. Mahajan and Jerry Wind, "New Product Models: Practice, Shortcomings, and Desired Improvements," *Journal of Product Innovation Management* 9 (1992): 129–39; Glen L. Urban, John R. Hauser, and Roberta A. Chicos, "Information Acceleration: Validation and Lessons from the Field," *Journal of Marketing Research* (February 1997): 143–53.

33. Jehoshua Eliashberg, Jedid-Jah Jonker, Mohanbir S. Sawhney, and Berend Wierenga, "Moviemod: An Implementable Decision-Support System for Prerelease Market Evaluation of Motion Pictures," *Marketing Science* 19 (Summer 2000): 226–43.

34. Corie Brown, "The Lizard Was a Turkey," *Newsweek*, June 15, 1998, p. 71; Tim Carvell, "How Sony Created a Monster," *Fortune*, June 8, 1998, pp. 162–70.

35. For further discussion, see Robert J. Thomas, "Timing: The Key to Market Entry," *Journal of Consumer Marketing* (Summer 1985): 77–87; Thomas S. Robertson, Jehoshua Eliashberg, and Talia Rymon, "New Product Announcement Signals and Incumbent Reactions," *Journal of Marketing* (July 1995): 1–15; Frank H. Alpert and Michael A. Kamins, "Pioneer Brand Advantages and Consumer Behavior: A Conceptual Framework and Propositional Inventory," *Journal of the Academy of Marketing Science* (Summer 1994): 244–36; and Barry L. Bayos, Sanjay Jain, and Ambar Rao, "Consequences: An Analysis of Truth or Vaporware and New Product Announcements," *Journal of Marketing Research* (February 2001): 3–13.

36. Mickey H. Gramig, "Coca-Cola Unveiling New Citrus Drink," *Atlanta Journal and Constitution*, January 24, 1998, p. E3.

37. Cooper and Kleinschmidt, *New Products*, pp. 35–38.

38. Erika Rasmusson, "Staying Power," *Sales & Marketing Management* (August 1998): 44–46.

39. Philip Kotler and Gerald Zaltman, "Targeting Prospects for a New Product," *Journal of Advertising Research* (February 1976): 7–20.

40. Jim Carlton, "From Apple, a New Marketing Blitz," *Wall Street Journal*, August 14, 1998, p. B1.

41. For details, see Keith G. Lockyer, *Critical Path Analysis and Other Project Network Techniques* (London: Pitman, 1984). Also see Arvind Rangaswamy and Gary L. Lilien, "Software Tools for New Product Development," *Journal of Marketing Research*, (February 1997): 177–84.

42. The following discussion leans heavily on Everett M. Rogers, *Diffusion of Innovations* (New York: The Free Press, 1962). Also see his third edition, published in 1983.

43. Gillian Newson and Eric Brown, "CD-ROM: What Went Wrong?" *NewMedia* (August 1998): 32–38; DVD Experiences "Success in the Living Room," *Business Wire*, December 15, 1999.

44. Rogers, *Diffusion of Innovations*, p. 192. Also see S. Ram and Hyung-Shik Jung, "Innovativeness in Product Usage: A Comparison of Early Adopters and Early Majority," *Psychology and Marketing* (January–February 1994): 57–68.

45. Claire Phoenix, "Red Bull—Fact and Function," *Soft Drinks World* (February 2001).

46. Hubert Gatignon and Thomas S. Robertson, "A Propositional Inventory for New Diffusion Research," *Journal of Consumer Research* (March 1985): 849–67; Vijay Mahajan, Eitan Muller, and Frank M. Bass, "Diffusion of New Products: Empirical Generalizations and Managerial Uses," *Marketing Science* 14, no. 3, part 2 (1995): G79–G89; Fareena Sultan, John U. Farley, and Donald R. Lehman, "Reflection on 'A Meta-Analysis of Applications of Diffusion Models,'" *Journal of Marketing Research* (May 1996): 247–49; Minhi Hahn, Sehoon Park, and Andris A. Zoltners, "Analysis of New Product Diffusion Using a Four-segment Trial-repeat Model," *Marketing Science* 13, no. 3 (1994): 224–47.

13

designing global market offerings

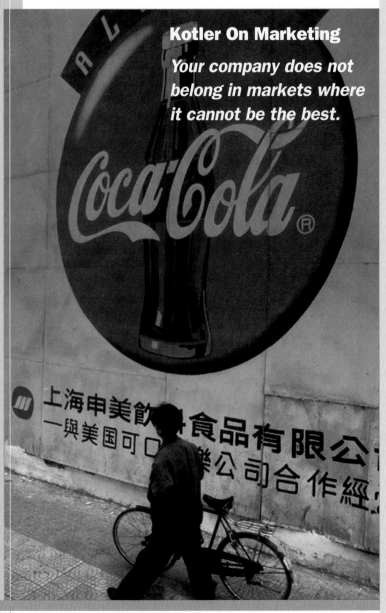

Kotler On Marketing

Your company does not belong in markets where it cannot be the best.

In this chapter, we will address the following questions:

- What factors should a company review before deciding to go abroad?
- How can companies evaluate and select specific foreign markets to enter?
- What are the major ways of entering a foreign market?
- To what extent must the company adapt its products and marketing program to each foreign country?
- How should the company manage and organize its international activities?

With faster communication, transportation, and financial flows, the world is rapidly shrinking. Products developed in one country—Gucci purses, Mont Blanc pens, McDonald's hamburgers, Japanese sushi, Chanel suits, German BMWs—are finding enthusiastic acceptance in others. A German businessman may wear an Armani suit to meet an English friend at a Japanese restaurant, who later returns home to drink Russian vodka and watch an American soap on TV.

Since 1969, the number of multinational corporations in the world's 14 richest countries has more than tripled, from 7,000 to 24,000. In fact, these companies today control one-third of all private sector assets and enjoy worldwide *sales of $6 trillion. International trade now accounts for one-quarter of U.S. GDP, up from 11 percent in 1970.*[1]

True, many companies have conducted international marketing for decades. Nestlé, Shell, Bayer, and Toshiba are familiar to consumers around the world; but global competition is intensifying: Domestic companies who never thought about foreign competitors suddenly find them in their backyards. Newspapers report on the gains of Japanese, German, Swedish, and Korean car imports in the U.S. market; and the loss of textile and shoe markets to Third World imports. Many companies that are thought to be American firms are really foreign firms: Bantam Books, Baskin-Robbins Ice Cream, Firestone Tires, Dr. Pepper soft drinks, and Pillsbury cake mixes, for example.

competing on a global basis

Although some U.S. businesses may want to eliminate foreign competition through protective legislation, the better way to compete is to continuously improve products at home and expand into foreign markets. Ironically, although companies need to enter and compete in foreign markets, the risks are high: huge foreign indebtedness, shifting borders, unstable governments, foreign-exchange problems, tariffs and other trade barriers, corruption, and technological pirating. Still, we argue that companies selling in global industries have no choice but to internationalize their operations. To do this, they must make a series of decisions (see Figure 13.1). Each of these decisions will be examined here.

A **global industry** is an industry in which the strategic positions of competitors in major geographic or national markets are fundamentally affected by their overall global positions.[2] A **global firm** is a firm that operates in more than one country and captures R&D, production, logistical, marketing, and financial advantages in its costs and reputation that are not available to purely domestic competitors. Global firms plan, operate, and coordinate their activities on a worldwide basis. Ford's "world truck" has a European-made cab and a North American–built chassis, is assembled in Brazil, and is imported into the United States for sale. Otis Elevator gets its door systems from France, small geared parts from Spain, electronics from Germany, and special motor drives from Japan; it uses the United States for systems integration. A company need not be large to sell globally. Small and medium-sized firms can practice global nichemanship. Even a sports league can be global:

The NBA   When the NBA season is over, basketball's big stars do not head to Florida for rest and recreation. Shaquille O'Neal is off to South Korea, Karl Malone to Hong Kong, Allen Iverson to Chile. Deployed by the NBA and global sponsors Coca-Cola, Reebok, and McDonald's, these well-paid traveling salesmen hawk soda, sneakers, burgers, and basketball to legions of young fans. The NBA, which has more than 100 global staff members, has emerged as the first American sports league to truly go global. In 2001, NBA games were broadcast to 210 countries in 42 languages. The league has signed on global sponsors such as Yahoo! and IBM; and the league and its partners have sold roughly $1 billion of NBA-licensed products outside the United States in the past five years.[3]

deciding whether to go abroad

Most companies would prefer to remain domestic if their domestic market were large enough. Managers would not need to learn other languages and laws, deal with volatile currencies, face political and legal uncertainties, or redesign their products to suit dif-

figure 13.1

Major Decisions in
International Marketing

Deciding whether
to go abroad

Deciding which
markets to
enter

Deciding how
to enter the
market

Deciding on
the marketing
program

Deciding on
the marketing
organization

ferent customer needs and expectations. Business would be easier and safer. Yet several factors are drawing more and more companies into the international arena:

- Global firms offering better products or lower prices can attack the company's domestic market. The company might want to counterattack these competitors in their home markets.
- The company discovers that some foreign markets present higher profit opportunities than the domestic market.
- The company needs a larger customer base to achieve economies of scale.
- The company wants to reduce its dependence on any one market.
- The company's customers are going abroad and require international servicing.

Before making a decision to go abroad, the company must weigh several risks:

- The company might not understand foreign customer preferences and fail to offer a competitively attractive product (Table 13.1 lists some famous blunders in this arena).
- The company might not understand the foreign country's business culture or know how to deal effectively with foreign nationals.
- The company might underestimate foreign regulations and incur unexpected costs.
- The company might realize that it lacks managers with international experience.
- The foreign country might change its commercial laws, devalue its currency, or undergo a political revolution and expropriate foreign property.

Because of the competing advantages and risks, companies often do not act until some event thrusts them into the international arena. Someone—a domestic exporter, a foreign importer, a foreign government—solicits the company to sell abroad, or the company is saddled with overcapacity and must find additional markets for its goods.

table **13.1**
Blunders in International Marketing

Hallmark cards failed when they were introduced in France. The French dislike syrupy sentiment and prefer writing their own cards.

Philips began to earn a profit in Japan only after it had reduced the size of its coffeemakers to fit into smaller Japanese kitchens and its shavers to fit smaller Japanese hands.

Coca-Cola had to withdraw its two-liter bottle in Spain after discovering that few Spaniards owned refrigerators with large enough compartments to accommodate it.

General Foods' Tang initially failed in France because it was positioned as a substitute for orange juice at breakfast. The French drink little orange juice and almost none at breakfast.

Kellogg's Pop-Tarts failed in Britain because the percentage of British homes with toasters was significantly lower than in the United States, and the product was too sweet for British tastes.

Procter & Gamble's Crest toothpaste initially failed in Mexico when it used the U.S. campaign. Mexicans did not care as much for the decay-prevention benefit, nor did scientifically oriented advertising appeal to them.

General Foods squandered millions trying to introduce packaged cake mixes to Japanese consumers. The company failed to note that only 3 percent of Japanese homes were equipped with ovens.

S. C. Johnson's wax floor polish initially failed in Japan. The wax made the floors too slippery, and Johnson had overlooked the fact that Japanese do not wear shoes in their homes.

deciding which markets to enter

In deciding to go abroad, the company needs to define its marketing objectives and policies. What proportion of foreign to total sales will it seek? Most companies start small when they venture abroad. Some plan to stay small; others have bigger plans. "Going abroad" on the Internet poses special challenges. (See "Marketing for the New Economy: *www.TheWorldIsYourOyster.com*: The Ins and Outs of Global E-Commerce.")

marketing for the new economy

www.TheWorldIsYourOyster.com: The Ins and Outs of Global E-Commerce

Companies small and large are taking advantage of the disappearance of traditional market boundaries. Major marketers doing global e-commerce range from automakers (GM) to direct-mail companies (L.L. Bean and Lands' End) to running-shoe giants (Nike and Reebok) to Internet start-ups like Amazon.com, which purchased three European companies to build its European book and video sales.

For some, marketing has been a hit-or-miss affair. They put up content in English for the American market, and if any international users stumble across the page and end up buying something, great. Hyperspace Cowgirls, a six-year-old New York City–based developer of children's multimedia software, has several European deals in the works, even though it has no marketing effort overseas. "We don't advertise overseas at all," says Susan Shaw, president of the company, whose Web address is www.hyperspacecowgirls.com. "People just find you."

Other marketers have made a strategic decision to become part of the cyberbazaar. They are using the Web to reach new customers outside their home countries, to support existing customers who live abroad, to source from international suppliers, and to build global brand awareness. Some of these companies adapt their Web sites to provide country-specific content and services to their best potential international markets, ideally in the local language. Reebok has launched a multilingual European Web site—available in English, French, German, Spanish, and Italian—in an attempt to increase brand awareness in its individual markets. The site, located at www.reebok.com, is aimed at sports and fitness enthusiasts and includes information on local events in each market.

Before companies decide to expand their Web presence internationally, they need to find the companies or regions with the largest potential online populations. The biggest area for growth today would be the Asia-Pacific region. The number of Internet users in the region is rising as access costs decline, local-language content increases, and infrastructure improves. By 2004, the number of Internet users in the Asia-Pacific region is expected to swell to 188 million. Europe is another hotspot for Internet growth. Internet penetration in Europe is expected to rise to 33 percent by 2003. By then, the five countries with the highest levels of Internet penetration—Germany, France, the Netherlands, the United Kingdom, and Sweden—will have online populations totaling 60 million, up from 34 million in 1999.

Despite these encouraging developments, however, Internet marketers sometimes overstate global opportunities. Although developed countries offer many choices for Internet access, less developed countries in Central and South America or Africa have fewer or none at all, forcing users to make international calls to go online. Only 6 percent of the world's population had Internet access in 2000. Even with adequate phone lines and PC penetration, high connection costs sharply restrict Internet use. In Asia, ISP subscriptions can run up to $60 a month, triple the average U.S. rate.

In addition, the global marketer may run up against governmental or cultural restrictions. In Germany, a vendor cannot accept payment via credit card until two weeks after an order has been sent. German law also prevents companies from using certain marketing techniques like unconditional lifetime guarantees. On a wider scale, the issue of who pays sales taxes and duties on global e-commerce is murkier still.

Finally, businesses need to realize that the Web does not offer complete solutions for transacting global business—and probably never will. Most companies will never cut a final deal via e-mail. People will still need to see and feel products at international trade shows. The Web will not surmount customs red tape or local regulation. The Web also cannot guarantee that goods will arrive in perfect condition.

What the Web can do is make foreign customers aware of one's business. The Web has certainly done that for upscale retailer and cataloger The Sharper Image, which now gets more than 25 percent of its online business from overseas customers. The company is thrilled about its global prospects but admits it is still overwhelmed by the logistical challenges of serving overseas markets.

Sources: Alice LaPlante, "Global Boundaries.com," *Computerworld*, October 6, 1997, pp. G6–G9; Roberta Maynard, "Trade Links via the Internet," *Nation's Business* (December 1997): 51–53; Michelle V. Rafter, "Multilingual Sites Give Companies Access to Global Revenue Sources," *Chicago Tribune*, May 11, 1998, Business Section, p. 9; Marla Dickerson, "Small Business Strategies; Technology; Foreign Concept; All Those Inflated Expectations Aside, Many Firms Are Finding the Internet Invaluable in Pursuing International Trade," *Los Angeles Times*, October 14, 1998, pp. C2, C10; Stephen Baker, "Finally, Europeans Are Storming the Net," *BusinessWeek*, May 11, 1998, p. 48; "Reebok Targets Its New Web Site at Euro Markets," *Marketing*, October 1, 1998, p. 16; "One In Three Europeans Will Embrace a Digital Lifestyle by 2003, According to Forrester," *Business Wire*, December 6, 2000; Brandon Mitchener, "E-Commerce: Border Crossings," *Wall Street Journal*, November 22, 1999, p. R41.

how many markets to enter

The company must decide whether to market in a few countries or many countries and determine how fast to expand. Consider Boo.com.

Boo.com   When online retailer Boo.com was founded in 1998, the company expressed the ambitious goal of becoming the "first truly global e-tailer, with worldwide sales, marketing and distribution capabilities." This bold plan attracted numerous investors, and the company raised $135 million in venture capital that it used to build high-tech e-commerce sites in seven languages in 18 countries. Boo.com constructed satellite offices in six cities, including Munich, Paris, and New York. After months of delays, the site went live in November 2000 and was immediately criticized for an interface that was too complicated and confusing. Monthly sales of $1.1 million a month could not make up for mounting expenses, which ran to an estimated $1 million a week by May 2000. In June of that year, American e-retailer fashionmall.com purchased the company at a liquidation auction for less than $500,000.[4]

In contrast, consider Amway's experience:

Amway   Consumer-product company Amway expanded into Australia in 1971. In the 1980s, Amway moved into 10 more countries. By 1999, Amway had evolved into a multinational juggernaut with a sales force of more than 3 million independent distributors hauling in $5 billion in sales. Today, Amway sells products in 43 countries worldwide. Its goal: to have overseas markets account for 80 percent of its sales. This is not an unrealistic or overly ambitious goal considering that Amway already gains 70 percent of its sales from markets outside North America.[5]

Generally speaking, it makes sense to operate in fewer countries with a deeper commitment and penetration in each. Ayal and Zif have argued that a company should enter fewer countries when

- Market entry and market control costs are high.
- Product and communication adaptation costs are high.
- Population and income size and growth are high in the initial countries chosen.
- Dominant foreign firms can establish high barriers to entry.[6]

The company must also decide on the types of countries to consider. Attractiveness is influenced by the product, geography, income and population, political climate, and other factors. The seller might have a predilection for certain countries or regions. Kenichi Ohmae recommends that companies concentrate on selling in the "triad markets"—the United States, Western Europe, and the Far East—because these markets account for a large percent of all international trade.[7] Although Ohmae's position makes short-run sense, it can spell disaster for the world economy in the long run. The unmet needs of the developing world represent huge potential markets for food, clothing, shelter, consumer electronics, appliances, and other goods. Many market leaders are now rushing into Eastern Europe, China, Vietnam, and Cuba, where there are many unmet needs to satisfy.

regional free trade zones

Regional economic integration—trading agreements between blocs of countries—has intensified in recent years. This development means that companies are more likely to enter entire regions overseas than do business with one nation at a time.

THE EUROPEAN UNION   Certain countries have formed free trade zones or economic communities—groups of nations organized to work toward common goals in the regulation of international trade. One such community is the European Union (EU). Formed in 1957, the European Union set out to create a single European market by reducing barriers to the free flow of products, services, finances, and labor among member countries, and by developing policies on trade with nonmember nations. Today, the European Union is one of the world's single largest markets. Its 15 member countries contain more than 370 million consumers and account for 20 percent of the world's exports. As more European nations seek admission to the EU, it could contain as many as 450 million people in 28 countries; and it is now using a common currency, the euro monetary system.

European unification offers tremendous trade opportunities for non-European firms. However, it also poses threats. European companies will grow bigger and more competitive. Witness the competition in the aircraft industry between Europe's Airbus consortium and Boeing in the United States. Perhaps an even bigger concern, however, is that lower barriers inside Europe will only create thicker outside walls. Some observers envision a "fortress Europe" that heaps favors on firms from EU countries but hinders outsiders by imposing obstacles such as stiffer import quotas, local content requirements, and other nontariff (nontax) barriers.

Also, companies that plan to create "pan-European" marketing campaigns directed to a unified Europe should proceed with caution. Even if the EU truly does manage to standardize its general trade regulations and implement the euro, creating an economic community will not create a homogeneous market. Companies marketing in Europe face 14 different languages, 2,000 years of historical and cultural differences, and a daunting mass of local rules. Consider the experience of the acclaimed Leo Burnett ad agency when it took on the goal of creating a single European campaign for United Distillers' Johnnie Walker account.

Johnnie Walker   In an ad with the headline "The Water of Life," a man attends the running of the bulls in Pamplona and, after narrowly escaping being trampled, celebrates with a glass of Johnnie Walker Red Label. In many countries, the Pamplona setting raised hackles because people said, "The Spanish don't know anything about whiskey." The ad was a total failure in Germany because to Germans it seemed simply reckless. "Also," said Jenny Vaughn, worldwide brand director for Johnnie Walker, "because of the German animal rights campaigners, you can't show a goldfish in a goldfish bowl on German television, so a bull run was just not on."[8]

The most successful pan-European ads are those that focus on the product and consumer and are aimed at one of the two audiences that market researchers really agree are turning into Euroconsumers—the young and the rich. One such ad is for TAG Heuer watches in which a swimmer races a shark, a hurdler leaps over an oversized razor blade, and a relay runner grabs a dynamite baton, all mind games that athletes everywhere use to rev up their performance.

NAFTA   Closer to home, in North America, the United States, and Canada phased out trade barriers in 1989. In January 1994, the North American Free Trade Agreement (NAFTA) established a free trade zone among the United States, Mexico, and Canada. The agreement created a single market of 360 million people who produce and consume $6.7 trillion worth of goods and services. As it is implemented over a 15-year period, NAFTA will eliminate all trade barriers and investment restrictions among the three countries. Prior to NAFTA, tariffs on American products entering Mexico averaged 13 percent, whereas U.S. tariffs on Mexican goods averaged 6 percent.

MERCOSUL   Other free trade areas are forming in Latin America. For example, MERCOSUL now links Brazil, Argentina, Paraguay, and Uruguay. Chile and Mexico have formed a successful free trade zone. It is likely that NAFTA will eventually merge with this and other arrangements to form an all-Americas free trade zone.

It is the European nations that have tapped Latin America's enormous potential. As Washington's efforts to extend NAFTA to Latin America have stalled, European countries have moved in with a vengeance. When Latin American countries instituted market reforms and privatized public utilities, European companies rushed in to grab up lucrative contracts for rebuilding Latin America's infrastructure. Spain's Telefonica de Espana has spent $5 billion buying phone companies in Brazil, Chile, Peru, and Argentina. European companies have moved rapidly into the private sector. In Brazil, seven of the ten largest private companies are European owned, compared to two controlled by Americans. Among the notable European companies operating in Latin America are automotive giants Volkswagen and Fiat, the French supermarket chain Carrefours, and the Anglo-Dutch personal care products group Gessy-Lever.

APEC   Twenty-one Pacific Rim countries, including the NAFTA member states, Japan, and China, are working to create a pan-Pacific free trade area under the auspices of the Asian Pacific Economic Cooperation forum (APEC). There are also active attempts at regional economic integration in the Caribbean, Southeast Asia, and parts of Africa.

Yet, however much nations and regions integrate their trading policies and standards, each nation still has unique features that must be understood. A nation's readiness for different products and services and its attractiveness as a market to foreign firms depend on its economic, political-legal, and cultural environments.

evaluating potential markets

Suppose a company has assembled a list of potential markets to enter. How does it choose among them? Many companies prefer to sell to neighboring countries because they understand these countries better, and they can control their costs better. It is not surprising that the largest U.S. market is Canada, or that Swedish companies first sold to their Scandinavian neighbors. As growing numbers of U.S. companies expand abroad, many are deciding the best place to start is next door, in Canada.

Mexico, also adjacent, is the second largest U.S. export market. The United States is encouraging small and medium-sized enterprises (SMEs) to sell to Mexico. However, SMEs are concerned about entry barriers: A study found that the two most worrisome barriers are collecting payment from Mexican customers and finding a reliable Mexican distributor or agent. Others include the difficulty of getting accurate and up-to-date information about Mexican markets and industries, fluctuating exchange rates between the peso and the dollar, the difficulty of adjusting to Mexican business practices, and confusing Mexican import regulations and procedures. All of this must be evaluated in deciding whether to enter a given market.[9]

At other times, *psychic proximity* determines choices. Many U.S. firms prefer to sell in Canada, England, and Australia—rather than in larger markets such as Germany and France—because they feel more comfortable with the language, laws, and culture.

In general, a company prefers to enter countries (1) that rank high on market attractiveness, (2) that are low in market risk, and (3) in which it possesses a competitive advantage. Here is how Bechtel Corporation, the construction giant, goes about evaluating overseas markets.

Bechtel Corporation   Before Bechtel ventures into new markets, the company starts with a detailed strategic market analysis. It looks at its markets and tries to determine where it should be in four or five years' time. A management team does a cost-benefit analysis that factors in the position of competitors, infrastructure, regulatory and trade barriers, and the tax situation (both corporate and individual). Ideally, the new market should be a country with an untapped need for its products or services; a quality, skilled labor pool capable of manufacturing the product; and a welcoming environment (governmental and physical).

Are there countries that meet Bechtel's requirements? Although Singapore has an educated, English-speaking labor force, basks in political stability, and encourages foreign

Marketing
MEMO

Going After Poor Markets Around the Globe

The developed nations and the prosperous parts of developing nations account for less than 15 percent of the world's population. Is there a way for marketers to profitably serve the other 85 percent, which has much less purchasing power? Some companies are now pioneering ways to serve these invisible consumers:

■ Grameen-Phone markets cell phones to 35,000 villages in Bangladesh by hiring village women as agents who lease phone time to other villagers, one call at a time.
■ Colgate-Palmolive rolls into Indian villages with video vans that show the benefits of toothbrushing; it expects to earn over half of its Indian revenue from rural areas by 2003.
■ An Indian-Australian car manufacturer created an affordable rural transport vehicle to compete with bullock carts rather than cars. The vehicle functions well at low speeds and carries up to two tons.
■ Fiat developed a "third-world car," the Palio, that far outsells the Ford Fiesta in Brazil and that will be launched in other developing nations.
■ Corporacion GEO builds low-income housing in Mexico. The two-bedroom homes are modular and can be expanded. The company is now expanding into Chile and southern U.S. communities.
■ A Latin-American building-supply retailer offers bags of cement in smaller sizes to customers building their own homes.

The challenge is to think creatively about how marketing can fulfill the dreams of most of the world's population for a better standard of living.

Source: Adapted from Vijay Mahajan, Marcos V. Pratini De Moraes, and Jerry Wind, "The Invisible Global Market," *Marketing Management* (Winter 2000): 31–35.

investment, it has a small population. Although many countries in central Europe possess an eager, hungry-to-learn labor pool, their infrastructures create difficulties. The team evaluating a new market must determine whether the company could earn enough on its investment to cover the risk factors or other negatives.[10] (For a neglected area of global market opportunity, see "Marketing Memo: Going After Poor Markets Around the Globe.")

deciding how to enter the market

Once a company decides to target a particular country, it has to determine the best mode of entry. Its broad choices are *indirect exporting, direct exporting, licensing, joint ventures,* and *direct investment.* These five market-entry strategies are shown in Figure 13.2. Each succeeding strategy involves more commitment, risk, control, and profit potential.

indirect and direct export

The normal way to get involved in a foreign market is through export. *Occasional exporting* is a passive level of involvement in which the company exports from time to time, either on its own initiative or in response to unsolicited orders from abroad. *Active exporting* takes place when the company makes a commitment to expand into a particular market. In either case, the company produces its goods in the home country and might or might not adapt them to the foreign market.

Companies typically start with *indirect exporting*—that is, they work through independent intermediaries. *Domestic-based export merchants* buy the manufacturer's products and then sell them abroad. *Domestic-based export agents* seek and negotiate foreign purchases and are paid a commission. Included in this group are trading companies. *Cooperative organizations* carry on exporting activities on behalf of several producers and are partly under their administrative control. They are often used by producers of primary products such as fruits or nuts. *Export-management companies* agree to manage a company's export activities for a fee. Indirect export has two advantages. First, it involves less investment; the firm does not have to develop an export department, an overseas sales force, or a set of foreign contacts. Second, it involves less risk; because international-marketing intermediaries bring knowhow and services to the relationship, the seller will normally make fewer mistakes.

Companies eventually may decide to handle their own exports. The investment and risk are somewhat greater, but so is the potential return. University Games of Burlingame, California, has blossomed into a $50-million-per-year international company through careful entry into overseas ventures.

University Games   Bob Moog, president and founder of University Games, says his company's international sales strategy relies heavily on third-party distributors and has a fair degree of flexibility. "We identify the foreign markets we want to penetrate," says Moog, "and then form a business venture with a local distributor that will give us a large degree of control. In Australia, we expect to run a print of 5,000 board games. These we will manufacture in the United States. If we reach a run of 25,000 games, however, we would then establish a sub-contracting venture with a local manufacturer in Australia or New Zealand to print the games."[11]

A company can carry on direct exporting in several ways:

■ *Domestic-based export department or division:* Might evolve into a self-contained export department operating as a profit center.
■ *Overseas sales branch or subsidiary:* The sales branch handles sales and distribution and might handle warehousing and promotion as well. It often serves as a display and customer service center.

- *Traveling export sales representatives:* Home-based sales representatives are sent abroad to find business.
- *Foreign-based distributors or agents:* These distributors and agents might be given exclusive rights to represent the company in that country, or only limited rights.

Whether companies decide to export indirectly or directly, many companies use exporting as a way to "test the waters" before building a plant and manufacturing a product overseas. This strategy worked well for IPSCO, Inc. In the early 1980s, this Saskatchewan-based steel producer exported its steel pipe and flat steel to the United States from Canada—despite significant transportation costs. Once the company realized there was a significant U.S. demand for its products, it decided to set up shop there.[12]

One of the best ways to initiate or extend export activities used to be to exhibit at an overseas trade show. With the World Wide Web, it is not even necessary to attend trade shows to show one's wares to overseas buyers and distributors. Electronic communication via the Internet is extending the reach of companies, particularly small ones, to worldwide markets. The Internet has become an effective means of everything from gaining free exporting information and guidelines, conducting market research, and offering customers several time zones away a secure process for ordering and paying for products.

Finding free information about trade and exporting has never been easier. Here are some places to start your search:

www.ita.doc.gov (the U.S. Department of Commerce's International Trade Administration).

www.exim.gov (the Export-Import Bank of the United States).

www.sba.gov (the U.S. Small Business Administration).

www.bxa.doc.gov (the Bureau of Export Administration, a branch of the Commerce Department).

www.tscentral.com (Trade Show Central, a Wellesley, Massachusetts, company).

Also, check with your state's export-promotion office to learn if it has online resources and allows businesses to link to its site. Then check "Marketing Memo: Making Your Web Site Worldwide and Worldly Wise" for tips on Web sites that attract, rather than frustrate, overseas customers.

licensing

Licensing is a simple way to become involved in international marketing. The licensor licenses a foreign company to use a manufacturing process, trademark, patent, trade secret, or other item of value for a fee or royalty. The licensor gains entry at little risk; the licensee gains production expertise or a well-known product or brand name. E-Trade Group, the Palo Alto, California, online broker-dealer, entered into a licensing agreement with Jerusalem Global Ltd., an Israeli investment banking operation. E-Trade's agreement with the Israeli firm is part of a strategy to form licensing agreements and international joint ventures in an effort to bring its brand of no-frills investing to people abroad. E-Trade has created E-Trade Australia, Canada, Denmark, Germany, Hong Kong, Japan, Korea, Norway, South Africa, Sweden, and U.K.[13]

Licensing has potential disadvantages. The licensor has less control over the licensee than it does over its own production and sales facilities. Furthermore, if the licensee is very successful, the firm has given up profits; and if and when the contract ends, the company might find that it has created a competitor. To avoid this, the licensor usually supplies some proprietary ingredients or components needed in the product (as Coca-Cola does); but the best strategy is for the licensor to lead in innovation so that the licensee will continue to depend on the licensor.

There are several variations on a licensing arrangement. Companies such as Hyatt and Marriott sell *management contracts* to owners of foreign hotels to manage these businesses for a fee. The management firm may even be given the option to purchase some share in the managed company within a stated period. Another variation is *contract manufacturing*, in which the firm hires local manufacturers to produce the product. When Sears opened department stores in Mexico and Spain, it found qualified local

figure **13.2**

Five Modes of Entry into Foreign Markets

Marketing
MEMO

Making Your Web Site Worldwide and Worldly Wise

Many companies that would never dream of launching an export initiative without careful planning are launching Web sites that are actually damaging their image with global customers. It may be something minor like using address fields that do not allow for European postal codes or as major as not translating a site aimed at Japanese customers. Here is a list of do's and don'ts for creating an export-friendly Web site:

1. *Be sure international customers can view your Web page at adequate speeds:* It may help to have your Web site hosted or mirrored overseas. You should also consider setting up a text-only version so overseas customers do not have to wait for graphics to download.

2. *Make sure every customer can experience your Web site and order products in the language, and culture, with which he or she feels comfortable:* You can set up e-commerce software to autodetect an international customer. Then you can automatically set up a dedicated country page, written in the language of that country. You can also link your Web site to a currency conversion calculator.

continued...

manufacturers to produce many of its products. Contract manufacturing gives the company less control over the manufacturing process and the loss of potential profits on manufacturing. However, it offers a chance to start faster, with less risk and with the opportunity to form a partnership or buy out the local manufacturer later.

Finally, a company can enter a foreign market through *franchising*, which is a more complete form of licensing. The franchiser offers a complete brand concept and operating system. In return, the franchisee invests in and pays certain fees to the franchiser. McDonald's, KFC, and Avis have entered scores of countries by franchising their retail concepts.

KFC Corporation   Although the initial reception in Japan was great, KFC still had a number of obstacles to overcome. The Japanese saw fast food as artificial, made by mechanical means, and unhealthy. KFC's ad agency in Japan, McCann-Erickson Japan, knew that it had to build trust in the KFC brand. Agency personnel flew to Kentucky to film an authentic version of Colonel Sanders' beginnings. To show the philosophy of KFC—the southern hospitality, old American tradition, and authentic home cooking—the commercial showed Colonel Sanders' mother making and feeding her children KFC chicken made with 11 secret spices. It conveyed the fact that "KFC chicken is not artificial. It's made by hand, and good enough for your children to eat." The campaign was hugely successful, and in less than 8 years KFC expanded its presence from 400 locations to more than 1,000.[14]

joint ventures

Foreign investors may join with local investors to create a **joint venture** company in which they share ownership and control. For instance:[15]

- Coca-Cola and Nestlé joined forces to develop the international market for "ready to drink" tea and coffee, which currently sell in significant amounts in Japan.
- Procter & Gamble formed a joint venture with its Italian arch-rival Fater to cover babies' bottoms in the United Kingdom and Italy.
- Whirlpool took a 53 percent stake in the Dutch electronics group Philips's white-goods business to leapfrog into the European market.

A joint venture may be necessary or desirable for economic or political reasons. The foreign firm might lack the financial, physical, or managerial resources to undertake the venture alone; or the foreign government might require joint ownership as a condition for entry. Even corporate giants need joint ventures to crack the toughest markets. When it wanted to enter China's ice cream market, Unilever joined forces with Sumstar, a state-owned Chinese investment company. The venture's general manager says Sumstar's help with the formidable Chinese bureaucracy was crucial in getting a high-tech ice cream plant up and running in just 12 months.[16]

Joint ownership has certain drawbacks. The partners might disagree over investment, marketing, or other policies. One partner might want to reinvest earnings for growth, and the other partner might want to declare more dividends. Joint ownership can also prevent a multinational company from carrying out specific manufacturing and marketing policies on a worldwide basis.

direct investment

The ultimate form of foreign involvement is direct ownership of foreign-based assembly or manufacturing facilities. The foreign company can buy part or full interest in a local company or build its own facilities. If the market appears large enough, foreign production facilities offer distinct advantages. First, the firm secures cost economies in the form of cheaper labor or raw materials, foreign-government investment incentives, and freight savings. Second, the firm strengthens its image in the host country because it creates jobs. Third, the firm develops a deeper relationship with government, customers, local suppliers, and distributors, enabling it to adapt its products better to the local environment. Fourth, the firm retains full control over its investment and therefore can develop manufacturing and marketing policies that serve its long-term international objectives. Fifth, the firm assures itself access to the market in case the host country starts insisting that locally purchased goods have domestic content.

The main disadvantage of direct investment is that the firm exposes a large investment to risks such as blocked or devalued currencies, worsening markets, or expropriation. The firm will find it expensive to reduce or close down its operations, because the host country might require substantial severance pay to the employees.

the internationalization process

Most countries lament that too few of their companies participate in foreign trade. This keeps the country from earning foreign exchange to pay for needed imports. It also raises the specter of domestic companies eventually being hurt or taken over by foreign multinationals. These countries are trying to encourage their domestic companies to grow domestically and expand globally. Many countries sponsor aggressive export-promotion programs to get their companies to export. These programs require a deep understanding of how companies become internationalized.

Johanson and Wiedersheim-Paul studied the *internationalization process* among Swedish companies.[17] They see firms moving through four stages:

1. No regular export activities
2. Export via independent representatives (agents)
3. Establishment of one or more sales subsidiaries
4. Establishment of production facilities abroad

The first task is to get companies to move from stage 1 to stage 2. This move is helped by studying how firms make their first export decisions.[18] Most firms work with an independent agent and enter a nearby or similar country. A company then engages further agents to enter additional countries. Later, it establishes an export department to manage its agent relationships. Still later, the company replaces its agents with its own sales subsidiaries in its larger export markets. This increases the company's investment and risk, but also its earning potential.

To manage these subsidiaries, the company replaces the export department with an international department. If certain markets continue to be large and stable, or if the host country insists on local production, the company takes the next step of locating production facilities in those markets, representing a still larger commitment and still larger potential earnings. By this time, the company is operating as a multinational company and is engaged in optimizing its global sourcing, financing, manufacturing, and marketing.

deciding on the marketing program

International companies must decide how much to adapt their marketing strategy to local conditions. At one extreme are companies that use a globally *standardized marketing mix* worldwide. Standardization of the product, advertising, and distribution channels promises the lowest costs. At the other extreme is an *adapted marketing mix*, where the producer adjusts the marketing-mix elements to each target market. For a discussion of the main issues, see "Marketing Insight: Global Standardization or Adaptation?"

Between the two extremes, many possibilities exist. Most brands are adapted to some extent. Even global brands, such as Pringles, Always, and Toyota, will undergo some changes in their product features, packaging, channels, pricing, or promotion in different foreign markets. (See "Marketing Memo: The Ten Commandments of Global Branding.")

3. *Avoid alphanumeric fields in forms, and make address fields internationally meaningful:* It sounds like a tiny detail, but people do get annoyed when registration or order forms do not recognize accents. Address fields should accommodate international postal codes.

4. *Provide enough information about your company, and make contact information prominent:* Providing details about your company's strengths is a good way to establish credibility. Also, do not bury contact information—names, telephone numbers, or fax numbers—deep within the site. Make it as clear and visible as possible.

5. *Do not leave site development to the technicians:* Involve your marketing people so you can ensure that your site is consistent with the image you want to project.

Sources: Eric J. Adams, "Electronic Commerce Goes Global," *World Trade* (April 1998): 90–92; Roberta Maynard, "Creating an Export-Friendly Site," *Nation's Business* (December 1997): 51; J. D. Mosely-Matchett, "Remember; It's the World Wide Web," *Marketing News*, January 20, 1997, p. 16.

marketing **insight**

Global Standardization or Adaptation?

The marketing concept holds that consumer needs vary and that marketing programs will be more effective when they are tailored to each target group. This also applies to foreign markets. Yet in 1983, in a groundbreaking article in the *Harvard Business Review*, Harvard Professor Theodore Levitt challenged this view and supplied the intellectual rationale for global standardization: "The world is becoming a common marketplace in which people—no matter where they live—desire the same products and lifestyles."

The development of the World Wide Web, the rapid spread of cable and satellite TV around the world, and the global linking of telecommunications networks have led to a convergence of lifestyles. A "global MTV generation" is what Joseph Quinlan, senior economist

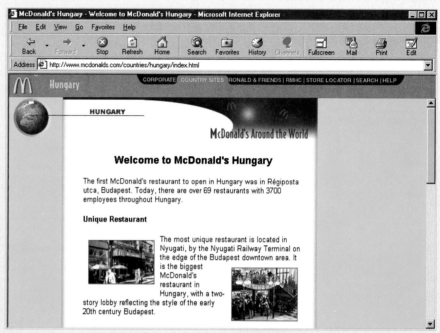

McDonald's around the world: Hungary.

at Dean, Witter Reynolds, calls these emerging consumers. Says Quinlan, "They prefer Coke to tea, Nikes to sandals, and Chicken McNuggets to rice, credit cards to cash." The convergence of needs and wants has created global markets for standardized products, particularly among the young middle class.

Levitt favors global corporations that try to sell the same product the same way to all consumers. They focus on similarities across world markets and "sensibly force suitably standardized products and services on the entire globe." These global marketers achieve economies through standardization of production, distribution, marketing, and management. They translate their efficiency into greater value for consumers by offering high quality and more reliable products at lower prices. Coca-Cola, McDonald's, Marlboro, Nike, the NBA, and Gillette are among the companies that have successfully marketed global products. Consider Gillette: Some 1.2 billion people use at least one Gillette product daily, according to the company's estimates. Gillette enjoys huge economies of scale by selling a few types of razor blades in every single market.

Many companies have tried to launch their version of a world product. Yet, most products require some adaptation. Toyota's Corolla will exhibit some differences in styling. McDonald's uses chili sauce instead of ketchup on its hamburgers in Mexico. Coca-

Cola is sweeter or less carbonated in certain countries. Rather than assuming that its domestic product can be introduced "as is" in another country, the company should review the following elements and determine which would add more revenue than cost:

- Product features
- Brand name
- Labeling
- Packaging
- Colors
- Materials

- Prices
- Sales promotion
- Advertising themes
- Advertising media
- Advertising execution

One study showed that companies made one or more marketing-mix adaptations in 80 percent of their foreign products and that the average number of adapted elements was four. So perhaps Levitt's globalization dictum should be rephrased. Global marketing, yes. Global standardization, not necessarily.

Sources: Theodore Levitt, "The Globalization of Markets," *Harvard Business Review* (May–June 1983): 92–102; Bernard Wysocki Jr., "The Global Mall: In Developing Nations, Many Youths Splurge, Mainly on U.S. Goods," *Wall Street Journal*, June 26, 1997, p. A1; "What Makes a Company Great?" *Fortune*, October 26, 1998, pp. 218–26; David M. Szymanski, Sundar G. Bharadwaj, and P. Rajan Varadarajan, "Standardization versus Adaptation of International Marketing Strategy: An Empirical Investigation," *Journal of Marketing* (October 1993): 1–17.

Marketing
MEMO

The Ten Commandments of Global Branding

Developing a global strategy is of paramount importance to brand builders everywhere. For many companies, however, global branding has been both a blessing and a curse. A global branding program can lower marketing costs, realize greater economies of scale in production, and provide a long-term source of growth; but if not designed and implemented properly, it may ignore important differences in consumer behavior and/or the competitive environment in the individual countries. Here are suggestions that can help a company retain many of the advantages of global branding while minimizing the potential disadvantages:

1. *Understand similarities and differences in the global branding landscape.* International markets can vary in terms of brand development, consumer behavior, competitive activity, legal restrictions, and so on, and yet there will be some similarities.
2. *Do not take shortcuts in brand-building.* Building a brand in new markets should be done from the "bottom-up," both strategically (building awareness before brand image) and tactically (creating sources of brand equity in new markets).
3. *Establish marketing infrastructure.* A company must either build marketing infrastructure "from scratch" or adapt to existing infrastructure in other countries.
4. *Embrace integrated marketing communications.* A company must often use many forms of communication in overseas markets, such as sponsorship, promotions, and merchandising, not just advertising.
5. *Establish brand partnerships.* Most global brands have marketing partners in their international markets; these partners help companies achieve advantages in distribution, profitability, and added value.
6. *Balance standardization and customization.* Some elements of a marketing program can be standardized (packaging, brand name); others typically require greater customization (distribution channels).
7. *Balance global and local control.* Companies must balance global and local control within the organization and distribute decision-making between global and local managers.
8. *Establish operable guidelines.* Brand definition and guidelines must be established, communicated, and properly enforced so that marketers everywhere know what they are expected to do and not do. The goal is to set rules for how the brand should be positioned and marketed.
9. *Implement a global brand equity measurement system.* A global brand equity system is a set of research procedures designed to provide timely, accurate, and actionable information for marketers so they can make the best possible short-run tactical decisions and long-run strategic decisions.
10. *Leverage brand elements.* Proper design and implementation of brand elements (brand name and trademarked brand identifiers) can be an invaluable source of brand equity worldwide.

Source: Adapted from Kevin Lane Keller and Sanjay Sood (2001), "The Ten Commandments of Global Branding," *Asian Journal of Marketing,* forthcoming.

product

Warren Keegan has distinguished five adaptation strategies of product and promotion to a foreign market (see Figure 13.3).[19]

Straight extension means introducing the product in the foreign market without any change. Straight extension has been successful with cameras, consumer electronics, and many machine tools. In other cases, it has been a disaster. General Foods introduced its standard powdered Jell-O in the British market only to find that British consumers prefer the solid wafer or cake form. Campbell Soup Company lost an estimated $30 million in introducing its condensed soups in England; consumers saw expensive small-sized cans

figure **13.3**

		Product		
		Do Not Change Product	Adapt Product	Develop New Product
Promotion	Do Not Change Promotion	Straight extension	Product adaptation	Product invention
	Adapt Promotion	Communication adaptation	Dual adaptation	

Five International Product and Promotion Strategies

and did not realize that water needed to be added. Straight extension is tempting because it involves no additional R&D expense, manufacturing retooling, or promotional modification; but it can be costly in the long run.

Product adaptation involves altering the product to meet local conditions or preferences. There are several levels of adaptation. A company can produce a regional version of its product, such as a Western European version. Finnish cellular phone superstar Nokia customized its 6100 series phone for every major market. Developers built in rudimentary voice recognition for Asia, where keyboards are a problem and raised the ring volume so the phone could be heard on crowded Asian streets; or it can produce a country version. In Japan, Mister Donut's coffee cup is smaller and lighter to fit the hand of the average Japanese consumer; even the doughnuts are a little smaller. Kraft blends different coffees for the British (who drink their coffee with milk), the French (who drink their coffee black), and Latin Americans (who want a chicory taste). A company can produce a *city version* of its product—for instance, a beer to meet Munich tastes or Tokyo tastes. Finally, a company can produce different retailer versions of its product, such as one coffee brew for the Migros chain store and another for the Cooperative chain store, both in Switzerland.

Although products are frequently adapted to local tastes, in some instances they must be adapted to local superstitions or beliefs, too. The concept of *feng shui* is a good example.

Hyatt Hotels A practice widely followed in China, Hong Kong, and Singapore, *feng shui* means "wind and water." Practitioners of *feng shui*, or geomancers, will recommend the most favorable conditions for any venture, particularly the placement of office buildings and the arrangement of desks, doors, and other items within. To have good *feng shui*, a building should face the water and be flanked by mountains. It also should not block the view of the mountain spirits. The Hyatt hotel in Singapore, designed without *feng shui*, had to be redesigned to boost business. Originally, the front desk was parallel to the doors and road, and this was thought to lead to wealth flowing out. Furthermore, the doors were facing northwest, which easily let in undesirable spirits. The geomancers recommended design alterations to keep wealth in and undesirable spirits out.[20]

Product invention consists of creating something new. It can take two forms. Backward invention is reintroducing earlier product forms that are well adapted to a foreign country's needs. The National Cash Register Company reintroduced its crank-operated cash register at half the price of a modern cash register and sold substantial numbers in Latin America and Africa. (This illustrates a good understanding of the international product life cycle, where countries stand at different stages of readiness to adopt a particular product.) **Forward invention** is creating a new product to meet a need in another country. There is an enormous need in less developed countries for low-cost, high-protein foods. Companies such as Quaker Oats, Swift, and Monsanto are researching these countries' nutrition needs, formulating new foods, and developing advertising campaigns to gain product trial and acceptance. Toyota produces vehicles specifically designed, with the help of local employees, to suit the tastes of these markets.[21] In globalization's latest twist, American companies are not only inventing new products for overseas markets, but also lifting products and ideas from their international operations and bringing them home.

Häagen-Dazs Häagen-Dazs had developed a flavor for sale solely in Argentina, called "dulce de leche," named for the caramelized milk that is one of the most popular flavors in Argentina. Just one year later, the company rolled out dulce de leche in supermarkets from Boston to Los Angeles to Paris. The co-opted flavor soon did $1 million a month in the United States and was particularly popular in Miami, where it sold twice as fast as any other flavor.[22]

Product invention is a costly strategy, but the payoffs can be great, particularly if a company can parlay a product innovation into other countries.

The world market for services is growing at double the rate of world merchandise trade. Large firms in accounting, advertising, banking, communications, construction, insurance, law, management consulting, and retailing are pursuing global expansion. Price Waterhouse, American Express, Citigroup, Club Med, Hilton, and Thomas Cook are known worldwide. U.S. credit-card companies have streamed across the Atlantic to convince Europeans of the joys of charge cards. In Britain, industry heavyweights Citibank and American Express have wrested a lot of business from big British banks like Barclay's.[23]

Many retailers are trying to make similar inroads.

Wal-Mart Faced with slowing growth in the United States, Wal-Mart is using cash flow from its domestic business to fuel the growth of its international division. In 1997 it purchased its Mexican joint venture partner CIFRA and then acquired German retailer Wertkauf. In 1998, it acquired another chain of German hypermarkets called Interspar. In 1999, Wal-Mart purchased the ASDA Group in Britain. Wal-Mart has more than 1,000 stores in Mexico, Canada, Germany, Argentina, China, Britain, South Korea, Brazil, and Puerto Rico. By 2005, Wal-Mart wants to have one-third of its revenues come from overseas, up from 12 percent in 2000.[24]

At the same time, countries have erected entry barriers or regulations. Brazil requires all accountants to possess a professional degree from a Brazilian university. Many Western European countries want to limit the number of U.S. television programs and films shown in their countries. Many U.S. states bar foreign bank branches. At the same time, the United States is pressuring South Korea to open its markets to U.S. banks. The General Agreement of Tariffs and Trade (GATT) is pressing for more free trade in international services, but the progress is slow.

Retailers who sell books, videos, and CD-ROMs, and entertainment companies have also had to contend with a culture of censorship in certain countries such as China and Singapore. In Singapore, for example, book retailers must submit potentially "hot" materials to the Committee on Undesirable Publications.[25] Clearly, ethics or ideals that are upheld in the home country may sometimes have to be compromised in order to do business in other countries.

promotion

Companies can run the same advertising and promotion campaigns used in the home market or change them for each local market, a process called **communication adaptation**. If it adapts both the product and the communication, the company engages in **dual adaptation**.

Consider the message. The company can use one message everywhere, varying only the language, name, and colors. Exxon used "Put a tiger in your tank" with minor variations and gained international recognition. Colors can be changed to avoid taboos in some countries. Purple is associated with death in Burma and some Latin American nations; white is a mourning color in India; and green is associated with disease in Malaysia.[26] Even names and headlines may have to be modified. When Clairol introduced the "Mist Stick," a curling iron, into Germany, it found that *mist* is slang for manure. Few Germans wanted to purchase a "manure stick." The Dairy Association brought its "Got milk?" advertising campaign to Mexico only to find that the Spanish translation read, "Are you lactating?" When Coors put its slogan "Turn it loose," into Spanish, it was read by some as "suffer from diarrhea." In Spain, Chevrolet's Nova translated as "it doesn't go." A laundry soap ad claiming to wash "really dirty parts" was translated in French-speaking Quebec to read "a soap for washing private parts."[27]

The second possibility is to use the same theme globally but adapt the copy to each local market. For example, a Camay soap commercial showed a beautiful woman bathing. In Venezuela, a man was seen in the bathroom; in Italy and France, only a man's hand was seen; and in Japan, the man waited outside. Danish beer company

Carlsberg's global Web site.

Carlsberg adapts copy not to countries, but to individual cities and even neighborhoods within those cities. The 151-year-old Danish beer is available in more than 140 countries around the world, but because of the competitiveness and maturity of the U.S. market, it has to take a local tack to win new customers. All advertisements feature the same single image of the Carlsberg bottle, along with a humorous message about the specific city. For example, in Manhattan, one headline on an ad reads: "Went all night without hearing car alarm. Celebrate special occasions with Carlsberg."[28]

The third approach consists of developing a global pool of ads, from which each country selects the most appropriate one. Coca-Cola and Goodyear use this approach. Finally, some companies allow their country managers to create country-specific ads—within guidelines, of course. Kraft uses different ads for Cheez Whiz in different countries, given that household penetration is 95 percent in Puerto Rico, where the cheese is put on everything; 65 percent in Canada, where it is spread on morning breakfast toast; and 35 percent in the United States, where it is considered a junk food.

The use of media also requires international adaptation because media availability varies from country to country. Norway, Belgium, and France (and now the United States) do not allow cigarettes and alcohol (except for beer in the United States) to be advertised on TV. Austria and Italy regulate TV advertising to children. Saudi Arabia does not want advertisers to use women in ads. India taxes advertising. Magazines vary in availability and effectiveness; they play a major role in Italy and a minor one in Austria. Newspapers have a national reach in the United Kingdom, but the advertiser can buy only local coverage in Spain.

Marketers must also adapt sales-promotion techniques to different markets. Several European countries have laws preventing or limiting sales-promotion tools such as discounts, rebates, coupons, games of chance, and premiums. In Germany, Lands' End could not advertise its money back guarantee, although it does accept returned merchandise. American Express could not award points based on charges to its card for redeeming merchandise. A German store could not advertise that it would contribute a small sum to the fight against AIDS for each transaction; a German law limits discounts to 3 percent of list price: However, these restrictions are under attack and are likely to crumble.

price

Multinationals face several pricing problems when selling abroad. They must deal with price escalation, transfer prices, dumping charges, and gray markets.

When companies sell their goods abroad, they face a **price escalation** problem. A Gucci handbag may sell for $120 in Italy and $240 in the United States. Why? Gucci has to add the cost of transportation, tariffs, importer margin, wholesaler margin, and retailer margin to its factory price. Depending on these added costs, as well as the currency-fluctuation risk, the product might have to sell for two to five times as much in another country to make the same profit for the manufacturer. Because the cost escalation varies from country to country, the question is how to set the prices in different countries. Companies have three choices:

1. *Set a uniform price everywhere:* Coca-Cola might want to charge 75 cents for Coke everywhere in the world, but then Coca-Cola would earn quite different profit rates in different countries. Also, this strategy would result in the price being too high in poor countries and not high enough in rich countries.

2. *Set a market-based price in each country:* Here Coca-Cola would charge what each country could afford, but this strategy ignores differences in the actual cost from country to country. Also, it could lead to a situation in which intermediaries in low-price countries reship their Coca-Cola to high-price countries.

3. *Set a cost-based price in each country:* Here Coca-Cola would use a standard markup of its costs everywhere, but this strategy might price Coca-Cola out of the market in countries where its costs are high.

Another problem arises when a company sets a **transfer price** (the price it charges another unit in the company) for goods that it ships to its foreign subsidiaries. If the company charges too high a price to a subsidiary, it may end up paying higher tariff duties, although it may pay lower income taxes in the foreign country. If the company charges too low a price to its subsidiary, it can be charged with dumping. **Dumping** occurs when a company charges either less than its costs or less than it charges in its home market, in order to enter or win a market. This example of dumping occurred in the steel industry.

Stelco   In 2000, Stelco, a Canadian steelmaker, successfully fought dumping of steel products by steelmakers in Brazil, Finland, India, Indonesia, Thailand, and Ukraine. A Canadian tribunal found that cut-price steel imports from these countries caused "material injury to Canadian producers, including Stelco." Stelco alleged in 2001 that several U.S. steel companies were guilty of dumping, but this claim has yet to be resolved.[29]

When the U.S. Customs Bureau finds evidence of dumping, it can levy a dumping tariff on the guilty company. Various governments are watching for abuses and often force companies to charge the **arm's-length price**—that is, the price charged by other competitors for the same or a similar product.

Many multinationals are plagued by the gray-market problem. A **gray market** occurs when the same product sells at different prices geographically. Dealers in the low-price country find ways to sell some of their products in higher-price countries, thus earning more. Here is an example.

GT Bicycles   In 1995, GT Bicycles signed a deal with a Moscow businessman that would send 2,600 mountain bikes to Russia to help the company break into that market. GT alleged in a lawsuit that the shipment of bikes wound up back in the United States, where domestic discounter Price/Costco sold them at prices far below what GT-authorized dealers were selling them for.[30]

figure **13.4**

Whole-Channel Concept
for International Marketing

Seller

↓

Seller's
international
marketing
headquarters

↓

Channels
between
nations

↓

Channels within
foreign nations

↓

Final
buyers

Very often a company finds some enterprising distributors buying more than they can sell in their own country and reshipping the goods to another country to take advantage of price differences. Multinationals try to prevent gray markets by policing the distributors, by raising their prices to lower-cost distributors, or by altering the product characteristics or service warranties for different countries. In the European Union, the gray market may disappear altogether with the transition to a single currency unit. Once consumers recognize price differentiation by country, companies will be forced to harmonize prices throughout the countries that have adopted the single currency. Companies and marketers that offer the most innovative, specialized, or necessary products or services will be least affected by price transparency. For instance, Mail Boxes, Etc., which has 350 stores in Europe, believes that customers who need to send faxes will not refuse to do so because it costs more in Paris than in Italy.[31]

The Internet will also reduce price differentiation between countries. When companies sell their wares over the Internet, price will become transparent: Customers can easily find out how much products sell for in different countries. Take an online training course, for instance. Whereas the price of a classroom-delivered day of training can vary significantly from the United States to France to Thailand, the price of an online-delivered day of training would have to be similar.[32]

Another global pricing challenge that has arisen in recent years is that countries with overcapacity, cheap currencies, and the need to export aggressively have pushed prices down and devalued their currencies. For multinational firms this poses challenges: Sluggish demand and reluctance to pay higher prices make selling in these emerging markets difficult. Instead of lowering prices, and taking a loss, some multinationals have found more lucrative and creative means of coping.[33]

General Electric Company Rather than striving for larger market share, GE's power systems unit focused on winning a larger percentage of each customer's expenditures. The unit asked its top 100 customers what services were most critical to them and how GE could provide or improve them. The answers prompted the company to cut its response time for replacing old or damaged parts from 12 weeks to 6. It began advising customers on the nuances of doing business in the diverse environments of Europe and Asia and providing the maintenance staff for occasional equipment upgrades. By adding value and helping customers reduce their costs and become more efficient, GE was able to avoid a move to commodity pricing and was actually able to generate bigger margins. These margins led to record revenues of $15 billion in 2000, a 50 percent rise from the previous year.[34]

place (distribution channels)

Too many U.S. manufacturers think their job is done once the product leaves the factory. They should pay attention to how the product moves within the foreign country. They should take a whole-channel view of the problem of distributing products to final users. Figure 13.4 shows the three major links between seller and ultimate user. In the first link, *seller's international marketing headquarters*, the export department or international division makes decisions on channels and other marketing-mix elements. The second link, *channels between nations*, gets the products to the borders of the foreign nation. The decisions made in this link include the types of intermediaries (agents, trading companies) that will be used, the type of transportation (air, sea), and the financing and risk arrangements. The third link, *channels within foreign nations*, gets the products from their entry point to final buyers and users.

Distribution channels within countries vary considerably. To sell soap in Japan, Procter & Gamble has to work through one of the most complicated distribution systems in the world. It must sell to a general wholesaler, who sells to a product wholesaler, who sells to a product-specialty wholesaler, who sells to a regional wholesaler, who sells to a local wholesaler, who finally sells to retailers. All these distribution levels can mean that the consumer's price ends up double or triple the importer's price. If P&G takes the soap to tropical Africa, the company might sell to an import wholesaler, who sells to several jobbers, who sell to petty traders (mostly women) working in local markets.

Another difference lies in the size and character of retail units abroad. Large-scale retail chains dominate the U.S. scene, but much foreign retailing is in the hands of small, independent retailers. In India, millions of retailers operate tiny shops or sell in open markets. Their markups are high, but the real price is brought down through haggling. Incomes are low, and people must shop daily for small amounts; they are limited to whatever quantity can be carried home on foot or on a bicycle. Most homes lack storage space and refrigeration. Packaging costs are kept low in order to keep prices low. In India, cigarettes are often bought singly. Breaking bulk remains an important function of intermediaries and helps perpetuate the long channels of distribution, which are a major obstacle to the expansion of large-scale retailing in developing countries.

When multinationals first enter a country, they prefer to work with local distributors who have good local knowledge, but friction often arises later. The multinational complains that the local distributor does not invest in business growth, does not follow company policy, does not share enough information; and the local distributor complains of insufficient corporate support, impossible goals, and confusing policies. The multinational must choose the right distributors, invest in them, and set up performance goals to which they can agree.[35]

deciding on the marketing organization

Companies manage their international marketing activities in three ways: through export departments, international divisions, or a global organization.

export department

A firm normally gets into international marketing by simply shipping out its goods. If its international sales expand, the company organizes an export department consisting of a sales manager and a few assistants. As sales increase, the export department is expanded to include various marketing services so that the company can go after business more aggressively. If the firm moves into joint ventures or direct investment, the export department will no longer be adequate to manage international operations.

international division

Many companies become involved in several international markets and ventures. Sooner or later they will create international divisions to handle all their international activity. The international division is headed by a division president, who sets goals and budgets and is responsible for the company's international growth.

The international division's corporate staff consists of functional specialists who provide services to various operating units. Operating units can be organized in several ways. First, they can be *geographical organizations*. Reporting to the international-division president might be regional vice presidents for North America, Latin America, Europe, Africa, the Middle East, and the Far East. Reporting to the regional vice presidents are country managers who are responsible for a sales force, sales branches, distributors, and licensees in the respective countries. The operating units may be *world product groups*, each with an international vice president responsible for worldwide sales of each product group. The vice presidents may draw on corporate-staff area specialists for expertise on different geographical areas. Finally, operating units may be *international subsidiaries*, each headed by a president. The various subsidiary presidents report to the president of the international division.

Many multinationals shift between types of organization.

IBM   Part of IBM's massive reorganization strategy has been to put 235,000 employees into 14 customer-focused groups such as oil and gas, entertainment, and financial services. This way a big customer will be able to cut one deal with a central sales office to have IBM computers installed worldwide. Under the old system, a corporate customer with operations in 20 countries had to contract with 20 little Big Blues, each with its own pricing structure and service standards.[36]

global organization

Several firms have become truly global organizations. Their top corporate management and staff plan worldwide manufacturing facilities, marketing policies, financial flows, and logistical systems. The global operating units report directly to the chief executive or executive committee, not to the head of an international division. Executives are trained in worldwide operations. Management is recruited from many countries; components and supplies are purchased where they can be obtained at the least cost; and investments are made where the anticipated returns are greatest.

These companies face several organizational complexities. For example, when pricing a company's mainframe computers to a large banking system in Germany, how much influence should the headquarters product manager have? And the company's market manager for the banking sector? And the company's German country manager? Bartlett and Ghoshal have proposed circumstances under which different approaches work best. In *Managing Across Borders*, they describe forces that favor "global integration" (capital-intensive production, homogeneous demand) versus "national responsiveness" (local standards and barriers, strong local preferences). They distinguish three organizational strategies:[37]

1. *A global strategy treats the world as a single market:* This strategy is warranted when the forces for global integration are strong and the forces for national responsiveness are weak. This is true of the consumer electronics market, for example, where most buyers will accept a fairly standardized pocket radio, CD player, or TV. Matsushita has performed better than GE and Philips in the consumer electronics market because Matsushita operates in a more globally coordinated and standardized way.
2. *A multinational strategy treats the world as a portfolio of national opportunities:* This strategy is warranted when the forces favoring national responsiveness are strong and the forces favoring global integration are weak. This is the situation in the branded packaged-goods business (food products, cleaning products). Bartlett and Ghoshal cite Unilever as a better performer than Kao and P&G because Unilever grants more decision-making autonomy to its local branches.
3. *A "glocal" strategy standardizes certain core elements and localizes other elements:* This strategy makes sense for an industry (such as telecommunications) where each nation requires some adaptation of its equipment, but the providing company can also standardize some of the core components. Bartlett and Ghoshal cite Ericsson as balancing these considerations better than NEC (too globally oriented) and ITT (too locally oriented).

One of the most successful "glocal" companies is ABB, formed by a merger between the Swedish company ASEA and the Swiss company Brown Boveri.[38]

ABB   ABB's products include power transformers, electrical installations, instrumentation, auto components, air-conditioning equipment, and railroad equipment. The company has annual revenues of $32 billion and 200,000 employees. Its motto: "ABB is a global company local everywhere." English is its official language (all ABB managers must be conversant in English), and all financial results must be reported in dollars. ABB aims to reconcile three contradictions: to be global and local; to be big and small; and to be radically decentralized with centralized reporting and control. ABB has fewer than 200 staff at company headquarters in Switzerland, compared to the 3,000 people who populate Siemens headquarters. The company's many product lines are organized into 8 business segments, 65 business areas, 1,300 companies, and 5,000 profit centers, with the average employee belonging to a profit center of around 50 employees. Managers are regularly rotated among countries and mixed-nationality teams are encouraged. Depending on the type of business, some units are treated as superlocal businesses with lots of autonomy, while others are governed with major central control and are considered global businesses.[39]

summary

1. Companies cannot simply stay domestic and expect to maintain their markets. Despite the many challenges in the international arena (shifting borders, unstable governments, foreign-exchange problems, corruption, and technological pirating), companies selling in global industries need to internationalize their operations.

2. In deciding to go abroad, a company needs to define its international marketing objectives and policies. The company must determine whether to market in a few countries or many countries. It must decide which countries to consider. In general, the candidate countries should be rated on three criteria: market attractiveness, risk, and competitive advantage.

3. Once a company decides on a particular country, it must determine the best mode of entry. Its broad choices are indirect exporting, direct exporting, licensing, joint ventures, and direct investment. Each succeeding strategy involves more commitment, risk, control, and profit potential.

4. In deciding on the marketing program, a company must decide how much to adapt its marketing mix (product, promotion, price, and place) to local conditions. At the two ends of the spectrum are standardized and adapted marketing mixes, with many steps in between. At the product level, firms can pursue a strategy of straight extension, product adaptation, or product invention. At the promotion level, firms may choose communication adaptation or dual adaptation. At the price level, firms may encounter price escalation and gray markets. At the distribution level, firms need to take a whole-channel view of the challenge of distributing products to the final users. In creating all elements of the marketing mix, firms must be aware of the cultural, social, political, technological, environmental, and legal limitations they face in other countries.

5. Depending on the level of international involvement, companies manage their international marketing activity in three ways: through export departments, international divisions, or a global organization.

applications

marketing debate – is the world coming closer together?

Many social commentators maintain that youth and teens are becoming more and more alike as time goes on. Others, while not disputing that fact, point out that the differences between cultures at even younger ages by far exceed the similarities.

Take a position: People are becoming more and more similar versus The differences between people of different cultures far outweigh their advantages.

marketing and advertising

1. Kellogg's ready-to-eat breakfast cereals are sold in many countries, including Germany, as the ad in Figure 1 shows. This ad highlights an in-package prize promotion rather than the taste or nutrition of the featured cereals. Kellogg's Frosties and Kellogg's Pops bear a strong resemblance to the U.S. products Kellogg's Frosted Flakes and Kellogg's Corn Pops.

   a. Neither Kellogg's Frosties Spice nor the cell-phone logos featured in this ad are available in the United States. Therefore, which of the five international product and promotion strategies does Kellogg's appear to be using?

   b. Which of the ten commandments of global branding are being applied in this ad? Why are these appropriate for Kellogg's international strategy?

   c. Can Kellogg be considered a global firm? Can ready-to-eat breakfast cereals be considered a global industry? Explain.

2. The ad in Figure 2 announces that HSBC, which is based in London, provides financial services (such as corporate banking, commercial lending, and personal banking) through 6,500 branches serving 25 million customers in 78 countries.

   a. Which distribution channels does HSBC have to use to make its financial services available to customers around the world?

   b. Do you think HSBC's financial services would tend to be more standardized or would they tend to require considerable adaptation for each country? Why?

   c. Does HSBC's global branch system represent a market entry strategy of licensing, joint venture, direct investment, or direct exporting?

Figure 1

Figure 2

online marketing today

Marketers participating in global e-commerce need to speak the languages and understand the customs and interests of their target customers. For example, the main Reebok.com Web site has links to country-specific sites for the United Kingdom and France. The Reebok brand name is prominently displayed on all three sites, but the specific products and promotions being highlighted differ from country to country.

Point your Web browser to the Reebok site (www.reebok.com), examine the U.S. site, then visit the U.K. and French sites. Bearing in mind the ten commandments of global branding, what differences and similarities do you notice when browsing these three Reebok sites? How does Reebok leverage key brand elements online? Which of the sites (if any) allow online purchases? What conclusions can you draw about Reebok's online balance of standardization and customization and its balance of global and local control?

you're the marketer: sonic pda marketing plan

Marketing Plan Pro

Global marketing offers a way for companies of all sizes to grow by expanding their customer base beyond the domestic market. However, the complexities of global marketing demand careful planning and proper implementation.

As Jane Melody's assistant, you are researching non–U.S. markets for Sonic's first personal digital assistant product. Review the data you previously collected and your other recommendations for Sonic's marketing plan. Then answer these questions about how Sonic can approach global marketing:

- Should Sonic use exporting, licensing, joint ventures, or direct investment to enter the Canadian market? To enter other markets?
- If Sonic wants to start marketing a PDA in other countries, which of the international product strategies is most appropriate? Why?

- What international markets seem most promising for Sonic? Using online or print sources (such as the Global Edge Web site at www.globaledge.msu.edu/ibrd/ibrd.asp or the U.S. Business Advisor at www.business.gov), identify at least one foreign market that Sonic could consider entering.
- Is global standardization or adaptation most appropriate for Sonic's entry into the market(s) identified above? To answer, you will have to research electronics standards in the chosen market(s) as well as consumer behavior and competitive products. How can you collect such data?
- What brand partnerships might be of most value to Sonic in entering one or more global markets? Why?

When you have examined potential global markets and strategies, summarize your ideas and additional research needs in a written marketing plan or enter them into the Markets, SWOT and Issue Analysis, Marketing Strategy, and Marketing Research sections of the *Marketing Plan Pro* software.

notes

1. John Alden, "What in the World Drives UPS?" *International Business* (April 1998): 6–71.
2. Michael E. Porter, *Competitive Strategy* (New York: The Free Press, 1980), p. 275.
3. "The NBA and Yahoo! Announce Groundbreaking Global Agreement," *Business Wire,* September 11, 2000.
4. Sarah Ellison, "Boo.com: Buried by Badly Managed Buzz," *Wall Street Journal,* May 23, 2000, p. B10; Stephanie Gruner, "Web Failure Boo.com Gets a New Lease on Life as a Unit of Fashionmall.com," *Wall Street Journal,* September 6, 2000, p. B8.
5. Yumiro Ono, "On a Mission: Amway Grows Abroad, Sending 'Ambassadors' to Spread the Word," *Wall Street Journal,* May 14, 1997, p. A1; <*www.amway.com*>.
6. Igal Ayal and Jehiel Zif, "Market Expansion Strategies in Multinational Marketing," *Journal of Marketing* (Spring 1979): 84–94.
7. Kenichi Ohmae, *Triad Power* (New York: The Free Press, 1985); Philip Kotler and Nikhilesh Dholakia, "Ending Global Stagnation: Linking the Fortunes of the Industrial and Developing Countries," *Business in the Contemporary World* (Spring 1989): 86–97.
8. John Heilemann, "All Europeans Are Not Alike," *The New Yorker,* April 28–May 5, 1997, pp. 174–81.
9. Richard T. Hise, "Overcoming Exporting Barriers to Mexico," *Marketing Management* (Spring 2000): 52–54.
10. Charlene Marmer Solomon, "Don't Get Burned by Hot Markets," *Workforce* (January 1998): 12–22.
11. Russ Banham, "Not-So-Clear Choices," *International Business* (November–December 1997): 23–25.
12. Ibid.
13. "In Brief: E-Trade Licensing Deal Gives It an Israeli Link," *American Banker,* May 11, 1998; <*www.etrade.com*>.
14. Cynthia Kemper, "KFC Tradition Sold Japan on Chicken," *Denver Post,* June 7, 1998, p. J4.
15. Laura Mazur and Annik Hogg, *The Marketing Challenge* (Wokingham, England: Addison-Wesley, 1993), pp. 42–44; Jan Willem Karel, "Brand Strategy Positions Products Worldwide," *Journal of Business Strategy* 12, no. 3 (May–June 1991): 16–19.
16. Paula Dwyer, "Tearing Up Today's Organization Chart," *Business Week,* November 18, 1994, pp. 80–90.
17. Jan Johanson and Finn Wiedersheim-Paul, "The Internationalization of the Firm," *Journal of Management Studies* (October 1975): 305–22.
18. Stan Reid, "The Decision Maker and Export Entry and Expansion," *Journal of International Business Studies* (Fall 1981): 101–12; Igal Ayal, "Industry Export Performance: Assessment and Prediction," *Journal of Marketing* (Summer 1982): 54–61; Somkid Jatusripitak, *The Exporting Behavior of Manufacturing Firms* (Ann Arbor: University of Michigan Press, 1986).
19. Warren J. Keegan, *Multinational Marketing Management,* 5th ed. (Upper Saddle River, NJ: Prentice Hall, 1995), pp. 378–81.
20. J. S. Perry Hobson, "Feng Shui: Its Impacts on the Asian Hospitality Industry,"*International Journal of Contemporary Hospitality Management* 6, no. 6 (1994): 21–26; Bernd H. Schmitt

and Yigang Pan, "In Asia, the Supernatural Means Sales," *New York Times,* February 19, 1995, pp. 3, 11.
21. "What Makes a Company Great?" *Fortune,* October 26, 1998, pp. 218–26.
22. David Leonhardt, "It Was a Hit in Buenos Aires—So Why Not Boise?" *BusinessWeek,* September 7, 1998, pp. 56–58.
23. Charles P. Wallace, "Charge!" *Fortune,* September 28, 1998, pp. 189–96.
24. "In Germany, Wal-Mart is Struggling," *Blooming News,* October 29, 2000; Wendy Zellner, "How Well Does Wal-Mart Travel," *BusinessWeek,* September 3, 2001.
25. Ben Dolven, "Find the Niche," *Far Eastern Economic Review,* March 26, 1998, pp. 58–59.
26. Thomas J. Madden, Kelly Hewett, and Martin S. Roth, "Managing Images in Different Cultures: A Cross-National Study of Color Meanings and Preferences," *Journal of International Marketing,* 8, no. 4 (2000): 90–107; Zeynep Gürhan-Canli and Durairaj Maheswaran, "Cultural Variations in Country of Origin Effects," *Journal of Marketing Research,* 37 (August 2000), pp. 309–17.
27. Richard P. Carpenter and the Globe Staff, "What They Meant to Say Was . . . ," *Boston Globe,* August 2, 1998, p. M6.
28. Carlos Briceno, "Labatt Believes Going 'Glocal' Will Melt the Ice for Carlsberg," *Beverage World,* September 30–October 31, 1988, p. 17. For discussion of the effects of brand development on advertising appeals, see Rajesh K. Chandy, Gerard J. Tellis, Deborah J. MacInnis, and Pattara Thaivanich, "What to Say When: Advertising Appeals in Evolving Markets," *Journal of Marketing Research,* 38 (November 2001): 399–414.
29. Tony Van Alphen, "Some U.S. Makers Dumping Steel in Canada," *Toronto Star,* May 2, 2001, p. E01.
30. Greg Johnson, "Gray Wail," *Los Angeles Times,* March 30, 1997, p. D1.
31. Maricris G. Briones, "The Euro Starts Here," *Marketing News,* July 20, 1998, pp. 1, 39.
32. Elliott Masie, "Global Pricing in an Internet World," *Computer Reseller News,* May 11, 1998, pp. 55, 58.
33. Ram Charan, "The Rules Have Changed," *Fortune,* March 16, 1998, pp. 159–62.
34. <*www.ge.com.*>
35. David Arnold, "Seven Rules of International Distribution," *Harvard Business Review* (November–December 2000): 131–37.
36. Dwyer, "Tearing Up Today's Organization Chart," pp. 80–90.
37. Christopher A. Bartlett and Sumantra Ghoshal, *Managing Across Borders* (Cambridge, MA: Harvard Business School Press, 1989).
38. Martha M. Hamilton, "Going Global: A World of Difference: DaimlerChrysler Joins Growing List of Titans That Must Find New Ways to Compete," *Washington Post,* May 10, 1998, p. H1; Jeremy Main, "Globe-zilla," *Working Woman* (October 1998): 9; Charles Fleming and Leslie Lopez, "The Corporate Challenge—No Boundaries: ABB's Dramatic Plan to Recast Its Business Structure along Global Lines: It May Not Be Easy— or Wise," *Wall Street Journal,* September 28, 1998, p. R16.
39. <*www.abb.com*>.

14

setting the product and branding strategy

In this chapter, we will address the following questions:

- What are the characteristics of products?
- How can a company build and manage its product mix and product lines?
- How can a company make better brand decisions?
- How can packaging and labeling be used as marketing tools?

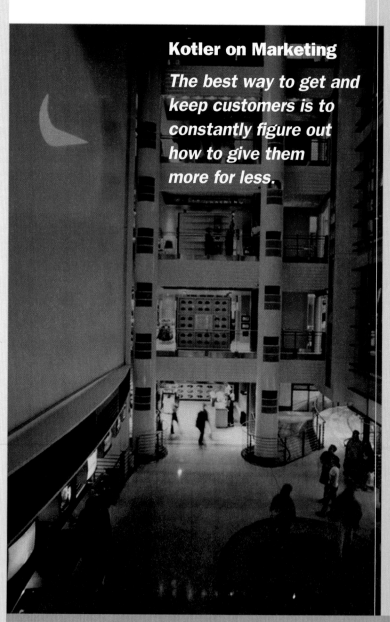

Kotler on Marketing

The best way to get and keep customers is to constantly figure out how to give them more for less.

W hat do business executives *Ray Kroc (McDonald's), Dave Thomas (Wendy's), and Colonel Sanders (Kentucky Fried Chicken)* have in common? They all have led or lead lives interesting enough to feature on A&E's award-winning television show *Biography. A&E's Biography offers excellent lessons in product and brand management.*

Arts & Entertainment Network A&E is steadily building *Biography*, its nightly look at famous figures, into its trademark masterbrand, one that is crossing a spectrum of media to reach a broad audience. So far, the cable series has profiled over 500 people. Executives at A&E are practicing line extension into new formats. Home video was the obvious first extension. Videos are sold through direct response, through catalogs, online, and in dedicated space at some 500 Barnes & Noble bookstores. A Biography Web site, born in 1996, has grown to include 22,000 personalities; its traffic surpasses that of A&E's own site; and A&E now offers a separate Biography cable channel, a Biography magazine, Biography books, and Biography CDs, which feature music from musicians profiled on the show.[1]

A&E's success story underscores the importance of the first and most important element of the marketing mix: the product. All the advertising and promotion in the world will not make consumers turn on a television show if they find it boring, irritating, or irrelevant.[2]

Product is a key element in the market offering. *Marketing-mix planning begins with formulating an offering to meet target customers' needs or wants. The customer will judge the offering by three basic elements: product features and quality, services mix and quality, and price (see Figure 14.1). In this chapter, we examine product; in Chapter 15, services; and in Chapter 16, prices. All three elements must be meshed into a competitively attractive offering.*

the product and the product mix

A **product** is anything that can be offered to a market to satisfy a want or need. Products that are marketed include *physical goods, services, experiences, events, persons, places, properties, organizations, information,* and *ideas.*

product levels

In planning its market offering, the marketer needs to think through five levels of the product (see Figure 14.2).[3] Each level adds more customer value, and the five constitute a **customer value hierarchy**. The most fundamental level is the **core benefit**: the fundamental service or benefit that the customer is really buying. A hotel guest is buying "rest and sleep." The purchaser of a drill is buying "holes." Marketers must see themselves as benefit providers.

At the second level, the marketer has to turn the core benefit into a **basic product**. Thus a hotel room includes a bed, bathroom, towels, desk, dresser, and closet.

At the third level, the marketer prepares an **expected product**, a set of attributes and conditions buyers normally expect when they purchase this product. Hotel guests expect a clean bed, fresh towels, working lamps, and a relative degree of quiet. Because most hotels can meet this minimum expectation, the traveler normally will settle for whichever hotel is most convenient or least expensive.

At the fourth level, the marketer prepares an **augmented product** that exceeds customer expectations. Consider BabyCenter.com.

BabyCenter.com BabyCenter.com's mission is to help mothers raise a healthy baby. Instead of simply setting itself up to sell baby products online, it has set itself up as a *metamediary* to provide a wide variety of information and services. Mothers will find helpful hints and checklists; a search engine for retrieving high-quality medical information; an opportunity to personalize the site; and access to a community of supportive fellow parents. As Elmer Wheeler once observed, "Don't sell the steak—sell the sizzle."

figure **14.1**

Components of the Market Offering

Five Product Levels

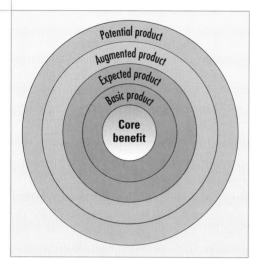

Today's competition essentially takes place at the product-augmentation level. (In less developed countries, competition takes place mostly at the expected product level.) Product augmentation leads the marketer to look at the user's total **consumption system**: the way the user performs the tasks of getting and using products and related services.[4] According to Levitt:

> The new competition is not between what companies produce in their factories, but between what they add to their factory output in the form of packaging, services, advertising, customer advice, financing, delivery arrangements, warehousing, and other things that people value.[5]

BabyCenter.com is not just an online merchant, it's a metamediary.

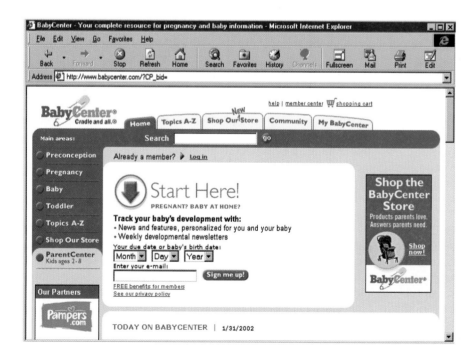

Some things should be noted about product-augmentation strategy. First, each augmentation adds cost. Second, augmented benefits soon become expected benefits. Today's hotel guests expect a remote-control television set. This means competitors will have to search for still other features and benefits. Third, as companies raise the price of their augmented product, some competitors offer a "stripped-down" version at a much lower price. Thus, alongside the growth of fine hotels like Four Seasons and Ritz Carlton, we see the emergence of lower-cost hotels and motels (Motel Six, Comfort Inn) catering to clients who simply want the basic product. Virgin Atlantic provides a good example of a company always searching to expand and differentiate its services from those offered by competitors.

Virgin Atlantic Airlines Virgin seeks to provide an integrated travel experience. It joined with limousine companies to provide free transportation for business-class passengers to airports. Once there, they check into Virgin's Clubhouse lounge. At the Clubhouse, passengers can shower, take a hydrotherapy bath, have a free manicure, pedicure, facial, or haircut. They can sit at the bar, in the restaurant, library, or music room. On certain planes, they can take a shower or use the Jacuzzi, sleep in a ship-style sleeper cabin, or surf the Internet.

At the fifth level stands the **potential product**, which encompasses all the possible augmentations and transformations the product or offering might undergo in the future. Here is where companies search for new ways to satisfy customers and distinguish their offer. Richard Branson of Virgin Atlantic is thinking of adding a casino and a shopping mall in the 600-passenger planes that his company will acquire in the next few years; and consider the customization platforms new e-commerce sites are offering, from which companies can learn by seeing what different customers prefer.

MyCereal.com, Personalblends.com, and Reflect.com General Mills' mycereal.com, which was available during 2000 and 2001, let users create their own cereal blends from ingredients that met their specific tastes or health needs. One woman received her cereal package with corn flakes, almond-coated raisins, sliced almonds, and dried banana bits; the package included the name she gave it: "Lisa's Yummy-to-My-Tummy" cereal. Proctor & Gamble has developed personalblends.com, where coffee lovers can customize their coffee by answering a few questions. P&G also developed Reflect.com, which offers customized beauty products created interactively on the Web site.

Successful companies add benefits to their offering that not only *satisfy* customers but also surprise and *delight* them. Delighting customers is a matter of exceeding expectations.

Ritz–Carlton Hotels Ritz-Carlton Hotels remember guests' preferences and assign rooms with these preferences in mind. They empower employees to make decisions and spend money to solve customer-service issues. They review the service delivery process to imagine everything that could go wrong and then take preventive steps.

product hierarchy

Each product is related to certain other products. The product hierarchy stretches from basic needs to particular items that satisfy those needs. We can identify six levels of the product hierarchy (here for life insurance):

1. *Need family:* The core need that underlies the existence of a product family. Example: security.
2. *Product family:* All the product classes that can satisfy a core need with reasonable effectiveness. Example: savings and income.
3. *Product class:* A group of products within the product family recognized as having a certain functional coherence. Example: financial instruments.

General Mills' Mycereal.com Web site, available in 2000 and 2001, allowed consumers to create their own cereal blend.

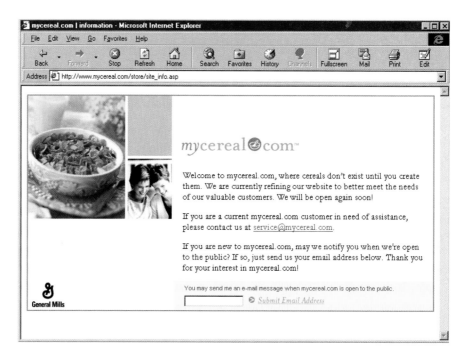

4. *Product line:* A group of products within a product class that are closely related because they perform a similar function, are sold to the same customer groups, are marketed through the same channels, or fall within given price ranges. Example: life insurance.

5. *Product type:* A group of items within a product line that share one of several possible forms of the product. Example: term life.

6. *Item (also called stockkeeping unit or product variant):* A distinct unit within a brand or product line distinguishable by size, price, appearance, or some other attribute. Example: Prudential renewable term life insurance.

Two other terms are frequently used with respect to the product hierarchy. A **product system** is a group of diverse but related items that function in a compatible manner. For example, the Handspring personal digital assistant comes with attachable Visor products including a phone, radio, pager, video games, e-books, MP3 player, digital camera, and voice recorder. A **product mix** (or product assortment) is the set of all products and items that a particular seller offers for sale to buyers.

product classifications

Marketers have traditionally classified products on the basis of characteristics: durability, tangibility, and use (consumer or industrial). Each product type has an appropriate marketing-mix strategy.[6]

DURABILITY AND TANGIBILITY   Products can be classified into three groups, according to durability and tangibility:

1. *Nondurable goods* are tangible goods normally consumed in one or a few uses, like beer and soap. Because these goods are consumed quickly and purchased frequently, the appropriate strategy is to make them available in many locations, charge only a small markup, and advertise heavily to induce trial and build preference.

2. *Durable goods* are tangible goods that normally survive many uses: refrigerators, machine tools, and clothing. Durable products normally require more personal selling and service, command a higher margin, and require more seller guarantees.

3. *Services* are intangible, inseparable, variable, and perishable products. As a result, they normally require more quality control, supplier credibility, and adaptability. Examples include haircuts and repairs.

CONSUMER-GOODS CLASSIFICATION   The vast array of goods consumers buy can be classified on the basis of shopping habits. We can distinguish among convenience, shopping, specialty, and unsought goods.

Convenience goods are those the customer usually purchases frequently, immediately, and with a minimum of effort. Examples include tobacco products, soaps, and newspapers. Convenience goods can be further divided. *Staples* are goods consumers purchase on a regular basis. A buyer might routinely purchase Heinz ketchup, Crest toothpaste, and Ritz crackers. *Impulse goods* are purchased without any planning or search effort. Candy bars and magazines are impulse goods. *Emergency goods* are purchased when a need is urgent—umbrellas during a rainstorm, boots and shovels during the first winter snowstorm. Manufacturers of emergency goods will place them in many outlets to capture the sale.

Shopping goods are goods that the customer, in the process of selection and purchase, characteristically compares on such bases as suitability, quality, price, and style. Examples include furniture, clothing, used cars, and major appliances. Shopping goods can be further divided. *Homogeneous shopping goods* are similar in quality but different enough in price to justify shopping comparisons. *Heterogeneous shopping goods* differ in product features and services that may be more important than price. The seller of heterogeneous shopping goods carries a wide assortment to satisfy individual tastes and must have well-trained salespeople to inform and advise customers.

Specialty goods have unique characteristics or brand identification for which a sufficient number of buyers is willing to make a special purchasing effort. Examples include cars, stereo components, photographic equipment, and men's suits. A Mercedes is a specialty good because interested buyers will travel far to buy one. Specialty goods do not involve making comparisons; buyers invest time only to reach dealers carrying the wanted products. Dealers do not need convenient locations; however, they must let prospective buyers know their locations.

Unsought goods are those the consumer does not know about or does not normally think of buying, like smoke detectors. The classic examples of known but unsought goods are life insurance, cemetery plots, gravestones, and encyclopedias. Unsought goods require advertising and personal-selling support.

INDUSTRIAL-GOODS CLASSIFICATION   Industrial goods can be classified in terms of how they enter the production process and their relative costliness. We can distinguish three groups of industrial goods: materials and parts, capital items, and supplies and business services. **Materials and parts** are goods that enter the manufacturer's product completely. They fall into two classes: raw materials and manufactured materials and parts.

Raw materials fall into two major classes: *farm products* (e.g., wheat, cotton, livestock, fruits, and vegetables) and *natural products* (e.g., fish, lumber, crude petroleum, iron ore). Farm products are supplied by many producers, who turn them over to marketing intermediaries, who provide assembly, grading, storage, transportation, and selling services. Their perishable and seasonal nature gives rise to special marketing practices. Their commodity character results in relatively little advertising and promotional activity, with some exceptions. At times, commodity groups will launch campaigns to promote their product—potatoes, prunes, milk. Some producers brand their product—Sunkist oranges, Chiquita bananas.

Natural products are limited in supply. They usually have great bulk and low unit value and must be moved from producer to user. Fewer and larger producers often market them directly to industrial users. Because the users depend on these materials, long-term supply contracts are common. The homogeneity of natural materials limits the amount of demand-creation activity. Price and delivery reliability are the major factors influencing the selection of suppliers.

Manufactured materials and parts fall into two categories: component materials (iron, yarn, cement, wires) and component parts (small motors, tires, castings). *Component* *material*s are usually fabricated further—pig iron is made into steel, and yarn is woven into cloth. The standardized nature of component materials usually means that price and supplier reliability are key purchase factors. *Component parts* enter the finished product with no further change in form, as when small motors are put into vacuum cleaners, and tires are put on automobiles. Most manufactured materials and parts are sold directly to industrial users. Price and service are major marketing considerations, and branding and advertising tend to be less important.

Capital items are long-lasting goods that facilitate developing or managing the finished product. They include two groups: installations and equipment. *Installations* consist of buildings (factories, offices) and equipment (generators, drill presses, mainframe computers, elevators). Installations are major purchases. They are usually bought directly from the producer, with the typical sale preceded by a long negotiation period. The producer's sales force includes technical personnel. Producers have to be willing to design to specification and to supply postsale services. Advertising is much less important than personal selling.

Equipment comprises portable factory equipment and tools (hand tools, lift trucks) and office equipment (personal computers, desks). These types of equipment do not become part of a finished product. They have a shorter life than installations but a longer life than operating supplies. Although some equipment manufacturers sell direct, more often they use intermediaries, because the market is geographically dispersed, the buyers are numerous, and the orders are small. Quality, features, price, and service are major considerations. The sales force tends to be more important than advertising, although the latter can be used effectively.

Supplies and business services are short-lasting goods and services that facilitate developing or managing the finished product. Supplies are of two kinds: *maintenance and repair items* (paint, nails, brooms), and *operating supplies* (lubricants, coal, writing paper, pencils). Together, they go under the name of MRO goods. Supplies are the equivalent of convenience goods; they are usually purchased with minimum effort on a straight rebuy basis. They are normally marketed through intermediaries because of their low unit value and the great number and geographic dispersion of customers. Price and service are important considerations, because suppliers are standardized and brand preference is not high.

Business services include *maintenance and repair services* (window cleaning, copier repair) and *business advisory services* (legal, management consulting, advertising). Maintenance and repair services are usually supplied under contract by small producers or are available from the manufacturers of the original equipment. Business advisory services are usually purchased on the basis of the supplier's reputation and staff.

product mix

A **product mix** (also called **product assortment**) is the set of all products and items that a particular seller offers for sale. Kodak's product mix consists of two strong product lines: information products and image products. NEC's (Japan) product mix consists of communication products and computer products. Michelin has three product lines: tires, maps, and restaurant-rating services.

A company's product mix has a certain width, length, depth, and consistency. These concepts are illustrated in Table 14.1 for selected Procter & Gamble consumer products.

- The *width* of a product mix refers to how many different product lines the company carries. Table 14.1 shows a product-mix width of five lines. (In fact, P&G produces many additional lines.)
- The *length* of a product mix refers to the total number of items in the mix. In Table 14.1, it is 25. We can also talk about the average length of a line. This is obtained by dividing the total length (here 25) by the number of lines (here 5), or an average product length of 5.
- The width of a product mix refers to how many variants are offered of each product in the line. If Crest comes in three sizes and two formulations (regular and mint), Crest has a depth of six. The average depth of P&G's product mix can be calculated by averaging the number of variants within the brand groups.

table **14.1**	Product-Mix Width and Product-Line Length for Procter & Gamble Products (Including Dates of Introduction)

			Product-Mix Width		
	Detergents	Toothpaste	Disposable Bar Soap	Diapers	Paper Tissue
PRODUCT-LINE LENGTH	Ivory Snow (1930)	Gleem (1952)	Ivory (1879)	Pampers (1961)	Charmin (1928)
	Dreft (1933)	Crest (1955)	Kirk's (1885)	Luvs (1976)	Puffs (1960)
	Tide (1946)		Lava (1893)		Banner (1982)
	Cheer (1950)		Camay (1926)		Summit (1992)
	Oxydol (1954)		Zest (1952)		
	Dash (1954)		Safeguard (1963)		
	Bold (1965)		Coast (1974)		
	Gain (1966)		Oil of Olay (1993)		
	Era (1972)				

- The *consistency* of the product mix refers to how closely related the various product lines are in end use, production requirements, distribution channels, or some other way. P&G's product lines are consistent insofar as they are consumer goods that go through the same distribution channels. The lines are less consistent insofar as they perform different functions for the buyers.

These four product-mix dimensions permit the company to expand its business in four ways. It can add new product lines, thus widening its product mix. It can lengthen each product line. It can add more product variants to each product and deepen its product mix. Finally, a company can pursue more product-line consistency.

product–line decisions

A product mix consists of various product lines. In General Electric's Consumer Appliance Division, there are product-line managers for refrigerators, stoves, and washing machines. At Northwestern University, there are separate academic deans for the medical school, law school, business school, engineering school, music school, speech school, journalism school, and liberal arts school.

In offering a product line, companies normally develop a basic platform and modules that can be added to meet different customer requirements. Car manufacturers build their cars around a basic platform. Homebuilders show a model home to which additional features can be added. This modular approach enables the company to offer variety while lowering production costs.

product-line analysis

Product-line managers need to know the sales and profits of each item in their line in order to determine which items to build, maintain, harvest, or divest. They also need to understand each product line's market profile.

SALES AND PROFITS   Figure 14.3 shows a sales and profit report for a five-item product line. The first item accounts for 50 percent of total sales and 30 percent of total profits. The first two items account for 80 percent of total sales and 60 percent of total profits. If these two items were suddenly hurt by a competitor, the line's sales and profitability

figure **14.3**

Product–Item
Contributions to a
Product Line's Total
Sales and Profits

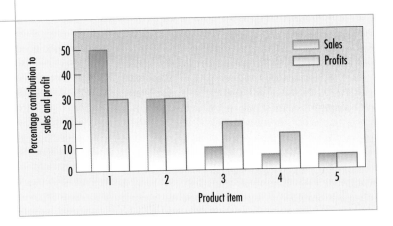

could collapse. These items must be carefully monitored and protected. At the other end, the last item delivers only 5 percent of the product line's sales and profits. The product-line manager may consider dropping this item unless it has strong growth potential.

Every company's product portfolio contains products with different margins. Supermarkets make almost no margin on bread and milk; reasonable margins on canned and frozen foods; and even better margins on flowers, ethnic food lines, and freshly baked goods. A local telephone company makes different margins on its core telephone service, call waiting, caller ID, and voice mail.

A company can classify its products into four types that yield different gross margins, depending on sales volume and promotion. To illustrate with personal computers:

- *Core product:* Basic computers that produce high sales volume and are heavily promoted but with low margins because they are viewed as undifferentiated commodities.
- *Staples:* Items with lower sales volume and no promotion, such as faster CPUs or bigger memories. These yield a somewhat higher margin.
- *Specialties:* Items with lower sales volume but which might be highly promoted, such as digital movie-making equipment; or might generate income for services, such as personal delivery, installation, or on-site training.
- *Convenience items:* Peripheral items that sell in high volume but receive less promotion, such as computer monitors, printers, upscale video or sound cards, and software. Consumers tend to buy them where they buy the original equipment because it is more convenient than making further shopping trips. These items can carry higher margins.

The main point is that companies should recognize that these items differ in their potential for being priced higher or advertised more as ways to increase their sales, margins, or both.[7]

MARKET PROFILE   The product-line manager must review how the line is positioned against competitors' lines. Consider paper company X with a paper-board product line.[8] Two paper-board attributes are weight and finish quality. Paper weight is usually offered at standard levels of 90, 120, 150, and 180 weight. Finish quality is offered at low, medium, and high levels. Figure 14.4 shows the location of the various product-line items of company X and four competitors, A, B, C, and D. Competitor A sells two product items in the extra-high weight class ranging from medium to low finish quality. Competitor B sells four items that vary in weight and finish quality. Competitor C sells three items in which the greater the weight, the greater the finish quality. Competitor D sells three items, all lightweight but varying in finish quality. Company X offers three items that vary in weight and finish quality.

figure **14.4**

Product Map for a
Paper–Product Line

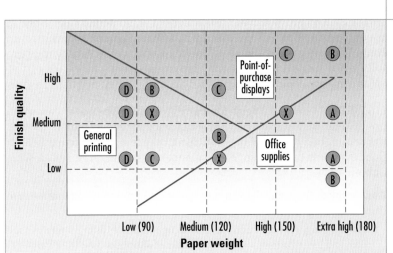

Source: Benson P. Shapiro, *Industrial Product Policy: Managing the Existing Product Line.* Cambridge, MA: Marketing Science Institute Report No. 77–110.

The product map shows which competitors' items are competing against company X's items. For example, company X's low-weight, medium-quality paper competes against competitor D's and B's papers, but its high-weight, medium-quality paper has no direct competitor. The map also reveals possible locations for new items. No manufacturer offers a high-weight, low-quality paper. If company X estimates a strong unmet demand and can produce and price this paper at low cost, it could consider adding this item to its line.

Another benefit of product mapping is that it identifies market segments. Figure 14.4 shows the types of paper, by weight and quality, preferred by the general printing industry, the point-of-purchase display industry, and the office-supply industry. The map shows that company X is well positioned to serve the needs of the general printing industry but is less effective in serving the other two industries.

After performing a product-line analysis, the product-line manager has to consider decisions on product-line length, line modernization, line featuring, and line pruning.

product-line length

A product line is too short if profits can be increased by adding items; the line is too long if profits can be increased by dropping items.

Company objectives influence product-line length. One objective is to create a product line to induce upselling: Thus BMW would like to move customers up from the BMW 3 series to the 5 to 7 series. A different objective is to create a product line that facilitates cross-selling: Hewlett-Packard sells printers as well as computers. Still another objective is to create a product line that protects against economic ups and downs; thus the GAP runs various clothing-store chains (Old Navy, GAP, Banana Republic) covering different price points in case the economy moves up or down. Companies seeking high market share and market growth will generally carry longer product lines. Companies that emphasize high profitability will carry shorter lines consisting of carefully chosen items.

Product lines tend to lengthen over time. Excess manufacturing capacity puts pressure on the product-line manager to develop new items. The sales force and distributors also pressure the company for a more complete product line to satisfy customers; but as items are added, several costs rise: design and engineering costs, inventory-carrying costs, manufacturing-changeover costs, order-processing costs, transportation costs, and new-item promotional costs. Eventually, someone calls a halt: Top management may stop development because of insufficient funds or manufacturing capacity. The controller may call for a study of money-losing items. A pattern of product-line growth followed by massive pruning may repeat itself many times.

A company lengthens its product line in two ways: by line stretching and line filling.

LINE STRETCHING   Every company's product line covers a certain part of the total possible range. For example, BMW automobiles are located in the upper price range of the automobile market. **Line stretching** occurs when a company lengthens its product line beyond its current range. The company can stretch its line downmarket, upmarket, or both ways.

Downmarket Stretch   A company positioned in the middle market may want to introduce a lower-priced line for any of three reasons:

1. The company may notice strong growth opportunities as mass-retailers such as Wal-Mart, Best Buy, and others attract a growing number of shoppers who want value-priced goods.
2. The company may wish to tie up lower-end competitors who might otherwise try to move upmarket. If the company has been attacked by a low-end competitor, it often decides to counterattack by entering the low end of the market.
3. The company may find that the middle market is stagnating or declining.

A company faces a number of naming choices in deciding to move downmarket. Sony, for example, faced three choices:

1. Use the name Sony on all of its offerings. (Sony did this.)
2. Introduce the lower-priced offerings using a sub-brand name, such as Sony Value Line. Other companies have done this, such as Gillette with Gillette Good News and United Airlines with United Express. The risks are that the Sony name loses some of its quality image and that some Sony buyers might switch to the lower-priced offerings.
3. Introduce the lower-priced offerings under a different name, without mentioning Sony; but Sony would have to spend a lot of money to build up the new brand name, and the mass-merchants may not even accept a brand that lacks the Sony name.

Moving downmarket carries risks. Kodak introduced Kodak Funtime film to counter lower-priced brands, but it did not price Kodak Funtime low enough to match the lower-priced film. It also found some of its regular customers buying Funtime, thereby cannibalizing its core brand. So it withdrew the product. On the other hand, Mercedes successfully introduced its C-Class cars at $30,000 without injuring its ability to sell other Mercedes cars for $100,000 and up. John Deere introduced a lower-priced line of lawn tractors called Sabre from John Deere while still selling its more expensive tractors under the John Deere name.

Upmarket Stretch   Companies may wish to enter the high end of the market for more growth, higher margins, or simply to position themselves as full-line manufacturers. Many markets have spawned surprising upscale segments: Starbucks in coffee, Haagen-Dazs in ice cream, and Evian in bottled water. The leading Japanese auto companies have each introduced an upscale automobile: Toyota's Lexus; Nissan's Infinity; and Honda's Acura. Note that they invented entirely new names rather than using or including their own names.

Other companies have included their own name in moving upmarket. Gallo introduced Ernest and Julio Gallo Varietals and priced these wines more than twice as high as their regular wines. General Electric introduced the GE Profile brand for its large appliance offerings in the upscale market.[9]

Two-Way Stretch   Companies serving the middle market might decide to stretch their line in both directions. Texas Instruments (TI) introduced its first calculators in the medium-price-medium-quality end of the market. Gradually, it added calculators at the

Marriott's Web site lists all the hotels in its product line.

lower end, taking market share away from Bowmar, and at the higher end to compete with Hewlett-Packard. This two-way stretch won TI early market leadership in the hand-calculator market.

The Marriott Hotel group also has performed a two-way stretch of its hotel product line. Marriott International develops lodging brands in the most profitable segments in the industry. In order to determine where these opportunities lie, Marriott conducts extensive consumer research to uncover distinct consumer targets and develop products targeted to those needs in the most profitable areas. Examples of this are the development of the JW Marriott line in the upper upscale segment, Courtyard by Marriott in the upper mid-scale segment and Fairfield Inn in the lower mid-scale segment. By basing the development of these brands on distinct consumer targets with unique needs, Marriott is able to ensure against overlap between brands.

LINE FILLING   A product line can also be lengthened by adding more items within the present range. There are several motives for *line filling*: reaching for incremental profits, trying to satisfy dealers who complain about lost sales because of missing items in the line, trying to utilize excess capacity, trying to be the leading full-line company, and trying to plug holes to keep out competitors.

Line filling is overdone if it results in self-cannibalization and customer confusion. The company needs to differentiate each item in the consumer's mind. Each item should possess a *just-noticeable difference*. According to Weber's law, customers are more attuned to relative than to absolute difference.[10] They will perceive the difference between boards 2 and 3 feet long and boards 20 and 30 feet long but not between boards 29 and 30 feet long. The company should also check that the proposed item meets a market need and is not being added simply to satisfy an internal need. The Edsel automobile, on which Ford lost $350 million, met Ford's internal positioning needs for a car between its Ford and Lincoln lines but not the market's needs.

line modernization, featuring, and pruning

Product lines need to be modernized. A company's machine tools might have a 1950s look and lose out to newer-styled competitors' lines. The issue is whether to overhaul the line piecemeal or all at once. A piecemeal approach allows the company to see how customers and dealers take to the new style. It is also less draining on the company's cash flow, but it allows competitors to see changes and to start redesigning their own lines.

In rapidly changing product markets, modernization is carried on continuously. Companies plan improvements to encourage customer migration to higher-valued, higher-priced items. Microprocessor companies such as Intel and Motorola, and software companies such as Microsoft and Lotus, continually introduce more advanced versions of their products. A major issue is timing improvements so they do not appear too early (damaging sales of the current line) or too late (after the competition has established a strong reputation for more advanced equipment).

The product-line manager typically selects one or a few items in the line to feature. Sears will announce a special low-priced washing machine to attract customers. At other times, managers will feature a high-end item to lend prestige to the product line. Sometimes a company finds one end of its line selling well and the other end selling poorly. The company may try to boost demand for the slower sellers, especially if they are produced in a factory that is idled by lack of demand. This situation faced Honeywell when its medium-sized computers were not selling as well as its large computers; but it could be counterargued that the company should promote items that sell well rather than try to prop up weak items.

Product-line managers must periodically review the line for deadwood that is depressing profits. Unilever recently cut down its portfolio of brands from 1,600 to 970 and may even prune more, to 400 by 2005. The weak items can be identified through sales and cost analysis. A chemical company cut down its line from 217 to the 93 products with the largest volume, the largest contribution to profits, and the greatest long-term potential. Pruning is also done when the company is short of production capacity. Companies typically shorten their product lines in periods of tight demand and lengthen their lines in periods of slow demand.

brand decisions

Branding is a major issue in product strategy. As Russell Hanlin, the CEO of Sunkist Growers, observed: "An orange is an orange . . . is an orange. Unless . . . that orange happens to be Sunkist, a name 80% of consumers know and trust." Well-known brands command a price premium. Japanese companies such as Sony and Toyota have built a huge brand-loyal market. At the same time, developing a branded product requires a great deal of long-term investment, especially for advertising, promotion, and packaging.

what is a brand?

Perhaps the most distinctive skill of professional marketers is their ability to create, maintain, protect, and enhance brands. Branding is the art and cornerstone of marketing. The American Marketing Association defines a **brand** as: a name, term, sign, symbol, or design, or a combination of them, intended to identify the goods or services of one seller or group of sellers and to differentiate them from those of competitors. Thus a brand identifies the seller or maker. Under trademark law, the seller is granted exclusive rights to the use of the brand name in perpetuity. Brands differ from other assets such as patents and copyrights, which have expiration dates.

A brand is a complex symbol that can convey up to six levels of meaning:[11]

1. *Attributes:* A brand brings to mind certain attributes. Mercedes suggests expensive, well-built, well-engineered, durable, high-prestige automobiles.
2. *Benefits:* Attributes must be translated into functional and emotional benefits. The attribute "durable" could translate into the functional benefit "I won't have to buy another car for several

years." The attribute "expensive" translates into the emotional benefit "The car makes me feel important and admired."

3. *Values:* The brand also says something about the producer's values. Mercedes stands for high performance, safety, and prestige.

4. *Culture:* The brand may represent a certain culture. The Mercedes represents German culture: organized, efficient, high quality.

5. *Personality:* The brand can project a certain personality. Mercedes may suggest a no-nonsense boss (person), a reigning lion (animal), or an austere palace (object).

6. *User:* The brand suggests the kind of consumer who buys or uses the product. We would expect to see a 55-year-old top executive behind the wheel of a Mercedes, not a 20-year-old secretary.

Companies need to research the position their brand occupies in the customers' minds. According to Kevin Keller, "What distinguishes a brand from its unbranded commodity counterparts is the consumer's perceptions and feelings about the product's attributes and how they perform. Ultimately, a brand resides in the minds of consumers." There are three commonly used research approaches to get at brand meaning:

1. *Word associations:* People can be asked what words come to mind when they hear the brand's name. In the case of McDonald's, they probably would mention hamburgers, fast food, friendly service, fun, and children. They may mention some negative words such as high calories and fatty food. They may mention some words unique to McDonald's such as Ronald McDonald, Golden Arches, and children's hospitals. McDonald's would try to emphasize the positive and unique words and try to reduce the causes giving rise to the negative words.

2. *Personifying the brand:* People can be asked to describe what kind of person or animal they think of when the brand is mentioned. For example, they may say that the John Deere brand makes them think of a rugged Midwestern male who is hardworking and trustworthy. The brand persona delivers a picture of the more human qualities of the brand.

3. *Laddering up to find the brand essence:* **Brand essence** relates to the deeper, more abstract goals consumers are trying to satisfy with the brand. Ask why someone wants to buy a Nokia cellular phone. "They look well built" (attribute). "Why is it important that the phone be well built?" "It suggests that the Nokia is reliable" (a functional benefit). "Why is reliability important?" "Because my colleagues or family can be sure to reach me" (an emotional benefit). "Why must you be available to them at all times?" "I can help them if they are in trouble" (brand essence). The brand makes this person feel like a Good Samaritan, ready to help others.

   These "why" questions constitute a technique known as **laddering up.** They help the marketer get a deeper understanding of the person's motivation. The answers suggest some possible campaigns. The campaign can center on the brand essence, or the marketer can ladder down and feature Nokia at a more concrete level, such as its emotional benefit (easy to be reached), functional benefit (reliability), or attribute (well built).

Marketers must decide at which level(s) to anchor the brand's identity. Scott Davis suggests visualizing a *brand pyramid* in constructing the image of a brand.[12] At the lowest level are the *brand attributes*, at the next level are the *brand's benefits*, and at the top are the brand's *beliefs and values*. Thus marketers of Dove soap can talk about its attribute of one-quarter cleansing cream; or its benefit of softer skin; or its value, being more attractive. The attribute is the least desirable level. First, the buyer is more interested in benefits. Second, competitors can easily copy attributes. Third, the current attributes may become less desirable.

Compaq In 1999, the computer manufacturer Compaq increased its global advertising budget by 50 percent to $300 million. The campaign was to promote the PC maker's "bigness" and the depth of its offerings. Bigness is an attribute that does not necessarily translate into a distinctive benefit. Furthermore, there are other "big" computer brands. This campaign failed to position Compaq with a "reason to prefer."

A brand can be better positioned by associating its name with a desirable benefit. Some successful brand positioning examples are Volvo (*safety*), Hallmark (*caring*),

Harley-Davidson (*adventure*), FedEx (*guaranteed overnight delivery*), Nike (*performance*), and Lexus (*quality*). These positionings work best when they are passionately felt by everyone in the organization, and the target market believes that the company is best at delivering that benefit.

Volvo   At Volvo, engineers think safety in every design decision. When they decided to add a Global Positioning System to the dashboard of a recent model, they wanted to be sure that the screen would be easy to read and close to the driver's viewing point so it would not act as a distraction; and when some customers asked Volvo to make a convertible car, the company decided against it because "convertible cars aren't safe."

At the same time, promoting a brand on only one benefit can be risky. Suppose Mercedes touts its main benefit as "high performance." Then several competitive brands emerge with high or higher performance; or suppose car buyers start placing less importance on high performance as compared to other benefits. Mercedes needs the freedom to maneuver into a new benefit positioning.

The strongest brands present more than a rational appeal; they pack an emotional wallop. Marc Gobe, author of *Emotional Branding*, argues that successful brands must engage customers on a deeper level, touching a universal emotion.[13] His brand design agency, Desgrippes Gobe, which has worked on such accounts as Starbucks, Victoria's Secret, Godiva, Versace, and Lancome, relies more on creating surprise, passion, and excitement surrounding a brand, and less on projecting tangible product attributes.

If the brand evokes a strong set of beliefs and values, the company must be careful not to stray from this. Thus Mercedes stands for high technology, performance, and success. Mercedes must project these qualities in its brand strategy. Some believe that Mercedes is taking a risk by making smaller and less expensive cars.

building brand identity

Building the brand identity requires additional decisions on the brand's *name, logo, colors, tagline,* and *symbol*. Here is what one new dot-com decided.

Gear.com   This e-tailer sells brand-name sporting goods at closeout prices. The name "gear" was chosen to suggest "hiking gear" or "fishing gear" clothing. The company used the tagline "The best sports deals on the planet." So far, the company has not chosen a symbol, although a symbol could be helpful in the image of the brand. Gear.com recently merged with Overstock.com, so its image may change.

At the same time, a brand is much more than a name, logo, colors, a tagline, or symbol. These are marketing tools and tactics. A brand is essentially a marketer's promise to deliver a specific set of features, benefits, and services consistently to the buyers. The marketer must establish a mission for the brand and a vision of what the brand must be and do. The marketer must think that he is offering a contract to the customer regarding how the brand will perform. The brand contract must be honest. Motel 6, for example, offers clean rooms, low prices, and good service but does not imply that the furniture is expensive or the bathroom is large.

At best, the brand campaign will create name recognition, some brand knowledge, maybe even some brand preference, but an ad campaign does not create brand bonding, no matter how much the company spends on advertising and publicity. **Brand bonding** occurs when customers experience the company as delivering on its benefit promise. The fact is that *brands are not built by advertising but by the brand experience.* All of the customers' contacts with company employees and company communications must be positive. The brand idea will not take unless *everyone in the company lives the brand.* Tosti and Stotz charge that too many companies make brand promises but fail to train employees to understand and deliver on the brand promise.[14] They suggest ways that companies can carry on *internal branding* with their employees to understand, desire, and deliver on the brand promise. Here are some examples.

Eli Lilly   In 2000, Eli Lilly launched a new brand-building initiative with the brandline "Answers that matter." The aim was to establish Eli Lilly as a pharmaceutical firm that could give doctors, patients, hospitals, HMOs, and government trustworthy answers to questions of concern to them. This brand-building initiative could not be launched before making sure that everyone at Eli Lilly received the training and knowledge to be able to deliver right answers.

Hewlett-Packard   Hewlett-Packard does not think that its job ends with carrying out advertising and personal selling. It has appointed a senior executive in charge of the *customer experience* in each of its two divisions, consumer and B2B. Their job is to monitor, measure, and improve the customer experience with H-P products. They report directly to the presidents of their respective divisions.

building brands in the new economy

Brand-building theory developed out of the practices of consumer packaged-goods companies in the last century. The theory called for creating a product difference, real or symbolic; spending a huge amount on advertising; and hoping this would lead to trial, adoption, and loyalty. Advertising played the crucial role and its effectiveness was judged by measures of awareness, recognition, recall, or intent to buy; but look at what happened to Pets.com using this theory:

Pets.com   This company did all the right things. It hired a top-flight advertising agency and created a highly recognized brand icon (Sock Puppet) that won all kinds of awards. Pets.com spent $2 million on the Super Bowl, marched in Macy's Thanksgiving Day Parade, and even developed its own line of merchandise. Although this created plenty of "industry buzz," on November 7, 2000, Pets.com shut its doors, having spent all this money without earning a dime.

Heidi and Don Schultz believe that the Consumer Packaged Goods (CPG) model for brand building is increasingly inappropriate, especially for service firms, technology firms, financial organizations, B2B brands, and even smaller CPG companies. They charge that the proliferation of media and message delivery systems has eroded massadvertising's power. They urge companies to use a different paradigm to build their brands in the new economy.

1. Companies should clarify the corporation's basic values and build the corporate brand. Companies such as Starbucks, Sony, Cisco Systems, Marriott, Hewlett-Packard, General Electric, and American Express have built strong corporate brands; their name on a product or service creates an image of quality and value.

2. Companies should use brand managers to carry out the tactical work, but the brand's ultimate success will depend on everyone in the company accepting and living the brand's value proposition. Prominent CEOs—such as Carly Fiorina (Hewlett-Packard) and John Chambers (Cisco)—are playing a growing role in shaping brand strategies.

3. Companies need to develop a more comprehensive brand-building plan to create positive customer experiences at every touchpoint—events, seminars, news, telephone, e-mail, person-to-person contact.

4. Companies need to define the brand's basic essence to be delivered wherever it is sold. Local executions can be varied as long as they deliver the feel of the brand.

5. Companies must use the brand-value proposition as the key driver of the company's strategy, operations, services, and product development.
6. Companies must measure their brand-building effectiveness not by the old measures of awareness, recognition, and recall, but by a more comprehensive set of measures including customer-perceived value, customer satisfaction, customer share of wallet, customer retention, and customer advocacy.[15]

brand equity

Brands vary in the amount of power and value they have in the marketplace. At one extreme are brands that are not known by most buyers. Then there are brands for which buyers have a fairly high degree of *brand awareness*. Beyond this are brands with a high degree of *brand acceptability*. Then there are brands that enjoy a high degree of *brand preference*. Finally, there are brands that command a high degree of *brand loyalty*. Tony O'Reilly, former CEO of H. J. Heinz, proposed this test of brand loyalty: "My acid test . . . is whether a housewife, intending to buy Heinz tomato ketchup in a store, finding it to be out of stock, will walk out of the store to buy it elsewhere."

Few customers are this brand-loyal. David Aaker distinguished five levels of a customer attitude toward a brand, from lowest to highest:

1. Customer will change brands, especially for price reasons. No brand loyalty.
2. Customer is satisfied. No reason to change the brand.
3. Customer is satisfied and would incur costs by changing brand.
4. Customer values the brand and sees it as a friend.
5. Customer is devoted to the brand.

Brand equity is highly related to how many customers are in classes 3, 4, or 5. It is also related, according to Aaker, to the degree of brand-name recognition, perceived brand quality, strong mental and emotional associations, and other assets such as patents, trademarks, and channel relationships.[16]

Customers will pay more for a strong brand. One study found that 72 percent of customers stated they would pay a 20 percent premium for their brand of choice relative to their closest competitive brand; 50 percent said they would pay a 25 percent premium; and 40 percent would pay up to a 30 percent premium.[17] Coke lovers are willing to pay a 50 percent premium over the closest competitor; Tide and Heinz users, a 100 percent premium; and Volvo users, a 40 percent premium; and although the Lexus and the Toyota Camry share the same exact engine, the Lexus brand commands $10,000 more than the Camry brand.[18]

VALUE OF BRAND EQUITY   Clearly, brand equity is an asset. We define **brand equity** as the positive differential effect that knowing the brand name has on customer response to the product or service. Brand equity results in customers showing a preference for one product over another when they are basically identical. The extent to which customers are willing to pay more for the particular brand is a measure of brand equity. Amazon.com, for example, is able to charge 7 to 12 percent more than lesser-known online book vendors.[19]

Brand equity needs to be distinguished from **brand valuation**, which is the job of estimating the total financial value of the brand. Certain companies base their growth on acquiring and building rich brand portfolios. Nestlé acquired Rowntree (U.K.), Carnation (U.S.), Stouffer (U.S.), Buitoni-Perugina (Italy), and Perrier (France), making it the world's largest food company.

The world's 10 most valuable brands in 2001 were (in rank order): Coca-Cola, Microsoft, IBM, General Electric, Nokia, Intel, Disney, Ford, McDonald's, and AT&T. Coca-Cola's brand value was $69 billion, Microsoft's $65 billion, and IBM's $53 billion.[20] With these well-known companies, brand value is typically over one-half of the total company market capitalization. U.S. companies do not list brand equity on their balance sheets because of the arbitrariness of the estimate. However, this is done by some companies in the United Kingdom, Hong Kong, and Australia. The estimate is based in part on the price premium the brand commands times the extra volume it moves over an average brand.[21] John Stuart, co-founder of Quaker Oats, said: "If this business were split up, I would give you the land and bricks and mortar, and I would take the brands and trade marks, and I would fare better than you."

High brand equity provides a number of competitive advantages:

- The company will have more trade leverage in bargaining with distributors and retailers because customers expect them to carry the brand.
- The company can charge a higher price than its competitors because the brand has higher perceived quality.
- The company can more easily launch extensions because the brand name carries high credibility.
- The brand offers the company some defense against price competition.

The power enjoyed by a strong brand is no better illustrated than by Virgin, the brainchild of England's flamboyant Richard Branson, now age 50.

Virgin   Starting with Virgin Music, Branson's Virgin Group Ltd. now spans three continents and 170 businesses, including Virgin Atlantic Airways, Virgin Mobile (cellular phones), Virgin Energy, Virgin Direct (insurance, mortgages, and investment funds), and Virgin Hotels. In 2001, Branson set up Virgin.com as the Web portal for everything from buying wine to booking airline tickets. The Web site is attracting 1.9 million visitors a month. Nearly 2 million Britishers book train tickets through Virgin and 1 million tap Virgin's help in managing $4 billion in assets.[22]

Clearly, Branson can create almost any business he wants and gain instant customers by simply attaching the name Virgin to it. Yet some marketing and financial critics point out that he is diluting the brand, that it covers too many businesses. Allen Adamson of the brand identity consultancy Landor Associates says: "(Branson) should get out of the businesses that don't fit the Virgin/Branson personality, such as beverages, cosmetics . . . the longer he keeps his name on businesses that are failing or neutral, the more damage it will do to his aura." Branson has had some fumbles, such as Virgin Clothing and the launch of Virgin Coke in the United States, but Branson replies: "We have a strategy of using the credibility of our brand to challenge the dominant players in a range of industries where we believe the consumer is not getting value for money. . . . If the consumer benefits, I see no reason why we should be frightened about launching new products."[23]

MANAGING BRAND EQUITY   A brand needs to be carefully managed so that its equity does not depreciate. This requires maintaining or improving brand awareness, perceived quality and functionality, and positive associations. These tasks require continuous R&D investment, skillful advertising, and excellent trade and consumer service. Procter & Gamble believes that well-managed brands are not subject to a brand life cycle. Many brand leaders of 70 years ago are still today's brand leaders: Kodak, Wrigley's, Gillette, Coca-Cola, Heinz, and Campbell Soup.

Some analysts see brands as outlasting a company's specific products and facilities. They see brands as the company's major enduring asset. Every powerful brand really represents a set of loyal customers. Brand equity is a major contributor to *customer equity*. The proper focus of marketing planning is to extend *customer lifetime value*, with brand management serving as a major marketing tool.

Unfortunately, many companies have mismanaged their brands. In the quest for ever-increasing profits, it is easy for a brand to lose its focus. This is what befell

Snapple Beverage Corporation almost as soon as Quaker Oats bought it for $1.7 billion in 1994.

Snapple Beverage Corporation Snapple had been a regional brand with an offbeat image available in only small outlets and convenience stores. Quaker bought the brand and attempted to make it a national brand with mass-market appeal. Quaker changed the ad campaign—abandoning the rotund and immensely popular Snapple Lady—and promoted it as an alternative to big brands like Coke and Pepsi. This turned off Snapple fans. According to one critic, "Quaker diluted the quirkiness." Snapple began losing money and sales plunged 23 percent in the next two years. Quaker finally sold the brand to Triarc, Inc., in 1997 at a $1.4 billion loss. The company revitalized Snapple by returning to clever advertising, using original distribution channels, creating throwback packaging, and reinstating the Snapple Lady as official spokesperson. Snapple's renewed success enabled Triarc to sell Snapple and its other beverages to Cadbury Schweppes for $1.5 billion in 2000.[24] (See "Marketing Insight: Can You Build a Cult Brand, and Do You Want To?")

In a nationwide study of companies in a wide range of industries, only 43 percent indicated that they even measured brand equity. Whereas 72 percent were confident enough in their brand equity to project that it would last two years with no financial support, over two-thirds of the respondents had no formal long-term brand strategy.[25] Also, while we normally think of brand equity as something accruing to the products of manufacturers, service companies also prize it. As Wall Street competition intensifies, financial service companies are spending millions on their brand names in order to attract investors. Just as Coke wants you to reach for a soda when you are thirsty, Merrill Lynch and Chase want you to call them when you need financial know-how.[26]

marketing **insight**

Can You Build a Cult Brand, and Do You Want To?

Some brands manage to achieve a cult status—Apple Computers, Mazda Miata automobiles, Harley-Davidson motorcycles, Krispy Kreme donuts, Ben & Jerry's ice cream, Palm personal digital assistants, Air Jordan Nike shoes. As many as 85,000 Apple Computer fans attend the annual four-day MacWorld expo in San Francisco. Every announced opening of another Krispy Kreme donut store brings long lines of fans camping out overnight waiting for the store opening.

What draws people to these brands? In part, people want to be part of something larger than themselves, something that may precede them and outlive them. Some cult brands offer a community experience, like that felt by the Hell's Angels who ride Harleys in groups and the Vespa fans who meet in Manhattan on Sundays and ride their scooters.

So why wouldn't every company launching a new product want it to gain cult status? For one thing, this is not easy to do. Most of it happens spontaneously. A cult brand captures the imagination of a small group and they spread the word to others.

A company can try to create a "buzz" around the product; it can deliberately keep the supply low so that people have to wait for it; and it can organize clubs and events. Whether these tactics work depends on how special the cult brand makes the small number of users feel, and how inclined they are to talk about it to friends and acquaintances.

A company can kill a cult brand by trying to rush it into the mass-market. Yet companies with a cult brand are sorely tempted to mass-market it. Coors beer used to sell in only 11 states; visitors from the Midwest, East, and South used to buy cases to bring back home. Once Coors expanded distribution to reach all 50 states, the brand lost its cult status and became another mainstream beer. This does not mean Coors made the wrong decision from a profit point of view, but companies must be careful. When Ford redesigned the Mustang to have broader market appeal, it lost many loyal Mustang fans.

Source: Adapted from Melanie Wells, "Cult Brands," *Forbes,* April 16, 2001, p. 150.

| figure **14.5** | An Overview of Branding Decisions |

Branding Decision	Brand-Sponsor Decision	Brand-Name Decision	Brand-Strategy Decision	Brand-Repositioning Decision
• Brand • No brand	• Manufacturer brand • Distributor (private) brand • Licensed brand	• Individual names • Blanket family name • Separate family names • Company–individual names	• Line extensions • Brand extensions • Multibrands • New brands • Cobrands	• Repositioning • No repositioning

branding challenges

Branding poses several challenges to the marketer. The key decisions are shown in Figure 14.5 and discussed in the following sections.

BRANDING DECISION: TO BRAND OR NOT TO BRAND? The first decision is whether to develop a brand name for a product. In the past, producers and intermediaries sold their goods out of barrels, bins, and cases, without any supplier identification. Buyers depended on the seller's integrity. The earliest signs of branding were the medieval guilds' efforts to require craftspeople to put trademarks on their products to protect themselves and consumers against inferior quality. In the fine arts, too, branding began with artists signing their works.

Today, branding is such a strong force that hardly anything goes unbranded. So-called commodities do not have to remain commodities. Salt is packaged in distinctive containers, oranges are stamped with growers' names, nuts and bolts are packaged in cellophane with a distributor's label, and automobile components—spark plugs, tires, filters—bear separate brand names from the automakers. Fresh food products—such as chicken, turkey, and salmon—are increasingly being sold under strongly advertised brand names. Even bricks do not have to be seen as commodities.

Acme Brick Acme Brick of Fort Worth, Texas, has managed to brand its bricks, with the result that it is able to charge 10 percent more and enjoy the largest market share in several of its metro markets. It makes high-quality bricks. It offers a 100-year guarantee (the norm is five years for bricks). Every time a home is built with Acme bricks, Acme contributes to the Troy Aikman Foundation for Children. Acme has also donated bricks to build 30 homes through Habitat for Humanity. A telephone survey in four major Acme markets revealed an 84 percent preference for Acme bricks, with no other supplier getting more than a 10 percent preference.[27]

In some cases, there has been a return to "no branding" of certain staple consumer goods and pharmaceuticals. Carrefours, the originator of the French hypermarket, introduced a line of "no brands" or generics in its stores in the early 1970s. Generics are unbranded, plainly packaged, less expensive versions of common products such as spaghetti, paper towels, and canned peaches. They offer standard or lower quality at a price that may be as much as 20 percent to 40 percent lower than nationally advertised brands and 10 percent to 20 percent lower than retailer private-label brands. The lower price is made possible by lower-quality ingredients, lower-cost labeling and packaging, and minimal advertising.

National brands have fought generics in a number of ways. Ralston-Purina increased its quality and targeted pet owners who identified strongly with their pets and cared most about quality. Procter & Gamble introduced its Banner paper products, a line offering lower quality than its higher lines but greater quality than generics and at a competitive price. Other companies simply have cut their prices to compete with generics.[28]

Why do sellers brand their products when doing so clearly involves costs? Branding gives the seller several advantages:

- The brand name makes it easier for the seller to process orders and track down problems.
- The seller's brand name and trademark provide legal protection of unique product features.
- Branding gives the seller the opportunity to attract a loyal and profitable set of customers. Brand loyalty gives sellers some protection from competition.
- Branding helps the seller segment markets. Instead of P&G's selling a simple detergent, it can offer eight detergent brands, each formulated differently and aimed at specific benefit-seeking segments.
- Strong brands help build the corporate image, making it easier to launch new brands and gain acceptance by distributors and consumers.

Distributors and retailers want brand names because brands make the product easier to handle, hold production to certain quality standards, strengthen buyer preferences, and make it easier to identify suppliers. Consumers want brand names to help them identify quality differences and shop more efficiently.

BRAND-SPONSOR DECISION A manufacturer has several options with respect to brand sponsorship. The product may be launched as a *manufacturer brand* (sometimes called a national brand), a *distributor brand* (also called reseller, store, house, or private brand), or a *licensed brand name*. Another alternative is for the manufacturer to produce some output under its own name and some under reseller labels. Kellogg, John Deere & Company, and IBM sell virtually all of their output under their own brand names. Hart Schaffner & Marx sells some of its manufactured clothes under licensed names such as Christian Dior, Pierre Cardin, and Johnny Carson. Whirlpool produces both under its own name and under distributors' names (Sears Kenmore appliances).

Although manufacturers' brands dominate, large retailers and wholesalers have been developing their own brands. Sears has created several names—Diehard batteries, Craftsman tools, Kenmore appliances—that command brand preference and even brand loyalty. Retailers such as The Limited, Benetton, The Body Shop, GAP, and Marks & Spencer carry mostly own-brand merchandise. In Britain, two large supermarket chains have developed popular store-brand colas—Sainsbury Cola (from Sainsbury) and Classic Cola (from Tesco). Sainsbury, Britain's largest food chain, sells 50 percent store-label goods; U.S. supermarkets average 19.7 percent private-brand sales. Some experts believe that 50 percent is the natural limit for carrying private brands because (1) consumers prefer certain national brands, and (2) many product categories are not feasible or attractive on a private-brand basis.

Why do intermediaries bother to sponsor their own brands? They have to hunt down qualified suppliers who can deliver consistent quality, order large quantities and tie up their capital in inventories, and spend money promoting a private label. Nevertheless, private brands offer two advantages. First, they are more profitable. Intermediaries search for manufacturers with excess capacity who will produce the private label at a low cost. Other costs, such as research and development, advertising, sales promotion, and physical distribution are also much lower. This means that the private brander can charge a lower price and yet make a higher profit margin. Second, retailers develop exclusive store brands to differentiate themselves from competitors. Many consumers do not distinguish between national and store brands.

In the confrontation between manufacturers' and private brands, retailers have many advantages and increasing market power. Because shelf space is scarce, many supermarkets now charge a *slotting fee* for accepting a new brand, to cover the cost of listing and stocking it. Retailers also charge for special display space and in-store advertising space. They typically give more prominent display to their own brands and make sure they are well stocked. Retailers are now building better quality in their store brands. Consider the following case.

Loblaw   Since 1984, when its President's Choice line of foods made its debut, it has been difficult to say "private label" without Loblaw and President's Choice coming instantly to mind. Toronto-based Loblaw's supermarket chain has demonstrated that store brands can match or even exceed the quality of other brands. A finely tuned strategy involving its trademarked President's Choice and "no name" labels has helped differentiate its stores and build the retailer into a powerhouse in Canada and the United States. By bringing out private labels in new product areas—such as frozen Jambalaya, frozen bread pudding, and frozen hors d'oeuvres—Loblaw stores reduce units of expensive national and secondary brands but still increase variety. Its store brands have become so successful that Loblaw is licensing them to noncompetitive retailers in other countries, thus turning a local store brand into— believe it or not—a global brand. Today, private label sales make up 32 percent of Loblaw's total sales, compared with a Canadian average of 22 percent.[29]

Manufacturers of national brands are frustrated by the growing power of retailer brands. Kevin Price put it well: "A decade ago, the retailer was a chihuahua nipping at the manufacturer's heels—a nuisance, yes, but only a minor irritant; you fed it and it went away. Today it's a pit bull and it wants to rip your arms and legs off. You'd like to see it roll over, but you're too busy defending yourself to even try."[30] Some marketing commentators predict that private brands will eventually knock out all but the strongest manufacturers' brands.

In years past, consumers viewed the brands in a category arranged in a *brand ladder*, with their favorite brand at the top and remaining brands in descending order of preference. There are now signs that this ladder is being replaced with a consumer perception of *brand parity*—that many brands are equivalent.[31] Instead of a strongly preferred brand, consumers buy from a set of acceptable brands, choosing whichever is on sale that day. As Joel D. Weiner, a former Kraft executive, said: "People don't think the world will come to a screeching halt if they use Tide instead of Cheer." A study by DDB Needham Worldwide reported that the percentage of packaged-goods consumers saying that they bought only well-known brands fell from 77 percent to 62 percent between 1975 and 1990. A Grey Advertising Inc., study reported that 66 percent of consumers said they were trading down to lower-priced brands, particularly store brands.

The growing power of store brands is not the only factor weakening national brands. Consumers are more price-sensitive. They are noting more quality equivalence as competing manufacturers and national retailers copy and duplicate the qualities of the best brands. The continuous barrage of coupons and price specials has trained a generation of shoppers to buy on price. The fact that companies have reduced advertising to 30 percent of their total promotion budget has weakened their brand equity. The endless stream of brand extensions and line extensions has blurred brand identity and led to a confusing amount of product proliferation.

Of course, one of the newest factors that is not necessarily weakening national brands but changing the entire branding landscape is the Internet. While some "born digital" companies, like Netscape and America Online, have used the Internet to gain brand recognition seemingly overnight, other companies have poured millions of dollars into online advertising with no significant effect on brand awareness. (See "Marketing for the New Economy: The Elusive Goal of Branding on the World Wide Web.")

Manufacturers have reacted by spending substantial amounts of money on consumer-directed advertising and promotion to maintain strong brand preference. Their price has to be somewhat higher to cover the higher promotion cost. At the same time, mass-

marketing for the **new economy**

The Elusive Goal of Branding on the World Wide Web

Ever had a day when you could not get a TV commercial out of your head? If you are like most people, you sop up a certain amount of TV advertising. Now, try to remember the last ad you saw while surfing the Web. Drawing a blank? That is not surprising. The issue of building brands through Web advertising has so confounded marketers that Procter & Gamble held a summit on the topic in the summer of 1998. Over 400 executives converged at P&G headquarters in Cincinnati, from Internet companies such as America Online and Agency.com to packaged-goods giants like Unilever and Kraft; their goal: to harness the interactivity of the Internet to build and maintain brands. Here are some of the challenges they confronted.

The one-to-one nature of the Web does not build mass brand awareness: On the World Wide Web, it is as if millions of private conversations are going on. It is not the same as when millions of people watch the Superbowl and see the same 30-second Budweiser spot at the same time. That is why tactics that have worked on TV have failed on the Web.

- *The format of Internet advertising has been ineffective:* So far, the two most common Internet ads are banner ads and interstitials. Banner ads are those tiny rectangular ads on which you can click for more information. In a discouraging Jupiter Communications survey, 21 percent of Internet users polled said they never clicked on banner ads and another 51 percent said they clicked only rarely. Interstitial ads, which flash in the browser window before the site is loaded, have proved annoying to most consumers.
- *In the digital world consumers are in control:* Even if advertisers put larger, richer ads on the Web, they would likely face a consumer backlash. Digital developments allow Web surfers to choose products solely on real value and not just intangibles, like brand associations. Already sites like Mysimon.com, which offers a free online buyer's guide that allows users to compare features and prices on products from more than 2,000 online stores, have gained popularity with consumers.

It is therefore not surprising that some of the biggest superstars of e-commerce still conduct most of their branding efforts off-line. Cisco spends ad money for full-page ads in the *Wall Street Journal* rather than on Web banners. At the same time, the almost overnight success of Netscape Communications, Amazon.com, and Yahoo! say that a brand can grow and secure customer loyalty on the Web. How? Companies that have powerful brand awareness on the Web all have sites that help consumers do something—whether it is configuring a computer system online at Dell.com or offering a host of options for customizing services at Yahoo.com. Marketers who are set on building their brands in the online world have to offer consumers an online experience or service.

The latest theory of how to do that involves something called "rational branding." The idea is to wed the emotional pitch of traditional brand marketing with a real service offered only online. Television ads for Saturn still offer the same old-fashioned appeal, but now they point viewers to the company's Web site, which offers lots of help and very little hype. Yet there is not much potential in using the Internet as a vehicle when you are selling soap or shampoo. Still, the packaged-goods powerhouses are hardly throwing in the towel. P&G, for instance, has put most of its small online marketing budget behind brands like Pampers diapers, which have narrow target audiences with more personal subject matter. The company has turned Pampers.com into the Pampers Parenting Institute, which addresses various issues of concern to new or expectant parents. One thing consumers can be sure of is that there will be more, not less, advertising and brand building on the Web as e-commerce develops.

Sources: Jeffrey O'Brien, "Web Advertising and the Branding Mission," *Upside* (September 1998): 90–94; Don Tapscott, "Net Culture Reshapes Brand Opportunities," *Advertising Age*, November 10, 1997; Saul Hansell, "Selling Soap without the Soap Operas, Mass Marketers Seek Ways to Build Brands on the Web," *New York Times*, August 24, 1998, p. D1; Ellen Neuborne, "Branding on the Net," *BusinessWeek*, November 9, 1998, pp. 76–86.

distributors pressure manufacturers to put more promotional money into trade allowances and deals if they want adequate shelf space. Once manufacturers start giving in, they have less to spend on advertising and consumer promotion, and their brand leadership starts spiraling down. This is the national brand manufacturers' dilemma.

To maintain their power, leading brand marketers need to invest in heavy and continuous R&D to bring out new brands, line extensions, features, and quality improvements. They must sustain a strong "pull" advertising program to maintain high consumer brand recognition and preference. They must find ways to "partner" with major mass-distributors in a joint search for logistical economies and competitive strategies that produce savings.

However, what if a company is small or just starting out and cannot pump millions into expensive advertising campaigns? Technology companies in particular have been adept at achieving levels of brand recognition through less conventional marketing approaches. Here is an example.[32]

America Online Inc.   Over half of U.S. households are familiar with America Online (AOL). That is because AOL gives away its software free. For several years AOL has been blanketing the country with diskettes and now CD-ROMs, offering consumers a one-month free trial. The company cuts deals that put its product in some unlikely places: inside Rice Chex cereal boxes, United Airlines in-flight meals, and Omaha Steaks packages. Because it is hard to describe the benefits of an online service to novices, AOL believes the best approach is to let them try it. Then, once consumers start using AOL, the company reasons that the user-friendly program will lure them to subscribe. So far, this philosophy has yielded remarkable results. In 2001, AOL had 29 million U.S. subscribers, more than four times as large as the nearest Internet service provider competitor.[33]

brand-name decision

Manufacturers and service companies who brand their products must choose which brand names to use. Four strategies are available:

1. *Individual names:* This policy is followed by General Mills (Bisquick, Gold Medal, Betty Crocker, Nature Valley). A major advantage of an individual-names strategy is that the company does not tie its reputation to the product's. If the product fails or appears to have low quality, the company's name or image is not hurt. A manufacturer of good-quality watches, such as Seiko, can introduce a lower-quality line of watches (called Pulsar) without diluting the Seiko name. The strategy permits the firm to search for the best name for each new product.
2. *Blanket family names:* This policy is followed by Heinz and General Electric. A blanket family name also has advantages. Development cost is less because there is no need for "name" research or heavy advertising expenditures to create brand-name recognition. Furthermore, sales of the new product are likely to be strong if the manufacturer's name is good. Campbell soup introduces new soups under its brand name with extreme simplicity and achieves instant recognition.
3. *Separate family names for all products:* This policy is followed by Sears (Kenmore for appliances, Craftsman for tools, and Homart for major home installations). Where a company produces quite different products, it is not desirable to use one blanket family name. Swift and Company developed separate family names for its hams (Premium) and fertilizers (Vigoro). When Mead Johnson developed a diet supplement for gaining weight, it created a new family name, Nutriment, to avoid confusion with its weight-reducing products, Metrecal. Companies often invent different family names for different quality lines within the same product class.
4. *Corporate name combined with individual product names:* This policy is followed by Kellogg (Kellogg's Rice Krispies, Kellogg's Raisin Bran, and Kellogg's Corn Flakes), as well as Honda, GE, and Hewlett-Packard. The company name legitimizes, and the individual name individualizes, the new product.

Once a company decides on its brand-name strategy, it faces the task of choosing a specific brand name. The company could choose the name of a person (Honda, Estée Lauder), location (American Airlines, Kentucky Fried Chicken), quality (Safeway, Duracell), lifestyle (Weight Watchers, Healthy Choice), or an artificial name (Exxon, Kodak). Among the desirable qualities for a brand name are the following:[34]

- *It should suggest something about the product's benefits:* Examples: Beautyrest, Craftsman, Accutron.
- *It should suggest the product or service category:* Examples: Ticketron, *Newsweek.*
- *It should suggest concrete, "high imagery" qualities:* Examples: Sunkist, Spic and Span, Firebird.
- *It should be easy to spell, pronounce, recognize, and remember:* Short names help. Examples: Tide, Crest, Puffs.
- *It should be distinctive:* Examples: Mustang, Kodak, Exxon.
- *It should not carry poor meanings in other countries and languages:* Example: Nova is a poor name for a car to be sold in Spanish-speaking countries; in Spanish it means "doesn't go."

Normally, companies choose brand names by generating a list of possible names, debating their merits, eliminating all but a few, testing them with target consumers, and making a final choice. Today many companies hire a marketing research firm to develop and test names. These companies use human brainstorming sessions and vast computer databases, catalogued by association, sounds, and other qualities. Name-research procedures include *association tests* (What images come to mind?), *learning tests* (How easily is the name pronounced?), *memory tests* (How well is the name remembered?), and *preference tests* (Which names are preferred?). Of course, the firm must also conduct searches through other databases to make sure the chosen name has not already been registered. The whole process, however, is not cheap. One of the best-known specialists in the "name game" is San Francisco–based Namelab Inc., whose average fee is $90,000. Namelab is responsible for such brand names as Acura, Compaq, and CompUSA.

Many firms strive to build a unique brand name that eventually will become intimately identified with the product category. Examples are Kleenex, Kitty Litter, Levis, Jell-O, Popsicle, Scotch Tape, Xerox, and Fiberglass. In 1994, Federal Express officially shortened its marketing identity to FedEx, a term that has become a synonym for "to ship overnight." Yet identifying a brand name with a product category may threaten the company's exclusive rights to that name. Cellophane and shredded wheat are now in the public domain and available for any manufacturer to use.

Given the rapid growth of the global marketplace, companies should choose brand names that work globally. One thing Compaq liked about the name Presario for its line of home computers is that it conjures up similar meanings in various Latin-influenced languages. In French, Spanish, Latin, or Portuguese, Presario has the same, or similar, association that it does in English. It makes one immediately think of an "impresario," the magical master of the whirl and fantasy of a stage production. Companies also should not change names owned by someone in another country. For example, Anheuser-Busch cannot use the name "Budweiser" in Germany.

brand-building tools

A common misconception is that brands are basically built by advertising. It is true that TV advertising in its early days was the most effective brand-building tool. There were very few TV stations and people watched the comedies, dramas, and ads with almost equal interest. Now, viewers may be watching one of dozens of TV stations, and many are zapping or ignoring the commercials. In fact, many more are simply not watching TV. They are busy on their computers or engaged in recreational activities.

Marketers are therefore turning to other tools for attracting attention to their brands. Among the most important are:

- *Public relations and press releases:* Brands can gain a lot of attention from well-placed newspaper and magazine stories, not to mention appearing visually in Hollywood films.
- *Sponsorships:* Brands are frequently promoted in sponsored events such as world-famous bicycle and car races.
- *Clubs and consumer communities:* Brands can form the center of a customer community, such as Harley-Davidson motorcycle owners or Bradford plate collectors.
- *Factory visits:* Hershey's and Cadbury's, two candy companies, have built theme parks at their factories and they invite visitors to spend a day.
- *Trade shows:* Trade shows represent a great opportunity to build brand awareness, knowledge, and interest.
- *Event marketing:* Many automobile companies make an event out of introducing their new car models.
- *Public facilities:* Perrier, the bottled water company, etched its identity in the public mind by building running tracks in public parks to promote healthful lifestyles.
- *Social cause marketing:* Brands can achieve a following by donating money to charitable causes. Ben & Jerry's Ice Cream turns over 7 percent of its profits to charity.

- *High value for the money:* Some brands create positive word of mouth by offering exceptional value for the money. Examples include IKEA and Southwest Airlines.
- *Founder's or a celebrity personality:* A colorful founder, such as Richard Branson, or a celebrity personality, such as Michael Jordan, can create positive affect for a brand.
- *Mobile phone marketing:* Customers in the future will hear about brands on their wireless mobile phones as m-commerce grows.

Many of these tools describe efforts to build a brand through "branded experiences" or "experiential communications," terms used by the Jack Morton Company. Businesses hire Morton to create memorable experiences that engage the hearts and minds of a target audience. Morton develops trade show experiences, traveling exhibits, worldwide Webcasts of major presentations and roundtables, corporate museums, entertainments, and other first-hand experiences that go deeper than just hearing or seeing an ad for a product.[35]

brand strategy decision

Brand strategy will vary with whether the brand is a functional brand, an image brand, or an experiential brand.[36] Consumers purchase a *functional brand* to satisfy a functional need such as to shave, to clean clothes, to relieve a headache. Functional brands have the best chance to satisfy customers if they are seen as providing superior performance (Tide) or superior economy (Wal-Mart). Functional brands rely heavily on "product" and or "price" features.

Image brands arise with products or services that are difficult to differentiate, or to assess quality, or convey a statement about the user. Strategies include creating a distinctive design (Mont Blanc pens), associating them with celebrity users (Armani suit wearers include Warren Beatty, Robert De Niro, and Tom Hanks), or creating a powerful advertising image (Marlboro Man). Typically, they are designed to say something positive about the brand user. Image brands include B2B products such as Intel, McKinsey & Company, and Goldman Sachs. Image brands rely heavily on "advertising creativity" and "high advertising expenditures."

Experiential brands involve the consumer beyond simply acquiring the product. The consumer encounters "people" and "place" with these brands, as happens in a Starbucks' coffee shop or a Barnes & Noble bookstore, visiting Disneyland or Niketown, going to the Golden Door spa, or visiting a California winery.

Over time, each type of brand can be developed further. A company can introduce **line extensions** (existing brand name extended to new sizes or flavors in the existing product category), **brand extensions** (brand names extended to new-product categories), **multibrands** (new brand names introduced in the same product category), **new brands** (new brand name for a new category product), and **co-branding** (combining two or more well-known brand names).

LINE EXTENSIONS   Line extensions consist of introducing additional items in the same product category under the same brand name, such as new flavors, forms, colors, added ingredients, and package sizes. Dannon introduced several Dannon yogurt line extensions, including fat-free "light" yogurt and dessert flavors such as "mint chocolate cream pie" and "caramel apple crunch." The vast majority of new-product introductions consist of line extensions.

Many companies are now introducing **branded variants**, which are specific brand lines supplied to specific retailers or distribution channels. They result from the pressure retailers put on manufacturers to enable the retailers to provide distinctive offerings. A camera company may supply its low-end cameras to mass-merchandisers while limiting its higher-priced items to specialty camera shops; or Valentino may design and supply different lines of suits and jackets to different department stores.[37]

Line extension involves risks and has provoked heated debate among marketing professionals.[38] On the downside, line extensions may lead to the brand name losing its specific meaning. Ries and Trout call this the "line-extension trap."[39] Michelob was an expensive, full-flavored premium beer; when it introduced Michelob Light and Michelob Dry, its brand suffered. In the past, when a person asked for a Coke, she received a 6.5-ounce bottle. Today the seller has to ask: New, Classic, or Cherry Coke? Regular or diet? Caffeine or caffeine-free? Bottle or can? Consider the following misfire.

Nabisco Even when a new line extension sells well, its sales may come at the expense of other items in the line. Although Fig Newton's cousins Cranberry Newtons, Blueberry Newtons, and Apple Newtons are all doing well for Nabisco, the original Fig Newton brand now seems like just another flavor. A line extension works best when it takes sales away from competing brands, not when it deflates or cannibalizes the company's other items.

However, line extensions can and often do have a positive side. They have a much higher chance of survival than brand-new products. Some marketing executives defend line extensions as the best way to build a business. Kimberly-Clark's Kleenex unit has had great success with line extensions. "We try to get facial tissue in every room of the home," says one Kimberly-Clark executive. "If it is there, it will get used." This philosophy led to 20 varieties of Kleenex facial tissues, including lotion-impregnated tissues, boxes with nursery-rhyme drawings for children's rooms, and a "man-sized" box with tissues 60 percent larger than regular Kleenex.

Line extensions are also fueled by fierce competition in the marketplace. Nabisco has had such success with its Snackwell Fat Free cookies that every competitor has had to extend its product line in defense. One study, by Reddy, Holak, and Bhat, examined what makes a line extension succeed or fail. Data on 75 line extensions of 34 cigarette brands over a 20-year period yielded these findings: Line extensions of strong brands, symbolic brands, brands given strong advertising and promotion support, and those entering earlier into a project subcategory are more successful. The size of the company and its marketing competence also play a role.[40]

BRAND EXTENSIONS A company may use its existing brand name to launch new products in other categories. Honda uses its company name to cover such different products as automobiles, motorcycles, snowblowers, lawnmowers, marine engines, and snowmobiles. This allows Honda to advertise that it can fit "six Hondas in a two-car garage." GAP stores now feature its name on soap, lotion, shampoo, conditioner, shower gel, bath salts, and perfume spray. A new trend in corporate brand building is that corporations are licensing their names to manufacturers of a wide range of products, from bedding to shoes. See "Marketing Insight: The Rise of Licensing and Corporate Branding" for a closer look at the new trend in corporate image branding.

Brand-extension strategy offers many of the same advantages as line extensions. Sony puts its name on most of its new electronic products and instantly establishes the new product's high quality. Ralph Lauren has successfully licensed his name to clothing lines, home furnishings, and even paints. Nike has successfully transitioned from sneakers to clothing, sports equipment, and watches.

Yet like line extension, brand extension also involves risks. Jack Daniels licensed its name for use as a mustard that failed; and Pierre Cardin put his name on a wine, and this failed. The brand name may be inappropriate to the new product—consider buying Shell Oil ketchup, Drano milk, or Boeing cologne. The new product might disappoint buyers and damage their respect for the company's other products. The brand name may lose its special positioning in the consumer's mind through overextension. **Brand dilution** occurs when consumers no longer associate a brand with a specific product or highly similar products and start thinking less of the brand.

Companies that are tempted to transfer their brand name must research how well the brand's associations fit the new product. The best result would occur when the brand name builds the sales of both the new product and the existing product. An

marketing **insight**

The Rise of Licensing and Corporate Branding

Corporations have seized on licensing to push the company name and image. In 1997 retail sales from licensing rights in the United States and Canada were $73.23 billion. Corporate brand licensing claimed 22 percent of that total, the same amount earned from licensing rights to entertainment properties. Licensing is a low-risk way for companies to increase revenue and raise brand awareness. Coke set up a licensing program, which started modestly but now consists of a large department overseeing more than 240 licensees and at least 10,000 products, including baby clothes, earrings, a fishing lure in the shape of a tiny coke can, and boxer shorts.

Caterpillar and John Deere are two companies with narrow markets that are now licensing a wide range of products. Caterpillar has a licensing agreement with Big Smith Brands to make Caterpillar work clothes, and Cat is also teaming up with Mattel to create a line of toys based on its construction equipment. David Aaker, author of *Building Strong Brands*, says the new branded offerings will help equipment makers reach out to younger people. Those who appreciate Deere's history "are getting older and older," he says. "They have to get people in their 20s and 30s to understand the tradition."

Sources: Adapted from Constance L. Hays, "No More Brand X: Licensing of Names Adds to Image and Profit," *New York Times*, June 12, 1998, p. D1; with additional information drawn from Carleen Hawn, "What's in a Name? Whatever You Make It," *Forbes*, July 27, 1998, pp. 84–88; Carl Quintanilla, "Advertising: Caterpillar, Deere Break Ground in Consumer-Product Territory," *Wall Street Journal*, June 20, 1996, p. B2. Also see David A. Aaker, *Building Strong Brands* (New York: The Free Press, 1995).

---

acceptable result would be one in which the new product sells well without affecting the sales of the existing product. The worst result would be one in which the new product fails and hurts the sales of the existing product.[41]

MULTIBRANDS, NEW BRANDS, AND CO-BRANDS A company will often introduce additional brands in the same product category. Sometimes the company is trying to establish different features or appeal to different buying motives. Consider Black & Decker.

Black & Decker In the 1990s, Black & Decker, a portable power-tool company, added a line of small kitchen appliances. This resulted in an image among professionals and tradesmen that the company's power tools were mainly for homeowners. Black & Decker decided to launch a separate line of power tools under a new brand name, DeWalt, and this brand soon captured leadership with professionals and tradesmen.

A **multibrand** strategy enables a company to lock up more distributor shelf space and to protect its major brand by setting up *flanker brands*. Seiko establishes different brand names for its higher-priced (Seiko Lasalle) and lower-priced watches (Pulsar) to protect its flanks. Sometimes the company inherits different brand names in the process of acquiring competitors. Electrolux, the Swedish multinational, owns a stable of acquired brand names (Frigidaire, Kelvinator, Westinghouse, Zanussi, White, Gibson) for its appliance lines.

A major pitfall in introducing multibrand entries is that each might obtain only a small market share, and none may be particularly profitable. The company will have dissipated its resources over several brands instead of building a few highly profitable brands. Ideally, a company's brands within a category should cannibalize the competitors' brands and not each other. At the very least, the net profits with multibrands should be larger even if some cannibalism occurs.[42]

When a company launches products in a new category, it may find that none of its current brand names are appropriate. If Timex decides to make toothbrushes, it is not likely to call them Timex toothbrushes. Yet establishing a new brand name in the U.S. marketplace for a mass-consumer-packaged good can cost $100 million.

A rising phenomenon is the emergence of **co-branding** (also called **dual branding**), in which two or more well-known brands are combined in an offer. Each brand sponsor expects that the other brand name will strengthen preference or purchase intention. In the case of co-packaged products, each brand hopes it might be reaching a new audience by associating with the other brand.

Co-branding takes a variety of forms. One is *ingredient co-branding*, as when Volvo advertises that it uses Michelin tires, or Betty Crocker's brownie mix includes Hershey's chocolate syrup. DuPont has achieved success marketing its products as ingredient brands.

DuPont Over the years, DuPont has introduced a number of innovative products for use in markets ranging from apparel to aerospace. Many products, such as Lycra® and Stainmaster® fabrics, Teflon® coating, and Kevlar® fiber, became household names as ingredient brands in consumer products manufactured by other companies. Several recent ingredient brands include Supro® isolated soy proteins used in food products, and RiboPrinter® genetic fingerprinting technology.[43]

Another form is *same-company co-branding*, as when General Mills advertises Trix and Yoplait yogurt. Still another form is *joint venture co-branding*, as in the case of General Electric and Hitachi lightbulbs in Japan and the Citibank AAdvantage credit card. Finally, there is *multiple-sponsor co-branding*, as in the case of Taligent, a technological alliance of Apple, IBM, and Motorola.[44]

Many manufacturers make components—motors, computer chips, carpet fibers—that enter into final branded products, and whose individual identity normally gets lost. Among the few component branders who have succeeded in building a separate identity are Intel, Nutrasweet, and Gortex. Intel's consumer-directed brand campaign convinced many personal computer buyers to buy only computer brands with "Intel Inside." As a result, major PC manufacturers—IBM, Dell, Compaq—purchase their chips from Intel at a premium price rather than buy equivalent chips from an unknown supplier. Searle has convinced many beverage consumers to look for Nutrasweet as an ingredient. Manufacturers of outerwear can charge a higher price if their garments include Gortex. However, most component manufacturers find it hard to convince buyers to insist on a certain component, material, or ingredient in the final product.

brand asset management

Although print and broadcast advertising have played a large role in building strong brands, other forces are now playing an increasing role. Customers come to know a brand through a range of contacts and touchpoints: personal observation and use, word of mouth, meeting company personnel, telephone experience, seeing the Web page, receiving invoices, and so on. Any of these experiences can be positive or negative. The company must put in as much quality in managing these experiences as it does in producing its ads.

Companies must balance their communication expenditures among the main communication media. These include the following seven communication vehicles: advertising, public relations, trade and sales promotion, consumer promotions, direct marketing, event marketing, and internal employee communications. Companies are increasingly moving their brand-building budgets to public relations, direct marketing, event marketing, and employee training.

One of the most potent influences on brand perception is the experience customers have with the company's personnel. If the telephone operator is curt, if the order taker is poorly informed, if the accountant will not explain the invoice—the brand image is compromised. Therefore the company needs to train its people to be customer-centered. Even better, the company should build pride in its employees regarding their products and service so that their enthusiasm will spill over to the customer. Companies such as Nordstrom and Harley-Davidson have succeeded in creating enthusiastic representatives.

Companies must go further and train and encourage their distributors and dealers to serve their customers well. Poorly trained dealers can ruin the best of efforts made by the company to build a strong brand image.

This suggests that managing a company's brand assets can no longer be entrusted to brand managers. Brand managers do not have enough power and scope to do all the things that are necessary to build and enhance their brands. Their incentive system drives them to pursue short-term results, whereas managing brands as assets calls for longer-term strategy and more inclusive teamwork.

Companies are beginning to establish brand asset management teams to manage their major brands. Canada Dry and Colgate-Palmolive have appointed *brand equity managers* to maintain and protect the brand's image, associations, and quality, and to prevent short-term tactical actions by overzealous brand managers from hurting the brand. Brand equity managers also have to handle unexpected negative publicity, as happened with the Exxon *Valdez*, Tylenol pill tainting, tainted Perrier, and Audi crashes. Coca-Cola's CEO recently resigned in part because of his slow and poor handling of Coke's contamination scare in Belgium. After all, Coca-Cola is a "giant image machine" and must handle itself as such.

Some companies are putting their branding in the hands of an entirely different company that can focus on brand management and nothing else. Henry Silverman of Cendant Corporation has made a business of managing—not owning—brands.

Cendant Corporation   Cendant's Henry Silverman has gone as far as anyone in arguing that brand is everything and in showing how a brand can even be split away from the operational aspect of the business. Cendant owns and manages brands, including motels (Days Inn, Super 8, Howard Johnson, Ramada), real estate franchises (Century 21, Coldwell Banker), and car rental agencies (Avis). The brands are all he owns. While other companies own and operate the messy, real-world parts of the business, Silverman spends his time and energy distilling, refurbishing, extending, linking, and leveraging brand names. For instance, he was able to change the brand image of Century 21. Old TV ads emphasized the company's vast real estate network, but Silverman's research showed that home buyers did not care how big Century 21 was; they cared about building good relationships with the company's real estate agents. Silverman launched a new campaign focusing on those more personal attributes, and Century 21's annual earnings have doubled.[45]

brand auditing and repositioning

Companies need to periodically audit their brands' strengths and weaknesses. Kevin Keller constructed a *brand report card* (see "Marketing Memo: The Brand Report Card") listing 10 characteristics based on his review of the world's strongest brands.[46]

A company will occasionally discover that it may have to reposition the brand because of changing customer preferences or new competitors. Consider the following repositioning stories.

Kmart   Kmart, which prospered in the 1970s as a leading discount store chain, came close to bankruptcy in the mid-1990s. It was losing out to Wal-Mart and better-looking stores such as Target. Kmart undertook a number of steps to relaunch itself as Big K. Critics saw the stores as old, dilapidated, unkept, with poor service. It built new stores that suggested it was young and hip, carried great brands and values, offered a high level of customer service, and was serving all classes. In spite of these changes, Kmart's performance remained much below its major competitors, Wal-Mart and Target. In late January 2002, Kmart filed for bankruptcy.

Marketing
MEMO

The Brand Report Card

The world's strongest brands share 10 attributes. How does your brand measure up?

1. *The brand excels at delivering the benefits consumers truly desire.* Do you focus relentlessly on maximizing your customers' product and service experiences?
2. *The brand stays relevant.* Are you in touch with your customers' tastes, current market conditions, and trends?
3. *The pricing strategy is based on consumers' perceptions of value.* Have you optimized price, cost, and quality to meet or exceed customers' expectations?
4. *The brand is properly positioned.* Have you established necessary and competitive points of parity with competitors? Have you established desirable and deliverable points of difference?
5. *The brand is consistent.* Are you sure that your marketing programs are not sending conflicting messages and that they have not done so over time?
6. *The brand portfolio and hierarchy makes sense.* Can the corporate brand create a seamless umbrella for all the brands in the portfolio? Do you have a brand hierarchy that is well thought out and well understood?

continued...

Schwinn   Schwinn, the leading U.S. bicycle manufacturer, had thrived since its beginnings in the late 1800s. It repositioned itself several times during the 1900s, first aiming its bikes at boys and their fathers, later positioning them as family bikes, then as fitness bikes. However, in the early 1980s, Schwinn paid little attention to two new markets—dirt bikes and mountain bikes. Schwinn started to become "uncool" and irrelevant in the minds of young bikers. Finally, in the 1990s, Schwinn repositioned itself by adding mountain bikes and sponsoring events featuring popular stunt riders sporting Schwinn equipment and gear. Schwinn built an image of fun and daring and its bikes were seen to be of the highest quality and durability.

packaging and labeling

Most physical products have to be packaged and labeled. Some packages—such as the Coke bottle and the L'eggs container—are world famous. Many marketers have called packaging a fifth P, along with price, product, place, and promotion. Most marketers, however, treat packaging and labeling as an element of product strategy.

packaging

We define **packaging** as all the activities of designing and producing the container for a product. The container is called the **package**, and it might include up to three levels of material. Old Spice aftershave lotion is in a bottle (*primary package*) that is in a cardboard box (*secondary package*) that is in a corrugated box (*shipping package*) containing six dozen boxes of Old Spice.

Well-designed packages can create convenience and promotional value. Various factors have contributed to the growing use of packaging as a marketing tool:

- *Self-service:* An increasing number of products are sold on a self-service basis. In an average supermarket, which stocks 15,000 items, the typical shopper passes by some 300 items per minute. Given that 53 percent of all purchases are made on impulse, the effective package operates as a "five-second commercial." The package must perform many of the sales tasks: attract attention, describe the product's features, create consumer confidence, and make a favorable overall impression.
- *Consumer affluence:* Rising consumer affluence means consumers are willing to pay a little more for the convenience, appearance, dependability, and prestige of better packages.
- *Company and brand image:* Packages contribute to instant recognition of the company or brand. The Campbell Soup Company estimates that the average shopper sees its familiar red-and-white can 76 times a year, creating the equivalent of $26 million worth of advertising.
- *Innovation opportunity:* Innovative packaging can bring large benefits to consumers and profits to producers. Companies are incorporating unique materials and features such as resealable spouts and openings. Toothpaste pump dispensers have captured 12 percent of the toothpaste market because they are more convenient and less messy. The fragrance industry is continuously developing unique bottle designs.

Developing an effective package requires several decisions. The first is to establish the packaging concept: defining what the package should basically *be* or *do* for the particular product. Decisions must be made on additional elements—size, shape, materials, color, text, and brand mark. Brian Wansink found, for example, that a larger package size will increase product usage between 7 and 43 percent.[47] Color must be carefully chosen: Blue is cool and serene, red is active and lively, yellow is medicinal and weak, pastel colors are feminine and dark colors are masculine. Decisions must also be made on the amount of text, on cellophane or other transparent films, on a plastic or a laminate tray, and so on. Decisions must be made on "tamperproof" devices. The various packaging elements must be harmonized. The packaging elements must also be harmonized with decisions on pricing, advertising, and other marketing elements. Consider this example.

Rhino Entertainment   Rhino, a music company based in Los Angeles, released a CD compilation with more than 100 songs called "Brain in a Box: The Science Fiction Collection." To get serious sci-fi fans to spend $100 for a collection of songs, Rhino designed unique packaging that would make the CD set a collector's item. Five CDs come in a box whose panels display three different views of the brain using three-dimensional holograms. The panels also show various clamps and wires attached to the brain that appear to connect with knobs and dials on the metallic lid. Since Rhino rarely records new bands, relying instead on reissues of older music, packaging has always been crucial to selling records.[48]

After the packaging is designed, it must be tested. *Engineering tests* are conducted to ensure that the package stands up under normal conditions; *visual tests*, to ensure that the script is legible and the colors harmonious; *dealer tests*, to ensure that dealers find the packages attractive and easy to handle; and *consumer tests*, to ensure favorable consumer response.

Developing effective packaging may cost several hundred thousand dollars and take several months to complete. Companies must pay attention to growing environmental and safety concerns about packaging. Shortages of paper, aluminum, and other materials suggest that marketers should try to reduce packaging. Many packages end up as broken bottles and crumpled cans littering the streets and countryside. Packaging creates a major problem in solid waste disposal, requiring huge amounts of labor and energy. Fortunately, many companies have gone "green": S. C. Johnson repackaged Agree Plus shampoo in a stand-up pouch using 80 percent less plastic. P&G eliminated outer cartons from its Secret and Sure deodorants, saving 3.4 million pounds of paper board per year.

Tetra Pak   Tetra Pak, a major Swedish multinational, provides an example of the power of innovative packaging and customer thinking. Tetra Pak invented an "aseptic" package that enables milk, fruit juice, and other perishable liquid foods to be distributed without refrigeration. So dairies can distribute milk over a wider area without investing in refrigerated trucks and facilities. Supermarkets can carry Tetra Pak packaged products on ordinary shelves, allowing them to save expensive refrigerator space. Tetra's motto is "the package should save more than it cost." Tetra Pak advertises the benefits of its packaging to consumers directly and even initiates recycling programs to save the environment. Its new American headquarters in Vernon, Illinois, used recycled materials and other environmentally sensitive building products and techniques.[49]

labeling

Sellers must label products. The label may be a simple tag attached to the product or an elaborately designed graphic that is part of the package. The label might carry only the brand name or a great deal of information. Even if the seller prefers a simple label, the law may require additional information.

Labels perform several functions. First, the label *identifies* the product or brand—for instance, the name Sunkist stamped on oranges. The label might also *grade* the product; canned peaches are grade labeled A, B, and C. The label might *describe* the product: who made it, where it was made, when it was made, what it contains, how it is to be used, and how to use it safely. Finally, the label might *promote* the product through its attractive graphics.

Labels eventually become outmoded and need freshening up. The label on Ivory soap has been redone 18 times since the 1890s, with gradual changes in the size and design of the letters. The label on Orange Crush soft drink was substantially changed when competitors' labels began to picture fresh fruits, thereby pulling in more sales. In response, Orange Crush developed a label with new symbols to suggest freshness and with much stronger and deeper colors.

7. *The brand makes use of and coordinates a full repertoire of marketing activities to build equity.* Have you capitalized on the unique capabilities of each communication option while ensuring that the meaning of the brand is consistently represented?
8. *The brand's managers understand what the brand means to consumers.* Do you know what customers like and do not like about your brand? Have you created detailed, research-driven portraits of your target customers?
9. *The brand is given proper, sustained support.* Are the successes or failures of marketing programs fully understood before they are changed? Is the brand given sufficient R&D support?
10. *The company monitors sources of brand equity.* Have you created a brand charter that defines the meaning and equity of the brand and how it should be treated? Have you assigned explicit responsibility for monitoring and preserving brand equity?

Source: Adapted from Kevin Lane Keller, "The Brand Report Card," *Harvard Business Review* (January 1, 2000), pp. 147–57.

There is a long history of legal concerns surrounding labels, as well as packaging. In 1914, the Federal Trade Commission Act held that false, misleading, or deceptive labels or packages constitute unfair competition. The Fair Packaging and Labeling Act, passed by Congress in 1967, set mandatory labeling requirements, encouraged voluntary industry packaging standards, and allowed federal agencies to set packaging regulations in specific industries. The Food and Drug Administration (FDA) has required processed-food producers to include nutritional labeling that clearly states the amounts of protein, fat, carbohydrates, and calories contained in products, as well as their vitamin and mineral content as a percentage of the recommended daily allowance. The FDA recently launched a drive to control health claims in food labeling by taking action against the potentially misleading use of such descriptions as "light," "high fiber," and "low fat." Consumerists have lobbied for additional labeling laws to require *open dating* (to describe product freshness), *unit pricing* (to state the product cost in standard measurement units), *grade labeling* (to rate the quality level), and *percentage labeling* (to show the percentage of each important ingredient).

summary

1. Product is the first and most important element of the marketing mix. Product strategy calls for making coordinated decisions on product mixes, product lines, brands, and packaging and labeling.

2. In planning its market offering, the marketer needs to think through the five levels of the product. The core benefit is the fundamental benefit or service the customer is really buying. At the second level, the marketer has to turn the core benefit into a basic product. At the third level, the marketer prepares an expected product, a set of attributes that buyers normally expect and agree to when they buy the product. At the fourth level, the marketer prepares an augmented product, one that includes additional services and benefits that distinguish the company's offer from that of competitors. At the fifth and final level, the marketer prepares a potential product, which encompasses all the augmentations and transformations the product might ultimately undergo.

3. Products can be classified in several ways. In terms of durability and reliability, products can be nondurable goods, durable goods, or services. In the consumer-goods category, products are convenience goods (staples, impulse goods, emergency goods), shopping goods (homogeneous and heterogeneous), specialty goods, or unsought goods. In the industrial-goods category, products fall into one of three categories: materials and parts (raw materials and manufactured materials and parts), capital items (installations and equipment), or supplies and business services (operating supplies, maintenance and repair items, maintenance and repair services, and business advisory services).

4. Most companies sell more than one product. A product mix can be classified according to width, length, depth, and consistency. These four dimensions are the tools for developing the company's marketing strategy and deciding which product lines to grow, maintain, harvest, and divest.

To analyze a product line and decide how many resources should be invested in that line, product-line managers need to look at sales and profits and market profile.

5. A company can change the product component of its marketing mix by lengthening its product via line stretching (downmarket, upmarket, or both) or line filling, by modernizing its products, by featuring certain products, and by pruning its products to eliminate the least profitable.

6. Branding is a major issue in product strategy. A brand is a complex symbol that can convey many levels of meaning. Branding is expensive and time-consuming, and it can make or break a product. The most valuable brands have a brand equity that is considered an important company asset and that must be carefully managed. In thinking about branding strategy, companies must decide whether or not to brand; whether to produce manufacturer brands, or distributor or private brands; which brand name to use; and whether to use line extensions, brand extensions, multibrands, new brands, or co-brands. The best brand names suggest something about the product's benefits; suggest product qualities; are easy to pronounce, recognize, and remember; are distinctive; and do not carry negative meanings or connotations in other countries or languages.

7. Many physical products have to be packaged and labeled. Well-designed packages can create convenience value for customers and promotional value for producers. In effect, they can act as "five-second commercials" for the product. Marketers develop a packaging concept and test it functionally and psychologically to make sure it achieves its desired objectives and is compatible with public policy and environmental concerns. Physical products also require labeling for identification and possible grading, description, and product promotion. Sellers may be required by law to present certain information on the label to protect and inform consumers.

applications

marketing debate – are line extensions good or bad?

Marketing consultants Al Ries and Jack Trout have vociferously denounced the practice of line extensions, referring to the "line extension trap." Others maintain that brand extensions are a critical growth strategy and source of revenue for the firm.

Take a position: Line extensions can endanger brands versus Line extensions are an important brand growth strategy.

marketing and advertising

1. Pepperidge Farm cookies are positioned as premium cookies. This magazine ad in Figure 1 features a larger-than-life Milano cookie, plus a simple headline, logo, and the tagline "Never have an ordinary day."

   a. Identify the basic, expected, and augmented products that Pepperidge Farm is offering.

   b. How would you classify this consumer product?

   c. How do the elements of this ad help convey the brand's attributes and benefits?

2. Binney & Smith is well known for marketing Crayola® crayons in a wide variety of colors, including jack-o-lantern orange, as shown in the seasonal ad in Figure 2.

   a. Can the Crayon Treat Pack be considered a line or brand extension? Why would Binney & Smith choose this strategy?

   b. Discuss Binney & Smith's packaging strategy for the Crayon Treat Pack. How does this strategy reinforce to the company's company and brand image?

   c. Are Crayola® crayons convenience goods, goods, specialty, or unsought goods? How does this classification affect Binney & Smith's marketing of its Crayon Treat Pack?

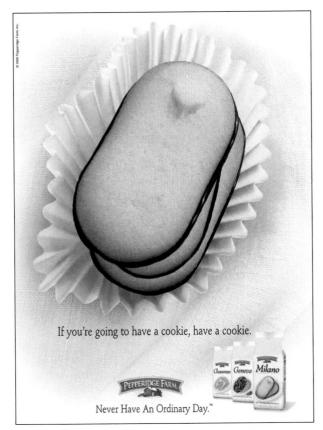

If you're going to have a cookie, have a cookie.

PEPPERIDGE FARM

Never Have An Ordinary Day.™

Figure 1

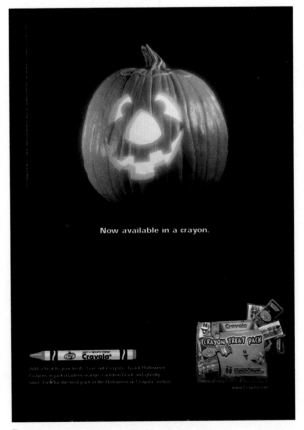

Now available in a crayon.

Figure 2

online marketing today

As noted earlier, Richard Branson is aggressively building his Virgin brand on and off the Internet. Virgin.com has evolved into a major U.K. portal with links to every Virgin company Web site and offers goods and services in numerous product categories, from travel and transport to house and home and business and finance. This site also serves as a central recruitment point for Virgin companies with job openings.

Visit the Virgin site (*www.virgin.com*), review the offers on the home page, and follow several links to featured offers and companies. Return to the home page and click to read about at least one "travel and transport" offer and one "house and home" offer. Which brand-name strategy is Virgin using? Why is this strategy appropriate for Virgin? Select two offers and determine whether they can be characterized as convenience goods, shopping goods, specialty goods, or unsought goods. Why would Virgin choose to highlight these types of products?

you're the marketer: sonic pda marketing plan

Marketing Plan Pro

Decisions about products and branding are critical elements of any marketing plan. During the planning process, marketers must consider a variety of issues related to product mix, product lines, brand equity, and brand strategies.

You are helping Sonic manage its soon-to-be-expanded line of personal digital assistant products, as well as branding for this line. After reviewing the company's current situation, target market, positioning, and other issues previously addressed in your marketing plan, consider the following questions:

- What is the core benefit of the first PDA product Sonic will soon introduce?
- What elements of the potential product should Sonic consider incorporating into the higher-end second product to be developed next year?

- What are the attributes and benefits suggested by the Sonic brand?
- How can Sonic use packaging and labeling to support its brand image and help its channel partners sell the PDA product more effectively?

Think about how your answers to these questions will influence Sonic's marketing activities. Now, as your instructor directs, summarize your ideas in a written marketing plan or type them into the Marketing Mix and Marketing Strategy sections of the *Marketing Plan Pro* software. Also indicate (in the Marketing Research section) any additional studies you will need to support decisions about managing the product line and brand.

notes

1. <*www.biography.com*>.
2. T. L. Stanley, "Brand Builders: Bio-Genetics at A&E," *Brandweek*, April 6, 1998, pp. 22–23.
3. This discussion is adapted from Theodore Levitt, "Marketing Success through Differentiation: of Anything," *Harvard Business Review* (January–February 1980): 83–91. The first level, core benefit, has been added to Levitt's discussion.
4. Harper W. Boyd Jr. and Sidney Levy, "New Dimensions in Consumer Analysis," *Harvard Business Review* (November–December 1963): 129–40.
5. Theodore Levitt, *The Marketing Mode* (New York: McGraw-Hill, 1969), p. 2.
6. For some definitions, see *Dictionary of Marketing Terms*, ed. Peter D. Bennett (Chicago: American Marketing Association, 1995). Also see Patrick E. Murphy and Ben M. Enis, "Classifying Products Strategically," *Journal of Marketing* (July 1986): 24–42.
7. Adapted from a Hamilton Consultants White Paper, December 1, 2000.
8. This illustration is found in Benson P. Shapiro, *Industrial Product Policy: Managing the Existing Product Line* (Cambridge, MA: Marketing Science Institute, September 1977), pp. 3–5, 98–101.
9. David A. Aaker, "Should You Take Your Brand to Where the Action Is?" *Harvard Business Review* (September–October 1997): 135–43; A. Kirmani, S. Sood, and S. Bridges, "The Ownership Effect in Consumer Responses to Brand Line

Stretches," *Journal of Marketing* 63 (1999): 88–101; T. Randall, K. Ulrich, and D. Reibstein, "Brand Equity and Vertical Product Line Extent," *Marketing Science* 17 (1998): 356–79.
10. Steuart Henderson Britt, "How Weber's Law Can Be Applied to Marketing," *Business Horizons* (February 1975): 21–29.
11. Jean-Noel Kapferer, *Strategic Brand Management: New Approaches to Creating and Evaluating Brand Equity* (London: Kogan Page, 1992), p. 38; Jennifer L. Aaker, "Dimensions of Brand Personality," *Journal of Marketing Research* (August 1997): 347–56. For an overview of academic research on branding, see Kevin Lane Keller, "Branding and Brand Equity," in *Handbook of Marketing*, eds., Bart Weitz and Robin Wensley (Sage Publications: in press).
12. Scott Davis, *Brand Asset Management: Driving Profitable Growth Through Your Brands* (San Francisco: Jossey-Bass, 2000); K. L. Keller, "Building Customer-Based Brand Equity: A Blueprint for Creating Strong Brands," *Marketing Management*, 10 (July/August 2001): 15–19.
13. Marc Gobe, *Emotional Branding* (New York: Allworth Press, 2001); B. H. Schmitt and A. Simonson, *Marketing Aesthetics: The Strategic Management of Brands, Identity and Image* (New York: Free Press, 1997); B. H. Schmitt, *Experiential Marketing: How to Get Customers to Sense, Feel, Think, Act and Relate to Your Company and Brands* (New York: Free Press, 1999).
14. Donald D. Tosti and Roger D. Stotz, "Building Your Brand from the Inside Out," *Marketing Management* (July–August

2001): 29–33; see also P. Berthon, J. M. Hulbert, and L. F. Pitt, "Brand Management Prognostications," *Sloan Management Review* (Winter 1999): 53–65.

15. Heidi F. Schultz and Don E. Schultz, "Why the Sock Puppet Got Sacked," *Marketing Management* (July–August 2001): 34–39.

16. David A. Akar, *Building Strong Brands* (New York: The Free Press, 1995). Also see Kavin Lane Keller, *Strategic Brand Management: Building, Measuring, and Managing Brand Equity* (Upper Saddle River, NJ: Prentice Hall, 1998); and D. A. Aaker and E. Joachimsthaler, *Brand Leadership* (New York; Free Press, 2000).

17. Scott Davis, *Brand Asset Management*; D. C. Bello and M. B. Holbrook, "Does an Absence of Brand Equity Generalize Across Product Classes?" *Journal of Business Research*, 34 (1996): 125–31.

18. Mary W. Sullivan, "How Brand Names Affect the Demand for Twin Automobiles," *Journal of Marketing Research* 35 (1998): 154–65.

19. Adrian J. Slywotzky and Benson P. Shapiro, "Leveraging to Beat the Odds: The New Marketing Mindset," *Harvard Business Review* (September–October 1993): 97–107.

20. Kurt Badenhausen with Joyce Artinian and Christopher Nikolov, "Most Valuable Brands," *Financial World* (September–October 1997): 62–63. "The Best Global Brands," *BusinessWeek*, August 6, 2001, pp. 50–64. The article ranks the 100 best global brands using a valuation method developed by Interbrand. For a discussion of methods of calculating brand value, see Kevin L. Keller, *Strategic Brand Management: Building, Measuring, and Managing Brand Equity* (Upper Saddle River, NJ: Prentice Hall, 1998), pp. 361–63.

21. Aaker, *Building Strong Brands*. Also see Patrick Barwise et al., *Accounting for Brands* (London: Institute of Chartered Accountants in England and Wales, 1990); Peter H. Farquhar, Julia Y. Han, and Yuji Ijiri, "Brands on the Balance Sheet," *Marketing Management* (Winter 1992): 16–22. Brand equity should reflect not only the capitalized value of the incremental profits from the current use of the brand name, but also the value of its potential extensions to other products.

22. Melanie Wells, "Red Baron," *Forbes*, July 3, 2000.

23. Kerry Capell, "Virgin Takes E-wing," *BusinessWeek e.biz*, January 22, 2001, pp. EB30–34; Melanie Wells, "Red Baron," *Forbes*, July 3, 2000, pp. 151–60.

24. Margaret Webb Pressler, "The Power of Branding," *Washington Post*, July 27, 1997, p. H1; "Cadbury Is Paying Triarc $1.45 Billion for Snapple Unit," *Baltimore Sun*, September 19, 2000.

25. Scott Davis and Darrell Douglass, "Holistic Approach to Brand Equity Management," *Marketing News*, January 16, 1995, pp. 4–5.

26. John F. Geer Jr., "Brand War on Wall Street," *Financial World*, May 20, 1997, pp. 54–63.

27. Bob Lamons, "Brick Brand's Mighty—Yours Can Be, Too," *Marketing News*, November 22, 1999, p. 16.

28. For further reading, see Brian F. Harris and Roger A. Strang, "Marketing Strategies in the Age of Generics," *Journal of Marketing* (Fall 1985): 70–81.

29. "President's Choice Continues Brisk Pace," *Frozen Food Age* (March 1998): 17–18; Warren Thayer, "Loblaw's Exec Predicts: Private Label to Surge," *Frozen Food Age* (May 1996): 1; Brian Dunn, "North Stars," *Supermarket News*, February 5, 2001.

30. Quoted in "Trade Promotion: Much Ado About Nothing," *Promo* (October 1991): 37.

31. Paul S. Richardson, Alan S. Dick, and Arun K. Jain, "Extrinsic and Intrinsic Cue Effects on Perceptions of Store Brand Quality," *Journal of Marketing* (October 1994): 28–36.

32. Patricia Nakache, "Secrets of the New Brand Builders," *Fortune*, June 22, 1998, pp. 167–70.

33. Marc Gunther, "Understanding AOL's Grand Unified Theory of the Media Cosmos, *Fortune*, January 8, 2001, p. 72.

34. Kim Robertson, "Strategically Desirable Brand Name Characteristics," *Journal of Consumer Marketing* (Fall 1989): 61–70; C. Kohli and D. W. LaBahn, "Creating Effective Brand Names: A Study of the Naming Process," *Journal of Advertising Research* (January/February 1997): 67–75.

35. Patricia Nakache, "Secrets of the New Brand Builders," *Fortune*, June 22, 1998, pp. 167–70.

36. Adapted from Alice M. Tybout and Gregory S. Carpenter, "Creating and Managing Brands," in *Kellogg on Marketing*, ed. Dawn Iacobucci (New York: John Wiley & Son, 2001), pp. 74–98; see also C. W. Park, S. Milberg, and R. Lawson, "Evaluation of Brand Extensions: The Role of Product Feature Similarity and Brand Concept Consistency," *Journal of Consumer Research*, 18 (1991): 185–93.

37. Steven M. Shugan, "Branded Variants," 1989 AMA Educators' Proceedings (Chicago: American Marketing Association, 1989), pp. 33–38. also M. Bergen, S. Dutta, and S. M. Shugan, "Branded Variants: A Retail Perspective," *Journal of Marketing Research*, 33 (February 1996): 9–21.

38. Robert McMath, "Product Proliferation," *Adweek* (Eastern Ed.) (Superbrands 1995 Supplement, 1995), pp. 34–40; John A. Quelch and David Kenny, "Extend Profits, Not Product Lines," *Harvard Business Review* (September–October 1994): 153–60; Bruce G. S. Hardle, Leonard M. Lodish, James V. Kilmer, and David R. Beatty et al., "The Logic of Product-Line Extensions," *Harvard Business Review* (November–December 1994): 53–62. J. Andrews and G. S. Low, "New But Not Improved: Factors That Affect the Development of Meaningful Line Extensions," Working Paper Report No. 98-124 (Cambridge, MA: Marketing Science Institute, November 1998).

39. Al Ries and Jack Trout, *Positioning: The Battle for Your Mind* (New York: McGraw-Hill, 1981).

40. From Srinivas K. Reddy, Susan L. Holak, and Subodh Bhat, "To Extend or Not to Extend: Success Determinants of Line Extensions," *Journal of Marketing Research* (May 1994): 243–62. See also Morris A. Cohen, Jehoshua Eliashberg, and Teck H. Ho, "An Anatomy of a Decision-Support System for Developing and Launching Line Extensions," *Journal of Marketing Research* (February 1997): 117–29; V. Padmanabhan, Surendra Rajiv, and Kannan Srinivasan, "New Products, Upgrades, and New Releases: A Rationale for Sequential Product Introduction," *Journal of Marketing Research* (November 1997): 456–72.

41. Barbara Loken and Deborah Roedder John, "Diluting Brand Beliefs: When Do Brand Extensions Have a Negative Impact?" *Journal of Marketing* (July 1993): 71–84; Deborah Roedder John, Barbara Loken, and Christohper Joiner, "The Negative Impact of Extensions: Can Flagship Products Be Diluted," *Journal of Marketing* (January 1998): 19–32; Susan M. Broniarcyzk and Joseph W. Alba, "The Importance of the Brand in Brand Extension," *Journal of Marketing Research* (May 1994): 214–28 (this entire issue of *JMR* is devoted to brands and brand equity). See also R. Ahluwalia and Z. Gürhan-Canli, "The Effects of Extensions on the Family Brand Name: An Accessibility-Diagnosticity Perspective,"

Journal of Consumer Research 27 (December 2000): 371–81; Z. Gürhan-Canli and M. Durairaj, "The Effects of Extensions on Brand Name Dilution and Enhancement," *Journal of Marketing Research* 35 (1998): 464–73; S. J. Milberg, C. W. Park, and M. S. McCarthy, "Managing Negative Feedback Effects Associated with Brand Extensions: The Impact of Alternative Branding Strategies," *Journal of Consumer Psychology* 6 (1997): 119–40.

42. Mark B. Taylor, "Cannibalism in Multibrand Firms," *Journal of Business Strategy* (Spring 1986): 69–75. For a general discussion of co-branding, see Shawn Clark, *The Co-Marketing Solution* (Chicago: American Marketing Association, 2000).

43. <*www.dupont.com*>.

44. Bernard L. Simonin and Julie A. Ruth, "Is a Company Known by the Company It Keeps? Assessing the Spillover Effects of Brand Alliances on Consumer Brand Attitudes," *Journal of Marketing Research* (February 1998): 30–42; see also C. W. Park, S. Y. Jun, and A. D. Shocker, "Composite Branding Alliances: An Investigation of Extension and Feedback Effects, " *Journal of Marketing Research* 33 (1996): 453–66.

45. Evan Schwartz, "The Brand Man," *Context* (Summer 1998): 54–58; Davis, *Brand Asset Management.*

46. Kevin Lane Keller, "The Brand Report Card," *Harvard Business Review* (January–February 2000): 147–57.

47. Brian Wansink, "Can Package Size Accelerate Usage Volume?" *Journal of Marketing* (July 1996): 1–14.

48. Queena Sook Kim, "This Potion's Power Is in Its Packaging," *Wall Street Journal*, December 21, 2000, p. B12.

49. "Tetra Pak Opens Innovative Environmentally Friendly Corporate Headquarters," *PR Newswire*, September 1, 1999.

designing and managing services

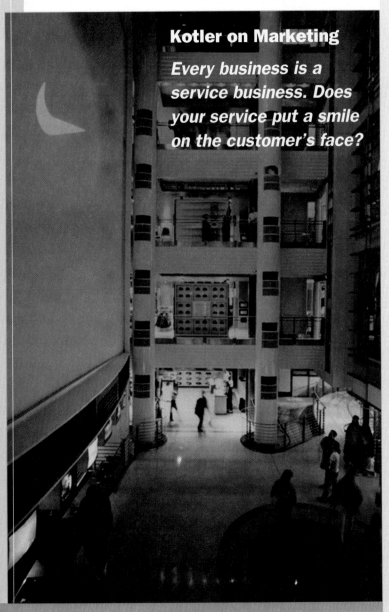

Kotler on Marketing

Every business is a service business. Does your service put a smile on the customer's face?

In this chapter, we will address the following questions:

- How are services defined and classified?
- How do services differ from goods?
- How can service firms improve their differentiation, quality, and productivity?
- How can goods-producing companies improve their customer support services?

A s companies find it harder to differentiate their physical products, they turn to service differentiation. Companies seek to develop a reputation for superior performance in on-time delivery, better and faster answering of inquiries, and quicker resolution of complaints. Service becomes the mantra, and many books have been written to point out the superior profitability of companies that manage to deliver superior service.[1]

Yet not all companies have invested to provide superior service, at least not to all of their customers. BusinessWeek, in its October 23, 2000, issue, carried a cover story, "Why Service Stinks."[2] Since 1994, customer satisfaction in the United States dropped 12.5 percent for airlines, 8.1 percent for banks, 6.5 percent for stores, and

4 percent for hotels. Customers are increasingly complaining about inaccurate information; unresponsive, rude, or poorly trained personnel; and long wait times. However, service is not uniformly bad for all customers. Airlines, hotels, and banks all pamper their best customers. Big spenders get special discounts, promotional offers, and lots of special service. Meanwhile, the rest of their customers get higher fees, stripped-down service, and at best a voice message to answer their inquiries.

In former times, service companies held out a welcoming hand to all customers, but these companies now have so much data on individuals that they are able to classify their customers into profit tiers. Companies assign larger staffs to handle their more profitable customers. Charles Schwab's best customers get their calls answered in 15 seconds; other customers can wait 10 minutes or more. Sears sends a repairperson to its best customers within two hours; other customers wait four hours.

This shift from a customer service democracy to a meritocracy was enabled by increasingly rich customer databases. It is also a response to lower profit margins resulting from customers becoming more price-driven and less loyal. Companies are now driven to seek ways to squeeze more profit out of the different customer tiers. Firms have decided to raise fees and lower service to customers who barely pay their way, and to coddle big spenders to retain their patronage as long as possible.

Companies that provide differentiated levels of service will not be able to claim superior service. This cannot be their value proposition, because the customers who receive poor treatment will bad-mouth the company and injure its reputation. Here we will examine how companies can deliver superior service to all customers, even though some companies will choose to direct superior service only to their more profitable customers.

the nature of services

One of the megatrends of recent years has been the phenomenal growth of services. In the United States, service jobs now account for 79 percent of all jobs and 74 percent of gross domestic product. According to the Bureau of Labor Statistics, service occupations will be responsible for all net job growth through the year 2005.[3] These numbers have led to a growing interest in the special problems of marketing services.[4]

Service industries are quite varied. The *government sector*, with its courts, employment services, hospitals, loan agencies, military services, police and fire departments, post office, regulatory agencies, and schools, is in the service business. The *private non-profit sector*, with its museums, charities, churches, colleges, foundations, and hospitals, is in the service business. A good part of the *business sector*, with its airlines, banks, hotels, insurance companies, law firms, management consulting firms, medical practices, motion-picture companies, plumbing-repair companies, and real estate firms, is in the service business. Many workers in the *manufacturing sector*, such as computer operators, accountants, and legal staff, are really service providers. In fact, they make up a "service factory" providing services to the "goods factory."

We define a service as follows: A **service** is any act or performance that one party can offer to another that is essentially intangible and does not result in the ownership of anything. Its production may or may not be tied to a physical product.

Manufacturers and distributors can pursue service excellence to differentiate themselves, as in the following example.

Acme Construction Supply   Located in Portland, Oregon, Acme has invested more than $135,000 in its Night Owl delivery service: Acme personnel deposit orders into lock boxes at construction sites during the nighttime hours, so materials are available first thing in the morning. Says the company's regional team leader, "People that are very, very price sensitive don't do business here. But people who see the www.keen.com is a virtual advice marketplace.

overall value we provide do. And it's very intimidating to our competition. They have to walk around our delivery boxes every day to make their sales calls."[5]

Many pure service firms are now using the Internet to reach customers. A little surfing on the Web will turn up a large number of virtual service providers. Here are some that dispense cyber-advice.

Dot-com Providers   Log on to Cyberdocs.com if you have a medical problem. Qualified physicians will answer your private questions with "Compassion, a Commitment to quality Care, and Confidentiality of your medical data." If you need adult or child counseling, click on http://adultandchildcounsel.uswestdex.com and talk with Bailey Molineaux or Bill Evans about marital and family therapy, children's problems, or job stress. If you want a psychic reading, click on Psychicrealm.com; and Keen, Inc. created a virtual advice marketplace at *www.keen.com*, where anyone can advertise his or her services and consumers pay a per-minute fee to receive live, immediate advice over the phone.

categories of service mix

A company's offering to the marketplace often includes some services. The service component can be a minor or a major part of the total offering. Five categories of offerings can be distinguished:

1. *Pure tangible good:* The offering consists primarily of a tangible good such as soap, toothpaste, or salt. No services accompany the product.
2. *Tangible good with accompanying services:* The offering consists of a tangible good accompanied by one or more services. Levitt observes that "the more technologically sophisticated the generic product (e.g., cars and computers), the more dependent are its sales on the quality and availability of its accompanying customer services (e.g., display rooms, delivery, repairs and maintenance, application aids, operator training, installation advice, warranty fulfillment). In this

Marketing
MEMO

Selling Services for Profit

As many companies experience shrinking profit margins on the products they sell, they are trying to make money on the services they sell. They sometimes charge fees for services they formerly provided free. In other cases, they are pricing their services higher. Companies can also add services. Here are seven ways manufacturers can create service businesses:

1. *Repackaging their product into a system solution:* Rather than selling only its products, a company can embed these products into service programs that meet more of customers' needs.[a]
2. *Packaging internal services into salable external services:* Some companies sell internal competence to other companies, such as employee training programs or IT capabilities.
3. *Servicing other companies from the company's physical facilities:* Companies that manage a physical facility often find they can sell the facility's services to others.
4. *Offering to manage other companies' physical facilities or business processes:* After installing equipment or other components of a business process, a company can use its experienced employee base to provide management services in an outsourcing arrangement.[b]

continued...

sense, General Motors is probably more service intensive than manufacturing intensive. Without its services, its sales would shrivel."[6] (See "Marketing Memo: Selling Services for Profit.")

3. *Hybrid:* The offering consists of equal parts of goods and services. For example, people patronize restaurants for both food and service.
4. *Major service with accompanying minor goods and services:* The offering consists of a major service along with additional services or supporting goods. For example, airline passengers buy transportation service. The trip includes some tangibles, such as food and drinks, a ticket stub, and an airline magazine. The service requires a capital-intensive good—an airplane—for its realization, but the primary item is a service.
5. *Pure service:* The offering consists primarily of a service. Examples include baby-sitting, psychotherapy, and massage.

Because of this varying goods-to-service mix, it is difficult to generalize about services without further distinctions. However, some generalizations seem safe:

First, services vary as to whether they are *equipment-based* (automated car washes, vending machines) or *people-based* (window washing, accounting services). People-based services vary by whether they are provided by unskilled, skilled, or professional workers.

Second, some services require the *client's presence* and some do not. Brain surgery involves the client's presence, a car repair does not. If the client must be present, the service provider has to be considerate of his or her needs. Thus beauty salon operators will invest in decor, play background music, and engage in light conversation with the client.

Third, services differ as to whether they meet a *personal need* (personal services) or a *business need* (business services). Service providers typically develop different marketing programs for personal and business markets.

Fourth, service providers differ in their *objectives* (profit or nonprofit) and *ownership* (private or public). These two characteristics, when crossed, produce four quite different types of organizations. The marketing programs of a private investor hospital will differ from those of a private charity hospital or a Veterans Administration hospital.[7]

characteristics of services and their marketing implications

Services have four major characteristics that greatly affect the design of marketing programs: *intangibility, inseparability, variability,* and *perishability.*

INTANGIBILITY Unlike physical products, services cannot be seen, tasted, felt, heard, or smelled before they are bought. The person getting a face-lift cannot see the exact results before the purchase, and the patient in the psychiatrist's office cannot know the exact outcome.

To reduce uncertainty, buyers will look for evidence of the service quality. They will draw inferences about quality from the place, people, equipment, communication material, symbols, and price that they see. Therefore, the service provider's task is to "manage the evidence," to "tangibilize the intangible."[8] Whereas product marketers are challenged to add abstract ideas, service marketers are challenged to add physical evidence and imagery to abstract offers. Consider the following images: "You are in good hands with Allstate"; "I've got a piece of the rock" (Prudential).

Suppose a bank wants to position itself as the "fast" bank. It could make this positioning strategy tangible through a number of marketing tools:

1. *Place:* The exterior and interior should have clean lines. The layout of the desks and the traffic flow should be planned carefully. Waiting lines should not get overly long.
2. *People:* Personnel should be busy. There should be a sufficient number of employees to manage the workload.
3. *Equipment:* Computers, copying machines, desks should be and look "state of the art."
4. *Communication material:* Printed materials—text and photos—should suggest efficiency and speed.
5. *Symbols:* The name and symbol should suggest fast service.
6. *Price:* The bank could advertise that it will deposit $5 in the account of any customer who waits in line for more than five minutes.

Service marketers must be able to transform intangible services into concrete bene-fits. Consider Dun & Bradstreet.

Dun & **Bradstreet**   Dun & Bradstreet is a $1.5 billion firm with an excellent reputa-tion. Its database of 28 million U.S. and global companies is so comprehensive that D&B has become something of a central intelligence agency for buyers and sellers. D&B's premier database, called the Million Dollar Database, contains detailed fi-nancial and corporate information on companies with 20 or more employees and sales exceeding $1 million annually. A split in 2000 separated the credit rating, re-search, and risk analysis company Moody's Corp., but D&B retained the business information service. In 2001, D&B added a new market segment when it unveiled a set of services specifically designed for small business customers:[9]

To aid in "tangibilizing the intangible," Carbone and Haeckel propose a set of con-cepts under the name *customer experience engineering*.[10] Companies must first develop a clear picture of what they want the customer's perception of an experience to be and then design a consistent set of *performance and context clues* to support that experience. In the case of a bank, whether the teller dispensed the right amount of cash is a perform-ance clue; a context clue is whether the teller was properly dressed. The context clues in a bank are delivered by people (*humanics*) and things (*mechanics*). The company assem-bles the clues in an *experience blueprint,* a pictorial representation of the various clues. To the extent possible, the clues should address all five senses. The Disney Company is a master at developing *experience blueprints* in its theme parks; so are companies such as McDonald's and Barnes & Noble in designing their respective retail stores.

INSEPARABILITY   Services are typically produced and consumed simultaneously. This is not true of physical goods, which are manufactured, put into inventory, distrib-uted through multiple resellers, and consumed later. If a person renders the service, then the provider is part of the service. Because the client is also present as the service is produced, provider–client interaction is a special feature of services marketing.

In the case of entertainment and professional services, buyers are very interested in the specific provider. It is not the same concert if Madonna is indisposed and replaced by Marie Osmond, or if a legal defense will be supplied by John Nobody because F. Lee Bailey is unavailable. When clients have strong provider preferences, price is raised to ration the preferred provider's limited time.

Several strategies exist for getting around this limitation. The service provider can learn to work with larger groups. Psychotherapists have moved from one-on-one ther-apy to small-group therapy to groups of over 300 people in a large hotel ballroom. The service provider can learn to work faster—the psychotherapist can spend 30 minutes with each patient instead of 50 minutes and can see more patients. The service organi-zation can train more service providers and build up client confidence, as H&R Block has done with its national network of trained tax consultants. Creative artists have also developed techniques to overcome the limits of inseparability.

Blue Man Group   The Blue Man Group got its start in 1988 when the three original members—Matt Goldman, Phil Stanton, and Chris Wink—began performing on the streets of New York City. The company eventually moved into a theater, and the three performed every show for three straight years without the help of understudies. When the group opened a second show in Boston, the founders decided to add more Blue Men to help carry the weight. There are now 33 different performers, including one woman, who make up the Blue Man Group. They enable the Blue Man Group to take on various projects, such as performing in Las Vegas, recording a Grammy-nominated album, and starring in a series of commercials for Intel's Pentium processors.[11]

---

5. *Selling financial services:* Equipment companies often discover that they can profit from financing customers' purchases.[c]
6. *Moving into distribution services:* Manufacturers can own and operate retail locations for their products, such as outlet stores, brand-name chains, or even restaurants.[d]
7. *Using the Internet to create new service offerings:* Many manufacturers are offering an array of customer services created on the Web, such as product support and value-added services.

Sources: Irving D. Canton, "Learning to Love the Service Economy," *Harvard Business Review* (May–June 1984): 89–97; Mack Hanan, *Profits without Products: How to Transform Your Product Business into a Service* (New York: Amacom, 1992); Ronald Henkoff, "Service Is Everybody's Business," *Fortune,* June 27, 1994, pp. 48–60.

[a]David Einstein, "Bigger and Bluer than Ever/Resurgent IBM Thrives by Meeting Technology Needs for U.S. Business," *San Francisco Chronicle,* November 30, 1998, p. E1.

[b]Del Jones, "Copying Chores Earn Xerox Recognition," *USA Today,* October 16, 1997, p. B4.

[c]Reed Abelson, "Hints of Change at GE Capital as Financial Companies Lose Favor," *New York Times,* October 2, 1998, p. D1.

[d]Richard Halverson, "Bypassing the Marketers in the Middle," *Discount Store News,* May 11, 1998, pp. 70, 108.

VARIABILITY   Because they depend on who provides them and when and where they are provided, services are highly variable. Some doctors have excellent bedside manner; others are less patient with their patients. Some surgeons are very successful in performing a certain operation; others are less successful. Service buyers are aware of this variability and often talk to others before selecting a service provider.

Service firms can take three steps toward quality control. The first is investing in good hiring and training procedures. Recruiting the right employees and providing them with excellent training is crucial, regardless of whether employees are highly skilled professionals or low-skilled workers. Here is an example.

The Horn Group   The California-based Horn Group does PR for high-powered Silicon Valley software makers and technology consultants. Founder Sabrina Horn invests heavily in training employees and building morale and enthusiasm. She has developed education programs that include lunchtime seminars on everything from how to write a press release to how to manage an account. Employees also receive tuition reimbursement for continuing education. To recognize hard-working, dedicated employees, awards are handed out at weekly staff meetings. On the fun side, the Horn Group sponsors bowling nights or scavenger hunts to foster creativity and teamwork and give employees a chance to build camaraderie and relax together.[12]

The second step is standardizing the service-performance process throughout the organization. This is done by preparing a *service blueprint* that depicts events and processes in a flowchart, with the objective of recognizing potential fail points. Figure 15.1 shows a service blueprint for a nationwide floral-delivery organization.[13] The customer's experience is limited to dialing the phone, making choices, and placing an order. Behind the scenes, the floral organization gathers the flowers, places them in a vase, delivers them, and collects payment. Any one of these activities can be done well or poorly.

The third step is monitoring customer satisfaction through suggestion and complaint systems, customer surveys, and comparison shopping.

figure **15.1**

A Service–Performance–Process Map: Nationwide Floral Delivery

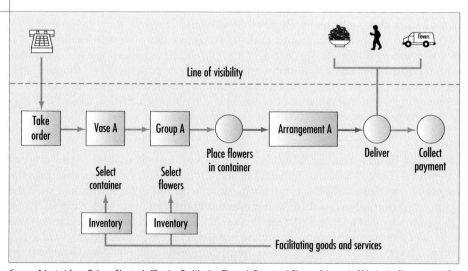

Source: Adapted from G. Lynn Shostack, "Service Positioning Through Structural Change," *Journal of Marketing* (January 1987): 39. Reprinted with permission of the American Marketing Association.

PERISHABILITY   Services cannot be stored. The perishability of services is not a problem when demand is steady. When demand fluctuates, service firms have problems. For example, public transportation companies have to own much more equipment because of rush-hour demand than if demand were even throughout the day. Some doctors charge patients for missed appointments because the service value existed only at that point.

Earl Sasser has described several strategies for producing a better match between demand and supply in a service business.[14]

On the demand side:

- *Differential pricing* will shift some demand from peak to off-peak periods. Examples include low early evening movie prices and weekend discount prices for car rentals.
- *Nonpeak demand* can be cultivated. McDonald's opened a breakfast service, and hotels developed minivacation weekends.
- *Complementary services* can be developed during peak time to provide alternatives to waiting customers, such as cocktail lounges in restaurants and automatic teller machines in banks.
- *Reservation systems* are a way to manage the demand level. Airlines, hotels, and physicians employ them extensively.

On the supply side:

- *Part-time employees* can be hired to serve peak demand. Colleges add part-time teachers when enrollment goes up, and restaurants call in part-time servers when needed.
- *Peak-time efficiency* routines can be introduced. Employees perform only essential tasks during peak periods. Paramedics assist physicians during busy periods.
- *Increased consumer participation* can be encouraged. Consumers fill out their own medical records or bag their own groceries.
- *Shared services* can be developed. Several hospitals can share medical-equipment purchases.
- *Facilities for future expansion* can be developed. An amusement park buys surrounding land for later development.

Club Med has come up with a unique solution to the perishability problem.

Club Med   Founded in 1955, Club Med operates hundreds of Club Med "villages" (resorts) around the world. If the company cannot sell its rooms and air packages, it loses out. Now Club Med uses e-mail to pitch unsold, discounted packages to the people in its database. These people are notified early to midweek on rooms and air seats available for travel that weekend. Discounts are typically 30 to 40 percent off the standard package price. Before the program, Club Med's only alternative was to rely on travel agents to sell last-minute packages. Today, the company also uses its global Web site to pitch discount packages.[15]

marketing strategies for service firms

Once service firms lagged behind manufacturing firms in their use of marketing because they were small, or professional businesses that did not use marketing, or faced large demand or little competition; but this has certainly changed. Consider the case of the U.S. Postal Service.

USPS   In 1992, Marvin Runyon was hired as postmaster general to overhaul the U.S. Postal Service. Since that time, the USPS has transformed itself into a lean, mean marketing machine. One memorable example of an effective USPS advertising campaign was the long-running Priority Mail series, which emphasized the low cost of shipping with the Postal Service instead of carriers like UPS and FedEx. In 1998, the USPS developed the "Fly Like an Eagle" image campaign, which used a popular song and the eagle mascot to emphasize the postal service as a whole. Today, the USPS has an annual advertising budget exceeding $300 million.[16]

three additional Ps

The traditional four Ps marketing approaches work well for goods, but additional elements require attention in service businesses. Booms and Bitner suggested three additional Ps for service marketing: *people, physical evidence,* and *process.*[17] Because most services are provided by *people*, the selection, training, and motivation of employees can make a huge difference in customer satisfaction. Ideally, employees should exhibit competence, a caring attitude, responsiveness, initiative, problem-solving ability, and goodwill. Service companies such as FedEx and Marriott empower their front-line personnel to spend up to $100 to resolve a customer problem.

Companies also try to demonstrate their service quality through *physical evidence* and *presentation.* A hotel will develop a look and style of dealing with customers that realizes its intended customer value proposition, whether it is cleanliness, speed, or some other benefit. Finally, service companies can choose among different *processes* to deliver their service. Restaurants have developed such different formats as cafeteria-style, fast-food, buffet, and candlelight service.

Service encounters are affected by several elements (see Figure 15.2). Consider a customer visiting a bank to get a loan (service X). The customer sees other customers waiting for this and other services. The customer also sees a physical environment consisting of a building, interior, equipment, and furniture. He or she sees bank personnel and deals with a loan officer. Not visible is a whole "backroom" production process and organization system that supports the visible business. Thus the service outcome, and whether or not people will remain loyal to a service provider, is influenced by a host of variables.[18]

In view of this complexity, Christian Gronroos has argued that service marketing requires not only external marketing, but also internal and interactive marketing (see

---

figure **15.2**

Elements in a Service Encounter

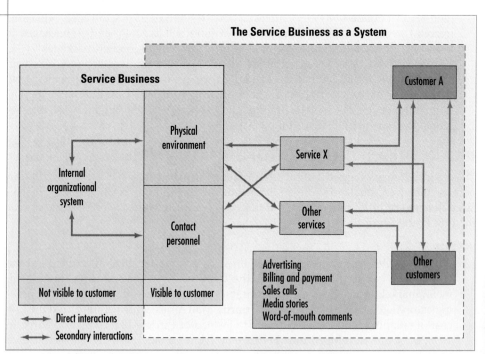

Source: Slightly modified from P. Eiglier and E. Langeard, "A Conceptual Approach to the Service Offering," in *Proceedings of the EAARM X Annual Conference*, ed. H. Hartvig Larsen and S. Heede (Copenhagen: Copenhagen School of Economics and Business Administration, 1981).

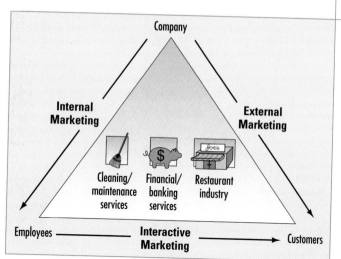

figure **15.3**

Three Types of Marketing
in Service Industries

Figure 15.3).[19] *External marketing* describes the normal work to prepare, price, distribute, and promote the service to customers. *Internal marketing* describes the work to train and motivate employees to serve customers well. Berry has argued that the most important contribution the marketing department can make is to be "exceptionally clever in getting everyone else in the organization to practice marketing."[20]

Radford Community Hospital   The Community Hospital in Radford, Illinois, set up a fund of $10,000 out of which it pays patients who have justified complaints ranging from cold food to overlong waits in the emergency room. Any money not paid out of the fund at the end of the year is divided among the hospital's employees. This plan has added a tremendous incentive for the staff to treat patients well. If there are 100 employees and no patients have to be paid by the end of the year, each employee gets a $100 bonus. In the first six months, the hospital had to pay out only $300 to patients.

Interactive marketing describes the employees' skill in serving the client. Because the client judges service not only by its *technical quality* (e.g., Was the surgery successful?) but also by its *functional quality* (e.g., Did the surgeon show concern and inspire confidence?),[21] service providers must deliver "high-touch" as well as "high-tech."[22] Consider Schwab.

Schwab.com   Charles Schwab, the nation's largest discount brokerage house, uses the Web to create an innovative combination of high-tech and high-touch services. One of the first major brokerage houses to provide online trading, Schwab today has 7.7 million accounts in its online trading network. It has avoided competing on price with low-priced competitors (e.g., Ameritrade.com) and instead has assembled the most comprehensive financial and company information resources to be found online. It offers account information and proprietary research from retail brokers; real-time quotes; an after-hours trading program; the Schwab learning center; live events; online chats with Customer Service representatives; a global investing service; and market updates delivered by e-mail. Schwab continues to lead its competitors by applying the three principles of superior service (online, via phone, and in local branch offices), innovative products, and discount prices.[23]

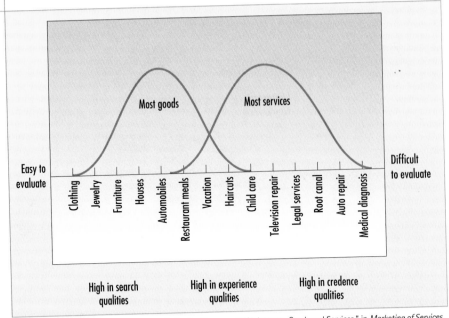

figure 15.4

Continuum of Evaluation for Different Types of Products

Source: Valarie A. Zeithaml, "How Consumer Evaluation Processes Differ between Goods and Services," in *Marketing of Services,* ed. James H. Donnelly and William R. George. Reprinted with permission of the American Marketing Association, 1981.

For some services, customers cannot judge the technical quality even after they have received the service. Figure 15.4 shows various products and services according to difficulty of evaluation.[24] At the left are goods high in *search qualities*—that is, characteristics the buyer can evaluate before purchase. In the middle are goods and services high in *experience qualities*—characteristics the buyer can evaluate after purchase. At the right are goods and services high in *credence qualities*—characteristics the buyer normally finds hard to evaluate even after consumption.[25]

Because services are generally high in experience and credence qualities, there is more risk in purchase. This has several consequences. First, service consumers generally rely on word of mouth rather than advertising. Second, they rely heavily on price, personnel, and physical cues to judge quality. Third, they are highly loyal to service providers who satisfy them.

Service companies face three tasks—increasing *competitive differentiation, service quality,* and *productivity.* Although these interact, we will examine each separately.

managing differentiation

Service marketers frequently complain about the difficulty of differentiating their services. The deregulation of several major service industries—communications, transportation, energy, banking—precipitated intense price competition. The success of budget-priced airlines has shown that many fliers care more about cost than service. The continued success of Charles Schwab in the discount brokerage service shows that many customers have little loyalty to the more established houses when they can save money. To the extent that customers view a service as fairly homogeneous, they care less about the provider than the price.

However, services can be differentiated. The alternative to price competition is to develop a differentiated offering, delivery, or image.

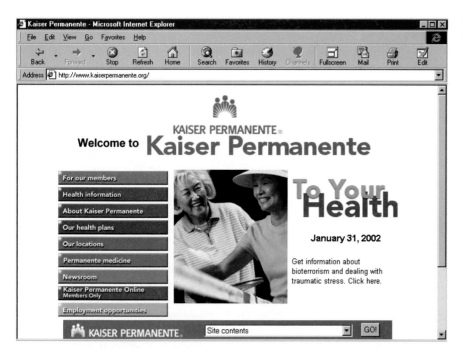

OFFERING   The offering can include innovative features. What the customer expects is called the *primary service package*. To this the provider can add *secondary service features*. In the airline industry, various carriers have introduced such secondary service features as movies, merchandise for sale, air-to-ground telephone service, and frequent-flier award programs. Marriott is setting up hotel rooms for high-tech travelers who need accommodations that will support computers, fax machines, and e-mail.

Many companies are using the Web to offer secondary service features that were never possible before:

> **Kaiser Permanente**   Like many health maintenance organizations (HMOs), Kaiser Permanente is seeking value-added services that will not break the bank. The largest HMO, with 8 million members in 11 states, in 1996 Kaiser rolled out a Web site called Kaiser Permanente Online that lets members register for office visits, e-mail questions to nurses and pharmacists (and get responses within 24 hours), participate in discussions monitored by health care professionals, and search for information in drug and health encyclopedias. Kaiser Permanente Online now has over 300,000 registered users.[26]

Sometimes the company achieves differentiation through the sheer range of its service offerings.

> **Bank of America**   The bank gets a new client who opens a checking and savings account. The banker mentions its low loan-interest rates, and the client subsequently takes out a loan. Not long after, the client is using a whole package of bank offerings, including a credit card, mutual fund, home mortgage, and auto and life insurance; but the bank's services do not stop there: It may notify the client of vacation opportunities, car leasing plans, and college loan programs, all as a result of the bank's deep knowledge of the customer's changing financial situation and requirements.

The major challenge is that most service offerings and innovations are easily copied. Still, the company that regularly introduces innovations will gain a succession of temporary advantages over competitors.

Marketing
MEMO

**Exceeding Customers'
Highest Hopes: A Service
Marketing Checklist**

Customers' expectations are the
true standards for judging service
quality. Berry and Parasuraman
propose that marketing managers
ask the following questions as
they seek to manage and exceed
expectations:

1. *Do we strive to present a realistic
   picture of our service to
   customers?* Do we always check
   the accuracy of our promotional
   messages prior to customers'
   exposure to them? Is there
   regular communication between
   employees who serve customers
   and those who make promises to
   customers? Do we assess the
   impact on customer expectations
   on cues such as price?

2. *Is performing the service right
   the first time a top priority in our
   company?* Do we stress to our
   employees that providing
   reliable service is an effective
   way of managing customers'
   expectations? Are our employees
   trained and rewarded for
   delivering error-free service? Do
   we regularly evaluate our service
   designs to identify and correct
   potential flaws?

3. *Do we communicate effectively
   with customers?* Do we
   periodically contact customers
   to ascertain their needs and let
   them know we appreciate their
   business? Do we train and
   require employees to
   demonstrate to customers that
   we care about and value them?
   continued...

Citigroup   Citigroup is respected and patronized because of its reputation for such innovations as automatic teller machines, nationwide banking, broad-spectrum financial accounts and credit cards, floating prime rates, and online banking.

Schneider National   Schneider National is the world's largest long-haul truckload freight carrier, with more than 40,000 bright orange trailers on the roads. Although the core benefit is to move freight from one location to another, Don Schneider is in the *customer solutions* business. His company is expert at providing a cost-minimizing trailer for each load. He offers service guarantees backed by monetary incentives for meeting tight schedules. He runs driver-training programs to improve driver performance. Dispatchers are assigned to large customers. Schneider was the first to introduce a computerized tracking system in each truck. Even painting the trucks orange was part of the branding strategy. If further innovations come into this industry, they will probably come from Schneider.

FASTER AND BETTER DELIVERY   A service company can differentiate itself by designing a better and faster delivery system. There are three levels of differentiation.[27] The first is *reliability:* Some suppliers are more reliable in their on-time delivery, order completeness, and order-cycle time. The second is *resilience:* Some suppliers are better at handling emergencies, product recalls, and answering inquiries. The third is *innovativeness*: Some suppliers create better information systems, introduce bar coding and mixed pallets, and in other ways help the customer.

Many distribution experts say that a company's money would be better spent on improving delivery performance than on advertising. They say that superior service performance is a more effective differentiator than image expenditures. Furthermore, it is harder for a competitor to duplicate a superior distribution system than to copy a competitor's advertising campaign.

Nordstrom   The Nordstrom department store chain, which began as a single shoe store in turn-of-the-century Seattle, prides itself on providing exceptional service. The company has a no-questions-asked return policy and free tailoring services for clothing items purchased in the store. Nordstrom's service is legendary: In his book *Thriving on Chaos*, Tom Peters tells the story of an executive who purchased two suits from Nordstrom before a business trip, but when he stopped in the following day to pick them up, they were not ready, as had been promised under Nordstrom's next-day alterations policy. When he arrived at his hotel the next day, he found a next-day air package from Nordstrom containing his suits, a gift of three silk ties, and a note of apology from the salesperson.[28]

Dial-A-Mattress   Napoleon Barragan started Dial-A-Mattress in 1976; by 1999, it had generated $80 million in annual sales. Customers can phone a toll-free number (1-800-Mattres) 24 hours a day, seven days a week, talk to a bedding consultant, have the right mattress delivered the same day, and receive a 30-day customer satisfaction guarantee trial period.

IMAGE   Service companies can also differentiate through symbols and branding. The Harris Bank of Chicago adopted the lion as its symbol and uses it on stationery, advertising, and even on the stuffed animals it offers to new depositors. The Harris lion confers an image of strength. Several hospitals have attained "megabrand" reputations for being the best in their field, such as the Mayo Clinic, Massachusetts General, and Sloan-Kettering. These hospitals could open clinics in other cities and attract patients on the strength of their brand reputation.

American Express is one of several highly branded service companies that have developed a successful international image.

American Express For years the charge-card division of American Express positioned itself as the Prince of Plastic. Ad lines such as "Membership Has Its Privileges" and "American Express: Don't Leave Home Without It" cultivated an affluent, upscale market consisting primarily of business professionals who could afford to pay off their Amex bill each month and pay high annual fees. In recent years, however, the company has needed to reinvent itself. Credit cards from Visa and Mastercard invaded Amex's turf in the 1980s and 1990s. Instead of prestige, customers now prefer value in the form of no-fee affinity credit cards with frequent-flier miles and other benefits. In an attempt to fight back, Amex has pushed out an astonishing number of new products, including new credit cards like the Blue Card aimed at upscale 25- to 35-year-olds. By April 2001, American Express Blue had 5.8 million cardholders, making it the fastest growing card portfolio at that time.[29]

managing service quality

The service quality of a firm is tested at each service encounter. If retail clerks are bored, cannot answer simple questions, or are visiting with each other while customers are waiting, customers will think twice about doing business again with that seller.

Customers form service expectations from past experiences, word of mouth, and advertising. Customers compare the *perceived service* with the *expected service*. If the perceived service falls below the expected service, customers are disappointed. If the perceived service meets or exceeds their expectations, they are apt to use the provider again. (See "Marketing Memo—Exceeding Customers' Highest Hopes: A Service Marketing Checklist.")

Parasuraman, Zeithaml, and Berry formulated a service-quality model that highlights the main requirements for delivering high service quality.[30] The model, shown in Figure 15.5, identifies five gaps that cause unsuccessful delivery:

1. *Gap between consumer expectation and management perception:* Management does not always correctly perceive what customers want. Hospital administrators may think that patients want better food, but patients may be more concerned with nurse responsiveness.
2. *Gap between management perception and service-quality specification:* Management might correctly perceive customers' wants but not set a performance standard. Hospital administrators may tell the nurses to give "fast" service without specifying it in minutes.
3. *Gap between service-quality specifications and service delivery:* Personnel might be poorly trained, or incapable or unwilling to meet the standard; or they may be held to conflicting standards, such as taking time to listen to customers and serving them fast.
4. *Gap between service delivery and external communications:* Consumer expectations are affected by statements made by company representatives and ads. If a hospital brochure shows a beautiful room, but the patient arrives and finds the room to be cheap and tacky looking, external communications have distorted the customer's expectations.
5. *Gap between perceived service and expected service:* This gap occurs when the consumer misperceives the service quality. The physician may keep visiting the patient to show care, but the patient may interpret this as an indication that something really is wrong.

The same researchers found five determinants of service quality. These are presented in order of importance.[31]

1. *Reliability:* The ability to perform the promised service dependably and accurately.
2. *Responsiveness:* The willingness to help customers and to provide prompt service.
3. *Assurance:* The knowledge and courtesy of employees and their ability to convey trust and confidence.
4. *Empathy:* The provision of caring, individualized attention to customers.
5. *Tangibles:* The appearance of physical facilities, equipment, personnel, and communication materials.

---

4. *Do we surprise customers during the service process?* Are our employees aware that the process of service delivery represents the prime opportunity to exceed customers' expectations? Do we take specific steps to encourage excellence during service delivery?

5. *Do our employees regard service problems as opportunities to impress customers, or as annoyances?* Do we prepare and encourage employees to excel in the service recovery process? Do we reward them for providing exceptional recovery service?

6. *Do we continuously evaluate and improve our performance against customers' expectations?* Do we perform consistently above the adequate service level? Do we capitalize on opportunities to exceed the desired service level?

Source: Excerpted from Leonard L. Berry and A. Parasuraman, *Marketing Services: Competing Through Quality* (New York: The Free Press, 1991), pp. 72–73. Also see Leonard L. Berry, *On Great Service: A Framework for Action* (New York: The Free Press, 1995), and his *Discovering the Soul of Service* (New York: The Free Press, 1999).

figure **15.5**
Service–Quality Model

Source: A. Parasuraman, Valarie A. Zeithaml, and Leonard L. Berry, "A Conceptual Model of Service Quality and Its Implications for Future Research," *Journal of Marketing* (Fall 1985): 44. Reprinted with permission of the American Marketing Association. The model is more fully discussed or elaborated in Valarie A. Zeithaml and Mary Jo Bitner, *Services Marketing* (New York: McGraw-Hill, 1996), ch. 2.

Various studies have shown that well-managed service companies share the following common practices: a strategic concept, a history of top-management commitment to quality, high standards, self-service technologies, systems for monitoring service performance and customer complaints, and an emphasis on employee satisfaction.

STRATEGIC CONCEPT   Top service companies are "customer obsessed." They have a clear sense of their target customers and their needs. They have developed a distinctive strategy for satisfying these needs.

TOP-MANAGEMENT COMMITMENT   Companies such as Marriott, Disney, and McDonald's have a thorough commitment to service quality. Their managements look not only at financial performance on a monthly basis, but also at service performance. Ray Kroc of McDonald's insisted on continually measuring each McDonald's outlet on its conformance to QSCV: quality, service, cleanliness, and value. Some companies insert a reminder along with employees' paychecks: BROUGHT TO YOU BY THE CUSTOMER. Sam Walton of Wal-Mart required the following employee pledge: "I solemnly swear and declare that every customer that comes within 10 feet of me, I will smile, look them in the eye, and greet them, so help me Sam."

HIGH STANDARDS   The best service providers set high service-quality standards. Citibank aims to answer phone calls within 10 seconds and customer letters within 2 days. The standards must be set *appropriately* high. A 98 percent accuracy standard may sound good, but it would result in FedEx losing 64,000 packages a day; 6 misspelled words on each page of a book; 400,000 misfilled prescriptions daily; and unsafe drinking water 8 days a year. One can distinguish between those companies offering "merely good" service and those offering "breakthrough" service, aimed at being 100 percent defect-free.[32]

SELF–SERVICE TECHNOLOGIES (SSTS)   Many person-to-person service interactions are being replaced by self-service technologies.[33] To the traditional vending machines we can add Automatic Teller Machines (ATMs), self-pumping at gas stations, self-checkout at hotels, self-ticket purchasing on the Internet, and self-customization of products on the Internet. Consider Myalert.com, which helps people quit smoking. Its 16,000 registered users will receive wireless alerts at the times of the day each is most likely to reach for a cigarette. The message: "Come on! You can do it!"

Not all SSTs improve service quality, but they have the potential of making service transactions more accurate, convenient, and faster. Every company needs to think about how it might improve its service using SSTs. Companies would be smart to enable customers to call the company when they need more information than the SST provides. Online hotel reservation Web sites often include a "Call Me" button. If the customer clicks on it, a service rep will immediately phone the person to answer a question. Even banks miss an opportunity to use their ATMs. A customer might draw money from the ATM and see the message: "Call 1-800-123-4567 to earn more interest"; but the customer goes home and forgets to call. The ATM's message could have been: "You have $6,000 over the required balance."

> Imagine an auto insurance company wanting to improve its claim service and assistance. Normally, a driver involved in an accident has to wait for a claim adjuster to show up, assess the damage, and offer a settlement. Instead, the insurance company's Web site could include step-by-step guidelines telling the insured

MyAlert.com provides access to any number of services that users can perform themselves.

figure **15.6**

Tracking Customer Service
Performance

person what to do. It would list the kinds of documents needed by the police, and by the hospital; suggest the names of reliable medical and legal professionals; and list reputable car rental firms and repair shops in the customer's area. Claim forms would be available to fill out on the Web site. The claims adjuster, when he visits the driver, can use a handheld mobile computing device and digital camera to photograph the damage, send a streaming video back to headquarters, get approval, and print out a check for repairing the car on the spot.

MONITORING SYSTEMS   Top firms audit service performance, both their own and competitors', on a regular basis. They collect *voice of the customer (VOC) measurements* to probe customer satisfiers and dissatisfiers. They use comparison shopping, ghost shopping, customer surveys, suggestion and complaint forms, service-audit teams, and letters to the president. General Electric sends out 700,000 response cards a year asking households to rate its service people's performance. Citibank checks continuously on measures of ART (accuracy, responsiveness, and timeliness). The First Chicago Bank employs a weekly Performance Measurement Program charting its performance on a large number of customer-sensitive issues. Figure 15.6 shows a typical chart to track the bank's speed in answering customer service phone inquiries. It will take action whenever performance falls below the minimum acceptable level. It also raises its performance goal over time.

When designing customer feedback mechanisms, marketers need to ask the right questions, as United Parcel Service discovered:

United Parcel Service   UPS always assumed that on-time delivery was its customers' paramount concern, and based its definition of quality on the results of time-and-motion studies. To get packages to customers faster, UPS would factor in such details as how long it took elevators to open on certain city apartment blocks. Surveys deluged customers with questions about whether they were pleased with delivery time and whether they thought the company could be any speedier. When the company began asking broader questions regarding how it could improve its service, it discovered that what customers wanted most was face-to-face contact with drivers. If drivers were less hurried and would answer questions, customers might get practical advice on shipping.[34]

Services can be judged on *customer importance* and *company performance. Importance-performance analysis* is used to rate the various elements of the service bundle and identify what actions are required. Table 15.1 shows how customers rated 14 service elements (attributes) of an automobile dealer's service department on importance and performance. For example, "Job done right the first time" (attribute 1) received a mean

table **15.1**

Attribute Number	Attribute Description	Mean Importance Rating[a]	Mean Performance Rating[b]
1	Job done right the first time	3.83	2.63
2	Fast action on complaints	3.63	2.73
3	Prompt warranty work	3.60	3.15
4	Able to do any job needed	3.56	3.00
5	Service available when needed	3.41	3.05
6	Courteous and friendly service	3.41	3.29
7	Car ready when promised	3.38	3.03
8	Perform only necessary work	3.37	3.11
9	Low prices on service	3.29	2.00
10	Clean up after service work	3.27	3.02
11	Convenient to home	2.52	2.25
12	Convenient to work	2.43	2.49
13	Courtesy buses and cars	2.37	2.35
14	Send out maintenance notices	2.05	3.33

Customer Importance and Performance Ratings for an Auto Dealership

[a]Ratings obtained from a four-point scale of "extremely important" (4), "important" (3), "slightly important" (2), and "not important" (1).

[b]Ratings obtained from a four-point scale of "excellent" (4), "good" (3), "fair" (2), and "poor" (1). A "no basis for judgment" category was also provided.

importance rating of 3.83 and a mean performance rating of 2.63, indicating that customers felt it was highly important but not performed well.

The ratings of the 14 elements are displayed in Figure 15.7 and divided into four sections. Quadrant A shows important service elements that are not being performed at the desired levels; they include elements 1, 2, and 9. The dealer should concentrate on improving the service department's performance on these elements. Quadrant B shows important service elements that are being performed well; the company needs to maintain the high performance. Quadrant C shows minor service elements that are being delivered in a mediocre way but do not need any attention. Quadrant D shows that a minor service element, "Send out maintenance notices," is being performed in an excellent manner. Perhaps the company should spend less on sending out maintenance notices and reallocate the savings toward improving the company's performance on important elements. The analysis can be enhanced by checking on the competitors' performance levels on each element.[35]

SATISFYING CUSTOMER COMPLAINTS   Studies of customer dissatisfaction show that customers are dissatisfied with their purchases about 25 percent of the time but that only about 5 percent complain. The other 95 percent either feel complaining is not worth the effort, or they do not know how or to whom to complain.

Of the 5 percent who complain, only about 50 percent report a satisfactory problem resolution. Yet the need to resolve a customer problem in a satisfactory manner is critical. On average, a satisfied customer tells three people about a good product experience, but the average dissatisfied customer gripes to 11 people. If each of them tells still other people, the number of people exposed to bad word of mouth may grow exponentially.

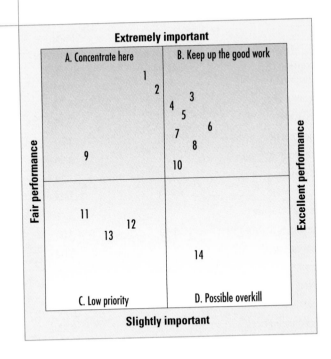

figure **15.7**

Importance–Performance
Analysis

Customers whose complaints are satisfactorily resolved often become more company-loyal than customers who were never dissatisfied. About 34 percent of customers who register major complaints will buy again from the company if their complaint is resolved, and this number rises to 52 percent for minor complaints. If the complaint is resolved quickly, between 52 percent (major complaints) and 95 percent (minor complaints) will buy again from the company.[36]

Every complaint is a gift if handled well. Tax and Brown have found that companies that encourage disappointed customers to complain—and also empower employees to remedy the situation on the spot—achieve higher revenues and greater profits than companies that do not have a systematic approach for addressing service failures.[37] Tax and Brown found that companies that are effective at resolving complaints:

- Develop hiring criteria and training programs that take into account employees' service-recovery role.
- Develop guidelines for service recovery that focus on achieving fairness and customer satisfaction.
- Remove barriers that make it difficult for customers to complain, while developing effective responses, which may include empowering employees to provide compensation for the failure. Pizza Hut prints its toll-free number on all pizza boxes. When a customer complains, Pizza Hut sends voice mail to the store manager, who must call the customer within 48 hours and resolve the complaint. Sometimes when a Virgin Atlantic Airways flight arrives several hours late at Heathrow Airport in London, CEO Richard Branson may personally come to apologize and distribute tickets for future flights.
- Maintain customer and product databases that let the company analyze types and sources of complaints and adjust its policies.

Hyatt hotels gets high marks on many of these criteria.

Hyatt Hotels   Hyatt Hotels excels at answering complaints in an extraordinarily short time. One business customer, for example, checked into the Denver Hyatt but did not like his room. He turned on the television and was greeted by a screen with the Hyatt customer survey. Using the TV remote, he punched in his evaluations. To his surprise and delight, within five minutes of receiving the electronic communication, the hotel manager called him to say that because the hotel was entirely booked and the room could not be changed, the guest could expect a hospitality gift for his inconvenience. By systematically analyzing customer surveys, Hyatt managers alert employees to problems. Whether it is a vending machine that eats quarters or a stale smell that greets a guest upon first entering a room, Hyatt can quickly channel service requests to thoroughly trained personnel who can resolve them.[38]

SATISFYING EMPLOYEES AS WELL AS CUSTOMERS   Excellent service companies know that positive employee attitudes will promote stronger customer loyalty. Sears found a high correlation between customer satisfaction, employee satisfaction, and store profitability. In companies such as Hallmark, John Deere, and Four Seasons Hotels, employees exhibit real pride in their companies.

Given the importance of positive employee attitudes, service companies must attract the best employees they can find. They need to market a career rather than just a job. They must design a sound training program and provide support and rewards for good performance. They can use the intranet, internal newsletters, daily reminders, and employee roundtables to reinforce customer-centered attitudes.

It is important to audit employee job satisfaction regularly. Karl Albrecht observed that unhappy employees can be "terrorists." Rosenbluth and Peters, in *The Customer Comes Second*, go so far as to say that the company's employees, not the company's customers, have to be made number one if the company hopes to truly satisfy its customers.[39]

Yet a company must be careful in training its employees to be friendly.

Safeway Stores   In the 1990s, supermarket chain Safeway instituted "Superior Service," an unusually aggressive program to build employee friendliness toward customers. Among the rules: Make eye contact with all customers, smile, greet each other, offer samples of products, make suggestions about other possible items to purchase. To ensure compliance, "mystery shoppers" secretly grade workers. Those who receive poor grades are sent to a training program. Although surveys show that customers are pleased with the program, many employees admit to being stressed out and several have quit in protest over the plan. "It's so artificial, it's unreal," said one second-generation Safeway employee who quit her job as cashier after 20 years with the chain, partly out of frustration with the Superior Service program. Several female employees even filed sexual harassment suits against Safeway, charging that the forced smiles were misinterpreted and led to unwelcome advances from male customers.[40]

managing productivity

Service firms are under great pressure to keep costs down and increase productivity. There are seven approaches to improving service productivity:

1. Have service providers work more skillfully. The company can hire and foster more skillful workers through better selection and training.
2. Increase the quantity of service by surrendering some quality. Doctors working for some HMOs have moved toward handling more patients and giving less time to each patient.
3. "Industrialize the service" by adding equipment and standardizing production. Levitt recommended that companies adopt a "manufacturing attitude" toward producing services, as represented by McDonald's assembly-line approach to fast-food retailing, culminating in the "technological hamburger."[41]

4. Reduce or make obsolete the need for a service by inventing a product solution, the way the wash-and-wear shirt reduced the need for commercial laundries, and certain antibiotics reduced the need for tuberculosis sanitariums.

5. Design a more effective service. How-to-quit-smoking clinics may reduce the need for expensive medical services later on. Hiring paralegal workers reduces the need for more expensive legal professionals.

6. Present customers with incentives to substitute their own labor for company labor. Banks have turned their customers into tellers; FedEx has turned customers into shippers; gas stations have turned customers into gas pumpers; and the phone company has turned customers into operators.

7. Harness the power of technology to give customers access to better service and make service workers more productive. Companies that use their Web sites to empower customers can lessen workloads, capture valuable data, and increase the value of their businesses.

See "Marketing for the New Economy: The Technologies of Customer Empowerment," for some real-world examples.

Technology has great power to make service workers more productive. For instance:[42]

San Diego Medical Center   Respiratory therapists at the University of California at San Diego Medical Center now carry miniature computers in their coat pockets. In the past, therapists had to wait at the nurses' station for patient records. Today, therapists call up the information on handheld computers, which pluck the data from a central computer. As a result, they can spend more time working directly with patients.

Companies must avoid pushing productivity so hard that they reduce perceived quality. Some methods lead to too much standardization and rob the customer of customized service; "high-touch" is replaced by "high-tech." Burger King challenged McDonald's by running a "Have it your way" campaign, where customers could get a "customized" hamburger, even though this offer reduced Burger King's productivity somewhat.

managing product support services

Thus far we have focused on service industries. No less important are product-based industries that must provide a service bundle. Manufacturers of equipment—small appliances, office machines, tractors, mainframes, airplanes—all have to provide *product support services*. In fact, product support service is becoming a major battleground for competitive advantage. Some equipment companies, such as Caterpillar Tractor and John Deere, make over 50 percent of their profits from these services. In the global marketplace, companies that make a good product but provide poor local service support are seriously disadvantaged. When Subaru entered the Australian market, it contracted to use the Australian Volkswagen dealer network to provide parts and service. Firms that provide high-quality service outperform their less service-oriented competitors.

The company must define customer needs carefully in designing its service support program. Customers have three specific worries:[43]

- They worry about reliability and *failure frequency*. A farmer may tolerate a combine that will break down once a year, but not two or three times a year.
- Customers worry about *downtime duration*. The longer the downtime, the higher the cost. The customer counts on the seller's *service dependability*—the seller's ability to fix the machine quickly, or at least provide a loaner.[44]
- Customers worry about *out-of-pocket costs* of *maintenance and repair*. How much does the customer have to spend on regular maintenance and repair costs?

A buyer takes all these factors into consideration in choosing a vendor. The buyer tries to estimate the **life-cycle cost**, which is the product's purchase cost plus the discounted

marketing for the **new economy**

The Technologies of Customer Empowerment

Internet-enabled applications do not have to be sophisticated or complex to drive major change in a business model. E-mail is proof of this fact. Real value is added by enabling customers to get information and interact with one another, and with a Web site's data. Here are some ways to engage the customer with an Internet site.

Content Creation

By allowing your customers to create their own content, you increase the value of your business and lessen your workload. Personalized applications let customers increase the worth of the product. Shared knowledge bases lead to increased learning and faster cycle times. *Real-world examples*: GeoCities (now owned by Yahoo!) gives users a free home page and then—for a fee—lets them upgrade that page or add a small business e-commerce site.

Audible.com's home page.

Ace Hardware's site features a "paint estimator" that determines how many gallons of paint to buy for a given project.

Collaboration

Using collaboration tools, customers can create and learn together. Forums and bulletin boards facilitate online communities. Conferencing and messaging tools enable globalization of activities. Group games and rating systems can provide information for e-commerce site owners. Polling, surveys, and collaborative filtering facilitate one-to-one marketing. *Real-world example*: E-Trade's game, E-Trade: The Game, lets players experience high-stakes trading and the thrill of competition without risking a dime—while at the same time transmitting information about product preferences and customer habits back to the company.

Teaching

Just-in-time learning and point-of-need information distribution, where information and instruction is made ready at the customer's demand, pay off for businesses because they improve and support the user's performance. If these services are performed correctly, users will soon depend on them and return. *Real-world examples*: Phoenix University demonstrates that real-world educational experiences can be duplicated online with diverse and specific classes, self-paced learning, and an instructor who is only an e-mail away. MIT may have started a new trend in 2001 when it decided to make materials for nearly all its courses freely available on the Internet through its OpenCourseWare program.

Commerce

Online transactions that create friction-free commerce should be the ultimate goal of any e-commerce site. If a site can offer a wide selection of merchandise, knowledgeable sales assistance, and no hassles or lines, it will be a desirable alternative to the mall. *Real-world examples:* Clothing cataloger Lands' End developed an e-commerce site with unique features that make it easy to shop for apparel and accessories. Shoppers can enter their measurements to create a 3-D model of themselves and then "try on" clothing using the site's Virtual Model. The site also uses interactive technology to provide real-time customer service via a chat window, where customers' questions are answered by a human customer service representative.

New Platforms

Soon personal assistants, cell phones, and dashboard computers will have the power and mobility to control all types of applications. New information appliances and smart cards offer great promise for customer-controlled applications. *Real-world examples:* Audible.com introduced a handheld mobile reader for its line of audio books. AirFlash makes applications for wireless devices that provide the user with content based on location, such as restaurant guides, driving directions, yellow pages, and entertainment information for a single city.

Source: Adapted from "The Technologies of Customer Empowerment," *New Media*, October 1998, p. 36.

marketing **insight**

Offering Guarantees to Promote Sales

All sellers are legally responsible for fulfilling a buyer's normal or reasonable expectations. *Warranties* are formal statements of expected product performance by the manufacturer. Products under warranty can be returned to the manufacturer or designated repair center for repair, replacement, or refund. Warranties, whether expressed or implied, are legally enforceable. Many sellers offer either *general guarantees* or *specific guarantees.* A company such as Procter & Gamble promises general or complete satisfaction without being more specific—"If you are not satisfied for any reason, return for replacement, exchange, or refund." Other companies offer specific guarantees and in some cases, extraordinary guarantees:

- General Motors' Saturn car division will accept the return of a new car within 30 days if the buyer is not satisfied.
- Hampton Inn motels guarantees a restful night or the customer does not have to pay.
- L.L. Bean promises its customers "100 percent satisfaction in every way, forever." If a customer buys a pair of boots and two months later finds that they scuff easily, L.L. Bean will refund the money or replace them.
- A. T. Cross guarantees its Cross pens and pencils for life. The customer mails the pen to A. T. Cross (mailing envelopes are provided at stores selling Cross writing instruments), and the pen is repaired or replaced at no charge.
- FedEx won its place in the minds and hearts of mailers by promising next-day delivery "absolutely, positively by 10:30 A.M."
- Oakley Millwork, a Chicago supplier of construction industry products, guaranteed that if any item in its catalog was

unavailable for immediate delivery, the customer would get the item free.
- BBBK, a pest extermination company, offers the following guarantee: (1) no payment until all pests are eradicated; (2) if the effort fails, the customer receives a full refund to pay the next exterminator; (3) if guests on the client's premises spot a pest, BBBK will pay for the guest's room and send an apology letter; and (4) if the client's facility is closed down, BBBK will pay all fines, lost profits, and $5,000.

Guarantees reduce the buyer's perceived risk. They suggest that the product is of high quality and that the company and its service performance are dependable. All this enables the company to charge a higher price than a competitor who is not offering an equivalent guarantee.

Guarantees are most effective in two situations. The first is where the company or the product is not well-known. For example, a company might sell a liquid claiming to remove the toughest spots. A "money-back guarantee if not satisfied" would provide buyers with some confidence in purchasing the product. The second situation is where the product's quality is superior to the competition. The company can gain by guaranteeing superior performance, knowing that competitors cannot match its guarantee.

Sources: "More Firms Pledge Guaranteed Service," *Wall Street Journal,* July 17, 1991, pp. B1, B6; Barbara Ettore, "Phenomenal Promises Mean Business," *Management Review* (March 1994): 18–23. Also see Christopher W. L. Hart, *Extraordinary Guarantees* (New York: Amacom, 1993); Sridhar Moorthy and Kannan Srinivasan, "Signaling Quality with a Money-Back Guarantee: The Role of Transaction Costs," *Marketing Science* 14, no. 4 (1995): 442–46.

cost of maintenance and repair less the discounted salvage value. Buyers ask for hard data in choosing among vendors.

The importance of reliability, service dependability, and maintenance vary. A one-computer office will need higher product reliability and faster repair service than an office where other computers are available if one breaks down. An airline needs 100 percent reliability in the air. Where reliability is important, manufacturers or service providers can offer guarantees to promote sales. (See "Marketing Insight: Offering Guarantees to Promote Sales.")

To provide the best support, a manufacturer must identify the services customers value most and their relative importance. In the case of expensive equipment, manufacturers offer *facilitating services* such as installation, staff training, maintenance and repair services, and financing. They may also add *value-augmenting services.* Herman Miller, a major office furniture company, offers the Herman Miller promise to buyers: (1) five-year product warranties; (2) quality audits after project installation; (3) guaranteed move-in dates; (4) trade-in allowances on systems products.

A manufacturer can offer and charge for product support services in different ways. One specialty organic-chemical company provides a standard offering plus a basic level of services. If the customer wants additional services, it can pay extra or increase its annual purchases to a higher level, in which case additional services would be included. As another alternative, many companies offer *service contracts* with variable lengths and different deductibles so that customers can choose the service level they want beyond the basic service package.

Companies need to plan product design and service-mix decisions in tandem. Design and quality-assurance managers should be part of the new-product development team. Good product design will reduce the amount of subsequent servicing needed. The Canon home copier uses a disposable toner cartridge that greatly reduces the need for service calls. Kodak and 3M designed equipment allowing the user to "plug in" to a central diagnostic facility that performs tests, locates the trouble, and fixes the equipment over the telephone lines.

postsale service strategy

The quality of customer service departments varies greatly. At one extreme are departments that simply transfer customer calls to the appropriate person or department for action, with little follow-up. At the other extreme are departments eager to receive customer requests, suggestions, and even complaints and handle them expeditiously.

In providing service, most companies progress through a series of stages. Manufacturers usually start out by running their own parts-and-service department. They want to stay close to the equipment and know its problems. They also find it expensive and time-consuming to train others, and discover that they can make good money running the parts-and-service business. As long as they are the only supplier of the needed parts, they can charge a premium price. In fact, many equipment manufacturers price their equipment low and compensate by charging high prices for parts and service. (This explains why competitors manufacture the same or similar parts and sell them to customers or intermediaries for less.)

Over time, manufacturers switch more maintenance and repair service to authorized distributors and dealers. These intermediaries are closer to customers, operate in more locations, and can offer quicker service. Manufacturers still make a profit on the parts but leave the servicing profit to intermediaries. Still later, independent service firms emerge. Over 40 percent of auto-service work is now done outside franchised automobile dealerships by independent garages and chains such as Midas Muffler, Sears, and JCPenney. Independent service organizations handle mainframes, telecommunications equipment, and a variety of other equipment lines. They typically offer a lower price or faster service than the manufacturer or authorized intermediaries.

Ultimately, some large customers handle their own maintenance and repair. A company with several hundred personal computers, printers, and related equipment might find it cheaper to have its own service personnel on-site. These companies typically press the manufacturer for a lower price, because they are providing their own services.

major trends in product support service

Lele has noted the following major trends in the customer service area:[45]

1. Equipment manufacturers are building more reliable and more easily fixable equipment. One reason is the shift from electromechanical equipment to electronic equipment, which has fewer breakdowns and is more repairable. Companies are adding modularity and disposability to facilitate self-servicing.

2. Customers are becoming more sophisticated about buying product support services and are pressing for "services unbundling." They want separate prices for each service element and the right to select the elements they want.

3. Customers increasingly dislike having to deal with a multitude of service providers handling different types of equipment. Some third-party service organizations now service a greater range of equipment.[46]

4. *Service contracts* (also called *extended warranties*), in which sellers agree to provide free mainten-ance and repair services for a specified period of time at a specified contract price, may di-minish in importance. Some new car warranties now cover 100,000 miles before servicing. The increase in disposable or never-fail equipment makes customers less inclined to pay from 2 per-cent to 10 percent of the purchase price every year for a service.

5. Customer service choices are increasing rapidly, and this is holding down prices and profits on service. Equipment manufacturers increasingly have to figure out how to make money on their equipment, independent of service contracts.

6. Companies are increasing the quality of their *call centers* and their *customer service representa-tives* (CSRs). By handling phone calls more efficiently, they will improve their service, reduce complaints, and extend customer longevity.

summary

1. A service is any act or performance that one party can offer to another that is essentially intangible and does not result in the ownership of anything. It may or may not be tied to a physical product.

2. Services are intangible, inseparable, variable, and perish-able. Each characteristic poses challenges and requires cer-tain strategies. Marketers must find ways to give tangibility to intangibles; to increase the productivity of service providers; to increase and standardize the quality of the service provided; and to match the supply of services dur-ing peak and nonpeak periods with market demand.

3. Service industries lagged behind manufacturing firms in adopting and using marketing concepts and tools, but this sit-uation has now changed. Service marketing strategy calls not only for external marketing but also for internal marketing to motivate employees and interactive marketing to emphasize the importance of both "high-tech" and "high-touch."

4. The service organization faces three tasks in marketing: (1) It must differentiate its offer, delivery, or image; (2) it must manage service quality in order to meet or exceed customers' expectations; (3) it must manage worker productivity by get-ting its employees to work more skillfully, increasing the quantity of service by surrendering some quality, industrial-izing the service, inventing new product solutions, design-ing more effective services, presenting customers with incen-tives to substitute their own labor for company labor, or using technology to save time and money.

5. Even product-based companies must provide postpurchase service. To provide the best support, a manufacturer must identify the services that customers value most and their rel-ative importance. The service mix includes both presale services (facilitating and value-augmenting services) and postsale services (customer service departments, repair and maintenance services).

applications

marketing debate – is service marketing different from product marketing?

Some services marketers vehemently maintain that services mar-keting is fundamentally different from product marketing and that different skills are involved. Some traditional product mar-keters disagree, saying "good marketing is good marketing."

Take a position: Product and services marketing are fundamentally different versus Product and services marketing are highly related.

marketing and advertising

1. CIGNA offers a range of financial services for individuals, businesses, and corporate employees. The ad in Figure 1 focuses on the benefits of buying the company's life, acci-dent, and disability insurance.

   a. Who is the target market for the CIGNA insurance prod-ucts featured in this ad? What does CIGNA do in this ad to make its services seem more tangible to this market?

   b. What elements of perishability and variability might CIGNA have to consider when marketing its services?

   c. What postsale service issues would be particularly vital for CIGNA customers?

2. Concierge.com, the travel planning Web site featured in the ad in Figure 2, provides informational services as "the online home of *Condé Nast Traveler*."

   a. Can Concierge.com be considered a pure tangible good or a pure service? Does it fall in between the two extremes? What are the implications for its marketing strategy?

   b. Why is inseparability a particularly important issue for online service providers like Concierge.com?

   c. How might Concierge.com use self-service technology to enhance its offering?

Figure 1

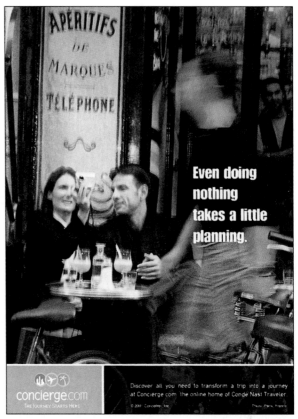

Figure 2

online marketing today

As discussed earlier, Schwab.com combines high-touch and high-tech services to allow its brokerage customers to place trades, research securities, or access account information at any hour. Geoff Penney, chief information officer, says the company's strategy emphasizes "people and technology working together" to deliver service "across all of our customer touch points . . . in our investment centers, on the phone, on the Web site, and with our software products." On the high-tech side, Schwab continually upgrades its technology for different customer segments, including special software for active traders.

On the high-touch side, the company focuses on hiring, training, and motivating its skilled workforce.[47]

To see Schwab's online approach to service, visit its home page at *www.schwab.com*. Note the different links for customers and noncustomers. Also look at the array of information available on the home page. How does Schwab make its services seem more tangible on this site? What aspects of the site would be particularly valuable to a very active trader? To a first-time investor? What are the implications for Schwab's service strategy?

you're the marketer: sonic pda marketing plan

Marketing Plan Pro

All marketers need to develop a service strategy when preparing their marketing plans. If they are marketing an intangible product, they will want to consider how to manage customers' expectations and satisfaction; if they are marketing something tangible, they will want to create suitable support services.

You are planning product support services for Sonic's new personal digital assistant. Start by looking over the information and decisions already documented in your marketing plan.

Then respond to the following questions to map your service strategy (indicating, where necessary, any additional data or research you may need):

- What support services do buyers of PDA products want and need? Review what you know about this market and its needs; also think about what Sonic's competitors are offering.
- How can Sonic manage gaps between expected and perceived service to satisfy customers?

- What postsale service arrangements must Sonic make to handle repairs and other issues that arise after the purchase?
- What kinds of guarantees should Sonic offer to be competitive?
- What type of internal marketing does Sonic need to be able to implement its service strategy?

Consider how your service strategy will support Sonic's overall marketing efforts. Summarize your recommendations in a written marketing plan or, if you are using *Marketing Plan Pro* software, enter the information under the Product Offering heading and the Service section under the Marketing Mix heading.

notes

1. Leonard L. Berry, *Discovering the Soul of Service: The Nine Drivers of Sustainable Business Success* (New York: The Free Press, 1999); Fred Wiersema, ed., *Customer Service: Extraordinary Results at Southwest Airlines, Charles Schwab, Lands' End, American Express, Staples, and USAA* (New York: HarperBusiness, 1998).

2. Diane Brady, "Why Service Stinks," *BusinessWeek,* October 23, 2000, pp. 119–28.

3. Ronald Henkoff, "Service Is Everybody's Business," *Fortune*, June 27, 1994, pp. 48–60.

4. G. Lynn Shostack, "Breaking Free from Product Marketing," *Journal of Marketing* (April 1977): 73–80; Leonard L. Berry, "Services Marketing Is Different," *Business* (May–June 1980): 24–30; Eric Langeard, John E. G. Bateson, Christopher H. Lovelock, and Pierre Eiglier, *Services Marketing: New Insights from Consumers and Managers* (Cambridge, MA: Marketing Science Institute, 1981); Karl Albrecht and Ron Zemke, *Service America! Doing Business in the New Economy* (Homewood, IL: Dow Jones-Irwin, 1986); Karl Albrecht, *At America's Service* (Homewood, IL: Dow Jones-Irwin, 1988); Benjamin Scheider and David E. Bowen, *Winning the Service Game* (Boston: Harvard Business School Press, 1995).

5. John R. Johnson, "Service at a Price," *Industrial Distribution* (May 1998): 91–94.

6. Theodore Levitt, "Production-Line Approach to Service," *Harvard Business Review* (September–October 1972): 41–42.

7. Further classifications of services are described in Christopher H. Lovelock, *Services Marketing*, 3rd ed. (Upper Saddle River, NJ: Prentice Hall, 1996). Also see John E. Bateson, *Managing Services Marketing: Text and Readings*, 3rd ed. (Hinsdale, IL: Dryden, 1995).

8. Theodore Levitt, "Marketing Intangible Products and Product Intangibles," *Harvard Business Review* (May–June 1981): 94–102; Berry, "Services Marketing Is Different."

9. "Dun & Bradstreet Files for Separation into 2 Companies," *Dow Jones News Service*, June 27, 2000.

10. Lewis P. Carbone and Stephan H. Haeckel, "Engineering Customer Experiences," *Marketing Management* (Winter) 1994.

11. "Mastering the Blues," *Times-Picayue*, March, 18, 2001, p. 1.

12. Carbone and Haeckel, "Engineering Customer Experiences"; "Creating a Corporate Culture," *PR Newswire*, May 17, 1999.

13. G. Lynn Shostack, "Service Positioning Through Structural Change," *Journal of Marketing* (January 1987): 34–43.

14. W. Earl Sasser, "Match Supply and Demand in Service Industries," *Harvard Business Review* (November–December 1976): 133–40.

15. Carol Krol, "Case Study: Club Med Uses E-mail to Pitch Unsold, Discounted Packages," *Advertising Age*, December 14, 1998, p. 40; <www.clubmed.com>.

16. Anthony Palazzo, "Postal Service Sees Shipping Customers in Internet Retailers Trying to Capitalize on Needs of High-Tech Marketers: 'Snail Mail' Meets E-Mail," *Wall Street Journal*, March 20, 1998, p. B7; Bill McAllister, "FedEx Delivers Blow to Ad Campaign by Postal Service," *Washington Post*, December 9, 1998, p. C11; Ira Teinowitz, "Postal Service Tries Image of Innovation," *Advertising Age*, October 19, 1988, p. 6.

17. B. H. Booms and M. J. Bitner, "Marketing Strategies and Organizational Structures for Service Firms," in *Marketing of Services*, ed. J. Donnelly and W. R. George (Chicago: American Marketing Association, 1981), pp. 47–51.

18. Keaveney has identified more than 800 critical behaviors of service firms that cause customers to switch services. These behaviors fit into 8 categories ranging from price, inconvenience, and core service failure to service encounter failure, failed employee response to service failures, and ethical problems. See Susan M. Keaveney, "Customer Switching Behavior in Service Industries: An Exploratory Study," *Journal of Marketing* (April 1995): 71–82. See also Michael D. Hartline and O. C. Ferrell, "The Management of Customer-Contact Service Employees: An Empirical Investigation," *Journal of Marketing* (October 1996): 52–70; Lois A. Mohr, Mary Jo Bitner, and Bernard H. Booms, "Critical Service Encounters: The Employee's Viewpoint," *Journal of Marketing* (October 1994): 95–106; Linda L. Price, Eric J. Arnould, and Patrick Tierney, "Going to Extremes: Managing Service Encounters and Assessing Provider Performance," *Journal of Marketing* (April 1995): 83–97; Jaishankar Ganesh, Mark J. Arnold, and Kristy E. Reynolds "Understanding the Customer Base of Service Providers: An Examination of the Differences Between Switchers and Sayers," *Journal of Marketing* 64 (July 2000): 65–87.

19. Christian Gronroos, "A Service Quality Model and Its Marketing Implications," *European Journal of Marketing* 18, no. 4 (1984): 36–44. Gronroos's model is one of the most thoughtful contributions to service-marketing strategy.

20. Leonard Berry, "Big Ideas in Services Marketing," *Journal of Consumer Marketing* (Spring 1986): 47–51. See also Walter E. Greene, Gary D. Walls, and Larry J. Schrest, "Internal Marketing: The Key to External Marketing Success," *Journal of Services Marketing* 8, no. 4 (1994): 5–13; John R. Hauser, Duncan I. Simester, and Birger Wernerfelt, "Internal Customers and Internal Suppliers," *Journal of Marketing Research* (August 1996): 268–80; Jagdip Singh, "Performance Productivity and Quality of Frontline Employees in Service Organizations," *Journal of Marketing* 64 (April 2000), pp. 15–34.

21. Gronroos, "Service Quality Model," 38–39; Michael D. Hartline, James G. Maxham III, and Daryl O. McKee, "Corridors of Influence in the Dissemination of Customer-Oriented Strategy to Customer Contact Service Employees," *Journal of Marketing* (April 2000): 35–50.

22. Philip Kotler and Paul N. Bloom, *Marketing Professional Services* (Upper Saddle River, NJ: Prentice Hall, 1984).

23. "USA: Charles Schwab Web Site Ready for Questioning," *Reuters English News Service*, May 22, 2001.

24. Valarie A. Zeithaml, "How Consumer Evaluation Processes Differ between Goods and Services," in *Marketing of Services*, eds. Donnelly and George, pp. 186–90.

25. Amy Ostrom and Dawn Iacobucci, "Consumer Trade-offs and the Evaluation of Services," *Journal of Marketing* (January 1995): 17–28.

26. Heather Green, "A Cyber Revolt in Health Care," *BusinessWeek*, October 19, 1998, pp. 154–56; Laura Landro, "Health Groups Push 'Information Therapy' to Help Treat Patients," *Wall Street Journal*, February 2, 2001, p. B1.

27. William C. Copacino, *Supply Chain Management* (Boca Raton, FL: St. Lucie Press, 1997).

28. Michael Fickes, "Word of Mouth Advertising," *Swimming Pool/Spa Age*, May 30, 1999.

29. Suzanne Bidlake, "John Crewe, American Express Blue Card," *Advertising Age International*, December 14, 1998, p. 10; Sue Beenstock, "Blue Blooded," *Marketing*, June 4, 1998, p. 14; Pamela Sherrid, "A New Class Act at AMEX," *U.S. News & World Report*, June 23, 1997, pp. 39–40; "AMEX Blue Totaling 5.8 Million Cardholders," *CardFAX*, April 25, 2001, p. 1.

30. A. Parasuraman, Valarie A. Zeithaml, and Leonard L. Berry, "A Conceptual Model of Service Quality and Its Implications for Future Research," *Journal of Marketing* (Fall 1985): 41–50. See also Susan J. Devlin and H. K. Dong, "Service Quality from the Customers' Perspective," *Marketing Research: A Magazine of Management & Applications* (Winter 1994): 4–13; William Boulding, Ajay Kalra, and Richard Staelin, "A Dynamic Process Model of Service Quality: From Expectations to Behavioral Intentions," *Journal of Marketing Research* (February 1993): 7–27; Michael K. Brady and J. Joseph Crorin Jr., "Some New Thoughts on Conceptualizing Perceived Service Quality," *Journal of Marketing* 65 (July 2001): 34–49.

31. Leonard L. Berry and A. Parasuraman, *Marketing Services: Competing Through Quality* (New York: The Free Press, 1991), p. 16.

32. James L. Heskett, W. Earl Sasser Jr., and Christopher W. L. Hart, *Service Breakthroughs* (New York: The Free Press, 1990).

33. Mary Jo Bitner, "Self-Service Technologies: What Do Customers Expect?" *Marketing Management* (Spring 2001): 10–11; Matthew L. Meuter, Amy L. Ostrom, Robert J. Roundtree, and Mary Jo Bitner, "Self-Service Technologies: Understanding Customer Satisfaction with Technology Based Service Encounters," *Journal of Marketing* 64 (July 2000): 50–64.

34. David Greising, "Quality: How to Make It Pay," *BusinessWeek*, August 8, 1994, pp. 54–59.

35. John A. Martilla and John C. James, "Importance-Performance Analysis," *Journal of Marketing* (January 1977): 77–79.

36. John Goodman, *Technical Assistance Research Program* (TARP), U.S. Office of Consumer Affairs Study on Complaint Handling in America, 1986; Albrecht and Zemke, *Service America!*; Berry and Parasuraman, *Marketing Services*; Roland T. Rust, Bala Subramanian, and Mark Wells, "Making Complaints a Management Tool," *Marketing Management* 1, no. 3 (1992): 41–45; Stephen S. Tax, Stephen W. Brown, and Murali Chandrashekaran, "Customer Evaluations of Service Complaint Experiences: Implications for Relationship Marketing," *Journal of Marketing* (April 1998): 60–76.

37. Stephen S. Tax and Stephen W. Brown, "Recovering and Learning from Service Failure," *Sloan Management Review* (Fall 1998): 75–88.

38. Robert Hiebeler, Thomas B. Kelly, and Charles Ketteman, *Best Practices: Building Your Business with Customer-Focused Solutions* (New York: Arthur Andersen/Simon & Schuster, 1997), pp. 184–85.

39. Hal F. Rosenbluth and Diane McFerrin Peters, *The Customer Comes Second* (New York: William Morrow, 1992).

40. Kirstin Downey Grimsley, "Service with a Forced Smile; Safeway's Courtesy Campaign Also Elicits Some Frowns," *Washington Post*, October 18, 1998, p. A1; Suzy Fox, "Emotional Value: Creating Strong Bonds with Your Customers," *Personnel Psychology*, April 1, 2001, pp. 230–34.

41. Theodore Levitt, "Production-Line Approach to Service," *Harvard Business Review* (September–October 1972): 41–52; also see his "Industrialization of Service," *Harvard Business Review* (September–October 1976): 63–74.

42. Nilly Landau, "Are You Being Served?" *International Business* (March 1995): 38–40.

43. Milind M. Lele and Uday S. Karmarkar, "Good Product Support Is Smart Marketing," *Harvard Business Review* (November–December): 124–32.

44. For recent research on the effects of delays in service on service evaluations, see Shirley Taylor, "Waiting for Service: The Relationship between Delays and Evaluations of Service," *Journal of Marketing* (April 1994): 56–69; Michael K. Hui and David K. Tse, "What to Tell Consumers in Waits of Different Lengths: An Integrative Model of Service Evaluation," *Journal of Marketing* (April 1996): 81–90.

45. Milind M. Lele, "How Service Needs Influence Product Strategy," *Sloan Management Review* (Fall 1986): 63–70.

46. However, see Ellen Day and Richard J. Fox, "Extended Warranties, Service Contracts, and Maintenance Agreement: A Marketing Opportunity?" *Journal of Consumer Marketing* (Fall 1985): 77–86.

47. Mary Schroeder, "Schwab Tech Group Focuses on Client Support," *Securities Industry News*, October 29, 2001; <www.securitiesindustry.com>.

16

developing price strategies and programs

In this chapter, we will address the following questions:

- How should a price be set on a product or service for the first time?
- How should the price be adapted to meet varying circumstances and opportunities?
- When should the company initiate a price change, and how should it respond to a competitor's price change?

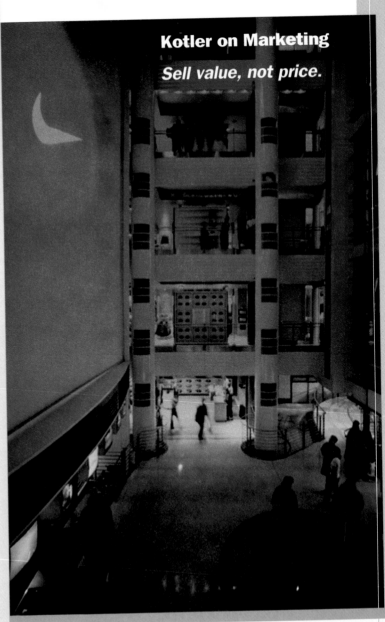

Kotler on Marketing

Sell value, not price.

P*rice is the one element of the marketing mix that produces revenue; the other elements produce costs. Prices are the easiest marketing-mix element to adjust; product features, channels, and even promotion take more time. Price also communicates to the market the company's intended value positioning of its product or brand.*

Today companies are wrestling with a number of difficult pricing tasks:

- *How to respond to aggressive price cutters*
- *How to price the same product when it goes through different channels*
- *How to price the same product in different countries*
- *How to price an improved product while still selling the previous version*

■ How to price different components of an offering when the customer wants to make his own choice of components

Price is not just a number on a tag or an item, it goes by many names:

> Price is all around us. You pay rent for your apartment, tuition for your education, and a fee to your physician or dentist. The airline, railway, taxi, and bus companies charge you a fare; the local utilities call their price a rate; and the local bank charges you interest for the money you borrow. The price for driving your car on Florida's Sunshine Parkway is a toll, and the company that insures your car charges you a premium. The guest lecturer charges an honorarium to tell you about a government official who took a bribe to help a shady character steal dues collected by a trade association. Clubs or societies to which you belong may make a special assessment to pay unusual expenses. Your regular lawyer may ask for a retainer to cover her services. The "price" of an executive is a salary, the price of a salesperson may be a commission, and the price of a worker is a wage. Finally, although economists would disagree, many of us feel that income taxes are the price we pay for the privilege of making money.[1]

Throughout most of history, prices were set by negotiation between buyers and sellers. "Bargaining" is still a sport in some areas. Setting one price for all buyers is a relatively modern idea that arose with the development of large-scale retailing at the end of the nineteenth century. F. W. Woolworth, Tiffany and Co., John Wanamaker, and others advertised a "strictly one-price policy," because they carried so many items and supervised so many employees.

Today the Internet is partially reversing the fixed pricing trend. On Priceline.com, the customer states the price he wants to pay for an airline ticket, hotel, or mortgage and Priceline checks whether any seller is willing to meet the customer's price. Online auction sites like eBay.com facilitate variable pricing on thousands of items—from refurbished computers to antique trains. Volume-aggregating sites combine the orders of many customers and press the supplier for a deeper discount.

Traditionally, price has operated as the major determinant of buyer choice. This is still the case in poorer nations, among poorer groups, and with commodity-type products. Although nonprice factors have become more important in recent decades, price still remains one of the most important elements determining market share and profitability. Consumers and purchasing agents have more access to price information and price discounters. Consumers put pressure on retailers to lower their prices. Retailers put pressure on manufacturers to lower their prices. The result is a marketplace characterized by heavy discounting and sales promotion.

Many companies do not handle pricing well. They make these common mistakes: Pricing is too cost-oriented; price is not revised often enough to capitalize on market changes; price is set independent of the rest of the marketing mix rather than as an intrinsic element of market-positioning strategy; and price is not varied enough for different product items, market segments, distribution channels, and purchase occasions.

Companies do their pricing in a variety of ways. In small companies, prices are often set by the boss. In large companies, pricing is handled by division and product-line managers. Even here, top management sets general pricing objectives and policies and often approves the prices proposed by lower levels of management. In industries where pricing is a key factor (aerospace, railroads, oil companies), companies will often establish a pricing department to set or assist others in determining appropriate prices. This department reports to the marketing department, finance department, or top management. Others who exert an influence on pricing include sales managers, production managers, finance managers, and accountants.

setting the price

A firm must set a price for the first time when it develops a new product, when it introduces its regular product into a new distribution channel or geographical area, and when it enters bids on new contract work. The firm must decide where to position its product on quality and price. In some markets, such as the auto market, as many as eight price points can be found:

Segment	*Example*
Ultimate	Rolls-Royce
Gold Standard	Mercedes-Benz
Luxury	Audi
Special Needs	Volvo
Middle	Buick
Ease/Convenience	Ford Escort
Me Too, but Cheaper	Hyundai
Price Alone	Kia

Marriott Hotels is good at developing different brands for different price points: Marriott Vacation Club—Vacation Villas (highest price), Marriott Marquis (high price), Marriott (high-medium price), Renaissance (medium-high price), Courtyard (medium price), Towne Place Suites (medium-low price), and Fairfield Inn (low price).

There can be competition between price-quality segments. Figure 16.1 shows nine price-quality strategies. The diagonal strategies 1, 5, and 9 can all coexist in the same market; that is, one firm offers a high-quality product at a high price, another offers an average-quality product at an average price, and still another offers a low-quality product at a low price. All three competitors can coexist as long as the market consists of three groups of buyers: those who insist on quality, those who insist on price, and those who balance the two.

Strategies 2, 3, and 6 are ways to attack the diagonal positions. Strategy 2 says, "Our product has the same high quality as product 1 but we charge less." Strategy 3 says the same thing and offers an even greater saving. If quality-sensitive customers believe these competitors, they will sensibly buy from them and save money (unless firm 1's product has acquired snob appeal).

Positioning strategies 4, 7, and 8 amount to overpricing the product in relation to its quality. The customers will feel "taken" and will probably complain or spread bad word of mouth about the company.

figure **16.1**

Nine Price–Quality Strategies

		Price		
		High	Medium	Low
Product Quality	High	1. Premium strategy	2. High-value strategy	3. Super-value strategy
	Medium	4. Overcharging strategy	5. Medium-value strategy	6. Good-value strategy
	Low	7. Rip-off strategy	8. False economy strategy	9. Economy strategy

figure **16.2**

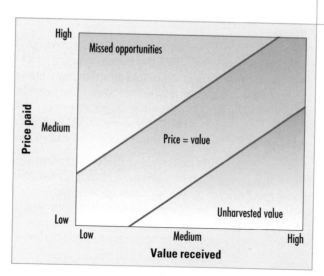

Price Should Align
with Value

The company must set its price in relation to the value delivered and perceived by the customer. If the price is higher than the value received, the company will miss potential profits; if the price is lower than the value received, the company will fail to harvest potential profits (see Figure 16.2).

The firm has to consider many factors in setting its pricing policy. We will describe a six-step procedure: (1) selecting the pricing objective; (2) determining demand; (3) estimating costs; (4) analyzing competitors' costs, prices, and offers; (5) selecting a pricing method; and (6) selecting the final price (see Figure 16.3).

step 1: selecting the pricing objective

The company first decides where it wants to position its market offering. The clearer a firm's objectives, the easier it is to set price. A company can pursue any of five major objectives through pricing: survival, maximum current profit, maximum market share, maximum market skimming, or product-quality leadership.

Companies pursue *survival* as their major objective if they are plagued with overcapacity, intense competition, or changing consumer wants. As long as prices cover variable costs and some fixed costs, the company stays in business. Survival is a short-run objective; in the long run, the firm must learn how to add value or face extinction.

Many companies try to set a price that will *maximize current profits*. They estimate the demand and costs associated with alternative prices and choose the price that produces maximum current profit, cash flow, or rate of return on investment. This strategy assumes that the firm has knowledge of its demand and cost functions; in reality, these are difficult to estimate. In emphasizing current performance, the company may sacrifice long-run performance by ignoring the effects of other marketing-mix variables, competitors' reactions, and legal restraints on price.

Some companies want to *maximize their market share*. They believe that a higher sales volume will lead to lower unit costs and higher long-run profit. They set the lowest price, assuming the market is price-sensitive. Texas Instruments (TI) practices this **market-penetration pricing**. TI will build a large plant, set its price as low as possible, win a large market share, experience falling costs, and cut its price further as costs fall. The following conditions favor setting a low price: (1) The market is highly price-sensitive, and a low price stimulates market growth; (2) production and distribution costs fall with accumulated production experience; and (3) a low price discourages actual and potential competition.

figure **16.3**

Setting Pricing Policy

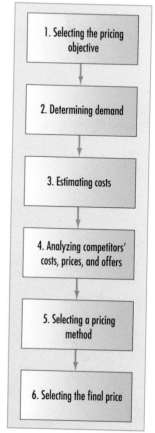

1. Selecting the pricing objective

2. Determining demand

3. Estimating costs

4. Analyzing competitors' costs, prices, and offers

5. Selecting a pricing method

6. Selecting the final price

Companies unveiling a new technology favor setting high prices to "skim" the market. Sony is a frequent practitioner of *market-skimming pricing.*

Sony   When Sony introduced the world's first high-definition television (HDTV) to the Japanese market in 1990, the high-tech sets cost $43,000. These televisions were purchased by customers who could afford to pay a high price for the new technology. Sony rapidly reduced the price over the next three years to attract new buyers, and by 1993 a 28-inch HDTV cost a Japanese buyer just over $6,000. In 2001, a Japanese consumer could buy a 40-inch HDTV for about $2,000, a price many could afford. In this way, Sony skimmed the maximum amount of revenue from the various segments of the market.[2]

Market skimming makes sense under the following conditions: (1) A sufficient number of buyers have a high current demand; (2) the unit costs of producing a small volume are not so high that they cancel the advantage of charging what the traffic will bear; (3) the high initial price does not attract more competitors to the market; (4) the high price communicates the image of a superior product.

A company might aim to be the *product-quality leader* in the market. Consider Maytag.

Maytag   Maytag has long built high-quality washing machines and priced them higher than competitors' products (its ads featured the Maytag repairman asleep at the phone because no customers ever call for service). Now, in a change of strategy, Maytag builds on its premium-brand strengths with innovative features and benefits. The objective is to get consumers to buy Maytag appliances with attractive features at a premium price, even though their old machines are still working. To lure the price-sensitive customer, Maytag ran commercials pointing out that washers are custodians of what is often a $400 load of clothes, making them worth the higher price tag. Maytag's new Neptune washers, for example, sell for double what most other washers cost, yet company marketers argue that they use less water and electricity and prolong the life of clothing by being less abrasive.[3]

Maytag's homepage presents its "corporate family of brands."

marketing **insight**

Power Pricers: How Smart Companies Use Price to Achieve Business Strategies

Executives continually complain that pricing is a big headache—and one that is getting worse by the day. Many firms have thrown up their hands with "strategies" like this: "We determine our costs and take our industry's traditional margins." Others have a different attitude: They use price as a key strategic tool. These "power pricers" have discovered the highly leveraged effect of price on the bottom line.

- *Pricing and the value perspective:* Pharmaceutical company Glaxo introduced its ulcer medication Zantac to attack market incumbent Tagamet. The conventional wisdom was that, as the "second one in," Glaxo should price Zantac 10 percent below Tagamet. CEO Paul Girolam knew that Zantac was superior to Tagamet in terms of fewer drug interactions and side effects and more convenient dosing. Glaxo introduced Zantac at a significant price premium over Tagamet and still gained the market-leader position.
- *Customizing price and service based on segment value:* Bugs Burger's Bug Killer price was about five times that of other

firms that do battle with rodents on a commercial property. Bugs got his price premium because he focused on a particularly quality-sensitive segment of the market (hotels and restaurants) and gave them what they valued most: guaranteed pest elimination. Superior value to this chosen segment guided his pricing and enabled him to train and compensate service technicians in a way that motivated them to deliver superior service.

- *Customizing price based on segment cost and competitive situation:* Progressive Insurance collects and analyzes loss data in automobile insurance better than anyone else. Its understanding of what it costs to service various types of customers enables it to serve the lucrative high-risk customer no one else wants to insure. Free of competition and armed with a solid understanding of costs, Progressive makes good profits serving this customer base.

Source: Adapted from Robert J. Dolan and Hermann Simon, "Power Pricers," *Across the Board* (May 1997): 18–19.

Nonprofit and public organizations may adopt other pricing objectives. A university aims for *partial cost recovery*, knowing that it must rely on private gifts and public grants to cover the remaining costs. A nonprofit hospital may aim for full cost recovery in its pricing. A nonprofit theater company may price its productions to fill the maximum number of theater seats. A social service agency may set a service price geared to the income of the client.

Whatever the specific objective, businesses that use price as a strategic tool will profit more than those who simply let costs or the market determine their pricing. (See "Marketing Insight: Power Pricers: How Smart Companies Use Price to Achieve Business Strategies.")

step 2: determining demand

Each price will lead to a different level of demand and therefore have a different impact on a company's marketing objectives. The relation between alternative prices and the resulting current demand is captured in a demand curve (see Figure 16.4). In the normal case, demand and price are inversely related: the higher the price, the lower the demand. In the case of prestige goods, the demand curve sometimes slopes upward. A perfume company raised its price and sold more perfume rather than less! Some consumers take the higher price to signify a better product. However, if the price is too high, the level of demand may fall.

PRICE SENSITIVITY   The demand curve shows the market's probable purchase quantity at alternative prices. It sums the reactions of many individuals who have different price sensitivities. The first step in estimating demand is to understand what affects price sensitivity. Generally speaking, customers are most price-sensitive to products that cost a lot or are bought frequently. They are less price-sensitive to low-cost items or items they buy infrequently. They are also less price-sensitive when price is only a small

figure **16.4**

Inelastic and Elastic
Demand

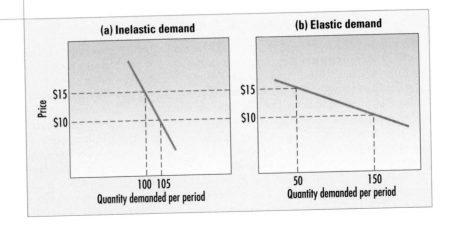

part of the total cost of obtaining, operating, and servicing the product over its lifetime. A seller can charge a higher price than competitors and still get the business if the company can convince the customer that it offers the lowest *total cost of ownership* (TCO).

Companies, of course, prefer to work with customers who are less price-sensitive. Tom Nagle offers the following list of factors associated with lower price sensitivity:

- The product is more distinctive
- Buyers are less aware of substitutes
- Buyers cannot easily compare the quality of substitutes
- The expenditure is a smaller part of the buyer's total income
- The expenditure is small compared to the total cost of the end product
- Part of the cost is borne by another party
- The product is used in conjunction with assets previously bought
- The product is assumed to have more quality, prestige, or exclusiveness
- Buyers cannot store the product[4]

On the other hand, the impact of the Internet has been to increase customers' price sensitivity. In buying a specific book online, for example, a customer can compare the prices offered by over two dozen online bookstores by just clicking mysimon.com. These prices can differ by as much as 20 percent. The Internet increases the opportunity for price-sensitive buyers to find and favor lower-price sites. At the same time, many buyers are not that price-sensitive. McKinsey conducted a study and found that 89 percent of Internet customers visited only one book site, 84 percent visited only one toy site, and 81 percent visited only one music site, which indicates that there is less price-comparison shopping taking place on the Internet than is possible.

Companies need to understand the price sensitivity of their customers and prospects and the trade-offs people are willing to make between price and product characteristics. In the words of marketing consultant Kevin Clancy, those who target only the price-sensitive are "leaving money on the table." Consider Green Mountain Power.

Green Mountain Energy Company   Green Mountain, a Vermont-based electric power company, has shown how a commodity, electric energy, can be brand-differentiated and price-differentiated. Green Mountain produces "green" energy in three grades: green (Eco-Smart), greener (EnviroBlend), and greenest (Nature's Choice). Each is blended differently from natural gas, hydro, wind, and solar energy. The greener the brand, the higher the kilowatt per hour price. Green Mountain conducted extensive marketing research and uncovered a large segment of prospects who would pay more for "greener" energy. It started an e-commerce site in 1997 called GreenMountain.com (now called Green Mountain Energy Company and head-quartered in Austin, Texas) that is currently selling electricity to more than 100,000 customers in Texas, Pennsylvania, New Jersey, and California.[5]

ESTIMATING DEMAND CURVES   Most companies make some attempt to measure their demand curves. They can use different methods.

The first involves statistically analyzing past prices, quantities sold, and other factors to estimate their relationships. The data can be longitudinal (over time) or cross-sectional (different locations at the same time). Building the appropriate model and fitting the data with the proper statistical techniques calls for considerable skill.

The second approach is to conduct price experiments. Bennett and Wilkinson systematically varied the prices of several products sold in a discount store and observed the results.[6] An alternative approach is to charge different prices in similar territories to see how sales are affected. Still another approach is to use the Internet. An e-business could test the impact of a 5 percent price increase by quoting a higher price to every fortieth visitor to compare the purchase response. However, it must do this carefully and not alienate customers, as happened when Amazon price-tested discounts of 30 percent, 35 percent, and 40 percent for DVD buyers, only to find that those receiving the 30 percent discount were upset.[7]

The third approach is to ask buyers to state how many units they would buy at different proposed prices,[8] but buyers might understate their purchase intentions at higher prices to discourage the company from setting higher prices.

In measuring the price–demand relationship, the market researcher must control for various factors that will influence demand. The competitor's response will make a difference. Also, if the company changes other marketing-mix factors besides price, the effect of the price change itself will be hard to isolate. Nagle presents an excellent summary of the various methods for estimating price sensitivity and demand.[9]

PRICE ELASTICITY OF DEMAND   Marketers need to know how responsive, or elastic, demand would be to a change in price. Consider the two demand curves in Figure 16.4. With demand curve (a), a price increase from $10 to $15 leads to a relatively small decline in demand from 105 to 100. With demand curve (b), the same price increase leads to a substantial drop in demand from 150 to 50. If demand hardly changes with a small change in price, we say the demand is *inelastic*. If demand changes considerably, demand is *elastic*. The higher the elasticity, the greater the volume growth with a 1 percent price reduction.

Demand is likely to be less elastic under the following conditions: (1) There are few or no substitutes or competitors; (2) buyers do not readily notice the higher price; (3) buyers are slow to change their buying habits; (4) buyers think the higher prices are justified. If demand is elastic, sellers will consider lowering the price. A lower price will produce more total revenue. This makes sense as long as the costs of producing and selling more units does not increase disproportionately.[10]

The effects of not considering the needs of customers for whom demand is most elastic is illustrated in the following case.

New York's Metropolitan Transit Authority   In 1997, the governor of New York announced that in the following year New York City subway riders would be able to purchase daily, weekly, or monthly passes. Riders who bought passes would also benefit from a discounted fare; for the monthly pass, the benefit kicked in if the pass was used at least 47 times. Yet a *Barron's* journalist pointed out that the special fare did not benefit those whose demand was most elastic, suburban off-peak riders who use the subway the least. Here is how he segmented New York City's subway riders in terms of price elasticity: Commuters' demand curve is perfectly inelastic; no matter what

figure **16.5**

Cost per Unit at Different
Levels of Production
per Period

**(a) Cost behavior in
a fixed-size plant**

Cost per unit

SRAC

1,000

Quantity produced per day

**(b) Cost behavior over
different-size plants**

Cost per unit

1 2 3 4 SRAC

LRAC

1,000 2,000 3,000 4,000

Quantity produced per day

happens to the fare, these people must get to work and get back home. There are also commuters who live in the city and who might use the subway for other activities if the fare were lowered. Their demand is more elastic. Suburban off-peak riders' demand is the most elastic.[11]

Price elasticity depends on the magnitude and direction of the contemplated price change. It may be negligible with a small price change and substantial with a large price change. It may differ for a price cut versus a price increase, and there may be a *price indifference band* within which price changes have little or no effect. A McKinsey pricing study estimated that the price indifference band can range as large as 17 percent for mouthwash, 13 percent for batteries, 9 percent for small appliances, and 2 percent for certificates of deposit.

Finally, long-run price elasticity may differ from short-run elasticity. Buyers may continue to buy from a current supplier after a price increase, but they may eventually switch suppliers. Here demand is more elastic in the long run than in the short run, or the reverse may happen: Buyers may drop a supplier after being notified of a price increase but return later. The distinction between short-run and long-run elasticity means that sellers will not know the total effect of a price change until time passes.

step 3: estimating costs

Demand sets a ceiling on the price the company can charge for its product. Costs set the floor. The company wants to charge a price that covers its cost of producing, distributing, and selling the product, including a fair return for its effort and risk.

TYPES OF COSTS AND LEVELS OF PRODUCTION A company's costs take two forms, fixed and variable. **Fixed costs** (also known as **overhead**) are costs that do not vary with production or sales revenue. A company must pay bills each month for rent, heat, interest, salaries, and so on, regardless of output.

Variable costs vary directly with the level of production. For example, each hand calculator produced by Texas Instruments involves a cost of plastic, microprocessing chips, packaging, and the like. These costs tend to be constant per unit produced. They are called variable because their total varies with the number of units produced.

Total costs consist of the sum of the fixed and variable costs for any given level of production. **Average cost** is the cost per unit at that level of production; it is equal to total costs divided by production. Management wants to charge a price that will at least cover the total production costs at a given level of production.

To price intelligently, management needs to know how its costs vary with different levels of production. Take the case in which a company such as TI has built a fixed-size plant to produce 1,000 hand calculators a day. The cost per unit is high if few units are produced per day. As production approaches 1,000 units per day, average cost falls. The reason is that the fixed costs are spread over more units. Average cost increases after 1,000 units, because the plant becomes inefficient: Workers have to queue for machines, machines break down more often, and workers get in each other's way (see Figure 16.5.[a]).

If TI believes it can sell 2,000 units per day, it should consider building a larger plant. The plant will use more efficient machinery and work arrangements, and the unit cost of producing 2,000 units per day will be less than the unit cost of producing 1,000 units per day. This is shown in the long-run average cost curve in Figure 16.5 (b). In fact, a 3,000-capacity plant would be even more efficient according to Figure 16.5 (b), but a 4,000-daily production plant would be less efficient because of increasing diseconomies of scale: There are too many workers to manage, and paperwork slows things down. Figure 16.5 (b) indicates that a 3,000-daily production plant is the optimal size if demand is strong enough to support this level of production.

ACCUMULATED PRODUCTION Suppose TI runs a plant that produces 3,000 hand calculators per day. As TI gains experience producing hand calculators, its methods

figure **16.6**

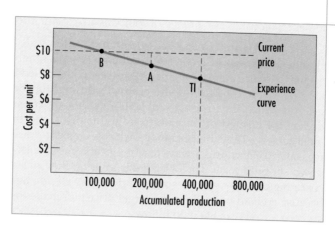

Cost per Unit as a
Function of Accumulated
Production:
The Experience Curve

improve. Workers learn shortcuts, materials flow more smoothly, procurement costs fall. The result, as Figure 16.6 shows, is that average cost falls with accumulated production experience. Thus the average cost of producing the first 100,000 hand calculators is $10 per calculator. When the company has produced the first 200,000 calculators, the average cost has fallen to $9. After its accumulated production experience doubles again to 400,000, the average cost is $8. This decline in the average cost with accumulated production experience is called the experience curve or **learning curve.**

Now suppose three firms compete in this industry, TI, A, and B. TI is the lowest-cost producer at $8, having produced 400,000 units in the past. If all three firms sell the calculator for $10, TI makes $2 profit per unit, A makes $1 per unit, and B breaks even. The smart move for TI would be to lower its price to $9. This will drive B out of the market, and even A will consider leaving. TI will pick up the business that would have gone to B (and possibly A). Furthermore, price-sensitive customers will enter the market at the lower price. As production increases beyond 400,000 units, TI's costs will drop still further and faster and more than restore its profits, even at a price of $9. TI has used this aggressive pricing strategy repeatedly to gain market share and drive others out of the industry.

Experience-curve pricing nevertheless carries major risks. Aggressive pricing might give the product a cheap image. The strategy also assumes that the competitors are weak. Finally, the strategy leads the company into building more plants to meet demand while a competitor innovates a lower-cost technology and obtains lower costs than the market-leader company, which is now stuck with the old technology.

Most experience-curve pricing has focused on manufacturing costs, but all costs, including marketing costs, can be improved on. If three firms are each investing a large sum of money in telemarketing, the firm that has used it the longest might achieve the lowest costs. This firm can charge a little less for its product and still earn the same return, all other costs being equal.[12]

DIFFERENTIATED MARKETING OFFERS   Today's companies try to adapt their offers and terms to different buyers. Thus a manufacturer will negotiate different terms with different retail chains. One retailer may want daily delivery (to keep stock lower) while another may accept twice-a-week delivery in order to get a lower price. The manufacturer's costs will differ with each chain, and so will its profits. To estimate the real profitability of dealing with different retailers, the manufacturer needs to use **activity-based cost (ABC) accounting** instead of standard cost accounting.[13]

ABC accounting tries to identify the real costs associated with serving each customer. Both variable and overhead costs must be tagged back to each customer. Companies that

figure **16.7**

The Three Cs Model for Price Setting

fail to measure their costs correctly are not measuring their profit correctly. They are likely to misallocate their marketing effort. Identifying the true costs arising in a customer relationship also enables a company to explain its charges to the customer.

TARGET COSTING   Costs change with production scale and experience. They can also change as a result of a concentrated effort by designers, engineers, and purchasing agents to reduce them. The Japanese use a method called **target costing**.[14] They use market research to establish a new product's desired functions. Then they determine the price at which the product will sell, given its appeal and competitors' prices. They deduct the desired profit margin from this price, and this leaves the target cost they must achieve. They then examine each cost element—design, engineering, manufacturing, sales. They consider ways to reengineer components, eliminate functions, and bring down supplier costs. The objective is to bring the final cost projections into the target cost range. If they cannot succeed, they may decide against developing the product because it could not sell for the target price and make the target profit. When they can succeed, profits are likely to follow.

step 4: analyzing competitors' costs, prices, and offers

Within the range of possible prices determined by market demand and company costs, the firm must take the competitors' costs, prices, and possible price reactions into account. The firm should first consider the nearest competitor's price. If the firm's offer contains positive differentiation features not offered by the nearest competitor, their worth to the customer should be evaluated and added to the competitor's price. If the competitor's offer contains some features not offered by the firm, their worth to the customer should be evaluated and subtracted from the firm's price. Now the firm can decide whether it can charge more, the same, or less than the competitor. The firm must be aware, however, that competitors can change their prices in reaction to the price set by the firm.

step 5: selecting a pricing method

Given the three Cs—the customers' demand schedule, the cost function, and competitors' prices—the company is now ready to select a price. Figure 16.7 summarizes the three major considerations in price setting. Costs set a floor to the price. Competitors' prices and the price of substitutes provide an orienting point. Customers' assessment of unique product features establishes the ceiling price.

Companies select a pricing method that includes one or more of these three considerations. We will examine seven price-setting methods: markup pricing, target-return pricing, perceived-value pricing, value pricing, going-rate pricing, auction-type pricing, and group pricing.

MARKUP PRICING   The most elementary pricing method is to add a standard **markup** to the product's cost. Construction companies submit job bids by estimating the total project cost and adding a standard markup for profit. Lawyers and accountants typically price by adding a standard markup on their time and costs.

Suppose a toaster manufacturer has the following costs and sales expectations:

Variable cost per unit	$ 10
Fixed cost	300,000
Expected unit sales	50,000

The manufacturer's unit cost is given by:

$$\text{Unit cost} = \text{variable cost} + \frac{\text{fixed cost}}{\text{unit sales}} = \$10 + \frac{\$300,000}{50,000} = \$16$$

Now assume the manufacturer wants to earn a 20 percent markup on sales. The manufacturer's markup price is given by:

$$\text{Markup price} = \frac{\text{unit cost}}{(1 - \text{desired return on sales})} = \frac{\$16}{1 - 0.2} = \$20$$

The manufacturer would charge dealers $20 per toaster and make a profit of $4 per unit. The dealers in turn will mark up the toaster. If dealers want to earn 50 percent on their selling price, they will mark up the toaster to $40. This is equivalent to a cost markup of 100 percent.

Markups are generally higher on seasonal items (to cover the risk of not selling), specialty items, slower-moving items, items with high storage and handling costs, and demand-inelastic items, such as prescription drugs. In the case of prescription drugs, generic (non-brand-name) drugs command an extraordinarily high markup:

Generic Drugs Drugstores and pharmacies are marking up the price of some generics by more than 1,000 percent. For example, stores charge an average of $18.08 for a prescription of the generic version of the antipsychotic drug Haldol, 2,800 percent more than the $.62 cost the generic manufacturer charges. A prescription for the generic version of Zovirax, an antiviral drug, sold at pharmacies for an average of $61.64, more than eight times the manufacturer's price of $7.22. Not only do pharmacies pocket a handsome profit, but they look like good guys when they encourage customers to use a generic to save money. Indeed, the generic is still cheaper than the brand-name counterpart. In 1999, a prescription for the generic version of the anti-anxiety drug Xanax cost an average of $17.23, versus $58.70 for the name-brand product, and the generic version of ulcer medication Zantac averaged $42.19 per prescription, versus $96.75 for the branded drug.[15]

Does the use of standard markups make logical sense? Generally, no. Any pricing method that ignores current demand, perceived value, and competition is not likely to lead to the optimal price. Markup pricing works only if the marked-up price actually brings in the expected level of sales.

Companies introducing a new product often price it high hoping to recover their costs as rapidly as possible, but this strategy could be fatal if a competitor is pricing low. This happened to Philips, the Dutch electronics manufacturer, in pricing its videodisc players. Philips wanted to make a profit on each player. Japanese competitors priced low and succeeded in building their market share rapidly, which in turn pushed down their costs substantially.

Still, markup pricing remains popular for a number of reasons. First, sellers can determine costs much more easily than they can estimate demand. By tying the price to cost, sellers simplify the pricing task. Second, where all firms in the industry use this pricing method, prices tend to be similar. Price competition is therefore minimized, which would not be the case if firms paid attention to demand variations. Third, many people feel that cost-plus pricing is fairer to both buyers and sellers. Sellers do not take advantage of buyers when the latter's demand becomes acute, and sellers earn a fair return on investment.

TARGET–RETURN PRICING In **target-return pricing**, the firm determines the price that would yield its target rate of return on investment (ROI). Target pricing is used by General Motors, which prices its automobiles to achieve a 15 to 20 percent ROI. This method is also used by public utilities, which need to make a fair return on their investment.

Suppose the toaster manufacturer has invested $1 million in the business and wants to set a price to earn a 20 percent ROI, specifically $200,000. The target-return price is given by the following formula:

$$\text{Target-return price} = \text{unit cost} + \frac{\text{desired return} \times \text{invested capital}}{\text{unit sales}}$$

$$= \$16 + \frac{.20 \times \$1,000,000}{\$50,000} = \$20$$

The manufacturer will realize this 20 percent ROI provided its costs and estimated sales turn out to be accurate, but what if sales do not reach 50,000 units? The manufacturer can prepare a break-even chart to learn what would happen at other sales levels (see Figure 16.8). Fixed

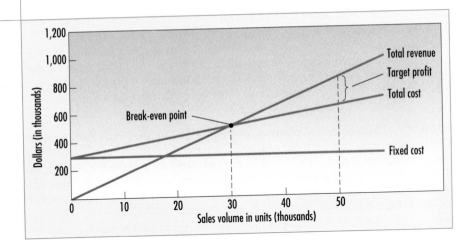

figure 16.8

Break–Even Chart for Determining Target–Return Price and Break–Even Volume

costs are $300,000 regardless of sales volume. Variable costs, not shown in the figure, rise with volume. Total costs equal the sum of fixed costs and variable costs. The total revenue curve starts at zero and rises with each unit sold.

The total revenue and total cost curves cross at 30,000 units. This is the break-even volume. It can be verified by the following formula:

$$\text{Break-even volume} = \frac{\text{fixed cost}}{(\text{price} - \text{variable cost})} = \frac{\$300,000}{\$20 - \$10} = 30,000$$

The manufacturer, of course, is hoping that the market will buy 50,000 units at $20, in which case it earns $200,000 on its $1 million investment, but much depends on price elasticity and competitors' prices. Unfortunately, target-return pricing tends to ignore these considerations. The manufacturer needs to consider different prices and estimate their probable impacts on sales volume and profits. The manufacturer should also search for ways to lower its fixed or variable costs, because lower costs will decrease its required break-even volume.

PERCEIVED-VALUE PRICING   An increasing number of companies base their price on the customer's **perceived value.** They must deliver the value promised by their value proposition, and the customer must perceive this value. They use the other marketing-mix elements, such as advertising and sales force, to communicate and enhance perceived value in buyers' minds.[16]

Perceived value is made up of several elements, such as the buyer's image of the product performance, the channel deliverables, the warranty quality, customer support, and softer attributes such as the supplier's reputation, trustworthiness, and esteem. Furthermore, each potential customer places different weights on these different elements, with the result that some will be *price buyers*, others will be *value buyers*, and still others will be *loyal buyers*. Companies need different strategies for these three groups. For price buyers, companies need to offer stripped-down products and reduced services. For value buyers, companies must keep innovating new value and aggressively reaffirming their value. For loyal buyers, companies must invest in relationship building and customer intimacy.

DuPont is a major practitioner of perceived-value pricing. When DuPont developed its new synthetic fiber for carpets, it demonstrated to carpet manufacturers that they could afford to pay DuPont as much as $1.40 per pound for the new fiber and still make their target profit. DuPont calls the $1.40 the *value-in-use price*, but pricing the new material at $1.40 per pound would leave the carpet manufacturers indifferent. So it set the price lower than $1.40 to induce manufacturers to adopt. DuPont did not use its manufacturing cost to set the price, but only to judge whether there was enough profit to go ahead in the first place. DuPont also embeds each chemical into a larger offering so that it is not seen as a commodity but rather as a solution to a customer's problem. Consider the following:

Attribute	Standard Offer	Premium Offer	Added Value
Quality	Impurities less than ten parts per million	Impurities less than one part per million	$1.40
Delivery	Within two weeks	Within one week	.15
System	Supply chemical only	Supply total system	.80
Innovation	Little R&D support	High level R&D support	2.00
Retraining	Train initially	Retrain on request	.40
Service	Through home office purchases	Locally available	.25
Price	$100/pound	$105/pound	$5.00

The chemical is part of a standard offer or a premium offer. The customer who wants the premium offer pays $105 instead of $100 a pound. The customer may end up requesting fewer added values. DuPont is willing to unbundle the premium offer and charge only for the chosen added values. Here is yet another example of DuPont's perceived value pricing approach.

DuPont DuPont educated its customers about the true value of its higher-grade polyethylene resin called Alathon. Instead of claiming only that pipes made from it were 5 percent more durable, DuPont produced a detailed analysis of the comparative costs of installing and maintaining in-ground irrigation pipe. The real savings came from the diminished need to pay the labor and crop damage costs associated with digging up and replacing the underground pipe. DuPont was able to charge 7 percent more and still see its sales double the following year.

Caterpillar also uses perceived value to set prices on its construction equipment. It might price its tractor at $100,000, although a similar competitor's tractor might be priced at $90,000. When a prospective customer asks a Caterpillar dealer why he should pay $10,000 more for the Caterpillar tractor, the dealer answers:

$ 90,000	is the tractor's price if it is only equivalent to the competitor's tractor
$ 7,000	is the price premium for Caterpillar's superior durability
$ 6,000	is the price premium for Caterpillar's superior reliability
$ 5,000	is the price premium for Caterpillar's superior service
$ 2,000	is the price premium for Caterpillar's longer warranty on parts
$ 110,000	is the normal price to cover Caterpillar's superior value
−$ 10,000	discount
$100,000	final price

The Caterpillar dealer is able to indicate why Caterpillar's tractor delivers more value than the competitor's. Although the customer is asked to pay a $10,000 premium, he is actually getting $20,000 extra value! He chooses the Caterpillar tractor because he is convinced that its lifetime operating costs will be lower.

The Scott Company is also a perceived-value marketer.

Scott Company Scott has created a new lawn care fertilizer that retards grass growth so that a homeowner can mow the lawn only once a month, instead of four times a month. If the homeowner spent $15 per week or $60 a month to cut the grass, he would be better off buying the new fertilizer if it is priced, say, at $40. He would save \$20 (\$60 − \$40 = \$20) a month. Note that Scott is basing its price on perceived value, not on the cost of producing the new fertilizer.

Yet even when a company claims that its offering delivers more total value, not all customers will respond positively. First, there is always a segment of buyers who care only about the price. Second, there are other buyers who suspect that the company is exaggerating its product quality and services. One company installed its software system in one or two plants operated by a company. The substantial and well-documented cost savings convinced the customer to buy the software for its other plants.

The key to perceived-value pricing is to deliver more value than the competitor and demonstrate this to prospective buyers. Basically, a company needs to research the customer's value drivers and understand the customer's decision-making process. The company can try to determine the value of its offering in several ways: managerial judgments within the company, value of analogous products, focus groups, surveys, experimentation, analysis of historical data, and conjoint analysis.[17]

VALUE PRICING   In recent years, several companies have adopted **value pricing**, in which they win loyal customers by charging a fairly low price for a high-quality offering. Among the best practitioners of value pricing are Wal-Mart, IKEA, and Southwest Airlines. Here are two other value pricers.

Enterprise Rent–A–Car   The world's largest car rental firm is not Hertz; Enterprise Rent-A-Car passed Hertz in 1996. Enterprise manages a rental fleet of nearly 500,000 vehicles from almost 4,000 rental offices that are no further than a 15-minute drive from 90 percent of the U.S. population. One of the chief draws of the company is that it charges less than its better-known competitors. It can do this for a number of reasons. First, it locates its offices in low-rent areas. Second, it works closely with insurance companies to rent cars to people whose cars have been in an accident; the typical rental period is 10 to 12 days, resulting in lower transaction costs. Third, its sales are steadier because accidents happen pretty much throughout the year.

Standard Hotel   This Los Angeles hotel has beige shag carpeting lining the lobby's floor and walls, Charles Eames tables, and minimalistic décor similar to nearby Sunset Boulevard hotels that charge \$400 a night. Rooms here start at \$99! Occupancy has been running at 95 percent since the hotel opened in March 1999, and the hotel plans to expand to New York and Chicago.

A few years ago Procter & Gamble created quite a stir by reducing prices on Pampers and Luvs diapers, liquid Tide detergent, and Folger's coffee to value price them. In the past, a brand-loyal family had to pay what amounted to a \$725 premium for a year's worth of P&G products versus private-label or low-priced brands. To offer value prices, P&G underwent a major overhaul. It redesigned the way it develops, manufactures, distributes, prices, markets, and sells products to deliver better value at every point in the supply chain.[18] Value pricing is not a matter of simply setting lower prices; it is a matter of reengineering the company's operations to become a low-cost producer without sacrificing quality, and lowering prices significantly to attract a large number of value-conscious customers.

An important type of value pricing is **everyday low pricing (EDLP)**, which takes place at the retail level. A retailer who holds to an EDLP pricing policy charges a constant low price with little or no price promotions and special sales. These constant prices eliminate week-to-week price uncertainty and can be contrasted to the "high-low" pricing of promotion-oriented competitors. In **high-low pricing**, the retailer charges higher prices on an everyday basis but then runs frequent promotions in which prices are temporarily lowered below the EDLP level.[19]

In recent years, high-low pricing has given way to EDLP at such widely different venues as General Motors' Saturn car dealerships and upscale department stores such as Nordstrom; but the king of EDLP is surely Wal-Mart, which practically defined the term. Except for a few sale items every month, Wal-Mart promises everyday low prices on major brands. "It's not a short-term strategy," says one Wal-Mart executive. "You have to be willing to make a commitment to it, and you have to be able to operate with lower ratios of expense than everybody else."

The most important reason retailers adopt EDLP is that constant sales and promotions are costly and have eroded consumer confidence in the credibility of everyday shelf prices. Consumers also have less time and patience for such time-honored traditions as watching for supermarket specials and clipping coupons. Yet, there is no denying that promotions create excitement and draw shoppers. For this reason, EDLP is not a guarantee of success. As supermarkets face heightened competition from their counterparts and from alternative channels, many find that the key to drawing shoppers is using a combination of high-low and everyday low pricing strategies, with increased advertising and promotions.[20]

GOING-RATE PRICING   In **going-rate pricing**, the firm bases its price largely on competitors' prices. The firm might charge the same, more, or less than major competitor(s). In oligopolistic industries that sell a commodity such as steel, paper, or fertilizer, firms normally charge the same price. The smaller firms "follow the leader," changing their prices when the market leader's prices change rather than when their own demand or costs change. Some firms may charge a slight premium or slight discount, but they preserve the amount of difference. Thus minor gasoline retailers usually charge a few cents less per gallon than the major oil companies, without letting the difference increase or decrease.

Going-rate pricing is quite popular. Where costs are difficult to measure or competitive response is uncertain, firms feel that the going price is a good solution because it is thought to reflect the industry's collective wisdom.

AUCTION-TYPE PRICING   Auction-type pricing is growing more popular, especially with the growth of the Internet. There are over 2,000 electronic marketplaces selling everything from pigs to used vehicles to cargo to chemicals. One major use of auctions is to dispose of excess inventories or used goods. Companies need to be aware of the three major types of auctions and their separate pricing procedures.

- *English auctions (ascending bids).* One seller and many buyers. The seller puts up an item and bidders raise the offer price until the top price is reached. English auctions are being used today for selling antiques, cattle, real estate, and used equipment and vehicles.
- *Dutch auctions (descending bids).* One seller and many buyers, or one buyer and many sellers. In the first kind, an auctioneer announces a high price for a product and then slowly decreases the price until a bidder accepts the price. In the other, the buyer announces something that he wants to buy and then potential sellers compete to get the sale by offering the lowest price. Each seller sees what the last bid is and decides whether to go lower. General Electric uses its Trade Processing Network (TPN) to announce items that it wants to buy and sets a time limit for receiving bids. It accepts the lowest bid providing that other things are equal. As another example, the state of Pennsylvania wanted to buy rock salt and went on FreeMarkets.com. Over 600 bids came in from 9 bidders during the day, reducing the cost of rock salt by 7 percent and saving $2.5 million for the taxpayers of Pennsylvania.
- *Sealed-bid auctions.* Would-be suppliers can submit only one bid and cannot know the other bids. The U.S. government often uses this method to procure supplies. A supplier will not bid below its cost but cannot bid too high for fear of losing the job. The net effect of these two pulls can be described in terms of the bid's *expected profit* (see Table 16.1). Suppose a bid of $9,500 would yield a high chance of getting the contract (say 81 percent) but only a low profit, say $100. The expected profit is therefore $81 (= $100 x .81). If the seller bid $11,000, its expected profit would only be $16 (= $1,600 x .01). According to Table 16.1, the best bid would be $10,000, for which the expected profit is $216. Using

table **16.1**				
Effect of Different Bids on Expected Profit	**Company's Bid**	**Company's Profit**	**Probability of Getting Award with This Bid (Assumed)**	**Expected Profit**
	$ 9,500	$ 100	0.81	$ 81
	10,000	600	0.36	216
	10,500	1,100	0.09	99
	11,000	1,600	0.01	16

expected profit for setting price makes sense for the seller that makes many bids. The seller who bids only occasionally or who needs a particular contract badly will not find it advantageous to use expected profit. This criterion does not distinguish between a $1,000 profit with a 0.10 probability and a $125 profit with an 0.80 probability. Yet the firm that wants to keep production going would prefer the second contract to the first.

GROUP PRICING   The Internet is facilitating a method whereby consumers and business buyers can join groups to buy at a lower price. Consumers can go to Volumebuy.com to buy electronics, computers, subscriptions, and other items. When a consumer finds a desired product, he or she will see the current *pool price*, which is a function of the number of orders received so far. The Web page may also indicate that if (say) three more orders were to come, the price would fall by a specified amount. A major drawback is that some buyers will not wait for the volume order to be executed.

www.volumebuy.com: group or pool pricing?

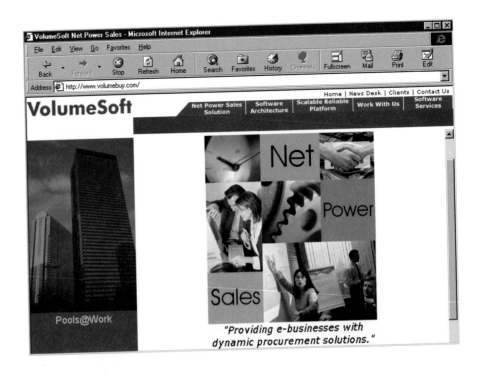

step 6: selecting the final price

Pricing methods narrow the range from which the company must select its final price. In selecting that price, the company must consider additional factors, including psychological pricing, gain-and-risk-sharing pricing, the influence of other marketing-mix elements on price, company pricing policies, and the impact of price on other parties.

PSYCHOLOGICAL PRICING   Many consumers use price as an indicator of quality. Image pricing is especially effective with ego-sensitive products such as perfumes and expensive cars. A $100 bottle of perfume might contain $10 worth of scent, but gift givers pay $100 to communicate their high regard for the receiver.

Price and quality perceptions of cars interact.[21] Higher-priced cars are perceived to possess high quality. Higher-quality cars are likewise perceived to be higher priced than they actually are. When alternative information about true quality is available, price becomes a less significant indicator of quality. When this information is not available, price acts as a signal of quality.

When looking at a particular product, buyers carry in their minds a **reference price** formed by noticing current prices, past prices, or the buying context. Sellers often manipulate these reference prices. For example, a seller can situate its product among expensive products to imply that it belongs in the same class. Department stores will display women's apparel in separate departments differentiated by price; dresses found in the more expensive department are assumed to be of better quality. Reference-price thinking is also created by stating a high manufacturer's suggested price, or by indicating that the product was priced much higher originally, or by pointing to a competitor's high price.[22]

Many sellers believe that prices should end in an odd number. Many customers see a stereo amplifier priced at $299 instead of $300 as a price in the $200 range rather than $300 range. Another explanation is that odd endings convey the notion of a discount or bargain, but if a company wants a high-price image instead of a low-price image, it should avoid the odd-ending tactic.[23]

GAIN-AND-RISK-SHARING PRICING   Buyers may resist accepting a seller's proposal because of a high perceived level of risk. The seller has the option of offering to absorb part or all of the risk if he does not deliver the full promised value. Consider the following.

Baxter Healthcare   Baxter, a leading medical products firm, approached Columbia/ HCA, a leading health care provider, with an offer to develop an information management system that would save Columbia several million dollars over an eight-year period. When Columbia balked, Baxter then offered to guarantee the savings; if they were not realized, Baxter would write a check for the difference. Baxter got the order!

Baxter could have gone further and proposed that if Baxter's information system saved Columbia more than the targeted amount, Baxter would share in 30 percent of the additional savings. This would amount to offering to share in the gain as well as the risk. An increasing number of companies, especially business marketers who promise great savings with their equipment, may have to stand ready to guarantee the promised savings, and possibly participate if the gains are much greater than expected.

THE INFLUENCE OF OTHER MARKETING-MIX ELEMENTS   The final price must take into account the brand's quality and advertising relative to competition. Farris and Reibstein examined the relationships among relative price, relative quality, and relative advertising for 227 consumer businesses, and found the following:

■ Brands with average relative quality but high relative advertising budgets were able to charge premium prices. Consumers apparently were willing to pay higher prices for known products than for unknown products.

- Brands with high relative quality and high relative advertising obtained the highest prices. Conversely, brands with low quality and low advertising charged the lowest prices.
- The positive relationship between high prices and high advertising held most strongly in the later stages of the product life cycle for market leaders.[24]

These findings suggest that price is not as important as quality and other benefits in the market offering. One study asked consumers to rate the importance of price and other attributes in using online retailing. Only 19 percent cared about price; far more cared about customer support (65 percent), on-time delivery (58 percent), and product shipping and handling (49 percent).[25]

COMPANY PRICING POLICIES   The price must be consistent with company pricing policies. At the same time, companies are not averse to establishing pricing penalties under certain circumstances.[26]

Airlines charge $75 to those who change their reservations on discount tickets. Banks charge fees for too many withdrawals in a month or for early withdrawal of a certificate of deposit. Car rental companies charge $50-100 penalties for no shows for specialty vehicles. Although these policies are often justifiable, they must be used judiciously so as not to unnecessarily alienate customers.

Many companies set up a pricing department to develop policies and establish or approve decisions. The aim is to ensure that the salespeople quote prices that are reasonable to customers and profitable to the company. Dell Computer has developed innovative pricing techniques.

Dell   Dell uses a high-tech "cost-forecasting" system that enables it to scale its selling prices based on consumer demand and the company's own costs. The company instituted this flexible pricing model in 2001 to maximize its margins during the economic slowdown. Dell managers get cost information from suppliers, which they then combine with knowledge about profit targets, delivery dates, and competition to set prices for business segments. On any given day, the same computer might sell at different prices depending on whether the purchaser is a government, small business, or home PC buyer. The cost-forecasting system may help to explain why Dell was the only U.S. PC maker among the top six to report a profit for the first quarter of 2001.[27]

IMPACT OF PRICE ON OTHER PARTIES   Management must also consider the reactions of other parties to the contemplated price. How will distributors and dealers feel about it? Will the sales force be willing to sell at that price? How will competitors react? Will suppliers raise their prices when they see the company's price? Will the government intervene and prevent this price from being charged?

In the last case, marketers need to know the laws regulating pricing. U.S. legislation states that sellers must set prices without talking to competitors: Price-fixing is illegal. Many federal and state statutes protect consumers against deceptive pricing practices. For example, it is illegal for a company to set artificially high "regular" prices, then announce a "sale" at prices close to previous everyday prices.

adapting the price

Companies usually do not set a single price, but rather a pricing structure that reflects variations in geographical demand and costs, market-segment requirements, purchase timing, order levels, delivery frequency, guarantees, service contracts, and other factors. As a result of discounts, allowances, and promotional support, a company rarely realizes the same profit from each unit of a product that it sells. Here we will examine several price-adaptation strategies: geographical pricing, price discounts and allowances, promotional pricing, discriminatory pricing, and product-mix pricing.

geographical pricing (cash, countertrade, barter)

Geographical pricing involves the company in deciding how to price its products to different customers in different locations and countries. For example, should the company charge higher prices to distant customers to cover the higher shipping costs or a lower price to win additional business? Another issue is how to get paid. This issue is critical when buyers lack sufficient hard currency to pay for their purchases. Many buyers want to offer other items in payment, a practice known as **countertrade**. American companies are often forced to engage in countertrade if they want the business. Countertrade may account for 15 to 25 percent of world trade and takes several forms:[28] barter, compensation deals, buyback agreements, and offset.

- *Barter:* The direct exchange of goods, with no money and no third party involved. In 1993, Eminence S.A., one of France's major clothing makers, launched a five-year deal to barter $25 million worth of U.S.–produced underwear and sportswear to customers in eastern Europe, in exchange for a variety of goods and services, including global transportation and advertising space in eastern European magazines.

- *Compensation deal:* The seller receives some percentage of the payment in cash and the rest in products. A British aircraft manufacturer sold planes to Brazil for 70 percent cash and the rest in coffee.

- *Buyback arrangement:* The seller sells a plant, equipment, or technology to another country and agrees to accept as partial payment products manufactured with the supplied equipment. A U.S. chemical company built a plant for an Indian company and accepted partial payment in cash and the remainder in chemicals manufactured at the plant.

- *Offset:* The seller receives full payment in cash but agrees to spend a substantial amount of the money in that country within a stated time period. For example, PepsiCo sells its cola syrup to Russia for rubles and agrees to buy Russian vodka at a certain rate for sale in the United States.

More complex countertrade deals involve more than two parties. For example, Daimler-Benz agreed to sell 30 trucks to Romania and accept in exchange 150 Romanian-made jeeps, which it sold in Ecuador for bananas, which in turn were sold to a German supermarket chain for Deutsche marks. Through this circuitous transaction, Daimler-Benz finally achieved payment in German currency. Deals such as this are carried on by a separate countertrade department within the company. Other companies rely on barter houses and countertrade specialists.

price discounts and allowances

Most companies will adjust their list price and give discounts and allowances for early payment, volume purchases, and off-season buying (see Table 16.2). Companies must do this carefully or find that their profits are much less than planned.[29]

Jack Trout, author of *Positioning*, cautions that some product categories tend to self-destruct by always being on sale. Mink coats and mattresses, says Trout, never seem to be sold at anything near list price, and when automakers get rebate-happy, the market just sits back and waits for a deal. (See "Marketing Memo: Commandments of Discounting" for Trout's discounting directives.) Discount pricing has become the modus operandi of a surprising number of companies offering both products and services. Even Pepsi and Coke, two of the most popular brands in the world, engaged in a price war that ultimately tarnished their brand equity.[30]

Kevin Clancy, chairman of Copernicus, a major marketing research and consulting firm, found that only between 15 and 35 percent of buyers in most categories are price-sensitive. People with higher incomes and higher product involvement willingly pay more for features, customer service, quality, added convenience, and the brand name. So it can be a mistake for a strong, distinctive brand to plunge into price discounting to respond to low-price attacks.[31]

Marketing MEMO

Commandments of Discounting

- Thou shalt not offer discounts because everyone else does.
- Thou should be creative with your discounting.
- Thou should use discounts to clear stocks or generate extra business.
- Thou should put time limits on the deal.
- Thou should make sure the ultimate customer gets the deal.
- Thou should discount only to survive in a mature market.
- Thou should stop discounting as soon as you can.

Source: Reprinted from Jack Trout, "Prices: Simple Guidelines to Get Them Right," *Journal of Business Strategy* (November–December 1998): 13–16.

<table>
<tr><td>table **16.2**

Price Discounts and Allowances</td></tr>
</table>

Cash Discount:	A price reduction to buyers who pay bills promptly. A typical example is "2/10, net 30," which means that payment is due within 30 days and that the buyer can deduct 2 percent by paying the bill within 10 days.
Quantity Discount:	A price reduction to those who buy large volumes. A typical example is "$10 per unit for less than 100 units; $9 per unit for 100 or more units." Quantity discounts must be offered equally to all customers and must not exceed the cost savings to the seller. They can be offered on each order placed or on the number of units ordered over a given period.
Functional Discount:	Discount (also called *trade discount*) offered by a manufacturer to trade-channel members if they will perform certain functions, such as selling, storing, and recordkeeping. Manufacturers must offer the same functional discounts within each channel.
Seasonal Discount:	A price reduction to those who buy merchandise or services out of season. Hotels, motels, and airlines offer seasonal discounts in slow selling periods.
Allowance:	An extra payment designed to gain reseller participation in special programs. *Trade-in allowances* are granted for turning in an old item when buying a new one. *Promotional allowances* reward dealers for participating in advertising and sales support programs.

Salespeople, in particular, are quick to give discounts in order to close a sale, but the word gets around fast that the company's list price is "soft," and discounting becomes the norm. The discounts undermine the value perceptions of the offerings.

At the same time, discounting can be a useful tool if the company can gain some concession in return:

- the customer agrees to sign a three-year contract
- the customer is willing to order electronically, thus saving the company money
- the customer agrees to buy in truckload quantities

Sales management needs to monitor the proportion of customers who are receiving discounts, the average discount, and the particular salespeople who are overrelying on discounting. Higher levels of management should conduct a **net price analysis** to arrive at the "real price" of their offering. The real price is affected not only by discounts, but by many other expenses (see promotional pricing below) that reduce the realized price: Suppose the company's list price is $3,000. The average discount is $300. The company's promotional spending averages $450 (15% of the list price). Co-op advertising money of $150 is given to retailers to back the product. The company's net price is $2,100, not $3,000.

Companies in an overcapacity situation are tempted to give discounts. For example, they may agree to supply a retailer with a store brand version of their product at a deep discount. The store brand, being priced lower, may start making inroads on the manufacturer's brand. Now the manufacturer has more overcapacity and may accept a larger order from the retailer. Eventually, the manufacturer's brand may wither away and the manufacturer may become totally dependent on supplying the store brand. Manufacturers should stop to consider the implications of supplying product at a discount to retailers because they may end up losing long-run profits in an effort to meet short-run volume goals.

promotional pricing

Companies can use several pricing techniques to stimulate early purchase:

■ *Loss-leader pricing:* Supermarkets and department stores often drop the price on well-known brands to stimulate additional store traffic. This pays if the revenue on the additional sales compensates for the lower margins on the loss-leader items. Manufacturers of loss-leader brands typically object because this practice can dilute the brand image and bring complaints from retailers who charge the list price. Manufacturers have tried to restrain intermediaries from loss-leader pricing through lobbying for retail-price-maintenance laws, but these laws have been revoked.

■ *Special-event pricing:* Sellers will establish special prices in certain seasons to draw in more customers. Every August, there are back-to-school sales.

■ *Cash rebates:* Auto companies and other consumer-goods companies offer cash rebates to encourage purchase of the manufacturers' products within a specified time period. Rebates can help clear inventories without cutting the stated list price.

■ *Low-interest financing:* Instead of cutting its price, the company can offer customers low-interest financing. Automakers have even announced no-interest financing to attract customers.

■ *Longer payment terms:* Sellers, especially mortgage banks and auto companies, stretch loans over longer periods and thus lower the monthly payments. Consumers often worry less about the cost (i.e., the interest rate) of a loan and more about whether they can afford the monthly payment.

■ *Warranties and service contracts:* Companies can promote sales by adding a free or low-cost warranty or service contract.

■ *Psychological discounting:* This strategy involves setting an artificially high price and then offering the product at substantial savings; for example, "Was $359, now $299." Illegitimate discount tactics are fought by the Federal Trade Commission and Better Business Bureaus. Discounts from normal prices are a legitimate form of promotional pricing.

Promotional-pricing strategies are often a zero-sum game. If they work, competitors copy them and they lose their effectiveness. If they do not work, they waste money that could have been put into other marketing tools, such as building up product quality and service or strengthening product image through advertising.

discriminatory pricing

Companies often adjust their basic price to accommodate differences in customers, products, locations, and so on. **Price discrimination** occurs when a company sells a product or service at two or more prices that do not reflect a proportional difference in costs. In first-degree price discrimination, the seller charges a separate price to each customer depending on the intensity of his or her demand. In second-degree price discrimination, the seller charges less to buyers who buy a larger volume. In third-degree price discrimination, the seller charges different amounts to different classes of buyers, as in the following cases:

■ *Customer-segment pricing:* Different customer groups are charged different prices for the same product or service. For example, museums often charge a lower admission fee to students and senior citizens.

■ *Product-form pricing:* Different versions of the product are priced differently but not proportionately to their respective costs. Evian prices a 48-ounce bottle of its mineral water at $2.00. It takes the same water and packages 1.7 ounces in a moisturizer spray for $6.00. Through product-form pricing, Evian manages to charge $3.00 an ounce in one form and about $.04 an ounce in another.

■ *Image pricing:* Some companies price the same product at two different levels based on image differences. A perfume manufacturer can put the perfume in one bottle, give it a name and image, and price it at $10 an ounce. It can put the same perfume in another bottle with a different name and image and price it at $30 an ounce.

- *Channel pricing:* Coca-Cola carries a different price depending on whether it is purchased in a fine restaurant, a fast-food restaurant, or a vending machine.
- *Location pricing:* The same product is priced differently at different locations even though the cost of offering at each location is the same. A theater varies its seat prices according to audience preferences for different locations.
- *Time pricing:* Prices are varied by season, day, or hour. Public utilities vary energy rates to commercial users by time of day and weekend versus weekday. Restaurants charge less to "early bird" customers. Hotels charge less on weekends. Hotels and airlines use **yield pricing,** by which they offer lower rates on unsold inventory just before it expires.[32]

Coca-Cola considered raising its vending machine soda prices on hot days using wireless technology, and lowering the price on cold days. However, customers so disliked the idea that Coke abandoned it.

For price discrimination to work, certain conditions must exist. First, the market must be segmentable and the segments must show different intensities of demand. Second, members in the lower-price segment must not be able to resell the product to the higher-price segment. Third, competitors must not be able to undersell the firm in the higher-price segment. Fourth, the cost of segmenting and policing the market must not exceed the extra revenue derived from price discrimination. Fifth, the practice must not breed customer resentment and ill will. Sixth, the particular form of price discrimination must not be illegal.[33]

As a result of deregulation in several industries, competitors have increased their use of discriminatory pricing. Airlines charge different fares to passengers on the same flight, depending on the seating class; the time of day (morning or night coach); the day of the week (workday or weekend); the season; the person's company, past business, or status (youth, military, senior citizen); and so on. Airlines are using yield pricing to capture as much revenue as possible.

Most consumers are probably not even aware of the degree to which they are the targets of discriminatory pricing. For instance, catalog retailers like Victoria's Secret routinely send out catalogs that sell identical goods except at different prices. Consumers who live in a more free-spending zip code may see only the higher prices. Office-product superstore Staples also sends out office supply catalogs with different prices.

Computer technology is making it easier for sellers to practice discriminatory pricing. For instance, they can use software that monitors customers' movements over the Web and allows them to customize offers and prices. New software applications, however, are also allowing buyers to discriminate between sellers by comparing prices instantaneously. (See "Marketing for the New Economy: How the Internet Is Revolutionizing Pricing—for Sellers and Buyers.")

Some forms of price discrimination (in which sellers offer different price terms to different people within the same trade group) are illegal. However, price discrimination is legal if the seller can prove that its costs are different when selling different volumes or different qualities of the same product to different retailers. Predatory pricing—selling below cost with the intention of destroying competition—is unlawful.[34]

product-mix pricing

Price-setting logic must be modified when the product is part of a product mix. In this case, the firm searches for a set of prices that maximizes profits on the total mix. Pricing is difficult because the various products have demand and cost interrelationships and are subject to different degrees of competition. We can distinguish six situations involving product-mix pricing: product-line pricing, optional-feature pricing, captive-product pricing, two-part pricing, by-product pricing, and product-bundling pricing.

PRODUCT-LINE PRICING   Companies normally develop product lines rather than single products and introduce price steps.

marketing for the new economy

E-commerce is arguably the Web's hottest application. Yet the Internet is more than simply a new "market-space." Internet-based technologies are actually changing the rules of the market. Here is a short list of how the Internet allows sellers to discriminate between buyers and allows buyers to discriminate between sellers.

Sellers can:

- Monitor customer behavior and tailor offers to individuals. Although shopping agent software and price comparison Web sites will tell consumers published prices, they may be missing out on the special deals consumers can get with the help of new technologies. Personify, a San Francisco–based start-up, has software that lets a Web-based merchant identify individual visitors to its Web site, studies the way the person navigates through the Web site, and instantaneously targets shoppers for specific products and prices.

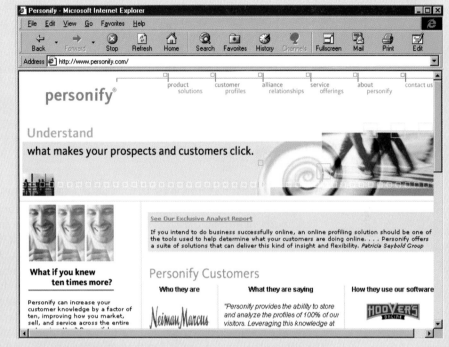

www.personify.com provides software that helps Web merchants find target customers.

- Give certain customers access to special prices. CDNOW, an online vendor of music albums, e-mails certain buyers a special Web site address with lower prices. Unless you know the secret address, you pay full price. Business marketers are already using extranets to get a precise handle on inventory, costs, and demand at any given moment—to adjust prices instantly.

Both buyers and sellers can:

- Negotiate prices in online auctions and exchanges. Want to sell hundreds of excess and slightly worn widgets? Post a sale on eBay. Want to purchase vintage baseball cards at a bargain price? Go to Boekhout's Collectibles Mall at *www.azww.com/mall*. Of the thousands of Internet auction sites, eBay is the largest, and unlike most Internet businesses, is actually turning a profit. About 19 million registered users bid on items in more than 20 general categories. The Internet has made the centuries-old art of haggling economical. In the brick-and-mortar world, it costs sellers too much in overhead to negotiate prices with individual buyers. Over the Internet, the cost per transaction is so low it becomes practical—even profitable—to auction an item for dollars rather than thousands of dollars. Sellers like auctions because they can get rid of excess inventory. Business marketers, whose transactions account for 68 percent of online auction sales, also use it to offer time-sensitive deals and gauge interest on possible price points for new products. Quite simply, buyers like the bargains they find.

Buyers can:

- Get instant price comparisons from thousands of vendors. New technologies make it possible to obtain price compar-isons with the click of a mouse. One site, PriceScan.com, lures thousands of visitors a day, most of them corporate buyers. Intelligent shopping agents ("bots") take price comparison a step further and seek out products, prices, and reviews from as many as 2,000 merchants.

- Name their price and have it met. Using complex software that shops bids to a number of airlines, Priceline.com has brokered around 7.5 million airline tickets since it opened in April 1998. Priceline extended its services to rental and new cars, accommodations, long distance telephone service, and home mortgages. Consumers can fix their own prices, and sellers can use it too: Airlines can fill in demand for empty seats, and hotels welcome the chance to sell vacant rooms.

Sources: Amy E. Cortese, "Good-Bye to Fixed Pricing?" *BusinessWeek*, May 4, 1998, pp. 71–84; Scott Woolley, "I Got It Cheaper than You," *Forbes*, November 2, 1998, pp. 82–84; Scott Woolley, "Price War!" *Forbes*, December 14, 1998, pp. 182–84; Michael Krauss, "Web Offers Biggest Prize in Product Pricing Game," *Marketing News*, July 6, 1998, p. 8; Julie Pitta, "Competitive Shopping," *Forbes*, February 9, 1998, pp. 92–95; Matthew Nelson, "Going Once, Going Twice . . . " *InfoWorld*, November 9, 1998, pp. 1, 64; Leslie Walker, "The Net's Battle of the Bots," *Washington Post*, December 10, 1998, p. B1; Heather Green, "A Cybershopper's Best Friend," *BusinessWeek*, May 4, 1998, p. 84; Rebecca Quick, "Buying the Goods—The Attack of the Robots: Comparison-Shopping Technology is Here—Whether Retailers Like It or Not," *Wall Street Journal*, December 7, 1998, p. R14. For a discussion of some of the academic issues involved, see Florian Zettelmeyer, "Expanding to the Internet: Pricing and Communication Strategies when Firms Compete on Multiple Channels," *Journal of Marketing Research*, 37 (August 2000): 292–308.

Intel   In the fall of 1997, Intel segmented its product line into microprocessors aimed at specific markets, such as cheap PCs, mid-tier "performance" PCs, and powerful servers. This strategy let Intel balance thin profits from chips like the Celeron—new models of which sell for as little as $150 and go into low-priced PCs—with cash cows like the Itanium workstation and server chips, which cost up to $4,200 each. The company's most profitable chips are the Pentium 4 chips, priced between $300 and $600, depending on processor speed.[35]

In many lines of trade, sellers use well-established price points for the products in their line. A men's clothing store might carry men's suits at three price levels: $200, $400, and $600. Customers will associate low-, average-, and high-quality suits with the three price points. The seller's task is to establish perceived-quality differences that justify the price differences.

OPTIONAL-FEATURE PRICING   Many companies offer optional products, features, and services along with their main product. The automobile buyer can order electric window controls, defoggers, light dimmers, and an extended warranty. Pricing is a sticky problem, because companies must decide which items to include in the standard price and which to offer as options. For many years, U.S. auto companies advertised a stripped-down model for $10,000 to pull people into showrooms. The economy model was stripped of so many features that most buyers left the showroom spending $13,000.

Restaurants face a similar pricing problem. Customers can often order liquor in addition to the meal. Many restaurants price their liquor high and their food low. The food revenue covers costs, and the liquor produces the profit. This explains why servers often press hard to get customers to order drinks. Other restaurants price their liquor low and food high to draw in a drinking crowd.

CAPTIVE-PRODUCT PRICING   Some products require the use of ancillary, or **captive, products**. Manufacturers of razors and cameras often price them low and set high markups on razor blades and film, respectively. AT&T may give a cellular phone free if the person commits to buying two years of phone service.

Hewlett-Packard   In 1996, Hewlett-Packard (H-P) began drastically cutting prices on its printers, by as much as 60 percent in some cases. H-P could afford to make such dramatic cuts because the high volume of sales of aftermarket products like replacement ink cartridges and specialty paper carried profit margins as high as 70 percent. As the price of printers dropped, printer sales rose, as did the number of aftermarket sales. Ink cartridges, which cost anywhere from $20 to $200, and other aftermarket consumables contributed 12 percent of H-P's total profit in 1996. Today, these consumables account for roughly two-thirds of H-P's $647 million annual profit.[36]

There is a danger in pricing the captive product too high in the aftermarket. Caterpillar, for example, makes high profits in the aftermarket by pricing its parts and service high. This practice has given rise to "pirates," who counterfeit the parts and sell them to "shady tree" mechanics who install them, sometimes without passing on the cost savings to customers. Meanwhile, Caterpillar loses sales.[37]

TWO-PART PRICING   Service firms often engage in **two-part pricing**, consisting of a fixed fee plus a variable usage fee. Telephone users pay a minimum monthly fee plus charges for calls beyond a certain area. Amusement parks charge an admission fee plus fees for rides over a certain minimum. The service firm faces a problem similar to captive-product pricing—namely, how much to charge for the basic service and how much for the variable usage. The fixed fee should be low enough to induce purchase of the service; the profit can then be made on the usage fees.

BY-PRODUCT PRICING   The production of certain goods—meats, petroleum products, and other chemicals—often results in by-products. If the by-products have value to a customer group, they should be priced on their value. Any income earned on the by-products will make it easier for the company to charge a lower price on its main product if competition forces it to do so.

Sometimes companies do not realize how valuable their by-products are. Until Zoo-Doo Compost Company came along, many zoos did not realize that one of their by-products—their occupants' manure—could be an excellent source of additional revenue.[38]

PRODUCT-BUNDLING PRICING   Sellers often bundle products and features. **Pure bundling** occurs when a firm only offers its products as a bundle. Michael Ovitz's company, Artists Management Group, will sign up a "hot" actor if the film company will also accept other talents that Ovitz represents (directors, writers, scripts). This is a form of *tied-in sales*. In **mixed bundling**, the seller offers goods both individually and in bundles. When offering a mixed bundle, the seller normally charges less for the bundle than if the items were purchased separately. An auto manufacturer might offer an option package at less than the cost of buying all the options separately. A theater company will price a season subscription at less than the cost of buying all the performances separately. Because customers may not have planned to buy all the components, the savings on the price bundle must be substantial enough to induce them to buy the bundle.[39]

Some customers will want less than the whole bundle. Suppose a medical equipment supplier's offer includes free delivery and training. A particular customer might ask to forgo the free delivery and training in exchange for a lower price. The customer is asking the seller to "unbundle" or "rebundle" its offer. If a supplier saves $100 by not supplying delivery and reduces the customer's price by $80, the supplier has kept the customer happy while increasing its profit by $20.

initiating and responding to price changes

Companies often face situations where they may need to cut or raise prices.

initiating price cuts

Several circumstances might lead a firm to cut prices. One is excess plant capacity: The firm needs additional business and cannot generate it through increased sales effort, product improvement, or other measures. It may resort to aggressive pricing, but in initiating a price cut, the company may trigger a price war. Another circumstance is declining market share. General Motors, for example, cut its subcompact car prices by 10 percent on the West Coast when Japanese competition kept making inroads.

Companies sometimes initiate price cuts in a *drive to dominate the market through lower costs*. Either the company starts with lower costs than its competitors or it initiates price cuts in the hope of gaining market share and lower costs; but a price-cutting strategy involves possible traps:

- *Low-quality trap:* Consumers will assume that the quality is low.
- *Fragile-market-share trap:* A low price buys market share but not market loyalty. The same customers will shift to any lower-priced firm that comes along.
- *Shallow-pockets trap:* The higher-priced competitors may cut their prices and may have longer staying power because of deeper cash reserves.

Companies may have to cut their prices in a period of economic recession. During hard times, consumers reduce their spending. Some possible company responses are given in Table 16.3.

initiating price increases

A successful price increase can raise profits considerably. For example, if the company's profit margin is 3 percent of sales, a 1 percent price increase will increase profits by 33 percent if sales volume is unaffected. This situation is illustrated in Table 16.4. The

table **16.3**	Marketing-Mix Alternatives	
Strategic Options	**Reasoning**	**Consequences**
1. Maintain price and perceived quality. Engage in selective customer pruning.	Firm has higher customer loyalty. It is willing to lose poorer customers to competitors.	Smaller market share. Lowered profitability.
2. Raise price and perceived quality.	Raise price to cover rising costs. Improve quality to justify higher prices.	Smaller market share. Maintained profitability.
3. Maintain price and raise perceived quality.	It is cheaper to maintain price and raise perceived quality.	Smaller market share. Short-term decline in profitability. Long-term increase in profitability.
4. Cut price partly and raise perceived quality.	Must give customers some price reduction but stress higher value of offer.	Maintained market share. Short-term decline in profitability. Long-term maintained profitability.
5. Cut price fully and maintain perceived quality.	Discipline and discourage price competition.	Maintained market share. Short-term decline in profitability.
6. Cut price fully and reduce perceived quality.	Discipline and discourage price competition and maintain profit margin.	Maintained market share. Maintained margin. Reduced long-term profitability.
7. Maintain price and reduce perceived quality.	Cut marketing expense to combat rising costs.	Smaller market share. Maintained margin. Reduced long-term profitability.
8. Introduce an economy model.	Give the market what it wants.	Some cannibalization but higher total volume.

assumption is that a company charged $10 and sold 100 units and had costs of $970, leaving a profit of $30, or 3 percent on sales. By raising its price by 10 cents (1 percent price increase), it boosted its profits by 33 percent, assuming the same sales volume.

A major circumstance provoking price increases is *cost inflation*. Rising costs unmatched by productivity gains squeeze profit margins and lead companies to regular rounds of price increases. Companies often raise their prices by more than the cost increase, in anticipation of further inflation or government price controls, in a practice called *anticipatory pricing*.

Another factor leading to price increases is *overdemand*. When a company cannot supply all of its customers, it can raise its prices, ration supplies to customers, or both. The price can be increased in the following ways. Each has a different impact on buyers.

■ *Delayed quotation pricing:* The company does not set a final price until the product is finished or delivered. This pricing is prevalent in industries with long production lead times, such as industrial construction and heavy equipment.

table **16.4**			
		Before	**After**
Profits Before and After a Price Increase	Price	$ 10	$10.10 (a 1 percent price increase)
	Units sold	100	100
	Revenue	$1000	$1010
	Costs	−970	−970
	Profit	$ 30	$ 40 (a 33⅓ percent profit increase)

- *Escalator clauses:* The company requires the customer to pay today's price and all or part of any inflation increase that takes place before delivery. An escalator clause bases price increases on some specified price index. Escalator clauses are found in contracts for major industrial projects, like aircraft construction and bridge building.
- *Unbundling:* The company maintains its price but removes or prices separately one or more elements that were part of the former offer, such as free delivery or installation. A joke in countries with high inflation is that the current price of a car no longer includes the tires and steering wheel.
- *Reduction of discounts:* The company instructs its sales force not to offer its normal cash and quantity discounts.

A company needs to decide whether to raise its price sharply on a one-time basis or to raise it by small amounts several times. Generally, consumers prefer small price increases on a regular basis to sudden, sharp increases.

In passing price increases on to customers, the company must avoid looking like a price gouger. Companies also need to think of who will bear the brunt of increased prices. Customer memories are long, and they will turn against companies they perceive as price gougers when the market softens. This happened to Kellogg, the breakfast cereal company.

Kellogg Throughout the 1980s, Kellogg pushed up the prices of its breakfast cereals and its stock price soared. Although the strategy worked for some time, in the early 1990s the company became embroiled in a bitter price war with rivals General Mills, Quaker Oats, and Post. Between 1993 and 1997, Kellogg cut prices by as much as 20 percent. The price cuts led to a 3.5 point drop in the company's U.S. market share between 1993 and 1998. To combat flagging sales, Kellogg began raising prices and used the profits to develop new products and boost advertising. Kellogg's $4 billion acquisition of Keebler in 2000 was a step toward less dependence on cereal sales, which dropped from 75 percent to 50 percent of Kellogg's $7 billion in sales.[40]

There are some techniques for avoiding this image: One is that a sense of fairness must surround any price increase, and customers must be given advance notice so they can do forward buying or shop around. Sharp price increases need to be explained in understandable terms. Making low-visibility price moves first is also a good technique: Eliminating discounts, increasing minimum order sizes, and curtailing production of low-margin products are some examples; and contracts or bids for long-term projects should contain escalator clauses based on such factors as increases in recognized national price indexes.[41]

Companies can also respond to higher costs or overdemand without raising prices. The possibilities include the following:

- Shrinking the amount of product instead of raising the price. (Hershey Foods maintained its candy bar price but trimmed its size. Nestlé maintained its size but raised the price.)
- Substituting less expensive materials or ingredients. (Many candy bar companies substituted synthetic chocolate for real chocolate to fight price increases in cocoa.)
- Reducing or removing product features. (Sears engineered down a number of its appliances so they could be priced competitively with those sold in discount stores.)
- Removing or reducing product services, such as installation or free delivery.
- Using less expensive packaging material or larger package sizes.
- Reducing the number of sizes and models offered.
- Creating new economy brands. (Jewel food stores introduced 170 generic items selling at 10 percent to 30 percent less than national brands.)

reactions to price changes

Any price change can provoke a response from customers, competitors, distributors, suppliers, and even government.

CUSTOMER REACTIONS   Customers often question the motivation behind price changes.[42] A price cut can be interpreted in different ways: The item is about to be replaced by a new model; the item is faulty and is not selling well; the firm is in financial trouble; the price will come down even further; the quality has been reduced.

A price increase, which would normally deter sales, may carry some positive meanings to customers: The item is "hot" and represents an unusually good value.

COMPETITOR REACTIONS   Competitors are most likely to react when the number of firms are few, the product is homogeneous, and buyers are highly informed.

How can a firm anticipate a competitor's reactions? One way is to assume that the competitor reacts in a set way to price changes. The other is to assume that the competitor treats each price change as a fresh challenge and reacts according to self-interest at the time. In this case, the company will have to figure out the competitor's self-interest. It will need to research the competitor's current financial situation, recent sales, customer loyalty, and corporate objectives. If the competitor has a market-share objective, it is likely to match the price change. If it has a profit-maximization objective, it may react by increasing the advertising budget or improving product quality.

The problem is complicated because the competitor can put different interpretations on a price cut: that the company is trying to steal the market, that the company is doing poorly and trying to boost its sales, or that the company wants the whole industry to reduce prices to stimulate total demand.

responding to competitors' price changes

How should a firm respond to a price cut initiated by a competitor? In markets characterized by high product homogeneity, the firm should search for ways to enhance its augmented product. If it cannot find any, it will have to meet the price reduction. If the competitor raises its price in a homogeneous product market, the other firms might not match it unless the increase will benefit the industry as a whole. Then the leader will have to rescind the increase.

In nonhomogeneous product markets, a firm has more latitude. It needs to consider the following issues: (1) Why did the competitor change the price? To steal the market, to utilize excess capacity, to meet changing cost conditions, or to lead an industrywide price change? (2) Does the competitor plan to make the price change temporary or permanent? (3) What will happen to the company's market share and profits if it does not respond? Are other companies going to respond? (4) What are the competitor's and other firms' responses likely to be to each possible reaction?

Market leaders frequently face aggressive price cutting by smaller firms trying to build market share. Using price, Fuji attacks Kodak, Bic attacks Gillette, and Compaq attacks IBM. Brand leaders also face lower-priced private-store brands. The brand leader can respond in several ways:

- *Maintain price:* The leader might maintain its price and profit margin, believing that (1) it would lose too much profit if it reduced its price, (2) it would not lose much market share, and (3) it could regain market share when necessary. However, the argument against price maintenance is that the attacker gets more confident, the leader's sales force gets demoralized, and the leader loses more share than expected. The leader panics, lowers price to regain share, and finds that regaining its market position is more difficult and costly than expected.
- *Maintain price and add value:* The leader could improve its product, services, and communications. The firm may find it cheaper to maintain price and spend money to improve perceived quality than to cut price and operate at a lower margin.
- *Reduce price:* The leader might drop its price to match the competitor's price. It might do so because (1) its costs fall with volume, (2) it would lose market share because the market is price-sensitive, and (3) it would be hard to rebuild market share once it is lost. This action will cut profits in the short run.

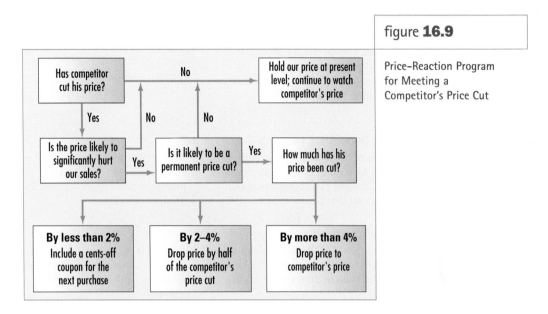

figure **16.9**

Price–Reaction Program for Meeting a Competitor's Price Cut

- *Increase price and improve quality:* The leader might raise its price and introduce new brands to bracket the attacking brand.
- *Launch a low-price fighter line:* It might add lower-priced items to the line or create a separate, lower-priced brand.

The best response varies with the situation. The company has to consider the product's stage in the life cycle, its importance in the company's portfolio, the competitor's intentions and resources, the market's price and quality sensitivity, the behavior of costs with volume, and the company's alternative opportunities.

An extended analysis of alternatives may not be feasible when the attack occurs. The company may have to react decisively within hours or days. It would make better sense to anticipate possible competitors' price changes and to prepare contingent responses. Figure 16.9 shows a *price-reaction program* to be used if a competitor cuts prices. Reaction programs for meeting price changes find their greatest application in industries where price changes occur with some frequency and where it is important to react quickly—for example, in the meatpacking, lumber, and oil industries.

summary

1. Despite the increased role of nonprice factors in modern marketing, price remains a critical element of the marketing mix. Price is the only one of the four Ps that produces revenue; the others produce costs.

2. In setting pricing policy, a company follows a six-step procedure. First, it selects its pricing objective. Second, it estimates the demand curve, the probable quantities that it will sell at each possible price. Third, it estimates how its costs vary at different levels of output, at different levels of accumulated production experience, and for differentiated marketing offers. Fourth, it examines competitors' costs, prices, and offers. Fifth, it selects a pricing method. Finally, it selects the final price.

3. Companies do not usually set a single price, but rather a pricing structure that reflects variations in geographical demand and costs, market-segment requirements, pur-

chase timing, order levels, and other factors. Several price-adaptation strategies are available: (1) geographical pricing; (2) price discounts and allowances; (3) promotional pricing; (4) discriminatory pricing; and (5) product-mix pricing, which includes setting prices for product lines, optional features, captive products, two-part items, by-products, and product bundles.

4. After developing pricing strategies, firms often face situations in which they need to change prices. A price decrease might be brought about by excess plant capacity, declining market share, a desire to dominate the market through lower costs, or economic recession. A price increase might be brought about by cost inflation or overdemand.

5. There are several alternatives to increasing price, including shrinking the amount of product instead of raising the

price, substituting less expensive materials or ingredients, and reducing or removing product features.

6. The firm facing a competitor's price change must try to understand the competitor's intent and the likely duration of the change. The firm's strategy often depends on whether it is producing homogeneous or nonhomogeneous products. Market leaders attacked by lower-priced competitors can choose to maintain price, raise the perceived quality of their product, reduce price, increase price and improve quality, or launch a low-priced fighter line.

applications

marketing debate – is the right price a fair price?

Prices are often set to satisfy demand or to reflect the premium that consumers are willing to pay for a product or service. Some critics shudder, however, at the thought of $2 bottles of water, $150 running shoes, and $500 concert tickets.

Take a position: Prices should reflect the value that consumers are willing to pay versus Prices should primarily just reflect the cost involved in making a product or service.

marketing and advertising

1. In the ad in Figure 1, 1-800-CONTACTS reaches out to price-sensitive contact-lens users with an offer to "Get the exact same contacts delivered for less than you're paying now."
   a. What specific elements might affect price sensitivity in the consumer market for contact lenses?
   b. What pricing method does 1-800-CONTACTS appear to be using in this ad?
   c. How might 1-800-CONTACTS use product-bundling pricing to increase sales to its target market?

2. The ad in Figure 2 shows how the online auction site eBay ™ attracts price-sensitive business buyers to auctions for electronic gear such as projectors, monitors, PCs, and television monitors.
   a. Since product prices are never mentioned, what benefits does eBay emphasize to encourage business buyers to visit its Web site?
   b. Is business demand for slide projectors likely to be elastic or inelastic? What are the implications for the auction prices of projectors sold to business customers on eBay's site?
   c. Which of Nagle's nine factors affecting price sensitivity are most applicable to business demand for slide projectors?

Figure 1

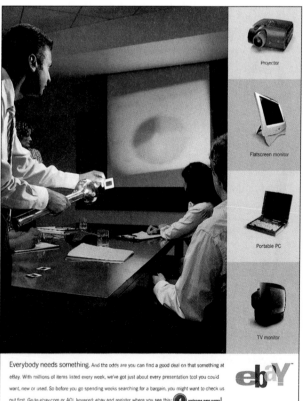

Figure 2

online marketing today

The online market for travel services will reach $63 billion within a few years, and Priceline.com is aiming to capture a significant share; already, it is high on the top-10 list of travel Web sites. After a brief period of diversification into name-your-price sales of groceries and gasoline, the company has refocused on its core travel and financial services offerings, including airline tickets, hotel rooms, rental cars, and mortgage loans. The company guarantees that a Priceline.com mortgage is the "lowest-cost loan on the market" and backs this up by paying $300 to any customer who finds a better price.[43]

See how the system works by visiting the Priceline Web site at *www.priceline.com*. Follow the link marked "How it works" to read about the name-your-price process. Then return to the home page and follow several of the links promoting discounted offerings. What can you say about the price sensitivity of Priceline's customers? What effect would Priceline's prices be likely to have on the reference prices customers bear in mind for travel and mortgage services? How does the company's lowest-cost loan guarantee affect a customer's perception of the product's value?

you're the marketer: sonic pda marketing plan

Marketing Plan Pro

Pricing is a critical element in any company's marketing plan, because it directly affects revenue and profit goals. To effectively design and manage pricing strategies, marketers must consider costs as well as the perceptions of customers and the reactions of competitors—especially in highly competitive markets.

You are in charge of pricing Sonic's first personal digital assistant for its launch early next year. Review your current situation, especially the SWOT analysis you previously prepared and your competitive environment. Also think about the markets you are targeting and the positioning you want to achieve. Now continue working on your marketing plan by responding to the following questions about pricing:

- What should Sonic's primary pricing objective be? Explain your reasoning.

- Are PDA customers likely to be price-sensitive? Is demand elastic or inelastic? What are the implications for your pricing decisions?
- How will the introductory product pricing work with the other parts of Sonic's marketing mix?
- What price adaptations (such as discounts, allowances, and promotional pricing) should Sonic include in its marketing plan?

After you have developed your pricing strategies and programs, document your recommendations in a written marketing plan or type them into the Marketing Mix section of the *Marketing Plan Pro* software, depending on your instructor's directions.

notes

1. David J. Schwartz, *Marketing Today: A Basic Approach*, 3rd ed. (New York: Harcourt Brace Jovanovich, 1981), p. 271.
2. Kara Swisher, "Electronics 2001: The Essential Guide," *Wall Street Journal*, January 5, 2001.
3. Steve Gelsi, "Spin-Cycle Doctor," *Brandweek*, March 10, 1997, pp. 38–40; Tim Stevens, "From Reliable to 'Wow,'" *Industry Week*, June 22, 1998, pp. 22–26; Juan Koncius, "A New Spin on Doing Your Laundry," *Washington Post*, April 12, 2001, p. A1.
4. Thomas T. Nagle and Reed K. Holden, *The Strategy and Tactics of Pricing*, 3rd ed. (Upper Saddle River, NJ: Prentice Hall, 2001), ch. 4. This is an excellent reference book for making pricing decisions.
5. Kevin J. Clancy, "At What Profit Price?" *Brandweek*, June 23, 1997, pp. 24–28; Monica Perin, "Vermont Energy Firm Green Mountain Moves to Texas with Increase in Capital," *Houston Business Journal*, May 12, 2000, p. 5A.
6. Sidney Bennett and J. B. Wilkinson, "Price-Quantity Relationships and Price Elasticity under In-Store Experimentation," *Journal of Business Research* (January 1974): 30–34.
7. Walter Baker, Mike Marn, and Craig Zawada, "Price Smarter on the Net," *Harvard Business Review* (February 2001): 122–27.
8. John R. Nevin, "Laboratory Experiments for Estimating Consumer Demand: A Validation Study," *Journal of Marketing Research* (August 1974): 261–68; Jonathan Weiner, "Forecasting Demand: Consumer Electronics Marketer Uses a Conjoint Approach to Configure Its New Product and Set the Right Price," *Marketing Research: A Magazine of Management & Applications* (Summer 1994): 6–11.
9. Nagle and Holden, *The Strategy and Tactics of Pricing*, ch. 13.
10. For summary of elasticity studies, see Dominique M. Hanssens, Leonard J. Parsons, and Randall L. Schultz, *Market Response Models: Econometric and Time Series Analysis* (Boston: Kluwer Academic Publishers, 1990), pp. 187–91.
11. Gene Epstein, "Economic Beat: Stretching Things," *Barron's*, December 15, 1997, p. 65.
12. William W. Alberts, "The Experience Curve Doctrine Reconsidered," *Journal of Marketing* (July 1989): 36–49.
13. Robin Cooper and Robert S. Kaplan, "Profit Priorities from Activity-Based Costing," *Harvard Business Review* (May–June 1991): 130–35. For more on ABC, see ch. 24.
14. "Japan's Smart Secret Weapon," *Fortune*, August 12, 1991, p. 75.
15. Elyse Tanouye, "Drugs: Steep Markups on Generics Top Branded Drugs," *Wall Street Journal*, December 31, 1998, p. B1; Julie Appleby, "Drugmakers Fight Back as Patents Near Expiration," *USA Today*, November 26, 1999, p. 4B.
16. Tung-Zong Chang and Albert R. Wildt, "Price, Product Information, and Purchase Intention: An Empirical Study," *Journal of the Academy of Marketing Science* (Winter 1994): 16–27. See also G. Dean Kortge and Patrick A. Okonkwo, "Perceived

Value Approach to Pricing," *Industrial Marketing Management* (May 1993): 133–40.

17. James C. Anderson, Dipak C. Jain, and Pradeep K. Chintagunta, "Customer Value Assessment in Business Markets: A State-of-Practice Study," *Journal of Business-to-Business Marketing* 1, no. 1 (1993): 3–29.

18. Bill Saporito, "Behind the Tumult at P&G," *Fortune*, March 7, 1994, pp. 74–82. For empirical analysis of its effects, see Kusom L. Ailawadi, Donald R. Lehmann, and Scott A. Neslin, "Market Response to a Major Policy Change in the Marketing Mix: Learning from Procter & Gamble's Value Pricing Strategy," *Journal of Marketing* 65 (January 2001): 44–61.

19. Stephen J. Hoch, Xavier Dreze, and Mary J. Purk, "EDLP, Hi-Lo, and Margin Arithmetic," *Journal of Marketing* (October 1994): 16–27; Rajiv Lal and R. Rao, "Supermarket Competition: The Case of Everyday Low Pricing," *Marketing Science* 16, no. 1 (1997): 60–80.

20. Becky Bull, "No Consensus on Pricing," *Progressive Grocer* (November 1998): 87–90.

21. Gary M. Erickson and Johny K. Johansson, "The Role of Price in Multi-Attribute Product-Evaluations," *Journal of Consumer Research* (September 1985): 195–99.

22. K. N. Rajendran and Gerard J. Tellis, "Contextual and Temporal Components of Reference Price," *Journal of Marketing* (January 1994): 22–34; Goromurthy Kalyanaram and Rossell S. Winer, "Empirical Generalizations from Reference Price Research," *Marketing Science*, 14(3), G161–G169.

23. Eric Anderson and Duncan Simester, "The Role of Price Endings: Why Stores May Sell More at $49 than at $44," an unpublished conference paper, April 2001.

24. Paul W. Farris and David J. Reibstein, "How Prices, Expenditures, and Profits Are Linked," *Harvard Business Review* (November–December 1979): 173–84. See also Makoto Abe, "Price and Advertising Strategy of a National Brand against Its Private-Label Clone: A Signaling Game Approach," *Journal of Business Research* (July 1995): 241–50.

25. J. P. Morgan Report, "eTailing and the Five C's."

26. Eugene H. Fram and Michael S. McCarthy, "The True Price of Penalties," *Marketing Management* (October 1999): 49–56.

27. Gary McWilliams, "How Dell Fine-Tunes Its PC Pricing to Gain Edge in a Slow Market," *Wall Street Journal*, June 8, 2001, p. A1.

28. Michael Rowe, *Countertrade* (London: Euromoney Books, 1989); P. N. Agarwala, *Countertrade: A Global Perspective* (New Delhi: Vikas Publishing House, 1991); Christopher M. Korth, ed., *International Countertrade* (New York: Quorum Books, 1987).

29. Michael V. Marn and Robert L. Rosiello, "Managing Price, Gaining Profit," *Harvard Business Review* (September–October 1992): 84–94. See also Gerard J. Tellis, "Tackling the Retailer Decision Maze: Which Brands to Discount, How Much, When, and Why?" *Marketing Science* 14, no. 3, pt. 2 (1995): 271–99; Kusom L. Ailawadi, Scott A. Neslin, and Karen Gedeak,

"Pursuing the Value-Conscious Consumer: Store Brands Versus National Brand Promotions," *Journal of Marketing* 65 (January 2001): 71–89.

30. Jack Trout, "Prices: Simple Guidelines to Get Them Right," *Journal of Business Strategy* (November–December 1998): 13–16.

31. Kevin J. Clancy, "At What Profit Price?" *Brandweek*, June 23, 1997.

32. Robert E. Weigand, "Yield Management: Filling Buckets, Papering the House," *Business Horizons* (September–October 1999): 55–64.

33. For more information on specific types of price discrimination that are illegal, see Henry Cheesman, *Contemporary Business Law* (Upper Saddle River, NJ: Prentice Hall, 1995).

34. Mike France, "Does Predatory Pricing Make Microsoft a Predator?" *BusinessWeek*, November 23, 1998, pp. 130–32. Also see Joseph P. Guiltinan and Gregory T. Gundlack, "Aggressive and Predatory Pricing: A Framework for Analysis," *Journal of Advertising* (July 1996): 87–102.

35. Andy Reinhardt, "Who Says Intel's Chips Are Down?" *BusinessWeek*, December 7, 1998, pp. 103–4; Therese Poletti, "Computer-Chip Price War Breaks Out," *San Jose Mercury News*, April 17, 2001.

36. Lee Gomes, "Computer-Printer Price Drop Isn't Starving Makers," *Wall Street Journal*, August 16, 1996, p. B4; Simon Avery, "H-P Sees Room for Growth in Printer Market," *Wall Street Journal*, June 28, 2001, p. B6.

37. Robert E. Weigand, "Buy In-Follow On Strategies for Profit," *Sloan Management Review* (Spring 1991): 29–37.

38. Susan Krafft, "Love, Love Me Doo," *American Demographics* (June 1994): 15–16.

39. See Gerald J. Tellis, "Beyond the Many Faces of Price: An Integration of Pricing Strategies," *Journal of Marketing* (October 1986): 155. This excellent article also analyzes and illustrates other pricing strategies. Also see Dilip Soman and John T. Gourville, "Transaction Decoupling: How Price Bundling Affects the Decision to Consume," *Journal of Marketing Research*, 38 (February 2001): 30–44.

40. "Costly Cornflakes," *New York Times*, January 12, 1999, p. A1; "Bowl of Kellogg Flakes to Cost More," *New Orleans Times-Picayune*, December 15, 1998, p. C2; Steven Pearlstein, "Making Shredded Wheat of Inflation," *Washington Post*, April 14, 1994, p. A1; "Why Cookies Look Grreat," *Newsweek*, November 6, 2000, p. 56.

41. Eric Mitchell, "How Not to Raise Prices," *Small Business Reports* (November 1990): 64–67.

42. For excellent review, see Kent B. Monroe, "Buyers' Subjective Perceptions of Price," *Journal of Marketing Research* (February 1973): 70–80.

43. Robert Julavits, "Priceline.com Sticking with Web Venture," *American Banker*, October 24, 2001, p. 16; Mike Beirne, "Upping the Ante," *Brandweek*, September 10, 2001, p. 31+.

C H A P T E R

17

designing and managing value networks and marketing channels

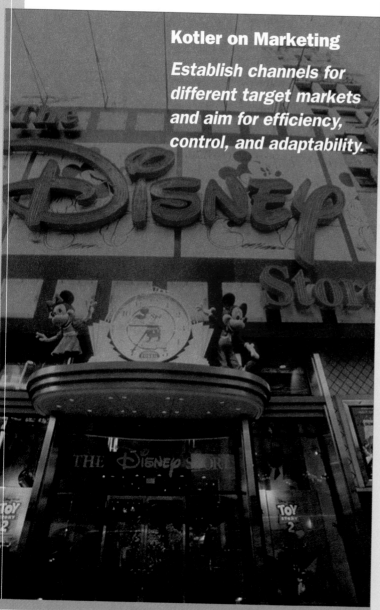

Kotler on Marketing

Establish channels for different target markets and aim for efficiency, control, and adaptability.

In this chapter, we will address the following questions:

- What is a value network and marketing-channel system?
- What work is performed by marketing channels?
- What decisions do companies face in designing, managing, evaluating, and modifying their channels?
- What trends are taking place in channel dynamics?
- How can channel conflict be managed?

Companies are increasingly taking a value network *view of their businesses. Instead of limiting their focus to their immediate* suppliers, distributors, and customers, they are examining the whole supply chain *that links raw material, components, and manufactured goods and shows how they are moved toward the final consumers. Companies are looking at their suppliers' suppliers upstream and at their distributors' customers downstream.*

Even the term supply chain *can be criticized for taking a make-and-sell view of the business. It suggests that raw materials, productive inputs, and factory capacity should serve as the starting point for market planning. A better term would be* demand chain *because it suggests a "sense-and-respond" view of the market. The planning starting point would be a customer segment with certain needs, to which the company responds by organizing resources.*

Experts are even beginning to say that a supply chain or demand chain view of a business is still too limited because it takes a linear or vertical view of purchase-production-consumption activities. With the advent of the Internet, companies are forming more numerous and complex relationships with other firms. For example, Ford not only manages numerous supply chains, but also sponsors or transacts on many B2B Web sites and exchanges as needs arise. Ford recently formed a buying alliance with GM and DaimlerChrysler to obtain lower prices by aggregating orders for common requirements from auto parts suppliers. Companies today are engaged in building and managing a continuously evolving value network.

what is a value network and marketing-channel system?

We define a value network as follows: A **value network** is a system of partnerships and alliances that a firm creates to source, augment, and deliver its offerings. Consider Palm's value network.

Palm, Inc. Palm, the leading manufacturer of handheld devices, is a whole community of suppliers and assemblers of semiconductor components, plastic cases, LCD displays, and accessories; of off-line and online resellers; and of 45,000 complementors who have created over 5,000 applications for the Palm operating systems.

This perspective yields several insights. First, the company can estimate whether more money is made upstream or downstream, in case it might want to integrate backward or forward. Second, the company is more aware of disturbances anywhere in the supply chain that might cause costs, prices, or supplies to change suddenly. Third, more companies are eager to go online with their business partners to carry on faster and more accurate communications, transactions, and payments; this will reduce costs, speed up information, and increase accuracy.

Managing this value network has required companies to make increasing investments in information technology (IT) and software. They have invited such software firms as SAP and Oracle to design comprehensive *enterprise resource planning* (ERP) systems to manage cash flow, manufacturing, human resources, purchasing, and other major functions within a unified framework. They hope to break up department silos and carry out core business processes more seamlessly. In most cases, however, companies are still a long way from truly comprehensive ERP systems.

Marketers, for their part, have traditionally focused on the side of the value network that looks forward toward the customer. Hopefully, they will increasingly participate in and influence their companies' upstream activities and become network managers, not only product and customer managers. Most producers do not sell their goods directly to the final users; between them stands a set of intermediaries performing a variety of functions. These intermediaries constitute a **marketing channel** (also called a trade channel or distribution channel).

Some intermediaries—such as wholesalers and retailers—buy, take title to, and resell the merchandise; they are called merchants. Others—brokers, manufacturers' representatives, sales agents—search for customers and may negotiate on the producer's behalf but do not take title to the goods; they are called agents. Still others—transportation companies, independent warehouses, banks, advertising agencies—assist in the distribution process but neither take title to goods nor negotiate purchases or sales; they are called facilitators.

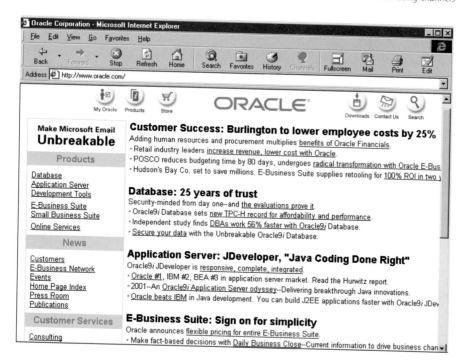

Oracle's home page.

Marketing channels are sets of interdependent organizations involved in the process of making a product or service available for use or consumption.[1] Marketing-channel decisions are among the most critical decisions facing management. The channels chosen intimately affect all the other marketing decisions. The company's pricing depends on whether it uses mass-merchandisers or high-quality boutiques. The firm's sales force and advertising decisions depend on how much training and motivation dealers need. In addition, the company's channel decisions involve relatively long-term commitments to other firms. When an automaker signs up independent dealers to sell its automobiles, the automaker cannot buy them out the next day and replace them with company-owned outlets. E. Raymond Corey observed:

> A distribution system . . . is a key external resource. Normally it takes years to build, and it is not easily changed. It ranks in importance with key internal resources such as manufacturing, research, engineering, and field sales personnel and facilities. It represents a significant corporate commitment to large numbers of independent companies whose business is distribution—and to the particular markets they serve. It represents, as well, a commitment to a set of policies and practices that constitute the basic fabric on which is woven an extensive set of long-term relationships.[2]

Today's companies are multiplying the number of "go-to-market" or **hybrid** channels:

- IBM uses its sales force to sell to large accounts, outbound telemarketing to sell to medium-sized accounts, direct mail with an inbound number for small accounts, retailers to sell to still smaller accounts, and the Internet to sell specialty items.
- Charles Schwab enables its customers to do transactions in its branches, over the phone, or on the Internet.
- Staples markets through its traditional retail channel, a direct-response Internet site, virtual malls, and 30,000 links on affiliated sites.

Companies that manage hybrid channels must make sure these channels work well together and match each target customer's preferred ways of doing business.

figure 17.1

How a Distributor Effects an Economy of Effort

(a) Number of contacts
M x C = 3 x 3 = 9

(b) Number of contacts
M + C = 3 + 3 = 6

M = Manufacturer
C = Customer
D = Distributor

WingspanBank.com   In June 1999, Bank One launched a spin-off venture called WingspanBank to get into the online banking business, but it developed Wingspan-Bank as a separate entity; WingspanBank customers could not use Bank One branches to do their banking in person. No wonder it only garnered 144,000 accounts and had to be closed down as a separate venture.

Customers expect *channel integration*, characterized by the following features:

- The ability to order a product online and pick it up at a convenient retail location.
- The ability to return an online-ordered product to a nearby store of the retailer.
- The right to receive discounts based on total online and off-line purchases.

We will examine marketing-channel issues from the perspective of retailers, wholesalers, and physical-distribution agencies in the next chapter.

what work is performed by marketing channels?

Why would a producer delegate some of the selling job to intermediaries? Delegation means relinquishing some control over how and to whom the products are sold, but producers do gain several advantages by using intermediaries:

- Many producers lack the financial resources to carry out direct marketing. For example, General Motors sells its cars through more than 8,100 dealer outlets in North America alone. Even General Motors would be hard-pressed to raise the cash to buy out its dealers.
- In some cases direct marketing simply is not feasible. The William Wrigley Jr. Company would not find it practical to establish small retail gum shops throughout the world or to sell gum by mail order. It would have to sell gum along with many other small products and would end up in the drugstore and grocery store business. Wrigley finds it easier to work through the extensive network of privately owned distribution organizations.
- Producers who do establish their own channels can often earn a greater return by increasing their investment in their main business. If a company earns a 20 percent rate of return on manufacturing and only a 10 percent return on retailing, it does not make sense to undertake its own retailing.

Intermediaries normally achieve superior efficiency in making goods widely available and accessible to target markets. Through their contacts, experience, specialization, and scale of operation, intermediaries usually offer the firm more than it can achieve on its own. According to Stern and El-Ansary:

> Intermediaries smooth the flow of goods and services. . . . This procedure is necessary in order to bridge the discrepancy between the assortment of goods and services generated by the producer and the assortment demanded by the consumer. The discrepancy results from the fact that manufacturers typically produce a large quantity of a limited variety of goods, whereas consumers usually desire only a limited quantity of a wide variety of goods.[3]

Figure 17.1 shows one major source of cost savings using intermediaries. Part (a) shows three producers, each using direct marketing to reach three customers. This system requires nine different contacts. Part (b) shows the three producers working through one distributor, who contacts the three customers. This system requires only six contacts. In this way, intermediaries reduce the number of contacts and the work.

channel functions and flows

A marketing channel performs the work of moving goods from producers to consumers. It overcomes the time, place, and possession gaps that separate goods and services from those who need or want them. Members of the marketing channel perform a number of key functions:

- They gather information about potential and current customers, competitors, and other actors and forces in the marketing environment.
- They develop and disseminate persuasive communications to stimulate purchasing.

| figure **17.2** | Five Marketing Flows in the Marketing Channel for Forklift Trucks |

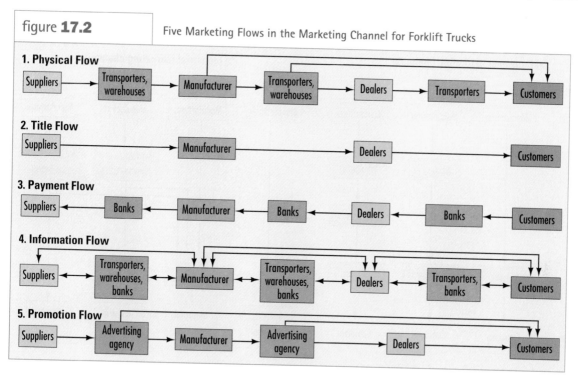

- They reach agreements on price and other terms so that transfer of ownership or possession can be effected.
- They place orders with manufacturers.
- They acquire the funds to finance inventories at different levels in the marketing channel.
- They assume risks connected with carrying out channel work.
- They provide for the successive storage and movement of physical products.
- They provide for buyers' payment of their bills through banks and other financial institutions.
- They oversee actual transfer of ownership from one organization or person to another.

Some functions (physical, title, promotion) constitute a *forward flow* of activity from the company to the customer; other functions (ordering and payment) constitute a *backward flow* from customers to the company. Still others (information, negotiation, finance, and risk taking) occur in both directions. Five flows are illustrated in Figure 17.2 for the marketing of forklift trucks. If these flows were superimposed in one diagram, the tremendous complexity of even simple marketing channels would be apparent. A manufacturer selling a physical product and services might require three channels: a *sales channel*, a *delivery channel*, and a *service channel*. Dell Computer uses the telephone and the Internet as sales channels, express mail services as the delivery channel, and local repair people as the service channel.

The question is not *whether* various channel functions need to be performed—they must be—but rather, *who* is to perform them. All channel functions have three things in common: They use up scarce resources; they can often be performed better through specialization; and they can be shifted among channel members. When the manufacturer shifts some functions to intermediaries, the producer's costs and prices are lower, but the intermediary must add a charge to cover its work. If the intermediaries are more efficient than the manufacturer, prices to consumers should be lower. If consumers perform some functions themselves, they should enjoy even lower prices.

Marketing functions, then, are more basic than the institutions that perform them at any given time. Changes in channel institutions largely reflect the discovery of more

| figure **17.3** | Consumer and Industrial Marketing Channels |

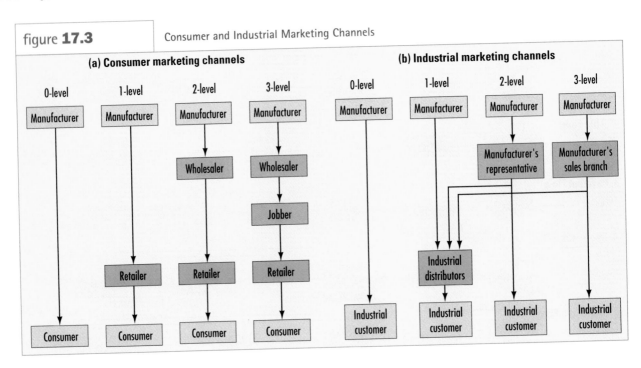

efficient ways to combine or separate the economic functions that provide assortments of goods to target customers.

channel levels

The producer and the final customer are part of every channel. We will use the number of intermediary levels to designate the length of a channel. Figure 17.3(a) illustrates several consumer-goods marketing channels of different lengths.

A **zero-level channel** (also called a *direct-marketing channel*) consists of a manufacturer selling directly to the final customer. The major examples are door-to-door sales, home parties, mail order, telemarketing, TV selling, Internet selling, and manufacturer-owned stores. Avon sales representatives sell cosmetics door-to-door; Tupperware representatives sell kitchen goods through home parties; Franklin Mint sells collectibles through mail order; Shearson-Lehman brokers use the telephone to prospect for new customers; some exercise equipment manufacturers sell through TV commercials or hour-long "infomercials"; Amazon sells books online; and Gateway sells computers through its own stores.

A **one-level channel** contains one selling intermediary, such as a retailer. A **two-level channel** contains two intermediaries. In consumer markets, these are typically a wholesaler and a retailer. A **three-level channel** contains three intermediaries. In the meatpacking industry, wholesalers sell to jobbers, who sell to small retailers. Longer marketing channels can be found. In Japan, food distribution may involve as many as six levels. From the producer's point of view, obtaining information about end users and exercising control becomes more difficult as the number of channel levels increases.

Figure 17.3(b) shows channels commonly used in industrial marketing. An industrial-goods manufacturer can use its sales force to sell directly to industrial customers; or it can sell to industrial distributors, who sell to the industrial customers; or it can sell through manufacturer's representatives or its own sales branches directly to industrial customers, or indirectly to industrial customers through industrial distributors. Zero-, one-, and two-level marketing channels are quite common in industrial marketing channels.

Channels normally describe a forward movement of products from source to user. One can also talk about *reverse-flow channels*. They are important in the following cases: (1) to reuse products or containers (such as refillable chemical-carrying drums); (2) to refurbish products (such as circuit boards or computers) for resale; (3) to recycle products (such as paper); and (4) to dispose of products and packaging (waste products). Zikmund and Stanton have commented on reverse-flow channels for recycling or disposal:

> The recycling of solid wastes is a major ecological goal. Although recycling is technologically feasible, reversing the flow of materials in the channel of distribution—marketing trash through a "backward" channel—presents a challenge. Existing backward channels are primitive, and financial incentives are inadequate. The consumer must be motivated to undergo a role change and become a producer—the initiating force in the reverse distribution process.[4]

Several intermediaries play a role in reverse-flow channels, including manufacturers' redemption centers, community groups, traditional intermediaries such as soft-drink intermediaries, trash-collection specialists, recycling centers, trash-recycling brokers, and central-processing warehousing.[5]

service sector channels

The concept of marketing channels is not limited to the distribution of physical goods. Producers of services and ideas also face the problem of making their output available and accessible to target populations. Schools develop "educational-dissemination systems" and hospitals develop "health-delivery systems." These institutions must figure out agencies and locations for reaching a population spread out over an area.

> Hospitals must be located in geographic space to serve the people with complete medical care, and we must build schools close to the children who have to learn. Fire stations must be located to give rapid access to potential conflagrations, and voting booths must be placed so that people can cast their ballots without expending unreasonable amounts of time, effort, or money to reach the polling stations. Many of our states face the problem of locating branch campuses to serve a burgeoning and increasingly well educated population. In the cities we must create and locate playgrounds for the children. Many overpopulated countries must assign birth control clinics to reach the people with contraceptive and family planning information.[6]

As Internet technology advances, service industries such as banking, insurance, travel, and stock buying and selling will take place through new channels.

Peoples.com Connecticut-based People's Bank, a brick-and-mortar bank, added an Internet site as early as 1995 to provide additional services and convenience to its customers. The site contains a "live banker now" feature that allows its customers to "live chat" with a representative any time during 11 hours of the day, Monday through Friday, about mortgages, CD rates, and other banking questions. The customer can hit a "Call Me Now" button to request a phone call. The bank is receiving about 20,000 e-mails per month and answering them within four hours, which is considered good service. The site contains easy-to-use mortgage and savings demos. Clients can integrate their banking and brokerage accounts, pay bills online, borrow money online, and access their credit card histories. While the site's primary role is to provide access and convenience to the bank's existing clients, it is also used to attract new clients.[7]

Marketing channels also keep changing in "person" marketing. Before 1940, professional comedians could reach audiences through seven channels: vaudeville houses, special events, nightclubs, radio, movies, carnivals, and theaters. Vaudeville houses have vanished and been replaced by comedy clubs and cable television stations. Politicians also must choose a mix of channels—mass-media, rallies, coffee hours, spot TV ads, faxes, Web sites—for delivering their messages to voters.[8]

The People's Bank Internet site, with the many services it offers to make banking easier for customers.

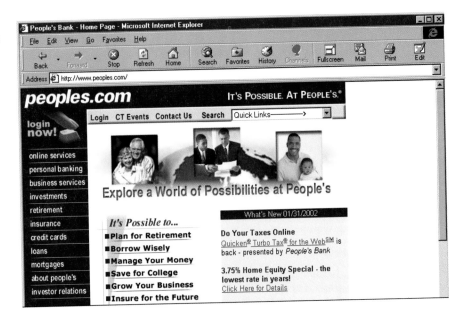

information highway channels

There was a time when information could only be passed from mouth to mouth, or by posters, or by mail. The invention of the telegraph made it possible to communicate over long distances by encrypting messages in dots and dashes. The telephone made it possible to communicate by voice using copper wires. Radio and television send voice and video signals through the wireless electromagnetic spectrum. Cable sends video content over coaxial cables. Satellite introduced the capability of beaming data, voice, text, and videos from satellites orbiting the earth.

Each information channel was originally designed to carry one type of information. Telephone carried voice, cable networks carried video programming, ATMs carried data. Today, there is a major drive to expand bandwidth so that these channels can effectively carry data, voice, video, and text. The rapid growth of the Internet, extranets, and intranets has created a huge demand for information channel capacity. Copper wires have too limited a bandwidth, so much hope lies in expanding the carrying capacity of fiber and in wireless transmission.

Marketers need to understand that these information channels require the inputs of four types of companies to function effectively: *content* companies (Disney, Time Warner, Prentice Hall), *consumer devices* companies (Nokia, Motorola, Sony, Palm), *components* companies (Lucent, Cisco), and *conduit* companies (AT&T, WorldCom, Verizon). These companies make up the information industry, and they face distinct marketing challenges in running their respective businesses.

channel-design decisions

A new firm typically starts as a local operation selling in a limited market, using existing intermediaries. The number of intermediaries in any local market is apt to be limited: a few manufacturers' sales agents, a few wholesalers, several established retailers, a few trucking companies, and a few warehouses. Deciding on the best channels might not be a problem. The problem might be to convince the available intermediaries to handle the firm's line.

If the firm is successful, it might branch into new markets. It might have to use different channels in different markets. In smaller markets, the firm might sell directly to retailers; in larger markets, it might sell through distributors. In rural areas, it might work with general-goods merchants; in urban areas, with limited-line merchants. In one part of the country, it might grant exclusive franchises; in another, it might sell through all outlets willing to handle the merchandise. In one country it might use international sales agents; in another, it might partner with a local firm.[9] In short, the channel system evolves in response to local opportunities and conditions.

In managing its intermediaries, the firm must decide how much effort to devote to push versus pull marketing. A **push strategy** involves the manufacturer using its sales force and trade promotion money to induce intermediaries to carry, promote, and sell the product to end users. Push strategy is appropriate where there is low brand loyalty in a category, brand choice is made in the store, the product is an impulse item, and product benefits are well understood. A **pull strategy** involves the manufacturer using advertising and promotion to induce consumers to ask intermediaries for the product, thus inducing the intermediaries to order it. Pull strategy is appropriate when there is high brand loyalty and high involvement in the category, when people perceive differences between brands, and when people choose the brand before they go to the store. Companies in the same industry may differ in their emphasis on push or pull.

Designing a channel system involves four steps: (1) analyzing customer needs, (2) establishing channel objectives, (3) identifying major channel alternatives, and (4) evaluating major channel alternatives.

analyze customers' desired service output levels

In designing the marketing channel, the marketer must understand the service output levels desired by target customers. Channels produce five service outputs:

1. *Lot size:* The number of units the channel permits a typical customer to purchase on one occasion. In buying cars for its fleet, Hertz prefers a channel from which it can buy a large lot size; a household wants a channel that permits buying a lot size of one.

2. *Waiting time:* The average time customers of that channel wait for receipt of the goods. Customers normally prefer fast delivery channels.

3. *Spatial convenience:* The degree to which the marketing channel makes it easy for customers to purchase the product. Chevrolet, for example, offers greater spatial convenience than Cadillac, because there are more Chevrolet dealers. Chevrolet's greater market decentralization helps customers save on transportation and search costs in buying and repairing an automobile.

4. *Product variety:* The assortment breadth provided by the marketing channel. Normally, customers prefer a greater assortment because more choices increase the chance of finding what they need.

5. *Service backup:* The add-on services (credit, delivery, installation, repairs) provided by the channel. The greater the service backup, the greater the work provided by the channel.[10]

The marketing-channel designer knows that providing greater service outputs means increased channel costs and higher prices for customers. The success of discount stores indicates that many consumers are willing to accept smaller service outputs if they can save money.

establish objectives and constraints

Channel objectives should be stated in terms of targeted service output levels. According to Louis Bucklin, under competitive conditions, channel institutions should arrange their functional tasks to minimize total channel costs with respect to desired levels of service outputs.[11] Usually, several market segments that desire differing service output levels can be identified. Effective planning requires determining which market segments to serve and the best channels to use in each case.

Channel objectives vary with product characteristics. Perishable products require more direct marketing. Bulky products, such as building materials, require channels that minimize the shipping distance and the amount of handling. Nonstandardized products, such as custom-built machinery and specialized business forms, are sold directly by company sales representatives. Products requiring installation or maintenance services, such as heating and cooling systems, are usually sold and maintained by the company or by franchised dealers. High-unit-value products such as generators and turbines are often sold through a company sales force rather than intermediaries.

Channel design must take into account the strengths and weaknesses of different types of intermediaries. For example, manufacturers' reps are able to contact customers at a low cost per customer because the total cost is shared by several clients, but the selling effort per customer is less intense than if company sales reps did the selling. Channel design is also influenced by competitors' channels.

Channel design must adapt to the larger environment. When economic conditions are depressed, producers want to move their goods to market using shorter channels and without services that add to the final price of the goods. Legal regulations and restrictions also affect channel design. U.S. law looks unfavorably on channel arrangements that may tend to substantially lessen competition or create a monopoly.

identify major channel alternatives

Companies can choose from a wide variety of channels for reaching customers—from sales forces to agents, distributors, dealers, direct mail, telemarketing, and the Internet. Each channel has unique strengths as well as weaknesses. Sales forces can handle complex products and transactions, but they are expensive. The Internet is much less expensive, but it cannot handle complex products. Distributors can create sales, but the company loses direct contact with customers.

The problem is further complicated by the fact that most companies now use a mix of channels. Each channel hopefully reaches a different segment of buyers and delivers the right products to each at the least cost. When this does not happen, there is usually channel conflict and excessive cost.

A channel alternative is described by three elements: the types of available business intermediaries, the number of intermediaries needed, and the terms and responsibilities of each channel member.

TYPES OF INTERMEDIARIES   A firm needs to identify the types of intermediaries available to carry on its channel work. Here are two examples:

A test-equipment manufacturer developed an audio device for detecting poor mechanical connections in machines with moving parts. Company executives felt this product would sell in all industries where electric, combustion, or steam engines were used, such as aviation, automobiles, railroads, food canning, construction, and oil. The sales force was small. The problem was how to reach these diverse industries effectively. The following alternatives were identified:

- Expand the company's direct sales force. Assign sales representatives to contact all prospects in an area, or develop separate sales forces for the different industries.
- Hire manufacturers' agents in different regions or end-use industries to sell the new equipment.
- Find distributors in the different regions or end-use industries who will buy and carry the device. Give them exclusive distribution, adequate margins, product training, and promotional support.

A consumer electronics company produces cellular car phones. It identified the following channel alternatives:

- The company could sell its car phones to automobile manufacturers to be installed as original equipment.
- The company could sell its car phones to auto dealers.
- The company could sell its car phones to retail automotive-equipment dealers through a direct sales force or through distributors.

- The company could sell its car phones to car phone specialist dealers through a direct sales force or dealers.
- The company could sell its car phones through mail-order catalogs.
- The company could sell its car phones through mass merchandisers such as Best Buy or Circuit City.

Companies should search for innovative marketing channels. The Conn Organ Company merchandises organs through department stores and discount stores, thus drawing more attention than it ever enjoyed in small music stores. The Book-of-the-Month Club merchandises books through the mail. Other sellers have followed with record-of-the-month clubs, candy-of-the-month clubs, flower-of-the-month clubs, fruit-of-the-month clubs, and dozens of others.

Sometimes a company chooses an unconventional channel because of the difficulty or cost of working with the dominant channel. The advantage is that the company will encounter less competition during the initial move into this channel. After trying to sell its inexpensive Timex watches through regular jewelry stores, the U.S. Time Company placed its watches in fast-growing mass-merchandise outlets. Avon chose door-to-door selling because it was not able to break into regular department stores. The company made more money than most firms selling through department stores.

Chiodo Candy Company   In the 1980s, Chiodo Candy was getting clobbered by candy mega-company E. J. Brach in the war for supermarket shelf space. The company began looking for alternative distribution channels. In 1988 it came up with a winner in the new club and warehouse stores. Club stores did not require any shelving fees and were receptive to new products. These stores wanted large packages, so Chiodo developed a plastic tub that could hold up to two pounds of penny candy. Soon club buyers were ordering more than 8,000 tubs at a time.[12]

NUMBER OF INTERMEDIARIES   Companies have to decide on the number of intermediaries to use at each channel level. Three strategies are available: exclusive distribution, selective distribution, and intensive distribution.

Exclusive distribution means severely limiting the number of intermediaries. It is used when the producer wants to maintain control over the service level and outputs offered by the resellers. Often it involves *exclusive dealing* arrangements. By granting exclusive distribution, the producer hopes to obtain more dedicated and knowledgeable selling. It requires greater partnership between seller and reseller and is used in the distribution of new automobiles, some major appliances, and some women's apparel brands. Relationships with intermediaries and the corporation can be strained when a company decides to alter an exclusive distribution relationship.

Avon   After 115 years of using only "Avon Ladies" to sell directly to consumers, in 2001, Avon Products, Inc., negotiated with Sears and JCPenney to develop in-store sales of the company's cosmetics. To avoid alienating its 500,000 U.S. representatives, the company moved cautiously at first. Avon planned to debut its in-store beauty centers, which resemble both mini-salons and typical cosmetic counters, in only 70 of JCPenney's 1,140 stores and only a few dozen of Sears' 860 stores. Avon also developed a new and separate product line called Avon Gold, which differs in price, packaging, and content from the products sold by Avon Ladies.[13]

Selective distribution involves the use of more than a few but less than all of the intermediaries who are willing to carry a particular product. It is used by established companies and by new companies seeking distributors. The company does not have to worry about too many outlets; it can gain adequate market coverage with more control and less cost than intensive distribution. Disney is a good example of selective distribution.

Disney Disney sells its videos through five different channels: Movie rental stores like Blockbuster; the company's proprietary retail stores, called Disney Stores; retail stores like Best Buy; online retailers like Amazon.com and Disney's own online Disney Stores; the Disney catalog and other catalog sellers. These varied channels afford Disney maximum market coverage, and enable the company to offer its videos at a number of price points.[14]

Intensive distribution consists of the manufacturer placing the goods or services in as many outlets as possible. This strategy is generally used for items such as tobacco products, soap, snack foods, and gum, products for which the consumer requires a great deal of location convenience.

Manufacturers are constantly tempted to move from exclusive or selective distribution to more intensive distribution to increase coverage and sales. This strategy may help in the short term, but often hurts long-term performance, as the Calvin Klein experience illustrates.

Calvin Klein In May 2000, designer Calvin Klein sued Linda Wachner, CEO of Warnaco Group Inc., for selling his jeans to cut-rate mass-market outlets without his permission. Warnaco, which has the license to make and distribute the jeans, was accused by Calvin Klein of making lower-quality jeans for these outlets, and therefore hurting his image. The suit was settled out of court in January 2001, and both sides said they "look forward to expanding jeanswear sales consistent with the image and prestige of Calvin Klein products." Warnaco would limit distributing jeanswear products to department and specialty stores.

TERMS AND RESPONSIBILITIES OF CHANNEL MEMBERS The producer must determine the rights and responsibilities of participating channel members. Each channel member must be treated respectfully and given the opportunity to be profitable.[15] The main elements in the "trade-relations mix" are price policies, conditions of sale, territorial rights, and specific services to be performed by each party.

Price policy calls for the producer to establish a price list and schedule of discounts and allowances that intermediaries see as equitable and sufficient.

Conditions of sale refers to payment terms and producer guarantees. Most producers grant cash discounts to distributors for early payment. Producers might also guarantee distributors against defective merchandise or price declines. A guarantee against price declines gives distributors an incentive to buy larger quantities.

Distributors' territorial rights define the distributors' territories and the terms under which the producer will enfranchise other distributors. Distributors normally expect to receive full credit for all sales in their territory, whether or not they did the selling.

Mutual services and responsibilities must be carefully spelled out, especially in franchised and exclusive-agency channels. McDonald's provides franchisees with a building, promotional support, a record-keeping system, training, and general administrative and technical assistance. In turn, franchisees are expected to satisfy company standards regarding physical facilities, cooperate with new promotional programs, furnish requested information, and buy supplies from specified vendors.

evaluate the major alternatives

Each channel alternative needs to be evaluated against economic, control, and adaptive criteria.

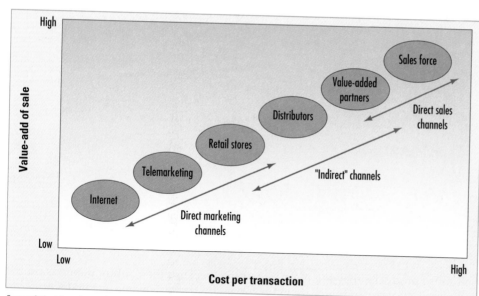

figure **17.4**

The Value–Adds Versus Costs of Different Channels

Source: Oxford Associates, adapted from Dr. Rowland T. Moriarty, Cubex Corp.

ECONOMIC CRITERIA Each channel alternative will produce a different level of sales and costs. Figure 17.4 shows how six different sales channels stack up in terms of the value added per sale and the cost per transaction. For example, in selling industrial products costing between $2,000 and $5,000, the cost per transaction is $500 (field sales), $200 (distributors), $50 (telesales), and $10 (Internet). Banks claim that in selling retail banking services, the cost per transaction is $2 (teller), $.50 (ATM), and $.10 (Internet). Clearly, sellers would try to replace high-cost channels with low-cost channels when the value added per sale was sufficient. When sellers discover a convenient lower-cost channel, they try to get their customers to use it. The company may reward customers for switching. SAS, the Scandinavian airline, gives bonus points to customers who order electronic tickets via the Internet. Other companies may raise the fees on customers using their higher-cost channels to get them to switch. Companies that are successful in switching their customers to lower-cost channels, assuming no loss of sales or deterioration in service quality, will gain a **channel advantage**.[16]

The lower-cost channels tend to be low-touch channels. This is not important in ordering commodity items, but buyers who are shopping for more complex products prefer high-touch channels such as salespeople.

As an example of an economic analysis of channel choices, consider the following situation:

A Memphis furniture manufacturer wants to sell its line to retailers on the West Coast. The manufacturer is trying to decide between two alternatives: One calls for hiring 10 new sales representatives who would operate out of a sales office in San Francisco. They would receive a base salary plus commissions. The other alternative would be to use a San Francisco manufacturers' sales agency that has extensive contacts with retailers. The agency has 30 sales representatives, who would receive a commission based on their sales.

The first step is to determine whether a company sales force or a sales agency will produce more sales. Most marketing managers believe that a company sales force will sell more. They concentrate on the company's products; they are better trained to

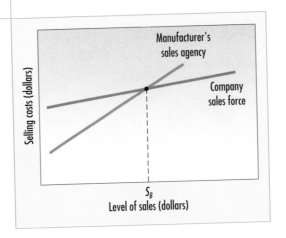

figure **17.5**

Break-even Cost Chart for the Choice Between a Company Sales Force and a Manufacturer's Sales Agency

sell those products; they are more aggressive because their future depends on the company's success; and they are more successful because many customers prefer to deal directly with the company. However, the sales agency could conceivably sell more. First, the agency has 30 representatives, not just 10. This sales force might be just as aggressive as a direct sales force, depending on the commission level. Some customers prefer dealing with agents who represent several manufacturers rather than with salespersons from one company; and the agency has extensive contacts and marketplace knowledge, whereas a company sales force would need to build these from scratch.

The next step is to estimate the costs of selling different volumes through each channel. The cost schedules are shown in Figure 17.5. The fixed costs of engaging a sales agency are lower than those of establishing a company sales office, but costs rise faster through an agency because sales agents get a larger commission than company salespeople. The final step is comparing sales and costs. As Figure 17.5 shows, there is one sales level (S_B) at which selling costs are the same for the two channels. The sales agency is thus the better channel for any sales volume below S_B, and the company sales branch is better at any volume above S_B. Given this information, it is not surprising that sales agents tend to be used by smaller firms, or by large firms in smaller territories where the volume is low.

CONTROL AND ADAPTIVE CRITERIA   Using a sales agency poses a control problem. A sales agency is an independent firm seeking to maximize its profits. Agents may concentrate on the customers who buy the most, not necessarily those who buy the manufacturer's goods. Furthermore, agents might not master the technical details of the company's product or handle its promotion materials effectively.

To develop a channel, members must make some degree of commitment to each other for a specified period of time. Yet these commitments invariably lead to a decrease in the producer's ability to respond to a changing marketplace. In rapidly changing, volatile, or uncertain product markets, the producer needs channel structures and policies that provide high adaptability.

channel-management decisions

After a company has chosen a channel alternative, individual intermediaries must be selected, trained, motivated, and evaluated. Channel arrangements must be modified over time.

selecting channel members

Companies need to select their channel members carefully. To customers, the channels are the company. Consider the negative impression customers would get of McDonald's, Shell Oil, or Ford if one or more of their outlets or dealers consistently appeared dirty, inefficient, or unpleasant.

Producers vary in their ability to attract qualified intermediaries. Toyota was able to attract many new dealers for its new Lexus. However, when Polaroid started up as a company, it could not get camera stores to carry its new cameras and was forced to use mass-merchandising outlets. Consider what happened at Epson.

Epson Japan's Epson Corporation, a leading manufacturer of computer printers, decided to add computers to its product line. Not happy with its current distributors nor trusting their ability to sell to new types of retail outlets, Epson quietly recruited new distributors. It gave Hergenrather, a recruiting company, the following instructions: (1) Search for applicants who have two-step distribution experience (factory to distributor to dealer). (2) Applicants have to be willing and able to set up their own distributorships. (3) They will be offered $80,000 yearly salary plus bonus and $375,000 to help them set up in business; each will add $25,000 of his or her own money, and each will get equity in the business. (4) They will handle only Epson products but may stock other companies' software. Each distributor will hire a training manager and run a fully equipped service center. The recruiting firm used the Yellow Pages to get the names of existing distributors and phoned the second-in-command managers. It arranged interviews and, after much work, produced a list of highly qualified individuals, from which it chose the 12 most qualified candidates. Epson's existing distributors were given a 90-day termination notice. Yet in spite of all these steps, Epson never succeeded as a computer manufacturer.[17]

Whether producers find it easy or difficult to recruit intermediaries, they should at least determine what characteristics distinguish the better intermediaries. They should evaluate the number of years in business, other lines carried, growth and profit record, financial strength, cooperativeness, and service reputation. If the intermediaries are sales agents, producers should evaluate the number and character of other lines carried and the size and quality of the sales force. If the intermediaries are department stores that want exclusive distribution, the producer should evaluate locations, future growth potential, and type of clientele.

training channel members

Companies need to plan and implement careful training programs for their intermediaries, because they will be viewed as the company by end users. Here are some examples of reseller training programs.

Microsoft Microsoft requires third-party service engineers to complete a set of courses and take certification exams. Those who pass are formally recognized as Microsoft Certified Professionals, and they can use this designation to promote business.

Mita Corporation Mita, producer of photocopying equipment, uses a specially created CD-ROM to train its dealers. A dealer's sales rep walks through all the steps in selling copier equipment, and because the CD-ROM program is interactive, the sales rep can "speak" to a hypothetical customer, make a sales presentation, handle objections, and ask for the sale. The rep's performance is scored and the CD-ROM program then offers suggestions for improvement.

Marketing
MEMO

Retail Cooperation Strategies

Alert manufacturers who want to develop stronger links with their retail customers are implementing a system called *efficient consumer response (ECR)*. Four tools are involved:

1. *Activity-based cost accounting.* This accounting method enables the manufacturer to measure and demonstrate the true costs of the resources consumed in meeting a retail chain's requirements.

2. *Electronic data interchange (EDI).* This data network technique improves the manufacturer's ability to manage inventory, shipments, and promotion.

3. *Continuous replenishment program (CRP).* Continuous replenishment enables manufacturers to replenish products on the basis of actual and forecasted store demand.

4. *Flow-through cross-dock replenishment.* This distribution method allows larger shipments headed for retailer distribution centers to be reloaded for shipment to individual stores, with little or no storage time lost at the distribution center.

Manufacturers that master ECR can gain an edge over their competitors.

Source: Gary Davies, *Trade Marketing Strategies* (London: Paul Chapman, 1993).

Ford Motor Company   Ford beams training programs and technical information via its satellite-based Fordstar Network to more than 6,000 dealer sites. Service engineers at each dealership sit around a conference table and view a monitor on which an instructor explains procedures such as repairing onboard electronics, and asks and answers questions. Increasingly, Ford is developing training programs that can be delivered to dealers over the Internet.

motivating channel members

A company needs to view its intermediaries in the same way it views its end users. It needs to determine intermediaries' needs and construct a channel positioning such that its channel offering is tailored to provide superior value to these intermediaries. (See "Marketing Memo: Retail Cooperation Strategies.")

The company should provide training programs, market research programs, and other capability-building programs to improve intermediaries' performance. The company must constantly communicate its view that the intermediaries are partners in a joint effort to satisfy end users of the product.

Brewski Brewing Company   When microbrewer Brewski Brewing Company launched its business, it offered attractive incentives to the large and small distributors who had signed on to sell its products. Once distributors began selling the product, they were rewarded with leather jackets valued at $300 for reaching distribution goals in a series of short-term incentive programs. In addition, distributors are empowered to offer top customers a solid wood, hand-carved, hand-painted tap handle that features the Brewski logo.[18]

Stimulating channel members to top performance starts with understanding their needs and wants. Philip McVey listed the following propositions to help understand intermediaries:

[The intermediary often acts] as a purchasing agent for his customers and only secondarily as a selling agent for his suppliers. . . . He is interested in selling any product which these customers desire to buy from him. . . .

The [intermediary] attempts to weld all of his offerings into a family of items which he can sell in combination, as a packaged assortment, to individual customers. His selling efforts are directed primarily at obtaining orders for the assortment, rather than for individual items. . . .

Unless given incentive to do so, [intermediaries] will not maintain separate sales records by brands sold. . . . Information that could be used in product development, pricing, packaging, or promotion planning is buried in nonstandard records of [intermediaries], and sometimes purposely secreted from suppliers.[19]

Producers vary greatly in skill in managing distributors. They can draw on the following types of power to elicit cooperation:

- *Coercive power:* A manufacturer threatens to withdraw a resource or terminate a relationship if intermediaries fail to cooperate. This power can be effective, but its exercise produces resentment and can lead the intermediaries to organize countervailing power.

- *Reward power:* The manufacturer offers intermediaries an extra benefit for performing specific acts or functions. Reward power typically produces better results than coercive power, but can be overrated. The intermediaries may come to expect a reward every time the manufacturer wants a certain behavior to occur.

- *Legitimate power:* The manufacturer requests a behavior that is warranted under the contract. As long as the intermediaries view the manufacturer as a legitimate leader, legitimate power works.

- *Expert power:* The manufacturer has special knowledge that the intermediaries value. Once the expertise is passed on to the intermediaries, however, this power weakens. The manufacturer must continue to develop new expertise so that the intermediaries will want to continue cooperating.
- *Referent power:* The manufacturer is so highly respected that intermediaries are proud to be associated with it. Companies such as IBM, Caterpillar, and Hewlett-Packard have high referent power.[20]

Intermediaries can aim for a relationship based on cooperation, partnership, or distribution programming.[21] Most producers see the main challenge as gaining intermediaries' cooperation. They often use positive motivators, such as higher margins, special deals, premiums, cooperative advertising allowances, display allowances, and sales contests. At times they will apply negative sanctions, such as threatening to reduce margins, slow down delivery, or terminate the relationship. The weakness of this approach is that the producer is using crude, stimulus-response thinking.

More sophisticated companies try to forge a long-term partnership with distributors. The manufacturer clearly communicates what it wants from its distributors in the way of market coverage, inventory levels, marketing development, account solicitation, technical advice and services, and marketing information. The manufacturer seeks distributor agreement with these policies and may introduce a compensation plan for adhering to the policies. Here are some examples of successful partner-building practices:

- Timken Corporation (roller bearings) has its sales reps make multilevel calls on its distributors.
- DuPont has a distributor marketing steering committee that meets regularly.
- Dayco Corporation (engineered plastics and rubber products) runs an annual week-long retreat with 20 distributors' executives and 20 Dayco executives.
- Vanity Fair, Levi Strauss, and Hanes have formed "quick response" partnerships with discounters and department stores.
- Rust-Oleum introduces a menu of marketing programs each quarter; distributors choose the programs that fit their needs.

Consider the program Ford implemented to motivate its dealers.

Ford   For dealerships that meet new standards for cleanliness, appearance, service, and training, Ford bestows the distinction Blue Oval Certified. To signal to customers which dealerships have been certified, Ford uses a blue thumbprint logo. As an incentive, certified dealers receive a 1.25 percent discount on cars from Ford. As of May 2001, 80 percent of Ford's 4,100 dealers in the United States had met the Blue Oval standards.[22]

The most advanced supply-distributor arrangement is **distribution programming**, which can be defined as building a planned, professionally managed, vertical marketing system that meets the needs of both manufacturer and distributors. The manufacturer establishes a department within the company called *distributor-relations planning*. Its job is to identify distributor needs and build up merchandising programs to help each distributor operate as efficiently as possible. This department and the distributors jointly plan merchandising goals, inventory levels, space and visual merchandising plans, sales-training requirements, and advertising and promotion plans. The aim is to convert the distributors from thinking that they make their money primarily on the buying side (through tough negotiation with the manufacturer) to seeing that they make their money on the selling side (by being part of a sophisticated, vertical marketing system). Kraft and Procter & Gamble are two companies with excellent distributor-relations planning.

Too many manufacturers think of their distributors and dealers as customers rather than working partners. Up to now, we have treated manufacturers and distributors as separate organizations, but many manufacturers are distributors of related products made by other manufacturers, and some distributors also own or contract for the manufacture of

Jeans by Any Other Name . . . Brand, or Label

Retailers and manufacturers struggle to differentiate brands by image and by distribution channel. Jeans—that staple of the American wardrobe—fall into four classes: national brands, designer labels, private labels, and retail store brands. Different types of brands have different impacts on profits.

National brands are owned by a manufacturer who advertises and sells them nationally. One of the first apparel brands to gain national recognition was Levi Strauss denim jeans in the 1870s. Examples of national brand jeans include Levi (still the number-one best-seller), Wrangler and Lee (both products of the VF Corporation), and Guess?. Levi saw great success in the 1980s and 1990s with its nondenim line of casual pants (Dockers) and its line of dress pants (Slates).

Designer labels carry the name of a designer and are usually sold at high prices ($100 and up) both nationally and internationally. The apparel industry's current mega-designers—Ralph Lauren, Calvin Klein, Tommy Hilfiger, and Donna Karan—all have their own jeans lines. Some foreign designer labels, such as Hugo Boss, are imported into the United States. Even some retired designers, such as Liz Claiborne and Gloria Vanderbilt, have active jeans lines.

A private label is owned by a retailer and found only in its stores. Examples are the Kathie Lee Gifford line sold by Wal-Mart, the Jaclyn Smith line sold by Kmart, and the Badge kids line sold by Federated Stores.

A retail store brand is the name of a chain that is used as the exclusive label on most of the items in the store or catalog. Examples include GAP, The Limited, J. Crew, L.L. Bean, and Lands' End. GAP successfully introduced the first complete store-brand jeans line in 1991. Private labels are usually priced well under national brands and far below designer brands. Store-brand prices, on the other hand, are usually close to those of national brands, and above those of private labels. Profit margins, however, are not always in proportion to selling price. The profit margin on store-brand merchandise is typically 5 to 15 percent greater than the profit on national brands.

Sources: "True Blue," *Esquire*, July 1, 1994, p. 102; George White, "Wall Street, California; Fashion Pushes Sales Forward," *Los Angeles Times*, September 8, 1998, p. B1; Sharon Haver, "Shedding Light on Denim's Dark Past," *Rocky Mountain News*, May 28, 1998, p. 6D; Stacy Perman, "Business: Levi's Gets the Blues," *Time*, November 11, 1997, p. 66.

in-house brands. "Marketing Insight: Jeans by Any Other Name . . . Brand, or Label" illustrates this situation in the jeans industry, but it is common in many others.

evaluating channel members

Producers must periodically evaluate intermediaries' performance against such standards as sales-quota attainment, average inventory levels, customer delivery time, treatment of damaged and lost goods, and cooperation in promotional and training programs. A producer will occasionally discover that it is paying too much to particular intermediaries for what they are actually doing. One manufacturer that was compensating a distributor for holding inventories found that the inventories were actually held in a public warehouse at its expense. Producers should set up functional discounts in which they pay specified amounts for the trade channel's performance of each agreed-upon service. Underperformers need to be counseled, retrained, remotivated, or terminated.

modifying channel arrangements

A producer must periodically review and modify its channel arrangements. Modification becomes necessary when the distribution channel is not working as planned, consumer buying patterns change, the market expands, new competition arises, innovative distribution channels emerge, and the product moves into later stages in the product life cycle. Consider Apple.

Apple   To combat its lowly 3.4 percent share of the U.S. personal computer market, Apple opened 25 retail locations in 2001. The stores sold Apple products exclusively and targeted tech-savvy customers with in-store product demonstrations, the full

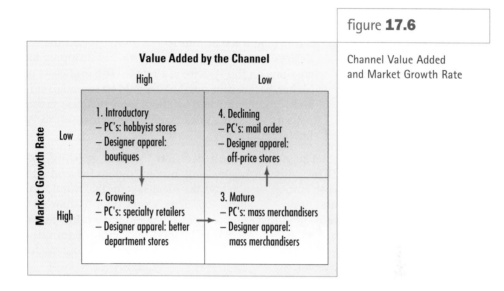

figure **17.6**

Channel Value Added
and Market Growth Rate

line of Macintosh computers, over 300 software titles, a "Genius Bar" staffed by an Apple specialist, and a host of compatible peripherals. Although the move upset existing retailers, Apple explained that since *www.apple.com* generates roughly 25 percent of sales, its own retail chain is a natural extension.[23]

No marketing channel will remain effective over the whole product life cycle. Early buyers might be willing to pay for high value-added channels, but later buyers will switch to lower-cost channels. Small office copiers were first sold by manufacturers' direct sales forces, later through office equipment dealers, still later through mass-merchandisers, and now by mail-order firms and Internet marketers.

Miland Lele developed the grid in Figure 17.6 to show how marketing channels have changed for PCs and designer apparel at different stages in the product life cycle:

- *Introductory stage:* Radically new products or fashions tend to enter the market through specialist channels (such as boutiques) that spot trends and attract early adopters.
- *Rapid growth stage:* As interest grows, higher-volume channels appear (dedicated chains, department stores) that offer services but not as many as the previous channels.
- *Maturity stage:* As growth slows, some competitors move their product into lower-cost channels (mass-merchandisers).
- *Decline stage:* As decline begins, even lower-cost channels emerge (mail-order houses, off-price discounters).[24]

In competitive markets with low entry barriers, the optimal channel structure will inevitably change over time. The change could involve adding or dropping individual channel members, adding or dropping particular market channels, or developing a totally new way to sell goods.

Adding or dropping individual channel members requires an incremental analysis. What would the firm's profits look like with and without this intermediary? An automobile manufacturer's decision to drop a dealer requires subtracting the dealer's sales and estimating the possible sales loss or gain to the manufacturer's other dealers.

Sometimes a producer considers dropping all intermediaries whose sales are below a certain amount. Consider the following.

Marketing
MEMO

**Designing a Customer–
Driven Distribution System**

Stern and Sturdivant have outlined
an excellent framework, called
*Customer-Driven Distribution
System Design*, for moving a poorly
functioning distribution system
closer to a customers' ideal system.
Companies have to reduce the
gaps between the service outputs
target customers desire, those the
existing channel system delivers,
and those management thinks are
feasible within the existing
constraints. Six steps are involved:

1. Research target customers'
   value perceptions, needs, and
   desires regarding channel
   service outputs.
2. Examine the performance of
   the company's and competitors'
   existing distribution systems in
   relation to customer desires.
3. Find service output gaps that
   need corrective action.
4. Identify major constraints that
   will limit possible corrective
   actions.
5. Design a "management-
   bounded" channel solution.
6. Implement the reconfigured
   distribution system.

Source: Louis W. Stern and Adel I. El-
Ansary, *Marketing Channels*, 5th ed.
(Upper Saddle River, NJ: Prentice Hall,
1996), p. 189.

Navistar   Navistar noted at one time that 5 percent of its dealers were selling fewer than three or four trucks a year. It cost the company more to service these dealers than their sales were worth, but dropping these dealers could have repercussions on the system as a whole. The unit costs of producing trucks would be higher, because the overhead would be spread over fewer trucks; some employees and equipment would be idled; some business in these markets would go to competitors; and other dealers might become insecure. All these factors must be taken into account.

The most difficult decision involves revising the overall channel strategy.[25] Distribution channels clearly become outmoded, and a gap arises between the existing distribution system and the ideal system that would satisfy target customers' needs and desires. Examples abound: Avon's door-to-door system for selling cosmetics had to be modified as more women entered the workforce, and IBM's exclusive reliance on a field sales force had to be modified with the introduction of low-priced personal computers. (See "Marketing Memo: Designing a Customer-Driven Distribution System.")

channel dynamics

Distribution channels do not stand still. New wholesaling and retailing institutions emerge, and new channel systems evolve. We will look at the recent growth of vertical, horizontal, and multichannel marketing systems and see how these systems cooperate, conflict, and compete.

vertical marketing systems

One of the most significant recent channel developments is the rise of vertical marketing systems. A **conventional marketing channel** comprises an independent producer, wholesaler(s), and retailer(s). Each is a separate business seeking to maximize its own profits, even if this goal reduces profit for the system as a whole. No channel member has complete or substantial control over other members.

A **vertical marketing system (VMS),** by contrast, comprises the producer, wholesaler(s), and retailer(s) acting as a unified system. One channel member, the *channel captain*, owns the others or franchises them or has so much power that they all cooperate. The channel captain can be the producer, the wholesaler, or the retailer. VMSs arose as a result of strong channel members' attempts to control channel behavior and eliminate the conflict that results when independent members pursue their own objectives. VMSs achieve economies through size, bargaining power, and elimination of duplicated services. They have become the dominant mode of distribution in the United States consumer marketplace, serving between 70 and 80 percent of the total market. There are three types of VMS: corporate, administered, and contractual.

CORPORATE AND ADMINISTERED VMS   A *corporate VMS* combines successive stages of production and distribution under single ownership. For example, Sears obtains over 50 percent of the goods it sells from companies that it partly or wholly owns. Sherwin-Williams makes paint but also owns and operates 2,000 retail outlets. Giant Food Stores operates an ice-making facility, a soft-drink bottling operation, an ice cream plant, and a bakery that supplies Giant stores with everything from bagels to birthday cakes.

An *administered VMS* coordinates successive stages of production and distribution through the size and power of one of the members. Manufacturers of a dominant brand are able to secure strong trade cooperation and support from resellers. Thus Kodak, Gillette, Procter & Gamble, and Campbell Soup are able to command high levels of cooperation from their resellers in connection with displays, shelf space, promotions, and price policies.

CONTRACTUAL VMS   A *contractual VMS* consists of independent firms at different levels of production and distribution integrating their programs on a contractual basis to obtain more economies or sales impact than they could achieve alone. Johnston and Lawrence call them "value-adding partnerships" (VAPs).[26] Contractual VMSs now constitute one of the most significant developments in the economy. They are of three types:

1. *Wholesaler-sponsored voluntary chains:* Wholesalers organize voluntary chains of independent retailers to help them compete with large chain organizations. The wholesaler develops a program in which independent retailers standardize their selling practices and achieve buying economies that enable the group to compete effectively with chain organizations.
2. *Retailer cooperatives:* Retailers take the initiative and organize a new business entity to carry on wholesaling and possibly some production. Members concentrate their purchases through the retailer co-op and plan their advertising jointly. Profits are passed back to members in proportion to their purchases. Nonmember retailers can also buy through the co-op but do not share in the profits.
3. *Franchise organizations:* A channel member called a *franchisor* might link several successive stages in the production-distribution process. Franchising has been the fastest-growing retailing development in recent years. Although the basic idea is an old one, some forms of franchising are quite new.

The traditional system is the *manufacturer-sponsored retailer franchise*. Ford, for example, licenses dealers to sell its cars. The dealers are independent businesspeople who agree to meet specified conditions of sales and services. Another is the *manufacturer-sponsored wholesaler franchise*. Coca-Cola, for example, licenses bottlers (wholesalers) in various markets who buy its syrup concentrate and then carbonate, bottle, and sell it to retailers in local markets. A newer system is the *service-firm-sponsored retailer franchise*. A service firm organizes a whole system for bringing its service efficiently to consumers. Examples are found in the auto rental business (Hertz, Avis), fast-food-service business (McDonald's, Burger King), and motel business (Howard Johnson, Ramada Inn).

THE NEW COMPETITION IN RETAILING   Many independent retailers that have not joined VMSs have developed specialty stores that serve special market segments. The result is a polarization in retailing between large vertical marketing organizations and independent specialty stores, which creates a problem for manufacturers. They are strongly tied to independent intermediaries, but must eventually realign themselves with the high-growth vertical marketing systems on less attractive terms. Furthermore, vertical marketing systems constantly threaten to bypass large manufacturers and set up their own manufacturing. *The new competition in retailing is no longer between independent business units but between whole systems of centrally programmed networks (corporate, administered, and contractual) competing against one another to achieve the best cost economies and customer response.* Consider the GAP:

The GAP   The GAP is a highly successful clothing chain store that has spun off additional branded store concepts. It created a lower priceline chain store called Old Navy and acquired Banana Republic to represent a higher priceline chain store. It also started GapKids, BabyGap, and GapMaternity. Each chain has captured significant market shares. The various properties must be managed so as not to cannibalize each other. However, many GAP customers have recently switched to Old Navy, where they find lower prices and see the quality as adequate.

horizontal marketing systems

Another channel development is the **horizontal marketing system**, in which two or more unrelated companies put together resources or programs to exploit an emerging marketing opportunity. Many supermarket chains have arrangements with local banks to offer in-store banking. Each company lacks the capital, know-how, production, or marketing resources to venture alone, or it is afraid of the risk. The companies might work with each other on a temporary or permanent basis or create a joint venture company. H&R Block, Inc., for example, entered into an agreement with GEICO insurance to provide car insurance information to Block customers. Customers now can contact GEICO through a special toll-free number. Here is another example.

Kmart and Fleming   In 2001, when Kmart needed to develop an efficient procurement and inventory system but could not afford to build one from the ground up, it turned to grocery wholesaler Fleming. The two companies formed a $4.5 billion supply-chain alliance governed by a joint team based in Kmart headquarters. Fleming uses its advanced procurement and distribution system to manage Kmart's buying, inventory, and logistics. Kmart expects the alliance will save $400 million during the first three years.[27]

multichannel marketing systems

Once, many companies sold to a single market through a single channel. Today, with the proliferation of customer segments and channel possibilities, more companies have adopted multichannel marketing. **Multichannel marketing** occurs when a single firm uses two or more marketing channels to reach one or more customer segments. Here are some examples.

Parker-Hannifin   The Parker-Hannifin Corporation (PHC) sells pneumatic drills to customers in the lumber, fishing, and aircraft industries. Instead of selling them through one industrial distributor, PHC established three separate channels—*forestry equipment distributors, marine distributors,* and *industrial distributors*. There appears to be little conflict because each type of distributor sells to a separate target segment.

Stihl's product lines. The Web site includes a link to dealerships in the USA and to company locations worldwide.

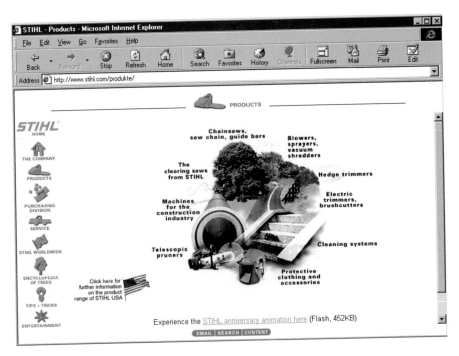

Stihl Stihl manufactures hand-held outdoor power equipment. All Stihl products are branded under one name and Stihl does not do private label for other companies. Stihl is best known for chain saws, but has expanded into string trimmers, blowers, hedge trimmers, and cut-off machines. It distributes products through a network of geographically exclusive distribution points, then through a network of independent servicing dealers. Stihl is one of the few outdoor power equipment companies that does not sell its products through mass merchants, catalogs, or the Internet.[28]

By adding more channels, companies can gain three important benefits. The first is increased market coverage. The second is lower channel cost—selling by phone rather than personal visits to small customers. The third is more customized selling—adding a technical sales force to sell more complex equipment. The gains from adding new channels come at a price, however. New channels typically introduce conflict and control problems. Two or more channels may end up competing for the same customers. The new channels may be more independent and make cooperation more difficult.

PLANNING CHANNEL ARCHITECTURE   Clearly, companies need to think through their channel architecture. Moriarty and Moran propose using the hybrid grid shown in Figure 17.7 to plan the channel architecture.[29] The grid shows several marketing channels (rows) and several demand-generation tasks (columns). The grid illustrates why using only one channel is not efficient. Consider using only a direct sales force. A salesperson would have to find leads, qualify them, presell, close the sale, provide service, and manage account growth. It would be more efficient for the company to perform the earlier tasks, leaving the salesperson to invest his or her costly time primarily to close the sale. The company's marketing department would generate leads through telemarketing,

figure **17.7**

The Hybrid Grid

		Demand-Generation Tasks						
		Lead Generation	Qualifying Sales	Presales	Close of Sale	Postsales Service	Account Management	
	Internet							
	National Account Management							
	Direct Sales							
	Telemarketing							
	Direct Mail							
	Retail Stores							
	Distributors							
	Dealers and Value-Added Resellers							
	Advertising							

Marketing Channels and Methods — VENDOR ... CUSTOMER

Source: Rowland T. Moriarty and Ursula Moran, "Marketing Hybrid Marketing Systems," *Harvard Besiness Review* (November–December 1990): 150.

Managing Vertical Channel Conflict

For many years, large consumer packaged-goods manufacturers enjoyed market power over retailers. Manufacturers spent huge amounts on advertising to build brand preference, and retailers were obliged to carry their brands. However, because of the growth of giant retailers, lower-priced store brands, lack of shelf space, and retailers' growing marketing sophistication, retailers are now in a position to exert more pressure on manufacturers for price, delivery, and promotional consideration. Manufacturers are trying to figure out how they can regain or hold on to their power. Market-share leaders are resorting to these strategies:

1. Focus on the brands that have a chance of being number one or two in their category and commit to continuous research to improve quality, features, and packaging.
2. Maintain an active program of line extensions and a careful program of brand extensions. Develop fighter brands to compete with store brands.
3. Spend as much time as possible on targeted advertising to build and maintain brand franchise.
4. Treat each major retail chain as a distinct target market, and treat each target retailer as a strategic partner. Be ready to customize products, packaging, services, benefits, and electronic linkups.
5. Provide a high level of service quality and new services such as order-cycle time reduction and emergency delivery capability.
6. Consider adopting everyday low pricing as an alternative to trade dealing.
7. Aggressively expand into alternative retail outlets such as membership warehouse clubs, discount merchandisers, convenience stores, and some direct marketing.

Source: Gary Davies, *Trade Marketing Strategies* (London: Paul Chapman, 1993).

direct mail, advertising, and trade shows. The leads would be sorted into hot, warm, and cool by using qualifying techniques such as checking whether a lead wants a sales call and has adequate purchasing power. The department would also run a preselling campaign informing prospects about the company's products through advertising, direct mail, and telemarketing. The salesperson comes to the prospect when the prospect is ready to talk business. This multichannel architecture optimizes coverage, customization, and control while minimizing cost and conflict.

Companies should use different channels for selling to different-size customers. A company can use its direct sales force to sell to large customers, telemarketing to sell to midsized customers, and distributors to sell to small customers; but these gains can be compromised by an increased level of conflict over who has account ownership. For example, territory-based sales representatives may want credit for all sales in their territories, regardless of the marketing channel used.

ROLES OF INDIVIDUAL FIRMS Each firm in an industry has to define its role in the channel system. Bert McCammon has distinguished five roles:[30]

1. *Insiders* are members of the dominant channel. They enjoy access to preferred sources of supply and high respect in the industry. They want to perpetuate the existing channel arrangements and are the main enforcers of industry codes of conduct.
2. *Strivers* are firms seeking to become insiders. They have less access to preferred sources of supply, which can handicap them in periods of short supply. They adhere to the industry code because of their desire to become insiders.
3. *Complementers* are not part of the dominant channel. They perform functions not normally performed by others in the channel, serve smaller segments of the market, or handle smaller quantities of merchandise. They usually benefit from the present system and respect the industry code of conduct.
4. *Transients* are outside the dominant channel and do not seek membership. They go in and out of the market and move around as opportunities arise. They have short-run expectations and little incentive to adhere to the industry code of conduct.
5. *Outside innovators* are the real challengers and disrupters of the dominant channels. They develop a new system for carrying out the marketing work of the channel. If successful, they force major channel realignments (see "Marketing for the New Economy: How CarMax Is Transforming the Auto Business").

conflict, cooperation, and competition

No matter how well channels are designed and managed, there will be some conflict, if for no other reason than the interests of independent business entities do not always coincide. Here we examine three questions: What types of conflict arise in channels? What causes channel conflict? What can be done to resolve conflict situations?

TYPES OF CONFLICT AND COMPETITION Suppose a manufacturer sets up a vertical channel consisting of wholesalers and retailers. The manufacturer hopes for channel cooperation that will produce greater profits for each channel member. Yet vertical, horizontal, and multichannel conflict can occur.

Vertical channel conflict means conflict between different levels within the same channel. General Motors came into conflict with its dealers in trying to enforce policies on service, pricing, and advertising. Coca-Cola came into conflict with bottlers who also agreed to bottle Dr. Pepper. (See "Marketing Memo: Managing Vertical Channel Conflict.")

Horizontal channel conflict involves conflict between members at the same level within the channel. Some Ford car dealers in Chicago complained about other Chicago Ford dealers advertising and pricing too aggressively. Some Pizza Inn franchisees complained about other Pizza Inn franchisees cheating on ingredients, providing poor service, and hurting the overall Pizza Inn image.

Multichannel conflict exists when the manufacturer has established two or more channels that sell to the same market. When Levi Strauss agreed to distribute its jeans

marketing for the **new economy**

How CarMax Is Transforming the Auto Business

For years, buying a used car was considered a dangerous and risky business; used-car salesmen were stock figures in comedy routines. Then CarMax emerged to change the face of the industry and its standards. Circuit City, a major retailer of electronic products, started CarMax, the Auto Superstore, in 1993. The first superstore opened in Richmond, Virginia: CarMax now operates 33 used-car stores and 22 new-car franchises.

What is so special about CarMax? The company locates its used-car superstores, each carrying around 500 cars, on large lots on the outskirts of a city near a major highway. Customers enter an attractive display room, where a sales associate finds out what kind of car they want and then escorts them to a computer kiosk. Using a touch screen, the associate retrieves a full listing of the cars in stock that meet the customer's criteria. A color display of each car can be shown along with the vehicle's features and its fixed selling price. There is no price negotiation. The salesperson, paid a commission on the number of cars sold rather than their value, has no incentive to push higher-priced cars. The customer is informed that CarMax mechanics carried out a 110-point inspection and made any necessary repairs beforehand. Furthermore, a car buyer receives a 5-day money-back guarantee and a 30-day comprehensive warranty. If the buyer wants financing, the CarMax associate can arrange it in 20 minutes. The entire process typically takes less than one hour.

A booming new-car market hurt CarMax at first. In fact, the company reported annual losses in each of its first six years. Recently, the company has found increased value by focusing on the used-car market. Given that today's cars are better and have longer life expectancies, many buyers now prefer to save money by buying a used car, and the substantial growth of car leasing has greatly inflated the supply of used cars. Banks are more willing to offer low-cost financing for used cars, especially when research revealed that default rates were lower for used-car buyers. Finally, dealers have reported earning a higher profit on used cars, up to $100 more than for a new car.

CarMax has been very successful in achieving even greater margins: The company's average selling price for a used vehicle is $15,000 and its average profit margin is 13 percent, compared with industry averages of $13,650 and 11 percent, respectively. As a result of these high margins, CarMax turned its first profit in fiscal 2000.

Sources: Gabriella Stern, "'Nearly New' Autos for Sale: Dealers Buff Up Their Marketing of Used Cars," *Wall Street Journal*, February 17, 1995, p. B1; Gregory J. Gilligan, "Circuit City's CarMax Superstores Pass $300 Million in Yearly Sales," *Knight-Ridder/Tribune Business News*, April 5, 1997, p. 19; Arlena Sawyers, "CarMax Is Out of the Red, In the Pink," *Automotive News*, April 16, 2001, p. 28; Mike Brennan, "Mavericks Are Changing Way Cars Are Sold," *Detroit Free Press*, January 6, 1998, p. 28.

through Sears and JCPenney in addition to its normal specialty store channel, the specialty stores complained. When clothing manufacturers like Ralph Lauren and Anne Klein opened their own stores, the department stores that carried their brands were upset. When Goodyear began selling its popular tire brands through Sears, Wal-Mart, and Discount Tire, it angered its independent dealers. (It eventually placated them by offering exclusive tire models that would not be sold in other retail outlets.) Multichannel conflict is likely to be especially intense when the members of one channel get a lower price (based on larger volume purchases) or work with a lower margin.

One of the major current examples of multichannel conflict is brick-and-mortar companies sweating over whether to add an online e-commerce channel. Barnes & Noble, Merrill Lynch, Compaq, and All State Insurance all resisted, but eventually succumbed after seeing how much online business was rushing to its competitors, Amazon, E*TRADE, Dell, and Direct Line, respectively. Yet adding an e-commerce channel creates the threat of a backlash from retailers, brokers, agents, and other intermediaries. For example, retailers were angered when Mattel decided to sell Barbie dolls via the Internet.

Mattel   Just before the 2000 holiday season, Mattel began selling a wide range of toys and children's apparel on its Barbie.com Web site. The company also mailed its first ever Barbie catalog to 4 million U.S households. Retailers perceived these moves as a clear case of channel conflict: "We're supposed to be partners and this is obviously competitive," said one toy retail executive. Mattel sought to placate retailers by noting that online and catalog sales would contribute less than 1 percent of Barbie's sales during the first year, and by not advertising the e-commerce features of the site. The company views its Web site as a "self-funding" marketing and advertising tool designed to foster relationships with customers.[31]

The question is how to sell both through intermediaries and online. There are at least three strategies for trying to gain acceptance from intermediaries. One, offer different brands or products on the Internet. Two, offer the off-line partners higher commissions to cushion the negative impact on sales. Three, take orders on the Web site but have retailers deliver and collect payment.

Here are some companies that have reconciled their off-line and online marketing channels:[32]

- **Talbots.** When Talbots, a specialty women's clothing chain, runs out of an item, the sales clerk will order it at a Talbots' catalog call center. Customers pay a flat $4 shipping charge, which is less than the normal charge on regular catalog orders. The store earns credit for the catalog sale.
- **Liberty Mutual.** Liberty Mutual asks its online customers if they might prefer to work though a financial advisor; if yes, their information will be routed to an advisor.
- **Avon.** Avon showed its reps that its online sales will not overlap with their sales from existing customers and even offered to help reps set up their own Web sites.
- **JCPenny.** JCPenny offers online coupons that can be printed and redeemed in its stores, and may even sell some items online that are not profitable to sell through its stores.
- **Gibson Guitars.** Gibson started by selling accessories such as guitar strings and parts online and is eager to overcome dealers' objections to selling guitars over the Internet. It may have to give some credit to the guitar store nearest the customer who bought online.

Ultimately, companies may need to decide whether to drop some or all of their retailers and go direct.

Dell and Compaq In selling direct, Dell is outperforming all other retailer-dependent competitors. Dell manufactures a PC only after receiving a Web site order from a customer who designs the desired computer on Dell's configurator choiceboard and who pays in advance by clicking in his or her credit card number. Dell gets paid before it makes the computer and uses the customer's cash, instead of its own, to pay suppliers, so it needs less working capital. Compaq, by contrast, has to guess the level of demand for its PCs, fill its warehouses and retailer pipelines with a sufficient number, and hope that they all sell in a reasonable time before Compaq introduces its next generation of PCs.

Given the superiority of Internet-based ordering, what is to stop an auto company from offering customers the ability to design a car on the Web site, and have it assembled and delivered to the customer's premises within a week? The cost of operating a *virtual dealership* would be considerably less than the present dealership systems, where cars sit in inventory for 70 days and companies have to spend about 10 percent of the car's price on ads and promotions to get customers to buy. Our prediction is that more companies in the economy will shift from build-for-stock to build-to-order.

CAUSES OF CHANNEL CONFLICT It is important to identify the causes of channel conflict. Some are easy to resolve, others are not.

One major cause is *goal incompatibility*. For example, the manufacturer may want to achieve rapid market penetration through a low-price policy. Dealers, in contrast, may prefer to work with high margins and pursue short-run profitability. Sometimes conflict arises from *unclear roles and rights*. IBM sells personal computers to large accounts through its own sales force, and its licensed dealers are also trying to sell to large accounts. Territory boundaries and credit for sales often produce conflict.

By adding new channels, a company faces the possibility of channel conflict. The following three channel conflicts arose at IBM:

1. *Conflict between the national account managers and field sales force:* National account managers rely on field salespeople to make calls at certain national account customers located in the salesperson's territory, sometimes on a moment's notice. Requests from several national

account managers to make such calls can seriously disrupt the salesperson's normal schedule and hurt commissions. Salespeople may not cooperate with national account managers when doing so conflicts with their own interests.

2. *Conflict between the field sales force and the telemarketers:* Salespeople often resent the company's setting up a telemarketing operation to sell to smaller customers. The company tells the salespeople that telemarketers free up their time to sell to larger accounts on which they can earn more commission, but the salespeople still object.

3. *Conflict between the field sales force and the dealers:* Dealers include value-added resellers, who buy computers from IBM and add specialized software needed by the target buyer, and computer retail stores, which are an excellent channel for selling small equipment to walk-in traffic and small businesses. These dealers frequently offer specialized software installation and training, better service, and even lower prices than IBM's direct sales force. The direct sales force becomes angry when these dealers go after large accounts: They want IBM to refuse to sell through dealers who try to sell to large accounts, but IBM would lose a lot of business if it dropped these successful resellers. As an alternative, IBM decided to give partial credit to salespeople for business sold to their accounts by aggressive resellers.

Conflict can also stem from *differences in perception.* The manufacturer may be optimistic about the short-term economic outlook and want dealers to carry higher inventory. Dealers may be pessimistic. Conflict might also arise because of the intermediaries' *dependence* on the manufacturer. The fortunes of exclusive dealers, such as auto dealers, are profoundly affected by the manufacturer's product and pricing decisions. This situation creates a high potential for conflict.

MANAGING CHANNEL CONFLICT Some channel conflict can be constructive and lead to more dynamic adaptation to a changing environment, but too much is dysfunctional. The challenge is not to eliminate conflict but to manage it better. There are several mechanisms for effective conflict management.[33]

One is the adoption of superordinate goals. Channel members come to an agreement on the fundamental goal they are jointly seeking, whether it is survival, market share, high quality, or customer satisfaction. They usually do this when the channel faces an outside threat, such as a more efficient competing channel, an adverse piece of legislation, or a shift in consumer desires.

A useful step is to exchange persons between two or more channel levels. General Motors executives might agree to work for a short time in some dealerships, and some dealership owners might work in GM's dealer policy department. Hopefully, the participants will grow to appreciate the other's point of view.

Co-optation is an effort by one organization to win the support of the leaders of another organization by including them in advisory councils, boards of directors, and the like. As long as the initiating organization treats the leaders seriously and listens to their opinions, co-optation can reduce conflict, but the initiating organization may have to compromise its policies and plans to win their support.

Much can be accomplished by encouraging joint membership in and between trade associations. For example, there is good cooperation between the Grocery Manufacturers of America and the Food Marketing Institute, which represents most of the food chains; this cooperation led to the development of the universal product code (UPC). Presumably, the associations can consider issues between food manufacturers and retailers and resolve them in an orderly way.

When conflict is chronic or acute, the parties may have to resort to diplomacy, mediation, or arbitration. *Diplomacy* takes place when each side sends a person or group to meet with its counterpart to resolve the conflict. *Mediation* means resorting to a neutral third party who is skilled in conciliating the two parties' interests. *Arbitration* occurs when the two parties agree to present their arguments to one or more arbitrators and accept the arbitration decision. Sometimes, when none of these methods proves effective, a company or a channel partner may choose to file a lawsuit. Levi Strauss and U.K. retailer Tesco became locked in a legal battle beginning in 1999.

Levi's Levi's filed a suit with the European Court of Justice against Tesco claiming the retailer's selling of low-priced Levi's jeans imported from outside Britain "undermines the product experience." Tesco offers genuine Levis at roughly half the price of other U.K. retailers, and Levi's also objects to the fact that its jeans appear in the same stores that sell produce and other food items. In order to win a decision, Levi's must prove that its brand suffered material damage by being sold at a discount in Tesco.[34]

legal and ethical issues in channel relations

For the most part, companies are legally free to develop whatever channel arrangements suit them. In fact, the law seeks to prevent companies from using exclusionary tactics that might keep competitors from using a channel. Here we briefly consider the legality of certain practices, including exclusive dealing, exclusive territories, tying agreements, and dealers' rights.

Many producers like to develop exclusive channels for their products. A strategy in which the seller allows only certain outlets to carry its products is called **exclusive distribution**, and when the seller requires that these dealers not handle competitors' products, this is called **exclusive dealing**. Both parties benefit from exclusive arrangements: The seller obtains more loyal and dependable outlets, and the dealers obtain a steady source of supply of special products and stronger seller support. Exclusive arrangements are legal as long as they do not substantially lessen competition or tend to create a monopoly, and as long as both parties enter into the agreement voluntarily.

Exclusive dealing often includes exclusive territorial agreements. The producer may agree not to sell to other dealers in a given area, or the buyer may agree to sell only in its own territory. The first practice increases dealer enthusiasm and commitment. It is also perfectly legal—a seller has no legal obligation to sell through more outlets than it wishes. The second practice, whereby the producer tries to keep a dealer from selling outside its territory, has become a major legal issue. An example of bitter lawsuits is one brought by GT Bicycles of Santa Ana, California, against the giant Price-Costco chain, which sold 2,600 of its high-priced mountain bikes at a huge discount, thus upsetting GT's other U.S. dealers. GT alleges that it first sold the bikes to a dealer in Russia and that they were meant for sale only in Russia. GT maintains that it constitutes fraud when discounters work with middlemen to get exclusive goods.[35]

Producers of a strong brand sometimes sell it to dealers only if they will take some or all of the rest of the line. This practice is called full-line forcing. Such **tying agreements** are not necessarily illegal, but they do violate U.S. law if they tend to lessen competition substantially.

Producers are free to select their dealers, but their right to terminate dealers is somewhat restricted. In general, sellers can drop dealers "for cause," but they cannot drop dealers if, for example, the dealers refuse to cooperate in a doubtful legal arrangement, such as exclusive dealing or tying agreements.

summary

1. Most producers do not sell their goods directly to final users. Between producers and final users stands one or more marketing channels, a host of marketing intermediaries performing a variety of functions. Marketing-channel decisions are among the most critical decisions facing management. The company's chosen channel(s) profoundly affect all other marketing decisions.

2. Companies use intermediaries when they lack the financial resources to carry out direct marketing, when direct mar-

keting is not feasible, and when they can earn more by doing so. The use of intermediaries largely boils down to their superior efficiency in making goods widely available and accessible to target markets. The most important functions performed by intermediaries are information, promotion, negotiation, ordering, financing, risk taking, physical possession, payment, and title.

3. Manufacturers have many alternatives for reaching a market. They can sell direct or use one-, two-, or three-level channels.

Deciding which type(s) of channel to use calls for analyzing customer needs, establishing channel objectives, and identifying and evaluating the major alternatives, including the types and numbers of intermediaries involved in the channel. The company must determine whether to distribute its product exclusively, selectively, or intensively, and it must clearly spell out the terms and responsibilities of each channel member.

4. Effective channel management calls for selecting intermediaries and training and motivating them. The goal is to build a long-term partnership that will be profitable for all channel members. Individual members must be periodically evaluated. Channel arrangements may need to be modified when market conditions change.

5. Marketing channels are characterized by continuous and sometimes dramatic change. Three of the most important trends are the growth of vertical marketing systems, horizontal marketing systems, and multichannel marketing systems.

6. All marketing channels have the potential for conflict and competition resulting from such sources as goal incompatibility, poorly defined roles and rights, perceptual differences, and interdependent relationships. Companies can manage conflict by striving for superordinate goals, exchanging people among two or more channel levels, co-opting the support of leaders in different parts of the channel, and encouraging joint membership in and between trade associations.

7. Channel arrangements are up to the company, but there are certain legal and ethical issues to be considered with regard to practices such as exclusive dealing or territories, tying agreements, and dealers' rights.

applications

marketing debate – should national brand manufacturers also supply private label brands?

One controversial move by some marketers of major brands is to actually supply private label makers. For example, Ralston-Purina, Borden, ConAgra, and Heinz have all admitted to supplying products—sometimes lower in quality—to be used for private labels. Other marketers, however, criticize this "if you can't beat them, join them" strategy, maintaining that these actions, if revealed, may create confusion or even reinforce a perception by consumers that all brands in a category are essentially the same.

Take a position: Manufacturers should feel free to sell private labels as a source of revenue versus National manufacturers should never get involved with private labels.

marketing and advertising

1. Ford has introduced a certification program to identify dealerships that are among the best in customer satisfaction. This ad alerts car and truck buyers to look for the blue thumbprint symbol at their local Ford dealerships.

   a. What type of vertical marketing system does the Blue Oval Certified Ford Dealership program represent?

   b. How might the Blue Oval certification program affect Ford's channel dynamics?

   c. Over time, how might Ford establish and apply criteria to evaluate its channel members?

Presenting
the blueprint for
the future of
Ford Dealerships.

When you come into a Blue Oval Certified Ford Dealership, you'll see the blue thumbprint.
It's something new. It means the dealership you're in has been
certified as among the best in customer satisfaction.
At Blue Oval Certified Ford Dealerships, we believe every experience you have should be a great one.
The blue thumbprint signifies the unique and personal dedication of every one
of our employees to get the job done right – whether you're buying, leasing or just in for service.
So come on in and see for yourself. We're certified to satisfy.

BlueOvalCertified
Ford

Come on in™

For your nearest Blue Oval Certified Dealer, call 866-BLUEOVAL or visit blueoval.fordvehicles.com.

online marketing today

As mentioned earlier, People's Bank, based in Connecticut, uses its Web site as a key channel for reaching individuals, business customers, and prospects. Not only can customers e-mail the bank with questions; they can click on a link to have a bank representative call them with further information or choose another link if they want to chat online. In addition, prospects can open new accounts online, print out and fax account applications, and even order printed checks with a few keystrokes. Now the company has expanded its financial services offerings by adding insurance products for consumers and businesses.

Visit the People's Web site (www.peoples.com). After looking at the home page, follow the link to read about Online Services and click for a demonstration of People's Online. Next, follow the Insurance link and dig deeper by clicking on Auto, Home, and Other Personal Insurance. What role is Peoples.com playing in the distribution of these insurance products? What is the length of the channel the bank uses to distribute its own checking account products? How would you describe the channel positioning of People's Bank?

you're the marketer: sonic pda marketing plan

Marketing Plan Pro

Manufacturers need to pay close attention to their value networks and marketing channels. By planning the design, management, evaluation, and modification of their marketing channels, manufacturers can ensure that their products are available when and where customers want to buy.

At Sonic, you have been asked to develop a channel strategy for the company's new personal digital assistant (PDA). Based on the information you previously gathered and the decisions you have already made about the target market, the product, and the pricing, answer the following questions about your marketing channels:

- What forward and backward channel flows should Sonic plan for?

- How many levels would be appropriate for the consumer and business markets you are targeting?
- In determining the number of channel members, should you use exclusive, selective, or intensive distribution? Why?
- What levels of service output do Sonic customers desire? How do these levels affect Sonic's channel strategy?
- How should Sonic support its channel members?

After you have answered the questions, document your recommendations about marketing channels and strategy in a written marketing plan. Alternatively, type them into the Marketing Mix and the Channels sections of the *Marketing Plan Pro* software.

notes

1. Louis W. Stern and Adel I. El-Ansary, *Marketing Channels*, 5th ed. (Upper Saddle River, NJ: Prentice Hall, 1996).

2. E. Raymond Corey, *Industrial Marketing: Cases and Concepts*, 4th ed. (Upper Saddle River, NJ: Prentice Hall, 1991), ch. 5.

3. Stern and El-Ansary, *Marketing Channels*, pp. 5–6.

4. William G. Zikmund and William J. Stanton, "Recycling Solid Wastes: A Channels-of-Distribution Problem," *Journal of Marketing* (July 1971): 34.

5. For additional information on backward channels, see Marianne Jahre, "Household Waste Collection as a Reverse Channel: A Theoretical Perspective," *International Journal of Physical Distribution and Logistics* 25, no. 2 (1995): 39–55; Terrance L. Pohlen and M. Theodore Farris II, "Reverse Logistics in Plastics Recycling," *International Journal of Physical Distribution and Logistics* 22, no. 7 (1992): 35–37.

6. Ronald Abler, John S. Adams, and Peter Gould, *Spatial Organizations: The Geographer's View of the World* (Upper Saddle River, NJ: Prentice Hall, 1971), pp. 531–32.

7. Described in *Inside 1-to-1*, Peppers and Rogers Group newsletter, May 14, 2001.

8. Irving Rein, Philip Kotler, and Martin Stoller, *High Visibility* (New York: Dodd, Mead, 1987).

9. For a technical discussion of how service-oriented firms choose to enter international markets, see M. Krishna Erramilli, "Service Firms' International Entry-Mode Approach: A Modified Transaction-Cost Analysis Approach," *Journal of Marketing* (July 1993): 19–38.

10. Louis P. Bucklin, *Competition and Evolution in the Distributive Trades* (Upper Saddle River, NJ: Prentice Hall, 1972). Also see Stern and El-Ansary, *Marketing Channels*.

11. Louis P. Bucklin, *A Theory of Distribution Channel Structure* (Berkeley: Institute of Business and Economic Research, University of California, 1966).

12. Teri Lammers Prior, "Channel Surfers," *Inc.* (February 1995): 65–68.

13. Emily Nelson, "Avon Goes Store to Store," *Wall Street Journal*, September 18, 2000, p. B1

14. <www.disney.com>; Edward Helmore, "Media: Why House of Mouse Is Haunted by Failures," *The Observer*, February 11, 2001, p. 10.

15. For more on relationship marketing and the governance of marketing channels, see Jan B. Heide, "Interorganizational Governance in Marketing Channels," *Journal of Marketing* (January 1994): 71–85.

16. Lawrence G. Friedman and Timothy R. Furey, *The Channel Advantage: Going to Marketing with Multiple Sales Channels* (Woburn, MA: Butterworth-Heinemann, 1999). They suggest measuring a channel's profitability by the expense-to-revenue ratio, or E/R. E/R is the average transaction cost divided by the average order size. The average transaction cost is found by dividing the total expense in operating the channel by the total number of transactions. The lower the E/R, the more profitable the channel because less money is spent on selling cost for each dollar of revenue.

17. Arthur Bragg, "Undercover Recruiting: Epson America's Sly Distributor Switch," *Sales and Marketing Management*, March 11, 1985, pp. 45–49.

18. Vincent Alonzo, "Brewski," *Incentive* (December 1994): 32–33.

19. Philip McVey, "Are Channels of Distribution What the Textbooks Say?" *Journal of Marketing* (January 1960): 61–64.

20. These bases of power were identified in John R. P. French and Bertram Raven, "The Bases of Social Power," in *Studies in Social Power*, ed. Dorwin Cartwright (Ann Arbor: University of Michigan Press, 1959), pp. 150–67.

21. Bert Rosenbloom, *Marketing Channels: A Management View*, 5th ed. (Hinsdale, IL: Dryden, 1995).

22. Earl Eldridge, "Ford Forces Dealers to Tidy Up—Or Pay Up," *USA Today*, April 6, 2001, p. B8.

23. Tobi Elkin, "Apple Gambles with Retail Plan," *Advertising Age*, June 24, 2001.

24. Miland M. Lele, *Creating Strategic Leverage* (New York: John Wiley, 1992), pp. 249–51.

25. For an excellent report on this issue, see Howard Sutton, *Rethinking the Company's Selling and Distribution Channels*, research report no. 885, Conference Board, 1986, p. 26.

26. Russell Johnston and Paul R. Lawrence, "Beyond Vertical Integration: The Rise of the Value-Adding Partnership," *Harvard Business Review* (July–August 1988): 94-101. See also Judy A. Siguaw, Penny M. Simpson, and Thomas L. Baker, "Effects of Supplier Market Orientation on Distributor Market Orientation and the Channel Relationship: The Distribution Perspective," *Journal of Marketing* (July 1998): 99–111; Narakesari Narayandas and Manohar U. Kalwani, "Long-Term Manufacturer–Supplier Relationships: Do They Pay Off for Supplier Firms?" *Journal of Marketing* (January 1995): 1–16; Arnt Bovik and George John, "When Does Vertical Coordination Improve Industrial Purchasing Relationships," *Journal of Marketing* 64 (October 2000): pp. 52–64.

27. Matthew Schifrin, "Partner or Perish," *Forbes*, May 21, 2001, p. 26.

28. "2001 Industry Forecasts," *Outdoor Power Equipment*, January 1, 2001.

29. Rowland T. Moriarty and Ursula Moran, "Marketing Hybrid Marketing Systems," *Harvard Business Review* (November–December 1990): 146–55. Also see Gordon S. Swartz and Rowland T. Moriarty, "Marketing Automation Meets the Capital Budgeting Wall," *Marketing Management* 1, no. 3 (1992); Sridhar Balasubramanian, "Mail versus Mall: A Strategic Analysis of Competition Between Direct Marketers and Conventional Retailers," *Marketing Science* 17, no. 3, 1998, pp. 181–95.

30. Bert C. McCammon Jr., "Alternative Explanations of Institutional Change and Channel Evolution," in *Toward Scientific Marketing*, ed. Stephen A. Greyser (Chicago: American Marketing Association, 1963), pp. 477–90.

31. Lisa Bannon, "Selling Barbie Online May Pit Mattel vs. Stores," *Wall Street Journal*, November 17, 2000, p. B1.

32. Some of these examples are found in Stanley A. Brown, *Customer Relationship Management* (New York: John Wiley and Sons, 2000), and Chuck Martin, *Net Future* (New York: McGraw-Hill, 1999).

33. This section draws on Stern and El-Ansary, *Marketing Channels*, ch. 6. See also Jonathan D. Hibbard, Nirmalya Kumar, and Louis W. Stern, "Examining the Impact of Destructive Acts in Marketing Channel Relationships," *Journal of Marketing Research* 38 (February 2001), pp. 45–61; Kersi D. Antia and Gary L. Frazier, "The Severity of Contract Enforcement in Interfirm Channel Relationships, "*Journal of Marketing* 65 (October 2001), pp. 67–81; James R. Brown, Chekitan S. Dev, and Dong-Jin Lee, "Managing Marketing Channel Opportunism: The Efficency of Alternative Governance Mechanisms," *Journal of Marketing* 64 (April 2001), pp. 51–65.

34. Allessandra Galloni, "Levi's Doesn't Fancy Selling With Cukes," *Wall Street Journal*, April 10, 2001, p. B10.

35. Greg Johnson, "Gray Wail: Southern California Companies Are among the Many Upscale Manufacturers Voicing Their Displeasure about Middlemen Delivering Their Goods into the Hands of Unauthorized Discount Retailers," *Los Angeles Times*, March 30, 1997, p. B1. Also see Paul R. Messinger and Chakravarthi Narasimhan, "Has Power Shifted in the Grocery Channel?" *Marketing Science* 14, no. 2 (1995): 189–223.

managing retailing, wholesaling, and market logistics

In this chapter, we will address the following questions:

- What major types of organizations occupy this sector?
- What marketing decisions do organizations in this sector make?
- What are the major trends in this sector?

Kotler on Marketing

Successful "go-to-market" strategies require integrating retailers, wholesalers, and logistical organizations.

I n the previous chapter, we examined marketing intermediaries from the viewpoint of manufacturers who wanted to build and manage marketing channels. In this chapter, we view these intermediaries—retailers, wholesalers, and logistical organizations—as requiring and forging their own marketing strategies. Some intermediaries dominate the manufacturers who deal with them. Many use strategic planning, advanced information systems, and sophisticated marketing tools. They measure performance more on a return-on-investment basis than on a profit-margin basis. They segment their markets, improve their market targeting and positioning, and aggressively pursue market expansion and diversification strategies.

retailing

Retailing includes all the activities involved in selling goods or services directly to final consumers for personal, nonbusiness use. A **retailer** or **retail store** is any business enterprise whose sales volume comes primarily from retailing.

Any organization selling to final consumers—whether it is a manufacturer, wholesaler, or retailer—is doing retailing. It does not matter *how* the goods or services are sold (by person, mail, telephone, vending machine, or Internet) or *where* they are sold (in a store, on the street, or in the consumer's home).

types of retailers

Consumers today can shop for goods and services in a wide variety of retail organizations. There are store retailers, nonstore retailers, and retail organizations. Perhaps the best-known type of retailer is the department store. Japanese department stores such as Takashimaya and Mitsukoshi attract millions of shoppers each year. These stores feature art galleries, cooking classes, and children's playgrounds

Retail-store types pass through stages of growth and decline that can be described as the *retail life cycle*.[1] A type emerges, enjoys a period of accelerated growth, reaches maturity, and then declines. Older retail forms took many years to reach maturity; newer retail forms reach maturity much more quickly. Department stores took 80 years to reach maturity, whereas warehouse retail outlets reached maturity in 10 years. The most important retail-store types are described in Table 18.1.

LEVELS OF SERVICE   The *wheel-of-retailing* hypothesis[2] explains one reason that new store types emerge. Conventional retail stores typically increase their services and raise their prices to cover the costs. These higher costs provide an opportunity for new store forms to offer lower prices and less service. New store types meet widely different consumer preferences for service levels and specific services.

Retailers can position themselves as offering one of four levels of service:

1. *Self-service:* Self-service is the cornerstone of all discount operations. Many customers are willing to carry out their own locate-compare-select process to save money.
2. *Self-selection:* Customers find their own goods, although they can ask for assistance.
3. *Limited service:* These retailers carry more shopping goods, and customers need more information and assistance. The stores also offer services (such as credit and merchandise-return privileges).
4. *Full service:* Salespeople are ready to assist in every phase of the locate-compare-select process. Customers who like to be waited on prefer this type of store. The high staffing cost, along with the higher proportion of specialty goods and slower-moving items and the many services, results in high-cost retailing.

By combining these different service levels with different assortment breadths, we can distinguish the four broad positioning strategies available to retailers, as shown in Figure 18.1 on page 537:

1. *Bloomingdale's:* Stores that feature a broad product assortment and high value added. Stores in this quadrant pay close attention to store design, product quality, service, and image. Their profit margin is high, and if they are fortunate enough to have high volume, they will be very profitable.
2. *Tiffany:* Stores that feature a narrow product assortment and high value added. Such stores cultivate an exclusive image and tend to operate on a high margin and low volume.
3. *Sunglass Hut:* Stores that feature a narrow line and low value added. Such stores keep their costs and prices low by centralizing buying, merchandising, advertising, and distribution.
4. *Wal-Mart:* Stores that feature a broad line and low value added. They focus on keeping prices low so that they have an image of being a place for good buys. They make up for low margin by high volume.

table **18.1**	Major Retailer Types

Specialty Store: Narrow product line with a deep assortment. A clothing store would be a *single-line store*; a men's clothing store would be a *limited-line store*; and a men's custom-shirt store would be a *superspecialty store*. *Examples:* Athlete's Foot, Tall Men, The Limited, The Body Shop.

Department Store: Several product lines—typically clothing, home furnishings, and household goods—with each line operated as a separate department managed by specialist buyers or merchandisers. *Examples:* Sears, JCPenney, Nordstrom, Bloomingdale's.

Supermarket: Relatively large, low-cost, low-margin, high-volume, self-service operation designed to serve total needs for food, laundry, and household products. *Examples:* Kroger, Food Emporium, Jewel.

Convenience Store: Relatively small store located near residential area, open long hours, seven days a week, and carrying a limited line of high-turnover convenience products at slightly higher prices, plus takeout sandwiches, coffee, soft drinks. *Examples:* 7-Eleven, Circle K.

Discount Store: Standard merchandise sold at lower prices with lower margins and higher volumes. Discount retailing has moved into specialty merchandise stores, such as discount sporting-goods stores, electronics stores, and bookstores. *Examples:* Wal-Mart, Kmart, Circuit City, Crown Bookstores.

Off-Price Retailer: Merchandise bought at less than regular wholesale prices and sold at less than retail: often leftover goods, overruns, and irregulars.

Factory outlets are owned and operated by manufacturers and normally carry the manufacturer's surplus, discontinued, or irregular goods. *Examples:* Mikasa (dinnerware), Dexter (shoes), Ralph Lauren (upscale apparel).

Independent off-price retailers are owned and run by entrepreneurs or by divisions of larger retail corporations. *Examples:* Filene's Basement, T. J. Maxx.

Warehouse clubs (or *wholesale clubs*) sell a limited selection of brand-name grocery items, appliances, clothing, and a hodgepodge of other goods at deep discounts to members who pay annual membership fees. Wholesale clubs operate in huge, low-overhead, warehouselike facilities and offer rock-bottom prices—typically 20 to 40 percent below supermarket and discount-store prices. *Examples:* Sam's Clubs, Max Clubs, Price-Costco, BJ's Wholesale Club.

Superstore: About 35,000 square feet of selling space traditionally aimed at meeting consumers' total needs for routinely purchased food and nonfood items, plus services such as laundry, dry cleaning, shoe repair, check cashing, and bill paying. A new group called *category killers* carry a deep assortment in a particular category and a knowledgeable staff. *Examples:* Borders Books and Music, Petsmart, Staples, Home Depot, IKEA.

Combination stores are combination food and drug stores that average 55,000 square feet of selling space. *Examples:* Jewel and Osco stores.

Hypermarkets range between 80,000 and 220,000 square feet and combine supermarket, discount, and warehouse retailing. Product assortment includes furniture, large and small appliances, clothing, and many other items. They feature bulk display and minimum handling by store personnel, with discounts for customers who are willing to carry heavy appliances and furniture out of the store. Hypermarkets originated in France. *Examples:* Carrefour and Casino (France); Pyrca, Continente, and Alcampo (Spain); Meijer's (Netherlands).

Catalog Showroom: Broad selection of high-markup, fast-moving, brand-name goods at discount prices. Customers order goods from a catalog, then pick these goods up at a merchandise pickup area in the store. *Example:* Service Merchandise.

Sources: For further reading, see Leah Rickard, "Supercenters Entice Shoppers," *Advertising Age*, March 29, 1995, pp. 1–10; Debra Chanil, "Wholesale Clubs: A New Era?" *Discount Merchandiser*, November 1994, pp. 38–51; Julie Nelson Forsyth, "Department Store Industry Restructures for the 90s," *Chain Store Age Executive* (August 1993): pp. 29A–30A; John Milton Fogg, "The Giant Awakens," *Success*, March 1995, p. 51; J. Douglas Eldridge, "Nonstore Retailing: Planning for a Big Future," *Chain Store Age Executive* (August 1993): 34A–35A.

Although the overwhelming bulk (97 percent) of goods and services is sold through stores, *nonstore retailing* has been growing much faster than store retailing. Nonstore retailing falls into four major categories: direct selling, direct marketing (which includes telemarketing and Internet selling), automatic vending, and buying services:

1. *Direct selling* (also called *multi-level selling, network marketing*) is a $9 billion industry, with over 600 companies selling door-to-door or at home sales parties. Well-known in one-to-one selling

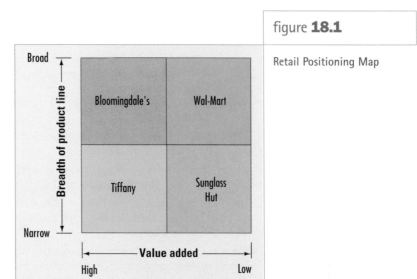

figure **18.1**

Retail Positioning Map

Source: William T. Gregor and Eileen M. Friars, *Money Merchandising: Retail Revolution in Consumer Financial Service* (Cambridge, MA: The MAC Group, 1982).

are Avon, Electrolux, and Southwestern Company of Nashville (Bibles). Tupperware and Mary Kay Cosmetics are sold one-to-many: A salesperson goes to the home of a host who has invited friends; the salesperson demonstrates the products and takes orders. Pioneered by Amway, the multilevel (network) marketing sales system consists of recruiting independent businesspeople who act as distributors. The distributor's compensation includes a percentage of sales of those the distributor recruits as well as earnings on direct sales to customers. These direct selling firms, now finding fewer consumers at home, are developing multidistribution strategies.

2. *Direct marketing* has roots in direct-mail and catalog marketing (Lands' End, L.L. Bean); it includes *telemarketing* (1-800-FLOWERS), *television direct-response marketing* (Home Shopping Network, QVC), and *electronic shopping* (Amazon.com, Autobytel.com). Of these, electronic shopping experienced a major take-off in the late 1990s as consumers flocked to dot-com sites to buy books, music, toys, electronics, and other products.

3. *Automatic vending* is used for a variety of merchandise, including impulse goods like cigarettes, soft drinks, coffee, candy, newspapers, magazines, and other products like hosiery, cosmetics, hot food, condoms, and paperbacks. Coinstar, a company started by a Stanford student, has placed over 8,500 machines in supermarkets. They take loose change and return bills, keeping 8.9 percent as a fee. Vending machines are found in factories, offices, large retail stores, gasoline stations, hotels, restaurants, and many other places. They offer 24-hour selling, self-service, and merchandise that is always fresh. Japan has the most vending machines per person and is experimenting with having vending machines take orders directly from the popular DoCoMo cell phones, cost to be charged against the customer's prepaid account.

4. *Buying service* is a storeless retailer serving a specific clientele—usually employees of large organizations—who are entitled to buy from a list of retailers that have agreed to give discounts in return for membership.

CORPORATE RETAILING   Although many retail stores are independently owned, an increasing number are part of some form of **corporate retailing**. Corporate retail organizations achieve economies of scale, greater purchasing power, wider brand recognition, and better-trained employees. The major types of corporate retailing—corporate chain stores, voluntary chains, retailer cooperatives, franchises, and merchandising

table **18.2**	
Major Types of Retail Organizations	**Corporate Chain Store:** Two or more outlets commonly owned and controlled, employing central buying and merchandising, and selling similar lines of merchandise. Their size allows them to buy in large quantities at lower prices, and they can afford to hire corporate specialists to deal with pricing, promotion, merchandising, inventory control, and sales forecasting. *Examples:* Tower Records, GAP, Pottery Barn.
	Voluntary Chain: A wholesaler-sponsored group of independent retailers engaged in bulk buying and common merchandising. *Examples:* Independent Grocers Alliance (IGA), True Value Hardware.
	Retailer Cooperative: Independent retailers who set up a central buying organization and conduct joint promotion efforts. *Examples:* Associated Grocers, ACE Hardware.
	Consumer Cooperative: A retail firm owned by its customers. In consumer co-ops residents contribute money to open their own store, vote on its policies, elect a group to manage it, and receive patronage dividends.
	Franchise Organization: Contractual association between a *franchiser* (manufacturer, wholesaler, service organization) and *franchisees* (independent businesspeople who buy the right to own and operate one or more units in the franchise system). Franchising has been prominent in dozens of product and service areas. *Examples*: McDonald's, Subway, Pizza Hut, Jiffy Lube, Meineke Mufflers, 7-Eleven.
	Merchandising Conglomerate: A free-form corporation that combines several diversified retailing lines and forms under central ownership, along with some integration of distribution and management. *Examples*: Allied Domeq PLC operates Dunkin' Donuts and Baskin-Robbins, plus a number of British retailers and a wine and spirits group.

conglomerates—are described in Table 18.2. Franchising is described in detail in "Marketing Insight: Franchise Fever."

marketing decisions

In the past retailers held customers by offering convenient location, special or unique assortments of goods, greater or better services than competitors, and store credit cards. All of this has changed. Today, national brands such as Calvin Klein, Izod, and Levi's are found in department stores, in their own shops, in merchandise outlets, and in off-price discount stores. In their drive for volume, national-brand manufacturers have placed their branded goods everywhere. The result is that retail-store assortments have grown more alike.

Service differentiation also has eroded. Many department stores have trimmed services, and many discounters have increased services. Customers have become smarter shoppers. They do not want to pay more for identical brands, especially when service differences have diminished; nor do they need credit from a particular store, because bank credit cards are almost universally accepted.

In the face of increased competition from discount houses and specialty stores, department stores are waging a comeback war. In addition to locations in the centers of cities, many have branches in suburban shopping centers, where parking is plentiful and family incomes are higher. Others run more frequent sales, remodel their stores, and experiment with mail-order and online marketing, and telemarketing. Supermarkets have opened larger stores, carry a larger number and variety of items, and upgrade facilities. Supermarkets have also increased their promotional budgets and moved heavily into private brands.

We will examine retailers' marketing decisions in the areas of target market, product assortment and procurement, services and store atmosphere, price, promotion, and place. (See also "Marketing Memo: Key Lessons on Shops, Shoppers, and Shopping.")

marketing **insight**

Franchise Fever

Franchises commanded over 40 percent of retail sales in the United States in 2000, up from 35 percent in 1998. This figure should not come as a surprise in a society where it is nearly impossible to stroll down a city block or drive on a suburban thoroughfare without seeing a Wendy's, a McDonald's, a Jiffy-Lube, or a 7-Eleven.

In a franchising system, individual *franchisees* are a tightly knit group of enterprises whose systematic operations are planned, directed, and controlled by the operation's innovator, called a *franchiser*. Franchises are distinguished by three characteristics:

1. *The franchiser owns a trade or service mark and licenses it to franchisees in return for royalty payments.*
2. *The franchisee pays for the right to be part of the system.* Start-up costs include rental and lease equipment and fixtures, and usually a regular license fee. McDonald's franchisees may invest as much as $750,000 in start-up costs. The franchisee then pays McDonald's a certain percentage of sales plus a monthly base rent.
3. *The franchiser provides its franchisees with a system for doing business.* McDonald's requires franchisees to attend "Hamburger University" in Oak Brook, Illinois, for three weeks to learn how to manage the business. Additionally, the franchisees must adhere to certain procedures in buying materials.

Franchising is mutually beneficial to both franchiser and franchisee. Among the benefits reaped by franchisers are the motivation and hard work of employees who are entrepreneurs rather than "hired hands," the franchisees' familiarity with local communities and conditions, and the enormous purchasing power of the franchiser. Franchisees benefit from buying into a business with a well-known and accepted brand name. They find it easier to borrow money from financial institutions, and they receive support in areas ranging from marketing and advertising to site selection and staffing.

The franchise explosion in recent years has increasingly saturated the domestic market. Some new directions that may deliver both franchiser growth and franchisee earnings are:

- *Strategic alliances with major outside corporations:* Fuji USA arranged with Moto Photo, a one-hour photo developer, to carry its film. Fuji won instant market penetration through Moto Photo's 400 locations, and Moto Photo franchisees enjoyed Fuji's name recognition and advertising reach.
- *Expansion abroad:* Fast-food franchises have become very popular throughout the world. Today McDonald's has over 15,000 restaurants in 119 countries outside the United States, which account for nearly 60 percent of the company's sales and profits.
- *Nontraditional site locations in the United States:* Franchises are opening in airports, sports stadiums, college campuses, hospitals, gambling casinos, theme parks, convention halls, and even riverboats.

Sources: Norman D. Axelrad and Robert E. Weigand, "Franchising—A Marriage of System Members," in *Marketing Managers Handbook* (3rd ed.), ed. Sidney Levy, George Frerichs, and Howard Gordon (Chicago: Dartnell, 1994), pp. 919–34; Meg Whittemore, "New Directions in Franchising," *Nation's Business* (January 1995): 45–52; "Trouble in Franchise Nation," *Fortune*, March 6, 1995, pp. 115–29; Carol Steinberg, "Millionaire Franchisees," *Success* (March 1995): 65–69; Deepak Agrawal and Rajiv Lal, "Contractual Agreements in Franchising: An Empirical Investigation," *Journal of Marketing Research* (May 1995): 213–21.

TARGET MARKET A retailer's most important decision concerns the target market. Until the target market is defined and profiled, the retailer cannot make consistent decisions on product assortment, store decor, advertising messages and media, price, and service levels.

Some retailers have defined their target markets quite well:

Wal-Mart The late Sam Walton and his brother opened the first Wal-Mart discount store in Rogers, Arkansas, in 1962. It was a big, flat, warehouse-type store selling everything from apparel to automotive supplies to small appliances at the lowest possible prices. More recently, Wal-Mart has been building stores in larger cities. Today, Wal-Mart operates 2,363 discount stores in the United States, including 454 Supercenters, 444 Sam's Clubs, and 41 distribution centers. It is expanding into the Wal-Mart Neighborhood Market supermarket-pharmacy business. Its annual sales exceed $165 billion, making it the largest U.S. private employer and the world's largest retailer. Its daily movement of goods is prodigious—474,000 pairs of shoes a day, 208,000 bras a day, 279,000 large boxes of diapers a day. Wal-Mart's secrets: Listen to customers, treat the employees as partners, push for lower prices from suppliers, keep a tight rein on

Marketing
MEMO

Key Lessons on Shops, Shoppers, and Shopping

In the pursuit of higher sales volume, retailers are studying their store environments for ways to improve the shopper experience. Paco Underhill, managing director of the retail consultant Envirosell Inc., writes about the art of selling in his book *Why We Buy: The Science of Shopping*. The book offers the following advice for fine-tuning the retail space in order to keep shoppers spending:

- *Attract shoppers and keep them in the store:* The amount of time shoppers spend in a store is perhaps the single most important factor in determining how much they will buy.
- *Honor the "transition zone":* On entering a store, people need to slow down and sort out the stimuli, which means that shoppers will likely be moving too fast to respond positively to signs, merchandise, or sales clerks in the zone they cross before making that transition.
- *Make merchandise available to the touch:* It is hard to overemphasize the importance of customers' hands to the world of shopping. A store can offer the finest, cheapest, sexiest goods, but if the shopper cannot pick them up, much of their appeal can be lost.
- *Men do not ask questions:* Men always move faster than women do through store's aisles. In many settings, it is hard to get them to look at anything they had not intended to buy. Men also do not like asking where things are. If a man cannot find the section he is looking for, he will wheel about once or twice, then leave the store without ever asking for help.
- *Behold the geriatrics:* By 2025, nearly one-fifth of the American people will be 65 or older. All of retailing is going to have to cater to seniors because there will be so many of them with money to spend.

Source: Keith Hammonds, "How We Sell," *Fast Company* (November 1999): 294.

expenses, and manage with the most advanced information systems. Wal-Mart's use of everyday low pricing and EDI for speedy stock replenishment has been benchmarked by other retailers, and it was the first U.S. mega merchant to take the plunge into global retailing. It already has stores in Argentina, Brazil, China, South Korea, and Mexico, and is adding more.[3]

The Limited   Leslie H. Wexner borrowed $5,000 in 1963 to create The Limited Inc., which started as a single store targeted to young, fashion-conscious women. All aspects of the store—clothing assortment, fixtures, music, colors, personnel—were orchestrated to match the target consumer. A decade later, his original customers were no longer in the "young" group. To catch the new "youngs," he started the Express. Over the years, he started or acquired other targeted store chains, including Lane Bryant, Victoria's Secret, Lerner's, and Bath and Body Works. Today, The Limited operates more than 5,300 stores in the United States plus global catalog operations. Sales totaled over $10 billion in 2000.[4]

PRODUCT ASSORTMENT AND PROCUREMENT   The retailer's product assortment must match the target market's shopping expectations. The retailer has to decide on product-assortment *breadth* and *depth*. Thus a restaurant can offer a narrow and shallow assortment (small lunch counters), a narrow and deep assortment (delicatessen), a broad and shallow assortment (cafeteria), or a broad and deep assortment (large restaurant). The real challenge begins after defining the store's product assortment, and that is to develop a product-differentiation strategy. Here are some possibilities:

- *Feature exclusive national brands that are not available at competing retailers:* Thus Saks might get exclusive rights to carry the dresses of a well-known international designer.
- *Feature mostly private branded merchandise:* Benetton and GAP design most of the clothes carried in their stores. Many supermarket and drug chains carry private branded merchandise.
- *Feature blockbuster distinctive merchandise events:* Bloomingdale's will run month-long shows featuring the goods of another country, such as India or China, throughout the store.
- *Feature surprise or ever-changing merchandise:* Benetton changes some portion of its merchandise every month so that customers will want to drop in frequently. T. J. Maxx offers surprise assortments of distress merchandise (goods the owner must sell immediately because it needs cash), overstocks, and closeouts.
- *Feature the latest or newest merchandise first:* The Sharper Image leads other retailers in introducing electronic appliances from around the world.
- *Offer merchandise customizing services:* Harrod's of London will make custom-tailored suits, shirts, and ties for customers, in addition to ready-made menswear.
- *Offer a highly targeted assortment:* Lane Bryant carries goods for the larger woman. Brookstone offers unusual tools and gadgets for the person who wants to shop in an "adult toy store."[5] Circuit City's decision to drop major appliances gave it more than 200 square feet to stock more units of higher-margin electronics. Remodeling also expanded total floor space by an additional 10,000 square feet, providing even more space for higher-margin home electronics.[6]

After deciding on the product-assortment strategy, the retailer must establish procurement sources, policies, and practices. In the corporate headquarters of a supermarket chain, specialist buyers (sometimes called *merchandise managers*) are responsible for developing brand assortments and listening to presentations by salespersons. In some chains, buyers have the authority to accept or reject new items. In other chains, they are limited to screening "obvious rejects" and "obvious accepts"; they bring other items to the buying committee for approval. Even when an item is accepted by a chain-store buying committee, individual stores in the chain may not carry it. About one-third of the items must be stocked and about two-thirds are stocked at the discretion of each store manager.

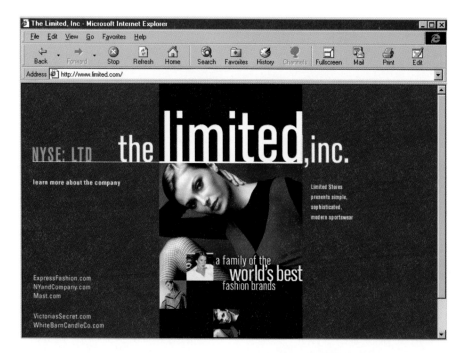

The Limited's home page presents "a family of the world's best fashion brands."

Manufacturers face a major challenge trying to get new items onto store shelves. They offer the nation's supermarkets between 150 and 250 new items each week, of which store buyers reject over 70 percent. Manufacturers need to know the acceptance criteria used by buyers, buying committees, and store managers. A. C. Nielsen Company interviewed store managers and found that they are most influenced (in order of importance) by strong evidence of consumer acceptance, a well-designed advertising and sales-promotion plan, and generous financial incentives to the trade.

Retailers are rapidly improving their skills in demand forecasting, merchandise selection, stock control, space allocation, and display. They are using computers to track inventory, compute economic order quantities, order goods, and analyze dollars spent on vendors and products. Supermarket chains are using scanner data to manage their merchandise mix on a store-by-store basis.

Stores are using **direct product profitability (DPP)** to measure a product's handling costs (receiving, moving to storage, paperwork, selecting, checking, loading, and space cost) from the time it reaches their warehouse until a customer buys it in their retail store. Resellers who have adopted DPP learn to their surprise that the gross margin on a product often has little relation to the direct product profit. Some high-volume products may have such high handling costs that they are less profitable and deserve less shelf space than low-volume products. Clearly, vendors are facing increasingly sophisticated retailers.

General Electric   Before the late 1980s, GE operated a traditional system of trying to load its dealers with GE appliances. This approach created problems for smaller independent dealers who could not afford to carry a large stock and who could not meet the price competition of multibrand dealers. So GE invented an alternative model called the Direct Connect system: GE dealers carry only display models and rely on a "virtual inventory" to fill orders. Dealers can access GE's order-processing system 24 hours a day, check on model availability, and place orders for next-day delivery. They get GE's best price, GE financing, and no interest charge for the first 90 days. In exchange, dealers must commit to selling 9 major GE product categories, generating 50 percent of their sales in GE products, opening their books to GE for review, and paying

marketing for the **new economy**

Extreme Retailing

Despite the failure of many dot-coms, customers continue to validate the concept of e-commerce with their wallets. Online business-to-consumer sales in the United States totaled $29 billion during 2000, nearly a 100 percent increase over 1999. E-commerce sites harbor advantages over brick-and-mortar retailers such as ease of use, product research and comparison tools, large inventories and better selection, and in-home purchasing. Brick-and-mortar retailers do have, however, several natural advantages, such as products shoppers can actually see, touch, and test, real-life customer service, no delivery lag time for small or medium-sized purchases, and they also provide the traditional shopping experience. Jeff Bezos, chief executive of Amazon.com, readily admits that "the physical world is still the best medium ever invented."

To further entice Internet-savvy consumers to visit their stores, real-life retailers are developing a host of new services and promotions designed to increase customer traffic. The change in strategy can be noticed in practices as simple as calling each shopper a "guest" (as many stores are beginning to do) or as grandiose as building an indoor amusement park. Still others are finding ways to update the customer service model. Several stores, such as the Banana Republic, offer free home delivery during the holidays for customers who spend above a certain amount. The flagship Banana Republic in San Francisco gives free rides home to shoppers who spend at least $100.

Retailers are also creating in-store entertainment in the hopes of attracting customers who want fun and excitement. The super-regional mall developer Mills Corp. has trademarked a word for this phenomenon: "shoppertainment." Mills Corp. built a mall in Las Vegas called The Forum Shops that treats shoppers to Vegas-style spectacles. Entertainment for shoppers helps The Forum Shops average $1,200 per square foot in annual sales, compared with a national average of about $300.

Super-regional malls often seek to anchor themselves with unique and interesting shops, rather than the brand-name department stores and national retailers that fill most traditional malls. Says Laurence C. Siegel, chairman and CEO at Mills Corp., "There are no Macy's at our centers. We want to create destination retail." One such destination is sporting-goods retailer Bass Pro Shops, which has aquariums, waterfalls, trout ponds, archery and rifle ranges, and putting greens in its stores. The Sony Style store, where Sony entertainment and electronics products are displayed in environments that encourage customers to test them, is another example of a mega-mall store.

Brick-and-mortar retailers are adding Internet content to their physical stores. Borders bookstores installed in-store kiosks called Title Sleuths that allow customers to view the full inventory from the company's Internet site and make online purchases. As the convenience of online shopping becomes more popular, more companies may adopt these Internet/brick-and-mortar in-store hybrids.

Despite the recent explosion of e-commerce, the vast majority of shoppers will do their purchasing in physical retail locations in the near future. By the highest estimate, online retail sales in the United States will be less than 5 percent of total estimated U.S. retail sales. If brick-and-mortar stores continue to find innovative ways to attract customers, this percentage could very well be lower.

Sources: Kenneth T. Rosen and Amanda L. Howard, "E-tail: Gold Rush or Fool's Gold?" *California Management Review* (April 1, 2000) 72-100; Moira Cotlier, "Census Releases First E-commerce Report," *Catalog Age*, May 1, 2001; Associated Press, "Online Sales Boomed at End of 2000," *Star-Tribune of Twin Cities*, February 17, 2001.

GE every month through electronic funds transfer. GE integrated Direct Connect with the Internet to create CustomerNet, which makes all the original Direct Connect services available on the Web. CustomerNet is also a B2B e-commerce site where GE provides Internet content for each of its 1,500 online dealers.[7]

SERVICES AND STORE ATMOSPHERE   Retailers must also decide on the *services mix* to offer customers:

- Prepurchase services include accepting telephone and mail orders, advertising, window and interior display, fitting rooms, shopping hours, fashion shows, trade-ins.
- Postpurchase services include shipping and delivery, gift wrapping, adjustments and returns, alterations and tailoring, installations, engraving.
- Ancillary services include general information, check cashing, parking, restaurants, repairs, interior decorating, credit, rest rooms, baby-attendant service.

The services mix is a key tool for differentiating one store from another; so is atmosphere. (See "Marketing for the New Economy: Extreme Retailing.") *Atmosphere* is another element in the store arsenal. Every store has a physical layout that makes it hard or easy to move around. Every store has a "look." The store must embody a planned atmosphere that suits the target market and draws consumers toward purchase. Consider Kohl's floor plan.

Kohl's   Retail giant Kohl's employs a floor plan modeled after a racetrack. Designed to smoothly convey customers past all the merchandise in the store, an eight-foot-wide main aisle moves them in a circle around the store. The design also includes a middle aisle that hurried shoppers can use as a shortcut. The racetrack loop yields higher spending levels than many competitors: Kohl's stores take in an average $279 per square foot, compared with $220 a square foot for Target and $147 for Dillard's.[8]

Victoria's Secret stores work on the concept of "retail theater": Customers feel they are in a romance novel, with lush music and faint floral scents in the background. Supermarkets have found that varying the tempo of music affects the average time spent in the store and the average expenditures. Retailers are now adding fragrances in their stores to stimulate certain moods in shoppers. London's Heathrow Airport sprays the scent of pine needles because it stimulates the sense of holidays and weekend walks. Automobile dealers will spray a "leather" scent in second-hand cars to make them smell "new."[9] Here are other examples of "packaged environments."[10]

Recreational Equipment Inc. (REI)   Seattle-based REI has been retailing outdoor equipment products since 1938 and today operates 57 stores in 23 states and Japan. Its stores work on the principle of "experiential retailing." Consumers are able to test climbing equipment on a huge wall in the store. They can test Gore-tex raincoats by going under a simulated rain shower.

Mall of America   The largest mall in the United States, the Mall of America (near Minneapolis) is a super-regional mall plus a seven-acre amusement park. Opened in 1992, it now has a total of over 500 stores that employ more than 12,000 people. Anchored by four major department stores—Nordstrom, Macy's, Bloomingdale's, and Sears—it has become a tourist destination for avid shoppers from around the world. It now attracts more than 40 million visitors yearly. Other attractions at the Mall of America include the four-story Lego Imagination Center, a miniature golf course, the UnderWater World aquarium, and a Chapel of Love, where thousands of couples have been married.[11]

PRICE DECISION   Prices are a key positioning factor and must be decided in relation to the target market, the product-and-service assortment mix, and competition. All retailers would like to achieve high volumes and high gross margins. They would like high *Turns x Earns*, but the two usually do not go together. Most retailers fall into the *high-markup, lower-volume* group (fine specialty stores) or the *low-markup, higher-volume* group (mass-merchandisers and discount stores). Within each of these groups are further gradations. Thus Bijan's on Rodeo Drive in Beverly Hills prices suits starting at $1,000 and shoes at $400. At the other extreme, Odd Lot Trading in New York City is a superdiscounter that sells odd lots and closeouts at prices below those of normal discounters.

Retailers must also pay attention to pricing tactics. Most retailers will put low prices on some items to serve as traffic builders or loss leaders. They will run storewide sales. They will plan markdowns on slower-moving merchandise. For example, shoe retailers expect to sell 50 percent of their shoes at the normal markup, 25 percent at a 40 percent markup, and the remaining 25 percent at cost. Recently, a classic pricing tactic experienced a revival.

Kmart   In 2001, as part of an initiative to revitalize ailing sales, Kmart reintroduced the classic Blue Light Specials, which it had discontinued in 1991. The Blue Light Specials, flashing blue police lights that announce unadvertised specials, were relaunched via a $25 million advertising campaign. The company anticipates the new Blue Lights will attract nostalgic shoppers who remember the specials from a decade ago.[12]

Some retailers have abandoned "sales pricing" in favor of everyday low pricing (EDLP). EDLP could lead to lower advertising costs, greater pricing stability, a stronger image of fairness and reliability, and higher retail profits. General Motors' Saturn division states a low list price for its cars and its dealers do not bargain. Wal-Mart also practices everyday low prices. Frank Feather cites a study showing that supermarket chains practicing everyday low pricing are often more profitable than those practicing sales pricing.[13]

PROMOTION DECISION   Retailers use a wide range of promotion tools to generate traffic and purchases. They place ads, run special sales, issue money-saving coupons, and run frequent shopper-reward programs, in-store food sampling, and coupons on shelves or at checkout points. Each retailer must use promotion tools that support and reinforce its image positioning. Fine stores will place tasteful full-page ads in magazines such as Vogue and Harper's. They will carefully train salespeople to greet customers, interpret their needs, and handle complaints. Off-price retailers will arrange their merchandise to promote the idea of bargains and large savings, while conserving on service and sales assistance.

PLACE DECISION   Retailers are accustomed to saying that the three keys to success are "location, location, and location." Customers generally choose the nearest bank and gas station. Department-store chains, oil companies, and fast-food franchisers exercise great care in selecting locations. The problem breaks down into selecting regions of the country in which to open outlets, then particular cities, and then particular sites. A supermarket chain might decide to operate in the Midwest; in the cities of Chicago, Milwaukee, and Indianapolis; and in 14 locations, mostly suburban, within the Chicago region. Two of the savviest location experts in recent years have been the off-price retailer T. J. Maxx and toy store giant Toys "R" Us. Both retailers put the majority of their new locations in areas with rapidly growing numbers of young families.

One retailer is adding stores in spite of a sales decline.

Staples Despite a recent downturn in the growth rate of small businesses and home offices and a decline in PC sales in the United States, Staples office-supply stores is seeking aggressive expansion. While its two major competitors (Office Depot and Office Max) are closing stores and cutting jobs, in 2001 Staples expanded its retail space 12 percent by opening 160 new stores. Explaining the aggressive expansion, Staples' head of real estate operations said, "We like to saturate markets. We want to be a convenience operator—our customers don't want to spend a lot of time trying to find a store or driving to a store."[14]

Retailers can locate their stores in the central business district, a regional shopping center, a community shopping center, a shopping strip, or within a larger store:

- *General business districts:* This is the oldest and most heavily trafficked city area, often known as "downtown." Store and office rents are normally high. Most downtown areas were hit by a flight to the suburbs in the 1960s, resulting in deteriorated retailing facilities; but in the 1990s, a minor renaissance of interest in downtown apartments, stores, and restaurants began in many cities.
- *Regional shopping centers:* These are large suburban malls containing 40 to 200 stores. They usually draw customers from a 5- to 20-mile radius. Typically, malls feature one or two nationally known anchor stores, such as JCPenney or Lord & Taylor, and a great number of smaller stores, many under franchise operation. Malls are attractive because of generous parking, one-stop shopping, restaurants, and recreational facilities. Successful malls charge high rents and may get a share of stores' sales.
- *Community shopping centers:* These are smaller malls with one anchor store and between 20 and 40 smaller stores.
- *Strip malls* (also called *shopping strips*): These contain a cluster of stores, usually housed in one long building, serving a neighborhood's needs for groceries, hardware, laundry, shoe repair, and dry cleaning. They usually serve people within a five- to ten-minute driving range.

- *A location within a larger store:* Certain well-known retailers—McDonald's, Starbucks, Nathan's, Dunkin' Donuts—locate new, smaller units as concession space within larger stores or operations, such as airports, schools, or department stores.

In view of the relationship between high traffic and high rents, retailers must decide on the most advantageous locations for their outlets. They can use a variety of methods to assess locations, including traffic counts, surveys of consumer shopping habits, and analysis of competitive locations.[15] Several models for site location have also been formulated.[16]

Retailers can assess a particular store's sales effectiveness by looking at four indicators: (1) number of people passing by on an average day; (2) percentage who enter the store; (3) percentage of those entering who buy; and (4) average amount spent per sale.

trends in retailing

At this point, we can summarize the main developments retailers and manufacturers need to take into account in planning competitive strategies.

1. *New retail forms and combinations.* Some supermarkets include bank branches. Bookstores feature coffee shops. Gas stations include food stores. Loblaw's Supermarkets have added fitness clubs to their stores. Shopping malls and bus and train stations have peddler's carts in their aisles.

2. *Growth of intertype competition.* Different types of stores—discount stores, catalog showrooms, department stores—all compete for the same consumers by carrying the same type of merchandise.

3. *Growth of giant retailers.* Through their superior information systems, logistical systems, and buying power, giant retailers are able to deliver good service and immense volumes of product at appealing prices to masses of consumers. They are crowding out smaller manufacturers who cannot deliver enough quantity and even dictating to the most powerful manufacturers what to make, how to price and promote, when and how to ship, and even how to improve production and management. Manufacturers need these accounts; otherwise they would lose 10 to 30 percent of the market. Some giant retailers are *category killers* that concentrate on one product category, such as toys (Toys "R" Us), home improvement (Home Depot), or office supplies (Staples). Others are *supercenters* that combine grocery items with a huge selection of nonfood merchandise (Kmart, Wal-Mart). (See "Marketing Insight: Category Killers vs. the Internet.")

4. *Growing investment in technology.* Retailers are using computers to produce better forecasts, control inventory costs, order electronically from suppliers, send e-mail between stores, and even sell to customers within stores. They are adopting checkout scanning systems,[17] electronic funds transfer, electronic data interchange,[18] in-store television, store traffic radar systems,[19] and improved merchandise-handling systems.

5. *Global presence of major retailers.* Retailers with unique formats and strong brand positioning are increasingly appearing in other countries.[20] U.S. retailers such as McDonald's, The Limited, GAP, and Toys "R" Us have become globally prominent. Wal-Mart operates over 700 stores abroad. Among foreign-based global retailers are Britain's Marks and Spencer, Italy's Benetton, France's Carrefour hypermarkets, Sweden's IKEA home furnishings stores, and Japan's Yaohan supermarkets.[21]

6. *Selling an experience, not just goods.* Retailers are now adding fun and community in order to compete with other stores and online retailers.[22] There has been a marked rise in establishments that provide a place for people to congregate, such as coffeehouses, tea shops, juice bars, bookshops, and brew pubs. Brew pubs such as New York's Zip City Brewing and Seattle's Trolleyman Pub offer tastings and a place to pass the time. Bass Pro Shops, a retailer of outdoor sports equipment, feature giant aquariums, waterfalls, trout ponds, archery and rifle ranges, putting greens, and classes in everything from ice fishing to conservation—all free. The Discovery Zone, a chain of children's play spaces, offers indoor spaces where kids can go wild without breaking anything and stressed-out parents can exchange stories. Denver's two Tattered Covered bookstores host more than 250 events annually, from folk dancing to women's meetings, and Barnes & Noble turned a once-staid bookstore industry into a fun-filled village green.

Barnes & Noble   Now the nation's largest bookseller, Barnes & Noble has over 500 locations across the United States. It reached this impressive size by making its stores attractive, sponsoring community and literary events, installing public rest

marketing **insight**

Category Killers vs. the Internet

One problem with the category killer model was that it was easy to copy, which meant that any specialty niche was subject to cutthroat competitors. For example, the office supply store market is currently occupied by three chains: Office Depot, Office Max, and Staples. Another problem was the success of superstore retailers like Wal-Mart. Wal-Mart's dominance of retail in the 1990s also led many experts to question the category killer concept: Why would consumers want to travel to a different store for each category purchase when they could buy all that they need at a single location? Wal-Mart demonstrated the power of its superstore concept when it surpassed Toys "R" Us in 1998 to become the largest toy seller in the United States.

Perhaps the biggest problem for category killers in recent years has been e-commerce. Internet sites with category killer business models, like online grocer Peapod.com, toy e-tailer eToys.com, and Internet pet supply site Pets.com, attracted much investor attention. By contrast, off-line retailers that moved to e-commerce were held to normal earnings criteria that did not reward a money-losing online venture, and as a result many brick-and-mortar retailers' stock prices were punished on Wall Street. With their high valuations, pure-click e-tailers were able to attract talented employees by offering lucrative stock options, and succeeded in building efficient delivery systems that fit the online business model. Traditional retailers had neither the cachet nor the soaring stock prices to attract the most creative talent, and often had to wrestle with delivery systems designed to bring products from warehouses to store shelves, not individual homes. Although many Internet pure-clicks did not survive the dot-com crash, they made the market much tougher for category killers.

The company that pioneered the category killer retail model, Toys "R" Us, struggled in the late 1990s against online competitors like eToys. In response, Toys "R" Us developed its own e-commerce site, called Toysrus.com, in 1998. The company invested more than $75 million in infrastructure to manage delivery of products ordered on the site. The number of visitors to Toysrus.com increased more than 300 percent from 1998 to 1999. Unfortunately, the site was overwhelmed by holiday season orders in 1999, and Toys "R" Us could not deliver many Christmas orders in time. In 2000, Toys "R" Us joined its e-commerce site with Amazon.com. The partnership illustrates one method for category killers to compete with Internet pure-plays. Another method is integrating the physical retail locations with the e-commerce site, known as a "clicks-and-mortar" strategy. For example, Barnes & Noble bookstores installed Internet terminals where customers can browse and purchase titles from the company's Web site, bn.com. The clicks-and-mortar approach has several advantages. For example, store-based retailers spent an average of less than $5 per person getting existing customers to shop online, while Internet start-ups spent an average of $45 per person building a customer base from square one. Moreover, customers who purchased online and off-line (the so-called "double channel") from the same retailer increased their total purchases by 10 percent.

Sources: John D. Calkins et al., "From Retailing to E-tailing," *The McKinsey Quarterly,* Janurary 1, 2000; John Peet, "Survey of E-commerce: Something Old, Something New," *The Economist,* February 26, 2000; William M. Bulkeley, " 'Category Killers' Go from Lethal to Lame," *Wall Street Journal Europe,* March 13, 2000; Steve Weiner, "With Big Selection and Low Prices, 'Category Killer' Stores Are a Hit," *Wall Street Journal,* June 17, 1996; "Toys 'R' Us Announces Aggressive Online Retailing Strategy," *PR Newswire,* April 27, 1999; Fran Silverman, "E-sales Overwhelm Toys 'R' Us," *Hartford Courant,* December 24, 1999.

rooms and Starbucks coffee bars, having storytelling for kids, comfortable reading areas, soft music, and a huge selection of books, magazines, and music. Barnes & Noble is also a major player on the Internet, with the largest free-standing inventory of any online bookseller. To better leverage the successful brick-and-mortar retail locations in building traffic to its Web sites, Barnes and Noble spent $20 million in 2000 to install counters with Internet access in its retail locations, which enable customers to order from the e-commerce site. This move helped Barnes & Noble.com's market share rise from 19 percent in the first quarter of 2000 to 27 percent in the first quarter of 2001.[23]

7. *Competition between store-based and non-store-based retailing.* Consumers now receive sales offers through direct mail letters and catalogs, and over television, computers, and telephones. These non-store-based retailers are taking business away from store-based retailers. Some store-based retailers initially saw online retailing as a definite threat. Home Depot shocked its top vendors (Black & Decker, Stanley Tools, etc.) by issuing a memo implying that if they started to sell online, Home Depot might drop them as suppliers; but now Home Depot is finding it advantageous to work with online retailers. Wal-Mart recently joined with America Online (AOL) so that AOL will provide a low-cost Internet access service that carries the Wal-Mart

brand, and Wal-Mart will promote the service and AOL in its stores and through TV advertising. Stores such as Wal-Mart and Kmart have developed their own online Web sites, and some online retailers are finding it advantageous to own or manage physical outlets, either retail stores or warehouses.

HomePoint.com   HomePoint.com, a Web-based home furnishings e-tailer, created HomePoint Advantage to link thousands of bricks-and-mortar furniture stores to its extranet. Customers visiting a furniture store can inspect items in the store or order items from the site's electronic catalog and arrange delivery. The local store thus becomes a giant furniture retailer. With HomePoint's huge inventory and regional warehouses, furniture items can be delivered in a week compared to the normal eight-week wait.

wholesaling

Wholesaling includes all the activities involved in selling goods or services to those who buy for resale or business use. Wholesaling excludes manufacturers and farmers because they are engaged primarily in production, and it excludes retailers. Wholesalers (also called *distributors*) differ from retailers in a number of ways. First, wholesalers pay less attention to promotion, atmosphere, and location because they are dealing with business customers rather than final consumers. Second, wholesale transactions are usually larger than retail transactions, and wholesalers usually cover a larger trade area than retailers. Third, the government deals with wholesalers and retailers differently in terms of legal regulations and taxes.

Why are wholesalers used at all? Why do manufacturers not sell directly to retailers or final consumers? In general, wholesalers are used when they are more efficient in performing one or more of the following functions:

- *Selling and promoting:* Wholesalers' sales forces help manufacturers reach many small business customers at a relatively low cost. Wholesalers have more contacts, and often buyers trust wholesalers more than they trust a distant manufacturer.
- *Buying and assortment building:* Wholesalers are able to select items and build the assortments their customers need, saving the customers considerable work.
- *Bulk breaking:* Wholesalers achieve savings for their customers through buying in large carload lots and breaking the bulk into smaller units.
- *Warehousing:* Wholesalers hold inventories, thereby reducing inventory costs and risks to suppliers and customers.
- *Transportation:* Wholesalers can often provide quicker delivery to buyers because they are closer to the buyers.
- *Financing:* Wholesalers finance customers by granting credit, and finance suppliers by ordering early and paying bills on time.
- *Risk bearing:* Wholesalers absorb some risk by taking title and bearing the cost of theft, damage, spoilage, and obsolescence.
- *Market information:* Wholesalers supply information to suppliers and customers regarding competitors' activities, new products, price developments, and so on.
- *Management services and counseling:* Wholesalers often help retailers improve their operations by training sales clerks, helping with store layouts and displays, and setting up accounting and inventory-control systems. They may help industrial customers by offering training and technical services.

the growth and types of wholesaling

Wholesaling has grown in the United States in recent years.[24] A number of factors explain this: the growth of larger factories located some distance from the principal buyers; production in advance of orders rather than in response to specific orders; an increase in the number of levels of intermediate producers and users; and the increasing

table **18.3**	Major Wholesaler Types

Merchant Wholesalers: Independently owned businesses that take title to the merchandise they handle. They are called *jobbers*, *distributors*, or *mill supply houses* and fall into two categories: full service and limited service.

Full-Service Wholesalers: Carry stock, maintain a sales force, offer credit, make deliveries, and provide management assistance. There are two types of full-service wholesalers: (1) *Wholesale merchants* sell primarily to retailers and provide a full range of services. *General-merchandise wholesalers* carry several merchandise lines. *General-line wholesalers* carry one or two lines. *Specialty wholesalers* carry only part of a line. (2) *Industrial distributors* sell to manufacturers rather than to retailers and provide several services—carrying stock, offering credit, and providing delivery.

Limited-Service Wholesalers: Offer fewer services to suppliers and customers. *Cash-and-carry wholesalers* have a limited line of fast-moving goods and sell to small retailers for cash. *Truck wholesalers* primarily sell and deliver a limited line of semi-perishable merchandise to supermarkets, small grocery stores, hospitals, restaurants, factory cafeterias, and hotels. *Drop shippers* operate in bulk industries, such as coal, lumber, and heavy equipment. Upon receiving an order, they select a manufacturer, who ships the merchandise directly to the customer on the agreed-upon terms and time of delivery. The drop shipper assumes title and risk from the time the order is accepted to its delivery to the customer. *Rack jobbers* serve grocery and drug retailers, mostly in nonfood items. They send delivery trucks to stores, and the delivery people set up displays, price the goods, keep them fresh, set up point-of-purchase displays, and keep inventory records. Rack jobbers retain title to the goods and bill retailers only for goods sold to consumers. *Producers' cooperatives* assemble farm produce to sell in local markets. Co-op profits are distributed to members at the end of the year. *Mail-order wholesalers* send catalogs to retail, industrial, and institutional customers featuring jewelry, cosmetics, specialty foods, and other small items. Main customers are businesses in small outlying areas. No sales force is maintained. Orders are filled and sent by mail, truck, or other means of transportation.

Brokers and Agents: Do not take title to goods, and perform only a few functions. Main function is to facilitate buying and selling, for which they earn a commission of 2 to 6 percent of the selling price. Generally specialize by product line or customer type.

Brokers: Chief function is bringing buyers and sellers together and assisting in negotiation. They are paid by the party who hired them and do not carry inventory, get involved in financing, or assume risk. The most familiar examples are food brokers, real estate brokers, insurance brokers, and security brokers.

Agents: Represent either buyers or sellers on a more permanent basis. *Manufacturers' agents* represent two or more manufacturers of complementary lines. They enter into a formal written agreement with each manufacturer covering pricing policy, territories, order-handling procedure, delivery service and warranties, and commission rates. Most manufacturers' agents are small businesses, with only a few skilled salespeople. *Selling agents* have contractual authority to sell a manufacturer's entire output in such product areas as textiles, industrial machinery and equipment, coal and coke, chemicals, and metals. *Purchasing agents* generally have a long-term relationship with buyers and make purchases for them, often receiving, inspecting, warehousing, and shipping merchandise to buyers. *Commission merchants* take physical possession of products and negotiate sales.

Manufacturers' and Retailers' Branches and Offices: Wholesaling operations conducted by sellers or buyers themselves rather than through independent wholesalers. Separate branches and offices can be dedicated to sales or purchasing. Sales branches and offices are set up by manufacturers to improve inventory control, selling, and promotion. Sales branches carry inventory and are found in such industries as lumber and automotive equipment and parts. *Sales offices* do not carry inventory and are most prominent in dry-goods and notions industries. *Purchasing offices* perform a role similar to that of brokers or agents but are part of the buyer's organization. Many retailers set up purchasing offices in major market centers.

Miscellaneous Wholesalers: A few specialized types of wholesalers are found in certain sectors of the economy. These include agricultural assemblers (which buy the agricultural output of many farms), petroleum bulk plants and terminals (which consolidate the petroleum output of many wells), and auction companies (which auction cars, equipment, and so forth, to dealers and other businesses).

need for adapting products to the needs of intermediate and final users in terms of quantities, packages, and forms. The major types of wholesalers are described in Table 18.3.

wholesaler marketing decisions

Wholesaler-distributors have faced mounting pressures in recent years from new sources of competition, demanding customers, new technologies, and more direct-buying programs by large industrial, institutional, and retail buyers. They have had to develop appropriate strategic responses. One major drive has been to increase asset productivity by managing their inventories and receivables better. They also have had to improve their strategic decisions on target markets, product assortment and services, price, promotion, and place.

TARGET MARKET   Wholesalers need to define their target markets. They can choose a target group of customers by size (only large retailers), type of customer (convenience food stores only), need for service (customers who need credit), or other criteria. Within the target group, they can identify the most profitable customers and design stronger offers to build better relationships with them. They can propose automatic reordering systems, set up management-training and advisory systems, and even sponsor a voluntary chain. They can discourage less profitable customers by requiring larger orders or adding surcharges to smaller ones.

PRODUCT ASSORTMENT AND SERVICES   The wholesalers' "product" is their assortment. Wholesalers are under great pressure to carry a full line and maintain sufficient stock for immediate delivery, but the costs of carrying huge inventories can kill profits. Wholesalers today are reexamining how many lines to carry and are choosing to carry only the more profitable ones. They are also examining which services count most in building strong customer relationships and which ones should be dropped or charged for. The key is to find a distinct mix of services valued by their customers.

PRICE DECISION   Wholesalers usually mark up the cost of goods by a conventional percentage, say 20 percent, to cover their expenses. Expenses may run 17 percent of the gross margin, leaving a profit margin of approximately 3 percent. In grocery wholesaling, the average profit margin is often less than 2 percent. Wholesalers are beginning to experiment with new approaches to pricing. They might cut their margin on some lines in order to win important new customers. They will ask suppliers for a special price break when they can turn it into an opportunity to increase the supplier's sales.

PROMOTION DECISION   Wholesalers rely primarily on their sales force to achieve promotional objectives. Even here, most wholesalers see selling as a single salesperson talking to a single customer, instead of a team effort to sell, build, and service major accounts. Wholesalers would benefit from adopting some of the image-making techniques used by retailers. They need to develop an overall promotion strategy involving trade advertising, sales promotion, and publicity. They also need to make greater use of supplier promotion materials and programs.

PLACE DECISION   In the past, wholesalers were typically located in low-rent, low-tax areas and put little money into their physical setting and offices. Often the materials-handling systems and order-processing systems lagged behind the available technologies. Today, progressive wholesalers have been improving materials-handling procedures and costs by developing *automated warehouses* and improving their supply capabilities through advanced information systems. Here is an example.[25]

McKesson   McKesson Corporation is a leading healthcare services company providing pharmaceutical and medical-surgical supply management, information solutions, pharmacy automation, and sales and marketing services to the healthcare industry. The company has unmatched depth, breadth, and reach delivering unique cost-saving and quality improvement solutions to pharmacies, hospitals, physicians, extended care sites, payor sites, and pharmaceutical and medical-surgical manufacturers. McKesson maintains a strong presence on the Internet through its Web site *www.mckesson.com*. The site offers access to information about the company, its people, products, and services. McKesson customers can use the Web site to access the company's healthcare software applications as well as order and track pharmaceutical and medical-surgical products.[26]

McKesson offers online supply management.

trends in wholesaling

Manufacturers always have the option of bypassing wholesalers or replacing inefficient wholesalers with better ones. Manufacturers' major complaints against wholesalers are as follows: They do not aggressively promote the manufacturer's product line, and act more like order takers; they do not carry enough inventory and therefore fail to fill customers' orders fast enough; they do not supply the manufacturer with up-to-date market, customer, and competitive information; they do not attract high-caliber managers and bring down their own costs; and they charge too much for their services.

It even appeared that wholesalers were headed for a significant decline as large manufacturers and retailers moved aggressively into direct buying programs. Savvy wholesalers rallied to the challenge and began to reengineer their businesses. The most successful wholesaler-distributors adapted their services to meet their suppliers' and target customers' changing needs. They recognized that they had to add value to the channel. They also had to reduce their operating costs by investing in more advanced materials-handling technology, information systems, and the Internet.

Grainger W. W. Grainger, Inc., is one of the largest B2B distributors of equipment, components, and supplies in the United States and Canada. It offers over 220,000 products to clients. It has developed and stocked one national, two regional, and seven zone distribution centers to guarantee product availability and quick service. The distribution centers are linked by satellite network, which has reduced customer-response time and boosted sales. Grainger also offers a Web site to provide 24-hour-a-day online ordering.[27]

Narus and Anderson interviewed leading industrial distributors and identified four ways they strengthened their relationships with manufacturers:

1. They sought a clear agreement with their manufacturers about their expected functions in the marketing channel.
2. They gained insight into the manufacturers' requirements by visiting their plants and attending manufacturer association conventions and trade shows.

3. They fulfilled their commitments to the manufacturer by meeting the volume targets, paying bills promptly, and feeding back customer information to their manufacturers.

4. They identified and offered value-added services to help their suppliers.[28]

The wholesaling industry remains vulnerable to one of the most enduring trends—fierce resistance to price increases and the winnowing out of suppliers based on cost and quality. The trend toward vertical integration, in which manufacturers try to control or own their intermediaries, is still strong. "Marketing Memo: Strategies of High-Performance Wholesaler-Distributors" outlines some of the strategies used by successful wholesale organizations.

market logistics

Physical distribution starts at the factory. Managers choose a set of warehouses (stocking points) and transportation carriers that will deliver the goods to final destinations in the desired time or at the lowest total cost. Physical distribution has now been expanded into the broader concept of **supply chain management (SCM).** Supply chain management starts before physical distribution: It involves procuring the right inputs (raw materials, components, and capital equipment); converting them efficiently into finished products; and dispatching them to the final destinations. An even broader perspective calls for studying how the company's suppliers themselves obtain their inputs. The supply chain perspective can help a company identify superior suppliers and distributors and help them improve productivity, which ultimately brings down the company's costs.

The supply chain view sees markets as destination points and amounts to a linear view of the flow. A broader view sees a company at the center of a *value network* that includes its suppliers and its suppliers' suppliers and its immediate customers and their end customers. The value network includes valued relations with others such as university researchers, government approval agencies, and so on. A company needs to orchestrate these parties to enable it to deliver superior value to the target market. The company should first think of the target market and then design the supply chain backward from that point. This view has been called **demand chain planning. Market logistics** involves planning the infrastructure to meet demand, then implementing and controlling the physical flows of materials and final goods from points of origin to points of use, to meet customer requirements at a profit.

Market logistics planning has four steps:[29]

1. Deciding on the company's value proposition to its customers. (What on-time delivery standard should be offered? What levels should be attained in ordering and billing accuracy?)

2. Deciding on the best channel design and network strategy for reaching the customers. (Should the company serve customers directly or through intermediaries? What products to source from which manufacturing facilities? How many warehouses to maintain and where should they be located?)

3. Developing operational excellence in sales forecasting, warehouse management, transportation management, and materials management.

4. Implementing the solution with the best information systems, equipment, policies, and procedures.

Market logistics leads to an examination of the most efficient way to deliver value:

■ A software company normally sees its challenge as producing and packaging software disks and manuals, then shipping them to wholesalers—who ship them to retailers, who sell them to customers. Customers bring the software package to home or office and download the software onto a hard drive. Market logistics would look at two superior delivery systems. The first involves ordering the software to be downloaded onto the customer's hard drive. Alternatively, software could be loaded onto a computer by the computer manufacturer. Both solutions eliminate the need for printing, packaging, shipping, and stocking millions of disks and manuals. The same solutions are available for distributing music, newspapers, video games, films, and other products that deliver voice, text, data, or images.

Marketing
MEMO

**Strategies for
High–Performance
Wholesaler–Distributors**

Lusch, Zizzo, and Kenderine
studied 136 wholesalers in North
America and concluded that the
progressive ones are renewing
themselves in five ways:

1. *Strengthening core operations:*
   Several wholesalers have put
   renewed focus on their core
   operations. They develop such
   expertise in distributing their
   particular product line that
   manufacturers and retailers
   cannot duplicate the efficiency.

2. *Expanding into global markets:*
   Wholesalers, especially in the
   chemical, electronics, and
   computer fields, have been
   expanding not only in Canada
   and Mexico but also in Europe
   and Asia. Many manufacturers
   prefer using these wholesaler
   networks to expand overseas.

3. *Doing more with less:*
   Wholesalers have been investing
   heavily in technology, including
   bar coding and scanning, fully
   automated warehouses,
   electronic data interchange
   (EDI), and advanced information
   technology. This has enabled
   them to serve manufacturers
   and retailers who have been
   unable or unwilling to make
   investments of their own.

   continued...

- At one time, German consumers purchased individual bottles of soft drinks. Then they said they would be willing to buy six bottles at a time in a six-pack. Retailers also favored this because the bottles could be loaded faster on the shelves, and more bottles would be purchased per occasion. A soft-drink manufacturer designed the six-packs to fit on store shelves. Then cases and pallets were designed to bring these six-packs to the store's receiving rooms. Factory operations were redesigned to produce the new six-packs. The purchasing department let out bids for the new materials. Once the six-packs hit the market, the manufacturer's market share rose substantially.

- The IKEA Retailers, franchisees of the world-famous IKEA concept for retail sale of furniture and home furnishings, are able to sell good-quality furniture and home furnishings at a much lower cost than competitors. The IKEA concepts cost savings stem from several sources: (1) The IKEA Retailers buy such large volumes of furniture and home furnishings that they get lower prices; (2) the furniture and home furnishings are designed in "knockdown" form and therefore shipped flat at a much lower transportation cost; (3) the customer drives the furniture home, which saves delivery cost; (4) the customer assembles the furniture; and (5) the IKEA concept works on a low markup and high volume. Altogether, the IKEA Retailers can charge 20 percent less than competitors for comparable furniture and home furnishings.

The market logistics task calls for **integrated logistics systems (ILS)**, involving materials management, material flow systems, and physical distribution, abetted by information technology (IT). Third-party suppliers, such as FedEx Logistics Services or Ryder Integrated Logistics, often participate in designing or managing these systems. Volvo, working with FedEx, set up a warehouse in Memphis with a complete stock of truck parts. A dealer, needing a part in an emergency, phones a toll-free number, and the part is flown out the same day and delivered that night either at the airport or at the dealer's office or even at the roadside repair site.

Information systems play a critical role in managing market logistics, especially computers, point-of-sale terminals, uniform product bar codes, satellite tracking, electronic data interchange (EDI), and electronic funds transfer (EFT). These developments have shortened the order-cycle time, reduced clerical labor, reduced the error rate in documents, and provided improved control of operations. They have enabled companies to make promises such as "the product will be at dock 25 at 10:00 A.M. tomorrow," and control this promise through information. Consider the following two examples.

Supervalu Supervalu, based in Eden Prairie, Minnesota, is a major wholesaler-retailer of dry groceries and the largest distributor to grocery retailers in the United States. It has been experimenting with "cross-docking," a system of moving products from the supplier's truck through the distribution center and onto a store-bound truck without putting them into pick or reserve bins. Attracted by the promise of savings on labor and time, Supervalu began cross-docking some high-volume products, such as paper products, and some milk and bread; about 12 percent of dry groceries were cross-docked in 1998. In 2000, the company expanded its cross-docking capabilities, which helped it to reduce the total number of inventory days on hand for the 1.5 billion cases of goods it shipped.[30]

Cutter & Buck Cutter & Buck, Inc., is a high-end fashion sportswear company founded in 1990. By 1996, after successful growth, the company realized it had a problem with the contract warehouse, further compounded by the lack of an in-house embroidery capability. About half of its knit shirts needed custom embroidery, and the logistics of dealing with 14 different embroidery suppliers were difficult. So Cutter & Buck built its own warehouse and put embroidery machines in it. Fast turnaround, especially for embroidered items, greatly improved the company's profit margins. In 2000, a new warehouse management system implemented by the company helped reduce total labor costs by 20 percent.[31]

Market logistics involves several activities. The first is sales forecasting, on the basis of which the company schedules distribution, production, and inventory levels. Production plans indicate the materials the purchasing department must order. These materials arrive through inbound transportation, enter the receiving area, and are stored in raw-material inventory. Raw materials are converted into finished goods. Finished-goods inventory is the link between customer orders and manufacturing activity. Customers' orders draw down the finished-goods inventory level, and manufacturing activity builds it up. Finished goods flow off the assembly line and pass through packaging, in-plant warehousing, shipping-room processing, outbound transportation, field warehousing, and customer delivery and servicing.

Management has become concerned about the total cost of market logistics, which can amount to 30 to 40 percent of the product's cost. The grocery industry alone thinks it can decrease its annual operating costs by 10 percent, or $30 billion, by revamping its market logistics. A typical box of breakfast cereal takes 104 days to get from factory to supermarket, chugging through a labyrinth of wholesalers, distributors, brokers, and consolidators.[32] With inefficiencies like these, it is no wonder that experts call market logistics "the last frontier for cost economies." Lower market-logistics costs will permit lower prices, yield higher profit margins, or both. Even though the cost of market logistics can be high, a well-planned program can be a potent tool in competitive marketing. Companies can attract additional customers by offering better service, faster cycle time, or lower prices through market-logistics improvements.

What happens if a firm's market logistics are not set up properly? Companies lose customers when they fail to supply goods on time. Kodak launched a national advertising campaign for a new instant camera before it had delivered enough cameras to the stores. Customers found that it was not available and bought Polaroid cameras instead.

Today's large customers are making stronger demands for logistical support that will increase the supplier's costs. Customers want more frequent deliveries so that they do not have to carry as much inventory. They want shorter order-cycle times, which means that suppliers will have to carry high in-stock availability. Customers often want direct store delivery rather than shipments to distribution centers. They want mixed

4. *Committing to TQM:* Instead of just measuring sales and product movement, progressive wholesalers are moving toward managing processes to improve outcomes as perceived by customers. This includes performing quality assessment of their suppliers' products and thereby adding value. As the wholesalers move toward zero-defect customer service, manufacturers and retailers will welcome this trend as contributing to their own capacity to satisfy customers.

5. *Marketing support philosophy:* Wholesalers are recognizing that their role is not simply to represent the suppliers' interests, or their customers' interests, but to provide marketing support to both, by acting as a valued member of the marketing value chain.

Sources: Robert F. Lusch, Deborah Zizzo, and James M. Kenderdine, "Strategic Renewal in Distribution," *Marketing Management* 2, no. 2 (1993): 20–29. Also see their *Foundations of Wholesaling—A Strategic and Financial Chart Book, Distribution Research Program* (Norman, OK: College of Business Administration, University of Oklahoma, 1996).

The IKEA-USA home page.

pallets of the goods they ordered rather than separate pallets. They want tighter prom-ised delivery times. They may want custom packaging, price tagging, and display building. Suppliers cannot say no to many of these requests, but at least they can set up different logistical programs with different service levels and customer charges.

Smart companies will abandon "one-size-fits-all" logistics service and adjust their offerings to each major customer's requirements. Some large retailers will want daily shipments of smaller volumes; others will accept less frequent shipments of larger vol-umes. The company's trade group will set up *differentiated distribution* by offering differ-ent bundled service programs for different customers.

market-logistics objectives

Many companies state their market-logistics objective as "getting the right goods to the right places at the right time for the least cost." Unfortunately, this objective pro-vides little practical guidance. No system can simultaneously maximize customer service and minimize distribution cost. Maximum customer service implies large inventories, premium transportation, and multiple warehouses, all of which raise market-logistics costs.

A company cannot achieve market-logistics efficiency by asking each market-logistics manager to minimize his or her own logistics costs. Market-logistics costs interact and are often negatively related. For example:

■ The traffic manager favors rail shipment over air shipment because rail costs less. How-ever, because the railroads are slower, rail shipment ties up working capital longer, delays customer payment, and might cause customers to buy from competitors who offer faster service.

■ The shipping department uses cheap containers to minimize shipping costs. Cheaper containers lead to a higher rate of damaged goods and customer ill will.

■ The inventory manager favors low inventories. This increases stockouts, back orders, paperwork, special production runs, and high-cost fast-freight shipments.

Given that market-logistics activities involve strong trade-offs, decisions must be made on a total system basis. The starting point is to study what customers require and what competitors are offering. Customers are interested in on-time delivery, supplier willingness to meet emergency needs, careful handling of merchandise, supplier will-ingness to take back defective goods and re-supply them quickly.

The company must then research the relative importance of these service outputs. For example, service-repair time is very important to buyers of copying equipment. Xerox developed a service-delivery standard that "can put a disabled machine any-where in the continental United States back into operation within three hours after receiving the service request." It then designed a service division of personnel, parts, and locations to deliver on this promise.

The company must also consider competitors' service standards. It will normally want to match or exceed the competitors' service level, but the objective is to maximize profits, not sales. The company has to look at the costs of providing higher levels of service. Some companies offer less service and charge a lower price; other companies offer more service and charge a premium price.

The company ultimately has to establish some promise to the market. Coca-Cola wants to "put Coke within an arm's length of desire." Lands' End, the giant clothing retailer, aims to respond to every phone call within 20 seconds, and to ship out every order within 24 hours of its receipt. Some companies define standards for each service factor. One appliance manufacturer has established the following service standards: to deliver at least 95 percent of the dealer's orders within seven days of order receipt, to fill the dealer's orders with 99 percent accuracy, to answer dealer inquiries on order status within three hours, and to ensure that damage to merchandise in transit does not exceed 1 percent.

Given the market-logistics objectives, the company must design a system that will minimize the cost of achieving these objectives. Each possible market-logistics system will lead to the following cost:

$$M = T + FW + VW + S$$

where M = total market-logistics cost of proposed system
T = total freight cost of proposed system
FW = total fixed warehouse cost of proposed system
VW = total variable warehouse costs (including inventory) of proposed system
S = total cost of lost sales due to average delivery delay under proposed system

Choosing a market-logistics system calls for examining the total cost (M) associated with different proposed systems and selecting the system that minimizes it. If it is hard to measure S, the company should aim to minimize $T + FW + VW$ for a target level of customer service.

market-logistics decisions

Four major decisions must be made with regard to market logistics: (1) How should orders be handled? (order processing); (2) Where should stocks be located? (warehousing); (3) How much stock should be held? (inventory); and (4) How should goods be shipped? (transportation).

ORDER PROCESSING   Most companies today are trying to shorten the *order-to-payment cycle*—that is, the elapsed time between an order's receipt, delivery, and payment. This cycle involves many steps, including order transmission by the salesperson, order entry and customer credit check, inventory and production scheduling, order and invoice shipment, and receipt of payment. The longer this cycle takes, the lower the customer's satisfaction and the lower the company's profits. Salespeople may be slow in sending in orders and use inefficient communications; these orders may pile up on the desk of order processors while they wait for credit department approval and inventory availability information from the warehouse.

Companies need to prepare criteria for the Perfect Order. Suppose the customer expects on-time delivery, order completeness, picking accuracy, and billing accuracy. Suppose the supplier has a 70 percent chance of delivering all four of these perfectly on any order. Then the probability that the supplier will fulfill perfect orders five times in a row to that customer would be $.70^5 = .168$. The customer's series of disappointments is likely to lead him to drop this supplier. A .70 standard is not good enough.

Companies are making progress, however. For example, General Electric operates an information system that checks the customer's credit standing upon receipt of an order, and determines whether and where the items are in stock. The computer issues an order to ship, bills the customer, updates the inventory records, sends a production order for new stock, and relays the message back to the sales representative that the customer's order is on its way—all in less than 15 seconds.

WAREHOUSING   Every company has to store finished goods until they are sold, because production and consumption cycles rarely match. The storage function helps to smooth discrepancies between production and quantities desired by the market. The company must decide on the number of inventory stocking locations. Consumer packaged-goods companies have been reducing their number of stocking locations from 10–15 to about 5–7; and pharmaceutical and medical distributors have cut their stocking locations from 90 to about 45. On the one hand, more stocking locations means that goods can be delivered to customers more quickly, but it also means higher warehousing and inventory costs. To reduce warehousing and inventory duplication costs, the company might centralize its inventory in one place and use fast transportation to fulfill orders. After National Semiconductor shut down its six storage warehouses and set up a central distribution warehouse in Singapore, its standard delivery time decreased by 47 percent, its distribution costs fell 2.5 percent, and its sales increased 34 percent.[33]

Some inventory is kept at or near the plant, and the rest is located in warehouses in other locations. The company might own private warehouses and also rent space in public warehouses. *Storage warehouses* store goods for moderate-to-long periods of time. *Distribution warehouses* receive goods from various company plants and suppliers and move them out as soon as possible.

The older, multistoried warehouses with slow elevators and inefficient materials-handling procedures are receiving competition from newer, single-story *automated warehouses* with advanced materials-handling systems under the control of a central computer. The computer reads store orders and directs lift trucks and electric hoists to gather goods according to bar codes, move them to loading docks, and issue invoices. These warehouses have reduced worker injuries, labor costs, pilferage, and breakage and improved inventory control. When the Helene Curtis Company replaced its six antiquated warehouses with a new $32 million facility, it cut its distribution costs by 40 percent.[34]

Some warehouses are now taking on some activities formerly done in the plant. These include assembly, packaging, and constructing promotional displays. By "postponing" finalization of the offering, savings can be achieved in costs and finer matching of offerings to demand.

INVENTORY   Inventory levels represent a major cost. Salespeople would like their companies to carry enough stock to fill all customer orders immediately. However, this is not cost-effective. *Inventory cost increases at an accelerating rate as the customer service level approaches 100 percent.* Management needs to know how much sales and profits would increase as a result of carrying larger inventories and promising faster order fulfillment times, and then make a decision.

Inventory decision making involves knowing when to order and how much to order. As inventory draws down, management must know at what stock level to place a new order. This stock level is called the *order (reorder) point.* An order point of 20 means reordering when the stock falls to 20 units. The order point should balance the risks of stockout against the costs of overstock.

The other decision is how much to order. The larger the quantity ordered, the less frequently an order has to be placed. The company needs to balance order-processing costs and inventory-carrying costs. *Order-processing costs* for a manufacturer consist of *setup costs* and *running costs* (operating costs when production is running) for the item. If setup costs are low, the manufacturer can produce the item often, and the average cost per item is stable and equal to the running costs. If setup costs are high, however, the manufacturer can reduce the average cost per unit by producing a long run and carrying more inventory.

Order-processing costs must be compared with *inventory-carrying costs.* The larger the average stock carried, the higher the inventory-carrying costs. These carrying costs include storage charges, cost of capital, taxes and insurance, and depreciation and obsolescence. Carrying costs might run as high as 30 percent of inventory value. This means that marketing managers who want their companies to carry larger inventories need to show that the larger inventories would produce incremental gross profit to exceed incremental carrying costs.

The optimal order quantity can be determined by observing how order-processing costs and inventory-carrying costs sum up at different order levels. Figure 18.2 shows that the order-processing cost per unit decreases with the number of units ordered because the order costs are spread over more units. Inventory-carrying charges per unit increase with the number of units ordered because each unit remains longer in inventory. The two cost curves are summed vertically into a total-cost curve. The lowest point on the total-cost curve is projected down on the horizontal axis to find the optimal order quantity Q^*.[35]

Companies are reducing their inventory costs by treating inventory items differently. They are positioning inventory items according to risk and opportunity. They distinguish between bottleneck items (high risk, low opportunity), critical items (high risk,

figure **18.2**

Determining Optimal Order
Quantity

high opportunity), commodities (low risk, high opportunity), and nuisance items (low risk, low opportunity).[36] They are also keeping slow-moving items in a central location while carrying fast-moving items in warehouses closer to customers.

Just-in-time production methods have changed inventory-planning practices. **Just-in-time production (JIT)** consists of arranging for supplies to come into the factory at the rate that they are needed. If the suppliers are dependable, then the manufacturer can carry much lower levels of inventory and still meet customer-order-fulfillment standards. The basic idea is to arrange for well-timed *flows*, not *stocks*. Consider the following example.

Tesco   Tesco, the large British supermarket chain, has set up an innovative JIT market-logistics system. Tesco's management wanted to greatly reduce costly backroom storage space. It accomplished this by arranging twice-a-day delivery of replenishment stock. Ordinarily, it would have needed three separate trucks to deliver frozen goods, refrigerated goods, and regular goods on each trip. Instead, it designed new trucks with three compartments to carry the three types of goods.

The ultimate answer to carrying *near-zero inventory* is to build for order, not for stock. Sony calls it SOMA, "sell-one, make-one." Dell, for example, gets the customer to order a computer and pay for it in advance. Then Dell uses the customer's money to pay suppliers to ship the necessary components. As long as customers do not need the item immediately, money can be saved by all.

TRANSPORTATION   Marketers need to be concerned with transportation decisions. Transportation choices will affect product pricing, on-time delivery performance, and the condition of the goods when they arrive, all of which affects customer satisfaction.

In shipping goods to its warehouses, dealers, and customers, the company can choose among five transportation modes: rail, air, truck, waterway, and pipeline. Shippers consider such criteria as speed, frequency, dependability, capability, availability, traceability, and cost. For speed, air and truck are the prime contenders. If the goal is low cost, then it is water and pipeline.

Shippers are increasingly combining two or more transportation modes, thanks to containerization. **Containerization** consists of putting the goods in boxes or trailers that are easy to transfer between two transportation modes. *Piggyback* describes the use of rail and trucks; *fishyback*, water and trucks; *trainship*, water and rail; and *airtruck*, air and trucks. Each coordinated mode offers specific advantages. For example, piggyback is cheaper than trucking alone, yet provides flexibility and convenience.

In deciding on transportation modes, shippers can choose from private, contract, and common carriers. If the shipper owns its own truck or air fleet, the shipper becomes a *private carrier*. A *contract carrier* is an independent organization selling transportation services to others on a contract basis. A *common carrier* provides services between predetermined points on a scheduled basis and is available to all shippers at standard rates.

Today billions of dollars are being invested to develop "last-mile delivery systems" to bring products to homes within a short delivery period. Domino's Pizza organized its franchised stores to be in locations where it could promise to deliver hot pizzas to homes within one-half hour. Peapod similarly offers to deliver online grocery orders within a few hours. Consumers may soon think twice about whether they should exert themselves to travel to stores to get their food, videos, or clothes or simply ask the stores to bring it to them in about the same amount of time. Everything, including flowers, can be delivered to their door, using the Internet.

1–800–flowers.com. A customer can order flowers from this site to send to an address book of recipients. 1-800-Flowers uses a sophisticated regional fulfillment system. If the flower is not available in the region, the customer is notified of the shipment delay and can approve or change the order. After ordering, the customer can use the site to track the order's location. The fulfillment capabilities have been designed to give customers confidence that their gifts will be delivered in the promised time.

organizational lessons

Experience with market logistics has taught executives three major lessons:

1. Companies should appoint a senior vice president of logistics to be the single point of contact for all logistical elements. This executive should be accountable for logistical performance on both cost and customer-satisfaction criteria.

The 1-800-Flowers.com site makes online ordering easy.

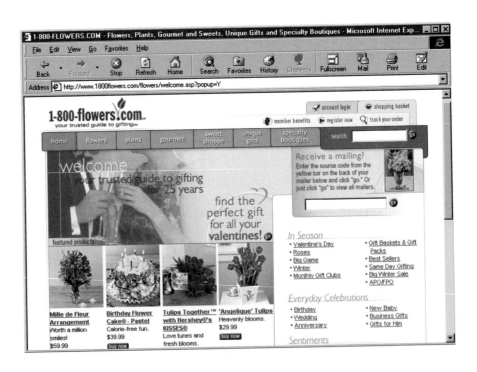

2. The senior vice president of logistics should hold periodic meetings (weekly, biweekly) with sales and operations people to review inventory, operating costs, and customer service and satisfaction, as well as to consider market conditions and whether changes should be made in production schedules.

3. New software and systems are the key to achieving competitively superior logistics performance in the future.

Here is how Sears is gaining through the use of better software:[37]

Sears   Sears, Roebuck & Company owns a huge credit-card company called Sears Credit, which serves over 60 million credit-card holders who use their cards to purchase more than 50 percent of all merchandise sold in Sears stores. To improve customer service, Sears formed a strategic alliance with Total Systems Services (TSYS), a third-party credit-card processing service. Alan J. Lacy, president of Sears Credit, stressed the ability of TSYS to track delinquent accounts more quickly and effectively, thus improving collections. The partnership with TSYS also yielded one of Sears' more successful credit-card launches—the Sears Gold MasterCard, which generated more than $1 billion in receivables within a year of its 2000 debut.[38]

Market-logistics strategies must be derived from business strategies, rather than solely from cost considerations. The logistics system must be information-intensive and establish electronic links among all the significant parties. Finally, the company should set its logistics goals to match or exceed competitors' service standards and should involve members of all relevant teams in the planning process.

summary

1. Retailing includes all the activities involved in selling goods or services directly to final consumers for personal, nonbusiness use. Retailers can be understood in terms of store retailing, nonstore retailing, and retail organizations.

2. Like products, retail-store types pass through stages of growth and decline. As existing stores offer more services to remain competitive, their costs and prices go up, which opens the door to new retail forms that offer a mix of merchandise and services at lower prices. The major types of retail stores are specialty stores; department stores; supermarkets; convenience stores; discount stores; off-price retailers (factory outlets, independent off-price retailers, and warehouse clubs); superstores (combination stores and supermarkets); and catalog showrooms.

3. Although most goods and services are sold through stores, nonstore retailing has been growing much faster than store retailing. The major types of nonstore retailing are direct selling (one-to-one selling, one-to-many-party selling, and multilevel network marketing); direct marketing (which includes e-commerce and Internet retailing); automatic vending; and buying services.

4. Although many retail stores are independently owned, an increasing number are falling under some form of corporate retailing. Retail organizations achieve many economies of scale, such as greater purchasing power, wider brand recognition, and better-trained employees. The major types of corporate retailing are corporate chain stores, voluntary chains, retailer cooperatives, consumer cooperatives, franchise organizations, and merchandising conglomerates.

5. Like all marketers, retailers must prepare marketing plans that include decisions on target markets, product assortment and procurement, services and store atmosphere, price, promotion, and place. These decisions must take into account the major trends in retailing.

6. Wholesaling includes all the activities involved in selling goods or services to those who buy for resale or business use. Manufacturers use wholesalers because wholesalers can perform functions better and more cost-effectively than the manufacturer can. These functions include, but are not limited to, selling and promoting, buying and assortment building, bulk breaking, warehousing, transportation, financing, risk bearing, dissemination of market information, and provision of management services and consulting.

7. There are four types of wholesalers: merchant wholesalers (full-service wholesalers like wholesale merchants and industrial distributors, and limited-service wholesalers like cash-and-carry wholesalers, truck wholesalers, drop shippers, rack jobbers, producers' cooperatives, and mail-order wholesalers); brokers and agents (including manufacturers' agents, selling agents, purchasing agents, and commission merchants); manufacturers' and retailers' sales branches, sales offices, and purchasing offices; and miscellaneous wholesalers such as agricultural assemblers and auction companies.

8. Like retailers, wholesalers must decide on target markets, product assortment and services, price, promotion, and place. The most successful wholesalers are those who adapt their services to meet their suppliers' and target customers' needs.

9. Producers of physical products and services must decide on market logistics—the best way to store and move their goods and services to market destinations. The logistical task is to coordinate the activities of suppliers, purchasing agents, manufacturers, marketers, channel members, and customers. Major gains in logistical efficiency have come from advances in information technology. Although the cost of market logistics can be high, a well-planned market-logistics program can be a potent tool in competitive marketing. The ultimate goal of market logistics is to meet customers' requirements in an efficient and profitable way.

applications

marketing debate – does it matter where you are sold?

Some marketers feel that the image of the retail store in which they sell their products does not matter—all that matters is that the right customers shop there and the product is displayed in the right way. Others maintain that store images can be critical and must be consistent with the image of the product.

Take a position: Store image does not really affect the brand images of the products they sell that much versus Store image must be consistent with the product image.

marketing and advertising

1. The Mayors jewelry store ad in Figure 1 focuses on a particular type of merchandise—the diamond engagement ring—and suggests how it helps to bring luxury to the recipient.

   a. What is the target market for this ad? How is the ad using the ad graphics and copy to appeal to this target market?
   b. Based on this ad, what services and atmosphere would a consumer expect to find at a Mayors store? At the Mayors Web site?
   c. Discuss the retailer's product-assortment strategy, as suggested by the item featured here.

2. Retailers need to plan market logistics for backward channels as well as forward channels. The ad shown in Figure 2 explains how online retailers can save time and money—and satisfy customers—by incorporating a UPS system to manage merchandise returns.

   a. What flows must an online retailer consider when preparing for customer returns?
   b. How would a system for managing returns be likely to affect an online retailer's decisions about warehousing and inventory?
   c. What market-logistics objectives might a retailer using this UPS system set for its merchandise returns?

Figure 1

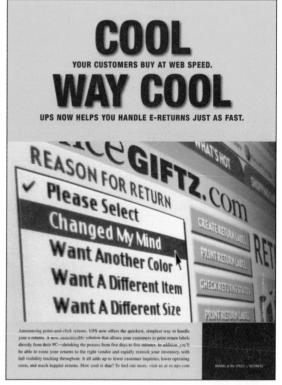

Figure 2

online marketing today

As discussed earlier, W. W. Grainger is a giant industrial wholesaler with branches throughout North America and a comprehensive Web site for online ordering at any hour. Despite competition from specialized Web marketplaces, Grainger.com draws more than one million users every month and rings up over $260 million in annual sales. After a months-long promotional campaign to attract online users, the site became so well established that Grainger was able to shift spending into advanced technology such as new search tools to help customers locate what they want even more quickly.[39]

Browse the home page of the Grainger Web site (www.grainger.com), noting the kinds of products that are highlighted here. Then follow the "About Us" link to read about the company's history, mission and values, and special promotions. Finally, follow the "Services" link and read about the various services being offered. Who is Grainger's target market, and what is its mission? How would you describe its product assortment and services? What is this wholesaler doing to build and strengthen customer relationships by adding extra value?

you're the marketer: sonic pda marketing plan

Marketing Plan Pro

Retailers and wholesalers play a critical role in marketing strategy because of their relationships with the final consumer. For this reason, manufacturers need to effectively manage their connections with these channel intermediaries.

You are responsible for channel management for Sonic's new personal digital assistant (PDA) product. Based on your previous strategic choices and your knowledge of the market, respond to the following questions in shaping your wholesaling and retailing decisions:

- What types of retailers would be most appropriate for distributing Sonic's PDA? What are the advantages and disadvantages of selling through these types of retailers?

- What role should wholesalers play in Sonic's distribution strategy? Why?
- What market-logistics issues must Sonic consider for the launch of its first PDA?
- What effect do your wholesale/retail decisions have on the other decisions you face about Sonic's marketing mix?

Now that you have examined Sonic's retail and wholesale opportunities and market logistics, summarize your ideas in a written marketing plan or type them into the Marketing Mix and Channels sections of the *Marketing Plan Pro* software.

notes

1. William R. Davidson, Albert D. Bates, and Stephen J. Bass, "Retail Life Cycle," *Harvard Business Review* (November–December 1976): 89–96.
2. Stanley C. Hollander, "The Wheel of Retailing," *Journal of Marketing* (July 1960): 37–42.
3. Bill Saporito, "And the Winner Is Still . . . Wal-Mart," *Fortune*, May 2, 1994, pp. 62–70; Lorrie Grant, "An Unstoppable Marketing Force: Wal-Mart Aims for Domination of the Retail Industry—Worldwide," *USA Today*, November 6, 1998, p. B1.
4. Hoover's Company Capsules, 1999; Limited Annual Report, 2001.
5. Laurence H. Wortzel, "Retailing Strategies for Today's Marketplace," *Journal of Business Strategy* (Spring 1987): 45–56.
6. Evan Ramstad, "Circuit City's CEO Gambles to Galvanize the Chain," *Wall Street Journal*, September 18, 2000, p. B4.
7. Michael Treacy and Fred Wiersema, "Customer Intimacy and Other Discipline Values," *Harvard Business Review* (January–February 1993): 84–93; "GE to Sell Appliances Online," *PR Newswire*, September 30, 1999.
8. Cametta Coleman, "Kohl's Retail Racetrack," *Wall Street Journal*, March 1, 2000.
9. Piet Vroon et al., *Smell : The Secret Seducer* (New York: Farrar, Straus & Giroux, 1997).
10. For more discussion, see Philip Kotler, "Atmospherics as a Marketing Tool," *Journal of Retailing* (Winter 1973–1974): 48–64; and Mary Jo Bitner, "Servicescapes: The Impact of Physical Surroundings on Customers and Employees," *Journal of Marketing* (April 1992): 57–71. Also see B. Joseph Pine II and

James H. Gilmore, *The Experience Economy* (Boston: Harvard Business School Press, 1999).
11. Mall of America Web site; Kristen Ostendorf, "Not Wed to Tradition," *Gannett News Service*, January 5, 1998; Carol Sottili, "Mall of America Has Stores Galore," *Plain Dealer*, April 23, 2000, p. 2K.
12. Joann Muller, "Kmart's Bright Idea," *Business Week*, April 9, 2001, p. 50.
13. Frank Feather, *The Future Consumer* (Toronto: Warwick Publishing, 1994), p. 171. Also see Stephen J. Hoch, Xavier Dreeze, and Mary E. Purk, "EDLP, Hi-Lo, and Margin Arithmetic," *Journal of Marketing* (October 1994): 1–15.
14. Paul Klebnikov, "Hair of the Dog," *Forbes*, April 16, 2001, p. 74.
15. R. L. Davies and D. S. Rogers, eds., *Store Location and Store Assessment Research* (New York: John Wiley, 1984).
16. Sara L. McLafferty, *Location Strategies for Retail and Service Firms* (Lexington, MA: Lexington Books, 1987).
17. Catherine Yang, "Maybe They Should Call Them Scammers," *BusinessWeek*, January 16, 1995, pp. 32–33; Ronald C. Goodstein, "UPC Scanner Pricing Systems: Are They Accurate?" *Journal of Marketing* (April 1994): 20–30.
18. For a listing of the key factors involved in success with an EDI system, see R. P. Vlosky, D. T. Wilson, and P. M. Smith, "Electronic Data Interchange Implementation Strategies: A Case Study," *Journal of Business & Industrial Marketing* 9, no. 4 (1994): 5–18.
19. "Business Bulletin: Shopper Scanner," *Wall Street Journal*, February 18, 1995, p. A1.

20. For further discussion of retail trends, see Louis W. Stern and Adel I. El-Ansary, *Marketing Channels*, 5th ed. (Upper Saddle River, NJ: Prentice Hall, 1996).

21. Shelley Donald Coolidge, "Facing Saturated Home Markets, Retailers Look to Rest of World," *Christian Science Monitor*, February 14, 1994, p. 7; Carla Rapoport with Justin Martin, "Retailers Go Global," *Fortune*, February 20, 1995, pp. 102–8.

22. Gherry Khermouch, "Third Places," *Brandweek*, March 13, 1995, pp. 36–40.

23. I. Jeanne Dugan, "The Baron of Books," *BusinessWeek*, June 29, 1998; Hoover's Company Profiles, 1999; Rebecca Quick, "CEO Steps Down at Barnes & Noble Online Concern," *Wall Street Journal*, January 13, 2000; Rebecca Quick, "Barnes & Noble and Its Online Sibling Enter Alliance Linking 'Bricks and Clicks,'" *Wall Street Journal*, October 27, 2000, p. B10; Erin White, "Barnes & Noble.com Expects to Report 23% Revenue Rise," *Wall Street Journal*, April 27, 2001, p. 25.

24. Bert McCammon, Robert F. Lusch, Deborah S. Coykendall, and James M. Kenderdine, *Wholesaling in Transition* (Norman: University of Oklahoma, College of Business Administration, 1989).

25. Hoover's Company Profiles, 1999; and company Web sites.

26. Michael Liedtke, "Online Goes Offline at McKesson HBOC," *Pittsburgh Post-Gazette*, February 27, 2001, p. B4.

27. <www.grainger.com>.

28. James A. Narus and James C. Anderson, "Contributing as a Distributor to Partnerships with Manufacturers, " *Business Horizons* (September–October 1987). Also see James D. Hlavecek and Tommy J. McCuistion, "Industrial Distributors—When, Who, and How," *Harvard Business Review* (March–April 1983): 96–101.

29. William C. Copacino, *Supply Chain Management* (Boca Raton, FL: St. Lucie Press, 1997).

30. Susan Reda, "Crossdocking: Can Supermarkets Catch Up?" *Stores* (February 1998); Supervalu 2001 *Annual Report*.

31. Diane Mayoros, "Cutter & Buck Chairman & CEO Interview," *Wall Street Corporate Reporter*, August 6, 1998; "Cutter & Buck Announces Two New Retail Locations;" *Business Wire*, August 21, 2000.

32. Ronald Henkoff, "Delivering the Goods," *Fortune*, November 28, 1994, pp. 64–78.

33. Ibid., pp. 64–78.

34. Rita Koselka, "Distribution Revolution," *Forbes*, May 25, 1992, pp. 54–62.

35. The optimal order quantity is given by the formula $Q^* = 2DS/IC$, where D=annual demand, S=cost to place one order, and I=annual carrying cost per unit. Known as the economic-order quantity formula, it assumes a constant ordering cost, a constant cost of carrying an additional unit in inventory, a known demand, and no quantity discounts. For further reading on this subject, see Richard J. Tersine, *Principles of Inventory and Materials Management*, 4th ed. (Upper Saddle River, NJ: Prentice Hall, 1994).

36. William C. Copacino, *Supply Chain Management* (Boca Raton, FL: St. Lucie Press, 1997), pp. 122–23.

37. "Darigold Selects IMI to Enhance Order Fulfillment and Customer Service," *Business Wire*, February 2, 1998.

38. Sears Press Release, "Sears Announces Strategic Alliance with Total Systems, Inc.," May 14, 1998; <www.tsys.com>; "TSYS Extends Retail Agreement with Sears." *PR Newswire*, January 18, 2000.

39. Don Steinberg, "W. W. Grainger—Grainger.com," *Ziff Davis Smart Business for the New Economy*, September 1, 2001, p. 64.

managing integrated marketing communications

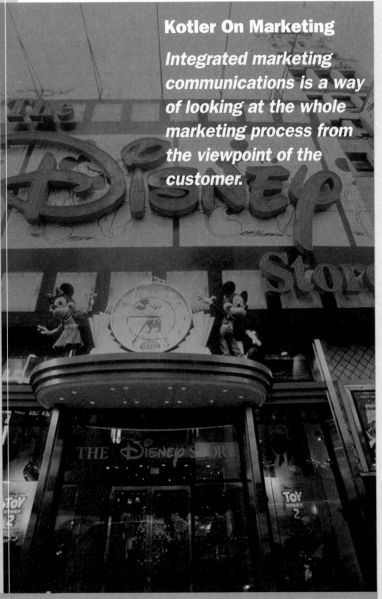

Kotler On Marketing

Integrated marketing communications is a way of looking at the whole marketing process from the viewpoint of the customer.

In this chapter, we will address the following questions:

- How does communication work?
- What are the major steps in developing an integrated marketing communications program?
- Who should be responsible for marketing communication planning?

Modern marketing calls for more than developing a good product, pricing it attractively, and making it accessible. Companies must also communicate with present and potential stakeholders, and the general public. Every company is inevitably cast into the role of communicator and promoter. For most companies, the question is not whether to communicate but rather what to say, to whom, and how often.

The **marketing communications mix** consists of five major modes of communication:

1. *Advertising: Any paid form of nonpersonal presentation and promotion of ideas, goods, or services by an identified sponsor.*

2. *Sales promotion: A variety of short-term incentives to encourage trial or purchase of a product or service.*

3. *Public relations and publicity: A variety of programs designed to promote or protect a company's image or its individual products.*

4. *Personal selling: Face-to-face interaction with one or more prospective purchasers for the purpose of making presentations, answering questions, and procuring orders.*

5. *Direct and interactive marketing: Use of mail, telephone, fax, e-mail, or Internet to communicate directly with or solicit response or dialogue from specific customers and prospects.*[1]

This chapter will describe the communication process; in the following chapters we will examine each of the communication tools.

the communications process

Today there is a new view of communications as an interactive dialogue between the company and its customers that takes place during the preselling, selling, consuming, and postconsuming stages. Companies must ask not only "How can we reach our customers?" but also, "How can our customers reach us?"

Table 19.1 lists numerous communication platforms. Thanks to technological breakthroughs, people can now communicate through traditional media (newspapers, magazines, radio, telephone, television, billboards), as well as through newer media (computers, fax machines, cellular phones, pagers, and wireless appliances). By decreasing communications costs, the new technologies have encouraged more companies to move from mass-communication to more targeted communication and one-to-one dialogue.

table **19.1**	Common Communication Platforms			
Advertising	**Sales Promotion**	**Public Relations**	**Personal Selling**	**Direct Marketing**
Print and broadcast ads	Contests, games, sweepstakes, lotteries	Press kits	Sales presentations	Catalogs
Packaging–outer		Speeches	Sales meetings	Mailings
Packaging inserts	Premiums and gifts	Seminars	Incentive programs	Telemarketing
Motion pictures	Sampling	Annual reports	Samples	Electronic shopping
Brochures and booklets	Fairs and trade shows	Charitable donations	Fairs and trade shows	TV shopping
Posters and leaflets	Exhibits	Sponsorships		Fax mail
Directories	Demonstrations	Publications		E-mail
Reprints of ads	Coupons	Community relations		Voice mail
Billboards	Rebates	Lobbying		
Display signs	Low-interest financing	Identity media		
Point-of-purchase displays	Entertainment	Company magazine		
Audiovisual material	Trade-in allowances	Events		
Symbols and logos	Continuity programs			
Videotapes	Tie-ins			

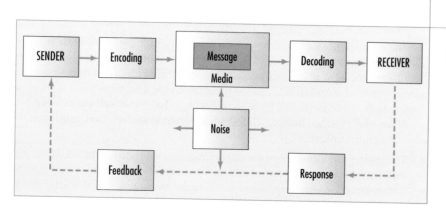

figure **19.1**

Elements in the
Communication Process

However, company communication goes beyond the specific platforms listed in Table 19.1. The product's styling and price, the shape and color of the package, the salesperson's manner and dress, the store decor, the company's stationery—all communicate something to buyers. Every *brand contact* delivers an impression that can strengthen or weaken a customer's view of the company. The whole marketing mix must be integrated to deliver a consistent message and strategic positioning.

The starting point is an audit of all the potential interactions target customers may have with the product and the company. For example, someone interested in purchasing a new computer would talk to others, see television ads, read articles, look for information on the Internet, and observe computers in a store. Marketers need to assess which experiences and impressions will have the most influence at each stage of the buying process. This understanding will help them allocate communications dollars more efficiently.

Marketers also need to understand the fundamental elements of effective communications. Figure 19.1 shows a communication model with nine elements. Two represent the major parties in a communication—sender and receiver. Two represent the major communication tools—message and media. Four represent major communication functions—*encoding, decoding, response,* and *feedback*. The last element in the system is *noise* (random and competing messages that may interfere with the intended communication).[2]

The model emphasizes the key factors in effective communication. Senders must know what audiences they want to reach and what responses they want to get. They must encode their messages so that the target audience can decode them. They must transmit the message through media that reach the target audience and develop feedback channels to monitor the responses. The more the sender's field of experience overlaps with that of the receiver, the more effective the message is likely to be.

The target audience may not receive the intended message for any of three reasons:

1. *Selective attention:* People are bombarded by about 1,600 commercial messages a day, of which 80 are consciously noticed and about 12 provoke some reaction. Selective attention explains why ads with bold headlines promising something, such as "How to Make a Million," have a high likelihood of getting attention.

2. *Selective distortion:* Receivers will hear what fits into their belief systems. As a result, receivers often add things to the message that are not there (amplification) and do not notice other things that are there (leveling). The communicator's task is to strive for simplicity, clarity, interest, and repetition to get the main points across.

3. *Selective retention:* People will retain in long-term memory only a small fraction of the messages that reach them. If the receiver's initial attitude toward the object is positive and he or she rehearses support arguments, the message is likely to be accepted and have high recall. If the initial attitude

figure **19.2**

Steps in Developing
Effective Communication

is negative and the person rehearses counterarguments, the message is likely to be rejected but to stay in long-term memory. Because persuasion requires the receiver's rehearsal of his or her own thoughts, much of what is called persuasion is actually self-persuasion.[3]

The communicator considers audience traits that correlate with persuasibility and uses them to guide message and media development. People of high education or intelligence are thought to be less persuasible, but the evidence is inconclusive. Those who accept external standards to guide their behavior and who have a weak self-concept appear to be more persuasible, as do those who have low self-confidence.[4]

Fiske and Hartley have outlined some general factors that influence the effectiveness of a communication:

■ The greater the influence of the communication source over the recipient, the greater the recipient's change or effect in favor of the source.
■ Communication effects are greatest where the message is in line with the receiver's existing opinions, beliefs, and dispositions.
■ Communication can produce the most effective shifts on unfamiliar, lightly felt, peripheral issues that do not lie at the core of the recipient's value system.
■ Communication is more likely to be effective if the source is believed to have expertise, high status, objectivity, or likability, but particularly if the source has power and can be identified with.
■ The social context, group, or reference group will mediate the communication and influence whether or not the communication is accepted.[5]

developing effective communications

Figure 19.2 shows the eight steps in developing effective communications that we discuss here.

identify the target audience

The process must start with a clear target audience in mind: potential buyers of the company's products, current users, deciders, or influencers; individuals, groups, particular publics, or the general public. The target audience is a critical influence on the communicator's decisions on what to say, how to say it, when to say it, where to say it, and to whom to say it.

IMAGE ANALYSIS   A major part of audience analysis is assessing the current image of the company, its products, and its competitors. **Image** is the set of beliefs, ideas, and impressions a person holds regarding an object. People's attitudes and actions toward an object are highly conditioned by that object's image.

The first step is to measure the target audience's knowledge of the object, using the *familiarity scale:*

Never Heard of	Heard of Only	Know a Little Bit	Know a Fair Amount	Know Very Well

If most respondents circle only the first two categories, the challenge is to build greater awareness.

Respondents who are familiar with the product can be asked how they feel toward it, using the *favorability scale:*

Very Unfavorable	Somewhat Unfavorable	Indifferent	Somewhat Favorable	Very Favorable

If most respondents check the first two categories, then the organization must overcome a negative image problem. The two scales can be combined to develop insight into the nature of the communication challenge. Suppose area residents are asked about their familiarity with and attitudes toward four local hospitals, A, B, C, and D. Their responses are averaged and shown in Figure 19.3. Hospital A has the most positive image: Most people know it and like it. Hospital B is less familiar to most people, but those who know it like it. Hospital C is viewed negatively by those who know it, but (fortunately for the hospital) not too many people know it. Hospital D is seen as a poor hospital, and everyone knows it!

Each hospital faces a different communication task. Hospital A must work at maintaining its good reputation and high awareness. Hospital B must gain the attention of more people. Hospital C must find out why people dislike it and must take steps to improve its quality while keeping a low profile. Hospital D should lower its profile, improve its quality, and then seek public attention.

Each hospital needs to research the specific content of its image. The most popular tool for this research is the **semantic differential**.[6] It involves the following steps:

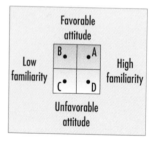

figure **19.3**

Familiarity–Favorability Analysis

1. *Developing a set of relevant dimensions:* The researcher asks people to identify the dimensions they would use in thinking about the object: "What things do you think of when you consider a hospital?" If someone suggests "quality of medical care," this dimension would be turned into a five- or seven-point bipolar adjective scale, with "inferior medical care" at one end and "superior medical care" at the other. A set of additional dimensions for a hospital is shown in Figure 19.4.

2. *Reducing the set of relevant dimensions:* The number of dimensions should be reduced to avoid respondent fatigue.

3. *Administering the instrument to a sample of respondents:* The respondents are asked to rate one object at a time. The bipolar adjectives should be randomly arranged so that the unfavorable adjectives are not all listed on one side.

4. *Averaging the results:* Figure 19.4 shows the results of averaging the respondents' pictures of hospitals A, B, and C (hospital D is left out). Each hospital's image is represented by a vertical "line of means" that summarizes average perception of that hospital. Hospital A is seen as a large, modern, friendly, and superior hospital. Hospital C, in contrast, is seen as small, dated, impersonal, and inferior.

5. *Checking on the image variance:* Because each image profile is a line of means, it does not reveal how variable the image is. Did everyone see hospital B this way, or was there considerable variation? In the first case, we would say that the image is highly specific; and in the second case, highly diffused. Some organizations prefer a diffused image so that different groups will see the organization in different ways.

figure **19.4**

Images of Three Hospitals (Semantic Differential)

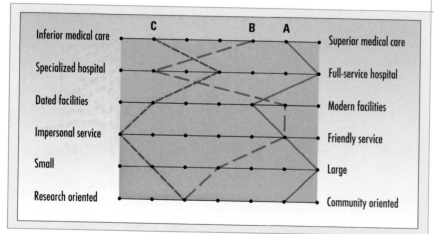

Management should now define a desired image if it differs from the current one. Suppose hospital C would like the public to view its medical care, facilities, and friendliness more favorably. Management must decide which image gaps it wants to close first. Is it more desirable to improve friendliness (through staff training programs) or the quality of its facilities (through renovation)? What would it cost to close a particular gap? How long would it take?

Images are "sticky"; they persist long after the organization has changed. Image persistence is explained by the fact that once people have a certain image, they perceive what is consistent with that image. It will take highly disconfirming information to raise doubts and open their minds, especially when people do not have continuous or new firsthand experiences with the changed object.

Wolverine Wolverine World Wide of Rockford, Michigan, discovered this when its Hush Puppies brand of casual shoes lost its fashionable image. Then a fashion designer used Hush Puppies dyed in bright colors. The Hush Puppies image went from stodgy to avant-garde, and once the "new" Hush Puppies were in demand, sales went from under 30,000 pairs in 1994 to 1.7 million pairs in 1996.[7]

determine the communication objectives

The marketer can be seeking a *cognitive, affective,* or *behavioral* response. That is, the marketer might want to put something into the consumer's mind, change an attitude, or get the consumer to act. Even here, there are different models of consumer-response stages. Figure 19.5 summarizes the four best-known *response hierarchy models.*

figure **19.5**

Response Hierarchy Models

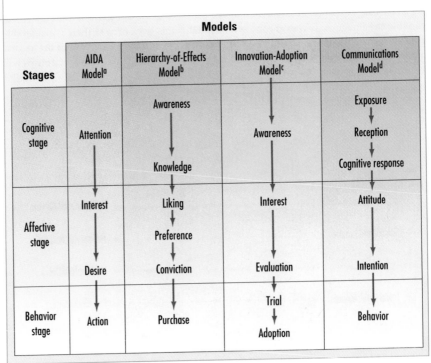

| | **Models** | | | |
Stages	AIDA Model[a]	Hierarchy-of-Effects Model[b]	Innovation-Adoption Model[c]	Communications Model[d]
Cognitive stage	Attention	Awareness ↓ Knowledge	Awareness	Exposure ↓ Reception ↓ Cognitive response
Affective stage	Interest ↓ Desire	Liking ↓ Preference ↓ Conviction	Interest ↓ Evaluation	Attitude ↓ Intention
Behavior stage	Action	Purchase	Trial ↓ Adoption	Behavior

Sources: [a]E. K. Strong, *The Psychology of Selling* (New York: McGraw-Hill, 1925), p. 9; [b]Robert J. Lavidge and Gary A. Steiner, "A Model for Predictive Measurements of Advertising Effectiveness," *Journal of Marketing* (October 1961): 61; [c]Everett M. Rogers, *Diffusion of Innovation* (New York: The Free Press, 1962), pp. 79–86; [d]various sources.

All these models assume that the buyer passes through a cognitive, affective, and behavioral stage, in that order. This "learn-feel-do" sequence is appropriate when the audience has high involvement with a product category perceived to have high differentiation, as in purchasing an automobile. An alternative sequence, "do-feel-learn," is relevant when the audience has high involvement but perceives little or no differentiation within the product category, as in purchasing aluminum siding. A third sequence, "learn-do-feel," is relevant when the audience has low involvement and perceives little differentiation within the product category, as in purchasing salt. By choosing the right sequence, the marketer can do a better job of planning communications.[8]

Here we will assume that the buyer has high involvement with the product category and perceives high differentiation within the category. We will illustrate the *hierarchy-of-effects model* (in the second column of Figure 19.5):

- *Awareness:* If most of the target audience is unaware of the object, the communicator's task is to build awareness, perhaps just name recognition, with simple messages repeating the product name. Suppose a small Iowa college named Pottsville seeks applicants from Nebraska but has no name recognition in Nebraska. Suppose there are 30,000 high school juniors and seniors in Nebraska who may potentially be interested in Pottsville College. The college might set the objective of making 70 percent of these students aware of Pottsville's name within one year.

- *Knowledge:* The target audience might have product awareness but not know much more. Pottsville may want its target audience to know that it is a private four-year college with excellent programs in English, foreign languages, and history. It needs to learn how many people in the target audience have little, some, or much knowledge about Pottsville. If knowledge is weak, Pottsville may decide to select product knowledge as its communication objective.

- *Liking:* If target members know the product, how do they feel about it? If the audience looks unfavorably on Pottsville College, the communicator has to find out why. If the unfavorable view is based on real problems, Pottsville will have to fix its problems and then communicate its renewed quality. Good public relations calls for "good deeds followed by good words."

- *Preference:* The target audience might like the product but not prefer it to others. In this case, the communicator must try to build consumer preference by promoting quality, value, performance, and other features. The communicator can check the campaign's success by measuring audience preference after the campaign.

- *Conviction:* A target audience might prefer a particular product but not develop a conviction about buying it. The communicator's job is to build conviction among interested students that Pottsville College is their best choice.

- *Purchase:* Finally, some members of the target audience might have conviction but may not quite get around to making the purchase. They may wait for more information or plan to act later. The communicator must lead these consumers to take the final step, perhaps by offering the product at a low price, offering a premium, or letting consumers try it out. Pottsville might invite selected high school students to visit the campus and attend some classes, or it might offer partial scholarships to deserving students.

design the message

Having defined the desired response, the communicator moves to developing an effective message. Ideally, the message should gain *attention*, hold *interest*, arouse *desire*, and elicit *action* (AIDA model—see the first column of Figure 19.5). In practice, few messages take the consumer all the way from awareness through purchase, but the AIDA framework suggests the desirable qualities of any communication.

Formulating the message will require solving four problems: what to say (message content), how to say it logically (message structure), how to say it symbolically (message format), and who should say it (message source).

MESSAGE CONTENT   In determining message content, management searches for an appeal, theme, idea, or unique selling proposition (USP). There are three types of appeals: rational, emotional, and moral.

Rational appeals engage self-interest: They claim the product will produce certain benefits. Examples are messages demonstrating quality, economy, value, or performance. It is widely believed that industrial buyers are most responsive to rational appeals. They are knowledgeable about the product, trained to recognize value, and accountable to others for their choices. Consumers, when they buy certain big-ticket items, also tend to gather information and estimate benefits.

Emotional appeals attempt to stir up negative or positive emotions that will motivate purchase. Marketers search for the right *emotional selling proposition* (ESP).

American Cancer Society (ACS)   The American Cancer Society launched a campaign in the 1990s to promote the use of SPF 15 sun block in order to help prevent skin cancer. It aimed the campaign at young men and women and used the selling line "Save your life!" This turned out to be too rational because young persons want to look attractive. ACS then changed the appeal to say that SPF 15 sun block would allow users to safely enjoy more time in the sun, get tan, and be more attractive.

Communicators work with both negative and positive emotional appeals. They use negative appeals such as fear, guilt, and shame to get people to do things (brush their teeth, have an annual health checkup) or stop doing things (smoking, alcohol or abuse, overeating). Fear appeals work best when they are not too strong. Research indicates that neither extremely strong nor extremely weak fear appeals are as effective as moderate ones. Furthermore, fear appeals work better when source credibility is high and when the communication promises to relieve, in a believable and efficient way, the fear it arouses.[9] Messages are most persuasive when they are moderately discrepant with what the audience believes. Messages that state only what the audience already believes at best only reinforce beliefs, and if the messages are too discrepant, they will be counterargued and disbelieved.

Communicators also use positive emotional appeals such as humor, love, pride, and joy. Advocates for humorous messages claim that they attract more attention and create more liking and belief in the sponsor. Others maintain that humor can detract from comprehension, wear out its welcome fast, and overshadow the product.[10] Here is an example of a successful use of humor.

E*TRADE   Online financial services company E*TRADE set itself apart from competitors and attracted traders to its site using humorous, high-profile advertising. During the 2000 Super Bowl, the company sponsored the halftime show and debuted a television spot that featured little more than a dancing chimpanzee and the tagline "We just wasted two million bucks. What are you doing with your money?" That year, E*TRADE spent $522 million—or nearly 40 percent of revenues—on marketing and generated 1.7 million new accounts. The company followed its Super Bowl success with an ad during the 2001 Super Bowl that poked fun at dot-com excesses and companies, such as Pets.com, that had not survived the bursting bubble. The ad earned high marks from critics and scored well in consumer polls.[11]

Moral appeals are directed to the audience's sense of what is right and proper. They are often used to exhort people to support social causes. An example is the appeal "Silence = Death," which is the slogan of Act-Up, the AIDS Coalition to Unleash Power.

Companies that sell their products in different countries must be prepared to vary their messages. In advertising its hair care products in different countries, Helene Curtis adjusts its messages. Middle-class British women wash their hair frequently, whereas

marketing for the **new economy**

Challenges in Global Advertising and Promotion

Multinational companies wrestle with a number of challenges in developing global communications programs: They must decide whether the product is appropriate for a country. They must make sure the market segment they address is both legal and customary. They must decide if the style of the ad is acceptable, and they must decide whether ads should be created at headquarters or locally.

1. **Product:** Many products are restricted or forbidden in certain parts of the world. Beer, wine, and spirits cannot be advertised or sold in Muslim countries. Tobacco products are subject to strict regulation in many countries. Sometimes a company is required to change the manner in which it sells its products. Avon China Inc., was forced to open retail stores after a resolution passed by the Chinese government banned selling directly to Chinese consumers. New advertising and promotion campaigns repositioned Avon as a retailer, rather than a direct marketer. (China and the United States reached an agreement in 1999 that would lift the ban on direct selling by 2003.)

2. **Market Segment:** Coca-Cola conducts business with more than 230 brands in 200 countries. The company has a pool of different commercials for different national market segments, and local segment managers decide which to use for which segments. When Douglas Daft took over as chairman and CEO in 2000, he gave Coca-Cola managers a new mantra: "Think locally and act locally." This local focus sometimes leaves Coke caught in the middle of a sensitive political issue. In 2000, Coca-Cola was running a campaign in mainland China featuring a popular female Taiwanese pop star. Authorities in China blacklisted the star after she sang Taiwan's national anthem at the inauguration of the island's new president. Coca-Cola had to replace all television, print, and radio advertising that used her voice.

   U.S. toy makers were surprised to learn that in many countries (Norway and Sweden, for example) no TV ads may be directed at children under 12. Sweden is lobbying to extend that ban to all EU member countries. To play it safe, McDonald's advertises itself as a family restaurant in Sweden.

3. **Style:** The style of the ad is also important. For instance, comparative ads, while acceptable and even common in the United States and Canada, are less commonly used in the United Kingdom, unacceptable in Japan, and illegal in India and Brazil. PepsiCo had a comparative taste test ad in Japan that was refused by many TV stations and eventually led to a lawsuit. China has restrictive censorship rules for TV and radio advertising; the words "the best" are banned, as are ads that "violate social customs" or present women in "improper ways."

4. **Local or Global:** Today, more and more multinational companies are attempting to build a global brand image by using the same advertising in all markets. When Daimler AG and Chrysler merged to become the world's fifth-largest automaker, they ran a three-week ad campaign in more than 100 countries consisting of a 12-page magazine insert, 9 newspaper spreads, and a 24-page brochure that was sent to business, government, and union leaders and to the news media. The campaign's tag line was "Expect the extraordinary," and it featured people from both companies working together.

Sources: Richard C. Morais, "Mobile Mayhem," *Forbes*, July, 6 1998, p. 138; Patti Bond, "Today's Topic: From Russia with Fizz, Coke Imports Ads," *Atlanta Journal and Constitution*, April 4, 1998, pp. E2; "Working in Harmony," *Soap Perfumery & Cosmetics*, July 1, 1998, p. 27; Rodger Harrabin, "A Commercial Break for Parents," *Independent*, September 8, 1998, p. 19; T. B. Song and Leo Wong, "Getting the Word Out," *The China Business Review*, September 1, 1998; "Avon Campaign Repositions Company in China," AdAgeInternational.com, July 1998; Naveen Donthu, "A Cross Country Investigation of Recall of and Attitude toward Comparative Advertising," *Journal of Advertising* 27 (June 22, 1998): 111; "EU to Try Again on Tobacco Advertising Ban," *Associated Press*, May 9, 2001; Betsy McKay, "Coca-Cola Restructuring Effort Has Yet to Prove Effective," *Asian Wall Street Journal*, March 2, 2001 p. N4; James Kynge and Mure Dickie, "Coke Forced to Dump Taiwanese Diva," *Financial Times*, May 25, 2000, p. C12.

---

the opposite is true among Spanish women. Japanese women avoid overwashing their hair for fear of removing protective oils. (See "Marketing for the New Economy: Challenges in Global Advertising and Promotion.")

MESSAGE STRUCTURE   Effectiveness depends on structure as well as content. For example, a credit-card company contacted customers who had not used the card for three months. To one group of nonusers it sent a message explaining the benefits of using the card. To another group it sent a message explaining the losses they could suffer by not using the card. The percentage of customers who started to use the card in the loss condition was more than double and, the charges of the former customers were more than twice that of the positive message receivers.[12]

Hovland's research at Yale has shed much light on message content and its relation to conclusion drawing, one- versus two-sided arguments, and order of presentation. Some early experiments supported stating conclusions for the audience rather than allowing the audience to reach its own. Subsequent research, however, indicates that the best ads ask questions and allow readers and viewers to form their own conclusions.[13]

Conclusion drawing might cause negative reactions if the communicator is seen as untrustworthy, or the issue is seen as too simple or highly personal. Drawing too explicit a conclusion can also limit appeal or acceptance. If Ford had hammered away that the Mustang was for young people, this strong definition might have blocked older age groups from buying it. Some stimulus ambiguity can lead to a broader market definition and more spontaneous purchases.

You would think that one-sided presentations that praise a product would be more effective than two-sided arguments that also mention shortcomings. Yet two-sided messages may be more appropriate, especially when some negative association must be overcome. In this spirit, Heinz ran the message "Heinz Ketchup is slow good" and Listerine ran the message "Listerine tastes bad twice a day."[14] Two-sided messages are more effective with more educated audiences and those who are initially opposed.[15]

Finally, the order in which arguments are presented is important.[16] In the case of a one-sided message, presenting the strongest argument first has the advantage of arousing attention and interest. This is important in newspapers and other media where the audience often does not attend to the whole message. With a captive audience, however, a climactic presentation might be more effective. In the case of a two-sided message, if the audience is initially opposed, the communicator might start with the other side's argument and conclude with his or her strongest argument.[17]

MESSAGE FORMAT   The message format needs to be strong. In a print ad, the communicator has to decide on headline, copy, illustration, and color. For a radio message, the communicator has to choose words, voice qualities, and vocalizations. The "sound" of an announcer promoting a used automobile has to be different from one promoting a new Cadillac. If the message is to be carried on television or in person, all these elements plus body language (nonverbal clues) have to be planned. Presenters have to pay attention to facial expressions, gestures, dress, posture, and hairstyle. If the message is carried by the product or its packaging, the communicator has to pay attention to color, texture, scent, size, and shape. BMW used a cinematic format to advertise its cars.

BMW   BMW blurred the line between advertising and entertainment when it developed a series of online minifilms that featured the company's cars. The company enlisted Hollywood heavyweights like John Frankenheimer and Ang Lee to direct the films, which starred actors such as Mickey Rourke and Madonna. To build traffic to the bmwfilms.com Web site, BMW used television spots that mirrored movie trailers. In the first six weeks after their April 2001 debut, the films attracted 3 million viewers. Although the Internet films intentionally did not use hard-sell tactics, a spokesperson for BMW said that many viewers requested information about cars after seeing the movies.[18]

MESSAGE SOURCE   Messages delivered by attractive or popular sources achieve higher attention and recall. This is why advertisers often use celebrities as spokespeople. Celebrities are likely to be effective when they personify a key product attribute. Catherine Deneuve's beauty did this for Chanel, and Paul Hogan's manliness did this for Subaru Outback. On the other hand, using James Garner and Cybill Shepherd to sell beef backfired: James had heart trouble and Cybill became a vegetarian.

What is important is the spokesperson's credibility. Pharmaceutical companies want doctors to testify about product benefits because doctors have high credibility. Antidrug crusaders will use ex-drug addicts because they have higher credibility for students than teachers do.

What factors underlie source credibility? The three most often identified are expertise, trustworthiness, and likability.[19] *Expertise* is the specialized knowledge the communicator possesses to back the claim. *Trustworthiness* is related to how objective and honest the source is perceived to be. Friends are trusted more than strangers or salespeople, and www.bmwfilms.com.

people who are not paid to endorse a product are viewed as more trustworthy than people who are paid.[20] *Likability* describes the source's attractiveness. Qualities like candor, humor, and naturalness make a source more likable. The most highly credible source would be a person who scores high on all three dimensions.

If a person has a positive attitude toward a source and a message, or a negative attitude toward both, a state of *congruity* is said to exist. What happens if the person holds one attitude toward the source and the opposite toward the message? Suppose a homemaker hears a likable celebrity praise a brand that she dislikes? Osgood and Tannenbaum posit that *attitude change will take place in the direction of increasing the amount of congruity between the two evaluations.*[21] The homemaker will end up respecting the celebrity somewhat less or respecting the brand somewhat more. If she encounters the same celebrity praising other disliked brands, she will eventually develop a negative view of the celebrity and maintain her negative attitudes toward the brands. The **principle of congruity** implies that communicators can use their good image to reduce some negative feelings toward a brand but in the process might lose some esteem with the audience.

select the communication channels

The communicator must select efficient channels to carry the message. For example, pharmaceutical company salespeople can rarely wrest more than five minutes' time from a busy physician. Their presentation must be crisp, quick, and convincing. This makes pharmaceutical sales calling extremely expensive. The industry has had to expand its battery of communication channels. These include placing ads in medical journals, sending direct mail (including audio and videotapes), passing out free samples, and even telemarketing. Pharmaceutical companies sponsor clinical conferences to which they invite and pay for a large number of physicians to spend a weekend listening to leading physicians extol certain drugs in the morning, followed by an afternoon of golf or tennis. Salespeople will arrange evening teleconferences where physicians are invited to discuss a common problem with an expert. Salespeople also will sponsor small group lunches and dinners. All of these channels are used in the hope of building physician preference for their branded therapeutic agent.

Communication channels may be personal and nonpersonal. Within each are many subchannels.

PERSONAL COMMUNICATION CHANNELS   Personal communication channels involve two or more persons communicating directly with each other face-to-face, person-to-audience, over the telephone, or through e-mail. Personal communication channels derive their effectiveness through individualized presentation and feedback.

A further distinction can be drawn among advocate, expert, and social communication channels. *Advocate channels* consist of company salespeople contacting buyers in the target market. *Expert channels* consist of independent experts making statements to target buyers. *Social channels* consist of neighbors, friends, family members, and associates talking to target buyers. In a study of 7,000 consumers in seven European countries, 60 percent said they were influenced to use a new brand by family and friends.[22]

Personal influence carries especially great weight in two situations. One is with products that are expensive, risky, or purchased infrequently. The other situation is where the product suggests something about the user's status or taste. In both cases, buyers will consult others for information or to avoid embarrassment.

Many companies are becoming acutely aware of the power of *word of mouth* or *buzz.* (See "Marketing Memo: Buzz Marketing.") Products and brands such as Beanie Babies, Pokemon, and the movie *The Blair Witch Project* were built through buzz. Companies such as Body Shop, USAA, Starbucks, Palm Pilot, BMW23 Roadster, and Amazon were essentially built by word of mouth, with very little advertising.

Amazon   Jeff Bezos, founder of Amazon.com, had noticed that the celebrated department store Nordstrom never advertised its customer service and yet had the most loyal customer following. Having no money to spend on advertising when he launched Amazon, Bezos trusted that good service would do the trick. "It was seeing how successful word-of-mouth was in that first year, that really led us on this path of being obsessively, compulsively, anal-retentively focused on customer service." According to Bezos, if you make a customer unhappy he will tell five friends; if you disappoint a customer on the Internet, he is capable of telling 5,000 or 50,000 people.[23]

In some cases, positive word of mouth happens in a natural way.

Kiehl   Kiehl's is a small, 148-year-old company that makes and sells hair and skin products, such as Kiehl's rosewater facial freshener-toner and pineapple papaya facial scrub. Its marketing practices defy normal wisdom. It does not advertise. Its packaging is bland and the text is difficult to read. It refuses to be carried by most stores, making exceptions only for the highest-priced stores such as Bergdorf Goodman and Barney's. It gives away vast amounts of free samples to anyone coming into its single store. It gets great coverage from the business press without ever soliciting attention. Kiehl's has the gift of being carried by word of mouth.[24]

In most cases, "buzz" is managed.[25] Regis McKenna advises a software company launching a new product to promote it initially to the trade press, opinion luminaries, and financial analysts, who can supply favorable word of mouth; then to dealers; and finally to customers.[26] MCI attracted customers with its Friends and Family program, which encourages MCI users to ask friends and family members to use MCI so that both parties will benefit from lower telephone rates.

Companies can take several steps to stimulate personal influence channels to work on their behalf:

■ *Identify influential individuals and companies and devote extra effort to them:*[27] In industrial selling, the entire industry might follow the market leader in adopting innovations.

■ *Create opinion leaders by supplying certain people with the product on attractive terms:* A new tennis racket might be offered initially to members of high school tennis teams at a special low price; or Toyota could offer its more satisfied customers a small gift if they are willing to advise prospective buyers.

- *Work through community influentials such as local disk jockeys, class presidents, and presidents of women's organizations:* When Ford introduced the Thunderbird, it sent invitations to executives offering them a free car to drive for the day. Of the 15,000 who took advantage of the offer, 10 percent indicated that they would become buyers, whereas 84 percent said they would recommend it to a friend.

- *Use influential or believable people in testimonial advertising:* Companies such as American Express, Nike, and Buick are using golf mega-star Tiger Woods to talk up the virtues of their respective products.

- *Develop advertising that has high "conversation value":* Ads with high conversation value often have a slogan that becomes part of the national vernacular. In the mid-1980s, Wendy's "Where's the Beef?" campaign (showing an elderly lady named Clara questioning where the hamburger was hidden in all that bread) created high conversation value. Nike's "Just do it" ads have created a popular command for those unable to make up their minds or take some action.

- *Develop word-of-mouth referral channels to build business:* Professionals will often encourage clients to recommend their services. Dentists can ask satisfied patients to recommend friends and acquaintances and subsequently thank them for their recommendations. (See "Marketing Memo: How to Develop Word-of-Mouth Referral Sources to Build Business.")

- *Establish an electronic forum:* Toyota owners who use an online service line such as America Online can hold online discussions to share experiences.

- *Use viral marketing:* Internet marketers are using **viral marketing** a form of word of mouth, to draw attention to their sites.[28] Viral marketing involves passing on company-developed products, services, or information from user to user. As a classic example, Hotmail, an Internet Service Provider (ISP), offered a free e-mail account to anyone who signed up. Each e-mail sent by a Hotmail subscriber included the simple tag at the bottom of each message: "Get your free private e-mail at *http://www.hotmail.com.*" Users were in effect advertising Hotmail to others. Hotmail spent less than $500,000 on marketing and within 18 months attracted 12 million subscribers. (See "Marketing Memo: Creating a Tipping Point" for further insight into factors that help spread word of mouth.)

Marketing MEMO

How to Develop Word-of-Mouth Referral Sources

People always ask others—friends, relatives, professionals—for a recommendation for a doctor, plumber, hotel, lawyer, accountant, architect, insurance agent, interior decorator, or financial consultant. If we have confidence in the recommendation, we normally act on the referral. In such cases, the recommender has potentially benefited the service provider as well as the service seeker. Service providers clearly have a strong interest in building referral sources.

The two chief benefits of developing referrals, or word-of-mouth sources, are:

1. *Word-of-mouth sources are convincing:* Word of mouth is the only promotion method that is of consumers, by consumers, and for consumers. Not only are satisfied customers repeat buyers, but they are also walking, talking billboards for your business.
2. *Word-of-mouth sources are low cost:* Keeping in touch with satisfied customers and making them providers costs the business relatively little. The business might reciprocate by referring business to the referrer, or by giving the referrer enhanced service or a discount, or by offering a small gift.

Marketing author Michael Cafferky's Word-of-Mouth Marketing Tips Web site offers many suggestions on how to build a network of referral sources; here are five:

1. *Involve your customers in the process of making or delivering your product or service.*
2. *Solicit testimonials from your customers:* Use a response form that asks for feedback—and permission to quote it.
3. *Tell true stories to your customers:* Stories are the central vehicle for spreading reputations because they communicate on an emotional level.
4. *Educate your best customers:* You can pick any topic that is relevant to your best customers and have them become the source of credible, up-to-date information on that topic.
5. *Offer fast complaint handling:* A speedy response is vital to preventing negative word of mouth from starting, because negative feelings about a product or service may linger for years.

Sources: Scott R. Herriott, "Identifying and Developing Referral Channels," Management Decision 30, no. 1 (1992): 4–9; Peter H. Riengen and Jerome B. Kernan, "Analysis of Referral Networks in Marketing: Methods and Illustration," Journal of Marketing Research (November 1986): 37–78; Jerry R. Wilson, *Word of Mouth Marketing* (New York: John Wiley, 1991); Cafferky's Free Word-of-Mouth Marketing Tips, 1999, available at www.geocities.com/wallstreet/cafferkys. Also see Emanuel Rosen, The Anatomy of Buzz (New York: Doubleday, 2000).

NONPERSONAL COMMUNICATION CHANNELS Nonpersonal channels include media, atmospheres, and events.

Media consist of print media (newspapers, magazines, direct mail), broadcast media (radio, television), network media (telephone, cable, satellite, wireless), electronic media (audiotape, videotape, videodisk, CD-ROM, Web page), and display media (billboards, signs, posters). Most nonpersonal messages come through paid media. Volvo attempted to market a car using only one channel, the Internet.

Volvo In 2000, Volvo developed an Internet-only launch for its new S60 sedan. The company signed an exclusive deal with America Online that placed banner ads for the car in prime locations on the AOL portal. The ads led viewers to a special Web site—called revolvolution.com—where they could learn more about the vehicle, configure a car to their tastes, and request a quote from a nearby dealer. Although over one million consumers visited the site, dealers across the nation were disappointed with the customer response: Only 2,994 vehicles were sold between the October introduction and the new year. Volvo replaced the Internet-only launch with an integrated campaign that included Web, wireless, television, and print advertising.[29]

Atmospheres are "packaged environments" that create or reinforce the buyer's leanings toward product purchase. Law offices are decorated with Oriental rugs and oak furniture to communicate "stability" and "success."[30] A five-star hotel will use elegant chandeliers, marble columns, and other tangible signs of luxury.

Events are occurrences designed to communicate particular messages to target audiences. Public-relations departments arrange news conferences, grand openings, and sports sponsorships to achieve specific communication effects with a target audience.

Sea-Doo Personal watercraft manufacturer Sea-Doo conducts a promotional tour each summer that offers consumers free test rides on a variety of Sea-Doo craft. The tour, called "Get Caught Doin' It" in a play on Sea-Doo's "Everybody's Doin' It" tagline, visits more than 40 domestic markets during the summer months. Sea-Doo works together with local dealers in each market to hold day-long events that include free food and drinks, prize giveaways, and remote radio broadcasts. About 15 percent of participants in the events become buyers of the $5,000 to $9,000 crafts.[31]

Although personal communication is often more effective than mass-communication, mass–media might be the major means of stimulating personal communication. Mass–communications affect personal attitudes and behavior through a two-step, flow-of-communication process. Ideas often flow from radio, television, and print to opinion leaders and from these to the less media-involved population groups. This two-step flow has several implications. First, the influence of mass-media on public opinion is not as direct, powerful, and automatic as supposed. It is mediated by opinion leaders, people whose opinions are sought or who carry their opinions to others. Second, the two-step flow challenges the notion that consumption styles are primarily influenced by a "trickle-down" or "trickle-up" effect from mass-media. People interact primarily within their own social groups and acquire ideas from opinion leaders in their groups. Third, two-step communication suggests that mass-communicators should direct messages specifically to opinion leaders and let them carry the message to others. Pharmaceutical firms should promote new drugs to the most influential physicians first.

Communication researchers are moving toward a social-structure view of interpersonal communication.[32] They see society as consisting of **cliques**, small groups whose members interact frequently. Clique members are similar, and their closeness facilitates effective communication but also insulates the clique from new ideas. The challenge is to create more system openness so that cliques exchange information with others in the society. This openness is helped by people who function as liaisons and bridges. A **liaison** is a person who connects two or more cliques without belonging to either. A **bridge** is a person who belongs to one clique and is linked to a person in another clique.

establish the total marketing communications budget

One of the most difficult marketing decisions is determining how much to spend on promotion. John Wanamaker, the department-store magnate, once said, "I know that half of my advertising is wasted, but I don't know which half."

Industries and companies vary considerably in how much they spend on promotion. Expenditures might amount to 30 to 50 percent of sales in the cosmetics industry and 5 to 10 percent in the industrial-equipment industry. Within a given industry, there are low- and high-spending companies. Philip Morris is a high spender. When it acquired the Miller Brewing Company, and later the 7-Up Company, it substantially increased total promotion spending. The additional spending at Miller raised its market share from 4 to 19 percent within a few years.

How do companies decide on the promotion budget? We will describe four common methods: the affordable method, percentage-of-sales method, competitive-parity method, and objective-and-task method.

AFFORDABLE METHOD Many companies set the promotion budget at what they think the company can afford. One executive said: "Why, it's simple. First, I go upstairs to the controller and ask how much they can afford to give us this year. He says a million and a half. Later, the boss comes to me and asks how much we should spend and I say, 'Oh, about a million and a half.' "[33]

The affordable method completely ignores the role of promotion as an investment and the immediate impact of promotion on sales volume. It leads to an uncertain annual budget, which makes long-range planning difficult.

PERCENTAGE-OF-SALES METHOD Many companies set promotion expenditures at a specified percentage of sales (either current or anticipated) or of the sales price. A railroad company executive said: "We set our appropriation for each year on December 1 of the preceding year. On that date we add our passenger revenue for the next month, and then take 2 percent of the total for our advertising appropriation for the new year."[34] Automobile companies typically budget a fixed percentage for promotion based on the planned car price. Oil companies set the appropriation at a fraction of a cent for each gallon of gasoline sold under their own label.

Supporters of the percentage-of-sales method see a number of advantages. First, promotion expenditures will vary with what the company can "afford." This satisfies financial managers, who believe that expenses should be closely related to the movement of corporate sales over the business cycle. Second, it encourages management to think of the relationship among promotion cost, selling price, and profit per unit. Third, it encourages stability when competing firms spend approximately the same percentage of their sales on promotion.

In spite of these advantages, the percentage-of-sales method has little to justify it. It views sales as the determiner of promotion rather than as the result. It leads to a budget set by the availability of funds rather than by market opportunities. It discourages experimentation with countercyclical promotion or aggressive spending. Dependence on year-to-year sales fluctuations interferes with long-range planning. There is no logical basis for choosing the specific percentage, except what has been done in the past or what competitors are doing. Finally, it does not encourage building the promotion budget by determining what each product and territory deserves.

COMPETITIVE-PARITY METHOD Some companies set their promotion budget to achieve share-of-voice parity with competitors. This thinking is illustrated by the executive who asked a trade source, "Do you have any figures which other companies in the builders' specialties field have used which would indicate what proportion of gross sales should be given over to advertising?"[35] This executive believes that by matching competitors, he will maintain his market share.

Two arguments are made in support of the competitive-parity method. One is that competitors' expenditures represent the collective wisdom of the industry. The other is that maintaining competitive parity prevents promotion wars. Neither argument is valid. There are no grounds for believing that competitors know better. Company reputations, resources, opportunities, and objectives differ so much that promotion budgets are hardly a guide. Furthermore, there is no evidence that budgets based on competitive parity discourage promotional wars.

OBJECTIVE-AND-TASK METHOD   The objective-and-task method calls upon marketers to develop promotion budgets by defining specific objectives, determining the tasks that must be performed to achieve these objectives, and estimating the costs of performing these tasks. The sum of these costs is the proposed promotion budget.

G. Maxwell Ule showed how the objective-and-task method could be used to establish an advertising budget. Suppose Helene Curtis wants to launch a new woman's anti-dandruff shampoo.[36]

1. *Establish the market-share goal:* The company estimates 50 million potential users and sets a target of attracting 8 percent of the market—that is, 4 million users.
2. *Determine the percentage of the market that should be reached by advertising:* The advertiser hopes to reach 80 percent (40 million prospects) with the advertising message.
3. *Determine the percentage of aware prospects that should be persuaded to try the brand:* The advertiser would be pleased if 25 percent of aware prospects (10 million) tried Clear. This is because it estimates that 40 percent of all triers, or 4 million people, would become loyal users. This is the market goal.
4. *Determine the number of advertising impressions per 1 percent trial rate:* The advertiser estimates that 40 advertising impressions (exposures) for every 1 percent of the population would bring about a 25 percent trial rate.
5. *Determine the number of gross rating points that would have to be purchased:* A gross rating point is one exposure to 1 percent of the target population. Because the company wants to achieve 40 exposures to 80 percent of the population, it will want to buy 3,200 gross rating points.
6. *Determine the necessary advertising budget on the basis of the average cost of buying a gross rating point:* To expose 1 percent of the target population to one impression costs an average of $3,277. Therefore, 3,200 gross rating points would cost $10,486,400 (= $3,277 × 3,200) in the introductory year.

The objective-and-task method has the advantage of requiring management to spell out its assumptions about the relationship among dollars spent, exposure levels, trial rates, and regular usage.

A major question is how much weight promotion should receive in relation to alternatives such as product improvement, lower prices, or better service. The answer depends on where the company's products are in their life cycles, whether they are commodities or highly differentiable products, whether they are routinely needed or have to be "sold," and other considerations. In theory, the total promotional budget should be established so that the marginal profit from the last promotional dollar just equals the marginal profit from the last dollar in the best nonpromotional use. Implementing this principle, however, is not easy.

deciding on the marketing communications mix

Companies must allocate the promotion budget over the five promotional tools—advertising, sales promotion, public relations and publicity, sales force, and direct marketing. Here is how one company touches several bases.

Select Comfort Corporation A mattress is a mattress, or is it? We have heard of waterbeds. Now Select Comfort offers an "air bed." The mattress is air-inflated, and sleepers can adjust firmness by changing the air level. Two sleepers can even call for different degrees of firmness on their respective sides of the mattress. To market the mattresses, Select Comfort, headquartered in Minneapolis, has put together a strong combination of channels and promotion initiatives: 300 retail stores where prospects can take a "Test Rest on Air"; demonstration videos and collateral material discussing "Sleep Science"; a company Web site (select comfort. com) describing the products and offering advice on how to sleep better; celebrity endorsements; and giving customers who recommend others who buy the mattress a merchandise certificate.

Within the same industry, companies can differ considerably in their media and channel choices. Avon concentrates its promotional funds on personal selling, whereas Revlon spends heavily on advertising. Electrolux spends heavily on a door-to-door sales force, whereas Hoover relies more on advertising.

Companies are always searching for ways to gain efficiency by replacing one promotional tool with others. Consider: "Procter & Gamble is urging its ad agencies to focus less on TV and embrace direct mail, staged events and the Internet . . . P&G no longer believes TV advertising provides the best value."[37] Many companies are replacing some field sales activity with ads, direct mail, and telemarketing. One auto dealer dismissed his five salespeople and cut his prices, and sales exploded. Companies are shifting advertising funds into sales promotion. The substitutability among promotional tools explains why marketing functions need to be coordinated. For an account of how companies set their budgets, in practice, see "Marketing Insight: How Do Companies Set and Allocate Their Marketing Communications Budgets?"

marketing **insight**

How Companies Set and Allocate Marketing Communications Budgets

Low and Mohr interviewed managers in consumer packaged-goods companies on how the marketing communications budget is set and allocated to advertising, sales promotion, and trade promotion. They found that a brand team is formed and, after performing an extensive situation analysis, establishes marketing objectives and a broad strategy. After forecasting brand sales and profits based on the broad strategy, the team develops an initial allocation to advertising, consumer promotion, and trade promotion. The team relies heavily on the previous year's budget allocation, which may make sense if the environment is stable but not if there is rapid environmental change. The brand plan is presented to senior management, required changes are made, and the revised plan is implemented.

During the year, the brand team will adjust allocations in response to the changing environment.

In their 1998 study, Low and Mohr also found that:

- As brands move to the more mature phase of the product life cycle, managers allocate less to advertising.

- When a brand is well-differentiated from the competition, managers allocate more to advertising.
- When managers are rewarded on short-term results, they allocate less of their budgets to advertising.
- As retailers gain more power, managers allocate less of their budgets to advertising.
- As managers gain greater experience with the company, they tend to allocate proportionately more of their budgets to advertising.

Sources: See George S. Low and Jakki J. Mohr, "The Advertising Sales Promotion Trade-Off: Theory and Practice" (Cambridge, MA: Marketing Science Institute, Report No. 92-127, October 1992); and their "Brand Managers' Perceptions of the Marketing Communications Budget Allocation Process" (Cambridge, MA: Marketing Science Institute, Report No. 98-105, March 1998). Also see Gabriel J. Beihal and Daniel A. Sheinen, "Managing the Brand in a Corporate Advertising Environment: A Decision-Making Framework for Brand Managers," *Journal of Advertising* 17 (June 22, 1998): 99.

the promotional tools

Each promotional tool has its own unique characteristics and costs.[38]

Advertising   Because of the many forms and uses of advertising, it is difficult to make generalizations.[39] Yet the following qualities can be noted:

- *Public presentation:* Advertising's public nature confers a kind of legitimacy on the product and also suggests a standardized offering.
- *Pervasiveness:* Advertising permits the seller to repeat a message many times. It also allows the buyer to receive and compare the messages of various competitors. Large-scale advertising says something positive about the seller's size, power, and success.
- *Amplified expressiveness:* Advertising provides opportunities for dramatizing the company and its products through the artful use of print, sound, and color.
- *Impersonality:* The audience does not feel obligated to pay attention or respond to advertising. Advertising is a monologue in front of, not a dialogue with, the audience.

Advertising can be used to build up a long-term image for a product (Coca-Cola ads) or trigger quick sales (a Sears ad for a weekend sale). Advertising can efficiently reach geographically dispersed buyers. Certain forms of advertising (TV advertising) can require a large budget, whereas other forms (newspaper advertising) do not. Just the presence of advertising might have an effect on sales: Consumers might believe that a heavily advertised brand must offer "good value."

Sales Promotion   Sales-promotion tools—coupons, contests, premiums, and the like—offer three distinctive benefits:

1. *Communication:* They gain attention and may lead the consumer to the product.
2. *Incentive:* They incorporate some concession, inducement, or contribution that gives value to the consumer.
3. *Invitation:* They include a distinct invitation to engage in the transaction now.

Companies use sales-promotion tools to draw a stronger and quicker buyer response. Sales promotion can be used for short-run effects such as to dramatize product offers and boost sagging sales.

Public Relations and Publicity   The appeal of public relations and publicity is based on three distinctive qualities:

1. *High credibility:* News stories and features are more authentic and credible to readers than ads.
2. *Ability to catch buyers off guard:* Public relations can reach prospects who prefer to avoid salespeople and advertisements.
3. *Dramatization:* Public relations has the potential for dramatizing a company or product.

Marketers tend to underuse public relations, yet a well-thought-out program coordinated with the other promotion-mix elements can be extremely effective.

Personal Selling   Personal selling is the most effective tool at later stages of the buying process, particularly in building up buyer preference, conviction, and action. Personal selling has three distinctive qualities:

1. *Personal confrontation:* Personal selling involves an immediate and interactive relationship between two or more persons. Each party is able to observe the other's reactions.
2. *Cultivation:* Personal selling permits all kinds of relationships to spring up, ranging from a matter-of-fact selling relationship to a deep personal friendship.
3. *Response:* Personal selling makes the buyer feel under some obligation for having listened to the sales talk.

Direct Marketing   The many forms of direct marketing—direct mail, telemarketing, Internet marketing—share four distinctive characteristics. Direct marketing is:

1. *Nonpublic:* The message is normally addressed to a specific person.
2. *Customized:* The message can be prepared to appeal to the addressed individual.

3. *Up-to-date:* A message can be prepared very quickly.

4. *Interactive:* The message can be changed depending on the person's response.

factors in setting the marketing communications mix

Companies must consider several factors in developing their promotion mix: type of product market, consumer readiness to make a purchase, and stage in the product life cycle. Also important is the company's market rank. Market leaders derive more benefit from advertising than from sales promotion. Conversely, smaller competitors gain more by using sales promotion in their marketing communications mix.

TYPE OF PRODUCT MARKET   Promotional allocations vary between consumer and business markets. Consumer marketers spend on sales promotion, advertising, personal selling, and public relations, in that order. Business marketers spend on personal selling, sales promotion, advertising, and public relations, in that order. In general, personal selling is used more with complex, expensive, and risky goods and in markets with fewer and larger sellers (hence, business markets).

Although advertising is used less than sales calls in business markets, it still plays a significant role:

- Advertising can provide an introduction to the company and its products.
- If the product embodies new features, advertising can explain them.
- Reminder advertising is more economical than sales calls.
- Advertisements offering brochures and carrying the company's phone number are an effective way to generate leads for sales representatives.
- Sales representatives can use tear sheets of the company's ads to legitimize their company and products.
- Advertising can remind customers of how to use the product and reassure them about their purchase.

A number of studies have underscored advertising's role in business markets. The Morrill study showed that advertising combined with personal selling increased sales 23 percent over what they had been with no advertising. The total promotional cost as a percentage of sales was reduced by 20 percent.[40] Cyril Freeman developed a formal model for dividing promotional funds between advertising and personal selling on the basis of the selling tasks that each performs more economically.[41] Levitt's research also showed the important role advertising can play in business markets. He found:

1. A company's reputation improves its sales force's chances of getting a favorable first hearing and an early adoption of the product. Corporate advertising that can build up the company's reputation will help the sales representatives.

2. Sales representatives from well-known companies have an edge if their sales presentations are adequate; but a rep from a lesser-known company who makes a highly effective presentation can overcome the disadvantage.

3. Company reputation helps most where the product is complex, the risk is high, and the purchasing agent is less professionally trained.[42]

Gary Lilien researched business marketing practices in a major project called ADVISOR and reported the following:[43]

- The average industrial company set its marketing budget at 7 percent of its sales. It spent only 10 percent of its marketing budget on advertising. Companies spent the remainder on sales force, trade shows, sales promotion, and direct mail.
- Industrial companies spent a higher-than-average amount on advertising if their products had higher quality, uniqueness, or purchase frequency, or if there was customer growth.
- Industrial companies set a higher-than-average marketing budget when their customers were more dispersed or the customer growth rate was higher.

Personal selling can also make a strong contribution in consumer-goods marketing. Some consumer marketers use the sales force mainly to collect weekly orders from dealers

figure **19.6**

Cost-Effectiveness of
Different Promotional
Tools at Different Buyer-
Readiness Stages

and to see that sufficient stock is on the shelf. Yet an effectively trained consumer company sales force can make four important contributions:

1. *Increased stock position:* Sales reps can persuade dealers to take more stock and devote more shelf space to the company's brand.
2. *Enthusiasm building:* Sales reps can build dealer enthusiasm by dramatizing planned advertising and sales-promotion backup.
3. *Missionary selling:* Sales reps can sign up more dealers.
4. *Key account management:* Sales reps can take responsibility for growing business with the most important accounts.

BUYER-READINESS STAGE   Promotional tools vary in cost-effectiveness at different stages of buyer readiness. Figure 19.6 shows the relative cost effectiveness of four promotional tools. Advertising and publicity play the most important roles in the awareness-building stage. Customer comprehension is primarily affected by advertising and personal selling. Customer conviction is influenced mostly by personal selling. Closing the sale is influenced mostly by personal selling and sales promotion. Reordering is also affected mostly by personal selling and sales promotion, and somewhat by reminder advertising.

PRODUCT LIFE-CYCLE STAGE   Promotional tools also vary in cost-effectiveness at different stages of the product life cycle. In the introduction stage, advertising and publicity have the highest cost-effectiveness, followed by personal selling to gain distribution coverage and sales promotion to induce trial. In the growth stage, demand has its own momentum through word of mouth. In the maturity stage, sales promotion, advertising, and personal selling all grow more important, in that order. In the decline stage, sales promotion continues strong, advertising and publicity are reduced, and salespeople give the product only minimal attention. An intriguing example of a promotion mix used in the introduction stage of the product or service life cycle is the privately held Best Friends Pet Care Company.

Best Friends Pet Care   Best Friends operates 28 pet care centers in 16 states, offering hotel services for dogs and cats, including grooming, day care, exercise, and overnight lodging. When opening a new site, the company takes out cable TV ads and sends direct mail invitations to come in and tour its state-of-the-art facility. At its grand opening in Milford, Connecticut, it brought in Beethoven, the canine movie star, and offered free pictures of him with visitors. The promotion attracted 7,000 visitors! Once on-site, a professionally trained staff used a highly personal selling approach.[44]

measure the communications' results

Senior managers want to know the *outcomes* and *revenues* resulting from their communications investments. Too often, however, their communications directors supply only *outputs* and *expenses:* press clipping counts, numbers of ads placed, media costs. In fairness, the communications directors try to translate outputs into intermediate outputs such as reach and frequency, recall and recognition scores, persuasion changes, and cost-per-thousand calculations. Ultimately, behavior change measures capture the real payoff from communications.

After implementing the promotional plan, the communicator must measure its impact on the target audience. Members of the target audience are asked whether they recognize or recall the message, how many times they saw it, what points they recall, how they felt about the message, and their previous and current attitudes toward the product and company. The communicator should also collect behavioral measures of audience response, such as how many people bought the product, liked it, and talked to others about it.

Figure 19.7 provides an example of good feedback measurement. We find that 80 percent of the consumers in the total market are aware of brand A, 60 percent have tried it, and only 20 percent who have tried it are satisfied. This indicates that the communications program is effective in creating awareness, but the product fails to meet consumer expectations. In contrast, only 40 percent of the consumers in the total market are aware of brand B, and only 30 percent have tried it, but 80 percent of those who have tried it are satisfied. In this case, the communications program needs to be strengthened to take advantage of the brand's power.

managing the integrated marketing communications process

Many companies still rely on one or two communication tools to achieve their communications aims. This practice persists in spite of the fragmenting of mass-markets into a multitude of minimarkets, each requiring its own approach; the proliferation of new types of media; and the growing sophistication of consumers. The wide range of communication tools, messages, and audiences makes it imperative that companies move toward **integrated marketing communications (IMC)**. As defined by the American Association of Advertising Agencies, IMC is a concept of marketing communications planning that recognizes the added value of a comprehensive plan. Such a plan evaluates the strategic roles of a variety of communications disciplines—for example, general advertising, direct response, sales promotion and public relations—and combines these disciplines to provide clarity, consistency, and maximum impact through the seamless integration of discrete messages.

Here are creative examples of integrated marketing communications.

Warner–Lambert Warner-Lambert wanted to promote its antihistamine Benadryl to allergy sufferers. The company used advertising and public relations to increase brand awareness and promote a toll-free number that provided people with the pollen count in their area. People who called the number more than once received free product samples, coupons, and in-depth materials describing the product's benefits. These people also received a newsletter that includes advice on how to cope with allergy problems.[45]

Beck's Beer Seeking a cost-effective campaign with which to compete against bigger spenders in the category, Beck's North America launched a $10 million integrated marketing campaign in late 1999. The company used 60 percent of the money to buy TV advertising on ESPN/ABC Sports networks. The remaining 40 percent went to Internet advertising on ESPN.com, radio advertising on ESPN radio, print

figure **19.7**

Current Consumer States for Two Brands

advertising in *ESPN Magazine*, and sponsorships and promotions at sporting events. The integrated, targeted approach enabled the company to "make an impact before its key audience," 21- to 34-year-old males.[46]

A study of top management and marketing executives in large consumer companies indicated that over 70 percent favored the concept of integrated marketing communications. Several large advertising agencies—Ogilvy & Mather, Young & Rubicam, Saatchi & Saatchi—acquired major agencies specializing in sales promotion, public relations, and direct marketing in order to provide one-stop shopping, but to their disappointment, most clients did not buy their integrated marketing communications package, preferring to put together the specialized agencies themselves.

Why the resistance? Large companies employ several communications specialists to work with their brand managers. Each specialist knows little about the other communication tools. Furthermore, the specialists usually have favorite outside agencies and oppose turning their responsibilities over to one superagency. They argue that the company should choose the best specialist agency for each purpose, not second- and third-rate agencies just because they belong to a superagency. They believe that the ad agency will still put most of the advertiser's money into the advertising budget.

Today, however, a few large agencies have substantially improved their integrated offerings. Many international clients have opted to put a substantial portion of their communications work through one agency. An example is IBM turning all of its advertising over to Ogilvy to attain uniform branding.

Integrated marketing communications does produce stronger message consistency and greater sales impact. It forces management to think about every way the customer comes in contact with the company, how the company communicates its positioning, the relative importance of each vehicle, and timing issues. It gives someone the responsibility—where none existed before—to unify the company's brand images and messages as they come through thousands of company activities. IMC will improve the company's ability to reach the right customers with the right messages at the right time and in the right place.[47] Duke Power, the North Carolina utility, found out how useful IMC can be.

Duke Power   To develop IMC, Duke Power conducted lengthy interviews with company officers, customer surveys, literature reviews, and "best practice" interviews with other companies. Out of this process came four recommendations: (1) that Duke manage its reputation as a corporate asset; (2) that the company develop and implement an integrated communications process to manage all aspects of its communications; (3) that the company train all its employees in how to communicate, because Duke's customers responded more to employees' actions than to specific planned programs; and (4) that the company develop and enhance a strategic database to help it anticipate customer interests and improve customer satisfaction and retention. Based on these recommendations, Duke Power developed integrated communications processes that are directly tied to the company's business processes.[48]

IMC advocates describe it as a way of looking at the whole marketing process instead of focusing on individual parts of it. Companies such as Motorola, Xerox, and Hewlett-Packard are bringing together their advertising, direct marketing, public relations, and employee communications experts into "supercouncils" that meet a few times each year for training and improved communication among them. Procter & Gamble recently revised its communications planning by requiring that each new program be formulated jointly, with its ad agency sitting together with P&G's public relations agencies, direct marketing units, promotion-merchandising firms, and Internet operations.

summary

1. Modern marketing calls for more than developing a good product, pricing it attractively, and making it accessible to target customers. Companies must also communicate with present and potential stakeholders, and with the general public. The marketing communications mix consists of five major modes of communication: advertising, sales promotion, public relations and publicity, personal selling, and direct marketing.

2. The communication process consists of nine elements: sender, receiver, message, media, encoding, decoding, response, feedback, and noise. To get their messages through, marketers must encode their messages in a way that takes into account how the target audience usually decodes messages. They must also transmit the message through efficient media that reach the target audience and develop feedback channels to monitor response to the message.

3. Developing effective communications involves eight steps: (1) Identify the target audience, (2) determine the communications objectives, (3) design the message, (4) select the communication channels, (5) establish the total communications budget, (6) decide on the communications mix, (7) measure the communications' results, and (8) manage the integrated marketing communications process.

4. In identifying the target audience, the marketer needs to close any gap that exists between current public perception and the image sought. Communications objectives may be cognitive, affective, or behavioral—that is, the company might want to put something into the consumer's mind, change the consumer's attitude, or get the consumer to act. In designing the message, marketers must carefully consider content, structure, format, and source. Communication channels may be personal (advocate, expert, and social channels) or nonpersonal (media, atmospheres, and events). The objective-and-task method of setting the promotion budget, which calls upon marketers to develop their budgets by defining specific objectives, is the most desirable.

5. In deciding on the marketing communications mix, marketers must examine the distinct advantages and costs of each promotional tool and the company's market rank. They must also consider the type of product market in which they are selling, how ready consumers are to make a purchase, and the product's stage in the product life cycle. Measuring the marketing communications mix's effectiveness involves asking members of the target audience whether they recognize or recall the message, how many times they saw it, what points they recall, how they felt about the message, and their previous and current attitudes toward the product and the company.

6. Managing and coordinating the entire communications process calls for integrated marketing communications (IMC): marketing communications planning which recognizes the added value of a comprehensive plan that evaluates the strategic roles of a variety of communications disciplines and combines these disciplines to provide clarity, consistency, and maximum impact through the seamless integration of discrete messages.

applications

marketing debate – what is the biggest obstacle to integrating marketing communications?

Although integrated marketing communications is a frequently espoused goal, truly integrated programs have been hard to come by. Some critics maintain the problem is an organizational one—the agencies have not done a good job of putting together all the different teams and organizations involved with a communications campaign. Others maintain that the biggest problem is the lack of managerial guidelines for evaluating IMC programs. How does a manager know when his or her IMC program is satisfactorily integrated?

Take a position: The biggest obstacle to effective IMC programs is a lack of agency coordination across communication units versus The biggest obstacle to effective IMC programs is a lack of understanding as to how to optimally design and evaluate such programs.

marketing and advertising

1. The magazine ad in Figure 1 promotes UpWords, a game marketed by the manufacturer of the Scrabble word game. Although the game is portrayed in the ad, other elements are more prominent.

    a. Who is the target audience for this advertising message? What image of the game would the advertiser like to create with this ad?

    b. How do selective attention, selective distortion, and selective retention apply to this advertising message?

    c. What communication objectives might the game manufacturer set for this advertising message?

2. Sharp incorporates a clever depiction of its imaging product's key benefit—using color to reach people—to attract attention and communicate with business decision makers in the ad shown in Figure 2.

    a. Analyze this ad in terms of the hierarchy-of-effects model.

    b. How is Sharp using message format to communicate with its target audience?

    c. How does Sharp establish source credibility in this advertisement?

Figure 1

Figure 2

online marketing today

VF, which makes Lee jeans, has used the Internet to create a word-of-mouth tidal wave around its jeans. It started by creating Web sites for Buddy Lee, a kewpie-doll character, and Curry, a fictional race-car driver, and encouraging consumers to discover the sites on their own or e-mail their friends about the sites. Weeks later, VF ran media ads revealing that the characters were part of an elaborate online computer game. To advance to higher levels in the game, players needed to input code numbers found only on Lee jeans—which meant visiting a store and looking at Lee's products. This integrated marketing communications campaign helped push Lee's sales 20 percent higher than in the previous year.[49]

VF continues to operate some of the sites. The Curry site is located at *www.rubberburner.com* and one of the Buddy Lee sites is at *www.buddylee.com*. Explore both sites. Also follow the "Lee Sites" link at the Buddy Lee home page and review one or two of the featured sites. How does Lee encourage consumer participation on these sites? What is the appeal of these sites? What objectives might Lee set for campaigns that rely on word of mouth?

you're the marketer: sonic pda marketing plan

Marketing Plan Pro

Every marketing plan must include a section showing how the company will use marketing communications to connect with customers, prospects, and other stakeholders. Web-based communications must be integrated into the overall communications strategy to ensure consistency of messages.

You are responsible for planning integrated marketing communications for Sonic's introduction of its personal digital assistant (PDA). Review the data, decisions, and strategies you have previously documented in your marketing plan. Now use your knowledge of communications to answer these questions:

- What audience(s) should Sonic be targeting? What image should it seek to create for its initial PDA product?

- What objectives are appropriate for Sonic's initial communications campaign?
- What message design and communication channel(s) are likely to be most effective for the target audience?
- How should Sonic establish its marketing communications budget?
- Which promotional tools would be most effective in Sonic's promotional mix? Why?

Be sure that your marketing communications plans will support Sonic's overall marketing efforts. Now, as your instructor directs, summarize your thoughts in a written marketing plan or type them into the Marketing Mix section of the *Marketing Plan Pro* software.

notes

1. The definitions are adapted from Peter D. Bennett, ed., *Dictionary of Marketing Terms* (Chicago: American Marketing Association, 1995).

2. For an alternate communication model developed specifically for advertising communications, see Barbara B. Stern, "A Revised Communication Model for Advertising: Multiple Dimensions of the Source, the Message, and the Recipient," *Journal of Advertising* (June 1994): 5–15. For some additional perspectives, see Tom Duncan and Sandra E. Moriarity, "A Communication-Based Marketing Model for Managing Relationships," *Journal of Marketing* (April 1998): 1–13.

3. Brian Sternthal and C. Samuel Craig, *Consumer Behavior: An Information Processing Perspective* (Upper Saddle River, NJ: Prentice Hall, 1982), pp. 97–102.

4. However, research by Cox and Bauer showed a curvilinear relation between self-confidence and persuasibility, with those moderate in self-confidence being the most persuasible. Donald F. Cox and Raymond A. Bauer, "Self-Confidence and Persuasibility in Women," *Public Opinion Quarterly* (Fall 1964): 453–66; Raymond L. Horton, "Some Relationships between Personality and Consumer Decision-Making," *Journal of Marketing Research* (May 1979): 233–46.

5. John Fiske and John Hartley, *Reading Television* (London: Methuen, 1980), p. 79. For the effects of expertise on persuasion, see also Elizabeth J. Wilson and Daniel L. Sherrell, "Source Effects in Communication and Persuasion Research: A Meta-Analysis of Effect Size," *Journal of the Academy of Marketing Science* (Spring 1993): 101–12.

6. The semantic differential was developed by C. E. Osgood, C. J. Suci, and P. H. Tannenbaum, *The Measurement of Meaning* (Urbana: University of Illinois Press, 1957).

7. John Bigness, "Back to Brand New Life," *Chicago Tribune*, October 4, 1998; Chris Reidy, "Putting on the Dog to be Arnold's Job," *Boston Globe*, August 28, 1998.

8. Michael L. Ray, *Advertising and Communications Management* (Upper Saddle River, NJ: Prentice Hall, 1982).

9. Michael R. Solomon, *Consumer Behavior*, 3rd ed. (Upper Saddle River, NJ: Prentice Hall, 1996), pp. 208–10 for references to research articles on fear appeals.

10. Kevin Goldman, "Advertising: Knock, Knock. Who's There? The Same Old Funny Ad Again," *Wall Street Journal*, November 2, 1993, p. B10. See also Marc G. Weinberger, Harlan Spotts, Leland Campbell, and Amy L. Parsons, "The Use and Effect of Humor in Different Advertising Media," *Journal of Advertising Research* (May–June 1995): 44–55.

11. Susanne Craig, "E*Trade to Cut Marketing Even as Its Losses Narrow," *Wall Street Journal*, April 12, 2001, p. B13; "Bank on It," *Brandweek*, December 11, 2000.

12. Yoav Ganzach and Nili Karashi, "Message Framing and Buying Behavior: A Field Experiment," *Journal of Business Research* (January 1995): 11–17.

13. James F. Engel, Roger D. Blackwell, and Paul W. Minard, *Consumer Behavior*, 8th ed. (Fort Worth, TX: Dryden, 1994).

14. Ayn E. Crowley and Wayne D. Hoyer, "An Integrative Framework for Understanding Two-Sided Persuasion," *Journal of Consumer Research* (March 1994): 561–74.

15. C. I. Hovland, A. A. Lumsdaine, and F. D. Sheffield, *Experiments on Mass Communication*, vol. 3 (Princeton, NJ: Princeton University Press, 1948), ch. 8; Crowley and Hoyer, "An Integrative Framework for Understanding Two-Sided Persuasion." For an alternative viewpoint, see George E. Belch, "The Effects of Message Modality on One- and Two-Sided Advertising Messages," in *Advances in Consumer Research*, ed. Richard P. Bagozzi and Alice M. Tybout (Ann Arbor, MI: Association for Consumer Research, 1983), pp. 21–26.

16. Curtis P. Haugtvedt and Duane T. Wegener, "Message Order Effects in Persuasion: An Attitude Strength Perspective," *Journal of Consumer Research* (June 1994): 205–18; H. Rao Unnava, Robert E. Burnkrant, and Sunil Erevelles, "Effects of Presentation Order and Communication Modality on Recall and Attitude," *Journal of Consumer Research* (December 1994): 481–90.

17. Sternthal and Craig, *Consumer Behavior*, pp. 282–84.

18. Michael McCarthy, "BMW Drives into New Ad World." *USA Today*, June 6, 2001, p. B3.

19. Herbert C. Kelman and Carl I. Hovland, "Reinstatement of the Communication in Delayed Measurement of Opinion Change," *Journal of Abnormal and Social Psychology* 48 (1953): 327–35.

20. David J. Moore, John C. Mowen, and Richard Reardon, "Multiple Sources in Advertising Appeals: When Product Endorsers Are Paid by the Advertising Sponsor," *Journal of the Academy of Marketing Science* (Summer 1994): 234–43.

21. C. E. Osgood and P. H. Tannenbaum, "The Principles of Congruity in the Prediction of Attitude Change," *Psychological Review* 62 (1955): 42–55.

22. Michael Kiely, "Word-of-Mouth Marketing," *Marketing* (September 1993): 6. See also Aric Rindfleisch and Christine Moorman, "The Acquistion and Utilization of Information in New Product Alliances: A Strength-of-Ties Perspective," *Journal of Marketing* (April 2001): 1–18.

23. Robert Spector, *Amazon.com: Get Big Fast* (New York: HarperBusiness, 2000), p. 149.

24. Hilary Stout, "Ad Budget: Zero. Buzz: Deafening." *Wall Street Journal*, December 29, 1999, B.1.

25. Renee Dye, "The Buzz on Buzz," *Harvard Business Review* (November–December 2000): 139–46.

26. Regis McKenna, *The Regis Touch* (Reading, MA: Addison-Wesley, 1985); Regis McKenna, *Relationship Marketing* (Reading, MA: Addison-Wesley, 1991).

27. Michael Cafferky has identified four kinds of people companies try to reach to stimulate word-of-mouth referrals: opinion leaders, marketing mavens, influentials, and product enthusiasts. Opinion leaders are people who are widely respected within defined social groups, such as fashion leaders. They have a large relevant social network, high source credibility, and a high propensity to talk. Marketing mavens are people who spend a lot of time learning the best buys (values) in the marketplace. Influentials are people who are socially and politically active; they try to know what is going on and influence the course of events. Product enthusiasts are people who are known experts in a product category, such as art connoisseurs, audiophiles, and computer wizards. See Cafferky, *Let Your Customers Do the Talking* (Chicago: Dearborn Financial Publishing, 1995), pp. 30–33.

28. Emanuel Rosen, *The Anatomy of Buzz* (New York: Currency, 2000), ch. 12; "Viral Marketing," *Sales & Marketing Automation* (November 1999): 12–14; George Silverman, *The Secrets of Word-of-Mouth Marketing* (New York: Amacom, 2001).

29. Suzanne Vranica, "Volvo Campaign Tests New Media Waters," *Wall Street Journal*, March 16, 2001 p. B5.; Karen Lundegaard. "Volvo's Web-Only Vehicle Launch Ends amid Ford Unit's Questioning of Tactic." *Wall Street Journal*, January 11, 2001, p. B13.

30. Philip Kotler, "Atmospherics as a Marketing Tool," *Journal of Retailing* (Winter 1973–1974): 48–64.

31. Theresa Howard, "Freebies Take on Brash New Form," *USA Today*, May 15, 2001, p. B1; "Sea-Doo's Plan: See It, Do It, Buy It," *Brandweek*, May 3, 1999, p. 12.

32. Everett M. Rogers, *Diffusion of Innovations*, 4th ed. (New York: The Free Press, 1995).

33. Quoted in Daniel Seligman, "How Much for Advertising?" *Fortune*, December 1956, p. 123. For a good discussion of setting promotion budgets, see Michael L. Rothschild, *Advertising* (Lexington, MA: D. C. Heath, 1987), ch. 20.

34. Albert Wesley Frey, *How Many Dollars for Advertising?* (New York: Ronald Press, 1955), p. 65.

35. Ibid., p. 49.

36. Adapted from G. Maxwell Ule, "A Media Plan for 'Sputnik' Cigarettes," *How to Plan Media Strategy* (American Association of Advertising Agencies, 1957 Regional Convention), pp. 41–52.

37. *New York Times*, July 6, 2000.

38. Sidney J. Levy, *Promotional Behavior* (Glenview, IL: Scott, Foresman, 1971), ch. 4.

39. Relatively little research has been done on the effectiveness of B2B advertising. For a survey, see Wesley J. Johnson, "The Importance of Advertising and the Relative Lack of Research," *Journal of Business & Industrial Marketing* 9, no. 2 (1994): 3–4.

40. *How Advertising Works in Today's Marketplace: The Morrill Study* (New York: McGraw-Hill, 1971), p. 4.

41. Cyril Freeman, "How to Evaluate Advertising's Contribution," *Harvard Business Review* (July–August 1962): 137–48.

42. Theodore Levitt, *Industrial Purchasing Behavior: A Study in Communication Effects* (Boston: Division of Research, Harvard Business School, 1965).

43. Gary L. Lilien and John D. C. Little, "The ADVISOR Project: A Study of Industrial Marketing Budgets," *Sloan Management Review* (Spring 1976): 17–31; Gary L. Lilien, "ADVISOR 2: Modeling the Marketing Mix Decision for Industrial Products," *Management Science* (February 1979): 191–204.

44. Danielle McDavitt, "Best Friends Pet Care CEO: Interview," CNBC-Dow Jones Business Video, October 19, 1998.

45. Paul Wang and Lisa Petrison, "Integrated Marketing Communications and Its Potential Effects on Media Planning," *Journal of Media Planning* 6, no. 2 (1991): 11–18.

46. Laurie Freeman, "Smaller Budget, Big Reach: Networks Sold on Integrated Marketing," *Electronic Media*, November 22, 1999, p. 12.

47. Don E. Shultz, Stanley I. Tannenbaum, and Robert F. Lauterborn, *Integrated Marketing Communications: Putting It Together and Making It Work* (Lincolnwood, IL: NTC Business Books, 1992); Ernan Roman, *Integrated Direct Marketing: The Cutting-Edge Strategy for Synchronizing Advertising, Direct Mail, Telemarketing, and Field Sales* (Lincolnwood, IL: NTC Business Books, 1995).

48. Don E. Schultz, "The Next Step in IMC?" *Marketing News*, August 15, 1994, pp. 8–9. Also see Birger Wernerfelt, "Efficient Marketing Communication: Helping the Customer Learn," *Journal of Marketing Research* (May 1996): 239–46.

49. Gerry Khermouch, "Buzz Marketing," *BusinessWeek*, July 30, 2001, pp. 50–56.

managing advertising, sales promotion, public relations, and direct marketing

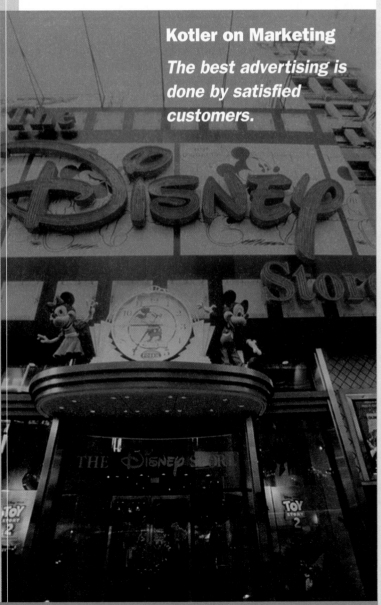

Kotler on Marketing

The best advertising is done by satisfied customers.

In this chapter, we will address the following questions:

- What steps are involved in developing an advertising program?
- What explains the growing use of sales promotion, and how are sales-promotion decisions made?
- How can companies exploit the potential of public relations and publicity?
- How can companies use integrated direct marketing for competitive advantage?
- How can companies do effective e-marketing?

I n this chapter, we examine the nature and use of four promotional tools—advertising, sales promotion, public relations, and direct marketing. We examine both traditional and online forms of these tools, and we look at the advantages of integrated direct marketing.

developing and managing an advertising program

Advertising is any paid form of nonpersonal presentation and promotion of ideas, goods, or services by an identified sponsor. Advertisers include not only business firms, but also museums, charitable organizations, and government agencies that direct messages to target publics. Ads are a cost-effective way to disseminate messages, whether to build brand preference for Coca-Cola or to educate people to avoid hard drugs.

Organizations handle advertising in different ways. In small companies, advertising is handled by someone in the sales or marketing department, who works with an advertising agency. A large company will often set up its own department, whose manager reports to the vice president of marketing. The advertising department's job is to propose a budget; develop advertising strategy; approve ads and campaigns; and handle direct-mail advertising, dealer displays, and other forms of advertising. Most companies use an outside agency to help create advertising campaigns and to select and purchase media.

Global companies that use a large number of ad agencies located in different countries and serving different divisions have suffered from uncoordinated advertising and image diffusion. Some large companies, such as IBM and Hewlett-Packard, now use only a few agencies or even one that can supply global advertising, public relations, sales promotion, and Web consulting. The result is integrated and more effective marketing communications and a much lower total communications cost.

Advertising agencies need to redefine themselves as *communication companies* and assist clients in improving their overall communication effectiveness. Yet many agencies have reduced the size of their research departments and therefore are less able to build a research-based brand strategy. Another criticism is that ad agencies are too oriented toward large-budget mass-advertising and less skilled in PR, and direct and database marketing. Procter & Gamble recently required that all its marketing programs be jointly planned with the various communication groups sitting together, instead of letting its advertising agency dominate the decision making. It changed ad agency compensation from a standard media commission to a percentage of how well its global sales perform.

In developing a program, marketing managers must always start by identifying the target market and buyer motives. Then they can make the five major decisions in developing an advertising program, known as "the five Ms" *Mission*: What are the advertising objectives? *Money*: How much can be spent? *Message*: What message should be sent? *Media*: What media should be used? *Measurement*: How should the results be evaluated? These decisions are summarized in Figure 20.1 and described in the following sections.

setting the advertising objectives

The advertising objectives must flow from prior decisions on target market, market positioning, and marketing mix.

Many specific communication and sales objectives can be assigned to advertising. Russell Colley lists 52 possible advertising objectives in his classic *Defining Advertising Goals for Measured Advertising Results*.[1] He outlines a method called DAG-MAR (after the book's title) for turning objectives into specific measurable goals. An **advertising goal** (or **objective**) is a specific communication task and achievement level to be accomplished with a specific audience in a specific period of time. Colley provides an example:

> To increase among 30 million homemakers who own automatic washers the number who identify brand X as a low-sudsing detergent and who are persuaded that it gets clothes cleaner–from 10 percent to 40 percent in one year.

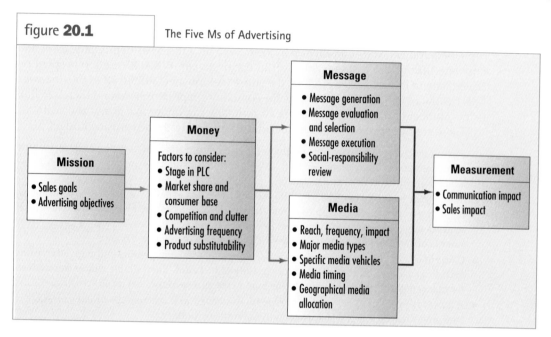

figure **20.1**   The Five Ms of Advertising

Advertising objectives can be classified according to whether their aim is to inform, persuade, remind, or reinforce. They aim at different stages in the *hierarchy of effects* discussed in Chapter 19.

- *Informative advertising* aims to create awareness and knowledge of new products or new features of existing products. When Subaru first introduced its cars in the United States, its advertising simply repeated the name Subaru.
- *Persuasive advertising* aims to create liking, preference, conviction, and purchase of a product or service. Thus Chivas Regal attempts to persuade consumers that it delivers more taste and status than other brands of Scotch whiskey. Some persuasive advertising uses comparative advertising, which makes an explicit comparison of the attributes of two or more brands.[2] The Burger King Corporation used comparative advertising for its attack on McDonald's (Burger King's burgers are flame-broiled; McDonald's are fried). Schering-Plough claimed that "New OcuClear relieves three times longer than Visine." Comparative advertising works best when it elicits cognitive and affective motivations simultaneously.[3]
- *Reminder advertising* aims to stimulate repeat purchase of products and services. Expensive, four-color Coca-Cola ads in magazines are intended to remind people to purchase Coca-Cola.
- *Reinforcement advertising* aims to convince current purchasers that they made the right choice. Automobile ads often depict satisfied customers enjoying special features of their new car.

The advertising objective should emerge from a thorough analysis of the current marketing situation. If the product class is mature, the company is the market leader, and brand usage is low, the proper objective should be to stimulate more usage. If the product class is new, the company is not the market leader, but the brand is superior to the leader, then the proper objective is to convince the market of the brand's superiority.

deciding on the advertising budget

How does a company know if it is spending the right amount? Some critics charge that large, consumer packaged-goods firms tend to overspend on advertising as a form of insurance against not spending enough, and that industrial companies underestimate the power of company and product image building and tend to underspend.[4]

Although advertising is treated as a current expense, part of it is really an investment that builds up an intangible asset called **brand equity**. When $5 million is spent on capital equipment, the equipment may be treated as a five-year depreciable asset and only one-fifth of the cost is written off in the first year. When $5 million is spent on advertising to launch a new product, the entire cost must be written off in the first year. This treatment of advertising reduces the company's reported profit and therefore limits the number of new-product launches a company can undertake in any one year.

There are five specific factors to consider when setting the advertising budget:[5]

1. *Stage in the product life cycle:* New products typically receive large advertising budgets to build awareness and to gain consumer trial. Established brands usually are supported with lower advertising budgets as a ratio to sales.

2. *Market share and consumer base:* High-market-share brands usually require less advertising expenditure as a percentage of sales to maintain share. To build share by increasing market size requires larger expenditures. On a cost-per-impression basis, it is less expensive to reach consumers of a widely used brand than to reach consumers of low-share brands.

3. *Competition and clutter:* In a market with a large number of competitors and high advertising spending, a brand must advertise more heavily to be heard. Even simple clutter from advertisements not directly competitive to the brand creates a need for heavier advertising.

4. *Advertising frequency:* The number of repetitions needed to put across the brand's message to consumers has an important impact on the advertising budget.

5. *Product substitutability:* Brands in a commodity class (cigarettes, beer, soft drinks) require heavy advertising to establish a differential image. Advertising is also important when a brand can offer unique physical benefits or features.

Marketing scientists have built a number of advertising-expenditure models that take these factors into account. Vidale and Wolfe's model called for a larger advertising budget, the higher the sales-response rate, the higher the sales-decay rate (the rate at which customers forget the advertising and brand), and the higher the untapped sales potential.[6] Unfortunately, this model leaves out other important factors, such as the rate of competitive advertising and the effectiveness of the company's ads.

John Little proposed an adaptive-control method for setting the advertising budget.[7] Suppose the company has set an advertising-expenditure rate based on its most current information. It spends this rate in all markets except in a subset of $2n$ markets randomly drawn. In n test markets the company spends at a lower rate, and in the other n it spends at a higher rate. This procedure will yield information on the average sales created by low, medium, and high rates of advertising that can be used to update the parameters of the sales-response function. The updated function can be used to determine the best advertising-expenditure rate for the next period. If this experiment is conducted each period, advertising expenditures will closely track optimal advertising expenditures.[8]

choosing the advertising message

Advertising campaigns vary in creativity. William Bernbach observed: "The facts are not enough. . . . Don't forget that Shakespeare used some pretty hackneyed plots, yet his message came through with great execution." Consider the following example.

Orkin In a recent ad, Orkin Pest Control, owned by Rollins, used creative imaging to emphasize the need for its services. The TV spot appeared to advertise "Sierra" brand fabric softener, then used a camera trick to make the audience think a real-life cockroach was crawling across the TV screen. The ad ended when an Orkin exterminator appears on-camera to get rid of the roach. Orkin received many complaints about the ad, but its effectiveness could not be questioned. Sales during the summer 2000 bug season rose 15 percent from the year before.[9]

Still, even a great execution must be updated before it gets outdated. Taco Bell learned this lesson when a popular campaign ceased to lift sales.

Taco Bell   In 1997, Taco Bell introduced television spots that featured a talking chihuahua. The hungry little dog, who became famous for his statement "Yo Quiero Taco Bell"—meaning in Spanish "I want some Taco Bell"—struck a chord with the chain's 18- to 35-year-old customers and helped increase revenues. The little pooch pushed Taco Bell's sales up 4.3 percent to $4.5 billion in 1997 and spawned an impressive array of chihuahua merchandise such as T-shirts, magnets, hats, and talking dolls. But after three years as official spokesdog, the chihuahua was unable to stop a decline in the fast-food industry that led Taco Bell sales during the fourth quarter of 2000 to drop 9 percent from the same quarter the previous year. Taco Bell fired its advertising agency and retired the dog, replacing him with a campaign featuring fun-loving twentysomethings singing and dancing at Taco Bell.[10]

Advertisers go through four steps to develop a creative strategy: message generation, message evaluation and selection, message execution, and social responsibility review.

MESSAGE GENERATION   Advertising people have proposed different theories for creating an effective message. Rosser Reeves of the Ted Bates Advertising Agency favored linking the brand directly to a single benefit, as in "Rolaids spells relief." Leo Burnett and his agency preferred to create a character that expressed the product's benefits: The Green Giant figure suggests that the brand's frozen vegetables are fresh frozen, vacuum-packed, and packed in butter sauce. His agency also created the Pillsbury Doughboy, the Marlboro Cowboy, and several other mythical personalities. The Doyle, Dane & Bernbach agency favored developing a narrative story with a problem, episodes related to the problem, and outcomes: A FedEx ad may show a person worried about on-time delivery who goes on FedEx's tracking system for assurance that the package will arrive on time.[11]

Whatever method is used, creative people should talk to consumers, dealers, and experts. Leo Burnett advocated "in-depth interviewing where I come realistically face-to-face with the people I am trying to sell. I try to get a picture in my mind of the kind of people they are—how they use this product and what it is."[12] However, when competitors all hear the same talk from members of the target market, they often end up using the same appeal. Many of today's ads for automobiles have a sameness about them—a car driving 90 miles an hour on a curved mountain road—with the result that only a weak link is established between the brand and the message.

Some creative people use a *deductive* framework for generating advertising messages. John Maloney proposed one framework.[13] He saw buyers as expecting one of four types of reward from a product: rational, sensory, social, or ego satisfaction. Buyers might visualize these rewards from results-of-use experience, product-in-use experience, or incidental-to-use experience. Crossing the four types of rewards with the three types of experience generates 12 types of advertising messages. For example, the appeal "gets clothes cleaner" is a rational-reward promise following results-of-use experience. The phrase "real gusto in a great light beer" is a sensory-reward promise connected with product-in-use experience.

How many alternative ad themes should the advertiser create before making a choice? The more ads that are independently created, the higher the probability of finding an excellent one. Yet the more time spent on creating alternative ads, the higher the costs. Under the present commission system, the agency does not like to go to the expense of creating and pretesting many ads. Fortunately, the expense of creating rough ads is rapidly falling due to computers. An ad agency's creative department can compose many alternative ads in a short time by drawing from computer files containing still and video images.

MESSAGE EVALUATION AND SELECTION   A good ad normally focuses on one core selling proposition. Dik Twedt suggested that messages be rated on *desirability*, *exclusiveness*, and *believability*.[14] The following is an example.

The March of Dimes   The March of Dimes searched for an advertising theme to raise money for its fight against birth defects. Several messages came out of a brainstorming session. A group of young parents was asked to rate each message for interest, distinctiveness, and believability, assigning up to 100 points for each. For example, "Seven hundred children are born each day with a birth defect" scored 70, 62, and 80 on interest, distinctiveness, and believability; whereas "Your next baby could be born with a birth defect" scored 58, 51, and 70. The first message outperformed the second on all accounts.[15]

The advertiser should conduct market research to determine which appeal works best with its target audience. Once an effective appeal is found, the advertiser should prepare a *creative brief*, typically covering one or two pages. It is an elaboration of the *positioning statement* (see Chapter 10, p. 8) and includes: key message; target audience; communication objectives (to do, to know, to believe); benefits to promise; supports for the promise; and media to be used. All the team members working on the campaign need to agree on the creative brief before investing in costly ads.

MESSAGE EXECUTION   The message's impact depends not only on what is said, but often more important, on how it is said. Some ads aim for *rational positioning* and others for *emotional positioning*. U.S. ads typically present an explicit feature or benefit designed to appeal to the rational mind: "gets clothes cleaner"; "brings relief faster." Japanese ads tend to be more indirect and appeal to the emotions: An example was Nissan's Infiniti ad, which showed not the car but beautiful scenes from nature aimed at producing an emotional association and response.

The choice of headlines and copy can make a difference in impact. Lalita Manrai created two ads for the same car. The first ad carried the headline "A New Car"; the second, the headline "Is This Car for You?" The second headline utilized an advertising strategy called *labeling*, in which the consumer is labeled as the type of person who is interested in that type of product. The two ads also differed in that the first ad described the car's features and the second described the car's benefits. In the test, the second ad far outperformed the first in terms of overall product impression, reader interest in buying the product, and likelihood of recommending it to a friend.[16]

Message execution can be decisive for highly similar products, such as detergents, cigarettes, coffee, and vodka. Consider the success of Absolut Vodka.

Absolut Vodka   Vodka is generally viewed as a commodity product, yet the amount of brand preference and loyalty in the vodka market is astonishing. Most of this preference and loyalty is attributed to brand image. When the Swedish brand Absolut entered the U.S. market in 1979, the company sold a disappointing 7,000 cases. By 1991, sales had soared to over 2 million cases. Absolut became the largest selling imported vodka in the United States, with 65 percent of the market, thanks in large part to its marketing strategy. In the U.S. market, Absolut has aimed for sophisticated, upwardly mobile, affluent drinkers. The vodka comes in a distinctive, oddly shaped clear bottle which is used as the centerpiece of every ad. Well-known artists—including Warhol, Haring, Scharf—designed Absolut ads, and the bottle image always fits with the caption in a clever way. By 1999, Absolut was selling more than $1 billion worldwide.[17]

In preparing an ad campaign, the advertiser usually prepares a *copy strategy statement* describing the objective, content, support, and tone of the desired ad. Here is the strategy statement for a Pillsbury product called 1869 Brand Biscuits.

Pillsbury   The advertising *objective* is to convince biscuit users they can buy a canned biscuit that is as good as homemade—Pillsbury's 1869 Brand Biscuits. The *content* consists of emphasizing the following product characteristics: They look like, have the same texture as, and taste like homemade biscuits. *Support* for the "good as homemade" promise will be twofold: (1) 1869 Brand Biscuits are made from a special kind of flour used to make homemade biscuits but never before used in making canned biscuits, and (2) the use of traditional American biscuit recipes. The tone of the advertising will be a news announcement, tempered by a warm, reflective mood emanating from a look back at traditional American baking quality.

Any message can be presented in a number of execution styles: slice-of-life, lifestyle, fantasy, mood or image, musical, personality symbol, technical expertise, scientific evidence, and testimonial. "Marketing Insight: Celebrity Endorsements as a Strategy" focuses on the use of testimonials, as does the following example.

Rogaine   Testimonial advertising is used by Rogaine extra-strength for men, which promises to grow back an average of 45 percent more hair than its predecessor. Noted sports figures deliver testimonials in television ads. Green Bay Packers football coach Mike Holmgren is seen prowling the sidelines during a Packers game, saying, "Every Sunday, I've got 60,000 friends staring at my head." After sneering at an old picture of himself with a noticeable bald spot, Holmgren adds, "Every hair's a big win." The Utah Jazz basketball star Karl Malone testifies that he used Rogaine extra-strength for five months and got good results. Manufacturer Pharmacia increased its advertising budget from $30 million in 1997 to between $50 million and $60 million in 1998.[18]

The following is a rare example of a celebrity seeking a product to endorse, rather than the other way around.

Jaguar   Rock musician Sting and his manager approached Jaguar in 2000 with a unique endorsement idea. The video for Sting's latest single, "Desert Rose," included shots of Sting riding in the new Jaguar S-Type. Television and radio stations had overlooked the single, however, and Sting's manager felt that using his artist's video in television ads to promote Jaguars would raise consumer awareness of both the cars and Sting. In exchange for the free exposure, Sting gave Jaguar the rights to the 30-second treatment of his video. Within six months of the ad's introduction, Sting's album cracked the *Billboard* top 10 and went platinum, and sales of the S-Type helped to rejuvenate Jaguar.[19]

The communicator must choose an appropriate tone for the ad. Procter & Gamble is consistently positive in its tone—its ads say something superlatively positive about the product, and humor is almost always avoided so as not to take attention away from the message. In contrast, ads for Staples office supply superstores focus on a humorous situation rather than on the products themselves.

Memorable and attention-getting words must be found. The themes listed on the left would have had much less impact without the creative phrasing on the right:[20]

Theme	Creative Copy
7-Up is not a cola.	The Un-Cola (7-Up).
Milk is good for you.	Got milk? (milk industry).
Our technology can help you do almost anything.	Where do you want to go today? (Microsoft).
No hard sell, just a good car.	Drivers wanted (Volkswagen).
We don't rent as many cars, so we have to do more for our customers.	We try harder.
Red Roof Inns offer inexpensive lodging.	"Sleep cheap at Red Roof Inns."

marketing **insight**

Celebrity Endorsements as a Strategy

A well-chosen celebrity can draw attention to a product or brand, as when Sarah, Duchess of York—better known as Fergie—showed how she slimmed down thanks to Weight Watchers or, more recently, starred in a Schwab ad during the 2001 Super Bowl; or, the celebrity's mystique can transfer to the brand—Bill Cosby entertains a group of kids while eating a bowl of Jell-O.

The choice of the celebrity is critical. The celebrity should have high recognition, high positive affect, and high appropriateness to the product. Dennis Rodman has high recognition but a negative affect among many groups. Bruce Willis has high recognition and high positive affect but might not be appropriate for advertising a World Peace Conference. Paul Newman, Meryl Streep, and Oprah Winfrey could successfully advertise a large number of products because they have extremely high ratings for well-knownness and likability (known as the Q factor in the entertainment industry).

Athletes are a particularly effective group for endorsing athletic products, beverages, and apparel. One of the premier athlete endorsers is golfer Tiger Woods. In 2000, Woods signed a blockbuster $100 million contract to endorse Nike products over the next five years. Woods endorses products from a number of companies, including Buick, Titleist, Rolex, American Express, and Wheaties. He earned an estimated $45 million from endorsements in 2000, second only to Michael Jordan, who earned $69 million. ESPN Magazine estimated that over the course of his lifetime, Woods's earnings from playing, endorsements, and appearance fees will total $6 billion.

Another sports star with an impressive endorsement portfolio is cyclist Lance Armstrong, who battled and beat testicular cancer on his way to winning two consecutive Tour de France championships.

He endorses a number of bicycle and sports products companies, including Trek, Shimano, Oakley, and Nike. Armstrong's improbable success story enabled him to win endorsement contracts from companies unaffiliated with sports, such as Bristol-Myers Squibb pharmaceuticals, AIM Mutual Funds, American General Insurance, BrainLab medical products, and WebMD. The total amount he earned from endorsements in 2000 topped $7 million.

Using celebrities poses certain risks. The celebrity might hold out for a larger fee at contract renewal time or withdraw; or the celebrity might gain weight or become anorexic; or the celebrity might get caught in a scandal or embarrassing situation. Football hero O. J. Simpson pitched Hertz rental cars for 20 years until he was charged with murdering his wife in 1994. Pepsi dropped Michael Jackson in the wake of child molestation charges. Cybill Shepherd embarrassed the Beef Council when she admitted she had stopped eating beef. Insurers are now selling policies to protect advertisers against such risks. One insurance company offers "death, disablement, and disgrace" insurance.

Some advertisers choose to use "spokescharacters." For nearly 20 years Owens-Corning has used the Pink Panther to endorse its insulation products, and Metropolitan Life has used the Peanuts gang to promote its insurance policies. Another way advertisers protect themselves is by using deceased celebrities. Through the wonders of technology, television viewers see screen legends John Wayne pitching Coors beer and Fred Astaire dancing with a Dirt Devil vacuum cleaner.

Sources: Irving Rein, Philip Kotler, and Martin Scoller, *The Making and Marketing of Professionals into Celebrities* (Chicago: NTC Business Books, 1997); Greg Johnson, "Woods Cautious Approach to the Green," *Los Angeles Times*, July 26, 2000, p. A1; Bruce Horovitz, "Armstrong Rolls To Market Gold," *USA Today*, May 4, 2000, p. 1B.

Creativity is especially required for headlines. There are six basic types of headlines: *news* ("New Boom and More Inflation Ahead . . . and What You Can Do About It"); *question* ("Have You Had It Lately?"); *narrative* ("They Laughed When I Sat Down at the Piano, but Then I Started to Play!"); *command* ("Don't Buy Until You Try All Three"); 1-2-3 ways ("12 Ways to Save on Your Income Tax"); and *how-what-why* ("Why They Can't Stop Buying").

Format elements such as ad size, color, and illustration will affect an ad's impact as well as its cost. A minor rearrangement of mechanical elements can improve attention-getting power. Larger-sized ads gain more attention, though not necessarily by as much as their difference in cost. Four-color illustrations increase ad effectiveness and ad cost. By planning the relative dominance of different elements, better delivery can be achieved. New electronic eye movement studies show that consumers can be led through an ad by strategic placement of dominant elements.

A number of researchers into print advertisements report that the *picture, headline,* and *copy* are important, in that order. The reader first notices the picture, and it must be strong enough to draw attention. Then the headline must propel the person to read the

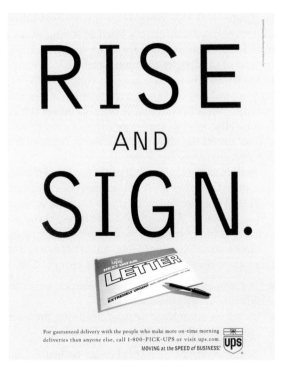

In this very effective UPS ad, the headline is what the reader notices first.

copy. The copy itself must be well composed. Even then, a really outstanding ad will be noted by less than 50 percent of the exposed audience. About 30 percent of the exposed audience might recall the headline's main point; about 25 percent might remember the advertiser's name; and less than 10 percent will read most of the body copy. Ordinary ads do not achieve even these results.

Ads are more effective when their message is congruent with their surroundings. A "happy" commercial placed within an upbeat television show is more likely to be effective than a downbeat commercial in the same place.[21] In addition, people are more likely to believe a TV or radio ad and to become more positively disposed toward the brand when the ad is placed within a program they like.[22] An industry study listed the following characteristics for ads that scored above average in recall and recognition: innovation (new product or new uses); "story appeal" (as an attention-getting device); before-and-after illustration; demonstrations; problem solution; and the inclusion of relevant characters that become emblematic of the brand.[23]

In recent years critics have bemoaned the spate of bland ads and slogans and, in particular, the frequent use of the nonreferential "it," as in "Coke is it"; Nike's popular "Just do it"; and the most egregious offender, Miller Lite's short-lived ad proclaiming, "It's it and that's that."[24] Why do so many ads look or sound alike? Norman W. Brown, former head of the advertising agency of Foote, Cone & Belding, says: "Many ads aren't creative because many companies want comfort, not creativity."

SOCIAL RESPONSIBILITY REVIEW   Advertisers and their agencies must be sure their "creative" advertising does not overstep social and legal norms. Most marketers work hard to communicate openly and honestly with consumers. Still, abuses occur, and public policy makers have developed a substantial body of laws and regulations to govern advertising.

Under U.S. law, companies must avoid false or deceptive advertising. Advertisers must not make false claims, such as stating that a product cures something when it does not. They must avoid false demonstrations, such as using sand-covered plexiglass instead of sandpaper to demonstrate that a razor blade can shave sandpaper. It is illegal in the United States to create ads that have the capacity to deceive, even though no one may actually be deceived. For example, a floor wax cannot be advertised as giving six months' protection unless it does so under typical conditions, and a diet bread cannot be advertised as having fewer calories simply because its slices are thinner. The problem is how to tell the difference between deception and "puffery"—simple exaggerations not intended to be believed.

Sellers in the United States are legally obligated to avoid bait-and-switch advertising that attracts buyers under false pretenses. Suppose a seller advertises a sewing machine at $149. When consumers try to buy the advertised machine, the seller cannot then refuse to sell it, downplay its features, show a faulty one, or promise unreasonable delivery dates in order to switch the buyer to a more expensive machine.[25]

To be socially responsible, advertisers must be careful not to offend ethnic groups, racial minorities, or special-interest groups. Consider the following examples.[26]

- A commercial for Black Flag insecticide was altered after a veterans group protested the playing of Taps over dead bugs.
- Ads for Calvin Klein apparel, featuring the waifish model Kate Moss, have come under attack from Boycott Anorexic Marketing.

Some companies have begun to build ad campaigns on a platform of social responsibility.

Ethical Funds When people buy shares in Ethical Funds, they know that fund managers will not invest in corporations involved in the production of military weapons, tobacco, nuclear power; and those with unfair employment practices, poor environmental records, or companies that support reactionary political regimes. A tough-talking advertising campaign for Ethical Funds shows scenes of child labor and people dying from cancer, presumably caused by smoking. The ad asks, "Do you know where your money goes?"

John Linthwaite, president of Vancouver-based Ethical Funds, Inc., says its emphasis is on research. It digs deep to weed out companies that do not meet its ethical standards while ensuring financially sound investments. Ethical Funds has grown from $100 million in assets to more than $2 billion over the last decade.[27]

deciding on media and measuring effectiveness

After choosing the message, the advertiser's next task is to choose media to carry it. The steps here are deciding on desired reach, frequency, and impact; choosing among major media types; selecting specific media vehicles; deciding on media timing; and deciding on geographical media allocation. Then the results of these decisions need to be evaluated.

deciding on reach, frequency, and impact

Media selection is finding the most cost-effective media to deliver the desired number and type of exposures to the target audience. What do we mean by the desired number of exposures? Presumably, the advertiser is seeking a specified advertising objective and response from the target audience—for example, a target level of product trial. The rate of product trial will depend, among other things, on level of brand awareness. Suppose the rate of product trial increases at a diminishing rate with the level of audience awareness, as shown in Figure 20.2(a). If the advertiser seeks a product trial rate of (say) T^*, it will be necessary to achieve a brand awareness level of A^*.

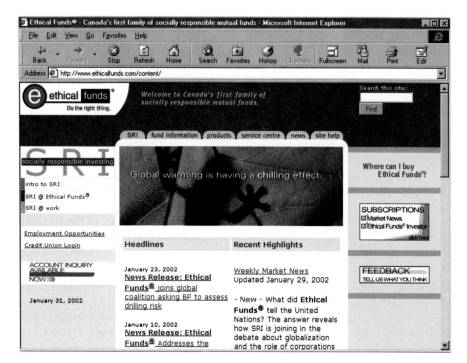

Ethical Funds' homepage carries its message: "Socially responsible investing."

The next task is to find out how many exposures, E^*, will produce a level of audience awareness of A^*. The effect of exposures on audience awareness depends on the exposures' reach, frequency, and impact:

- *Reach (R):* The number of different persons or households exposed to a particular media schedule at least once during a specified time period.
- *Frequency (F):* The number of times within the specified time period that an average person or household is exposed to the message.
- *Impact (I):* The qualitative value of an exposure through a given medium (thus a food ad in Good Housekeeping would have a higher impact than in the Police Gazette).

Figure 20.2(b) shows the relationship between audience awareness and reach. Audience awareness will be greater, the higher the exposures' reach, frequency, and

figure **20.2**

Relationship Among Trial, Awareness, and the Exposure Function impact. There are important trade-offs among reach, frequency, and impact. Suppose the planner has an advertising budget of $1,000,000 and the cost per thousand exposures of average quality is $5. This means the advertiser can buy 200,000,000 exposures ($1,000,000 ÷ [$5/1,000]). If the advertiser seeks an average exposure frequency of 10, then the advertiser can reach 20,000,000 people (200,000,000 ÷ 10) with the given budget. But if the advertiser wants higher-quality media costing $10 per thousand exposures, it will be able to reach only 10,000,000 people unless it is willing to lower the desired exposure frequency.

The relationship between reach, frequency, and impact is captured in the following concepts:

- *Total number of exposures (E):* This is the reach times the average frequency; that is, $E = R \times F$. This measure is referred to as the *gross rating points* (GRP). If a given media schedule reaches 80 percent of the homes with an average exposure frequency of 3, the media schedule is said to have a GRP of 240 (80×3). If another media schedule has a GRP of 300, it is said to have more weight, but we cannot tell how this weight breaks down into reach and frequency.
- *Weighted number of exposures (WE):* This is the reach times average frequency times average impact, that is $WE = R \times F \times I$.

The media planner has to figure out the most cost-effective combination of reach, frequency, and impact. Reach is most important when launching new products, flanker brands, extensions of well-known brands, or infrequently purchased brands; or going after an undefined target market. Frequency is most important where there are strong competitors, a complex story to tell, high consumer resistance, or a frequent-purchase cycle.[28]

Many advertisers believe a target audience needs a large number of exposures for the advertising to work. Others doubt the value of high frequency. They believe that after people see the same ad a few times, they either act on it, get irritated by it, or stop noticing it. Herbert Krugman asserted that three exposures might be enough:

> The first exposure is by definition unique. As with the initial exposure to anything, a "What is it?" type of cognitive response dominates the reaction. The second exposure to a stimulus . . . produces several effects. One may be the cognitive reaction that characterized the first exposure, if the audience missed much of the message the first time around. . . . More often, an evaluative "What of it?" response replaces the "What is it?" response. . . . The third exposure constitutes a reminder, if a decision to buy based on the evaluations has not been acted on. The third exposure is also the beginning of disengagement and withdrawal of attention from a completed episode.[29]

Krugman's thesis has to be qualified. He means three actual impressions or *advertising exposures*—the person sees the ad three times. These exposures should not be confused with *vehicle exposures*. If only half the magazine readers look at magazine ads, or if the readers look at ads only every other issue, then the advertising exposure is only half of the vehicle exposures. Most research services estimate vehicle exposures, not ad exposures. A media strategist would have to buy more vehicle exposures than three to achieve Krugman's three "hits."[30] Another factor arguing for repetition is that of forgetting. The job of repetition is partly to put the message back into memory. The higher the forgetting rate associated with a brand, product category, or message, the higher the warranted level of repetition. However, repetition is not enough; ads wear out and viewers tune out. Advertisers should not coast on a tired ad but insist on fresh executions by their advertising agency.

choosing among major media types

The media planner has to know the capacity of the major media types to deliver reach, frequency, and impact. The major advertising media along with their costs, advantages, and limitations are profiled in Table 20.1.

Media planners make their choice among media categories by considering the following variables:

table **20.1**	Profiles of Major Media Types	
Medium	**Advantages**	**Limitations**
Newspapers	Flexibility; timeliness; good local market coverage; broad acceptance; high believability	Short life; poor reproduction quality; small "pass-along" audience
Television	Combines sight, sound, and motion; appealing to the senses; high attention; high reach	High absolute cost; high clutter; fleeting exposure; less audience selectivity
Direct mail	Audience selectivity; flexibility; no ad competition within the same medium; personalization	Relatively high cost; "junk mail" image
Radio	Mass use; high geographic and demographic selectivity; low cost	Audio presentation only; lower attention than television; nonstandardized rate structures; fleeting exposure
Magazines	High geographic and demographic selectivity; credibility and prestige; high-quality reproduction; long life; good pass-along readership	Long ad purchase lead time; some waste circulation; no guarantee of position
Outdoor	Flexibility; high repeat exposure; low cost; low competition	Limited audience selectivity; creative limitations
Yellow Pages	Excellent local coverage; high believability; wide reach; low cost	High competition; long ad purchase lead time; creative limitations
Newsletters	Very high selectivity; full control; interactive opportunities; relative low costs	Costs could run away
Brochures	Flexibility; full control; can dramatize messages	Overproduction could lead to runaway costs
Telephone	Many users; opportunity to give a personal touch	Relative high cost unless volunteers are used
Internet	High selectivity; interactive possibilities; relatively low cost	Relatively new media with a low number of users in some countries

- *Target-audience media habits:* For example, radio and television are the most effective media for reaching teenagers.
- *Product characteristics:* Media types have different potentials for demonstration, visualization, explanation, believability, and color. Women's dresses are best shown in color magazines, and Polaroid cameras are best demonstrated on television.
- *Message characteristics:* Timeliness and information content will influence media choice. A message announcing a major sale tomorrow will require radio, TV, or newspaper. A message containing a great deal of technical data might require specialized magazines or mailings.
- *Cost:* Television is very expensive, whereas newspaper advertising is relatively inexpensive. What counts is the cost-per-thousand exposures.

NEW MEDIA   Ideas about media impact and cost must be reexamined periodically. For a long time, television was dominant. Then researchers began to notice reduced effectiveness, which was due to increased commercial clutter (advertisers beamed shorter and more numerous commercials at the audience), increased "zipping and zapping" of commercials (aided by the arrival of new TV systems such as TiVo and Replay TV), and lower viewing owing to the growth in cable TV and VCRs. Furthermore, television advertising costs rose faster than other media costs. Several companies found that a combination of print ads and television commercials often did a better job than television commercials alone.

Another reason for review is the continuous emergence of new media. **Advertorials** are print ads that offer editorial content and are difficult to distinguish from newspaper or magazine contents; **infomercials** are TV commercials that appear to be 30-minute TV shows but are advertisements for products. Advertisers have substantially increased their spending on outdoor media over the last decade. Outdoor advertising provides an excellent way to reach important local consumer segments. Cable television now reaches a majority of U.S. households and produces billions of dollars in advertising revenue a year. Cable systems make it easier to reach select groups. (See "Marketing for the New Economy: New Ad Formats.")

Rust and Oliver see proliferation of new media as hastening the death of traditional mass-media advertising as we know it. They see a greater amount of direct producer–consumer interaction, with benefits to both parties. Producers gain more information about their customers; customers gain greater control because they can choose whether to receive an advertising message or not.[31]

ALLOCATING THE BUDGET   Given the abundance of media, the planner must first decide how to allocate the budget to the major media types. In launching a new biscuit,

marketing for the new economy

New Ad Formats

Marketers are using creative and unexpected ad placements that they hope will grab consumers' attention. One new strategy from Captivate Network involves equipping office and hotel elevators with television monitors that display news, weather, and advertising. The Pump Radio Network installed speakers next to gas pumps at filling stations. They broadcast 120 seconds of ads to captive drivers. Internet service provider EarthLink placed ads in restrooms of restaurants and bars touting its Internet privacy policy with the slogan "EarthLink protects your privates." Coca-Cola mounted illuminated rectangular displays called "light boxes" on New York subway tunnel walls to advertise its Dasani brand water.

Companies are even taking to the seas to get their message out: Software company Oracle used a boat to tow a floating banner bearing the company's logo across San Francisco Bay. Guerrilla marketing—or street-level marketing—is another new technique, illustrated by a campaign from ABC Television. As part of its "Yellow" campaign promoting its fall 2000 prime-time lineup, ABC went to grocery stores and put stickers reading "Another fine use of yellow: ABC" on bunches of bananas. ABC also placed signs on trash cans at beaches across the nation that read "It's a beautiful day, what are you doing outside?"

Earthlink: high-speed Internet Service Provider.

Fearing commercial-zapping technology, marketers are finding inventive ways to advertise during actual television broadcasts. Sports fans are familiar with the virtual logos networks add digitally to the playing field. Invisible to spectators at the event, these ads look just like painted-on logos to home viewers. Product placements, a classic marketing tactic, are also now being added digitally to programs.

Pillsbury might decide to allocate $3 million to daytime network television, $2 million to women's magazines, $1 million to daily newspapers in 20 major markets, and $50,000 to maintaining its home page on the Internet.

All of this must be planned with the awareness that people are increasingly time-starved. People are assaulted daily by ads and information from traditional media plus e-mail, voice mail, and instant messages. There is little time for giving thought to one's experiences, let alone time for hobbies and other diversions. Attention is becoming a scarce currency, and advertisers will need strong devices to capture people's attention.[32] As one example of how more money has to be spent attracting attention than on the product itself, the film *The Blair Witch Project*, which cost only $350,000 to make, cost $11 million to market.

selecting specific vehicles

The media planner must search for the most cost-effective vehicles within each chosen media type. The advertiser who decides to buy 30 seconds of advertising on network television can pay $154,000 for a popular prime-time show such as *Law and Order*,

Traditional in-show product placements are becoming more obvious. Many companies, including Target, Reebok, PepsiCo, GM, and Anheuser-Busch, spent $12 million per season to sponsor CBS's reality-TV show *Survivor*. In return, they received exclusive product placements. For example, contestants competed for a bag of Doritos, or spent the night in the camper-like Pontiac Aztec. Some television shows even revolve around a central product placement: Ford and the WB network created a commercial-free program in 2001 called *No Boundaries*, which features Ford SUVs during the show.

Another promising new media site is the store itself. Some supermarkets are selling space on their floors for company logos, experimenting with talking shelves, and introducing "video-carts," which contain a computerized screen that carries consumer-benefit information ("cauliflower is rich in vitamin C") and advertiser promotions ("20¢ off on White Star Tuna this week"). Ads also appear in best-selling paperback books, sports arenas, movie theaters, and movie videotapes. Written material such as annual reports, data sheets, catalogs, and newsletters increasingly carry ads. Many companies include advertising inserts in monthly bills. Some companies mail audiotapes or videotapes to prospects.

Here are other emerging media:

- *Digital magazines (or digizines):* Magazines such as *Salon* and *Launch* are available only on the Internet. Digizines are much cheaper to start up and operate than print magazines.
- *Interactive TV:* Combined computer, telephone, and TV hookups have made it possible for people to participate in two-way communication via their television sets. Interactive TV allows consumers to use a computer keyboard to communicate directly with sellers on their TV screens. (The technology is still in the testing phase.)

- *Fax on demand:* Fax-on-demand technology allows businesses to store information in a fax technology program. Customers who need information call a toll-free number, and the program automatically faxes the information to them within a few minutes. Customers can access information 24 hours a day, 7 days a week, and the service can be set up for as little as $1,000.
- *Wireless information on demand:* Users of wireless devices (mobile phones, personal digital assistants) can pay a monthly fee and retrieve stock market activity, sports scores, city maps, daily humor, and newspaper headlines.

These new marketing strategies and tactics must be judged for how they contribute to brand equity. Unique ad placements designed to break through clutter may also be perceived as invasive and obtrusive. There has been consumer backlash when people see ads in traditionally ad-free spaces, such as in schools, on police cruisers, and in doctor's waiting rooms. Consumer advocate Ralph Nader says, "What these people on Madison Avenue don't understand is consumers will reach a saturation point." Not all Americans are turned off, however, by the proliferation of advertising. One marketing consultant says, "Kids 18 and under aren't thinking twice about it. Branded merchandise is just the landscape of their lives." Still, marketers must keep a careful eye on the consumer reaction to new techniques.

Sources: James Betzold, "Jaded Riders Are Ever-Tougher Sell," *Advertising Age*, July 9, 2001; Michael McCarthy, "Ads Are Here, There, Everywhere," *USA Today*, June 19, 2001; Kipp Cheng, "Captivating Audiences," *Brandweek*, November 29, 1999; Michael McCarthy, "Critics Target 'Omnipresent' Ads," *USA Today*, April 16, 2001; Beth Snyder Bulik, "Who Wants to Use AT&T," *Business 2.0*, July 10, 2001; Douglas A. Blackmon, "New Ad Vehicles: Police Car, School Bus, Garbage Truck," *Wall Street Journal*, February 20, 1996.

$650,000 for especially popular programs like *Frasier* and *ER*, or $1.3 million for an event like the Super Bowl.[33] In making choices, the planner has to rely on measurement services that provide estimates of audience size, composition, and media cost.

Audience size has several possible measures:

- *Circulation:* The number of physical units carrying the advertising.
- *Audience:* The number of people exposed to the vehicle. (If the vehicle has pass-on readership, then the audience is larger than circulation.)
- *Effective audience:* The number of people with target audience characteristics exposed to the vehicle.
- *Effective ad-exposed audience:* The number of people with target audience characteristics who actually saw the ad.

Media planners calculate the cost per thousand persons reached by a vehicle. If a full-page, four-color ad in *Newsweek* costs $84,000 and *Newsweek*'s estimated readership is 3 million people, the cost of exposing the ad to 1,000 persons is approximately $28. The same ad in *BusinessWeek* may cost $30,000 but reach only 775,000 persons—at a cost-per-thousand of $39. The media planner ranks each magazine by cost-per-thousand and favors magazines with the lowest cost-per-thousand for reaching target consumers. The magazines themselves often put together a "reader profile" for their advertisers, summarizing the characteristics of the magazine's readers with respect to age, income, residence, marital status, and leisure activities.

Several adjustments have to be applied to the cost-per-thousand measure. First, the measure should be adjusted for *audience quality*. For a baby lotion ad, a magazine read by 1 million young mothers would have an exposure value of 1 million; if read by 1 million old men, it would have almost a zero exposure value. Second, the exposure value should be adjusted for the *audience-attention probability*. Readers of *Vogue* pay more attention to ads than do readers of *Newsweek*. Third, the exposure value should be adjusted for the magazine's *editorial quality* (prestige and believability). Fourth, the exposure value should be adjusted for the magazine's *ad placement policies and extra services* (such as regional or occupational editions and lead-time requirements).

Media planners are increasingly using more sophisticated measures of effectiveness and employing them in mathematical models to arrive at the best media mix. Many advertising agencies use a computer program to select the initial media and then make further improvements based on subjective factors.[34]

deciding on media timing

In choosing media, the advertiser faces both a macroscheduling and a microscheduling problem. The macroscheduling problem involves scheduling the advertising in relation to seasons and the business cycle. Suppose 70 percent of a product's sales occur between June and September. The firm can vary its advertising expenditures to follow the seasonal pattern, to oppose the seasonal pattern, or to be constant throughout the year. Most firms pursue a seasonal policy. Yet some years ago, a soft-drink manufacturer put more money into off-season advertising. This resulted in increased nonseasonal consumption of its brand, while not hurting seasonal consumption. Other soft-drink manufacturers started to do the same, and the result was a more balanced consumption pattern.

Jay Forrester has proposed using his "industrial dynamics" methodology to test cyclical advertising policies.[35] He believes that advertising has a delayed impact on consumer awareness; awareness has a delayed impact on factory sales; and factory sales have a delayed impact on advertising expenditures. These time-lag relationships can be studied and formulated mathematically into a computer-simulation model. The model can simulate alternative timing strategies to assess varying impacts on company sales, costs, and profits. Rao and Miller also developed a lag (delay) model to relate a brand's share to advertising and promotional expenditures on a market-by-market basis. They tested their model successfully with 5 Lever brands in 15 districts, relating market share to dollars spent on TV, print, price-off, and trade promotions.[36]

Alfred Kuehn developed a model to explore how advertising should be timed for frequently purchased, highly seasonal, low-cost grocery products.[37] He showed that the appropriate timing pattern depends on the degree of advertising carryover and the amount of habitual behavior in customer brand choice. **Carryover** refers to the rate at which the effect of an advertising expenditure wears out with the passage of time. A carryover of 0.75 per month means that the current effect of a past advertising expenditure is 75 percent of its level in the previous month. **Habitual behavior** indicates how much brand holdover occurs independent of the level of advertising. High habitual purchasing, say 0.90, means that 90 percent of the buyers repeat their brand choice in the next period.

Kuehn found that when there is no advertising carryover or habitual purchasing, the decision maker is justified in using a percentage-of-sales rule to budget advertising. The optimal timing pattern for advertising expenditures coincides with the expected seasonal pattern of industry sales. But if there is advertising carryover or habitual purchasing, it would be better to time advertising to lead sales. Advertising expenditures should peak before sales peak. Lead time should be greater the higher the carryover; furthermore, the advertising expenditures should be steadier the greater the habitual purchasing.

The microscheduling problem calls for allocating advertising expenditures within a short period to obtain maximum impact. Suppose the firm decides to buy 30 radio spots in the month of September. Figure 20.3 shows several possible patterns. The left side shows that advertising messages for the month can be concentrated ("burst" advertising), dispersed continuously throughout the month, or dispersed intermittently. The top side shows that the advertising messages can be beamed with a level, rising, falling, or alternating frequency.

The most effective pattern depends on the communication objectives in relation to the nature of the product, target customers, distribution channels, and other marketing factors. The timing pattern should consider three factors. *Buyer turnover* expresses the rate at which new buyers enter the market; the higher this rate, the more continuous the advertising should be. *Purchase frequency* is the number of times during the period that

figure **20.3**

Classification of Advertising Timing Patterns

the average buyer buys the product; the higher the purchase frequency, the more continuous the advertising should be. The *forgetting rate* is the rate at which the buyer forgets the brand; the higher the forgetting rate, the more continuous the advertising should be.

In launching a new product, the advertiser has to choose among ad continuity, concentration, flighting, and pulsing. **Continuity** is achieved by scheduling exposures evenly throughout a given period. Generally, advertisers use continuous advertising in expanding market situations, with frequently purchased items, and in tightly defined buyer categories. **Concentration** calls for spending all the advertising dollars in a single period. This makes sense for products with one selling season or holiday. **Flighting** calls for advertising for some period, followed by a hiatus with no advertising, followed by a second period of advertising activity. It is used when funding is limited, the purchase cycle is relatively infrequent, and with seasonal items. **Pulsing** is continuous advertising at low-weight levels reinforced periodically by waves of heavier activity. Pulsing draws on the strength of continuous advertising and flights to create a compromise scheduling strategy.[38] Those who favor pulsing feel that the audience will learn the message more thoroughly, and money can be saved.

deciding on geographical allocation

A company has to decide how to allocate its advertising budget over space as well as over time. The company makes "national buys" when it places ads on national TV networks or in nationally circulated magazines. It makes "spot buys" when it buys TV time in just a few markets or in regional editions of magazines. These markets are called *areas of dominant influence* (ADIs) or *designated marketing areas* (DMAs), and ads reach a market 40 to 60 miles from a city center. The company makes "local buys" when it advertises in local newspapers, radio, or outdoor sites. Consider the following example.

Pizza Hut Pizza Hut levies a 4 percent advertising fee on its franchisees. It spends half of its budget on national media and half on regional and local media. Some national advertising is wasted because of low penetration in certain areas. Even though Pizza Hut may have a 30 percent share of the franchised pizza market nationally, this share may vary from 5 percent in some cities to 70 percent in others. The franchisees in the higher market-share cities want much more advertising money spent in their areas, but Pizza Hut does not have enough money to cover the whole nation by region. National advertising offers efficiency but fails to address the different local situations effectively.

evaluating advertising effectiveness

Good planning and control of advertising depend on measures of advertising effectiveness. Yet the amount of fundamental research on effectiveness is appallingly small. According to Jay Forrester, "probably no more than 1/5 of 1% of total advertising expenditure is used to achieve an enduring understanding of how to spend the other 99.8%."[39]

Most measurement of advertising effectiveness deals with specific ads and campaigns. Most of the money is spent by agencies on pretesting ads, and much less is spent on evaluating their effectiveness. A proposed campaign should be tested in one or a few cities first and its impact evaluated before rolling it out nationally. One company tested its new campaign first in Phoenix. The campaign bombed, and the company saved all the money that it would have spent by going national.

Most advertisers try to measure the communication effect of an ad—that is, its potential effect on awareness, knowledge, or preference. They would also like to measure the ad's sales effect.

COMMUNICATION-EFFECT RESEARCH **Communication-effect research** seeks to determine whether an ad is communicating effectively. Called *copy testing*, it can be done before an ad is put into media and after it is printed or broadcast.

There are three major methods of advertising pretesting. The *consumer feedback method* asks consumers for their reactions to a proposed ad. They respond to such questions as these:

1. What is the main message you get from this ad?
2. What do you think they want you to know, believe, or do?
3. How likely is it that this ad will influence you to undertake the implied action?
4. What works well in the ad and what works poorly?
5. How does the ad make you feel?
6. Where is the best place to reach you with this message? Where would you be most likely to notice it and pay attention to it? Where are you when you make decisions about this action?

Portfolio tests ask consumers to view or listen to a portfolio of advertisements, taking as much time as they need. Consumers are then asked to recall all the ads and their content, aided or unaided by the interviewer. Recall level indicates an ad's ability to stand out and to have its message understood and remembered.

Laboratory tests use equipment to measure physiological reactions—heartbeat, blood pressure, pupil dilation, galvanic skin response, perspiration—to an ad; or consumers may be asked to turn a knob to indicate their moment-to-moment liking or interest while viewing sequenced material. These tests measure attention-getting power but reveal nothing about impact on beliefs, attitudes, or intentions. Table 20.2 describes some specific advertising research techniques.

Haley, Stafforoni, and Fox argue that current copy-testing methods have become so familiar and well-established that it is easy to overlook their sizable limitations. These methods tend to be excessively rational and verbal, and they tend to rely primarily on respondents' playback in one form or another. They argue that marketers need to take more account of ads' nonverbal elements, which can be very strong influences on behavior.[40]

Advertisers are also interested in posttesting the overall communication impact of a completed campaign. If a company hoped to increase brand awareness from 20 percent to 50 percent and succeeded in increasing it to only 30 percent, then the company is not spending enough, its ads are poor, or some other factor has been ignored.

---

table 20.2

Advertising Research Techniques

For Print Ads. Starch and Gallup & Robinson, Inc. are two widely used print pretesting services. Test ads are placed in magazines, which are then circulated to consumers. These consumers are contacted later and interviewed. Recall and recognition tests are used to determine advertising effectiveness.

For Broadcast Ads. *In-home tests:* A videotape is taken into the homes of target consumers, who then view the commercials.

Trailer tests: In a trailer in a shopping center, shoppers are shown the products and given an opportunity to select a series of brands. They then view commercials and are given coupons to be used in the shopping center. Redemption rates indicate commercials' influence on purchase behavior.

Theater tests: Consumers are invited to a theater to view a potential new television series along with some commercials. Before the show begins, consumers indicate preferred brands in different categories; after the viewing, consumers again choose preferred brands. Preference changes measure the commercials' persuasive power.

On-air tests: Respondents are recruited to watch a program on a regular TV channel during the test commercial or are selected based on their having viewed the program. They are asked questions about commercial recall.

figure 20.4

Formula for Measuring
Sales Impact of Advertising

SALES-EFFECT RESEARCH   What sales are generated by an ad that increases brand awareness by 20 percent and brand preference by 10 percent? Advertising's sales effect is generally harder to measure than its communication effect. Sales are influenced by many factors, such as the product's features, price, and availability, as well as competitors' actions. The fewer or more controllable these other factors are, the easier it is to measure effect on sales. The sales impact is easiest to measure in direct-marketing situations and hardest to measure in brand or corporate image-building advertising.

Companies are generally interested in finding out whether they are overspending or underspending on advertising. One approach to answering this question is to work with the formulation shown in Figure 20.4.

A company's *share of advertising expenditures* produces a *share of voice* (i.e., percentage of company advertising of that product to all advertising of that product) that earns a *share of consumers' minds and hearts* and ultimately, a *share of market*. J. O. Peckham studied the relationship between share of voice and share of market for several consumer products over a number of years and found a 1:1 ratio for established products and a 1.5–2.0:1.0 ratio for new products.[41]

Researchers try to measure the sales impact through analyzing either historical or experimental data. The *historical approach* involves correlating past sales to past advertising expenditures using advanced statistical techniques. Kristian Palda studied the effect of advertising expenditures on the sales of Lydia Pinkham's Vegetable Compound between 1908 and 1960.[42] He calculated the short-term and long-term marginal sales effects of advertising. The marginal advertising dollars increased sales by only $.50 in the short term, suggesting that Pinkham spent too much on advertising; but the long-term marginal sales effect was three times as large. Palda calculated a posttax marginal rate of return on company advertising of 37 percent over the whole period.

Montgomery and Silk estimated the sales effectiveness of three communication tools used in the pharmaceutical industry.[43] A drug company spent 38 percent of its communication budget on direct mail, 32 percent on samples and literature, and 29 percent on journal advertising. Yet the sales-effects research indicated that journal advertising, the least-used communication tool, had the highest long-run effectiveness, followed by samples and literature, and then by direct mail.

Other researchers use an *experimental design* to measure advertising's sales impact. Here is an example.

Information Resources, Inc.   Information Resources offers a service called BehaviorScan that provides marketers in the United States with data about advertising effectiveness by tracking consumer purchases tied to specific advertising. Consumers in test markets who sign up to be members of IRI's "Shoppers Hotline" panel agree to have microcomputers record when the TV set is on and to which station it is tuned, while electronic scanners record UPC codes of their household purchases at supermarkets. IRI has the capability to send different commercials to different homes. The company also conducts in-store tests in most chains and in most markets in the United States to study the effects of promotions, displays, coupons, store features, and packaging. An IRI review of 389 research studies found that although advertising could have long-term effects on sales, promotion effects were almost always short-term.[44]

A growing number of researchers are striving to measure the sales effect of advertising expenditures instead of settling for communication-effect measures.[45] Millward Brown International has conducted tracking studies in the United Kingdom for many years to provide information to help advertisers decide whether their advertising is benefiting their brand.[46] The findings are not always positive. Gerald Tellis analyzed household purchases of 12 key brands of a frequently purchased consumer product and concluded that advertising appears effective in increasing the volume purchased by loyal buyers, but less effective in winning new buyers. Advertising appears unlikely to have some cumulative effect that leads to loyalty; rather, features, displays, and especially price have a stronger impact on response than does advertising.[47] These findings did not sit well with the advertising community, and several people attacked Tellis's data and methodology.

sales promotion

Sales promotion, a key ingredient in marketing campaigns, consists of a diverse collection of incentive tools, mostly short term, designed to stimulate quicker or greater purchase of particular products or services by consumers or the trade.[48]

Whereas advertising offers a *reason* to buy, sales promotion offers an *incentive* to buy. Sales promotion includes tools for *consumer promotion* (samples, coupons, cash refund offers, prices off, premiums, prizes, patronage rewards, free trials, warranties, tie-in promotions, cross-promotions, point-of-purchase displays, and demonstrations); *trade promotion* (prices off, advertising and display allowances, and free goods); and *business* and *sales-force promotion* (trade shows and conventions, contests for sales reps, and specialty advertising). These tools are used by most organizations, including nonprofit organizations. Churches, for example, often sponsor bingo games, theater parties, testimonial dinners, and raffles.

A decade ago, the advertising-to-sales-promotion ratio was about 60:40. Today, in many consumer packaged-goods companies, sales promotion accounts for 65 to 75 percent of the combined budget. Sales-promotion expenditures have been increasing as a percentage of budget expenditure annually for the last two decades. Several factors contribute to this rapid growth, particularly in consumer markets.[49] Promotion is now more accepted by top management as an effective sales tool; more product managers are qualified to use sales-promotion tools; and product managers are under greater pressure to increase current sales. In addition, the number of brands has increased; competitors use promotions frequently; many brands are seen as similar; consumers are more price-oriented; the trade has demanded more deals from manufacturers; and advertising efficiency has declined because of rising costs, media clutter, and legal restraints.

The rapid growth of sales-promotion media has created clutter similar to advertising clutter. Manufacturers have to find ways to rise above the clutter—for instance, by offering larger coupon-redemption values or using more dramatic point-of-purchase displays or demonstrations.

purpose of sales promotion

Sales-promotion tools vary in their specific objectives. A free sample stimulates consumer trial, whereas a free management-advisory service aims at cementing a long-term relationship with a retailer.

Sellers use incentive-type promotions to attract new triers, to reward loyal customers, and to increase the repurchase rates of occasional users. Sales promotions often attract brand switchers, who are primarily looking for low price, good value, or premiums. Sales promotions are unlikely to turn them into loyal users. Sales promotions used in markets of high brand similarity produce a high sales response in the short run but little permanent gain in market share. In markets of high brand dissimilarity, sales promotions can alter market shares permanently.

Farris and Quelch cite a number of sales-promotion benefits flowing to manufacturers and consumers.[50] Sales promotions enable manufacturers to adjust to short-term variations in supply and demand. They enable manufacturers to test how high a list price they can charge, because they can always discount it. They induce consumers to try new products instead of never straying from current ones. They lead to more varied retail formats, such as the everyday-low-price store and the promotional-pricing store. They promote greater consumer awareness of prices. They permit manufacturers to sell more than they would normally sell at the list price. They help the manufacturer adapt programs to different consumer segments. Consumers themselves enjoy some satisfaction from being smart shoppers when they take advantage of price specials.

Today, many marketing managers first estimate what they need to spend in trade promotion, then what they need to spend in consumer promotion. Whatever is left they will budget for advertising. There is a danger, however, in letting advertising take a back seat, because advertising typically acts to build brand loyalty. The question of whether or not sales promotion weakens brand loyalty is subject to different interpretations. Sales promotion, with its incessant prices off, coupons, deals, and premiums, may devalue the product offering in buyers' minds. Buyers learn that the list price is largely a fiction. However, before jumping to any conclusion, we need to distinguish between price promotions and added-value promotions. These examples show how certain types of sales promotion can actually enhance brand image.

Pine-Sol   The makers of Pine-Sol, a general liquid cleaning agent, ran a "Pine-Sol in Pine Valley" sweepstakes in which Pine Valley was the habitat of the TV soap opera *All My Children*. Sweepstake winners would travel to Los Angeles to meet the stars and watch four days of filming. This association of an ordinary cleaning agent with glamorous stars enhanced the Pine-Sol brand image.

AKAI   AKAI, a Japanese manufacturer of stereo equipment and TV sets, managed to become a TV-set market leader in India by running value-added sales promotions. It offered good trade-in value on black-and-white TV sets at the purchase of a new color TV set. At other times, it would offer a free watch, or calculator or radio, along with the purchase of a new TV set. This steady promotion made AKAI a very popular brand in India, and competitors such as Sony were not free to compete in the same way.

However, usually, when a brand is price promoted too often, the consumer begins to devalue it and buy it mainly when it goes on sale. So there is risk in putting a well-known brand leader on promotion over 30 percent of the time.[51] Dominant brands offer deals less frequently, because most deals only subsidize current users. Brown's study of 2,500 instant-coffee buyers concluded that:

- Sales promotions yield faster and more measurable responses in sales than advertising does.
- Sales promotions do not tend to yield new, long-term buyers in mature markets because they attract mainly deal-prone consumers who switch among brands as deals become available.
- Loyal brand buyers tend not to change their buying patterns as a result of competitive promotion.
- Advertising appears to be capable of deepening brand loyalty.[52]

There is also evidence that price promotions do not build permanent total-category volume.
Small-share competitors find it advantageous to use sales promotion, because they cannot afford to match the market leaders' large advertising budgets; nor can they obtain shelf space without offering trade allowances or stimulate consumer trial without offering incentives. Price competition is often used by a small brand seeking to enlarge its share, but it is less effective for a category leader whose growth lies in expanding the entire category.[53] The upshot is that many consumer packaged-goods companies feel they are forced to use more sales promotion than they wish. They blame the heavy use of sales promotion for decreasing brand loyalty, increasing consumer price-sensitivity, brand-quality-image dilution, and a focus on short-run marketing planning.

major decisions in sales promotion

In using sales promotion, a company must establish its objectives, select the tools, develop the program, pretest the program, implement and control it, and evaluate the results.

ESTABLISHING OBJECTIVES   Sales-promotion objectives are derived from broader promotion objectives, which are derived from more basic marketing objectives developed for the product. For consumers, objectives include encouraging purchase of larger-sized units, building trial among nonusers, and attracting switchers away from competitors' brands. For retailers, objectives include persuading retailers to carry new items and higher levels of inventory, encouraging off-season buying, encouraging stocking of related items, offsetting competitive promotions, building brand loyalty, and gaining entry into new retail outlets. For the sales force, objectives include encouraging support of a new product or model, encouraging more prospecting, and stimulating off-season sales.[54] (See "Marketing Memo: Sales Promotions as Brand Builders.")

SELECTING CONSUMER-PROMOTION TOOLS   The promotion planner should take into account the type of market, sales-promotion objectives, competitive conditions, and each tool's cost-effectiveness.

The main consumer-promotion tools are summarized in Table 20.3. We can distinguish between *manufacturer promotions* and *retailer promotions*. The former are illustrated by the auto industry's frequent use of rebates, gifts to motivate test-drives and purchases, and high-value trade-in credit. The latter include price cuts, feature advertising, retailer coupons, and retailer contests or premiums. We can also distinguish between sales-promotion tools that are "consumer-franchise building," which reinforce the consumer's brand preference, and those that are not. The former impart a selling message along with the deal, as in the case of free samples, frequency awards, coupons when they include a selling message, and premiums when they are related to the product. Sales-promotion tools that are not consumer-franchise building include price-off packs, consumer premiums not related to a product, contests and sweepstakes, consumer refund offers, and trade allowances.

Sales promotion seems most effective when used together with advertising. In one study, a price promotion alone produced only a 15 percent increase in sales volume. When combined with feature advertising, sales volume increased 19 percent; when combined with feature advertising and a point-of-purchase display, sales volume increased 24 percent.[55]

Many large companies have a sales-promotion manager whose job is to help brand managers choose the right promotional tool. The following example shows how one firm determined the appropriate tool.

Coolsavings.com   Consumers can click on coolsavings.com, which has 17 million members, and select and print out coupons of their choice redeemable at local stores. The most popular coupon categories are groceries, books, health, music, beauty, fast food, apparel, and toys. The fact that consumers are choosing the coupons is resulting in a 57 percent redemption rate, compared to the normal 1.2 percent redemption rate of Sunday paper coupons. Merchants are pleased because they can build a relationship with the customers that initially buy from them with coupons. E-couponing also covers cases where consumers see a code in a print ad that they can type into an online site such as CDNow and get a further discount.[56]

SELECTING TRADE-PROMOTION TOOLS   Manufacturers use a number of trade-promotion tools (Table 20.4). Surprisingly, a higher proportion of the promotion pie is devoted to trade-promotion tools (46.9 percent) than to consumer promotion (27.9 percent), with media advertising capturing the remaining 25.2 percent. Manufacturers award money to the trade (1) to persuade the retailer or wholesaler to carry the brand; (2) to persuade the retailer or wholesaler to carry more units than the normal amount; (3) to induce retailers to promote the brand by featuring, display, and price reductions; and (4) to stimulate retailers and their sales clerks to push the product.

The growing power of large retailers has increased their ability to demand trade promotion at the expense of consumer promotion and advertising.[57] These retailers depend on promotion money from the manufacturers. No manufacturer could unilaterally stop offering trade allowances without losing retailer support. The company's sales force and its brand managers are often at odds over trade promotion. The sales force says that

Marketing MEMO

Sales Promotions as Brand Builders

Building brand awareness is a long-term process. What a brand does today predicts what it will do tomorrow. Sales promotions are short term and temporary. Here are some tips on how to make a sales promotion an effective brand-building tool.

- *Make sure the promotion is justified:* A new store opening, a company anniversary, and other kinds of celebrations are all good reasons for running a promotion. They put the brand name in the forefront. Celebrating spring or back-to-school time are not good reasons to run a promotion; they are too generic.
- *Tie the promotion to a brand's image:* Birth dates and anniversaries are good. For example, Haagen-Dazs could run a promotion on or around July 9 for its Dulce de Leche ice cream to coincide with Argentine National Day. (The flavor and name originated in Argentina.)
- *Look at every promotion both for the sales job it can do and as a communications tool:* A promotion is one of a brand's many voices; it can help build brand awareness if it says the right things. For example, Bayer aspirin could run a coupon promotion, thus offering a price reduction, and use the promotion to reinforce the name Bayer.

Source: Adapted from Jacques Chevron, "Branding and Promotion: Uneasy Cohabitation," *Brandweek*, September 14, 1998, p. 24.

table **20.3**	
Major Consumer–Promotion Tools	**Samples:** Offer of a free amount of a product or service delivered door to door, sent in the mail, picked up in a store, attached to another product, or featured in an advertising offer.
	Coupons: Certificates entitling the bearer to a stated saving on the purchase of a specific product: mailed, enclosed in other products or attached to them, or inserted in magazine and newspaper ads.
	Cash Refund Offers (rebates): Provide a price reduction after purchase rather than at the retail shop: consumer sends a specified "proof of purchase" to the manufacturer who "refunds" part of the purchase price by mail.
	Price Packs (cents-off deals): Offers to consumers of savings off the regular price of a product, flagged on the label or package. A *reduced-price pack* is a single package sold at a reduced price (such as two for the price of one). A *banded pack* is two related products banded together (such as a toothbrush and toothpaste).
	Premiums (gifts): Merchandise offered at a relatively low cost or free as an incentive to purchase a particular product. A *with-pack premium* accompanies the product inside or on the package. A *free in-the-mail* premium is mailed to consumers who send in a proof of purchase, such as a box top or UPC code. A *self-liquidating premium* is sold below its normal retail price to consumers who request it.
	Frequency Programs: Programs providing rewards related to the consumer's frequency and intensity in purchasing the company's products or services.
	Prizes (contests, sweepstakes, games): *Prizes* are offers of the chance to win cash, trips, or merchandise as a result of purchasing something. A *contest* calls for consumers to submit an entry to be examined by a panel of judges who will select the best entries. A *sweepstake* asks consumers to submit their names in a drawing. A *game* presents consumers with something every time they buy—bingo numbers, missing letters—which might help them win a prize.
	Patronage Awards: Values in cash or in other forms that are proportional to patronage of a certain vendor or group of vendors.
	Free Trials: Inviting prospective purchasers to try the product without cost in the hope that they will buy.
	Product Warranties: Explicit or implicit promises by sellers that the product will perform as specified or that the seller will fix it or refund the customer's money during a specified period.
	Tie-in Promotions: Two or more brands or companies team up on coupons, refunds, and contests to increase pulling power.
	Cross-Promotions: Using one brand to advertise another noncompeting brand.
	Point-of-Purchase (POP) Displays and Demonstrations: POP displays and demonstrations take place at the point-of-purchase or sale.

the local retailers will not keep the company's products on the shelf unless they receive more trade-promotion money, whereas the brand managers want to spend the limited funds on consumer promotion and advertising. Manufacturers face several challenges in managing trade promotions. First, they often find it difficult to police retailers to make sure they are doing what they agreed to do. Manufacturers are increasingly insisting on proof of performance before paying any allowances. Second, more retailers are doing *forward buying*—that is, buying a greater quantity during the deal period than they can sell during the deal period. Retailers might respond to a 10-percent-off-case allowance by buying a 12-week or longer supply. The manufacturer has to schedule

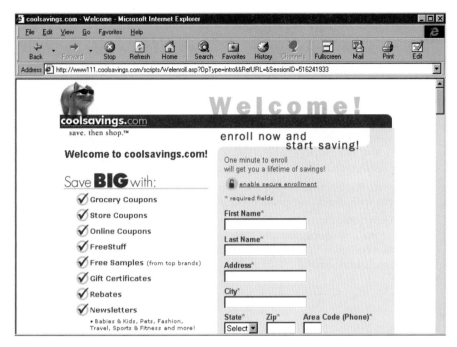

Coolsavings.com's home page.

more production than planned and bear the costs of extra work shifts and overtime. Third, retailers are doing more diverting, buying more cases than needed in a region in which the manufacturer offered a deal, and shipping the surplus to their stores in non-deal regions. Manufacturers are trying to handle forward buying and diverting by limiting the amount they will sell at a discount, or producing and delivering less than the full order in an effort to smooth production.[58]

All said, manufacturers feel that trade promotion has become a nightmare. It contains layers of deals, is complex to administer, and often leads to lost revenues. Kevin Price describes trade promotion in the following way:

> A decade ago, the retailer was a chihuahua nipping at the manufacturer's heels—a nuisance, yes, but only a minor irritant; you fed it and it went away. Today it's a pit bull and it wants to rip your arms and legs off. You'd like to see it roll over, but you're too busy defending yourself to even try. . . . Today management of trade promotions is a president-level issue.[59]

table **20.4**
Major Trade-Promotion Tools

Price-Off (off-invoice or off-list): A straight discount off the list price on each case purchased during a stated time period.

Allowance: An amount offered in return for the retailer's agreeing to feature the manufacturer's products in some way. An *advertising allowance* compensates retailers for advertising the manufacturer's product. A *display allowance* compensates them for carrying a special product display.

Free Goods: Offers of extra cases of merchandise to intermediaries who buy a certain quantity or who feature a certain flavor or size.

Source: For more information, see Betsy Spethman, "Trade Promotion Redefined," *Brandweek*, March 13, 1995, pp. 25–32.

table **20.5**	
Major Business- and Sales-Force-Promotion Tools	**Trade Shows and Conventions:** Industry associations organize annual trade shows and conventions. Business marketers may spend as much as 35 percent of their annual promotion budget on trade shows. Over 5,600 trade shows take place every year, drawing approximately 80 million attendees. Trade show attendance can range from a few thousand people to over 70,000 for large shows held by the restaurant or hotel-motel industries. Participating vendors expect several benefits, including generating new sales leads, maintaining customer contacts, introducing new products, meeting new customers, selling more to present customers, and educating customers with publications, videos, and other audiovisual materials.
	Sales Contests: A sales contest aims at inducing the sales force or dealers to increase their sales results over a stated period, with prizes (money, trips, gifts, or points) going to those who succeed.
	Specialty Advertising: Specialty advertising consists of useful, low-cost items bearing the company's name and address, and sometimes an advertising message that salespeople give to prospects and customers. Common items are ballpoint pens, calendars, key chains, flashlights, tote bags, and memo pads.

SELECTING BUSINESS- AND SALES-FORCE-PROMOTION TOOLS Companies spend billions of dollars on business- and sales-force-promotion tools (Table 20.5). These tools are used to gather business leads, impress and reward customers, and motivate the sales force to greater effort. Companies typically develop budgets for each business-promotion tool that remain fairly constant from year to year.

DEVELOPING THE PROGRAM In planning sales-promotion programs, marketers are increasingly blending several media into a total campaign concept. Kerry E. Smith describes a complete sales-promotion program:

> A sports trivia game to create pull-through at taverns for a premium beer brand would use TV to reach consumers, direct mail to incentivize distributors, point-of-purchase for retail support, telephones for consumer call-ins, a service bureau for call processing, live operators for data entry, and computer software and hardware to tie it all together. . . . Companies use telepromotions not only to pull product through at retail but also to identify customers, generate leads, build databases and deliver coupons, product samples, and rebate offers.[60]

In deciding to use a particular incentive, marketers have several factors to consider. First, they must determine the *size* of the incentive. A certain minimum is necessary if the promotion is to succeed. Second, the marketing manager must establish *conditions* for participation. Incentives might be offered to everyone or to select groups. Third, the marketer has to decide on the *duration* of promotion. According to one researcher, the optimal frequency is about three weeks per quarter, and optimal duration is the length of the average purchase cycle.[61] Fourth, the marketer must choose a *distribution vehicle*. A fifteen-cents-off coupon can be distributed in the package, in stores, by mail, or in advertising. The following is an example of a sales promotion that was distributed via the Web.

Twentieth Century Fox To promote its teen comedy *Dude Where's My Car* during the 2000 holiday season, Twentieth Century Fox targeted 25,000 young adults from its database with an e-mail "viral marketing" campaign. The e-mails contained information about the movie, as well as a movie-editing software package called the

Dude Movie-Maker. Recipients of the e-mail could use actual footage from the film, type in speech bubbles to create a personalized movie, and send the results to as many friends as they wanted. The movie, which cost only $15 million to make, reaped $25 million at the box office in its opening two weeks.[62]

Fifth, the marketing manager must establish the *timing* of promotion. Finally, the marketer must determine the *total sales-promotion budget*. The cost of a particular promotion consists of the administrative cost (printing, mailing, and promoting the deal) and the incentive cost (cost of premium or cents-off, including redemption costs), multiplied by the expected number of units that will be sold on the deal. In the case of a coupon deal, the cost would take into account the fact that only a fraction of the consumers will redeem the coupons.

PRETESTING, IMPLEMENTING, CONTROLLING, AND EVALUATING THE PROGRAM
Although most sales-promotion programs are designed on the basis of experience, pretests should be conducted to determine if the tools are appropriate, the incentive size optimal, and the presentation method efficient. Roger Strang maintains that promotions usually can be tested quickly and inexpensively and that large companies should test alternative strategies in selected market areas with each national promotion.[63] Consumers can be asked to rate or rank different possible deals, or trial tests can be run in limited geographic areas.

Marketing managers must prepare implementation and control plans for each individual promotion that cover lead time and sell-in time. *Lead time* is the time necessary to prepare the program prior to launching it: initial planning, design, and approval of package modifications or material to be mailed or distributed; preparation of advertising and point-of-sale materials; notification of field sales personnel; establishment of allocations for individual distributors; purchasing and printing of special premiums or packaging materials; production of advance inventories in preparation for release at a specific date; and, finally, the distribution to the retailer.[64] *Sell-in time* begins with the promotional launch and ends when approximately 95 percent of the deal merchandise is in the hands of consumers.

To evaluate the program, manufacturers can use three methods: sales data, consumer surveys, and experiments. The first method involves using scanner sales data, which are available from companies such as Information Resources Inc. and Nielsen Media Research. Marketers can analyze the types of people who took advantage of the promotion, what they bought before the promotion, and how they behaved later toward the brand and other brands. Suppose a company has a 6 percent market share in the pre-promotion period. The share jumps to 10 percent during the promotion, falls to 5 percent immediately after, and rises to 7 percent in the post-promotion period. The promotion evidently attracted new triers and also stimulated more purchasing by existing customers. After the promotion, sales fell as consumers worked down their inventories. The long-run rise to 7 percent indicates that the company gained some new users.

In general, sales promotions work best when they attract competitors' customers to try a superior product and these customers switch. If the company's product is not superior, the brand's share is likely to return to its pre-promotion level. One study of more than 1,000 promotions concluded that only 16 percent paid off.[65] If more information is needed, *consumer surveys* can be conducted to learn how many recall the promotion, what they thought of it, how many took advantage of it, and how the promotion affected subsequent brand-choice behavior.[66] Sales promotions can also be evaluated through *experiments* that vary such attributes as incentive value, duration, and distribution media. For example, coupons can be sent to half of the households in a consumer panel. Scanner data can be used to track whether the coupons led more people to buy the product immediately and in the future.

Beyond the cost of specific promotions, management must recognize additional costs. First, promotions might decrease long-run brand loyalty by making more consumers deal-prone rather than advertising-prone. Second, promotions can be more expensive than they appear. Some are inevitably distributed to the wrong consumers.

Third, there are the costs of special production runs, extra sales-force effort, and handling requirements. Finally, certain promotions irritate retailers, who may demand extra trade allowances or refuse to cooperate.[67]

public relations

Not only must the company relate constructively to customers, suppliers, and dealers, but it must also relate to a large number of interested publics. A **public** is any group that has an actual or potential interest in or impact on a company's ability to achieve its objectives. **Public relations (PR)** involves a variety of programs designed to promote or protect a company's image or its individual products.

Public relations has often been treated as a minor element in the promotion mix, but the wise company takes concrete steps to manage successful relations with its key publics. Most companies have a public-relations department that monitors the attitudes of the organization's publics and distributes information and communications to build goodwill. The best PR departments spend time counseling top management to adopt positive programs and to eliminate questionable practices so that negative publicity does not arise in the first place. They perform the following five functions:

1. *Press relations:* Presenting news and information about the organization in the most positive light.
2. *Product publicity:* Sponsoring efforts to publicize specific products.
3. *Corporate communication:* Promoting understanding of the organization through internal and external communications.
4. *Lobbying:* Dealing with legislators and government officials to promote or defeat legislation and regulation.
5. *Counseling:* Advising management about public issues and company positions and image during good times and crises.

marketing public relations

Marketing managers and PR specialists do not always talk the same language. Marketing managers are much more bottom-line-oriented, whereas PR practitioners see their job as preparing and disseminating communications; but these differences are disappearing. Many companies are turning to **marketing public relations (MPR)** to directly support corporate or product promotion and image making. MPR, like financial PR and community PR, serves a special constituency, namely, the marketing department.[68]

The old name for MPR was **publicity**, which was seen as the task of securing editorial space—as opposed to paid space—in print and broadcast media to promote or "hype" a product, service, idea, place, person, or organization. However, MPR goes beyond simple publicity and plays an important role in the following tasks:

- *Assisting in the launch of new products:* The amazing commercial success of toys such as Teenage Mutant Ninja Turtles, Mighty Morphin' Power Rangers, Beanie Babies, and Pokemons owes a great deal to clever publicity.
- *Assisting in repositioning a mature product:* New York City had extremely bad press in the 1970s until the "I Love New York" campaign.
- *Building interest in a product category:* Companies and trade associations have used MPR to rebuild interest in declining commodities such as eggs, milk, beef, and potatoes, and to expand consumption of such products as tea, pork, and orange juice.
- *Influencing specific target groups:* McDonald's sponsors special neighborhood events in Latino and African American communities to build goodwill.
- *Defending products that have encountered public problems:* PR professionals must be adept at managing crises, such as the Coca-Cola incident in Belgium over allegedly contaminated soda, and Firestone's crisis with regard to the tire tread separation problem.
- *Building the corporate image in a way that reflects favorably on its products:* Lee Iacocca's speeches and his autobiography created a whole new winning image for the Chrysler Corporation.

As the power of mass-advertising weakens, marketing managers are turning more to MPR. In a survey of 286 U.S. marketing managers, three-fourths reported that their companies used MPR. They found it particularly effective in building awareness and brand knowledge, for both new and established products. MPR is also effective in blanketing local communities and reaching specific groups. In several cases, MPR proved more cost-effective than advertising. Nevertheless, it must be planned jointly with advertising.[69] In addition, marketing managers need to acquire more skill in using MPR resources. Gillette is a trendsetter here: Each brand manager is required to have a budget line for MPR and to justify not using it.

Clearly, creative public relations can affect public awareness at a fraction of the cost of advertising. The company does not pay for the space or time obtained in the media. It pays only for a staff to develop and circulate the stories and manage certain events. If the company develops an interesting story, it could be picked up by the media and worth millions of dollars in equivalent advertising. The Body Shop, for example, has spent very little money on advertising; its success has been almost entirely due to publicity. Some experts say that consumers are five times more likely to be influenced by editorial copy than by advertising.

Here are examples of creative MPR.

Brita When Brita Water Filtration Systems sought to promote its brand using public relations, the company monitored papers throughout the country for editorials and stories about poor water quality. The company expected that readers of these stories would be concerned about the safety of their local water supply and therefore receptive to Brita advertising. Within a day or two of a story's appearance, Brita would place an advertisement in the same paper touting its water filtration technology.[70]

Yahoo! Yahoo! founders Jerry Yang and David Filo enlisted the services of a public relations agent months in advance of the public unveiling of their Web site. The PR campaign focused on Yahoo!'s user-friendliness and downplayed its technological aspects, in part because few journalists from mainstream publications covered the Internet at that point. In its first six months of operation, Yahoo! garnered 600 press mentions. By the time the company was set to go public, the media were fighting for the opportunity for exclusive coverage. Yang and Filo had become poster children for the dot-com craze, and Yahoo! no longer had to generate buzz on its own.[71]

major decisions in marketing pr

In considering when and how to use MPR, management must establish the marketing objectives, choose the PR messages and vehicles, implement the plan carefully, and evaluate the results. The main tools of MPR are described in Table 20.6.[72]

ESTABLISHING THE MARKETING OBJECTIVES MPR can build *awareness* by placing stories in the media to bring attention to a product, service, person, organization, or idea. It can build *credibility* by communicating the message in an editorial context. It can help boost sales-force and dealer enthusiasm with stories about a new product before it is launched. It can hold down *promotion cost* because MPR costs less than direct-mail and media advertising.

Some product launches are able to garner publicity without much effort.

Pfizer Viagra, Pfizer's anti-impotence drug, was the most successful prescription drug launch in history, racking up $788 million in sales during the first nine months after its 1998 introduction. Pfizer used PR to inform consumers about the drug before the launch and spent $21 million on advertising, but as the small blue pill grew

table **20.6**	
Major Tools in Marketing PR	**Publications:** Companies rely extensively on published materials to reach and influence their target markets. These include annual reports, brochures, articles, company newsletters and magazines, and audiovisual materials.
	Events: Companies can draw attention to new products or other company activities by arranging special events like news conferences, seminars, outings, trade shows, exhibits, contests and competitions, and anniversaries that will reach the target publics.
	Sponsorships: Companies can promote their brands and corporate name by sponsoring sport and cultural events and highly regarded causes.
	News: One of the major tasks of PR professionals is to find or create favorable news about the company, its products, and its people, and get the media to accept press releases and attend press conferences.
	Speeches: Increasingly, company executives must field questions from the media or give talks at trade associations or sales meetings, and these appearances can build the company's image.
	Public-Service Activities: Companies can build goodwill by contributing money and time to good causes.
	Identity Media: Companies need a visual identity that the public immediately recognizes. The visual identity is carried by company logos, stationery, brochures, signs, business forms, business cards, buildings, uniforms, and dress codes.

into a genuine pop-culture phenomenon, Viagra got vast quantities of PR gratis. The pill got unofficial endorsements from celebrities like Hugh Hefner and newspaper columnists all over the country who "test-drove" the drug, and almost nightly coverage during Leno and Letterman's monologues. Former senator Bob Dole appeared on Larry King Live and revealed that he had taken Viagra following prostate surgery. Dole then appeared in television ads for the drug. Three years after the launch, Pfizer had sold over 240 million Viagra pills.[73]

Whereas PR practitioners reach their target publics through the mass media, MPR is increasingly borrowing the techniques and technology of direct-response marketing to reach target audience members one on one. MPR expert Thomas L. Harris offers suggestions for how PR and direct-response marketing can work together to achieve specific marketing objectives:[74]

- *Build marketplace excitement before media advertising breaks:* The announcement of a new product offers a unique opportunity for obtaining publicity and for dramatizing the product.
- *Build a core consumer base:* Marketers recognize the value of maintaining consumer loyalty, because it costs far less to keep a consumer than to get a new one.
- *Build a one-to-one relationship with consumers:* Marketers can use telephone hot lines and 800 numbers, plus the Internet, to build and maintain relationships with individual consumers.
- *Turn satisfied customers into advocates:* Customer databases and profiles can yield satisfied customers who can become role models and spokespeople for the product.
- *Influence the influentials:* The influencer may be an authority figure like a teacher, doctor, or pharmacist, but it also can be someone who has a different kind of one-to-one relationship with the consumer, such as a hair stylist or personal trainer.

CHOOSING MESSAGES AND VEHICLES The MPR manager must identify or develop interesting stories to tell about the product. Suppose a relatively unknown college wants more visibility. The MPR practitioner will search for possible stories. Do any faculty members have unusual backgrounds, or are any working on unusual projects? Are any new and unusual courses being taught? Are any interesting events taking place on campus? If there are no interesting stories, the MPR practitioner should propose newsworthy events the college could sponsor. Here the challenge is to create news. PR ideas include hosting major academic conventions, inviting expert or celebrity speakers, and developing news conferences. Each event is an opportunity to develop a multitude of stories directed at different audiences.

Event creation is a particularly important skill in publicizing fund-raising drives for nonprofit organizations. Fund-raisers have developed a large repertoire of special events, including anniversary celebrations, art exhibits, auctions, benefit evenings, bingo games, book sales, cake sales, contests, dances, dinners, fairs, fashion shows, parties in unusual places, phonathons, rummage sales, tours, and walkathons. No sooner is one type of event created, such as a walkathon, than competitors spawn new versions, such as readathons, bikeathons, and jogathons.[75]

For-profit organizations also use events to call attention to products and services. Fuji Photo Film Company flew its blimp over the renovated Statue of Liberty during the reopening celebration, outdoing its rival Kodak, which had mounted a permanent photo exhibit at the site. Anheuser-Busch sponsored a Black World Championship Rodeo in Brooklyn that attracted more than 5,000 spectators.

The best MPR practitioners are able to find or create stories even for mundane products such as pork ("the other white meat"), garlic, and potatoes. Here is an example of an unglamorous product around which a successful MPR campaign was built.

Random House   In 1998, Modern Library, a division of Random House, used a survey of its editorial board to create a list of the top 100 novels of the Twentieth century. The list was then published on the Modern Library Web site. A swarm of press coverage ensued, in part because of a squabble over the selection criteria between Random House and the editorial board. Five months after the list appeared, over 1,000 articles and editorials had been written about it, and traffic to the Modern Library Web site increased 7,000 percent. This free coverage generated by the list and the surrounding controversy helped four of the top five books reach Amazon.com's bestseller list. Since Modern Library published an edition of each book on the top 100, many viewed the creation of the list as a shrewd, and successful, PR move.[76]

IMPLEMENTING THE PLAN AND EVALUATING RESULTS   Implementing public relations requires care. A great story is easy to place, but most stories are less than great and might not get past busy editors. One of the chief assets of publicists is their personal relationship with media editors. PR people look at media editors as a market to satisfy so that these editors will continue to use their stories.

MPR's contribution to the bottom line is difficult to measure, because it is used along with other promotional tools. The three most commonly used measures of MPR effectiveness are number of exposures; awareness, comprehension, or attitude change; and contribution to sales and profits.

The easiest measure of MPR effectiveness is the number of *exposures* carried by the media. Publicists supply the client with a clippings book showing all the media that carried news about the product and a summary statement such as the following:

Media coverage included 3,500 column inches of news and photographs in 350 publications with a combined circulation of 79.4 million; 2,500 minutes of air time of 290 radio stations and an estimated audience of 65 million; and 660 minutes of air time on 160 television stations with an estimated audience of 91 million. If this time and space had been purchased at advertising rates, it would have amounted to $1,047,000.[77]

Marketing
MEMO

The Public and Ethical Issues in Direct Marketing

Direct marketers and their customers usually enjoy mutually rewarding relationships. Occasionally, however, a darker side emerges:

- *Irritation:* Many people do not like the increasing number of hard-sell direct-marketing solicitations. Especially bothersome are dinnertime or late-night phone calls, poorly trained callers, and computerized calls placed by auto-dial recorded- message players.
- *Unfairness:* Some direct marketers take advantage of impulsive or less sophisticated buyers. TV shopping shows and infomercials may be the worst culprits with their smooth-talking hosts and claims of drastic price reductions.
- *Deception and fraud:* Some direct marketers design mailers and write copy intended to mislead buyers. They may exaggerate product size, performance claims, or the "retail price." The Federal Trade Commission receives thousands of complaints each year about fraudulent investment scams or phony charities.

continued...

This measure is not very satisfying because it contains no indication of how many people actually read, heard, or recalled the message and what they thought afterward; nor does it contain information on the net audience reached, because publications overlap in readership. Because publicity's goal is reach, not frequency, it would be more useful to know the number of unduplicated exposures.

A better measure is the change in product awareness, comprehension, or attitude resulting from the MPR campaign (after allowing for the effect of other promotional tools). For example, how many people recall hearing the news item? How many told others about it (a measure of word of mouth)? How many changed their minds after hearing it? In a Potato Board campaign, the board found that the number of people who agreed with the statement "Potatoes are rich in vitamins and minerals" went from 36 percent before the campaign to 67 percent after the campaign, a significant improvement in product comprehension.

Sales-and-profit impact is the most satisfactory measure. For example, 9-Lives Cat Food sales increased 43 percent by the end of the Morris the Cat PR campaign. However, advertising and sales promotion had also been stepped up. Suppose total sales have increased $1,500,000, and management estimates that MPR contributed 15 percent of the total increase. Then the return on MPR investment is calculated as follows:

Total sales increase	$1,500,000
Estimated sales increase due to PR (15 percent)	225,000
Contribution margin on product sales (10 percent)	22,500
Total direct cost of MPR program	−10,000
Contribution margin added by PR investment	$ 12,500
Return on MPR investment ($12,500/$10,000)	125%

direct marketing

Direct marketing is the use of consumer-direct (CD) channels to reach and deliver goods and services to customers without using marketing middlemen. These channels include direct mail, catalogs, telemarketing, interactive TV, kiosks, Web sites, and mobile devices. Direct marketing is one of the fastest growing avenues for serving customers.

Direct marketers seek a measurable response, typically a customer order. This is sometimes called **direct-order marketing**. Today, many direct marketers use direct marketing to build a long-term relationship with the customer (**customer relationship marketing**).[78] They send birthday cards, information materials, or small premiums to select customers. Airlines, hotels, and other businesses build strong customer relationships through frequency award programs and club programs.

the growth of direct marketing

Sales produced through traditional direct-marketing channels (catalogs, direct mail, and telemarketing) have been growing rapidly. Whereas U.S. retail sales grow around 3 percent annually, catalog and direct-mail sales grow at about double that rate. Direct sales include sales to the consumer market (53 percent), B2B (27 percent), and fundraising by charitable institutions (20 percent). Total media spending for all direct marketing in 2000 (including direct mail, telephone, broadcast, Internet, newspaper, magazine, etc.) was over $421 billion.[79]

Electronic marketing is showing even more explosive growth. In 2001, the Internet user population in the United States numbered over 100 million, and there were over 2 million Web sites. In the week ending January 30, 2001, 6.8 million orders took place over the Internet, adding up to an amount spent of $785 million.[80]

The extraordinary growth of direct marketing is the result of many factors. *Market demassification* has resulted in an ever-increasing number of market niches. Higher costs of driving, traffic congestion, parking headaches, lack of time, a shortage of retail sales help, and lines at checkout counters all encourage at-home shopping. Consumers appreciate direct marketers' toll-free phone numbers available 24 hours a day, 7 days a week, and their commitment to customer service. The growth of next-day delivery via FedEx, Airborne, and UPS has made ordering fast and easy. In addition, many chain stores have dropped slower-moving specialty items, creating an opportunity for direct marketers to promote these items to interested buyers. The growth of the Internet, e-mail, mobile phones, and fax machines has made product selection and ordering much simpler. More and more business marketers have turned to direct mail and telemarketing in response to the high and increasing costs of reaching business markets through a sales force.

the benefits of direct marketing

Direct marketing benefits customers in many ways. Home shopping is fun, convenient, and hassle-free. It saves time and introduces consumers to a larger selection of merchandise. They can do comparative shopping by browsing through mail catalogs and online shopping services. They can order goods for themselves or others. Business customers also benefit by learning about available products and services without tying up time in meeting salespeople.

Sellers also benefit. Direct marketers can buy a mailing list containing the names of almost any group: left-handed people, overweight people, millionaires. They can customize and personalize their messages. Direct marketers can build a continuous relationship with each customer. The parents of a newborn baby will receive periodic mailings describing new clothes, toys, and other goods as the child grows. Nestlé's baby-food division continuously builds a database of new mothers and mails six personalized packages of gifts and advice at key stages in the baby's life.

Direct marketing can be timed to reach prospects at the right moment, and direct-marketing material receives higher readership because it is sent to more interested prospects. Direct marketing permits the testing of alternative media and messages in search of the most cost-effective approach. Direct marketing also makes the direct marketer's offer and strategy less visible to competitors. Finally, direct marketers can measure responses to their campaigns to decide which have been the most profitable. (However, see "Marketing Memo: The Public and Ethical Issues in Direct Marketing.")

integrated direct marketing

Although direct and online marketing are booming, a large number of companies still relegate them to minor roles in their communication/promotion mix. Advertising and sales-promotion departments receive most of the communication dollars and jealously guard their budgets. The sales force may also see direct marketing as a threat when it has to turn over smaller customers and prospects to direct mailers and telemarketers.

However, companies are increasingly recognizing the importance of integrating their marketing communications. Some companies are appointing a chief communications officer (CCO) in addition to a CIO (chief information officer). The CCO supervises specialists in advertising, sales promotion, public relations, and direct marketing. The aim is to establish the right overall communication budget and the right allocation of funds to each communication tool. This movement has been variously called *integrated marketing communications* (IMC), *integrated direct marketing* (IDM), and *maximarketing*.[81]

How can different communication tools be integrated in campaign planning? Imagine a marketer using a single tool in a "one-shot" effort to reach and sell a prospect. An example of a *single-vehicle, single-stage campaign* is a one-time mailing offering a cookware item. A *single-vehicle, multiple-stage campaign* would involve successive mailings to the same prospect. Magazine publishers, for example, send about four renewal notices to a household before giving up. A more powerful approach is the *multiple-vehicle, multiple-stage campaign*. Consider the following sequence:

News campaign about a new product→Paid ad with a response mechanism→Direct mail→Outbound telemarketing→Face-to-face sales call→Ongoing communication.

■ *Invasion of privacy:* It seems that almost every time consumers order products by mail or telephone, enter a sweepstakes, apply for a credit card, or take out a magazine subscription, their names, addresses, and purchasing behavior may be added to several company databases. Critics worry that marketers may know too much about consumers' lives, and that they may use this knowledge to take unfair advantage.

People in the direct-marketing industry are attempting to address these issues. They know that, left unattended, such problems will lead to increasingly negative consumer attitudes, lower response rates, and calls for greater state and federal regulation. In the final analysis, most direct marketers want the same thing that consumers want: honest and well-designed marketing offers targeted only to those consumers who appreciate hearing about the offer.

Ernan Roman says that the use of response compression, whereby multiple media are deployed within a tightly defined time frame, increases message reach and impact. The underlying idea is to deploy a sequence of messages with precise timing intervals in the hope of generating incremental sales and profits that exceed the costs involved. Roman cites a Citibank campaign to market home equity loans. Instead of using only "mail plus an 800 number," Citibank used "mail plus coupon plus 800 number plus outbound telemarketing plus print advertising." Although the second campaign was more expensive, it resulted in a 15 percent increase in the number of new accounts compared with direct mail alone. Roman concluded:

> When a mailing piece that might generate a 2% response on its own is supplemented by a toll-free 800-number ordering channel, we regularly see response rise by 50-125%. A skillfully integrated outbound telemarketing effort can add another 500% lift in response. Suddenly our 2% response has grown to 13% or more by adding interactive marketing channels to a "business as usual" mailing. The dollars and cents involved in adding media to the integrated media mix is normally marginal on a cost-per-order basis because of the high level of responses generated. . . . Adding media to a marketing program will raise total response . . . because different people are inclined to respond to different stimuli.[82]

Rapp and Collins's Maximarketing model makes direct-marketing techniques the driving force in the general marketing process.[83] This model recommends the creation of a customer database and advocates making direct marketing a full partner in the marketing process. Maximarketing consists of a comprehensive set of steps for reaching the prospect, making the sale, and developing the relationship. Citigroup, AT&T, IBM, Ford, and American Airlines have used integrated direct marketing to build profitable relations with customers over the years. Retailers such as Nordstrom, Nieman Marcus, Saks Fifth Avenue, and Bloomingdale's regularly send catalogs to supplement in-store sales. Direct-marketing companies such as L. L. Bean, Eddie Bauer, Franklin Mint, and The Sharper Image made fortunes in the direct-marketing mail-order and phone-order business, then opened retail stores after establishing strong brand names as direct marketers.

major channels for direct marketing

Direct marketers can use a number of channels for reaching individual prospects and customers. These include face-to-face selling, direct mail, catalog marketing, telemarketing, TV and other direct-response media, kiosk marketing, and e-marketing.

FACE-TO-FACE SELLING   The original and oldest form of direct marketing is the field sales call. Today most industrial companies rely heavily on a professional sales force to locate prospects, develop them into customers, and grow the business; or they hire manufacturers' representatives and agents to carry out the direct-selling task. In addition, many consumer companies use a direct-selling force: insurance agents, stockbrokers, and distributors working for direct-sales organizations such as Avon, Amway, Mary Kay, and Tupperware.

DIRECT MAIL   Direct-mail marketing involves sending an offer, announcement, reminder, or other item to a person. Using highly selective mailing lists, direct marketers send out millions of mail pieces each year—letters, flyers, foldouts, and other "salespeople with wings." Some direct marketers mail audiotapes, videotapes, CDs, and computer diskettes to prospects and customers. Ford sends a computer diskette called "Disk Drive Test Drive" to consumers responding to its ads in computer publications. The diskette's menu provides technical specifications and attractive graphics about Ford cars, and answers frequently asked questions. Here is how another company uses direct mail.

Tesco   Fourteen million shoppers at Tesco, the U.K.'s largest retailer, have a Tesco Clubcard and use it when paying for their groceries. Tesco has accumulated massive data on its customers and has identified 5,000 needs segments. Instead of mailing standardized promotions to all customers, Tesco sends personalized letters and coupon assortments. Its coupon redemption rate averages 90 percent. Tesco also mails a mass-customized quarterly magazine with hundreds of thousands of combinations of third-party advertisements.

Direct mail is a popular medium because it permits target market selectivity, can be personalized, is flexible, and allows early testing and response measurement. Although the cost per thousand people reached is higher than with mass-media, the people reached are much better prospects. Over 45 percent of Americans purchased something through direct mail in 1993. The same year, charities raised over $50 billion via direct mail. The power of a well-designed direct-mail piece to garner contributions can be seen in this campaign for an ailing public TV-radio station in Indianapolis.

WFYI–TV (Indianapolis, Indiana)   The results of a pair of startlingly graphic support pieces, created by the ad agency Young and Laramore for Indianapolis public TV-radio station WFYI, outpaced all internal projections. The capital improvement campaign raised $3.5 million in its first nine months, when the five-year goal was $5 million. Only 500 pieces were mailed, so the average per-piece return was $7,000. The agency went out on a limb by using an approach that was brutally frank about the station's financial straits: Cardboard, rubber stamps, and duct tape were used to create an introductory mailer. A follow-up brochure offered a timeline of the station's 18-year history. Above the line in black were milestones and accomplishments. Below, in red, equipment failures. When the timeline hit 1996, expenses had become an angry, unreadable blotch of red ink.[84]

Until recently, mail was paper-based and handled by the U.S. Postal Service, telegraphic services, or for-profit mail carriers such as FedEx, DHL, or Airborne Express. Then three new forms of mail delivery appeared:

- *Fax mail:* Fax machines enable one party to send a paper-based message to another party over telephone lines. Marketers have begun to send fax mail announcing offers, sales, and events to prospects and customers.
- *E-mail:* E-mail (short for *electronic mail*) allows users to send a message or file from one computer directly to another. The message arrives almost instantly but is stored until the receiving person turns on the computer. Marketers send sales announcements, offers, and other messages to e-mail addresses—sometimes to a few individuals, sometimes to large groups.
- *Voice mail:* Voice mail is a system for receiving and storing oral messages at a telephone address. Telephone companies sell this service as a substitute for answering machines. Some marketers have set up programs that will dial a large number of telephone numbers and leave the selling message in the recipients' voice mailboxes.

Direct marketing has passed through a number of stages:

- *"Carpet bombing":* Direct mailers gather or buy as many names as possible and send out a mass-mailing. Usually the response rate is very low.
- *Database marketing:* Direct marketers mine the database to identify the prospects who would have the most interest in an offer.
- *Interactive marketing:* Direct marketers include their telephone number and Web address, and offer to print coupons from the Web site. Recipients can contact the company with questions. The company uses the interaction as an opportunity to up-sell, cross-sell, and deepen the relationship.

Marketing
MEMO

When Your Customer Is a Committee . . .

One of the many advantages of database marketing and direct mail is that they allow you to tailor format, offer, and sell messages to the target audience(s). Business marketers can create a series of interrelated and reinforced mailings to decision makers and decision influencers. Here are some tips for increasing success in selling to a customer-by-committee:

- When creating lead generation and follow-up mailings, remember that most business mailings are screened once, twice, or even more before reaching your targeted audience.
- Plan and budget for a series of mailings to reach each of your customer-by-committee members. Timing and multiple exposures are critical in reaching these audiences.
- Whenever possible, mail to individuals by name and title. Using the title helps the in-office mail screener reroute your mailing if the individual addressed has moved on to another job.
- Do not necessarily use the same format and size for reaching all your targeted audiences. A more expensive-looking envelope may reach the president or CEO, but it may be equally effective to use a less expensive, less personal format to reach other decision influencers.

continued...

- *Real-time personalized marketing:* Direct marketers know enough about each customer to customize and personalize the offer and message.
- *Lifetime value marketing:* Direct marketers develop a plan for lifetime marketing to each valuable customer, based on knowledge of life events and transitions.

CONSTRUCTING A DIRECT-MAIL CAMPAIGN   In constructing an effective direct-mail campaign, direct marketers must decide on their objectives, target markets, and prospects; offer elements, means of testing the campaign, and measures of campaign success.

Objectives   Most direct marketers aim to receive an order from prospects. A campaign's success is judged by the response rate. An order-response rate of 2 percent is normally considered good, although this number varies with product category and price.

Direct mail can achieve other communication objectives as well, such as producing prospect leads, strengthening customer relationships, informing and educating customers, reminding customers of offers, and reinforcing recent customer purchase decisions.

Target Markets and Prospects   Direct marketers need to identify the characteristics of prospects and customers who are most able, willing, and ready to buy. Most direct marketers apply the R-F-M formula (*recency, frequency, monetary amount*) for rating and selecting customers. For any proposed offering, the company selects customers according to how much time has passed since their last purchase, how many times they have purchased, and how much they have spent since becoming a customer. Suppose the company is offering a leather jacket. It might make this offer to customers who made their last purchase between 30 and 60 days ago, who make 3 to 6 purchases a year, and who have spent at least $100 since becoming customers. Points are established for varying R-F-M levels, and each customer is scored. The higher the score, the more attractive the customer. The mailing is sent only to the most attractive customers.[85]

Prospects can also be identified on the basis of such variables as age, sex, income, education, and previous mail-order purchases. Occasions provide a good departure point for segmentation. New parents will be in the market for baby clothes and baby toys; college freshmen will buy computers and small television sets; newlyweds will be looking for housing, furniture, appliances, and bank loans. Another useful segmentation variable is consumer lifestyle groups, such as computer buffs, cooking buffs, and outdoor buffs. For business markets, Dun & Bradstreet operates an information service that provides a wealth of data.

In B2B direct marketing, the prospect is often not an individual but a group of people or a committee that includes both decision makers and multiple decision influencers. See "Marketing Memo: When Your Customer Is a Committee…" for tips on crafting a direct-mail campaign aimed at business buyers.

Once the target market is defined, the direct marketer needs to obtain specific names. The company's best prospects are customers who have bought its products in the past. Additional names can be obtained by advertising some free offer. The direct marketer can also buy lists of names from list brokers, but these lists often have problems, including name duplication, incomplete data, and obsolete addresses. The better lists include overlays of demographic and psychographic information. Direct marketers typically buy and test a sample before buying more names from the same list.

Offer Elements   Nash sees the offer strategy as consisting of five elements—the *product*, the *offer*, the *medium*, the *distribution method*, and the *creative strategy*.[86] Fortunately, all of these elements can be tested.

In addition to these elements, the direct-mail marketer has to decide on five components of the mailing itself: the outside envelope, sales letter, circular, reply form, and reply envelope. Here are some findings:

1. The outside envelope will be more effective if it contains an illustration, preferably in color, or a catchy reason to open the envelope, such as the announcement of a contest, premium, or

benefit. Envelopes are more effective when they contain a colorful commemorative stamp, when the address is hand-typed or handwritten, and when the envelope differs in size or shape from standard envelopes. Other envelopes employ "fascinations," as they were called by the late Mel Martin, a copywriter for Boardroom, Inc. Catchy headlines like these worked year after year after year on envelopes for Boardroom, Inc.'s promotions: "What Credit Card Companies Don't Tell You" or "What Never to Eat on an Airplane."[87]

2. The sales letter should use a personal salutation and start with a headline in bold type. The letter should be printed on good-quality paper and be brief. A computer-typed letter usually outperforms a printed letter, and the presence of a pithy P.S. increases the response rate, as does the signature of someone whose title is important.

3. In most cases, a colorful circular accompanying the letter will increase the response rate by more than its cost.

4. Direct mailers should feature a toll-free number and also send recipients to their Web site. Coupons should be printed out at the Web site.

5. The inclusion of a postage-free reply envelope will dramatically increase the response rate.

Direct mail should be followed up by an e-mail, which is less expensive and less intrusive than a telemarketing call.

Testing Elements One of the great advantages of direct marketing is the ability to test, under real marketplace conditions, different elements of an offer strategy, such as products, product features, copy platform, mailer type, envelope, prices, or mailing lists.

Direct marketers must remember that response rates typically understate a campaign's long-term impact. Suppose only 2 percent of the recipients who receive a direct-mail piece advertising Samsonite luggage place an order. A much larger percentage became aware of the product (direct mail has high readership), and some percentage may have formed an intention to buy at a later date (either by mail or at a retail outlet). Furthermore, some of them may mention Samsonite luggage to others as a result of the direct-mail piece. To derive a more comprehensive estimate of the promotion's impact, some companies are measuring direct marketing's impact on awareness, intention to buy, and word of mouth.

Measuring Campaign Success: Lifetime Value By adding up the planned campaign costs, the direct marketer can figure out in advance the needed break-even response rate. This rate must be net of returned merchandise and bad debts. Returned merchandise can kill an otherwise effective campaign. The direct marketer needs to analyze the main causes of returned merchandise (late shipment, defective merchandise, damage in transit, not as advertised, incorrect order fulfillment).

By carefully analyzing past campaigns, direct marketers can steadily improve their performance. Even when a specific campaign fails to break even, it can still be profitable. Consider the following situation:

> Suppose a membership organization spends $10,000 on a new-member campaign and attracts 100 new members, each paying annual dues of $70. It appears that the campaign has lost $3,000 ($10,000−$7,000). But if 80 percent of the new members renew their membership in the second year, the organization gets another $5,600 without any effort. It has now received $12,600 ($7,000 + $5,600) for its investment of $10,000.

This example illustrates the concept of customer lifetime value (CLV), which we first mentioned in Chapter 2.[88] A customer's ultimate value is not revealed by his or her purchase response to a particular mailing. Rather, it is the expected profit made on all future purchases net of customer acquisition and maintenance costs. For an average customer, one would calculate the average customer longevity,[89] average customer annual expenditure, and average gross margin, minus the average cost of customer

- Tell your customer-by-committee that you are communicating with others in the organization.
- Make your decision influencers feel important. They can be your biggest advocates.
- When communicating with different audiences, make sure you anticipate—and address—their individual buying objectives and objections.
- When your database or mailing lists cannot help you reach all the key people, ask the individual you are addressing to pass along your information.
- When doing a lead-generation mailing, make sure to ask for the names and titles of those who might be interested and involved in the buying decision. Enter this information into your database.
- Even though it may seem like a lot of work (and expense) to write different versions of the same letter and create different offers, there is a big payoff. The final decision maker may be interested in having a payback calculated, but others may be interested in day-to-day benefits such as safety, convenience, and time savings. Tailor your offer to your targets.

Source: Adapted from Pat Friesen, "When Your Customer Is a Committee," *Target Marketing* (August 1998): 40.

acquisition and maintenance (properly discounted for the opportunity cost of money). Various estimates have been made for different products and services.

- Carl Sewell, and Paul Brown in their book *Customers for Life*, estimated that a customer entering his dealership for the first time represents a potential lifetime value of over $300,000.[90]
- If the customer is satisfied, and buys several automobiles from the dealership over his or her buying lifetime, and subtracting the cost of selling and serving the customer, this may be the figure. If the satisfied customer brings in other customers, the figure would be higher.
- Mark Grainer, former chairman of the Technical Assistance Research Programs Institute (TARP), estimated that a loyal supermarket customer is worth $3,800 annually.[91]

Of course, a company needs, in addition to an average customer estimate, a way of estimating CLV for each individual customer. This is because the company must decide how much to invest in each customer.

After assessing customer lifetime value, the company can focus its communication efforts on the more attractive customers. These efforts include sending communications that do not "sell" anything but rather maintain interest in the company and its products. Such communications may include newsletters, booklets, and brochures, all of which build a stronger customer relationship.

catalog marketing

In catalog marketing, companies may send full-line merchandise catalogs, specialty consumer catalogs, and business catalogs, usually in print form but also sometimes as CDs, videos, or online. JCPenney and Spiegel send general merchandise catalogs. Saks Fifth Avenue sends specialty clothing catalogs to the upper-middle-class market. Through its catalogs, Avon sells cosmetics, W. R. Grace sells cheese, and IKEA sells furniture. Thousands of small businesses issue specialty catalogs. Large businesses such as Grainger, Merck, and others send catalogs to business prospects and customers.

Catalogs are a huge business—the $87 billion catalog industry jumped 8 percent annually from 1993 to 1998. The Direct Marketing Association estimates that there are currently up to 10,000 mail-order catalogs of all kinds. Someone who frequently buys from catalogs can easily receive 70 catalogs in a single week over the holiday season. However, the number of catalogs streaming into consumers' mailboxes is not the only measure of growth in this business. Catalogers have gotten a big boost from the Internet—about three-quarters of catalog companies present merchandise and take orders over the Internet. The Lands' End Web site, which debuted in 1995, now gets 180,000 e-mail queries a year, surpassing the print-mail response.[92]

The success of a catalog business depends on the company's ability to manage its customer lists carefully so that there is little duplication or bad debts, to control its inventory carefully, to offer quality merchandise so that returns are low, and to project a distinctive image. Some companies distinguish their catalogs by adding literary or information features, sending swatches of materials, operating a special hot line to answer questions, sending gifts to their best customers, and donating a percentage of the profits to good causes. The editorial content of Wisconsin-based Lands' End's catalogs has certainly set it apart from competitors.

Lands' End   In 1985 the company began adding essays and informative stories by such well-known writers as Garrison Keillor and David Mamet in order to cater to its well-educated customers. The resulting "magalog" style creates anticipation for the next catalog and helps distinguish the catalog from the countless others that clutter customers' mailboxes, particularly during the holiday season. The copy in Lands' End catalogs is also distinguished by its exhaustive attention to product details. "The more customers know about the product they're buying, the better it is for Lands' End," says the company's creative director.[93]

In addition, some catalog houses (Neiman Marcus, Spiegel) mail video catalogs to their best customers and prospects or put their catalog on the Internet, in which case they save considerable printing and mailing costs.[94]

Global consumers in Asia and Europe are also catching on to the catalog craze. In the 1990s, U.S. catalog companies such as L.L. Bean, Lands' End, Eddie Bauer, and Patagonia began setting up operations in Japan—and with great success. In just a few years foreign catalogs—mostly from the United States and a few from Europe—have won 5 percent of the $20 billion Japanese mail-order catalog market. A full 90 percent of L.L. Bean's international sales come from Japan. One reason the American companies have flourished in Japan is that they offer high-quality merchandise aimed at specific groups. For decades Japanese consumers shunned Japanese catalogs because they were a hodgepodge of everything from cheap dresses and necklaces to diapers and dog food. American catalogs also often contain two other items unusual in Japan: a lifetime, no-questions-asked guarantee and pictures of top models.

Consumer catalog companies such as Tiffany & Co., Patagonia, Eddie Bauer, and Lands' End are also entering Europe. Business marketers are making inroads as well. Sales to foreign (mainly European) markets have driven earnings increases at Viking Office Products and computer and network equipment cataloger Black Box Corporation. Viking has had success in Europe because, unlike the United States, Europe has fewer superstores and is very receptive to mail order. Black Box owes much of its international growth to its customer service policies, which are unmatched in Europe. The company, now operating in nearly 132 countries, provides technical support around the clock, seven days a week at no charge, ships 89 percent of orders within the same day, and offers extended two-year to lifetime warranties on its products.[95]

By putting their entire catalogs online, catalog companies have better access to global consumers than ever before. They also save considerable printing and mailing costs and offer some unique services.

Eddie Bauer Inc.   Seattle-based casual apparel maker Eddie Bauer is letting customers enter a "virtual dressing room" on its Web site. Although visitors to Eddiebauer.com will find the same khaki, denim, and knit basics found in the retailer's catalogs and in its stores, the site is more than just an electronic sales flyer. If customers want to see how that holiday sweater will look with khakis or try a sports jacket with the plaid pants, they can just click and drag the items to see how they look together. Because half the consumers who visit the Web site have never shopped at Eddie Bauer before, their experience online is an important first contact with the company. The virtual dressing room as well as other special services ensure that the first contact is a memorable one.[96]

telemarketing and m-commerce

Telemarketing involves the use of the telephone and call centers to attract prospects, sell to existing customers, and provide service by taking orders and answering questions. Telemarketing helps companies increase revenue, reduce selling costs, and improve customer satisfaction.

Companies use call centers for *inbound telemarketing* (receiving calls from customers) and *outbound telemarketing* (initiating calls to prospects and customers). In fact, companies carry out four types of telemarketing:

- *Telesales:* Taking orders from catalogs or ads and also doing outbound calling.
- *Telecoverage:* Calling customers to maintain and nurture key account relationships.
- *Teleprospecting:* Generating and qualifying new leads for closure by another sales channel.
- *Customer service and technical support:* Answering service and technical questions.

Here are two successful examples of telemarketing.

USAA USAA, located in San Antonio, Texas, proves that a company can successfully conduct its entire insurance business over the phone without ever meeting customers face-to-face. From its beginnings, USAA focused on selling auto insurance, and later other insurance products, to those with military service. It increased its share of each customer's business by launching a consumer bank, issuing credit cards, opening a discount brokerage, and offering a selection of no-load mutual funds. In spite of transactions taking place on the phone, USAA boasts one of the highest customer satisfaction ratings of any company in the United States.

First Direct (Midland Bank) The telephone brought home banking to Great Britain. First Direct, set up in 1989 by Britain's Midland Bank, operates entirely by telephone (subsequently adding fax and Internet channels as well) and has no branches or physical presence. With 850,000 customers and adding 12,500 new ones each month, Midland represents the future for the financial industry.[97]

Telemarketing has become a major direct-marketing tool. In 1998, telemarketers sold $482 billion worth of products and services to consumers and businesses. The average household receives 19 telemarketing calls each year and makes 16 calls to place orders.

Telemarketing is increasingly used in business as well as consumer marketing. Raleigh Bicycles uses telemarketing to reduce the amount of personal selling needed for contacting its dealers. In the first year, sales-force travel costs were reduced by 50 percent and sales in a single quarter went up 34 percent. Telemarketing, as it improves with the use of videophones, will increasingly replace, though never eliminate, more expensive field sales calls. An increasing number of salespeople have made five- and six-figure sales without ever meeting the customer face-to-face. Effective telemarketing depends on choosing the right telemarketers, training them well, and providing performance incentives.

Telemarketers should have pleasant voices and project enthusiasm. Women are more effective than men for selling many products. Telemarketers should initially train with a script and then move toward more improvisation. The telemarketer needs to know how to end the conversation if the prospect seems to be a poor one. The call should be made at the right time, which is late morning and afternoon to reach business prospects, and evening hours between 7:00 and 9:00 P.M. to reach households. The telemarketing supervisor can build enthusiasm by offering prizes to the first one who gets an order or to the top performer. Given privacy issues and the higher cost per contact, precise list selection is critical.

other media for direct-response marketing

Direct marketers use all the major media to make direct offers to potential buyers. Newspapers and magazines carry abundant print ads offering books, articles of clothing, appliances, vacations, and other goods and services that individuals can order by dialing a toll-free number. Radio ads present offers to listeners 24 hours a day. Television is used by direct marketers in three ways to promote direct sales:

1. *Direct-response advertising:* A classic example is Dial Media's ads for Ginsu knives, which ran for seven years and sold almost 3 million sets of knives worth over $40 million in sales. Some companies prepare 30- and 60-minute infomercials, which resemble documentaries (on quitting smoking, curing baldness, or losing weight), carry testimony from satisfied users of the product or service, and include a toll-free number for ordering or getting further information. Chrysler developed "Chrysler Showcase," a 30-minute infomercial touting Chrysler's brand heritage and the exterior design, performance, handling, and premium features in the new Chrysler 300M, LHS, and Concorde. It aired on national cable networks as well as United Airlines SkyTV. Infomercials are more profitable than most people realize and are used to good effect to sell high-ticket items. They share the product's story and benefits with millions of

additional prospects at a cost-per-lead or cost-per-order that usually matches or beats direct mail or print ads. In 1998, an estimated $1.5 billion in sales was generated by infomercials.[98]

2. *At-home shopping channels:* Some television channels are dedicated to selling goods and services. Home Shopping Network (HSN), which broadcasts 24 hours a day, consists of the program's hosts offering bargain prices on such products as jewelry, lamps, collectible dolls, and power tools. Viewers call in their orders on a toll-free number and receive delivery within 48 hours. Millions of adults watch home shopping programs, and close to half of them buy merchandise from a home shopping program.

3. *Videotext and interactive TV:* Here the consumer's TV set is linked with a seller's catalog by cable or telephone lines. Consumers can place orders via a special keyboard device connected to the system. Much research is now going on to combine TV, telephones, and computers into interactive TV.

kiosk marketing

A kiosk is a small building or structure that might house a selling or information unit. The term describes newsstands, refreshment stands, and free-standing carts whose vendors sell watches, costume jewelry, and other items often seen along the aisles in a mall. The term also covers computer-linked vending machines and "customer-order-placing machines" that one sees in stores, airports, and other locations. All of these are direct-selling tools.

e-marketing

The newest channels for direct marketing are electronic. E-business describes a wide variety of electronic platforms, such as the sending of purchase orders to suppliers via electronic data interchange (EDI) or extranets; the use of fax and e-mail to conduct transactions; the use of ATMs, EFTPOS, and smart cards to facilitate payment and obtain digital cash; and the use of the Internet and online services. All of these involve doing business in a "marketspace" as compared to a physical "marketplace."[99]

The Internet today functions as an information source, an entertainment source, a communication channel, a transaction channel, and even a distribution channel. One can use it as a shopping mall, a TV set, a newspaper, a library, or a phone. Users can send e-mail, exchange views, shop for products, and access news, recipes, art, and business information. The Internet itself is free, though individual users need to pay a monthly fee to an Internet service provider (ISP) such as AOL or EarthLink to be hooked up to it.

The Internet provides marketers and consumers with opportunities for much greater *interaction* and *individualization*. Companies in the past would send standard media—magazines, newsletters, ads—without any individualization or interaction. Today these companies can send individualized content and consumers themselves can further individualize the content; and today companies can interact and dialogue with much larger groups than ever in the past.

PERMISSION MARKETING   According to Seth Godin, former CEO of Yoyodyne Inc., now part of Yahoo!, most company promotion amounts to "interruption marketing," and interruption marketing is becoming less effective. As companies offer more products, they have to increase their promotional spending to get attention; but this leads to more ad clutter, less reach, and lower profits. The Catch-22: The more marketers spend on interruption marketing, the less it works; the less it works, the more companies spend.

Godin came up with the term **permission marketing**. Permission-based marketing uses the interactivity of the Internet to let consumers have a say in what is sent to them. Godin compares permission-based marketing to dating; if a company conducts itself well in its first contact with consumers, it will build up the trust that encourages them to open up to subsequent offers. Godin distinguishes five permission levels:

1. *No Permission Level:* They want nothing to do with the companies.
2. *Low Permission Level:* They do not really know the companies, but they might want to look at their offerings and prices.

3. *Medium Permission Level:* They know the companies. They have neutral feelings about these companies, and they are not sure they want to spend any time in a dialogue; but if companies asked politely, they would probably let companies send them a catalog or flyer.

4. *High Permission Level:* They have not yet done any business with these companies, but they are confident these companies will send them something relevant and interesting to see, read, or hear. They are not reluctant to give companies a lot of data about themselves to get some interesting offers or a special catalog.

5. *Transaction Level:* They do transactions with these companies. They are customers. They are satisfied with the products and services. They trust the companies, and the companies do not hassle them or clutter up their mailboxes with junk mail.

E-MARKETING GUIDELINES   If a company does an e-mail campaign right, it can not only build customer relationships, but also reap additional profits. E-mail involves only a fraction of the cost of a "d-mail," or direct-mail, campaign. For example, Microsoft spent approximately $70 million a year on paper-driven campaigns. Now, it sends out 20 million pieces of e-mail every month at a significant savings over the cost of paper-based campaigns. Also, compared to other forms of online marketing, e-mail is a hands-down winner. Click-through rates for ad banners have dropped to less than 1 percent whereas click-through rates for e-mail are running around 80 percent.

Here are some important guidelines followed by pioneering e-mail marketers:

■ *Give the customer a reason to respond:* Companies should offer surfers powerful incentives for reading e-mail pitches and online ads, like e-mail trivia games, scavenger hunts, and instant-win sweepstakes.

■ *Personalize the content of your e-mails:* IBM's "Focusing on You News Digest" is distributed directly to customers' office e-mail, delivering only "the news they choose." Customers who agree to receive the newsletter select from topics listed on an interest profile.

■ *Offer something the customer could not get via direct mail:* Because e-mail campaigns can be carried out quickly, they can offer time-sensitive information. Travelocity sends frequent e-mails pitching last-minute cheap airfares. Club Med uses e-mail to pitch unsold, discounted vacation packages to the 34,000 people in its database.

■ *Make it easy for customers to "unsubscribe."*[100]

Online merchants will face many challenges in expanding the public's use of e-commerce. Customers will have to feel that the information they supply is confidential and not to be sold to others. Customers will need to trust that online transactions are secure, and they will need to get better and faster responses when they send an inquiry to an online company.

summary

1. Advertising is any paid form of nonpersonal presentation and promotion of ideas, goods, or services by an identified sponsor. Advertisers include not only business firms but also charitable, nonprofit, and government agencies that advertise to various publics.

2. Developing an advertising program is a five-step process: (1) Set advertising objectives; (2) establish a budget that takes into account stage in product life cycle, market share and consumer base, competition and clutter, advertising frequency, and product substitutability; (3) choose the advertising message, determine how the message will be generated, evaluate alternative messages for desirabil-

ity, exclusiveness, and believability; and execute the message with the most appropriate style, tone, words, and format and in a socially responsible manner; (4) decide on the media by establishing the ad's desired reach, frequency, and impact and then choosing the media that will deliver the desired results in terms of circulation, audience, effective audience, and effective ad-exposed audience; and (5) evaluate the communication and sales effects of advertising.

3. Sales promotion consists of a diverse collection of incentive tools, mostly short term, designed to stimulate quicker or greater purchase of particular products or services by con-

sumers or the trade. Sales promotion includes tools for consumer promotion (samples, coupons, cash refund offers, prices off, premiums, prizes, patronage rewards, free trials, warranties, tie-in promotions, cross-promotions, point-of-purchase displays, and demonstrations); trade promotion (prices off, advertising and display allowances, and free goods); and business and sales-force promotion (trade shows and conventions, contests for sales reps, and specialty advertising).

4. In using sales promotion, a company must establish its objectives, select the tools, develop the program, pretest the program, implement and control it, and evaluate the results.

5. Public relations (PR) involves a variety of programs designed to promote or protect a company's image or its individual products. Many companies today use marketing public relations (MPR) to support the marketing departments in corporate or product promotion and image making. MPR can affect public awareness at a fraction of the cost of advertising, and is often much more credible. The main tools of PR are publications, events, news, speeches, public-service activities, and identity media. In considering when and how to use MPR, man-

agement must establish the marketing objectives, choose the PR messages and vehicles, implement the plan carefully, and evaluate the results.

6. Direct marketing is an interactive marketing system that uses one or more media to effect a measurable response or transaction at any location. Direct marketing, especially electronic marketing, is showing explosive growth.

7. Companies are recognizing the importance of integrating their marketing communications in systems called integrated marketing communications, integrated direct marketing, and maximarketing. The aim is to establish the right overall communications budget and the right allocation of funds to each communication tool.

8. Direct marketers must plan campaigns by deciding on objectives, target markets and prospects, offers and prices, followed by testing the campaign and establishing measures to determine the campaign's success.

9. Major channels for direct marketing include face-to-face selling, direct mail, catalog marketing, telemarketing and M-commerce, direct-response marketing, kiosk marketing, and e-marketing.

applications

marketing debate – has tv advertising lost power?

Long deemed the most successful advertising medium, television advertising has received increased criticism as being too expensive and, even worse, no longer as effective as it once was. Critics maintain that consumers tune out too many ads by zipping and zapping and that is difficult to make a strong impression. The future, claim some, is with online advertising. Supporters of TV advertising disagree,

contending that the multisensory impact of TV is unsurpassed and that no other media option offers the same potential impact.

Take a position: TV advertising has faded in importance versus TV advertising is still the most powerful advertising medium.

marketing and advertising

1. Absolut Vodka's ads always feature its distinctive bottle, as shown in Figure 1. For this holiday ad, the company commissioned a specially designed bottle cover to suggest that sipping Absolut is a warm holiday experience, and photographed the ad in the knit designer's New York City apartment.

   a. How would you classify this magazine ad in terms of its advertising objective?

   b. Analyze this ad in terms of message execution, style, tone, and format.

   c. What is the most striking part of the ad? Would the ad be as effective if the headline and copy were more prominent? Why?

2. The ad in Figure 2 invites advertisers to advertise on the Ask Jeeves search site, Ask.com. The message states that an ad on Ask Jeeves will reach consumers "when they are most receptive to your message."

   a. Analyze this ad in terms of the reach, frequency, and impact an advertiser might expect from using Ask Jeeves as an advertising vehicle.

   b. Discuss how a media planner might look at the four media variables of media habits, product characteristics, message characteristics, and cost when considering Ask Jeeves as an Internet advertising vehicle.

   c. What additional questions would a media planner ask when making a decision about whether to advertise on the Ask Jeeves site?

Figure 1

Figure 2

online marketing today

More manufacturers are working with Web-based companies to mount targeted consumer sales promotions on the Internet. StartSampling, for example, helped Golden Books Publishing distribute samples of a new book to mothers of young children. In exchange for receiving a free sample, the mothers filled out a brief online survey. The results far exceeded the company's expectations: Although Golden Books projected a 25 percent response rate from this online sampling program, it actually achieved a 67 percent response rate—and it obtained valuable marketing research at the same time.[101]

To see how StartSampling operates, visit its home page (*www.startsampling.com*). What benefits does this site emphasize for participants? How does it encourage consumers to continue returning for additional samples? How can manufacturers become involved with this site? Why would a manufacturer choose to offer samples through StartSampling rather than through another method (such as in-store sampling, for example)?

you're the marketer: sonic pda marketing plan

Advertising, sales promotion, public relations, and direct marketing—both online and off—are among the most visible outcomes of any marketing plan. Marketers plan these programs with special care because of the support they provide for the product, pricing, and distribution strategies described in the marketing plan.

At Sonic, you are starting to plan the promotional support for launching the new personal digital assistant (PDA) product next year. After reviewing your earlier marketing-mix decisions and thinking about the current situation (especially your competitive circumstances), respond to the following questions as you decide on your promotion strategy:

- Based on the overall promotion decisions you made in the previous chapter, should Sonic use advertising to support the PDA introduction? If so, what advertising goals will you set, and how will you measure your results?

- What message(s) do you want to communicate to your target audience? What media are most appropriate, and why?
- Should you use consumer or trade promotion or both? Which promotion tools would be most appropriate for your new-product introduction?
- Should you use public relations to promote Sonic and its products? If so, what objectives will you set, and which tools will you plan to use?
- How can you use integrated direct marketing to support your new-product introduction?

- Which of the direct-marketing channels are most appropriate for reaching PDA buyers?
- What role should e-marketing plan in your new-product launch?

Consider how the promotion programs you are planning will fit with the other decisions you have made and with Sonic's goals and objectives. As your instructor directs, summarize your programs in a written marketing plan or type them into the Marketing Mix section of the *Marketing Plan Pro* software.

notes

1. Russell H. Colley, *Defining Advertising Goals for Measured Advertising Results* (New York: Association of National Advertisers, 1961).
2. William L. Wilkie and Paul W. Farris, "Comparison Advertising: Problem and Potential," *Journal of Marketing* (October 1975): 7–15.
3. Randall L. Rose, Paul W. Miniard, Michael J. Barone, Kenneth C. Manning, and Brian D. Till, "When Persuasion Goes Undetected: The Case of Comparative Advertising," *Journal of Marketing Research* (August 1993): 315–30; Sanjay Putrevu and Kenneth R. Lord, "Comparative and Noncomparative Advertising: Attitudinal Effects under Cognitive and Affective Involvement Conditions," *Journal of Advertising* (June 1994): 77–91; Dhruv Grewal, Sukumar Kavanoor, and James Barnes, "Comparative versus Noncomparative Advertising: A Meta-Analysis," *Journal of Marketing* (October 1997): 1–15; Dhruv Grewal, Kent B. Monroe, and P. Krishnan, "The Effects of Price-Comparison Advertising on Buyers' Perceptions of Acquisition Value, Transaction Value, and Behavioral Intentions," *Journal of Marketing* (April 1998): 46–59.
4. For a good discussion, see David A. Aaker and James M. Carman, "Are You Overadvertising?" *Journal of Advertising Research* (August–September 1982): 57–70.
5. Donald E. Schultz, Dennis Martin, and William P. Brown, *Strategic Advertising Campaigns* (Chicago: Crain Books, 1984), pp. 192–97.
6. M. L. Vidale and H. R. Wolfe, "An Operations-Research Study of Sales Response to Advertising," *Operations Research* (June 1957): 370–81.
7. John D. C. Little, "A Model of Adaptive Control of Promotional Spending," *Operations Research* (November 1966): 1075–97.
8. For additional models for setting the advertising budget, see Gary L. Lilien, Philip Kotler, and K. Sridhar Moorthy, *Marketing Models* (Upper Saddle River, NJ: Prentice Hall, 1992), ch. 6.
9. Vanessa O'Connell, "Edgy Spots Stir Controversy, and Results," *Wall Street Journal*, January 11, 2001, p. B13.
10. Jennifer Ordonez, "Managers & Managing: Taco Bell's President Set to Improve Sales," *Wall Street Journal*, February 27, 2001, p. 27.
11. These methods were contrasted in Brian Sternthal, "Advertising Strategy," in *Kellogg on Marketing*, ed. Dawn Iacobucci (New York: John Wiley & Sons, 2001): 218–71.
12. "Keep Listening to That Wee, Small Voice," in *Communications of an Advertising Man* (Chicago: Leo Burnett Co., 1961), p. 61.
13. John C. Maloney, "Marketing Decisions and Attitude Research," in *Effective Marketing Coordination*, ed. George L. Baker Jr. (Chicago: American Marketing Association, 1961): 595–618.
14. Dik Warren Twedt, "How to Plan New Products, Improve Old Ones, and Create Better Advertising," *Journal of Marketing* (January 1969): 53–57.
15. William A. Mindak and H. Malcolm Bybee, "Marketing Application to Fund Raising," *Journal of Marketing* (July 1971): 13–18.
16. Lalita Manrai, "Effect of Labeling Strategy in Advertising: Self-Referencing versus Psychological Reactance" (Ph.D. dissertation, Northwestern University, 1987).
17. James B. Amdorfer, "Absolut Ads Sans Bottle Offer a Short-Story Series," *Advertising Age*, January 12, 1998, p. 8; Shelly Branch, "Absolut's Latest Ad Leaves Bottle Behind," *Wall Street Journal*, May 3, 2001 p. B9.
18. Yumiko Ono, "Bulletins from the Battle of Baldness Drug—Sports Figures Tout Rogaine for Pharmacia," *Wall Street Journal*, December 19, 1997, p. B1.
19. Lori L. Tharps, "Hollywood Shills," *Entertainment Weekly*, September 8, 2000, p. 24.
20. L. Greenland, "Is This the Era of Positioning?" *Advertising Age*, May 29, 1972.
21. Michael A. Kamins, Lawrence J. Marks, and Deborah Skinner, "Television Commercial Evaluation in the Context of Program Induced Mood: Congruency versus Consistency Effects," *Journal of Advertising* (June 1991): 1–14.
22. Kenneth R. Lord and Robert E. Burnkrant, "Attention versus Distraction: The Interactive Effect of Program Involvement and Attentional Devices on Commercial Processing," *Journal of Advertising* (March 1993): 47–60; Kenneth R. Lord, Myung-Soo Lee, and Paul L. Sauer, "Program Context Antecedents of Attitude Toward Radio Commercials," *Journal of the Academy of Marketing Science* (Winter 1994): 3–15.
23. David Ogilvy and Joel Raphaelson, "Research on Advertising Techniques That Work—And Don't Work," *Harvard Business Review* (July–August 1982): 14–18.
24. Joanne Lipman, "It's It and That's a Shame: Why Are Some Slogans Losers?" *Wall Street Journal*, July 16, 1993, p. A4; Paul Farhi, "The Wrong One Baby, Uh-Uh: Has Madison Avenue Lost It?" *Washington Post*, February 28, 1993, p. C5.

25. For further reading, see Dorothy Cohen, *Legal Issues in Marketing Decision Making* (Cincinnati, OH: South-Western, 1995).

26. Ibid.

27. Adapted from Sandra Cordon, "Where High Road Meets Bottom Line: Ethical Mutual Funds Avoid Companies Deemed Socially Irresponsible," *The London Free Press*, October 9, 1998, p. D3.

28. Schultz et al., *Strategic Advertising Campaigns*, p. 340.

29. Herbert E. Krugman, "What Makes Advertising Effective?" *Harvard Business Review* (March–April 1975): 98.

30. Peggy J. Kreshel, Kent M. Lancaster, and Margaret A. Toomey, "Advertising Media Planning: How Leading Advertising Agencies Estimate Effective Reach and Frequency" (Urbana: University of Illinois, Department of Advertising, paper no. 20, January 1985). Also see Jack Z. Sissors and Lincoln Bumba, *Advertising Media Planning*, 3rd ed. (Lincolnwood, IL: NTC Business Books, 1988), ch. 9.

31. Roland T. Rust and Richard W. Oliver, "Notes and Comments: The Death of Advertising," *Journal of Advertising* (December 1994): 71–77.

32. Thomas H. Davenport and John C. Beck, *The Attention Economy: Understanding the New Currency of Business* (Boston: Harvard Business School Press, 2000).

33. Gene Accas, "Prime Prices Fall with Shares," *Broadcasting & Cable*, September 28, 1998, p. 36; "Hilfilger Hikes Ads to New Level: First Designer to Go Super Bowl Route," *Daily News Record* 28, no. 7 (January 16, 1998): 2.

34. Roland T. Rust, *Advertising Media Models: A Practical Guide* (Lexington, MA: Lexington Books, 1986).

35. Jay W. Forrester, "Advertising: A Problem in Industrial Dynamics," *Harvard Business Review* (March–April 1959): 100–10.

36. Amber G. Rao and Peter B. Miller, "Advertising/Sales Response Functions," *Journal of Advertising Research* (April 1975): 7–15.

37. Alfred A. Kuehn, "How Advertising Performance Depends on Other Marketing Factors," *Journal of Advertising Research* (March 1962): 2–10.

38. Hani I. Mesak, "An Aggregate Advertising Pulsing Model with Wearout Effects," *Marketing Science* (Summer 1992): 310–26; Fred M. Feinberg, "Pulsing Policies for Aggregate Advertising Models," *Marketing Science* (Summer 1992): 221–34.

39. Forrester, "Advertising," p. 102. For one review of what's known about advertising effectiveness, see Demetrios Vakratsas and Tim Ambler, "How Advertising Works: What Do We Really Know," *Journal of Marketing* 63 (January 1991): 26–43.

40. Russell I. Haley, James Staffaroni, and Arthur Fox, "The Missing Measures of Copy Testing," *Journal of Advertising Research* (May–June 1994): 46–56. (Also see this May–June 1994 issue of the *Journal of Advertising Research* for more articles on copy testing.)

41. J. O. Peckham, *The Wheel of Marketing* (Scarsdale, NY: privately printed, 1975), pp. 73–77.

42. Kristian S. Palda, *The Measurement of Cumulative Advertising Effect* (Upper Saddle River, NJ: Prentice Hall, 1964), p. 87.

43. David B. Montgomery and Alvin J. Silk, "Estimating Dynamic Effects of Market Communications Expenditures," *Management Science* (June 1972): 485–501.

44. <www.infores.com>, Leonard M. Lodish, Magid Abraham, Stuart Kalmenson, Jeanne Livelsberger, Beth Lubetkin, Bruce Richardson, and Mary Ellen Stevens, "How T.V. Advertising Works: A Meta Analysis of 389 Real World Split Cable T.V. Advertising Experiments," *Journal of Marketing Research*, 32 (May 1995): pp. 125–139.

45. In addition to the sources cited below, see David Walker and Tony M. Dubitsky, "Why Liking Matters," *Journal of Advertising Research* (May–June 1994): 9–18; Abhilasha Mehta, "How Advertising Response Modeling (ARM) Can Increase Ad Effectiveness," *Journal of Advertising Research* (May–June 1994): 62–74; Karin Holstius, "Sales Response to Advertising," *International Journal of Advertising* 9, no. 1 (1990): 38–56; John Deighton, Caroline Henderson, and Scott Neslin, "The Effects of Advertising on Brand Switching and Repeat Purchasing," *Journal of Marketing Research* (February 1994): 28–43; Anil Kaul and Dick R. Wittink, "Empirical Generalizations about the Impact of Advertising on Price Sensitivity and Price," *Marketing Science* 14, no. 3, pt. 1 (1995): G151–60; Ajay Kalra and Ronald C. Goodstein, "The Impact of Advertising Positioning Strategies on Consumer Price Sensitivity," *Journal of Marketing Research* (May 1998): 210–24; Gerard J. Tellis, Rajesh K. Chandy, and Pattana Thaivanich, "Which Ad Works, When, Where, and How Often? Modeling the Effects of Direct Television Advertising," *Journal of Marketing Research*, 37 (February 2000): 32–46.

46. Nigel Hollis, "The Link between TV Ad Awareness and Sales: New Evidence from Sales Response Modelling," *Journal of the Market Research Society* (January 1994): 41–55.

47. Gerald J. Tellis, "Advertising Exposure, Loyalty, and Brand Purchase: A Two-Stage Model of Choice," *Journal of Marketing Research* (May 1988): 134–44. Also see "It's Official: Some Ads Work," *The Economist* (April 1, 1995): 52; Dwight R. Riskey, "How TV Advertising Works: An Industry Response," *Journal of Marketing Research* (May 1997): 292–93.

48. From Robert C. Blattberg and Scott A. Neslin, *Sales Promotion: Concepts, Methods, and Strategies* (Upper Saddle River, NJ: Prentice Hall, 1990). This text provides the most comprehensive and analytical treatment of sales promotion to date.

49. Roger A. Strang, "Sales Promotion: Fast Growth, Faulty Management," *Harvard Business Review* (July–August 1976): 116–19.

50. Paul W. Farris and John A. Quelch, "In Defense of Price Promotion," *Sloan Management Review* (Fall 1987): 63–69.

51. For a good summary of the research on whether promotion erodes the consumer franchise of leading brands, see Blattberg and Neslin, *Sales Promotion*.

52. Robert George Brown, "Sales Response to Promotions and Advertising," *Journal of Advertising Research* (August 1974): 36–37. Also see Carl F. Mela, Sunil Gupta, and Donald R. Lehmann, "The Long-Term Impact of Promotion and Advertising on Consumer Brand Choice," *Journal of Marketing Research* (May 1997): 248–61; Purushottam Papatla and Lakshman Krishnamurti, "Measuring the Dynamic Effects of Promotions on Brand Choice," *Journal of Marketing Research*

(February 1996): 20–35; Kandel Jedidi, Carl F. Mela, and Sunil Gupta, "Managing Advertising and Promotion for Long-Rum Profitability," *Marketing Science*, 18(1), (1999): 1–22.

53. F. Kent Mitchel, "Advertising/Promotion Budgets: How Did We Get Here, and What Do We Do Now?" *Journal of Consumer Marketing* (Fall 1985): 405–47.

54. For a model for setting sales-promotions objectives, see David B. Jones, "Setting Promotional Goals: A Communications Relationship Model," *Journal of Consumer Marketing* 11, no. 1 (1994): 38–49.

55. See John C. Totten and Martin P. Block, *Analyzing Sales Promotion: Text and Cases*, 2nd ed. (Chicago: Dartnell, 1994), pp. 69–70.

56. Roger O. Crockett, "Penny-Pinchers' Paradise: E-coupons are Catching on Fast—and Companies are Learning How to Use Them," *BusinessWeek E.Biz*, January 22, 2001, p. EB12.

57. Paul W. Farris and Kusum L. Ailawadi, "Retail Power: Monster or Mouse?" *Journal of Retailing* (Winter 1992): 351–69.

58. "Retailers Buy Far in Advance to Exploit Trade Promotions," *Wall Street Journal* October 9, 1986, p. 35; Rajiv Lal, J. Little, and J. M. Vilas-Boas, "A Theory of Forward Buying, Merchandising, and Trade Deals," *Marketing Science* 15, no. 1 (1996): 21–37.

59. Kevin Price, "Trade Promotion: Much Ado about Something," *Promo* (October 1991): 15, 37, 40.

60. Quoted from Kerry E. Smith, "Media Fusion," *Promo* (May 1992): 29.

61. Arthur Stern, "Measuring the Effectiveness of Package Goods Promotion Strategies" (paper presented to the Association of National Advertisers, Glen Cove, NY, February 1978).

62. Mary Cowlett, "Consumer PR: Infectious Marketing," *PR Week*, March 2, 2001, p. 12.

63. Strang, "Sales Promotion," p. 120

64. Kurt H. Schaffir and H. George Trenten, *Marketing Information Systems* (New York: Amacom, 1973), p. 81.

65. Magid M. Abraham and Leonard M. Lodish, "Getting the Most Out of Advertising and Promotion," *Harvard Business Review* (May–June 1990): 50–60.

66. Joe A. Dodson, Alice M. Tybout, and Brian Sternthal, "Impact of Deals and Deal Retraction on Brand Switching," *Journal of Marketing Research* (February 1978): 72–81.

67. Books on sales promotion include Totten and Block, *Analyzing Sales Promotion: Text and Cases*; Don E. Schultz, William A. Robinson, and Lisa A. Petrison, *Sales Promotion Essentials*, 2nd ed. (Lincolnwood, IL: NTC Business Books, 1994); John Wilmshurst, *Below-the-Line Promotion* (Oxford, England: Butterworth/Heinemann, 1993); Robert C. Blattberg and Scott A. Neslin, *Sales Promotion: Concepts, Methods, and Strategies* (Upper Saddle River, NJ: Prentice Hall, 1990). For an expert systems approach to sales promotion, see John W. Keon and Judy Bayer, "An Expert Approach to Sales Promotion Management," *Journal of Advertising Research* (June–July 1986): 19–26.

68. For an excellent account, see Thomas L. Harris, *The Marketer's Guide to Public Relations* (New York: John Wiley, 1991). Also see Harris, *Value-Added Public Relations* (Chicago: NTC Business Books, 1998).

69. Tom Duncan, *A Study of How Manufacturers and Service Companies Perceive and Use Marketing Public Relations* (Muncie, IN: Ball State University, December 1985). For more on how to contrast the effectiveness of advertising with the effectiveness of PR, see Kenneth R. Lord and Sanjay Putrevu, "Advertising and Publicity: An Information Processing Perspective," *Journal of Economic Psychology* (March 1993): 57–84.

70. From Ken Sacharin, *Attention!: How to Interrupt, Yell, Whisper, and Touch Customers*. As quoted in "Grand Entrance," *Adweek*, November 27, 2000, p. 38.

71. Tia O'Brien, "Secrets of Spin," *Upside*, June 1, 1999.

72. For further reading on cause-related marketing, see P. Rajan Varadarajan and Anil Menon, "Cause-Related Marketing: A Co-Alignment of Marketing Strategy and Corporate Philanthropy," *Journal of Marketing* (July 1988): 58–74.

73. Dave Hill, "Viagra Nation," *The Independent*, July 15, 2001, pp. 22–26; Peter Carlson, "Potent Medicine," *Washington Post*, March 26, 1999, p. C1.

74. Material adapted from Thomas L. Harris, "PR Gets Personal," *Direct Marketing* (April 1994): 29–32.

75. Dwight W. Catherwood and Richard L. Van Kirk, *The Complete Guide to Special Event Management* (New York: John Wiley, 1992).

76. Renée Dye, "The Buzz on Buzz," *Harvard Business Review* (November–December 2000).

77. Arthur M. Merims, "Marketing's Stepchild: Product Publicity," *Harvard Business Review* (November–December 1972): 111–12. Also see Katerine D. Paine, "There Is a Method for Measuring PR," *Marketing News*, (November 6): 1987, p. 5.

78. The Terms *direct-order marketing* and *direct-relationship marketing* were suggested as subsets of direct marketing by Stan Rapp and Tom Collins in *The Great Marketing Turnaround* (Upper Saddle River, NJ: Prentice Hall, 1990).

79. Figures supplied by Direct Marketing Magazine, Tel 516-716-6700.

80. *Industry Standard*, February 12, 2001, p. 86.

81. Don E. Schultz, Stanley I. Tannenbaum, and Robert F. Lauterborn, *Integrated Marketing Communications* (Lincolnwood, IL: NTC Business Books, 1993); Ernan Roman, *Integrated Direct Marketing: The Cutting Edge Strategy for Synchronizing Advertising, Direct Mail, Telemarketing, and Field Sales* (Lincolnwood, IL: NTC Business Books, 1995); *Beyond Maximarketing: The New Power of Caring and Daring* (New York: McGraw-Hill, 1994).

82. Roman, *Integrated Direct Marketing*, p. 3.

83. Rapp and Collins, *Maximarketing*.

84. Debra Ray, "'Poor Mouth' Direct Mail Brochure Nets $3.5 Million in Contributions," *Direct Marketing* (February 1998): 38–39.

85. Bob Stone, *Successful Direct Marketing Methods*, 6th ed. (Lincolnwood, IL: NTC Business Books, 1996). Also see David Shepard Associates, *The New Direct Marketing*, 2nd. ed. (Chicago: Irwin, 1995); Amiya K. Basu, Atasi Basu, and Rajeev Batra, "Modeling the Response Pattern to Direct Marketing Campaigns," *Journal of Marketing Research* (May 1995): 204–12.

86. Edward L. Nash, *Direct Marketing: Strategy, Planning, Execution*, 3rd ed. (New York: McGraw-Hill, 1995).

87. Rachel McLaughlin, "Get the Envelope Opened!" *Target Marketing* (September 1998): 37–39.

88. Also see Richard J. Courtheoux, "Calculating the Lifetime Value of a Customer," in Roman, *Integrated Direct Marketing*, pp. 198–202. Also see Rob Jackson and Paul Wang, *Strategic Database Marketing* (Lincolnwood, IL: NTC Business Books, 1994), pp. 188–201.

89. The *average customer longevity* (N) is related to the *customer retention rate* (CR). Suppose the company retains 80% of its customers each year. Then the average customer longevity is given by:

$$N = \frac{1}{10CR} = \frac{1}{10.8} = 5 \text{ years}$$

90. Carl Sewell and Paul Brown, *Customers for Life* (New York: Pocket Books, 1990), p. 162.

91. Cited in Don Peppers and Martha Rogers, *The One To One Future* (New York: Currency, 1993), pp. 37–38.

92. Bruce Horovitz, "Catalog Craze Delivers Holiday Deals," *USA Today*, December 1, 1998, p. 3B.

93. Erika Rasmussen, "The Lands' End Difference," *Sales & Marketing Management* (October 1988): 138.

94. For more reading, see Janice Steinberg, "Cacophony of Catalogs Fill All Niches," *Advertising Age*, October 26, 1987, pp. S1–S2.

95. Mari Yamaguchi, "Japanese Consumers Shun Local Catalogs to Buy American," *Marketing News*, December 2, 1996, p. 12; Cacilie Rohwedder, "U.S. Mail-Order Firms Shake Up Europe—Better Service, Specialized Catalogs Find Eager Shoppers," *Wall Street Journal*, January 6, 1998; Kathleen Kiley, "B-to-B Marketers High on Overseas Sales," *Catalog Age* (January 1997): 8.

96. De'Ann Weimer, "Can I Try (Click) That Blouse (Drag) in Blue?" *BusinessWeek*, November 9, 1998, p. 86.

97. David Woodruff, "Twilight of the Teller?" *BusinessWeek*, European Edition, July 20, 1998, pp. 16–17.

98. "Infomercial Offers Multiple Uses," *Direct Marketing* (September 1998): 11; Tim Hawthorne, When and Why to Consider Infomercials," *Target Marketing* (February 1998): 52–53.

99. Jeffrey F. Rayport and John J. Sviolka, "Managing in the Marketplace," *Harvard Business Review* (November–December 1994): 78–85. Also see their "Exploiting the Virtual Value Chain," *Harvard Business Review* (November–December 1994): 141–50.

100. Seth Godin, *Permission Marketing: Turning Strangers into Friends and Friends into Customers* (New York: Simon & Schuster, 1999).

101. "Money for Nothing, Hits for Free," *Business 2.0*, June 2001, p. 36.

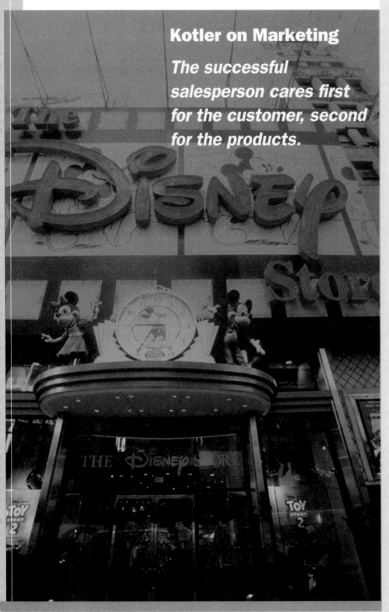

21

managing the sales force

Kotler on Marketing

The successful salesperson cares first for the customer, second for the products.

In this chapter, we will address the following questions:

- What decisions do companies face in designing a sales force?
- How do companies recruit, select, train, supervise, motivate, and evaluate a sales force?
- How can salespeople improve their skills in selling, negotiating, and carrying on relationship marketing?

U.S. firms spend over a trillion dollars annually on sales forces and sales-force materials—more than they spend on any other promotional method. Nearly 12 percent of the total workforce work full time in sales occupations. Sales forces are found in nonprofit as well as for-profit organizations. College recruiters are the university's sales-force arm. Churches use membership committees to attract new members. The U.S. Agricultural Extension Service sends agricultural specialists to sell farmers on new farming methods. Hospitals and museums use fund-raisers to contact donors and solicit donations.

The term **sales representative** *covers a broad range of positions. Robert McMurry distinguished six sales positions, ranging from the least to the most creative types of selling:*[1]

1. Deliverer: *A salesperson whose major task is the delivery of a product (milk, bread, fuel, oil).*

2. Order taker: *A salesperson who acts predominantly as an inside order taker (the salesperson standing behind the counter) or outside order taker (the soap salesperson calling on the supermarket manager).*

3. Missionary: *A salesperson who is not expected or permitted to take an order but whose major task is to build goodwill or to educate the actual or potential user (the medical "detailer" representing an ethical pharmaceutical house).*

4. Technician: *A salesperson with a high level of technical knowledge (the engineering salesperson who is primarily a consultant to the client companies).*

5. Demand creator: *A salesperson who relies on creative methods for selling tangible products (vacuum cleaners, refrigerators, siding, encyclopedias) or intangibles (insurance, advertising services, or education).*

6. Solution vendor: *A salesperson whose expertise is in the solving of a customer's problem, often with a system of the company's products and services (for example, computer and communications systems).*

No one debates the importance of the sales force in the marketing mix. However, companies are sensitive to the high and rising costs (salaries, commissions, bonuses, travel expenses, and benefits) of maintaining a sales force. Because the average cost of a personal sales call ranges from $250 to $500, and closing a sale typically requires four calls, the total cost can range from $1,000 to $2,000. Not surprisingly, companies are seeking to substitute mail- and phone-based selling units to reduce field sales expenses. They also are trying to increase the productivity of the sales force through better selection, training, supervision, motivation, and compensation.

designing the sales force

Sales personnel serve as the company's personal link to the customers. The sales representative *is* the company to many of its customers. It is the sales rep who brings back much-needed information about the customer. Therefore, the company needs to carefully consider issues in sales force design—namely, the development of sales force objectives, strategy, structure, size, and compensation. (See Figure 21.1.)

sales-force objectives and strategy

The old idea was that the sales force should "sell, sell, and sell." At IBM, salespeople would "push metal" and at Xerox they would "sell boxes." Salespeople had quotas, and the better salespeople met or exceeded their quotas. Later, the idea arose that sales reps should know how to diagnose a customer's problem and propose a solution. Salespeople show a customer-prospect how their company can help the customer improve its profitability. They seek to join their company with the customer's company as "partners for profit."

Companies need to define the specific objectives they want their sales force to achieve. For example, a company might want its sales representatives to spend 80 percent of their time with current customers and 20 percent with prospects, and 85 percent of their time on established products and 15 percent on new products. The specific allocation scheme depends on the kind of products and customers, but regardless of the selling context, salespeople will have one or more of the following specific tasks to perform:

- *Prospecting:* Searching for prospects, or leads.
- *Targeting:* Deciding how to allocate their time among prospects and customers.
- *Communicating:* Communicating information about the company's products and services.
- *Selling:* Approaching, presenting, answering objections, and closing sales.
- *Servicing:* Providing various services to the customers—consulting on problems, rendering technical assistance, arranging financing, expediting delivery.
- *Information gathering:* Conducting market research and doing intelligence work.
- *Allocating:* Deciding which customers will get scarce products during product shortages.

Because of the expense, most companies are moving to the concept of a *leveraged sales force*. A sales force should focus on selling the company's more complex and customized products to large accounts and the company should turn over low-end selling to inside sales people and to Web ordering. Tasks such as lead generation, proposal writing, order fulfillment, and postsale support should be turned over to others. Salespeople should handle fewer accounts, and be rewarded for key account growth. This is far different from expecting salespeople to sell to every possible account, which is usually the weakness of geographically based sales forces.[2]

The sales representative's focus varies with the state of the economy. During product shortages, reps have no problem selling. During periods of product abundance, reps compete vigorously to win customer preference. Companies are increasingly judging their sales reps not only on their sales volume, but also on their ability to create customer satisfaction and profit. Here is an example.

Tiffany & Co. The name *Tiffany* brings to mind expensive jewelry, and this image is cultivated in every aspect of the retailer's marketing. A purchase on the selling floor can be like an investment, so management trains its retail sales staff to be consultants. Because the consumer is not typically an expert, salespeople are trained to offer advice and information about the quality and cut of stones, the suitability of various settings, and the choices available in various price ranges. Even when selling less expensive items, such as a box of stationery or a scarf, the salespeople know that part of the purchase is the experience and prestige of shopping at Tiffany. They also know that a satisfied customer is a potential return customer.

In addition to its retail sales staff, Tiffany has 155 field reps to serve corporate customers. An initial training program for the corporate sales staff lasts for six to eight weeks, and only when new hires have demonstrated mastery of skills, knowledge, and products are they allowed to deal with customers.[3]

Companies must deploy sales forces strategically so that they call on the right customers at the right time and in the right way. Today's sales representatives act as "account managers" who arrange fruitful contact between various people in the buying and selling organizations. Selling increasingly calls for teamwork requiring the support of other personnel, such as top management, especially when national accounts or major sales are at stake; technical people, who supply technical information and service to the customer before, during, or after product purchase; customer service representatives, who provide installation, maintenance, and other services; and an office staff, consisting of sales analysts, order expediters, and secretaries.

DuPont When DuPont heard that corn growers needed a herbicide that could be applied less often, it appointed a team of chemists, sales and marketing executives, and regulatory specialists to solve the problem. They created a product that topped $57 million in sales its first year.[4]

figure **21.1**

Designing a Sales Force

Designing the sales force → Sales force objectives → Sales force strategy → Sales force structure → Sales force size → Sales force compensation

To maintain a market focus, salespeople should know how to analyze sales data, measure market potential, gather market intelligence, and develop marketing strategies and plans. Sales representatives need analytical marketing skills, and these skills become especially important at the higher levels of sales management. Marketers believe that sales forces will be more effective in the long run if they understand marketing as well as selling.

Once the company decides on an approach, it can use either a direct or a contractual sales force. A **direct (company) sales force** consists of full- or part-time paid employees who work exclusively for the company. This sales force includes inside sales personnel who conduct business from the office using the telephone and receive visits from prospective buyers, and field sales personnel who travel and visit customers. A **contractual sales force** consists of manufacturers' reps, sales agents, and brokers, who are paid a commission based on sales.

sales-force structure

The sales-force strategy has implications for the sales-force structure. If the company sells one product line to one end-using industry with customers in many locations, it would use a territorial sales-force structure. If the company sells many products to many types of customers, it might need a product or market sales-force structure. Table 21.1 summarizes

table **21.1**	
Sales–Force Structures	**Territorial:** Each sales representative is assigned an exclusive territory. This sales structure results in a clear definition of responsibilities. It increases the rep's incentive to cultivate local business and personal ties. Travel expenses are relatively low because each rep travels within a small area.
	Territory size: Territories can be designed to provide equal sales potential or equal workload. Territories of *equal potential* provide each rep with the same income opportunities and provide the company with a means to evaluate performance. Territories can also be designed *to equalize the sales workload* so that each rep can cover the territory adequately.
	Territory shape: Territories are formed by combining smaller units, such as counties or states, until they add up to a territory of a given potential or workload. Companies can use computer programs to design territories that optimize such criteria as compactness, equalization of workload or sales potential, and minimal travel time.
	Product: The importance of sales reps' knowing their products, together with the development of product divisions and product management, has led many companies to structure their sales forces along product lines. Product specialization is particularly warranted where the products are technically complex, highly unrelated, or very numerous.
	Market: Companies often specialize their sales forces along industry or customer lines. Separate sales forces can be set up for different industries and even different customers. The advantage of market specialization is that each sales force can become knowledgeable about specific customer needs. The major disadvantage is that customers are scattered throughout the country, requiring extensive travel.
	Complex: When a company sells a wide variety of products to many types of customers over a broad geographical area, it often combines several structures. Reps can be specialized by territory-product, territory-market, product-market, and so on. A sales rep might then report to one or more line and staff managers. Motorola, for example, manages four types of sales forces: (1) a strategic market sales force composed of technical, applications, and quality engineers and service personnel assigned to major accounts; (2) a geographic sales force calling on thousands of customers in different territories; (3) a distributor sales force calling on and coaching Motorola distributors; and (4) an inside sales force doing telemarketing and taking orders via phone and fax.

marketing **insight**

Major Account Management—What It Is and How It Works

Major accounts (also called key accounts, national accounts, global accounts, or house accounts) are typically singled out for special attention. Important customers who have multiple divisions in many locations are offered *major account contracts*, which provide uniform pricing and coordinated service for all customer divisions. A **major account manager (MAM)** supervises field reps calling on customer plants within their territories. Large accounts involving collaborative work are handled by *major account programs* consisting of cross-functional personnel who handle all aspects of the relationship. The company's largest accounts may get a strategic account management team, consisting of cross-functional personnel permanently assigned to one customer, that often maintains offices at the customer's facility. For example, in 1992 Procter & Gamble stationed a strategic account management team to work with Wal-Mart in its Bentonville, Arkansas, headquarters. By 1998, P&G and Wal-Mart had already jointly saved $30 billion through supply chain improvements. Today, the P&G team in Bentonville consists of approximately 100 staffers dedicated to serving Wal-Mart.

If a company has several such accounts, it is likely to organize a major account management division. The average company manages about 75 key accounts. In a typical major account management division, the average MAM handles nine accounts. MAMs typically report to the national sales manager who reports to the vice president of marketing and sales, who in turn reports to the CEO.

Major account management is growing. As buyer concentration increases through mergers and acquisitions, fewer buyers account for a larger share of a company's sales. Many buyers are centralizing their purchases for certain items, which gives them more bargaining power. Sellers in turn need to devote more attention to these major buyers. Still another factor is that as products become more complex, more groups in the buyer's organization become involved in the purchase process. The typical salesperson might not have the skill, authority, or coverage to be effective in selling to the large buyer.

In organizing a major account program, a company faces a number of issues, including how to select major accounts; how to manage them; how to select, manage, and evaluate major account managers; how to organize a structure for major account managers; and where to locate major account management in the organization. In selecting major accounts, companies look for accounts that purchase a high volume (especially of more profitable products), purchase centrally, require a high level of service in several geographic locations, may be price-sensitive, and may want a long-term partnering relationship.

Major account managers have a number of duties: acting as the single point of contact; developing and growing customer business; understanding customer decision processes; identifying added-value opportunities; providing competitive intelligence; negotiating sales; and orchestrating customer service. MAMs are typically evaluated on their effectiveness in growing their share of the account's business and on their achievement of annual profit-and-sales volume goals. Companies often make the mistake of selecting their most productive salespeople as MAMs, but different sets of skills are required for the two jobs. One MAM said, "My position must not be as a salesman, but as a 'marketing consultant' to our customers and a salesman of my company's capabilities as opposed to my company's products."

Major accounts normally receive more favorable pricing based on their purchase volume, but marketers cannot rely exclusively on this incentive to retain customer loyalty. There is always a risk that competitors can match or beat a price or that increased costs may necessitate raising prices. Many major accounts look for added value more than for a price advantage. They appreciate having a single point of dedicated contact; single billing; special warranties; EDI links; priority shipping; early information releases; customized products; and efficient maintenance, repair, and upgraded service. In addition to these practical considerations, there is the value of goodwill. Personal relationships with personnel who value the major account's business and who have a vested interest in the success of that business are compelling reasons for being a loyal customer.

Sources: S. Tubridy, "Major Account Management," in *AMA Management Handbook* (3rd ed.), ed. John J. Hampton (New York: Amacom, 1994), pp. 3-25, 3-27; Sanjit Sengupta, Robert E. Krapfel, and Michael A. Pusateri, "The Strategic Sales Force," *Marketing Management* (Summer 1997): 29–34; Robert S. Duboff and Lori Underhill Sherer, "Customized Customer Loyalty," *Marketing Management* (Summer 1997): 21–27; Tricia Campbell, "Getting Top Executives to Sell," *Sales & Marketing Management* (October 1998): 39. More information can be obtained from NAMA (National Account Management Association), <*www.nasm.com*>; "Promotion Marketer of the Decade: Wal-Mart," *Promo*, December 1, 1999.

the most common sales-force structures, and "Marketing Insight: Major Account Management—What It Is and How It Works" discusses major account management, a specialized form of sales-force structure.

Established companies need to revise their sales-force structure as market and economic conditions change. British Airways is an excellent example.

British Airways   British Airways hired a team of consultants in 2000 to evaluate its sales force. The results of the evaluation revealed that British Airways excelled in business-to-consumer sales, but needed to focus more on B2B sales. The company kept its basic sales structure intact, under which separate sales teams cover leisure sales, field sales, and the top 200 corporate accounts. To improve its business-to-business sales, the company added "key account" managers to "focus on accounts that delivered the most value."[5]

sales-force size

Once the company clarifies its strategy and structure, it is ready to consider sales-force size. Sales representatives are one of the company's most productive and expensive assets. Increasing their number will increase both sales and costs.

Once the company establishes the number of customers it wants to reach, it can use a *workload approach* to establish sales-force size. This method consists of the following five steps:

1. Customers are grouped into size classes according to annual sales volume.
2. Desirable call frequencies (number of calls on an account per year) are established for each class.
3. The number of accounts in each size class is multiplied by the corresponding call frequency to arrive at the total workload for the country, in sales calls per year.
4. The average number of calls a sales representative can make per year is determined.
5. The number of sales representatives needed is determined by dividing the total annual calls required by the average annual calls made by a sales representative.

Suppose the company estimates that there are 1,000 A accounts and 2,000 B accounts in the nation. A accounts require 36 calls a year, and B accounts require 12 calls a year. The company needs a sales force that can make 60,000 sales calls a year. Suppose the average rep can make 1,000 calls a year. The company would need 60 full-time sales representatives.

The Internet has enabled companies to reduce their sales forces without sacrificing relationships with customers.

Bethlehem Steel   Bethlehem Steel had 220 salespeople in 1990, a number it cut in half by 2000. The company was able to reduce the number of salespeople so drastically because it embraced e-commerce early. It set up a proprietary e-commerce site, *www.bethsteel.com*, where customers can view product inventories, view order status, and track orders. Bethlehem Steel also sells its products via MetalSite, a steel trading portal. Customers are pleased with Bethlehem's e-commerce offerings, and the company plans on reducing its sales force even further.[6]

sales-force compensation

To attract top-quality sales reps, the company has to develop an attractive compensation package. Sales reps would like income regularity, extra reward for above-average performance, and fair payment for experience and longevity. Management would like to achieve control, economy, and simplicity. Some management objectives will conflict with sales rep objectives. No wonder compensation plans exhibit a tremendous variety from industry to industry and even within the same industry.

The level and components of an effective compensation plan must bear some relation to the "going market price" for the type of sales job and required abilities. For example, the average earnings of a typical U.S. sales and marketing manager in 1998 was $110,000.[7] If the market price for salespeople is well-defined, the individual firm has little choice but to pay the going rate. However, published data on industry sales-force compensation levels are infrequent and generally lack sufficient detail.

The company must next determine the four components of sales-force compensation—a fixed amount, a variable amount, expense allowances, and benefits. The *fixed amount*, a salary, is intended to satisfy the reps' need for income stability. The *variable amount*, which might be commissions, bonus, or profit sharing, is intended to stimulate and reward greater effort. *Expense allowances* enable sales reps to meet the expenses involved in travel, lodging, dining, and entertaining. Benefits, such as paid vacations, sickness or accident benefits, pensions, and life insurance, are intended to provide security and job satisfaction.

A popular rule favors making about 70 percent of the salesperson's total income fixed and allocating the remaining 30 percent among the other elements. Fixed compensation receives more emphasis in jobs with a high ratio of nonselling to selling duties and in jobs where the selling task is technically complex and involves teamwork. Variable compensation receives more emphasis in jobs where sales are cyclical or depend on individual initiative. Fixed and variable compensation give rise to three basic types of compensation plans—straight salary, straight commission, and combination salary and commission. Only one-fourth of all firms use either a straight-salary or straight-commission method. Three-quarters use a combination of the two, though the relative proportion of salary versus incentives varies widely.[8]

Straight-salary plans provide sales reps with a secure income, make them more willing to perform nonselling activities, and give them less incentive to overstock customers. From the company's perspective, they provide administrative simplicity and lower turnover. Straight-commission plans attract higher performers, provide more motivation, require less supervision, and control selling costs. On the negative side, commission plans overemphasize getting the sale rather than building the relationship. Combination plans feature the benefits of both plans while reducing their disadvantages.

With compensation plans that combine fixed and variable pay, companies may link the variable portion of a salesperson's pay to a wide variety of strategic goals. Some see a new trend toward deemphasizing volume measures in favor of factors such as gross profitability, customer satisfaction, and customer retention. For example, IBM now partly rewards salespeople on the basis of customer satisfaction as measured by customer surveys.[9]

Some companies are basing the rep's reward partly on a sales team's performance or even companywide performance. This should get reps to work more closely together for the common good. Yet some talented reps may resent carrying weaker team members.

managing the sales force

Once the company has established objectives, strategy, structure, size, and compensation, it has to recruit, select, train, supervise, motivate, and evaluate sales representatives. Various policies and procedures guide these decisions (see Figure 21.2).

recruiting and selecting representatives

At the heart of a successful sales force is the selection of effective representatives. One survey revealed that the top 27 percent of the sales force brought in over 52 percent of the sales. Beyond differences in productivity is the great waste in hiring the wrong people. The average annual turnover rate for all industries is almost 20 percent. When a salesperson quits, the costs of finding and training a new person—plus the cost of lost sales—can run as high as $50,000 to $100,000. A sales force with many new people is less productive.[10]

The financial loss due to turnover is only part of the total cost. If a new representative receives $50,000 a year, another $50,000 goes into fringe benefits, expenses, supervision, office space, supplies, and secretarial assistance. Consequently, the new representative needs to produce sales on which the gross margin at least covers the selling expenses of $100,000. If the gross margin is 10 percent, the new salesperson will have to sell at least $1,000,000 for the company to break even.

Selecting sales reps would be simple if one knew what traits to look for. One good starting point is to ask customers what traits they prefer. Most customers say they want

figure **21.2**

Managing the Sales Force

the rep to be honest, reliable, knowledgeable, and helpful. Another approach is to look for traits common to the most successful salespeople in the company. Here are some findings:

- Charles Garfield, in his study of superachievers, concluded that supersales performers exhibit the following traits: risk taking, powerful sense of mission, problem-solving bent, care for the customer, and careful call planning.[11]
- Robert McMurry wrote: "It is my conviction that the possessor of an effective sales personality is a habitual 'wooer,' an individual who has a compulsive need to win and hold the affection of others."[12] He listed five additional traits: "A high level of energy, abounding self-confidence, a chronic hunger for money, a well-established habit of industry, and a state of mind that regards each objection, resistance, or obstacle as a challenge."[13]
- Mayer and Greenberg offered one of the shortest lists of traits. They concluded that the effective salesperson has two basic qualities: *empathy*, the ability to feel as the customer does; and *ego drive*, a strong personal need to make the sale.[14]

After management develops its selection criteria, it must recruit. The human resources department seeks applicants by various means, including soliciting names from current sales representatives, using employment agencies, placing job ads, and contacting college students. Unfortunately, few students decide to go into selling as a career. Reasons include "Selling is a job and not a profession," and "There is insecurity and too much travel." To counter these objections, company recruiters emphasize starting salaries, income opportunities, and the fact that one-fourth of the presidents of large U.S. corporations started out in marketing and sales.

Selection procedures can vary from a single informal interview to prolonged testing and interviewing, not only of the applicant but of the applicant's spouse.[15] If the spouse is not ready to support the "away-from-home" lifestyle of the salesperson, the hire will not be a good one. Many companies give sales applicants formal tests. Although test scores are only one information element in a set that includes personal characteristics, references, past employment history, and interviewer reactions, they are weighted quite heavily by such companies as IBM, Prudential, Procter & Gamble, and Gillette. Gillette claims that tests have reduced turnover by 42 percent and have correlated well with the subsequent progress of new reps in the sales organization.

training sales representatives

Many companies send their new reps into the field almost immediately, supplied with samples, order books, and a description of the territory. Much of their selling is ineffective. A vice president of a major food company once spent a week watching 50 sales presentations to a busy buyer for a major supermarket chain. Here is what he observed:

> The majority of salesmen were ill prepared, unable to answer basic questions, uncertain as to what they wanted to accomplish during the call. They did not think of the call as a studied professional presentation. They didn't have a real idea of the busy retailer's needs and wants.[16]

Today's customers expect salespeople to have deep product knowledge, to add ideas to improve the customer's operations, and to be efficient and reliable. These demands have required companies to make a much higher investment in sales training.

One of the main problems is that salespeople give in too often when customers demand a discount. One company pinpointed this as a problem when it recognized that its sales revenue had gone up by 25 percent but its profit had remained flat. The company decided to retrain its salespeople to "sell the price," rather than "sell through price." Salespeople were given richer information about each customer's sales history and behavior. They received training to recognize value-adding opportunities rather than price-cutting opportunities. As a result, the company's sales revenue climbed further and so did its margins.[17]

Today, new reps may spend a few weeks to several months in training. The median training period is 28 weeks in industrial-products companies, 12 in service companies, and 4 in consumer-products companies. Training time varies with the complexity of the selling task and the type of person recruited into the sales organization. At IBM, new reps receive extensive initial training and may spend 15 percent of their time each year in additional training. (IBM has now switched 25 percent of the training from classroom to e-learning, saving a great deal of money in the process.)

Sales training programs have several goals:

- Sales representatives need to know and identify with the company.
- Sales representatives need to know the company's products.
- Sales representatives need to know customers' and competitors' characteristics.
- Sales representatives need to know how to make effective sales presentations.
- Sales representatives need to understand field procedures and responsibilities.

New methods of training are continually emerging, such as role playing and sensitivity training; the use of cassette tapes, videotapes, and CD-ROMs; and programmed learning, distance learning, and films on selling.

IBM IBM uses a self-study system called Info-Window that combines a personal computer and a laser videodisc. A trainee can practice sales calls with an on-screen actor who portrays a buying executive in a particular industry. The actor-buyer responds differently depending on what the trainee says.

Whirlpool In order to increase its sales reps' understanding of its appliances, Whirlpool rented an eight-bedroom farmhouse near its headquarters in Benton Harbor, Michigan, and outfitted it with Whirlpool dishwashers, microwaves, washers, dryers, and refrigerators. It sent eight new salespeople to live in the house, to cook and do laundry and household chores. When they emerged, they knew a great deal about Whirlpool appliances and gained more confidence than if they had taken the traditional two-week classroom training course.[18]

supervising sales representatives

Companies vary in how closely they supervise sales reps. Reps paid mostly on commission generally receive less supervision. Those who are salaried and must cover definite accounts are likely to receive substantial supervision.

norms for customer calls

The average salesperson makes about four calls a day, down from five in the previous decade. The downward trend is due to the increased use of the phone, fax machines, and e-mail; the increased reliance on automatic ordering systems; and the drop in cold calls owing to better market research information.

How many calls should a company make on a particular account each year? Magee described an experiment where similar accounts were randomly split into three sets.[19] Sales representatives were asked to spend less than five hours a month with accounts in the first set, five to nine hours a month with those in the second set, and more than nine hours a month with those in the third set. The results demonstrated that additional calls produced more sales, leaving only the question of whether the magnitude of the sales increase justified the additional cost. Some later research has suggested that today's sales reps are spending too much time selling to smaller, less profitable accounts when they should be focusing more of their efforts on selling to larger, more profitable accounts.[20]

NORMS FOR PROSPECT CALLS Companies often specify how much time reps should spend prospecting for new accounts. Spector Freight wants its sales representatives to spend 25 percent of their time prospecting and to stop calling on a prospect after three unsuccessful calls.

Companies set up prospecting standards for a number of reasons. Left to their own devices, many reps will spend most of their time with current customers, who are known quantities. Reps can depend on them for some business, whereas a prospect might never deliver any business. Some companies rely on a missionary sales force to open new accounts.

USING SALES TIME EFFICIENTLY   Studies have shown that the best sales reps are those who manage their time effectively.[21] One effective planning tool is configurator software, a program that automates the order preparation process. DAA Solutions of Hartford, Connecticut, is a producer of an online version of this time-saving product.

DAA Solutions   DAA Solutions Configurator software is intended especially for companies with highly complex engineered products that require drawings. DAA Solutions software links the customer to all the resources of the seller, but the software operates through the sales reps. On a sales call, reps can present product specifications to experts on a customer's staff without having to develop their own technical expertise. The reps can also access pricing information and production schedules, as well as input customization information on behalf of the customer. The configurator software integrates all this information and writes up a virtual order in a matter of minutes. In addition to saving time, the software builds goodwill by reducing errors. DAA Solutions offers all these features using its online configurator software, Design-To-Order, which enables the customer to write an order without necessitating a visit from a sales rep. The sales rep achieves greater efficiency by monitoring the order over the Internet.[22]

Another tool is *time-and-duty analysis*, which helps reps understand how they spend their time and how they might increase their productivity. Sales reps spend time in the following ways:

■ *Preparation:* Getting information and planning call strategy.
■ *Travel:* In some jobs, travel time amounts to over 50 percent of total time. Travel time can be cut down by using faster means of transportation—but this will increase costs.

DAA Solutions' home page describes its Design-to-Order™ software application.

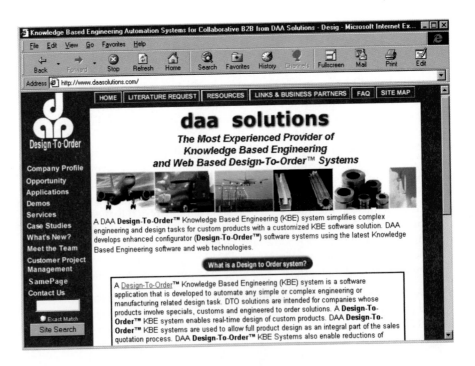

- *Food and breaks:* Some portion of the workday is spent in eating and taking breaks.
- *Waiting:* Time spent in the buyer's outer office, which is dead time unless the representative uses it to plan or to fill out reports.
- *Selling:* Time spent with the buyer in person or on the phone.
- *Administration:* Time spent in report writing and billing, attending sales meetings, and talking to others in the company about production, delivery, billing, sales performance, and other matters.

With so many duties, it is no wonder that actual face-to-face selling time amounts to as little as 29 percent of total working time![23] Companies are constantly seeking ways to improve sales-force productivity. Their methods take the form of training sales representatives in the use of "phone power," simplifying record keeping and administrative time, and using the computer and the Internet to develop call and routing plans and to supply customer and competitive information.

Owens–Corning   Owens-Corning recently put its sales force online with FAST—its newly developed Field Automation Sales Team system. FAST gives its salespeople a constant supply of information about the company and the people they are dealing with. Using laptop computers, each salesperson can access three types of programs. First, FAST gives them a set of *generic tools*, everything from word processing to fax and e-mail transmission to creating presentations online. Second, it provides *product information*—tech bulletins, customer specifications, pricing information, and other data that can help close a sale. Finally, it offers up a wealth of *customer information*—buying history, types of products ordered, and preferred payment terms. Salespeople can prime themselves on backgrounds of clients; call up prewritten sales letters; transmit orders and resolve customer service issues on the spot during customer calls; and have samples, pamphlets, brochures, and other materials sent to clients with a few keystrokes.

To reduce time demands on their outside sales force, many companies have increased the size and responsibilities of their inside sales force. In a survey of 135 electronics distributors, Narus and Anderson found that an average of 57 percent of the sales force's members were inside salespeople.[24] As reasons for the growth of the internal sales force, managers cited the escalating cost of outside sales calls and the growing use of computers and innovative telecommunications equipment.

Inside salespeople are of three types. There are *technical support people*, who provide technical information and answers to customers' questions. There are *sales assistants*, who provide clerical backup for the outside salespersons. They call ahead and confirm appointments, carry out credit checks, follow up on deliveries, and answer customers' questions. *Telemarketers* use the phone to find new leads, qualify them, and sell to them. Telemarketers can call up to 50 customers a day compared to the four an outside salesperson can contact. They can cross-sell the company's other products; upgrade orders; introduce new products; open new accounts and reactivate former accounts; give more attention to neglected accounts; and follow up and qualify direct-mail leads.

The inside sales force frees the outside reps to spend more time selling to major accounts, identifying and converting new major prospects, placing electronic ordering systems in customers' facilities, and obtaining more blanket orders and systems contracts. The inside salespeople spend more time checking inventory, following up orders, and phoning smaller accounts. The outside sales reps are paid largely on an incentive-compensation basis, and the inside reps on a salary or salary plus bonus pay.

Another dramatic breakthrough is the new high-tech equipment—desktop and laptop PCs, videocassette recorders, videodiscs, automatic dialers, e-mail, fax machines, and teleconferencing and videophones. The salesperson has truly gone "electronic." Not only is sales and inventory information transferred much faster, but specific computer-based

marketing for the **new economy**

Automation for the Personal Touch

The array of technological resources available to the contemporary sales representative—Web sites, laptop computers, software, printers, modems, fax-copiers, e-mail, cellular phones, and pagers—is giving reps more time for personal interaction with customers. The old paradigm of the sales presentation in which the rep discerns the customer's needs and then offers the product or service that comes closest to meeting them has been replaced by a new model. In **relationship marketing**, a rep sells a long-term partnership in which both parties collaborate on identifying needs and developing, maintaining, and updating products and services customized to fulfill them.

One of the most valuable electronic tools for the sales rep is the company Web site, and one of its most useful applications is as a prospecting tool. Company Web sites can help define the firm's relationships with individual accounts and identify those whose business warrants a personal sales call. The Web site provides an introduction to self-identified potential customers. Depending on the nature of the business, the initial order may even take place online. For more complex transactions, the site provides a way for the buyer to contact the seller. Pall Corporation, a manufacturer of fluid filtration and purification technologies, has all e-mail directed to company headquarters, with leads going directly to the appropriate sales rep.

Not every company has achieved immediate success in using a Web site for sales and sales support. Grainger, an industrial-supply company, had less encouraging results with its initial efforts. Less than 1 percent of its customers registered to open a Web account during its first year in operation, and less than 1 percent of the company's revenue in fiscal 1998 came from Web sales. Still, Grainger anticipated that its Internet customer base would grow, and spent more than $25 million over the next year bringing its full catalog of 220,000 products to the Web. Customers began flocking to Grainger.com, and in 2000 the company's digital businesses contributed

$337 million—or 6 percent—of total sales, growth of 150 percent from the previous year.

Making a Web site an effective selling tool requires experts in both the medium and the content of the site. The site can attract and keep customers only if the information is kept up-to-date and presented in a way that is easily accessible and appealing to visitors, both technically and in terms of communication style. Selling over the Internet supports relationship marketing by solving problems that do not require live intervention and thus allowing more time to be spent on issues that are best addressed face-to-face.

Sources: Charles Waltner, "Pall Corp. Wins Business with Info-Driven Web Site," *Net Marketing* (October 1996); Beth Snyder, "Execs: Traditional Sales Still Key," *Net Marketing* (May 1998); John Evan Frok, "Grainger's Buy-in Plan," *Business Marketing* (November 1998): 1, 48; "Grainger Reports EPS of 51 Cents for the 2000 Fourth Quarter," *Business Wire*, January 30, 2001; "10 Companies That Get It," *Fortune*, November 8, 1999.

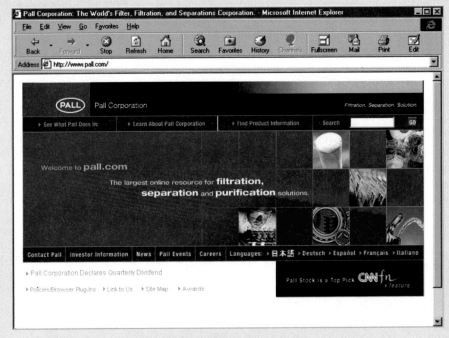

Company Web site as a prospecting tool: Pall's site helps customers find solutions and contact the company.

---

decision support systems on CDs have been created for sales managers and sales representatives. (See "Marketing for the New Economy: Automation for the Personal Touch.")

motivating sales representatives

Some sales representatives will put forth their best effort without any special coaching from management. To them, selling is the most fascinating job in the world; they are ambitious and self-starters. However, the majority require encouragement and special incentives. This is especially true of field selling: Reps usually work alone, their hours are irregular, and they are often away from home. They confront aggressive, competing sales reps; they have an inferior status relative to the buyer; they often do not have the authority to do what is necessary to win an account; and they sometimes lose large orders they have worked hard to obtain.

The problem of motivating sales representatives has been studied by Churchill, Ford, and Walker.[25] Their basic model says that the higher the salesperson's motivation, the greater the effort. Greater effort will lead to greater performance; greater performance will lead to greater rewards; greater rewards will lead to greater satisfaction; and greater satisfaction will reinforce motivation. The model thus implies the following:

- *Sales managers must be able to convince salespeople that they can sell more by working harder or by being trained to work smarter:* But if sales are determined largely by economic conditions or competitive actions, this linkage is undermined.
- *Sales managers must be able to convince salespeople that the rewards for better performance are worth the extra effort:* But if the rewards seem to be set arbitrarily or are too small or of the wrong kind, this linkage is undermined.

The researchers went on to measure the importance of different rewards. The reward with the highest value was pay, followed by promotion, personal growth, and sense of accomplishment. The least-valued rewards were liking and respect, security, and recognition. In other words, salespeople are highly motivated by pay and the chance to get ahead and satisfy their intrinsic needs, and less motivated by compliments and security. However, the researchers also found that the importance of motivators varied with demographic characteristics: Financial rewards were mostly valued by older, longer-tenured people and those who had large families. Higher-order rewards (recognition, liking and respect, sense of accomplishment) were more valued by young salespeople who were unmarried or had small families and usually more formal education.

Motivators also vary across countries. Whereas money is the number-one motivator of 37 percent of U.S. salespeople, only 20 percent of salespeople in Canada feel the same way. Salespeople in Australia and New Zealand were the least motivated by a fat paycheck.[26]

SALES QUOTAS Many companies set annual sales quotas. Quotas can be set on dollar sales, unit volume, margin, selling effort or activity, and product type. Compensation is often tied to degree of quota fulfillment.

Sales quotas are developed from the annual marketing plan. The company first prepares a sales forecast. This forecast becomes the basis for planning production, workforce size, and financial requirements. Management then establishes quotas for regions and territories, which typically add up to more than the sales forecast. Quotas are set higher than the sales forecast to encourage managers and salespeople to perform at their best levels. If they fail to make their quotas, the company nevertheless might reach its sales forecast.

Each area sales manager divides the area's quota among the area's reps. There are three schools of thought on quota setting. The *high-quota school* sets quotas higher than what most sales reps will achieve but that are attainable. Its adherents believe that high quotas spur extra effort. The *modest-quota school* sets quotas that a majority of the sales force can achieve. Its adherents feel that the sales force will accept the quotas as fair, will attain them, and gain confidence. The *variable-quota school* thinks that individual differences among sales reps warrant high quotas for some, modest quotas for others.

One general view is that a salesperson's quota should be at least equal to the person's last year's sales plus some fraction of the difference between territory sales potential and last year's sales. The more the salesperson reacts favorably to pressure, the higher the fraction should be.

Setting sales quotas creates certain problems. If the company underestimates sales potential, and the sales reps easily achieve their quotas, the company has overpaid its reps. If the company overestimates sales potential, the sales people will find it very hard to reach their quotas, and be frustrated or quit.

Another problem: If a sales rep covers 50 products, should he "sell everything in the bag" or should he focus his selling effort on a few of the more important products and not worry about missing quotas on the rest? Should he visit every customer or focus on the more profitable customers? The general wisdom is that profits are maximized by sales reps focusing on the major products and customers.

Reps are not likely to achieve their quotas when the company is launching several new products at the same time. New-product launches demand a sizeable selling effort. Sales reps will have less time for meeting their quotas on the company's established products. The company will need to expand its sales force whenever it is launching major new products.

Some companies are dropping quotas.[27] Quotas drive reps to get as much business as possible—often resulting in the reps ignoring the service side of the business. The company gains short-term results at the cost of long-term customer satisfaction. Companies such as Siebel, Nortel, and AT&T Worldnet prefer to use a larger set of measures for motivating and rewarding sales reps.

Siebel Systems   Siebel, the leading supplier of sales automation software, does not set quotas for its reps. Siebel judges its sales reps using a number of metrics, such as customer satisfaction, repeat business, and profitable revenues. Almost 40 percent of sales reps' incentive compensation is based on their customers' reported satisfaction with service and product. According to Siebel's vice president, Steve Mankoff, "[If reps] close a contract with a customer, continue to follow up with that customer, and make sure that customer is successful, chances are that customer will come back for more." The main point is to set guidelines for sales reps that drive the kind of rep behavior the company wants to see.

Siebel uses its own software to monitor the responsiveness of the sales staff and measure customer satisfaction. Each rep is required to enter into a database all information about a sales call, including conversations with customers and price quotes. The sales call data is compared with sales goals and customer satisfaction, and the rep is evaluated using a scoring system. Bonuses and commissions are scaled according to the score. The company's close scrutiny of the sales process leads to satisfied customers: Over 50 percent of Siebel's revenue comes from repeat business.[28]

SUPPLEMENTARY MOTIVATORS   Companies use additional motivators to stimulate sales-force effort. Periodic *sales meetings* provide a social occasion, a break from routine, a chance to meet and talk with "company brass" and each other, and a chance to air feelings and to identify with a larger group. Sales meetings are an important tool for education, communication, and motivation.

Companies also sponsor *sales contests* to spur the sales force to a special selling effort above what is normally expected. The contest should present a reasonable opportunity for enough salespeople to win. At IBM, about 70 percent of the sales force qualifies for the 100 percent Club. The reward is a holiday trip that includes a recognition dinner and a blue-and-gold pin. The contest period should not be announced in advance. If it is, some salespersons will defer sales and others pad their sales during the period with customer promises to buy that do not materialize after the contest period ends.

Whether a sales contest is focused on selling a specific product or products during a limited time period or is a more general recognition of top revenue earners for the quarter, the reward should be commensurate with the achievement. Reps who are well paid and whose earnings are based in large part on commissions are more likely to be motivated by a trip, a trophy, or merchandise than by a check of equal value. Consider Okidata's program.

Okidata   Okidata Printers of Mt. Laurel, New Jersey, knows that recognition is part of the prize. Merchandise won in a sales contest is a reminder of the rep's success each time the item is used. Its President's Club is another strong incentive. Reps who achieve their annual goal, and their spouses, are rewarded with five-day vacations at world-class tourist destinations. A poll of salespeople taken by *Incentive* magazine suggests that Okidata knows how to motivate its employees. Respondents whose earnings top $100,000 indicate a preference for prizes of group travel with other winners. They value the recognition and companionship of other top sellers.[29]

evaluating sales representatives

We have been describing the *feed-forward* aspects of sales supervision—how management communicates what the sales reps should be doing and motivates them to do it; but good feed-forward requires good *feedback*, which means getting regular information from reps to evaluate performance.

SOURCES OF INFORMATION   The most important source of information about reps is sales reports. Additional information comes through personal observation, customer letters and complaints, customer surveys, and conversations with other sales representatives.

Sales reports are divided between *activity plans* and *write-ups of activity results*. The best example of the former is the salesperson's work plan, which reps submit a week or month in advance. The plan describes intended calls and routing. This report forces sales reps to plan and schedule their activities, informs management of their whereabouts, and provides a basis for comparing their plans and accomplishments. Sales reps can be evaluated on their ability to "plan their work and work their plan."

Many companies require representatives to develop an annual territory marketing plan in which they outline their program for developing new accounts and increasing business from existing accounts. This type of report casts sales reps into the role of market managers and profit centers. Sales managers study these plans, make suggestions, and use them to develop sales quotas. Sales reps write up completed activities on *call reports*. Sales representatives also submit expense reports, new-business reports, lost-business reports, and reports on local business and economic conditions.

These reports provide raw data from which sales managers can extract key indicators of sales performance: (1) average number of sales calls per salesperson per day, (2) average sales call time per contact, (3) average revenue per sales call, (4) average cost per sales call, (5) entertainment cost per sales call, (6) percentage of orders per hundred sales calls, (7) number of new customers per period, (8) number of lost customers per period, and (9) sales-force cost as a percentage of total sales.

FORMAL EVALUATION   The sales force's reports along with other observations supply the raw materials for evaluation. There are several approaches to conducting evaluations. One type of evaluation compares current performance to past performance. An example is shown in Table 21.2

The sales manager can learn many things about a rep from this table. Total sales increased every year (line 3). This does not necessarily mean that the person is doing a better job. The product breakdown shows that he has been able to push the sales of product B further than the sales of product A (lines 1 and 2). According to his quotas for the two products (lines 4 and 5), his success in increasing product B sales could be at the expense of product A sales. According to gross profits (lines 6 and 7), the company earns more selling A than B. The rep might be pushing the higher-volume, lower-margin product at the expense of the more profitable product. Although he increased total sales by $1,100 between 2001 and 2002 (line 3), the gross profits on total sales actually decreased by $580 (line 8).

Sales expense (line 9) shows a steady increase, although total expense as a percentage of total sales seems to be under control (line 10). The upward trend in total dollar expense

table **21.2**

Form for Evaluating
Sales Representative's
Performance

Territory: Midland Sales
Representative: John Smith

	1999	2000	2001	2002
1. Net sales product A	$251,300	$253,200	$270,000	$263,100
2. Net sales product B	423,200	439,200	553,900	561,900
3. Net sales total	674,500	692,400	823,900	825,000
4. Percent of quota product A	95.6	92.0	88.0	84.7
5. Percent of quota product B	120.4	122.3	134.9	130.8
6. Gross profits product A	$50,260	$50,640	$54,000	$52,620
7. Gross profits product B	42,320	43,920	55,390	56,190
8. Gross profits total	92,580	94,560	109,390	108,810
9. Sales expense	$10,200	$11,100	$11,600	$13,200
10. Sales expense to total sales (%)	1.5	1.6	1.4	1.6
11. Number of calls	1,675	1,700	1,680	1,660
12. Cost per call	$6.09	$6.53	$6.90	$7.95
13. Average number of customers	320	24	328	334
14. Number of new customers	13	14	15	20
15. Number of lost customers	8	10	11	14
16. Average sales per customer	$2,108	$2,137	$2,512	$2,470
17. Average gross profit per customer	$289	$292	$334	$326

does not seem to be explained by any increase in the number of calls (line 11), although it might be related to success in acquiring new customers (line 14). There is a possibility that in prospecting for new customers, this rep is neglecting present customers, as indicated by an upward trend in the annual number of lost customers (line 15).

The last two lines show the level and trend in sales and gross profits per customer. These figures become more meaningful when they are compared with overall company averages. If this rep's average gross profit per customer is lower than the company's average, he could be concentrating on the wrong customers or not spending enough time with each customer. A review of annual number of calls (line 11) shows that he might be making fewer annual calls than the average salesperson. If distances in the territory are similar to other territories, this could mean that he is not putting in a full workday, he is poor at sales planning and routing, or he spends too much time with certain accounts.

The rep might be quite effective in producing sales but not rate high with customers. Perhaps he is slightly better than the competitors' salespeople, or his product is better, or he keeps finding new customers to replace others who do not like to deal with him. An increasing number of companies are measuring customer satisfaction not only with their product and customer support service, but also with their salespeople. The customers' opinion of the salesperson, product, and service can be measured by mail questionnaires or telephone calls.

Evaluations can also assess the salesperson's knowledge of the company, products, customers, competitors, territory, and responsibilities. Personality characteristics can be rated, such as general manner, appearance, speech, and temperament. The sales manager can review any problems in motivation or compliance.[30]

The sales manager can also check that the representative knows and observes the law. For example, it is illegal for salespeople to lie to consumers or mislead them about the advantages of buying a product. Under U.S. law, salespeople's statements must match advertising claims. In selling to businesses, salespeople may not offer bribes to purchasing agents or others influencing a sale. They may not obtain or use competitors' technical or trade secrets through bribery or industrial espionage. Finally, salespeople must not disparage competitors or competing products by suggesting things that are not true.[31]

principles of personal selling

Personal selling is an ancient art. It has spawned a large literature and many principles. Effective salespersons have more than instinct; they are trained in methods of analysis and customer management. We will examine three major aspects of personal selling: sales professionalism, negotiation, and relationship marketing.[32] Figure 21.3 shows these aspects in schematic form.

professionalism

Today's companies spend hundreds of millions of dollars each year to train salespeople in the art of selling. Over a million copies of books, cassettes, and videotapes on selling are purchased annually, with such tantalizing titles as *Questions That Make the Sale; Green Light Selling: Your Secret Edge to Winning Sales and Avoiding Dead Ends; You'll Never Get No for an Answer; Secrets of Power Persuasion; What They Don't Teach You in Sales 101; Close! Close! Close! How to Make the Sale; How to Make Money Tomorrow Morning; Samurai Selling;* and *World Class Selling.* One of the most enduring books is Dale Carnegie's *How to Win Friends and Influence People.*

Sales-training approaches try to convert a salesperson from a passive order taker into an active order getter. Order takers operate on the assumption that customers know their own needs, resent attempts to influence them, and prefer courteous and self-effacing salespersons. There are two basic approaches in training salespersons to be order getters, a sales-oriented approach and a customer-oriented approach. The *sales-oriented approach* trains the person in the stereotyped high-pressure techniques used in selling encyclopedias or automobiles. This form of selling assumes that customers are not likely to buy except under pressure, that they are influenced by a slick presentation, and that they will not be sorry after signing the order—or, if they are, that it does not matter.

The *customer-oriented approach* trains salespeople in customer problem solving. The salesperson learns how to listen and question in order to identify customer needs and come up with sound product solutions. Presentation skills are secondary to customer-need analysis skills. This approach assumes that customers have latent needs that constitute opportunities, that they appreciate constructive suggestions, and that they will be loyal to sales reps who have their long-term interests at heart. The problem solver is a much more congruent concept for the salesperson under the marketing concept than the hard seller or order taker.

Two vocal exponents of the customer-oriented approach are Neil Rackham and Sharon Drew Morgen. Neil Rackham has developed a method that he calls *SPIN selling* (Situation, Problem, Implication, Need-Payoff). Gone is the script of the slick salesperson, and in its place is the salesperson who knows how to raise good questions and listen and learn. Neil Rackham trains salespeople to raise four types of questions with the prospect:

1. *Situation questions:* These ask about facts or explore the buyer's present situation. For example, "What system are you using to invoice your customers?"
2. *Problem questions:* These deal with problems, difficulties, and dissatisfactions the buyer is experiencing. For example, "What parts of the system create errors?"
3. *Implication questions:* These ask about the consequences or effects of a buyer's problems, difficulties, or dissatisfactions. For example, "How does this problem affect your people's productivity?"
4. *Need-payoff questions:* These ask about the value or usefulness of a proposed solution. For example, "How much would you save if our company could help reduce the errors by 80 percent?"

figure **21.3**

Managing the Sales Force: Improving Effectiveness

figure **21.4**

Major Steps in Effective
Selling

Prospecting
and qualifying

Preapproach

Approach

Presentation
and
demonstration

Overcoming
objections

Closing

Follow-up
and
maintenance

Rackham suggests that companies, especially those selling complex products or services, should have their salesperson move from *preliminaries*, to *investigating* the prospect's problems and needs, to *demonstrating* the supplier's superior capabilities, and then *obtaining* a long-term commitment. This approach reflects the growing interest of many companies in moving from pursuing an immediate sale to developing a long-term customer relationship.[33]

Sharon Drew Morgen takes Rackham's approach a step further with what she calls the Buying Facilitation Method.[34] She holds that the job of a salesperson is to help prospects go through a process to decide first whether their company's performance can be improved, and second whether the seller's offering would provide a solution. Prospects only buy when they realize they have a problem, that they lack resources to solve their problem, and that the seller's offering can add value. The salesperson uses a questioning and listening process to help buyers navigate through their unique decision process. The seller thus becomes a true consultant not only in regard to the seller's product, but in regard to the buyer's need to function more efficiently. The seller willingly terminates the sales call if it is clear that the buyer cannot benefit from the seller's products and services.

No approach works best in all circumstances. Yet most sales-training programs agree on the major steps involved in any effective sales process. These steps are shown in Figure 21.4, and their application to industrial selling is discussed next.[35]

PROSPECTING AND QUALIFYING   The first step in selling is to identify and qualify prospects. Historically, most companies have left it to their salespeople to find leads. Now, more companies are taking responsibility for finding and qualifying leads so that the salespeople can use their expensive time doing what they can do best: selling. Companies can generate leads in the following ways:

- Examining data sources (newspapers, directories, CD-ROMs) in search of names. Firms can acquire company and industry information from commercial list vendors such as Dun & Bradstreet, R. L. Polk, and TRW.
- Putting up a booth at trade shows to encourage drop-bys.
- Inviting current customers to suggest the names of prospects.
- Cultivating other referral sources, such as suppliers, dealers, noncompeting sales representatives, bankers, and trade association executives.
- Contacting organizations and associations to which prospects belong.
- Engaging in speaking and writing activities that will draw attention.
- Using the telephone, mail, and the Internet to find leads.
- Dropping in unannounced on various offices (cold canvassing).

Companies can then qualify the leads by contacting them by mail or phone to assess their level of interest and financial capacity. The leads can be categorized as hot prospects, warm prospects, and cool prospects, with the hot prospects turned over to the field sales force and the warm prospects turned over to the telemarketing unit for follow-up. Even then, it usually takes about four calls on a prospect to consummate a business transaction.

Sometimes companies develop original sales prospecting approaches.

John Deere   In 1993, the dwindling demand for farm equipment and the aggressive actions of competitors pushed Deere's managers to create a strategy that involved its hourly assembly workers in finding and approaching prospects. Deere sent some of its more experienced and knowledgeable workers to regional trade exhibits across North America to pitch the company's equipment to dealers and farmers. The workers also made unscheduled visits to local farmers to discuss their special problems. Customers perceived these new "reps" as presenting an honest, grassroots view of what goes into making Deere products. Once the new reps had wooed potential customers with their expertise in advanced manufacturing methods and total quality programs, the company could decide how to introduce sales reps to make further presentations or close the sale.[36]

PREAPPROACH The salesperson needs to learn as much as possible about the prospect company (what it needs, who is involved in the purchase decision) and its buyers (their personal characteristics and buying styles). The salesperson can consult standard sources (Moody's, Standard & Poor's, Dun & Bradstreet), acquaintances, and others to learn about the company. The salesperson should set call objectives: to qualify the prospect, gather information, make an immediate sale. Another task is to decide on the best contact approach, which might be a personal visit, a phone call, or a letter. The best timing should also be considered because many prospects are busy at certain times. Finally, the salesperson should plan an overall sales strategy for the account.

APPROACH The salesperson should know how to greet the buyer to get the relationship off to a good start. The salesperson might consider wearing clothes similar to what buyers wear (for instance, in California, office clothing is more casual than in Washington, DC); show courtesy and attention to the buyer; and avoid distracting mannerisms, such as staring at the customer. The opening line should be positive; for example, "Mr. Smith, I am Alice Jones from the ABC Company. My company and I appreciate your willingness to see me. I will do my best to make this visit profitable and worthwhile for you and your company." This opening line might be followed by key questions and active listening to understand the buyer's needs. (For new approaches being used to reach doctors, see "Marketing Insight: Drug Salespeople Rely on New Technology to Reach Doctors.")

PRESENTATION AND DEMONSTRATION The salesperson now tells the product "story" to the buyer, following the AIDA formula of gaining *attention*, holding *interest*, arousing *desire*, and obtaining *action*. The salesperson uses a *features, advantages, benefits, and value* approach (FABV). Features describe physical characteristics of a market offering, such as chip processing speeds or memory capacity. Advantages describe why the features provide an advantage to the customer. Benefits describe the economic, technical, service, and social benefits delivered by the offering. Value describes the summative worth (often in monetary terms) of the offering. Too often, salespeople spend too much time dwelling on product features (a product orientation) and not enough stressing the offering's benefits and value (a customer orientation).

Companies have developed three different styles of sales presentation. The oldest is the *canned approach*, which is a memorized sales talk. It is based on stimulus-response thinking; that is, the buyer is passive and can be moved to purchase by the use of the right stimulus words, pictures, terms, and actions. The *formulated approach* is also based on stimulus-response thinking but first identifies the buyer's needs and buying style and then uses a formulated approach to this type of buyer. The *need-satisfaction approach* starts with a search for the customer's real needs by encouraging the customer to do most of the talking. The salesperson takes on the role of a knowledgeable business consultant hoping to help the customer save money or make more money.

Sales presentations can be improved with demonstration aids such as booklets, flip charts, slides, movies, audio- and videocassettes, product samples, and computer-based simulations. Visual aids can show how a product performs and provide other information about it. Booklets and brochures remain useful as "leave behinds" for customer reference. For group presentations, Powerpoint and similar software have replaced the flip chart. These programs enable reps to project professionally prepared visuals on a screen or download them to the laptops of audience members. Johnson & Johnson's Advanced Sterilization Products division uses a visual aid that includes a small video player with five headsets, all easily transported in a briefcase-sized package. Computer animation shows the viewer the inner workings of the Sternad Sterilization System, providing more information in a more engaging way than could be done by displaying the actual machinery—even if the system were portable.[37]

marketing **insight**

Drug Salespeople Rely on New Technology to Reach Doctors

Over 63,000 U.S. sales reps "detail" doctors every day, hoping to get five minutes of a busy doctor's time. Some 40 percent of the calls do not even result in the doctor being available. As a result, pharmaceutical companies are employing new technologies to reach doctors. Among them:

- EPocrates sends brief product information to the handheld devices now used by 130,000 doctors who can e-mail to request more detailed product information.
- RxCentric, an online marketing solutions company, provides doctors with online services that include interactive learning programs like Continuing Medical Education, market research, and promotion presentations. Through these programs, pharmaceutical companies can more effectively detail doctors and gather research information. Doctors can participate whenever they have access to the Internet, 24 hours a day, 7 days a week, not just when a sales rep is available.
- IPhysicianNet has installed free computers, high-speed phone lines, and videoconferencing equipment in the offices of 7,000 high-prescribing doctors in exchange for each doctor agreeing to participate in one video-detailing session per month where nine drug firms will

present their latest products. These drug firms bear the cost of the equipment and videocast time. Doctors can request a video call at a time that is convenient. Video callcenters are typically open 12 hours a day Monday through Friday. A live office visit costs nearly twice as much as a video session, and pilot trials have increased new prescriptions by 14 percent over office visits.

Source: "Rebirth of a Salesman," *The Economist*, April 14, 2001.

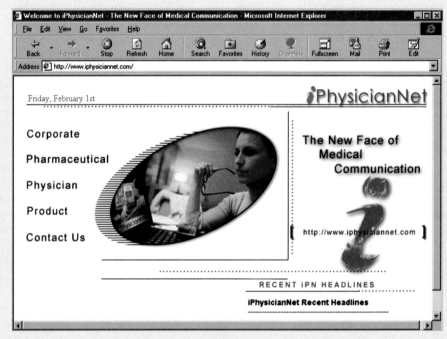

iPhysicianNet's home page shows a video detailing session.

OVERCOMING OBJECTIONS Customers typically pose objections during the presentation or when asked for the order. *Psychological resistance* includes resistance to interference, preference for established supply sources or brands, apathy, reluctance to giving up something, unpleasant associations created by the sales rep, predetermined ideas, dislike of making decisions, and neurotic attitude toward money. *Logical resistance* might consist of objections to the price, delivery schedule, or certain product or company characteristics. To handle these objections, the salesperson maintains a positive approach, asks the buyer to clarify the objection, questions the buyer in a way that the buyer has to answer his or her own objection, denies the validity of the objection, or turns the objection into a reason for buying. Handling and overcoming objections is a part of the broader skills of negotiation.

CLOSING Now the salesperson attempts to close the sale. Some salespeople do not get to this stage or do not do it well. They lack confidence or feel uncomfortable about asking for the order or do not recognize the right psychological moment. Salespersons need to know how to recognize closing signs from the buyer, including physical actions, statements or comments, and questions. There are several closing techniques. They can ask for the order, recapitulate the points of agreement, offer to help the secretary write up the order, ask whether the buyer wants A or B, get the buyer to make minor choices such as the color or size, or indicate what the buyer will lose if the order is not placed now. The salesperson might offer the buyer specific inducements to close, such as a special price, an extra quantity, or a token gift.

FOLLOW-UP AND MAINTENANCE   Follow-up and maintenance are necessary if the salesperson wants to ensure customer satisfaction and repeat business. Immediately after closing, the salesperson should cement any necessary details on delivery time, purchase terms, and other matters that are important to the customer. The salesperson should schedule a follow-up call when the initial order is received to make sure there is proper installation, instruction, and servicing. This visit or call will detect any problems, assure the buyer of the salesperson's interest, and reduce any cognitive dissonance that might have arisen. The salesperson should also develop a maintenance and growth plan for the account.

negotiation

Much B2B selling involves negotiating skills. The two parties need to reach agreement on the price and the other terms of sale. Salespersons need to win the order without making concessions that will hurt profitability.

Marketing is concerned with exchange activities and the manner in which the terms of exchange are established. In *routinized exchange*, the terms are established by administered programs of pricing and distribution. In *negotiated exchange*, price and other terms are set via bargaining behavior, in which two or more parties negotiate long-term binding agreements. Although price is the most frequently negotiated issue, other issues include contract completion time; quality of goods and services offered; purchase volume; responsibility for financing, risk taking, promotion, and title; and product safety.

Marketers who find themselves in bargaining situations need certain traits and skills to be effective. The most important are preparation and planning skill, knowledge of subject matter being negotiated, ability to think clearly and rapidly under pressure and uncertainty, ability to express thoughts verbally, listening skill, judgment and general intelligence, integrity, ability to persuade others, and patience.[38]

WHEN TO NEGOTIATE   Dobler has listed the following circumstances where negotiation is an appropriate procedure for concluding a sale:

1. When many factors bear not only on price, but also on quality and service.
2. When business risks cannot be accurately predetermined.
3. When a long period of time is required to produce the items purchased.
4. When production is interrupted frequently because of numerous change orders.[39]

Negotiation is appropriate whenever a *zone of agreement* exists,[40] when there are simultaneously overlapping acceptable outcomes for the parties. This concept is illustrated in Figure 21.5. Suppose two parties are negotiating a price. The seller has a *reservation prices*, s, which is the minimum he will accept. Any final-contract value, x, that is below s is worse than not reaching an agreement at all. For any $x > s$, the seller receives a surplus. Obviously, the seller desires as large a surplus as possible while maintaining good relations with the buyer. Likewise, the buyer has a reservation price, b, that is the maximum he will pay; any x above b is worse than no agreement. For any $x < b$, the buyer receives a surplus. If the seller's reservation price is below the buyer's— that is, $s < b$—then a zone of agreement exists, and the final price will be determined through bargaining.

There is an obvious advantage in knowing the other party's reservation price and in making one's own reservation price seem higher (for a seller) or lower (for a buyer) than

figure **21.5**
The Zone of Agreement

Source: Reprinted by permission of the publishers from Howard Raiffa, *The Art and Science of Negotiation,* (Cambridge, MA: The Belknap Press of Harvard University Press, copyright 1982 by the President and Fellows of Harvard College).

it really is. The openness with which buyers and sellers reveal their reservation prices depends on the bargainers' personalities, the negotiation circumstances, and expectations about future relations.

FORMULATING A NEGOTIATION STRATEGY   Negotiation involves preparing a strategic plan before meeting the other party and making good tactical decisions during the negotiation sessions. A **negotiation strategy** is a commitment to an overall approach that has a good chance of achieving the negotiator's objectives.

Some negotiators pursue a "hard" strategy with opponents, whereas others maintain that a "soft" strategy yields more favorable results. Fisher and Ury propose another strategy, that of "principled negotiation," described in "Marketing Memo: The Principled-Negotiation Approach to Bargaining."

Marketing
MEMO

The Principled–Negotiation Approach to Bargaining

In a research program known as the Harvard Negotiation Project, Roger Fisher and William Ury arrived at four points for conducting principled negotiations:

1. *Separate the people from the problem:* Each party must understand the other side's viewpoint and the level of emotion with which they hold it, but the focus should be on the parties' interests rather than their differences. Active listening to opposing arguments and addressing the problem in response improve the chance of reaching a satisfactory conclusion.
2. *Focus on interests, not positions:* The distinction between positions and interests is similar to that between solutions and desired outcome or means and end. By focusing on interests rather than positions, the negotiators are more likely to find a mutually agreeable means of achieving common interests.
3. *Invent options for mutual gain:* Search for a larger pie rather than arguing over the size of each side's slice. Looking for options that offer mutual gain helps identify shared interests.
4. *Insist on objective criteria:* Insist that the agreement reflect fair objective criteria independent of either side's position. This approach avoids a situation in which one side must yield to the position of the other. Instead, both sides are yielding to a fair solution based on criteria they both accept.

Source: Adapted from Roger Fisher and William Ury, *Getting to Yes: Negotiating Agreement without Giving In,* rev. ed. (Boston: Houghton Mifflin, 1992), p. 57.

Negotiators use a variety of tactics when bargaining. Bargaining tactics are maneuvers made at specific points in the bargaining process. Several classic bargaining tactics are listed in Table 21.3. Fisher and Ury have offered tactical advice that is consistent with their strategy of principled negotiation. If the other party is more powerful, the best tactic is to know one's BATNA—Best Alternative to a Negotiated Agreement. By identifying the alternatives if a settlement is not reached, the company sets a standard against which any offer can be measured. Knowing its BATNA protects the company from being pressured into accepting unfavorable terms from a more powerful opponent.

table **21.3**

		Classic Bargaining Tactics
Acting Crazy	Put on a good show by visibly demonstrating your emotional commitment to your position. This increases your credibility and may give the opponent a justification to settle on your terms.	
Big Pot	Leave yourself a lot of room to negotiate. Make high demands at the beginning. After making concessions, you will still end up with a larger payoff than if you started too low.	
Get a Prestigious Ally	The ally can be a person or a project that is prestigious. You try to get the opponent to accept less because the person/object he or she will be involved with is prestigious.	
The Well Is Dry	Take a stand and tell the opponent you have no more concessions to make.	
Limited Authority	You negotiate in good faith with the opponent, and when you are ready to sign the deal, you say, "I have to check with my boss."	
Whipsaw/Auction	You let several competitors know you are negotiating with them at the same time. Schedule competitors' appointments with you for the same time and keep them all waiting to see you.	
Divide and Conquer	If you are negotiating with the opponent's team, sell one member of the team on your proposals. That person will help you sell the other members of the team.	
Get Lost/Stall for Time	Leave the negotiation completely for a while. Come back when things are getting better and try to renegotiate then. Time period can be long (say you are going out of town) or short (go to the bathroom to think).	
Wet Noodle	Give no emotional or verbal response to the opponent. Do not respond to his or her force or pressure. Sit there like a wet noodle and keep a "poker face."	
Be Patient	If you can afford to outwait the opponent, you will probably win big.	
Let's Split the Difference	The person who first suggests this has the least to lose.	
Trial Balloon	You release your possible/contemplated decision through a so-called reliable source before the decision is actually made. This enables you to test reactions to your decision.	
Surprises	Keep the opponent off balance by a drastic, dramatic, sudden shift in your tactics. Never be predictable—keep the opponent from anticipating your moves.	

Another set of bargaining tactics are responses intended to deceive, distort, or otherwise influence the bargaining. What tactic should be used when the other side uses a take-it-or-leave-it tactic or seats the other party on the side of the table with the sun in his eyes? A negotiator should recognize the tactic, raise the issue explicitly, and question the tactic's legitimacy and desirability—in other words, negotiate over it. If negotiating fails, the company should resort to its BATNA and terminate the negotiation until the other side ceases to employ these tactics. Meeting such tactics with defending principles is more productive than counterattacking with tricky tactics.

relationship marketing

The principles of personal selling and negotiation thus far described are transaction-oriented because their purpose is to close a specific sale, but in many cases the company is not seeking an immediate sale, but rather to build a long-term supplier–customer relationship. The company wants to demonstrate that it has the capabilities to serve the account's needs in a superior way. Today's customers are large and often global. They prefer suppliers who can sell and deliver a coordinated set of products and services to many locations; who can quickly solve problems that arise in different locations; and who can work closely with customer teams to improve products and processes. Salespeople working with key customers must do more than call when they think customers might be ready to place orders. They should call or visit at other times, take customers to dinner, and make useful suggestions about their business. They should monitor key accounts, know their problems, and be ready to serve them in a number of ways.

When a relationship management program is properly implemented, the organization will begin to focus as much on managing its customers as on managing its products. At the same time, companies should realize that while there is a strong and warranted move toward relationship marketing, it is not effective in all situations. Ultimately, companies must judge which segments and which specific customers will respond profitably to relationship management. (For some guidelines, see "Marketing Memo: When—and How—to Use Relationship Marketing.")

Marketing
MEMO

When—and How—to Use Relationship Marketing

Barbara Jackson argues that relationship marketing is not effective in all situations but is extremely effective in the right situations. She sees transaction marketing as more appropriate with customers who have a short time horizon and low switching costs, such as buyers of commodities. Relationship marketing pays off handsomely with customers who have long time horizons and high switching costs, such as buyers of office automation systems. The customer for a major system carefully researches competing suppliers and chooses one from whom it can expect good long-term service and state-of-the-art technology. Both the customer and the supplier invest a lot of money and time in the relationship.

Anderson and Narus believe that transaction versus relationship marketing is not so much an issue of the type of industry as of the particular customer's wishes. Some customers value a high service bundle and will stay with that supplier for a long time. Other customers want to cut their costs and will switch suppliers for lower costs. In this case, the company can still retain the customer by agreeing to reduce the price, provided the customer is willing to accept fewer services. This customer would be treated on a transaction basis rather than on a relationship-building basis.

Sources: Barbara Bund Jackson, *Winning and Keeping Industrial Customers: The Dynamics of Customer Relationships* (Lexington, MA: D. C. Heath, 1985); James C. Anderson and James A. Narus, "Partnering as a Focused Market Strategy," *California Management Review*, (Spring 1991): 95–113.

summary

1. Sales personnel serve as a company's link to its customers. The sales rep is the company to many of its customers, and it is the rep who brings back to the company much-needed information about the customer.

2. Designing the sales force requires decisions regarding objectives, strategy, structure, size, and compensation. Objectives may include prospecting, targeting, communicating, selling, servicing, information gathering, and allocating. Determining strategy requires choosing the mix of selling approaches that is most effective. Choosing the sales-force structure entails dividing territories by geography, product, or market (or some combination of these). Estimating how large the sales force needs to be involves estimating the total workload and how many sales hours (and hence salespeople) will be needed. Compensating the sales force entails determining what types of salaries, commissions, bonuses, expense accounts, and benefits to give, and how much weight customer satisfaction should have in determining total compensation.

3. There are five steps involved in managing the sales force: (1) recruiting and selecting sales representatives; (2) training the representatives in sales techniques and in the company's products, policies, and customer-satisfaction orientation; (3) supervising the sales force and helping reps to use their time efficiently; (4) motivating the sales force, and balancing quotas, monetary rewards, and supplementary motivators; (5) evaluating individual and group sales performance.

4. Effective salespeople are trained in the methods of analysis and customer management, as well as the art of sales professionalism. No approach works best in all circumstances, but most trainers agree that selling is a seven-step process: prospecting and qualifying customers, preapproach, approach, presentation and demonstration, overcoming objections, closing, and follow-up and maintenance.

5. Another aspect of selling is negotiation, the art of arriving at transaction terms that satisfy both parties. A third aspect is relationship marketing, which focuses on developing long-term, mutually beneficial relationships between two parties.

applications

marketing debate – are great salespeople born that way?

One difference of opinion with respect to sales concerns the potential impact of training versus selection in developing an effective sales force. Some observers maintain that the best salespeople are "born" that way and are effective due to their personalities and all the interpersonal skills they have developed over their lifetimes. Others disagree and contend that application of leading-edge sales techniques can make virtually anyone a sales star.

Take a position: The key to developing an effective sales force is selection versus The key to developing an effective sales force is training.

marketing and advertising

1. Saab uses ads such as the one in Figure 1, which appeared in a national business magazine, to bring prospects into its dealers' showrooms. Note that Sweden-based Saab, owned by General Motors, is promoting GM's OnStar navigation system as a standard feature in this convertible.

   a. What kind of training do you think Saab's dealers' sales reps need to successfully sell to consumers?
   b. How can Saab dealers qualify prospects for this convertible?
   c. Why are good follow-up and maintenance skills important for dealers' sales reps?

2. The Anthro direct-response ad shown in Figure 2 is geared toward businesses that need office furniture for their employees. The headline refers to follow-up calls placed by Anthro reps to check on customer satisfaction, and the fine print invites business buyers to call to discuss needs or request a product catalog.

   a. Which of the six types of sales representatives are prospects likely to speak with when they call Anthro's toll-free phone number?
   b. Which of the specific sales tasks is this sales rep likely to perform?
   c. Why would Anthro's advertising put so much emphasis on its follow-up call policy?

Figure 1

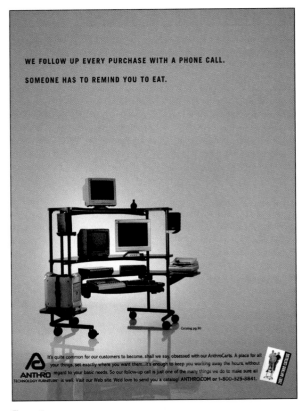

Figure 2

online marketing today

As noted earlier in this chapter, Siebel Systems uses its own sales-management software to monitor its sales reps' activities, manage the sales process, and assess customer satisfaction. In the past, Siebel worked with 20 resellers who sold the company's software, as well as with 760 other "Siebel Partners" who provide support in the form of installation, customization, upgrading, and other services. Now, however, the company has eliminated indirect sales in favor of its direct sales force. "When we analyzed customer feedback from the reseller channel, the results were not living up to the standards that we expected," explains Siebel's vice president and general manager for alliances. "The customers were effectively telling us that they would rather have Siebel involved in the sale." Partners still have an opportunity to build sales and profits because customers spend at least $7 in implementation, training, hardware, and other items for every $1 spent on Siebel software.[41]

Go to Siebel's Web site (*www.siebel.com*) and review the products, events, and customized views available on the home page. Then follow the link to information for sales professionals (or, if this is unavailable, locate the information about Siebel's sales management software). What benefits does Siebel highlight for its sales management offerings? Why are these benefits important for business customers? How do both Siebel and its prospects gain from the company's online product demonstrations? From attendance at the company's product seminars?

you're the marketer: sonic pda marketing plan

Many marketers have to consider sales-force management in their marketing plans. However, because of the high cost of maintaining a direct sales force, some companies are substituting online, mail, and telephone sales for some of their personal sales calls.

In your marketing role at Sonic, you are planning a sales strategy for the company's new personal digital assistant (PDA). After reviewing the data you previously gathered and the deci-

sions you made about other marketing-mix activities, answer these questions about Sonic's use of personal selling:

- Does Sonic need a direct sales force or can it sell through agents and other outside representatives?
- Toward whom should Sonic's sales activities be geared? How can the company's sales activities support the rest of the marketing plan and the goals that have been set?
- What kinds of sales objectives should Sonic set for its sales personnel?

- What kind of training will sales representatives need to sell the new Sonic PDA?

Once you have answered these questions and looked at how your sales management ideas will work with Sonic's goals and objectives, either summarize your programs in a written marketing plan or type them into the Marketing Mix, Marketing Organization, and Sales Forecast sections of the *Marketing Plan Pro* software.

notes

1. Adapted from Robert N. McMurry, "The Mystique of Super-Salesmanship," *Harvard Business Review* (March–April 1961): 114. Also see William C. Moncrief III, "Selling Activity and Sales Position Taxonomies for Industrial Salesforces," *Journal of Marketing Research* (August 1986): 261–70.

2. Lawrence G. Friedman and Timothy R. Furey, *The Channel Advantage: Going to Marketing with Multiple Sales Channels* (Oxford, UK: Butterworth-Heinemann, 1999).

3. Sarah Lorge, "A Priceless Brand," *Sales & Marketing Management* (October 1998): 102–10.

4. Christopher Power, "Smart Selling: How Companies Are Winning Over Today's Tougher Customer," *BusinessWeek*, August 3, 1992, pp. 46–48.

5. "BA Shake-up 'Not Due to New Scheme'," *Travel Trade Gazette UK & Ireland*, May 7, 2001.

6. Philip B. Clark and Sean Callahan, "Sales Staffs: Adapt or Die," *B to B*, April 10, 2000.

7. For estimates of sales reps' salaries, see *Sales & Marketing Management* (October 1998): 98.

8. Luis R. Gomez-Mejia, David B. Balkin, and Robert L. Cardy, *Managing Human Resources* (Upper Saddle River, NJ: Prentice Hall, 1995), pp. 416–18.

9. "What Salespeople Are Paid," *Sales & Marketing Management* (February 1995): 30–31; Power, "Smart Selling," pp. 46–48; William Keenan Jr., ed., *The Sales & Marketing Management Guide to Sales Compensation Planning: Commissions, Bonuses & Beyond* (Chicago: Probus Publishing, 1994).

10. George H. Lucas Jr., A. Parasuraman, Robert A. Davis, and Ben M. Enis, "An Empirical Study of Sales Force Turnover," *Journal of Marketing* (July 1987): 34–59.

11. Charles Garfield, *Peak Performers: The New Heroes of American Business* (New York: Avon Books, 1986); "What Makes a Supersalesperson?" *Sales & Marketing Management* (August 1984): 86; "What Makes a Top Performer?" *Sales & Marketing Management* (May 1989): Timothy J. Trow, "The Secret of a Good Hire: Profiling," *Sales & Marketing Management* (May 1990): 44–55.

12. McMurry, "The Mystique of Super-Salesmanship," p. 117.

13. Ibid., p. 118.

14. David Mayer and Herbert M. Greenberg, "What Makes a Good Salesman?" *Harvard Business Review* (July–August 1964): 119–25.

15. James M. Comer and Alan J. Dubinsky, *Managing the Successful Sales Force* (Lexington, MA: Lexington Books, 1985), pp. 5–25.

16. From an address given by Donald R. Keough at the 27th Annual Conference of the Super-Market Institute, Chicago, April 26–29, 1964. Also see Judy Siguaw, Gene Brown, and Robert Widing II, "The Influence of the Market Orientation of the Firm on Sales Force Behavior and Attitudes," *Journal of Marketing Research* (February 1994): 106–16.

17. Joel E. Urbany, "Justifying Profitable Pricing," Working Paper Series, Marketing Science Institute, Report No. 00-117, 2000, pp. 17–18.

18. "Welcome to the Real Whirled: How Whirlpool Training Forced Salespeople to Live with the Brand," *Sales & Marketing Management* (February 2001): 87–88.

19. John F. Magee, "Determining the Optimum Allocation of Expenditures for Promotional Effort with Operations Research Methods," in *The Frontiers of Marketing Thought and Science,* ed. Frank M. Bass (Chicago: American Marketing Association, 1958), pp. 140–56.

20. Michael R. W. Bommer, Brian F. O'Neil, and Beheruz N. Sethna, "A Methodology for Optimizing Selling Time of Salespersons," *Journal of Marketing Theory and Practice* (Spring 1994): 61–75. See also, Lissan Joseph, "On the Optimality of Delegating Pricing Authority to the Sales Force," *Journal of Marketing* 65 (January 2001): 62–70.

21. Thomas Blackshear and Richard E. Plank, "The Impact of Adaptive Selling on Sales Effectiveness within the Pharmaceutical Industry," *Journal of Marketing Theory and Practice* (Summer 1994): 106–25.

22. Paul Mann, "Success Mode," *Manufacturing Systems* (September 2000).

23. Dartnell Corporation, 30th Sales Force Compensation Survey. Other breakdowns show that 12.7 percent is spent in service calls, 16 percent in administrative tasks, 25.1 percent in telephone selling, and 17.4 percent in waiting/traveling.

24. James A. Narus and James C. Anderson, "Industrial Distributor Selling: The Roles of Outside and Inside Sales," *Industrial Marketing Management* 15 (1986): 55–62.

25. Gilbert A. Churchill Jr., Neil M. Ford, and Orville C. Walker Jr., *Sales Force Management: Planning, Implementation and Control*, 4th ed. (Homewood, IL: Irwin, 1993). Also see Jhinuk Chowdhury, "The Motivational Impact of Sales Quotas on Effort," *Journal of Marketing Research* (February 1993): 28–41; Murali K. Mantrala, Prabhakant Sinha, and Andris A. Zoltners, "Structuring a Multiproduct Sales Quota-Bonus Plan for a Heterogeneous Sales Force: A Practical Model-Based Approach," *Marketing Science* 13, no. 2 (1994): 121–44; Wujin Chu, Eitan Gerstner, and James D. Hess, "Costs and Benefits of Hard-Sell," *Journal of Marketing Research* (February 1995): 97–102; Manfred Krafft, "In Empirical Investigation of the Antecedents of Sales Force Control Systems," *Journal of Marketing* 63 (July 1999): 120–34.

26. "What Motivates U.S. Salespeople?" *American Salesman,* (February 1994): 25, 30.

27. Eilene Zimmerman, "Quota Busters," *Sales & Marketing Management* (January 2001): pp. 59–63.

28. Melanie Warner, "Confessions of a Control Freak," *Fortune,* September 4, 2000, p. 30; Peter Burrows, "The Era of Efficiency," *BusinessWeek*, June 18, 2001, p. 92.

29. Kenneth Heim and Vincent Alonzo, "This Is What We Want!" *Incentive* (October 1998): 40–49.

30. Philip M. Posdakoff and Scott B. MacKenzie, "Organizational Citizenship Behaviors and Sales Unit Effectiveness," *Journal of Marketing Research* (August 1994): 351–63. See also, Andrea L. Dixon, Rosann L. Spiro and Magbul Jamil, "Successful and Unsuccessful Sales Calls: Measuring Salesperson Attributions and Behavioral Intentions," *Journal of Marketing* 65 (July 2001): 64–78. Willem Verbeke and Richard P. Bagozzi, "Sales Call Anxiety: Exploring What It Means When Fear Rules a Sales Encounter," *Journal of Marketing* 64 (July 2000): 88–101.

31. For further reading, see Dorothy Cohen, *Legal Issues in Marketing Decision Making* (Cincinnati, OH: South-Western, 1995).

32. For an excellent summary of the skills needed today by sales representatives and sales managers, see Rolph Anderson and Bert Rosenbloom, "The World Class Sales Manager: Adapting to Global Megatrends," *Journal of Global Marketing* 5, no. 4 (1992): 11–22.

33. Neil Rackham, *SPIN Selling* (New York: McGraw-Hill, 1988). Also see his *The SPIN Selling Fieldbook* (New York: McGraw-Hill, 1996); and his latest book, co-authored with John De Vincentis, *Rethinking the Sales Force* (New York: McGraw-Hill, 1996).

34. Sharon Drew Morgen, *Selling With Integrity: Reinventing Sales Through Collaboration, Respect, and Serving* (New York: Berkeley Books, 1999).

35. Some of the following discussion is based on W. J. E. Crissy, William H. Cunningham, and Isabella C. M. Cunningham, *Selling: The Personal Force in Marketing* (New York: John Wiley, 1977), pp. 119–29.

36. Norton Paley, "Cultivating Customers," *Sales & Marketing Management* (September 1994): 31–32.

37. "Notebook: Briefcase Full of Views: Johnson and Johnson Uses Virtual Reality to Give Prospects an Inside Look at Its Products," *Marketing Tools* (April 1997).

38. For additional reading, see Howard Raiffa, *The Art and Science of Negotiation* (Cambridge, MA: Harvard University Press, 1982); Max H. Bazerman and Margaret A. Neale, *Negotiating Rationally* (New York: The Free Press, 1992); James C. Freund, *Smart Negotiating* (New York: Simon & Schuster, 1992); Frank L. Acuff, *How to Negotiate Anything with Anyone Anywhere Around the World* (New York: American Management Association, 1993); Jehoshua Eliashberg, Gary L. Lilien, and Nam Kim, "Searching for Generalizations in Business Marketing Negotiations," *Marketing Science* 14, no. 3 (pt. 1) (1995): G47–G60.

39. Donald W. Dobler, *Purchasing and Materials Management*, 5th ed. (New York: McGraw-Hill, 1990).

40. This discussion of zone of agreement is fully developed in Raiffa, *Art and Science of Negotiation*.

41. "Siebel Systems Cuts Sales Agents' Network," *Sunday Business,* October 30, 2001, <*www.sundaybusiness.co.uk*>.

managing the total marketing effort

Kotler on Marketing

The marketing organization will have to redefine its role from managing customer interactions to integrating and managing all the company's customer-facing processes.

In this chapter, we will address the following questions:

- What are the trends in company organization?
- How are marketing and sales organized in companies?
- What steps can a company take to build a stronger customer-focused culture?
- How can a company improve its marketing-implementation skills?
- What tools are available to help companies monitor and improve their marketing activities?

We now turn from the strategic and tactical management of marketing to its administration. Our goal is to examine how firms organize, implement, evaluate, and control marketing activities.

trends in company organization

Companies often need to restructure their business and marketing practices in response to significant changes in the business environment, such as globalization, deregulation, computer and telecommunications advancements, and market fragmentation. The main responses of business firms to a rapidly changing environment have included these:

- *Reengineering:* Appointing teams to manage customer-value-building processes and trying to break down walls between departments.
- *Outsourcing:* Greater willingness to buy more goods and services from outside vendors when they can be obtained more cheaply and better this way.
- *Benchmarking:* Studying "best practice companies" to improve performance.
- *Supplier partnering:* Increased partnering with fewer but better value-adding suppliers.
- *Customer partnering:* Working more closely with customers to add value to their operations.
- *Merging:* Acquiring or merging with firms in the same or complementary industries to gain economies of scale and scope.
- *Globalizing:* Increased effort to "think global" and "act local."
- *Flattening:* Reducing the number of organizational levels to get closer to the customer.
- *Focusing:* Determining the most profitable businesses and customers and focusing on them.
- *Empowering:* Encouraging and empowering personnel to produce more ideas and take more initiative.

The role of marketing in the organization is also changing. Traditionally, marketers have played the roles of middlemen, charged with understanding customer needs and transmitting the voice of the customer to various functional areas in the organization; but in a networked enterprise, every functional area can interact directly with customers. Marketing no longer has sole ownership of customer interactions; rather, marketing needs to integrate all the customer-facing processes so that customers see a single face and hear a single voice when they interact with the firm.

Companies are also showing a renewed interest in analyzing marketing profitability and connecting it with shareholder value. Marketers are responding by developing financial tools for measuring brand equity, channel equity, customer equity, and other key marketing assets. Among the best current expositions are those of Peter Doyle, Roger Best, and Tim Ambler, as described in "Marketing Insight: Seeing the Big Picture and Getting to the Bottom Line in Marketing."

marketing organization

Over the years, marketing has grown from a simple sales department into a complex group of activities. We will examine how marketing departments have evolved in companies, how they are organized, and how they interact with other company departments.

the evolution of the marketing department

Marketing departments have evolved through six stages: simple sales department, sales department with marketing functions, separate marketing department, modern marketing department, effective marketing company, process- and outcome-based company (see Figure 22.1).

SIMPLE SALES DEPARTMENT   Small companies typically appoint a sales vice president, who manages a sales force and also does some selling. When the company needs marketing research or advertising, the sales vice president hires help from the outside (see Figure 22.1[a]).

SALES DEPARTMENT WITH ANCILLARY MARKETING FUNCTIONS   As the company expands, it needs to add or enlarge certain functions. For example, an East Coast

marketing **insight**

Seeing the Big Picture and Getting to the Bottom Line in Marketing

To provide a financial overview of marketing activity, several authors have developed new approaches to thinking about marketing. Here are three notable ones.

Peter Doyle maintains that

value-based marketing is not primarily about numbers. . . . [Rather,] it consists of three main elements. First is a set of *beliefs* about the objectives of marketing. The . . . primary task is to develop strategies that will maximize shareholder return. . . . Second is a set of *principles* for choosing marketing strategies and making marketing decisions that are consistent with these beliefs. These principles are based on estimating the future cash flow associated with a strategy to calculate the shareholder value added. Finally, it is a set of *processes* that ensure that marketing develops, selects, and implements a strategy that is consistent with these beliefs and principles. These processes concern management of the financial, marketing and organizational value drivers of the business. The financial value drivers are those key ratios that have the most significant impact on shareholder value. The marketing drivers are the customer-oriented plans necessary to drive improvement in the financial ratios. The organizational value drivers are the core capabilities, systems and leadership styles needed to create and implement the shareholder value orientation in the business.

According to Doyle, financial value drivers relate to sales growth, operating margin, and investment; marketing value drivers relate to strong brands, customer loyalty, strategic relationships, market selection, and differential advantage.

According to Roger Best,

Market-based management is at the base of a business with a strong market orientation. A strong market orientation translates into a strong customer focus, competitor orientation, and a team approach that cuts across organizational functions. The result is a market-based business that is in a strong position to develop and deliver market-based strategies designed to attract, satisfy, and retain customers. Implemented successfully across a wide range of market situations, a market-based approach . . . will deliver higher levels of profitability, cash flow, and shareholder value than will a cost-based approach.

Best maintains that the only source of positive cash flow is the customer and therefore the customer must be the focus of market-based management.

Tim Ambler suggests that if firms think they are already measuring marketing performance adequately, they should ask themselves five questions:

1. Do you routinely research consumer behavior (retention, acquisition, usage, etc.) and why consumers behave that way (awareness, satisfaction, perceived quality, etc.)?
2. Are the results of this research routinely reported to the board in a format integrated with financial marketing metrics?
3. In those reports, are the results compared with the levels previously forecasted in the business plans?
4. Are they also compared with the levels achieved by your key competitor using the same indicators?
5. Is short-term performance adjusted according to the change in your marketing based asset(s)?

Ambler believes firms must give priority to measuring and reporting marketing performance, or "marketing metrics." He believes evaluation can be split into two parts: (1) short-term results and (2) changes in brand equity. Short-term results often reflect profit and loss concerns as shown by sales turnover, shareholder value, or some combination of the two. Brand-equity measures include awareness, market share, relative price, number of complaints, distribution/availability, total number of customers, perceived quality, and loyalty/retention. Ambler also recommends developing employee measures and metrics, arguing that "End users are the ultimate customers, but your own staff are your first; you need to measure the health of the internal market."

Sources: Peter Doyle, *Value-Based Marketing: Marketing Strategies for Corporate Growth and Shareholder Value* (Chichester, England: John Wiley & Sons, 2000); Roger J. Best, *Market-Based Management: Strategies for Growing Customer Value and Profitability*, 2nd ed. (Upper Saddle River, NJ: Prentice Hall, 2000); Tim Ambler, *Marketing and the Bottom Line: The New Methods of Corporate Wealth* (London: Financial Times/Prentice Hall, 2000).

---

firm that plans to open in the West will need to conduct marketing research to learn about customer needs and market potential. It will have to advertise its name and products in the area. The sales vice president will hire a marketing research manager and an advertising manager to handle these activities. He might hire a *marketing director* to manage these and other marketing functions (see Figure 22.1[b]).

SEPARATE MARKETING DEPARTMENT   The continued growth of the company will warrant additional investment in marketing research, new-product development, advertising and sales promotion, and customer service. Yet the sales vice president normally focuses time and resources on the sales force. Eventually, the CEO will see the

figure **22.1**

Stages in the Evolution of
the Marketing Department

**(a) Stage 1:
Simple Sales Department**

President

Sales VP

Sales force

Other marketing functions (hired from outside)

**(b) Stage 2: Sales Department
with Ancillary
Marketing Functions**

President

Sales VP

Sales force

• Marketing Director
• Other marketing functions (internal staff and external support)

**(c) Stage 3: Separate
Marketing Department**

President

Sales VP

Marketing VP

Sales force

Other marketing functions

advantage of establishing a separate marketing department headed by a marketing vice president, who reports, along with the sales vice president, to the president or executive vice president (see Figure 22.1[c]). At this stage, sales and marketing are separate functions that are expected to work closely together.

This arrangement permits the CEO to obtain a more balanced view of company opportunities and problems. Suppose sales start slipping. The sales vice president might recommend hiring more salespeople, raising sales compensation, running a sales contest, providing more sales training, or cutting the price so the product will be easier to sell. The marketing vice president will want to analyze the forces affecting the marketplace. Is the company going after the right segments and customers? Are changes in features, styling, packaging, services, distribution, or promotion warranted?

MODERN MARKETING DEPARTMENT/EFFECTIVE MARKETING COMPANY Although the sales and marketing vice presidents should work together, their relationship is often strained and marked by distrust. The sales vice president resents efforts to make the sales force less important in the marketing mix, and the marketing vice president seeks a larger budget for non-sales-force activities. The marketing manager's task is to identify opportunities and prepare marketing strategies and programs. Salespeople are responsible for implementing these programs. Marketers rely on marketing research, try to identify and understand market segments, spend time in planning, think long term, and aim to produce profits and gains in market share. Sales people, in contrast, rely on street experience, try to understand each individual buyer, spend time in face-to-face selling, think short term, and try to meet their quotas.

If there is too much friction between sales and marketing, the company president might place marketing activities back under the sales vice president, instruct the executive vice president to handle conflicts, or place the marketing vice president in charge of everything, including the sales force. This last solution is the basis of the modern marketing department, a department headed by a sales and marketing executive vice president with managers reporting from every function, including sales management (see Figure 22.1[d]).

A company can have an excellent marketing department and yet fail at marketing. Much depends on how the other departments view customers. If they point to the marketing department and say, "They do the marketing," the company has not implemented effective marketing. Only when all employees realize that their jobs are to create, serve, and satisfy customers does the company become an effective marketer.[1]

PROCESS- AND OUTCOME-BASED COMPANY Many companies are now refocusing their structures on key processes rather than departments. Departmental organization is increasingly viewed as a barrier to the smooth performance of fundamental business processes. To achieve customer-related process outcomes, companies appoint process leaders who manage cross-disciplinary teams. Marketing and sales people spend an increasing percentage of their time as process team members. As a result, marketing personnel may have a solid-line responsibility to their teams and a dotted-line responsibility to the marketing department. The marketing department is also responsible for training its marketing personnel, assigning them to new teams, and evaluating their overall performance (see Figure 22.1[e]).

organizing the marketing department

Modern marketing departments may be organized by function, by geographic area, by products, or by customer markets.

FUNCTIONAL ORGANIZATION The most common form of marketing organization consists of functional specialists reporting to a marketing vice president, who coordinates their activities. Figure 22.2 shows five specialists. Additional specialists might include a customer service manager, a marketing planning manager, a market logistics manager, a direct marketing manager, and an Internet marketing manager.

It is quite a challenge to develop smooth working relations within the marketing department. Frank Cespedes has urged companies to improve the critical interfaces among *field sales*, *customer service*, and *product management* groups, because they collectively have a major impact on customer satisfaction. He has proposed several ways to set up tighter links among these three key marketing groups.[2]

The main advantage of a functional marketing organization is its administrative simplicity. However, this form loses its effectiveness as products and markets increase. First, a functional organization often leads to inadequate planning for specific products and markets. Products that are not favored by anyone are neglected. Second, each functional group competes with the others for budget and status. The marketing vice president constantly has to weigh the claims of competing functional specialists and faces a difficult coordination problem.

GEOGRAPHIC ORGANIZATION   A company selling in a national market often organizes its sales force (and sometimes other functions, including marketing) along geographic lines. The national sales manager may supervise four regional sales managers, who each supervise six zone managers, who in turn supervise eight district sales managers, who supervise ten salespeople.

Several companies are now adding *area market specialists* (regional or local marketing managers) to support the sales efforts in high-volume markets. One such market might be Miami, Florida, where 46 percent of the households are Latino, compared to neighboring Fort Lauderdale, where 6.7 percent of the households are Latino. The Miami specialist would know Miami's customer and trade makeup, help marketing managers at headquarters adjust their marketing mix for Miami, and prepare local annual and long-range plans for selling all the company's products in Miami.

Several factors have fueled the move toward regionalization and localization. The U.S. mass-market has slowly subdivided into a profusion of minimarkets along demographic lines: baby boomers, senior citizens, African Americans, single mothers.[3] Improved information and marketing research technologies have also spurred regionalization. Data from retail-store scanners allow instant tracking of product sales, helping companies pinpoint local problems and opportunities. Retailers themselves strongly prefer local programs aimed at consumers in their cities and neighborhoods. To keep retailers happy, manufacturers now create more local marketing plans.

Campbell Soup   Campbell has created many successful regional brands. It sells its spicy Ranchero beans in the Southwest, Creole soup in the South, and red bean soup in Latino areas. Brands appealing to regional tastes add substantially to Campbell's annual sales. Campbell has divided its domestic market into 22 regions, each responsible for planning local programs. The company has allocated 15 to 20 percent of its total marketing budget to support local marketing. Within each region, Campbell's sales managers and salespeople create advertising and promotions geared to local needs and conditions.[4]

figure **22.1 (cont.)**

(d) Stages 4 and 5: Modern/ Effective Marketing Company

(e) Stage 6: Process- and Outcome-Based Company

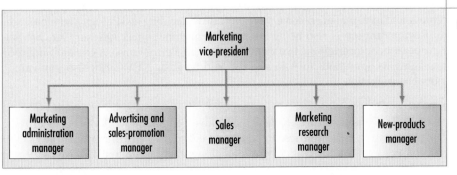

figure **22.2**

Functional Organization

Krispy Kreme's Web site promotes new store openings.

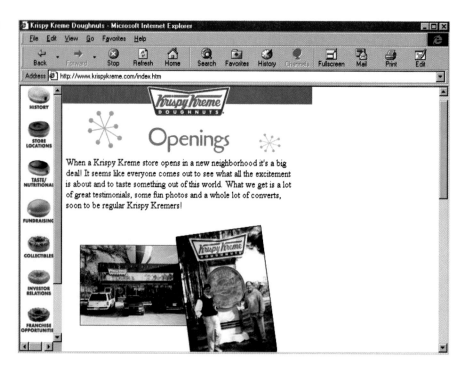

Krispy Kreme   Krispy Kreme doughnuts uses local marketing to enhance customer loyalty. When the company enters a new market, it works with local PR firms to build brand awareness; delivers thousands of doughnuts to local businesses and media; and holds a grand opening celebration at each new store. Instead of hiring a single national ad agency, Krispy Kreme encourages its Area Developers to contract with local PR firms. These local marketing efforts have a positive effect on customers. "That's one way we try to build a long-term relationship with the customer and the community," says Krispy Kreme's Marketing Director Steve Bumgarner. Its ever-growing customer base has helped the company's shares rise 78 percent in the year following its April 2000 initial public offering.[5]

Other companies that have shifted to regional marketing are McDonald's, which now spends about 50 percent of its total advertising budget regionally; American Airlines, which realized the that the travel needs of Chicagoans and Southwesterners are very different in the winter months; and Anheuser-Busch, which has subdivided its regional markets into ethnic and demographic segments, with different ad campaigns for each.

Regionalization may be accompanied by a move toward branchising. **Branchising** means empowering the company's districts or local offices to operate more like franchises. IBM told its branch managers to "make it your business." The branches resemble profit centers, and local managers have more latitude in deciding on strategy and more incentive.

Regionalization is also being adopted by multinationals. Quaker Oats has set up a European headquarters in Brussels, and British Petroleum has chosen Singapore for managing its operations in Asia and the Middle East.[6] KPMG has also innovated in its global organization.

KPMG   Consulting firm KPMG maintains a global network of offices in 760 cities, representing 150 countries. To better serve its clients in different regions, in 1999 the company restructured its operations along geographic lines. KPMG's 19 member firms in Latin America, Mexico, and the Caribbean combined with the U.S. parent to form the new "Americas" group. The company also formed a group comprised of national offices from Europe, the Middle East, and Africa (EMA), and an Asia Pacific group. The new structure enabled the company to focus on local and regional issues, while still retaining the breadth of a global organization.[7]

PRODUCT- OR BRAND-MANAGEMENT ORGANIZATION Companies producing a variety of products and brands often establish a product- (or brand-) management organization. The product-management organization does not replace the functional management organization, but serves as another layer of management. A product manager supervises product category managers, who in turn supervise specific product and brand managers. A product-management organization makes sense if the company's products are quite different, or if the sheer number of products is beyond the ability of a functional marketing organization to handle. Kraft uses a product-management organization in its Post division. Separate product category managers are in charge of cereals, pet food, and beverages. Within the cereal product group, there are separate subcategory managers for nutritional cereals, children's presweetened cereals, family cereals, and miscellaneous cereals.

Product and brand managers have these tasks:

- Developing a long-range and competitive strategy for the product.
- Preparing an annual marketing plan and sales forecast.
- Working with advertising and merchandising agencies to develop copy, programs, and campaigns.
- Stimulating support of the product among the sales force and distributors.
- Gathering continuous intelligence on the product's performance, customer and dealer attitudes, and new problems and opportunities.
- Initiating product improvements to meet changing market needs.

These tasks are common to both consumer- and industrial-product managers. However, consumer-product managers typically manage fewer products and spend more time on advertising and sales promotion. They are often younger and MBA-educated. Industrial-product managers spend more time with customers and laboratory and engineering personnel, think more about the technical aspects of their product and possible design improvements, and work more closely with the sales force and key buyers.

The product-management organization introduces several advantages. The product manager can concentrate on developing a cost-effective marketing mix for the product. The product manager can react more quickly to products in the marketplace. The company's smaller brands have a product advocate (see Figure 22.3).

However, this organization has some disadvantages. First, product managers and specifically brand managers are not given enough authority to carry out their responsibilities. They have to rely on persuasion to get the cooperation of other departments. They are told they are "minipresidents" but are often treated as low-level coordinators. Second, product and brand managers become experts in their product area but rarely achieve functional expertise. They vacillate between posing as experts and being cowed by real experts. This is unfortunate when the product or brand depends on a specific type of expertise, such as advertising.

Third, the product management system often turns out to be costly. One person is appointed to manage each major product or brand. Soon managers are appointed to manage even minor products and brands. Each brand manager, usually overworked, pleads for an associate brand manager. Payroll costs climb. In the meantime, the company continues to increase its functional specialists in copy, packaging, media, sales promotion, market surveys, and statistical analysis. The business is soon saddled with a large and costly structure. Fourth, brand managers normally manage a brand for only a short time. Either they move up in a few years to another brand, or they transfer to

figure **22.3**

The Product Manager's
Interactions

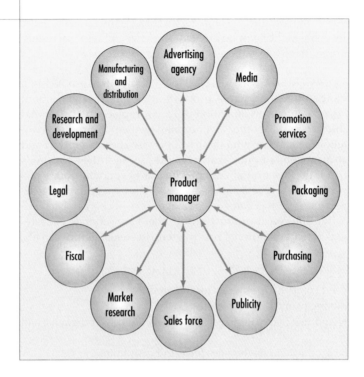

another company. Short-term involvement with the brand leads to short-term planning and plays havoc with building long-term strengths.

Fifth, the fragmentation of markets makes it harder to develop a national strategy from headquarters. Brand managers must increasingly please their regional and local sales groups, resulting in a transfer of power from marketing to sales. Sixth, product and brand managers cause the company to focus on building market share rather than building the customer relationship. Brand management can be seen as antagonistic to customer relationship management. *Today we believe that the customer relationship, not the brand, is the primary lever for value creation.*

Pearson and Wilson have suggested five steps to make the product-management system work better:[8]

1. Clearly delineate the limits of the product manager's role and responsibility.
2. Build a strategy-development-and-review process to provide a framework for the product manager's operations.
3. Take into account areas of potential conflict between product managers and functional specialists when defining their respective roles.
4. Set up a formal process that forces to the top all conflict-of-interest situations between product management and functional line management.
5. Establish a system for measuring results consistent with the product manager's responsibilities.

A second alternative is to switch from product managers to product teams. There are three types of product-team structures in product management (see Figure 22.4):

1. *Vertical product team:* Product manager, associate product manager, and product assistant (see Figure 22.4[a]). The product manager is the leader and deals with other managers to gain their cooperation. The associate product manager assists in these tasks and also does some paperwork. The product assistant carries out most of the paperwork and routine analysis.

2. *Triangular product team:* Product manager and two specialized product assistants, one who takes care of marketing research and the other, marketing communications (see Figure 22.4[b]). The Hallmark Company uses a "marketing team" consisting of a market manager (the leader), a marketing manager, and a distribution manager.

3. *Horizontal product team:* Product manager and several specialists from marketing and other functions (Figure 22.4[c]). 3M has teams consisting of a team leader and representatives from sales, marketing, laboratory, engineering, accounting, and marketing research. Dow Corning sets up teams of five to eight people; each team manages a specific product, market, and process.

The second and third approaches are favored by those who advocate brand asset management. They believe that each major brand should be run by a **brand asset management team (BAMT)** consisting of key representatives from major functions affecting the brand's performance. The company would be comprised of several BAMTs which would periodically report to a BAMT Directors Committee, which itself would report to a Chief Branding Officer. This is quite different from the way brands have traditionally been handled.

A third alternative is to eliminate product manager positions for minor products and assign two or more products to each remaining manager. This is feasible where two or more products appeal to a similar set of needs. A cosmetics company does not need separate product managers for each product because cosmetics serve one major need—beauty. A toiletries company needs different managers for headache remedies, toothpaste, soap, and shampoo, because these products differ in use and appeal. A fourth alternative is to introduce category management, in which a company focuses on product categories to manage its brands. Here is one example.

Kraft   Kraft has changed from a classic brand-management structure, in which each brand competed for original resources and market share, to a category-based structure in which category business directors (or "product integrators") lead cross-functional teams composed of representatives from marketing, R&D, consumer promotion, and finance. The category business directors have both broad responsibility and bottom-line accountability. No longer viewed solely as marketers, they are as responsible for identifying opportunities to improve the efficiency of the supply chain as they are for developing the next advertisement. Kraft's category teams work in conjunction with process teams dedicated to each product category and with customer teams dedicated to each major customer (see Figure 22.5).[9]

Category management is not a panacea. It is still a product-driven system. Colgate has moved from brand management (Colgate toothpaste) to category management (toothpaste category) to a new stage called "customer-need management" (mouth care). This last step finally focuses the organization on a basic customer need.[10]

MARKET–MANAGEMENT/CUSTOMER MANAGEMENT ORGANIZATION   Many companies sell their products to many different markets. Canon sells its fax machines to consumer, business, and government markets. U.S. Steel sells its steel to the railroad, construction, and public utility industries. When customers fall into different user groups with distinct buying preferences and practices, a **market-management organization** is desirable. A *markets manager* supervises several market managers (also called market-development managers, market specialists, or industry specialists). The market managers draw on functional services as needed. Market managers of important markets might even have functional specialists reporting to them.

Market managers are staff (not line) people, with duties similar to those of product managers. Market managers develop long-range and annual plans for their markets. Their performance is judged by their market's growth and profitability. This system carries many of the same advantages and disadvantages of product-management systems. Its strongest advantage is that the marketing activity is organized to meet the needs of

figure **22.4**

Three Types of Product Teams

(a) **Vertical product team**

(b) **Triangular product team**

(c) **Horizontal product team**

PM = product manager
AP = associate product manager
PA = product assistant
R = market researcher
C = communication specialist
S = sales manager
D = distribution specialist
F = finance/accounting specialist
E = engineer

Managing Through
Teams at Kraft

Process teams
(dedicated to each
product category)

Category teams
(dedicated to each
product category)

Customer teams
(dedicated to each
major customer)

Source: Michael George, Anthony Freeling, and David Court, "Reinventing the Marketing Organization," *The McKinsey Quarterly,*
No. 4 (1994): 43–62.

distinct customer groups rather than being focused on marketing functions, regions, or products. Many companies are reorganizing along market lines and becoming *market-centered organizations*. Xerox has converted from geographic selling to selling by industry, as have IBM and Hewlett-Packard.

In a **customer-management organization**, companies can organize themselves to understand and deal with individual customers rather than with the mass-market or even market segments.

Providian   Providian Bank of San Francisco has done away with product and brand managers and even with classic marketing research. Marketing consists of two groups: Marketing Management and Customer Relationships. The job of the Marketing Management group is to identify new customers and new products. The group gets its ideas from analyzing latent, unmet needs as revealed by customer behavior. If marketing research is used at all, it is to confirm new product ideas, not to discover them. The marketers do not use mass-media but rather target the kinds of new customers who match the profile of their best customer. The job of the Customer Relationships group is to maximize the potential business from each current customer. Customers are grouped into customer behavior segments rather than demographic segments. The marketers use state-of-the art analytical tools to track the usage patterns and profitability of each customer and to set pricing and service levels. In essence, Providian is designing a separate product plan for each of its customers.[11]

PRODUCT-MANAGEMENT/MARKET-MANAGEMENT ORGANIZATION   Companies that produce many products flowing into many markets may adopt a matrix organization. DuPont was a pioneer in developing the matrix structure (see Figure 22.6).

DuPont   DuPont's textile fibers department consists of separate product managers for rayon, acetate, nylon, orlon, and dacron; and separate market managers for men's wear, women's wear, home furnishings, and industrial markets. The product managers plan the sales and profits for their respective fibers. They ask market managers to estimate how much of their fiber they can sell in each market at a proposed price.

figure **22.6**

	Market managers			
	Men's wear	Women's wear	Home furnishings	Industrial markets
Rayon				
Acetate				
Product managers Nylon				
Orlon				
Dacron				

Product- /Market-Management Matrix System

The market managers, however, are more interested in meeting their market's needs than pushing a particular fiber. In preparing their market plans, they ask each product manager about the fiber's planned prices and availabilities. The final sales forecast of the market managers and the product managers should add to the same grand total.

Companies like DuPont can go one step further and view the market managers as the main marketers, and their product managers as suppliers. The menswear market manager, for example, would be empowered to buy textile fibers from DuPont's product managers or, if DuPont's price is too high, from outside suppliers. This system would force Dupont product managers to become more efficient. If a DuPont product manager cannot match the "arm's length pricing" levels of competitive suppliers, then perhaps Dupont should not continue to produce that fiber.

A matrix organization would seem desirable in a multiproduct, multimarket company. The rub is that this system is costly and often creates conflicts. There is the cost of supporting all the managers. There are also questions about where authority and responsibility should reside. Here are two of many dilemmas:

1. *How should the sales force be organized?* Should there be separate sales forces for rayon, nylon, and other fibers? Or should the sales forces be organized into men's wear, women's wear, and other markets? Or should the sales force not be specialized? (The marketing concept favors organizing the sales force by markets, not product.)
2. *Who should set the prices for a particular product or market?* Should the nylon product manager have final authority for setting nylon prices in all markets? What happens if the men's wear market manager feels that nylon will lose out on this market unless special price concessions are made?

   Matrix management is resurfacing because companies provide the context in which a matrix can thrive—flat, lean team organizations focused around business processes that cut horizontally across functions.[12]

CORPORATE–DIVISIONAL ORGANIZATION   As multiproduct-multimarket companies grow, they often convert their larger product or market groups into separate divisions. The divisions set up their own departments and services. This raises the question of what marketing services and activities should be retained at company headquarters. Divisionalized companies have reached different answers to this question:

- *No corporate marketing:* Some companies lack a corporate marketing staff. They do not see any useful function for marketing at the corporate level. Each division has its own marketing department.
- *Moderate corporate marketing:* Some companies have a small corporate marketing staff that performs a few functions, primarily (1) assisting top management with overall opportunity

evaluation, (2) providing divisions with consulting assistance on request, (3) helping divisions that have little or no marketing, and (4) promoting the marketing concept throughout the company.

- *Strong corporate marketing:* Some companies have a corporate marketing staff that, in addition to the preceding activities, also provides various marketing services to the divisions, such as specialized advertising services, sales-promotion services, marketing research services, and sales-administration services.

The potential contribution of a corporate marketing staff varies in different stages of the company's evolution. Most companies begin with weak marketing in their divisions and often establish a corporate staff to bring stronger marketing into the divisions through training and other services. Some members of the corporate marketing staff might be transferred to head divisional marketing departments. As divisions become strong in their marketing, corporate marketing has less to offer them. Some companies then decide corporate marketing has done its job and proceed to eliminate the department.[13]

marketing relations with other departments

In principle, all business functions should interact harmoniously to pursue the firm's overall objectives. In practice, however, interdepartmental relations are often characterized by deep rivalries and distrust. Some conflict stems from differences of opinion as to what is in the company's best interests, some from real trade-offs between departmental well-being and company well-being, and some from unfortunate stereotypes and prejudices.

In the typical organization, each business function has a potential impact on customer satisfaction. Under the marketing concept, all departments need to "think customer" and work together to satisfy customer needs and expectations. The marketing department must drive this point home. The marketing vice president has two tasks: (1) to coordinate the company's internal marketing activities and (2) to coordinate marketing with finance, operations, and other company functions to serve the customer.

Yet there is little agreement on how much influence and authority marketing should have over other departments. Typically, the marketing vice president must work through persuasion rather than authority. Other departments often resist changing their efforts to meet the customer's interests. Inevitably, departments define company problems and goals from their viewpoint. As a result, conflicts of interest are unavoidable.

Perhaps the best solution is for marketing to periodically propose a *function-to-function* meeting with each department where greater understanding and collaboration is warranted. Even if each function indulges in stereotypical charges and complaints about the other, such a meeting can lead to a clearing of the air and a basis for a more constructive collaboration.

Each department needs to understand the operating logic of the other departments.

R&D The company's drive for successful new products is often thwarted by weak working relations between R&D and marketing. In many ways, these groups have different cultures.[14] R&D is staffed with scientists and technicians who pride themselves on scientific curiosity and detachment, who like to work on challenging technical problems without much concern for immediate sales payoffs and prefer to work without much supervision or accountability. The marketing-sales department is staffed with business-oriented people who pride themselves on a practical understanding of the marketplace, who like to see many new products with promotable sales features and feel compelled to pay attention to product cost.

A balanced company is one in which R&D and marketing share responsibility for successful market-oriented innovation. The R&D staff must take responsibility not only for innovation but also for a successful product launch. The marketing staff must take responsibility not only for new sales features but also for correctly identifying customer needs and preferences.

R&D–marketing cooperation can be facilitated in several ways:[15]

- Sponsor joint seminars to build understanding and respect for each other's goals, working styles, and problems.
- Assign each new project to functional teams including an R&D person and a marketing person, who work together through the project's life. R&D and marketing jointly establish the development goals and marketing plan.
- Encourage R&D participation into the selling period, including involvement in preparing technical manuals, participating in trade shows, carrying out postintroduction marketing research with customers, and even doing some selling.
- Work out conflicts by going to higher management, following a clear procedure. In one company, R&D and marketing both report to the same vice president.

Merck is a company that recognizes the strong connection between marketing and R&D.

Merck The description on its Web site reveals the importance of Merck's R&D department: "Merck is a worldwide research-intensive company that discovers and develops, manufactures and markets human and animal health products and services." The research focus at Merck is on the development of prescription drugs—Merck is the world's largest seller of these products—and much of its marketing effort involves dissemination of medical and pharmaceutical information. Proprietary publications include *The Merck Index*, a widely used single-volume medical text; *The Merck Manual*, said to be the world's most widely used medical text; *The Merck Manual of Medical Information—Home Edition*, a plain-English version of *The Merck Manual*; and *The Merck Veterinary Manual*. In addition, the company places articles in professional journals to publicize its research efforts. Like its competitors, Merck provides advertising brochures and videotapes to doctors and other health professionals, informing them about the benefits of its drugs. Merck's research focus enabled the company to develop new products, such as the anti-inflammatory drug Vioxx, which pushed its profits higher than all other pharmaceuticals in 2000.[16]

ENGINEERING AND PURCHASING Engineering is responsible for finding practical ways to design new products and production processes. Engineers are interested in achieving technical quality, cost economy, and manufacturing simplicity. They come into conflict with marketing executives when the latter want several models produced, often with product features requiring custom components. Engineers often think of marketing people as inept technically, as continually changing priorities, and as not fully credible or trustworthy. These problems are less pronounced in companies where marketing executives have engineering backgrounds and can communicate effectively with engineers.[17]

Purchasing executives are responsible for obtaining materials and components in the right quantities and quality at the lowest possible cost. They see marketing executives pushing for several models in a product line, which requires purchasing small quantities of many items rather than large quantities of few items. They think that marketing insists on too high a quality for materials and components. They also dislike marketing's forecasting inaccuracy, which causes them to place rush orders at unfavorable prices or to carry excessive inventories.

MANUFACTURING AND OPERATIONS Manufacturing people are responsible for the smooth running of the factory to produce the right products in the right quantities at the right time for the right cost. They have spent their lives in the factory, with its attendant problems of machine breakdowns, inventory stockouts, and labor disputes. They see marketers as having little understanding of factory economics or politics. Marketers complain about insufficient capacity, delays in production, poor quality control, and poor customer service. Yet marketers often turn in inaccurate sales forecasts, recommend features that are difficult to manufacture, and promise more factory service than is reasonable.

Marketers do not see the factory's problems, but rather the problems of the customers, who need the goods quickly, who receive defective merchandise, and who cannot get factory service. The problem is not only poor communication, but also an actual conflict of interest.

Companies settle these conflicts in different ways. In *manufacturing-driven companies*, everything is done to ensure smooth production and low costs. The company prefers simple products, narrow product lines, and high-volume production. Sales campaigns calling for a hasty production buildup are kept to a minimum. Customers on back order have to wait. In *marketing-driven companies*, the company goes out of its way to satisfy the customers. In one large toiletries company, marketing personnel call the shots and manufacturing people have to fall in line, regardless of overtime costs or short runs. The result is high and fluctuating manufacturing costs, as well as variable product quality.

Companies need to develop a balanced orientation in which manufacturing and marketing jointly determine what is in the company's best interests. Solutions include joint seminars to understand each other's viewpoints, joint committees and liaison personnel, personnel exchange programs, and analytical methods to determine the most profitable course of action.[18]

Company profitability depends on achieving effective working relations. Marketers need to understand the marketing potentials of new manufacturing strategies—the flexible factory, automation and robotization, just-in-time production, and total quality management. Manufacturing strategy depends on whether the company wants to win through low cost, high quality, high variety, or fast service. Manufacturing is also a marketing tool insofar as potential customers may want to visit the factory to assess how well it is managed.

The term *manufacturing* is used for industries making physical products. The term *operations* is used for industries that create or provide services. In the case of a hotel, for example, the operations department includes front-desk people, doormen, and restaurant servers. Because marketing makes promises about service levels, it is extremely important that marketing and operations work together. If operations personnel lack a customer orientation and motivation, negative word of mouth will eventually destroy the business. Marketing people must fully understand the capabilities and mind-set of those delivering the service and continuously try to improve attitudes and capabilities.

FINANCE Financial executives pride themselves on being able to evaluate the profit implications of different business actions. Marketing executives ask for substantial budgets for advertising, sales promotions, and sales force, without being able to prove how much revenue these expenditures will produce. Financial executives suspect the forecasts are self-serving. They think marketers are too quick to slash prices to win orders, instead of pricing to make a profit. They claim that marketers "know the value of everything and cost of nothing."

However, marketing executives often see financial people as "knowing the cost of everything and the value of nothing." They see finance as controlling the purse strings too tightly and refusing to invest in long-term market development. They think financial people see marketing expenditures as *expenses* rather than *investments* and are overly conservative and risk averse, causing many opportunities to be lost. The solution lies in giving marketing people more financial training and financial people more marketing training. Financial executives need to adapt their financial tools and theories to support strategic marketing.

ACCOUNTING AND CREDIT Accountants see marketing people as lax in providing sales reports on time. They dislike the special deals salespeople make with customers because these require special accounting procedures. Marketers dislike the way accountants allocate fixed-cost burdens to different products in the line. Brand managers may feel that their brand is more profitable than it looks, the problem being that it is assigned too high an overhead burden. They would also like accounting to prepare special reports on sales and profitability by segments, important customers, individual products, channels, territories, order sizes, and so on.

Credit officers evaluate potential customers' credit standing and deny or limit credit to the more doubtful ones. They think marketers will sell to anyone, including those from whom payment is doubtful. Marketers, in contrast, often feel that credit standards are too high. They think "zero bad debts" really means the company lost a lot of sales and profits. They feel they work too hard to find customers to hear that they are not good enough to sell to.

building a companywide marketing orientation

Many companies are beginning to realize that they are not really market- and customer-driven—they are product-and-sales driven. Companies such as Baxter, General Motors, Shell, and J.P. Morgan are attempting to transform themselves into true market-driven companies. This will require:

1. Developing a companywide passion for customers.
2. Organizing around customer segments instead of around products.
3. Developing a deep understanding of customers through qualitative and quantitative research.

The payoffs are considerable. Two researchers recently concluded: "We found that the more aggressive a company's customer-focused strategy, the higher its productivity. Those with a customer focus were almost 7 percent more productive than their competitors."[19]

The task is not easy. It will not happen as a result of the CEO making speeches and urging every employee to "think customer." The change will require a change in job and department definitions, responsibilities, incentives, and relationships. "Marketing Memo—Audit: Characteristics of Company Departments That Are Truly Customer-Driven" shows an audit instrument that can be used to evaluate which company departments are truly customer-driven.

What steps can a CEO take to create a market- and customer-focused company?

1. *Convince senior management of the need to become customer-focused:* The CEO personally exemplifies strong customer commitment and rewards those in the organization who do likewise. For example, former CEO Jack Welch of GE and CEO Lou Gerstner of IBM are said to spend 100 days a year visiting with customers, in spite of the many strategic, financial, and administrative burdens they bear; and IBM's top 470 executives are personally responsible for more than 1,300 customer accounts.

2. *Appoint a senior marketing officer and marketing task force:* The marketing task force should include the CEO; the vice presidents of sales, R&D, purchasing, manufacturing, finance, and human resources; and other key individuals.

3. *Get outside help and guidance:* Consulting firms have considerable experience in helping companies move toward a marketing orientation.

4. *Change the company's reward measurement and system:* As long as purchasing and manufacturing are rewarded for keeping costs low, they will resist accepting some costs required to serve customers better. As long as finance focuses on short-term profit, it will oppose major investments designed to build satisfied, loyal customers.

5. *Hire strong marketing talent:* The company needs a strong marketing vice president who not only manages the marketing department but also gains respect from and influence with the other vice presidents. A multidivisional company would benefit from establishing a strong corporate marketing department.

6. *Develop strong in-house marketing training programs:* The company should design well-crafted marketing training programs for corporate management, divisional general managers, marketing and sales personnel, manufacturing personnel, R&D personnel, and others. GE, Motorola, and Accenture run these programs.

7. *Install a modern marketing planning system:* The planning format will require managers to think about the marketing environment, opportunities, competitive trends, and other forces. These managers then prepare strategies and sales and profit forecasts for specific products and segments and are accountable for performance.

8. *Establish an annual marketing excellence recognition program:* Business units that believe they have developed exemplary marketing plans should submit a description of their plans and results.

Marketing
MEMO

Audit: Characteristics of Company Departments That Are Truly Customer-Driven

R&D	___ They spend time meeting customers and listening to their problems.
	___ They welcome the involvement of marketing, manufacturing, and other departments on each new project.
	___ They benchmark competitors' products and seek "best of class" solutions.
	___ They solicit customer reactions and suggestions as the project progresses.
	___ They continuously improve and refine the product on the basis of market feedback.
Purchasing	___ They proactively search for the best suppliers rather than choose only from those who solicit their business.
	___ They build long-term relations with fewer but more reliable high-quality suppliers.
	___ They do not compromise quality for price savings.
Manufacturing	___ They invite customers to visit and tour their plants.
	___ They visit customer factories to see how customers use the company's products.
	___ They willingly work overtime when it is important to meet promised delivery schedules.
	___ They continuously search for ways to produce goods faster and/or at lower costs.
	___ They continuously improve product quality, aiming for zero defects.
	___ They meet customer requirements for "customization" where this can be done profitably.
Marketing	___ They study customer needs and wants in well-defined market segments.
	___ They allocate marketing effort in relation to the long-run profit potential of the targeted segments.
	___ They develop winning offerings for each target segment.
	___ They measure company image and customer satisfaction on a continuous basis.
	___ They continuously gather and evaluate ideas for new products, product improvements, and services to meet customers' needs.
	___ They influence all company departments and employees to be customer-centered in their thinking and practice.
Sales	___ They have specialized knowledge of the customer's industry.
	___ They strive to give the customer "the best solution."
	___ They make only promises that they can keep.
	___ They feed back customers' needs and ideas to those in charge of product development.
	___ They serve the same customers for a long period of time.
Logistics	___ They set a high standard for service delivery time and they meet this standard consistently.
	___ They operate a knowledgeable and friendly customer service department that can answer questions, handle complaints, and resolve problems in a satisfactory and timely manner.
Accounting	___ They prepare periodic "profitability" reports by product, market segment, geographic areas (regions, sales territories), order sizes, and individual customers.
	___ They prepare invoices tailored to customer needs and answer customer queries courteously and quickly.
Finance	___ They understand and support marketing expenditures (e.g., image advertising) that represent marketing investments that produce long-term customer preference and loyalty.
	___ They tailor the financial package to the customers' financial requirements.
	___ They make quick decisions on customer creditworthiness.
Public Relations	___ They disseminate favorable news about the company and they "damage control" unfavorable news.
	___ They act as an internal customer and public advocate for better company policies and practices.
Other Customer Contact Personnel	___ They are competent, courteous, cheerful, credible, reliable, and responsive.

The winning teams would be rewarded at a special ceremony. The plans would be disseminated to the other business units as "models of marketing thinking." Such programs are carried on by Accenture, Becton-Dickenson, and DuPont.

9. *Shift from a department focus to a process-outcome focus:* After defining the fundamental business processes that determine its success, the company should appoint process leaders and cross-disciplinary teams to reengineer and implement these processes.

10. *Empower the employees:* Progressive companies encourage and reward their employees for coming up with new ideas. They also empower them to settle customer complaints in order to save the customer's business. IBM, for example, lets its frontline employees spend up to $5,000 to solve a customer problem on the spot.

DuPont successfully made the transition from an inward-looking to an outward-looking orientation. Under CEO Richard Heckert's leadership, DuPont undertook a number of initiatives to build a "marketing community." Several divisions were reorganized along market lines. The company held a series of marketing-management training seminars, which were ultimately attended by 300 senior people, 2,000 middle managers, and 14,000 employees. It established a corporate marketing excellence recognition program and honored 32 employees from around the world who had developed innovative marketing strategies and service improvements.[20] It takes a great amount of planning and patience to get managers to accept the fact that customers are the foundation of the company's business and its future, but it can be done.

injecting more creativity into the organization

Although it is necessary in a hypercompetitive economy that an organization be customer-oriented, it is not enough. The organization must also be creative. Companies today copy each other's advantages and strategies with increasing speed. Strategies converge and strategies decay more rapidly. Differentiation gets harder to achieve, let alone maintain. Margins fall when firms become more alike. The only answer is for the firm to build a capability in strategic innovation and imagination. This capability comes from assembling tools, processes, skills and measures that will enable the firm to generate more and better new ideas than its competitors.[21] And some argue that marketers should not emphasize satisfying customers at the expense of imaginative strategies (see Marketing Insight: "Do Marketers Give Too Much Allegiance to the Marketing Concept?").

Companies must watch trends and be ready to capitalize on them. Motorola was 18 months late in moving from analog to digital cellular phones, giving a big lead to Nokia and Ericsson. Barnes & Noble was late in recognizing online ordering of books and music, giving the lead to Amazon. Coca-Cola was slow in recognizing beverage trends toward fruit-flavored drinks such as Snapple, energy drinks such as Gatorade, and designer water brands (Nestlé is the leader here). Yet Nestlé was late in recognizing the trend toward coffee houses such as Starbucks.

Market leaders tend to miss trends when they are risk averse, obsessed about protecting their existing markets and physical resources, and more interested in efficiency than innovation. They give lip service to innovation but keep it at the periphery of their business, not at the center.

marketing **insight**

Do Marketers Give too Much Allegiance to the Marketing Concept?

Professor Stephen Brown of Ulster University has challenged a number of fundamental assumptions underlying the marketing concept. He thinks that marketers make too much of researching and satisfying consumers, and as a result, risk losing marketing imagination and significant consumer impact. Here are his criticisms:

1. If marketers pay too much attention to what consumers say they need or want, marketers will simply make products similar to those that already exist. Consumers normally start from what they know, not from what might be possible. For example, they might say they want a smaller cellular phone but would not ask for one that includes a Palm Pilot or voice recognition. It is the marketer's job to go beyond what customers say they want.

2. The marketing concept assumes that consumers have clear goals and pursue them rationally. But consumers are buffeted by all kinds of forces. Many respond to hyped products and stories. Therefore marketers need skills beyond APIC—analysis, planning, implementation, and control. Marketers need to be able to create dramas, new realities, artificial scarcities, celebrations, and the like.

3. The marketing concept implies that marketer must be submissive to customers, and go all out to please them. Any suggestion that marketers might "play" with the customer, even manipulate the public, is taboo. Yet some of the greatest marketers of the past, such as P. T. Barnum, teased the public, overdramatized offerings, and yet the public loved it. Why should the customer be dominant and the marketer always be submissive?

Source: For more on Brown's views, see Stephen Brown, *Marketing—The Retro Revolution* (Thousand Oaks, CA: Sage Publications, 2001).

How can companies build a capability for strategic innovation? Here are some approaches:

- Hire some marketers who are unusually creative to counterbalance the majority who do marketing by the textbook. These people may be more unconventional, more rule-breaking, more risk-taking, and even more argumentative, but their ideas will at least present a challenge.
- Train your employees in the use of creativity techniques, including group techniques (brainstorming, synectics) and individual techniques (visualization, attribute listing, forced relationships, morphological analysis, mind-mapping).[22]
- List observable trends such as longer working hours, single parents, and new life styles, and tease out their implications for your firm.
- List unmet needs and imagine new offerings or solutions: how to help people lose weight, stop smoking, relieve stress, meet others, and so on.
- Set up rewards and prizes for new ideas. Run a "best idea" competition once a month. Give a cash reward, extra vacation time, or travel awards to those who come up with the best ideas.
- Senior managers should take small sets of employees out to lunch or dinner once a week to discuss ideas they might have on improving the business. Sometimes take them into new settings, such as a wrestling match, a drug rehabilitation center, a poor neighborhood.
- Set up groups of employees to critique the company's and competitors' products and services. Also have them critique the company's cherished beliefs and consider turning them upside down.
- Occasionally hire creative resources from outside the firm. BrightHouse (*www.brighthouse.com*) employs a number of highly creative people and charges $500,000 to spend 10 weeks on each assignment to come up with breakthrough ideas. Faith Popcorn (*www.brainreserve.com*), author of *The Popcorn Report* and *Clicking*, runs a *brain reserve* where she will select a half-dozen creative people to meet with a company to generate new ideas. Many large advertising agencies, such as Leo Burnett, run a creativity service for clients.

Here is a company that is serious about injecting more creativity into employees' thinking.

Strategic innovation resource: BrightHouse.

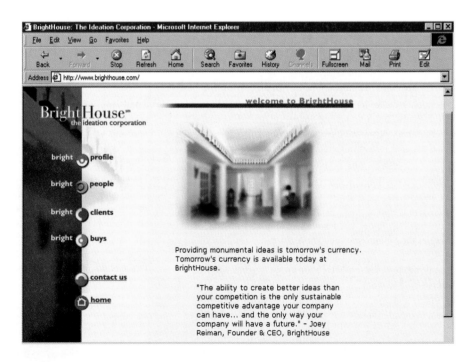

Clorox   Clorox runs a project called THINC (Tools and Habits for Inspiring and Nurturing Creativity). The aim is to enlist all departments and employees in thinking up new ideas. One program is called "Food for Thought": small groups of employees are treated to lunch where they brainstorm solutions to particular problems. Clorox features a large creativity bulletin board in the company's main lobby, and has placed white boards along the hallways where employees can scribble ideas.

marketing implementation

We now ask how marketing managers can effectively implement marketing plans.[23] **Marketing implementation** is the process that turns marketing plans into action assignments and ensures that such assignments are executed in a manner that accomplishes the plan's stated objectives.[24]

A brilliant strategic marketing plan counts for little if it is not implemented properly. Consider the following example:

> A chemical company learned that the customers were not getting good service from any of the competitors. The company decided to make customer service its strategic thrust. When this strategy failed, a postmortem revealed a number of implementation failures. The customer service department continued to be held in low regard by top management; it was understaffed; and it was used as a dumping ground for weak managers. Furthermore, the company's reward system continued to focus on cost containment and current profitability. The company had failed to make the changes required to carry out its strategy.

Whereas strategy addresses the *what* and *why* of marketing activities, implementation addresses the *who*, *where*, *when*, and *how*. Strategy and implementation are closely related in that one layer of strategy implies certain tactical implementation assignments at a lower level. For example, top management's strategic decision to "harvest" a product must be translated into specific actions and assignments.

Thomas Bonoma has identified four sets of skills for implementing marketing programs:

1. *Diagnostic skills:* When marketing programs do not fulfill expectations, was it the result of poor strategy or poor implementation? If implementation, what went wrong?
2. *Identification of company level:* Implementation problems can occur in three levels: the marketing function, the marketing program, and the marketing policy level.
3. *Implementation skills:* To implement programs successfully, marketers need other skills: *allocating skills* for budgeting resources, *organizing skills* to develop an effective organization, and *interaction skills* to motivate others to get things done.
4. *Evaluation skills:* Marketers also need monitoring skills to track and evaluate marketing actions.[25]

Companies today are striving to make their marketing operations more efficient and their return on marketing investments more measurable. Marketing costs can amount to 20 to 40 percent of a company's total operating budget. Companies recognize the high amount of waste in many practices: too many meetings lasting too long, undue time spent in looking for documents, delays in receiving approvals, and difficulties in coordinating vendor partners.

Most marketing departments use a limited number of unconnected technology tools such as e-mail, spreadsheets, project management software, and customer databases; but unconnected tools cannot deal with the increasingly complex nature of business, the increased number of collaborators, and the global scope of operations. Companies use information technology to improve the management of their marketing resources. They need better templates for marketing processes, better management of marketing assets, and better allocation of marketing resources.

Aprimo's customized software packages help companies "manage the business of marketing."

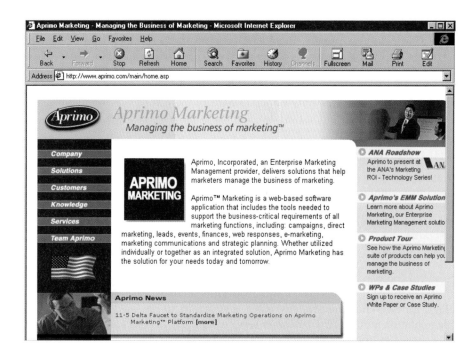

Certain repetitive processes can be automated. This drive is going under such names as *marketing resource management* (MRM), *enterprise marketing management* (EMM), and *marketing automation systems* (MAS).[26]

Several software companies—Aprimo, Emmperative, Kickfire, and Blue Scope (all have Web sites)—now offer software packages to help companies better manage their marketing processes, assets, and resources. The packages are customized so different marketing managers—vice president of marketing, product and brand managers, field sales managers, marketing communications managers—can carry on their planning, implementation, and control. Marketing resource management (MRM) software provides a set of Web-based applications that automate and integrate such activities as project management, campaign management, budget management, asset management, brand management, customer-relationship management, and knowledge management. The knowledge management component consists of process templates, how-to wizards, and best practices.

The software packages are Web-hosted and available to users with passwords. They add up to what some have called *desktop marketing* in that marketers can find whatever information and decision structures they need on their computers. The computer will work as a "dashboard" on which marketers manage their activities. In the next few years, MRM software will enable marketers to greatly improve their spending and investment decisions, bring new products to market more quickly, and reduce decision time and costs.

evaluation and control

In spite of the need to monitor and control marketing activities, many companies have inadequate control procedures. A study of 75 companies turned up these findings:

- Smaller companies do a poorer job of setting clear objectives and establishing systems to measure performance.
- Less than half the companies studied knew their individual products' profitability. About one-third had no regular review procedures for spotting and deleting weak products.

table **22.1**	Types of Marketing Control

Type of Control	Prime Responsibility	Purpose Of Control	Approaches
I. Annual-plan control	Top management Middle management	To examine whether the planned results are being achieved	■ Sales analysis ■ Market-share analysis ■ Sales-to-expense ratios ■ Financial analysis ■ Market-based scorecard analysis
II. Profitability control	Marketing controller	To examine where the company is making and losing money	Profitability by: ■ product ■ territory ■ customer ■ segment ■ trade channel ■ order size
III. Efficiency control	Line and staff management Marketing controller	To evaluate and improve the spending efficiency and impact of marketing expenditures	Efficiency of: ■ sales force ■ advertising ■ sales promotion ■ distribution
IV. Strategic control	Top management Marketing auditor	To examine whether the company is pursuing its best opportunities with respect to markets, products, and channels	■ Marketing-effectiveness rating instrument ■ Marketing audit ■ Marketing excellence review ■ Company ethical and social responsibility review

■ Almost half of the companies failed to compare their prices with those of the competition, to analyze their warehousing and distribution costs, to analyze the causes of returned merchandise, to conduct formal evaluations of advertising effectiveness, and to review their sales force's call reports.

■ Many companies take four to eight weeks to develop control reports, which are occasionally inaccurate.

Table 22.1 lists four types of marketing control needed by companies: annual-plan control, profitability control, efficiency control, and strategic control.

annual-plan control

Annual-plan control aims to ensure that the company achieves the sales, profits, and other goals established in its annual plan. The heart of annual-plan control is management by objectives. Four steps are involved (see Figure 22.7). First, management sets monthly or quarterly goals. Second, management monitors its performance in the marketplace. Third, management determines the causes of serious performance deviations. Fourth, management takes corrective action to close the gaps between goals and performance.

This control model applies to all levels of the organization. Top management sets annual sales and profit goals that become specific goals for lower levels of management. Each product manager is committed to attaining specified levels of sales and costs; each regional district and sales manager and each sales representative is also committed to specific goals. Each period, top management reviews and interprets the results.

figure **22.7**

The Control Process

Marketers today are showing a growing interest in developing better *marketing metrics* for measuring marketing performance.[27] Managers use five tools to check on the plan performance: sales analysis, market-share analysis, marketing expense-to-sales analysis, financial analysis, and market-based scorecard analysis.

SALES ANALYSIS   **Sales analysis** consists of measuring and evaluating actual sales in relation to goals. Two specific tools are used in sales analysis.

Sales-variance analysis measures the relative contribution of different factors to a gap in sales performance. Suppose the annual plan called for selling $4,000 widgets in the first quarter at $1 per widget, for total revenue of $4,000. At quarter's end, only 3,000 widgets were sold at $.80 per widget, for total revenue of $2,400. How much of the sales performance is due to the price decline and how much to the volume decline? The following calculation answers this question:

$$\text{Variance due to price decline} = (\$1.00 - \$.80)\ (3{,}000) = \quad \$600 \qquad 37.5\%$$
$$\text{Variance due to volume decline} = (\$1.00)\ (4{,}000 - 3{,}000) = \underline{\$1{,}000 \qquad 62.5\%}$$
$$ \$1{,}600 \qquad 100.0\%$$

Almost two-thirds of the variance is due to failure to achieve the volume target. The company should look closely at why it failed to achieve expected sales volume.

Microsales analysis looks at specific products, territories, and so forth that failed to produce expected sales. Suppose the company sells in three territories and expected sales were 1,500 units, 500 units, and 2,000 units, respectively. The actual sales volume was 1,400 units, 525 units, and 1,075 units, respectively. Thus territory 1 showed a 7 percent shortfall in terms of expected sales; territory 2, a 5 percent improvement over expectations; and territory 3, a 46 percent shortfall! Territory 3 is causing most of the trouble. The sales vice president needs to check into territory 3: maybe territory 3's sales rep is loafing or has a personal problem; a major competitor has entered this territory; or business is in a recession in this territory.

MARKET-SHARE ANALYSIS   Company sales do not reveal how well the company is performing relative to competitors. For this purpose, management needs to track its market share. Market share can be measured in three ways: **Overall market share** is the company's sales expressed as a percentage of total market sales. **Served market share** is its sales expressed as a percentage of the total sales to its served market. Its **served market** is all the buyers who are able and willing to buy its product. Served market share is always larger than overall market share. A company could capture 100 percent of its served market and yet have a relatively small share of the total market. **Relative market share** can be expressed as market share in relation to its largest competitor. A relative market share over 100 percent indicates a market leader. A relative market share of exactly 100 percent means that the company is tied for the lead. A rise in relative market share means a company is gaining on its leading competitor.

Conclusions from market-share analysis, however, are subject to certain qualifications:

- The assumption that outside forces affect all companies in the same way is often not true: The U.S. Surgeon General's Report on the harmful consequences of cigarette smoking caused total cigarette sales to falter, but not equally for all companies.
- The assumption that a company's performance should be judged against the average performance of all companies is not always valid: A company's performance should be judged against the performance of its closest competitors.
- If a new firm enters the industry, then every existing firm's market share might fall: A decline in market share might not mean that the company is performing any worse than other companies. Share loss depends on the degree to which the new firm hits the company's specific markets.
- Sometimes a market-share decline is deliberately engineered to improve profits: For example, management might drop unprofitable customers or products.

■ Market share can fluctuate for many minor reasons: For example, it can be affected by whether a large sale occurs on the last day of the month or at the beginning of the next month. Not all shifts in market share have marketing significance.[28]

A useful way to analyze market-share movements is in terms of four components:

$$
\begin{matrix}
\textit{Overall} \\
\textit{market} \\
\textit{share}
\end{matrix}
=
\begin{matrix}
\textit{Customer} \\
\textit{penetration}
\end{matrix}
\times
\begin{matrix}
\textit{Customer} \\
\textit{loyalty}
\end{matrix}
\times
\begin{matrix}
\textit{Customer} \\
\textit{selectivity}
\end{matrix}
\times
\begin{matrix}
\textit{Price} \\
\textit{selectivity}
\end{matrix}
$$

where:

■ *Customer penetration* is the percentage of all customers who by from the company.
■ *Customer loyalty* is the purchases from the company by its customers expressed as a percentage of their total purchases from all suppliers of the same products.
■ *Customer selectivity* is the size of the average customer purchase from the company expressed as a percentage of the size of the average customer purchase from an average company.
■ *Price selectivity* is the average price charged by the company expressed as a percentage of the average price charged by all companies.

Now suppose the company's dollar market share falls during the period. The overall market-share equation provides four possible explanations: The company lost some of its customers (lower customer penetration); existing customers are buying less form the company (lower customer loyalty); the company's remaining customers are smaller in size (lower customer selectivity); or the company's price has slipped relative to competition (lower price selectivity).

MARKETING EXPENSE-TO-SALES ANALYSIS   Annual-plan control requires making sure that the company is not overspending to achieve sales goals. The key ratio to watch is *marketing expense-to-sales.* In one company, this ratio was 30 percent and consisted of five component expense-to-sales ratios: sales force-to-sales (15 percent); advertising-to-sales (5 percent); sales promotion-to-sales (6 percent); marketing research-to-sales (1 percent); and sales administration-to-sales (3 percent).

Management needs to monitor these ratios. Fluctuations outside the normal range are cause for concern. The period-to-period fluctuations in each ratio can be tracked on a *control chart* (see Figure 22.8). This chart shows that the advertising expense-to-sales ratio

figure **22.8**

The Control-Chart Model

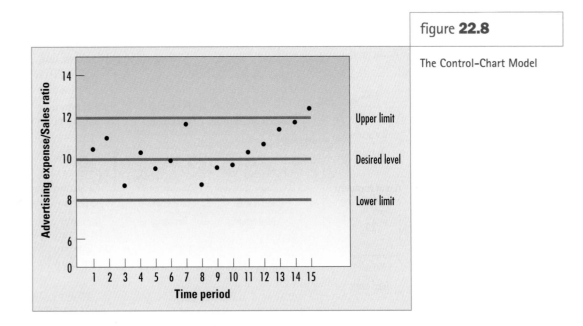

normally fluctuates between 8 percent and 12 percent, say 99 out of 100 times. In the fifteenth period, however, the ratio exceeded the upper control limit. One of two hypotheses can explain this occurrence: (1) The company still has good expense control, and this situation represents a rare chance event. (2) The company has lost control over this expense and should find the cause. If no investigation is made, the risk is that some real change might have occurred, and the company will fall behind. If the environment is investigated, the risk is that the investigation will uncover nothing and be a waste of time and effort.

The behavior of successive observations even within the upper and lower control limits should be watched. Note in Figure 22.8 that the level of the expense-to-sales ratio rose steadily from the ninth period onward. The probability of encountering six successive increases in what should be independent events is only 1 in 64.[29] This unusual pattern should have led to an investigation sometime before the fifteenth observation.

FINANCIAL ANALYSIS The expense-to-sales ratios should be analyzed in an overall financial framework to determine how and where the company is making its money. Marketers are increasingly using financial analysis to find profitable strategies beyond sales building.

Management uses financial analysis to identify the factors that affect the company's *rate of return on net worth*.[30] The main factors are shown in Figure 22.9, along with illustrative numbers for a large chain-store retailer. The retailer is earning a 12.5 percent return on net worth. The return on net worth is the product of two ratios, the company's *return on assets* and its *financial leverage*. To improve its return on net worth, the company must increase its ratio of net profits to its assets or increase the ratio of its assets to its net worth. The company should analyze the composition of its assets (i.e., cash, accounts receivable, inventory, and plant and equipment) and see if it can improve its asset management.

The return on assets is the product of two ratios, the *profit margin* and the *asset turnover*. The profit margin in Figure 22.9 seems low, whereas the asset turnover is more normal for retailing. The marketing executive can seek to improve performance in two ways: (1) Increase the profit margin by increasing sales or cutting costs; and (2) increase the asset turnover by increasing sales or reducing assets (e.g., inventory, receivables) that are held against a given level of sales.[31]

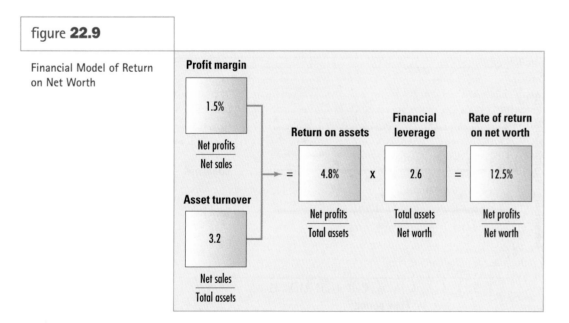

figure **22.9**

Financial Model of Return on Net Worth

Executives also want to know the rate of return on marketing investment. Tim Matanovich suggests the following formula:

$$ROMI = \frac{NMC}{ME}$$

where:

ROMI = Return-on-marketing investment.
 NMC = Net marketing contribution. This is the difference between total revenue and total variable costs. (Leave out operating expenses and overhead because they can be somewhat arbitrary.)
  ME = Marketing expenditures.

Matanovich hopes ROMI will lead senior management to view marketing expenditures as an investment yielding a certain rate of return rather than as simple expenses.[32]

MARKET-BASED SCORECARD ANALYSIS   Most company measurement systems amount to preparing a financial-performance scorecard at the expense of more qualitative measures. Companies would do well to prepare two market-based scorecards that reflect performance and provide possible early warning signals.

A **customer-performance scorecard** records how well the company is doing year after year on such customer-based measures as:

- Percentage of new customers to average number of customers
- Percentage of lost customers to average number of customers
- Percentage of win-back customers to average number of customers
- Percentage of customers falling into very dissatisfied, dissatisfied, neutral, satisfied, and very satisfied categories
- Percentage of customers who say they would repurchase the product
- Percentage of customers who say they would recommend the product to others
- Percentage of target market customers who have brand awareness or recall
- Percentage of customers who say that the company's product is the most preferred in its category
- Percentage of customers who correctly identify the brand's intended positioning and differentiation
- Average perception of company's product quality relative to chief competitor
- Average perception of company's service quality relative to chief competitor

Norms should be set for each measure, and management should take action when results get out of bounds.

The second measure is called a **stakeholder-performance scorecard**. Companies need to track the satisfaction of various constituencies who have a critical interest in and impact on the company's performance: employees, suppliers, banks, distributors, retailers, stockholders. Again, norms should be set for each group and management should take action when one or more groups register increased levels of dissatisfaction.[33] Consider Hewlett-Packard's program.

Hewlett-Packard   Each division of Hewlett-Packard evaluates its performance on a customer-based scorecard that monitors 18 to 20 "business fundamentals." Some, such as customer satisfaction and on-time delivery, are rated for all divisions; other indicators are tracked according to the nature of the division's business. The company is thus able to gauge the effects of its marketing strategies on sales and profits and to identify areas where improvements in performance can lead to improved quantitative results.[34]

profitability control

Here are some disconcerting findings from a bank profitability study:

> We have found that anywhere from 20 to 40 percent of an individual institution's products are unprofitable, and up to 60 percent of their accounts generate losses.
>
> Our research has shown that, in most firms, more than half of all customer relationships are not profitable, and 30 to 40 percent are only marginally so. It is frequently a mere 10 to 15 percent of firm's relationships that generate the bulk of its profits.
>
> Our profitability research into the branch system of a regional bank produced some surprising results . . . 30 percent of the bank's branches were unprofitable.[35]

Clearly, companies need to measure the profitability of their products, territories, customer groups, segments, trade channels, and order sizes. This information will help management determine whether any products or marketing activities should be expanded, reduced, or eliminated.

MARKETING-PROFITABILITY ANALYSIS　　We will illustrate the steps in marketing-profitability analysis with the following example:

> The marketing vice president of a lawnmower company wants to determine the profitability of selling its lawnmower through three types of retail channels: hardware stores, garden supply shops, and department stores. The company's profit-and-loss statement is shown in Table 22.2.

Step 1: Identifying Functional Expenses　　Assume that the expenses listed in Table 22.2 are incurred to sell the product, advertise it, pack and deliver it, and bill and collect for it. The first task is to measure how much of each expense was incurred in each activity.

Suppose that most of the salary expense went to sales representatives and the rest went to an advertising manager, packing and delivery help, and an office accountant. Let the breakdown of the $9,300 be $5,100, $1,200, $1,400, and $1,600, respectively. Table 22.3 shows the allocation of the salary expense to these four activities.

Table 22.3 also shows the rent account of $3,000 allocated to the four activities. Because the sales reps work away from the office, none of the building's rent expense is assigned to selling. Most of the expenses for floor space and rented equipment are for packing and delivery. The supplies account covers promotional materials, packing materials, fuel purchases for delivery, and home office stationery. The $3,500 in this account is reassigned to the functional uses made of the supplies.

Step 2: Assigning Functional Expenses to Marketing Entities　　The next task is to measure how much functional expense was associated with selling through each type of

table **22.2**			
A Simplified Profit–and–Loss Statement	Sales		$60,000
	Cost of goods sold		39,000
	Gross margin		$21,000
	Expenses		
	Salaries	$9,300	
	Rent	3,000	
	Supplies	3,500	
			15,800
	Net profit		$5,200

Natural Accounts	Total	Selling	Advertising	Packing and Delivery	Billing and Collecting
Salaries	$9,300	$5,100	$1,200	$1,400	$1,600
Rent	3,000	–	400	2,000	600
Supplies	3,500	400	1,500	1,400	200
	$15,800	$5,500	$3,100	$4,800	$2,400

channel. Consider the selling effort. The selling effort is indicated by the number of sales made in each channel. This number is found in the selling column of Table 22.4. Altogether, 275 sales calls were made during the period. Because the total selling expense amounted to $5,500 (see Table 22.3), the selling expense per call averaged $20.

Advertising expense can be allocated according to the number of ads addressed to different channels. Because there were 100 ads altogether, the average ad cost $31.

The packing and delivery expense is allocated according to the number of orders placed by each type of channel. This same basis was used for allocating billing and collection expense.

Step 3: Preparing a Profit-and-Loss Statement for Each Marketing Entity   A profit-and-loss statement can now be prepared for each type of channel (see Table 22.5). Because hardware stores accounted for half of total sales ($30,000 out of $60,000), this channel is charged with half the cost of goods sold ($19,500 out of $39,000). This leaves a gross margin from hardware stores of $10,500. From this must be deducted the proportions of the functional expenses hardware stores consumed. According to Table 22.4, hardware stores received 200 out of 275 total sales calls. At an imputed value of $20 a call, hardware stores have to be charged with a $4,000 selling expense. Table 22.4 also shows that hardware stores were the target of 50 ads. At $31 an ad, the hardware stores are charged with $1,550 of advertising. The same reasoning applies in computing the share of the other functional expenses to charge to hardware stores. The result is that hardware stores gave rise to $10,050 of the total expenses. Subtracting this from the gross margin, the profit of selling through hardware stores is only $450.

This analysis is repeated for the other channels. The company is losing money in selling through garden supply shops and makes virtually all of its profits through department stores. Notice that gross sales is not a reliable indicator of the net profits for each channel.

Channel Type	Selling	Advertising	Packing and Delivery	Billing and Collecting
Hardware	200	50	50	50
Garden supply	65	20	21	21
Department stores	10	30	9	9
	275	100	80	80
Functional expense	$5,500	$3,100	$4,800	$2,400
÷ No. of Units	275	100	80	80
Equals	$ 20	$ 31	$ 60	$ 30

table **22.5**

Profit–and–Loss
Statements for
Channels

	Hardware	Garden Supply	Dept. Stores	Whole Company
Sales	$30,000	$10,000	$20,000	$60,000
Cost of goods sold	19,500	6,500	13,000	39,000
Gross margin	$10,500	$ 3,500	$ 7,000	$21,000
Expenses				
Selling ($20 per call)	$ 4,000	$ 1,300	$ 200	$ 5,500
Advertising ($31 per advertisement)	1,550	620	930	3,100
Packing and delivery ($60 per order)	3,000	1,260	540	4,800
Billing ($30 per order)	1,500	630	270	2,400
Total Expenses	$10,050	$ 3,810	$ 1,940	$ 15,800
Net profit or loss	$ 450	$ (310)	$ 5,060	$ 5,200

DETERMINING CORRECTIVE ACTION   It would be naive to conclude that the company should drop garden supply shops and possibly hardware stores so that it can concentrate on department stores. The following questions need to be answered first:

- To what extent do buyers buy on the basis of type of retail outlet versus brand?
- What are the trends with respect to the importance of these three channels?
- How good are the company marketing strategies directed at the three channels?

On the basis of the answers, marketing management can evaluate five alternatives:

1. Establish a special charge for handling smaller orders.
2. Give more promotional aid to garden supply shops and hardware stores.
3. Reduce the number of sales calls and the amount of advertising going to garden supply shops and hardware stores.
4. Do not abandon any channel entirely, but only the weakest retail units in each channel.
5. Do nothing.

In general, marketing-profitability analysis indicates the relative profitability of different channels, products, territories, or other marketing entities. It does not prove that the best course of action is to drop the unprofitable marketing entities, nor does it capture the likely profit improvement if these marginal marketing entities are dropped.

DIRECT VERSUS FULL COSTING   Like all information tools, marketing-profitability analysis can lead or mislead marketing executives, depending on how well they understand its methods and limitations. The lawnmower company showed some arbitrariness in its choice of bases for allocating the functional expenses to its marketing entities. "Number of sales calls" was used to allocate selling expenses, when in principle "number of sales working hours" is a more accurate indicator of cost. The former base was used because it involves less record keeping and computation.

Far more serious is another judgmental element affecting profitability analysis. The issue is whether to allocate full costs or only direct and traceable costs in evaluating a marketing entity's performance. The lawnmower company sidestepped this problem by assuming only simple costs that fit in with marketing activities, but the question cannot be avoided in real-world analyses of profitability. Three types of costs have to be distinguished:

1. *Direct costs:* These are costs that can be assigned directly to the proper marketing entities. Sales commissions are a direct cost in a profitability analysis of sales territories, sales representa-

tives, or customers. Advertising expenditures are a direct cost in a profitability analysis of products to the extent that each advertisement promotes only one product. Other direct costs for specific purposes are sales-force salaries and traveling expenses.

2. *Traceable common costs:* These are costs that can be assigned only indirectly, but on a plausible basis, to the marketing entities. In the example, rent was analyzed this way.

3. *Nontraceable common costs:* These are common costs whose allocation to the marketing entities is highly arbitrary. To allocate "corporate image" expenditures equally to all products would be arbitrary, because all products do not benefit equally. To allocate them proportionately to the sales of the various products would be arbitrary because relative product sales reflect many factors besides corporate image making. Other examples are top management salaries, taxes, interest, and other overhead.

No one disputes including direct costs in marketing cost analysis. There is a small amount of controversy about including traceable common costs, which lump together costs that would change with the scale of marketing activity and costs that would not change. If the lawnmower company drops garden supply shops, it would probably continue to pay the same rent. In this event, its profits would not rise immediately by the amount of the present loss in selling to garden supply shops ($310).

The major controversy concerns whether the nontraceable common costs should be allocated to the marketing entities. Such allocation is called the *full-cost approach*, and its advocates argue that all costs must ultimately be imputed in order to determine true profitability. However, this argument confuses the use of accounting for financial reporting with its use for managerial decision making. Full costing has three major weaknesses:

1. The relative profitability of different marketing entities can shift radically when one arbitrary way to allocate nontraceable common costs is replaced by another.

2. The arbitrariness demoralizes managers, who feel that their performance is judged adversely.

3. The inclusion of nontraceable common costs could weaken efforts at real cost control.

Operating management is most effective in controlling direct costs and traceable common costs. Arbitrary assignments of nontraceable common costs can lead them to spend their time fighting arbitrary cost allocations rather than managing controllable costs well.

Companies are showing a growing interest in using marketing-profitability analysis or its broader version, **activity-based cost accounting (ABC)**, to quantify the true profitability of different activities. According to Cooper and Kaplan, ABC "can give managers a clear picture of how products, brands, customers, facilities, regions, or distribution channels both generate revenues and consume resources."[36] To improve profitability, managers can then examine ways to reduce the resources required to perform various activities, or make the resources more productive or acquire them at lower cost. Alternatively, management may raise prices on products that consume heavy amounts of support resources. The contribution of ABC is to refocus management's attention away from using only labor or material standard costs to allocate full cost, and toward capturing the actual costs of supporting individual products, customers, and other entities.

Companies are showing a renewed interest in analyzing marketing profitability and connecting it with shareholder value. Marketers are responding by developing financial tools for measuring brand equity, channel equity, customer equity, and other key marketing assets of the firm. Among the best current expositions are those of Peter Doyle, Roger Best, and Tim Ambler.[37]

efficiency control

Suppose a profitability analysis reveals that the company is earning poor profits in certain products, territories, or markets. Are there more efficient ways to manage the sales force, advertising, sales promotion, and distribution in connection with these marketing entities?

Some companies have established a *marketing controller* position to improve marketing efficiency. Marketing controllers work out of the controller's office but specialize in the marketing side of the business. At companies such as General Foods, DuPont, and

Johnson & Johnson, they perform a sophisticated financial analysis of marketing expenditures and results. They examine adherence to profit plans, help prepare brand managers' budgets, measure the efficiency of promotions, analyze media production costs, evaluate customer and geographic profitability, and educate marketing personnel on the financial implications of marketing decisions.[38]

SALES-FORCE EFFICIENCY   Sales managers need to monitor the following key indicators of efficiency in their territories:

- Average number of calls per salesperson per day
- Average sales call time per contact
- Average revenue per sales call
- Average cost per sales call
- Entertainment cost per sales call
- Percentage of orders per 100 sales calls
- Number of new customers per period
- Number of lost customers per period
- Sales-force cost as a percentage of total sales

When a company starts investigating sales-force efficiency, it often finds areas for improvement. General Electric reduced the size of one of its divisional sales forces after discovering that its salespeople were calling on customers too often. When a large airline found that its salespeople were both selling and servicing, they transferred the servicing function to lower-paid clerks. Another company conducted time-and-duty studies and found ways to reduce the ratio of idle-to-productive time.

ADVERTISING EFFICIENCY   Many managers believe it is almost impossible to measure what they are getting for their advertising dollars; but they should try to keep track of at least the following statistics:

- Advertising cost per thousand target buyers reached by media vehicle
- Percentage of audience who noted, saw, or associated and read most of each print ad
- Consumer opinions on the ad's content and effectiveness
- Before and after measures of attitude toward the product
- Number of inquiries stimulated by the ad
- Cost per inquiry

Management can take a number of steps to improve advertising efficiency, including doing a better job of positioning the product, defining objectives, pretesting messages, using computer technology to guide the selection of media, looking for better media buys, and doing posttesting.

SALES-PROMOTION EFFICIENCY   Sales promotion includes dozens of devices for stimulating buyer interest and product trial. To improve sales-promotion efficiency, management should record the costs and sales impact of each promotion. Management should watch the following statistics:

- Percentage of sales sold on deal
- Display costs per sales dollar
- Percentage of coupons redeemed
- Number of inquiries resulting from a demonstration

A sales-promotion manager can analyze the results of different promotions and advise product managers on the most cost-effective promotions to use.

DISTRIBUTION EFFICIENCY   Management needs to search for distribution economies in inventory control, warehouse locations, and transportation modes. It should track such measures as:

- Logistics costs as a percentage of sales
- Percentage of orders filled correctly

- Percentage of on-time deliveries
- Number of billing errors

Management should strive to reduce inventory while at the same time speeding up the order-to-delivery cycle. That both can be done simultaneously is shown by Dell Computer.

Dell   A customer-customized computer that is ordered from Dell's Web site at 9:00 A.M. on Wednesday can be on the delivery truck by 9:00 P.M. Thursday. In that short period, Dell electronically orders the computer components from its suppliers' warehouses. Equally impressive, Dell gets paid electronically within 24 hours while Compaq, supplying its computers to retailers, receives payment on an average of 35 days later.

One problem is that distribution efficiency declines when the company experiences strong sales increases. Peter Senge describes a situation in which a strong sales surge causes the company to fall behind in meeting delivery dates (see Figure 22.10).[39] This leads customers to bad-mouth the company and eventually sales fall. Management responds by increasing sales-force incentives to secure more orders. The sales force succeeds, but once again the company slips in meeting delivery dates. Management needs to identify the real bottleneck and invest in more production and distribution capacity.

strategic control

From time to time, companies need to undertake a critical review of overall marketing goals and effectiveness. Each company should periodically reassess its strategic approach to the marketplace with marketing effectiveness reviews and marketing audits. Companies can also perform marketing excellence reviews and ethical/social responsibility reviews.

THE MARKETING EFFECTIVENESS REVIEW   Here is an actual situation: The president of a major industrial equipment company reviewed the annual business plans of various divisions and found several lacking in marketing substance. He called in the corporate vice president of marketing and said:

> I am not happy with the quality of marketing in our divisions. It is very uneven. I want you to find out which of our divisions are strong, average, and weak in marketing. I want to know if they understand and are practicing customer-oriented marketing. I want a marketing score for each division. For each deficient division, I want a plan for improving marketing effectiveness over the next several years. I want evidence next year that each deficient division is improving its capabilities.

The corporate marketing vice president agreed. His first inclination was to base the evaluation on each division's performance in sales growth, market share, and profitability. His thinking was that high-performing divisions had good marketing leadership and poor-performing divisions had poor marketing leadership; but good results could be due to a division's being in the right place at the right time. Another division might have poor results in spite of excellent marketing planning.

A company's or division's marketing effectiveness is reflected in the degree to which it exhibits the five major attributes of a marketing orientation: *customer philosophy, integrated marketing organization, adequate marketing information, strategic orientation,* and *operational efficiency* (see "Marketing Memo: Marketing Effectiveness Review Instrument"). Most companies and divisions receive scores in the fair-to-good range.[40]

THE MARKETING AUDIT   The average U.S. corporation loses half of its customers in five years, half of its employees in four years, and half of its investors in less than one year.[41] Clearly, this points to some weaknesses. Companies that discover weaknesses should undertake a thorough study known as a marketing audit.[42] A **marketing audit** is a comprehensive, systematic, independent, and periodic examination of a company's or

figure **22.10**

Dynamic Interactions Between Sales Orders and Distribution Efficiency

Source: Adapted from Peter M. Senge, *The Fifth Discipline.* ©1990 by Peter M. Senge. Used by permission of Doubleday, a division of Bantam Doubleday Dell Publishing Group, Inc.

Marketing
MEMO

Marketing Effectiveness Review Instrument

(Check One Answer to Each Question)

Customer Philosophy

A. *Does management recognize the importance of designing the company to serve the needs and wants of chosen markets?*
   0 __ Management primarily thinks in terms of selling current and new products to whomever will buy them.
   1 __ Management thinks in terms of serving a wide range of markets and needs with equal effectiveness.
   2 __ Management thinks in terms of serving the needs and wants of well-defined markets and market segments chosen for their long-run growth and profit potential for the company.
B. *Does management develop different offerings and marketing plans for different segments of the market?*
   0 __ No.   1 __ Somewhat.   2 __ To a large extent.
C. *Does management take a whole marketing-system view (suppliers, channels, competitors, customers, environment) in planning its business?*
   0 __ No. Management concentrates on selling and servicing its immediate customers.
   1 __ Somewhat. Management takes a long view of its channels, although the bulk of its effort goes to selling and servicing the immediate customers.
   2 __ Yes. Management takes a whole marketing-systems view, recognizing the threats and opportunities created for the company by changes in any part of the system.

Integrated Marketing Organization

D. *Is there high-level marketing integration and control of the major marketing functions?*
   0 __ No. Sales and other marketing functions are not integrated at the top and there is some unproductive conflict.
   1 __ Somewhat. There is formal integration and control of the major marketing functions but less than satisfactory coordination and cooperation.
   2 __ Yes. The major marketing functions are effectively integrated.
E. *Does marketing management work well with management in research, manufacturing, purchasing, logistics, and finance?*
   0 __ No. There are complaints that marketing is unreasonable in the demands and costs it places on other departments.
   1 __ Somewhat. The relations are amicable, although each department pretty much acts to serve its own interests.
   2 __ Yes. The departments cooperate effectively and resolve issues in the best interest of the company as a whole.
F. *How well organized is the new-product development process?*
   0 __ The system is ill-defined and poorly handled.
   1 __ The system formally exists but lacks sophistication.
   2 __ The system is well structured and operates on teamwork principles.

Adequate Marketing Information

G. *When were the latest marketing research studies of customers, buying influences, channels, and competitors conducted?*
   0 __ Several years ago.   1 __ A few years ago.   2 __ Recently.
H. *How well does management know the sales potential and profitability of different market segments, customers, territories, products, channels, and order sizes?*
   0 __ Not at all.   1 __ Somewhat.   2 __ Very well.
I. *What effort is expended to measure and improve the cost-effectiveness of different marketing expenditures?*
   0 __ Little or no effort.   1 __ Some effort.   2 __ Substantial effort.

Strategic Orientation

J. *What is the extent of formal marketing planning?*
   0 __ Management conducts little or no formal marketing planning.
   1 __ Management develops an annual marketing plan.
   2 __ Management develops a detailed annual marketing plan and a strategic long-range plan that is updated annually.
K. *How impressive is the current marketing strategy?*
   0 __ The current strategy is not clear.
   1 __ The current strategy is clear and represents a continuation of traditional strategy.
   2 __ The current strategy is clear, innovative, data-based, and well reasoned.
L. *What is the extent of contingency thinking and planning?*
   0 __ Management does little or no contingency thinking.
   1 __ Management does some contingency thinking but little formal contingency planning.
   2 __ Management formally identifies the most important contingencies and develops contingency plans.

Operational Efficiency

M. *How well is the marketing strategy communicated and implemented?*
   0 __ Poorly.   1 __ Fairly.   2 __ Successfully.
N. *Is management doing an effective job with its marketing resources?*
   0 __ No. The marketing resources are inadequate for the job to be done.
   1 __ Somewhat. The marketing resources are adequate but they are not employed optimally.
   2 __ Yes. The marketing resources are adequate and are employed efficiently.

continued...

0. *Does management show a good capacity to react quickly and effectively to on-the-spot developments?*
   0 __ No. Sales and market information is not very current and management reaction time is slow.
   1 __ Somewhat. Management receives fairly up-to-date sales and market information; management reaction time varies.
   2 __ Yes. Management has installed systems yielding highly current information and fast reaction time.

Total Score
The instrument is used in the following way. The appropriate answer is checked for each question. The scores are added—the total will be somewhere between 0 and 30. The following scale shows the level of marketing effectiveness:

0–5 = None	11–15 = Fair	21–25 = Very good
6–10 = Poor	16–20 = Good	26–30 = Superior

business unit's marketing environment, objectives, strategies, and activities with a view to determining problem areas and opportunities and recommending a plan of action to improve the company's marketing performance.

Let us examine the marketing audit's four characteristics:

1. *Comprehensive:* The marketing audit covers all the major marketing activities of a business, not just a few trouble spots. It would be called a *functional audit* if it covered only the sales force, pricing, or some other marketing activity. Although functional audits are useful, they sometimes mislead management. Excessive sales-force turnover, for example, could be a symptom not of poor sales-force training or compensation but of weak company products and promotion. A comprehensive marketing audit usually is more effective in locating the real source of problems.

2. *Systematic:* The marketing audit is an orderly examination of the organization's macro- and micromarketing environments, marketing objectives and strategies, marketing systems, and specific activities. The audit indicates the most-needed improvements, which are then incorporated into a corrective action plan involving both short-run and long-run steps to improve overall effectiveness.

3. *Independent:* A marketing audit can be conducted in six ways: self-audit, audit from across, audit from above, company auditing office, company task-force audit, and outsider audit. Self-audits, in which managers use a checklist to rate their own operations, lack objectivity and independence.[43] The 3M Company has made good use of a corporate auditing office, which provides marketing audit services to divisions on request.[44] Generally speaking, however, the best audits come from outside consultants who have the necessary objectivity, broad experience in a number of industries, some familiarity with the industry being audited, and the undivided time and attention to give to the audit.

4. *Periodic:* Typically, marketing audits are initiated only after sales have turned down, sales-force morale has fallen, and other problems have occurred. Companies are thrown into a crisis partly because they failed to review their marketing operations during good times. A periodic marketing audit can benefit companies in good health as well as those in trouble.

A marketing audit starts with a meeting between the company officer(s) and the marketing auditor(s) to work out an agreement on the audit's objectives, coverage, depth, data sources, report format, and time frame. A detailed plan regarding who is to be interviewed, the questions to be asked, the time and place of contact, and so on is prepared so that auditing time and cost are kept to a minimum. The cardinal rule in marketing auditing is: Do not rely solely on company managers for data and opinions. Customers, dealers, and other outside groups must also be interviewed. Many companies do not really know how their customers and dealers see them, nor do they fully understand customer needs.

The marketing audit examines six major components of the company's marketing situation. The major questions are listed in Table 22.6.

table **22.6**	Components of a Marketing Audit

Part I. Marketing Environment Audit

Macroenvironment

A. Demographic	What major demographic developments and trends pose opportunities or threats to this company? What actions has the company taken in response to these developments and trends?
B. Economic	What major developments in income, prices, savings, and credit will affect the company? What actions has the company been taking in response to these developments and trends?
C. Environmental	What is the outlook for the cost and availability of natural resources and energy needed by the company? What concerns have been expressed about the company's role in pollution and conservation, and what steps has the company taken?
D. Technological	What major changes are occurring in product and process technology? What is the company's position in these technologies? What major generic substitutes might replace this product?
E. Political	What changes in laws and regulations might affect marketing strategy and tactics? What is happening in the areas of pollution control, equal employment opportunity, product safety, advertising, price control, and so forth, that affects marketing strategy?
F. Cultural	What is the public's attitude toward business and toward the company's products? What changes in customer lifestyles and values might affect the company?

Task Environment

A. Markets	What is happening to market size, growth, geographical distribution, and profits? What are the major market segments?
B. Customers	What are the customers' needs and buying processes? How do customers and prospects rate the company and its competitors on reputation, product quality, service, sales force, and price? How do different customer segments make their buying decisions?
C. Competitors	Who are the major competitors? What are their objectives, strategies, strengths, weaknesses, sizes, and market shares? What trends will affect future competition and substitutes for the company's products?
D. Distribution and Dealers	What are the main trade channels for bringing products to customers? What are the efficiency levels and growth potentials of the different trade channels?
E. Suppliers	What is the outlook for the availability of key resources used in production? What trends are occurring among suppliers?
F. Facilitators and Marketing Firms	What is the cost and availability outlook for transportation services, warehousing facilities, and financial resources? How effective are the company's advertising agencies and marketing research firms?
G. Publics	Which publics represent particular opportunities or problems for the company? What steps has the company taken to deal effectively with each public?

Part II. Marketing Strategy Audit

A. Business Mission	Is the business mission clearly stated in market-oriented terms? Is it feasible?
B. Marketing Objectives and Goals	Are the company and marketing objectives and goals stated clearly enough to guide marketing planning and performance measurement? Are the marketing objectives appropriate, given the company's competitive position, resources, and opportunities?
C. Strategy	Has the management articulated a clear marketing strategy for achieving its marketing objectives? Is the strategy convincing? Is the strategy appropriate to the stage of the product life cycle, competitors' strategies, and the state of the economy? Is the company using the best basis for market segmentation? Does it have clear criteria for rating the segments and choosing the best ones? Has it developed accurate profiles of each target segment? Has the company developed an effective positioning and marketing mix for each target segment? Are marketing resources allocated optimally to the major elements of the marketing mix? Are enough resources or too many resources budgeted to accomplish the marketing objectives?

Part III. Marketing Organization Audit

A. Formal structure	Does the marketing vice president have adequate authority and responsibility for company activities that affect customers' satisfaction? Are the marketing activities optimally structured along functional, product, segment, end-user, and geographical lines?

B. Functional Efficiency	Are there good communication and working relations between marketing and sales? Is the product-management system working effectively? Are product managers able to plan profits or only sales volume? Are there any groups in marketing that need more training, motivation, supervision, or evaluation?
C. Interface Efficiency	Are there any problems between marketing and manufacturing, R&D, purchasing, finance, accounting, and/or legal that need attention?

Part IV. Marketing Systems Audit

A. Marketing Information System	Is the marketing intelligence system producing accurate, sufficient, and timely information about marketplace developments with respect to customers, prospects, distributors and dealers, competitors, suppliers, and various publics? Are company decision makers asking for enough marketing research, and are they using the results? Is the company employing the best methods for market measurement and sales forecasting?
B. Marketing Planning Systems	Is the marketing planning system well conceived and effectively used? Do marketers have decision support systems available? Does the planning system result in acceptable sales targets and quotas?
C. Marketing Control System	Are the control procedures adequate to ensure that the annual plan objectives are being achieved? Does management periodically analyze the profitability of products, markets, territories, and channels of distribution? Are marketing costs and productivity periodically examined?
D. New-Product Development System	Is the company well organized to gather, generate, and screen new-product ideas? Does the company do adequate concept research and business analysis before investing in new ideas? Does the company carry out adequate product and market testing before launching new products?

PART V. Marketing Productivity Audit

A. Profitability Analysis	What is the profitability of the company's different products, markets, territories, and channels of distribution? Should the company enter, expand, contract, or withdraw from any business segments?
B. Cost-Effectiveness Analysis	Do any marketing activities seem to have excessive costs? Can cost-reducing steps be taken?

Part VI. Marketing Function Audits

A. Products	What are the company's product-line objectives? Are they sound? Is the current product line meeting the objectives? Should the product line be stretched or contracted upward, downward, or both ways? Which products should be phased out? Which products should be added? What are the buyers' knowledge and attitudes toward the company's and competitors' product quality, features, styling, brand names, and so on? What areas of product and brand strategy need improvement?
B. Price	What are the company's pricing objectives, policies, strategies, and procedures? To what extent are prices set on cost, demand, and competitive criteria? Do the customers see the company's prices as being in line with the value of its offer? What does management know about the price elasticity of demand, experience-curve effects, and competitors' prices and pricing policies? To what extent are price policies compatible with the needs of distributors and dealers, suppliers, and government regulation?
C. Distribution	What are the company's distribution objectives and strategies? Is there adequate market coverage and service? How effective are distributors, dealers, manufacturers' representatives, brokers, agents, and others? Should the company consider changing its distribution channels?
D. Advertising, Sales Promotion, Publicity, and Direct Marketing	What are the organization's advertising objectives? Are they sound? Is the right amount being spent on advertising? Are the ad themes and copy effective? What do customers and the public think about the advertising? Are the advertising media well chosen? Is the internal advertising staff adequate? Is the sales-promotion budget adequate? Is there effective and sufficient use of sales-promotion tools such as samples, coupons, displays, and sales contests? Is the public relations staff competent and creative? Is the company making enough use of direct, online, and database marketing?
E. Sales Force	What are the sales force's objectives? Is the sales force large enough to accomplish the company's objectives? Is the sales force organized along the proper principles of specialization (territory, market, product)? Are there enough (or too many) sales managers to guide the field sales representatives? Do the sales-compensation level and structure provide adequate incentive and reward? Does the sales force show high morale, ability, and effort? Are the procedures adequate for setting quotas and evaluating performance? How does the company's sales force compare to competitors' sales forces?

table **22.7**			
The Marketing Excellence Review: Best Practices	**Poor**	**Good**	**Excellent**
	Product-Driven	Market-Driven	Market-Driving
	Mass-Market Oriented	Segment Oriented	Niche Oriented and Customer Oriented
	Product Offer	Augmented Product Offer	Customer Solutions Offer
	Average Product Quality	Better Than Average	Legendary
	Average Service Quality	Better Than Average	Legendary
	End-Product Oriented	Core-Product Oriented	Core-Competency Oriented
	Function Oriented	Process Oriented	Outcome Oriented
	Reacting to Competitors	Benchmarking Competitors	Leapfrogging Competitors
	Supplier Exploitation	Supplier Preference	Supplier Partnership
	Dealer Exploitation	Dealer Support	Dealer Partnership
	Price-Driven	Quality-Driven	Value-Driven
	Average Speed	Better Than Average	Legendary
	Hierarchy	Network	Teamwork
	Vertically Integrated	Flattened Organization	Strategic Alliances
	Stockholder-Driven	Stakeholder-Driven	Societally-Driven

THE MARKETING EXCELLENCE REVIEW   Companies can use another instrument to rate their performance in relation to the best practices of high-performing businesses. The three columns in Table 22.7 distinguish among poor, good, and excellent business and marketing practices. Management can place a checkmark to indicate its perception of where the business stands. The resulting profile exposes weaknesses and strengths, highlighting where the company might make changes to become a truly outstanding player in the marketplace.

THE ETHICAL AND SOCIAL RESPONSIBILITY REVIEW   Several forces are driving companies to practice a higher level of corporate social responsibility: rising customer expectations, changing employee expectations, government legislation and pressure, the inclusion of social criteria by investors, and changing business procurement practices. Companies need to evaluate whether they are truly practicing ethical and socially responsible marketing. Business success and continually satisfying the customer and other stakeholders are closely tied to adoption and implementation of high standards of business and marketing conduct. The most admired companies in the world abide by a code of serving people's interests, not only their own. (See "Marketing for the New Economy: Marketing Fair Labor Practices.")

Business practices are often under attack because business situations routinely pose tough ethical dilemmas. One can go back to Howard Bowen's classic questions about the responsibilities of businesspeople:

> Should he conduct selling in ways that intrude on the privacy of people, for example, by door-to-door selling....? Should he use methods involving bally-hoo, chances, prizes, hawking, and other tactics which are at least of doubtful good taste? Should he employ "high pressure" tactics in persuading people to buy? Should he try to hasten the obsolescence of goods by bringing out an end-less succession of new models and new styles? Should he appeal to and attempt to strengthen the motives of materialism, invidious consumption, and "keeping up with the Joneses?"[45]

marketing for the **new economy**

Marketing Fair Labor Practices

Globalization is a fact of life in the apparel industry. Labels bearing the names of U.S.–owned companies commonly indicate that the items are produced in other countries, often less developed nations of Latin America and the Pacific Rim. A series of news reports in the mid-1990s brought to public attention the fact that many of these products were made by underpaid, overworked, and sometimes underage employees in sweatshops. One of the most highly publicized labor controversies involved Nike.

In 1997, a labor watchdog agency published the results of Ernst & Young's 1996 audit of a Nike factory in Vietnam that found unsafe working conditions. Workers were forced to work 65-hour weeks and were improperly compensated for overtime labor; they worked in areas with poor ventilation while being exposed to dangerous levels of carcinogens, and earned little more than $10 a week. As the media reported further findings, human rights and workers' rights groups lined up to attack Nike. In response, Nike implemented comprehensive changes in its corporate labor policy.

In 1998, the company formally announced the implementation of new global labor standards. The same year, Nike created a Corporate Responsibility Division that consolidated the labor, environmental, and community action groups already part of the company. The stated mission of this new division was "to lead in corporate citizenship through programs that reflect caring for the world family of Nike, our teammates, our consumers, and those who provide services to Nike." Nike became a charter member of the Fair Labor Association (FLA), a White House initiative that established a code of conduct for global manufacturers and accredited monitoring processes in the industry. Nike enlisted FLA-approved PricewaterhouseCoopers to conduct annual audits of each of its 500 global factories.

Nike's measures to improve and monitor its global manufacturing conditions met with decidedly mixed responses. While some commended Nike for its community involvement, its environmental consciousness, and its comparatively high wages and clean factories, others continued to condemn the company. Some activists claimed that scheduled annual audits paint an inaccurate portrait of actual conditions. Others complained that Nike employees' yearly pay did not constitute a "living wage." To respond to the continuing accusations, Nike initiated measures to provide the public with access to information about its labor practices and the results of audits. The company referred to this project as "Transparency 101," and the first step was an agreement to disclose the results of all audits by posting them on Nike's Web site starting in May 2000. During college spring break the same year, the company sent 16 undergraduates, each of whom had applied for the opportunity to tour Nike's global factories, to a total of 32 factories worldwide. The company then made full-text copies of every report available on the Internet.

In addition, not every labor group was satisfied with the government's oversight of workers' rights issues. In 1998, UNITE, the apparel workers' union, withdrew from the FLA in protest. The American Apparel Manufacturers Association, impatient with the progress of the FLA, developed its own program, called Worldwide Responsible Apparel Production (WRAP), with similar standards and its own certification agency. Since WRAP officially started operations in June 2000, over 225 factories from around the world have registered with the agency.

Although UNITE and its allies fear that manufacturers will make only superficial improvements and that certification will be a misrepresentation, the disagreements between the two sides reveal their common convictions: Labor must be recognized as an important stakeholder in every employer's business. Fair labor practices are a critical marketing issue as well as a matter of corporate ethics.

Sources: Vanessa Groce, "Chronicle," *Earnshaw's Infants', Toddlers', and Girls' and Boys' Wear Review* (October 1996): 36; Steven Greenhouse, "Voluntary Rules on Apparel Labor Prove Hard to Set," *New York Times,* February 1, 1997, pp. A1, A7; "No Sweat? Sweatshop Code Is Just a First Step to End Worker Abuse," *Solidarity* (June–July 1997): 9. See also the Web sites of UNITE, Corporate Watch, and the American Apparel Association, plus: <www.wrapaparrel.com>; <www.nikebiz.com>; Aaron Bernstein, "Nike Opens Its Books on Sweatshop Audits," *BusinessWeek,* April 27, 2000; "Nike Offers Students Chance to See Conditions in Third-World Factories," *DowJones.com,* November 11, 1999.

The issues raised are complicated. Drawing a clear line between normal marketing practice and unethical behavior is not easy. At the same time, certain business practices are clearly unethical or illegal. These include bribery or stealing trade secrets; false and deceptive advertising; exclusive dealing and tying agreements; quality or safety defects; false warranties; inaccurate labeling; price-fixing or undue discrimination; and barriers to entry and predatory competition.

Companies today that do not perform are at greater risk of being exposed, thanks to the Internet. In the past, a disgruntled customer might bad-mouth a manufacturer or merchant to 12 other people; today he or she can reach thousands of people on the Internet. Microsoft, for example, has attracted over 100 anti-Microsoft sites, including Hate Microsoft and Boycott Microsoft.

Raising the level of socially responsible marketing calls for a three-pronged attack. First, society must use the law to define, as clearly as possible, those practices that are illegal, antisocial, or anticompetitive. Second, companies must adopt and disseminate a written code of ethics, build a company tradition of ethical behavior, and hold its people fully responsible for observing ethical and legal guidelines. Third, individual marketers must practice a "social conscience" in their specific dealings with customers and various stakeholders.

The future holds a wealth of opportunities for companies. Technological advances in solar energy, online networks, cable and satellite television, biotechnology, and telecommunications promise to change the world as we know it. At the same time, forces in the socioeconomic, cultural, and natural environments will impose new limits on marketing and business practices. Companies that are able to innovate new solutions and values in a socially responsible way are the most likely to succeed. Consider Working Assets.

Working Assets Working Assets long-distance telephone service competes with AT&T, MCI, and Sprint in the same way the major carriers compete with each other: low rates, clear transmission over fiber optic lines, efficient operators, and convenient calling cards. However, it adds a unique appeal to its selected market niche: Working Assets donates at least 1 percent of annual revenues to charity and lets customers vote on which nonprofit groups receive money. The customers addressed in the company's clever tagline "We make your voice heard" are people who identify themselves as supporters of progressive causes. On its monthly bills, the company provides information about two current issues along with the names and phone numbers of influential people the customer is invited to call free of charge. For a fee, the customer may have a prepared letter sent to these leaders on his or her behalf. In all its business practices, the company has a consistent policy of corporate citizenship that matches the ethical concerns of its target market. Working Assets' corporate idealism has had a favorable effect on the bottom line. Revenue shot up from $2 million in 1991 to $140 million in 1999, and the company made *Inc.*'s list of the fastest-growing corporations for five consecutive years between 1992 and 1997.[46]

summary

1. The modern marketing department evolved through six stages, and today companies can be found in each stage. In the first stage, companies simply start out with a sales department. In the second stage, they add ancillary marketing functions, such as advertising and marketing research. In the third stage, a separate marketing department is created to handle the increased number of ancillary marketing functions. In the fourth stage, both sales and marketing report to a sales and marketing vice president. In the fifth stage, all of a company's employees are market and customer centered. In the sixth stage, marketing personnel work mainly on cross-disciplinary teams.

2. Modern marketing departments can be organized in a number of ways. Some companies are organized by functional specialization, while others focus on geography and regionalization. Still others emphasize product and brand management or market-segment management. Some companies establish a matrix organization consisting of both product and market managers. Finally, some companies have strong corporate marketing, others have limited corporate marketing, and still others place marketing only in the divisions.

3. Effective modern marketing organizations are marked by a strong cooperation and customer focus among the company's departments: marketing, R&D, engineering, purchasing, manufacturing, operations, finance, accounting, and credit.

4. A brilliant strategic marketing plan counts for little if it is not implemented properly. Implementing marketing plans calls for skills in recognizing and diagnosing a problem, assessing the company level where the problem exists, implementation skills, and skills in evaluating the results.

5. The marketing department has to monitor and control marketing activities continuously. The purpose of *annual-plan control* is to ensure that the company achieves the sales, profits, and other goals established in its annual plan. The main tools of annual-plan control are sales analysis, market-share analysis, marketing expense-to-sales analysis, financial analysis, and market-based scorecard analysis.

6. *Profitability control* seeks to measure and control the profitability of various products, territories, customer groups, trade channels, and order sizes. An important part of controlling for profitability is assigning costs and generating profit-and-loss statements.

7. *Efficiency control* focuses on finding ways to increase the efficiency of the sales force, advertising, sales promotion, and distribution.

8. *Strategic control* entails a periodic reassessment of the company and its strategic approach to the marketplace, using the tools of the marketing effectiveness review and the marketing audit. Companies should also undertake marketing excellence reviews and ethical/social responsibility reviews.

applications

marketing debate – is marketing management an art or a science?

Some marketing observers maintain that good marketing is something that is more than anything an art and does not lend itself to rigorous analysis and deliberation. Others strongly disagree and contend that marketing management is a highly disciplined enterprise that shares much in common with other business disciplines.

Take a position: Marketing management is largely an artistic exercise and therefore highly subjective versus Marketing management is largely a scientific exercise with well-established guidelines and criteria.

marketing and advertising

1. When Bumble Bee introduced the new vacuum-sealed pouch highlighted in the ad in Figure 1, it had to coordinate the work of the marketing department with the work of many other departments within the company.

   a. How would the marketing department have needed to interact with purchasing in the course of developing and launching this new product package?

   b. In creating this new package, what kinds of interactions would the product manager have had with his or her counterparts in the manufacturing department?

   c. Outline how Bumble Bee's marketing managers would have interacted with employees in finance, accounting, and credit as they planned and implemented the marketing of this product.

2. The ad in Figure 2 uses a first-person story to show how Iomega's Zip technology can help a company move more quickly—and make the employee look good, as well.

   a. What measurements could Iomega use to determine the efficiency of its print advertising campaign?

   b. What implementation issues would Iomega's marketers need to consider when planning this advertisement?

   c. What questions should Iomega marketers ask in determining whether corrective action is needed if this advertising campaign does not meet expectations?

Figure 1

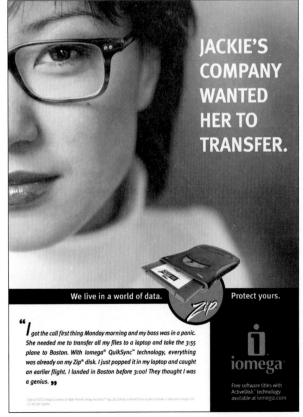

Figure 2

online marketing today

BrightHouse, as noted earlier, specializes in helping companies generate innovative marketing ideas. By hiring outside experts to jump-start the innovation process, management can gain valuable insights and identify new ways of exploiting market opportunities. For example, BrightHouse helped Coty create "ghost myst" perfume—a product that became the best-selling perfume in the market during its first year. BrightHouse uses a four-step process to come up with innovative ideas, starting with investigation (to learn more about the situation) and incubation (to allow time for different thoughts to surface), then continuing with illumination and illustration (the steps in which the ideas are elaborated and brought to life with detail).[47]

Learn more about BrightHouse by visiting its Web site (*www.brighthouse.com*). Review the home page and then follow the "bright profile" link to read about how this company approaches its assignments. Also look at the glossary at the bottom of the page. How do BrightHouse's techniques help a company innovate on a more systematic basis? What are the pros and cons of hiring an outside firm to help with innovation?

you're the marketer: sonic pda marketing plan

Marketing Plan Pro

No marketing plan is complete without provisions for organizing, implementing, evaluating, and controlling the total marketing effort. In addition to measuring progress toward financial targets and other objectives, marketers need to plan how to audit and improve their marketing activities.

Sonic has asked you to plan the management of the marketing effort for the launch of the company's new personal digital assistant (PDA) product. Look back over the parts of the marketing plan that you have already developed, especially the goals, strategies, and programs. Now answer these questions about managing Sonic's marketing activities:

- What is the most appropriate organization for Sonic's marketing and sales departments?

- What can Sonic do to create a more market- and customer-focused organization?
- What control measures should Sonic incorporate into its marketing plan?
- What can Sonic do to evaluate its marketing?
- How can Sonic evaluate its level of ethically and socially responsible marketing?

After you have answered these questions, summarize your recommendations in a written marketing plan or type them into the Marketing Organization and Implementation sections of the *Marketing Plan Pro* software. To complete your marketing plan, write the Executive Summary of the plan's highlights.

notes

1. Frederick E. Webster Jr., "The Changing Role of Marketing in the Corporation," *Journal of Marketing* (October 1992): 1–17. Also see Ravi S. Achrol, "Evolution of the Marketing Organization: New Forms for Turbulent Environment," *Journal of Marketing* (October 1991): 77–93; John P. Workman Jr., Christian Homburg, and Kjell Gruner, "Marketing Organization: An Integrative Framework of Dimensions and Determinants," *Journal of Marketing* (July 1998): 21–41. For some contemporary perspectives, see Special Issue 1999 of *Journal Marketing Fundamental Issues and Directions for Marketing*.

2. Frank V. Cespedes, *Concurrent Marketing: Integrating Product, Sales, and Service* (Boston: Harvard Business School Press, 1995); and *Managing Marketing Linkages: Text, Cases, and Readings* (Upper Saddle River, NJ: Prentice Hall, 1996).

3. Robert E. Lineman and John H. Stanton Jr., "A Game Plan for Regional Marketing," *Journal of Business Strategy* (November–December 1992): 19–25.

4. Scott Humes, "Execs Favor Regional Approach," *Advertising Age*, November 2, 1987, p. 36; "National Firms Find That Selling to Local Tastes Is Costly, Complex," *Wall Street Journal*, February 9, 1987, p. B1; Paul A. Herbig, *Handbook of Cross-Cultural Marketing* (New York: International Business Press, 1998), pp. 45–46.

5. Emily Fromm, "Steve Bumgarner: Field Marketing Coordinator, Krispy Kreme Doughnut Corp.," *Brandweek*, March 26, 2001, p. 21.

6. "... and Other Ways to Peel the Onion," *The Economist*, January 7, 1995, pp. 52–53.

7. "KPMG Combining Firms in Americas, Europe," *PR Newswire*, March 29, 1999; <www.kpmg.com>.

8. Andrall E. Pearson and Thomas W. Wilson Jr., *Making Your Organization Work* (New York: Association of National Advertisers, 1967), pp. 8–13.

9. Michael George, Anthony Freeling, and David Court, "Reinventing the Marketing Organization," *The McKinsey Quarterly*, no. 4 (1994): 43–62.

10. For further reading, see Robert Dewar and Don Shultz, "The Product Manager, an Idea Whose Time Has Gone," *Marketing Communications* (May 1998): 28–35; "The Marketing Revolution at Proctor & Gamble," *BusinessWeek*, July 25, 1988, pp. 72–76; Kevin T. Higgins, "Category Management: New Tools Changing Life for Manufacturers, Retailers," *Marketing News*, September 25, 1989, pp. 2, 19; George S. Low and Ronald A. Fullerton, "Brands, Brand Management, and the Brand Manager System: A Critical Historical Evaluation," *Journal of Marketing Research* (May 1994): 173–90; Michael J. Zanor, "The Profit Benefits of Category Management," *Journal of Marketing Research* (May 1994): 202–13.

11. Sam I. Hill, David L. Newkirk, and Wayne Henderson, "Dismantling the Brandocracy," *Strategy & Business*, no. 1 (Fall 1995): 4–17.

12. Richard E. Anderson, "Matrix Redux," *Business Horizons* (November–December 1994): 6–10.

13. For further reading on marketing organization, see Nigel Piercy, *Marketing Organization: An Analysis of Information Processing, Power and Politics* (London: George Allen & Unwin, 1985); Robert W. Ruekert, Orville C. Walker, and Kenneth J. Roering, "The Organization of Marketing Activities: A Contingency Theory of Structure and Performance," *Journal of Marketing* (Winter 1995): 13–25; Tyzoon T. Tyebjee, Albert V. Bruno, and Shelly H. McIntyre, "Growing Ventures Can Anticipate Marketing Stages," *Harvard Business Review* (January–February 1983): 2–4; Andrew Pollak, "Revamping Said to Be Set at Microsoft," *New York Times*, February 9, 1999, p. C1.

14. Gary L. Frankwick, Beth A. Walker, and James C. Ward, "Belief Structures in Conflict: Mapping a Strategic Marketing Decision," *Journal of Business Research* (October–November 1994): 183–95.

15. William E. Souder, *Managing New Product Innovations* (Lexington, MA: D. C. Health, 1987), chs. 10 and 11; William L. Shanklin and John K. Ryans Jr., "Organizing for High-Tech Marketing," *Harvard Business Review* (November–December 1984): 164–71; Robert J. Fisher, Elliot Maltz, and Bernard J. Jaworski, "Enhancing Communication between Marketing and Engineering: The Moderating Role of Relative Functional Identification," *Journal of Marketing* (July 1997): 54–70.

16. David J. Morrow, "Struggling to Spell R-E-L-I-E-F," *New York Times*, December 29, 1998, pp. C1, C18; "JAMA Study Shows Merck-Medco's Partners for Healthy Aging Program Significantly Reduces the Use of Potentially Harmful Medication by Seniors," *Business Wire,* October 12, 1998; Gardiner Harris, "The Cure: With Big Drugs Dying, Merck Didn't Merge," *Wall Street Journal*, January 10, 2001, p. A1.

17. Fisher, Maltz, and Jaworski, "Enhancing Communication," pp. 54–70.

18. Benson P. Shapiro, "Can Marketing and Manufacturing Coexist?" *Harvard Business Review* (September–October 1977): 104–14. Also see Robert W. Ruekert and Orville C. Walker Jr., "Marketing's Interaction with Other Functional Units: A Conceptual Framework with Other Empirical Evidence," *Journal of Marketing* (January 1987): 1–19.

19. Erik Brynjolfsson and Lorin Hitt, "The Customer Counts," *Information Week*, September 9, 1996.

20. Edward E. Messikomer, "DuPont's 'Marketing Community,'" *Business Marketing* (October 1987): 90–94. For an excellent account of how to convert a company into a market-driven organization, see George Day, *The Market-Driven Organization: Aligning Culture, Capabilities, and Configuation to the Market* (New York: The Free Press, 1989).

21. Gary Hamel, *Leading the Revolution* (Boston: Harvard Business School Press, 2000).

22. Michael Michalko, *Cracking Creativity: The Secrets of Creative Genius* (Berkeley, CA: Ten Speed Press, 1998); James M. Higgins, *101 Creative Problem Solving Techniques* (New York: New Management Publishing Company, 1994); and all of the books by Edward DeBono.

23. For more on developing and implementing marketing plans, see H. W. Goetsch, *Developing, Implementing, and Managing an Effective Marketing Plan* (Chicago: NTC Business Books, 1993).

24. Ibid.

25. Thomas V. Bonoma, *The Marketing Edge: Making Stategies Work* (New York: The Free Press, 1985). Much of this section is based on Bonoma's work.

26. C. Marcus, "Marketing Resource Management: Key Components," Gartner Research Note, August 22, 2001, and also the Web sites of various MRM vendors mentioned in text.

27. Marion Debruyne and Katrina Hubbard, "Marketing Metrics," working paper series, Conference Summary, Marketing Science Institute, Report No. 00-119, 2000.

28. Alfred R. Oxenfeldt, "How to Use Market-Share Measurement," *Harvard Business Review* (January–February 1969): 59–68.

29. There is a one-half chance that a successive observation will be higher or lower. Therefore, the probability of finding six successively higher values is given by (1/2) to the sixth, or 1/64.

30. Alternatively, companies need to focus on factors affecting shareholder value. The goal of marketing planning is to increase shareholder value, which is the present value of the future income stream created by the company's present actions. Rate-of-return analysis usually focuses on only one year's results. See Alfred Rapport, *Creating Shareholder Value*, rev. ed. (New York: The Free Press, 1997).

31. For additional reading on financial analysis, see Peter L. Mullins, *Measuring Customer and Product Line Profitability* (Washington, DC: Distribution Research and Education Foundation, 1984).

32. Timothy Matanovich, "Value Measures in the Executive Suite," *Marketing Management* (Spring 2000): 35–40.

33. Robert S. Kaplan and David P Norton, *The Balanced Scorecard* (Boston: Harvard Business School Press, 1996).

34. Richard Whiteley and Diane Hessan, *Customer Centered Growth* (Reading, MA: Addison-Wesley, 1996), pp. 87–90; Adrian J. Slywotzky, *Value Migration: How to Think Several Moves Ahead of the Competition* (Boston: Harvard University Press, 1996), pp. 231–35.

35. The MAC Group, *Distribution: A Competitive Weapon* (Cambridge, MA: MAC Group, 1985), p. 20.

36. Robin Cooper and Robert S. Kaplan, "Profit Priorities from Activity-Based Costing," *Harvard Business Review* (May–June 1991): 130–35.

37. Peter Doyle, *Value-Based Marketing: Marketing Strategies for Corporate Growth and Shareholder Value* (Chichester, England: John Wiley & Sons; 2000); Roger J. Best, *Market-Based Management: Strategies for Growing Customer Value and Profitability*, 2nd. ed. (Upper Saddle River, NJ: Prentice Hall, 2000); Tim Ambler, *Marketing and the Bottom Line: The New Methods of Corporate Wealth* (London: Financial Times/Prentice Hall, 2000).

38. Sam R. Goodman, *Increasing Corporate Profitability* (New York: Ronald Press, 1982), ch. 1. Also see Bernard J. Jaworski, Vlasis Stathakopoulos, and H. Shanker Krishnan, "Control Combinations in Marketing: Conceptual Framework and Empirical Evidence," *Journal of Marketing* (January 1993): 57–69.

39. Peter M. Senge, *The Fifth Disipline: The Art and Practice of the Learning Organization* (New York: Doubleday Currency, 1990), ch. 7.

40. For further discussion of this instrument, see Philip Kotler, "From Sales Obsession to Marketing Effectiveness," *Harvard Business Review* (November–December 1977): 67–75.

41. Frederick Reichheld, *The Loyalty Effect* (Boston: Harvard Business School Press, 1996).

42. Philip Kotler, William Gregor, and William Rodgers, "The Marketing Audit Comes of Age," *Sloan Management Review*

(Winter 1989): 49–62. For an interesting alternative approach, see the Copernican Decision Navigator, available from Copernican at (617) 630-8705.

43. Useful checklists for a marketing self-audit can be found in Aubrey Wilson, *Abrey Wilson's Marketing Audit Checklists* (London: McGraw-Hill, 1982); Mike Wilson, *The Management of Marketing* (Westmead, England: Gower Publishing, 1980). A marketing audit software program is described in Ben M. Enis and Stephen J. Garfein, "The Computer-Driven Marketing Audit," *Journal of Management Inquiry* (December 1992): 306–18.

44. Kotler, Gregor, and Rodgers, "The Marketing Audit,"

45. Howard R. Bowen, *Social Responsibilities of the Businessman* (New York: Harper and Row, 1953), p. 215. Also see N. Craig Smith and Elizabeth Cooper-Martin, "Ethics and Target Marketing: The Role of Product Harm and Consumer Vulnerability," *Journal of Marketing* (July 1997): 1–20.

46. Todd Wallack, "Conscience Calls," *San Francisco Chronicle*, September 21, 2000.

47. Curtis Sittenfeld, "This Old House Is a Home for New Ideas," *Fast Company* (July–August 1999): 58.

Chapter 1
14 reprinted by permission of Harvard Business School Press/copyright © 1996 by Corporate Decision, Inc./all rights reserved; 30 (left) courtesy of TK Maxx (right) courtesy of Nexen, Inc.

Chapter 2
37 courtesy of Reflect.com; 41 courtesy of Calyx and Corolla; 44 courtesy of Transora; 46 courtesy of Carpoint; 51 courtesy of Infogate; 57 (left) courtesy of Interlink Electronics (right) used courtesy of Garmin Ltd. or its subsidiaries. © Garmin Corp.

Chapter 3
65 courtesy of Dell Computer Corporation; 74 © Lands' End, Inc. used with permission; 79 courtesy of Harley-Davidson; 86 (left) copyright © 2001 Hilton Hospitality, Inc. reprinted by permission (right) copyright © Blue Martini Software reprinted by permission.

Chapter 4
100 courtesy of Starbucks Corporation; 107 courtesy of Travelocity.com; 119 (left) courtesy of AeroMexico (right) courtesy of Ernst & Young.

Chapter 5
126 courtesy of the Marriott Vacation Club; 127 courtesy of CEOExpress Company; 132 compliments of Focus Suites of Philadelphia; 136 reprinted by permission of Dr. Brian Wansink; 152 courtesy of AcuPoll®; 155 (left) courtesy of National Cattleman's Beef Association (right) courtesy of Mutual of America.

Chapter 6
162 courtesy of Colgate-Palmolive; 172 (left) courtesy of Paul Howell/Liaison Agency, Inc. (right) courtesy of Dan Lamont/Matrix International, Inc.; 179 (left) courtesy of Schering-Plough Health/Care

Products (right) reprinted by permission of PRACO and Oi2.

Chapter 7
187 courtesy of Levi.com; 193 courtesy of SRI Consulting; 200 courtesy of Bozell Worldwide, Inc.; 203 courtesy of Edmunds.com, Inc.; 212 (left) courtesy of The Quaker Oats Company (right) Blackberry Wireless e-mail solution print advertisement courtesy of Research in Motion (RIM).

Chapter 8
218 courtesy of mylifepath.com; 224 courtesy of Plastics.com, Inc.; 225 courtesy of Covisint; 239 (left) courtesy of Ford Motor Company (right) courtesy of Cessna Aircraft Company.

Chapter 9
244 courtesy of Owners.com; 245 courtesy of GetThere; 257 The "IGT" spade design, "MegaJackpots" and Quartermania are trademarks of IGT/web site screen shot courtesy of and © IGT, a wholly-owned subsidiary of International Game Technology; 267 courtesy of SCA; 275 (left) courtesy of Lever Brothers Company (right) courtesy of Pfizer Consumer Group, Pfizer Inc.

Chapter 10
284 courtesy of Mattel; 285 courtesy of ChemStation; 289 courtesy of Sega.com; 304 (left) courtesy of Bahlsen USA (right) reprinted by permission of Hertz and Getty Images/photograph © Stephen Derr/ Getty Images/ The Image Bank.

Chapter 11
314 courtesy of PepsiCo, Inc.; 322 courtesy of Peapod, Inc.; 324 courtesy of Hewlett-Packard Company; 341 courtesy of the LEGO Group; 344 (left) courtesy of T-FAL (right) courtesy of the United States Postal Service.

Chapter 12
353 courtesy of 3M; 367 © Lands' End, Inc. Used with permission; 373 courtesy of Philips Consumer Electronics; 375 courtesy of Apple Computer, Inc.; 379 (left) courtesy of Alberto-Culver USA, Inc. (right) reprinted by permission of Steelcase, Inc.

Chapter 13
394 used with permission from McDonald's Corporation; 398 courtesy of Carlsberg A/S; 404 (left) courtesy of Kellogg Deutschland GMBH (right) courtesy of HSBC Holdings plc.

Chapter 14
408 courtesy of BabyCenter.com; 410 courtesy of Procter & Gamble; 417 courtesy of Marriott Corporation; 439 (left) courtesy of Pepperidge Farm (right) Crayola, chevron, and serpentine designs are registered trademarks, the rainbow/swash is a trademark of Binney & Smith, used with permission.

Chapter 15
445 courtesy of Keen, Inc.; 453 courtesy of Kaiser Permanente; 457 courtesy of MyAlert; 463 courtesy of Audible; 467 (left) courtesy of CIGNA, Brad Harris and Creative Management Partners, Craig Anthony Grant and Oppenheim-Christy, and Mr. and Mrs. Victor Frierson (right) Concierge.com ©2001 CondèNet/all rights reserved/reprinted with permission.

Chapter 16
474 courtesy of Maytag Corporation; 486 courtesy of Volumebuy, Inc.; 493 courtesy of Personify, Inc.; 500 (left) courtesy of 1-800-CONTACTS (right) courtesy of eBay. eBay and the eBay logo are trademarks of eBay Inc.

Chapter 17
505 copyright © 2002, Oracle Corporation/all rights reserved;

510 courtesy of People's Bank; 524 courtesy of STIHL, Inc.; 531 (left) courtesy of Ford Motor Company.

Chapter 18
541 courtesy of The Limited, Inc.; 550 courtesy of McKesson HBOC; 553 © Inter IKEA Systems B.V. 2001/used with permission; 558 courtesy of 1-800-Flowers.com; 560 (left) reprinted by permission of Mayors Jewelers (right) courtesy of United Parcel Service, Inc.

Chapter 19
573 2001 BMW of North America/used with permission. The BMW name and logo are registered trademarks; 586 (left) UPWORDS® & © Hasbro, Inc. used with permission (right) courtesy of Sharp Electronics Corporation.

Chapter 20
597 courtesy of United Parcel Service; 599 courtesy of Ethical Funds; 602 courtesy of Earthlink; 613 courtesy of Coolsavings.com; 632 (left) under permission of V&S Vin & Sprit AB. Absolut Country of Sweden Vodka & logo, Absolut, Absolut bottle design and Absolut calligraphy are trademarks owned by V& S Vin & Sprit AB/ copyright © 2001 V&S Vin & Sprit AB (right) courtesy of Ask Jeeves.

Chapter 21
646 courtesy of DAA Solutions; 648 courtesy of Pall Corporation; 656 courtesy of PhysicianNet; 662 (left) reprinted by permission of Saab Cars USA (right) courtesy of Anthro Corporation.

Chapter 22
670 courtesy of Krispy Kreme; 682 courtesy of BrightHouse; 684 courtesy of Aprimo; 703 (left) copyright © Bumble Bee Seafoods, Inc. courtesy of ConAgra (right) courtesy of Iomega Corporation.

company/
brand index

subject index

beyond 2000: key concepts for marketing success

The Eleventh Edition is dedicated to helping companies, groups, and individuals adapt their marketing strategies and management to the new technological and global realities.

Philip Kotler

Customer Relationship Management: *"It is no longer enough to satisfy customers; you must delight them."*

Technology Revolution/Internet: *"The future isn't ahead of us. It has already happened."*